John Murray

Handbook for Travelers in Northern Italy

John Murray

Handbook for Travelers in Northern Italy

ISBN/EAN: 9783742892881

Manufactured in Europe, USA, Canada, Australia, Japa

Cover: Foto ©Andreas Hilbeck / pixelio.de

Manufactured and distributed by brebook publishing software (www.brebook.com)

John Murray

Handbook for Travelers in Northern Italy

HANDBOOK

FOR

TRAVELLERS IN NORTHERN ITALY.

COMPRISING

PIEDMONT, LIGURIA, LOMBARDY, VENETIA, PARMA, MODENA, AND ROMAGNA.

Eighth Edition,

CAREFULLY REVISED TO THE PRESENT TIME.

WITH A TRAVELLING MAP AND FIFTEEN PLANS OF TOWNS.

LONDON:

JOHN MURRAY, ALBEMARLE STREET.

PARIS: A. W. GALIGNANI & CO.; AND STASSIN & XAVIER.
FLORENCE: GOODBAN. MILAN: MEINERS.
VENICE: MÜNSTER. ROME: PIALE; SPITHÖVER; GALLERINI.

1860.

The right of Translation is reserved.

PREFACE.

SINCE the publication of the last editions of the *Handbooks of North and Central Italy*, the Editor has had occasion to revisit nearly every part of the countries described in them, the most considerable portion during the present year, and, while correcting some inaccuracies that remained, to add much new information useful to the traveller.

The changes that have taken place in the political map of the Peninsula, arising out of the events of last year, have rendered necessary a different arrangement of the routes; and to adopt one more natural in a geographical point of view, whilst it will prove more convenient to the traveller. Instead of including Tuscany in the description of North Italy, and the Romagna amongst the Central Italian Provinces, the *Handbook of North Italy* will now embrace the great natural division comprised between the Alps, the Apennines, and the Adriatic, with the Ligurian Provinces on the Mediterranean; and that of *Central Italy*, Tuscany, the Papal States, and the Island of Sardinia.

The interest which Sardinia offers for the Antiquarian, the Naturalist, and the Sportsman, coupled with the daily increasing facilities for reaching and travelling through it, induced the Editor in 1856 to include a description of it in these Handbooks. For this he was in a great measure indebted to his lamented friend, the late General Count de Collegno, one of the most distinguished members of the Piedmontese senate, and well known as one of the most eminent geologists on the Continent, who had then recently visited in great detail that island. This description has been since extended from information derived from General Alberto della Marmora, both personally and from his lately published 'Itinéraire.'

As regards the continental portion of the Peninsula described in these volumes, considerable pains have been taken to point out the easiest means of communication between different places, of late years so much facilitated by the extension of railways.

The Catalogues of all the Public Galleries, and of the most important Private Collections of Pictures, and of objects generally connected with the Fine Arts, have been carefully revised on the spot; and ground-plans of all not likely to undergo for some years changes in their arrangement inserted from the Editor's personal examinations. A still more important addition has been also made to the present volumes, by completing the series of Plans of the principal Cities, upon which all the objects worthy of the tourist's notice have been inserted, so as to enable him, unattended by a guide, to discover everything described and most deserving of attention. All the railways in operation, or projected, have been laid down upon the Map from the most trustworthy sources.

It has been the Editor's endeavour to render the *Handbooks of Northern and Central Italy* as complete guides, to the countries they profess to describe, as exist in any language; and it is his duty again to express his acknowledgments to the numerous friends both in Italy and at home, and to the several correspondents, who have aided him in his task by the information they have transmitted to him. It is in a great measure by such means that works of this nature can lay claim to that degree of accuracy which the travelling public has a right to expect; and he begs still to solicit of travellers, who may use these Handbooks of Travel, to transmit to him through the Publisher any alterations they may consider advisable to make hereafter, founded upon information of a practical and useful nature obtained on the spot.

London, September, 1860.

CONTENTS.

INTRODUCTION.

                     PAGE

1. Plan of the Work — 2. Passports and Custom-houses — 3. Routes — 4. Modes and Expenses of Travelling — 5. Couriers — 6. Sight-seeing; Laquais de Place and Ciceroni — 7. Money — 8. Inns and Accommodations — 9. Books — 10. Maps of Italy — 11. Objects to be noticed — 12. Music — 13. Skeleton Tours -   · · · · ix

Tables of Foreign Coins reduced into the different Currencies of Italy, at the par of exchange - · · · · · · · · xxxi

Table 1. English Money reduced to an equivalent Value in the Money of the several States of North Italy · · · · · · xxxii

Table 2. Currency of the different Italian States reduced into English Money, at the par of exchange - · · · · · · xxxiii

Table 3. Showing the Value of the different Measures of Distances employed in Italy, reduced to English statute Miles, Furlongs, and Yards xxxiv

Abbreviations, &c., employed in the Handbook · · · · xxxiv

SECT. I.—PIEDMONT AND SARDINIAN LOMBARDY.

Preliminary Information — Tables of Money, Weights, and Measures · 1
Routes · · · · · · · · · · · · · 7

SECT. II.—SARDINIAN DOMINIONS ON THE MEDITERRANEAN — THE RIVIERA DI PONENTE, AND RIVIERA DI LEVANTE — TERRITORIES OF NICE, MONACO, AND DUCHY OF GENOA.

Preliminary Information · · · · · · · · 71
Routes · · · · · · · · · · · 76

SECT. III.—LOMBARDY.

Preliminary Information · · · · · · · · 131
Routes · · · · · · · · · · · 140

Sect. IV.—VENETIAN PROVINCES.

	PAGE
Preliminary Information	260
Routes	263

Sect. V.—DUCHIES OF PARMA AND PIACENZA.

Preliminary Information	395
Routes	396

Sect. VI.—DUCHY OF MODENA.

Preliminary Information	425
Routes	426

Sect. VII.—LA ROMAGNA.

Preliminary Information	435
Routes	436

INDEX . . . . 54?

LIST OF PLANS, &c.

	PAGE
Plan of Turin	to face 12
" Genoa	" 98
" Milan	" 157
" Brera Gallery at Milan	192
" Pavia	215
" Brescia	238
" Verona	to face 263
" Mantua	280
" Ducal Palace in Mantua	293
" Vicenza	302
" Padua	312
" Venice	to face 329
" Pinacoteca at Venice	374
" Parma	408
" Galleria at Parma	416
" Modena	429
" Ferrara	439
" Bologna	to face 455
" Pinacoteca at Bologna	459
" Ravenna	510
" Pinacoteca at Forli	536
Map of North Italy	at the end.

INTRODUCTION.

1. *Plan of the Work.* — 2. *Passports and Custom-houses.* — 3. *Routes.* — 4. *Modes and Expenses of Travelling.* — 5. *Couriers.* — 6. *Sight-seeing; Laquais de Place and Ciceroni.* — 7. *Money.* — 8. *Inns and Accommodations.* — 9. *Books.* — 10. *Maps of Italy.* — 11. *Objects to be noticed.* — 12. *Music.* — 13. *Skeleton Tours.* — *Tables of Foreign Coins reduced into the different Currencies of Italy.*

1.—PLAN OF THE WORK.

THE new edition of this Handbook has been revised with a view of making it a guide to the most remarkable places of Northern Italy, and drawing the attention of the traveller to the objects best worthy of being noticed. Reflections not contributing to this end have been excluded: those who desire remarks upon Italy can find books containing them in plenty, from Forsyth down to the latest modern tourist. Of the objects here pointed out to the traveller, most have long been thought worthy of inspection and admiration; some, however, have not, but have risen into notice through a periodical fluctuation of taste and opinions. These latter are inserted, because some travellers will wish to see them, and others ought, in order that they may judge for themselves, and avoid being imposed upon.

The compiler of a Handbook is happily relieved, by the necessity of being useful, from the pursuit of that originality of a tourist which consists in omitting to notice great works because they have been noticed by others, and in crying up some object which has hitherto been deservedly passed over. It would, moreover, be out of place for the editor of a Guidebook of Italy to be ambitious of composing an original work. Italy has been so long studied, that all its most interesting sites and works have been repeatedly and carefully described; and so much has been written, and by persons of ability and acquirements, that the most difficult task is that of compiling and of selecting materials.

Although the Editor has had the benefit of repeated personal examination, he has not scrupled to use freely the numerous works which treat upon the subject. As it is scarcely possible, in the compass of a Handbook, where space is so valuable, to indicate where passages have been extracted from, the following works are here mentioned as those which have been chiefly used, in order to protect the Editor from the charge of borrowing without acknowledgment, and that the traveller may, if he wishes, seek in them further information. In architecture, Mr. Gally Knight's work on the Ecclesiastical Architecture of Italy has been referred to in all cases in which the buildings mentioned in this work have been described by him, and his descriptions and observations are frequently given. Passages from Woods' 'Letters from an Architect' have been sometimes inserted, particularly those relating to the architecture of Palladio and Scamozzi at Vicenza and Venice, a subject he seems to have particularly studied. Some of Mr. Gwilt's descriptions of celebrated buildings have been taken from his Encyclopedia of Architecture. For much of the description of the

1.—Plan of the Work.

Certosa of Pavia and the palaces at Mantua, and of some other places, the Editor is indebted to the magnificent volume entitled 'La Certosa de Pavia,' published at Milan, and to the work on 'Fresco Decorations and Stuccoes of Churches and Palaces in Italy during the Fifteenth and Sixteenth Centuries,' by Mr. Lewis Gruner.

As some travellers have a curiosity to be informed respecting the produce and agriculture of Italy, and as such details usually lie in large unreadable books, a short summary of information on these subjects, taken chiefly from the Papers presented to Parliament by the Board of Trade, is inserted.

Considerable assistance has been derived from the Guides produced for the use of the Scienziati Italiani, at their annual meetings. Those of Genoa, Milan, Padua, and Venice are elaborate works, and full of useful and interesting matter: those of Florence, Pisa, and Lucca, being less detailed, are more convenient as guide-books.

A few remarks are inserted on works of art, derived from persons whose opinions are of weight; and, although the remarks may not be assented to by some travellers, at least they are worthy of consideration. Flaxman's Lectures have supplied some remarks on sculpture; and for others the Editor is indebted to artists whose names will be found appended to their remarks.

Although we have endeavoured to apportion the extent of our remarks to the importance of the subjects described, we have considered it useful to place in the hands of our readers more detailed catalogues of the different galleries than appeared in the former editions of the Handbook, in many cases there being no printed catalogue at all (as in those of the Galleries at Verona, Parma, &c.), and in others where these catalogues are hand-lists which the traveller cannot carry away; whilst many may be glad to preserve in their own language a kind of record of the objects they have seen during their artistical peregrinations, without being put to the inconvenience of making unnecessary notes. Ground-plans of all the most remarkable galleries, made by the editor on the spot, have been also added in the present edition.

We have extended our descriptions and explanations of some of the allegorical and Scriptural paintings of the middle ages, as in *Giotto's chapel* at Padua, the *Capella degli Spagnuoli* in Santa Maria Novella at Florence, and the *Campo Santo* at Pisa, in order to enable the traveller to understand the subjects of those interesting compositions. Many incidents are taken from the Apocryphal Gospels, others are allegorical: and the allegories, in many cases, would be quite unintelligible, had not the meaning been preserved by tradition. Unless they are fully understood, the traveller will only obtain a vague and unsatisfactory impression of the forms, without appreciating the mind and genius of the artists.

The historical and literary notices have been rendered as brief as possible. In a subsequent section (9) we have pointed out from what sources our deficiencies may be partly supplied. A few anecdotes and citations have been occasionally introduced, which, by creating an additional interest, may be useful in fixing the scene in the traveller's memory.

2.—Passports and Custom-houses.

Every English traveller proceeding to Italy, or indeed to any part of the continent, before leaving London ought to procure a passport from the

Foreign Office, which costs 2s., *it being the best certificate of his nationality*, and to obtain IN LONDON the visas of the Ministers of all the principal powers through whose territories he intends to pass: a great deal of trouble is thus saved. A Foreign Office passport is most essential for entering the Austrian territories, and is admitted without visa into the kingdom of Northern Italy. The diplomatic agents of Austria never issue an original passport except to their own countrymen, nor can the visa be obtained in England (which ought when possible to be procured) excepting upon the passport of the British Secretary of State. In France, whatever passport you carry, it may be taken from you at the port where you land, in exchange for a provisional one (*passe provisoire*), which costs 2 francs, and forwarded to your place of destination. But the *British Secretary of State's* passport is generally re-delivered to you without a provisional one, on your stating that you do not intend remaining in Paris, and you have thus all your credentials in your own possession. At the same time it should be recollected that this is a matter of courtesy, and can only be solicited as such, and not as a right. If this plan be not adopted before leaving England, a passport can be obtained at Paris, at the British Embassy, taking care to obtain the needful visas of the legations of those states through which you will have to pass; if you intend to embark at Marseilles for Italy, it may be necessary to have the visa of the French Foreign Office, which costs 10 francs, although of late years it has not been insisted upon. These regulations, which, however, are constantly varying, we have noticed under the heads of the principal towns which the traveller is likely to visit. Should the traveller embark at Marseilles, that of the Consul of the State to which he is proceeding will also be required, for which a fee is charged.*

IT SHOULD BE BORNE IN MIND THAT the signature of an Austrian minister or diplomatic agent on the passport is essential before entering THE AUSTRIAN DOMINIONS. It will also be advisable to have inserted in the passport the number of persons composing a family, with the names of the servants, stating whether British subjects or foreigners. The Papal authorities require the visa of their own agents, which may be obtained gratuitously at the mission in Paris, but for which a fee is charged by their consuls at Marseilles and other ports. The Government of North Italy has abolished the necessity of all visas to passports issued by the British Secretary of State.

With respect to *Custom-houses*:—When travellers arrive by a public conveyance, it is in most places usual to have all the luggage opened, and, if any cause for suspicion arises, carefully searched. But, in the case of persons travelling either by vetturino or posting, the conduct of the officers is usually different. They do make a distinction; and if you give them an assurance that there is no prohibited article or book in the luggage, —and a fee,—the examination will probably be dispensed with: you proffer the keys, and a few of the trunks are opened and closed again. Should any object appear out of the common way, it is possible that the officer may ask an explanation, but merely out of curiosity.

---

* Passports are issued daily at the Foreign Office, on the recommendation of any banking firm or constituted authority addressed to the Secretary of State. In order to save the traveller trouble, agencies have been established for procuring the several visas and the passport itself on transmitting to them the recommendation above alluded to, and for a trifling remuneration. Amongst those agents Messrs. Lee, 440, West Strand, and Messrs. Dorrell & Son, 15, Charing Cross, can be recommended as careful and trustworthy.

As to administering fees, however, to custom-house officers, it is difficult to lay down any positive rules. The Austrian and Sardinian officers would consider it an insult to be offered money; they are in general civil, but sometimes rather troublesome in their search for books, newspapers, arms, &c.

3.—ROUTES.

In the Handbooks of France, Switzerland, Savoy, and Southern Germany, most of the Routes leading into Italy have been described. Of late years the means of travelling over them have been materially facilitated, both as regards time and expence, by the extension of railways; most can now be travelled by railroad and by steamers, so that, even for a family, that once indispensable comfort for an English party, a travelling carriage, will now prove an almost useless and expensive incumbrance.

The following embrace all the Routes by which the traveller can now approach Italy; the principal Stations have been inserted, with the time employed *on the road*, whether by rail, coach, posting, or steamer. From this list the traveller will be able to select his own Itinerary—the expense of each will of course depend on the number of miles gone over, and which will be in proportion nearly to the times stated opposite each of the principal stations. Our calculations are made on the supposition that the traveller uses the quickest or express trains. On an average the expenditure for living at hotels may be estimated at 13 or 14 francs (10*s.* 6*d.* or 11*s.* 3*d.*) per diem for one person.

ROUTE 1.—*London, by Paris, Mont Cenis, to Turin.*

	Hours.
London to Paris, by Dover or Folkestone	11
Paris to St. Jean de Maurienne (Rail)	17
St. Jean de M. to Susa (Coach or Post) over the Mont Cenis pass	14
Susa to Turin (Rail)	1½
	43½

Or, including detention at St. Jean de Maurienne and Susa 46 hrs.

The most expeditious of all the highways into Italy. From Turin Genoa can be reached in 4 hrs., Milan in 3½, Venice in 15, Bologna in 9, and Florence in 25.

ROUTE 2.—*By Paris, Geneva, the Simplon, and Lago Maggiore.*

London to Paris (Rail and Steam)	11
Paris to Geneva (Rail)	15
Bouveret & Martigny (Steam or Rail)	3
Sion (Rail)	2½
Arona (Coach or Post)	18
Milan (Rail)	2¼
	52

ROUTE 3.—*London to Milan, by Ostend, Cologne, Basle, Lucerne, the St. Gothard, and Lago Maggiore.*

	Hours.
London to Cologne, by Ostend (Rail and Steam)	13
Basle (Rail)	13½
Lucerne (Rail)	3
Fluellen (Steam)	3
Locarno or Magadino (Coach or Post)	17
Arona (Steam)	4½
Milan (Rail)	2½
	56½

ROUTE 4.—*London to Milan, by Paris, Basle, Lucerne, the St. Gothard, &c.*

London to Paris	11
Paris to Basle direct (Rail)	13½
Basle to Milan, as by Rte. 3	30
	54½

ROUTE 5.—*London to Milan*, by Paris, Basle, Zurich, the Splugen, and Lake of Como.

	Hours.
London to Basle, as in Rte. 4 ..	24½
Zurich (Rail)	3½
Rappenschwyl (Steam)	1½
Coire (Rail)	3½
Splugen to Colico (Coach & Post)	16
Como (Steam)	3½
Milan (Rail)	1½
	64

Or, by Belinzona, Lago Maggiore, &c.

To Coire, by last Route	33
Belinzona (Coach)	14
Arona (Diligence and Steam)	6
Milan	2½
	55½

ROUTE 6.—*London to Verona*, by Ostend, Cologne, Munich, Inspruck, and the Brenner Pass.

London to Cologne, by Ostend (Rail and Steam)	13
Munich (Rail)	15½
Inspruck (Rail)	3½
Botzen (Coach)	18
Verona (Rail)	5½
	55½

ROUTE 7.—*London to Verona*, by Paris, Munich, through Strasbourg, Stuttgard, Augsbourg, Inspruck, and the Brenner.

London to Paris (Rail)	11
Munich (Rail)	24¾
Inspruck (Rail)	3¼
Botzen (Coach and Post)	18
Verona (Rail)	5½
	63

ROUTE 8.—*London to Trieste and Venice*, by Ostend, Cologne, Berlin, Dresden, Vienna, Laibach.

London to Cologne (Rail and Steam)	13
Berlin (Rail)	14½
Dresden (Rail)	5½
Vienna (Rail)	19½
Trieste (Rail)	22½
	74

	Hours.
From Trieste to Venice by steam.	6
Or, by Coach and Rail	10
Shortest time to Venice by Vienna	80
By Turin (Rte. 1)	61

ROUTE 9.—*London to Trieste and Venice*, by Paris, Munich, Vienna, and Laibach.

London to Munich, as in Rte. 7	35¾
Saltzburg .. .. } Rail.	
Linz .. .. }	15
Vienna .. .. }	
Trieste	22½
	73¼
To Venice	79¼

ROUTE 10.—*London to Nice*, by Paris, Marseilles, and Toulon.

London to Paris (Rail and Steam)	11
Marseilles (Rail)	19½
Toulon (Rail)	2
Nice (Coach or Post)	20
	52½

Or, from Toulon to Nice by Vetturino in 2½ days.

ROUTE 11.—*London to Florence*, by Paris, Marseilles, and Leghorn.

London to Marseilles, as in Rte. 10	30½
Leghorn (Steam)	44
Florence (Rail)	3
	77½

ROUTE 12.—*London to Florence*, by Turin, Bologna, Pietramala.

London to Turin (Rail and Coach)	46
Bologna (Rail)	9
Florence (Coach)	16
	71

ROUTE 13.—*London to Florence*, by Turin and Genoa.

London to Turin (Rail & Coach)	46
Genoa (Rail)	4
Leghorn (Steam)	8
Florence	3
	61

ROUTE 14.—*London to Rome, by Marseilles and Civita Vecchia.*

	Hours.
London to Marseilles	30½
Marseilles to Civita Vecchia	30
Rome	2¼
	63¾

Or, in 86 hrs., including stopping a day in Paris, and 6 hrs. at Marseilles.

Shortest Routes to different towns in Italy—from Paris—in time absolutely employed in travelling.

	Hours.
To Turin	35½
Genoa	39½
Milan	38½
Venice	50½
Bologna	45½
Florence	61
Rome	62

4.—MODES OF TRAVELLING—EXPENSES.

The posting in Italy is inferior to that of France. The horses often look half starved, and are wretchedly used, but on the whole one gets on with reasonable expedition. The postmasters frequently attempt various petty acts of imposition, which they seldom practise in the North Italy States, where the custom of issuing the *Bolletone* (a printed bill, which contains your route, length of posts, and the posting regulations) prevents all disputes, and is, in fact, the *Livre des Postes.* For the Austrian dominions there are official post-sheets, which will be delivered upon application at the offices at Verona and Venice. Although the extension of railways renders every day the study of these rules less necessary, we have given an abstract of them under the head of Venetia, Sect. IV., sufficient for the wants of the traveller, and in the introductory information at the head of each section of the Handbook.

Vetturini.—From the same cause fewer families find it now necessary to encumber themselves with their own carriages, and have recourse to those of vetturini, which, as to neatness and comfort, are improved, although their charges have risen in proportion. In making an agreement it is the custom for the vetturino to give his employer a deposit, *caparra,* or handsel, a small sum as a security for the due performance of his contract; and, whether the journey be shorter or longer, this precaution should *never* be neglected. There are three varieties in this mode of travelling:—1st, Taking a seat in a carriage jointly with other parties. These are usually people of the country; and it is a mode of journeying which can only suit a single male traveller, and even he must be one who is not very particular as to comforts. You must of course take your meals entirely at the discretion of the driver, who contracts to furnish you with board and lodging: your companions are frequently disagreeable; and none of the regulations which prevent annoyance in a diligence apply to these private vehicles. 2nd, Hiring a carriage for a party,—a very convenient mode of travelling for those who are not much pressed for time. A party of six persons may be conveyed in a very decent carriage, with good horses, and an intelligent and civil driver, at an expense of about 50 francs per diem, going from 30 to 40 miles; and if you get a return carriage (which at Nice, Turin, or Milan one sometimes can) for a little less. When a carriage is thus hired, the vetturino will, if required, contract to provide board and lodging. In Tuscany and the Roman states this answers very well. In other parts it is neither needful nor advisable, and you should stipulate that you are to go to what houses you please. Also *always* sign an agreement in writing expressing the hire, the time within which the vetturino is to perform the journey, the stay he is to make at each place, and the daily indemnity to which he will be entitled in case of detention on the part of the traveller, and make the vetturino sign the duplicate. Two forms of such documents, with directions for filling them up, will be found in Murray's 'Handbook of Travel Talk'—one for a traveller who engages a single place, the other for a party contracting for the hire of a whole carriage. If the driver gives you satisfaction, he expects a *buona mano*, about 3 or 4 francs per diem. The 3rd mode is for one or two individuals to hire a *calessa* or other small and light carriage, generally for short distances, and for not more than a day or two. This is often very convenient in making out *pieces* of a journey, particularly for the purpose of seeing places where the diligence does not stop, but it is liable to some inconvenience. The vetturini who do these jobs are usually of an inferior class, and will often attempt to play tricks upon the traveller, sometimes refusing to go as far as the intended point, sometimes transferring him to another vetturino, and generally contriving, with much ingenuity, to find a pretext for placing some other companion in the vacant seat beside you.

Diligences.—The number of these conveyances has very much diminished in consequence of the extension of railways. The most important now are :—From St. Jean de Maurienne, where the Victor Emanuel Railway ends for the present, to Susa over the Mont Cenis ; between Turin and Nice, or rather from the railway at Cuneo, crossing the Col di Tenda ; from Toulon to Nice, and from thence to Genoa, along the Riviera di Ponente ; from Genoa to Lucca and Pisa, along the Riviera di Levante ; from Milan to Lodi and Cremona ; from Brescia to Cremona ; from Como to Lecco and Bergamo ; from Parma to Sarzana across the Cisa Pass ; from Bologna to Florence, by the passes of the Collina, and Covigliajo ; and from Bologna to Ferrara, in correspondence with another from Ferrara to Rovigo and Padua. There are regular conveyances from almost all the larger towns to the localities in the vicinity. Such are the so-called diligences from Milan to Pavia, Bergamo to the Val Brembana, Brescia to the Val Camonica and Lake of Iseo, Vicenza to Scio and Bassano, Treviso to Belluno, Mantua to Este, Bologna to Ravenna, Forli to Florence, &c.

Railways.—Numerous *railroads* have been opened of late years in Northern Italy; indeed this country now is little behind other states of the Continent as regards railway communication. A short line from Milan to Monza and Como (28 English miles). The great line from Milan to Venice, through Bergamo, Brescia, Verona, Vicenza, and Padua, to Venice, with branch-lines from Mestre to Trieste and Vienna, by Treviso, Pordenone, and Udine; from Verona to Mantua; and from Verona to Bolzano (Botzen) in the Tyrol by Roveredo and Trento. The railway from Turin to Genoa (102 English miles) passes by Asti, Alessandria, and Novi, and, piercing the central ridge of the Apennines by the great tunnel of Busalla, performs the whole distance from Turin in 4 hours. The prolongation of the railway from Alessandria to Piacenza, Parma, Modena, and Bologna is also open, and ere long will be extended to Rimini. The line from Alessandria to Arona, on the Lago Maggiore, crossing the Po at Valenza, from the main Turin and Genoa trunk, is in activity, and, when prolonged into Switzerland as is proposed, will secure to Genoa a great part of the trade of that country, to the detriment of Marseilles. The line from Turin to Cuneo is also open, as well as those from Turin to Susa and Pinerolo. The railway from Turin to Vercelli, Novara, and Milan, with branches to Ivrea and Biella on one side, and from Vercelli to Casale, Valenza, and Alessandria, afford, with the branch to Arona, the quickest means of reaching the Lago Maggiore and the eastern parts of Switzerland. A short line has been opened between Genoa and Voltri along the Riviera di Ponente; and lines are projected from Nice to Genoa, and from the latter to the Tuscan frontier; from Milan to Pavia; from Pavia to Valenza; from Monza to Bergamo; from Treviglio to Cremona; and from Faenza or Forli to Ravenna.

In Tuscany the Leopolda railroad between Leghorn and Florence is completed (3 hours), and from Empoli to Sienna:—by means of the latter the journey from Leghorn to Sienna may be performed in 4, and to Rome in 30 hours—and from Sienna to Asinalunga and the Val di Chiana. Another line (the Maria Antonia) from Florence to Lucca, passing by Prato and Pistoia, is also in operation. The branch of the Centro-Italian railway which is to connect Bologna and the valley of the Po with Tuscany, is now in progress, and will join the Maria Antonia line at Pistoia; when completed there will be an unbroken railway communication between Turin, Milan, Venice, and Florence. Lines are in progress or projected from Florence to Arezzo; from Asinalunga to Arezzo and Chiusi; and a great artery to extend parallel to the sea-coast from Leghorn to Civita Vecchia, with a branch to Volterra.

Expenses of Travelling in Italy.—No question is more frequently asked, and few so difficult to answer, as that relative to the expenditure to be incurred in a journey through, or an excursion into, Italy. Now that people of all classes are obliged to adopt the same means of locomotion, railways, a nearer approximation can be reached. This will, however, depend on the length of ground gone over in a given time. For bachelors, who travel for the purpose of seeing the country, whose railway expenses each day will consequently be inconsiderable, we should say that 20 francs ought to cover all expenses. On this subject we cannot convey more practical information than what has been transmitted to us by one of our correspondents, respecting the outlay for himself and party during an autumnal tour last year.

"Three gentlemen spent five weeks in Italy in the months of August and September. They started from Paris, went across the Mont Cenis through Turin and Genoa (staying at each place two nights); by Spezzia to Pisa, to Florence (stayed four nights); to Bologna (stayed two nights), Mantua, Venice (stayed five nights), Padua, Verona, Milan (two nights); crossed the St. Gothard, Lucerne (two nights), Basle, Vesone, and Paris; and the total expenses averaged 23 francs per day for each person. They travelled by rail, first and second class, by vettura, and by diligence; and went to the best inns, and generally had a bottle of wine, beside the *vin ordinaire* at dinner. The travelling expenses amounted to 913 francs; the living expenses to 1225 francs; and the sundries, sights, visâs of passports to 95 francs. The distance travelled exceeded 2000 miles."—(*H. C.*)

5.—COURIERS.

Couriers are almost an indispensable incumbrance to families, and to bachelors even, when ignorant of the language. In another of these Handbooks (N. Germany) we have entered into some detail on the uses of such servants, and on their necessary qualifications. As regards Italy, the best are certainly those born in the country; and we should strongly insist on a courier, to accompany a family into Italy, being an Italian. The Italian courier is in general active, ready to do or attend to any and every thing, good-humoured, and devoted to his employer; he will serve if required as a personal servant, and, understanding the language, will not refuse to act as guide in the large towns—a thing rarely to be obtained of a German or a Swiss; besides, at the present moment there is such a prejudice against everything German in Italy, that inconveniences might arise from being accompanied by a servant of that country.

As to honesty, they are all ready to take advantage of their masters. In addition to receiving very high wages, 10 guineas a month, they are lodged and fed at his expence in reality, *i. e.* the masters of hotels are obliged to lodge and feed them, and, as a general rule, they are more difficult to satisfy in their requirements than their employers.

6.—SIGHT-SEEING—LAQUAIS DE PLACE AND CICERONI.

There are few things more disagreeable than being led about by a *laquais de place;* and as good plans of all the principal towns of Northern Italy are given in the present volume, his help will be by no means indispensable; although, for persons ignorant of the language, his services may be useful, and in all cases lead to a saving of time, which to most travellers will be a saving in money.

If you do take a laquais de place—1st, Make him conduct you to every place *you* wish to see, not allowing yourself to be put off with, "*non c'è niente da vedere;*" or the like; for he has no notion of the value of any object; and caprice, or some plan of his own, or mere laziness, will often make him try to put you off. 2nd, If you have plenty of time on your hands, it is as well to go and see every object which *he* recommends, unless it should be evidently something quite absurd. For though in so doing he may have a job in view—some shop kept by a friend into which he wishes to seduce you, some ally of a custode, for whom he wants to secure a *buona mano*, and thus usually occasions you a waste of time and money—yet he is sometimes the means of conducting you to an object which you would have been sorry to have lost. A laquais de place should never be allowed to make bargains for you, as the commission which the shopkeeper allows him will be of course added to what you pay.

The churches, excepting some of the cathedrals, are, upon week-days, usually closed from twelve to three; and during this interval, when the sacristan takes his dinner and his nap, it is hardly possible to obtain admittance; and, when open, there is frequently quite as much difficulty in finding any one who can or will conduct you. Your guide is usually one of the lowest grade of attendants. The fact is, that the clergy do not like to have the churches considered as shows, nor are the congregations at all indifferent, as has been asserted, to the conduct of strangers, in walking about and talking during Divine service. It might perhaps too be suggested to our Protestant countrymen, that they are not protesting against Roman Catholic errors by behaving indecorously in churches; and to reflect how they would like to see their own places of worship made objects of show during Divine service.

In order to enable the tourist to dispense as much as possible with local guides, we have inserted in the description of every town of importance a list of the objects worth seeing, arranged in topographical order, by means of which, and the plans annexed, persons not pressed for time can visit, unaided by a laquais de place, the principal sights.

It is always a most useful preliminary to the examination of any city to obtain a bird's-eye view from some tall steeple or tower.

7.—MONEY.

The traveller will find it to his advantage in Italy, even more than elsewhere, *always to make his payments in the current coin of the country in which he is travelling*. If he does otherwise, and pays in French francs for example, he will not only pay rather more, but he will be more liable to trouble and annoyance from attempts at imposition, because those with whom he has to deal, perceiving his ignorance of the money in which their transactions should be reckoned, will draw their conclusion that he is equally ignorant as to the amount to which they are fairly entitled. Of all foreign money, French gold Napoleons are the best to carry, as they pass current everywhere, and in many towns their value in the currency of the place is fixed by the authorities.. The traveller going to Italy through France would do well to take as many with him as he conveniently can, for, when cashing his letters of credit, he will have to pay an increasingly high premium for gold the further he advances on his journey. He should get rid of his English sovereigns at Paris, Geneva, or Marseilles, where he will generally obtain 25 fr. for them. French money is current through all parts of the Sardinian territory, as the Austrian, the Zwanziger (*beware of taking Austrian paper into Italy*), is in Modena, the Papal States, and Tuscany. A very objectionable system has been adopted by several of the innkeepers in the larger towns, Padua, Venice, &c., of making out their bills in French money, as the difference between it and the current Austrian coin is nearly 12 per cent. to the loss of the traveller.

The French Napoleon, and its fractional parts, is now the current coin throughout all Northern Italy, except Venetia, where it is almost equally so, although florins, zwanzigers, &c., are the official currency. In the ancient provinces of Sardinia francs and Napoleons, with the old Savoy lire, equal to 40 centimes, are alone current. In Lombardy the Austrian currency still exists to a considerable degree, as it does in Parma and Modena. In the Romagna the Papal currency of pauls and scudi is also current, but in Venetia Austrian money is the most abundant.

In proceeding to Northern Italy, if the traveller should not have taken bills of exchange, circular notes, or a letter of credit, the best money he can carry with him will be French gold Napoleons.

8.—INNS AND ACCOMMODATIONS.

In the large towns of Italy the hotels are vastly superior to those in French provincial cities, being comfortable and well kept, as at Turin, Milan, Verona, Venice, Genoa, Pisa, the Bagni di Lucca, Leghorn, and Florence. In all these places the resort of foreigners has enabled the proprietors to meet the expenses required for such establishments; but this, of course, cannot be the case in places which are not equally frequented, and here the traveller will very frequently have to content himself with the accommodation of a national or *Italian* inn.

He must, firstly, when this contingency arrives, not expect a choice and well-furnished larder. The stock of provisions is on the average but scanty, and the choice in this scanty stock limited. Most of the country wines are indifferent, poor, and sour, especially of late years, since the vine-disease has nearly destroyed the plant. Even in towns where the houses are very decent, he may be compelled to submit to meagre fare, if he arrives after others have been served. It must always be recollected also, that every chance of inconvenience is exceedingly increased by coming in late :—" *Chi tardi arriva mal' alloggia,*" as the proverb truly says. Even in the smaller towns, however, the hotels have been much improved of late years, and are fully on a par with those of France similarly situated.

Another source of annoyance, namely, the demand made upon your purse at inns, is sometimes more particularly vexatious in Italy, in consequence of the exactions being so often accompanied either by such good humour or such appeals to your generosity, almost to your charity, as to be more difficult to parry than downright rudeness or extortion. The best hotels, though not cheap, are not (compared with an English standard) extravagant, and, if any ladies are of the party, no house except a first-rate one should be used; but bachelor travellers may frequently be quite comfortably accommodated, and at a lower charge, at houses of a second grade. One great secret of keeping down bills is to avoid having anything out of the common way. The *table-d'hôte* (*tavola rotonda*), where it exists (for it is not common in Italy, except in large towns), should be preferred.

Ask the price of everything beforehand, and never scruple to bargain. This is an unpleasant operation to our English tastes, but it is the custom of the country: no offence is taken, or even suspected, and you are only considered an inexperienced traveller if you do not. Amongst other reasons, innkeepers always suppose that every Englishman likes to have the best of everything, especially at dinner: and therefore, even where no overcharge is practised, you are often put to needless expense by having more, and greater variety, than you desire or care for; thus, by explaining the number of dishes you want, you bring them within bounds. In ordering wines, when you have chosen your *kind,* order the cheapest *quality,* for in small towns the chance is ten to one that they have no other, and you only pay for the name. If exorbitant charges be made, the best plan, if you have nerve enough, is to refuse to pay them putting down a reasonable sum upon the table. Where expostulations have proved ineffectual, travellers not unfrequently enter cautions against the offending party in the travellers' books at other inns along the road, so as to warn others, and sometimes communicate their complaints to the Editor of these Handbooks, requesting him to endeavour to redress the grievance by noting the offence in future editions. *Where the complaint has been properly attested, and the case shows very palpable injustice on the part of the innkeeper, we have agreed, in some instances, to place a note against the name of the house, or to omit it altogether.* Travellers, however, who resort to this expedient, ought to consider beforehand whether they are quite in the right, and the innkeeper in the wrong; weighing well, that a hasty accusation may inflict serious injury on an honest man and his family. The simple threat of making such a complaint may, in some cases, infuse a salutary terror, so as to produce the desired effect—a remedy of the abuse.

The *buona-mano* to servants and waiters is a source of constant trouble; to those who travel with couriers advice is needless: to those who must decide for themselves what to give, the following suggestions are offered. The best plan is to give (in the presence of some other servant) a sum to the head-waiter to be distributed. In the principal towns, for a single day, for one person, a franc, a zwanziger, and 2 pauls are sufficient. If the traveller has to distribute his *buona-mano* among the servants, he can hardly give less than 1 franc, or 2 pauls, to the waiter, and about ¼ franc to the *facchino*, who brushes clothes, &c. Of course the rate of payment is proportionally reduced when the traveller's stay is prolonged, or where several persons are travelling in the same party; and in small country inns about two-thirds of the above is quite enough. After a certain stay, the chambermaid, too, receives a gratuity. The excellent system of charging the gratuity to servants in the bill is become very general in Italy, *and ought to be encouraged by travellers.* When dining at a Trattoria, 25 cts., or 3 crazie, are enough for the waiter.

" Ladies should be aware that they may always be attended by a female in the Italian inns, by expressing a wish to this effect. At the best inns, in some of the great towns, a female attends regularly to the arrangements of the bedrooms."—*Mrs. M.*

9.—Books.

A traveller whose mind is not previously prepared for a visit to Italy is deprived of the greatest portion of the pleasure (to say nothing of the instruction) which he would otherwise derive. This observation is true of every part of the world; but the extent and variety of interest attaching to the scenery, the cities, the churches, the castles, the palaces, the works of art in Italy, renders the amount of loss much heavier than in any other country; we shall therefore venture to give a short list of the works which we would recommend, for the purpose of affording a small portion of the information which may be required.

History.—To those who are willing to devote the time we should strongly recommend the attentive perusal of Sismondi's great work, *Histoire des Républiques Italiennes.* As a narrator, Sismondi has peculiar clearness: without attempting effect, he is always interesting. The great difficulty in affording a general view of Italian history arises from the necessity which the historian is under of constantly shifting the scene, from Florence to Venice, from Naples to Milan, &c. &c. Sismondi, with singular ability, has interwoven the history of the several states without perplexing the narrative. There is hardly a place of any importance in Italy which is not more or less noticed in this work, which contains the very pith of Italian history in more modern times.

For the history of particular states, the following may be noticed:—

Venice.—*Daru's* history is very entertaining and clear, but must be read with caution, for it was written with the feeling of placing the extinct republic in an unfavourable light, and thus justifying the faithless conduct of Napoleon in subverting it, and delivering it over to Austria.

Tuscany,—*Pignotti.*—No depth of thought, and by no means impartial, but perhaps the best as regards the Grand Ducal period. *Machiavelli* should be read, but he is rather a difficult writer. *Reppetti's* geographical dictionary of Tuscany is a model of such works, and contains almost everything the traveller can wish to know on the different localities; and the *Osservatore Fiorentino* is a very entertaining historical guide for Florence. The Chronological Tables of Tuscan History, by *M. de Reumont* (published at Florence), will be found most useful, as they are an invaluable manual to modern Italian chronology.

Milan.—*Verri's* history is the best of his native city; the style is elegant as to language, the remarks philosophical, and the narrative impartial.

Fine Arts.—The work of Vasari is both entertaining and full of valuable information, not to be obtained elsewhere; and the book, heretofore so unreadable, has been reprinted in an economical and portable form by Lemonnier of Florence, 1850-53. This edition is by far the most useful hitherto published, each Life being accompanied by copious notes, pointing out, amongst other things, where the different works of art mentioned by Vasari are now to be found.*

" The plan of the book was suggested in a familiar conversation which took place at Naples, somewhile in the year 1544, at a supper in the house of the Cardinal Farnese. Amongst the company was Paolo Giovio, who had then composed his well-known work, the 'Vitæ Illustrium Virorum.' The book does not appear to have been published, but it had probably been circulated in manuscript, as was then much the custom in the literary world. Giovio wished to append a biography of artists from the time of Cimabue, upon whose productions, as Vasari says, he began to discourse with judgment and knowledge of art, making, however, terrible mistakes with respect to the artists themselves, confounding names, surnames, birth-places, and specimens. In reply to a question put by the Cardinal, Vasari replied that such a biography would be very instructive, if compiled with accuracy; and the company, amongst whom was Annibal Caro, joined in urging him to undertake the task of giving a better outline to Giovio. This he did. And he performed his task so satisfactorily, that, when the sketch was presented to Giovio, the latter declined using it, and advised Vasari to complete the book for himself.

" Vasari, ever since his youth, had been collecting materials for such a work, yet the instinct of authorship was not strong upon him. He hesitated—asked advice—a rare thing in authors—and what is still more rare, he took it; and his advisers were sound—Annibal Caro, Molza, Tolomei ; and he worked diligently, until, being urged by Cosmo to bring it out, the first edition was printed at the grand-ducal press, and under the special auspices of his patron. In this first edition he inserted no Life of any contemporary, excepting that of Michael Angelo, who received the presentation

---

* An English translation of Vasari, by Mr. I. Forster, in a cheap and portable form, has been published by Bohn in 1851, but it only contains the original text. We may take the opportunity here of recommending to our Italian readers the collection of Classical Works published by Lemonnier at Florence: great pains have been taken in editing each work—the most approved texts have been adopted, and the publication superintended by very eminent literary characters in their different departments; in addition to which the works are printed in a clear type, and in a portable (12mo.) form: the collection embraces Dante, Petrarch, Tasso, Ariosto, Guarini amongst the poets; Machiavelli, Verri, Amari, Colletta, Farini, Gualterio amongst the Historians; Vasari, Cellini, Balbo of the Biographers; and most of the recent authors on Historical Romance who have cast so much splendour on the Italian literature of the 19th century—Manzoni, Grossi, Rossini, Azeglio, Guerrazzi, &c. &c.

copy with great pleasure, testifying his gratitude by a sonnet, a thing, like most complimentary poems, a column of fine words, containing an infinitesimal quantity of meaning. Still the sonnet was a high token of approbation, and it increased the intimacy subsisting between them; and this friendship enabled Vasari to profit the more by the verbal information received from Michael Angelo, as well as by his correspondence. Other valuable materials Vasari obtained from the manuscripts of Ghirlandajo, Ghiberti, Rafael d'Urbino, and many more who are not named. It was the custom in Florence for the heads of families to keep a book of remembrances—'ricordi,' as they were termed—of the events happening to themselves, their children, and kindred; and from these memorials he gleaned abundantly. Vasari was also well versed in the general and particular history of Tuscany and the adjoining states; but besides these sources, all the traditions of art were yet rife and lively, and much information of the greatest importance had been handed down from mouth to mouth. The chain of tradition, if once broken, can never be replaced. Interesting as such traditions of art may be in relation to the personal anecdotes they preserve, they were perhaps even more important with respect to the knowledge which they imparted of the mechanical proceedings employed by the artists, the identification of the portraits introduced in historical subjects, and the meaning of allegorical compositions, without which many would have remained unintelligible mysteries—enigmas to be gazed at, and nothing more—like hieroglyphics of which the key is lost. For example, the great fresco of Simon Memmi in the ancient chapterhouse of Santa Maria Novella, representing the Church Militant, in which the portraits of Petrarch and Laura are introduced, would, without this aid, be completely inexplicable."—*Quart. Review,* vol. lxvi. art. 1.

Vasari is, however, unmethodical, and much prejudiced in favour of the Tuscan school: dates are frequently wanting or given incorrectly, and his works need a continuation through subsequent periods. Those who require a succinct compendium of the history of Italian painting will find what they need in Kugler's *Handbook of Painting,* edited by Sir Charles Eastlake, P.R.A., with numerous and well-executed illustrations of the most celebrated paintings referred to in it.

Lanzi gives more ample particulars, and is especially useful in the manner in which the different schools are grouped together by him, and an edition has been published in small and portable volumes; but his more methodical work does not possess the charm or interest of Vasari's biographies.

As a portable compendium on Italian painters the traveller will find no work in a small space so useful as the *Biographical Catalogue of Italian Painters,* by Miss Farquhar (1 vol. 12mo., Murray, 1855): indeed it may be considered as a necessary companion or supplement to the Handbooks of Italy; except in rare cases the artist even will find in it all the biographical details necessary for his purpose, with indications of the principal works of each painter, and a very clear view of the connexion of the different schools with each other.

The publications of the *Arundel Society* ought to be in the possession of every lover of Italian art. The execution of the drawings, and coloured copies of paintings of the great masters, make them acceptable to all, and their marvellously low price places them within the means of most travellers.

Ticozzi's Dictionary of Painters, in 2 vols., will be found useful.

A very interesting work on the *History of Painting* (*Storia della Pittura*), on the same plan as that of Cicognara on *Sculpture*, was published by the late Professor *Rossini* of Pisa; the portion that has already appeared, embracing the earlier artists who preceded Perugino, is very interesting, and accompanied by well-executed outline engravings of some characteristic works of each master.

In Italy each great school has had its historian; and there is scarcely an artist of note who has not had his separate biographer, who may be usefully consulted by the traveller. The Italian translation of *Quatremère de Quincy's* Life of Raphael, by Longhena, is valuable, from the annotations of the translator.

Those who read German will derive much information from *Rumohr's Italienische Forschungen*, which contain a great deal of curious matter respecting early Tuscan art; and Passavant's *Life of Raphael*. Muller's *Archäologie der Kunst* is also a good guide for the works of art generally.

Cicognara is the principal authority on Italian sculpture; there is no other general one that can be recommended. It is bulky, expensive, and incomplete: we notice it merely as a book to be consulted.

Literature.—*Ginguené* is an interesting, though not always a faithful guide; but perhaps, for the general reader, none better can be found.

The reputation acquired by Roscoe's *Lorenzo de' Medici* was, in some degree, owing to the novelty of the subject. But Roscoe is always elegant, and, so far as literary history is concerned, fairly correct. The Italian edition of Roscoe's *Leo X.* is valuable from the notes appended to it by Ticozzi.

Manzoni's Novel, The Promessi Sposi, will add much interest to the scenery of Milan and its vicinity.

Dante's Divina Commedia, the small edition with notes by Costa and Bianchi, Florence, published by Lemonnier at Florence, will be found the most convenient.

10.—MAPS OF ITALY.

General.—The best general Maps of Italy are those of Cerri and Orgiazzi, but they are both incorrect in the topographical details. The same observation applies to nearly all the Maps of Italy published in England, Germany, and France. We have endeavoured to render those annexed to the Handbooks as accurate as possible, and from the latest surveys.

General Collegno published some years since, at Paris, a useful Geological Map of Italy, founded on all that was then known; recent discoveries, and particularly the labours of our countryman Sir R. Murchison, call for a new edition of it.

Piedmont and Sardinia.—The Sardinian Government has published a very beautiful Map of its Continental States, in 6 sheets, founded on a trigonometrical survey; and a reduction of the same in 1 sheet, which will answer every object of most travellers: it is also now issuing a detailed Map of its Continental territories on a scale of $\frac{1}{50000}$; and Professor Sismonda is about to give a Geological Map of the same kingdom, based upon the topographical ones above referred to.

General Alberto de la Marmora has published a magnificent Map of the Island of Sardinia, in two large sheets, which reflects the highest credit on the talents, patriotism, and liberality of that nobleman, who has been for several years engaged on it, and completed the whole of the surveys, almost at his own expense.

Venetian-Lombardy.—The Austrian Government has published a very detailed and beautiful Map of the Lombardo-Venetian Kingdom in 80 sheets, on a scale of $\frac{1}{86400}$, and a reduction of it in 4 on that of $\frac{1}{288000}$; the latter contains everything necessary for the ordinary traveller, like all the Maps published by the Imperial Corps of Geographical Engineers at Vienna; they may be procured at Artaria's, Via di St. Margarita, Milan.

Parma and Piacenza, Modena.—Very accurate Maps of these duchies, on a similar scale to that of the great Map of the Lombardo-Venetian kingdom, have been also published by the Austrian Government.

Tuscany.—The Austrian Government has completed the publication, on a scale of $\frac{1}{86400}$, of its surveys of Central Italy. The Map of Tuscany by the late Padre Inghirami, in 4 sheets, is very good, and, before the Austrian Survey, was by far the best: it is sometimes erroneous in its topographical details; but when it is considered that it was the work of a single individual, who, almost unaided by his Government, not only made a trigonometrical survey of the country, but executed the topographical drawing, the highest praise is to be given to its reverend author, one of a family whose members have been long known for their learning, and their services to Italian literature and science. A very useful reduction in one sheet of Inghirami's Map has been published at Florence by *Segato.*

Signor Zuccagni Orlandini published some years since an Atlas of Tuscany, divided into valleys, a convenient arrangement enough, with very useful statistical details at the time respecting each valley; the Map or topographical part is copied from Inghirami.

As to Zuccagni's voluminous and expensive work on the Geography of Italy (*Corografia dell' Italia*), the Maps are compiled from more original works, often with little criticism or judgment, and have been rendered obsolete by the more recent Austrian surveys.

The French Dépôt de la Marine has recently completed the survey of the coasts of Italy from the Var to the Bay of Naples, and has published the Charts of Liguria and Tuscany, with detailed plans of their harbours, &c.; they embrace not only the coast-line of the continent, but the islands of the Tuscan Archipelago lying off it—Gorgona, Elba, Giglio, Monte Cristo, Pianosa, and Gianutri.

The traveller will find at Artaria's shop in Milan, and in Turin at Maggi's, most of the Maps of Italy that have been published, save those of Tuscany and Naples, which can rarely be procured out of their respective capitals.

11.—OBJECTS TO BE NOTICED.

Within the districts described in this volume, the supposed Phœnician edifices in Sardinia, and some few Celtic remains in Piedmont and the

Euganean hills, are the only vestiges anterior to the Roman domination.

To the era of the Empire belong the amphitheatre and gates of Verona, the theatre at Vicenza, the villa of Catullus on the Lake of Garda, the arch of Susa, the ruins of Velleja, the columns of San Lorenzo at Milan, the temple at Brescia, and the amphitheatre of Padua. Amongst the edifices of the Roman period, the amphitheatre at Verona is the most remarkable; the arch of Susa is the oldest; the other vestiges belong to the later Emperors; but none are in a very pure style of architecture. The only ones which we can ascribe to the Augustan age (the arch of Susa, and the Trophæa of Augustus at Turbia near Nice) are rude in taste. To the Imperial times belong the buried city of Velleia—the Pompeii of Northern Italy—and the ruins of Industria and of Luni.

Amongst the museums of antiquities, the *Galleria Reale* of Florence stands pre-eminent. Turin, inferior in other departments, has one of the richest collections in Europe of Egyptian antiquities. The museums of Parma, Bologna, and Verona, and particularly of Brescia, are of considerable local importance. The *Campo Santo* of Pisa, though not, strictly speaking, a museum, is a precious depository of ancient art. Of Christian antiquities during Roman times, or of the remoter period of the middle ages, Ravenna stands pre-eminent for its early ecclesiastical edifices; Milan, Verona, and Pisa offer also remarkable vestiges. The Baptisteries of Ravenna, Novara, and Parma, perhaps, also belong to this class, but there is much difficulty about their date.—St. Mark's Church, at Venice, forms a class of its own.

Although frequently much altered, northern Italy abounds in magnificent specimens of the Lombard style, so strangely called *Romanesque*, a variety of which is familiarly known amongst us as Norman. The cathedrals of Verona, Parma, and Modena, and the conventual churches of San Zeno (Verona), San Miniato (Florence), San Michele (Pavia), are peculiarly remarkable. Most of the larger Lombard churches are interesting from the symbolical sculptures on the façades, as well as from their impressive grandeur. This Lombard style was never entirely superseded in Italy till the revival of classical architecture: and, generally speaking, so many schools and styles had a coeval existence in Italy, that the data by which we judge of the age of a building in French or England lose much of their certainty when applied here.

Gothic or *Pointed* architecture in Italy exhibits itself in many marked varieties, and four distinct schools may be observed: (1.) The *Tuscan-Gothic*, remarkable in the earlier periods for its simplicity, and in the latter for the extreme beauty of its forms. (2.) The *Venetian-Gothic*, of which the great type is the Palazzo Ducale at Venice, and which may be traced as far west as Brescia. (3.) The *Genoese-Gothic*, more than any other disclosing an imitation of the Arabian or Saracenic models. (4.) The *Lombard-Gothic*, an exuberant variety of the French and German, and which, in the Duomo of Milan, and Certosa of Pavia, attained transcendent excellence.*

---

* For more detailed information on the different styles of architecture met with in Italy and its monuments, we must refer our readers to Mr. Fergusson's beautiful 'Illustrated Handbook of Architecture' (2 vols. 8vo., 1855); to Mr. Ruskin's 'Stones of Venice,' and Signor Selvatico's work, for the edifices of that city; to Mr. Street's work entitled 'Brick and Marble Architecture in Italy' (1 vol. 8vo., 1855); and for the early Christian edifices to Mr. Gally Knight's large work on the Ecclesiastical Architecture of Italy, and to Canina's 'Tempi Christiani,' 1 vol. fol.

Connected with the Italian churches, the *Campanili*, or bell-towers, often detached, constitute a remarkable feature. Those of Venice and of Florence are familiarly known; the latter has no equal for beauty. The Campanili of Cremona and Modena deserve attention, and in all cases they form a characteristic and pleasing feature in the scenery of Italy. The Circular Bell-towers of Ravenna, probably the most ancient of all, are peculiar to that celebrated city.

So much for the styles which we commonly, though not quite accurately, term mediæval. During their prevalence in Italy an imitation of Roman or classical architecture had never ceased to exist. But it had not been usefully reintroduced till the times of *Brunelleschi* and of *L. B. Alberti*. The churches of San Lorenzo and Santo Spirito at Florence are noble examples of the genius of the first of these great men. He also possessed great influence throughout Italy, though few direct imitations of his style appear out of his native city. Brunelleschi's tendency is to assimilate his Italian to the Lombard. But others united the Italian to somewhat of Gothic feeling, after the manner which in France has been termed the style of the *Renaissance;* and this style in Italy has great elegance. The façade of the Certosa of Pavia may be mentioned as an example; but it is more generally discernible in subsidiary portions, in chapels, and in tombs. *Leon Battista Alberti,* one of whose best works will be found at Mantua (Sant' Andrea), bestowed extraordinary thought upon church architecture: whilst *Sanmicheli, Scammozzi,* and *Palladio* more peculiarly excelled in their civil buildings, which form the chief ornaments of Vicenza and Venice. The traveller should observe the edifices of Turin which belong to a much later period.

Domestic architecture, in Italy, affords a high interest. Its progress may be traced at least from the 15th century. The interiors of the period of the *Renaissance,* which are frequently well preserved—and Mantua may be instanced as affording a remarkable example—should be well examined, and will well repay this study; as also will some of the palaces of Genoa. In Venice, besides the great beauty of the buildings, the ingenuity of the architect in adapting his plans to their confined and untoward sites will often be found peculiarly interesting. At Verona buildings of this class have a character of their own, of strength and elegance united in the details. Florence excels in the colossal grandeur of its palaces.

The *municipal buildings* of Lombardy are of great and varied merit. In the Town-halls, or *Broletlos,* of *Como, Bergamo, Monza,* and *Brescia,* the beauty of the structures is enhanced by their varied styles of decoration.

The ancient *military architecture* of Italy has been little attended to by travellers. Northern Italy abounds in noble mediæval strongholds and fortifications. The Scaligerian castles in and about Verona are peculiarly grand; and the Modenese are not only curious in themselves, but interesting as being amongst the objects which first tinged the mind of Ariosto with his fondness for tales of chivalry. In Italy, also, will be found the earliest examples of regular fortification, by which all the ancient modes of defence were superseded.

Sculpture in Italy offers a vast number of objects of the highest interest. The names of Niccolo and Giovanni da Pisa, of Mino da Fiesole, of Bambaja, of Donatello, of Orgagna, of Ghiberti, and of Michel Angelo, are of world-wide celebrity; but the merits of many second-rate Italian sculptors have not yet attracted the notice they deserve by the traveller from beyond the Alps.

Of all the more remarkable works of sculpture we believe that we have given sufficient notices; and the traveller should recollect that of some of the best of the Italian sculptors so few specimens exist, that, unless he avails himself of the opportunity of examining them where they now stand, he will never meet with them again. Thus, there is scarcely a first-rate fragment of *Luca della Robbia* out of Tuscany, or of *Bambaja* out of Milan and Pavia; very few works of *Mino da Fiesole* out of Florence and Fiesole; no work of *Begarelli* out of Parma and Modena. They have rarely been multiplied by casts, and, when engraved, the representations have been most inadequate.

Working in the *precious metals* was a branch of the sculptor's art, or, as would be better said, trade, for, in the earlier periods at least, they followed it as a craft. Some magnificent specimens, in which enamelled work and jewels are introduced, exist as *pale*, or *palliotti*, altar-fronts or coverings. Those of San Marco at Venice, of Sant' Ambrogio at Milan, of the Baptistery at Florence, and the Cathedral of Pistoia, are amongst the most remarkable. Many specimens of the same description, together with votive offerings, cups, vessels, and the like, are still preserved in the sacristies of the churches.

Very early and fine specimens of *mosaic*, formed of prisms of coloured or gilded opaque glass, or enamel, will be found at Milan (San Ambrogio and San Lorenzo), Lucca (San Frediano), Pisa (Duomo), Florence (Baptistery and San Miniato), Venice (San Marco and Torcello), and especially at Ravenna, where the finest and oldest works of the kind exist, dating as far back as the 6th cent. The art continued to be practised at Venice till the 16th century, but not so late in Lombardy or in Tuscany. At Novara and Cremona, also, are some curious specimens of early Christian tesselated pavements. In Tuscany, about the 13th century, a richer kind of working was introduced, employing serpentine, porphyry, and various coloured marbles, as at Pisa (Duomo and Baptistery), Florence (Baptistery and San Miniato), which mode of workmanship seems to have been improved into the present beautiful Florentine mosaic in *pietra dura*. This is composed of rich natural mineral productions, and of the finest marbles, and may be seen in the greatest perfection in the Medicean Chapel of San Lorenzo (Florence), and at the Certosa of Pavia.

The stained glass of Italy is exceedingly beautiful. In the cathedrals of Milan, Bologna, Lucca, Pisa, and Florence, it is most brilliant. In Venice the colours are not so good. Stained glass, however, does not appear to have become common: there are few examples of it in the smaller churches or in civil buildings.

12.—MUSIC.

"There is no feature of Italy in which the traveller is more liable to disappointment than its music; a vague idea still pervading many persons that Grisis are to be found at every country town opera,—that the streets are never empty of singing,—and that 'all those churches, open from morning to night,' must mean organ-playing and choral performance of some sort or other. Now, without stopping to point out how a sweeping denial of all this would be as unfair to the genius of a country which has been always spontaneous, no less than elaborate, as the sweeping expectation is ridiculous, a word or two may in some degree protect the tourist from disappointment. In the first place, he must prepare himself for a declamatory style of dramatic singing, in which the old French usages (reviled by the Burneys and Walpoles) are more nearly approached than is agreeable to cultivated taste. Next he must recollect that, save in the winter and at Carnival times, he will fall upon the bad opera season at the great theatres of Milan and Venice ('La Fenice' indeed is not open in autumn). At the fairs a 'star or two' are generally secured to add their attractions to the manager's bill of fare; and at the second-class towns, such as Verona, Vicenza, Padua, there is a chance of tolerable average companies, but hardly singers of 'primo cartello.' The best assemblage, I have been told, is generally at Trieste, early in September. In the churches, even the Duomo at Milan, and St. Mark's, Venice, the performances on high days and holidays are nothing short of disastrous. All trace, moreover, of the fine unaccompanied church music of Italy, most of which was perpetuated by MS. copies, has vanished from the shops. Lastly, though Italy produces surpassing instrumentalists, the taste for instrumental music hardly secures sufficient to maintain them at home. I never heard of an orchestral concert, or saw sign of a single new composition, save fantasias on the favourite opera themes. This does not sound very tempting: and yet the dilettante who troubles himself to seek, will, I think, discern that the sense of tune among the people is still living; and when he recollects that Rossini sprang up to amaze Europe, at a time little more promising than the present, will pause ere he echoes the common *growl*, 'There is no more music in Italy.'"—*H. F. C.*

13.—A FEW SKELETON TOURS THROUGH NORTH ITALY.

∗∗∗ The figures after each station denote the number of days employed not only in arriving from the last place noted, but the time to be employed in sight-seeing. In the description of all the larger towns, a list of the objects most deserving of the traveller's attention is given in their topographical order.

First Tour—of about Three Months in the North of Italy; visiting everything most deserving of notice.

	Days.
Paris to Turin	2
Turin .. .. stay	2
Pinerolo and Vaudois Valleys ..	3
Excursions in the vicinity of Turin—to Raconigi, Carmagnola, and Cuneo	3
Turin to Asti and Alexandria ..	2
Alexandria to Acqui	1
Alexandria to Vercelli by Casale	1
Battle-fields of Palestro to Novara	1
Novara to Magenta, and return to Novara and Arona	1
Excursions on the Lago Maggiore; journey to Laveno, Varese, and Como	2
Excursions on the Lake of Como and Lugano, and journey to Milan	3
Milan .. .. stay	3
Milan to Pavia	1
Milan to Monza and Lecco ..	1
Lecco to Bergamo	1
Bergamo to Lovere, and Lake of Isco	2
Brescia	1
Cremona	1
Desenzano, and excursions to Solferino, and on the Lake of Garda	2
Peschiera and Verona.. .. stay	2
Mantua	1
Vicenza to Padua	1
Padua and Euganean Hills ..	3
Venice .. .. stay	3
Excursions to Treviso, Conegliano, Udine, and Trieste ..	3

	Days.
Return to Venice by Steamer or Rail	1
Journey to Ferrara .. and stay	2
Bologna .. .. stay	2
Journey to Ravenna .. and stay	3
Ravenna to Rimini	1
Rimini to Cesena, Forli, Faenza, and Imola, and return to Bologna	3
Bologna to Modena and Parma	1
Parma (stay), with excursion to Colorno, &c.	2
Parma to Piacenza, stopping at Borgo S. Donino, with excursion to Velleija	2
Piacenza to Genoa, stopping at Tortona and Casteggio	1
Genoa .. .. stay	3
Genoa to Leghorn and Florence	1
Pisa and Florence	1
Florence and environs, including excursion to Valombrosa ..	7
Florence to Lucca, stopping at Pistoia and Prato	1
Lucca	1
Pietrasanta, Massa Carrara, and Spezzia	3
Spezzia to Genoa	1
Genoa to Nice	2
Nice	1
Toulon, stopping at Fréjus and Toulon	3
Toulon to Marseilles	1
Marseilles to Paris	1
	90

13.—Skeleton Tours.

Second Tour—of about Seven Weeks in North Italy.

	Days.
Paris to Turin .. .. and stay	4
Turin to Novara, by Vercelli	1
Vercelli to Alexandria, by Casale	1
Novara and Arona	1
Excursion on Lago Maggiore ..	2
Arona to Milan, by Magenta ..	1
Milan (stay), with excursions to Como, Monza, and Pavia ..	6
Milan to Bergamo and Brescia ..	1
Brescia to Desenzano, with excursion to Solferino, and on the Lago di Garda	3
Verona .. .. and stay	1
Mantua	1
Verona to Padua (and stay), by Vicenza, and to Venice	2

	Days.
Venice	3
Venice to Ferrara .. and stay	2
Bologna	3
Bologna to Ravenna	2
Ravenna to Rimini	1
Rimini to Bologna	2
Bologna to Modena and Parma	2
Parma to Piacenza	1
Piacenza to Genoa, by Alexandria	1
Genoa	2
Genoa to Nice	2
Nice to Toulon	2
Nice to Paris, by Marseilles ..	2
	49

Third Tour—of about Six Weeks, entering Italy by Venice.

	Days.
Venice	3
Padua	1
Ferrara	1
Bologna	2
Ravenna	2
Forli and Faienza	1
Bologna and Modena	1
Modena, Parma, and Piacenza ..	3
Piacenza to Alessandria and Milan	1
Milan (stay), and visits to Monza, Como, and Pavia	5
Milan to Bergamo and Brescia ..	2
Brescia to Lake of Garda, Solferino, and Verona	2

	Days.
Verona to Vicenza and back ..	1
Verona to Mantua	1
Mantua to Cremona	1
Cremona to Milan, by Lodi ..	1
Milan to Novara and Lago Maggiore, Magenta, &c.	2
Novara to Turin, by Vercelli ..	1
Turin	2
Turin to Genoa .. .. and stay	3
Genoa to Nice	2
Nice to Toulon and Marseilles ..	2
Marseilles, by Lyons, to Paris ..	2
	42

Tour of about Three Weeks through a part of Northern Italy, after visiting Switzerland, and returning to England through Germany.

	Days.
Turin from Geneva .. and stay	3
Milan (and stay), visiting Novara and Magenta	3
Pavia	1
Bergamo and Brescia	1½
Solferino and Verona	2
Mantua	1
Vicenza, Padua, to Venice (and stay)	3

	Days.
Treviso, Udine, and Trieste ..	2
Vienna	1
To London or Paris, by Munich, Augsbourg, Frankfort, Heidelberg, Mayence, Cologne, and Ostend	5
	21

Tables of Foreign Coins reduced into the different Currencies of Italy, at the par of exchange.

I. INTO FRENCH AND NORTH ITALIAN CURRENCY.

	Francs.	Centimes.		Francs.	Centimes.
English Sovereign	25	21	Tuscan Scudo of 10 Pauls	5	60
Crown of 5 Shillings	6	25	Dena of 15 Pauls	8	40
Shilling	1	25	Paul	0	56
French Napoleon d'Or			Florin	1	40
20 frs	20	00	Roman Doppia, gold	26	87
5 franc piece	5	00	Scudo, 10 Pauls	5	37
1 ditto	1	00	Paul	0	54
Austrian or Milanese Lira	0	87	Neapolitan Oncia of 3		
Crown of 6 Lira	5	22	Ducats	12	99
Gold Sovrana	34	80	Scudo of 12 Carlini	5	09
Tuscan Zecchino	11	20	Carlino	0	42½

II. INTO VENETIAN (AUSTRIAN) CURRENCY.

	Aust. Lira.	Centimes.		Aust. Lira.	Centimes.
English Sovereign	29	00	Tuscan Paul	0	67
Crown	7	25	Florin	1	67
Shilling	1	49	Roman Doppia	30	87
French Napoleon d'Or	23	00	Scudo of 10 Pauls	6	17
5 franc piece	5	75	Paul	0	62
1 ditto	1	15	Neapolitan Oncia	14	93
Tuscan Zecchino	13	33	Scudo of 12 Carlini	5	85
Scudo of 10 Pauls	6	66	Carlino	0	49

III. INTO TUSCAN CURRENCY.

	Pauls.	Grazie.		Pauls.	Grazie.
English Sovereign	45	00	Roman Paul	0	7 7/10
Crown	11	2	Neapolitan Oncia	23	1¼
Shilling	2	2½	Scudo of 12 Carlini	9	0 7/10
French Napoleon	35	5½	Carlino	0	6
5 franc piece	8	7½	Milanese Sovrana, gold	62	1
1 franc ditto	1	6½	Scudo of 6 Lira	9	2¼
Roman Doppia since 1839	46	7½	Lira	1	5½
Scudo of 10 Pauls	9	47¼			

TABLE 1.—*English Money reduced to an equivalent Value in the Money of the several States of North Italy.*

English Money.			Lira Nova or Franc.		Austrian Lira.		Tuscan Scudi, Pauls, and Grazie.			English Money.			Lira Nova or Franc.		Austrian Lira.		Tuscan Scudi, Pauls, and Grazie.		
£.	s.	d.	Lira	cent.	Lira	cent.	Sc.	pl.	gr.	£.	s.	d.	Lira	cent.	Lira	cent.	Sc.	pl.	gr.
0	0	1	0	10¼	0	12	0	0	1¼	5	0	0	126	5	145	00	22	5	0
0	0	2	0	21	0	24	0	0	3	6	0	0	151	26	174	00	27	0	0
0	0	4	0	42	0	48	0	0	6	7	0	0	176	47	203	00	31	5	0
0	0	6	0	63	0	72	0	1	1	8	0	0	201	68	232	00	36	0	0
0	1	0	1	26	1	44	0	2	2	9	0	0	226	89	261	00	40	5	0
0	2	0	2	52	2	89	0	4	4	10	0	0	252	10	290	00	45	0	0
0	3	0	3	78	4	33	0	6	6	20	0	0	504	20	580	00	90	0	0
0	4	0	5	04	5	80	0	9	0	30	0	0	756	30	870	00	135	0	0
0	5	0	6	30	7	25	1	1	2	40	0	0	1008	40	1160	00	180	0	0
0	10	0	12	60	14	50	2	2	4	50	0	0	1260	50	1455	00	225	0	0
0	15	0	18	90	21	75	3	3	6	60	0	0	1512	60	1740	00	270	0	0
1	0	0	25	21	29	00	4	5	0	70	0	0	1764	70	2030	00	315	0	0
2	0	0	50	42	58	00	9	0	0	80	0	0	2016	80	2320	00	360	0	0
3	0	0	75	63	87	00	13	5	0	90	0	0	2268	90	2610	00	405	0	0
4	0	0	100	84	116	00	18	0	0	100	0	0	2521	00	2900	00	450	0	0

The Lira Nuova d'Italia, equivalent to the French Franc, is the current coin throughout the kingdom of North Italy.

The Austrian Lira, equal to 84 centimes of the Lira Nova, and the Florin of 3 Lire, are current in the Venetian provinces, and are taken, without deduction, in Modena, Tuscany, and the adjoining parts of the Papal States.

The above Table has been calculated at the par of exchange, *i. e.* at the comparative intrinsic values of the precious metals contained in the English sovereign and the different foreign coins comprised in it.

TABLE 2.—*Currency of the different Italian States reduced into English Money, at the par of exchange.*

LOMBARDY AND VENICE.		ENGLISH.			TUSCANY.			ENGLISH.			ROME.			ENGLISH.			NAPLES.			ENGLISH.		
Lire or Aust. Swanziger.	Centimes.	£.	s.	d.	Scudi.	Pauls.	Grazie.	£.	s.	d.	Scudi.	Pauls.	Baiocchi.	£.	s.	d.	Ducats.	Carlini.	Grani.	£.	s.	d.
0	1	0	0	0 8/100	0	0	1	0	0	0 7/10	0	0	1	0	0	0 8/10	0	0	1	0	0	0 4/10
0	10	0	0	0 8/10	0	0	4	0	0	1 8/10	0	0	5	0	0	2 6/10	0	0	5	0	0	2
0	50	0	0	4 15/100	0	1	0	0	0	5 3/10	0	1	0	0	0	5 3/10	0	1	0	0	0	4
1	00	0	0	8¼	0	2	0	0	0	10 6/10	0	2	0	0	0	10 6/10	0	2	0	0	0	8
2	00	0	1	4½	0	3	0	0	1	3 9/10	0	3	0	0	1	3 9/10	0	3	0	0	1	0
3	00	0	2	0¾	0	4	0	0	1	9 2/10	0	4	0	0	1	9 2/10	0	4	0	0	1	4
4	00	0	2	9	0	5	0	0	2	2 6/10	0	5	0	0	2	2 5/10	0	5	0	0	1	8
5	00	0	3	5¼	1	0	0	0	4	5 3/10	1	0	0	0	4	3½	1	0	0	0	3	4¼
10	00	0	6	10½	2	0	0	0	8	10 6/10	2	0	0	0	8	6½	2	0	0	0	6	8½
15	00	0	10	4	3	0	0	0	13	3 9/10	3	0	0	0	12	9¾	3	0	0	0	10	0¾
20	00	0	13	9½	4	0	0	0	17	9 2/10	4	0	0	0	17	0½	4	0	0	0	13	5
30	00	1	0	8½	5	0	0	1	2	2 5/10	5	0	0	1	1	3¾	5	0	0	0	16	9¼
40	00	1	7	7	10	0	0	2	4	5	10	0	0	2	2	7½	10	0	0	1	13	6½
50	00	1	14	5¾	15	0	0	3	6	7 5/10	15	0	0	3	3	10¼	15	0	0	2	10	3¾
60	00	2	1	4½	20	0	0	4	8	10	20	0	0	4	5	2½	20	0	0	3	7	1
70	00	2	8	3¾	30	0	0	6	13	3	30	0	0	6	7	9¾	30	0	0	5	0	7½
80	00	2	15	2	40	0	0	8	17	8	40	0	0	8	10	5	40	0	0	6	14	2
90	00	3	1	10¾	50	0	0	11	2	1	50	0	0	10	13	0½	50	0	0	8	7	8½
100	00	3	9	0¾	60	0	0	13	6	6	60	0	0	12	15	5½	60	0	0	10	1	3
200	00	6	18	0½	70	0	0	15	10	11	70	0	0	14	18	2¾	70	0	0	11	14	9½
300	00	10	7	0¾	80	0	0	17	15	4	80	0	0	17	0	10	80	0	0	13	5	4
400	00	13	16	1	90	0	0	19	19	9	90	0	0	19	3	5¾	90	0	0	15	1	10½
500	00	17	5	1¼	100	0	0	22	4	2	100	0	0	21	6	0½	100	0	0	16	15	5
600	00	20	14	1½	200	0	0	44	8	4	200	0	0	42	12	1	200	0	0	33	10	10
700	00	24	3	1¾	300	0	0	66	12	6	300	0	0	63	18	1½	300	0	0	50	6	3
800	00	27	12	2	400	0	0	88	16	8	400	0	0	85	4	2	400	0	0	67	1	8
900	00	31	1	2¼	500	0	0	111	0	10	500	0	0	106	10	2½	500	0	0	83	17	1
1000	00	34	10	2½	1000	0	0	222	1	8	1000	0	0	212	0	5	1000	0	0	167	14	2

TABLE 3.—*Showing the Value of the different Measures of Distances employed in Italy, reduced to English statute Miles, Furlongs, and Yards.*

Foreign Distances.	Reduced to English.				Foreign Distances.	English.		
	Yards.	Miles.	Furl.	Yds.		Miles.	Furl.	Yds.
Geographical mile	2,025¼	1	1	45¼				
French Myriamètre	10,936	6	1	156	Piedmontese Post	4	4	168
Piedmontese Mile	2,697	1	4	60	Milanese Post	8	6	200
Milanese Mile	1,952	1	0	192	Tuscan Post of 8 Miles	8	1	164
Venetian Mile	2,114	1	1	134	Roman Post of 8 Miles	7	3	40
Parma & Piacenza M.	1,619	0	7	79	Neapolitan Post of 8 Miles	11	0	112
Tuscan Mile	1,808	1	0	48				
Roman Mile	1,628	0	7	88				
Neapolitan Mile	2,435	1	3	15				
Austrian Mile of 4000 klafter	8,297	4	5	155				

ABBREVIATIONS, &c., EMPLOYED IN THE HANDBOOK.

The points of the compass are marked by the letters N. S. E. W.

(*rt.*) right, (*l.*) left,—applied to the banks of a river. The right bank is that which lies on the right hand of a person looking down the stream, or whose back is turned towards the quarter from which the current descends.

Miles.—Distances are, as far as possible, reduced to English miles; when miles are mentioned without any other designation, they are understood to be English.

The names of Inns precede the description of every place (often in a parenthesis), because the first information needed by a traveller is where to lodge.

Instead of designating a town by the vague words "large" or "small," the amount of its population, according to the latest census, is almost invariably stated, as presenting a more exact scale of the importance and size of the place.

In order to avoid repetition, the Routes are preceded by a chapter of preliminary information; and to facilitate reference to it, each division or paragraph is separately numbered.

Each Route is numbered with Arabic figures, corresponding with those attached to the Route on the Map, which thus serves as an Index to the Book.

A HANDBOOK

FOR

TRAVELLERS IN NORTHERN ITALY.

SECTION I.

PIEDMONT AND SARDINIAN LOMBARDY.

PRELIMINARY INFORMATION.

1. *Territory, Government.*—2. *Nature of the Country, Extent, Population.*—3. *Language.*—4. *Fine Arts, Literature.*—5. *Posting.*—6. *Railways.*—7. *Money, Weights, Measures, &c.*

ROUTES.

[In the tables of contents throughout this work the names of places are printed *in italics* only in those routes where they are *described*.]

ROUTE	PAGE	ROUTE	PAGE
1. *Susa* to *Turin*—RAIL.	7	7. Alessandria to Piacenza, by *Tortona, Voghera*, and *Casteggio*	54
2. Turin to Milan, by *Vercelli, Novara*, and *Magenta*—RAIL.	33	8. Turin to Nice, by Cuneo and the *Col di Tenda*	58
3. Turin to Milan, by *Casale, Mortara*, and *Vigevano*	44	9. Turin to Oneglia, by *Cherasco*	63
4. Turin to Asti, by *Chieri*	47	10. Turin to Oneglia, by *Fossano* and *Mondovi*	66
5. Turin to Genoa, by *Asti, Alessandria.*, and *Novi*—RAIL.	48	11. Alessandria to Savona, by *Acqui* and *Dego*	67
6. Alessandria to *Mortara*, Novara, and Arona on the Lago Maggiore—RAIL.	53	12. Turin to Savona, by *Millesimo*	70

§ 1. TERRITORY.—GOVERNMENT.

WHAT Frederick said of Prussia, that it was made up of *pièces rapportées*, is most particularly applicable to the continental dominions of the King of Sardinia. On this side of the Alps, the following are the component parts, united under

N. *Italy*—1860. B

the authority of the present dynasty:—*Piedmont proper*, the nucleus of the present kingdom, gained from the Counts of Provence, by Peter Count of Savoy, in 1220, and inherited from the Marchioness Adelaide, and subsequently an Imperial donation. The *Marquisate of Susa*, which, at an earlier period, included the greater part of Piedmont, but which was afterwards restrained to narrower bounds. The *Principality of Carignano*, a modern dismemberment of the Marquisate of Susa. The *Marquisate of Ivrea*, ceded to Savoy by the Emperors Frederick II. in 1248, and Henry VII. in 1313. The small *Marquisate of Ceva*, at the foot of the Apennines. The *County of Nice* in 1388. The *Lordship of Vercelli*, which, after several changes of masters, was ceded by Milan to Savoy in 1427. The *County of Asti*, ceded by Charles V. to Duke Charles IV. in 1531. The *Marquisate of Saluzzo*, long contested by the French, and which, though cutting into the heart of Piedmont, was not fully acquired by the Dukes of Savoy till 1588. The *Duchy of Montferrat*, obtained by the Dukes of Savoy in 1630; Val Sesia from the Emperor Leopold in 1703; the County of Arona and the Province of Duomo d'Ossola in 1743 by the treaty of Worms. Several dismemberments of the Duchy of Milan, namely, the Provinces of *Alessandria*, *Tortona*, and *Novara*, with the *Lomellina*, in 1736,; the *Oltro Po Pavese* in 1743, subsequently confirmed by the treaty of Aix-la-Chapelle in 1748; and, lastly, *Oneglia*, and the *Genoese* territories, by the treaty of *Vienna* in 1814.

Previously to the occupation of Italy by the French, these territories were all respectively governed by their local laws. Under Napoleon, Piedmont continued annexed to the French Empire; and, since the restoration of the House of Savoy, much of the French administration has been retained, in connexion, however, with the original institutions, which have been partially restored. The government since 1848 is a constitutional monarchy, consisting of a king, a senate, and a chamber of representatives. The Dukes of Savoy, as is well known, acquired the regal title at the beginning of the last century. The following is their succession from the time of Emanuele Filiberto (1553), by whom the fortunes of the House were restored, and who may be considered as the founder of the Monarchy:—

1580. Carlo Emanuele I.
1630. Vittorio Amedeo I.
1637. Francesco Giacinto.
1638. Carlo Emanuele II.
1675. Vittorio Amedeo II.
1730. Carlo Emanuele III.

1773. Vittorio Amedeo III.
1796. Carlo Emanuele IV.
1802. Vittorio Emanuele.
1821. Carlo Felice.
1831. Carlo Alberto.
1849. Vittorio Emanuele II.

At the Congress of Vienna, the right of succession, in the event (which happened) of the failure of male issue in the direct royal line of Vittorio Amedeo II., was secured to the collateral branch of Savoy Carignan. The founder of this branch was Prince Tomaso Francesco (born 1596, died 1656), the fourth son of Carlo Emanuele I.; and upon the death of Carlo Felice, without male issue, the late king, as the descendant of Tomaso Francesco, obtained the crown accordingly. Defeated by the Austrians at Novara on the 23rd of March, 1849, he abdicated in favour of his son, the reigning Monarch, and retired to Oporto, where he died soon afterwards. The royal family now consists of his Majesty Vittorio Emanuele, King of Sardinia, Cyprus, and Jerusalem; Duke of Savoy, Genoa, &c. &c.; born March 14, 1820; ascended the throne March 23, 1849; married April 12, 1842;—and several children by the late Queen, Maria Adelaide Francesca, Archduchess of Austria, and daughter of the Archduke Renier; born June 3, 1822;—the eldest, Humbert Carlo Emanuele, Prince of Piedmont and prince royal, born March 14, 1844.

The constitutional government which has now existed eight years in Piedmont has gone on working as favourably as the best friends of liberal institutions could have desired, affording a gratifying contradiction to those who have supposed the Italians unfitted for representative institutions. In no country on the continent of Europe has the representative system taken so firm a root as in the Sardinian dominions, and, thanks to it, and the good feeling and prudence of its inhabitants, whilst many other states in the Peninsula were groaning under political and ecclesiastical oppression, Piedmont is prosperous under its constitutional monarchy. The supporters of the new order of things have had many difficulties to overcome, arising out of the war of 1849, as they still have from the jealousy of powerful neighbours, from the openly avowed hostility of the Court of Rome, and at home from the intrigues of an ignorant aristocracy and a bigoted clergy, the enemies of progress and of liberal government. Many of these obstacles must ere long disappear before the firmness of a popular sovereign who has his country's good at heart, and from an administration like that of Count Cavour's, founded on public and commercial liberty.

§ 2. NATURE OF THE COUNTRY.—EXTENT.—POPULATION.

What may be now called Piedmont is the country that extends from the Alps proper to the Maritime Alps and Apennines, as far as the Ticino and Trebbia rivers on the E., and including the provinces of Turin, Coni, Alexandria, Ivrea, Vercelli, and Novara, with a small stripe of the former Duchy of Piacenza, having a population of about 3,100,000 inhabitants. Like Lombardy, it offers three well-marked regions; a higher one which extends to the snow-capped peaks of the Alps, where it blends with France (now) and Switzerland, and to the tops of the Maritime Alps and Ligurian Apennines; an intermediate one consisting of subalpine and subapennine hills, and of the valleys through which descend the tributaries of the Po; and of a lower region bordering on that great river, and on the lower course of the rivers that empty themselves into it—the Dora, the Sesia, the Ticino, the Tanaro, the Bormida, and the Scrivia. The most fertile region is the latter. In respect to cultivation, the principal products are, in the more elevated region, timber, barley, potatoes; in the middle one, vines, wheat—and, in its lower part, maize, mulberry-trees; and in the flat region bordering on its great watercourses, corn, rice, mulberry-trees, maize. The central region is the favoured one of the vine in Piedmont, with the grain crops, and the silkworms, the most important of the agricultural productions of the country. The quantity of grain produced is not sufficient for the sustenance of its population; hence a good deal is imported from Lombardy and the neighbouring districts of the Emilian Provinces and Romagna.

The nature of the agricultural produce consumed for food varies in different parts of the country. In the towns wheat is extensively used. The inhabitants of the plains and low hills of Piedmont consume at least as much Indian corn and rye as wheat. In the Alpine valleys wheat is an article of luxury, and Indian corn, potatoes, rye, and buckwheat are the food of the great majority of the inhabitants. In the Apennines and the hills of Montferrat chestnuts form an important article of sustenance; and lastly, rice, produced in large quantity in the provinces of Vercelli, Novara, and Lomellina, is consumed in the country, and exported beyond the Alps.

Manufactures.—Piedmont proper has few manufactures, and none on a large scale—none of any importance as articles of export, the great wealth of the country consisting in its wines, which are sent in large quantities to the sea-coast and into Lombardy; and its silk, which is exported, almost all in an unmanufactured state, to France, Switzerland, and especially to England. Of late years its mining industry has attracted more attention, some works of importance having been opened in the higher Alpine valleys of the Dora, the Sesia, and the Ticino.

The Piedmontese peasantry are not handsome, but they are strong and well built, very active and industrious, and form excellent soldiers; and, in the rural districts, are very simple and honest. The Roman Catholic religion is the established and dominant creed. It may be noticed that, unlike in many parts of the Continent, the Sunday is very strictly observed in the Sardinian states. Since the accession of the present sovereign, the Protestants of the Alpine valleys are no longer persecuted as formerly; they have been even permitted to erect a handsome church at Turin, towards which the Government has very liberally contributed.

§ 3. LANGUAGE.

The Piedmontese dialect has much more analogy with the Provençal than any other of the Northern dialects of the Italian. But this similarity is not the effect of mixture or corruption: it holds, in some degree, a middle place between the Provençal and Italian, with certain peculiar intonations and vowels, which, in addition to its vocabulary, render it perfectly unintelligible to a stranger, however well versed he may be in the sister tongues. The Piedmontese is the universal speech of the country, and employed by high and low; though, of course, all persons of education speak Italian. French is in very common use at Turin; first introduced by the court and followers of the Dukes of Savoy, and kept up by the frequent occupations of the country by its Gallic neighbours.

§ 4. FINE ARTS.*—LITERATURE.

The manner in which the dominions of the House of Savoy have been compacted renders it rather difficult in some cases to define who are the great men whom it can claim. The best painters that were naturalised here, such as *Gaudenzio Ferrari*, a native of Val Sesia (see Vercelli), *Lanini*, and *Solari*, really belong to the Milanese school. The last, Solari (fl. 1530), was born at Alessandria. He was an imitator of Raphael, and not without success. *Guglielmo Caccia*, otherwise called *Moncalvo* (1568-1625), worked much at Turin, Novara, and Vercelli. Some consider him as a follower of the Caracci. The eighteenth century produced a host of inferior artists. The Dukes of Savoy were liberal and splendid collectors of works of art, and they also invited many foreign artists, as *Balthazar Matthew* of Antwerp, *Jan Miel*, a pupil of Vandyke, and *Daniel Seyter* of Vienna. Very recently the Academy, founded in 1678, has received much encouragement. A certain number of pupils are sent to Rome, and are there maintained at the expense of the government. It was re-organised by the King Carlo Felice in 1824, and was afterwards denomi-

---

* On this subject consult Kugler's 'Handbook of Painting in Italy,' edited by Eastlake, 2 vols. 1855—a work designed for the information of travellers; and the 'Biographical Catalogue of the Principal Italian Painters,' by a Lady, 1 vol. 12mo. 1855.

nated the *Accademia Albertina*, after the then reigning sovereign. No painter of any eminence has been produced. One of the distinguished sculptors of the present day, Baron *Marochetti*, is a Piedmontese by birth. The Piedmontese school of architecture in the last century exhibits some originality, if not genius.

Literature is flourishing; offering as good if not a better prospect than in any other state of Italy. French literature is losing much of its influence. German has been hitherto little cultivated from the anti-Teutonic feelings of the Piedmontese. Printing is carried on to a great extent, and forms a very important branch of national industry, especially at Turin. It is in history, belles-lettres, and science, that the Piedmontese have most distinguished themselves. Botta, Manno, Balbo, Cibrario, Bertolotti, Pellico, Massimo d'Azeglio, Nota, Gioberti, Sclopis, Peyron, Plana, Collegno, Alberto della Marmora, Lorenzo Pareto, Moris, Gené, Sismonda, do great honour to the intellectual fame of their country.

§ 5. Posting.

The posting regulations in the kingdom of Sardinia generally have been recently assimilated to those of France, the distances being reckoned in kilomètres, and the charges being nearly the same, viz. 20 centimes for each horse, and 12 for postilions, for every kilomètre; on the mountain-passes of Mt. Cenis, the Simplon, and Tenda, the charge for each horse is increased one-third, or to 30 c.

The number of horses which the postmasters can put on is regulated according to the nature of the carriage, for which purpose all vehicles are arranged under three classes:—*1st:* cabriolets on two wheels, light calèches without a seat in front, broughams, &c., to which only 2 horses are required, provided the number of persons does not exceed 2; if 3 or 4, then 3 horses, and for each additional passenger 15 centimes per kilomètre must be paid. *2nd class:* limonières, large calèches with a double seat inside, chariots or *coupés*, clarences, &c., 3 horses and one postilion; should the number of persons exceed 3, an additional charge of 15 c. for each per kilomètre. *3rd class*, heavy landaus, barouches, berlines, whether closed or open, 4 horses and 2 postilions, if above 4 passengers, 15 c. per kil. for the 5th; if 6 passengers, 6 horses and 2 postilions (it is usual to pay for the 2 additional horses without yoking them to), and every additional person 15 c. per kilomètre.

One child under 10 years is not reckoned, but if two they are considered as equivalent to one full-grown person, in the above regulations.

The postmasters of Turin and Genoa are allowed to charge for 4 kilomètres in addition to the real distance, and as *postes de faveur*, on all carriages leaving these cities.

Each postmaster is obliged to be provided with carriages for the use of travellers (in general very rickety concerns), for the hire of which they are authorised to charge, for a cabriolet on two wheels 10 c., and a four-wheeled vehicle 15 c. per kilomètre.

At the posthouses on the passes of the Monts Cenis, Simplon, and Col di Tenda, the masters must provide sledges during the winter season, for the hire of which they are entitled to charge 15 c. per kilomètre; they are also authorised to demand 3 and 4 francs for dismounting and placing each carriage on the sledge, according to the class to which it may be referable.

Chevaux de renfort.—Except on the mountain passes, for which there are special regulations noted in our description of these routes, carriages of the first and second classes, with one person, are not obliged to take a *cheval de renfort;* but if more than one passenger, carriages of the 1st class, one additional horse; of the 2nd and 3rd classes, two additional horses; and carriages of the 3rd class and 6 horses, 3 additional ones and another postilion.

For the other posting regulations the traveller is referred to the 'ARTICLES DE RÉGLEMENT SUR LE SERVICE DES POSTES AUX CHEVAUX, APPROUVÉS PAR LE DÉCRET ROYAL DU 8 DÉCEMBRE.' Turin, 1854.

The stations for post-horses have of late years been considerably reduced, and entirely done away with on the lines of communication where railways have been opened.

§ 6. RAILWAYS.

Considerable progress has been made in the construction of Railroads in Piedmont. More than 600 miles have been completed up to the present time. *Lines already open :*—From Turin to Genoa, 103¾ miles; Turin to Susa, 33 miles; Turin to Pinerolo, 21¾ miles; Alessandria to Novara, 41 miles; Novara to Arona, 22½ miles; Turin by Savigliano and Fossano to Cuneo, with a branch to Bra, 54½ miles; Turin to Novara and the Lombard frontier, through Vercelli, 68 miles, with branches to Ivrea, Biella, and to Valenza by Casale; from Mortara to Vigevano, 7 miles; from Alessandria by Tortona to Piacenza, joining the Centro-Italian line connecting Milan, Parma, and Bologna; from Alessandria to Acqui; and from Novi to Tortona; whilst others are projected from Arona across the Alps by the Lukmanier into the Valley of the Rhine, and from Susa to Modane, traversing the central chain of the Alps by an immense tunnel.

§ 7. MONEY, WEIGHTS, MEASURES.

The coinage is exactly the same as in France—on the decimal system; the old coinage of 40 and 20 centime pieces is, however, still current.

SILVER COINS.

1 franc	= 100 centimes	=		9¼d.	English.	
½	„ = 50	„	=	4¾d.	„	
¼	„ = 25	„	=	2⅜d.	„	
5	„ = 500	„	=	3s. 11¼d.	„	

GOLD COINS.

Pieces of 20 francs or Napoleons = 15s. 10d.

VALUE OF SOME OF THE COINS OF THE NEIGHBOURING COUNTRIES IN THE CURRENCY OF SARDINIA.

A Zwanziger or Lira Austriaca is equal to 87 centimes; 5¾ zwanzigers are current as equal to 5 francs.. An Austrian florin is equal to 2 francs 60 centimes.

GOLD AND SILVER WEIGHT.				VALUES IN ENGLISH TROY-WEIGHT.		
Mark.	Oncie.	Denari.	Grani.	Ounces.	Pennywts.	Grains.
1 =	8 =	192 =	4608 =	7	18	3
	1 =	24 =	576 =		19	18¾
		1 =	24 =			19¹³⁄₁₆

The Rubbo, commercial weight, is 25 pounds. This pound or libra contains 1¼ Mark or 12 ounces of the gold and silver weight. Therefore, 100 pounds of Turin = 81·32 lb. Avoirdupois.

WINE MEASURE.

The Brenta is divided into 36 Pente and 72 Boccale. The Brenta =14·88 Gallons English; and the Boccale is rather more than a pint and a half; but the Litre is now generally used in all liquid measures.

LONG MEASURE.

The mètre (with its divisions) is now universally adopted throughout the Kingdom of North Italy;—of the measures formerly used—
The foot = 12·72 English inches, or 0·323 of a mètre. The raso or ell = 23·3 English inches, or 0·5915 of a mètre.

The Piedmontese mile is reckoned at 2466 mètres = 2697 English yards = 1½ mile and 57 yards English. 45$\frac{1}{10}$ Piedmontese miles are equal to 1 mean degree of latitude.

ROUTES.

ROUTE 1.

SUSA TO TURIN—RAIL.

(33* m. or 53 kilomètres.)—The Railway was opened in April, 1854. Trains to Turin at 3·30, 6·15, and 11·10 A.M., and at 4·20 and 7·13 P.M., in 1 h. 40 m.†
(For the road from Pont de Beauvoisin to Susa, see *Handbook for Switzerland*, Rte. 127.) Luggage is examined, on arriving from France and Savoy, at the Susa rly. station.

Susa (Hôtel de France; the hotel near the bridge, reasonable).

This very ancient city, the Segusium of the Romans, is now reduced to a small extent, scarcely numbering 3300

* The miles used throughout the Handbooks of Italy, when not otherwise expressed, are English statute miles of 1760 yards each.
† The times of the railway trains throughout this volume are given on the authority of the latest Orarii, or bills published by the several Governments and companies.

Inhab. It is still the seat of a bishopric, the only token of its former importance. It is surrounded with lovely scenery. The Dora-Susina, so called to distinguish it from the Dora-Baltea, in the valley of Aosta, runs by the side of the city.

The *Arch* or *City Gate*, erected by Julius Cottius, the son of King Donnus, about B.C. 8 (A.U.C. 745), in honour of Augustus, is the most remarkable historical feature of the city; it is on a road leading from behind the Cathedral to the Old Castle outside the town, and is supposed to have stood on the Roman road which crossed the Alps of Mont Genèvre. This chieftain of the Alpine tribes, having submitted to the Roman authority, records his dignity under the humbler title of Prefect: the inscription, now nearly effaced, states the names of his 14 mountain clans; whilst the basso-rilievos represent the sacrifices (Suovetaurilia) and other ceremonies by which the treaty was ratified and concluded. The order is Corinthian, in a good style for a provincial town, and worthy of the study of the architect. The bas-reliefs, of coarse execution, represent colossal rams and swine followed by horsemen armed with spears, and the sacrifice of bulls—sculptures which were perhaps the work of native artists; the bas-reliefs on the lesser sides have been destroyed.

"The arch is a fine but simple building of white marble. The upper part is destroyed, but enough of the attic remains to exhibit the inscription. On the upper course, in a single line, are the following letters, which remain very perfect:—IMP. CAESARI AUGUSTO DIVI F. PONTIFICI MAXVMO TRIBUNIC. POTESTATE XV. IMP. XIII. The second course seems to have contained three lines of inscription, but the upper is so nearly destroyed as to suggest the idea that the line above it must have been restored; the part most exposed could hardly have remained perfect while that below it suffered so much. Many letters of the third line (the middle line of the second course of stones) are distinguishable, but I could not make out the words reported by Millin. The general proportions are not unpleasing, but it is rather singular that the columns are set on a pedestal which raises them considerably above the pilasters of the arch. This diminishes their size and apparent importance. The details of the entablature are in bad taste, and the frieze is ornamented with a bas-relief of men and monsters rudely executed."—*Woods.*

Near this arch two fine torsos of figures in armour were discovered, which, without any authority, were supposed to have belonged to statues of Augustus and Cottius. They were sent to Paris for deposit in the Louvre, where they were repaired and completed by the addition of heads, arms, and legs. After the peace these statues were restored to the Sardinian government, and are now in the cortile of the university of Turin.

The *Cathedral* of St. Justus is of the 11th centy. The great bell-tower, in the Lombard style, is one of the loftiest of its kind. In the cathedral the centre arches and massy piers of the nave belong to a more ancient fabric; the rest is of a simple Gothic. In the Chapel of the Virgin is a gilded statue in wood of the 12th centy. of Adelaide Countess of Susa, the princess through whom the House of Savoy acquired the dominions which became the origin of its power in Italy. This celebrated lady was thrice married; first to Herman Duke of Suabia; secondly, to Henry Marquis of Montferrat; and thirdly, to Otho, son of Humbert I., Count of Maurienne. It is said that she is buried here; but others suppose that her body rests at Turin. In one of the chapels is a curious mediæval group in bronze of our Lady of Roccia Melone with S. George and Bonifacio Rotari, a Crusader of the 12th centy. A magnificent font, hollowed out of a single block of green Susa marble, stands in the baptistery. This font is a work of the 11th century, with an ambiguous inscription, leaving it doubtful whether "Guigo" was the workman or the donor (supposed, according to the latter interpretation, to be Guigo V., first Count of the Viennois). In the sacristy is shown a large silver cross, said to have been given by Charlemagne.

Ancient towers, gateways (one very noble near the cathedral, called the Capitol), and Gothic porticoes, add to the picturesque effect of the city, contrasting with the modern edifices and improvements rapidly going on here.

Above Susa are the extensive ruins of *La Brunetta*, once a very important fortress, and considered as the key of the valley. The road from the Mont Cenis passes near them. The defence which La Brunetta formerly afforded to Piedmont on the side of Savoy was effected by Fort Lesseillon, near Modane, on the other side of Mont Cenis, until its recent cession to France. The *Brunetta*, which with the fortresses of Exiles and Fenestrelles formed the line of defence of Piedmont on the side of France, was destroyed by the French in 1798, in virtue of a stipulation in the treaty with Sardinia of that year, and the demolition is said to have cost 600,000 francs.

The *Monte di Roccia Melone* (*Mons Romulea*), also above Susa, is 11,139 feet in height. Upon the summit is a chapel, founded by *Bonifaccio di Asti*, a crusader, who, having been taken prisoner by the Mahometans, made a vow that, if set free, he would erect an oratory here in honour of the Virgin. The fetters which bound him are preserved in the chapel. An annual procession takes place to this chapel on the 5th of August, the feast of the Assumption. It is not to be accomplished without much difficulty: all the pilgrims are equipped with spiked staves and shoes.

It is to the top of the Roccia Melone that some of the writers who erroneously maintain that Hannibal crossed the Alps by the pass of Mont Cenis, believe him to have led his army, in order to encourage his soldiers by the view of Italy.

3 m. from Susa is the celebrated Abbey of *Novalesa*, situated upon the old and now almost abandoned road to the Hospice. Here are the remains of the monastery founded by Abbo, lord of Susa, about the year 739. It was ruined by the Saracens not long after its foundation, when the monks withdrew to Turin, carrying with them their precious collection of MSS. which formed a part of the library of S. Salvatore: it was again rebuilt in the 10th century. The convent is now inhabited by a few Benedictine monks.

Just outside of Susa, the view, looking back upon the town, in which the Roman arch is conspicuous, is very beautiful. It is equally so on looking down the long valley. The furthest extremity of this valley appears closed by the lofty Monte Pirchiriano, upon the summit of which may be descried the tower of the Abbey of *San Michele*. The Roman road over the Alps, which was constructed when Cotius submitted to Augustus, passed up this valley, and, turning to the S.W.

at Susa, along the valley of the Dora, crossed by the pass of Mt. Genèvre. This became the road most frequented by the Romans between Italy and Gaul. The military road of Pompey and Cæsar passed through Oulx, and over the Col de Sestrieres.

The Rly. and post-roads skirt to

8 kil. *Bussoleno Stat.*, a small town surrounded by walls and towers. Before reaching this place, at Foresto on the l., are quarries of the greenstone called marble of Susa, a kind of serpentine, very much like the verd' antique, but possessing less durability. The road again skirts

8 kil. *Borgone Stat.* Between Bussoleno and this stat. on the rt. is

San Giorio, displaying its array of walls and towers, and an ancient fortress ascending the hill which crowns it, standing out boldly, and rising stage above stage with great beauty.

The road next crosses the Dora Susina by a good bridge.

3 kil. *Sant' Antonino Stat.*, a small town, in which the principal feature is a very ancient Lombard tower.

3 kil. *Condove Stat.*, on the l. bank of the Dora. The gorge here narrows, and becomes exceedingly picturesque. From the beginning of the traveller's progress down the valley of Susa, he will have seen before him, in the distance, a very lofty hill, upon the summit of which a building, apparently a tower, can be faintly discerned, the whole mass appearing to close the valley. This mountain is the *Monte Pirchiriano*, between which and the *Monte Caprasio* was the ancient fortified line erected A.D. 774 by Desiderius King of the Lombards, by which he vainly endeavoured to defend his kingdom against Charlemagne; but of these defences no traces are now to be found, except in the name of the neighbouring hamlet of *Chiusa*. The wall was defended by bulwarks and towers; but Charlemagne did not attack them—a minstrel from the Lombard camp betrayed the existence of a secret and unfortified path, through which the forces of the King of the Franks pene-

trated. Desiderius fled to Pavia, and the Lombard monarchy was overthrown.

On the mountain on the E. stands the monastery of the "*Sagra di San Michele*," one of the most remarkable religious monuments of Piedmont. It is supposed to have been originally an oratory, founded by Amisone Bishop of Turin, in the 10th century. Beams of fire descending from heaven marked, it was said, the spot, and lighted the tapers employed for its consecration. As a monastery, it was rebuilt by Hugh de Montboissier, a nobleman of Auvergne (between the years 970 and 998), who for some heinous crime had been enjoined the penance of founding a monastery in the Alps. In its flourishing age the Sagra contained 300 monks of the order of St. Benedict, who kept up the "laus perennis," or perpetual service, in the choir; and its history is connected with several of the most important personages and events in that of Piedmont and Savoy.

The mountain can be ascended most easily from S. Ambrogio, but only on foot or mule-back. Its summit is 2880 feet above the level of the sea. The higher portion is covered with fine groves of chestnut-trees, through which you pursue a winding path. Still higher up are secluded and picturesque farms, which, with the woods, constitute almost all the property that this once opulent monastery retains. Like most of the monasteries dedicated to St. Michael, this *Sagra* has the character at once of a castle and a church: great masses of ruins surround the habitable portion. A rock near it is called the *Salto della Bella Alda*. The fair Alda leaped from the summit and reached the ground in safety, under the protection of the Virgin. Vainglorious and rash, she attempted the leap a second time, and perished by the fall. Injudicious repairs have diminished the effects of the building; but it is yet a complete castle of romance,—walls growing out of rocks, and rocks built in and forming walls and foundations of the edifice.

Passing by a ruined outwork, whose circular windows bespeak its early date, we traverse a low vaulted gallery, and reach a small terrace. Before us is a tower, rising out of, and also abutting or leaning against the rock: the lower part contains the staircase by which we ascend to the monastery; the upper portion of the tower forms the extremity of the choir, and terminates in an open Lombard gallery of small circular arches supported by pillars: this is one of the oldest and most curious features of the building. The height, looking down from the outer gallery, is great: an iron balustrade has been fitted into the interstices. This staircase is supported by an enormous central pier: here and there the rocks against which the edifice is built jut out, and portions of sepulchres are dimly seen. At the summit is a great arch, filled with desiccated corpses. Until recently these corpses were placed sitting upon the steps of the stairs; and as you ascended to the church you had to pass between the ranks of these ghastly sentinels. Whence the corpses came, or why they were placed there, is not known: respected, if not venerated, the peasants used to dress them up and adorn them with flowers, which must have rendered them still more hideous. The extremely beautiful circular arch, by which we pass from the staircase to the corridor leading to the church, is a vestige of the original building. It is composed of grey marble, Lombard in style, and sculptured with the signs of the zodiac and inscriptions in very early Longobardic characters. The church itself is in a plain Gothic style: the choir retains vestiges of an earlier age. A fine Gothic tomb, representing an abbot, has excited much controversy.

The late king caused the remains of Carlo Emanuele II. (the father of Vittorio Amedeo, the first King of Sardinia, whose monument is in the cathedral at Turin), and of several other members of the royal family, to be removed hither from Turin; and it was supposed that he intended to render San Michele the future place of burial of the royal family. The remainder of the Sagra is composed of a wilderness of ruined halls and corridors, and of the cells and other apartments inhabited by the confraternity to whom the monastery is now assigned. The Benedictines have disappeared; and long before the Revolution their possessions had been much dilapidated. It was considered as one of those good "pieces of preferment" which the crown might dispose of; and the celebrated Prince Eugene, all booted and spurred, appears in the list of abbots. The monastery has been given over within the last three or four years to the priests of the *Instituto della Carità*, called *Rosminians*, from the name of their founder—an order of recent origin, and belonging to a class of regulars now much encouraged by the Church of Rome, as better suited to the exigencies of the age than the more ancient ascetic confraternities. They are principally employed in education.

The views from the summit of the mountain, and more particularly from the outer gallery of the choir, are of the greatest beauty, and would alone repay the traveller for the toil of the ascent.

4 kil. *Sant' Ambrogio Stat*., a village at the foot of the Monte Pirchiriano. The houses with their projecting galleries are pleasing objects; and there is a decent small inn at the place. The church is rather remarkable. A little beyond, by the side of the road, is seen *Avigliana*, with a fine feudal castle standing out boldly above the tower, and forming with it a beautiful group.

3 kil. *Avigliana Stat.*

Avigliana is a very unaltered town, and full of shattered fragments. The church of *San Pietro* is of very high antiquity, and supposed, like many buildings of the same class, to have been a heathen temple. The *Monte Musino* in the neighbourhood furnishes some remarkable minerals, amongst others the *Hydrophane*, which, opaque when dry, has the property of becoming transparent when immersed in water. The neighbouring woods also furnish much game, both for the sportsman and the ornithologist. Near Avigliana are two small pleasing and secluded lakes, the *Lago della Madonna* and the *Lago di San Bartolommeo*. The Dora adds greatly to the beauty of the scenery in this vicinity. About this spot the Alpine valley of Susa ends, and the traveller now enters the great valley of the Po.

At some little distance from the road is seen the church of *Sant' Antonio di Rinverso*, anciently belonging to the Knights Hospitallers, and consecrated in 1121 by Pope Calixtus V. It is Gothic, and built of moulded brick; the pinnacles and all other ornaments being formed with much delicacy. This is a specimen of a style almost peculiar to Lombardy, of which the traveller will find the full display at Milan, Piacenza, and Pavia. The roof is of brilliant painted tiles; and both within and without are many interesting frescoes. The high altar is of the 15th century. The country is pleasantly wooded.

5 kil. *Rosta Stat.* in the plain below the hill of Rivoli.

Rivoli, a town of about 5200 Inhab., pleasantly situated, above which towers the great unfinished palace begun by Juvara, and exhibiting many of his peculiarities. This palace was one of the places of confinement in which Vittorio Amedeo II. was incarcerated during the short interval which elapsed between the unfortunate attempt which he made to re-ascend the throne and his death. He had abdicated (1730) in favour of his son Carlo Emanuele III., and had retired to Chambery, taking the title of Conte di Tenda. He was a wise and good monarch; and in his person the House of Savoy obtained the island of Sardinia and the regal title; but a short time after his retirement he grew weary of a private life, and formed a scheme for repossessing himself of the royal authority. Some say that his intellect was impaired; others, that he was instigated by the ambition of the Countess of Sommariva, for whom he had renounced the crown, and whom he married immediately after his abdication. The royal *revenant* was speedily laid. The council of Carlo Emanuele readily concurred in the opinion that Vittorio should be seized — a determination which was probably not retarded by his boast that he would take good care to behead all his son's ministers. He was accordingly brought to Rivoli, Sept. 1731, and kept in what was equivalent to solitary confinement. His attendants and guards were strictly prohibited from speaking to him; and, if he addressed them, they maintained the most inflexible silence, answering only by a very low and submissive bow — a miserable mockery of respect. He was afterwards permitted to have the company of his wife, and remove to another prison; but, on the 31st of October, 1732, he died. Some of the rooms have recently been fitted up for the late king. There are many pictures in the palace — a collection of views in Piedmont by the brothers *Cignaroli*, landscapes by *Vanloo*, and a series of historical scenes from the lives of Amedeo VII. and VIII., Counts of Savoy.

The air of Rivoli is remarkably pure, and the place is very healthy. Hence the town and its vicinity abound in villas. Amongst others is the residence of the Avvocato Colla, to which is annexed a botanic garden, with hot-houses and conservatories.

At Rivoli begins an avenue of pollard elms, leading to Turin, about six miles in length, the distant extremity of the *vista* being terminated by the Superga.

6 kil. *Alpignano Stat.* near the large village of Pianezza, on the opposite side of the river. The railway has constantly on the rt. the long alley of elms leading from Rivoli to the capital.

4 kil. *Collegno Stat.*, a small town on the Dora, in the most fertile part of the plain: it gives a count's title to the Provana family. Here is a large Carthusian monastery; the fine Ionic façade was added to it in 1727. The knights of the Order of the Annunciad (the Garter of Piedmont) are interred under the ch. annexed to this monastery. The large château belongs to the Provana family. From Collegno to the capital the railway crosses the plain for 10 kil., passing on the l. the *Citadel* and the *Place. d'Armes* before reaching

9 kil. *Turin Terminus*, at the S. extremity of the town. Omnibuses convey travellers from the Rly. to the different hotels.

TURIN. *Inns:* Hôtel de l'Europe, kept by Trombetta, in the Piazza del Castello; very comfortable and well managed — excellent table-d'hôte at 4 fr.; and restaurant dinner in apartments 5 fr.; breakfast with eggs 1-50 to 1-75; bed-rooms 2-0 to 3-0. Hôtel de la Grande Bretagne, in the Contrada del Po, with a table-d'hôte. Hôtel Feder, in the Contrada di S. Francesco di Paola; tables-d'hôte at half-past 1 and at 5, 4 francs. Il dei Liguri, near the railway (to Genoa) station. Hôtel de la Ville, formerly the Pension Suisse. La Bonne Femme, tolerably good as a second-rate inn.

Cafés and *Restaurateurs:* The *Cafés* of Turin are numerous and good; the Fiorio, the San Carlo, and Café Nationale in the Contrada del Po, are the best. The prices at the cafés are not high: *e. g.* coffee, 20 cents; chocolate, 25 cents; ice, 25 cents; good white wine, 60 cents the bottle; red 50 cents. There are *restaurateurs* on the French plan: l'Universo; il Pastore; le Indie; and la Verna. At these establishments dinners may be had from 2 to 5 francs. The best restaurants, however, are at the Hôtel de l'Europe and the Grande Bretagne. The chocolate of Turin is reckoned the best in Italy. The Piedmontese bread, in long thin wands, called "grissini," is remarkably good. It was introduced by a physician, who found it in his own case more digestible than the ordinary bread. It takes its name from him.

The Post-office is in the Via delle Finanze, behind the Palazzo Carignano. The letters for Genoa and Tuscany, Rome and Naples, leave at an early hour, so that letters must be posted before 8 P.M. on the preceding day, or before 5 A.M. at the railway station.

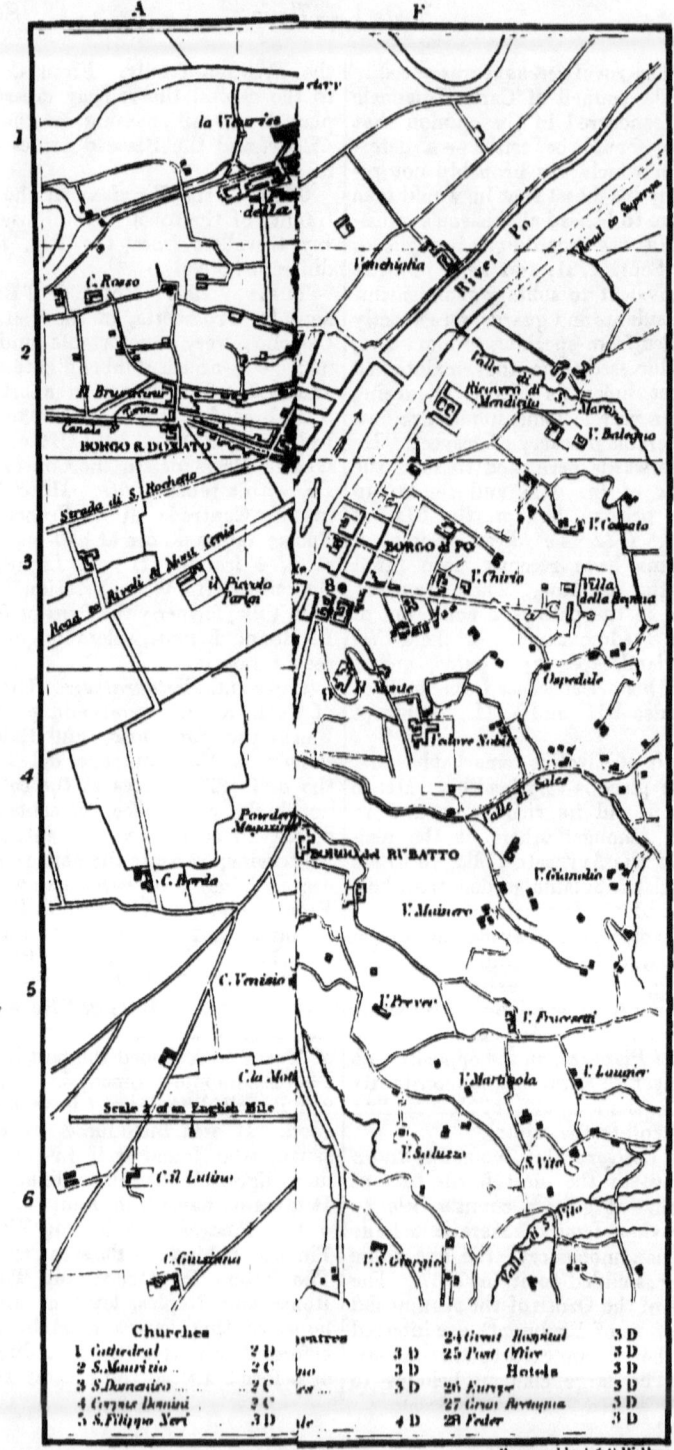

For France, England, and all countries to the north, the office closes at 8 P.M., and the courier leaves at 9. Letters to England may be prepaid or not: postage 60 c.; to the United States 1-20; to France 50 c.: letters not prepaid are charged double the prepayment on delivery in England and France, and *vice versâ* on arriving in Piedmont.

There are regular hackney coaches, or fiacres—*cittadini*; fares, 1 horse 1·50, 2 horses 3 francs an hour; private carriages 10 francs for half a day, 15 for the whole; excursion to the Superga 30 francs with 4 horses, with 2 horses 20 francs. For most purposes of excursion in and about the city, the fiacres answer quite as well as the more expensive carriages hired at the hotels. The owner of the Hôtel de l'Europe furnishes carriages at the same rates as the hackney ones.

Diligences, Mallespostes, &c.—Most of the public conveyances out of Turin are now in connection with the railways; the first in importance to the general traveller being those that cross the Mont Cenis into France. A malleposte starts every evening from the Post-office at 9½; and as its fares are very nearly the same (33 fr.) as by the ordinary diligences to St. Jean de Maurienne, it is to be preferred, especially in the winter season, as, from the state of the roads, the latter overloaded vehicles sometimes arrive too late for the express railway train. The malleposte takes 3 passengers, 2 inside, and 1 in the cabriolet. The administration of the Victor Emanuel Railway, whose offices are opposite the Post-office, despatch every day by the 7 P.M. train as many diligences as are necessary to convey its passengers over the Mont Cenis; they are in correspondence with the express trains for Paris, Lyons, and Geneva. Seats in the coupés can be secured at a trifling extra charge, the whole fare being to Paris 104 fr. and 106·50; and passengers can have their luggage registered for their destination by sending it a few hours before, which will save them much trouble. In ordinary weather these diligences arrive at St. Jean de Maurienne a couple of hours before the departure of the trains, giving the traveller time to breakfast. *Diligences* and a *Malleposte for Nice* start every evening from Cuneo on the arrival of the last railway train from Turin, crossing the Col di Tenda by daylight, and reaching Nice at 5 P.M. Places may be secured at the office in the Via dell' Arcivescovado at Turin; to *Aosta* by railway as far as Ivrea: the office for securing places in the coach is at the Albergo del Pozzo.

Vetturini and Private Carriages over the Mont Cenis.—Borgo, who may be heard of at the Hôtel de l'Europe, will undertake to convey travellers from the Rly. stat. at Susa to that of St. Jean de Maurienne, which can now be performed in a day, leaving Turin by the early morning train, and by changing horses at Modane, in which case a small additional charge of 20 francs is made; or with the same horses to St. Michel, where there is a fair inn, and the next morning to the rly. in time for the express train, which leaves at 12·30 for Paris, Lyons, and Geneva: the charge for a comfortable carriage will vary from 150 fr. for 2 persons to 200 and 220 for a small diligence that can accommodate a family of 8 or 9 persons with a large quantity of luggage. The same arrangements can be made at St. Jean de Maurienne for the journey to Turin, by writing to Borgo beforehand; his carriages are very good. The Messageries Impériales in connection with the rly. administration furnish carriages and post-horses under the denomination of *extra poste*, but their charges are much higher, without commensurate advantage, and their carriages in general far from comfortable—the charges being for 2 persons 220 fr.; for 3, 260; for 4, 280, in inconvenient open calèches; for 5, 320, for 6, 360, in closed carriages. But, we repeat, families especially will find it almost equally expeditious, and more economical and comfortable, besides the advantage of crossing the Mont Cenis by daylight, to employ respectable vetturini like Borgo, and to apply to the masters of the principal hotels to arrange the fares. It may be as well to add that there is now a very good hotel (l'Europe) close to the station at St. Jean de Maurienne.

Railways are now open in every direction from Turin :—Between Turin and *Genoa* 4 times a day (5·35, 9·50 A.M.; 3·15, 5·55 P.M.), in 4 and 5½ hrs., passing by Alexandria, Novi, and Asti: to *Susa* 5 times a day (6·10, 9·40 A.M.; 1, 7·10, and 10 P.M.; the latter in correspondance with the express train to Paris), in 1½ and 2 hrs. : to *Pinerolo* 4 times a day, in 1 hr. 10 m. : to *Cuneo* 4 times a day, in 2 hrs. 30 m., with branches to Bra and Saluzzo : to Milan 4 times a day (5·15, 8·37 A.M.; 1·30, 6·35 P.M.), in 3 hrs. 35 m. and 4 hrs. 30 m. ; with branches to Ivrea and the Val d'Aosta : to Biella: to Arona on the Lago Maggiore : to Casale and Mortara : to Piacenza, Parma, Modena, and Bologna, 3 times a day (at 5·35, 9·50 A.M., and 5·55 P.M.).

There are 2 Rly. stats. at Turin : that for Alexandria, Genoa, Bologna, Pinerolo, and Cuneo, at the extremity of the Contrada Nuova, S. of the town; and that for Novarra, Arona, Milan, Casale, Ivrea, and Biella, on the W. side, at the extremity of the Via di Santa Teresa and beyond the Old Citadel. Omnibuses run to meet the trains from the hotels. For details respecting the times of starting and fares see the several routes.

Physicians. Dr. J. Sapolini (Contrada di Goito, No. 9) has studied in England the English modes of treatment. Dr. Pacchiotti, who also speaks English.

Homœopathic Physician. Dr. Ajmini, Maison Natta, Piazza S. Carlo.

Apothecary. Thomassini, Via di S. Filippo.

The *English Protestant Service* is performed every Sunday, in an apartment in the rear of the Vaudois Ch. in the Stradale del Rò.

There are now no suburbs to Turin : what were the suburbs are taken into the town, and continuously built upon. It may be said to be one of the most flourishing cities of Europe.

Under the French, the population in 1813 sank to 65,000 : it is now 150,000 exclusive of the military, and is increasing yearly.

Turin is now unfortified ; the citadel, which is almost abandoned, and its outworks rased—to make room for the station of the Novara Rly. and the new portion of the town rapidly extending in that direction—was a remarkable monument of military architecture. It was built by Emanuele Filiberto in 1565 ; and, preceding Antwerp by two or three years, was the earliest specimen of regular fortification in Europe.

In Italy, the land the most rich in recollections of the past, Turin is perhaps the poorest city in this respect. Its history, whether under the Empire or during the middle ages, is almost a blank. Some of its marquises are obscurely noticed; Claudius Bishop of Turin (died 840) was distinguished by his opposition to the use of images in Divine worship, as a breach of the second commandment, and to the veneration of relics.

Turin has been repeatedly ruined: the last ravages it sustained were from Francis I., in 1536, who demolished the extensive suburbs, and reduced the limits of its ancient walls; destroying at the same time the amphitheatre and several other Roman remains. It is therefore almost denuded of any vestiges of classical or mediæval antiquity. A portion of the walls of the Palazzo delle Torri, at the N. extremity of the city, and so called from the two mediæval towers which were added, and some of the lower part of the Palazzo Madama, are perhaps the only exceptions. The reconstruction of the city, begun by Emanuele Filiberto and Carlo Emanuele I., is more due to Carlo Emanuele II. and Vittorio Amedeo II. Still further improvements have been more recently made, under the three late kings and the reigning monarch. At least one fourth of the city has been erected since the restoration of the royal family, and of later years nearly one third has been added to it on the

S. side, where entire streets and squares are rising as if by magic; a proof of the great prosperity of the country under its liberal institutions, which have made Turin the refuge of the persecuted and oppressed all over Italy. The streets, or *contrade*, are all in straight lines, intersecting each other at right angles. The blocks, or masses, of buildings, formed by these intersections, are called *isole*, an architectural Latinism retained here and also in Provence. The houses are of brick intended for stucco. They are large, the windows and doors are ornamented, and crowned with a cornice. Through the perspective of the streets, the hills which surround the city, and the more distant Alps, are continually in view.

Turin is situated in the plain which forms the angle between the Dora Riparia and the Po, just above the junction of these two rivers: the first is a fine mountain torrent; the latter a deep and rapid river.

" Cosi scendendo dal natio suo monte
Non empie umile il Pò l' angusta sponda;
Ma sempre più, quanto è più lunge al fonte,
Di nove forze insuperbito abonda.
Sovra i rotti confini alza la fronte
Di tauro, e vincitor d' intorno inonda:
E con più corna Adria respinge, e pare
Che guerra porti, e non tributo, al mare."—
Tasso, Gier. Lib., ix. st. 46.

It is supposed to have been founded by a Ligurian tribe called the Taurini; the earliest mention we find of it is for its resistance to Hannibal after his celebrated passage of the Alps. At a later period it became a Roman colony under the name of *Augusta Taurinorum*. Destroyed by Constantine for having espoused the cause of Maxentius, sacked and ruined successively by Stilicho, Attila, and Odoacer, we find it in the hands of its dukes at the invasion of the Lombards. In the 11th century it was the capital of a county, the chief of which and last of the male branch, Manfred III., married his only daughter Adelaide to Otho of Savoy in 1045, the origin of its possession by the present royal family. The most remarkable events in the more modern history of Turin are the two memorable sieges it stood in 1649 and 1706 : the first during the contest between the French and Spaniards, when the latter, headed by Prince Tomasso of Savoy, capitulated to Marshal d'Harcourt: the second during the war of the Succession, when, Piedmont siding against Louis XIV., V. Amadeo was besieged in his capital, which he defended heroically for 3 months before a very superior force, until the arrival of Prince Eugene and the imperialist army, which was followed by the signal defeat of the French (Sept. 7, 1706), and their being forced to raise the siege.

Beyond the Po is the lovely range of hills called the *Collina di Torino*, rising to the height of nearly 1600 feet. They are sparkling with villas; their valleys are richly clothed with vegetation; and advantage has been taken of these varieties of surface in many of the beautiful gardens and grounds attached to the villas.

The climate of Turin is influenced by the vicinity of the Alps; the winters are cold and foggy, the quantity of rain is considerable; and hail-storms are frequent in summer, when the crops are sometimes literally cut in pieces by them; hence the institution of insurance offices against this risk.

The architect principally employed at Turin by Carlo Emanuele II. was *Guarini* (1624-1683), a Theatine monk, an able mathematician, and who well used his mathematical knowledge in his bold and daring constructions. *Juvara*, a Sicilian by birth (1685-1735), was much patronised by Vittorio Amedeo II. There is a great difference in the style of these two architects, but both have in common a neglect of the rules of Vitruvius or Palladio; more moderated perhaps in Juvara, but carried to the utmost extent in Guarini. Hence both have been much criticised.

The *Cathedral*, or *Duomo*, is the oldest of the ecclesiastical edifices in Turin. The original structure was founded by Agilulph King of the Lombards, about 602. The present building was begun 1498, and consecrated in 1505.

The architect's name is unknown, Baccio Pintelli by some being supposed to have designed it, whilst others attribute it to *Meo del Caprino:* it has been much altered, and some arabesques in the pilasters of the façade are the only remarkable portions of the original structure. The interior has been very recently decorated with frescoes. The vaulting contains the Scripture history, from the expulsion of Adam and Eve from Paradise to the giving of the Law. Over the arches are the principal events in the life of St. John the Baptist; at the west end is a copy of the Cenacolo of Leonardo da Vinci, also in fresco. The older pictures are not very remarkable. The best are the following: *Albert Durer,* the Virgin and Saints, in the 2nd chapel. — *F. Zucchero,* the Resurrection.—*Casella,* St. Cosmo and St. Damiano.—Two statues, by *Pierre le Gros,* of Sta. Teresa and Sta. Christina, have been much praised; but except in their mechanical execution they have not great merit.

There are few sepulchral monuments in this church. The most remarkable is that in the winter choir, of Claude Seyssell, who, after filling successively the places of professor in the university of Turin, and of Master of Requests in France, where he was employed by Louis XII. on several diplomatic missions, became Bishop of Marseilles, and, subsequently, Archbishop of Turin, where he died in 1520.

The high altar is ornamented by a most splendid display of church plate : by the side of it, in the l. transept, is the tribune, or gallery for the royal family.

The sacristy contains several magnificent crosses, vases, reliquiaries, and the like, of which the chief is a large statue of the Virgin, crowned, and standing under a silver-gilt canopy. On the festival of the Nativity of the Virgin (8th Sept.) a procession takes place, equally in honour of the Virgin and in commemoration of the delivery of the city from the French (see *Superga,* p. 31) in 1706. Vittorio Amedeo, assisted by the Imperial and Prussian troops, under Prince Eugene and Field Marshal Daun, who occupied Turin, and the Prince of Anhalt, gained a complete and decisive victory. The French lost 153 pieces of cannon and 60 mortars; this victory was the salvation of the house of Savoy, whose destruction was sought by Louis XIV. with the most inveterate antipathy. Of late years this procession has been so much reduced in splendour as to be now scarcely worth the traveller's putting himself out of the way to witness it. Another procession takes place on the festival of *Corpus Domini.*

Behind the cathedral, seen through the arch over the high altar, and entered by a flight of stairs on the rt., is the chapel of the *Santo Sindone,* or *Sudario,* said to be the masterpiece of Guarini. Its cupola is formed of arched ribs, from the summits of which others spring in succession, thus forming a sort of dome. The capitals of the columns, and some other ornamental portions, are of bronze. In these capitals the crown of thorns is introduced amidst the leaves of the acanthus. The pavement is inlaid with bronze stars. In the centre is the altar, of black marble, upon which is placed the shrine, brilliant with gold, silver, and precious stones. Four silver lamps, given by the late queen, are suspended on either side. The *Santo Sudario,* according to the ecclesiastical legend, is one of the folds of the shroud in which our Lord was wrapped by Joseph of Arimathea, and on which an impression was left of his body; other folds being preserved at Rome, at Besançon, and at Cadouin in Périgord. This one was brought from Cyprus, and presented in 1452, by Margherite de Charni, the descendant of a nobleman of Champagne, who was said to have obtained it during the Crusades : but there is no mention of its existence until the fifteenth century, when, having been given by Margherite to Duke Louis II., it was first deposited at Chambéry, from which it was brought to Turin, in 1578, by Emanuel Philibert, for the purpose of enabling St. Carlo

Borromeo to venerate it without the fatigue of crossing the Alps. While it was at Chambéry it was invoked by Francis I. previously to the battle of Marignano, and on his return to France he went on foot from Lyons to worship it. A sitting statue of the late Queen Maria Adelaide, by *Revelli*, a Genoese sculptor, has been recently erected in this chapel. In the niches round the sanctuary have been placed by the late King Charles Albert monuments to four of the most renowned members of the house of Savoy—viz. to Emanuel Philibert, whose remains are beneath—a very fine work by *Marchesi*; to Prince Thomas of Savoy, from whom descend the present Sovereigns of Piedmont, of the branch of Carignano, by *Gaggini*, a Genoese and pupil of Canova; to Charles Emanuel II., by *Fracaroli*; and to Amedeo VIII., by *Cacciatori*. The inscriptions are from the pen of Cavaliere Cibrario.

Many of the other churches of Turin are splendidly decorated: amongst these may be noticed—

Ch. of La Consolata, which derives its name from a supposed miraculous painting of the Virgin, the object of much veneration. The picture is, in the opinion of Lanzi, the production of a pupil of the school of Giotto, though attributed by the legend to the age of St. Eusebius, Bishop of Vercelli, in the fourth century. This church is a combination of three churches opening into each other; the most ancient founded in the 10th centy. by the monks of the abbey of Novalesa, after their expulsion by the Saracens, and dedicated to St. Andrew. The present edifice dates from the end of the 17th centy.; the architect was Guarini. Juvara subsequently erected the high altar. It is richly decorated with marbles, many of which are very beautiful. The corridor leading to one of the churches of the Consolata is covered with *ex votos*, chiefly paintings of the rudest kind. On the Piazza opposite the church stands a handsome column of Biella granite, erected in 1835, surmounted by a statue of the Virgin of the Consolata, to record the cessation of the cholera.

Ch. del Corpus Domini (one of the finest in Turin), built by Vitozzi in 1607; but the whole of the interior is from the designs of Count Alfieri. It is very rich, and is a characteristic specimen of the architect and of his age. In the centre is a railed-in marble slab, with an inscription, to commemorate the miraculous recovery of a piece of Sacramental plate containing the blessed wafer, which, being stolen during the pillage of Exilles by a soldier, and hidden in one of his panniers, the ass carrying it refused to pass the church door; the sacred vase fell to the ground, and the wafer, rising into the air, remained suspended there, encircled with rays of light, until the bishop and his clergy came out to receive it. This singular miracle, said to have taken place in 1453, is represented in 3 paintings on the vault of the church.

Ch. of San Domenico contains a picture of the Virgin and Child presenting the rosary to the patron saint, by *Guercino*.

Ch. of San Filippo. This church was one of the trials of skill of Guarini, but here it failed him; and the cupola, which was somewhat upon the plan of that of the Santo Sudario, with a great part of the church, fell in 1714. It was rebuilt by *Juvara*. San Filippo is one of the finest churches in Turin. Over the heavy high altar, supported by 6 barbarous torse columns, is a painting of the Virgin and Child with S. John and S. Eusebius, and 2 holy persons of the House of Savoy, by *Carlo Maratta*. In other parts of the church are pictures of S. Philip before the Virgin, by *Solimena*, and of S. John Nepomucene, by *Seb. Conca*.

Ch. of San Lorenzo, on the Piazza del Castello, an extreme example of the fancy of Guarini, is curious from its fantastical dome, formed on ribs, each of which is the chord of 3-8ths of a circle; in this may readily be traced the architect of the Chapel of the Sudario. It was erected by Emmanuele Filiberto in consequence of a row for his success at the battle of St. Quentin.

La gran Madre di Dio, opposite the bridge over the Po, was begun 1818 in commemoration of the restoration of the royal family, and finished about 1840. The building is an imitation of the Pantheon at Rome, the architect Buonsignore. This edifice is said to have cost 100,000*l*. sterling, chiefly contributed by king Carlo Felice, and forms a fine close to the vista at the extremity of the Contrada del Po.

Ch. of San Maurizio, belonging to the military order of St. Maurizio and S. Lazzaro, with an oval cupola; and a recent façade by *Mosca*.

There are nearly 40 other churches in Turin, none very remarkable for their architecture, their historical interest, or the objects of art which they contain.

A handsome *Protestant church* was commenced in 1851, and consecrated 2 years afterwards, in the fine *Viale dei Platani* of the Stradale del Re, chiefly for the use of the Vaudois, of whom there is a considerable number settled at Turin. The service is performed in French, according to the Vaudois rite. The building, by the architect Formento, is in a Lombardo-Norman style. The principal part of the expense was contributed by the government, which, for this, and for even having assented to the erection of such an edifice, has been visited with great animadversion by the bigoted party, and by the ever illiberal councils of the Vatican.

The *Piazza Castello*, containing some of the principal public edifices, is surrounded by lofty palaces, which extend also along the Strada del Po, a noble perspective, terminating with the green slopes of la Collina ; in the same manner as the Contrada Dora Grossa, on the other side of the Piazza, terminates in the opposite direction with the prospect of the snowy peaks of the Alps about Mont Cenis.

The *Royal Palace*, on the N. side of the Piazza, was raised by Carlo Emanuele II., from the designs of the Count di Castellamonte. The exterior has no pretension to magnificence, except from its size. The fine iron railing and gates which separate it from the Piazza are from designs by Palagi ; the bronze statues of Castor and Pollux by Sangiorgio. The interior is well arranged, and, besides the usual apartments for the state and residence of a sovereign, contains within it many of the public offices. On the principal staircase is an equestrian statue of Vittorio Amedeo I., commonly called "*Il Cavallo di Marmo*," the animal being much more prominent than his rider. The figures of captives at the feet of the horse are by Adriano Frisio, a scholar of Giov. da Bologna. The great old-fashioned hall, formerly appropriated to the Swiss Guards, is open to the public. The large hall or anteroom of the Guards is covered with paintings of battle-scenes : opening out of it on the rt. is the suite of royal apartments. In the first room is a large picture of the Judgment of Solomon, by *Podesti;* in the second a large painting of the battle of St. Quentin, attributed to *Palma Giovane*. The state apartments are splendidly furnished ; modern luxury being united to the heavy magnificence of the last century. They were restored and newly decorated during the reign of Charles Albert, under the directions of Cav. Palagi. The inlaid floors, in woods of different colours, are remarkably beautiful. In the King's *Salle de Travail* are a series of modern paintings of members of the House of Savoy remarkable for their piety, or who were members of religious orders. The *Great Gallery*, a splendid apartment overlooking the gardens, contains portraits of sovereigns of the reigning family, and of men of eminence in every department, natives of the country. Beyond this is the *apartment of the Queen*, with magnificent boudoirs. In the room called the *Guardaroba della Regina* are some good Etruscan vases, and a large picture of Taormina, with Ætna in the distance, by Cav. *Massimo d' Azeglio;* near this is the *Chapel,* gaudy and heavy. The *State Dining-room* contains several indifferent historical pictures—one of a tournament at the Court of France between Amadeus VIII. of Savoy and the three English Earls of Harrington, Arundel, and Pembroke. The *Salle de Reception de la Reine* is richly decorated with a profusion of Chinese and Japan porcelain vases. The last apartment is the *State Ball-room,* which offers nothing remarkable. The *Chapel of the Santo Sudario,* generally closed during the afternoon on the side of the Cathedral, can always be entered from the palace, near the anteroom of the State apartments. The King's *Private Library,* on the ground floor, is a very handsome hall, containing 40,000 printed vols. and 2000 MSS. Amongst the latter are some curious documents and correspondence :—the materials sent by Frederick "the Great" to Count Algarotti as the basis for the history of the seven years' war ; letters of Emanuel Filibert, Prince Eugene, and Napoleon ; many Arabic and Syrian manuscripts. Cavaliere Promis is the librarian. There is also a valuable collection of drawings by old masters, formed by Volpato. In the passage leading into the library are several early Christian inscriptions from the Catacombs at Rome, a few in Greek characters. The palace communicates by a wing, called the Galerie di Beaumont, with the offices of the Secretaries of State.

Under the roof of the palace, and adjoining the state apartments, but entered from the side of the Piazza, is the *Armeria Regia.* This collection was formed in 1834, partly from the arsenals of Turin and Genoa, and partly from private collections purchased by the late king, especially that of the Martinengo family of Brescia. It contains several pieces of historical interest, and is considered as one of the principal *shows* of Turin. It has been judiciously arranged by the late director, Count Seyssell d'Aix. Permission to visit it is obtainable in the library below, from the concierge. The following are amongst the chief objects :—

20, 33. Two suits which belonged to Antonio di Martinengo in the 15th century, both ornamented with damasquine and other engravings of excellent design : the latter (33) is the finest in the collection.

35. The full suit of the Duke Emanuele Filiberto, or Tête de Fer, and worn by him on the great day of the battle of St. Quentin. (See Piazza di San Carlo.) Emanuele himself was a very good armourer, not only in the coarse smith's work, but in the finer departments of inlaying with silver, or damasquining, and it is said that the armour which he wore was his own manufacture. Pacific as he was in the later years of his life, he never went into public except in his panoply, and bearing his good sword under his arm. This armour is copied in Marochetti's fine statue in the Piazza S. Carlo.

37. A suit fit for a giant, respecting which there have been many conjectures. Nothing is known of its history or owner ; it bears a ducal coronet and the letter F.

67. The staff of command of Alfonso di Ferrara (1515).

104. The like of the celebrated burgomaster Tiepolo.

239. A magnificent suit of damasquined steel.

275. The cuirass of Prince Eugene, with three deep bullet indentations in front, worn by him at the battle of Turin, where, as before mentioned, the French were totally defeated ; and (990) his sword worn on the same memorable occasion.

288. Cuirass worn by Carlo Emanuele III. at the battle of Guastalla, 19th September, 1734.

292-294. Helmets in the style of the Renaissance. The last belonged to the celebrated surgeon and anatomist Scarpa of Pavia, who, towards the close of his life, was as fond of it as Dr. Woodward was of his shield, and made it the subject of a special dissertation, which he printed privately for his friends, illustrated with beautiful engravings. It is covered with imagery, representing Jove thundering upon the Titans. 381-385, 394, 395. Shields and targets in the same style. 380 is exceedingly rich, embossed with subjects representing the contests between Marius and Jugurtha. Amongst the ornaments is introduced a crescent, supposed to be the device of Diana of Poitiers; but more probably the armorial bearings of its owner. It is of the best period of modern art, and has been attributed to Benvenuto Cellini, the reputed father of all works of this description. 394 is also very splendid, representing the labours of Hercules. 819-821. Three very delicate triangular-bladed stilettoes, which, it is said, were carried by Italian ladies for the purpose of ridding themselves of husbands or lovers. 943. Sword of Duke Emanuele Filiberto, formerly preserved in the "Camera de' Conti," and upon which the officers of state were sworn. Amongst the other objects worthy of notice in the armoury may be mentioned an ancient Roman eagle, bearing the inscription Leg: VIII., found in Savoy, and the two Imperial eagles of Napoleon's Italian Guard, presented by one of its commanders, General Lecchi. The sword worn by Napoleon at Marengo; several Russian flags taken by the Piedmontese during the siege of Sebastopol; the sword of the leader of the Theban Legion, given to Duke Charles Emanuel by the Abbey of Agauno in 1571; and the rostrum of an ancient galley in bronze, in the form of a wild boar's head, found in the port of Genoa, have been lately added to the collection.

The collection of Oriental arms is extensive, as also of S. American. Amongst the former is a sword of Tippoo Saib, given by him to Gen. de Boigne, a Savoyard officer, who had been much employed by the native princes of India. The series of fire-arms of different periods is also considerable, and very many interesting as works of manufacture and art, amongst which may be particularised—1534, the arquebuse which belonged to Emmanuel Philibert; 1547, another, incrusted with ivory, with designs of mythological subjects; and, 1548, a third, having exceedingly beautiful subjects sculptured on ivory, representing Meleager and Atalanta In the anteroom are busts of some Sardinian military celebrities, and models of warlike engines and apparatus.

At the extremity of the armoury is a smaller apartment; over the door is a marble bust of King Carlo Alberto, with his swords, and two Austrian standards, captured, at Somma Campagna, during the campaign of 1849. This cabinet contains the private collection of medals formed by the late king: it is particularly rich in those of the house of Savoy, and of the Italian States in modern times; over the cases of the medals are several bronzes found in the Island of Sardinia, supposed to be of Phœnician origin, and a series of Roman bronzes discovered in the ruins of the Roman station of Industria, amongst which the statue of a youthful Cupid is very beautiful.

Adjoining the palace, and, in fact, forming part of it, for there is a continued series of internal communications, are the following buildings and establishments:—

The *Reali Segretarie*, containing the offices of secretaries of state and the principal departments of government.

The *Archivi*, in which is deposited a very rich collection of diplomas and charters; a selection from these is in course of publication. Annexed to these archives is a very select library of early printed books and manuscripts.

The *Accademia Militare* forms also a part of the same pile. It encloses a large quadrangle, of handsome and scenic effect. The institution, which was re-organized in 1839, is said to be very complete and efficient.

Lastly, the *Teatro Regio*. It was built from the designs of the Count Alfieri, and was the building which made his fortune. Alfieri, born at Rome, was educated as an advocate; but his exceeding love for architecture soon induced him to abandon the bar. He never mentioned the name of Michael Angelo without taking off his hat or beretta. Having been employed at Tortona, when Carlo Emanuele II. happened to pass through that town, the monarch was so pleased with his work, that he took the young advocate into his service, and at once intrusted the building of this theatre to him; and so satisfactory was the production, that Alfieri was forthwith appointed court architect, and became the object of every species of favour. He obtained the reputation of the best architect of his time.

In the centre of the Piazza del Castello is the ancient castle, now converted into the *Palazzo Madama*. Of the old castle, founded by Ludovico d'Acaya in the early part of the 14th century, the principal vestiges are the two towers, which have been before mentioned. Two others exist, concealed by the modern buildings. When restored by Amedeo VIII., 1416, this castle was at the extremity of the city. The principal front was added to the old structure in 1720, after the designs of Juvara. It is an excellent piece of street architecture. The other three were to have been completed after the same design. It was fitted up as a palace for *Madama Reale*, mother of King Victor Amadeus II., in 1718. It now contains the Hall of Assembly and Bureaus of the Senate, the Royal Gallery of Pictures, and the Astronomical Observatory on the summit of one of its towers. In front of the P. Madama, and facing the wide Via di Dora Grossa, the entrance from Mont Cenis, stands a statue of a Piedmontese soldier, a good work by Vela, the Lugano sculptor, erected by the Lombard emigrants to the Piedmontese army, in memory of its heroic deeds for the liberation of their country in 1849.

The *Royal Gallery of Pictures* formed by Carlo Alberto with paintings formerly scattered through the Royal Palaces. The great entrance hall remains nearly as it was when the building was used as a palace: it is adorned with paintings representing the deeds of the house of Savoy.

The gallery is open daily; on Sundays from 9 till 2, and on other days from 9 till 4. The rooms are plainly but appropriately fitted up. Some of these being used as committee rooms by the Senate, the paintings are seen with difficulty during the session of the Parliament (Dec. to June); indeed many of them are entirely removed during this period to prevent their being injured by the fires necessary for heating the apartments. By a decree of the government a new building is to be erected for a picture gallery, the direction of which has been confided to the Cavaliere Massimo Azeglio, himself a most talented artist. In the mean time the principal paintings are the following; but their arrangement has been so often altered that it is difficult to give a correct description of the objects contained in each room. That which follows is as it existed in 1859. There are two good printed catalogues. The three first apartments, occupied by the Senate, are entirely closed to the visitor in the Parliamentary Session, and the best pictures in them removed to others. During the sittings of the Senate the gallery can only be seen before 12 o'clock.

ROOM 1. *Sala Piemontese.* — Gaudenzio Ferrari, a Crucifixion in distemper, on canvas, being the design for one of the frescoes at Vercelli (see Vercelli),—very rich, although only a sketch, and offering scarcely any variation from the fresco, which is much damaged;—an Entombment, on wood, very fine;—a subject called the Conversion of St. Paul, but more probably a legend of some other saint; St. Peter and a devotee; a Resurrection, with Saints. *Bernardino Lanini*, a Holy Family and Saints on wood, 1564; Deposition from the Cross, 1545; Deposition with Saints, 1558. *Giovenone*, Resurrection; a Virgin and Saints. *Olivieri*, a Crucifixion.

ROOM 2.—RAPHAEL, *La Madonna della Tenda*, on wood,—a very beautiful picture, whether it be really by Raphael or not; for there are at least three repetitions, all claiming to be originals : one is at Munich, another is or was in Spain, and this is the third. Its history is said to be as follows :— a certain Cardinal delle Lanze gave it as a present to a Countess Porporate : upon her death it came to the Countess of Broglio, who sold it for 800 francs. It then passed, no one knows exactly how, to Professor Boucheron, who kindly "relinquished it," as the phrase is, to the late king, when Prince of Carignano, for 75,000 francs (3000*l*.). Passavant says that competent judges consider it to be a good copy by Pierino del Vaga.—TITIAN, the Supper at Emmaus, a noble picture, bought by Cardinal Maurice of Savoy in 1660, and said to be the original of that in the Louvre; a portrait. —*Palma Vecchio*, Holy Family and Saints, the Virgin crowning a Figure in front.—*Guercino*, Virgin and Child; a Figure, half naked, with a red Beretta, and bearing a great Sword, called David; a Virgin and Child.—*Panini*, Interiors of the Basilicas of San Paolo fuori le Mura, and of St. Peter's, at Rome.—*Bassano*, a Market.—*Guido*, Sta. Caterina with a lamb.—*Cignani*, Venus and Cupid.—*Crespi*, a Confessional.—*Cesare da Sesto*, Virgin and Child.

ROOM 3.—*Mantegna*, Holy Family and Saints.—PAUL VERONESE, Pharaoh's Daughter finding Moses, a splendid picture, in which the artist has introduced his own portrait; Magdalene washing our Lord's Feet at the table of the Pharisee. This fine picture formed until recently one of the principal ornaments of the collection at the Palazzo Reale or Durazzo at Genoa; Queen of Sheba's Visit to Solomon.—*Bassano*, Rape of the Sabines; a Fair.—*Titian*, Adoration of the Shepherds; Fall of Troy; Judgment of Paris; Rape of Helen; Æneas sacrificing : all in Titian's early style.—*Salvator Rosa*, a very fine Landscape, with the Baptism of our Lord.—*Canaletti*, Turin from the N.E.; Old Bridge at Turin; fine.—*Badile*, Presentation in the Temple.—*Beltraffio*, Angels singing.— *Vanni*, a Magdalene.—*Bronzino*, Portrait of Cosimo I., very characteristic. —*Carlo Dolce*, Mater Dolorosa.—*C. Maratta*, the Angel Gabriel.—*Velasquez*, Portrait of Maria Colonna Spinola. —*Guercino*, Head of St. Elizabeth of Hungary.—*Pompeo Battoni*, Æneas carrying Anchises.—*Solimena*, four pictures.

ROOM 4.—*Guercino*, Sta. Francesca Romana.—*L. Spada*, David. — *Spagnoletto*, Homer.—*Bassano*, Venus and Cupid superintending the forging of the Armour of Mars.—*Andrea del Sarto*, Holy Family.—*Semino*, Adoration of the Shepherds, on wood, 1584. —*Cignani*, Adonis and his Dog.—*Spagnoletto*, St. Jerome. — *Mazzuchelli*, Lucretia. — *Procaccini*, Virgin with Saints; S. Carlo Borromeo and S. Francis.—*Guido*, Combat between three Sons of Venus and three of Bacchus; Samson, the same subject as in the Pinacotheca at Bologna.—*P. Battoni*, Return of the Prodigal Son. — *Annib. Caracci*, St. Peter.—*Carlo Dolce*, Head of Christ.—*Sasso Ferrato*, Virgin and Child.—*Giorgione*, a Portrait.— *Domenichino*, Three Children, as emblems of Architecture, Astronomy, and Agriculture.—*Guercino*, Return of the Prodigal Son, very beautiful.—*Velasquez*, Portrait of Philip IV.—*Carlo Dolce*, Mater Dolorosa. — *Bernardino Luini*, Herodias' Daughter receiving the Head of St. John the Baptist.— *Lomi*, the Annunciation. — *Moroni*, Carlo III., Duke of Savoy, and his Wife.

ROOM 5. Circular Sala in the N.E. tower.—*Cagnacci*, Magdalene.—*Piola*, Bacchante.—*Schidone*, two subjects of Children's Heads.—*Raphael* (?), Virgin and Child, in his very early manner. —*Panini*, three pictures of Ruins.— *Guercino*, Head of our Lord.—*Seiter*, a dead Christ.—*Moroni*, Portraits of a Doge of Venice and his Wife.—*Bassano*, the Deposition of our Saviour in the Sepulchre; an Ecce Homo.— *Guido*, Lucretia; Fame on a Globe. —*Ricci*, Magdalene washing the Saviour's Feet; Abraham dismissing Hagar; Solomon sacrificing to Idols.— *Bernardino Luini*, Holy Family. — *Cesare d'Arpino*, Adam and Eve driven from Paradise.—*Sementi*, Cleopatra.— *Daniel da Volterra* a Crucifixion, fine. —*Garofalo*, Christ disputing with the Doctors, a beautiful picture. — *Ciro Ferri*, the Agony in the Garden.—*C. Allori*, Jacob's Vision. — *Beltraffio*, Marriage of St. Catherine.—*Giorgione*, Herodias' Daughter receiving the Head of St. John, fine.—*Vanni*, a Crucifixion, with Saints.

ROOM 6.—*Baltoni*, a Nativity.—*Tintoretto*, our Lord on the Cross received into Heaven by the Father. —*Titian*, a fine Portrait of Paul III.—*Pietro da Cortona*, Rebecca at the Well.—*L. Cambiasi*, the Wise Men's Offering. —*Giovanni Bellini*, Virgin and Child, and Saints, a fine picture. — *Tiarini*, St. Peter.—*Morazzone*, Virginia stabbing herself.—*Pordenone*, Holy Family and Saints. — *Guido*, St. John Baptist; Apollo flaying Marsyas, a very disagreeable painting; St. Jerome. — *Franciabigio*, Holy Family and Saints.— *Dan. da Volterra*, Decollation of St. John.—*Piola*, St. Paul.—*F. Francia*, an Entombment.—*Salviati*, the Wise Men's Offering.—*Grechetto*, Satyrs in a Landscape. —*Elisabetta Sirani*, Cain killing Abel.—*Caravaggio*, Reading at Night.—*Bronzino*, Portrait of Elleonora of Toledo.

ROOM 7.—*Albani*, Earth, Air, Fire, Water. These allegorical paintings are among the finest works of Albani. They were painted for Cardinal Maurice of Savoy; and Albani in two of his letters, written in 1626, has explained the meaning of his allegories with much clearness and originality. Venus represents *fire*. The Cardinal had directed the painter to give him "*una copiosa quantità di amoretti;*" and Albani served him to his heart's content. The amoretti in this and the other companion pictures are exquisitely playful. *Juno* is the representative of Air; and her nymphs are, with much odd ingenuity, converted into the atmospheric changes. Dew, rain, lightning, and thunder form one group. *Water* is figured by the triumph of Galatea: at the bottom of the picture are nymphs and Cupid fishing for pearls and coral. *Earth* is personified by Cybele, whose car is surrounded by three seasons, winter being excluded. Here the Cardinal's Cupids are occupied in various agricultural labours.

ROOM 8.—Male and female portraits, incorrectly called Cromwell and his wife, in the catalogue, and attributed to Sir P. Lely — *Vandyke*, Holy Family, a rich painting.—*Vanloo*, Louis XV.—*Luca da Leida*, Crowning of a Sovereign.—*Rubens*, 4 heads.—*Jan Miel*, a Market.—*Valentin*, our Lord hound.—*Vandyke*, Virgin and Child.— *Mytens*, Charles I. of England.—*Rubens*, an unknown portrait in armour.—*Angelica Kauffman*, a portrait.—*Rubens*, a Magdalene.—*Mignard*, Louis XIV.— *Teniers*, Peasants dancing.—*Jan Miel*, a Royal Chace.—*Rembrandt*, the Wise Men's Offering.—*Rubens*, Holy Family. —*Vandyke*, three Children of Charles I. (fine); six Heads of Children of the House of Savoy.—*Porbus*, Portrait of a Lady of the same Family.

ROOM 9.—*Rothenhammer*, the Nativity.—*Bernhardt*, a Family at Supper. —*Wouvermans*, a Battle-piece, *la Bicoque*, good.—*Rubens*, our Lord and the Magdalene.—*Holbein*, Portrait of Calvin. — *Vandyke*, Assumption of the

Virgin.—*C. Moor*, Pyramus and Thisbe. —*Ravenstein*, Portrait of Catherine of Savoy. — *Rubens*, a Burgomaster. — *Poussin*, Peasants. — *Luca da Leida*, Crucifixion, altarpiece in 3 compartments. — *Mabuse*, an excellent Crucifixion.—*Siffert*, Holy Family.—*Geldorp*, Portrait of a Lady.—*Rubens*, two Heads. — *Vandyke*, Holy Family. — *Rubens*, Boar and Dogs.—*Vander Werf*, Adam and Eve lamenting the Death of Abel.—*Rembrandt*, Resurrection of Lazarus.—*C. Netscher*, a Knife-grinder. —*Ostade*, old Man and Woman.— *Lustermans*, a Head. — *Rembrandt*, a Rabbin.

ROOM 10.— *Rubens*, three Heads.— *Vandyke*, Nymphs and Bacchantes.— *Fytt*, two Fruit and Game pieces.— *F. Mieris, sen.*, three Heads.—*G. Crayer*, our Lord teaching the Doctors; an Entombment.—*Holbein*, Portrait of Erasmus; ditto of himself.—*Teniers*, two Interiors of Taverns. — *P. Potter*, four Oxen, a well-studied and carefully executed work.—*G. Honthorst*, Samson shorn.—*Vander Werf*, Shepherd and Shepherdess.—*G. le Duc*, a Head.— *G. Terburg*, a Head.—*G. Dow*, Woman looking out at a Window; Head of a Man; Boy and Girl at a Window.— *Holbein*, Portrait of a Man; ditto of a Lady. — *Wouvermans*, Battle-piece. — *Hans Hemling*, History of our Lord's Passion, a most singular succession of scenes, in the same style as the Nativity in the Boisserée collection.

ROOM 11.—Flower-pieces, by *Breughel*, *Van Huysum*, and *Snyders*.

ROOM 12.—*A. Durer*, the Salutation by St. Elizabeth; Man praying.—*Holbein*, a Portrait called Luther and his Wife, dated 1542.—*Jordaens*, Our Lord and Angels; raising of Lazarus.—*Vandyke*, a Holy Family.—*Teniers*, a Lady and Music, in his best manner; Interior of a Tavern, with Music.—*Rubens* and *Breughel*, Venus and Cupid in a Landscape.—*Breughel, sen.*, Village Dance. —*Mignard*, St. John; Scene in an Arbour. — *Teniers, sen.*, a Countryman and his Wife talking with a Lawyer.—*Rembrandt*, a striking Portrait of an old Man.—*Poussin*, St. Margaret.—*Wouvermans*, Halt of Horsemen.—*Rubens*, Portrait of himself when very old.

ROOM 13.—*Of the Battles*. *Hugtemberg*, 12 pictures of battles, between 1697 and 1716, in which Prince Eugene of Savoy commanded; amongst others the Battle of Turin, which is historically and locally very interesting. —*De la Pegna*, 4 battle-pieces.—*Vandermeulen*, 4 battle-pieces, in which princes of the house of Savoy played a conspicuous part.

ROOM 14. — *Breughel de Velours*, River scene; ditto, with Ruins.—*Willingen*, Interior of a Church.—*Jan Miel*, Modeller's Studio.—*Peter Neefs*, Interior of a Cathedral.—*Teniers*, a Man playing.—*Jordaens*, Diana and Nymphs bathing.—*Van Vitelli*, Port of Naples; the Coliseum.—*A. Durer*, Deposition from the Cross; a fine Holy Family— *Lucas da Leida*, Death of the Virgin.— *Jordaens*, Boar-hunting.—*Gagnereau*, Cupids and Lion.—*Jan Miel*, Roman Ruins.—*Rubens*, Sketch for one of the series of the life of Mary de' Medici in the Louvre.—*Schalken*, View near a Ruin, with figures.—*Holbein*, Portrait (?).— *Breughel de Velours*, Passage of the Red Sea; a Fair.

ROOM 15.—*Constantin*, 18 modern copies of celebrated pictures in the galleries of Florence, upon porcelain.

ROOM 16.—Landscapes: by *Breughel de Velours*; *Claude Lorraine*; *Both*; *Vanloo*; *Greffier*; *Vander Meulen*; *Gaspar Poussin*; *Tempesta*; *Brill*; *Vries*; *Manglard*; *Peter Neefs*, Interior of a Cathedral; *Vries*; and 5 views of places about Turin by *Vanloo*.

ROOM 17.—Family Portraits of the Royal House of Savoy.—*Vanschuppen*,

Prince Eugene. — *P. de Champagne*, Prince Tomaso and his wife.—*Argenta*, Emmanuele Filiberto in his childhood. *Horace Vernet*, portrait of the late king Carlo Alberto.—Copy of *Guido*, Cardinal Maurice of Savoy. — *Vandyke*, Portrait on horseback of Prince Thomas of Savoy.—*Jan Miel*, Portrait of the wife of Carlo Emmanuele II.; Statues of Mars, Mercury, Ceres, and Flora, and Busts of Emmanuele Filiberto, Carlo Emmanuele II., and Cardinal Maurice of Savoy, by *Collini*.

The Royal Gallery of Pictures at Turin has been well illustrated in the Marquis Roberto Azeglio's work, entitled 'La R. Galleria di Torino, 1835,' *et seq.* That nobleman was the first director of the collection, and has been recently replaced by his brother Massimo Azeglio, as an artist, a writer, a patriot, and a statesman, one of the brightest ornaments of Italy.

Upon the northern tower of the Palazzo is the Royal Observatory, established in 1822, and now under the able direction of Baron Plana.

Accademia Albertina delle Belle Arti, in the Via della Posta, No. 10, formerly in the buildings of the University; it was removed here in 1832. Besides the different schools connected with the Fine Arts, the Academy contains a collection of pictures arranged in 5 rooms, the gift of Monsignore Mosse; amongst which may be noticed a Madonna di Loreto, attributed to *Raphael*; the same subject, by *Andrea del Sarto*; St. Alexis, by *Ghirlandajo*; St. John, by *Francia*; the Communion of St. Francis, by *Moncalvo*; a Holy Family, by *Caravaggio*; the Last Judgment, by *Heemskerk*; the Youth of Bacchus, by *Rubens*; an Ecce Homo, by *Elisabetta Sirani*; and 12 views of Venice by *Canaletti*. Among the drawings is a fine collection of 24 cartoons by *Gaudenzio Ferrari*, formed by Cardinal Maurice of Savoy; and a Virgin, by *Leonardo da Vinci*.

The *Palazzo dell' Accademia Reale delle Scienze* contains the museums of antiquities and natural history, as well as the apartments where the Academy holds its sittings, the library of the Academy, &c.

The *Museum of Antiquities* (open from 10 to 4, except on holidays) has acquired much importance of late years by the addition of the *Museo Egizzio*, composed in great part of the collections formed by Cavaliere Drovetti, a Piedmontese by birth, whilst he was Consul-General of France in Egypt, and which was purchased by King Carlo Felice in 1820, after negotiations had failed for securing it for the British Museum. It is entered from the Piazza di Carignano, and is open to the public on Mondays and Thursdays; but the *custode* will be found in attendance on the other days. The antiquities are arranged in two suites of apartments: one on the ground floor, where the more massive objects, statues, sphinxes sarcophagi, and inscriptions, are placed; the other on the upper floor of the palace, containing the smaller Egyptian objects, Roman bronzes, &c.

The division on the ground floor consists of three large halls: the two first are exclusively occupied by the Egyptian monuments, the greater part from Drovetti's collection; they are well arranged, and an excellent catalogue of them by the deputy keeper, Signor Occurti, may be purchased at the door, in which their description is preceded by a notice on the present state of our knowledge on hieroglyphical interpretation, Egyptian chronology, &c.

It may be useful to state that the greater part of Drovetti's specimens, having been collected about Thebes, Luxor, &c., belong, like the massive objects in our British Museum, to the period of the 18th and 19th Dynasties, or from the 17th to the 13th centuries B.C. They are classed under the four heads of—A, Divinities and Religious Monuments; B, Kings, Royal Monuments, Sphinxes, &c.; C, Civil Monuments; D, *varia*, Sarcophagi, Steles or Votive Tablets, Bas-reliefs, &c. The following are the objects best worthy of the attention of the visitor, as he will pass them in review, adopting Signor Occurti's classification:

1st Hall.—A 5, fragment of a marble statue of the goddess Neith; A 9, 10, 11, 12, four lion-headed female statues of Pasht, or Bubastes; A 4, group of Ammon Rha and Horus; A 2, sitting statue of Phtah, the Vulcan of the Greeks, of the time of the 18th Dynasty (1500 years B.C.); A 20, granite statue of Pasht; B 2, sitting statue of Thothmes III., in black granite (16th century B.C.); B 3, crouching colossal statue in granite of Amenophis II., the contemporary of Moses (16th century B.C.); C 1, statue in basalt of Amenophis III., or Memnon (1430 years B.C.), the most powerful of Egypt's kings; C 23, a group of two statues of the period of Amenophis I.; D 1 and 3, a very beautiful sarcophagus with its cover in green basalt; D 24, pedestal of an altar in black granite (this is perhaps the most interesting relic in the whole collection, for its remote date: it bears the name of Meri of the 12th dynasty, who lived 3000 years B.C.); D 37, a hollow marble plinth with a Greek inscription in honour of Ptolemy Epiphanes, 200 years B.C.); D 56, 57, two groups of the Greek period with inscriptions. On the floor of this hall have been let into the pavement several Mosaics of the Roman period, discovered at Stampace in Sardinia, offering good representations of several animals, such as lions, bears, and antelopes, with a male figure playing on a lyre, who formed the centre of the group, supposed to be Orpheu.

2nd Hall.—A 1, statue of Phtha with a Nilometer; A 3, group of three sitting statues in granite of Rhamses II. (Sesostris) between Ammon Rha and Mut (14th century B.C.); A 7, 13, female statues with a lion's head of the goddess Pasht (Bubastes); A 30, colossal head of a ram in sandstone; B 4, group of Horus and his daughter Muthmet (15th century B.C.); B 5, 6, statues in granite of Rhamses II., Meiamoun, or Rhamses the Great, or Sesostris, who reigned in the 14th century B.C.; B 7, foot of a colossal statue o Menepthah, or Amenophis, son o Rhamses the Great; B 8, colossal statue in red sandstone, of Seti or Se Ptah, son of Menepthah; B 16, 17, two colossal sphinxes in sandstone from before the palace at Karnac, erected in the 17th century B.C.; D 4, lid of a sarcophagus in granite of Thothmes, son of Isis; D 8, a curious bilingual inscription on a slab of granite, in *demotic* and Greek characters, containing a decree of the priests in honour of Callimachus during the reign of Cleopatra, and of Ptolemy Cæsarion, her son by Julius Cæsar (B.C. 44); D 22, a circular altar, dedicated to several divinities—probably of the 28th dynasty, in the 5th century B.C. In this room are several models of Egyptian ruins: D 40, of the temples of Ipsamboul; D 41, of Derry; D 43, of Essebuah; D 45, 46, of Dakke; D 47, of Ghirscich; D 49, of Talmis—of Tafah, Debodeh, Balagua, &c.

Out of this Egyptian Hall opens that of the *Greek and Roman statues*, a poor collection compared to those of most other Italian capitals; it has been recently removed here from the University. The following are most worthy of notice: a Sleeping Cupid or Genius is perhaps the finest object in the collection; it has been supposed to be Greek; although there are persons who consider it a copy made in the 16th centy. of some ancient work; a colossal Oracle Head of Juno, found at Alba in Piedmont, so arranged as to be fixed to a wall, and hollowed out, behind which the priest could remain concealed; Busts of Vespasian entire, and of the Emperor Julian, the latter good, considering the period at which it was executed.

The portion of the Museum of Antiquities on the upper floor consists of a series of eight rooms, the three first of which are exclusively devoted to the smaller objects of the Egyptian collection; in the first, or *long saloon*, is a very interesting series of human mummies, with their chests or cases, some highly decorated, whilst on the walls are placed, in frames, numerous papyri, and below several smaller Egyptian statues, votive tablets, &c.

In the second large hall the most striking object is the celebrated *Isiac Table*, a tablet in bronze covered with Egyptian figures and hieroglyphics, engraved or sunk, part of the outlines being filled with silvering—forming a kind of *Niello*. Considerable uncertainty exists as to its history: it would appear to have been first discovered on the Aventine at Rome, near where a Temple of Isis once stood, and given by Pius III. to a son of Cardinal Bembo; having disappeared during the pillage of Rome by the Connétable de Bourbon, little is known of what became of it until 1709, when it was discovered at Turin amongst some lumber; it was carried off to Paris in 1797, and restored to Italy at the peace. The Isiac Table is interesting as being one of the first objects of Egyptian antiquity in recent times that led to inquiry as regarded the interpretation of hieroglyphics, successively explained by Olaus Magnus as representing the mythology of Edda; by Father Kircher as containing the entire cosmogony of Hermes Trismegistus: by Jablonski, Montfaucon, and Winckelman, it is now clearly ascertained that its hieroglyphics have no meaning at all, and that it is one of those pseudo-Egyptian productions so extensively fabricated during the reign of Hadrian. There are also doubts whether any real signification is conveyed by the imagery upon it. In this room are several glass cases containing Egyptian ornaments of every kind; a very complete collection of the smaller divinities in terracotta, enamel, and glass; a very extensive series of nearly 2000 scarabœi with inscriptions, amulets, and some beautiful specimens of jewellery mounted with precious stones; whilst in presses around are several mummies of animals, such as monkeys, cats, heads of calves and bulls (without doubt of Apis), of the ibis, falcons, crocodiles, and of several species of fishes from the Nile. *Articles of food:* bread, corn, eggs, onions, dates, &c.—even to ducks ready for the spit of some Egyptian chef 3000 years ago. *Clothing for the dead:* masks to cover the faces of mummies; sandals, upon the soles of which are painted captives—some negroes, others Jews—with their hands bound; a singular mode of expressing a posthumous triumph.

Amongst the numerous illustrated Papyri hung on the walls, two are remarkable: the celebrated Book of the Kings, first published and ably illustrated by our countryman, Sir Gardner Wilkinson, and the funerary roll, 40 ft. in length, on which is represented the trial of a Soul before the tribunal of Amentis, where Osiris is seen acting as President, and the divinity Tot as Secretary, with a court of 42 judges, before whom the goddess of Justice leads the accused Soul. This curious papyrus has been recently illustrated by Dr. Lepsius of Berlin.

In the small room leading from the 2nd Egyptian Saloon is an extensive series of *steles* or votive tablets, some of which are said to belong to as remote a period as the 8th dynasty, at least thirty centuries B.C.

Rooms of Roman Bronzes.—Here have been lately placed several Roman bronzes, formerly in the Numismatic collection, and belonging to the Academy of Sciences. In the first are worthy of remark, a collection of silver vessels discovered lately in Savoy; a Roman inscription on bronze found at Industria; a Minerva with a handsome brazier on a tripod from the ruins at the same place; a good statue of a Faun found in the bed of the river Staffora, near Tortona; a few engraved pateræ; a good head of Claudius; and several small Roman bronzes and utensils from Industria. In the passage between the two rooms of the *ancient bronzes* are some large specimens of ivory carvings by German artists of the 18th centy.: they represent the Judgment of Solomon and the Sacrifice of Abraham, and are more remarkable for their size than for their sculpture. Finally, in the last room of the museum is an indifferent *collection of Etruscan vases* from the

South of Italy, and a series of earthenware of the Roman period from the ruins near *Pollenzo* (the ancient Pollentia: see p. 64).

Numismatic collection.—Attached to the Section of Antiquities is the Cabinet of Medals, consisting of a collection bequeathed by Cavaliere Lavy to the Academy of Sciences, of others added by the King, and modern acquisitions. It is said to contain 18,000 specimens, of which 5000 are Greek, 6000 Roman, and 7000 modern and of the middle ages.

The *Museum of Natural History* is also in the Palace of the Academy, but at the opposite extremity of the building from that of the antiquities. The entrance is by the great portal in the Contrada dell' Accademia; it contains a very complete mineralogical collection; the specimens from Savoy and the valleys descending from the Mont Blanc are perhaps unique, and particularly interesting to the foreign mineralogist. The geological and paleontological collections are very extensive as regards the Sardinian territory, having been formed by Professor Sismonda during his labours for the geological map of the continental portion of the kingdom, and by General Alberto de la Marmora for that of the island of Sardinia. The fossil organic remains of the tertiary formations of the Montferrat are perhaps unique; amongst which deserves particular notice the skeleton of a Mastodon found recently in a freshwater deposit near Baldichieri. But the most remarkable objects of this part of the collection are an almost entire skeleton of the *Megatherium*, from Buenos Ayres, the most perfect hitherto discovered of this extraordinary gigantic species of Sloth—more so than that in the British Museum; and of the gigantic armadillo, called Glyptodon. The zoological department has been greatly improved of late years under the care of Professor de Filippi; the series of birds of Piedmont is particularly good.

Università Reale, Contrada del Po, a very extensive and magnificent building. The cortile is an example of the effect produced by columns encircled by bands, story above story; and is a species of lapidary museum. Until recently, the greater part of the Roman and Greek remains now in the museum were in the university. Here are still the Torsos found at Susa, to which heads, legs, and arms were added by the French sculptor, Cartellier, on their removal to Paris in 1809. Many of the inscriptions and monuments are sepulchral. Upon the cippus of Quintus Minutius Faber, a wheelwright, he is represented, at bottom, working upon a wheel; and at the top, lying in bed. The inscription on an altar raised to an almost hitherto unknown divinity by a certain Sempronia Eutychia does not speak well for the modesty of the devotee. There are also several mediæval inscriptions: some of the times of the Lombard kings, Grimoald, Aripert, and Lothair.

The *Library* contains upwards of 120,000 volumes of printed books, and a valuable ·collection of MSS., many of which belonged to the Dukes of Savoy. It was placed here by Carlo Emanuele I.; and many collections have been successively added. The celebrated Calusio, the author of the Hebrew Concordance, bequeathed his Oriental manuscripts to it; and it also contains a part of those from the Benedictine monastery of Bobbio. These latter are very ancient and authentic, and probably include palimpsests; but they do not seem to have been examined. A very numerous collection of the Greek writers on alchemy, mostly inedited. A manuscript of the ' De Imitatione Christi,' the celebrated work commonly attributed to Thomas à Kempis, but with more probability to Gersen, abbot of the Benedictines of Vercelli, who lived a century before. This codex was found in a Benedictine convent at Arona in 1604. Several Bibles, from the 10th to the 16th centy., some curiously and richly illuminated; a *Catena Patrum*, probably of the 9th centy., with portraits of the 12 minor prophets, interesting for the time when they were executed, showing the long prevalence of Roman art. A Book of Offices, with miniatures of the Flemish school, of great beauty; four or five seem to be by Hemling. ("I know nothing so fine in this class of art—the Kiss of Judas is a marvel of its kind."—*H. A. L.*) Seyssell's translation of Appian, illuminated, and in which is his portrait presenting the work to Louis XII. Hebrew MSS., several inedited. The University of Turin is now very flourishing, and forms with that of Genoa the two great educational establishments of the monarchy ; there are upwards of 60 professorships. The lecture-rooms, and other parts of the building appropriated to the business of the university, offer nothing remarkable.

The *Piazza di San Carlo* is the finest square at Turin: one side is formed by the churches of Sta. Christina and of San Carlo Borromeo, from the latter of which it derives its name. It became necessary, after the houses were first erected, to strengthen the columns of the façades by a species of pilaster; and this accidental alteration has produced a better effect than the architect originally contemplated. In this piazza is the statue of Emanuele Filiberto, presented to the city by King Carlo Alberto, and executed by Baron Marochetti, of whose works it is perhaps the finest. The bronze basso-rilievos on the pedestal represent the two great events in the life of Emanuele Filiberto,—the battle of St. Quentin, and the treaty of Câteau Cambresis (1557, 1559).

The *Piazza de Emanuele Filiberto* and the *Piazza di Milano*, at the N. extremity of the city, form the largest open space in Turin; here are held two of the principal markets.

The *Piazza Susina* or *Paesana* is remarkable for the fine granite obelisk erected in its centre in 1853, to commemorate the abolition of the ecclesiastical jurisdiction in civil affairs in Piedmont, the first cause of the unworthy persecution exercised against the kingdom of Sardinia and its rulers by the Court of Rome; on the sides of the obelisk are engraved the names of the members of the legislature who took part in the vote of the Chambers on this most important measure for the liberties of Italy.

The Piazza del Palazzo della Citta is a small square surrounded by porticoes on 3 sides, with the Hôtel de Ville on the 4th ; in the centre is a bronze group by Pelagi, representing Duke Amadeo VI. of Savoy, better known as the Conte Verde; and on each side of the gate marble statues of Prince Eugene of Savoy and of the late Duke of Genoa.

The *Piazza Vittorio Emanuele*, at the extremity of the fine Contrada del Po is principally remarkable for its extent and regularity, and the fine view which it commands of the Po, and the Collina covered with villas and churches, and the Superga towering over all. At its eastern extremity is the bridge which connects this Piazza with the opposite bank of the river, in front of the church of La gran Madre di Dio. The bridge was begun by the French in 1810, under the direction of the engineer Pertinchamp, and completed by King Vittorio Emanuele II. It has five elliptic arches, each of about 80 feet span. The granite used in its construction is from the quarry of Cumiana. The bridge on the road to Chivasseo, a little beyond the Piazza Emilio Filiberto, is much bolder and finer. It is erected over the Dora Riparia, a river ordinarily shallow, but liable to heavy floods, and during these extremely rapid. It consists of a single arch of granite, resting on solid abutments of the same material from the quarries of Malanaggio, near Pinerolo. This bridge was constructed under the direction of the Cavaliere Mosca, and to this day not the least settling has taken place. The cost of the bridge, with the approaches, was 56,000*l*.

There is also a suspension bridge a little above the stone bridge over the Po.

Palaces.—There are very many excellent mansions in Turin, but none which need to be particularly remarked for outward appearance, except, perhaps, the unfinished *Palazzo Carignano*, one of the specimens of the fancy of Guarini, and in which he has carried his powers of invention to the greatest extreme. Several of its rooms contain allegorical frescoes of Gallcari and Leguarineo, painters of the last century: this palace has considerable historical interest of late years; it was the residence of King Carlo Alberto before his accession to the throne. In the piazza in front of the palace has been lately placed a very fine statue of the celebrated writer Gioberti, by the Piedmontese sculptor *Albertoni*, erected in 1859 at the public expense. It was here that the Constitution was proclaimed in 1821, and it is in it that the Chamber of Deputies or Lower House of the North Italian monarchy holds its sittings. Behind the P. Carignano, in the newly opened piazza of Carlo Alberto, is to be erected the colossal equestrian statue of the late king, by *Marochetti*; forming one side of this square is the *Institute Teanico*, containing the industrial schools, and a collection of objects connected with arts and manufactures.

Theatres.—In addition to the *Royal Theatre* already noticed, there are the *Teatro Carignano*, which is open for operas and ballets during the autumn, and for the regular drama in the spring and summer; it was built by the Count Alfieri; and here the first tragedy of Vittorio Alfieri was first represented. The *Teatro d'Angennes*, remarkable for the good arrangement of the scenes and stage, is an elegant but not a large theatre. It is open for the regular drama during the Carnival, and for the opera buffa in spring and summer. French plays are generally represented here during several months in the year. The *Teatro Sutera* in the Contrada del Po is open for the opera buffa during the Carnival, and for comedy at other times. There are also two theatres of *fantoccini*. The Piedmontese claim the honour of being the inventors of puppet-shows, which are carried to high perfection in the performances of these wooden companies. The buffoon characters *Girolamo* and *Gianduja* are of Piedmontese origin, as *Arlequino* is Bergamasque. There are several other theatres: the T. Nazionale, built in 1848, in the Contrada La Marmora; and two for diurnal representations, the Circo Salles and the T. Gerbino in the Via dei Tintori. The charitable institutions of Turin are numerous and opulent. As a detail of them would be foreign to the object of this work, we shall only notice a few of the most remarkable.

The *Ritiro delle Rosine* was founded by Rosa Govona, a poor girl of Mondovi, who, in 1740, collected a number of other girls of her own class for the purpose of living as a semi-religious community, maintaining themselves by their own labour. In 1745 she removed her institution to Turin, and settled here, under the patronage of Carlo Emanuele III. She died in 1776, and is buried in the simple oratory, or chapel, of the Ritiro; on her tomb being inscribed "*Le figlie grate alla Benedetta Madre hanno posto questo monumento.*" The inmates of the Ritiro may quit if they think fit, but few avail themselves of this privilege. This interesting establishment, which now contains 350 inmates, was under the special patronage of the late lamented Queen, who deputed one of the ladies of her court to look after it: the income, which arises entirely from the work of the inmates, amounts to 80,000 francs, with which they are most comfortably maintained. Over the principal entrance is engraved the very appropriate inscription—"*Tu vivrai del lavoro delle tue mani.*" There are several houses of the *Rosine* in other parts of the Sardinian states.

The *Reale Albergo di Virtù* is what we should term an industrial school. It was founded, in 1580, by Carlo Emanuele I.

The *Regio Manicomio*, a lunatic asylum, arose out of the voluntary contributions of the fraternity of the Santo Sudario, about the year 1728; and the Prior of the fraternity, with the approbation of the Crown, names the directors. The number of inmates is about 500, who are received from the different provinces, their maintenance being defrayed by the several localities in the proportion of four-fifths, the rest paid by the government. Its management is very mild and judicious: the patients, as far as possible, dine at a common table, and many of the improvements in the treatment of these unfortunate objects recently adopted in England and France have been long practised here.

The *Casa della Divina Providencia* is a very interesting establishment of modern foundation (1828), which owes its origin to a benevolent ecclesiastic, the Canon Cottolengo; it receives the infirm poor without distinction of country, religion, or malady, and is entirely supported by voluntary contributions. The number of admissions annually is nearly 1500.

The *Grande Ospedale di S. Giovanni*, founded in the 14th century, may be called the Great Hospital of Turin. It is managed by a congregation composed of six canons of the cathedral and six decurions of the city: about 6000 patients are annually received in it. The revenues before the French invasion were very large; and now, partly from estates, and also from voluntary contributions, they amount to about 300,000 francs per annum: the contributions being nearly one half. In the centre of the wards is an altar, so placed that it can be seen from every bed. The clinical school and the anatomical theatre attached to the university are in this hospital, now one of the most flourishing medical schools of Italy: forming a part of the establishment are wards for nearly 100 incurable cases, and apartments for persons who are admitted on paying a trifling retribution.

The hospital of *San Luigi Gonzaga*, founded in 1797, and wholly supported by voluntary contributions, is also a dispensary. The out-patients are maintained at their own homes for a fortnight *after* they are discharged as cured, in order that they may fully recover their strength, and have an opportunity of obtaining employment. The in-patients (about 80) are those who are refused admittance into the other hospitals, from their maladies being incurable. Upwards of 12,000 out-patients are annually relieved, and fed if they require it. This noble institution owes its origin to the late Padre Barucchi, a parish priest of Turin, who began by establishing a fraternity for the purpose of assisting the poor at their own houses; and, in the course of twenty years, collected a sufficient sum to erect the present edifice.

La Maternità, at the same time a lying-in and foundling hospital, well managed under the direction of the Sisters of Charity; it generally contains about 80 women and 40 children; about 2000 foundlings are deposited here annually, who, after being kept a short time in a ward for the purpose, are sent out to nurse in the country.

The *Rifugio di Madama Barol*, a kind of Magdalen hospital, founded by a benevolent lady, the Baroness Barol, and supported by her and contributing friends; it admits all unfortunate females, either in sickness or who wish to abandon their evil course of life, who are maintained, and after several years of probation allowed to take the veil. They are employed in taking care of the sick inmates, and in other works for the benefit of the establishment. We would recommend any of our countrywomen interested in charitable institutions to visit this Rifugio, still managed by the benevolent lady by whom it was founded 25 years ago.

ENVIRONS OF TURIN.

In the *vicinity of Turin* is the *Superga*, with which the traveller becomes acquainted before he enters the city. The easiest mode of reaching it will be, for the pedestrian, from the *Madonna del Pilone*, to which omnibuses run every half-hour from Turin ; and from which a very agreeable walk, although constantly ascending, leads to the ch. ; families and ladies must proceed in carriages, for the hire of which, as four horses are necessary, the hotel-keepers charge 25 and 30 francs. The Basilica of La Superga was erected by Vittorio Amadeo in the accomplishment of a vow made previously to the battle of Turin. On the 2nd Sept. 1706, he advanced with Prince Eugene from Chieri ; and taking their station upon the summit of the Collina, they looked down upon his capital, blockaded by the army of Louis XIV. Vittorio vowed to erect a church here in honour of the Virgin, if it should please the Lord of Hosts to grant him and his people deliverance from the hands of the enemy. (These are the words of the vow.) The result of the battle of Turin has been before noticed. The name of *Superga* is said to be derived from its situation, *super terga montium*.

The Basilica was begun by Juvara in 1717, and completed in 1731. The interior is circular : 8 pilasters, and an equal number of columns, support the cupola ; between the pilasters are chapels of an elliptical form. Through the interpilaster, opposite the principal entrance, is the access to a large octangular chapel, at the extremity of which is the high altar. The flight of steps on the outside is continued all round the building. The cupola, which is of good proportions, is flanked by two elegant quadrangular bell-towers. The front of the ch. is formed by a fine portico of 8 Corinthian columns in front. The high altar is decorated with a profusion of statues and bas-reliefs, one representing the siege of Turin—Vittorio Amadeo, Prince Eugene, and the Duke of Anhalt pursuing the enemy. The subterranean ch. is in the form of a Latin cross, and contains the remains of most of the members of the royal house, King Carlo Felice alone having been interred at Haute Combe in Savoy. The monuments most worthy of being noticed are those of Vittorio Amadeo II., decorated with allegorical figures in the taste of the last century, and of Carlo Emanuele III., having on it a bas-relief of the battle of Guastalla by Collini. In the centre of the cross stands the temporary monument of the late king, whose body was deposited here in 1850, when brought from Oporto, in the place always occupied by the last-departed sovereign. Adjoining the Basilica is the college upon a large scale. The halls and staircases are grand from their proportions and rich marbles, and the solid decorations of the architect. A series of portraits of the popes, the majority of course imaginary, is placed in the apartments appropriated to the sovereign, who visits the Superga annually, upon the 8th September, the feast of the Nativity of the Virgin. A congregation of secular priests, endowed by the state, has been established at the Superga, its members being chosen among the most meritorious of the parochial clergy, and those who have rendered the greatest services to the church and state. No traveller who visits the Superga should omit to ascend to the top of the building, from which opens perhaps the most magnificent panorama of the Alps, extending from Mont Viso at the extremity of the Cottian portion of the chain to the Simplon, including the whole of the Greek and Pennine Alps, with the beautiful hills of Montferrat below, the plains of Lombardy, of the Po, and the first portion of the Apennines beyond. The top of the cupola is 2405 feet above the level of the sea.

La Vigna della Regina. This palace overlooks Turin, being on the side of the Collina, immediately above the Po. It was built by Cardinal Maurice of Savoy, when he had ceased to be a cardinal for the purpose of marrying his niece Ludovica, the daughter of Vittorio Amadeo I. The views of the city from hence are very beautiful.

Il Valentino, at the S.E. extremity

of Turin, built by Christine of France, the wife of Vittorio Amadeo I., and daughter of Henri IV. and Marie de Medicis. As far as the design of the original building has been executed, it is a regular French château; the decorations of the apartments are in the heavy and extreme bad taste of the 17th centy. The gardens are very agreeable; one part of them is set apart as the *Botanic Garden* of the university. The grounds are pleasantly situated on the banks of the Po, to which you descend from the palace by a subterranean staircase. The palace is now uninhabited; the state apartments are used periodically for the exhibition of arts and manufactures.

Stupinigi, about 5 m. from Turin. A fine avenue leads from the city to this unfinished hunting lodge or palace, of which the object is announced by the bronze stag which crowns the roof. It was erected by Carlo Emanuele III. from the designs of Juvara. The elevation is finely varied by the masses, semi-castellated in form, of which it is composed. Napoleon lodged here in his way to Milan, when about to receive the iron crown. It contains some tolerable paintings: a good *Vanloo,* representing Diana bathing.

Castello di Aglie. The favourite country residence of King Carlo Felice, remarkable for the extreme purity of the air. It contains a small collection of Roman antiquities, chiefly from the excavations made at Veii and Tusculum by Maria Christina, the queen dowager of Victor Emanuel.

TURIN to Cormayeur and the Val d'Aosta. (*Swiss Handbook.* Rte. 107.)

TURIN to Romagnano and Biella. (*Ibid.* Rte. 103.)

ROUTE 2.

TURIN TO MILAN, BY VERCELLI, NOVARA, AND MAGENTA—RAIL.

90 miles.

KIL.		KIL.	
12	Settimo.	78	Borgo Vercelli.
19	Brandizzo.	85	Ponzana.
23	Chivasso.	95	Novara.
30	Torrazza.	104	Trecate.
35	Saluggia.	109	Ticino.
42	Livorno.	116	Magenta.
46	Bianze.	123	Vittuone.
51	Tronzano.	131	Rho.
54	Santhia.	138	Musocco.
60	S. Germano.	145	Milan.
73	Vercelli.		

Since the opening of the direct railway from Turin to the Lombard frontier, by Vercelli and Novara, this is the shortest and most interesting route between Turin and Milan, as it will enable the traveller to visit Vercelli and Novara, and to pass through a lovely country at the foot of the Alps. Trains leave 4 times a-day for Milan, employing 3½, 4½ and 5 hrs.; travellers who wish to visit Vercelli will be able to sleep at Novara, where there are 2 good Inns.

The Stat. is at the W. extremity of the city, beyond the citadel, and at the extremity of the *Contrada di Santa Teresa.*

The rly. runs parallel to the l. bank of the Po, after crossing the Dora Riparia, as far as *Chivasso,* passing by

12 kil. *Settimo Stat.,* a village on rt., bearing in its name the reminiscence of its Roman origin, *ad septimam.*

8 kil. *Brandizzo Stat.,* the village on the rt., of great antiquity. It is noticed in the ancient itineraries as one of the stations where the pilgrims to Jerusalem were accustomed to change horses. On leaving Brandizzo,

Cross the *Malone* and *Orco* torrents, which, like the other streams already passed, flow into the Po, and, like that river, frequently inundate the adjoining lands.

3 kil. *Chivasso Junction Stat.,* a small city on the l. bank of the Po, at one time of some military importance. Pop. 7841. It was long considered as the key of Piedmont, and in 1798 it opposed a considerable resistance to Mar-

shal Joubert when executing the decree of the Directory, by which he was ordered to dethrone the House of Savoy. The fortifications were destroyed by the French in 1804, when their possession of Lombardy placed Chivasso in the midst of their territory. Chivasso was the ordinary court residence of the Marquises of Montferrat, who, as sovereigns, held so conspicuous a place in the mediæval history of Italy, though Casale was their capital. The Marquis Giovanni, surnamed the Just, who was much loved by his people, died here in 1305. He had been attended during his malady by Manuel di Vercelli, a physician of great reputation. Manuel followed as one of the mourners. There is an old jest in Joe Miller of an M.D. in a similar situation being told that he was "carrying his work home." The people of Chivasso believed it. Suspicions had been spread that the good marquis had died in consequence of the want of skill, or that somehow or another the doctor had despatched his employer; they rushed upon him and literally tore him in pieces. The Marquis Giovanni had no children; and his dominions devolved to his sister Violante (Irene the Greeks called her), the Empress of the East, wife of Andronicus Comnenus Palæologus. Their second son, Teodoro, was selected to exercise his mother's rights, and in his person began the dynasty of the Montferrat-Palæologi, which became extinct in 1553.

The town consists of two adjoining groups of streets and buildings, and which once, probably, formed two distinct jurisdictions. The church of *San Pietro* dates as early as 1425. The front is decorated with ornaments and statues in terracotta, of great elegance, but much defaced.

The remains of the ancient palace, or castle, of the Counts of Montferrat, consist of a high tower, upon the summit of which grow two mulberry-trees. Chiavasso is celebrated for its lampreys.

[The Rly. to Ivrea branches off here, ascending the Valley of the Dora for 33 kil. in an hour, the stations being—6 kil. Montanaro, 5 kil. Rodallo, 3 kil. Caluso, 4 kil. Candia, 2 kil. Mercenasco, and 4 kil. Strambino. 9 kil. to Ivrea.]

7 kil. *Torazza Stat.* Soon after leaving, the Dora Baltea, descending from Ivrea, is crossed.

5 kil. *Saluggia Stat.* The town is upon a rising ground in the midst of canals derived from the Dora Baltea.

7 kil. *Livorno Stat.*, a good-sized village, not far from which, on the l., is *Cigliano*. This town, which is now dismantled, was once surrounded with walls and towers. The old church is rather an interesting object; but the main beauty of this vicinity is the view of Monte Rosa, which is seen from hereabouts in great magnificence.

4 kil. *Bianze Stat.*

5 kil. *Tronzano Stat.*

3 kil. *Santhia Junction Stat.*, a town on the high road from Ivrea to Vercelli. [The Rly. to *Biella* (18½ m. or 30 kil.) branches off here : trains go in 60 min. : the stations are—11 kil. *Saluzzola*, 6 kil. *Vergnasco*, 3 kil. Sandigliari, and 4 kil. *Candele*.] Henceforward our Rly. follows the direction of the old post-road.

6 kil. *San Germano Stat.*, once fortified, but now dismantled. In this neighbourhood the women wear a peculiar ornament in the hair, which we shall meet, with more or less variation, throughout Lombardy. It consists of rows of large pins (spiloni) radiating round the back of the head. Here these pins terminate in balls, either gilt or of polished brass. The dialect of the people is Milanese; and the style of all the ancient buildings shows that the traveller has entered, at least, historical Lombardy. Monte Rosa is seen in all its grandeur between S. Germano and Vercelli.

13 kil. *Vercelli Junction Stat.* (*Inns*: Leone d'Oro, the best; La Posta; but both indifferent and dirty. The less the traveller has to do with inns here the better; he will be able to see everything at Vercelli in the interval between the departure of two successive

rlwy.-trains, and get on to Turin or Novara, where he will find more comfortable quarters.) A city near the l. bank of the Sesia, the seat of a bishopric, of great importance in the middle ages, and still containing a population of 18,000 Inhab., and with great appearance of activity. It covers a wide extent of ground, and is surrounded by boulevards, of which those on the N.W. command the finest view of the Alps. At this extremity of the city are the *Duomo* or Cathedral, the church of San Andrea, and the Rly. stat. The Duomo was built by Pellegrino Tibaldi, towards the middle of the 16th century, and is in the best style of Italian architecture. During the French occupation this building was exposed to ruin. They turned it into a stable, burned all the wood-work of the choir, and defaced the tomb of St. Amadeus of Savoy. All this damage has been repaired. The tomb of St. Amadeus was richly decorated with silver, at the expense of King Carlo Felice, in 1823, from the designs of Savesi, an artist of Turin. The wood-work of the choir was restored in 1822, from a design of Ranza, an architect of Vercelli; it is so contrived that it holds together without nails, and can be taken down in a very short time. The portico, by Count Alfieri, is original and bold. In this church are interred St. Eusebius, the first bishop of the see, and St. Amadeus. The sepulchral chapels, in which their bodies are deposited, are sumptuously ornamented.

The library of the cathedral has escaped spoliation, and contains a collection of manuscripts of great antiquity and value. The most remarkable is a copy of the Gospels written by St. Eusebius, the founder of the see in the fourth century, and which, being much decayed, even in the reign of Berengarius King of Italy (see *Monza*), was, by order of that monarch, bound in silver; and it yet remains in this cover, with the inscription, testifying the name of the donor, in the following verses :—

"Presul hoc Eusebius scripsit, solvitque vetustas;
Rex Berengarius sed reparavit idem."

The silver cover is ornamented with rude chasings: it represents our Lord seated upon a species of throne composed of two zones ornamented with gems, and which have been explained as representing the earth and the heavens. Upon his knees is an open book, the Gospel, presented to mankind. Olive-branches surround the tablet, as the emblems of peace. On the other side is St. Eusebius in his robes, but merely designated as "Eusebius Episcopus;" the absence of the epithet *Sanctus* being conformable to the usages of high antiquity. This manuscript is considered as of the greatest importance in biblical criticism. It is a Latin version, and supposed to be the most authentic copy of that called "Itala" by St. Augustine, and employed in the earliest ages of the Western Church, until its use was superseded by the Vulgate; and this being older than any Greek manuscript now extant, it is in one sense the most ancient copy of the Gospels existing. The Gospels are arranged in the following order :—St. Matthew, St. John, St. Luke (here called "Lucanus"), and St. Mark. It is written in capitals, in two columns; the writing is much faded, and the evanescent character can scarcely be traced except by the indentation of the pen in the mouldering vellum. St. Eusebius always carried this volume about with him; it is one of the earliest authentic autographs in existence. Besides the injuries which the manuscript has sustained from time, it has been strangely mutilated to gratify the former devotion of the people of Lausanne, who in the 15th century erected a church in honour of St. Eusebius, and in whose favour Bonifazio Ferreri, the then Bishop of Vercelli, detached a leaf, which he sent to them as a relic of the holy prelate whom they thus revered. Lalande stated this manuscript to be an autograph of St. Luke, though it is a Latin version! Amongst the other manuscripts are *Anglo-Saxon poems*, including one in honour of St. Andrew, and very possibly brought from England by Cardinal Guala, of whom we shall shortly have occasion to speak; the *Recognitions of St. Clement*, a very early manuscript, but whether the work be really the production of this apostolic father is a question upon which theological critics are much divided; the Laws of the *Lombard Kings*, written in the reign of King Liutprand, and therefore not later than the year 744.

The church of *Sant' Andrea*, at a short distance from the Rly. stat., was erected by Cardinal Guala de' Bicchieri, who filled the office of papal legate in England in the reigns of John and Henry III., and whose name is connected with some very important transactions during that turbulent period of our history. He was born and educated at Vercelli, and was a canon of its cathedral. Over one of the lateral doors he is represented as in the act of dedicating the church; and his merits are recorded in rhyming Leonines, in the first of which, by a poetical figure, called Epenthesis, familiar to the students of the Westminster and Eton Latin grammars, one word is inserted in the centre of another, that is to say, the word Car——dinalis is split into two, and the word Guala inserted in the gap between, for the sake of the metre:—

"Lux cleri patriæque decus Carg*uala*dinalis
Quem canon atque artes, quem Sanctio canonicalis,
Quem lux dotavit, quom pagina spiritualis."

The Cardinal left all his property to the Church, and amongst the relics which he deposited there was the *oblationarium* of Saint Thomas à Becket. Cardinal Guala was a most strenuous ally of King John; he excommunicated Stephen Langton and Prince Lewis, when the latter was called in by the barons of Runnymede (1215); and on the accession of Henry III. he was one of the ministry by whose exertions the royal authority was in a great measure supported and restored. The gratitude of the new monarch bestowed upon Guala much preferment, and among others the rich benefice of Chesterton near Cambridge. He made heavy demands upon the clergy generally, besides sequestrating (to his own use) the benefices and preferments of those who were in opposition to him; and he thus amassed the fortune, amounting, it is said, to 12,000 marks of silver, with which this fabric was raised and endowed.

On his return to Italy through France, in 1218, he engaged in his service an ecclesiastic, a native of Paris, skilled in architecture, and in 1219 began his new church, which he dedicated to St. Andrew. The career of the founder accounts for the style of St. Andrea. Having passed many years in France and England, Cardinal Guala imbibed a taste for the style of architecture which had recently come into fashion in those countries. St. Andrea is far from pure. It is curious from the transition it offers between the Lombard and Pointed styles, greatly inferior as regards the latter to the ch. of S. Francesco at Assisi. In parts of the exterior, perhaps from compliance with the habits of the native masons, round forms are used. The façade is Lombard; but the interior presents the exact appearance of a French or English building, in the early Gothic style. The arches are pointed. Light pillars, with foliage capitals, run up to support the roof, which is vaulted and groined. The windows in the chancel are lancet. The interior has been much injured by the recent injudicious restorations, and painting in the worst possible taste. The material of the walls is brick, with stone joints, windows, and doors. The campanile was added by Pietro del Verme in 1399.

The ancient tombs formerly here have been destroyed, with the exception of that of the first abbot, and architect of the church, Tomaso Gallo, a French ecclesiastic (ob. 1246), upon which is a curious fresco, where he is represented as surrounded by his disciples; amongst others, St. Anthony of Padua, distinguished by a halo of glory: below, in a contemporary bas-relief, Gallo is seen kneeling before the Virgin, while St. Dionysius the Areopagite lays his hand on his head. The church has lately had the addition of painted glass and Gothic confessionals, not in the best taste.

The *Hospital*, founded by Cardinal Guala, retains its original endowment and destination. It contains a picturesque cloister, with the arms of its benefactors; and a Museum, not of much interest.

The ch. of *San Cristofero* contains some excellent frescoes by Gaudenzio Ferrari, an artist much less known beyond the Alps than many inferior ones, owing to his best works being in fresco, and not removable. He was born in 1484, in Valdugia, about 40 m. from Vercelli; and not being able to find a teacher of the art he loved in his native place, he came to Vercelli for the sake of instruction. Giovenone was his first master; and so proud was he of his pupil, that in some of his paintings he signs himself "Geronimo Giovenone, maestro di Gaudenzio." He afterwards studied under Perugino and Raphael. The magistrates of Vercelli conferred on him the municipal freedom; and the city where Gaudenzio was thus instructed and adopted claims him as her own.

This church was anciently attached to a convent of the Umiliati, and afterwards belonged to the Jesuits. The paintings by Gaudenzio were chiefly executed for two brothers of the former order, by name Corradi, about the year 1532, and are so remarkable as to merit a more than ordinarily detailed description. Most of them were executed by Gaudenzio's own hand, in some he was assisted by his pupil Lanini.

Looking towards the altar, and on the l. of the spectator, the principal subject, forming one composition from top to bottom, is—1. the *Assumption of the Virgin*, very fine and grand. The group of the apostles divides the composition.

As introductory to the Assumption, and painted in smaller compartments on the wall forming the extremity of the transept, are—2. the *Birth of the Virgin*; 3. her *Marriage*, or the *Sposalizio*. In the background the painter has introduced the Presentation in the Temple. 4. The *Nativity of our Lord*. The Virgin is kneeling before the infant Saviour, to whom she is presented by angels, perhaps the finest part of all the frescoes here. The Annunciation, and the Visitation of St. Elizabeth, are introduced in the background. 5. The *Adoration of the Magi*. Many portraits are evidently introduced into this composition, particularly a prominent figure with a cap and feathers. So also the bearded king kneeling before the Virgin. This fresco contains portraits of the painter, of his master Giovenone, and of his pupil Lanini. Groups of pages, esquires, and attendants fill the scene. Between the Nativity and the Adoration the painter has introduced a group, representing S. Catherine of Siena and S. Nicholas of Bari presenting to the Virgin and Child two novices of the Lignara family.

Passing to the rt.-hand transept, the principal composition is—1. the *Crucifixion*, perhaps too crowded and confused, but full of expressive figures and faces, wonderfully foreshortened; the converted Centurion and the Magdalene are the most conspicuous; the former a most singular figure, clad nearly in the fashion of the court of Henry VIII., in the second row. In the right-hand corner is the portrait of Padre Angelo Corradi. The angels hovering about the cross, one receiving the soul of the good thief "Gestas" (according to the legend), and another weeping for the loss of the soul of the impenitent thief "Dysmas." Upon the adjoining wall is the history of the Magdalene, consisting of the following subjects: 2. The *Conversion of the Magdalene*, who is represented seated, with her sister Martha, listening to the preaching of our Lord. This fresco is damaged. 3. *Our Lord at the table of Simon the Pharisee*, the Magdalene kissing his feet. Very many figures are introduced, but nearly destroyed.

4. The *Arrival and Preaching at Marseilles*, a scene from the legendary life of the Magdalene; according to which, St. Mary Magdalene, St. Matthew, St. Lazarus, with some other disciples of our Lord, after his ascension, being expelled by the Jews, embarked from Judea, and landed at Marseilles, of which place St. Lazarus became the first bishop, and where they were received by St. Maximinus, afterwards Bishop of Aix, and St. Marcella. The city is seen in the distance. This and the following fresco, which are attributed entirely to Lanini, are very fine, and the best preserved of the whole. 5. The *Assumption of the Magdalene*: she is carried up by angels to pray; her death and burial are seen in the background. These two last frescoes have been much injured by shells and cannon-balls.

Other works of Gaudenzio Ferrari are —the *Madonna enthroned*, on panel, attended by saints, amongst whom St. Cristopher, as patron of the church, is conspicuous in front. The painter has followed the popular legend by representing this saint larger than the other figures. St. John the Baptist is seen in the background. Two portraits of Umiliati monks, probably the donors, are introduced.

In the sacristy is a good *Lanini*, a Virgin enthroned, with St. Peter Martyr and another monk; thorough monastic faces.

The frescoes are all more or less injured. The first damage occurred during the siege in 1638, although the young Marquis de Leganez forbade his artillerymen to fire on the church of St. Christopher, lest the masterpiece of Ferrari should be injured. But they suffered more from the French, who converted the church into a place of custody for refractory conscripts.

Ch. of Santa Caterina. Here is the Marriage of the patron saint, by G. Ferrari: in this painting St. Francis, St. Agapetus, and St. Anthony are introduced.

San Bernardino has a fresco representing Our Lord about to be nailed to the Cross. This church has some curious remains of Lombard architecture.

In the *Casa Mariano* is a fine fresco by Lanini—the Feast of the Gods, and some other allegorical and mythological figures. The hall in which it is painted is now a granary.

There is a handsome theatre at Vercelli. A railway to Valenza branches off at Vercelli (26 m.): the stations are —8 kil. Asigliano; 4, Pertengo; 5, Balzola; 6, *Casale*; 7, Borgo S. Martino; 5, Giarole; 7, Valenza.

On leaving Vercelli we cross the Sesia. Monte Rosa appears again with great beauty, and hence to Novara, generally, the Alps are seen in great majesty. This mountain view is much enhanced in effect by the peculiar characteristics of the great plain of Lombardy. The open face of Flanders is not more level; and the soil, much intersected by ditches and canals, is teeming with exuberant fertility. We have the contrast of the richest plain and grandest mountain scenery.

[About 4 m. on the rt., after crossing the Sesia, a road by Torrione leads to Vinaglio and Palestra, scenes of very brilliant actions, especially the latter, between the Piedmontese and the Austrians, on the 30th and 31st May 1859, and in which the King of Sardinia showed himself most heroically at the head of his little army. The Austrians, who had invaded Piedmont in May of last year, pushing their advances as far as the Dora, and threatening the capital, had occupied very strongly Vercelli and the line of the Sesia, until the 28th of that month, when, in consequence of the great flank movement of the French Emperor from the S. bank of the Po, the Allied Army occupied Vercelli, with the intention of invading Lombardy on the side of the Mincio. No time was lost therefore in crossing the Sesia: on the 30th the Piedmontese, who formed the advanced guard of the army, occupied the villages of *Vinzaglio*, *Confienza*, and *Palestro*, after a very serious resistance on the part of the Austrians. On the 31st the latter made a strong effort to retake Palestro, but sustained a signal defeat from the Piedmontese, on this occasion, however, aided by 3000 French Zouaves, who fought with extraordinary bravery, leaving on the field of battle 2100 between killed and wounded, 950 prisoners, and 6 pieces of cannon. On the same day Marshal Canrobert crossed the Sesia at Prarola, and General M'Mahon at Vercelli, with their two corps d'armée; the main body of the Austrians under Giulay retreating on Mortara, and subsequently crossing the Ticino, as we shall see presently in speaking of the great battles which decided the first part of this extraordinary campaign, at Buffalora and Magenta.]

5 kil. *Borgo Vercelli Stat.*, and 5 m. farther

7 kil. *Ponzana Stat.*

A mile beyond *Torrion Balducco*, where meadows and mulberry-tree plantations succeed to marshes and ricefields, cross the Agogna torrent, and soon after reach

10 kil. *Novara Junct. Stat.* (*Inns:* Albergo de' tre Rè; a very tolerable inn; Albergo d'Italia, formerly the Pesce d'Oro, recently fitted up on an extensive scale, and good), a flourishing city of 16,000 Inhab. Novara is situated on a rising ground above the plain of the Terdoppio; there are some good streets in it, well paved on the Lombard system. The town was formerly surrounded by fortifications, which had witnessed many an onslaught; but nearly all have now disappeared. There is no point from which Monte Rosa is seen to greater advantage than from here, especially from the N. extremity of the street leading to the Rly. Stat. Around extends the plain, cultivated like a rich garden; but the soil is marshy, and the neighbourhood rather unhealthy.

The *Duomo* is an early Lombard building, somewhat damaged on the outside by neglect and weather, and more so within by recent repairs and adornments. The choir and transepts are masked by the stucco, the paintings, and the gildings introduced within the last 20 years. The high altar, though quite out of place, is a splendid structure. It has some angels executed by Thorwaldsen. The nave remains nearly in its original state; many ancient columns are inserted.

In the chapel of St. Joseph are several frescoes by Luini. The Sibyls: portions of the history of the Virgin, partly scriptural and partly legendary. They are rather injured by damp; but enough remains to show that they fully deserve the praises which have been bestowed upon them by those who saw them when they were more perfect. Of the six subjects on the walls, the Adoration of the Magi, and the Flight into Egypt, are the best preserved. In the sacristy are a Marriage of St. Catherine, by Gaudenzio Ferrari; an Adoration of the Magi, by Lanini; and a Last Supper, by Cesare da Sesto, a pupil of L. da Vinci or Morosoni.

The pavement of the Duomo is a relic of the original structure. It is of Mosaic, worked and laid in the Roman manner, probably by Byzantine artists of the 9th or 10th century: only two colours are employed, black and white. The compartments are divided by borders of frets and grotesques, such as are usually found in the tesselated pavements of Roman baths. The figures in the medallions are all birds:—the pelican, an emblem of the love of the Saviour; the phœnix, of the resurrection; the stork, of filial piety. They are very remarkable as early specimens of Christian allegory.

There is a square atrium, or cloistered court, in front of the cathedral, in the walls of which are inserted many Roman and mediæval inscriptions, including one in what appears to be a barbarous or colloquial corruption of Greek. From the side opposite to the great door of the cathedral opens the curious circular baptistery, supported, as is the case with almost all the very early edifices of the kind, by ancient columns; and hence the tradition, almost invariably annexed to these buildings, of their having been Pagan temples. These columns of white marble are fluted and of the Corinthian order, and have originally belonged to an edifice of a good Roman period; in the centre of the floor is a circular Roman urn, bearing an inscription to Umbrena Polla: it is now used as a font.

In the recesses between the columns are representations of the events of the Passion. The figures, in plastic work, are as large as life, and painted in gaudy colours; and in some cases the resemblance to life is completed by the addition of real hair. They have been attributed to Gaudenzio Ferrari, but, if so, they do little honour to him as compositions, although many of the figures are of fair workmanship. The two finest groups are the Garden of Olives and the Scourging of our Lord; one of the executioners is sitting down, tired with his work; the Roman soldier looks on with pity; the other can no longer look, and turns away.

The archives of the Duomo contain some curious specimens of the antiquities of the Lower Empire and the middle ages, and some very old documents. There are two remarkably fine ivory diptychs, both consular: on the first the consul is represented at full-length, under a species of cupola supported by columns, in the style of which we may see most evidently the transition which produced the Lombard or Norman style. This diptych contains a list of the bishops from Gaudentius to the year 1170; the second bears the bust of a consul, and contains another list of the bishops from St. Gaudentius to William of Cremona, in 1343. There is also a life of St. Gaudentius, and other saints of Novara, written in 700, and a petition to Bishop Grazioso, in 730, for the consecration of an altar erected to St. Michael. The library of the seminary, which is open to the public 3 days a-week, contains about 12,000 vols.

The Duomo of Novara is known in Italy as a distinguished school of music; and the office of Maestro di Capella has usually been given to eminent composers. In more recent times the place has been held by Generali and Mercadante.

The *Basilica of San Gaudenzio*, the patron saint of Novara and its first bishop, was entirely rebuilt by Pellegrini in the 16th centy., and is a noble structure; the sepulchral chapel of the patron saint is very magnificent: the high altar was erected in 1725, and betrays the bad taste of that time. This church contains one of the finest works of Gaudenzio Ferrari. It was originally over the high altar; but, upon the latter being re-constructed, it was placed in the 2nd chapel on l. on entering the ch. It consists of six compartments, enclosed in a framework richly carved and gilt, also executed by the painter. The date of this work (1515) is exactly fixed by the contract between the artist and the chapter in the archives of the church. The principal compartments contain the Nativity above, with the Madonna and Child and four saints with attending angels below. Much gilding is introduced into the garments of the figures; and this adornment is the subject of a special clause in the contract. This was his largest work before he went to Rome, and the last in his earlier style. In the 4th chapel on the rt. is a crucifix modelled by Ferrari. The church also contains—the Deposition from the Cross, by *Moncalvo;* *Morazzone*, the Last Judgment; and some recent frescoes by *Sabatelli*. The archives of San Gaudenzio are valuable. A consular diptych of great beauty, on which are sculptured two Roman consuls giving the signal for the public games, and some early manuscripts, are worthy of notice. The bell-tower of S. Gaudenzio is fine, and so lofty as to form a very conspicuous object, being visible from a great distance.

Ch. of San Pietro al Rosario, formerly annexed to a Dominican convent, now suppressed, was finished in 1618. It contains some good wall-paintings in oil by a Novarese artist of the last century: and the Virgin, St. Peter Martyr, and St. Catherine, in the chapel of the Rosary, by *Giulio Cesare Procaccini*. Here, in 1307, sentence was passed on Frate Dolcino, who preached the tenets of Manes, and a community of goods and women. Having retreated to the mountains above Vercelli, at the head of 5000 disciples, he was defeated on Maundy Thursday, in a pitched battle, by the Novarese, and taken prisoner. He and his concubine, the beautiful Margaret, a nun whom he had abducted from her convent, were burnt alive (March 23, 1307). They both behaved with extraordinary firmness at their execution, which was accompanied with circumstances of most revolting cruelty. Dante introduces Mahomet requesting him to warn Dolcino of his approaching fate:—

"Or di' a fra Dolcin dunque, che s' armi,
Tu, che forse vedrai il sole in breve,
(S' egli non vuol qui tosto seguitarmi)
Sidi vivanda, che stretta di neve
Non rechi la vittoria al Novarese,
Ch' altrimenti acquistar non saria leve."
Inferno, xxviii. 55-60.

"Thou who perhaps the sun wilt shortly see,
Exhort Friar Dolcin, that with store of food
(Unless he wish full soon to follow me)
He arm himself; lest, straiten'd by the snow,
A triumph to Novara be allow'd
O'er him whom else he could not overthrow."

There is rather a good theatre at Novara, which is open for operas and ballets during the carnival and the autumn.

Much building is now in progress at Novara, exhibiting the prosperous state of the country. The new *Mercato*, which also contains the offices of the Tribunal of Commerce, has been built from the designs of Professor Orelli of Milan.

The *Ospedale Maggiore*, with its cortile supported by 88 columns of granite, less ornamented than the *Mercato*, is also a great ornament to the city. The ancient streets of low cloistered arches are disappearing fast before lofty arcades like those of Turin.

A statue of Carlo Emanuele III., by Marchesi, has been lately erected near the *Palazzo della Giustizia*. The extension of the Rly. to Novara has added greatly to its prosperity and commercial activity. Placed as it now is within a few hours' distance of Turin, Milan, and Genoa, it forms the point where all the communications to the Lago Maggiore, and, the most important now, across the Alps, converge.

The Rly. Stat. is in the plain of the Terdoppio, a few hundred yds. beyond the N.E. extremity of Novara.

It was to the S. of the town of Novara, almost in its suburbs, that took place on the 23rd of March, 1849, the sanguinary action between the Austrians and the Piedmontese, which terminated in the defeat of the latter, and the abdication of the brave and chivalrous Carlo Alberto. That unfortunate sovereign, pressed by the democratic party at Turin, denounced the armistice into which he had entered in August of the preceding year, after his unsuccessful campaign on the Adige and the Mincio, and prepared to invade the Austrian territory by crossing the Ticino on the 21st March. On the same day the veteran Radetsky invaded the Piedmontese territory by crossing the same river at Pavia, with a well-equipped army of 60,000 men, in 4 divisions. Without losing a moment his advanced guard was put into motion in the direction of the headquarters of the Piedmontese army, then lying between Novara and Trecate. After a hard-fought action at Mortara, on the 21st, in which the Piedmontese were worsted, the Austrians advanced upon Novara, where both armies engaged on the 23rd, the Austrians under Radetsky, the Piedmontese commanded by the Polish General Chernowski, under the King in person. The site of the battle is a little S. of the town in the plain separating the Agogna and Terdopio streams. The heat of the action was between Olengo and the chapel of La Bicocca, about 2½ m. S. of Novara, on the road to Mortara: the Piedmontese performed prodigies of valour, led on by Carlo Alberto and his sons the Dukes of Savoy (the present King Victor Emanuel) and Genoa. The conflict lasted during the whole day, and at its close the Piedmontese retired through the town, committing some acts of pillage and disorder. On the 26th of March an armistice was signed, in which Radetsky showed much generosity as a victor — the whole campaign, from the crossing of the Ticino at Pavia, having only lasted 5 days.

Leaving Novara, the rly. crosses the plain to

9 kil. *Trecate* Stat., a large village. 2 m. farther is San Martino, situated on the highest point of the escarpment on the W. side of the valley of the Ticino. From San Martino less than a mile brings us to the Ticino, crossing, before reaching it, 2 canals, which, derived about 2 m. higher up, irrigate the districts of Vigevano and S. Martino.

5 kil. *Ticino Stat.*, on the river.

The *Ticino*, until recently the boundary between the dominions of Sardinia and Austrian Lombardy, is here a fine river, with a wide gravelly bed which is frequently changing. The bridge or Ponte Nuovo, by which it is crossed, is of the granite of Montorfano, and has 11 arches all of the same size; its length is 997 feet; it cost 128,603*l.* It was begun by the French in 1810, afterwards stopped by political events, resumed in 1823, and completed in 1827 by the two sovereigns whose territories it joined. It is one of the finest works of the kind in Italy. The Austrians attempted, in their retreat from Piedmont, to blow up the eastern arches on the 2nd of May, 1859, but not sufficiently so as to prevent the French crossing it on the day following. 1 m. farther, by a very gradual ascent, brings us to the Canal or *Naviglio Grande*, which is here rapid and clear, and which is crossed by the *Ponte di Magenta*, the former Austrian custom-house station.

The *Naviglio Grande*, which derives its water from the Ticino at the village of Tornavento about 8 m. higher up, after first reaching Milan, connects the Ticino and the Po, and is remarkable as being the earliest artificial canal in Europe, with the exception (not quite certain) of that between Ghent and Bruges. It was begun in the 12th century. The first portion ended at Abbiategrasso, and was intended principally for the purposes of irrigation. In 1259 it was continued to Milan by Napoleone della Torre, and also deepened and better adapted for navigation. It is still mainly useful for its original purpose. The country on either side is irrigated by the numerous watercourses which derive from it. The flood-gates are locked and opened when required, under particular regulations, so as to secure to the adjoining landowners their due share of the fertilising waters. 3 m. higher up the Ticino is Turbigo, opposite which Marshal M'Mahon crossed the river on the 3rd of June, the first entrance of the allied army into Lombardy in the late memorable campaign.

7 kil. *Magenta Stat.* It was founded by the Emperor Maximilian, and destroyed by Barbarossa. It is in the midst of a most fertile district of mulberry-trees and corn.

As Magenta and its environs were the scene of one of the greatest battles during the late war, it will not be out of place here to say a few words on the military operations of which it was the culminating event.

Our readers need scarcely be informed that after the entrance of the Austrians into Piedmont, in the spring of 1859, advancing as far as the Dora, and to within a few miles of Turin, they continued to occupy the country between the Dora, Sesia, and Ticino, covering Lombardy from invasion on the W., whilst the Sardo-French army occupied the country S. of the Po, and especially the line extending from Alexandria to the frontier of the duchy of Piacenza, receiving their supplies from Genoa, and supported by Alexandria and Casale; the Allies menacing thus the whole line of the Po from Valenza to La Stradella, where the Lombard frontier was strongly defended; the Austrians crossing at times the river. It was in one of these expeditions, a kind of gigantic reconnaissance that was fought the brilliant action of Montebello, near Casteggio, so honourable to the Piedmontese army (p. 57).

The French Emperor towards the close of May, having become persuaded that an invasion of Lombardy from the S. would be attended with insuperable obstacles, all at once changed his plan of operations, and by a rapid flank movement in a few days transferred the greater part of the Allied army into the plains of the Sesia, thus turning almost unperceived and unsuspected the right wing of the Austrian army; in this rapid transfer, for it can scarcely be called a march, the railway from Alexandria offered the greatest facilities. On the 28th of May this flank movement commenced, crossing the Po at Casale, where was the only bridge, and on the 30th the great mass of the Allies was encamped on the W. side of the Sesia, having their head-quarters at Vercelli; the Austrians under Giulay holding the opposite bank, and all the country between it and the Ticino. On the 30th the Piedmontese commenced their onward march, occupying Borgo Vercelli, and attacked with success the Austrians at Confienza, Vinzaglio, and Palestro; but the latter returning to occupy their former positions on the following day, the Piedmontese, aided by the French Zouaves, gained a very important victory at Palestro, the consequence of which was the Austrians retreating to Mortara, in the direction of Boreguardo and Pavia. The French army crossed the Sesia on the same day, and on the day following occupied without opposition Novara. On the 2nd of June General M'Mahon advanced from Novara, crossed the Ticino with scarcely any opposition at Turbigo, and established himself there and in the adjoining village of Robechetto, the Sardinian army following on the 3rd. On the same day the Emperor of the French, with the Imperial guard, moved from Novara, by the high road to Milan, through Trecate and S. Martino, at the W. extremity of the fine bridge of Buffalora or Ponte Nuovo.

On the morning of the 4th of May took place the combined movements from Turbigo on the N., and S. Martino on the S., which ended after a long day's contest in the total defeat of the Austrians,—the battle which bears the name of Magenta, although it might equally bear that of Buffalora. The plan of Napoleon was that General M'Mahon should advance from Turbigo by way of Buffalora, the Emperor at the head of the Imperial guard by the Ponte Nuovo, parallel to the line of railway, both armies to form a junction at Magenta. This plan was punctually followed; M'Mahon engaging the Austrians at Buffalora, where they were strongly posted. About 2 o'clock M'Mahon was engaged at Buffalora, on hearing the cannon from which the Emperor ordered the bridge to be crossed, beyond which the Imperial guard, under the orders of Marshal Baraguay d'Hilliers, met with an obstinate resistance, and were more than once obliged to fall back, in which the General commanding the attacking force, Cler, was killed. The contest here lasted several hours, with very doubtful issue, until M'Mahon, having driven back the right wing of the Austrians by his flank movement on Buffalora, advanced on Magenta. About 6 o'clock the Austrians occupied the village, defending it most obstinately for 2 hours against the combined forces of M'Mahon, of Canrobert, and of the Imperial guard, which, after a most sanguinary conflict, had succeeded in making its way from the river; each house being defended and stormed as a fortress. Here more than 10,000 men were put hors de combat, and General Espinasse, commanding the Imperial guard, and one of the bravest officers in the French army, was killed. It was not until 8½ P.M. that the firing ceased, by the arrival of the reserves of Niel's and Canrobert's divisions, the Austrians retreating on Rebecco with the intention of recommencing the contest on the morrow. During the long and arduous contest along the line, from the Ponte Nuovo to Magenta, Napoleon was constantly in the midst of the fight; his principal station being at the top of one of the large buildings at the hamlet of Ponte di Magenta, a bridge which crosses the canal or Naviglio about half-way between the Ticino and Magenta. The losses in this sanguinary conflict were very great on both sides; according to the French bulletins, theirs amounting to 3700 and 735 prisoners, and those of the Austrians to 13,000 killed and wounded and 7000 prisoners, out of 55,000 engaged on one side and 75,000 on the other. The result was that the Austrians, being demoralized, and the corps of their right wing so much cut up by M'Mahon's flank movement, instead of attacking on the morrow, retreated in a southerly direction towards Abbiategrasso and the Adda, leaving the road to Milan open, which the Emperor and his Royal Ally entered in triumph on the .

The result of this memorable campaign is well told in the closing paragraph of the Imperial bulletin, dated from S. Martino the day after the battle of Magenta.

"In 5 days after its departure from Alexandria the Allied army have fought 3 actions, gained a great battle, cleared Piedmont of the Austrians, and opened the gates of Milan. Since the combat of Montebello the Austrian army has lost 25,000 men in killed and wounded, 10,000 prisoners, and 17 guns"—although there is a good deal of exaggeration in the number of the casualties.

By military men Marshal Giulay's tactics have been much blamed, for allowing the Allies to cross the Ticino almost without firing a shot, and for giving battle on his own instead of on the enemy's ground; but the fact appears to be that he was quite unprepared for Napoleon's sudden change from the bank of the Po to that of Ticino, and unable to bring up in time his reserves from the vicinity of Pavia and the Oltro Po Pavese to oppose the French attack in this new position. Giulay was soon relieved of his command, almost with disgrace, and M'Mahon, to whose able strategy this great victory was chiefly due, created almost on the battle-field Marshal of France and Duke of Magenta.

Leaving Magenta, the rlwy. and post-road diverge.

4 m. *Vettuone Stat.*, leaving which we pass on the rt. where Desiderius, the King of the Lombards, had a villa.

6 m. *Rho Stat.*, before reaching which the river Olona is crossed, and afterwards the Lura, near where they join. Rho is a large village in a productive district; it has a large church from the designs of Pellegrini.

5 m. *Musocco Stat.* Here the rly. crosses the carriage-road from Varese, Saronno, and Bollate.

5 m. *Milan Stat.* The station is the same as that of the Monza and Como Rlwy., near the Porta Nuova, where omnibuses from the different hotels, and flys, will be found waiting on the arrival of every train; but as the former are generally crammed with passengers, and take a circuitous route, the traveller will find it more convenient, and generally as economical, as a charge is made by the omnibus for every parcel of luggage, to take a carriage, the fare for which to his hotel will be 1 fr. 35 c.

Hotels. Hôtel de la Ville, kept by Baur, and Hôtel Royal, by Bruschetti, the best; both excellent, with landlords and servants who speak English.

ROUTE 3.

TURIN TO MILAN, BY CASALE, MORTARA, AND VIGEVANO.

This road follows the rt. bank of the Po in nearly the whole of its extent through a rich alluvial country, having on the rt. hand the hilly region of the Montferrat, and on the other the plain extending to the foot of the Alps. There are no post relays upon it. The Rly. from Vercelli to Casale causes this route to be now seldom followed by travellers.

11 kil. *Settimo Stat.*
12 kil. *Chivasso Stat.*

Verolengo, containing 5000 Inhab. Half-way before reaching here the old post-road to Vercelli branches off on the l.

Near this place, but on the opposite side of the Po, is *Monteu Po,* occupying the site of the Roman station of *Industria.* This city, mentioned by Pliny and other ancient writers, had been in a manner lost. Many antiquaries supposed that Casale had risen upon its ruins ; but in 1744 the discovery of remains in this neighbourhood, and some fragments of inscriptions, led to further excavations. The result was, as has been before mentioned, the discovery of many of the finest objects in the Museum of Turin. The excavations have not been recently prosecuted with much vigour.

21 kil. *Crescentino,* beyond the junction of the Dora Baltea with the Po, 4300 Inhab., in the midst of a marshy territory. Its plan indicates a Roman station ; and some remains discovered in the last centy. seem to confirm this supposition. The principal church, the *Assunta,* is ancient, but has been recently decorated and altered. It contains some paintings by *Moncalvo.*

Beyond the Po, opposite to Crescentino, but not in the road, rises *Verrua,* formerly strongly fortified, but now dismantled. Situated upon an abrupt and insulated hill, it is a most defensible position : it opposed an obstinate resistance to the Emperor Frederick II. In more recent times (1704) the Duke of Vendôme attacked it without success. The defences were destroyed by the French during their first occupation of Piedmont.

The road continues skirted by the Po, passing through a rich but unhealthy country, full of swamps, and constantly liable to inundations. The marshy meadows feed abundance of cattle, and hence the cultivation of rice is not so much resorted to here as farther on.

18 kil. *Trino,* 7000 Inhab. This place was formerly much better peopled ; its decrease is attributed to the insalubrity of the country. Great herds of swine are reared in the marshes, and the hams of Trino are celebrated throughout Piedmont. Trino was the birthplace of Bernardino Gioleto, a celebrated printer, who established himself at Venice in 1487, and who became the father of a long line of typographers. Trino originally belonged to Vercelli ; and was the constant object of contention between it and its dangerous neighbours the marquises of Montferrat. When Victor Emanuel asserted his claims to the marquisate, he laid siege to and took it, assisted by his two sons Victor Amedeus and Francis Thomas. This achievement was commemorated by the following jingling epigram :—

"Trina dies Trinum trino sub principe cepit.
Quid mirum? numquid Mars ibi trinus erat."

The road follows the l. bank of the Po, which it crosses by a suspension bridge before entering

20 kil. *Casale,* an important city, 21,000 Inhab., the capital of the ancient marquisate of Montferrat. In later times it was a position exceedingly contested ; and the citadel, founded in 1590 by Duke Vicenzo, was one of the strongest places in Italy. The castle or palace is yet standing : it was embellished by the Gonzagas. Many Roman remains have been found here ; amongst others, coins of the earliest ages of the republic. The fortifications of Casale have been recently greatly increased and strengthened, and, with Alessandria and Genoa, it is now one of the great military strongholds of the kingdom of Sardinia ; it forms as it were the frontier barrier on the side of Lombardy.

The *Cathedral* or *Duomo* is said to have been founded by Liutprand, King of the Lombards, in 742 ; and the archives of the chapter contain a singular muniment, a charter engraved upon a tablet of lead, supposed to confirm this opinion. The cathedral, by whomsoever founded, is of high antiquity as a Lombard building ; but in 1706 the repairs and decorations bestowed upon it effaced many of its original features. It contains some good paintings: the best is the Baptism of our Lord by *Gaudenzio Ferrari*, a portion of a larger picture which was destroyed by fire. The chapel of Sant' Evasio has been recently decorated with much splendour; the shrine is of silver. In the sacristy (though the French removed a large portion of its contents) are still some very curious specimens of art. A cross taken from the inhabitants of Alessandria, covered with silver plates set with gems. Another of exceedingly rich workmanship in enamel, given by the Cardinal Theodore Palæologus. A statue by Bernini, forming part of a group of the *Spasimo*, from the suppressed convent of Santa Chiara. The altar, with alto-rilievos, was formerly in the chapel of Sant' Evasio. Amongst the archives, besides Liutprand's charter-tablet, are some valuable manuscripts of the 10th centy., and an ancient sacrificial vase in silver representing the Triumph of Bacchus.

The church of *San Domenico* is one of the last bequests of the Palæologi, having been begun by them in 1469, and consecrated in 1513. The stags which form a part of their armorial bearings, and which ornamented the façade, have been removed; but the memory of this family is preserved by the tomb erected by the late king in 1835, and in which the remains of several of its princes have been deposited. The building is supposed to be after the designs of Bramantino, and from the elegance of its proportions and the richness of its ornaments, especially of the façade, it may rank among the finest of the sacred edifices in this country. It contains paintings by Pompeo Battoni and Moncalvo. Here is the fine Mausoleum of Benvenuto di San Giorgio, who died in 1527. This individual wrote an excellent chronicle of Montferrat, of much importance also in the general history of Italy; he was a knight of Malta, and he is represented upon his tomb in the habit of his order. Quaint allegorical bas-reliefs adorn other portions of it; it is surmounted by a canopy; and the style of the whole is interesting, as being the parent of that which prevailed in England in the days of Elizabeth.

Sant' Ilario enjoys the reputation of having been once a pagan temple. It is said to have been consecrated by St. Hilary in the 4th centy. It did contain many good paintings of early date: the best have been removed to Turin, but some curious specimens still remain.

Many of the ancient civil edifices of Casale are remarkable. The old *Torre del grand' Orologio* was built before the year 1000. It was altered in 1510 by William IV., Marquis of Montferrat, whose arms are cast upon the great bell. The *Palazzo della Città* was originally the property of the noble family of Blandrate. Having been confiscated in 1535, it was made over to the municipal body. It is attributed to Bramante; and the portal and porticoes are not unworthy of his reputation. The paintings which it contained have been removed, but some frescoes yet ornament the roof and walls. *Palazzo Delavalle* contains some frescoes by *Giulio Romano*. In the *Palazzo Callori* is a portrait of Gonzaga, abbot of Sant' Andrea, at Mantua, by *Titian*.

The central position of Casale has always given it importance as a military position, and this has been turned to good account by the present government in adding greatly to its defences. Rlwys. branch from it to Vercelli, Novara, Valenza, and Alessandria; and a good road to Mortara and Vigevano by *Caudia*, where there are some frescoes in the ch. of Sta. Maria, by Lanini; and *Cozzo*, said to have been founded by king Cottius, across the rich country bordering on the Sesia and the Lomellina.

18 kil. *Mortara*, 4070 Inhab.; the chief town of a district called the Lomellina. It is said to have derived its name from its unhealthiness—*Mortis ara*, the altar of death. According to another tradition, it derives its funereal appellation from the slaughter of the

Lombards, who were here defeated by Charlemagne, A.D. 774. The whole district is intersected by rivers, watercourses, and canals; and the rice-plantations add to the insalubrity of the marsh-lands around.

The Rly. is open from Mortara to *Vigevano*, 12 kil., 14,000 Inhab.; a place of considerable trade, but not otherwise remarkable. The ancient castle of the Sforzas was altered in 1492 by Bramante; and having been formed into a palace, it is now employed as a barrack. The cathedral is a good building; it has recently been repaired and decorated. Public conveyances for Milan start on the arrival of each Rly. train, employing 3½ to 4 hrs.

Cross the Ticino upon a flying bridge, and enter Lombardy.

Abbiategrasso (first Lombard station), a considerable borgo upon the *Naviglio Grande*. It contains a large establishment in the nature of an infirmary, dependent upon the great hospital of Milan.

Gaggiano.

Corsico. Much of the cheese exported under the name of Parmesan, but known in the country by the name of *formaggio di grana*, is made in this neighbourhood.

MILAN. (Route 21.)

Chieri (the ancient *Carrea Potentia*), which contains about 12,000 Inhab. The ch. of *Santa Maria della Scala* is one of the largest Gothic buildings in Piedmont. It was erected in 1405. Annexed to it is a very ancient baptistery, which, as usual, is said to have been a pagan temple.

The *Church of St. Dominico*, built in 1260, has some good paintings by *Moncalvo*. This convent has been restored. It once contained a singular inmate. In the month of October, 1664, the knights of Malta captured a Turkish galley, on board of which was one of the sultanas of Ibrahim, the then reigning Padishah, with her son, the young Osman. The boy was educated at Rome; but it was judged expedient to send him to France, when, chancing to stop at Turin, he determined to become a friar, and he entered this convent, where he professed under the name of Padre Domenico Ottoman di San Tomaso. Some members of the Broglia family, and amongst them Francesco Broglia, who served under Louis XIV., ancestor of the family of de Broglie in France, are buried in this church. The de Broglies came originally from this neighbourhood.

The cupola of the Cistercian monastery is considered one of the best works of Juvara.

Chieri is one of the most ancient manufacturing towns in Europe. The manufactories of fustians and cotton stuffs date from 1422, and upwards of 100,000 pieces were annually made towards the middle of the 15th century. The manufactories still exist, and also some silk-works.

Riva di Chieri, to the Stat. of *Valdechiesa*, on the railway to Asti, or by the road to *Villanova*.

Asti. (See Rte. 5.)

ROUTE 4.

TURIN TO ASTI, BY CHIERI.

This is a good road of about 40 m. Chieri is about 17 m. from Turin.

La Madonna del Pilone. From this point the road ascends the Collina, S. of the Superga, to

Pino, on the highest part of the range, whence it descends for 4 m. to

ROUTE 5.

TURIN TO GENOA, BY ASTI, ALESSANDRIA, AND NOVI—RAIL.

166 kil., 103¾ m.

KIL.		KIL.	
8	Moncalieri.	91	Alessandria.
13	Trofarello.	101	Frugarolo.
17	Cambiano.	113	Novi.
22	Pessione.	121	Serravalle.
30	Villanova.	125	Arquata.
42	Villafranca.	134	Isola di Cantone.
47	Baldichieri.	139	Ronco.
50	San Damiano.	144	Busalla.
57	Asti.	154	Pontedecimo.
67	Annone.	158	Bolzanetto.
71	Cerro.	161	Rivarolo.
77	Felizzano.	163	San Pier d'Arena.
83	Solero.	166	Genoa.

The railway from Turin to Genoa was opened Dec. 1853. Trains start 4 times a day for Genoa, performing the journey in from 4h. 5 min. to 5h. 30 min.; the fares are moderate: 1st class 16f. 60c. (13s. 3d.); 2nd 11f. 60c. (9s. 4d.); 3rd 8f. 30c. (6s. 7d.) No allowance of free weight of luggage is made, so that every pound is charged for. The traveller may take a small parcel or bag with him in the carriage.

The station in Turin is at the extremity of the Strada Nuova. The Rly. runs parallel to the old post-road in a great portion of its extent from Turin to Genoa.

Leaving Turin, the line follows the l. bank of the Po and crosses it at

8 kil. *Moncalieri* (the first station), pleasantly situated on the declivity of the southern extremity of the range of the Collina. The palace, which crowns the hill above the town, was built by Vittorio Amedeo I., on the site of a far older building, dating from the days of Jolanda: it is fine and commanding from every point of view. This palace was the last prison of Vittorio Amedeo II.; here he died after his removal from Rivoli. The gallery contains a long succession of family portraits, and also a curious series representing the hunting parties of Carlo Emanuele II. The influence of French costume is singularly marked in the fashions of the court: with respect to the countenances, the descendants of *Humbert aux blanches mains*, the founder (or nearly so) of the family, may be said to be generally a handsome race. The little town has some vestiges of antiquity in its collegiate church. The name of the place is said to be derived from *Mont Caillier*, the hill of qunils, in the provincial language; but these birds are not more common here than in other parts of the range. Ariosto has made Moncalieri the seat of one of the Paladins of Charlemagne, —slain, when sleeping, by Clorinda:—

"Dopo essi Palidon da Moncalieri
Che sicuro dormia fra due destrieri."

The fair of Moncalieri is held on the 29th of October, and lasts for a week. It is one of the greatest cattle-markets of Piedmont; but it is also a pleasure fair, and a favourite holiday-time with both the country folks and the citizens. The road onwards is varied by beautiful undulations: mulberry-trees abound in the fields. On the W. the noble mass of the *Monte Viso* towers above the rest of the alpine range. On the S.E. the distant Apennines, or rather the mountains which, connecting Alps and Apennines, may be said to belong to both, are seen blue and clear in the extreme distance.

5 kil. *Troffarello Stat.* Here the Rly. to Savigliano and Cuneo branches off on the rt.; the road from here to the next stat. runs along the base of the Collina, studded with villas and farm-houses.

4 kil. *Cambiano Stat.* The village of Cambiano, on a gentle rise, about ¼ m. on the l. Here the line separates from the post-road, running through the plain of Riva Chieri and Poirino, and crossing several streams to

5 kil. *Pessione Stat.*

Valdechiesa, 2 miles from Villanova, and an equal distance from Riva di Chieri (Rte. 4). Valdechiesa was founded in 1248 by the inhabitants of several townships which had been destroyed by the citizens of Asti and other more powerful places. The road from Turin to Asti, by Chieri (Rte. 4), here crosses the railway. The view of the snowy Alps is very fine from this part of the route, extending from Monte Viso to Monte Rosa; the declivities of the hills in the foreground are covered with villas and farms. Beyond the stat. the country becomes hilly to

8 kil. *Villanova Stat.*, situated on the highest part of the plain that separates the waters flowing towards the Po on the one side, and the Tanaro on the E.; The country hitherto passed through is chiefly laid out in corn-fields, with few mulberry or vine plantations; the view of Monte Viso is very fine from Dusino. The Rly. descends rapidly through deep cuttings to Villa Franca, the difference of level being 350 ft. The geologist will here find himself in the midst of the tertiary subapennine formation, abounding in marine shells; several remains of large fossil mammalia have been found here, near Baldechieri, in the Val d'Andona, &c. In this neighbourhood is produced much of the wine commonly called *vino d'Asti*, the most drinkable of Piedmont. The vineyards are principally upon the undulating hills; and other crops are grown amongst the vines.

12 kil. *Villafranca Stat.*
5 kil. *Baldichieri Stat.*
3 kil. *San Damiano*, near the confluence of the Triversa and Borbore torrents, in the same valley. Vines become more abundant here, on the declivities of the hills.

7 kil. *Asti Stat.*

ASTI (Albergo Reale; indifferent). Population 24,500. An ancient city of some celebrity (Hasta Pompeija), situated near the confluence of the Borbore and Tanaro, surrounded by fertile and picturesque hills. The original *Duomo* fell down in 1323, and the present ample Gothic edifice was begun shortly afterwards, and completed about 1348. It is a fine and venerable building, filled with much painting, which unfortunately begins to suffer by decay. The choir was painted by *Carloni*,—a Nativity is said to be by *Bassano*; but its parentage may be doubted. In a chapel to the l. of the high altar is an ancient painting, German or Flemish, representing the Nativity. This picture was much admired by Gaudenzio Ferrari,

N. Italy—1860.

who has made a careful copy of it. By *Moncalvo* is a Resurrection: the terror of the soldiers is expressed with ability.

Ch. of San Secondo. Also a fine Gothic building. It is a collegiate church; and here also is a good ancient Flemish painting, representing the Purification; and another, in the same style, in the church of *Sta. Maria Nuova.*

Ch. of San Pietro in Concava, probably an ancient baptistery; it has, as usual, the perplexing appearance of classical antiquity. It is supposed, but without any reason, to have been a temple of Diana.

In this town is a printing-office in which the business has been carried on since 1479 without interruption.

The *Seminary* is a fine building, by Count Alfieri, the cousin of the poet. It is rich and picturesque in effect, and contains a good library.

In the *Palazzo Alfieri*, also built by the Count, is shown the room where Vittorio Alfieri was born, January 17th, 1749: his portrait, and the following autograph addressed to his sister, decorate the apartment.

" Oggi ha sei lustri, appiè del colle ameno
Che al Tanaro tardissimo sovrasta,
Dove Pompeo piantò sua nobil asta,
L' aure prime io bevea del dì sereno.
Nato e cresciuto a rio servaggio in seno,
Pur dire osai; servir, l' alma mi guasta;
Loco, ove solo un contra tutti basta,
Patria non m' è benchè natio terreno.
Altre leggi, altro cielo, infra altra gente
Mi dian scarso, ma libero ricetto,
Ov' io pensare e dir possa altamente.
Esci dunque, o timore, esci dal petto
Mio, che attristagli già sì lungamente;
Meco albergar non dei sotto umil tetto."
Son. xxxvii.

The churches of the *Certosa* and *San Bartolommeo*, outside the town, were ruined by the French. In both are some remains of good paintings: about half the other churches in and about Asti were destroyed.

The *Astigiano*, or territory about Asti, contains several mineral and thermal springs. At *Castel Alfieri* are two wells, which, until the earthquake of Lisbon, were of pure water. After the earthquake they became su' phureted, and wholly unfit for (

D

mestic purposes, and continued so until 1807, when, a sharp earthquake having been felt at Pinerolo, but which did not extend to this province, the waters became sweet again. This part of the country abounds with fossil organic remains. They are most numerous in the Val d' Andona, and all the way from Dusino, about Rochetta and Castel Nuovo.

Leaving Asti, the railway follows the valley of the Tanaro to

10 kil. *Anone* (*Stat.*), i. e. *ad Nonam;* the ninth mile station from Asti on the banks of the Tanaro; it is unhealthy, and the inhabitants are a good deal affected with the disease called *Pellagra*, common throughout Lombardy. Poor and unwholesome food, and exclusive feeding on Indian corn, is supposed to be the principal cause of it.

4 kil. *Cerro Stat.* The village is on a gentle rising on the L.; here the Plain of the Tanaro opens, Felizzano being upon one of the last spurs of the Astesan hills.

6 kil. *Felizzano* (*Stat.*); burnt three times in the 17th century, besides sustaining many previous destructions. The country around is frequently inundated by the Tanaro.

6 kil. *Solero Stat.* In the plain of the Tanaro.

8 kil. *Alessandria Junction Stat.* (The Albergo Nuovo, late Albergo Reale, is the best hotel: a good character is also given to the Albergo d' Italia: the Albergo dell' Universo.) Alessandria is 58 m. from Turin. Its population is 19,000, and, with the suburbs, about 40,000. This city stands between the Tanaro and the Bormida, near their junction, and is the most remarkable monument of the great Lombard league. This alliance, so powerful, so memorable, and yet so ineffectual for the preservation of the national liberties, began in 1164 by the confederacy of Verona, Vicenza, Padua, and Treviso, and included in 1167, besides these four cities, Ferrara, Brescia, Bergamo, Cremona, Lodi, Parma, Piacenza, Modena, Bologna, Novara, Vercelli, Como, Venice, and, lastly, Milan, ;—all bound by solemn oath and covenant to defend their mutual rights and privileges. The most powerful allies and willing subjects of the Emperor Frederick were the citizens of Pavia and the Marquis of Montferrat; and to keep these in check, the cities of the League determined to erect a new city, at once a fortress for their defence and a memorial of their liberties.

On the confines of the marquisate of Montferrat and the Pavezano, or country of Pavia, was a small castle called Robereto; this was chosen as the site of the new city. The ground was carefully surveyed by the engineers, for military architecture had already become a study among the Italians, and the expanse of the country and the course of the streams, not deep, but frequently inundating the adjoining plains, appeared excellently adapted for defence against the German cavalry. The astrologer stood by with his astrolabe, and the first stone was laid at the fortunate moment. The blessing of the Pontiff was asked and obtained; and in a general congress of the League it was determined that the new city should be called Alessandria, in honour of Pope Alexander III., the protector of the Guelfs, and the head of Catholic Christendom. The building of the city was more peculiarly intrusted to the Milanese, the Cremonese, and the Placentines: Genoa sent large sums of money. So earnestly did they labour, that before the close of the year the city was completed. The Ghibellines scornfully called it "Alessandria della Paglia," either in allusion to the materials of the newly erected buildings, earth mixed with chopped straw, or in prognostication of its being speedily destroyed like stubble or chaff; but Alessandria rapidly rose to great power. The inhabitants of the surrounding villages and towns, Castellazzo, Marengo, Solerio, Bergoglio, Quargnento, Villa del Foro, and Origlio, removed into it. From Asti came 3000, including some of the most noble families. Milan furnished a large contingent; and the siege laid to Alessandria by the incensed Emperor in 1174 ended in a disgraceful retreat from before the newly erected walls. Subsequently, when he made peace with the city, he stipulated that it should assume the name of *Cesarea*, but the Guelfic appellation prevailed over the Ghibelline; and Alessandria continued to retain its original denomination.

Alessandria has been strongly fortified by the sovereigns of the House of Savoy. The citadel, built in 1728, is now the most interesting and the most prominent feature of the city. The road winds round it, passing over a covered bridge, under which the Tanaro seems to be lost. This fortress is larger than many towns, with a regular *Place* in the centre, a parish church, and very extensive barracks and armouries. The French added to the fortifications of the city; and much more was projected by Napoleon, by whose orders extensive lines were begun, but the unfinished works left by him were afterwards destroyed. Modern engineers have skilfully availed themselves of the advantages afforded by the position chosen by those of the middle ages; and, after Verona, Alessandria is now the strongest place in Italy; by means of the sluices of the Tanaro the whole surrounding country can be inundated, and rendered quite unapproachable by the enemy.

The *Duomo* is richly decorated; its principal work of art is a colossal statue of St. Joseph, by *Parodi*.

The Church of the Madonna di Loreto, recently completed, says little for the talent of the architect.

Palazzo Ghilino, built by Count Alfieri, and amongst the best examples of his style. It now belongs to the king. On the whole, Alessandria offers less than the average interest of Italian cities, partly the result of its modern foundation.

Two great business fairs are held here annually, in April and in October. The goods are sold in a species of bazaar erected for the purpose. The traveller who consults his purse and his comfort must not attempt to stop at Alessandria during these fairs.

The Rly. between Alessandria and Arona, by Valenza, Mortara, and Novara, is now open throughout the entire distance. By it and by the line between Genoa and Alessandria, the journey from Genoa to Milan is reduced to 5½ hrs. By these lines also the traveller is enabled to reach the shores of the Lago Maggiore in 5¼ hrs. from Genoa—a great convenience for persons going into Switzerland and down the Rhine to England. From Alessandria a Rly. branches off to Acqui, 21 m., up the valley of the Bormida (Rte. 11, p. 68), and to Piacenza by Tortona, Voghera, and Stradella (Rte. 7).

Before arriving at the Station of Alessandria the railway crosses the Tanaro, and, soon after leaving it, the Bormida: it then runs along the western side of the battle-field of Marengo (see Rte. 7), distant about two miles from and parallel to the old post-road to

10 kil. *Frugarolo Stat.*, near the village of Bosco, in the extensive plain of Marengo, richly cultivated in corn, mulberry-trees, &c.

12 kil. *Novi Stat.* (*Inns*: l'Europa, very tolerable; the Aquila Nera is also good and clean.) Novi is the best sleeping-place between Milan and Genoa. It is a town of 10,800 Inhab., with a considerable trade, but offering nothing remarkable, except some picturesque old houses. The silk produced about Novi is amongst the most celebrated in Italy. The old post-road from Milan to Genoa, by Pavia and Tortona, joins at Novi, and the Rly. from Tortona (12 m.), forming the most direct communication with Pavia, Piacenza, Parma, Modena, and Bologna.

Beyond Novi we approach the Apennines, and the country becomes very beautiful. Fine hills in the distance, curiously stratified rocks nearer the road, and beautiful groves of chestnut-trees, cheer and enliven the way.

8 kil. *Serravalle Stat.* Near the entrance to the mountain valley of the

Scrivia, which flows close to the village, and which is crossed by a bridge: the hills rise picturesquely on either side, and the geologist will here observe an interesting section of the tertiary marine strata dipping away from the central range. The Rly. follows the sinuosities of the valley, passing through a long tunnel after leaving Serravalle. A tunnel is traversed before—

4 kil. *Arquata Stat.* A fine ruined castle surmounts the hill, and the road continues increasing in beauty.

9 kil. *Isola del Cantone Stat.*, near a small village of that name, on a promontory at the junction of the Scrivia and another stream. A fine new bridge has been thrown over the former river at this point.

5 kil. *Ronco Stat.* A romantic village, from which, before the completion of the Rly., commenced the ascent of the Apennines by the post-road.

5 kil. *Busalla Stat.*, on the Scrivia, the last station on the northern declivity of the Apennines, and the summit level of the entire line of Rly. between Turin and Genoa. The carriage-road, which runs through the village, ascends to the Pass or Col di Giove, the culminating point from which the traveller will descry the Mediterranean, a considerable portion of the valley of the Polcevera, leading to Genoa, and the peaks behind that city crowned with their detached forts.

The great *Tunnel* which traverses the central ridge of the Apennines commences at Busalla; it is 3470 yards, or very little short of 2 English miles, in length; the whole of this distance is not however excavated in the mountain; the first part being a great artificial tube or archway parallel to the Scrivia, it having, from the friable nature of the rock, been found impossible to form a cutting that would exclude the river, and prevent infiltrations from torrents descending from the hills above to empty themselves into the Scrivia: the rest of the tunnel (about 3000 yards) is excavated in the rock, a friable calcareous schistus; the whole is walled, and 14 shafts descend from the surface to convey air. A portion of the stream of the Scrivia has been diverted through the tunnel to supply Genoa with water. Notwithstanding the very steep incline, the passage through the tunnel, as well as that along the rest of the line leading to Genoa, is very safely effected by engines of a peculiar construction, made by Messrs Stephenson of Newcastle. Emerging from the tunnel we enter the valley of the Polcevera, which the Rly. follows, to near the gates of Genoa. The works of the railroad in all this extent have been admirably constructed, the greater portion of the line being on terraces of solid masonry, or on gigantic embankments; the following being the stations beyond *Busalla:—*

10 kil. *Pontedecimo Stat.*
4 kil. *Bolzanetto Stat.*
3 kil. *Rivarolo Stat.*
2 kil. *San Pier d' Arena Stat.*
3 kil. GENOA.

Once on the S. declivity of the chain, the entire appearance of the country and the people changes: vines grow luxuriantly at Ponte Decimo near the S. opening of the tunnel, and are soon succeeded by olive-trees; and before reaching Genoa, the traveller arriving from beyond the Alps will, for the first time, see oranges growing in the open air; the villages he passes through have also quite a southern appearance, and the language spoken is different, being the Genoese dialect. As Genoa is approached, the villas of the Genoese aristocracy succeed; the Rly. runs along the base of a ridge crowned by fortifications on the l., and after passing through San Pier d'Arena it enters the tunnel of the Lanterna to emerge from it a few hundred yards before reaching the station in Genoa, situated near the Palazzo Doria and the Piazza di Aqua Verde.

GENOA TERMINUS. (Rte. 13.)

Hotels: Hôtel d'Italie, kept by Ten; H. Royal, by Perosio. The Hôtels de la Ville, Croix de Malte, Feder, all good. Omnibuses are in attendance to take travellers to these different hotels.

PIEDMONT.   *Route 6.—Alessandria to Novara and Arona.*   53

ROUTE 6.
ALESSANDRIA TO MORTARA, NOVARA, AND ARONA, ON THE LAGO MAGGIORE—RAIL.
63 m.

KIL.		KIL.	
9	Val Madonna.	51	Vespolate.
14	Valenza.	66	Novara.
11	Torreberetti.	79	Bellinzago.
27	Sartirana.	82	Oleggio.
29	Valle.	90	Varallo Pombia.
37	Olevano.	93	Borgo Ticino.
41	Mortara.	102	Arona.
49	Borgo Lavezzaro.		

The Rly. is now open from Alessandria to Arona, 63¼ m. (4 trains daily in 2¾ hrs.), thus furnishing the easiest mode of reaching Switzerland from the shores of the Mediterranean, and Milan, by means of the line from Novara by Magenta.

The first part of the Rly., as far as the Po, is through an irregular hilly country, the E. angle of the group of tertiary hills of the Astigiano, between the Po and the Tanaro: a gradual ascent of 75 ft. brings us to

9 kil. *Val Madonna Stat.*, nearly at the summit level, from which an equally gradual descent, after passing through a long tunnel, leads to

5 kil. *Valenza Junction Stat.*, a short way on the l. of the town, which contains a population of 4000. A Rly. branches off to Casale (14 m.) and Vercelli (26 m.). Soon after leaving Valenza the Po is crossed by a fine bridge of 20 arches.

7 kil. *Torreberetti Stat.* A Rly. is projected from here to Pavia.

6 kil. *Sartirana Stat.*, near a considerable town in a fine agricultural district.

2 kil. *Valle Stat.* 3 m. on the l. is the town of Candia, on the carriage-road from Casale to Mortara.

After *Valle* the Rly. crosses numerous streams and canals, the country being highly irrigated, and laid out in pasturage and rice-fields, to

8 kil. *Olevano Stat.*, near the l. bank of the *Agogna*, descending from Novara.

4 kil. *Mortara* (4070 Inhab.), the chief town of the Lomellina, the district between the rivers Ticino and Sesia; its name is supposed by some to be derived from *Mortis Ara*, the altar of death, by others from the slaughter of the Lombards by Charlemagne, whom he defeated here in A.D. 774; the country around being unhealthy, from its luxuriant vegetation and irrigation.

Santa Maria, the principal church, has been a good specimen of Italian Gothic, it is now much dilapidated. In this neighbourhood took place a severe action between the Piedmontese and the Austrians on the 21st of March, 1849, when the former, overpowered by numbers, were obliged to fall back on Novara.

A Rly. is open from Mortara to *Vigevano*, about 8 m. distant, and from which conveyances are ready on the arrival of each train to take passengers to Milan in 3½ hrs. (See Rte. 3.) From Mortara the Rly. follows the course of the *Arboroso* stream nearly to Novara.

8 kil. *Borgo Lavezzaro Stat.* 3 m. on the rt. is the town of *Gravellona*, in the plain of the Terdoppio.

5 kil. *Vespolate Stat.* From here the Rly. has a steeper incline than hitherto, running parallel to the post-road passing from

Garbagna to *Olegno.* It was about here, and over the fields reaching to the hamlet of la Bicocca, ½ m. on the l., that the battle raged most violently on the 23rd of March, 1849. (See p. 41.)

12 kil. *Novara Stat.* (See Rte. 2.) Between Novara and Arona the Rly. runs close to the post-road, and parallel to the Ticino and the W. shore of the Lago Maggiore. Persons proceeding to Milan change carriages here (see Rte. 2).

13 kil. *Bellinzago Stat.*

3 kil. *Oleggio Stat.*, a large village about 3 m. W. of the Ticino.

8 kil. *Varallo Pombia Stat.* A ro-

from here strikes off on the rt. to Somma, crossing the Ticino by a ferry-boat.
3 kil. *Borgo Ticino Stat.* Following the shores of the lake,
9 kil. *Arona Stat.* The Rly. Stat. is at the S. extremity of the town, close to the lake and to the quay where the steamers start from.
Inns: Albergo d'Italia, near the harbour; A. della Posta; both good, the latter nearer to the Rly. station and landing-place from the steamers. Hôtel Royal.

Steamers leave Arona on the arrival of the Rly. trains, ascending the lake at 7 a.m., 12·30 and 3·15 p.m., corresponding with the trains that leave Genoa at 5·40 and 10 a.m., and Turin by the Vercelli and Novara line at 8·37 a.m., and by the Alessandria and Mortara line at 8·45 and 12·15. These steamers stop, in going and returning, at Belgirate, Stresa, the Borromean Islands, Baveno (for the road by the Simplon), Pallanza, and Intra; and one daily at Laveno.

Steamers arrive from the head and more northern parts of the lake at 8·25 and 11·50 a.m., and 5·30 p.m., in correspondence with the Rly. trains which reach Alessandria at 11·22 a.m., 5 and 7·40 p.m., Genoa at 1·57, 8·55, and 10·15 p.m., Turin at 12·10 and 6·29 p.m., and Milan at 12 12, 6·29, and 11·26 p.m.

ROUTE 7.

ALESSANDRIA TO PIACENZA, BY TORTONA, VOGHERA, CASTEGGIO, AND THE TREBBIA.

60 m.

KIL.		KIL.	
8	La Spinetta.	64	Stradella.
14	S. Giuliano.	68	Arena Po.
22	Tortona.	75	Castel S. Giovanni.
31	Ponte Curone.	79	Sarmato.
39	Voghera.	84	Rottofreno.
48	Casteggio.	88	S. Nicolo.
53	San Giulletta.	97	Piacenza.
60	Broni.		

For the journey by Rly. between Turin and Alessandria, see Rte. 5. The railway to Piacenza, Parma, and Bologna—at 4·30, 8·45 a.m., 12·10, 8·20 p.m.— proceeds in a direct line, passing by Tortona, Casteggio, and La Stradella. Soon after leaving Alessandria the Bormida is crossed, the line to Genoa branching off on the rt.

The village of Marengo is passed on the l. soon after crossing the Bormida, and the road continues through the plain of the battle-field. "On the evening of the 13th of June, 1800, the whole Austrian army mustered in front of Alessandria, having only the river Bormida between them and the plain of Marengo; and early in the following morning they passed the stream at three several points, and advanced towards the French position in as many columns.

"The Austrians were full forty thousand strong; while, in the absence of Dessaix and the reserve, Napoleon could at most oppose to them twenty thousand, of whom only two thousand five hundred were cavalry. He had, however, no hesitation about accepting the battle. His advance, under Gardanne, occupied the small hamlet of Padre Bona, a little in front of Marengo. At that village, which overlooks a narrow ravine, the channel of a rivulet, Napoleon stationed Victor with the main body of his first line, the extreme right of it resting on Castel Ceriolo, another hamlet almost parallel with Marengo. Kellerman, with a brigade of cavalry, was posted immediately behind Victor for the protection of his flanks. A thousand yards in the rear of Victor was the second line, under Lannes, protected in like fashion by the cavalry of Champeaux. At about an equal distance, again, behind Lannes, was the third line, consisting of the division of St. Cyr, and the consular guard under Napoleon in person. The Austrian heavy infantry, on reaching the open field, formed into two lines, the first, under General Haddick, considerably in advance before the other, which Melas himself commanded, with General Zach for his second. These moved steadily towards Marengo, while the light infantry and cavalry, under

General Elsnitz, made a détour round Castel Ceriolo, with the purpose of outflanking the French right.

"Such was the posture of the two armies when this great battle began. Gardanne was unable to withstand the shock, and, abandoning Padre Bona, fell back to strengthen Victor. A furious cannonade along the whole front of that position ensued. The tirailleurs of either army posted themselves along the margin of the ravine, and fired incessantly at each other, their pieces almost touching. Cannon and musketry spread devastation everywhere, for the armies were but a few toises apart. For more than two hours Victor withstood singly the vigorous assaults of a far superior force; Marengo had been taken and retaken several times ere Lannes received orders to reinforce him. The second line at length advanced; but they found the first in retreat, and the two corps took up a second line of defence considerably to the rear of Marengo. Here they were again charged furiously, and again, after obstinate resistance, gave way. General Elsnitz, meantime, having effected his purpose, and fairly marched round Castel Ceriolo, appeared on the right flank with his splendid cavalry, and began to pour his squadrons upon the retreating columns of Lannes. That gallant chief formed his troops *en échelon*, and retired in admirable order: but the retreat was now general; and, had Melas pursued the advantage with all his reserve, the battle was won. But that aged general (he was 84 years old) doubted not that he had won it already; and at this critical moment, being quite worn out with fatigue, withdrew to the rear, leaving Zach to continue what he considered as now a mere pursuit.

"At the moment when the Austrian horse were about to rush on Lannes' retreating corps, the reserve under Dessaix appeared on the outskirts of the field. Dessaix himself, riding up to the First Consul, said, 'I think this a battle lost.' 'I think it is a battle won,' answered Napoleon. 'Do you push on, and I will speedily rally the line behind you.' And, in effect, the timely arrival of this reserve turned the fortune of the day.

"Napoleon in person drew up the whole of his army in a third line of battle, and rode along the front, saying, 'Soldiers, we have retired far enough— let us now advance—you know it is my custom to sleep on the field of battle.' The enthusiasm of the troops appeared to be revived, and Dessaix prepared to act on the offensive. He led a fresh column of 5000 grenadiers to meet and check the advance of Zach. The brave Dessaix fell dead at the first fire, shot through the head. 'Alas! it is not permitted to me to weep,' said Napoleon: and the fall of that beloved chief redoubled the fury of his followers. The first line of the Austrian infantry charged, however, with equal resolution. At that moment Kellerman's horse came on them in flank, and, being by that unexpected assault broken, they were, after a vain struggle, compelled to surrender. General Zach himself was here made prisoner. The Austrian columns behind, being flushed with victory, were advancing too carelessly, and proved unable to resist the general assault of the whole French line, which now pressed onwards under the immediate command of Napoleon. Post after post was carried. The noble cavalry of Elsnitz, perceiving the infantry broken and retiring, lost heart; and, instead of forming to protect their retreat, turned their horses' heads and galloped over the plain, trampling down everything in their way. When the routed army reached at length the Bormida, the confusion was indescribable. Hundreds were drowned—the river rolled red amidst the corpses of horses and men. Whole corps, being unable to effect the passage, surrendered; and, at ten at night, the Austrian commander with difficulty rallied the remnant of that magnificent array on the very ground which they had left the same morning in all the confidence of victory."

The portion of the plain on which the

battle was fought was purchased some years ago by M. Giovanni Delavo, who in 1847 erected there a Museum, and a monument to the memory of Napoleon. From Marengo the rlway runs across the plain, here richly cultivated, for 12 m., passing by

8 kil. *La Spinetta Stat.*
6 kil. *San Giuliano Stat.*
8 kil. *Tortona Junction Stat.*, the *Dertona* of the Romans, a town of 12,500 Inhab., situated at the base of the last spurs of the sub-Apennine hills, about ¼ m. beyond the rt. bank of the Scrivia (*Inn*: St. Marsano, where a good dinner and clean bed may be had); one of the most ancient cities of Northern Italy; it was one of the towns of the Lombard league, and was levelled to the ground by Frederick Barbarossa. In recent times it was fortified by Vittore Amadeo II.; but the French blew up the citadel in 1796, after its surrender, in virtue of the stipulations of the treaty of Cherasco. The Duomo contains a remarkable ancient sarcophagus, on which are inscriptions in Greek and Latin, to the memory of P. Ælius Sabinus, and a curious mixture of Pagan and Christian emblems. The former are by far the most prominent. Castor, Pollux, and the fall of Phaëton stand out boldly; whilst the lamb and the vine more obscurely indicate the faith of the mother who raised the tomb. This curious amalgamation of Pagan mythology and of Christianity is explained by supposing that the family were afraid to manifest their belief.

In the church of *San Francesco* is the rich chapel of the Garofali family. The other churches do not offer anything remarkable.

9 kil. *Ponte Curone Stat.*, a village so named from the torrent which runs close to it. The rly. continues across the plain, having the hills on the rt., passing through

8 kil. *Voghera Stat.*, the Tria of the Romans. (The Moro, the principal Inn, is thoroughly Italian. H. d'Italie, tolerable, but high charges unless you bargain.) 11,450 Inhab. The country around Voghera, which is situated in the plain at some distance from the sub-Apennine hills, is very fertile. The church of *S. Lorenzo* is an elegant building of the 17th centy. Near the altar is the tomb of a certain Count Taddeo de Vesme, whose body was found entire 200 years after his death, in 1458—a fact commemorated in a strange inscription placed over his tomb, announcing that when it was opened, in 1646, his body was found entire, and, on separating one of the arms, blood flowed from it. This count, despoiled of his possessions by Ludovico Sforza, died in odour of sanctity. Here is preserved, in a curious *ostensoir*, a thorn of the crown of our Saviour, presented in 1436 to this ch. by Archbishop Pietro de Giorgi, whose tomb is in the middle of the aisle. There is also another ostensoir, weighing 25 lbs., made at Milan about the same period. This is one of the earliest Italian towns in which printing was introduced; and the books produced here are of the greatest rarity. Voghera having been a station on the Via Emilia, several Roman antiquities have been found near it. There is a small collection of them at the Canon Manfredi's: amongst others a large cameo of a female, supposed to be Eudoxia or Theodora. Leaving Voghera, the railway approaches gradually the hilly region, the foot of which it reaches, about a mile before reaching Casteggio, at Montebello

9 kil. *Casteggio Stat.* (*Inn*: Albergo d'Italia); 2900 Inhab.; the ancient Clastidium, a town of importance in Cisalpine Gaul, celebrated as the place where Claudius Marcellus gained the *spolia opima*, by defeating and slaying Virdomarus King of the Gæsatæ. It has been an important military position from the time of the Gallic and Punic wars down to the last great European conflict. It was besieged by Hannibal, and might have defied his power; but 200 pieces of gold paid to Publius Darius, the commander, purchased the fortress; and the provisions and stores found therein were of the greatest utility to the Car-

thaginian army. Of the Carthaginian general there is yet a remarkable memorial. About a quarter of a mile from the town is a spring of very pure and clear water, called, by immemorial tradition, "the Fontana d'Annibale," and girt by a wall which he is said to have built. It is close to the track of the Roman army, and about 100 yards from the modern road to Piacenza. It was near Casteggio that, on the 9th of June, 1800, the great battle between the French and the Austrians was fought, usually called the battle of Montebello, from the village on the hill, about 1 m. W. of it, where the French finally routed the *corps de reserve* of the enemy. The Austrians defended themselves in Casteggio with the greatest valour; and the hills near the town were constantly occupied and re-occupied by the contending parties; but the fortune of the day was decided by Victor, who broke the centre of the enemy; and when Napoleon came up to the assistance of the French vanguard, the victory had been already gained. It was nearly on the same site that the united armies of the French and Piedmontese defeated the Austrians in May, 1859: the first great success of the allied armies during the late Italian war. A few fragments of walls and towers are the only remaining vestiges of antiquity in this town; but many curious Roman inscriptions, bronzes, and coins, have been found here. A good road of about 10 m. leads from Casteggio to Pavia, crossing the Po at *Mezzana Corti* and the Ticino at *San Martino*. Conveyances will be easily procured at the Rly Stat., and diligences in correspondence with the early trains from Turin, Genoa, and Piacenza run between the two places. From Casteggio the railway follows the base of the hilly region, through cornfields, the hills being covered with vines, passing by

5 kil. S. Giulietta Stat.

7 kil. *Broni Stat.*, a town of 4500 Inh ab. Its situation, a plain at the roots of the Apennines, is very beautiful. The collegiate church, founded by Azzo Marquis of Este and Ferrara, in the 13th century, is a building of various ages and styles: some portions are of the 10th century. It has recently been richly fitted up by the inhabitants: it boasts a silver shrine, containing the relics of San Contardo, the son of the founder. Very good wine is made in this neighbourhood, which, when old, has some resemblance to Malaga.

4 *Stradella Stat.*, at the extreme northern point of the hills, which here approach within 2 m. of the Po. A road leads from Stradella to Milan, by *Corte Olona*, crossing the Po (2½ m.) at the ferry of *Portalbera*.

From La Stradella the Rly., following the base of the hills, approaches gradually the Po.

4 kil. *Arena Po Stat.* The village of this name is at some distance on the l. Half-way between this Stat. and the next cross the Bardonezza torrent, formerly the boundary between Piedmont and the duchy of Piacenza.

7 kil. *Castel S. Giovanni.* Formerly the frontier-town of the Duchies, on the l. bank of the Corona.

4 kil. *Sarmato Stat.* Here the line separates from the hills on the rt., and soon crosses the Tidone stream.

5¼ kil. *Rottofreno Stat.*

3 kil. *San Nicolo Stat.*, near the l. bank of the Trebbia, on leaving which the river is crossed on the magnificent bridge erected in 1825 by the Empress Maria Louisa, under the direction of the engineer Coccanelli, at an expense of 47,200*l*. sterling. It consists of 23 arches, its length 500 yards, and the width between the parapets 26 ft. A column at its extremity recalls the 3 great battles which took place in the neighbourhood. By an act of useless precaution, for the river was dry at the time, the Austrians blew up some of the arches on the eastern side, in their retreat from Piacenza, in May, 1859.

The lower course of the Trebbia is celebrated in the military history of Italy, as having witnessed three great battles, each of which decided the fate of Italy for the time; the first, between

Hannibal and the Romans under the Consul Sempronius, B.C. 218, which opened Central and Southern Italy to the Carthaginian invader; the second, in 1746, between the united armies of France and Spain on the one side, and the allied Austro-Piedmontese, which led to the momentary expulsion of the Bourbons from Parma and Piacenza; and the last, in June, 1799, when the French army, under Macdonald, after a prolonged struggle of 3 days, and a loss of 15,000 men, was obliged to retreat before the Russians and Imperialists commanded by Suwarrow. It is difficult to fix, with any degree of precision, the site where Hannibal defeated Sempronius, or where the force of Mago was placed in ambuscade, which so greatly contributed to that disaster. It is probable, however, that, Hannibal being encamped on the l. bank, the Romans attacked him nearly on the same spot where, by a similar manœuvre, Macdonald, 2000 years afterwards, made a last effort to defeat his Russian antagonist—about 5 m. to the S. of the modern bridge. The battle of 1746 took place nearly under the walls of Piacenza, the great feat of the day being Prince Lichtenstein's charge on Maillebois' columns near to San Lazzaro. The battle-field on the last occasion (June 20, 1799), between the French under Macdonald, and the Austro-Russians commanded by Suwarrow, occupied the l. bank of the river from Grignano upwards to Rivalta, the first being about 3 m. on the rt. of the village of St. Nicolo, on the post-road, before arriving at Maria Louisa's bridge. Macdonald, being forced to retire from Tuscany, crossed the Apennines into the upper valley of the Trebbia, hoping to be joined by Moreau, then in the Genoese territory. Suwarrow, however, managed, by his great activity, to prevent this junction, and to place himself between the two Republican armies. Attacked by Macdonald during 3 days, he opposed to him an energetic resistance, the whole ending by one of the most disastrous defeats that the Republican armies of France had yet experienced.

Soon after crossing the bridge the spires of Piacenza come into view, and the rly., after running parallel to the half-ruined walls of the city, and the elegant ch. of La Madonna della Campagna on the rt., reaches the Stat., situated at the E. extremity of the city, close to the Porta di S. Lazzaro.

9 kil. PIACENZA Stat. (See Rte. 40.)
Hotels: La Croce Bianca, and San Marco. Omnibuses to the different hotels.

ROUTE 8.

TURIN TO NICE, BY CUNEO AND THE COL DI TENDA.
143 m.

The Railroad as far as Cuneo is now open. There are 4 trains a day: they perform the journey in rather less than 2½ h. The diligence from Nice starts on the arrival of the evening train, which leaves Turin at 5 p.m. in winter and 6 p.m. in summer, crossing the Col di Tenda by daylight, and reaching Nice about 5 p.m. on the day following.

The *railway* follows the line from Turin to Genoa as far as

13 kil. *Troffarello Stat.*

7 kil. *Villastellone Stat.*, at the junction of the Molinasso and Stellone torrents. A road of about 6 m. leads from this Stat., crossing the Po, to

[*Carignano*, a town of 7800 Inhab., not far from the river, and on the high carriage-road from Turin to Nice. The country around is beautiful, dotted with villages, towns, and hamlets. Much silk is produced in the vicinity. The principal ornaments of this little city are its churches; and the Carignanesi are said to be distinguished for the care bestowed upon their places of worship. *San Giovanni Batista*, built by Count Alfieri. The principal façade is noble. The entrance of the building is lighted almost entirely from above, by windows placed over the cornice. The bas-reliefs of the four doctors of the church, St. Chrysostom, St. Jerome, St. Ambrose, and St. Augustine, come out under the glaring rays. *Sta. Maria delle Grazie*, annexed to a monastery of Franciscan friars. It was endowed by the Duchess Bianca Palæologus, wife of Duke Charles I., and contains her monument. She was the daughter of William IV. Marquis of Montferrat; as a widow, Bianca was distinguished for her *gentilezza* and beauty; and Bayard, who had been brought up as a youth in the household of the duke, gained great honour in a tournament held before her in this place when she was becoming advanced in years. After many mutations Carignano was severed from the rest of Piedmont, or rather from the marquisate of Susa, and granted as an appanage, with the title of a principality, to Thomas, second son of Charles Emanuel I., from whom the present reigning family of Sardinia is descended.]

9 kil. *Carmagnola Stat.* contains upwards of 13,000 Inhab. The principal church is that of *Sant' Agostino.* It is Gothic, though much altered. The Campanile, with its pointed spire, is the most unchanged portion. In the cloister annexed to the church are the remains of the tomb of James Turnbull, a Scottish *condottiere* in the French service, who died here when the army was returning from Naples in 1496. The collegiate church of *San Pietro e San Paolo* is also Gothic, but more altered than the other; it was consecrated in the year 1514. Carmagnola stood on the extreme frontier of the marquisate of Saluzzo, and, as the border town, was defended by a very strong castle, of which only one massive tower remains, now forming the steeple of the church of *San Filippo.* The walls are upwards of 7 feet in thickness. It was built in 1435; and the city, when the marquis required an aid, gave him his choice, 300,000 bricks or 300 ducats. Bricks now cost in Piedmont 35 fr. per thousand. The female peasantry in and about Carmagnola are gaily dressed, wearing round their necks rows of large metal beads, often of gold, which are manufactured in the town. The name of Carmagnola is associated with the horrible orgies of the French Revolution, though no one can explain exactly how. The inhabitants most sturdily disclaim the disgrace of being the inventors of the too celebrated " Danse de la Carmagnole," the prelude to so many fearful tragedies.

Here was born, in 1390, the celebrated *condottiere*, Francesco Bussone, the son of a poor herdsman, who became so renowned under the name of Conte di Carmagnola, which he assumed from his birthplace. He began his career in the service of Filippo Maria Visconti, Duke of Milan, and, rapidly rising in power, he served his master most effectually, regaining a great part of Lombardy and of the dominions of Giovanni Galeazzo, which had escaped from his successor. Suspicions of his loyalty were entertained by the duke; Carmagnola was unthankfully banished, his property confiscated, his wife and children cast into prison, whilst he passed into the service of the republic of Venice, by which he was appointed generalissimo. He conquered Brescia for it from the Duke of Milan; and at the battle of Macalo, 1427, he entirely routed the ducal army. But the aristocracy of Venice, as suspicious as the despot of Milan, also distrusted the soldier bound by no tie of allegiance; and having seduced him to Venice by a vote of thanks and confidence, he was cast into prison, tortured, and beheaded on the 5th May, 1432. " between the two columns" in the Piazzetta of San Marco,

9 kil. *Racconigi (Stat).* Pleasantly situated, and in the days of Trissino was famed for the beauty of its women.

" E quei di Scarnafesso e Racconigi,
   Ch' han bellissime donne."

The palace of Racconigi is one of the country residences of the royal family. It was given as an appanage by Charles Emmanuel I. to his son Thomas, the head of the branch of Carignan of the house of Savoy, in whose possession it has since remained. It was the favourite sojourn of the late king, Charles Albert, by whom it underwent great repairs, and is now one of the most comfortable *villegiaturas* of the royal family. The small park which surrounds it is handsomely laid out. Following the rt. bank of the river Maira is

7 kil. *Cavaller Maggiore Junct. Stat.*, a large and flourishing town of 5300 Inhab., formerly fortified; but there is hardly a vestige of the two castles and the lofty walls which once surrounded it. A Rly. branches off from here to Bra in 20 min.

7 kil. *Savigliano Junct. Stat. (Inn:* the Corona, tolerably comfortable), a pleasant and cheerful town; 14,500 Inhab. In the ch. are several paintings by Molinieri, a native artist of the 17th centy., a scholar of the Carracci; others are in the Palazzo Taffino, representing the battles of C. Emanuel I. The principal street terminates in a species of triumphal arch, erected in honour of the marriage between Victor Amadeo and Christina of France. A branch strikes off from Savigliano to Saluzzo, passing by Lagnasco, in 25 min.

12 kil. *Fossano—Stat.* See Rte. 10.

7 kil. *La Maddalena—Stat.*, in the middle of the plain between the Stura and the Grana.

4 kil. *Centallo*, 4900 Inhab.; also a large place in the midst of a fertile though not a healthy country: remains of walls and towers mark its importance in the middle ages. Roman inscriptions are found on the site; but, as is generally the case in the north of Italy, there is nothing above ground to prove its antiquity.

12 kil. *Cuneo* or *Coni*, 1500 ft. above the sea (*Inn:* the Barre de Fer, a dismal and dirty auberge: there is another, the H. de Londres, said to be no better), a city of 20,500 Inhab., situated between the Stura and Gesso torrents, at their junction. Cuneo was, in its origin, a species of city of refuge. About the year 1100, Boniface Marquis of Savoy had conquered, or rather occupied, this district, which formed a part of the marquisate of Susa; but his authority, hardly strong enough to enable him to retain his usurpation, was entirely inadequate to enforce the observance of the laws, or to ensure tranquillity; and the lords of the adjoining castles so plundered the inhabitants of the surrounding country, that they determined upon resistance.

Such outrages, a few centuries later, gave rise to the republics of Switzerland and the Grisons; but Piedmont was not yet ripe for a revolution. The people came together under the colour of a pilgrimage to a sanctuary of the Virgin, called Our Lady of the Wood, now included in the city; and there determined to take vengeance, if, as usual, any of their wives and daughters were insulted by the petty tyrants of the surrounding castles. The anticipated cause of offence was soon given; the peasants assembled again, destroyed the castles, slew the oppressors, and, retreating in a body to the present site of the city, a *wedge-like* piece of land between the two rivers, they began to build. The abbot of San Dalmazzo, to whom the woods belonged, gladly permitted a settlement which gave him the prospect of such a numerous vassalage; and the "*nuova villa di Cuneo*" rapidly rose into consequence. In the 16th century Cuneo was strongly fortified, and its history from then is a succession of sieges. No place was more celebrated in the military history of Piedmont, until 1800, when, after the battle of Marengo, the three consuls decreed, on the 5th July, that the fortifications of Cuneo, the citadels of Milan and Tortona, the fortress of Cera, and the gates and bastions of Turin, should all be destroyed; and, before the end of the month, those massy girdles of Cuneo were riven from their foundations, to the great comfort and advantage of the inhabitants. The *Duomo*, or cathedral, of Coni is the ancient sanctuary of the "Madonna del Bosco," but it offers nothing remarkable beyond its historical interest. The picture of St. John and St. Michael, over the chief altar, is by the Jesuit P. Pozzi. *San Francesco*, belonging to a Capuchin convent: a regular Gothic church of the 12th century, said to have been built in the time of the saint himself. It is remarkable that the Franciscans, both in Italy and beyond the Alps, employed the Gothic style of architecture more than the other religious orders. Cuneo suffered much from the cholera in 1835, and amongst its numerous charitable establishments is one for the reception of the children who were deprived of their parents by the disease. At first there were 200. There is a pleasant public walk at the junction of the Gesso and Stura.

In the Alpine valley of the Pesio, about 10 m. from Coni, is the Certosa of Val Pesio, founded in 1173, in a very picturesque situation. An hydropathic establishment has lately been formed there by Dr. Brandeis, on the Graffenberg or Preisnitz system. The situation is represented as very salubrious, and the water, which is in abundance, is excellent. In the Val di Gesso are the baths of *Valdieri*, now much resorted to, although the accommodation hitherto has been indifferent: pension 7 fr. a day, everything included. These waters are similar in their properties to those of Aix in Savoy; from their increasing repute, a new establishment, by a joint-stock company formed at Turin, to accommodate 400 or 500 persons, has been partially opened, and will be completed in 1861. Valdieri is 25 m. or 5 hrs. distant from Cuneo, from which carriages start twice every day for the Baths, during the season, from the middle of June until the end of August. There are hot springs which are used for the baths, and a slighty saline tepid one, called *Acqua Magnesiaca*, which some patients use internally; but it appears that the most efficacious remedy supplied by nature arises from a cryptogamic plant which grows in thick gelatinous masses in the streams from the hot springs. This substance, called *Le Muffe*, is applied, while hot, to wounds, and in cases of internal inflammation, and is frequently found to be very efficacious. Valdieri has great natural advantages, being situated in the finest part of the chain of the Maritime Alps, whose jagged granitic peaks rise on every side to the height of 8000 to 9000 ft. above the sea-level. The climate is cool, and sometimes even cold in the height of summer; and it is the resort of good Piedmontese society. Up to the present time (Aug., 1860) the accommodation has been indifferent, and the charges for lodging high. Two meals are supplied daily at the table-d'hôte—charge 5 fr.; attendance indifferent. The shooting of chamois, &c., in this district is reserved exclusively for the king, who frequently pitches his tent in the valleys adjoining. The road from Cuneo to Valdieri, which passes through Borgo San Dalmazzo, has but lately been extended to the Baths. It is in parts narrow and wanting in parapets.

The pedestrian may make various excursions from the Baths of Valdieri through the range of the Maritime Alps. Perhaps the most interesting will be that to San Martino di Lantosca, on the S. side of the chain. This may be reached in seven or eight hours by the pass of *La Fumna Morta*, or in a shorter time over the Col delle Ceresc, but by a steeper and rougher track over snow and rocks. The aspect of the inn at San Martino is very discouraging; but a clean bed and tolerable fare may be had there as at most of the villages in these valleys.

From San Martino di Lantosca the tourist may return to Entraque, on the N. side of the chain, by the *Col delle Finestre*, and thence regain the carriage-road to the Baths a little above the village of Valdieri; or else, sleeping at the little inn on the S. side of the Col delle Finestre, he may make his way to Tenda through a wild part of the range; but this will probably be a long day's walk. It is also practicable to cross the mountains which separate the valley of the Vesubia from that of the Roja, ascending from Rocca Bighera or Bollena, descending into the Val di Caros, and sleeping at Saorgio, or at the little village of Fontano, on the high road to Tenda, 2 m. N. of Saorgio. These valleys may equally well be visited from Nice, and would offer a resource to many a sufferer from the heat and dust of that city.

The Rly. for the present ending at Cuneo, the rest of the journey must be performed by the ordinary road, which, on leaving the town, ascends gradually, offering much beauty.

Borgo di San Dalmazzo, a village, supposed to be the remains of the city of Pedone, destroyed by the Milanese in 1250. 4 m. after leaving Cuneo the post-road enters the valley of the Vermanagna, along which it runs to the bottom of the Col di Tenda.

14 kil. *Robillante*. (An extra horse from Cuneo to Robillante from the 1st of Nov. to the 1st of May, but not in the opposite direction.) Hitherto the road has passed through the great plain of Piedmont, watered by the Po, the Maira, the Grana, and the Stura; but it now enters the mountains and begins to ascend, and the noble masses of the maritime Alps, crowned by the Monte Viso, more than 12,000 feet above the level of the sea, become more clearly visible. The plains themselves are very fertile, and nothing can be more beautiful than the little streams by which they are irrigated and crossed. The hills abound with bright and aromatic flowers.

15 kil. *Limone*, 3340 feet above the sea. (An extra horse from Robillante to Limone from Nov. 1st to May 1st, but not in the opposite direction.) *Inn:* the Hôtel de la Poste; a civil and obliging landlord. The traveller hence ascends rapidly, and by a good alpine road, though constructed with less skill than those of more recent date. The abrupt turns of the terraces are often almost alarming in their aspect, nor are they so well defended as could be wished. The danger, or rather the semblance of it, is, of course, more felt in the descent from Nice. The difficulty is greater this way. About half way from the summit an attempt was made by the former princes of Savoy, and continued down to the French occupation in 1794, to bore a tunnel through the mountain, and thus avoid altogether the passage over its crest. If completed, it would have been more than half a mile long, and would have surpassed any similar work in the Alps. The summit is a narrow ridge, 6158 feet above the level of the sea. It commands a very fine view of the Alps, from Monte Viso to Monte Rosa, the latter appearing like a cloud; while, on the south, the Mediterranean may be faintly discovered. During more than three months in the year, and not unfrequently during five, the Col di Tenda is impassable for wheel carriages, though it can always be crossed by sledges, and generally by mules, provided there be no storms; for the wind is so violent that the mules themselves can hardly keep their footing, and are compelled to wind round a more sheltered path. The descent on the S. side is by a succession of 75 zigzags from the house of refuge near the summit.

30 kil. *Tenda*, at the southern foot of the Col (between Limone and Tenda an extra horse. both ways all the year); 2600 Inhab. (*Inns:* Hôtel Royal; Hôtel National, dirty.) Tenda is an excellent station for sketching and fishing. It is a place of much note in the feudal history of Italy. From the family of Facino Cane it became vested in the unfortunate Beatrice di Tenda, the luckless wife of Filippo Maria Visconti, by whose commands she was cruelly tortured and condemned to death. (See Binasco, p. 210.) There are some picturesque remains of the castle.

The road from Tenda is amongst the earliest of the alpine roads. It was made by Carlo Emanuele I., 1591; and improved in 1780 by Vittore Amadeo III., as is commemorated in two inscriptions near its commencement. Fine scenery and good chamois-hunting in the mountain-range W. of the Col di Tenda.

3 m. after leaving Tenda is the Abbey of *S. Dalmazzo*, recently converted into a hydropathic establishment; the situation is rather hot, but the neighbourhood abounds in picturesque scenery. Beyond this the road becomes exceedingly striking with alpine scenery of peculiar boldness, and by the side is the Roya, a torrent scarcely leaving room for a carriage to pass. Wherever the rocks fall back ever so little out of the perpendicular—enough to allow the possibility of raising a wall—you see a little village in the cleft, like the nest of a bird. The finest of these savage defiles of the Roja is below Saorgio, a town of 2600 Inhab., where a fort, perched upon a rocky knoll, commands the passage of the gorge. It was taken by the French in the campaign of 1794. The Roya abounds with excellent trout. The upper portion of this valley remains in the hands of the Piedmontese; but the strong position of Saorgio and the valley of the Roja is occupied by the French. The Italian Custom-house Stat. is at Fontano, on the N. side of the pass of Saorgio.

19 kil. *Giandola*, which forms the boundary between Piedmont and France, the first French custom-house station in the county of Nice, 1250 feet above the sea. (From Giandola to Tenda an extra horse all the year, but not *vice versâ*.) *Inns:* Hôtel des Etrangers affords decent accommodation, and a civil landlady; Hôtel de la Poste, said to be good. The town is grandly situated at the foot of high schistose rocks, which look as if they were on the point of crushing the inhabitants. The road has been recently altered, and leaves on the l. *Breglio*, a town of 2500 Inhab., near which are the ruins of the castle of Trivella; and ascends the mountain of *Brouis* by a very steep road to the pass of the same name,

the sides of which are covered with wild lavender.

21 kil. *Sospello*, 1175 ft. above the sea (between Giandola and Sospello an extra horse both ways all the year—*Inn:* Hôtel Carenco, said to be the best between Turin and Nice), 4300 Inhab., is the sleeping-place for travellers by vetturino. Its situation is very beautiful. Through it rushes the Bevera, a roaring mountain stream; and all around rise the mountains out of an exceedingly fertile plain. The valley abounds in thick woods of olives and figs. The Bevera forms a junction with the Roya about 4 m. before entering the sea at Vintimiglia. A cross road branches off from Sospello to Vintimiglia, by the ravine of the Bevera.

The road commences to ascend from the inn door at Sospello until we pass the Col di Braus, about 4000 feet above the sea. In the autumn a good deal of lavender-water is made on the sides of this mountain by the peasantry, whose rude apparatus for that purpose, which you see on the road-sides, is curious.

22 kil. *Scarena* (between Sospello and Scarena, an extra horse both ways all the year), 2000 Inhab. After crossing another hill we descend along the Escarena, one of the tributaries of the Paglione, which is followed to Nice, and to the full luxuriance of the Riviera, passing by the villages of Pallaren, Drap, and La Trinita.

23 kil. *Nice* (from Nice to Scarena an extra horse all the year, but not *vice versâ*). (Rte. 13.)

ROUTE 9.

TURIN TO ONEGLIA, BY BRÀ, CHERASCO, ALBA, AND CEVA.

Distance about 107 m. The first part of this road is now performed by Rly. as far as *Cavaller Maggiore*, 29 kil., from whence a railroad is in progress as far as Cherasco: beyond this the only mode of conveyance is by vetturino, there being no post stations. The distance from Cavaller Maggiore to Brà is about 10 m.

Brà, or Brauda, 12,500 Inhab.; in the vale of the Stura, and about 2 m. N. of it. The principal object of interest in this town is the church of *Sta. Chiara*, built in 1742 by Vettone. It is in the most luxuriant style of the Piedmontese churches. A fine avenue leads to the *Santuario di nostra Donna de' Fiori*. According to the legend, a miraculous appearance of the Virgin in the copse hard by, on the 29th December, 1336, was the means of rescuing a peasant girl from the daggers of assassins; since which event the sloe-bushes with which the copse abounds are said to flower three times in the year—in spring, autumn, and the depth of winter. It is yet much resorted to, especially on the 8th of September, the feast of the Nativity of the Virgin.

2 m. S.E. of Brà, on the l. bank of the Tanaro, is *Pollenzo*, a castle and a village, replacing the Roman municipium of *Pollentia*. Here the armies of the Triumvirate frequently assembled. It was celebrated for its wool, as well as for its manufactures of terra-cotta, praised by Pliny as being scarcely inferior to those of Samos. In the age of the Antonines Pollentia was very flourishing; and it is supposed that the edifices, of which there are still considerable vestiges, belonged to that era. An amphitheatre and a theatre can be distinguished; and the walls of both are still standing to a considerable height. Upon the ridges of the Colle di San Vittorio are the ruins of four small edifices, called by the peasants the "*Turilie*," supposed by antiquaries to be the ruins of a temple of Diana, and the buildings which were annexed thereto. On the old road to Alba are the supposed remains of the Villa Martis, the birthplace of the Emperor Pertinax, who together with his father carried on what we should call an earthenware manufactory. Hard by is a field called "*Ciupelle*," of which the ground is quite covered with fragments of earthenware, the confirmation (or perhaps the origin) of the opinion by which the spot is identified. Pollenzo was erected into a county by Wenzel or Wenceslaus (the emperor who was deposed by the electors in consequence of his sluggishness and vice), in favour of Antonio Pirro, a condottiere, who had served under Galeazzo Visconti of Milan in 1383; and with the assent of the Antipope, Clement, he erected, in 1385, a castle upon the site of a monastery. Most of this building is standing, and it is exceedingly picturesque, with its overhanging machicolations and lofty dungeon tower. It has lately been fitted up and judiciously restored, and is a favourite residence of the present king. A good road (10 m.) branches off from the road to Cherasco at Brà, and proceeding along the l. bank of the Tanaro, by San Vittorio, leads to

Alba (Alba Pompeia), a very ancient episcopal town of 8500 Inhab., on the rt. bank of the Tanaro, where the Querazza empties itself into it. The town is in a plain, surrounded by very fertile hills, producing much wine and silk. The Cathedral, dedicated to San Lorenzo, and founded in 1486, is attributed to Bramante, and contains in its choir a handsome mausoleum of the founder, Andrea Novelli. Alba was an Imperial fief, granted successively to the Counts of Saluzzo and the Viscontis, and as such it formed a part of the marriage-portion given by Gian Galeazzo to his daughter Violante on her marriage with Lionel Duke of Clarence.

The road from Brà continues in the plain of the Stura; crossing that river 3 m. farther to

Cherasco : 10,000 Inhab. The quadrangular form of this town indicates its position upon the site of a Roman town. At each end of the principal street is a fine modern arch. Of the five churches, three, *San Pietro*, *San Martino*, and *San Giorgio*, are Gothic; the fourth, the *Madonna del Popolo*, was built in 1693-1702. Its interior is of rustic work, and heavy. It has, however, a good cupola. In the *Palazzo del Commune* are some paintings by *Torrico*. There are others in the Palazzo Gotti. They are scriptural and historical; in the landscape portion Torrico was a successful imitator of G. Poussin.

Numerous organic remains are found in the tertiary marls and sands in this neighbourhood. In the Colle di San Bartolomeo is petrified wood. The fortifications of Cherasco, once exceedingly strong, were destroyed by the French in 1801. After the battle of Mondovi, April 22nd, 1796 (see Rtes. 10, 11), the Piedmontese troops fell back upon Cherasco, and made a show of resistance. Cherasco was well provisioned, and in an excellent state of defence; but, after very few shells had been thrown into the town, the garrison surrendered, not without suspicions of treachery. The Sardinians now proposed a suspension of arms; and on the 28th of April their commissioners concluded with Napoleon the "armistice of Cherasco," by which, and the treaty that followed, the King of Sardinia renounced the coalition with Austria; ceded to the French Republic Savoy, Nice, and the whole possessions of Piedmont to the westward of the highest ridge of the Alps (extending from Mount St. Bernard by Mount Genevre to Roccabarbona near Genoa); and granted a free passage through his dominions to the troops of the Republic.

The road, which here enters the upper valley of the Tanaro as far as Monchiero, now passes through

18 kil. *Dogliani*, 2000 Inhab.; a village, standing partly upon the banks of the Rea torrent, and partly upon a bold hill. The road from Dogliani to Ceva is very hilly. About 5 m. before arriving at the latter, at Montezzemolo, the road from Turin to Savona, through Millesimo and the Cadibona pass, strikes off to the l. (see Rte. 12).

There is a road from Cherasco to Fossano (see Rte. 10), on which is the town of

Bene, upon a pleasant rising on the Mondalavia torrent: it has arisen out of the ruins of the ancient Augusta Bagiennorum, destroyed by Alaric, and of which many interesting vestiges are found at *Roveglia*, about half a mile off. The ruins of an aqueduct, amphitheatre, baths, and other buildings, extend over a considerable tract of ground. To the N. of Bene is the district of Salmour, anciently Sarmatia, so called from the Sarmatians settled there during the Lower Empire, who had a Prefect of their own.

22 kil. *Ceva*, a town of 4500 Inhab., on the rt. bank of the Tanaro: the capital of the marquisate of Ceva, whose lords held rather a conspicuous place in the history of this part of Italy. They traced their origin to Aleramo, the hero of many a traditionary tale; but the first of whom there is any real account is Anselmo, the fourth son of Boniface Marquis of Savona, about 1142. The place is much decayed; and recent demolitions have deprived it of all its feudal towers. The chief feature of the landscape is a rock towering above the town, and upon which are the remains of the dismantled citadel. The Piedmontese cheese, called Robiole, is made in this neighbourhood.

11 kil. *Bagnasco*. We are now fairly entering the Maritime Alps. The mountains surrounding Bagnasco are bold and picturesque, and the streams and torrents are limpid and beautiful. The castle was destroyed by the Maréchal de Brissac in 1555. The ruins of its ancient fortifications are fine, spreading widely above and around. On the E. are the remains attributed to the Saracens: it is recorded that the present town was originally built with the materials of the Saracenic castle. According to a most apocryphal tradition, the historian Valerius Maximus was buried here; and a stone, with the inscription "Hic jacet Valerius," found, or *made* to be found, has been adduced in support of this tradition. It is now at Turin.

11 kil. *Garessio*, once the capital of a small marquisate, which, in 1509, was

sold to the Spinola family. It is nearly 2000 feet above the sea. A good road, leading from Garessio to Albenga, crosses the Col di Bernardo to descend into the valley of the Nerva.

Hence the road to Oneglia passes through wild and picturesque scenery, by Ormea and the Ponte di Nava, where it crosses, for the last time, the Tanáro. The rocks are often of marble, the variety called *Persigliano* being quarried here.

The *source of the Tanaro* is of difficult access, but the path is practicable. The mountain from which it rises is called the *Tanarelo;* the rush of waters is magnificent. The mountain scenery of this part of the Apennines is entirely distinct in character from the Alps on the N., or from the central range further S. It is more verdant and luxuriant than either.

Near this is the *Cavern of Aleramo*, where he and Adelasio took refuge with their seven sons, who, in process of time, became seven marquises. The traditions of this country deserve quite as much attention as the "*Deutsche Sagen*," of which we have heard so much of late years.

11 kil. *Ormea.* It was once well inhabited, but, having been nearly depopulated by the plague in 1630, it has never recovered. From Ponte di Nava the road ascends to the Col of the same name, the culminating point of the Apennines on this road (3150 ft. above the sea), to descend into the valley of the Arrosia at

20 kil. *Pieve*, in a lonely valley. The mountains around are singular and bold. The principal church has some frescoes of *Luca Cambiaso*. The Arrosia, which is crossed on leaving Pieve, falls into the sea at Albenga.

Pass over the Col of San Bartolomeo, which separates the waters of the Arrosia and Impera torrents: along the l. bank of the latter a wide and easy road leads to

28 kil. *Oneglia.* (See Rte. 12.)

ROUTE 10.

TURIN TO ONEGLIA, BY FOSSANO AND MONDOVI.

About 116 Eng. m.; by Rly. as far as Fossano (see Rte. 8); 64 kil. Like the last route, this is not comprised amongst those on which there are post relays with horses.

Fossano, on the l. bank of the Stura, the seat of a bishopric, 16,000 Inhab., offers a very beautiful prospect from without. Seated upon a lofty hill, surrounded by ramparts, and crowned by the still lofty feudal castle, it is as fine a picture as can be imagined. Within, it is singularly antique and gloomy. The houses stand upon ranges of arches, which in many parts are so low that you can hardly walk through them upright, contrasting strongly with the very charming walk planted with trees which surrounds the town. It is said to derive its name from some salubrious fountain, *Fonte Sano*, in its vicinity. The city was founded in the 13th cent., by the inhabitants of the villages of the adjoining conutry; burnt during the wars of the Guelphs and Ghibellines. Constantly exposed to the attacks of the Counts of Saluzzo on the one side and of Asti on the other, the Fossanese ended by placing themselves, in 1314, under the protection of Philip of Savoy, Prince of Achaia. The cathedral is a fine building by Guarini, with some decent modern paintings. In the Palazzo Grimbaldi are frescoes by Giovanni Boetto, who was also a good engraver. After crossing the Stura, pass

La Trinità, a village of 2500 Inhab., the head of a very ancient barony.

22 kil. *Mondovi*, on the rt. bank of the *Ellero*, 1810 feet above the sea, the seat of a bishop, 17,300 Inhab. A portion of this city is on a commanding hill. Here are the cathedral of San Donato and the principal public buildings. The three other portions, Brea, Carazzone, and Piano, are partly

on the side of the hill and partly in the plain below. Mondovì is comparatively a modern city, having been founded in the 12th century. Like Coni, Fossano, and several other of the Apennine towns, Mondovì was a city of refuge; that is to say, built by the inhabitants of the villages of the open country flying from the contentions of Guelphs and Ghibellines. Near Mondovi is the sanctuary of the *Madonna di Vico*. This church, built by Vitozzi, is one of the innumerable adaptations of the main idea of St. Peter's. In one of the chapels is the tomb of Charles Emanuel I., who died at Savigliano in 1630; it is by the brothers Cellini. This church has been a favourite place of pilgrimage of many Sovereigns of the house of Savoy; it is richly decorated by royal and private munificence, and is said to have cost 9,000,000 francs (360,000*l.*); it has only been recently finished.

It is said that the people assembled here when they determined to abandon their houses and to found the new city. They governed themselves as an independent republic until, in 1396, they submitted to Amadeo, Prince of Achaia.

Here, 22nd April, 1796, was fought the decisive battle between Napoleon and the Sardinian troops under Colli. The Sardinians occupied this strong position, while Beaulieu, with the Austrians and an army still formidable, was in the rear of the French, and might have resumed offensive operations. The French therefore determined to renew the attack on the following day, but, on arriving at the advanced posts at daybreak they found them abandoned by the Piedmontese, who had retired in the night to Mondovi. Colli was overtaken, however, in his retreat, near Mondovi, by the indefatigable Victor, who had seized a strong position, where he hoped to arrest the enemy. The Republicans immediately advanced to the assault, attacked and carried the redoubt of La Bicoque, the principal defence of the position, and gained a decisive victory. Colli lost 2000 men, eight cannon, and eleven standards. Great as the loss was, yet, coming in accumulation upon the preceding defeats, the moral effect was still greater. Colli retreated to Cherasco, whither he was followed by Napoleon. The result has been already told. (See Rte. 9.)

In 1799 the people of Mondovì rose against the French. This offence was cruelly punished by Moreau, whose troops committed acts of violence such as no provocation could excuse.

From Mondovì the road ascends to the village of Vico, and descends to the bridge of San Michele, on the Corsaglia torrent, where Colli repulsed Joubert and Serrurier on the 19th of April, but retreated on Mondovi in the night: continuing on its rt. bank to Lesegno, near where the Corsaglia joins the Tanaro, to Ceva, and from thence along the l. bank of the Tanaro as far as *Ponte di Nava*, between which and *La Pieve* it crosses the Apennines; the relays between Mondovi and Oneglia being

Ceva.
Bagnasco.
Garessio.
Ormea.
La Pieve, and
Oneglia.
} (Rte. 9.)

ROUTE 11.

ALESSANDRIA TO SAVONA, BY ACQUI, DEGO, AND MONTENOTTE.

There are no relays of post-horses between Alessandria and Savona. A Rly. is open as far as Acqui, 21 m.

This is a very interesting road to the military traveller, as it is over ground rendered celebrated by Napoleon's first Italian campaign of 1796; the greater part of it is up the valley of the Bormida to the passes of Montenotte and Cadibona.

8 kil. *Cantalupo Stat.*, in the plain. The road enters the hilly country at

3 kil. *Borgorato Stat.*, following the l. bank of the Bormidato.

3 kil. *Gamalero Stat.*, a small village in a pleasant country, and thence to 2 kil. *Sezze Stat.*

6 kil. *Cassine Stat.*, 4000 Inhab., situated upon a height overlooking the fine valley of the Bormida. This small town maintained many a sturdy conflict with its more powerful neighbour Alessandria.

6 kil. *Strevi Stat.*

6 kil. *Acqui Stat.* (the *Aquæ Statielæ* of the Romans): 8200 Inhab. This city the seat of a bishop, was the ancient capital of the Statielli, a Ligurian nation, and acquired much celebrity under the Romans from its hot springs. The whole country abounds with them; and, like those at Aix-la-Chapelle, they are partly within the city and partly without. Within the walls is the spring called the "Bollente." The heat, on the average, is 167° Fahrenheit. The flow is most abundant, and never diminishes, and the water is used by the inhabitants for the purposes of washing, though, both to taste and smell, disagreeably impregnated with sulphuretted hydrogen. The bath-houses are outside of the city, on the opposite bank of the river, where several springs issue from the ground, their temperature varying from 111° to 124° Fahrenheit. They were built in the 16th century, by the Duke of Mantua, but have recently been much improved. The mud of the baths is considered as having most efficacy. Gout, paralysis, and rheumatic affections, are the complaints in which they are peculiarly useful. Dr. Cantu, a celebrated Piedmontese physician, has discovered iodine in the waters, to which he attributes much of their virtues, and also a trace of bromine. The waters of the Bormida are, or at least have been, supposed to possess the same efficacy as the hot springs.

Roman remains are found at Acqui. The few which have escaped the destruction of the city by the Goths attest its ancient magnificence. Four arches of a massive yet elegant aqueduct are the most conspicuous. Several reservoirs and other portions of the thermæ may be traced. One spring retains, by tradition, the name of "the fountain of Pallas." The block or nucleus of a large sepulchral monument is called the *Carné* by the common people, a name having a curious, though perhaps accidental, similarity to the Gaelic and Cymric *cairn* or *Carnedd*. Numerous sepulchral and other inscriptions have been found near the branch of the Via Emilia which ran by the city, relating to the Lollian, Mettian, Rutilian, Petronian, Rubrian, Mennian, and Plautian families, as well as urns, lamps, brazen and other idols. Coins are also found, extending from Augustus to Theodosius.

The *Duomo* was begun in the 12th century. The front has a fine and venerable porch; and an ample flight of stone steps adds to its effect. The interior is divided into a nave with four aisles. The church of *San Francesco*, a Gothic building scarcely inferior to the Duomo, is in ruins, having been reduced to this state by the French. The other churches have nothing remarkable.

The *Monte Stregone*, or Mountain of the Great Wizard, rises above the city. Here the hot springs have their sources. The air is exceedingly pure and pleasant; the Baths of Acqui are much frequented, and would be more so if their efficacy was better known, and the accommodation for visitors improved. The wine produced in this neighbourhood is very good.

Acqui was the capital of the Upper Montferrat, and some of the towers erected by the Palæologi yet remain. It suffered much during the revolutionary wars.

On leaving Acqui the road follows the l. bank of the Bormida, which it crosses at Terzo, on the site of a Roman station—ad Tertium—which represents very accurately its present distance from Acqui: from thence it follows the rt. bank of the river, leaving Bistagno, a village of 2000 Inhab., on the rt. The two branches forming the Bormida unite opposite *Bistagno*—the Bormida di Spigno descending from the

Altare or Cadibona Pass, and the Bormida di Millesimo, which rises at the foot of Monte Calvo. The road to Savona follows the first of the two, nearly in a true south direction, for 9 m. to *Spigno*, a village of 3000 Inhab., 12 m. from Acqui, in a fertile territory, producing much silk and wine; and 10 m. further is

Dego (Degus), a village of 2300 Inhab., which has little to interest the traveller, except its historical recollections. It is situated in a bend, and on the l. bank of the Bormida: its territory produces a good deal of wine and some silk.

Dego, from its situation on one of the high roads into the plains of Lombardy and of Piedmont, has suffered severely on several occasions from military operations, but especially in Sept. 1794, when it was occupied by Massena, and in 1796, when it was the scene of one of the sanguinary battles that opened to Napoleon the conquest of Italy. The French general, having succeeded by a most masterly movement in cutting through the centre of the allied army of the Piedmontese and Austrians at Montenotte on the 12th of April, lost no time in following up his success by attacking each in turn. The Austrians, after their disaster at Montenotte, retreated along the Bormida, and occupied Dego, where their conquered division received reinforcements from the main body of the Imperial army, then about Genoa. After beating the Piedmontese under Colli at Millesimo, and forcing them to retreat on Ceva and Mondovi, Napoleon, having under his orders Laharpe and Massena, attacked the Austrians at Dego. After a series of hard-fought actions during two days, the Imperial general was obliged to retreat upon Acqui, leaving 3000 prisoners and 13 cannon in the hands of the French. Two days afterwards, however, a most gallant attempt was made by General Wickasowich, at the head of 6000 Austrian grenadiers, to retrieve the past disaster of his countrymen. Dego was retaken with 600 French in it; but Napoleon, uniting his forces, pounced upon Wickasowich unexpectedly, and soon recovered it, making 1600 Imperialists prisoners. The results of the battle of Dego were — the impossibility of the Imperialists forming a junction with, or relieving, their Piedmontese allies, already hard pressed by Napoleon at Ceva, and ultimately defeated at Mondovi (see Rte. 10), and their being obliged to retreat on Alessandria to cover Milan from an attack by Napoleon. It was at the battle of Dego that Lannes, afterwards celebrated as Duc de Montebello, was first distinguished by General Bonaparte, who for his gallant conduct made him a colonel on the field of battle.

Cairo (Cairum), 5 m. S. of Dego, is supposed to have been a station on the Via Emilia, which from Rimini led to Savona. It has a population of 3500 souls, and some iron-furnaces in the neighbourhood. It is the principal town in this upper valley of the Bormida. The old road to Savona by the *Pass of Montenotte*, now abandoned, struck off to the left from this point, passing by the battle-field of Montenotte. A mule-path, frequented by the Genoese fishermen, still exists over that celebrated pass. Since the new road has been opened, a handsome stone bridge of 7 arches has been thrown over the Bormida at Cairo. This new road was commenced in 1800 by Napoleon; and, instead of crossing a difficult col, as that of Montenotte was, now penetrates into Liguria by that between Altaro and Cadibona, perhaps the lowest pass or depression in the whole chain of the Apennines, for the Apennines may be considered to commence hereabouts.

As we have already mentioned, it was at Montenotte that Napoleon, on the 12th of April, 1796, succeeded in piercing the centre of the allied army by a masterly movement. Encamped at Savona, having the Austrian commander-in-chief in front, at Voltri, he had detached a corps of 1200 men, under Colonel Rampon, to occupy the pass of Montenotte. The latter was vigorously attacked by a vastly superior force of the Imperialists under General Roccavina, who being severely wounded, the command devolved on Argenteau. Forced to shut himself up in the dismantled redoubt of Monte Legino, the French commander defended himself with heroism until night closed in, exacting from his soldiers an oath that they would conquer or die. Napoleon, hearing of Rampon's critical position, immediately broke up from Savona, unobserved owing to the darkness of the night, with the greater part of his forces, and by daybreak the next morning was able to relieve Rampon. The Austrians were completely beaten, losing 1000 killed, 2000 prisoners, and 5 pieces of cannon; but, what was more serious still, having their centre forced, and their main body obliged to retreat on Dego.

Leaving Cairo, some remains of the Roman road are seen about a mile beyond the town, and the ruins of a convent, said to have been founded by St. Francis himself, but burned down by the French in 1799.

4 m. farther is the village of *Carcare*, where the valley widens. The road from Turin to Savona, by Ceva and Millesimo, here joins that from Alessandria. Carcare has a population of 1500, and in a military point of view occupies an important position; for this reason it was selected by Napoleon, after the battle of Montenotte, as his head-quarters, from which he directed his operations against the Austrians in the valley of the Bormida, and the Piedmontese at Millesimo, and in that of the Tanaro. Beyond Carcare the road rises from the torrent over a ridge which separates the two branches of the upper Bormida, to reach

Altare, the last village on the northern declivity of the Apennines, and only 7 Piedmontese m. as the crow flies from the shores of the Mediterranean at Savona. The ascent to Cadibona is very easy, and the road generally in good condition.

The very great depression of this part of the Ligurian Apennines gave rise to the project of the French government in 1805, of establishing a water communication by a canal between the valley of the Po and the Mediterranean. Altare was in that project selected as the site of an immense reservoir to supply the canal in its descent, through the valley by which we have travelled, to Alessandria, from whence the Tanaro is navigable to the Po.

The road attains its culminating point near *Cadibona*, from which it descends to the hamlet of Montemore, at the head of the Vanestra torrent, which it follows to Savona. There are mines of a lignite coal in the environs of Cadibona belonging to the tertiary geological epoch. This coal contains bones of an extinct quadruped, the *Anthracotherium*, also found in the tertiary strata of the Paris basin, of Alsace, the Isle of Wight, &c.

For Savona see Rte. 13.

ROUTE 12.

TURIN TO SAVONA, BY MILLESIMO.

The first part of this road, as far as Dogliani, has been described under Rte. 9.

From Dogliani the road follows that to Ceva, as far as Montezzemolo, a mountain village 2500 ft. above the sea; from whence striking off to the l., after 6 m. of rapid ascents and descents, over the Alpine spur that separates the upper valleys of the Tanaro and Bormida, it reaches

Millesimo, a poor village of less than 1000 Inhab., on the Upper Bormida, 1490 ft. above the sea, memorable for the battle between the French under Augereau, and the Piedmontese commanded by General Provera, in which the latter were defeated and forced to retire on Ceva and Mondovi, whilst at the same moment Bonaparte was forcing the Austrians at Dego (p. 69) from Millesimo. The road crosses a high ridge for 5 m. to reach Carcare, where it joins that from Alessandria to Savona (Rte. 11).

SECTION II.

SARDINIAN DOMINIONS ON THE MEDITERRANEAN.—THE RIVIERA DI PONENTE, AND RIVIERA DI LEVANTE.—TERRITORIES OF NICE, MONACO, AND DUCHY OF GENOA.*

PRELIMINARY INFORMATION.

1. *Political Changes and Character of the Country.*—2. *Agriculture, Towns.*—3. *Roads.*—4. *Posting, Modes of Travelling.*—5. *Money, Weights, Measures.*—6. *Character of the Population.*—7. *Inns.*—8. *Fine Arts.*

ROUTES.

ROUTE		PAGE
13.	Nice to *Genoa*, by the Riviera di Ponente	76
14.	Genoa to *Sarzana*, by the Riviera di Levante	121

§ 1. POLITICAL CHANGES.—CHARACTER OF THE COUNTRY.

At the beginning of the present century the dominions of Sardinia on this coast consisted of the county of Nice (ceded to France by the Treaty of March 24, 1860), the principality of Oneglia, and some smaller *enclavures;* the remainder belonged to the republic of Genoa. What were called the "imperial fiefs" in the interior were, as the name imports, small feudal sovereignties; but they all belonged to Genoese nobles, and, though by law subject to the empire, still, politically speaking, they had no independent existence, and had become mere private domains. After the transitory duration of the Ligurian republic (1797), the whole was incorporated with the French empire (1805). The congress of Vienna transferred it to the king of Sardinia; and the House of Savoy thus not only regained their old possessions, but also obtained the territories for which they had more than once struggled. A nominal existence has been given to the "duchy of Genoa," and the title of duke was taken by the sovereign; but the whole is politically united to the rest of the Sardinian, now *North Italian*, states, though it is very distinct in its physical features and the national character of its population. Between the Var, fixed in the time of Augustus as the boundary of Italy on the W., and the Magra, the ancient boundary of Tuscany, the greater part of this territory is situated. We say "the greater part," for a small district beyond the Magra, won by the Genoese from their ancient rivals of Lucca, and composing a part of the Tuscan Lunigiana, is retained by the Sardinian monarch as the successor of the republic.

* Notwithstanding the recent political union of Nice to France, we have considered it would be more convenient for travellers to continue to include its description in the Handbook of Italy, and the more so as it has not been inserted in the latest edition of our Handbook of France; besides, the most zealous annexionist will not question that Nice is much more Italian than French by its history, language, manners, &c., as it is by its geographical position.

The country is a continued series of mountain ridges, valleys, and ravines, formed by the spurs of the Maritime Alps and the Apennines. The breadth of the district, which is now denominated "Maritime Liguria," varies (always supposing the central ridge of the Maritime Alps and Apennines to form its N. limit) from 25 m. at Nice, to 5 m. between Arenzano and Voltri, where the latter chain (at Monte Reisa) approaches nearest to the shores of the Mediterranean. The climate is most agreeable, the atmosphere remarkable for its transparency and purity. In several of the districts on the sea-side, which are protected from the N. and N.E. winds, the thermometer rarely falls below the freezing-point; and hence the singular beauty of the vegetation, in which the botany of the temperate zone of the southern coasts of Europe, and of the northern coasts of Africa, is combined with that of the tropics. Where the ravines open into the mountains the sharp wind occasionally penetrates, and sometimes the winters are severe; but the olive rarely suffers on this coast, and this affords a test of the mildness of the climate. These transient variations of temperature, or perhaps some less perceptible cause, render pulmonary complaints common amongst the inhabitants of the Riviera; and the foreign invalid who resorts hither in search of health finds the natives mowed down by the disease from which he seeks to fly. The mountains abound in valuable marbles, furnishing many of those with which the palaces of Genoa are adorned. The most remarkable of these are that of Polcevera di Genova, a mixture of serpentine with granular limestone, and the black marble of Porto Venere, quarried at the cape of that name, in the Gulf of Spezia. The first of these marbles was formerly much employed in Italy, France, and England, for chimney-pieces, but its sombre appearance has put it out of fashion. Taken as a whole, nearly all the beauties which the traveller admires in the Alps of Switzerland, or on the shores of the bay of Naples, are here combined.

§ 2. AGRICULTURE—TOWNS.

The coast of the Mediterranean from Sarzana to the frontier of France rises abruptly to the Maritime Alps and the Apennines. Facing the S., with generally a warm aspect, the vine and the olive are extensively cultivated. Wheat and maize are grown in rotative crops. Beans, some potatoes, and other vegetables are also produced, which, with roasted chestnuts and Indian corn meal made into pollenta, form the chief food of the lower classes in the mountain districts. Generally the rural inhabitants, as well as the labouring classes in the towns, are poor. The farms are small, held chiefly on leases of from three to seven years, and slovenly husbandry prevails. Along some parts of the sea-coast, and inland up the valleys and hills, the Métayer system predominates.

The towns along the Mediterranean, from the Var to Genoa, with the exception of Nice (which strangers have enriched), appear strikingly picturesque and beautiful from the sea; but, on entering them, dirt and discomfort, windows without glass, a want of all that we consider convenient within doors, dilapidation and a general absence of completeness without and within, and a prevalence of what may serve as a slovenly expedient for the moment, are their ordinary characteristics. Improvement is, however, making advances. It commenced under the late king, and it is making rapid progress under the present constitutional sovereign.

The chief ports are Spezia, Genoa, Savona, Porto Maurizio, Mentone, Villa Franca, and Nice.

§ 3. Roads.

At the beginning of the present century there were only two roads practicable for carriages, and those but indifferent—the road from Nice to Turin by the Col di Tenda, and the road from Alessandria to Genoa over the Pass of the Bocchetta; all the rest were mountain paths, some of which could not be crossed, even on mules, without danger. The present great thoroughfare which connects France with Tuscany was planned and executed as far as Mentone by Napoleon I., but was completed by the Sardinian government, which has also opened most of the other carriage-roads by which the traffic of the country is carried on, and to which its rapid improvement is to be in part ascribed. The road along the coast is intersected by fifty or sixty torrents, the passage of some of which is occasionally not unattended with danger. Bridges have already been thrown over many of them, as at Ventimiglia, Oneglia, Pegli, and St. Pier d'Arena. From Genoa to Sarzana the road is excellent: a bridge over the Magra recently erected has been a great improvement. The only Rly. yet completed is the short line from Voltri to Genoa, although one along the whole line of the two Rivieras, from Nice to Pisa and Lucca, is projected.

§ 4. Posting, Modes of Travelling, &c.

The post regulations are the same as in the other parts of the Sardinian dominions. The relays are good and well served. From the nature of the roads, persons who wish to see the country will prefer the vetturini, which are good, though much more expensive than formerly; or the diligences, which are excellent, all the way from Nice to Pisa. The journey, from point to point, may also be performed by water, by the steamers between Marseilles, Nice, Genoa, and Spezia.

§ 5. Money.

The Sardinian currency is the same as the French. The following coins of the republic of Genoa are also current, though not very common. Those most current are of mixed metal: pieces of 40 and of 20 centimes.

Gold:—Quadruplo di Genova, 79 francs.
Doppia di Genova, 39 francs 50 cents.

Among the small dealers calculations are still in use in the old currency of Genoa, the lira and soldo. Their value in the present currency is as follows:—
A lira of Genoa contains 20 soldi, and is equal to 80 centimes of the present currency. A soldo = 4 centimes.
A French franc is equal to 25 soldi of Genoa.

Weights.

The pound, gold and silver weight, is divided into 12 ounces; the ounce into 24 denari; the denaro into 24 grani.
The pound = $4891\frac{1}{2}$ grains Troy = 10 ounces 3 pennyweights $13\frac{1}{2}$ grains.
The ounce = 16 „ $23\frac{3}{5}$ „

N. Italy—1860.

This weight, called *peso sottile*, is used not only for gold and silver, but for all commodities of small bulk. Other goods are weighed with the peso grosso.

  100 lbs. peso grosso = 76·875 lbs. avoirdupois.
  100 lbs. peso sottile = 69·89 lbs. avoirdupois.

Measures of Length.

The palmo = 9·725 English inches.

The canna is of three sorts; the piccola, which tradesmen and manufacturers use, is 9 palmi, or 87·5 English inches. The canna grossa, which is used by merchants, is 12 palmi, or 116·7 English inches. The canna used at the custom-house is 10 palmi, or 97·6 English inches.

The braccio contains 2¼ palmi; but in all large towns, and in general through the country, the *mètre* is in general use, and the only official measure.

§ 6. Character of the Population.

The Ligurian tribes were amongst the last of the inhabitants of Italy incorporated in the Roman empire. We are not acquainted with the government and constitution of the people prior to that event; it seems probable, however, that, being Celts, they constituted a confederacy of clans and tribes bound by their own laws and customs, but not acknowledging any common head or superior. Having allied themselves to the Carthaginians, the Romans, after the second Punic war, assailed them with eighty years' hostility, and they were for a time rendered obedient; yet they were not finally subjugated until they were conquered by Augustus, who commemorated his triumph by the remarkable trophy of which the ruins are still existing at Turbia. By him—or, at least, during his reign—the Alps became the limits of Italy; and that fair country acquired the boundaries by which it was known and characterised by its great poet—

    . . . . Il bel paese
  Che l' Appenin' parte, e 'l mar' circonda e l' Alpe—

until the recent cession of the territory of Nice to France.

But this conquest did not break up the nationality, nor indeed the government, of the Ligurian states. They continued to retain their identity, though under Roman supremacy; and this corporate succession (as in the large cities of the south of France) was continued, in a great measure, until the great European revolution of the 19th centy. Thus Noli, Savona, Albenga, San' Remo, Porto Maurizio, and Vintimiglia, were rather the allies than the subjects of Genoa; and even much smaller communities enjoyed a species of independence. The inhabitants of this coast possess a very decided national character, and present all the physical characteristics of a pure and unaltered race, excepting at Genoa, where there appears to have been a considerable mixture of Lombard blood; and in the district between Nice and Mentone, where the Provençals have intermingled.

From the earliest period the Ligurians have been a nation of sailors and merchants. Mago the Carthaginian reduced the city of Genoa B.C. 205. The ancestors of Doria and of Columbus were distinguished by their aptness for maritime enterprise. In the middle ages Genoa alone vied with Venice; and at the present day she has recovered her ancient commercial prosperity, and far surpassed her rival of the Adriatic.

The Genoese are said to be parsimonious: this reputation they had of old;

but in acts of charity, and indeed in every call which can be made on public spirit, their liberality has been unbounded, and still continues very eminent. The lower orders are remarkably hard-working and industrious.

§ 7. INNS.

The inns between Nice and Genoa, and between Genoa and Pisa, have perhaps rather declined since the steamers between Marseilles, Nice, Genoa, and Leghorn have been established, the number of travellers by land having very considerably diminished. They are still, however, good in almost all the places in which, according to the usual arrangement, a traveller requires to stop. Iron bedsteads, for the manufacture of which Genoa is celebrated, are now in general use, greatly to the comfort of the traveller.

§ 8. FINE ARTS.

Little is known respecting the arts of Genoa in the middle ages. There are Roman remains at Cimies, near Nice; others exist at Turbia and at Albenga; but the ancient masters of the world have left few traces of their domination in Liguria. The "Gothic" architecture of the country is of a peculiar character, and, in Genoa at least, exhibits more *orientalism* than perhaps in any other part of W. Europe. But, in the 16th century, architecture burst out in Genoa with peculiar splendour. The palaces of Genoa exhibit fine specimens of domestic architecture. Galeazzo Alessi (1500-1572), by whom the best of them were designed, gave the impulse which continued till the last century, when the art declined, giving way to extravagant decoration.

Nowhere has painting been more closely allied to architecture than at Genoa. In the first era the earliest known Genoese artist is the individual who bears the somewhat romantic appellation of the "Monk of the Golden Islands" (1321-1408). The golden islands are said to be the isles d'Hyères, where he took the vows. This monk, who is thought to have belonged to the noble family of Cibo, was also a Troubadour of no mean powers; and he gave what may be termed a new edition of the works of his predecessors, by making correct copies of them, which had been much corrupted by the ignorance of transcribers. As an artist he was chiefly distinguished as a miniature painter or illuminator. There appears also to have been a class of artists who flourished in this district, either Germans, or who followed German models; to this class belong Giusto d'Allemagna, who painted at Genoa in 1451, and Ludovico Brea, who, flourishing between the years 1483 and 1515, is perhaps to be considered as the father of the Genoese school, of which the principal of the more early masters were, Robertelli (1499), Nicolo Corso (about 1503), Pietro Francesco Sacchi (1512-1526), and Lorenzo Moreno (about 1544).

The second era was formed by Pierino del Vaga (died 1547) and his scholars, and may be considered as an offset from the Roman school. The calamities of Rome compelled Pierino to seek a refuge at Genoa at the time when those palaces were rising which have conferred such splendour upon the Città Superba. Patronised by the great Andrea Doria, he was employed upon the decoration of his palace; and by him, and by the native Genoese who were either directly or indirectly his pupils, were those frescoes produced. To this period belong Lazzaro Calvi (born 1502, and who attained the patriarchal age of 105 years) and Pantaleon Calvi his brother (died 1509), Antonio Semini, a follower of Perugino (died 1547), and his son Andrea (1578), Giovanni Cambiaso and Luca Cambiaso his son (died 1585), Tavarone (1556-1641), and Bernardo Castelli (died 1629).

E 2

Giovanni Cambiaso is the chief of these artists. All were exceedingly prized in their own country; and the Genoese republic conferred an honour upon painting which no other Italian state had bestowed. By a special decree, they raised painting from a *trade* to a *profession*, declaring that it was a liberal art, and that it might be practised without derogating from nobility.

In the third era, which partly includes some who may also be considered as belonging to the preceding age, Domenico Fiasella, surnamed "Sarzaha," from his birthplace (1584-1669), holds a conspicuous station. The Piola family produced many artists of high merit, one of whom, Pellegro (died 1640), had he not been prematurely cut off, would probably have attained the highest rank in art. Eight of the Piola family were artists, the series extending from 1625 to 1774. The Carlone family also formed a clan of painters. Giovanni Battista Carlone (died 1680) must perhaps be considered as the greatest master of this period; and his elder brother, Giovanni, was scarcely inferior. During the earlier part of this period Genoa was visited by many foreign artists, more, certainly, than any other state in Italy. Both Rubens and Vandyke were much encouraged here, and had a good deal of influence on the Genoese school of painting in the early part of the 18th centy. During the great plague of 1657 many of the principal painters died. This is assigned as one of the causes of the sudden decline of the Genoese school; but the main cause was the general decline in art, in which all Italy participated. Many young men went to Rome to pursue their studies; and, on their return, constituted what is considered as the fourth era. The greater number of these students became the pupils of Carlo Maratta; the most distinguished were, Andrea Carlone (died 1697), Paol' Girolamo Piola (1724), Domenico Parodi (1740), and the Jesuit Padre Pozzi (ob. 1709). The later artists are of no great importance, nor does Genoa at the present day form any exception to the general observation—that Italy exhibits no real symptoms of any efficient revival in painting.

ROUTES.

ROUTE 13.

NICE TO GENOA, BY THE RIVIERA DI PONENTE.

206 kilomètres (129 English miles). Nice may be reached from Marseilles and Toulon by 2 diligences daily, in 24 and 20 hours, distance 138 m., and by steamer, twice a week, in 15; from Turin, by the railway as far as Cuneo, and from thence over the Col di Tenda, by the mail diligence, in 26 hours.

Inns.—Hôtel Victoria, a large new establishment, recently opened by Zicchitelli, on the sea-shore to the W. of the town, having a fine southern exposure, and convenient in winter for invalids, and in summer for bathers, from being outside of the town, and near the sea-beach. Hôtel de la Grande Bretagne, kept by Brizzi, in the centre of the great square of the Public Gardens, one of the best managed hotels in Nice; charges more moderate than at the Victoria, with an excellent table-d'hôte. Hôtel d'Angleterre, kept by Vincenzo Palmieri, excellent, and praised by families who have lived in it, near the latter. Hôtel de France, and Hôtel Chauvain, also very good, with gardens and a S.E. exposure, and nearer the old town: table-d'hôte 4 frs. Hôtel des

Etrangers, kept by Schmitz, the owner of the Hôtel de la Ville at Genoa, in the town at some distance from the sea, is much frequented by travellers arriving at Nice, and is well spoken of for its moderate charges: the Office of the Messageries Générales Diligence is here, and the street in which it is situated contains the gayest shops in the town. Hotel Royal, kept by Mrs. Santi, an Englishwoman, clean, comfortable, and well situated on the new Boulevard. Hôtel de l'Univers, in the Piazza S. Domenico, kept by How, much improved, near where the Courrier to Turin has its office. Hôtel de l'Europe, in the Rue de France; and the Hôtel des Princes, at the E. extremity of the town, near the sea, "very clean and comfortable," and in a good situation under the Castle-hill, protected from the N. winds. Hôtel di Paradis. The hotels at Nice have been much improved of late years, and most of those above-mentioned are as good as in any other part of the Continent: at the Grande Bretagne, Angleterre, and Victoria visitors can make economical arrangements for a prolonged stay, avoiding thus many of the inconveniences attending furnished lodgings. Bachelors in Zicchitelli's new establishment, and at the Grande Bretagne, on paying about 10 frs. a day are furnished with bed-room, breakfast, dinner, servants' fees, lights, &c.: similar arrangements may be made in many of the other first-rate hotels.

Lodgings. — Comfortably furnished houses and lodgings may be had to suit every purse, and number of persons, both in the town and the environs, a list of which will be found at Lattes' and Jougla's House Agency Offices (p. 79); persons who can be recommended for their honesty, and whose services will save the stranger much trouble. The price of lodgings varies from 6000 frs. downwards; excellent apartments for families in the best quarter may be procured for 4000 frs., and very comfortable ones for smaller families from 800 to 1200 frs., always for the season, which includes from the commencement of the winter until the end of April. Bachelors' apartments, consisting of a small sitting-room and bedroom, with a S. aspect, may be hired for from 40 to 60 frs. per month, with 15 frs. additional for attendance. All persons taking lodgings at Nice will do well to have an inventory of the furniture carefully made out, which ought to be done at the joint expense of the landlord and tenant. Lattes, Jougla, the house-agents, undertake for a small remuneration to attend to this and deliver back the furniture. There are several handsome villas about Nice let to foreigners, the rent for the season varying from 3000 to 12,000 francs.

Servants.—As persons taking private lodgings must necessarily employ native servants, the following is the usual scale of wages:—for men-servants, 60 to 70 frs. per month; men-cooks, 60 to 80; female cooks, 40 to 50; house-maids, 25 to 35. Lists of servants may be procured at Lattes', or at Jougla's offices.

Restaurants.—None very good; several send out dinners on the Roman system. The best are Lavit's, Rue Longchamps, and Escoffier, Restaurans Francais, Quai Massena. Bachelors will always find it as economical and with better fare to frequent the table-d'hôte (3½ frs.) at the principal hotels.

Cafés.—The best cafés are on the Corso, near the theatre. The Café Américain is elegantly fitted up. Café de l'Univers, Boulevard du Pont Neuf, with an excellent Neapolitan Glacier. Café Royal. Café du Commerce. The principal local and French newspapers are taken in at all, and good cigars may be obtained from the waiters.

Carriages.—Private carriages with 2 horses of the best kind may be hired at 500 frs. a month, less elegant for 400 to 320, the coachman's allowance not being included in the above sums; *fiacres* or *voitures de place* abound, with 2 horses, at 2½ frs. for the first and 2 for every successive hour; with 1 horse 2 fr. and 20 sols.

Vetturini.—The Nice vetturini are

good and attentive; and as persons proceeding to Genoa and Marseilles must either employ this mode of conveyance or posting, the following are the ordinary charges: from Nice to Genoa with a good carriage drawn by 4 horses, 15 to 16 Napoleons; with 2 horses, 10 to 12; the same time and charge to Marseilles or Aix, and to Turin. Plana near the Croix de Marbre, and Felice near the Palace, can be recommended as worthy of confidence. Return vetturini may sometimes be found at more reasonable prices; the keepers of the respectable hotels will make every necessary arrangement, and their intervention will save much trouble to the traveller. The journey to Genoa will generally require 3½ days, to Toulon 2½, to Turin 3, i.e. to Cuneo, and from thence by railway to Turin.

Passports must be signed at the Prefecture, for which no fee is exacted, nor is the visa of the Consul previously necessary.

British Consul.—A. Lacroix, Esq., in the Place St. Dominique.

Bankers.—The principal bankers are MM. Avigdor and Co.; Lacroix and Co., at the British Consulate; and Etienne, Carlone, and Co.; all of whom are very useful and obliging to their English customers. The rates of exchange on England are stuck up at the principal reading-rooms.

Physicians.— Dr. Travis and Dr. Gurney, in the Piazza del Giardino Publico, near the Hôtel de la Grande Bretagne; Dr. P. Fitzpatrick; Dr. de Pascale.

Apothecaries.—Ferrari's, on the Quai Massena, in the foreign quarter; the business is conducted by Mr. Turner, his partner, from London. Musso, Rue du Pont Neuf; the business is also conducted by an English partner and assistant. This establishment is also celebrated for its dried fruits and syrups, which it exports largely. Paulain, in the Rue du Pont Neuf, also good.

Libraries and Reading Rooms.— Giraud, on the Place du Jardin des Plantes, in the centre of the English quarter, keeps a reading-room, where the principal London papers are taken in: charges, 5 frs. per month, 13 for 3 months, 24 for 6 months. Attached to the reading-room is a circulating library. This establishment is the most convenient from its situation for foreign residents, and the owner is a very intelligent and obliging person. Visconti's establishment, in the Via di San Francesco di Paolo, is one of the largest and best managed of the kind in Italy. Dalbecchi, in the Rue du Pont Neuf, bookseller and stationer, and the best supplied with articles necessary for drawing and painting.

Club or *Cercle.*—There is a club or cercle called the Société Philharmonique, formed of the principal inhabitants of Nice, where foreign residents are admitted on being presented by one of the members, gratuitously for 10 days, and afterwards on payment for 1 month of 10 francs, for 3 of 25, and for 6 months or longer of 50 francs. Balls and concerts are frequently given here during the winter season, to which subscribers can bring their families; the principal Italian and French newspapers are taken in, as well as several English; and attached to the establishment is a circulating library.

PUBLIC CONVEYANCES.—*Diligences, Steamers, &c.*—Diligences leave Nice daily, at 8 a.m. and 4 p.m., from the offices of the Messageries Impériales et Générales de France, for Marseilles, performing the journey in 24 hours; for Antibes every morning in 3 hours; for Genoa two diligences daily at 8 a.m. and 10 p.m. in 26 hours. Travellers, however, who do not wish to travel by night, thus losing a portion of the beautiful scenery of the Riviera, by giving notice 2 days beforehand may secure places to Oneglia by the diligence of the Messageries Impériales that leaves Nice at 8 a.m. and arrives in the evening, and proceed from thence on the following morning to Genoa; an additional charge is made for effecting this arrangement. Malleposte from Nice to Turin, daily in 24 hours, by the Col di Tenda to Cuneo, and from thence to Turin by railway.

Steamers to Genoa on Monday and Thursday evenings, arriving at Genoa the next morning, fare 28 and 18 francs (these steamers are small and not over well appointed); to Marseilles twice a week also, but more irregular in their days of departure.

TRADESMEN. — *Grocers.* — Berlandina, Rue St. François de Paule, keeps a good warehouse for tea, wines, groceries, and English articles in general; he is a very obliging person, and will give information as to lodgings, servants, &c.; Gent, on the same quay, equally good.

Tailors.—Thibaut is a good tailor, and makes ladies' habits; Gavarry frères are considered the Stultz of Nice; Morrison, an English tailor, in the Jardin Public.

Bootmakers.—Bouchon, Brun.

Hatter.—Cordiglia keeps French and English hats.

Dressmakers.—The best are Madame Baud (an Englishwoman) and Madame Davin, who work for the different courts.

Straw Hats.—Nice is celebrated for a peculiar form of straw hat for ladies, of late become so fashionable, perhaps the best in Italy for protection from the sun; the principal shop where they may be purchased is at Tori et Fils, in the Place St. Dominique.

Turnery, Marqueterie, &c.—Nice is also celebrated for its inlaid work, a kind of mosaic in woods of different colours, something resembling that made at Tunbridge Wells; the best shops for it, and for turnery, which is largely manufactured at Nice, are, Ciaudo's in the Rue St. François de Paule, who obtained a medal at the Great Exhibition of 1851; Gimeele, Place Charles Albert; and Nicolas and Lacroix's, in the Rue des Ponchettes, near the Hôtel des Princes.

House Agents.—Lattes, whose office is near the Pont Neuf, and Charles Jougla, 13, Quai Massena, are represented as very active and honest persons; most of the furnished lodgings at and about Nice are confided to their letting, and lists of them may be seen at their offices. Jougla, who speaks English fluently, is an agreeable person to deal with, and is generally recommended. The general system is, that the person letting the lodging pays the commission of the agent as well as the charge of the inventory, *which ought never to be omitted;* but on leaving it is usual for the hirer to give a small gratuity to the latter for delivering up the furniture, and arranging all squabbles and differences with the proprietors as to damage done, breakages, &c., during the occupation.

English Church.—The English Ch. is situated near the Rue de la Croix de Marbre, and is supported chiefly by the subscriptions of the British residents and visitors; the contribution for seats is as follows :—Families, 105 francs for the season, and 15 francs additional for each servant; single persons, 10 francs for 1 month, 15 for 2 months, and 25 for the season, and half the same rates for children. Divine service is performed twice a day on Sundays and holidays; the present clergyman is Mr. Childers. Annexed to the church is the English burying-ground. There is also a French and German Reformed church, where the service is performed alternately in these languages.

Masters.—It is difficult to give a list of the various masters: the best way for foreigners will be to apply at Giraud or Visconti's libraries, or at the principal music-shops. M. Mallard is represented as a good teacher of French. Belgrand is a good master for the piano, and moderate in his terms. For persons wishing to take lessons in elementary botany, the Abbé Montolivo, librarian of the municipal library, gives lessons in that science, interesting at Nice from the great variety of the vegetable products of its environs.

Nice, in Italian Nizza, called also Nizza di Mare, and Nizza Maritima, to distinguish it from Nizza della Paglia, in the province of Alessandria, was formerly the capital of a small independent sove_ reignty governed by its counts in the middle ages. It passed successively into the hands of the Counts of Provence, of the Angevin sovereigns of Naples, until the end of the 14th century, when it was sold by Ladislaus to Amadeus VII. of Savoy, in whose family it has since remained, except during the French revolutionary war and empire, to which it was attached, until the present year, when it was ceded to France; it is now the chief town of the French Département des Alpes Maritimes. Considerable doubt exists as to the first foundation of Nice and the origin of its name, but it is generally believed to have been peopled by a Phocean colony from Marseilles, as early as the 5th century of Rome; during the imperial period it was a port of some importance, from its vicinity to Cemenelum (the modern Cimies), the Roman capital of the Maritime Alps. The name of Nice is derived by some philologists from Nike, in memory of a victory gained by its early Phocean colonists over some neighbouring Ligurian tribes.

Modern Nice offers no remains of ancient art; we must seek this on the hills above it, near where the capital of the Maritime Alps stood. The mediæval town appears to have been entirely situated on the left bank of the Paglione torrent, and round the base of the hill on which its castle stood, the whole of that on the right bank being of very modern date, chiefly during the present century, and since the great influx of foreigners; of late years the town has been much extended also in a northerly direction, and the quarter bordering on its little port much enlarged and embellished.

The city consists of three principal portions: that on the rt. bank of the Paglione, called the Quartier de la Croix de Marbre; the Old Town, with its modern additions; and the Port. The quarter of the Croix de Marbre is that principally occupied by foreigners; it borders the river with a handsome quay filled with gay shops. The great square called the Jardin Public is surrounded by handsome buildings, at the extremity of which is the street leading towards the French frontier, and a new parade, the Passeggiata degli Inglesi, facing the sea, constructed by subscriptions chiefly of the English visitors, to employ the poor during a year of scarcity. The English church and cemetery is in this part of the town, which derives its name of Croix de Marbre from a marble cross erected in 1538, on the occasion of the arrival of Paul III. to bring about a reconciliation between Charles V. and Francis I., "when so great was the difficulty of adjusting the ceremonial, or such the remains of rancour and distrust on each side, that they refused to see one another, and everything was transacted by the intervention of the Pope, who visited them alternately."—*Robertson's Charles V.* The obelisk opposite this cross was put up in 1823 to commemorate the two visits of Pius VII. in 1809 and 1814.

The quarter of the Old Town extends from the Paglione to the foot of the Castle-hill; on the side of the sea it is bordered by a very handsome quay or parade, affording a delightful walk, in the direction of the port, of more than a mile. Parallel to this are the Rue St. François de Paule and the Corso, where the theatre, public library, and principal cafés are situated. Farther N. is the Rue du Pont Neuf and Place St. Dominique, the principal centre of business; and at its N. extremity the large Piazza Vittorio, which forms the entrance from the sides of Turin and Genoa. The dirty quarter close under the hill is the oldest part of Nice. Near this are the market, the cathedral, principal churches, &c.

Between this quarter and that of the port is the Castle-hill, an insulated mass of limestone, which rises to an elevation of 800 ft. It was formerly crowned by a strong castle, destroyed by the Duke of Berwick, a general of Louis XIV., in 1706. This hill has been recently laid out as a public promenade, the entrance to which is towards the Piazza Vittorio. From the summit the view is most extensive, Corsica being easily seen, in clear weather, early in the morning and before sunset.

The quarter of the port, until lately a low crowded place, has been recently greatly improved, and is approached by the beautiful parade of the Ponchettes from the W., and by the Rue Cassini from the N. It is chiefly inhabited by seafaring persons. The little port itself, capable of admitting vessels drawing 15 ft. water, is protected by 2 moles, at the extremity of the outer one of which is a small lighthouse and a strong battery. The entrance is somewhat difficult, and at no time can it be considered as a place of refuge, from the difficulty of its approach in heavy weather.

The principal objects worthy of the traveller's notice at Nice are—

The *Cathedral* or Ch. of S. Reparata, the principal ecclesiastical edifice of the town: it is in the ordinary Italian style of the 17th cent., and offers nothing remarkable as a work of art. The same observation applies to the pictures over the principal altars.

The *Public Library*, in the Rue St. François de Paule, is open daily from 10 till 4. It contains about 40,000 volumes, and is well supplied with works of modern Italian and French literature. In one of the rooms are preserved fragments of 3 milestones, of the reigns of Augustus and Adrian, discovered on the Via Aurelia, near Turbia. The most perfect, indicating the DCV. mile, was discovered and presented by our countryman Sir John Boileau. Annexed to the public library is the Zoological Museum, also supported by the municipality, and chiefly formed by Dr. Verrani: it is rich in ornithological specimens. It contains some interesting fossil bones found in the crevices of the limestone rock of the Castle-hill.

Liceo Nazionale, or College, near the Ponte Vecchio, a large educational establishment on the plan of the French lycées or colleges, and containing several hundred pupils. Annexed to it is a small Botanic Garden, which contains a gigantic specimen of Melaleuca, perhaps the largest in Europe. The geological collection, formed by Dr. Perez, is very rich in fossils of the environs of Nice, and will be well worthy of a visit to those interested in natural science.

It may not be out of place here to give a general sketch of the different formations which constitute the environs of Nice, as many of our readers may wish to occupy themselves in their walks around with geological investigations. "Commencing in the ascending order, the oldest rock in this part of the Maritime Alps is a metamorphic conglomerate, called *Verruccano* by the Tuscan geologists, which may be seen about San Dalmazzo and on the road to Tenda. On this lies, at Isola, an extensive calcareous deposit referable to the lias and inferior oolite of England and to our Oxford clay, and with the characteristic fossils of the latter beds in the Vallée de St. André. The *Coral rag* constitutes the greater part of the range of hills that separate the bays of Nice and Villefranche, and the promontory of Montboron, on which is situated the lighthouse. To this portion of the oolitic series belong the deposits of gypsum which exist close to the town. The limestone of this period is frequently converted into *dolomite*, as may be seen at the foot of Montalbano and in the Castle-hill of Nice. The only fossils hitherto discovered have been corals and the Diceras Arietina, near to S. Pons. Upon the coral rag, near the small bay *des Fosses*, lies a series of beds of a compact limestone, without fossils, which may be referred to the Portland system. The Neocomian and Cretaceous systems are well developed about Nice. The *gault* exists, with its characteristic fossils, in the valley of the Madonna del Laghetto, in the ravines W. of the village of Esa, and on the Mont Chauve, N. of Nice.

E 3

In the two former places good collections of its fossils may be procured. *Green-sand.*—The best points for studying this formation will be perhaps along the E. side of the peninsula of San Ospizio, as we shall notice in our excursion to Villefranche and that promontory. The same may be said of the upper cretaceous rocks, which abound in the most characteristic chalk fossils, Gryphœa columba, Ananchites ovatus, about the village of S. Jean, and on the headland of San Ospizio itself. *Tertiary System.*—The members of the tertiary period, the most developed about Nice, are the eocene and pleiocene formations. The eocenic strata are well characterised by their fossils in the escarpments along the E. side of the peninsula of S. Ospizio, between Beaulieu and the village of S. Jean, especially in the small Baie des Fourmis. The richest localities, however, for these fossils are in the vicinity of Drap and Pallarea, on the road from Nice to Turin, where about 400 species have been already found and described by Signor Bellardi. The pleiocene strata, with the exception of a small patch near La Trinité, are confined to the W. side of the Paglione, and occupy all the low hilly region between it and the Var, so remarkable for its rich olive-plantations, and which presents so marked a contrast with the bare and arid region of the limestone hills on the E. side of the first-mentioned river. The pleiocene strata appear identical with those of the Subapennine hills, and of the patches which exist along the Corniche road and at Genoa. *Quaternary.*—An interesting quaternary deposit, which rises to upwards of 50 ft. above the present sea-level, and containing marine shells identical with those now living in the Mediterranean, may be seen covering the eocene beds between Beaulieu and S. Jean, on the E. side of the promontory. The dolomitized coral rag, which forms the greater part of the insulated hill on which stood the castle of Nice, is penetrated at its S.E. extremity with fissures and caverns, in which bones of extinct quadrupeds have been frequently found. These remains are accompanied by bones of fresh-water turtle and some marine shells, as may be seen in the museum of the municipality. The bones of quadrupeds are referable to the elephant, hippopotamus, rhinoceros, horse, hog, several species of ruminants, &c."

Climate of Nice.—When Nice first became the resort of British residents, the salubrity and advantages of its climate were perhaps overrated, but at present there is too great a tendency in a contrary direction, in comparing it with other places adopted as a residence for invalids. With its few drawbacks as regards climate, Nice offers advantages from its situation, its resources, its vicinity to England, &c., vastly superior to most of the places which have been placed in competition with it. Situated at the opening of a mountain valley, enclosed by hills which in winter are often covered with snow, the wind descending from them is sometimes cold and stimulant; but the greatest drawback perhaps is the dry N.W. wind or *mistral*, which, crossing Provence from the Pyrenees, is very trying to invalids while it lasts, and is attended with another inconvenience, clouds of dust, which no amount of watering can prevent. The great advantage which the climate of Nice offers in winter is its clear atmosphere and bright sun, which always renders the chamber of the invalid cheerful. The temperature seldom falls below freezing during the clear, serene winter nights, and is then produced more by radiation than by an absolute diminished temperature. The daytime is warm, sometimes inconveniently so, even in December; and persons subject to nervous headaches, or determination of blood to the head, will do well not to expose themselves too much to the sun, or in doing so to use the grey linen parasols so generally adopted. The mean temperature of Nice, deduced from 15 years' observation, has been found to be $60\frac{1}{2}°$ Fahrenheit. The greatest heat in July and August, $88\frac{1}{4}°$; the greatest cold in January, $27\frac{1}{2}°$; the mean temperature during the 3 winter months, $48\frac{3}{4}°$; during the 3 spring ditto, $58°$; in June, July, and August, $78°$; in the autumn, $62°$: January being the coldest, and August the hottest months. In speaking of the climate, it may not be out of place to add that the sea-bathing at Nice is good, something similar to that at Brighton, on a shingle beach. Bathing machines on the English system have been lately introduced; those who prefer a sandy beach will find some beautiful situations in the deep coves, near Villefranche, and round the peninsula of Saint Hospice.

Among the low hills on the W. side of the Paglione and behind Nice the air is said to be milder and less stimulant than in the lower situation about the town and nearer the sea; and a large boarding establishment is now in progress near Cimies, to enable invalids to enjoy its more equable temperature. The climate of some of the towns along the *Riviera* is undoubtedly milder than that of Nice, as is also that round the bay of Villefranche, owing to their more protected situation by headlands from the sharp mistral, and not being at the mouths of valleys descending from the Alps; Mentone and San Remo are peculiarly favoured in this respect.

The advantages of Nice may be summed up in a few words: a delightful winter climate, except during the few days that the mistral blows; a town possessing all the resources of many capitals as to lodgings, masters, recreations, tradespeople, supplies, a Protestant church, English medical men, and abundant society for those inclined to take part in its gaieties; house-rent and provisions, and, we may add, hotel charges, moderate; and, what will be the case as soon as the railway to Toulon is opened, at the easy distance of 3 days' journey from England. The climates of Pisa and Hyères are perhaps more equable, but certainly damper, than that of Nice, and consequently more relaxing, and with fewer social advantages and resources; the same may be said of Cannes, which to other drawbacks unites those of being a dirty town, the country around comparatively bare and arid, and the principal residences for foreigners near a high road, from which there rise clouds of dust in the dry season.

EXCURSIONS IN THE ENVIRONS OF NICE.

One of the most interesting, in an antiquarian point of view, is to Cimies, the Civitas Cemenliensis of the Romans, and once the capital of the Maritime Alps. Cimies is less than 3 m. from Nice, and may be reached in an hour either on foot or in a carriage. The pedestrian can combine in the same excursion other interesting points, as St. Pons, returning by the Fontaine du Temple, the Vallée Obscure, and St. Barthélemy. The road to Cimies branches off from the rt. bank of the Paglione at the N. extremity of the town, and, ascending rapidly between high walls which exclude all view, and bordered by villas, at the end of 2 m. reaches the well-preserved ruins of a small Roman Amphitheatre, called by the peasantry the *Tino delle Fade*, or Bath of the Fairies; it is 210 ft. by 175, and could have contained about 8000 spectators. A short distance further on on the rt. is the Franciscan Convent of Cimies, which is supposed to occupy the site of the ancient *Cemenelum*. The ch., which has been newly repaired, contains a picture by Ludovico Brea, the only artist of any eminence whom Nice has produced. In front of the ch. is a square planted with gigantic ilexes, and an interesting Gothic marble cross of the 15th centy. Annexed to the convent is a burying-ground, a favourite spot of repose for the inhabitants of Nice. Not far from here, in the villa of Count Garin, are some Roman ruins, the supposed remains of a Temple of Apollo.

At St. Pons, about a mile from Cimies, by an abrupt stony path, is an extensi-

convent over the rt. bank of the Paglione. It stands on the site of one where Charlemagne is said to have dwelt on his way to Rome in 777. The place is more celebrated as having witnessed the assembly of the inhabitants of Nice in 1388, when they declared for Amadeus VII. of Savoy.

La Fontaine du Temple, and the Fontaine de Mouraille, both in very picturesque situations, may be reached by the pedestrian from Cimies, or more easily from Nice, combined with a visit to St. Barthélemy and the Vallée Obscure. The Fontaine du Temple derives its name from the ch. of St. Marie du Temple, founded by the Templars. The neighbouring Vallée Obscure is a fine gorge, a Via Mala on a diminutive scale.

CHÂTEAU DE S. ANDRÉ, FALICON AND ITS GROTTO.

This excursion may be performed in a carriage by the road running along the rt. bank of the Paglione as far as St. Pons, and from thence along the same side of the torrent of S. André by the road to Levens. The Castle of S. André is a very picturesque ruin, surrounded by plantations of aloes and cacti: the Grotto is at a short distance beneath the Castle, from which a path leads to it. Crossing the torrent, the pedestrian will soon reach the village of Falicon, from which, following the road to Levens, he will arrive, about a mile further, at the Grotto of Falicon, at the base of Mont Cavo or Mont Chauve, one of the elevated limestone peaks which bound the district of Nice towards the N. The grotto is very picturesque, and lined with stalactites; it is of a circular form: there are some remote smaller chambers which have not yet been explored.

The geologist will find much to interest him in the excursion to S. André and Falicon.

EXCURSION TO VILLEFRANCHE, CAPE ST. HOSPICE, ETC.

This excursion, the most interesting for beautiful scenery, may be easily performed in a day. To the geologist it offers a great variety of objects for observation, as during it all the formations found about Nice may be seen in a limited space. The best mode of proceeding for ladies will be to reach Villefranche (about 2½ m.) in their carriage, and from thence to cross the bay in a boat, or to walk round the head of the bay along the beautiful Corniche road which leads to Beaulieu. There is a good Inn at Villefranche; but we would advise travellers to lunch or dine at old Gianetta's homely Locanda, at the pretty little cove of St. Jean, on the S. side of the peninsula of St. Hospice, where they will find a comfortable meal and a good bed, should they desire to prolong their stay. A new Inn, the Victoria, of greater pretensions, has been lately opened near to St. Jean.

The road to Villefranche leaves the Piazza Vittorio on the rt., and, after passing a kind of faubourg, reaches the bottom of the hill which separates the Bay of Nice from that of Villefranche. An ascent of 450 ft. through olive groves leads to the summit of the low neck or pass called the Col de Villefranche. Instead of proceeding immediately to Villefranche, the lover of the picturesque will do well to take a path on the rt., which in a few minutes will bring him to the Fort of Montalban, on the highest point of the range of Montboron, which separates the two bays, and from which, or a little further S. near some ruined buildings, he will discover the whole coast-line from near S. Remo, on the E., passing by Mentone, Ventimiglia, Monaco, to St. Tropez, on the W. passing by Antibes, the islands of St. Marguerite, the mouth of the Var and its low delta. The Fort de Montalban commands the Bays of Nice and Genoa, and from its height (950 ft.) a magnificent view of the valley of the Paglione, Nice, and of the rich district between it and the Var, covered with one continuous olive forest extending to the foot of the last spurs of the Alps. Returning to the Col of Villefranche, an excellent, well-managed road leads to the pretty town of that name, which from its cleanliness offers a striking contrast with the older parts of Nice, and with the other towns along the sea-coast. Villafranca, or Villefranche, owes its foundation to Charles II. of Anjou, King of Naples and Count of Provence, in the 13th centy. It is near the head of a most lovely land-locked bay, which offers a secure anchorage for vessels of the largest size. Before the Government of Piedmont became possessed of Genoa and its maritime territory, Villefranche was the naval arsenal of the House of Savoy: it contains a good dock, storehouses, &c.; but since then, Genoa having become the great naval station, Villefranche was almost abandoned as a naval post. Commanding the dock is an extensive fortified castle, and a Lazzaretto. Though so close to Nice the climate is much milder, scarcely ever feeling the inconvenience of the cutting mistral, or of the blasts from the snow-capped Alps. Orange, lemon, and carouba trees abound in its territory, and its beautiful gulf is not only rich in fish for the table, but furnishes a very ample field for the student in zoology, from the abundance and variety of its marine mollusca and zoophytes; indeed, Villefranche will always prove the best locality for the naturalist wishing to study the varied animals of the Mediterranean, as the fishermen are the most expert, and furnish the greater proportion of fish for the market at Nice. A very beautiful road leads from Nice to Beaulieu along the N. side of the bay, on a ledge overhanging the Mediterranean, and passing through woods of orange-trees, olives, carouba, pistachio, &c.: at the distance of about a mile it suddenly emerges on the Bay of St. Jean, and a very agreeable path, which strikes off on the rt. and along the top of the cliff, will carry the tourist to the small village of St. Jean, on the E. side of the peninsula of St. Ospizio: or a boat may be hired at Villefranche, which will enable him to cross the bay to Passable, from which a stony path across the isthmus leads to the same village; but, although less fatiguing, this route offers nothing of the beauty or interest of the former. St. Jean consists of an Inn (Gianneta's), where a fair fish dinner may always be had; and while this is preparing, a walk of half an hour will bring the tourist to the S.E. extremity of the peninsula, crowned by a circular fort, at the foot of which is the chapel of the patron saint, a recluse, who died in the tower where he was here immured in the 6th centy. It was on this portion, called *Fraxinet*, that the Saracens established themselves, and were only expelled in the 10th centy. In the bay between Cape St. Ospizio and Beaulieu, opposite to St. Jean, is the Madrague or Tunnyfishery of Nice; it is in activity from February until the autumn, and, being the one most accessible to the passing traveller along the shores of the Mediterranean, will well repay the trouble of a visit; no other exists until we arrive near Genoa. Instead of returning by the same route, let the tourist take the path S. of St. Jean, leading to the lighthouse, along the E. declivity of Mont Canferrat, and along the W. side of the wild bay des Fosses: a different path will take him from the lighthouse to Passable, where boats will generally be found to carry him across the bay to Villefranche in 10 minutes; or he will find a pleasant path round the head of the bay, amidst olive and carouba trees. The little bay of Passable is by some antiquaries supposed to be the Olivula Portus of the Ancient Itineraries.

GEOLOGICAL EXCURSION TO THE PENINSULA OF ST. HOSPICE, &c.

However foreign to the object of this work to enter into details on dry scientific subjects, as many of our countrymen during their sojourn at Nice may be disposed to turn their attention to the interesting geological features of the country around, no part of it is better calculated to show the succession of the formations which enter into its structure than the environs of Villefranche and the Peninsula of St. Hospice. "The tourist, on leaving the Faubourg de Villefranche, at Nice, begins to ascend the chain of Montboron, which is composed of highly inclined strata of limestone of the oolitic series, probably of the age of our great oolite of the West of England, and of the coral rag. The Château or Fort of Montalbano is perched on strata changed into dolomite, a metamorphism very common in the environs of Nice, the effect probably of the porphyritic eruptions of the chain of Estrelles. If the geologist, before arriving at the Col, at a small oratory or chapel, will turn off to the l., the path will lead him to a ravine excavated in the gypsum, which is evidently a part of the oolitic series, although its origin as a metamorphic rock (produced by the action of sulphureous emanations on the limestone) is probably posterior to the deposit of the cretaceous formation, and even of the eocene beds. At the Col de Villefranche the green beds of the cretaceous rock lie on the dolomite. On arriving near Villefranche, let the pedestrian take the road on the l. to Beaulieu, and, rounding the N. side of the bay, he will soon find himself on the same rocks of the cretaceous system as he had seen at the Col de Villefranche; before arriving at the lowest part of the neck of land which separates the two bays, these latter are covered by a quaternary deposit containing shells still living in the Mediterranean, and which continues to the escarpment of the bay of Beaulieu, where it attains an elevation of 50 ft. above the level of the sea. Having reached this point, let him descend the escarpment to the thick bed of seaweed which covers this part of the beach, and he will find under the quaternary deposit a cliff of inclined strata of sandy marls abounding in *Foraminiferæ*, and farther S. of *nummulites* and other well-characterised fossils of the Eocene period; following the sea-beach at the foot of the escarpment, he will be able to make a large collection of fossils. This Eocenic deposit, here very limited in extent, lies on the cretaceous rocks in a kind of *gorge*, the latter reappearing in the Baie des Fourmis, where it contains numerous fossils, amongst others the Exogyra Haliotidea in great abundance; and in the ledge of inclined beds which form the N. side of the little Bay of St. Jean, millions of that most characteristic shell of the upper chalk, the Gryphæa columba, with Spatangi, &c. These cretaceous beds form the whole of the small peninsula of St. Hospice, and may be seen resting on the oolitic ones behind the village of St. Jean. From the latter place let the geologist take the path leading to the *Baie des Fosses*, and following its W. side he will discover successively the lower beds of the Neocomian series, with Nautilus pseudo-elegans, Belemnites dilatatus, Ammonites intermedius, &c.; and beneath a compact limestone, which probably represents our English Portland beds, resting on the coral rag full of madrepores, and which forms the whole southern portion of the peninsula on which the lighthouse stands, the Mont Canferrat as far as the small Bay of Passable, the bareness and aridity of which contrast so singularly with the richly wooded region situated upon the cretaceous and tertiary rocks."

GEOLOGICAL EXCURSION TO LA TRINITÉ, DRAP, AND PALLAREA.

"This excursion may be made easily in a carriage, as the principal points of interest lie close to the high post-road leading from Nice to Turin. Following the l. bank of the Paglione, the road runs along the base of the Mont Vinnigrier, and Mont Gros, formed of Jurassic limestones, as far as the chapel of Notre Dame du Bon Voyage, where the Paglione

Route 13.—*Nice to Genoa.*

bends to the N.E., and from which to the village of La Trinité we pass over the cretaceous system. This village is at the W. extremity of a kind of island of Pleoconic marls, extending for a short distance on either side of the torrent of the Magnan, and offers perhaps the best point in the environs of Nice for studying this modern marine deposit. After leaving La Trinité, the road continues for about 2 m. farther to the village of Drap, still on the cretaceous or Neocomian beds, which about the latter village contain a great variety of our English greensand fossils. Continuing along the banks of the Paglione, we at length reach Pallarea, a short distance on the rt., in the environs of which abound fossils of the Eocene period, of which nearly 400 species have been collected, and described in Signor Bellardi's work on the 'Fossils of Nice.'"

ROUTE FROM NICE TO GENOA.

184 kil. = 120 miles.

KIL.		KIL.	
18	Turbia.	108	Alassio.
31	Mentone.	115	Albenga.
42	Ventimiglia.	134	Finale.
59	S. Remo.	159	Savona.
71	S. Stefano.	184	Voltri.
86	Oneglia.	194	Genoa by Rlway.

There are several modes of performing this journey: with post-horses it may be done in 2 days, but more comfortably in 3; starting not very early, Mentone, where there are good inns, may be reached the first night, Savona the second, and Genoa early on the third. Vetturini generally employ 3½ days, sleeping at Mentone, Oneglia, and Savona; this is by far the most convenient way for families, the charge for a carriage with 4 horses being from 15 to 16 napoleons. 2 good diligences start daily, morning and evening, performing the journey in 26 hours. Steamers sail twice a week from Nice; but as they are small, performing the voyage by night, and seldom employing less than 15 hours, and with fares nearly as high as by the diligences, the former mode of conveyance is infinitely preferable for those not pressed for time.

Leaving Nice by the Piazza Vittorio and the fine alley of plane-trees which leads also to the road of the Col di Tenda and Turin, the road soon commences to rise, and for the next 10 miles is one continuous ascent: this route, which has replaced the once dangerous Corniche, was commenced by the French, who, before the fall of Napoleon, carried it nearly to Ventimiglia, from which it has been completed by the Sardinian government to Genoa, under circumstances of great engineering difficulties. The views during the ascent to Turbia are very fine, especially over the subjacent lovely bays of Villefranche, St. Jean, Beaulieu, and the village, with its castle on a high peak, of Esa. The road attains its greatest elevation (2100 ft.) 2 m. before reaching Turbia: soon after passing a column on the road-side, called the *Colonna del Rè*, from its having been erected to commemorate the visit of one of the late kings of Sardinia, a road turns off on the L leading to the sanctuary of La Madonna del Laghetto, in a romantic valley at the foot of Monte Sembola, and through which the branch of the Via Aurelia passed between Turbia and Cimies: several remains of Roman antiquities have been discovered hereabouts; the most remarkable is the Milliarium, now preserved in the library at Nice, marking the DCV mile. A very gradual descent brings us to

18 kil. *Turbia*, a village at an ele-

vation of 1900 feet above the sea, upon a col or saddleback between two limestone peaks. Turbìa, a corruption of Trophæa, is celebrated for the Trophæa Augusti, which stands close to and S. of the village; and was probably a Roman station on the branch of the Via Aurelia called *Julia*, from having been continued from Tuscany to Arles by Augustus. The Trophæa Augusti was erected by Augustus, and may be considered as marking the limit between Liguria and Gaul; it is now a mass of ruins: the mediæval tower by which it is surmounted forms a remarkable object in the landscape. Of the Roman construction only the basement remains, which offers some fine blocks of quadrilateral masonry, and which is supposed to have been surmounted by successive stories, tapering to a point, decorated with sculptures and statues like some of the sepulchral monuments on the Via Appia. On this basement was an inscription commemorating the victories of Augustus over the Alpine tribes, of which only some detached fragments have been discovered: one contains the letters RVM-PILI, forming part of the name of one of the vanquished tribes (Trumpili), which is recorded in Pliny's description. It is not known at what period the Gothic tower which surmounts the Trophæa Augusti was erected, but it long served as a mountain fastness, and was reduced to its present dilapidated state in the 17th century by the Maréchal de Villars, who blew it up, thus destroying what man and 17 centuries had spared, at the instigation of Louis XIV.'s ally, the Prince of Monaco. In some of the itineraries Turbìa is assigned as the limit or boundary between Italy and Gaul, and is certainly naturally so, being placed on the pass over the most inaccessible spur of the Maritime Alps, which descends to the shores of the Mediterranean, and round the base of which neither the ancient nor modern rulers of Italy have succeeded in carrying a line of communi-

cation. Leaving Turbìa the road constantly descends. Soon after emerging from the village a splendid view, embracing Monaco, Mentone, and the blue Mediterranean, opens, and a road branches off to the former town, but with so rapid a descent as to be only suited for mules or pedestrians, the traveller who may wish to reach Monaco by carriage being obliged to go round by Mentone.

Monaco, the capital of the smallest European monarchy, is now reduced to the town itself and to a very small territory near the promontory on which it stands: seen from the N. it presents a good appearance, surrounded by fortifications, and flanked with batteries commanding its little bay; indeed the view as you look down upon the town, with its fortifications, towers, and quiet port, is peculiarly beautiful. Monaco contains a population of about 1500 souls, and is the only part of its prince's dominions over which he still retains any authority: his flag, a shield, *en échiquier*, supported by two monks, in allusion to the name of Monaco (Monachus), may be seen floating over its half-ruined castle. The town is garrisoned by French soldiers.

The principality of Monaco embraced the towns and territory of Mentone and Roccabruna: its history is obscure; it seems, however, to have been one of those allodial domains which escaped feudalization in the middle ages, and over which the Emperor had no authority; we find one Carlo Grimaldi in possession of this little sovereignty in the middle of the 14th century, but this seems only to have been an Imperial restitution, for the dominion appears to have been granted as early as the 10th century to one of his ancestors by the Emperor Othò, for the part he took in the expulsion of the Saracens from Provence and this part of Liguria. The reigning family became extinct in the male line in 1731, in the person of Antonio Grimaldi, whose only daughter married into the French family of Thorigny, and from whom the present Prince of Monaco, Charles Honoré, of the Matignon family, and who has assumed the name and arms of the Grimaldis, is descended. Considerable discussion has arisen as to his being really the legitimate heir: by the exertions, however, of Prince Talleyrand his title was acknowledged at the Congress of Vienna, in spite of the protests of the then existing Grimaldis, one of the most ancient families of Genoa, also now extinct in the male line, and the principality placed under the protection of the King of Sardinia, as suzerain. In 1848 the inhabitants of Mentone and Roccabruna, who had much to complain of the exactions and misgovernment of this petty sovereign, annexed themselves to the Sardinian monarchy, which was subsequently confirmed by a decree of King Charles Albert, and by placing Piedmontese garrisons at Mentone and Monaco. An attempt of the late prince to re-establish his authority at Mentone, in 1854, was met by his expulsion. France has stepped into Sardinia's shoes as regards the principality, and this petty sovereign is allowed to exercise a certain authority at Monaco alone.

The town of Monaco covers a considerable extent of ground. In the centre is a large *place d'armes* and the Prince's palace. The place is of remote antiquity, its foundation being attributed by some writers to the Greeks, even to Hercules, who undertook several expeditions to the coasts of Liguria; it is frequently alluded to as the Monœci Portus, and is noticed in the Antonine Itinerary, under the name of Portus Herculis Monœci. Lucan gives an accurate description of its situation:—

Quaque sub Herculeo sacratus nomine Portus
Urget rupe cava pelagus; non Corus in
illum
Jus habet aut Zephyrus; solus sua littora
turbat
Circius, et tuta prohibet statione Monœci.

Monaco was fortified by Louis XIV. for his protégé, the duke; the works are now falling into ruin.

A continuous descent of 8 miles leads from Turbia to Mentone; about 3 m. from the former we pass on the l. the village of Roccabruna, one of the former possessions of the Prince of Monaco, perched upon a mass of tertiary breccia, of which two large pyramids are seen standing amongst the houses of the village; there are remains of an old castle and of some mediæval towers and walls.

All this part of the country is highly romantic; every inch of ground capable of cultivation is attended to; gigantic olives rise to a considerable height on the mountain sides, and Mentone is approached by a handsome alley of plane-trees, on the l. of which, before entering the town, one of the ducal residences is passed.

13 kil. *Mentone.* (*Inns:* Hôtel Victoria, a new and excellent hotel, on entering the town from Nice; the Hôtel de Turin, much improved, with a fine view over the sea; the Pension Anglaise, kept by Clerici, is well spoken of; the Hôtel de Londres, newly opened by Boggi.) Mentone will be found the best resting-place for the first night on leaving Nice. This little city, of 6000 Inhab., is situated in a fertile district, and carries on a large trade in oil, oranges, lemons, the produce of its territory. It has a clean, neat appearance, and a look of more prosperity and comfort than most of the towns of the Riviera. French is generally spoken here, and the traveller, on arriving from the side of Genoa, will see the sign-boards for the first time in that language. On the hill above are the remains of an old castle and walls; at a short distance, under the Cape Martino, is its little port, resorted to by the coasters employed in carrying off its produce. The climate of Mentone is one of the mildest on the Ligurian seabord, and perhaps better calculated for invalids than Nice, as the N. wind, or mistral, is seldom felt. It is surrounded by gardens of lemon and olive-trees, the former blossoming during the greater part of the winter. Of late Men-

tone has become a favourite residence for invalids, and numerous villas in the vicinity and houses in the town have been fitted up for their accommodation. Hitherto it has had the additional advantage of being more economical than Nice. The service of the Church of England is performed in a house near the Hôtel Victoria on Sundays and Wednesdays, by the resident clergyman, the Rev. Mr. Morgan. Dr. Bottini is recommended as a good physician here. Dr. Berryer, son of the celebrated French Advocate, practices homœopathy. A good road (5 m.) leads from Mentone to Monaco, and forms a very agreeable drive. Mentone being a part of the territory lately ceded by Sardinia to France, it is now the frontier custom-house station, where luggage is examined on coming from Genoa.

Soon after leaving Mentone we enter the Sardinian territory; the road passes near to St. Louis; the Sardinian Custom-house is in the valley of Garavan, near the latter place; a steep ascent leading from the plain to

11 kil. *Ventimiglia* (*Inn :* the Croce di Malta, an indifferent Italian locanda), the ancient Albium Intermelium, and the capital of the Intermelians, a Ligurian tribe. From its position on the brow of a hill, commanding the road along the sea-coast, Ventimiglia was an important military position, and its possession much contested in the middle ages by the Genoese, the Counts of Provence, and the Dukes of Savoy. Before the French Revolution it formed the frontier town of Piedmont on the side of Genoa. It is an episcopal see, and boasts of having had S. Barnabas for its first bishop. The Cathedral has been much modernized in the interior; the principal entrance and some parts inside present good specimens of the Gothic peculiar to the churches of the Riviera. In the ch. of S. Michel are two Roman milestones found here, one bearing the number DXC., and inscriptions of Augustus and Antoninus Pius. Above the town is a castle strongly fortified, which, with the approaches on the eastern side, have been recently repaired and greatly strengthened, constituting the principal stronghold between Nice and Genoa. Several Roman inscriptions found here are built into the walls of the cathedral and of other public edifices. A very steep and dangerous descent from the square before the cathedral leads to the gate on the side of Genoa, a short way beyond which the river Roya is crossed on a long bridge, the arches of which having been frequently carried away have been replaced by wooden ones. A sandy flat is now traversed, in which runs the river Nervia, over which a new elegant stone bridge of 3 arches has been lately built, approached by an elevated causeway. N. of Ventimiglia is the Monte Appio, one of the principal spurs of the Maritime Alps. Upon one of its heights stands a castle consisting of 2 towers, supposed to be of Roman construction. At 5 m. from the road, up the valley of the Nervia, is the castle of Dolce Acqua, a fine feudal relic ; and on one of the heights above the same valley may be seen the village of *Perinaldo*, the birthplace of the great astronomer, Gian Domenico Cassini, and of Moualdi, his nephew, also eminent in the same branch of science. A flat sandy plain, formed by the detritus of the neighbouring sandstone (tertiary) hills which extend from Ventimiglia, is followed nearly as far as Bordighera. Here the date-palm is extensively cultivated, the nature of the soil being particularly suited for that semi-tropical plant. These trees give an oriental aspect to the country around : they form groups of quite a tropical character, and most of them will be seen bound up or swathed at their summits in order to exclude the light, so as to prevent their leaves becoming green, as this palm is cultivated here exclusively for its leaves, used in the ceremonies of the Church on the Sunday before Easter, hence denominated Palm Sunday. They are sent in

large quantities every year to Rome, and the inhabitants of Bordighera possess the privilege of furnishing them to the Chapter of St. Peter's, where they are distributed in such large numbers by the Pope. This exclusive right is said to have been accorded by Sixtus V. to reward the ingenious suggestion of a sailor from this place, during the erection of the great obelisk of the Vatican, who, seeing all efforts useless to raise the column when it had reached a certain height, suddenly called out to wet the cables, by which the desired effect, well known to all seafaring people, was instantly procured, of shortening them. Bordighera is situated on the declivity of the range terminating in the promontory of Capo di S. Ampoglio. It once constituted, with the adjoining districts of San Biagio, Soldano, Vallebona, and Sasso, a republic independent in some degree of Genoa, but under its protection. A delightful drive along the coast leads to

17 kil. *St. Remo* (*Inn:* La Palma, in the Lower Town, improved), a large and flourishing town of 11,000 Inhab., and chief place of the province. It is beautifully situated on a declivity descending to the sea-shore, covered by a thick wood of olive-trees. Except the post-road, at the bottom of the town, the streets are narrow, tortuous, and steep. The principal church is very ancient, and of the ordinary Gothic style of the country. St. Remo is perhaps the mildest situation on all the Riviera. Here palms, lemon and orange trees grow with the greatest luxuriance; and the fruit of the date-palm almost attains maturity. On the outskirts of the town are several gardens planted with palms, and during the summer season the traveller will not fail to remark the odoriferous effect of the orange and jessamine flowers as he passes through. There is no part of the Riviera to which Ariosto's description of the voyage of the traitor Gan di Maganza from Marseilles can better apply (*Giunta all' Orlando Furioso,* canto 1, st. 71) :—

"Poiche licenza dal Rè tolto avea,
  Uscì del porto, e dei sicuri stagni.
Restare addietro, anzi fuggir parea,
  Il lito, ed occultar tutti i vivagni.
Indi l' Alpe a sinistra apparea lunge,
  Ch' Italia in van da' Barbari disgiunge.

72.

"Indi i monti Ligustici, e Riviera,
  Che con aranci, e sempre verdi mirti,
Quando avendo perpetua primavera,
  Sparge per l' aria i bene olenti spirti.

73.

. . . . .
"Dove un miglio discosto da l' arena
  D' antiche palme era una selva amena:

74.

"Che per mezzo da un' acqua era partita
  Di chiaro flumicel, fresco e giocondo,
Che l' una e l' altra proda avea florita,
  Dei più soavi odor che siano al mondo,
Era di là dal bosco una salita,
  D' un picciol monticel quasi rotondo,
Sì facile a montar, che prima il piede
  D' aver salito, che salir si vede."

An excursion may be made, on leaving S. Remo, to the ch. of La Madonna della Guardia on the Capo Verde, from which there is a magnificent panoramic view of the coast. The high-road continues along the beach through Arma, with an old square castle before entering the village, to Riva, 2 m. before reaching which the dangerous torrent of la Taggia is crossed by a handsome new bridge. The village of Taggia is seen on a height to the l. higher up the valley, to

12 kil. *San Stefano al Mare*, a fishing-village lying along the beach, on which a heavy surf generally breaks. Looking back towards Capo Verde the view is very pleasing.

San Lorenzo, a small town with its ch. on a low point, backed by rounded hills, covered with olive-trees. Vines are grown in the plain, which are said to produce a sweet wine something like Cyprus, and nearly equal to it. A gradual ascent leads from the sea-shore up the promontory, on which stands

Porto Maurizio. (*Inn:* Hôtel du Commerce, tolerable.) The town is upon a hill on the rt., the post-road running below over a kind of neck of land, the lowest part of the promontory that separates the bays of Oneglia and S. Stefano. P. Maurizio is one of the most characteristic towns of the

Riviera, standing on a high promontory projecting boldly into the sea, and overlooking its little tranquil port, generally crowded with the picturesque coasting-vessels of the Mediterranean. In the centre is a lofty ch. painted in brilliant colours, whilst towards the N. noble mountains form the background. The neighbourhood of Porto Maurizio produces much oil, and a considerable trade in this and in other agricultural produce is carried on from it. 2 m. farther we arrive at

15 kil. *Oneglia*. (*Inn:* Hôtel Victoria; clean and comfortable.) Oneglia is a good halting-place for the night; it is about half way between Genoa and Nice. The town was bombarded and burnt by the French under Admiral Truguet in 1792. Andrea Doria, the great Genoese admiral, was born here in 1468. Here, in the autumn, the fronts of the houses are often seen hung with the inflated pigs' skins in which the wine is kept. A fine suspension-bridge, with the piers which support the chains of white marble, has been thrown across the Impero torrent, and forms a noble addition to the approach to the town. A toll of 2½ frs. is paid on crossing it. (For the roads from Oneglia to Turin see Rtes. 9 and 10.)

From Oneglia the road becomes very beautiful; far and near the landscape is dotted with bright towns and villages. In one part you descend into the valley of Diano, celebrated for its growth both of olives and vines.

Diano Marina, as its name imports, upon the shore, and through which the road passes. *Diana Calderina* and *Diano Castello* are upon the hills on the l.

Cervo.

Cross the *Merula*, a sluggish stream, which often swamps and floods the neighbouring valley. The country is unhealthy, and consequently not well peopled. About a mile onward is the haunted *Castle of Andora*, a ruin. Here, it is said, a papal Nuncio was murdered; and the curse pronounced in consequence is the cause of the decay of the adjoining territory.

2 m. beyond the mouth of the Merula the *Capo delle Mele* advances boldly into the sea. This cape divides the Riviera di Ponente into two nearly equal parts. The aspect of the coast changes. There is a perceptible difference in the quality of the crops, particularly of the olive, of which the oil is of an inferior quality.

From the *Capo delle Mele* to the *Capo di Santa Croce* the coast encircles a beautiful bay, on the shores of which are the towns of

Laigueglia and

22 kil. *Alassio*. (An extra horse from Oneglia to Alassio and *vice versâ* all the year. *Inns:* Hôtel de la belle Italic, clean and comfortable — 1854; Albergo Reale; Albergo della Posta.) The road runs through both of these towns. Both are places of much commercial activity. The inhabitants are excellent sailors. Alassio has 6500 Inhab. It is said to derive its name from Alassia, a daughter of the Emperor Otho the Great, who fled to the forests in this part of the Riviera with her betrothed Aleramo, where they lived after the fashion of Lord Richard and Alice Brand.

On rounding Cape Santa Croce we come in sight of the island of *Gallinaria*. The name of this island is said by Varro and Columella to have arisen from its containing a particular species of the fowls now called domestic, or, according to another explanation mentioned by the first of these writers, from fowls having been left here by some navigators, which so multiplied as to overrun the island.

Enter the beautiful valley of *Albenga*, splendid in its varied vegetation and rich cultivation. It is watered by the river *Centa*, one of the few streams of the Riviera which are perennial. This valley contains many pleasant villages. In one, *Lusignano*, Madame de Genlis lived some time, and she considered the valley as a perfect Arcadia. The vines are often allowed to hang in festoons from the trees, a practice which, whenever it prevails, improves the landscape at the expense of the liquor. The female peasantry arrange their hair with much taste, usually adding small bunches of natural flowers.

Lusignano is 2 m. from *San Fedele*, which possesses a ruined feudal castle. So does *Villanuova*, situated at the confluence of the torrents by which the Centa is formed.

After passing over a marshy plain, frequently overflowed by the Lerone, one of these torrents, you reach

Garlenda. The church of this sequestered spot contains some good paintings. The martyrdom of St. Erasmus (*N. Poussin*) is a fine composition, though the subject is so horrible as to render it almost disgusting. The Virgin and Child, between St. Benedict and St. Maur (*Domenichino*), painted with great delicacy and sweetness. It was intended to remove this painting to Paris. More recently, the curate, and what we should call the vestry, were in treaty to dispose of it for 20,000 francs, with which they intended to purchase an organ, and otherwise to embellish the church, but the peasantry rose *en masse* and prevented the completion of the bargain. After this excursion out of the main road, we must return to

7 kil. *Albenga* (Inns: Albergo della Posta, said to be lately improved; Albergo d'Italia, tolerable, but rather dirty), a city, the "capoluogo" of the province, and containing nearly 5000 Inhab. Both within and without, the aspect of this ancient metropolis of a republic which was of sufficient importance to be courted as an ally by Carthage is very striking. Three very lofty towers, besides many smaller structures of the same nature, frown over its narrow streets in all the sternness of the feudal ages. Of these, the loftiest is that called the *Torre del Marchese Malespina*, in front of which, at the basement, are three fine statues of lions couchant. The second is the *Torre dei Guelfi*. The third is annexed to the Casa del Commune. These towers derive much of their effect from their bold machicolations and battlements, the peculiar features of Italian castellated architecture, and of which these are the first examples which the traveller will see on this road. They have the aspect of castles of romance; and here Madame de Genlis has localized her story of the Duchess of Cerifalco, immured nine long years in a dungeon by her barbarous husband.

The cathedral is an ancient Gothic building: over the doorways are some bas-reliefs in a singular style, exhibiting runic knots and imagery not unlike what are found on the runic pillars of Penrith or Bewcastle. The interior is modernised. The baptistery is an octangular building, supported within by Corinthian pillars, and supposed to have been a heathen temple. It contains early Christian mosaics, with a curious recessed monument enclosing a sarcophagus. Many unquestionable Roman antiquities, however, have been discovered in and about Albenga; and the "*Ponte Lungo*," at the distance of about a quarter of a mile, is of Roman construction, at least in the piers. It was built by the Emperor Honorius. Albenga is one of the unhealthy spots of the Riviera. The frequent inundations of the Centa rendered the ground about it marshy; and the insalubrity was increased by the numerous flax-steeping grounds. "Hai faccia di Albenga," *You have an Albenga face*, is a proverbial expression, addressed to those who look out of sorts, or out of condition. This insalubrity has, however, recently been diminished by draining; and the steeping-grounds are now confined to the vicinity of the sea, and are at some distance from the town.

Albenga was occupied by the French in 1794, and became the centre of their military operations; and in 1796 Napoleon made it his head-quarters. During this period the adjoining country suffered greatly from the ravages of the contending armies, and also from epidemic diseases. In 1797 it formed a part of the Ligurian republic, an incorporation which terminated its political existence; for, although previously subjected to the supremacy of Genoa, Albenga had continued to be governed by its own magistrates and laws.

The road now runs close upon the shore, passing, after 5 m., through *Ceriale*, a place abounding in pleasant gardens. 1 m. farther is *Borghetto di Santo Spirito*, above which lies *Toirano*. The cave of Sta. Lucia in the adjoining hill is filled with stalactites, and beautiful of its kind; one of its recesses is fitted up as a chapel.

Loano, a small city, a title claimed for it by the inhabitants. It was the principal fief of Luigi Fieschi, so celebrated for his unfortunate conspiracy. Loano was the scene of the first victory of the French Republicans in Italy, on the 24th Nov. 1795, when Scherer and Massena defeated the Austrians with great loss.

Pietra, a small town, the principal church of which contains some curious wood carvings. (*Inn:* H. d'Italie.)

A new road has been made close to the sea, to avoid going over the mountains; a tunnel leads to Finale. There is a fine view of Genoa before reaching Finale. A toll of 2¼ francs is paid at the barrier before entering on this new piece of road.

Pass the Headland or Capo di Capra zoppa. The road is carried up a causeway to the middle of the rock, through which a tunnel has been cut. The rock here is constantly disintegrating and falling down upon the shore.

19 kil. *Finale Marina*, on the sea-coast (to distinguish it from Finale Borgo, situated higher up the valley in the interior). (*Inns:* Hôtel de Londres; Hôtel de la Chine, new and good, but not cheap.) Finale was the capital of a marquisate, which anciently belonged to the family of del Caretto. Towards the end of the 15th centy. the town, passing to the kings of Spain, was strongly fortified by them. The ruins of the numerous forts which they built are still seen upon the adjoining heights: they were mostly dismantled by the Genoese when, after a series of contests, they acquired the marquisate, by purchase in 1713, from the Emperor Charles VI.; but their title was not considered as established until it was confirmed by Maria Theresa in 1743. Bernini was the architect of the principal church, a collegiate foundation, dedicated to St. John the Baptist. On the heights above is the *Castello Gavone*, a picturesque ruin. One of the towers is fronted with stone cut in facettes, like Tantallon in Scotland.

Varigotti, an inconsiderable village; soon after leaving which, the road passes through the fine tunnel or gallery of the *Capo di Noli*, on emerging from which a most lovely prospect opens.

Noli, anciently an episcopal city, and picturesque from its walls and towers, terminated by the castle, commanding the town. Noli, like Albenga, was a republic, and preserved its own government under the Genoese, until both were equally devoured by their Gallic invaders.

The rocks bordering the road are here lofty and beautiful, overhanging the path; the splendid aloes rising in the rifts, and flourishing in gigantic vigour. A view of Genoa is gained after you have passed the gallery of Noli, when you discover the lofty lighthouse, the long line of the Mole, and the fortifications which crown the hills behind.

Spotorno, opposite to which is a small island bearing the name of Isola dei Bergeggi, now uninhabited, but upon which are the ruins of an abbey and a castle.

Pass *Bergeggi*. At the foot of the cliff is a stalactitical cavern, praised by the Genoese in prose and verse. From Bergeggi the road runs along the seashore under Capo di Vado, on the top of which is a ruined fort.

Vado, anciently the seat of a bishop, now a small village; it has been proposed to form a great maritime arsenal under the Cape. From Vado the road continues near the sea, passing through the villages of *Zinola* and *I Fornacci.*

25 kil. *Savona.* (*Inns:* Grand Hôtel Royal, situated near the harbour; clean; baths on the premises. Hôtel Suisse, near the theatre and the seaside; clean and good. An omnibus runs daily to Genoa, and at times a small steamer, which performs the voyage in about 3 hours. For the roads from Savona to Turin, see Rtes. 11 and 12.)—A flourishing city, the third in importance on the Riviera, Genoa being the first, and Nice the second. The town exhibits much appearance of activity and prosperity. Large quantities of pottery are made here. It is of high antiquity; here Mago, the Carthaginian, deposited his spoils after the capture of Genoa. The acropolis of the Ligurian city is thought to have been the site of the fort on the "rupe di San' Giorgio." Savona is close upon the sea; but its once ample port was spoiled by the Genoese in 1528. They blocked it up by sinking hulks filled with stones, and the deposit of sand and silt did the rest; and though it has been partly cleared and repaired, it cannot admit vessels of more than 200 tons.

The *Cathedral* was built in 1604, an older and more curious structure having been demolished to make way for the fortifications. This former cathedral had been enriched by the munificence of Pope Julius II. (Giulio della Rovere), who, born at Albisola close by, was bishop of this see at the time of his election to the papal dignity. Some of the ornaments of the present cathedral are his gifts, having been saved from the demolished structure; as, for example, the fine wood-work of the choir. It contains some good paintings. A Virgin and Child, by *Lodovico Brea*; the Annunciation and Presentation, by *Albani*; the Scourging of our Lord, by *L. Cambiasi*; La Madonna della Colonna, by *Robertelli.* The last is a fresco, and so called because it was painted on a pillar in the ancient Duomo, from which it was ingeniously detached, and placed in its present situation. In the chapel of the Madonna is a large painting in seven compartments, the Virgin and several Saints in a richly-sculptured framework, representing the front of a church, and exhibiting the allusive arms of the house of Rovere,—an oak-tree, surmounted with the cardinal's hat. It was the gift of Pope Julius; and as almost every picture in Italy has its story, it is said with respect to this, that Julius, who, when Pope, threatened Michael Angelo with a halter, or something as bad, because he did not paint fast enough, employed seven painters upon this work, in order to get it soon out of hand. The best compartment is the St. John by *Lodovico Brea.* There is a curious painted and gilt bas-relief of the Assumption of the Virgin in the N. transept, brought from the old cathedral. Near the cathedral stands the Sistine Chapel, founded by Sixtus IV. (1471-1484), also of the family of La Rovere, and uncle of Julius II., as a place of sepulture for his ancestors. His father was, however, but a poor fisherman, though descended from a noble family.

Savona is the birthplace of *Chiabrera*, one of the best poets of the 17th century. He was highly successful as a lyric poet: "and though the Grecian robe is never cast away, he imitated Anacreon with as much skill as Pindar." Chiabrera also wrote much poetry of a devotional character; and over his tomb in the church of San' Giacomo he caused this impressive inscription to be engraved:—

"Amico, Io, vivendo, cercava conforto
Nel Monte Parnasso:
Tu, meglio consigliato, cercalo
Nel Calvario."

In the Dominican church is a painting attributed to *Albert Durer.* The Nativity, by *Antonio Semini.* Lanzi says of this picture that it is sufficient to see it to be convinced that Semini rivals not only Perugino, but Raphael himself. In the cloister of this church is a bust to the memory of Chiabrera, beneath which is an inscription written by Pope Urban VIII. The villa in which Chiabrera lived is near the ch. of *San' Giacomo*, his burial-place. The house in which he was born is in the town, with the significant motto which he chose, "*Nihil ex omni parte beatum.*" And the newly-erected theatre is dedicated to him.

One of the towers of the port is decorated by a colossal statue of the Virgin, beneath which, in large characters, is engraved the following inscription, which may (after a sort) be read either in Latin or Italian.

"In mare irato, in subita procella,
Invoco te, nostra benigna stella."

This conceit has been attributed to Chiabrera; but there is not the slightest authority for supposing him to be its author. It is part of a popular hymn sung by the sailors and fishermen on this coast.

The sanctuary of *Nostra Signora di Misericordia*, situated about 5 miles from Savona, is a celebrated place of pilgrimage, and well worthy of a visit, though the road is only practicable for light carriages. It is embosomed in the mountains. The church is built over the spot where a miraculous appearance of the Madonna is said to have taken place in 1536; and, though of such recent origin, the devotion of the Riviera so increased its treasures, that they were thought only second to those of Loretto. The greater part of these disappeared under the French; but the sanctuary has been somewhat replenished, particularly by a crown of silver studded with gems, placed on the head of the image by Pope Pius VII. Marino and Chiabrera in poetry, and *Bernardo Castello* in painting, vied with each other in exercising their talents in honour of this sanctuary. The church is filled with paintings by Castello, containing nearly the whole life, legendary as well as scriptural, of the Virgin. They are much faded. Castello was the intimate friend of Tasso; and one of the most prized editions of the Gerusalemme is adorned with engravings, partly executed by Agostino Caracci from his designs. Other objects in this church are a Presentation of the Virgin by *Domenichino;* and an alto-rilievo of St. Elizabeth and the Virgin by *Bernini*. The valley of the sanctuary is properly called the Valley of San' Bernardo. In the small chapel of the village is a very curious and well-preserved painting of an early date (1345), containing 14 figures upon a gold ground.

Leaving Savona for Genoa, the road runs more inland as far as Albissola; in several parts tunnelled through the rock where the last abutments of the hills come down into the sea, and in some parts supported by terraces. Along this part of the Riviera may be seen villas, sometimes high above the road, sometimes on its level, with their gardens gay with bowers, terraces, trellis walks, and the brightest profusion of trees, and shrubs, and flowers. These gardens are generally in the old-fashioned, regular style, and are mostly entered by a lofty gate, once surmounted by armorial bearings. Almost all the buildings were originally painted on the outside, but these paintings are all more or less washed off, or faded, by exposure to the rain and sun. The traveller will have seen the first specimens at Nice of this kind of decoration.

Albissola Marina, at the opening of a pleasant valley, stretches along the shore. The town of Albissola Superiore, 1 m. on l., contains a fine palace of the Della Rovere family, not the building in which Pope Julius was born, though he was a native of the town. In the principal church, the Madonna della Concordia, are some good paintings by *Fiasella* and *Ansaldo*.

Celle. In the church of St. Michael is a picture of the Archangel by *Pierino del Vaga*, painted by him in fulfilment of a vow made during a storm. Following the coast-line, we reach

Varazze, or *Voragine*, a large town of importance, stretching along the coast for more than a mile. Here are built a large proportion of the mercantile marine of Genoa, the slips for which along the beach form a busy and interesting scene. It is the birthplace of Jacopo di Voragine, the author or compiler of the well-known

Golden Legend, a collection of monkish legends of saints, miracles, and adventures of the devil, which was most popular in the 13th, 14th, and 15th centuries. It has the fame of being the chief book which transformed Loyola from a soldier to a religious enthusiast. In 1292 its author became Archbishop of Genoa, where he excelled in charity and benevolence, and was most useful in putting down the factions by which the city was disturbed. In the hills above Voragine is a very singular monastery, most appropriately called "Il Deserto." It was founded by a noble lady of the family of Balbo Pallavicini. According to fame, she was exceedingly beautiful, and is said to be somewhat profanely represented in the character of the Madonna, though in the Genoese dress of the 16th cent., in an exquisite altar-piece by *Fiasella*.

Pass the cape or headland of

Cogoletto. Before entering this town is an extensive foundry of shot and shells. Cogoletto is by tradition the birthplace of Columbus; and if faith is to be given to inscriptions, we may see the house in which he was born. On the other hand, the house of his father Domenico can be proved by title-deeds to have been situated in the suburbs of Genoa, and he himself states that he was born in Genoa, an expression which, however, was quite compatible with his being born within the territory. The family can be traced in Savona, Oneglia, and all about the neighbourhood; and the fact of his being a Ligurian is unquestionable.

The country through which the road passes between Cogoletto and Arenzana offers the most picturesque and varied scenery, and the most luxurious richness of vegetation, fine woods of pinasters and evergreen oaks, with an undergrowth of myrtles and various kinds of the most beautiful heaths, astragals, and lilies rearing their tall stems and snow-white blossoms among the shrubs. The view on descending towards Arenzana is enchanting.

20 kil. *Arenzana*, a pleasant village.

N. Italy—1860.

Voltri, a flourishing town of 8000 Inhab., with churches richly adorned. Much paper is manufactured in this town and its neighbourhood. Anciently the Genoese supplied most parts of Europe with paper, and a considerable quantity is still exported to S. America. It is said to have the property of resisting the worm better than any other, a quality supposed to be derived from the sulphureous impregnation of the water with which it is made. This is particularly the case with the mills in the valley of *the Leira*, about three miles off. The paper made there used to be much in request in Spain. In this valley are the sulphureous springs of the *Aqua Santa*, as it is called, which rush out very copiously near the chapel dedicated to the "*Madonna della Aqua Santa*," to whose intercession the healing powers of the waters have been ascribed. A bath-house has been recently erected here. The waters are very clear at the source, and are considered very efficacious in cutaneous diseases, and are much frequented by the Genoese during the summer months. There is a villa of the Marchese Brignole at Voltri, in a lovely situation. A railway between Voltri and Genoa was opened in 1856, to be continued to Savona and Nice; and the post station is now here: the distance to Savona reckoned 30 kil. (The distance by Rly. from Voltri to Genoa is 9½ m., performed in 35 min.; it runs close to the sea the whole way until it joins the line from Turin, before entering the tunnel beyond San Pierdarena.)

3 kil. *Pra* (Stat.), which almost joins on to

2 kil. *Pegli* (Stat.), another town. The *villa Grimaldi* has a small Botanic Garden. The *villa Doria* is fine. It was built by Adamo Centurione, one of the richest merchants of Genoa in the time of Charles V. When the emp. was preparing for his expedition, his treasurer borrowed 200,000 crowns from Centurione, who immediately paid over the amount in ready money, and then forthwith sent a receipt in full to Charles V., who cast it into the flames,

F

determining not to be outdone in confidence and generosity. A story not dissimilar in spirit is told of the Fuggers of Augsburgh. The *Villa Pallavicini* at Pegli well deserves a visit; the grounds have recently been laid out at great expense, large artificial grottos constructed with stalactitic masses brought from a great distance, and subterranean lakes formed, over which the visitor is conducted in a boat. As an order to visit this villa is required, it may be more conveniently done from Genoa, from which it is an hour and a half's drive. Orders may be obtained at the Palazzo Pallavicini, in the Strada Carlo Felice.

The church of *Mont' Oliveto* is on a hill above. Here is a remarkable picture by *Francesco Succhi* of Pavia, with the date 1527. The subject is the Descent from the Cross; it is in excellent preservation. The background, an extensive landscape, retreating in perspective, is painted with Flemish accuracy.

3 kil. *Sestri di Ponente* (Stat.), a flourishing town of 6000 Inhab. In the principal church is a painting of the bark of St. Peter, by *Fiasella*. Behind Sestri rises the hill of La Madonna del Gazo, crowned by a chapel, with a colossal statue of the Virgin. From this point, in every direction, the view is magnificent. The *Villa Serra*, with its terraces and hanging gardens, is very striking.

Pass the monastery of *Sant' Andrea*, now the *Villa Vivaldi*. 4 kil. *Cornigliano Stat.*, a flourishing town. Like many others on this coast it is composed of two—the "'longshore" town, and the one more inland. Here are rather extensive manufactures of printed calicos. The *Serra Palace* has a fine elevation. On the height above Cornigliano is the church of Santa Maria Incoronata, which contains a Holy Family by Pierino del Vaga, of great sweetness, but in a bad condition. Below this church is an oratory attached to a convent, which contains some frescoes of merit; the ceiling is attributed to P. del Vaga.

Cross the *Polcevera*. The bridge over the river was built at the expense of the Durazzo family. Herr Masséna signed his capitulation with Lord Keith and the Austrians for the surrender of Genoa.

1 kil. *San Pierdarena Stat.* may be considered a suburb of Genoa, but which is not seen until passing the gate of the Lanterna, or emerging from the railway tunnel, when the city, its harbour, and the shipping burst in all their beauty on the traveller. In the principal church of S. Pierdarena are some good paintings. The Flight into Egypt, by *Cambiaso;* the Virgin, by *Castello ;* and some frescoes, by *Fiasella*. The *Palazzo Spinola* is an excellent specimen of a Genoese villa. The great saloon on the first floor is painted in fresco by *Carlone*. The *Villa Imperiale* also contains frescoes. *Palazzo Saüli*, smaller, but a good specimen of architectural skill.

4 kil. GENOA Stat., Ital. Genova, and called "La Superba." *Inns:* Albergo d' Italia, or Hôtel de l'Italic, in the Raggi palace, is perhaps the cleanest and best in Genoa; it has been fitted up recently in a way to insure every English and foreign comfort; table-d'hôte; the front windows command a view over the harbour, the lighthouse, and the eastern part of the town : charges—single rooms, 2 fr.; breakfast, with eggs, 2 fr.; table-d'hôte at 5 P.M., 3½ fr., including vin ordinaire; servants, 1 fr. per diem; servant's board, 4 fr. per diem; dinners in apartments, 5 fr. Hôtel Royal, formerly Albergo di Londra, near the Italia, kept by Perosio, newly fitted up; the landlady is English; comfortable and well managed. Hôtel de la Ville, on the Port, kept by Schmitz; this hotel is well spoken of. Hôtel Feder, formerly the Palace of the Admiralty, contains some fine rooms, is clean, and in general good, with moderate charges (table-d'hôte, 4 fr.). Croce di Malta, also good, with table-d'hôte; this house once belonged to the Order whose name it bears; forming part

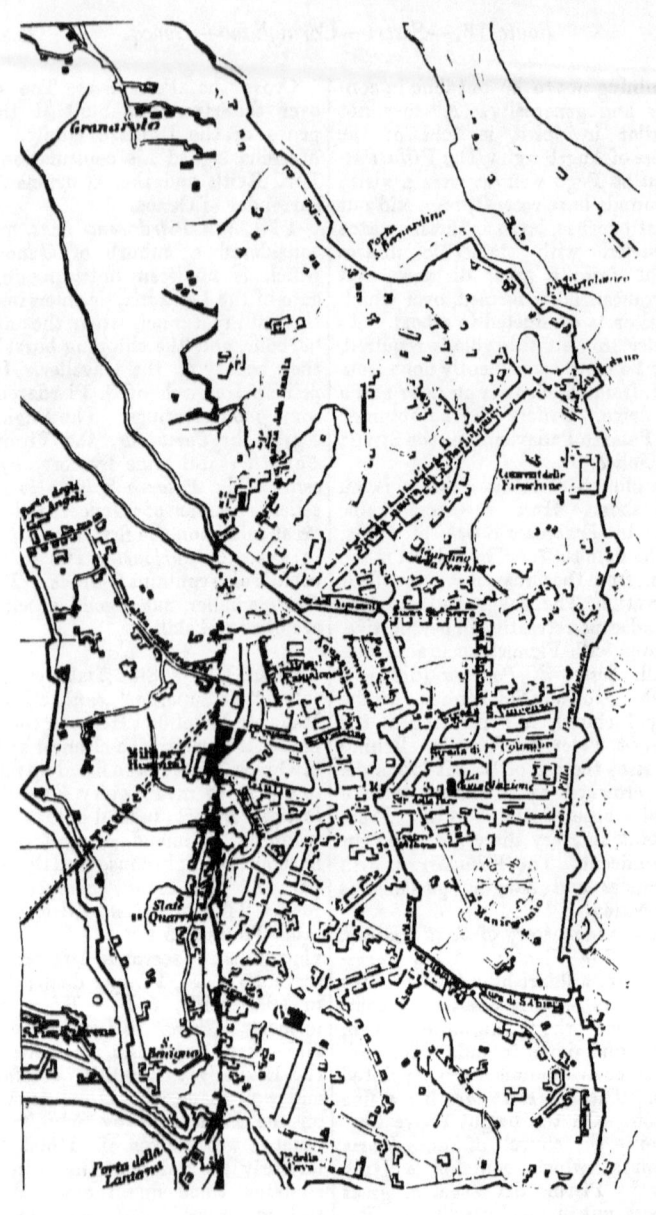

of it is a lofty tower, from which its inmates may enjoy a very extensive panoramic view of Genoa, its harbour, lighthouse, &c. In this hotel Mr. Massa keeps one of the principal shops of filigree-work, for which he received a medal at the great Exposition of 1851; comfortable and moderate. Hôtel des Etrangers; Albergo delle Quattro Nazioni—good, and reasonable charges. Hôtel de la Grande Bretagne. Hôtel de France, opposite the H. Feder. The *Alb. della Vittoria*, in the Piazza dell' Annunziata; the Lega Italiana, and the Albergo Nazionale, in the Piazza dell' Acqua Verde, the nearest to the Rly. Stat.; and the Pensione Suizzera, are said to be comfortable second-rate houses.

The Italie, Royal, la Ville, Croce di Malta, Quattro Nazioni, and Feder, all overlook the harbour, but the view of it from the lower floors is shut out by the terrace on the top of the arcade, which has been constructed along the quay to separate the port from the town. Complaints having been made lately of frequent robberies in the hotels at Genoa, travellers may do well to keep their doors locked at night, and on going out to deposit their keys in the office or at the porter's; otherwise the landlord's responsibility to make good any losses may be disputed.

Cafés.—La Concordia, in the Strada Nuova, with the best restaurant in Genoa, and a garden, and the Café Gran Cairo, near the Exchange, are very good; Galignani and the French newspapers are to be seen at the former. Gran Corso is a new café splendidly fitted up, opposite the Carlo Felice theatre.

Consuls.—Great Britain, M. Y. Brown, Esq. The British consular office is in the Salita di Santa Caterina. The Consul's visa is no longer necessary to a Secretary of State's Passport; that of the U. S. Consul, in the Piazza di Acqua Sola, whose charge is 3½ francs, is still necessary.

Steamers.—There is communication by steam-vessels between Genoa and Leghorn, Civitá Vecchia, Naples, Messina, Palermo, Malta, and Marseilles. The days and hours of the sailing of the steamers are announced by posted bills, and must be learned from these or at the respective offices. The voyager may generally reckon on the sailing of a steamer belonging to one or other of the several companies every second day, both for Leghorn and Marseilles. The only steamers that arrive and depart on fixed days belong to the French Messageries Impériales Company. They arrive from Marseilles on the morning of Friday, and sail on the same evng. for Leghorn, Civita Vecchia, Naples, and Malta; and returning from these places on the Friday, they sail for Marseilles the same day at 3 p.m. The Neapolitan Company's steamers sail for Leghorn every Wednesday at 6 p.m., and for Marseilles on Sunday. Steamers leave Genoa for Spezzia, Savona, and Nice several times a week, for the island of Sardinia, landing at Porto Torres, on the Wednesdays at 9 A.M., and for Cagliari on Saturday at 6 P.M.; in connection with the latter, a steamer sails from Cagliari to Tunis on the days of their arrival from Genoa, corresponding to the sailings of the 1st and 3rd Saturday of every month, and to Tunis from Genoa on the 10th and 25th, at 6 P.M.

Malle Postes, Diligences.—Malle Postes daily to Nice, at 3 P.M., in 26 hours, from the offices of the French Messageries Impériales; fares 50 and 45 francs, but constantly varying. The easiest mode of reaching Milan will be by Rly. by Novara and Magenta, for which trains start 3 times a day; in this way the journey may be performed in 6 hours, fares 19 fr. 35 c. and 13 fr. 75 c. To Lucca, by Spezzia, Massa, and Carrara, a malleposte daily, at 12·30 P.M. (fare 50 fr.); also a diligence 3 times a week in 27 hrs. By the last-mentioned conveyance the traveller may reach Florence on the following evening.

Vetturini.—Plenty and good. They

Route 13.—*Genoa—Port Regulations.*

may be found in the Piazza della Annunziata, and on inquiry of the masters at the principal hotels.

Railway. Trains leave Genoa for Turin, Novara, and Arona (fares to Turin, 16 fr. 60 c. and 11 fr. 60 c.; and to Novara, 14 fr. 20 c. and 9 fr. 85 c.) four times, and for Alessandria five times a-day. The Rly. station is near the Doria palace and the Piazza di Acqua Verde. Omnibuses from the hotels meet each train; fare with luggage, 1 fr.: there are very good broughams, by which the long delay in the starting of the omnibus can be avoided; fare, 1 fr. 50 c.: a Rly. is just finished along the coast, as far as Voltri, 10 m., and others are projected towards Tuscany and Nice.

Post Office in the Piazza delle Fontane Amorose. Letters arrive from England, the N. of France, and N. of Italy, at 10 A.M.; from S. Italy, Nice, S. of France, Spain, &c., early in the morning; and are despatched for England and the N. of Europe at 5 P.M.; for Nice and the S. of France and Spain at 2 P.M.; for Tuscany, the Roman States, and Naples at mid-day; for Turin and Switzerland at 11 A.M. and 5 P.M.; besides, letters are received and forwarded by all the steamers: those, however, for which bags are always made up are the French mail-boats; on Fridays for S. Italy, Malta, and the Levant, as well as to Marseilles; for the island of Sardinia by Porto Torres every Wednesday, by Cagliari every Saturday; and for Tunis on the 1st and 3rd Saturdays of each month. Letters from England cost 60 c., and in sending may or may not be prepaid. But letters for Piedmont generally, if not prepaid in England, are charged double on delivery here, and *vice versâ*.

English Church.—A large room has been fitted up in the Via S. Giuseppe, where the service is regularly performed by the Rev. Mr. Strettle, of the Established Church. An Hospital for English Protestants has been lately opened in the Salita di S. Girolamo, under the direction of the British residents and the clergymen of the Established Church. It is well deserving of the support of our travelling fellow countrymen. A book to receive the names of subscribers will be found at the principal hotels.

Bankers.—Messrs. Gibbs are particularly civil and obliging to their English customers.

Physicians.—Dr. Gilioli, an Edinburgh M.D., who practised some years in London—a very respectable man— he lives in Casa Tagliavacche, Salita all' Acqua Sola, No. 894; and Dr. A. Millingen, an English Physician, 59, Strada Carlo Alberto San Tomasso, 3° Piano.

English Pharmacy, kept by Aurelio, in the Piazzetta delle Vigne, near the Banchi and Hôtel Feder.

Port regulations, Passports. In these respects Genoa offers an agreeable contrast with the worries and annoyances which the traveller will experience in some of the other seaports of Italy. Passengers arriving are now allowed to land at all hours., and are detained but a short time on board. Travellers proceeding to sea,—if to Marseilles, their passports must bear the visa of the French Consul, which costs 3 fr.; to Civita Vecchia, of the Papal Consul, 3 fr. 20 c.; and to Naples, of the Neapolitan Consul, 6 fr. Passengers to Malta and the Levant require no Consular visa. The passport of the British Secretary of State does not require any visa at Genoa except that of the foreign consuls to whose States the traveller is proceeding.

Boatmen. The charge for embarking and landing passengers from steamers at Genoa is 1 fr. per person, including luggage; the fee for carrying it to the hotels by the porters is 1 fr. each porter, but the traveller who has several parcels will do well to make his bargain beforehand; the charge for a boat in the port, or for an excursion round the moleheads and lighthouse, is 2 fr. an hour.

The expenses for embarking carriages are—for a calèche, 15 fr.; for a chariot, or Berline, 20 fr., everything included.

Antiquities and Articles of Vertu.— Wannenes, Contrada Canetta, Piazza

Stampa, No. 1374, behind the ch. of S. Giorgio; and Maggi, in the Strada Carlo Felice, have very good collections of curiosities, antique articles, &c.; the latter asks unreasonable prices, which he has been known to abate 50 per cent.

Silks, Velvets, &c.—The best shops for velvets are those of Ferrari, Via degli Orefici, No. 352; and of Piccini, Piazza Campetto, No. 14. The best qualities of Genoese velvet cost from 18 to 22 fr. a mètre, about 13s. 6d. to 16s. 6d. a yard.

Bookseller.—Bœuf, Strada Novissima, No. 574, has a good assortment of Guide-books and Maps; there is a circulating library and a news-room in the same establishment, where Galignani and the French and Italian newspapers are taken in.

Jewellery, Filigree Work.—Parodi, Via degli Orefici, and Brazi, at No. 109 in the same street; Massa, in the Hôtel della Croce di Malta; Schmitz, Hôtel de la Ville.

English Warehouse, Teas, &c.—An establishment well furnished with English articles has been opened by Pellegrini in the Palazzo de' Mari, Piazza Annunziata, where the traveller going into Italy will be able to obtain, at prices not exceeding those in England, most articles of comfort.

Confectionery.—Romanengo, Via degli Orefici, is celebrated for his candied fruits.

Sedan-chairs are common, and are generally used by ladies going out in the evening, although not so much employed as formerly, the new streets having rendered the town more easy of access to carriages.

Genoa is now in a flourishing state. It is not an economical residence; especially with respect to house-rent, which is high within the city. Villas may be hired in the country, but the rents are by no means moderate; the best winter situations for invalids are about Nervi and Recco, the declivities of the Apennines along the Riviera di Levante being much less exposed to the cold northerly winds from the mountains than in the opposite direction. It is difficult to hire lodgings here, except by the year. Signor Noli, who lives near the post-office, is a good house-agent. Provisions are abundant. Beef, poultry, and fish are good, but of the latter there is only a scanty supply; so that there is some truth in the old vituperative Tuscan proverb, which says of Genoa,—*Mare senza pesce,—montagne senza alberi,—uomini senza fede, —e donne senza vergogna.* The climate is fine and the atmosphere clear, but the winds in winter are so piercing, that great caution is needed for strangers, especially invalids.

Genoa has a Porto Franco, where goods may be warehoused and re-exported free of duty. It is the chief outlet on the Mediterranean for the manufactures of Switzerland, Lombardy, and Piedmont; and Lombardy receives many of its imported foreign articles through it. The harbour, which is not of great extent, is deep, and protected by two moles. The width of the opening between the heads of the moles is 595 yards. The port is exposed to the south-west wind (the Libeccio), and to the heavy swell which follows gales from that quarter. The opening of the Rly. to Turin and the Lago Maggiore, and ultimately across the Alps into Savoy and Switzerland, is likely to make Genoa one of the first commercial ports in the Mediterranean, and a very dangerous rival to Marseilles, especially when the judicious plans proposed by the Government for the construction of docks, and the enlargement of the accommodation for the mercantile marine, by the removal of the naval arsenal to Spezzia, have been carried into effect.

The resident population of the town, within the walls, excluding the garrison and seamen, amounts to 105,000. Manufactures of silks, velvets, damasks, thrown silks, paper, soap, and the usual trades of a seaport town, employ many of the inhabitants.

The shops are good: the articles of manufacture peculiar to Genoa are gold and silver objects, especially filigree work, the three-piled velvet, artificial flowers, and coral ornaments. The velvet is still an excellent article; and embroidery on cambric and muslin is carried to much perfection. Bedsteads of iron are well made, and, to the great comfort of the traveller, are coming very much into use.

The Genoese are laborious, and a robust and well-looking people; but the Ligurian character, both physical and mental, is very peculiar; and they have yet a strong feeling of nationality. Their dialect is almost unintelligible to a stranger. One national peculiarity will, it is to be hoped, long remain unaltered—the exceedingly simple, graceful head-dress of the women, consisting in the higher classes of a muslin scarf (*pezzotto*) pinned to the hair and falling over the arms and shoulders, allowing the beautiful faces and hair of the wearers to be seen through it; this costume is general amongst the higher and middle classes during the summer, but in the colder season is replaced by the French bonnet. The lower orders wear a long calico scarf printed in most gaudy colours, called *Mezzaro*, manufactured in large quantities about Genoa.

To the beautiful road of the Riviera through which the traveller has passed, Genoa forms a very worthy termination. "I have now seen," says a competent observer, "all the most beautiful cities of the South, and have no hesitation in ranking this after Naples and Constantinople. But the charm of the latter ceases on landing, whereas the interior of Genoa does not disappoint our expectations. The streets indeed are narrow; but, to say nothing of the obvious convenience of this in a hot climate, it does not of course produce the gloom which it does in our northern cities. We too naturally attach the idea of small mean houses to narrow streets, whereas these are lined with magnificent palaces. In this respect, as well as in the massive and florid character of these edifices, Genoa bears a considerable resemblance to La Valletta, in Malta; but in that island architecture has something of an oriental cast; here it has adopted a more festive character."—*Rose*.

The port, round which "Genova la Superba" extends, is terminated at either extremity by two piers, the *Molo Vecchio* and the *Molo Nuovo*. Near the land end of the western pier stands the Fanalò, or lighthouse, built 1547; the tower rises out of the rock, to the height of 247 feet above its base, or 385 feet above the level of the sea. Several towers had previously stood here. The last, called the *Briglia*, or *Bridle*, was erected in 1507 by Louis XII., for the purpose of securing the authority which he had acquired. The lighthouse should be ascended for the extensive view which it commands. The arrangement of the light is excellent, being on the Dioptric or Fresnel principle now so generally in use in Great Britain. It exhibits a revolving, flashing light, and in clear weather may be seen from a distance of 30 marine miles; in addition to this principal light there is a smaller one on the extremity of the E. or old mole, and another, a coloured one, on the W. or new mole head. Close to the foot of the lighthouse is the quarantine establishment. On the N. side of the harbour is the *Darsena* (dockyard and arsenal), which was established in 1276; the first expenses of the works being furnished by the spoils taken by Tomaso Spinola, in 1276. It now exhibits considerable activity. A fine dry dock has been added to it, capable of admitting the longest steam or line-of-battle ship; it was constructed by Col. Sauli, an eminent engineer officer, at an expense of 2,725,000 fr., and as a work of engineering would do honour to any country. Here also is the *Bagne*, or prison for the convicts, who are still called galley-slaves, although galleys no longer exist. They, now 800 in number, are employed, in gangs, in the public works in different parts of the city, and are dressed in red clothes and caps. The caps of those who have committed murders have a band of black, while those whose caps have a yellow one have been condemned for theft or other crimes. The great majority of the first come from the island of Sardinia. It is the custom, if they behave well, to pardon them at the expiration of half their sentence.

The small but respectable Navy of Sardinia is on the English model, and is as superior in efficiency to that of any other Power, except France, on the shores of the Mediterranean, as the Genoese sailors are to all other Italians. Young men of family are much encouraged to enter the service.

The *Porto Franco*, which is on the E. side of the harbour, near the end of the Molo Vecchio, is a collection of bonded warehouses, surrounded by high walls, and with gates towards the sea and the city: the most recent portions were built in 1642. It contains 355 warehouses, which are filled with goods. According to ancient regulations, entrance is forbidden (except by special permission) to the military, the priesthood, and womankind; all these being, as it would seem, equally liable to suspicion. The Porto Franco is under the management of the Chamber of Commerce. The Facchini, or porters employed in the Porto Franco, form a privileged corporation. There are two classes, the *Facchini di Confidenza*, who are employed in the interior of the warehouses, and the *Facchini di Caravana*, who carry out the goods. The latter were formerly *Bergamaschi*, and the calling hereditary in their families. They enjoyed an exclusive privilege since 1340. They were recruited, not from Bergamo itself, but from certain towns in the Val Brembana, to the N. of it. They sold their privileges to their fellow-countrymen at high prices. Of late years this system has fallen into disuse, and the porters are now recruited from the Genoese.

Close to the Porto Franco is the Dogana (custom-house), and from this to the Darsena, along the quay of the port, extends the new portico, constructed in 1839, under which are shops; above is a terrace on which is an agreeable walk affording a full view of the harbour. The branch Rly. from the principal station to the Portofranco runs along the line of these arcades.

The city has been repeatedly increased in size, and its walls as often enlarged. It is said that some traces of the Roman walls are discernible. The first modern fortifications were erected in 935, extending from the Fort of S. Giorgio above the modern Rly. station to San Andrea. In 1155 the Genoese raised another circuit, for the purpose of resisting the threatened attacks of Frederick Barbarossa. Some of the gates are yet standing. Such is the *Porta Vacca*, or *Cowgate*, near the Darsena, a fine and lofty arch, between two towers. Above are pendent huge links of the chain that closed the Porto Pisano, carried off by the Genoese as a trophy of the great naval victory which they gained over their commercial and political rivals.

Another circuit was begun in 1327. In this many of the previous suburbs were included. It is in the semi-modern style of fortification, but very strong. The ramparts afford very agreeable promenades, and are connected on the E. with a public garden, called the *Acqua Sola*, which affords a delightful walk. The last portions of this second line of fortifications, *the Casteletto*, which only served to overawe the town, or was considered in that light by the popular party in 1849, has been destroyed, and the site covered with tall dwelling-houses; as well as the Porta di San Giorgio, above the Piazza dell' Acqua Verde, to make room for the Rly. station.

The third circuit, at a considerable distance from the second, encircles all the heights that immediately command the town and harbour: planned in 1627, it was begun in 1630, and completed in 1632, and forms an immense triangle, having the harbour for its base, and the great fort of the *Sperone* for its apex: the circuit occupies an extent of several miles, and is strengthened at different points by stronger works in the form of forts, which command the approaches to the city and the valleys of the Bisagno and Polcevera; the principal of these forts are the redoubts of La Lanterna and S. Benigno on the W., commanding the entrances on the side of Turin and Nice, the Tenaglia, the valley of the Polcevera higher up; the forts of *il Begato* and *la Specola*, near the summit of the triangle, which are of recent construction; and the great citadel of *il Sperone*, which, from a height of 1650 ft., completely commands the town and harbour. In addition to these forts on the line of the wall which surrounds Genoa, an extensive system of detached redoubts has been added on every peak from which the city or its defences can possibly be threatened; to the N. are the forts of the *Diamante i Fratelli* and *Puino*, which form such picturesque objects as seen by the traveller descending the Apennines from the Pass of i Giove, and on the E. of the valley of the Bisagno Forts Richelieu and Tecla—in fact, the military works round Genoa constitute at present the largest town fortifications in Europe, those of Paris excepted; since 1815 they have been greatly strengthened; and should the city again sustain a siege, it will be on these lines its principal defence must depend; but so large must be the attacking force, that, with the approaches by sea open, Genoa may be now considered impregnable, a rigorous and long-continued blockade by sea and land being alone capable of reducing it.

The fortifications in the first instance were erected to protect the city against the present dynasty, when the Gallo-Sardinian army, under Carlo Emanuele Duke of Savoy, threatened the very existence of the Republic; and they were, in great measure, raised by voluntary contributions and voluntary labour. Upwards of 10,000 of the inhabitants worked upon them, without receiving either provisions or pay. All the citizens contributed individually, besides the donations made by the different trades, public bodies, and corporations. One Carmelite friar raised 100,000 lire by collections after his sermons. Within these walls Masséna sustained the famous siege of 1800. The city was invested on the land-side by the Austrian troops, the British fleet, under Lord Keith, blockading the port. Masséna was at length starved out, and he evacuated the city on the 4th of June 1800, after a blockade of 60 days, during which the garrison, and still more the inhabitants, suffered the greatest misery from famine. Of the 7000 troops under Masséna, only 2000 were fit for service when they surrendered. The number of the inhabitants who died of the famine, or of disease produced by it, exceeded 15,000. The present garrison amounts to 7000 men, but treble that number would be necessary to man its works, in the event of a siege by any great continental power.

An interesting excursion may be made by the pedestrian round the fortifications, following the road on the inner side, from the Porta della Lanterna to the Porta delle Chiappe, during which he will enjoy some of the finest prospects over the town and harbour; emerging from the latter gate, a walk of little more than an hour will enable him to reach by a good road the Diamante and the fort of il Fratello Maggiore, from both of which the views over the encircling valleys of the Polcevera and Bisagno are splendid, with that of the whole line of sea-coast, from the rugged promontory of Portofino on the E. to the Capo delle Melle on the W., lined by the towns of Sestri, Voltri, Savona, &c., and the high mountains of Corsica on the extreme southern horizon. No one can enter the forts without an order from the military authorities.

Genoa is, like Bath, very up and down. Many parts of the city are inaccessible to wheel-carriages; nor are the smaller *vicoli* convenient for foot-passengers. Through these the trains of mules, with their bells and trappings, add to the busy throng. In the older parts of the town the houses have an appearance of antique solidity, whilst those in the more modern streets, the *Strada Nuova*, the *Strada Nuovissima*, the *Strada Balbi*, the *Strada Carlo Felice*, and the *Strada Carlo Alberto*, are all distinguished for their magnitude; and the first, in the *Strada Nuova*, for their unparalleled splendour.

"Genoa may justly be proud of her palaces: if you walk along the three continuous streets of Balbi, Nuovissima, and Nuova, looking into the courts and staircases on each hand as you proceed, you may indeed think yourself in a city of kings. The usual disposition exhibits a large hall supported partly on columns leading to a court surrounded by arcades, the arches of which likewise rest upon columns. Sometimes, on one side of the street, these courts are on a level with the external pavement; while on the other the rapid rise of the ground is compensated by a flight of marble steps. Beyond this court is the great staircase rising on each hand, and further still is frequently a small garden, shaded with oranges; so far the composition is admirable. It is invariably open to public view; and the long perspective of halls, courts, columns, arches, and flights of steps, produces a most magnificent effect; and this is still further enhanced when the splendour of the marble is contrasted with the dark shades of the orange-groves. But the chief merit of the buildings lies in these parts. There are internally fine apartments, but by no means of magnificence corresponding to that of the entrance. The other streets of Genoa are mostly narrow and dark: but even here some noble edifices are found."—*Woods.*

The objects *most* worthy of the attention of the passing traveller who has but little time to devote to Genoa are—the Strade Nuova, Nuovissima, Balbi, and Carlo Felice; the Piazza delle Fontane Amorose; the Brignole, Serra, Balbi, Reale, and del Principe Palaces and Galleries; the Cathedral and the Strada degli Orefici; the churches of S. Ambrogio, Carignano, and San Matteo. Most of these may be visited in the course of one day, indeed between the arrival of the steamer in the morning and its departure in the afternoon.

The *Strada Nuova* was built in 1552, on ground purchased by the republic. This street, the most splendid in this CITY OF PALACES, contains on entering from the W. on the l. or N. side the Brignole, Doria Tursi, Spinola, Lercari-Imperiale, and Cambiaso palaces, and on the rt. Durazzo, Brignole Sale or Rosso, Serra, Adorno, Doria (Giorgio), Cattaneo, and Gambara. Of these, all except two are by Alessio.

Just at the entrance of the *Strada Nuova,* but in the *Strada Nuovissima,* is the *Palazzo Brignole* (now Durazzo), the vestibule of which is decorated with modern arabesques and frescoes: the portal is supported by two gigantic Terms. In this palace is preserved one of the most extensive collections of rare engravings in Italy, said to exceed 50,000 in number.

Palazzo Brignole Sale, also called the *Palazzo Rosso,* from the outside being painted red, is in the Strada Nuova, No. 53: its front is very extensive, and, were it not for its colour, the architecture would appear to advantage. The apartments on the second floor contain the most extensive collection of pictures in Genoa. We shall notice the most remarkable, following the order in which the visitor is generally shown over the rooms. Very full hand-catalogues are to be found in each, as is generally the case in all the Genoese palaces containing collections of pictures, and which are most liberally thrown open to the stranger from 10 A.M. until 3 P.M.—
First Room. *Sala delle Arti Liberali.* A kind of ante-room containing copies of portraits of Doges of the Brignole family; the frescoes on the roof by Carlone.—II. *Salone della Vita dell' Uomo. Paolo Veronese,* a portrait of a Woman holding a fan; *A. Sacchi,* Dædalus and Icarus; *Guercino,* the Almighty looking on a Globe; *Ann. Caracci,* Christ bearing the Cross; *Carlo Dolce,* Christ sweating Blood; VANDYKE, a beautiful full-length portrait of Jeronima Brignole Sale and her

F 3

Daughter, and another by the same painter of a handsome young Man in a Spanish costume: both are beautiful specimens of Vandyke's finest style.—III. *Sala dell' Inverno.* *Piola,* a Holy Family; *Strozzi* or *Il Cappuccino,* a Madonna and Child; *Carlo Marratta,* the Flight into Egypt; *F. Barroccio,* the Virgin and St. Catherine; *Domenichino,* San Rocco in a Scene of the Plague; *P. Veronese,* Judith holding the Head of Holofernes just cut off—a disagreeable picture, without expression on the face of the murderess; *Piola,* Sant' Orsola; *Procaccini,* the Virgin, Child, St. John, Joseph, and Elizabeth: a good picture; *Spagnoletto,* a Philosopher; *L. da Vinci,* more probably by Luini, St. John the Baptist; *Rubens,* a good male portrait, very like Vandyke in style.—IV. *Sala d' Autunno.* *Giorgione,* an excellent portrait of Doctor Franciscus Philetus (Fileto); *Guido,* half-figure of S. Marco; *Tintoretto,* male portrait; *Bonifazio Veneziano,* the Adoration of the Magi, a fine specimen of the master—it has by some been attributed to Palma Vecchio; *Guido,* 2 heads of Our Saviour and the Virgin; GUERCINO, Madonna, Infant Christ, St. John the Baptist and Evangelist, and St. Bartholomew—a fine picture of Guercino's richest colouring; *Andrea del Sarto,* Virgin and Child, a *replica,* similar to that in Lord Westminster's gallery; *Luca Cambiaso,* a dead Christ: *Il Cappuccino* (B. Strozzi), Christ on the Cross, with St. Francis in Adoration before it. The frescoes in this saloon are chiefly by *Piola.*—V. *Sala di Estate.* *M. A. Caravaggio,* the Resurrection of Lazarus; *Guido,* St. Sebastian; *Lanfranco,* Christ bearing the Cross; *Luca Giordano,* Olinda and Sophronia, the same subject as that of the picture at the Palazzo Reale (p. 102), but inferior to the latter; *Guercino* (?), the Suicide of Cato; *P. Veronese,* a spirited sketch for his large picture of the Adoration of the Shepherds; *Luca di Olanda,* portrait of a middle-aged Man with a long beard; GUERCINO, Christ expelling the Merchants from the Temple—a fine composition, two of the female figures in the foreground on the right particularly; *Procaccini,* a Holy Family with St. Thomas; *Luca di Olanda* (or L. da Leida, as he is generally called by the Italians), St. Jerome.—VI. *Sala della Primavera.* VANDYKE, a fine portrait of a Prince of Orange; id., a portrait of Antonio Brignole Sale on horseback; id., a full-length portrait of the Marchesa Paolina Adorno-Brignole — the two latter are amongst the finest works of Vandyke at Genoa, where so many of his best portraits exist; *Scipione Gaetani,* portrait of a Cardinal; *Tintoretto,* good portrait of a Warrior; *Moretto da Brescia,* portrait of a Botanist; *Tilian,* portrait of Philip II.; *Vandyke,* Our Saviour on the Cross; *Paris Bordone,* portraits of a Venetian Lady and Gentleman; *Francia,* a small male portrait; *Giov. Bellini,* id. The four Halls of the Seasons through which we have passed are decorated with frescoes allusive to the names they bear, by Piola, de Ferrari, Haffner, Canzio, &c. — VIII. *Salone* or *Sala Grande,* a magnificent square hall, the roof decorated with the armorial bearings of the Brignoles and the aristocratic families of Genoa with whom they have formed alliances, and with frescoes by de Ferrari and Canzio. Over the doors are 5 pictures representing events in the life of Abraham and Lot, by the priest *Guidobono da Savona,* and a large composition by *Domenico Piola,* called the Chariot of the Sun. On one of the *consoles* stands a large model in white marble and bronze of a monument to Columbus, executed at the expense of the Marquis Brignole.

Palazzo Doria Tursi, in the Strada Nuova, now occupied by the Municipality of Genoa; it formerly belonged to the Queen Dowager of Sardinia, who bequeathed it to the Jesuits, by whom it was occupied until their expulsion. The façade is grand, and is flanked by terraced gardens. The architect was Rocca Lurago, of Como, who built it for Nicolo Grimaldi, from whom it passed to one of the Doria family, created Duke of Tursi. In the lower cortile are some very mediocre frescoes relative to the visit to Genoa of Don John of Austria, removed from the Ducal Palace. On the first floor in the ante-room of the hall, where the town council assembles, is a marble pedestal, on which stands a bust of Columbus, and in a recess under it a box containing some interesting MSS. of that great navigator; especially 3 autograph letters, one to the Bank of St. George transmitting his will (1502), by which he bequeathed one-tenth of all he possessed to that establishment and an authenticated copy of all the documents connected with the honours conferred upon him by the Kings of Spain; a second letter on the same subject; and the third to Oderigo, the Genoese agent in Spain, complaining that the bank had never acknowledged the receipt of the will. It may not be out of place to state that no trace of the will has been discovered amongst the records of the Banco di S. Giorgio, and that the only record of the last wishes of the discoverer of the new world is a copy in the archives of his Spanish descendant, the Duke di Veraguas, at Madrid. These precious MSS. were discovered among the papers of the Cambiaso family some years since, having been fraudulently obtained from the archives of S. Giorgio, a too common practice of late years in Italy; they are now preserved under triple lock and key. In another room of the Municipality are a few good Dutch pictures, formerly in the ducal palace; one by *Albert Durer*, another by *Mabuse*, and a third probably by *Van Eyck*: as they are in the apartments of the Mayor (Sindaco), they can only be seen when his *worship* has left his office.

Here is kept one of the most remarkable monuments of the history of Genoa — a bronze table, containing the award made A. U. C. 633, by Quintus Marcus Minutius and Q. F. Rufus, between the *Genuenses* and the *Viturii*, supposed to be the inhabitants of Langasco and Voltaggio, in the upper valley of the Polcevera, who had been disputing about the extent of their respective territories, and had petitioned the Senate in an appeal from the jurisdiction of the local Genoese authorities. This boundary question was most carefully investigated: the landmarks are set out with great minuteness, and clauses are inserted respecting rights of common and commutation rents, with as much accuracy as we should now find in an Inclosure Bill. The table was discovered in 1506 by a peasant when digging his land at Isosecco, near Pedemonte, 6 m. from Genoa. He brought it to Genoa for the purpose of selling it as old metal; but the matter coming to the knowledge of the senate, they purchased it for the commonwealth.

Palazzo Serra, Strada Nuova, No. 49, by Alessio. The entrance, which is modernised, is richly decorated; and *Semini* and *Galeotti*, Genoese artists, painted the ceilings, &c., of the principal rooms. The saloon is particularly rich: the gilding, said to have cost a million of francs, the white marble bas-reliefs, the caryatides, the mirrors, the mosaic pavement, procured for this palace its name of the Palazzo del Sole. The entresol has been recently fitted up by a member of the family, in a style of richness and magnificence seldom to be met with, even in the dwellings of royalty.

Palazzo Adorno contains some good frescoes by *Taveroni*, of subjects from Genoese history.

Palazzo Spinola (Ferdinando), formerly Palazzo Grimaldi, Strada Nuova, No. 44, opposite the last, a large and fine building, with good pictures. THE HALL.—Frescoes by *Semino;* a man on horseback by *Vandyke.* FIRST SALOON.—Two fine portraits by *Andrea del Sarto;* a remarkable portrait of a Philosopher in a black dress, by *Sebastiano del Piombo;* a finely preserved and beautifully painted circular picture of the Virgin and Child, by *Beccafumi;* a Venus, by *Titian;* and a fine head, by *Vandyke.* THIRD SALOON.— A Crucifixion by *Vandyke;* a Holy Family, *Gian. Bellini;* and the same subject, with two Saints, by *Luini.*

Palazzo Lercaro Imperiale. A striking façade, opening into a handsome cortile. The first floor is now occupied by the club or Casino, where strangers remaining at Genoa for some time can easily obtain admittance.

The *Palazzo Spinola (Giov. Batt.)*; containing the following pictures:— *Carlone*, Æneas and the Cumæan Sibyl; *Vandyke*, Madonna and Child; *Le Sueur*, Joseph before Pharaoh; *Guido*, St. Sebastian; *Guercino*, Madonna and Child sleeping; *Domenichino*, the Family of Tobias; *Borgognone*, Holy Family, and Abraham's Sacrifice; *Bassano*, the Marriage of Cana; *Parmeggiano*, the Adoration of the Kings; *Guido*, the Flight into Egypt; *Ann. Caracci*, a Woman and Child, and a Woman with two Men; *Luca Giordano*, the Woman of Samaria.

Palazzo Doria (Giorgio), Strada Nuova, contains a fine full-length portrait of a Lady of this noble house, by *Vandyke;* and a remarkably fine one of a Duchess of Sforza Cesarini, by *Leonardo da Vinci*.

The *Strada Nuova* opens into an irregular open space, called the *Piazza delle Fontane Amorose*, containing some fine buildings, of which the principal are the

Palazzo Negroni, No. 24, a wide-spreading and noble front; there are here some good pictures—Tarquin and Lucretia, by *Guercino;* and some interesting frescoes, relating to the deeds of the Negroni family, by *Parodi*. Next to it is the P. Pallavicini with its painted façade, and close to the latter, forming the entrance to the Strada Nuova, the handsome *P. Cambiaso* with its marble front.

Palazzo Spinola dei Marmi, Piazza delle Fontane Amorose, an edifice of the 15th century, built of alternate courses of white and black marble; in front are four niches containing full-length statues of members of the family with inscriptions in Gothic characters beneath. This palace is said to have been built from the materials of that of the Fieschi, near Santa Maria in Via Lata, pulled down by order of the Senate after their Conspiracy in 1336. It contains some of the earliest frescoes of *Cambiaso*, in particular the Combat of the Titans, which he executed at eighteen years of age.

The *Strada Carlo Felice*, which connects the Piazza delle Fontane Amorose with the Piazza Carlo Felice, is of recent date and has less architectural splendour than the Strada Nuova: it is broad and regular, and is chiefly occupied by shops.

Palazzo Pallavicini, Strada Carlo Felice, No. 12. The name of Pallavacini, one of the most ancient in Genoa, has by some been derived from Pela vicino, or "strip my neighbour," but without any foundation, the appellation being derived from the district of the same name, the *Stato Pallavicino*, situated near the Po, between Parma and Cremona (see p. 404). A member of this family acted in England in conformity to the supposed signification of his patronyme. This was

———" Sir Horatio Palvasene.
Who robb'd the Pope to pay the Queen."

He was receiver and banker of the court of Rome during the reign of Mary; and having a good balance in his hands at the accession of Elizabeth, could not then reconcile himself to the iniquity of letting so much money go out of the country to be employed against his new sovereign. He built Babraham in Cambridgeshire, and became afterwards allied by marriage with the Cromwells. The palace contains a collection of pictures, many of which are of great merit. The collection may be considered the second in Genoa. As there are no hand-catalogues, and as the person who shows strangers over the apartments is little versed in the history of the paintings, we shall enter into greater details in describing the Pallavicini gallery than would have been otherwise necessary.—I. SALA or GALLERY. *Guercino*, an Ecce Homo; *E. Sirani*, Santa Cæcilia; *Brevghel*, a Flower Garden; *Albani*, a Magdalen and Our Saviour.—II. SALA DELLA CAMMINA. *A. del Sarto*, Adoration of the Magi; *B. Strozzi* or *Il Cappuccino*, Sta. Caterina; *Luca Giordano*, a large picture of a Holy Family; *Luca di*

Olanda, a curious picture representing the Crucifixion, with the family of the Donatario kneeling below.—III. SALA DEL CARDINALE, from a portrait of a Cardinal of the Pallavacini family over the chimney; *Luca di Olanda*, Madonna and Child, with the Donatarii in the lateral compartments; *Franceschini*, Diana; *Luca di Olanda*, a dead Christ; *Albani* (?), Diana in the Bath: in the passage leading from this to the next room is a good picture of Madonna and Saints attributed to A. del Sarto. — IV. SALONE DI LEVANTE. *Rubens*, the Angel liberating St. Peter; *Romanelli*, a very pretty Magdalene; *Schidone*, a good Madonna and Child; *Il Cappuccino*, an *Adolorata*; *Franceschini*, the Ascension of St. Mary Magdalen; *Guido*, Christ on the Cross, with St. Francis; RAPHAEL (?), the *Madonna della Colonna*, so called from the column introduced in the picture—somewhat injured by restorations, still it is a lovely picture: the central portion, containing the Virgin and Child, appears to form a separate piece from the rest, the greater part of the column being on what appears a part subsequently added. It is very doubtful that Raphael painted this picture. *Guercino*, St. Jerome; *A. Caracci*, St. John the Baptist; *Bassano*, the Journeying of Jacob and his family; *M. A. Caravaggio*, an Ecce Homo.—V. SALONE DEL DIVANO. *Vandyke*, five circular family portraits, four of females, all very fine paintings.— VI. SALONE DI CONVERSAZIONE. *Castiglione*, a large picture of Pan and Animals. VANDYKE, the beautiful picture known by the name of Coriolanus and Veturia, generally considered to represent James I. of England, his wife and children. The costumes are quite Hispano-Dutch of the 17th cent.; the portraits of the females lovely. *Guercino*, octagonal picture of Music; *Luca Cambiaso*, Venus and Cupid; *Salaino* (?), Cleopatra; *Castiglione*, the finding of Romulus.—VII. SALA DI PONENTE. *Guercino*, Mutius Scævola before Porsenna; *Luca di Olanda*, Descent from the Cross, with portraits of the Donatorio and family in the lateral compartments, the men on the l. and the females on the rt.; *Spagnoletto*, the Woman taken in Adultery; *Franceschini*, Bathsheba in the Bath, a good painting; *Ann. Caracci*, a pretty small Magdalen on copper; *Vandyke*, portrait of one of the Pallavacinis; *Bassano*, two pictures of Cattle and Sheep.

The beautiful Villa Pallavicini at Pegli (see p. 89) belongs to the owner of this palace, one of the most wealthy of the Genoese aristocracy, where orders to visit it may be obtained.

The *Strada Balbi*, which forms a continuation of the *Piazza dell' Annunziata*, derives its name from the noble family by whom some of its palaces were built, the principal of which are —on the rt. side, *P. Durazzo della Scala* and *P. Balbi*, now the University; and on the l. another P. Balbi, which was once the Durazzo Palace, but which, having been sold to the government, now forms the residence of the sovereign, under the name of *Palazzo Reale*.

Palazzo Balbi, a fine palace built in the early part of the 17th century from the designs of Bartolommeo Bianco. The court is surrounded by 3 tiers of porticoes, the uppermost of which forms part of the family apartments, being enclosed with glass. This suite of rooms is very richly decorated, and, being at all times open to the stranger, will give him a good idea of the dwellings of the wealthy Genoese aristocracy: the vaulted ceilings are highly ornamented and painted by native artists. The rooms contain a very good collection of pictures, many of which are first-rate; indeed the Balbi gallery may be considered the third in importance in Genoa.

The first room entered from the quadrangular closed portico is the GREAT HALL, or SALONE, a magnificent square room.—*Vandyke*, an equestrian portrait, very fine; *Bernadino Strozzi*, or *Il Cappuccino*, Joseph interpreting the chief Butler's dream— one of the artist's best works—he was a Genoese Capuchin friar, and in a great measure self-taught.

2ND ROOM.—6. *Guido*, Lucretia; 7.

Albani, a Bacchanalian scene; *Ann. Caracci*, Sta. Caterina — very pretty picture; *Ag. Caracci*, a Martyr; 18. *Mantegna*, Madonna and Child; 19. *Michel Angelo*, Our Saviour and the Apostles—more than doubtful—called by some Christ's Agony in the Garden, said to be designed by M. Angelo, and finished by Seb. del Piombo; 20. *Vandyke*, A Holy Family.

3RD ROOM.—23. *Vandyke*, fine female portrait; 24. *id.* equestrian portrait of Paolo Balbi the senator, to which was subsequently added by Velasquez the head of Philip II. of Spain, to save it from destruction when Balbi was disgraced and banished from Genoa; 25. *Luca Cambiaso*, family portrait.

4TH ROOM. — 31. *Michel Angelo Caravaggio*, Conversion of St. Paul; 32. *Luca di Olanda*, a Holy Family; *Guido*, St. Jerome; *Ann. Caracci*, a Magdalen.

5TH ROOM, *Library.*—39. *Guido*, Andromeda; 41. *Guercino*, Cleopatra; 45. *Bassano*, a large picture of a Market.

6TH ROOM, *Gallery.*—Although this beautiful room contains nearly as many paintings as all the others united, none are very remarkable; *Spagnoletto*, two pictures called the Philosopher and Mathematician; *Tintoretto*, a fine male portrait; *Pierino del Vaga*, Madonna and Child; 73. *Vandyke*, A Holy Family; 75. *Vandyke*, Portrait of a Spanish Gentleman on horseback; 76. *Breughel*, The Temptation of St. Anthony—a singular composition; 82. *Hemling*, Our Saviour on the Cross; 85. *Garofalo*, A Holy Family; 87. *Filippo Lippi*, The Communion of St. Jerome; *Guido*, a Magdalene; *Paolo Veronese*, Portrait of a Venetian Doge.

Palazzo Reale. Formerly belonging to the Durazzo family, was purchased by the king in 1815, and splendidly fitted up by Charles Albert in 1842, as a royal residence. The front is nearly 300 feet in length; it was built from the designs of G. A. Falcone and P. F. Cantone. It contained a fine collection of pictures, the greater part of which have been removed to the Royal Gallery at Turin. The fine portraits of the Durazzo family, and the other pictures relative to that noble house, by Piola and Barloletto, are however still at Genoa in possession of their descendants. The P. Reale is open to strangers every day except during the occasional visits of the court.

Entering from the great staircase on the second floor, the 1st room has 2 large Marinas by *Burrasca;* the 2nd, called the *Salotto della Pace,* a Carita Romana by *Carloni;* the 3rd, the *Salotto di Paolo,* contains an ancient copy of the fine picture which is now in the gallery of Turin, by *Paul Veronese,* representing the Feast of Our Lord in the house of the Pharisee, with the Magdalene at his feet. Opening out of this room is the GRAN GALLERIA, painted by Parodi: there are some indifferent antique statues, busts of Apollo, Venus, Bacchus, &c., but all much made up: 2 modern ones of Flora and Zephyr by *Filippo Parodi,* and a group of the Rape of Proserpine by *Schiaffone.* Recrossing the Salotto di Paolo, we enter the PICCOLA GALLERIA, forming a passage to what formerly was called the *Salone di Giordano,* but which is now the THRONE ROOM, newly and magnificently decorated and containing the 2 celebrated pictures by *Luca Giordano,* of Olinda and Sophronia, and the Transformation of Phineas by Perseus. Next to this is the king's *Audience Room,* having only some indifferent modern pictures and tapestry; copies of St. Peter and St. Paul by Fra Bartolommeo: followed by the bed-room and study of the unfortunate king Carlo Alberto, the floors formed of very handsome inlaid work in coloured woods. In the *Sala della Cappella* there is a Last Supper by *Bonnano di Ferrara;* San Bernardo by *Spagnoletto;* San Antonio by *Ann. Caracci;* a Dead Man by *Honthorst;* a Sibilla Cumœa by *Ann. Caracci.* In the *Salone di Tapisseria* are some very old Gobelins and several portraits of kings of the House of Savoy, which replace those of the Durazzo family that once stood in these spaces, and which were not alienated with the palace. SALOTTA DI AURORA contains a Crucifixion and a portrait of Caterina Durazzo, said to be by *Vandyke*; 2 pictures of saints by *Il Cappuccino*, &c.: this room opens on the beautiful terrace overlooking the harbour, from which the view is so interesting. At the opposite side of this terrace is a room called the SA-LOTTA DEL TEMPO, corresponding with the S. di Aurora, in which there is a good Madonna and Child with St. John by *D. Piola*; 2 doubtful portraits by *Tintoretto*; 2 battle-pieces by *Borgognone*; and several pictures with animals by *il Grechetto*; the Woman taken in Adultery by *Moretto da Brescia*; a pretended head by *Titian*, &c. The modern *Salle-à-manger*, newly fitted-up, is a splendid apartment.

Palazzo della Università, Strada Balbi. This building was erected at the expense of the Balbi family. The vestibule and the cortile are amongst the finest specimens of the kind. Two huge lions are placed at the top of the staircase. The halls are decorated with frescoes by Genoese painters and with oil pictures. The Hall of Medicine contains some bronze statues by Giovanni di Bologna, and in the Great Hall are six of the Cardinal Virtues by the same sculptor, whilst in a third room above are a number of his bas-reliefs in bronze. The museum of natural history is interesting, as containing a good collection of the birds and fishes of this part of Italy. The library, which is open to the public, contains about 45,000 vols. The University consists of three faculties, Law, Medicine, and Humanities. In each there is a senate composed of twelve doctors, by whom the degrees are conferred. In the church belonging to the University is a bas-relief in bronze, and in the sacristy another, a good Descent from the Cross, both by *Giov. di Bologna*. Behind the University Palace is a small *Botanic Garden*; in the court leading to it several curious inscriptions removed here from suppressed churches, and on the top of the palace the Meteorological Observatory.

Palazzo Durazzo, or *della Scala* (of the Stairs), in the Via Balbi, is one of the finest of the Genoese palaces: it was erected in the 17th century for the Balbis, by *Bart. Bianco*. The court is surrounded by a Doric colonnade of white marble, from a corner of which opens the magnificent flight of stairs which has rendered it so celebrated. The 2 statues of Union and Force, in the lower vestibule, are by F. Rovaschio. The Palace contains several good pictures.

1st room on the left: *Ludovico Caracci*, an Ecce Homo; *Annibale Caracci*, St. Peter; *Paolo Veronese*, S. Catherine; *Rubens* and *Vandyck*, 2 circular portraits.

2nd saloon: *Guercino*, Christ and the Pharisees, or the Tribute Money; *Simone da Pesaro*, the Flight into Egypt; *Pellegrini*, the Oath of Gertrude, mother of Hamlet; *Titian*, a Magdalen, injured by restorers; *Procaccini*, the Woman taken in Adultery.

3rd saloon: *Vandyck*, 4 fine portraits of the Durazzo family; *Rubens*, Philip IV.; *Domenichino*, Jesus appearing to Mary, the Martydom of St. Sebastian, and Venus weeping over Adonis; *Spagnoletto*, 3 pictures of Philosophers.

Palazzo Imperiale, near the Piazza del Campetto. This palace is much decayed. In the soffit are frescoes, with mythological subjects in the compartments.

To describe the palaces of Genoa would be out of place in the present work, yet one more must be noticed, which, from its situation, is the most striking of them all: the *Palazzo Doria*, called also *P. del Principe*, situated beyond the Piazza di Aqua Verde, outside the Porta di San Tomaso, and the gardens of which extend to the sea. These gardens, with the palace in their centre, form a noble feature in the panorama of the port of Genoa.

This magnificent pile, originally the Palazzo Fregoso, was given to the great Andrea Doria, in 1522, and improved, or rather rebuilt, and brought to its present form, by him. The stately feelings of this Doria, who is emphatically called

"Il Principe" (for that title of dignity had been granted to him by Charles V.), are expressed in the inscription which is engraved on the exterior of the edifice: "Divino munere, Andreas D'Oria Cevæ F. S. R. Ecclesiæ Caroli Imperatoris Catolici maximi et invictissimi Francisci primi Francorum Regis et Patriæ classis triremium IIII. præfectus ut maximo labore jam fesso corpore honesto otio quiesceret, ædes sibi et successoribus instauravit. M.D.XXVIII." The architect who directed Doria's alterations was Montorsoli, a Florentine, but many portions were designed by Pierino del Vaga, who has here left some of the best productions of his pencil. Pierino, poor, sorrowful, and needy, driven from Rome by the calamities which had befallen the Eternal City when stormed by the Imperialists in 1527, was kindly received by Doria, who became his patron, giving him constant employment. He worked here, not merely as a painter, but as a general decorator; and it was Doria's express wish to reproduce in his palace, as much as possible, the magnificence of the buildings which Raphael had adorned at Rome.

The decorations introduced by Pierino in this palace were exceedingly admired; and he became, in fact, the founder of the peculiar style which prevails in the other palaces by which Genoa has been so much adorned. In the gallery that leads to the terraced garden are the portraits of Andrea Doria and his family. The figures are in a semi-heroic costume; Andrea Doria is grey-headed, his sons are helmeted, and supporting themselves upon their shields. Beyond this gallery you look upon the garden, where are walks of cypress and orange, fountains, statues, and vases. In the background are the moles, the lighthouse, and the sea. The fountain in the centre represents Andrea in the character of Neptune. Over another fountain is a fanciful mermaid or merman, the portrait of one which, according to popular belief, was caught at Genoa. Opposite to the palace, on the street front, is another garden belonging to it, bordered by a grapery. In this garden is the monument raised by Doria to "*Il gran' Roldano*," a great dog which had been given to him by Charles V.: here also is a grotto built by Alessio, in its time much admired, but now almost a ruin. The successive employments held by Doria enabled him to acquire great wealth. With these riches he was able to keep a fleet of 22 galleys; a force with which he turned the scale against the French, and accomplished the deliverance of Genoa, 11th Sept. 1528, from the heavy yoke which they imposed.

"Questo è quel Doria, che fa dai Pirati
Sicuro il vostro mar per tutti i lati.

Non fù Pompeio a par di costui degno,
Se ben vinse, e cacciò tutti i Corsari;
Però che quelli al più possente regno
Che fosse mai, non poteano esser pari;
Ma questo Doria sol col proprio ingegno
E proprie forze purgherà quei mari;
Sì che da Calpe al Nilo, ovunque s' oda
Il nome suo, tremar veggio ogni proda.

Questi, ed ognaltro che la patria tenta
Di libera far serva, si arrossisca;
Nè dove il nome d' Andrea Doria senta,
Di levar gli occhi in viso d' uomo ardisca.
Veggio Carlo, che 'l premio gli augmenta;
Ch' oltre quel che in commun vuol che fruisca,
Gli dà la ricca terra, ch' ai Normandi
Sarà principio a farli in Puglia grandi."
Orlando Furioso, cant. xv. 30-34.

It was under Doria's influence and counsel that the form of government was established in Genoa which lasted till the French revolution. He was offered the ducal authority for life, and there is no doubt but that he might have acquired the absolute sovereignty. The Dorias are still numerous at Genoa, but the elder branch, since its alliance with the Papal family of Pamphili, resides at Rome; the palace is generally let, and is in good preservation. The statements that the decorations by P. del Vaga had been injured of late years are unfounded.

The *Duomo* or *Cathedral of St. Lorenzo* was built in the 11th century, consecrated in 1118 by Pope Gelasius II., and restored about 1300. The front belongs to the latter date. The intention was, probably, to erect two towers, but of these only one has been executed, and that at a later period. There are traces in this edifice of the taste which prevailed at Pisa and Lucca. Some of the columns of the portal were taken from Almeria, as part of the spoils won at the capture of that city, 1148: among the vestiges of an earlier period are the curious ornaments on the N., exhibiting monsters and runic knots, and some rude basso-rilievos encrusted in the outer walls. Over the principal entrance is a bas-relief representing the Martyrdom of S. Lorenzo, with some quaint figures of the 13th or 14th cents.; and into several parts of the outer walls are let Pagan bas-reliefs, which formed the front of sarcophagi, of the Roman period.

In some parts of the church are inscriptions, from which we ascertain that the N. side was completed in 1307, and the S. in 1312; furthermore it is on one related how the city was founded by Janus I. King of Italy, the grandson of Noah; and how Janus II. Prince of Troy took possession of the city founded by his namesake and ancestor. These inscriptions are engraved in capital letters exactly in the form employed in coeval manuscripts, and are fine specimens of lapidary calligraphy.

Internally the nave is preceded by a very elegant inner Gothic porch with a groined roof, and which, as well as the pilasters that support it, is formed of alternate courses of black and white marble: over this porch is what was originally the organ-loft. The nave is separated from the aisles by Corinthian columns supporting pointed arches, each column being formed of alternate courses of that variety of serpentine called Polcevera breccia and of white marble: upon these pointed arches rests an entablaturo with a long inscription in Gothic letters, over which rises a second tier of round arches, supported by alternate stumpy columns and pilasters, the latter in the early Italian-Gothic style.

The choir and side chapels have been modernised, and covered with carving, paintings, and gilding. The architecture is by Alessio. The high altar is decorated with a fine statue in bronze of the Madonna and Child, by G. P. Bianchi, a work of the 17th cent.

The paintings are not first-rate; the principal are—*Barroccio*, St. Sebastian, in the chapel on the rt. at the end of the nave; *Ferrari*, the Virgin; *Piola*, the Ascension; and, *L. Cambiaso*, Saints adoring the Infant Saviour, good. The stalls of the choir behind the high altar are in very handsome wood carving with backs of coloured *intarsia*-work: the choir, according to the inscription, was restored to its present form in 1624. The ancient manuscript choir-books are yet in use, and they are fine volumes of their kind. In the *Pallavacini chapel*, corresponding to the left-hand transept, is a curious detached marble statue of a man kneeling before the altar, a good figure. An altarpiece by Gaggini, of Genoa, has lately been put up in the chapel on the rt. of the high altar.

The richest portion of this church is the *Chapel of St. John the Baptist*, into which no female is permitted to enter except on one day of the year, an exclusion imposed by Pope Innocent VIII., as it is said, in recollection of the daughter of Herodias. The screen which divides it from the church is of rich *cinquecento* Gothic, and was completed about 1496. The canopy over the altar, supported by four porphyry pillars, covering the sarcophagus in which the so-called relics of the Baptist are contained, was erected in 1532 at the expense of Filippo Doria. The eleven statues, and the bas-reliefs which adorn the external façade, are by *Guglielmo della Porta*. Eight niches in the interior of the chapel are also filled with statues, six of which are by *Matteo Civitale* (1435-1501), that of Zaccharias is peculary fine; and two, the Madonna, and the Baptist, by *Sansovino*. The altar is by *Giacomo* and *Guglielmo della Porta*. The relics of the saint are contained in an iron-bound chest, which is seen through the apertures of the marble covering. On the day of his nativity they are carried in procession, being placed in the *Cassone di San' Giovanni*, a shrine preserved in the treasury of the cathedral. It was made in 1437 by *Daniele di Terramo*, of silver gilt, a combination of Gothic panels, tracery, and finials of the most delicate workmanship. The sides are covered with imagery of the history of St. John; the figures being all but completely detached from the background.

In the treasury is preserved a more interesting relic, the *Sacro Catino*, long supposed to be composed of a single piece of emerald. It was part of the spoils taken at Cæsarea, 1101. The Crusaders and their allies divided the booty; and the Genoese, under the command of Guglielmo Embriaco, selected this precious vessel as their portion. The supposed intrinsic worth of the material was infinitely enhanced by the fond traditions annexed to the vessel, whether as a gift from the Queen of Sheba to Solomon, or as the dish which held the Pascal Lamb at the Last Supper, or the vessel in which Joseph of Arimathea received the blood flowing from the side of the Redeemer. Three times each year was the *Catino* brought out of the sacristy, and exposed to the veneration of the faithful. A prelate of high rank exhibited it to the multitude; and around him were ranged the Clavigeri, to whose care the relic was committed. No stranger was allowed to touch the *Catino* under heavy penalties; and the attempt to try the material by steel or diamond, gem or coral, or any real or supposed test of its genuineness or hardness, was punishable with heavy fines, imprisonment, or even death. Acute and somewhat sceptical travellers, as Keysler and the Abbé Barthélemy, in spite of these precautions, saw enough to lead them to suppose that the *Catino* was glass, a fact which is now fully confirmed. But the extraordinary perfection of the material, as well as of the workmanship, must always cause it to be considered as a very remarkable monument, and of remote antiquity. The dish is hexagonal, with some slight ornaments, which appear to have been finished with the tool, as in gem engraving. The colour is beautiful, the transparency perfect; but a few air-bubbles sufficiently disclose the substance of which it is made. The *Catino* was sent to Paris; and was reclaimed in 1815, with other objects of art. It was so carelessly packed that it broke by the way. The fragments have been united by a setting of gold filigree. The keys of the cabinet are kept by the municipal authorities, and a fee of about 5 francs is expected, at least from Englishmen, by the officer who opens the door.

Near the cathedral is the *Baptistery*, no longer used as such; and a large *cloister*, in which are the residences of the canons, but it has nearly lost all vestiges of antiquity.

Many of the churches of Genoa were demolished during the French occupation. Amongst those which remain, the most conspicuous are

Sant' Agostino, now desecrated, a good specimen of the Genoese Gothic of the 14th centy. The campanile, which, like the rest of the church, is built of alternate courses of white and black marble, is remarkable.

Sant' Ambrogio or *di Gesù*, entirely built at the expense of the Pallavacini family. The interior is covered with rich marbles and paintings; from the vaulting down to the pavement all is gold and colours. Here are several fine paintings:—The Assumption, by *Guido*, in the 3rd chapel on the rt.: the Virgin surrounded by hosts of angels. The commission for this picture was sent to Bologna, and offered to the *Caracci* and to *Guido;* when the latter, being willing to execute it for half the price demanded by his competitors, obtained the order. The *Caracci* were much vexed; but when the picture was exhibited, they fully acknowledged its excellence. The Circumcision, over the High Altar, by *Rubens*, painted before he came to Genoa; and St. Ignatius healing a Demoniac, painted in this city. The altarpiece was executed whilst he was in ignorance of the height and the position whence it would be seen; but in the second picture he was able to adapt his figures accurately to their site. Beneath is a small painting of the Virgin and Child, which belonged to St. Ignatius. St. Peter in Prison, by *Wael*. The frescoes in the cupolas are principally by *Carloni* and *Galeotto*. The four very fine Corinthian columns at the high altar are of Porto Venere marble.

L'Annunciata is, like many other churches we have noticed, a monument of private munificence. It was built and decorated at the expense of the Lomellini family, formerly sovereigns of the island of Tabarca off the N. coast of Africa, which they held until 1741, when it was taken by the Bey of Tunis. The very rich marbles of the interior give it extraordinary splendour. The roof has been recently regilt, and the church magnificently restored. Here is the "Cena" of *Procaccini*, a noble painting, but unfavourably placed over the principal entrance.

The *Ch. of San Donato*, built on the site of a more ancient edifice of the 11th centy. In the interior are some columns, in granite and cippolino, of a pagan edifice, which support the round arches of the nave. In front are links of the chains of the Porto Pisano, which were distributed among the different parish churches of the city after its capture by the Genoese. The octagonal bell-tower is of an early period.

San Giovanni di Prè, near the dockyard, formerly the Church of the Knights of St. John, built in the 13th century; some of the round arches of the original edifice are still visible; the present entrance has been cut into the tribune at the E. extremity of the old church, at a comparatively recent period. It was in the rich convent to which this church was attached that Urban V. resided on his return from Avignon. Some remains of the ancient cloisters may be yet seen, with a head of St. John of the 12th centy. over one of the doors. It was in the convent of *S. Giovanni* that Urban VI. caused to be barbarously executed 5 cardinals of his opponents, made prisoners at the siege of Lucera in 1386; the sixth, being an Englishman, Cardinal Adam of Hertford, is said to have been spared in consequence of the intercession of his countrymen, then influential at Genoa. In making some excavations years ago the skeletons of these unfortunate martyrs of Papal vengeance were discovered.

Santa Maria di Carignano, finely situated on a hill, built from the ground about 1552, and endowed by the Sauli family. It is in the form of a Greek cross, with a lofty dome in the centre. It was built by Alessio. Two colossal statues by *Puget*, and two by *David*, are placed beneath the cupola. They represent St. Sebastian, St. John, St. Bartholomew, and the blessed Alessandro Sauli. *Paintings.*—*Guercino*, St. Francis receiving the stigmata—originally good, though now damaged; *Procaccini*, the Virgin and Saints; *Piola*, St. Peter and St. John healing the Man afflicted with Palsy; *Cambiaso*, Three subjects, of which the best is a Pietà; *Carlo Maratta*, The Martyrdom of St. Biagio; *Vanni of Sienna*, St. Catherine receiving the Sacrament; *Fiasella*, Bishop Sauli going in Procession.

A fine view of Genoa is obtained from the top of the cupola, which is ascended with tolerable ease. Opposite to the church is a noble bridge or viaduct, also built by the munificence of the Saulis, begun 1718, by an architect named Langlade. It joins two hills, crossing the street and houses below. Some of these houses are seven stories high (adding to the reminiscence which the bridge gives of Edinburgh); the bridge rises far above their roofs, and affords a cool and pleasant evening walk.

Santa Maria di Castello, supposed to be built on the site of a temple of Diana. The present church is not very ancient: some parts of it may go back as far as 1350. The interior consists of a handsome nave, separated from the aisles by 6 round arches, supported by granite columns with Corinthian and composite capitals, and which formed a part of some Roman edifice, possibly of the Temple of Diana. There are some good paintings of the Genoese school here. In the 3rd chapel on the rt. a curious specimen by *Ludovico Brea*, representing a number of quaint figures in the costume of his time; and an Adoration of the Virgin;—a picture, in 6 compartments, of the 14th centy., the Annunciation, with Saints on either side. The choir contains tombs of the Giustinianis, great protectors of this church and convent, belonging to the order of St. Dominick. In the adjoining cloister are some early frescoes, one signed by a certain *Justus de Allemania*, in 1451.

Santa Maria in Via Lata, on the hill beyond the Ch. of Carignano, is a very old church, now desecrated, the walls being of alternate courses of black and white marble. It is chiefly interesting as having belonged to the Fieschis, and annexed to their palace, which covered a large space hereabouts, and which was razed after the unsuccessful attempt of Luca Fieschi, who in the celebrated conspiracy which bears his name here assembled his followers in 1336, to subvert the power of the Dorias.

San' Matteo. This interesting little ch., which has always remained under the patronage of the Dorias, was founded in 1125 by Martino D., an ecclesiastic of the family: the front, which dates from 1278, is a good specimen of Genoese-Gothic, formed of alternate courses of black and white marble.* Five of the white courses bear inscriptions relating to the achievements of the family. The pilasters at either extremity of the façade, and on each side of the entrance, support the shields of Genoa and of the Dorias, the red cross on a white ground and an eagle

———
* This mode of construction was confined at Genoa to public edifices and to buildings erected by the Commune. The four great families of Doria, Grimaldi, Spinola, and Fieschi, alone among the patricians, had the privilege of employing it.

erect. The uppermost of the inscriptions commemorates the great naval victory of Scarzola, September 7, 1298, over the Venetian fleet, commanded by Andrea Dandolo, by the Genoese, under Lamba Doria, both being the most honoured names in the military annals of Italy. In the ancient Roman urn above, with bas-reliefs of children and dead animals, were deposited the remains of Lamba Doria, who died in 1323. Above the principal door of the ch. is one of the very few mosaics still existing in Genoa. It is in the ancient Greek style. The interior was splendidly reconstructed at the expense of the great Andrea Doria; it consists of a small nave and aisles, separated by 5 arches supported by composite columns of white marble: behind the altar is a small choir with a good pietà and saints by Montorsoli, who was also the architect of the ch.; and on each side, chapels containing sepulchral urns of the Dorias, and the remains of Saints Maurus, Eleuterius, and Maximus, brought here from Istria by Pagano Doria. In the crypt beneath the high altar is the tomb of Andrea Doria, also by Montorsoli. In the adjoining cloister, erected in the early part of the 14th century, have been of late arranged several sepulchral inscriptions of the Doria family, brought from the suppressed church of S. Dominick, and others; and all that remained of the two colossal statues of Gianetto Doria, who commanded at Lepanto, and of another member of the family, which formerly stood before the Ducal palace, and which were erected there in 1577 by the Senate: they were thrown down and mutilated by the revolutionary rabble in 1797. In the adjoining Piazza are some curious specimens of domestic architecture — three palaces of the 15th century, over the door of one of which is an inscription stating that it was given to Andrea Doria by the Republic: *Senat. Cons. Andreæ de Oria Patriæ Liberatori Munus Publicum.* Here A. Doria lived—it was in the small square on which it opens that he assembled his fellow-citizens in 1528, to consult on the means for driving off the French, by whom Genoa was then beseiged; it was in the ch. of S. Matteo that Doria deposited the sword sent to him in 1535, by Paul III., for the services he had rendered in the cause of the Church. The door-sides of the Casa Doria have some beautifully sculptured arabesques. Over the door of one of the neighbouring palaces is a curious bas-relief of the combat of St. George and the Dragon, in presence of the Virgin and of a Doge of Genoa; and on the third a long Gothic inscription relative to the victories gained by one of the Doria family, to whom it belonged.

San' Siro. The most ancient Christian foundation in Genoa, and associated with important events in its history. It was originally the cathedral, under the title of the Basilica *dei Dodici Apostoli,* but San' Siro, or Cyrus, an ancient bishop, became its patron; in 904 the episcopal throne was translated to St. Lorenzo. In this church the assemblies of the people were held. Here Guglielmo Boccanegra was proclaimed Capitano del Popolo in 1257. Hitherto the powers of government, and its profits and pleasures also, had been wholly enjoyed by the aristocracy. This revolution first broke down the barrier; and although the office of Capitano del Popolo did not continue permanent, it prepared the way for the great changes which the constitution afterwards sustained. Here, in 1339, Simone Boccanegra was created the first Doge of Genoa, amidst cries of "*Viva il popolo!*" marking the influence by which he had been raised. His election was, in fact, the crisis of another revolution: the government was completely transferred from the nobles to the people. All traces of the original building are destroyed, or concealed by recent adjuncts and reconstructions. The roof is painted by *Carloni.* This Carloni was born at Genoa in 1594, and died at an advanced age. Some of the other paintings are—*Bernardo Castello,* the Saviour disputing in the Temple; *Pomarancio,* the Adoration of the Shepherds; *Castello,* Saint Catherine of Sienna.

St. Stefano della Porta, in the Piazza S. Stefano, at the end of the Strada Giulia, a very ancient edifice; the present building does not date later than the 13th century. The only object worth notice in the interior is the picture, over the high altar, of the martyrdom of the patron Saint, considered by some to be the joint production of *Raphael* and *Giulio Romano:* Raphael it is said made the design for the whole, and finished the upper part, and Giulio Romano executed the remainder after his death. Others attribute the whole to the latter. In its present position (it is concealed by an unsightly tabernacle and candlesticks) the unbounded praise accorded to this picture will to many persons appear extravagant. It was sent to Paris by Napoleon, and the head of the saint and other parts were there retouched by Girodet. It was a gift to the Genoese republic by Leo X. It is said that in 1814 a negotiation was opened for its purchase by an Englishman for 100,000 fr. The fee demanded for showing it is 1 fr.

The great *Albergo de' Poveri* is to the N. of the city, just outside the Porta Carbonara. It was founded in 1564, by Emanuel Brignole, and unites the care of the poor within its walls to the administration of many charitable endowments for their benefit. Thus, for example, the girls who marry out of the hospital receive a decent dowry. The house is very clean, and the proportion of deaths remarkably small. It is a stately palace, extending above 560 feet each way, and enclosing four courts, each about 170 feet square. The ranges of buildings, dividing the courts, form a cross, in the middle of which is the chapel, or at least the altar; the different inmates occupying the arms during the time of public service. It boasts a Pietà of Michael Angelo. In the chapel is also a statue of the Virgin ascending to heaven, by *Puget,* one of his best works. This establishment will contain 2200 persons.

The *Ospedale di Pammatone* stands

on the W. side of the public gardens of the Acquasola. It was originally a private foundation by Bartolomeo del Bosco, a Doctor of Laws, 1430; and was built from the designs of Andrea Orsolini. It is a large building, and contains statues of benefactors of the establishment. It has within its walls, on an average, 1000 patients and 3000 foundlings, and is open to the sick of all nations. The Institution for the Deaf and Dumb (*Sordi Muti*), founded by Ottavio Assarotti, a poor monk, in 1801, is celebrated in Italy.

The hospital for the insane, or *Regio Mancicomio*, situated outside of the Porta Romana, is a very extensive foundation recently erected, consisting of six wings converging towards a central edifice; it is said to be very well conducted, and contains 700 patients.

In and about Genoa there are as many as 15 *Conservatorie*. They are all intended for females, and all are religious foundations, and regulated according to the monastic system, though none of the inmates take vows. Some are houses of refuge for the unmarried; some penitentiaries for those who wish to abandon their evil courses; some are schools for the higher branches of education; some asylums for girls who are either orphans or the children of parents unable to maintain them. Of these, the largest is that of the *Fieschine*, founded in 1762 by Domenico Fieschi, for orphan girls, natives of Genoa, and which now contains about 250 inmates: they are employed upon various light works, such as lace and embroidery, but principally in the manufacture of artificial flowers. Half the profits belong to the workers; and with these they are often enabled, not only to relieve their relations, but even to accumulate a small dowry. The situation of the house, to which large gardens are annexed, is very beautiful. The whole establishment is conducted kindly and affectionately, under the patronage of the descendants of the family.

Theatres.—The *Teatro Carlo Felice* is the principal theatre, and is an elegant structure. It was opened in 1828, and ranks the third in size in Italy, the Scala at Milan and the S. Carlo at Naples alone being larger. It is open for operas and ballets during the carnival and spring seasons, for the opera buffa in the autumn, and for the regular drama in the summer and the early part of December. The *Teatro Sant' Agostino* is open during the carnival for the regular drama, the *Teatro Colombo* for Italian comedy, and the *Teatro Apollo*, where a French company generally perform during the winter: the two latter houses are near the Porta dell' Arco.

The *Accademia Ligustica delle Belle Arti* was founded by private munificence, having been instituted by the Doria family. The society consists of *protettori*, or subscribing patrons, and of working academicians. It is situated in a large building in the Piazza di Carlo Felice, of which it forms one of the sides, near the theatre, and contains numerous schools in the different departments of art, resorted to by a large body of pupils; it has contributed in improving not only the designs used in manufactures, but the architecture employed in the numerous recent buildings erected throughout the city. Attached to the schools of painting is a collection of pictures, mostly by eminent artists of the Genoese school—*Ansaldo, the Piolas, Fiasella, de Ferrari, Benedetto Strozzi, Luca Cambiaso*, &c.; and a large series of casts from the finest antique sculptures. On the stairs leading to the Accademia are four fine columns of Porto Venere marble, from the suppressed church of San Domenico.

The *Public Library*, on the first floor of the same building, has been formed out of various collections bequeathed to the town and to the king, and made over by him to the municipality, who very liberally provide for its support. It contains nearly 50,000 vols.; and nowhere does there exist a library opened with such liberality,—in summer from 7 A.M. to 10 P.M., in winter from 8 to 11. Its chief merit is to contain the most useful modern works. It is much frequented in the evenings.

Palazzo Ducale. The interior of the principal range of the building, which contained the hall of the senate and the state apartments, was destroyed by fire in 1777. The present interior was reconstructed by Carloni. The vestibule is supported by 80 columns of white marble: a fine staircase leads, on the rt. hand, to the apartments of the governor, on the l. to the hall of the senate. The latter is decorated by paintings, not of a high order, representing subjects connected with the history of Genoa. Of these, the best are copies from pictures of *Solimena,* that existed before the fire, the deposition of the relics of St. John the Baptist, and the discovery of America by Columbus. There is also a large picture by *I. David,* representing the Battle of Meloria. The hall also contained statues of the great men of Genoa. These were destroyed by the republicans of 1797; and upon occasion of the fête given to Napoleon as the restorer of the liberties of Italy, their places were supplied by statues of straw and wicker-work, coated with plaster of Paris, which still remain. This building was formerly the residence of the Doges of the republic, who held office for two years; it has been recently made over by the City to the Government. The front is now well laid open, and the space converted into an open piazza. The palace now contains the law-courts, and several other offices connected with the public administration. The great dungeon tower, with its grated windows, is the only part of the residence of the Doges of earlier times that now remains.

The Archiepiscopal Palace has some good frescoes by *L. Cambiaso.*

The garden of the Marquis Negri near the Acquasola is worth a visit. It contains some curious exotic plants, and commands a fine view over the city.

In the *Land Arsenal,* near the Piazza d'Acquaverde, are many curious objects. These were formerly deposited in the Ducal Palace, with others which were stolen or dispersed in 1797: the residue was here collected. A rostrum of an ancient galley, some say Roman, others Carthaginian, found in the port; but, though its origin may be uncertain, its antiquity and value are undoubted. A cannon of wood bound round with iron, said to have been employed by the Venetians in the defence of Chioggia, when attacked by the Genoese fleet. A good store of halberts, partizans, and other weapons, many of unusual forms.

The *Loggia de' Banchi* (in the Piazza de' Banchi) is an interesting monument of the ancient commercial splendour of Genoa. It consists of a large hall, the sides of which are supported by sixteen columns, now glazed in, built by Galeazzo Alessi (1570, 1596), being about 110 feet in length and 60 in breadth. The roof is skilfully constructed, the tie-beams being concealed in the concave of the ceiling; and the quantity of wall upon which the roof rests is so small, that the whole is considered as a very bold effort in construction. This Loggia is now used as the exchange, where the merchants meet for business; in front of it is the place of meeting of the corn and oil merchants, a very animated scene during the hours of business at Genoa.

Hard by is the *Strada degli Orefici* (Goldsmiths' Street), being filled with the shops of that trade. Before the revolution they formed a guild or company, possessing many privileges and possessions, all of which are lost. One relic they yet preserve — a picture of the *Holy Family,* with the addition of St. Eloy, the patron saint of the smiths' craft, whether in gold, silver, or iron. It is upon stone, a tablet framed and glazed, in the middle of the goldsmiths' street, and surmounted by a wrought canopy. This picture, attributed to *Pellegrino Piola,* is of a deep and harmonious colour, and beautifully drawn. It is said that Pellegrino was a pupil of Castello; that he was only 22 years of age when he painted this picture, and that it excited so much envy on the part of the master, that he caused his pupil to be assassinated. Others say that Pellegrino was assassinated by Giovan' Batista Carloni. Be this as it may, two things are certain—his violent death at an early age, and the extraordinary rarity and excellence of his paintings. It is impossible, says Lanzi, to define the style of the artist so early cut off; he was yet only a student, and a student employed in imitating the best models, preferring those which had most grace. He tried several manners, and worked in all of them with surpassing taste and care. When Napoleon was here, he desired much to remove this picture to the Louvre. "We cannot oppose you by force," said the goldsmiths, "but we will never surrender it;" and accordingly he yielded, and the picture remains.

The goldsmiths of Genoa excel in a beautiful fine filigree, either of gold or silver, which they work into bunches of flowers, butterflies, and other articles, principally designed for female ornaments. They sell them by weight, at a price of about 15 per cent. above the value of the metal. These ornaments are very pretty, and are hardly to be procured out of Genoa; but the workmanship is scarcely equal to that of Malta, or of Cuttack in Bengal. They may be passed at the French custom-house at a small duty. Parodi in the Strada degli Orefici, and Loleo at the Albergo della Croce di Malta, can be recommended for their excellent assortments.

The *Compera*, or *Banco di San Giorgio* (Bank of St. George), of which the hall is now used as the *Long Room* of the custom-house, was the most ancient establishment of this description in Europe. It was a combination, so to speak, of the Bank of England and the East India Company, being both a banking and a trading company. The colonies of Kaffa in the Crimea, several ports in Asia Minor, and also Corsica, were under its administration, and the latter island is still studded with towers and block-houses upon which the arms of the Bank are engraved. The Bank was managed with great ability and integrity; and most of the charitable and public institutions had their funds placed here at interest, which was considered, and justly, as a most secure investment. The French passed the sponge over the accounts, and ruined the individuals and the communities. The Bank of St. George was founded in 1346, in consequence of the trouble which the republic experienced from the exiled nobles who had been expelled from the city. Fortifying themselves at Monaco, they collected a numerous train of others discontented and banished, having nothing to lose and nothing to fear. They plundered the shores of the republic; and this marauding warfare became so profitable, that they were enabled to fit up a fleet of 30 galleys, with crews amounting to upwards of 20,000 men. The republic, not having the means of meeting the expenses of resisting them, negotiated with the richest merchants for a loan, which was *funded;* that is to say, the revenues of the state were permanently pledged for the re-payment. With the money so raised the republic fitted out a fleet. The insurgents abandoned their position; and the result is curiously connected with English history. Many of them entered the service of Philippe de Valois; and they were the Genoese crossbow men engaged in the battle of Crécy, whose rout so greatly contributed in the accomplishment of the victory by the English.

"Genova la Superba" appears most proudly in this old hall. All around are the statues of the nobles and citizens whose munificence and charities are here commemorated—the Spinolas, the Dorias, Grimaldis, Fieschis, and others, whose names are so familiar in the annals of the republic. The statues are in two ranges, the uppermost standing, the lower sitting, all as large as life; most of them are of an earlier date than the 17th century, some of the 15th, and a few as late as the

18th; rendering the edifice one of the finest monumental halls that can be imagined. The ample, flowing dress of the times contributes to this magnificent effect, combined with the truth and simplicity of the attitudes. Beneath each statue is a tablet or inscription, recounting the actions of those whom they commemorate:—one had founded an hospital; another had bought off a tax upon provisions which pressed heavily upon the poor; another had left revenues for endowing poor maidens. In this hall was the celebrated mediæval group, in marble, of a griffin holding in his claws an eagle and a fox (the latter two being allegorical representations of the Emperor Frederic II. and the city of Pisa). The inscription, still remaining, is—

"Gryphus ut has angit,
Sic hostes Genua frangit."

In the smaller apartments adjoining are other statues of the same description, and some curious ancient, though barbarous, pictures of St. George. In one room is a Madonna of *Domenico Piola.*

On the exterior of the Dogana, fronted by three Gothic arches, were links of the chains of the Porto Pisano, long suspended here as trophies, but now restored to Pisa since the union of that city to the same constitutional monarchy. All this portion of the city is one continued monument of the ancient Genoese commerce. The lofty houses are supported by massive, crypt-like arches and vaulted apartments; on the other side is the rampart of the port.

Public Promenades.—The principal is the *Acquasola,* a large esplanade, on the old fortifications, the favourite resort of the Genoese of all classes. The gardens are handsomely planted and laid out. On certain days of the week the military bands play here. The view from the Acquasola, over the valley of the Bisagno and the mountains E. of the city, is very fine.

Beyond the Bisagno torrent, and close to the sea, is the Government yard, where ships of war are built.

N. Italy—1860.

The Genoese, or Ligurians, from the time of Virgil to Dante, and since, have been the subject of vituperation.

" Ahi Genovesi, uomini diversi
D' ogni costume, e pieni d' ogni magagna ;
Perchè non siete voi del mondo spersi ?"
Inferno, xxxiii. 150—154.

" Ah Genoese, of every grace devoid !
So full of all malevolence and guile,
Why are ye not at one fell swoop destroy'd ?"
WRIGHT'S *Translation of Dante.*

But those who have resided here speak well of them now; and the splendid memorials of the charity of past generations raise a strong presumption in their favour, and against the poet's appreciation of their character.

ROUTE 14.

GENOA TO SARZANA, BY THE RIVIERA DI LEVANTE.

KIL.		KIL.	
19	Recco.	75	Mattarana.
31	Rapallo.	87	Borghetto.
43	Chiavari.	110	Spezzia.
63	Bracco.	129	Sarzana.

129 kilomètres = 80 miles.

This beautiful road, which, besides its connection with the preceding route, is the great high road to Tuscany from Turin and Milan, passes through a larger proportion of mountainous scenery than that of the Riviera di Ponente, and therefore has less of a southern aspect, nor is it so thickly studded with those picturesque towns and villages which adorn the shore between Nice and Genoa; but it has the same beauties of wide-spreading views over the loveliest land and water; it is also finely indented by gulfs and bays, affording good anchorage for the many vessels which enliven the brilliant sea.

The road, which is excellent, was begun by the French, and has been completed by the Sardinian government. Before it was made, Genoa was, in great measure, deprived of direct communication with Tuscany, which perhaps it was neither the wish nor the interest of the earlier governments to encourage. The best stopping-places for persons travelling post by this road will be—in summer; 1st day, Borghetto, or, by leaving Genoa early, even La Spezzia ; 2nd day, Pietra Santa, Lucca, or Pisa: in winter, 1st day, Sestri ; 2nd day, La Spezzia; 3rd day, Lucca, Pisa, or Florence, taking the railroad at either of the first 2 places.

The Vetturini generally employ 3½ days, stopping for the night at Sestri, Spezzia, and Pietra Santa, at each of which places there are good Inns, thus arriving on the 4th at Pisa, in time for the second Rly. train to Florence. The usual charge for a carriage with 4 horses from Genoa to Pisa is from 12 to 15 napoleons.

There are 2 public conveyances—the mail courier, which takes 4 passengers in 24 hrs., leaving Genoa about midday, fare 50 fr. as far as Pisa ; and a good diligence 3 times a-week, in 28 hrs. during favourable weather, leaving Genoa at 1 P.M., and reaching Lucca for the last train to Leghorn and Florence —36, 32, and 28 fr. Both these conveyances, except as regards time, will be found preferable to the steamers, by which the traveller will scarcely be able to get to Florence, including the railway fare, for less than 60 fr. It may be remarked, *en passant*, that the fares by the steamers all along the coast of Italy are exorbitant, and between no two stations more so than between Genoa and Leghorn; the distance 80 m., and the charge nearly 4*d*. a mile.

The road begins to ascend soon after quitting Genoa ; and, from the first summit, the view of the city and the white houses dotted around and ascending the hill sides is as lovely a sight as can be seen. Hedges of the aloe mix with vines, olives, and fig and orange trees.

Crossing the Bisagno torrent, we arrive at *San' Martino d'Albaro*, from where the road descends and runs near the shore. This town may be considered as a suburb of Genoa. The *Colle d'Albaro* is one of the most beautiful spots. Here are some magnificent villas ; the principal is the Villa Cambiaso, built by Alessio (1557), it is said, from the designs of Michael Angelo. It has frescoes by *Taormino*, representing the triumphs of Alexander Farnese, Prince of Parma, and two by *Pierino del Vaga*, Night and Day. The views from *Albaro*, looking over Genoa, are particularly beautiful. The Villa dell Paradiso is in a fine situation.

Cross the *Sturla* torrent before reaching

Quarto and Quinto. The names of these villages, which follow in succession, bespeak their Roman origin,— " ad quartum," " ad quintum:" they were probably Roman stations. Quinto is also one of the claimants for the honour of the birthplace of Columbus.

Nervi; gay with its bright painted houses. The gardens around are peculiarly luxuriant and fragrant. The church of *San' Siro* has much gilding and some tolerable paintings. An old palace, now in ruins, with decaying frescoes on the walls, is a picturesque object. There are several handsome villas here, that of the Gropallo family in particular. Beyond Nervi is the village of Bogliasc. The village and bridge of Sori (a fine arch) are passed about 2 miles before arriving at

19 kil. *Recco.* An additional distance of 4 kil. is paid on leaving and arriving at Genoa. (Inn tolerable.) Rather a handsome little town. The white houses and the high campanile of the church, backed by the hilly promontory of Porto Fino, which, stretching into the sea, forms the western shore of the bay of Rapallo, have a charming effect. Leaving Recco, the road traverses Camogli, and then ascends for about 1 mile, at the culminating point of which

from which the slate is extracted, though not very picturesque in form or colour, are striking from their extent. The laminated structure of the rock enables the workmen in some of these caverns to dispense with the pillars usually required in extensive excavations. The slate is of a good quality, and, if the workmen chose, slabs might be split of 10 or 12 ft. in length; but, for convenience of carriage, they split them in regular sizes, the largest being about 3 ft. by 4. An argument for the antiquity of the employment of this material is found in the name of the *Tegullii*, the Ligurian tribe who inhabited this part of the coast previous to the Roman conquest. There are other quarries between Lavagna and Sestri, but nearer the seashore.

We now resume the main road to Lavagna, a thriving and cheerful town, with about 6500 Inhab. The road is bordered by the slate rock. A strange red palace, with bartizan towers, is here a conspicuous object. The *principal church* is amongst the most splendid on the Riviera di Levante. From the slates being found about the town, they are called in Italian *pietre di Lavagna*. From this place the celebrated family of the Fieschi derived their title of Count.

Sestri à Levante, a town on an isthmus at the foot of a wooded promontory. (*Inns*: Hôtel de l'Europe, good: Albergo d'Inghilterra.) Sestri has the sea on either side, and the promontory is supposed to have been once an island. In the church of *San Pietro* is a painting attributed to *Pierino del Vaga*, a Holy Family. It is Raffaelesque in style. A more unquestionable specimen of a good artist is the Descent of the Holy Ghost, by *Fiasella*, in the church of the Nativity. The surrounding scenes are full of varied beauties. At the Hôtel de l'Europe are machines for sea-bathing, for which Sestri is well suited, from its excellent beach and its delightful situation. Travelling with a vetturino, you sleep the first night at Sestri, and the next at Spezia: but although the former place is not a post-station, the hotel-keeper will make arrangements with the neighbouring postmasters for travellers stopping here, without any additional charge.

Soon after leaving Sestri the road, which runs inland, commences to ascend, the island-like promontory being left on the rt. hand. It first winds through hills of olive-trees, and in the clefts of which the myrtle grows wild. Hence many headlands stretching into the sea, and white houses and churches dotting the hills, are seen. The pass of Bracco, however, leads above fig-trees and vines, and even above chestnuts and fir-trees; and the finely made road, winding amongst summits of rocks scantily covered with grass, continues to ascend to

20 kil. *Bracco*. (From Chiavari to Bracco an extra horse all the year.) The post-house (1350 ft. above the sea) is placed in a comparatively fertile nook, screened by still higher summits, and looking down a long green vista on the blue sea far below. The view is exceedingly fine, embracing the bay of Moneglia, Sestri, and its high promontory, and the Bay of Rapallo, with the headland of Porto Fino beyond. The ascent still continues by a good and well-traced road for 3 or 4 m. beyond the Post-house of Bracco, until it attains an elevation of about 2100 ft. above the sea, at the Col or Pass of Velva: here all cultivation nearly ceases; the views both towards the sea and inland are very fine from this elevation; a well-managed descent leads from the Pass to Matarana.

[The geologist will find much to interest him in this part of his journey, between Sestri and the Velva Pass, where he will be able to examine one of the finest eruptions of serpentine in Italy. On the ascent the serpentine may be seen piercing through the beds of calcareous slate, of the age of our British chalk. Some good sections may be observed near the pass: in the cuttings made for the post-road the serpentine and diallage rocks will be seen

of a painting cast on shore from a shipwrecked vessel, and to which the superstition of the Rappallese attributed miraculous powers. The picture is of Greek workmanship, and execrable as a work of art.

The road from Rapallo to Chiavari is exceedingly varied; sometimes you mount long rocky heights, covered with arbutus and frequent stone pines. Many apparently good and picturesque houses are scattered high up on the hill-sides, where there is no visible road to them from below. Churches, with white and often elegant campaniles, are frequent all along the road. Towards the evening these numerous churches add perhaps more to the interest of the landscape than at any other time, the bells sounding and the light streaming through the windows. Sometimes we are many hundred feet above the level of the Mediterranean, looking down upon its blue waters; sometimes you pass vast surfaces of rock sloping down to the sea with as even a surface as a revêtement wall; and sometimes, as at Rapallo, you are on the very level of the shore. There are two short tunnels or galleries near the top of the ascent between Rapallo and Chiavari. In one of the beautiful nooks lies a most picturesquely situated village, with its white tall houses in the midst of olive groves. About a mile before reaching Chiavari the road descends into the plain extending to Sestri, and in the midst of which is situated

12 kil. *Chiavari.* An extra horse between Rapallo and Chiavari, both ways, all the year. (*Inns:* La Posta; diligences to Genoa run from this house once a day: the other inn, La Fenice, is good.) The chief city of the province, with more than 10,000 Inhab., situated in the centre of the bay. It is one of the most considerable towns of the ancient Genoese territory. It has the aspect of an old Italian town; the houses generally are built on open arcades which skirt the narrow streets; the arches are pointed and circular, and with capitals which would puzzle an architect by their similarity to our early Norman, but which are probably not *older* than the 13th centy. There are several fine churches. In that of *San' Francesco* is a painting attributed to Velasquez, representing a miracle wrought for the patron saint—an angel, at his prayer, causing water to flow from the rock. This picture was removed by the French to the Louvre. Another picture with St. Francis in the centre, and the history of his life in small compartments around, is curious.

The *Madonna del' Orto*, the principal church, is annexed to the ecclesiastical seminary. The cupola was shattered by lightning some years ago. The front is unfinished; the portico will be upon a magnificent scale, with columns six feet in diameter. It is said that the work will cost 700,000 francs. Old and picturesque towers are dotted about the town. The largest, a castle in fact, is now used for the offices of the municipality.

There is the same luxuriant vegetation at Chiavari as on other parts of this coast. The aloe, in particular, grows luxuriantly, even in the very sand of the shores; and in some points of view, when they constitute the foreground, and the fantastic, mosque-like cupolas of the churches are seen in the distance, the scene assumes almost an oriental character. This place is noted for the manufacture of furniture, and especially of handsome and very light chairs, made chiefly of cherry-wood, costing 10 or 12 fr. apiece.

2 m. beyond Chiavari runs the river *Lavagnaro*, or "*Fiume di Lavagna*," the *Entella* of ancient geographers.

The Lavagnaro winds amongst agreeable groves, and the walks along its banks are pleasing. The vines throw their graceful festoons over poplars and mulberries. Along these banks is the path leading to the slate-quarries of Lavagna, which are worthy of a visit. It passes near to the Ch. of *San Salvatore*, founded by Innocent IV. (1243-1254), and completed by Adrian V. Ascending further, you reach the slate-quarries. The quarries from which the slate is extracted, though not very picturesque in form or colour, are striking from their extent. The laminated structure of the rock enables the workmen in some of these caverns to dispense with the pillars usually required in extensive excavations. The slate is of a good quality, and, if the workmen chose, slabs might be split of 10 or 12 ft. in length; but, for convenience of carriage, they split them in regular sizes, the largest being about 3 ft. by 4. An argument for the antiquity of the employment of this material is found in the name of the *Tegullii*, the Ligurian tribe who inhabited this part of the coast previous to the Roman conquest. There are other quarries between Lavagna and Sestri, but nearer the seashore.

We now resume the main road to Lavagna, a thriving and cheerful town, with about 6500 Inhab. The road is bordered by the slate rock. A strange red palace, with bartizan towers, is here a conspicuous object. The *principal church* is amongst the most splendid on the Riviera di Levante. From the slates being found about the town, they are called in Italian *pietre di Lavagna*. From this place the celebrated family of the Fieschi derived their title of Count.

Sestri à Levante, a town on an isthmus at the foot of a wooded promontory. (*Inns:* Hôtel de l'Europe, good: Albergo d'Inghilterra.) Sestri has the sea on either side, and the promontory is supposed to have been once an island. In the church of *San Pietro* is a painting attributed to *Pierino del Vaga*, a Holy Family. It is Raffaelesque in style. A more unquestionable specimen of a good artist is the Descent of the Holy Ghost, by *Fiasella*, in the church of the Nativity. The surrounding scenes are full of varied beauties. At the Hôtel de l'Europe are machines for sea-bathing, for which Sestri is well suited, from its excellent beach and its delightful situation. Travelling with a vetturino, you sleep the first night at Sestri, and the next at Spezia; but although the former place is not a post-station, the hotel-keeper will make arrangements with the neighbouring postmasters for travellers stopping here, without any additional charge.

Soon after leaving Sestri the road, which runs inland, commences to ascend, the island-like promontory being left on the rt. hand. It first winds through hills of olive-trees, and in the clefts of which the myrtle grows wild. Hence many headlands stretching into the sea, and white houses and churches dotting the hills, are seen. The pass of Bracco, however, leads above fig-trees and vines, and even above chestnuts and fir-trees; and the finely made road, winding amongst summits of rocks scantily covered with grass, continues to ascend to

20 kil. *Bracco*. (From Chiavari to Bracco an extra horse all the year.) The post-house (1350 ft. above the sea) is placed in a comparatively fertile nook, screened by still higher summits, and looking down a long green vista on the blue sea far below. The view is exceedingly fine, embracing the bay of Moneglia, Sestri, and its high promontory, and the Bay of Rapallo, with the headland of Porto Fino beyond. The ascent still continues by a good and well-traced road for 3 or 4 m. beyond the Post-house of Bracco, until it attains an elevation of about 2100 ft. above the sea, at the Col or Pass of Velva: here all cultivation nearly ceases; the views both towards the sea and inland are very fine from this elevation; a well-managed descent leads from the Pass to Matarana.

[The geologist will find much to interest him in this part of his journey, between Sestri and the Velva Pass, where he will be able to examine one of the finest eruptions of serpentine in Italy. On the ascent the serpentine may be seen piercing through the beds of calcareous slate, of the age of our British chalk. Some good sections may be observed near the pass: in the cuttings made for the post-road the serpentine and diallage rocks will be seen not only forming veins or dykes in the limestone, but in each other: the country E. of the Velva Pass is cut into deep ravines, and wherever the serpentine shows itself it is characterized by the bareness and desolation so characteristic of this rock in every part of the world.]

12 kil. *Matarana* is a poor village, 1600 ft. above the sea. (From Bracco to Matarana an extra horse all the year.) The women here wear their hair in nets, hanging on their backs, and often a folded cloth on their heads, which at Spezia is superseded by a little straw hat, placed on the top of the head, and only used as an ornament. The road winds along the steep sides of the valley on descending from Matarana, the hills around being thinly clad with chestnut-trees; a low pass near the village of Beruviana (where there is an interesting contact of the serpentine and secondary strata) leads into the ravine, near which, at its junction with the Vara, is situated the village of Borghetto.

12 kil. *Borghetto* (between Matarana and Borghetto an extra horse both ways all the year). There is a fair *Inn* (Hôtel de l'Europe) at the neighbouring village of Pogliano, which the vetturini make their dining-station.

The road hence lies for a time near the bed of the Vara, a tributary of the Magra, and, after ascending the Recco torrent to San Benedetto, or La Foce di Spezia, a long descent, during which the traveller will enjoy many beautiful peeps over the subjacent bay and the distant mountains of Carara, leads to

23 kil. *La Spezia*. (Between Borghetto and La Spezia an extra horse both ways all the year.)

[The coast-road from Sestri to La Spezia possesses equal interest, but is a mere mule-path; indeed the principal means of communication between the different places is by sea.

Moneglia, a town of about 2000 Inhab., with remains of its mediæval fortifications and battlemented wall on the hill to the W. Farther on are the towns of *Deiva, Framura,* and *Bonasola*.

Levanto, a large but dirty town of 4600 Inhab., surrounded by overhanging hills. To reach it in any carriage you must go through Bracco. A road strikes off to the rt. from the post-road to Spezia at *La Baracca*, the highest point of the mountain, half way between Bracco and Matarana. In the ch. of the Minor Friars is a painting attributed to Andrea del Castagno, one of the first who practised oil-painting in Italy. The subject is St. George and the Dragon, and the action is that for which Pistrucci was so much criticised in his design on the sovereigns of Geo. III. The spear is broken, and St. George is despatching the monster with his sword. The picture was carried off by the French, and the Louvre numbering is yet upon the frame. The *principal church*, which was consecrated in 1463, is after the model of the cathedral of Genoa; and is still a fine building, though sadly modernised. Several of the houses bear marks of antiquity. A small district below the headlands of Mescolo and Montenero, belonging to five villages or communities, Monte Rosso, Vernazza, Corniglia, Manarola, and Rio Maggiore, known by the collective name of the *Cinque Terre*, is remarkable for the beauty of the scenery and the primitive simplicity (at least in outward appearance) of its inhabitants. Much wine is grown here, the vineyards in some places overhanging the sea. The "vino amabile" of this district had anciently a very high character. From Vernazza came the *Vernaccia*, quoted by Boccaccio and Sacchetti as the very paragon of good liquor. The present growth, however, seems to have declined in quality. Oranges and lemons grow here in great perfection; and the fan-palm and the cactus opuntia flourish with tropical luxuriance.

Monterosso. The church, built in 1307, is also after the Genoese model. Near Monterosso is the sanctuary of the Madonna *di Soviore*. The rock upon which it stands commands a most extensive prospect, reaching to the island of Corsica. The annual feast of the Virgin, held on the 15th and 16th of August, is attended by great numbers of country people from the adjoining ports. The coast between the Capes of Monterosso and Porto Venere is extremely bold and arid, without any place of importance.]

Gulf of Spezia. By the ancients the Gulf of Spezia was known as the Gulf of *Luna*. Its situation is accurately described by Strabo as a geographer, and its climate by Persius, who found a retreat on its shores.

" Mihi nunc Ligus ora
Intepet, hybernatque meum mare ; qua latus
ingens
Dant scopuli, et multa littus se valle receptat.
Lunai portum est operæ cognoscere, cives.
Cor jubet hoc Enni, postquam destertuit esse
Mæonides Quintus pavone ex Pythagoreo."
Persius, vi.
"To me, whilst tempests howl and billows rise,
Liguria's coast a warm retreat supplies ;
Where the huge cliffs an ample front display,
And, deep within, recedes the sheltering bay.
The port of Luna, friends, is worth your note.
Thus in his sober moments Ennius wrote,
When, all his dreams of transmigration past,
He found himself plain Quintus at the last."

Not less remarkable for its beauty than its security is this gulf, capable of containing all the fleets of Europe, and possessing from nature more advantages than the art of man could possibly bestow. Hence Napoleon, in the triumphant stage of his career, intended to render it *the* naval station of his empire in the Mediterranean. The plan, it is said, was frustrated by the intrigues of the French ministry, jealous of the injury which would have resulted to Toulon. The Sardinian government has now in contemplation to remove the Naval Arsenal from Genoa to La Spezia, in order to increase the accommodation for the rapidly increasing trade and shipping at the former place ; but there are strong objections to this, arising from its position, close to the extreme frontier of the kingdom.

La Spezia (*Inns:* Croce di Malta: very good ; a new Hotel on the shore, opened by the brothers Lenzi, with Bath-house, and every accommodation for sea-bathers; clean and comfortable.—Hôtel d'Odessa, a large and new hotel outside the town, and close to the sea). Of late years, La Spezia having become a much-frequented watering-place, the bathing being excellent, the inns and lodging-houses are greatly improved. Families coming here for the bathing season may make arrangements on equitable terms for board and lodging at the two principal hotels. Spezia has about 10,000 Inhab., and is situated in the deepest part of its bay, formed by the branches of the Apennines, advancing into the sea. There is some commerce in wine, and oil, which is produced abundantly from the olive-clad hills around; also in thick slabs of marble for paving-stones, like those of Genoa. Oranges and lemons are exported to the ports of the Black Sea. Steamers ply twice or three times a week between Spezia and Genoa, employing, as they are small, about 10 hours, and starting in the evening. There is a British Consul, Mr. Lever (Harry Lorrequer), at Spezia.

To those who are inclined to boating amusement at Spezia, the brothers Moscova can be recommended as boatmen. They speak good Italian, and are intelligent and civil fellows.

All around Spezia the country is beautiful. It is studded with villas, each in its own thicket of luxuriant foliage, intermingled with the olive and the vine. The town has not many prominent edifices. An ancient castle or tower, upon which the " biscia," or viper, of the Viscontis is yet to be seen, and a round citadel built by the Genoese, are conspicuous objects. The church has nothing remarkable. Whatever importance is possessed by Spezia results from the Genoese, who acquired it in 1276 by the then not unusual means of purchase from Nicolo de' Fieschi, Count of Lavagna. At a short distance from the shore, to the S. of Spezia, the water of the gulf offers the remarkable phenomenon called the *Polla*, resulting from the gush of an abundant submarine freshwater spring. It occupies a circular space 25 ft. in circumference, and sometimes rises above the adjoining sea-level. On the surface, at least, it is however not sufficiently fresh to be drinkable. Various contrivances have been suggested for conducting the water to the shore, or otherwise enabling vessels to fill their casks.

Neighbourhood of Spezia. — The beautiful scenery of the gulf of Spezia can be best seen by coasting along its shores in a boat. The road on the western side is very good, and affords a beautiful drive as far as Porto Venere.

There are seven fine coves on the western side of the gulf. Beginning at the northern end near la Spezia, and proceeding along the shore to the southward, they occur in the following order:—1. Cala di Marc, in the mouth of which rises the *Polla* spring : 2. Fezzano: 3. Panigaglia, where Napoleon wished to make his dockyard : 4. Delle Grazzie : 5. Varignano, where are, the quarantine ground for vessels arriving at Genoa, an extensive lazaretto, and fortifications : 6. La Castagna : 7. *Porto Venere*, 2200 Inhab., at the extremity of the S.W. promontory of the gulf of Spezia, one of the most picturesque places on the coast. The temple of Venus, from which this town is supposed to derive its name, may, as antiquaries suppose, be traced in the dilapidated Gothic church of *San Pietro*, which boldly overlooks the sea, and from which there is a magnificent view. Another church worth notice is that of *San Lorenzo*. The marble of the rock upon which Porto Venere stands, black, with gold-coloured veins, is exceedingly beautiful. The Genoese acquired Porto Venere in the year 1113, and encircled it with walls and towers, of which some portions remain. Four of the then most illustrious families of Genoa—De' Negri, Giustiniani, Demarini, and De' Fornari — were sent to rule the colony; and it is probable that they were accompanied by others of inferior rank, the dialect of the inhabitants being still pure Genoese, whilst in the vicinity another dialect is in use.

Immediately opposite to Porto Venere is the island of Palmaria, a mile across, and S. of it the two still smaller ones of Tino and Tinetto. In it are quarries of one of the most highly esteemed varieties of the Genoese marbles, called *Portor*, which has brilliant yellow veins on a deep black ground, like that of Porto Venere. Louis XIV. caused a great deal of it to be worked for the decoration of Versailles. The beds dip about eight degrees to the N., or a little to the E. of N. The island commands fine views of the gulf of Spezia.

Palmaria contains but one house, properly so called, which, for several years, was tenanted by Mr. Brown, British consul at Genoa, and his family. Upon Tino is a lighthouse, the persons having the care of it being the only inhabitants of the island.

On the eastern side of the gulf is *Lerici*, anciently belonging to the Pisans, who fortified it against their rivals both of Lucca and of Genoa. Upon the principal gateway an inscription was affixed, remarkable as being one of the earliest examples known of the lapidary application of the "lingua volgare." It was to the following effect :—

" Scopa boca al Zenoese,
Crepacuore al Porto Venerese,
Streppa borsello al Lucchese."

The wit, if it can be so called, is clumsy enough; but it produced the effect of annoying those against whom it was directed; and when the Genoese won Lerici in 1256, they carried off the inscription in triumph; but this was not enough : they replied in their turn by some strange rhyming Leonines of rather a higher tone, which are yet existing upon one of the towers of the castle. This castle is picturesquely situated on an advancing point, which, sheltering the little cove behind it, forms the harbour. It was at Lerici that Andrea Doria transferred his services from Francis I. to Charles V., and thus gave that preponderance to the influence of the house of Austria in Italy which has affected the political situation of the country up to the present time. The terrors of the old *corniche* roads from Lerici to Turbia are alluded to by Dante in his Purgatorio, when, speaking of the difficulty of ascending the rock, he says

"Tra Lerici e Turbia la più diserta
La più romita via è una scala
Verso di quella, agevole e aperta."

There is a road connecting Lerici with that leading from la Spezia and Sarzana, and which falls into it near the ferry over the Magra.

The extreme S.E. point of this beautiful gulf is Punta Bianca, or White Cape, being formed of white marble. A little within it is the Punta del *Corvo* or Cape Crow, although one side of it is white, being formed of the same limestone. The entrance to the gulf is guarded by forts, one upon the Punta di Santa Teresa, N.W. of Lerici, and two on the W. side, the batteries of Pessino and Santa Maria, near the Lazzaretto. A very beautiful chart of this great haven has been recently published by the French Depôt de la Marine.

The Ligurian commentators unanimously maintain that the well-known description in Virgil of the gulf in which Æneas took refuge after the storm was suggested by the gulf of Spezia. But that description is closely imitated from the Odyssey, and excepting the island, which Virgil has added, the gulf of Spezia resembles Homer's harbour quite as much as Virgil's. The two passages are Æn. i. 159-169, and Odyssey, N. 96-112.

The road from Spezia runs along a rising ground at the head of the bay, ascending gradually the ridge of hills that separates it from the valley of the Magra, and descending to the river near the village of Vezzano, which it follows, on the rt. bank, to the bridge, about 1 m. before reaching Sarzana. A road from the ferry to Lerici strikes off to the rt.

———

Cross the Magra, now on a fine bridge: its construction was attended with much difficulty, owing to the instability of the foundation for the piers. The Magra, the Macra of the Romans, divides the territory of Liguria from the Lunigiana, and the ancient Liguria from Etruria, as it did in more modern times the Genoese from the Tuscan possessions.

"Macra che per cammin corto
Lo Genovese parte dal Toscano."
Paradiso, ix. 89.

On the rt. of the Magra, just before crossing it, the town of *Arcola*, perched on a mountain, with a high tower and fine walls, and *Trebbiano*, equally well situated a little lower down, are attractive objects to the traveller, if he has time to leave the beaten track.

The province of the *Lunigiana*, which we now enter, belongs geographically to Tuscany, though politically separated from it. It was unequally divided between Sardinia, Massa, and Carrara (united until lately to the possessions of the Duke of Modena), and Parma; but the character and lineage of the inhabitants continue to mark it as a distinct province, and to connect it with its ancient history.

19 kil. *Sarzana.* From Spezia to Sarzana an extra horse both ways from Nov. 1 to May 1. (*Inns:* Albergo di Londra. The Bibolini, father and son, of the Albergo di Londra, are also the postmasters. The Hôtel della Nuova York, a new hotel on the ramparts, is kept by a brother of Bibolini the postmaster.) This city, which is the capital of the province of Levante, contains 9000 Inhab. It appears to have risen out of the decay of Luni, from whence the bishopric was removed. Its ancient government, which subsisted till the French invasion, was rather remarkable, being vested in an assembly called the "Parlamento," not, like the Parlamento of Florence, a primary or democratic meeting, but

Route 14.—*Sarzana*.   Sect. II.

mixed aristocratic representative body, composed of nobles, artificers, and peasants from the district included within the jurisdiction of the municipality. All these constitutional forms were swept away by the republicans; and when the Sardinian government was restored, the French forms of administration were substantially retained, as in most other parts of the kingdom.

The Duomo, built of white marble, begun in 1355, but not completed till a century later, is a fine specimen of the Italian-Gothic. In the centre of the west front is a good and unaltered rose window. The façade is remarkable for its simplicity. The interior has been much modernised, but the transepts contain two rich and florid Gothic altars. There is a Massacre of the Innocents, by *Fiasella*, surnamed *Sarzana*, from this his birthplace. In the façade are three statues, one of which represents Pope Nicholas V. (1447-1455), Thomas of Sarzana, who was a native of this town: his mother, Andreola de' Calandrini, is buried within. Though born of poor and humble parents, he was entirely free from the weakness of nepotism. He was the munificent protector of the Greeks when driven into Italy after the fall of Constantinople; an event which, as it is said, he took so much to heart, that it hastened his end. He was also the founder of the greatest literary repository of Italy—the Vatican Library. It was also from Sarzana that the reigning family of France appears to have derived its origin, as shown by the curious researches of Signor Passerrini, the director of the Archivio della Nobilta at Florence. The name of Buonaparte, a kind of sobriquet in its origin (as Malaparte was in the Gherardesca family), became the patronymic of a junior branch of the Cadolingis, Lords of Fucecchio, which had settled in the province of Lunigiana, and neighbourhood of Sarzana, where, as proved by contemporary documents, a certain notary called Buonaparte lived in 1264. It was the chief of this branch who emigrated to Corsica (Ajaccio), and from whom descended the family of Napoleon. The genealogy of the Counts of Fucecchio can be traced as far back as the middle of the 10th centy., so that the Imperial family of France may boast of an origin almost as remote as that of their Bourbon predecessors on the throne of that country. The Buonaparte family of S. Miniato was of Siennese origin, and was supposed generally before Signor Passerrini's researches, and by the first Napoleon himself, to be that from which the Imperial house derived its origin.

The castle and the ancient fortifications of the city form an extensive mass of buildings.

In this neighbourhood the peasant-girls wear hats which would not be too large for a full-sized doll, and are whimsically placed on the crown of the head.

Sarzanetta, a "rocca," or fortress, built by Castruccio degli Antelminelli, the celebrated Lord of Lucca, for the purpose of defending the territory against the Malaspinas, from whom it was won. It is a finely preserved specimen of ancient military architecture, with its commanding keep harmonising with the fortifications of the town.

12 kil. AVENZA.   (See Rte. 76.)

The distance from Avenza to Lucca is 52 m., passing through Carrara, Massa, and Pietra Santa (Rte. 76); from Lucca to Florence, by Rly., 48½ m. (Rte. 77); from Lucca to Pisa, 17 m. (Rte. 78); Leghorn to Pisa and Florence, 58½ m. (Rte. 79).

SECTION III.

LOMBARDY.

1. *Passports, Posting.*—2. *Money.*—3. *Weights, Measures.*—4. *Territory.*—5. *Nature of the Country, Agriculture, Productions.*—6. *Language.*—7. *Fine Arts of Lombardy.*

ROUTES.

ROUTE	PAGE	ROUTE	PAGE
17. Sesto Calende to Milan	141	25. Milan to *Mantua*, by *Cremona*	223
18. Laveno to *Varese* and *Como*	142	27. Milan to the Austrian Frontier at Peschiera, by *Treviglio, Bergamo, Brescia, Solferino*, &c.—Rail	229
19. Como to *Lecco* and Bergamo	150		
20. Lecco to Milan	152		
21. Como to *Milan*, by *Monza*—Rail	153		
22. Milan to Varese, by *Saronno*	208	28. Milan to Bergamo, by the post-road through *Gorgonzola* and *Vaprio*	258
23. Milan to Genoa, by *Pavia*	209		
24. Milan to Piacenza, by *Melegnano* and *Lodi*	219		

PRELIMINARY INFORMATION.

§ 1. PASSPORTS.—POSTING.

The regulations as to passports are on the same liberal system as in Piedmont. The Sardinian measures of distances, and rules as to post-horses, are now adopted on the few roads of Lombardy near which railway travelling has not yet penetrated.

§ 2. MONEY.

Money calculations are rather perplexing in consequence of payments being made in three currencies—in Lire Austriache, Lire Milanesi, and Lire Italiane. The Lira Italiana is that now used in all official and commercial transactions.

The Lira Milanese is a nominal coin: it is divided into 20 soldi, and each soldo is divided into 12 denari; its average value is 77 French centimes. The Lira Austriaca is the *zwanziger* of the German provinces of Austria, being the third part of a florin, and containing, therefore, 20 kreutzers, or 100 *centesimi*; ten centesimi are sometimes called a soldo, and in Venetia a piece of 5 centesimi, which is equivalent to the kreutzer of Germany, is called a carantano; but this name is hardly known at Milan. The Lira Italiana is of the same value and subdivisions as the French franc; in fact, the coins current under this name are the francs of France, Sardinia, and Switzerland.

§ 2. *Money.* Sect. III.

The following are the comparative average values of these coins:—

I.

Lira Italiana, or French Franc.		Lira Austriaca, or Zwanziger.		Lira Milanese.	
Lir.	Cent.	Lir.	Cent.	Lir.	Soldi.
1	—	1	19	1	8
2	—	2	38	2	16
3	—	3	57	4	4
4	—	4	76	5	12
5	—	5	95	7	—
10	—	11	90	14	—

II.

L. Austriache.		L. Ital.		L. Milan.	
Lir.	Cent.	Lir.	Cent.	Lir.	Soldi.
1	—	—	84	1	4
2	—	1	68	2	8
3	—	2	52	3	12
4	—	3	36	4	16
5	—	4	20	6	—
10	—	8	40	12	—

III.

Milanese.			Austrian.		Italian.	
Lir.	Soldi.	Den.	Lir.	Cent.	Lir.	Cent.
1	—	—	—	88	—	77
2	—	—	1	76	1	54
3	—	—	2	64	2	31
4	—	—	3	52	3	8
5	—	—	4	40	3	85
6	—	—	5	28	4	62
7	—	—	6	16	5	39
8	—	—	7	4	6	16
9	—	—	7	92	6	93
10	—	—	8	80	7	70

At present the currency of Lombardy, being the same as that of Sardinia, consists *in gold*, of Napoleons, and 40 and 80 franc pieces, and *in silver* of 5, 2, 1, and ½ franc pieces.

The Napoleon at the money-changers' is usually worth from 23½ to 24 Lire Austriache.

§ 3. WEIGHTS.—MEASURES.

Weights.—Although the metrical division is the only recognised standard, there are several local weights and measures which it is important to know the equivalents of. Those of Lombardy are extremely various and confused. Until within a few years there were in use, 11 units of money, 100 of linear measure, 120 of superficial measure, and a still greater number of measures of capacity. Some clearness has been gained by the use of, and by reference to, the French metrical system, which is still used in some of the government transactions. Some of the most commonly occurring measures are here given.

The *libbra piccola*, the ordinary commercial weight, is divided into 12 once, 288 danari, and 6912 grani, and equals 5044 English grains, or 0·32679 kilogrammes. Thus 100lb. of Milan = 72·06lb. avoirdupois, or 32·68 kilogrammes.

The *libbra grossa* is equal to 28 once, or 2·33 of the libbra piccola. Hence 3 libbra grossa equal 7 libbra piccola, and 100 libbra grossa equal 168·2lb. avoirdupois, or 76·25 kilogrammes.

Liquid Measures.—The *brenta* is divided into 3 staia, 6 mine, 12 quartari, 96 boccali, and 384 zaine or terzeruole, and contains 18·86 English gallons.

Land or Superficial Measures.—The *Pertica* consists of 1849 square braccie, and is equal to 783 square English yards, and to 654$\frac{7}{10}$ metres.

    1 *Pertica* is equal to   • • •   1$\frac{8}{5}$ Roods.
    1 English acre equal to • • •   6$\frac{1}{10}$ Pertiche.

Measures of length.—The *braccio* is divided into 12 once, 144 punti, and 1728 atomi, and is equal to 23·42 English inches, or 1·95 feet, or 0·5949 of a French mètre.

The Lombard mile contains 3000 *braccia da legname*, and is equal to 1952 English yards, or 1 mile and 190 yards, or 1784 mètres.

The Italian mile, which is sometimes used, is the same as the geographical or nautical mile, and is equal to 2025 English yards, and 1852 mètres. Eight of the Milanese or common Lombard miles make a post. As the post is reckoned and charged not merely in reference to the length of the road, the number of posts does not afford a satisfactory indication of its length.

§ 4. TERRITORY.

The ancient kingdom possessed by the Longobardi, or *Longbeards*, extended from the Apennines and the Po to the Alps, excepting Venice and some few border districts. From this great and opulent territory large portions were detached at various times by the Venetians, constituting nearly the whole of their *terra firma* dominions. A considerable portion was taken by the dukes of Savoy on the W. Mantua, Modena, Parma, Piacenza, Guastalla, all were dismembered from Lombardy, and erected into Imperial or Papal fiefs. The Swiss appropriated the Valtellina; and the Italian Balliages of Switzerland, now the canton Ticino (which still retains so many features of ancient Lombardy), resulted from this acquisition. The republic of Milan became subject to the lordship of Matteo Visconti I. in 1288. The Viscontis gained a great extent of territory which had belonged to the other Lombard republics; and their domains were erected into the "Duchy of Milan" by the Emperor Sigismund, in 1395. Milan, when acquired by the Spanish branch of the House of Austria, was thus reduced within comparatively narrow bounds. The treaty of Vienna, in 1814, restored to Austria all the possessions enjoyed by that house before the wars arising out of the French revolution, and also gave a great deal more—Venice, and the whole of the Venetian *terra firma*, the Valtellina, and some smaller districts. These possessions were erected into a distinct kingdom, and still possess a national character widely different from the rest of Italy, which continued to be possessed by Austria until last year, when Lombardy was ceded to France by the Treaties of Villafranca and Zurich, after the disastrous campaign of 1859, and by France transferred to Sardinia.

The population, according to the last census, amounts to 2,949,000, divided into seven provinces: Milan, including Crema and Lodi, 800,000 Inhab.; Brescia, 453,000; Como, 432,000; Bergamo, 410,000; Pavia, 400,000; Cremona, 350,000; Sondrio and the Valtelline, 104,000: each province having at its head a Governor, and the subdivisions Deputy Governors or Intendentes.

§ 5. NATURE OF THE COUNTRY.—AGRICULTURE.—PRODUCTIONS.

In the earliest times of the history of Italy, the whole of that rich country which now bears the name of Lombardy was possessed by the ancient and powerful nation of the Tuscans. Subsequently numerous hordes from Gaul poured successively over the Alps into Italy, and drove by degrees the Tuscans from these fertile plains. At about the beginning of the second century before Christ it became a Roman province. Large tracts of country, which, from being swampy or covered with forests, were uninhabited and unfit for cultivation, were now drained and levelled, and the whole assumed an appearance of prosperity and opulence which was not surpassed by any part of the Empire. The splendour of Verona may be traced in its remains; yet Verona was less celebrated than Padua, Milan, or Ravenna. But from the reign of Tiberius the decay of agriculture was felt in Italy. In the division and decline of the Empire the country was exhausted by the irretrievable losses of war, famine, and pestilence. St. Ambrose has deplored the ruin of a populous region, which had been once adorned with the flourishing cities of Bologna, Modena, Regium, and Placentia. The barbarians who took possession of Italy on the fall of the Western Empire were compelled by necessity to turn their attention to agriculture, which had been long in such a state of progressive but rapid depression, that the country could not furnish the imposts on which the pay of the soldiery depended, nor even a certain supply of the necessaries of life. After the occupation of Northern Italy by the Lombards, and the restoration of a tolerable degree of security and quiet, agriculture gradually improved. In spite of the constant warfare of the neighbouring cities during the existence of the Italian republics, both the towns and country advanced in population and wealth. Though the greatest territorial improvement of Lombardy took place, perhaps, at an æra rather posterior to that of her republican government, yet from this it primarily sprang, owing to the perpetual demand upon the fertility of the earth by an increasing population. The rich Lombard plains, still more fertilised by irrigation, became a garden, and agriculture seems to have reached the excellence which it still retains. Though Lombardy was extremely populous in the thirteenth and fourteenth centuries, she exported large quantities of corn. Many canals were cut: the *Naviglio Grande* was commenced in 1177, and completed in 1272; that of Pavia, though only recently brought into its present complete state, was begun in 1359; that which runs through Milan, in 1440, and finished in 1497; those of Bereguardo and the Martesana were begun in 1457; and that of Paderno in 1518. These canals, and the general character of the land, give to the districts of the plain a considerable similarity to Flanders.

At the present time this fertile section of the Sardinian kingdom, situated between the northern and the maritime Alps, and stretching from the Cottian and Pennine Alps to the Mincio and the Adriatic, comprises the most generally productive part of Italy. It is distinguished for its mulberry-trees and silk, its rice, Indian corn, wheat, and cheese. The vine, olive, chestnut, and a great variety of fruits are raised. Potatoes and various vegetables are also grown; and the peasantry are in a better condition than in most parts of the Peninsula. The farm-houses are often large, but inconveniently and scantily furnished, and, generally speaking, there is a great absence of completeness about the dwellings and in the implements of husbandry: many things are found out of order; and we seldom fail to observe a prevalence of the *make-shift* system in agriculture.

There is, however, a great variety in the pursuits, as well as in the habitations, of the people. Those in the mountain or hilly regions live and work very differently from those in the low countries of Lombardy and Venice. The flat countries derive their fertility from the mountain regions which fill those great subalpine reservoirs the lakes of Maggiore, Como, and Garda with the water which is carried downwards by the rivers, and serves to flood the lands of the plain requiring irrigation.

1. *The Mountainous Region* comprises the northern parts of the provinces of Bergamo, Brescia, and Como, and the province of Sondrio. The lower heights of the Alps consist of woodland and pastures. The trees are chiefly fir, larch, birch, oaks, and chestnut; the pastures in the mountain slopes and valleys. The herds ascend with their families, horses, and cattle to great elevations on the Alps during summer, and descend gradually, as in Switzerland, when winter approaches, to the valleys and low country. Cultivation is attended to with great labour on the southern declivities of the mountain region; the ground being formed in terraces, and the earth frequently carried up to supply what has been washed away by the rains. The vine is cultivated on the slopes. Walnut and mulberry trees are also grown. Common fruits, some hemp and flax, barley, rye, Indian corn, buckwheat, potatoes, common and kitchen vegetables, are all cultivated, though not in great abundance. Wax and honey are collected; the latter, especially that of Bormio, is delicious.

2. *The Littoral Region* (that bordering on the lakes) comprehends the districts of Gravedona, Dongo, Bellaggio, Menaggio, Bellano, and Lecco, in the province of Como; Lovere and Sarnico, in Bergamo; and Isco, Gargnano, Salò, and Dezenzano, in Brescia. It belongs to the elevated region, and forms the sides of high mountains, which shelter it in a great measure from the cold winds. It is exposed to the warm air from the S. and from the lakes; it is rarely subject to frost or snow; and in these districts the climate is much more temperate than on the hills and plains situated at a lower level. The lemon is cultivated in a few places, not only for ornament, but for its fruit.

These districts produce much wine and silk; the country is covered with villas and gardens, adorned with cypresses, magnolias, or acacias.

Properties are much divided on the Lake of Garda; a few yards of ground set apart for the cultivation of lemons suffice to maintain a whole family. The peasants there, are, properly speaking, gardeners. In this district are produced 15 millions of lemons and 40,000 lbs. of oil from the berry of the laurel. The lemon-trees are covered in winter by sheds. This region is chiefly dependent on the neighbouring mountains for timber. The cultivation of the mulberry is greatly extending, and that of the olive decreasing.

It must be noticed that for several years the mulberry has by degrees supplanted the olive, because the product of the mulberry-tree is more constant, and the time of crop less distant, whilst with the olive there are alternate years of abundance and scarcity. The olive crop is gathered towards the end of the year, and remains long exposed to accidents. In the province of Brescia, within these last 36 years, the production of silk has greatly increased; that of oil having diminished.

3. *Hilly*, or *Subalpine Region*. This region, forming a rather narrow belt of country, immediately N. of the low country, extends along the upper parts of the provinces of Milan, Como, Bergamo, and Brescia.

The chief productions of the hill country are the finest silk, wines, maize, millet, chestnuts, fruit, and vegetables.

The properties are less divided than in the mountain region; still they are often split into small farms (*Massarie*), of the value of from 15,000 to 20,000 francs.

Few peasants are proprietors; the greater part are simple tenants, and pay in kind. They keep cows and oxen, but milk, cheese, and butter are scarce: part of these articles are introduced from the mountains, and part from the low country.

The inhabitants attend principally to the cultivation of silk, and with the money gained from this they provide themselves with the necessaries of life. The houses in general are large, well aired, and clean, which they owe chiefly to the use these rooms are put to in rearing silkworms, as the worms are always more healthy in well-ventilated apartments. Here, as everywhere in the Lombardian provinces, the abodes of the peasantry are built of brick with tiled roofs.

The climate is salubrious, mild, and free from fogs. Hail-storms are frequent. In this region there are often clear days, when the adjacent flat country is enveloped in fog.

4. *The upper flat country* comprehends part of Somma, Gallarate, Busto, Cuggionno, Saronno, Barlassina, Desio, Monza, in the province of Milan; Verdello, Treviglio, Martinengo, and Romano, in Bergamo; Ospitaletto, Castiglione, and Montechiaro, in Brescia.

This region is traversed by gentle undulations which branch from the hills; the soil is in many places dry, and not of natural fertility. The districts to which irrigation does not reach are often to a great extent covered with heath. There are still some forests of oak, pine, and chestnut trees.

The subterranean waters are very deep, and the wells, for the greater part, are some hundred feet below the surface, as in the environs of Gallarate, Saronno, and Desio. The peasantry, when they have not some water-course in the neighbourhood, are obliged to collect the rain-water in tanks, called *foppe*, or large square ditches embedded with a clayey stratum, which contain the rain-water for the use of the cattle, and which in dry weather becomes green and unwholesome. The ground is cultivated in wheat, rye, Indian corn (which last suffers much from the drought), a little buckwheat, millet, melons, and, above all, in mulberry and fruit trees.

In situations near the water the apple-tree flourishes. Meadow land is obtained by means of artificial irrigation. The peasants are less active, less cordial, and less cleanly than in the hilly country. Instead of *massarie*, or stewardships, as in the hills, it is customary to have tenants who pay a money-rent for the house, and a rent in kind for the ground. When in want of fodder for the cattle, the deficiency is made up by an abundant supply of lupins and heath, which latter substance is collected for this purpose; it is cut from a portion of heath-ground, and given as an appendage to a certain quantity of cultivated land.

5. *The low flat country* comprehends Bollate, Gorgonzola, Melzo, Melegnano, and Corsico, in Milan; the provinces of Pavia, Lodi, Crema, and Cremona; Orzi-Novo, Verola-nuova, Bagnolo, and Leno, in that of Brescia; Marcaria, Bozzolo, Sabbioneta, Viadana, Borgo Forte, Mantua, Ostiglia, Lazarra, Gonzaga, Rèvere, and Sermide, in Mantua.

A grayelly soil prevails also in this region; but the same aridity does not exist as in the upper flat region. Rills of good water are easily formed by digging a very moderate depth. *Fontanili*, or Artesian wells on a small scale, are circular excavations dug in the earth, in which are placed long tubs, from the bottom of which bubble up copious streams of water. The water flows from the *fontanili* into a canal or ditch, along which it runs to irrigate the fields. The *fontanili* abound chiefly about Milan.

Water is also drawn from the rivers by canals. The smaller canals, *cavi* and *rugie*, are innumerable, and were cut at different times. They often encroach on each other, mixing their waters, or avoiding them by means of bridges, canals, or by syphons, called *salte di gatto*.

The waters are diligently measured by rules deduced from the law of hydrostatics, which have passed into an habitual practice. The canals are provided with graduated sluices (*incastri*), which are raised or lowered according as the case may be. The measure is called *oncia*, and corresponds to the quantity of water which passes through a square hole, three Milanese inches high (an oncia of Milan equals two inches English) and four inches wide, open one inch below the surface of the water, which, with its pressure, determines a given velocity. The value of a property depends on the command, the conveniency, and the goodness of the water. Hence the distribution of the waters is the object of local statutes, of diligent care and keeping.

The best irrigation is that in the low lands of Milan, Lodi, and Pavia.

In the country between Milan, Lodi, and Pavia, the cheese called in the country *Grana*, and by us Parmesan, is made. The provinces of Lodi and Pavia are the chief seats of its production.

In the eastern part of Lodi and Crema flax is largely cultivated, and exported to foreign countries by way of Venice and Genoa. In the marshy districts of the provinces of Milan and Cremona the cultivation of rice is on the increase.

In the more elevated parts of the Cremonese country, where irrigation is impossible, the cultivation of various kinds of grain, flax, mulberry-trees, and the vine is followed. In the low parts, along the Po, towards Casal maggiore, wine is the principal production.

The inhabitants of the low country are less inclined to be industrious, or to engage in commerce, than those of the upper. Hence in the lower countries manufacturing industry is greatly restricted. Nevertheless, in the Cremonese territory much linen is manufactured about Viadana; and at Pralboino, in the province of Brescia. Some classes of the peasantry, and chiefly those who tend large flocks, often change masters, and show a little-settled disposition.

In the Milanese districts the rich cheese called Stracchino is made from cream and unskimmed cow's milk. The best is produced about Gorgonzola, 12 m̃. E. of Milan.

Silk.—The culture of the mulberry, and the rearing of the silkworm, have, in commercial value, become the most important branch of Lombard industry. The white mulberry grows chiefly in rows, surrounding grounds under other cultivation, over a great extent of Lombardy. In most places it is pollarded, and is a dwarf thickly-leaved tree. When allowed to grow naturally it attains a tolerable size.

All things considered, Italy ranks higher for her silk than any other country. She supplies her own manufactures, and exports largely. In thirty years the production has grown from a small value to the enormous amount of 300,000,000 Austrian livres (more than 10,000,000*l.*). In 1800 the whole produce of the Lombardo-Venetian kingdom did not exceed 1,800,000 lbs. of silk; in 1856 it reached 2,512,500 lbs. avoird., valued at 3,333,000*l.* sterl. The value of the silk exported from the whole Lombardo-Venetian territory amounts to nearly 5,000,000*l.* sterling.

In Lombardy it is not found advantageous to raise more than one brood of worms during the year. The eggs are hatched in May, before the beginning of which a supply of leaves cannot be reckoned upon. The reeling the cocoons takes place in the autumn. A woman seated at a caldron containing hot water prepares and arranges the cocoons, while a girl turns the wheel on which the silk is wound. Considerable skill is required to manage the reeling. It is usually carried on in large buildings, with machinery adapted to the purpose, and is a very animated spectacle during the autumn.

§ 6. LANGUAGE.

The Lombard dialects are, perhaps, the harshest in all Italy. The sound of the French *u* is generally found in them. It is not merely unknown, but quite unpronounceable, beyond the Apennines; and Verri, the able historian of Milan, supposes it was left behind by the Gauls.

§ 7. FINE ARTS OF LOMBARDY.

For painting we must refer our readers to Kugler's Handbook of the Italian Schools, ed. Eastlake; for Architecture, to Mr. Fergusson's Handbook of Architecture, Mr. Street's Marble and Brick Architecture of North Italy, which is specially dedicated to a class of edifices almost peculiar to Lombardy.*

* Kugler's Handbook of the Italian Schools, 2 vols. 8vo., edited by Sir C. Eastlake, P.R.A., 1855. Fergusson—The Illustrated Handbook of Architecture, with 850 Illustrations on wood, 2 vols. 8vo., 1855. The Marble and Brick Architecture of North Italy during the Middle Ages, by G. E. Street, 1 vol. 8vo., 1855.

§ 7. *Fine Arts of Lombardy.*

Of ancient sculpture little has been found in Lombardy, except at Brescia. The earliest specimens of the sculpture of the middle ages are remarkably rude; fully as coarse as those of our Saxon ancestors; of which the bas-reliefs of the Porta Romana, at Milan, executed about the year 1169, immediately after the rebuilding of the city, are a striking specimen. About a hundred years afterwards sculpture produced a class of figures almost peculiar to Lombardy. These are frequently colossal, of lions and other animals, supporting the pillars of the portals of the churches, or sepulchral urns. In the 14th century several Tuscan sculptors were called in; but there appear to have been also many Lombards, though few of their names have been preserved, as they do not seem to have adopted the custom, so much practised in other parts of Italy, of inscribing them upon their works. The records of the Certosa of Pavia, begun in 1473, suddenly afford us ample information respecting the artists employed upon that splendid building—*Amadeo, Brioschi, Ettore d'Alba, Antonio di Locate, Battista* and *Stefano da Sesto, Piontello, Nava, Agrate, Fusina, Solari,* and others; but without giving us the means of distinguishing, at least in this building, the parts upon which they were severally employed. They have, however, one uniform character, extraordinary delicacy of finish in the details, and a pictorial management of their figures in bas-relief; so that it seems as if the works of Mantegna, or Pietro Perugino, were transferred to marble. Many of these sculptors were also architects, and in estimating the works of this school it must be recollected that sculpture was seldom used by them as a detached ornament, but was always attached to some architectural structure.

The pride, however, of Lombard sculpture is *Agostino Busti*, also called *Bambaja, Bambara,* or *Zarabaja,* who flourished in the early part of the 16th century; and by whom the cinque-cento style, or that of the Renaissance, was carried to perfection. The minute ornaments in which he excelled are usually arabesques of elegant invention, intermixed with fanciful ornament—animals, weapons, pieces of armour, flowers, insects. Busti is supposed to have died about the year 1540. *Brambilla*, who worked some time before the death of Busti, has much of his character. The colossal *terms* of the Doctors of the Church in Milan cathedral, supporting one of the great pulpits, are by him: his minuter ornaments are scarcely inferior to those of Busti. The great and interminable work of the cathedral of Milan, by furnishing constant employment, has maintained a school of sculpture of considerable merit, which subsists to the present day. A majority of the workmen and artists have always been from the neighbourhood of Como, where the profession has been hereditary in families from the time of the Lombards. In recent times *Marchesi* and the *Monti* family have given a well-deserved reputation to the Milanese school of sculpture.

The monuments of Roman architecture in the territory of ancient Lombardy are not numerous. Few of them are in accordance with the rules of classical architecture: the sculpture and the ornaments are indifferent; most of them belong to the lower empire, and have what may be considered a provincial character.

In mediæval architecture Lombardy offers much, both in civil and ecclesiastical buildings. The town-halls are interesting: they usually stand upon open arches; and above is the *Ringhiera*, or balcony, from which the magistrates addressed the people.

Military architecture also exists in great variety—the rude tower of the periods of Queen Theodolinda or King Berengarius; the castellated palace of the *Signori*, in the ages of the Italian republics; and the regular fortifications which, invented in Italy, have become universal throughout Europe.

§ 8. *Fine Arts of Lombardy.*

The earlier Lombard churches exhibit a very peculiar character, allied to that which we find in many of those of Germany, especially near the Rhine. It is very marked, and will be found to exist in almost every structure of that class. Of Pointed architecture there are two distinct styles : the one simple and bearing much analogy to the Italian Gothic of Tuscany ; the other florid or highly ornamented and introduced from Germany : to the latter belongs the Duomo of Milan.

Many of the Gothic and some of the cinque-cento buildings are of moulded brick, to which are added terra-cotta bas-reliefs. This kind of work has been carried to a degree of excellence which can only be appreciated in Lombardy. The colour is a shade lighter than that of our Tudor buildings ; the durability of the material is such as to be nearly as lasting as marble. In the style of the Renaissance Lombardy excels. The works of Bramante and Solari are full of imagination and effect. In later times Palladio had comparatively little influence; in civil architecture, the palaces of Milan, Pavia, and Cremona, are inferior to those of Vicenza or Genoa. At present the most eminent architects have been formed, either directly or indirectly, by the French and Roman schools.

In the middle ages Lombardy was the great instructress of Christendom in civil law and in medicine ; and in modern times science has been cultivated here with success ; while, in imaginative literature, Monti was one of the most elegant of modern Italian poets, and the name of Manzoni is an honour, not only to Lombardy, but to the Italian tongue. His historical novel, the Promessi Sposi, should be in the traveller's hands in his excursions in and about Milan. It is a real guide-book both to the scenery and the history of that lovely land.

ROUTES.

FROM THE LAGO MAGGIORE TO MILAN.

As a great number of persons who visit Northern Italy arrive by way of the Simplon, the St. Gothard, and the Bernardino passes from Switzerland, they will find it convenient to examine the shores of the Lago Maggiore before entering Lombardy, either by stopping at Baveno, or at the Isola Bella, where there is now a very fair inn (the Delfino), if they have crossed the Simplon, or at Bellinzona if they have come over the St. Gothard. We will suppose therefore that the traveller, after having visited the great attraction of the Lago Maggiore, the Borromean Islands, wishes to proceed into Lombardy: for this purpose he may choose between two routes, by Sesto Calende, or by the far more agreeable one through Laveno, Varese, and Como; by adopting the latter he will be able to visit the Lake of Como and its magnificent scenery.

ROUTE 17.
SESTO CALENDE ON LAGO MAGGIORE TO MILAN.

4¾ Austrian posts=40 m.

The road from the Simplon to Sesto Calende is described in the *Handbook for Switzerland* (Rte. 59). Railway from Arona to Borgo Ticino (employing ¼ hr.), from which an omnibus runs to the ferry-boat at Sesto. Since the opening of the rly. from Novara to Milan, it will afford the most expeditious means of reaching the Lombard capital from the shores of the Lago Maggiore. See Rtes. 2 and 6.

There are three lines of steamers daily ascending and descending the Lake, all in correspondence with the rly. trains from Milan, Genoa, and Turin; but as their hours of starting vary with the season, the traveller must have recourse to the local time-tables for the necessary information. The boats belong to the Sardinian Government and are well appointed; that which leaves Magadino at 5·50 A.M. calls at Laveno and Isola Bella, arriving at Arona at 11·50, in time for the trains to Milan, Genoa, Bologna, and Turin. The boat that leaves Sesto at 5·15 A.M., and Arona at 7, calls also at Laveno about 9½ A.M., and reaches Magadino at 11 A.M. Nearly all the boats, both in ascending and descending, stop off the Borromean Islands to land passengers.

Sesto Calende. (*Inn:* La Posta, very indifferent.) Public conveyances start for Milan on the arrival of each steamer, and a regular diligence at midday. The distance, about 40 English miles, requires at least 6 hours, and in rainy weather longer; but as the same distance can be performed in 3½ hrs. passing by Novara, this road is now seldom used by travellers. Except the mediæval church of San Donato, there is nothing to detain the traveller at Sesto.

On leaving Sesto the road crosses the plain of the Ticino by a very gradual rise to the foot of the hills of La Somma, as we approach which large deposits of erratic blocks are seen on either side: the village of *Somma* is situated on the top of this ridge, 500 feet above the Lago Maggiore. The view of the chain of the Alps, and of Monte Rosa in particular, from here and during the ascent from Sesto, is magnificently grand. There is a mediæval castle bearing the arms of the Viscontis at Somma; but the object most interesting is an enormous cypress-tree, so old as to be said to date from the time of Julius Cæsar. It is in an angle formed by the bend of the road, which Napoleon is said to have caused to be diverted from its straight course in order to prevent the destruction of the tree, at first decided on by his engineers. It was in this neighbourhood that took place the battle between Scipio and Hannibal, wherein the latter was victorious.

Somma is situated at the top of a ridge parallel to the course of the Ticino, consisting of sand and gravel, with huge boulders, and which, from its elevation, cannot be irrigated. In many parts it forms a waste, covered with heath, and known as the *Bruguiera* of Somma and Gallarate. Efforts have been made at different times to bring it into cultivation, but to little purpose. A plan has been recently brought forward to convey a canal of irrigation from the Lake of Lugano, the only one of the great Alpine reservoirs whose superior level would allow of its waters reaching here.

1¼ *Gallarate*, a large town on the eastern side of the Somma hills, at the commencement of the fertile region that extends to Milan; good roads branch off from here to Varese on the

N. and to Busto Arsizio on the S. A very rich district, cultivated in Indian corn and mulberry-trees, extends from Gallarate to

⅞ *Cascina Buon Jesu*, a short distance beyond which the road descends to the Olonna, which it crosses at *Castellanza*, around which there are some large villas. From this point it follows at a short distance the l. bank of that river as far as Milan. At *Busto*, 1 m. from Cascina, are some frescoes by G. Ferrari, in a church built from the designs of Bramante.

1¼ *Rho*, near the confluence of the Lura and Olonna. There is a large church here, designed by Pellegrini, and only recently completed. From here the country is one continuous garden of mulberry-trees, maize-fields, and meadows, until at the termination of a fine avenue we arrive opposite the Triumphal Arch of the Simplon, close to which is the gate by which Milan is entered.

1¼ MILAN (see Rte. 21).

ROUTE 18.

LAVENO TO VARESE AND COMO.
30 m.

This route may easily be performed in a day, enabling the traveller to visit Varese and Como, or in two, to visit not only the town of Como, but its Lake, and to reach Milan by railway on the second evening. By persons pressed for time Milan may be reached from Laveno in 7 hours, as expeditiously as by the preceding route, whilst in every respect it is more agreeable and equally economical; leaving the Borromean Islands or Baveno by the steamboat, which calls at the former about 8 A.M., and lands its passengers at Laveno at 9, from which a good public conveyance starts for Varese and Como, and for which places can be secured on board the steamboat. As the steamers do not generally embark carriages from the Borromean Islands or Baveno, it will be necessary for those who have arrived at the latter place by the Simplon road to send them round to Pallanza, or Arona, or to embark them on board one of the large lake boats, which will generally make the passage across in 1½ hr. The advantages of this over the preceding route are that it traverses a very beautiful country, and will enable the traveller to visit Varese, to make a diversion to Lugano from Como, to examine its lovely lake, and to see Monza before proceeding to the capital of Lombardy.

The distance by water from the Borromean Islands to Laveno is about 4 m.

Laveno (*Inns:* La Posta, very fair; il Moro), the principal town on the eastern side of the Lago Maggiore, is situated on the shores of a small, well-protected bay; it had of late years been selected as the naval station for the Austrian war steamers, and had been fortified by the erection of two strong redoubts and an extensive casemated barrack. Laveno is supposed to occupy the site of the Roman station of Labienum. The distance from Laveno to Varese is 13 m., and is performed in about 2 hrs., although for a part of the way the road constantly ascends. Leaving the town we skirt the base of the mountain of Laveno, or Monte Boscero, which forms so fine an object in the landscape from the central parts of the Lago Maggiore, rising gradually to Gavirate: half way between these towns a road up the Val Cuvio branches off on the l. to Luino.

Gavirate is a large village on a rising ground near the W. extremity of the Lake of Varese, over which the view from here is very beautiful. A great deal of silk is produced hereabouts, and in the neighbourhood are quarries of the variety of marble called *marmo majolica* by the Milanese, extensively used for ornamental purposes: it is a variety of compact limestone of the age of our lower English chalk-beds. Between Gavirate and Varese, 7 m., the road ascends as far as *Comerio*, where it attains an elevation of about 750 ft. above the Lago Maggiore, passing through *Luinate* in a charming position, commanding a magnificent prospect over the Lakes of Commabbio, Monate, and Varese; there are some handsome villas about Comeria; a gradual descent of 3 m. from here brings us to Varese, passing on the l., but at some distance, the hill on which is situated the Sanctuary of the Madonna del Monte, or the Sagro Monte of Varese.

13 m. VARESE. *Inns: La Stella* and *l'Angelo*, both bad, and the less the traveller has to do with them the better; persons, however, who may wish to visit the Sagro Monte will be able to do so, and on their return proceed to Como, or to arrive at Camerlata in time for the last train to Milan. The public conveyances from Laveno generally stop here for 2 hrs., which will enable the traveller to go over the town.

Coaches leave Varese for Camerlata (the Stat. of the Como and Milan Rly.) and Como 3 times a day, at 4 and 8·30 A.M. and 2·45 P.M., performing the journey in about 3 hrs., fare 3 lire; and others start regularly for Laveno and Luino, corresponding with the calling at these places of the steamboats on the Lago Maggiore. A public conveyance, but of an inferior description, for Milan, by the way of Saronno, in 5 hrs.

All round Varese are numerous villas of the wealthy Milanese, of whom many reside here during the autumn. Varese is a city of 8000 Inhab., and has an hospital, schools, a theatre, and several factories for the winding of silk from the cocoons. The principal church, *St. Vittore*, was built from the designs of *Pellegrini:* the façade was completed in 1791, by *Polack*. It contains frescoes, and a Magdalene, by *Morazzone;* a St. George by *Cerano*. The adjoining octagonal baptistery is in the Lombard style.

The chief object of attraction here is the celebrated Sanctuary of the Virgin, called La Madonna del Monte, which is situated on a lofty hill about 5 m. to the N.W. of the city. It is said to have been founded in 397 by St. Ambrose, to commemorate a great victory,—not in argument, but in arms,—gained by him on this spot over the Arians. The slaughter is said to have been so great that the heterodox party were exterminated. It was dedicated to the Virgin, and her statue, which was consecrated by St. Ambrose, is still preserved. At the end of the 16th centy. Agaggiari, a Capuchin monk, built, out of funds raised by his exertions, the 14 chapels which stand by the side of the road which leads to the church on the summit. A good road leads to Robarello, a village about 2½ m. from Varese, where ponies or sedan-chairs may be hired to make the ascent. A pony costs 1 fr. 50 c.; a chair 4 fr. The walk up will be, to most people, easy. The entrance to the road is through a species of triumphal arch.

The fourteen chapels represent the mysteries of the Rosary; the first five represent the mysteries of joy, the second five the mysteries of grief, the last four the mysteries of glory. They contain coloured statues in stucco, like those at Varallo and Orta (see *Swiss Handbook*), and frescoes, by *Morazzone, Bianchi, Nuvolone, Legnani,* and others of the painters of the Milanese school of the 16th century. Over the fountain, near the last chapel, is a fine colossal statue of Moses, by *Gaetano Monti*. Connected with the church is a convent of Augustinian nuns. There are several inns at the top, the number of pilgrims being very considerable. Those who are not tempted by the religious objects may be perhaps induced to visit the Santuario by being told that the ascent affords the most magnificent views of the rich plain of Lombardy as far as the Apennines, of the higher and lower chains of the Alps, and the lakes of Varese, Comabbio, Biandrone, Monate, Maggiore, and Como.

Five roads branch off at Varese : one to the S., which joins the Simplon road at Gallarate ; a second, 13 m. to Laveno, where the Lago Maggiore may be crossed to the Borromean Islands, and to Stresa, and Baveno on the Simplon road ; a third to Como, hilly, about 17 m. ; a fourth by Arcisate to Porto on the lake of Lugano, the last very interesting to geologists ; and a fifth to Milan by Saronno. (See Rte. 22.)

On leaving Varese for Como we pass through the suburb of Biume, which contains several handsome villas of the Milanese aristocracy, and soon descends into the pretty valley of the Olonna. After crossing the river a steep ascent brings us to the town of *Malnate*, on the edge of the escarpment which bounds the valley on the E. ; a gradual ascent during the next 6 m., as far as the village of *Olgiate*, leads to the highest point of the road, about 730 ft. above the Lake of Como. The scenery on the l. towards the Alps is very fine ; a deep depression marks the site of the Lake of Lugano, through which may be descried the church of San Salvatore, which from the summit of its dolomitic peak towers over the capital of the canton of Ticino. As we approach Como the road runs near the foot of a lower range of subalpine hills, at the E. extremity of which is the Monte Baradello, remarkable for its fine ruined mediæval castle, and close to which is the rapidly-increasing village of Camerlata, where the Stat. of the Como and Milan Rly. is situated. Travellers proceeding to the latter place will stop here, whilst those going to Como will continue by a steep but a well-managed descent of less than a mile, entering the town by the new gate behind the cathedral, after passing through the long suburb of S. Abondio.

COMO, 20,000 Inhab. (*Inns :* the *Angelo*, kept by Sala, has been greatly improved of late, and is now excellent ; charges moderate—bed-rooms 1½ and 2 fr., very good table-d'hote 3 fr., and breakfasts 1½ fr. ; it is pleasantly situated on the edge of the quay, on the E. side of the little port. On the opposite side of the harbour is the *Albergo d' Italia*, tolerably good. The *Corona*, outside the town, second-rate. Families who wish to remain some time at Como may make an economical arrangement, during their stay, at the Angelo. There is a very comfortable hotel, with moderate charges, the *Albergo della Regina d' Inghilterra*, near the Villa d' Este at Cernobbio, about 3 m. from Como, and in a delightful situation ; attached to it are baths, large pleasure-grounds, and a water-cure establishment ; an omnibus runs between it and the rly. stat.)

Steamboats leave Como at 8 a.m. and 5·30 p.m. for Colico and the different places on the lake, and return to Como at 1 and 8·30 p.m., performing the voyage each way in 3 hrs. Other steamers leave Como on market-days, Tues., Thurs., and Sat., at 1·30 p.m., for the several villages on the lake, and at early hours on Sat. for Lecco, returning in the afternoon—the latter will afford the best opportunity for seeing the Lecco branch of the lake.

Diligences. A coach leaves at 2·30 p.m. daily, for Lecco in 3 hrs., returning every morning at 10. To Varese 3 times a day, in 3 hrs., fare 3 francs.

Railway to Milan. The station is at Camerlata, about a mile S. of Como, for which omnibuses start to meet every train (3 or 4 a day), fare 50 centimes; but an exorbitant charge is made for luggage, one-half the amount charged for its conveyance by rly. to Milan.

Pleasure-boats for excursions may be hired opposite the Angelo: there is no tariff; 3 fr. an hr. is the understood charge, but by bargaining may be reduced to 2.

Como, situated at one end of the lake called by the ancients the Lacus Larii, was anciently a town of considerable importance. A Greek colony having been settled in this district by Pompeius Strabo and Cornelius Scipio, and subsequently by J. Cæsar, *Comum* was made the chief seat of this colony. It had hitherto been an inconsiderable place, but from that time it rose to a great degree of prosperity under the name of Comum Novum. It appears from the letters of the younger Pliny, who was born at Comum, that his native city was, in his time, in a very flourishing state, and in the enjoyment of all the privileges which belonged to a Roman *municipium*. There are traces of this Greek colony in the names of many places on the lake, *e. g.* Nesso, Pigra, Lenno, Dorio, &c. Como does not figure in history after the fall of the Empire till the year 1107, about which time it became an independent city, and engaged in wars with Milan, which ended in its total destruction in 1127. It was rebuilt by Frederic Barbarossa in 1155, and four years afterwards was fortified. It remained a republic for two centuries, until it fell under the dominion of the Viscontis. Since that time Como has followed the fortunes of Milan.

Como is a place of considerable trade and industry. Its silk fabrics formerly stood next in rank to those of Milan. The stuffs known by the names of *mantini* and *amorelle* had a wide reputation. Time was when the number of looms at work at Como exceeded those of Lyons. Como has manufactures of silks, woollens, cotton, yarn and soap. It trades from its port on the lake chiefly with Switzerland. It exports rice, corn, and other agricultural produce for the mountain districts, and large quantities of raw silk in transit through Switzerland, for Germany and England, by the routes over the Splugen and St. Gothard.

The view of Como from the N. is peculiarly striking, the city being spread out on the undulating shore of the lake; and in the background is the ancient picturesque tower of the *Baradello*, connected with one of the most important passages in the history of Milan. Ugo Foscolo used to say that it was impossible to study in the neighbourhood of Como; for the beauty of the landscape, always tempting you to the window, quite prevented you from giving proper attention to your book.

The *Cathedral*, or *Duomo*, is a fine building, the beauty of the architecture being heightened by the richness and solidity of the material used in its construction. It is of marble. A long series of architects, of whom *Lorenzo de' Spazi* was the first, from 1396 to the last century, have been engaged upon it, and hence a corresponding variety in the style of its different parts. The façade was begun by *Lucchino di Milano*, in 1460, and completed, between 1487 and 1526, by *Tomaso Rodario*, of Maroggia. This architect was also a sculptor, and an excellent workman. Many of the statues were executed by his own hand. But he was criticised by a fellow artist, the celebrated *Cristoforo Solaro*, nicknamed *Il Gobbo*, or the Hunchback; by whose advice the designs for the other parts were altered, perhaps improved. The cupola, or dome, was completed about 1732, by *Juvara*. The façade is Gothic with the exception of "the three entrance doors, which are round-headed, and of the richest Lombard style: the façade is divided by slips, or pilasters, with statues all the way up, enclosing a most magnificent rose window, and studded with rich tribunes and canopies; elegant trefoil corbels circulate round the cornice and pinnacles, the centre of which chiefly presents a circular temple of small columns on brackets, rising from a tall pedestal and supporting a diadem of lesser pinnacles, and is unique."—*Hope.* The lower portions of the pilasters, and of the façade, are covered with curious emblems, some *masonic*, some religious, interspersed with texts and inscriptions in beautiful Gothic letters. Many of these bas-reliefs are types; *e.g.* a fountain, a vine, a lily, a church upon a hill. Amongst the larger bas-reliefs, the Adoration of the Magi in the arch of the door should be noticed; but the most remarkable ornaments of this front are the statues of the two Plinys, erected by the Comaschi in the 16th centy. to their "fellow citizens." They are placed under canopies in an ornamental style by Rodario. The younger Pliny was much attached to Como, and he resigned a considerable legacy in its favour, founded a school, built a temple, and fully deserves commemoration as a benefactor. Verona has also claimed the honour of being the birthplace of the elder Pliny; but all the ancient authorities are in favour of Como, where the Plinian family was long established. Of the younger Pliny, there is no doubt that he was born here. Very many inscriptions have been found at Como relating to the family: one, much mutilated, is built into the wall of the S. side of the Duomo, relating to a Caius Plinius Cæcilius Secundus, who may be (though some doubt has been raised by antiquaries) the individual of whom Como is so justly proud.

The other sides of the exterior are in the style of the Renaissance. The lateral doorways, particularly that on the northern side, with angels and fanciful columns, are elegant. Both these doorways were executed by Rodario.

The arabesques are interspersed with birds, animals, serpents, and children. The 3 windows of each aisle are splendidly ornamented with arabesques and portraits, in relief, of illustrious men, in the best *cinquecento* style, and the buttresses between them surmounted by elegant pinnacles. The cupola is in the complicated and overloaded style of the French architecture of the 18th century.

In the interior of the Duomo the nave and two aisles are *Italian Gothic*, with finely-groined vaults; the transepts and choir are the Italian of the Renaissance. The choir is circular, with 5 windows on two tiers, each separated by Corinthian pilasters; around are placed statues of the patron saints of Como. The painting of the vault of the choir and nave has been recently restored. The large wheel window over the W. door, with those on each side containing stained glass paintings of the patron saints in three tiers or compartments, produce a very fine effect, especially with the evening sun shining through them.

Paintings, altars, and monuments.—Luini. The Adoration of the Magi, in distemper. In this painting the artist has introduced a giraffe, drawn with tolerable correctness. This seems to show that the animal had then been seen in Italy.—St. Jerome, or rather the history of his life, in compartments.—The Nativity, also in distemper. In this painting Luini's sweetness of conception is exemplified in the expression of the Virgin mother.—Another picture, St. Christopher and St. Sebastian, attributed to *Luini*, is probably only a copy. *Gaudenzio Ferrari.* The Marriage of the Virgin, a fine and unaltered specimen of this master.—The Flight into Egypt, in distemper. Some of the altars and chapels are worthy of notice.

The Altar of Santa Lucia, by *Tomaso di Rodario*, who has inscribed his name, 1492. The smaller statues at this altar are beautiful; so also are the candelabras, which, however, are partially and injudiciously concealed.

Altar of St. Abondio, third Bishop of Como; his statue in the centre; his miracles in compartments around. *Altar of Santa Apollonia*, erected by Ludovico di Montalto, a canon of the cathedral, in the same rich and singular style. *Altar of Sant' Ambrosio*, erected in 1482, by John de Veludino, another canon. *Altar of the Vergine dell' Angelo*, a fine altarpiece, representing St. Jerome, St. Francis, St. Carlo, and St. Anthony. In front, the Canon Raimundi, by whom it was presented.

Chapel of the Vergine dell' Assunta, called the Altar of the Marchese Gallo. The Baldachino of marble is splendid.

A modern altarpiece, by *Marchesi*. St. Joseph and our Lord as a child; considered as one of the best works of this artist. *Altar of the Mater Doloarrosa — Alt of the Cenacolo —* both with fine sculptures: the first has an Entombment over it.

Tomb of Bishop Boniface, of the 14th century. The statue of the bishop, sleeping in death, is striking. *Monument of Benedetto Giovio*, the historian of Como. Benedetto was the brother of the more celebrated Paolo Giovio. He was the first exact archæologist who appeared during the revival of letters. One of his most important works, yet in manuscript, is a *Thesaurus* of Roman inscriptions found in this country; and it is said that not one spurious inscription has been detected in these collections. He died in 1544, and was buried here with great solemnity. This tomb was erected by his brother in 1556.

In the *Sacristy* is a fine picture by *Luini*—a Virgin and Child, with SS. Jerome, Augustine, Anthony, and Nicholas.

There are two organs; one built in 1596, but afterwards much improved; the other, in 1650, by Father Hermann, a German Jesuit. The former is rather out of repair, the tone of the latter is exquisite. Just as you enter the Duomo are two animals, neither lions nor tigers, but something between, supporting the basins for holy water. These, without doubt, are remains of the porch of the original cathedral, and supported its columns.

The circular Battisterio, on the l. of the entrance into the church, is attributed to Bramante; it consists of 8 Corinthian columns of Breccia marble, with the font in the centre, but, having neither dome nor cupola, has an unfinished look. The ornaments exhibit the last gradation of the Renaissance.

The Bishop of Como has an extensive diocese, extending over a great portion of Italian Switzerland. The Duomo was wholly built by voluntary contributions, the Comaschi taking great pride in this chief ornament of their town and diocese, and the manner in which the edifice was begun by the people is recorded in the inscriptions upon it.

By the side of the Duomo stands the *Broletto*, or town-hall, built of alternate courses of black and white marble, and with one entire course and a few red patches. This building, completed in 1215, is interesting as a memorial of the ancient days of the independence of the Italian republics; as such a Broletto is, or has existed, in every Lombard city. The lower story is a *Loggia* upon 4 open arches. Above is a floor with large windows, where the chiefs of the municipality assembled; and from the middle window projects the "*ringhiera*," from which they addressed the crowd of citizens convened in *parliament* below; for, in the constitutional language of ancient Italy, the *parliamento* was the primary assembly of the democracy, from whence the powers of government originated, and to which the ultimate appeal was to be made.

The lower arches here are pointed, the upper circular.

Como possesses some other curious mediæval antiquities,—none more remarkable than the church of *San Fedele*. This building is considered to be of the era of the Lombard kings, and the exterior is nearly unaltered.

H 2

It was for some time used as a cathedral before the erection of the present one: it has a triangular arch with straight sides over the entrance, octagonal cupola, and round apsis, small galleries outside under the cupola, and a triforium or gallery inside for the women. The style is not unlike that of the oldest churches of Cologne. It contains some very rude but remarkable imagery; *e. g.* a conflict between a dragon and a serpent, flanking a doorway (itself most singular) at the N. side of the apse. The interior has been modernised. In the unaltered parts serpents and lions abound. One monster sustains the basin for holy-water. There are some good frescoes here by *Camillo Procaccini*.

Ch. of *St. Abondio*. In the suburb of the Annunciata, and "on the site of the ancient city, at a short distance from the present one, is the church of San Carpofero, first Bishop of Como, reckoned the oldest of the place, with a round apse and square tower. The church was first dedicated to St. Peter and St. Paul, and after the death of St. Abondius, third Bishop of Como, in 469, to that holy prelate, buried within its precincts. It was the cathedral of the old city, presents single round-headed windows, with small pillars and arches, again enclosed in broad flat borders of the richest arabesque and basket-work. Though small, it has double aisles, and of the outermost range the pillars are smaller and the arches lower than of the innermost."— *Hope*. It contains the tombs of several of the bishops of Como. In the apse are some curious old frescoes, representing scenes from the life of our Lord. This church now serves as the chapel of an ecclesiastical seminary.

The *Theatre*, standing behind the Duomo upon the site of the old castle, is a handsome building.

The *Liceo Imperiale e Reale*, recently completed. The front is adorned with busts of the great men whom Como has produced. It contains reading-rooms, a bust of the celebrated singer Madame Pasta, a collection of natural history, a laboratory, &c., and is well organized and conducted.

The *Piazza Volta*, so called from the eminent philosopher, whose statue, by Marchesi, stands in the centre of it, opposite the house in which he lived. Como gave birth to Pinzzi the astronomer, the discoverer of the planet Ceres, and to Volta, whose discoveries seem to pervade the whole system of physical science. Alessandro Volta was born at Como, February 19th, 1745: he was intended for the law; but his first work, published in 1769, and which treated upon electricity, sufficiently announced the direction which his mind had permanently received. He died in 1819.

Palazzo Giovio, still belonging to the family, contains a number of Roman inscriptions and other antiquities —a collection begun by Paolo Giovio. Later times have added several interesting relics from suppressed churches and convents. The library contains several of the inedited works and papers of Paolo Giovio and of Benedetto the historian.

The gateways of the city are fine specimens of the military architecture of the middle ages, and add much to its picturesque appearance: that which opens towards Milan is the most perfect.

The little *Port* of Como is formed by two piers, each ending in a square pavilion, the view up the lake from which is pleasing. The lake abounds with fish. Of these the most numerous are the trout, pike, perch, and the *agone*, a species of *clupea*. The agoni migrate periodically from one end of the lake to the other.

The plan of the city of Como has been assimilated to the shape of a crab, the city being the body, and the two suburbs of *Vico* and *St. Agostino* being the claws. Vico is on the N.: it abounds with pleasant walks and handsome villas. The *Raimondi* or *Odescalchi*, *Visconti*, and *Rezzonico Villas* are amongst the most splendid, and further on the *Villa d' Este*, long inhabited by Queen Caroline of England.

Near here is the *Gallia,* supposed to be upon the site of one of Pliny's villas.

The *Borgo di St. Agostino* is the manufacturing suburb of Como. The church and the Casa Gallietta, containing some tolerable pictures, are its principal objects of note. In the hill above is the grotto of *St. Donato,* much visited by pilgrims; and still higher is *Brunate,* also a place of fond devotion; the object of popular veneration being an ancient, uncouth image called the *Beata Guglielmina,* an English princess unknown to history, and who, flying from her native home, became a recluse and died here. The peasant women believe that by her intercession they obtain help in nursing their children.

The inhabitants of Como and its vicinity have been celebrated as masons ever since the days of the Lombards. In the laws of Rothar, one of the earliest of the Lombard kings, mention is made of the "Magistri Comacini," who travelled the country as masons, which they continue to do at the present day.

There is a charming walk from Como to Blevio, on the E. shore of the lake.

Above *Camerlata,* about a mile to the S. of Como, upon a sandstone rock, stands the lofty tower of *Baradello.* Some ascribe this building, whose castellated walls run down the abrupt sides of the steep, to the Lombard kings. It is more probably of the age of Barbarossa. It is interesting as the monument that witnessed the fall of the first of the dynasties which successively tyrannised over Milan. This city, one of the first which asserted its independence, was the first amongst the Italian republics to lose it. Her freedom dates from the peace of Constance in 1183; her thraldom from 1246, when *Pagano della Torre,* the chief of that once powerful family, was inaugurated as the protector of the republic. In the hands of the Torriani the power continued until the accession of Napoleone della Torre, who, created *Anziano Perpetuo* by the people, and Vicar of the Empire by Rodolph of Hapsburgh, governed with absolute authority. The nobles whom he had exiled, guided by Ottone Visconti, were in possession of the city of Como, and on the 21st of January, 1277, Napoleone and his troop fell into the power of their enemy. The victors spared the lives of Napoleone and of all the members of his family whom they captured; but the prisoners were put in separate iron cages in the Baradello. What ultimately became of the others is not known; but Napoleone, after lingering several years, devoured by vermin, and suffering the most extreme misery, probably maddened by it, ended his captivity with his life by dashing his head against the bars of his prison. Upon the fall of the Torriani arose the power of the Viscontis.

Great numbers of erratic blocks are to be seen in the neighbourhood of Como. The material of these boulders is usually granite or gneiss. Many are found in the mountains between Como and Lecco. One of the most celebrated is on the mountain-pastures of San Primo, which stands above the bend of the lake, near Carvagnana and Nesso. This boulder is 59 ft. long, 39½ ft. wide, and 26 ft. high. There is another at a short distance from it, smaller, which the country people call the Sasso della Luna. Many have been broken up for building-stones. The pillars of the church at Valmadrera, near Lecco, which are 46½ ft. high, and 3 ft. 8 in. in diameter, were cut from an erratic block found upon Mount Valmadrera at the height of 1065 ft. above the level of the lake. The geologist Curioni observed a mass of granite of about 710 cubic ft. some hundred yards above Camnago, 2 m. to the eastward of Como.

[Although few now travel otherwise than by the Railway, it may suit persons travelling with vetturino or their own horses to continue along the old post-road 25 m. (there are no longer post-stations upon it), which passes by

Fino. The country here has the full character of the plain of Lombardy—level, exceedingly fertile, and dotted with villas: maize and millet are the prevailing crops. The road is often bordered by rows of trees, and mulberry trees are interspersed in the fields.

Barlassina, a town of some extent. The church which belonged to the suppressed convent of Dominicans, is now converted into an ecclesiastical seminary. The convent annexed to it was founded upon the spot where St. Peter Martyr was slain, as commemorated in Titian's celebrated picture. About 2 m. further on the road is *Cesano*, belonging to the Borromeo family, who have a large villa on the outskirts of the village.

About 3 m. beyond Barlassina, near Bovisio, and on a slight eminence about a mile on the rt. of the road, stands the Villa of *Mombello*. It commands a fine view of the plain of Lombardy. Here Napoleon established himself after the fall of Venice. "Negotiations for a final peace were there immediately commenced; before the end of May the powers of the plenipotentiaries had been verified, and the work of treaties was in progress. There the future Emperor of the West held his court in more than regal splendour; the ambassadors of the Emperor of Germany, of the Pope, of Genoa, Venice, Naples, Piedmont, and the Swiss republics assembled to examine the claims of the several states which were the subject of discussion; and there weightier matters were to be determined, and dearer interests were at stake, than had ever been submitted to European diplomacy since the iron crown was placed on the brows of Charlemagne. Josephine there received the homage due to the transcendent glories of her youthful husband; Pauline displayed those brilliant charms which afterwards shone with so much lustre at the court of the Tuileries; and the ladies of Italy, captivated by the splendour of the spectacle, hastened to swell the illustrious train, and vied with each other in admiration of those warriors whose deeds had filled the world with their renown. Already Napoleon acted as a sovereign prince; his power exceeded that of any living monarch; and he had entered on that dazzling existence which afterwards entranced and subdued the world."

MILAN (see Route 21).]

ROUTE 19.

COMO TO LECCO AND BERGAMO.

This route, whilst it passes through perhaps the most lovely country in the N. of Italy, will enable the traveller who has visited the lakes to proceed to Venice without passing through Milan. As we have already remarked, most travellers who now enter Northern Italy from the side of Switzerland do so by the great Alpine passes of the Simplon and the St. Gothard; to those this route may be preferable, as enabling them to continue their examination of the subalpine region and of the other lakes on the southern declivity of the Alps before proceeding to Venice. We have already described in the preceding route the first part of this subalpine region between Laveno and Como.

The distance from Como to Lecco is 17 m., the road rather hilly, but in every other respect excellent. A good public conveyance leaves Como every day at 2·30 P.M., arriving at 7. Here the traveller will find another on the following morning for Bergamo, at 7·30, from which the Rly. is now open to Venice.

Leaving Como by the Porta Milanese, we soon begin to ascend the hills on the E. of the town, until the road attains its highest level opposite the village of *Tavernerio* on the l., before which it passes near *Camnago*, in the modest church of which is the tomb of the celebrated Volta. Further on, and upon the rt., rises the pointed ridge of *Montorfano*, which will well repay the geologist for visiting it (it consists of strata of a calcareous breccia of the Eocene period): the view from the summit is splendid. Continuing our road, we pass through the villages of *Cassano* and *Albese*; at the entrance of the former, on the l., is a curious leaning bell-tower. Beyond Albese we soon reach the top of a ridge, from which the panorama over the Pian d'Erba, the Lakes of Alserio, Pusiano, and Anone, backed by the serrated Alpine peaks of Canzo and of the Resegone di Lecco, is extremely beautiful. A gradual descent of 2 m. brings us to *Erba*, one of the largest towns of the district, and which gives its name to it, the *Pian d'Erba*, renowned as the most fertile in the upper or hilly region of Lombardy: there are several handsome villas here, especially the Villa Amalia, celebrated by Parini, from the grounds of which the view over the Brianza is incomparable. There is a very fair inn at Erba, where the tourist not pressed for time can take up quarters and make excursions, amongst which the most interesting, especially to the geologist, will be to the cavern called the Buco del Piombo, 3 m., excavated in the secondary oolitic limestone; to the *Pian di S. Primo*, celebrated for its huge erratic blocks; and in the opposite direction to the beautiful villas of *Sordo* and *Inverigo*, the latter the masterpiece of the Marquis Cagnola, the celebrated architect; to *Incino*, with its tall Lombard *campanile*, on the site of the Roman Forum Licinii; and to *Canzo*, and even to Bellagio on the Lake of Como, ascending the very picturesque *Valassina*. Two m. beyond Erba the *Lambro* torrent, which soon afterwards empties itself into the Lake of Pusiano, is crossed, the road approaching the latter and that of Anone, passing through the villages of Cesana and Suello, and afterwards over a gentle rising ground; it follows from thence the Ritorto stream, the natural emissary of the Lake of *Anone*, to Malgrate opposite to Lecco. A road of about ½ m. down the rt. bank of the Adda, leads to the bridge at a short distance from the town.

17 m. *Lecco* (*Inns:* Leone d'Oro; Croce di Malta), a town of 8000 Inhab. on the l. bank of the Adda, where it emerges from the lake at the foot of an elevated range of mountains called the Resegone (saw), from its serrated summit, and which forms so picturesque an object in the landscape of the Brianza and Pian d'Erba. Lecco is situated on the shores of the lake, which sometimes inundates its streets: it is a place of considerable trade in silk and iron, of which it has manufactures. The market on Saturdays is a busy scene, and in the Villegiatura season is the place of rendezvous of the rich Milanese families from their villas in the neighbouring Brianza and Pian d'Erba. The branch of the Lake of Como at the extremity of which Lecco is situated is much wilder than the W. arm, and offers little to attract the tourist. A steamer traverses it once a week, on Saturday, arriving from Como early for the market, and returning in the afternoon. Diligences start daily to meet the rly. at Monza.

The distance from Lecco to Bergamo is about 16 m., and, as both towns are post stations, travellers with their own carriages will have no difficulty in getting on. A fair public conveyance leaves here every morning at 7·30, arriving in 4 hrs., in time for the rly. train that reaches Brescia at 2·30, Verona at 6·15, and Venice at 10·30 P.M.

Leaving Lecco, the road follows the l. bank of the Adda, which here widens so as to form a narrow lake called the Lago di Olginate, and the river itself for 3 m. further, from whence it runs in a more easterly direction through *Cisano*, close to the larger village of Caprino.

Crossing a low hilly country, the

eastern continuation of the Brianza, beyond the Adda, we reach *Ponte San Pietro*, on the Brembo, a stream which, rising on the S. declivity of the high alpine ridge that bounds the Valtellina on the S., empties itself into the Adda near *Vaprio* after a long course through the Val Brembana: 4 m. beyond P. S. Pietro we reach the lower town of Bergamo (see Rte. 28).

ROUTE 20.

LECCO TO MILAN.

32 m.

Lecco. (See Rte. 19.)

The road which connects Lecco with Milan is called the *Strada militare*, being a continuation of the great military road across the Stelvio, which is carried along the eastern shore of the Lake of Como. (See *Handbook for South Germany*, Rte. 214.) There are diligences at 5·15 A.M. and 2·15 P.M. to meet the rly. at Monza. On leaving Lecco, the road crosses the Adda, by a bridge of 10 arches, built by Azzo Visconti in 1335. The river is here flowing from the Lake of Lecco into the Lake of Olginate, or Pescate. About six miles from Lecco, a little to the rt. of the road, is the village of Greghentino, which gives its name to the neighbouring valley. Not far from this place, in descending to the Lake of Olginate, may be seen an enormous assemblage of erratic boulders. A geologist has described the spot by saying that it looks like a battle-field in the war of the giants.

The road all the way from Lecco to Monza skirts the district which is known by the name of La Brianza, the last elevations of the Alps, or what may be called the Subalpine hills, towards the great plain of Lombardy. Its boundaries are not exactly fixed, but generally the Brianza is held to include the hilly country between the Adda and the Lambro, from Lecco and Valmadrera, down to Monza, and on the W. of the Lambro, from the neighbourhood of Arosio to Como, and the foot of the mountains lying between the Lakes of Como and Lecco. These mountains enclose the head valley of the Lambro, called the Vallasina. The Brianza is celebrated for its richness and beauty: its intelligent inhabitants are masters of the art of cultivating the mulberry and rearing the silkworm, as well as in the preparation of the raw article for manufacture. The finest silk in Lombardy is produced in this district.

1½ Carsaniga. To the eastward of this lies the Montorobbio, which produces the best wine of the Milanese.

Arcore. There is a fine villa belonging to the Count Giov. d'Adda here. The chapel near the park gate is a handsome modern building in the cinquecento style: in it is a beautiful monument to a young Countess d'Adda, by the Swiss sculptor Vela, and a fine Madonna over the altar by the same distinguished artist. Before reaching Monza the road runs along the vice-regal park on the rt.

1 Monza. See Rte. 21.

The Strada militare for half the distance to Milan runs nearly parallel to, and at a short distance from, the railroad. Half way to Milan it crosses it, and from thence runs in a straight line to Loreto, where it falls into the Bergamo and Brescia road, which enters Milan by the Porta Orientale. The old post-road enters Milan by the Porta Nuova, running during the last two miles close by the side of the canal of the Martesana. To the rt. of the road, about two miles after having crossed the railroad, is La Bicocca, where the French, under Lautrec, were defeated by the Imperialists, 27th April, 1522.

1¼ MILAN. See Route 21.

ROUTE 21.

COMO TO MILAN, BY MONZA—RAIL.

KIL.		KIL.	
6	Cucciago.	32	Monza.
16	Camnago.	38	Sesto.
23	Seregno.	46½	Milan.
25	Desio.		

29 miles.

Railway from Camerlata near Como to Milan: trains four times a-day; the stations are Cucciago, Camnago, Seregno, Desio, Monza, Sesto, and Milan: the distance, 30 m., is performed in an hour and a half: the fares 6 and 3·90 A. l. An omnibus leaves Como to meet every train, by which a very exorbitant charge is made for conveying passengers' luggage. Omnibuses are in attendance at all the stations to convey passengers to the towns in the Brianza.

The old post-road is more agreeable and varied than that by Barlassina, and, although nearly parallel to the railway, may, from its more beautiful scenery, be preferred by many. The roots of the Alps extend in successive ranges before us; and the foregrounds, especially near Como, are beautiful. The vegetation is luxuriant, and, like all in the neighbourhood of the lake, more *southern* than that which the traveller will find at Milan. Mulberry-trees abound, the district being celebrated for its silk; and the exotics, naturalised by the more wealthy inhabitants, who delight in their gardens, flourish in the utmost luxuriance. The *Catalpa* is very common. Leaving Camerlata, the Rlwy. runs through a beautiful country, covered with rich vegetation, to

6¼ kil. *Cucciago* Stat., about 2 m. on the l. of which is

Cantù, in a rich district of the Brianza. The bell-tower of the church, with its projecting battlements, is slender and tall. In the middle ages it was used as a beacon, corresponding with that upon the Monte di Baradello. The fires blazing on the summit have often announced the advance of the Milanese against the Comaschi during their frequent wars; and the Baradello, equally by its fires, gave notice of the approach of any enemy on the side of the lake.

Galliano, near Cantù, has a curious Lombard church, now a barn. It contains Christian inscriptions of the 4th centy. Some ancient frescoes, executed in the 11th, were painted by order of Arimbert, the celebrated Archbishop of Milan. They contain, as it is supposed, portraits of the Emperor Henry and his wife Cune-

H 3

gunda. The baptistery is remarkable. The building was sold as national property during the French occupation. From Cucciago the rlwy. follows the Severo torrent as far as

10 kil. *Camnago* Stat. At *Meda*, a short distance on the l., are the ruins of an extensive monastery.

7 kil. *Seregno* Stat. 2 m. on the l. is the village of *Carate*, on a rising ground above the Lambro; an agreeable excursion may be made from here to *Inverigo*, the beautiful villa of the Marquis Cagnola, a fine specimen of his architecture. The view from the top of it commands the entire region of the Brianza.

2 kil. *Desio* Stat. Here the Torriani were entirely routed by the Viscontis in 1277. The Villa *Traversa*, with a fine garden, is the principal object to be visited in Desio. It contains some curious Roman inscriptions.

7 kil. MONZA Stat. at the S. extremity of the town. (*Inns:* Il Falcone, tolerable; l'Angelo.) This city, the ancient Modœtia, is divided into two nearly equal parts by the Lambro. It has a Pop. of 16,000.

The *Broletto*, or town-hall, is attributed to Frederick Barbarossa: some say it was a portion of a palace built by him. It is of Italian Gothic, with a *Ringhiera* between two handsome windows on the S. side. Annexed to it is a fine and lofty campanile, with forked battlements.

The *Cathedral* or *Duomo*. "On the spot where this building now stands Theodolinda erected, in 595, a splendid temple in honour of St. John the Baptist. The church of Theodolinda was not on the Latin plan, but on the Byzantine. It was an equilateral cross, surmounted by a dome. For above 600 years this building remained unaltered. At the close of the 13th centy. Matteo Magno Visconti, Lord of Milan, with the assistance of the oblations of the people, undertook the reconstruction of the church upon a larger scale. But he left his work unfinished; for the façade was not commenced till the year 1396. In that year the celebrated architect, Matteo di Campione, was employed to give a design for the façade and he constructed it in the form which it exhibits at present. This façade is a curious specimen of the *cabinet* style prevalent in Italy at that period; a style which attempts to please the eye rather by a subdivision of parts, and a variety of patterns, in marbles of different shapes and colours, than by the form of the building itself. In the interior some of the capitals of the pillars are ornamented with barbarous figures, and must be older than the 14th centy. Frisi is of opinion that they formed no part of the Lombard church, but had belonged to some 11th centy. building, and were removed from thence to their present situation."—*G. Knight.*

The *Pallioto*, or front of the altar, of silver-gilt, perhaps of the 10th centy., is entirely covered with Scripture histories, inlaid with enamel and coarse gems. The *Cantorie*, or galleries for the singers, on either side of the nave, are of rich Gothic work, and are worthy of attention, as well as the Gothic woodwork of the choir. In the chapel in the adjoining cemetery is the shrivelled corpse of Ettore Visconti (a natural son of Bernabò), a partisan, who became, for a short time, one of the leaders of Milan. Expelled by Duke Filippo Maria, he seized the Castle of Monza, where a shot from a springall broke his leg, an injury of which he died (1413): he was buried in this basilica; and his body having been accidentally disinterred, it has remained above ground.

Theodolinda, whose memory, like Bertha in Switzerland, or Elizabeth in England, was cherished by the people beyond that of any male sovereign, Charlemagne himself scarcely excepted, and whose beauty, wisdom, and piety were all equally transcendent, was the daughter of Garibold King of the Bavarians, and became the wife of Autharis King of the Lombards (589). Upon the death of Autharis, which happened six years after their marriage, the Lombards offered the crown to Theodolinda, with the intimation that whomsoever she would select for her husband they would acknowledge as their sovereign. She chose Agelulphus (sometimes called Astolf) Duke of Turin. Valiant and ambitious, he contemplated becoming master of Rome; but Theodolinda diverted him from this enterprise. She thus earned the gratitude and the friendship of Pope Gregory the Great, who dedicated his Dialogues to her.

The *Sacristy of the Duomo* is one of the most curious of mediæval museums. It has been much plundered, especially during the republican rule at the end of the last centy. The following are some of the more remarkable objects which it still contains:—*Theodolinda's fan*, or *flabellum*, of painted leather, with a massive, metallic, enamelled handle. Her *comb*, ornamented with gold filigree and emeralds. Her *crown*, a plain diadem set with coarse gems. *Theodolinda's hen and chickens*, a species of tray of silver gilt, upon which are the figures of the *Chioccia*, or *Chucky*, and her seven chickens. The hen's eyes are of rubies. It is said by antiquarians to typify either the arch-priest and chapter of the church of Monza, or the seven provinces of the Lombard kingdom. The probability is that this gift of the Queen was in fact only a plateau or ornament for her banquet table. *The list of relics sent by Pope Gregory the Great to Theodolinda*, written upon papyrus: some say it is his autograph. The celebrated antiquary Maffei calls this the " king of papyri." One of these relics consists of drops of oil taken from the lamps burning before the tombs of the martyrs in the catacombs. *Theodolinda's Evangelistarium* or *Gospel-book*. The binding is of gold and silver gilt, rudely set with rough stones, glass placed over coloured foil, and fine ancient intaglios, characteristic of the age of transition from the Roman to mediæval times. A *cross*, given to the Queen by the Pope upon the occasion of the baptism of her eldest child: it is now worn by the arch-priest on certain great occasions and festivals. It is composed, in front, of rock crystal; the back is worked in gold filigree. *Theodolinda's cup*, said to be hollowed out of a solid sapphire. It is about three inches in diameter. The colour of the material (probably very fine glass, like the catino of Genoa) is exceedingly rich. The Gothic setting bears the date of 1490.

In a curious bas-relief over the centre doorway of the church *Theodolinda* is represented offering her gifts.

The *Cross*, or *pectoral*, employed in the coronation of the kings of Italy, and which it was the custom to hang round the neck of the sovereign. It is massive, and richly decorated—not merely with uncut stones, but with ancient engraved gems; amongst others, there is appended to it an amethyst, exhibiting a Diana, of excellent workmanship.

The *Sacramentary of Berengarius King of Italy*. This monarch is sometimes reckoned as Berengarius I. amongst the Roman emperors. The son of Everard Duke of Friuli, Berengarius obtained his authority upon the division of the empire which took place on the death of Charles the Fat, in 888. The coverings of this book are of pierced ivory, plates of gold placed beneath shining between the interstices. On one side are scrolls interlaced, springing from birds; on the other are runic knots, elaborately interlaced, springing from a central ornament composed of four grotesque animals, from whose mouths the root of each knot is seen to issue. These singular carvings are clearly Teutonic; for, excepting a greater delicacy in the workmanship, they are exactly such as are found upon Scandinavian monuments. The services which the book contains stand as they were composed by Pope Gregory; and in it may be found the collects of our own Liturgy.

Another very curious volume is the *Evangelistarium* of Aribert or Heribert, Archbishop of Milan (1018-1045).

Three *ivory diptychs*, of much better workmanship than is usually the case with sculptures of this description. The first and most curious represents, on one leaf, a poet or a philosopher in his study; on the other a muse striking the lyre with her *plectrum*. The whole is finely carved. Claudian and Ausonius are both candidates for the portrait. Antiquaries give it to Boethius, upon conjecture. The second represents two figures in consular robes, with the Roman eagle, and other insignia. The original names have been effaced, and those of Pope Gregory and David substituted. The third is remarkable for the boldness of the relief. The principal figures are an emperor with the *paludamentum*, and a female in rich attire.

The celebrated *Iron Crown* is no longer here; it was removed by the Austrians to Mantua in May, 1859, and since then to Vienna. Formerly the sight of it was conceded only to persons of high rank; an exact model of it has been retained, as well as some pieces of the true cross, of the sponge, of the Holy Sepulchre, and of the reed held by Christ; and one of the thorns of the crown. The thin plate or fillet of iron which lined the diadem, and whence the crown derived its name, is supposed to have been hammered from one of the nails employed at the crucifixion; and hence the crown is also called *Il sacro Chiodo*. It may be readily supposed that there is not the slightest foundation for the belief in such an origin, and the Church of Milan opposed the tradition; but their objections were overcome by the congregation "*dei sacri riti*" at Rome, by whom the relic was pronounced to be authentic, and, when it was exhibited, tapers were lighted and much ceremony observed. The workmanship of the outer crown, which is of gold, with enamelled flowers, is plain, but very peculiar. The traditions of Monza relate that this crown was given by Gregory the Great to Queen Theodolinda; yet nothing is really known respecting its origin, nor was it regularly used in the coronation of the kings of Italy. Henry VII. (or Henry of Luxemburg) is the first who is known with any certainty to have worn it, 1311. The crown was carried for that purpose to Milan, in spite of the remonstrances of the inhabitants of Monza. Charles V. was the last of the later emperors crowned with it; and the crown remained quietly as a relic in the Tesoro, until Napoleon, anxious to connect his dignity with the recollections of the past, placed it with his own hands upon his head, disdaining to receive it from the Bishop, and using the words, "*Dieu me l'a donné, gare à qui la touche.*" It has been since used at the coronation of the two last Emperors of Austria, and formed part of the royal insignia of the Lombardo-Venetian kingdom, until its recent removal.

A curious *bas-relief* in the chapel of *San Stefano* represents the coronation of an Emperor. The six Electors assisting are the Archbishop of Cologne, as Arch-Chancellor of Italy; the Duke of Saxony; the Archbishop of Trèves; the Landgrave or Count Palatine of the Rhine; the Archbishop of Mayence; and the Elector of Brandenburg. The seventh Elector, the King of Bohemia, is absent, and this circumstance shows that the bas-relief is earlier than 1290, when he was admitted into the Electoral College. It will be noticed that the crown which the Arch-Priest of Monza is here represented to place on the head of the Emperor is *not* the Iron Crown, but one decorated with fleurons. This bas-relief seems, from its inscription, to have been put up by the people of Monza as a memorial of *their* right to have the coronation performed here, in preference to Milan. The chapel of S. Maria del Rosario contains some curious frescoes, representing events in the history of S. Theodolinda, by one *Trosi* of Monza, bearing the date of 1444.

The only other ch. of Monza worth notice, and this desecrated, is *Santa*

ior wa
ition of L
or Henr
ho is kno
worn it
for that p
e remon
fonza. C
later em
the cro
in the I
to cont
ionsof th
ands up
ive it fre
words,
ui la l
t the c
erors of
the ron
enetian
val.
the ch
covet
Elector
of Col
the l
of Tr
Palati
p of M
Brave
the L
his cir
s-reli
was
llege.
ru vis
her
d o
wn,
1
rio

References

1 Cathedral ... G f
2 S. Alessandro ... F g
3 S. Ambrogio ... C g
4 S. Antonio ... G g
5 S. Bernardino ... G g
6 S. Celso ... F i
7 S. Eufemia ... F h
8 S. Eustorgio ... D i
9 S. Fedele ... G e
10 S. Giorgio ... E g
11 S. Giovanni ... F g
12 S. Lorenzo ... E h
13 S. Marco ... F c
14 S. Maria del Carmine ... E d
15 ... presso S. Celso ... F i
16 ... della Grazie ... B f
17 ... Incoronata ... F b
18 ... della Passione ... I f
19 ... S. Carlo ... H f
20 S. Maurizio ... D f
21 S. Nazzaro ... G h
22 S. Paolo ... F h
23 S. Pietro ... I g
24 S. Satiro ... F g
25 S. Sebastiano ... F g
26 S. Sepolcro ... E g
27 S. Simpliciano ... E c
28 S. Stefano ... H g
29 S. Tomaso ... E c
30 S. Vittore ... B g
31 Ambrosian Library ... E f
32 Arcivescovado ... G f
33 Brera ... F d
34 Ospedale Maggiore ... G g
35 Ospizio Trivulzi ... H g
36 Palazzo Imp.le ... G g
37 Piazza Borromeo ... E f
38 ... della Fontana ... G f
39 ... de' Mercanti ... F f
40 Post Office ... F g

Theatres

41 la Scala ... F e
42 della Canobbiana ... G y
43 Carcano ... H h
44 Filodrammatico ... F c
45 Fiando ... G f
46 Albergo de la Villa ... G f
47 ... Reale ... E g
48 ... Reichmann ... F g

Maria in Strada, remarkable for its very elaborate W. front in terracotta, and fine rose window.

The Palace of Monza is an extensive edifice, but has nothing in or about it (excepting the size of the apartments) above a country mansion. The park is large, well laid out, and abounds in game. The gardens are very rich in exotic plants. It was in former times the country residence of the Viceroy, and is now occasionally that of the King of Sardinia.

The *Railroad* has rendered Monza almost a suburb of Milan. Trains run six times a day in 20 minutes.

6 kil. *Sesto Stat.*, in a very fertile plain, with many country-seats around.

8 kil. MILAN.—The Railway Station is outside the Porta Nuova. Omnibuses and hackney coaches are in attendance on the arrival of every train. The fare for each person from the station to his hotel in the former is 85 centimes, including a moderate quantity of luggage; but as these omnibuses are generally very crowded, and take a circuitous route, depositing passengers on their way, the traveller will find it much more comfortable, expeditious, and nearly as economical, to hire a hackney cab; the fares of which are 1 fr. 35 cent., including luggage.

Hotels. The Hôtel de la Ville, kept by Baër, in the Corso Francesco, the best situation in Milan, open and airy, is an excellent house, and handsomely fitted up; it affords every cleanliness and comfort. A good table-d'hôte at 4 francs; coffee and reading room, master and waiters speaking English; and baths in the house.—The Albergo Reale, in the Contrada dei Tre Rè, kept by Bruschetti, is also a first-rate hotel, clean and quiet, with a very obliging landlord and a good table-d'hôte. Bruschetti is also a dealer in pictures, articles of vertu, majolica; he has a large gallery of paintings, and speaks English as well as his servants. Both these hotels are well suited to English families.—La Gran Bretagna, in the Contrada della Palla, in the centre of the city, improved of late, is comfortable.—The Hôtel Reichman, in the Corso di Porta Romana, is much frequented by Germans and commercial travellers, but inferior to the two first, and without their comforts, although with as high charges.—The Albergo del Marino, in a central situation near La Scala theatre, is well spoken of for its cleanliness and cuisine. La Bella Venezia, La Pension Suisse, and San Marco, all three comfortable, frequented more by Italian families: the latter, which is near the post-office, is well spoken of. It has a good table-d'hôte at 3 fr.

Good Vetturini, for all parts of Italy and Switzerland, may be found at Milan. The innkeepers can be trusted to negotiate the bargain.

Carriages may be hired for the day or job. A good carriage for half a day for about 12 fr., and the drink-money of 1 fr. to the driver.

Fiacres are very good. Lists of the fares are placed inside; 1 lira a course, and 1½ an hour.

Omnibuses. There are numerous lines of these vehicles to every quarter of the town; fares, 25 c. within the walls.

During the summer the fashionable evening drive is in the Corso di Porta Orientale, and along the Boulevard between it and Porta Nuova; particularly on Sundays and Thursdays, the greatest Corso being on the first Sunday in Lent.

This city is the centre of business; and all pecuniary transactions can be well managed here: such as obtaining further letters of credit, and the like. The *Cambia Monete*, or money-changers, are numerous; most live near the Duomo. As the monetary transactions at Milan are extensive, this is a very lucrative business. The value of foreign coins is printed daily, with the rates of exchange on different countries, so that the traveller runs little risk of being cheated.

The Post-Office, from which the Government diligences start, is in the Contrada dei Rastrelli, near the Duomo. It opens at 8 A.M., when letters are delivered, and shuts at 8 P.M; on

Sundays at 3. The mail which carries the English letters (through Paris) is that by Turin: it leaves daily at 2 P.M., and arrives about midday. Between Milan and London a letter takes 3 days. Prepayment is not absolutely necessary, but unpaid letters to the different parts of Italy are charged double on delivery.

The principal *Public Conveyances* are the following:—

Lucerne, by Bellinzona and the St. Gothard. By rly. to Camerlata near Como, at 6 A.M., and from thence by diligence. Places may be secured at Milan or Camerlata. This goes on direct, and arrives at Fluellen on the Lake of Lucerne in 25 hrs.

Chiavenna, Coire, and *Zurich*, by the Rly. to Como, at 6 A.M. and 2·30 P.M., from thence by the steamboat to Colico, whence the diligence starts by Chiavenna and the Splugen Pass—Diligence daily at 6 A.M.; by Bellinzona and the Bernardino Pass every day. The latter diligence, like that to Lucerne, now starts from Camerlata.

Geneva. To Arona by rly., and from thence by diligence by Domo d'Assola, the Simplon, Vevay, and Lausanne; the coach leaves Arona at 1 P.M., corresponding with the rly. train of 8·37 A.M. from Milan.

Piacenza, Parma, Modena, Bologna, Rome, by Lodi.—Diligences to Piacenza every morning and evening at 7 a.m. and p.m., and from thence by rly. to Bologna.

The rly. trains to Monza run 6, and to Como 4, times a-day.

The railroad to Venice is now open all the way, by Bergamo, Brescia, Verona, Padua, Venice, and from the latter to Treviso, Conegliano, and Udine. There are two trains daily, which leave Milan at 6·10 and 11·15 A.M., reaching Venice at 5·55 and 10·30 P.M.

Physicians.—There is at Milan a physician who has lived in England and speaks English—Dr. Capelli; he lives in the Corsia del Giardino. This gentleman is stated by those who have consulted him to be worthy of confidence.

Apothecary and chemist, Monteggia, Corso Francesco, opposite the Hôtel de la Ville.

Restaurateurs and Cafés. Canetta (successor to Cova), Contrada San Giuseppe, near La Scala Theatre, is the best; this café is well supplied with newspapers. Martini. La Colonna. Café *Reale* and *dell' Europa,* in the Piazza del Duomo. *St..Carlo,* in the Corso Francesco.

Booksellers.—Artaria and Co., in the Via Santa Margarita, No. 1110, for Guide-books, maps of the Austrian Ordnance Survey, engravings, &c.; Messrs. Artaria are obliging, and well supplied with all works necessary for travellers in Italy and Switzerland, Handbooks, &c., and are agents for Sinigaglia's photographic views of Milan, perhaps the best, and for Santi's of the drawings of the old masters which are preserved in the Brera and Ambrosian Libraries. Dumolard frères, in the Corso Francesco, *French booksellers.* Meisner and Son are good *foreign booksellers* in the same street, nearer the cathedral, and Laenger in the Galleria di Cristoferis.

The traveller will find at Mannini's shop under the Arcades of the Piazza del Duomo an assortment of Italian and foreign jewellery, English and French articles, &c.,; and a great variety of jewellery in the shops of the Strada degli Orefici, &c.

The Pop. of Milan is now about 187,000.

Milan, founded by the Insubrian Gauls, became, in point of splendour, the second city of Italy, filled with temples, baths, theatres, statues, and all the structures required for the dignity and luxury of a great capital. Ausonius, who flourished under the Emperor Gratian, towards the end of the fourth century, assigns to it the rank of the sixth city in the Empire. He describes it in these lines:—

" Et Mediolani mira omnia,—copia rerum:
Innumerae, cultaeque domus, fecunda virorum
Ingenia, antiqui mores. Tum duplice muro
Amplificata loci species, populique voluptas
Circus, et inclusi moles cuneata theatri:

Templa, Platinæque arces, opulensque moneta,
Et regio Herculei celebris sub honore lavacri,
Cunctaque marmoreis ornata peristyla signis,
Mœniaque in valli formam circumdata labro;
Omnia, quæ magnis operum velut æmula
formis
Excellunt: nec juncta premit vicinia Romæ."

Procopius, a century later, speaks of Mediolanum as one of the first cities of the West, and inferior only to Rome in population and extent. Its ancient edifices and monuments have all disappeared, save one portico (*see* San Lorenzo); a column (*see* Sant' Ambrogio); a piece of massive wall, forming part of the Monasterio Maggiore; two rather dubious heads, called Quintus and Rufus, in the arches of the Corsia di Porta Nova; and, lastly, the *Uomo di Pietra*, or in Milanese *Homin de Pree*, now inserted in the wall of a house in the Corsia de Servi, between the first and second stories. So far as can be judged, he is a Roman of the lower empire.

The paucity of Roman remains at Milan must be attributed to the calamities which the city has sustained. It was sacked by Attila, A.D. 452, in the invasion which occasioned the foundation of Venice. But the great destruction was effected after the surrender of Milan to Frederick I., 1162; when his vengeance, co-operating with, or rather instigated by, the jealousies of the surrounding cities, Pavia, Cremona, Lodi, Como, Novara, rased it to the ground. On Palm Sunday, in that fatal year when the Emperor departed in triumph for Pavia, the site of the great city was to be recognised only by the Basilica of Sant' Ambrogio, and some other churches, which were left standing in the midst of the ruins; and the inhabitants being dispersed in four adjoining villages, the name of Milan was effaced from the Lombard community.

But this event was followed by the great Lombard league, the confederacy against the imperial authority; and in the diet, or parliament, held at Pontida, 1167, the deputies of the combined cities determined to bring back the Milanese to their ancient seat, which, on the 27th April, 1167, was effected by the combined forces of Cremona, Brescia, Bergamo, Mantua, and Verona, and the city speedily rose again with unwonted energy and power. This remarkable event was commemorated in the coeval bas-reliefs of the *Porta Romana*, a venerable gateway which stood till 1810-12.

These sculptures have, however, been preserved by being let into the walls of a house (near the bridge) erected on the site of the gate, and are curious as illustrating one of the most memorable passages in the chronicles of mediæval Italy. The Milanese around, on foot and on horseback, are seen proceeding to the re-erected city, with an inscription pointing out that there they are to make their stay. "Fata vetant ultra procedere, stabimus ergo." The cities of "Cremona," "Brixia," and "Bergamum" are represented by turreted gateways, out of which come forth their allies.—"Fra' Giacobo," thus written, bears the banner of Milan. The artist "Anselmus" has also represented himself, adding an inscription, in which he either assumes to himself the appellation of Dædalus, or ascribes to himself Dædalian skill; a whimsical vanity, the sculpture being of the rudest kind. In another part is a figure in a consular or magisterial robe, surmounting a strange monster with a huge grinning face and bats' wings, which, according to the tradition of Milan, represents the Emperor Frederick Barbarossa.

This *Porta Romana* stood in the line of walls erected by the Milanese when they rebuilt the city.

About eighty years after the rebuilding of the city commenced the rule of the family of della Torre, by the election of Pagano, lord of Vall Assina, as protector; and then followed that of the Viscontis and Sforzas. During the later part of this period Milan attained a state of great prosperity, and became celebrated for its manufactures of armour, dress, and ornaments.

" Well was he arm'd, from head to heel,
In mail and plate of Milan steel."

Milan then set the fashion to the rest of Europe; hence the word *milliner*. After the extinction of the family of Sforza, Milan fell, in 1535, under the power of the Emperor Charles V., who, in 1549, fixed the succession to the duchy of Milan in his son Philip II. It remained under the government of the Spaniards until the death of the last King of Spain of the Austrian line, when it became an object of contention between France and Austria, and was finally given to the latter by the treaty of Utrecht, 1713. In the hands of Austria it remained, until May, 1859, with a few interruptions, the principal one of which was the occupation of Milan by the French, and the establishment of the kingdom of Italy, of which Milan was made the capital.

The extent of Milan, when it was rebuilt after its destruction by Frederick Barbarossa, is marked by the canal, which, entering on the N. side, runs nearly round the central part of the modern city. The wall or rampart, called the *bastione*, which now encircles Milan, except on that side which was protected by the Castle, was built by the Spaniards in 1555. The greater portion of the ground between this wall and the canal is occupied by gardens. All round, just outside this wall, runs the road called the *Strada di Circonvallazione*. The circuit of the modern city is about 7¾ m.

Certain wider streets which radiate from the centre of the town are called "*corsi;*" the continuations of these beyond the bridges which cross the canal to the present line of wall generally are called *borghi*. The streets, in many places which run parallel to and immediately within the canal, retain the name of *terrazi*, or terraces. The Piazze or squares before the churches are in Milanese called "pasquée" (pascua), and some open spaces, where several streets meet, are called "carobbio" (quadrivium).

The average height of Milan above the sea is 450 feet.

Milan has now ten gates. On the N. side is the *Porta Comasina*, erected in 1826-1828 by the merchants, from a design of *Moraglia*.

Next to this, towards the E., is the *Porta Nuova*, built in 1810, from a design of *Zanoia*. The view of the Alps from the rampart near this gate is very fine.

At the N.E. angle of the rampart is the *Porta Orientale*, begun in 1828, from a design of *Vantini*, the architect of the Campo Santo at Brescia.

Near the centre of the E. side is the *Porta Tosa*.

At the S.E. angle of the rampart is the *Porta Romana*, built by the Milanese, from a design of *Bassi*, in 1598, to welcome the arrival of Margaret of Austria, the wife of Philip III. of Spain. Just within the gate is the ancient emporium (*sciostra romana*) for merchandize coming from Cremona and Piacenza.

In the S. side of the rampart, next to the Porta Romana, is the *Porta Vigentina*, so called from the village of Vigentino, which lies on this road, at a short distance. This gate will give an idea of the architecture of all the others a few years ago.

The gate situated nearly in the centre of the S. side of the rampart is the *Porta Ludovica*, so called from Ludivico il Moro.

Near the W. end of the S. face of the rampart, and to where it forms an angle with the S.W. face, is the *Porta Ticinese*, the gate leading to Pavia, and by which Bonaparte entered after the battle of Marengo, whence for a short time it was called the Porta Marengo. Its Ionic portico was built in 1815, from a design of the Marquis Cagnola.

The *Porta Vercellina*, at the W. extremity of the city, was built in great haste, with materials from the Castello, from a design of Canonica, to receive Napoleon when he came to assume the iron crown.

Porta Tanaglia, the N.W. gate leading to the Simplon road, received its name from a fortified work, so called, which once stood near it.

Between the Porta Tanaglia and the Porta Vercellina there is no rampart, the city having been protected on this side by the *Castello.* Here stood the ancient ducal castle, built by Galeazzo Visconti II. in 1358, to keep the Milanese in subjection. Upon his death they insisted on its demolition; it was, however, rebuilt with increased strength by Gian Galeazzo. Thus it remained till the death of the Duke Filippo Maria, when the Milanese rose (Aug. 30, 1447), and, having proclaimed the "*Aurea respublica Ambrosiana,*" destroyed the castle. It was soon rebuilt by Francesco Sforza, for the ornament (he said) of the city and its safety against enemies; and he promised that its governors should be always Milanese. This is the building now standing. In the interior is a keep, where the dukes often resided. Remains of paintings have been discovered under the whitewash in the stables. Philip II. added very extensive modern fortifications, and cut down all the bell-towers which overlooked them. The advanced works reached to the edge of what is now open space. The castle was taken by the French in 1796; and again in 1800, when Napoleon ordered the fortifications to be rased. It has since been converted into a barrack, the approaches to which were strengthened after the outbreak of 1848, when a large Austrian force was obliged to evacuate it. A strong lunette mounting 6 guns defends each gate: there are two half-moon batteries, loop-holed, and mounting 6 guns, on the S.E. and N.E.: the four round towers at the angles have been altered, in doing which the fine marble shields of the Sforzas have been mutilated; and a line of loopholed defences has been carried nearly all round the castle, and the square in which it is situated considerably opened. During the government of Eugene Beauharnois a Doric gateway of granite, with a portico or line of arches on each side, and in the same style, was erected on the N.W. side.

The space gained by the demolition of the fortifications was meant to be covered by splendid buildings and monuments, for which Antolini prepared a design in 1804. Two only of the edifices planned have been erected— the Arena and the Arco della Pace. The space on which it was intended to erect a forum has been converted into a *Piazza d'Armi,* for the purpose of exercising the military.

Arco della Pace. A triumphal arch having been erected with wood and canvas, in 1806, at the Porta Orientale, from a design of the Marquis Cagnola, upon the marriage of the Viceroy Eugene with the Princess Amalia of Bavaria, it was so much admired, that the municipal council resolved that it should be executed in white marble from Crevola, on the Simplon road, the expense to be defrayed out of 200,000 francs assigned by Napoleon for adorning the city. It was begun in 1807, but, on the fall of the kingdom of Italy in 1814, had not risen above the impost of the smaller arches. The works were resumed in 1816 and completed in 1838, in which year the arch was inaugurated at the time of the coronation of the Emperor Ferdinand I. It was originally intended to have been called the Arch of the Simplon, and to have been embellished with a statue of Victory, in commemoration of the battle of Jena, and with bas-reliefs representing the events of Napoleon's campaigns. When it fell into the hands of the Austrians its name was changed to that of Arch of Peace, and the sculptures underwent a transformation to make them represent the events which preceded the general pacification of 1815. On the top of the arch is a bronze figure of Peace, in a car drawn by six horses. Four figures of Fame, one at each angle, announce her arrival. These latter are by *Giovanni Putti,* a Bolognese. The central group is by *Sangiorgio.* The subjects of the sculpture and the names of the artists are as follows:—Side towards the city. The colossal figure to the l. of the inscription represents the river Po, that on the rt. the Ticino;

both are by *Cacciatori*. The subject of the bas-relief on the l. side immediately below the entablature is the battle of Culm, by *G. Monti*. The large bas-relief below this is intended to represent the entry of the Emperor Francis I. into Milan; it is by *Cacciatori*. Below this is the capitulation of Dresden, by *C. Pacetti*. On the rt. below the entablature is the passage of the Rhine. The large bas-relief below this represents the foundation of the Lombardo-Venetian kingdom, and the lowest one the occupation of Lyons; these three are by *Marchesi*. Each of the pedestals of the columns has an allegorical figure in half-relief:—they are Hercules, by *G. Monti*; Mars and Minerva, by *E. Pacetti*; Apollo, modelled by *Pizzi*. Under the great central arch, a large bas-relief on the rt.-hand side represents the conference of the three allied sovereigns of Russia, Prussia, and Austria; it is by *G. Monti*. A corresponding one opposite was begun by *Acquisti*, and completed by *Somaini*.— Side towards the country. The colossal reclining figure to the l., above the entablature, represents the river Tagliamento; the one on the rt. the Adige: they are both by *Marchesi*. The bas-relief immediately under the entablature, on the l. hand of the spectator, represents the re-institution of the order of the Iron Crown. The subject of the large bas-relief is the Congress of Vienna; both these are by *G. B. Perabò*. Below is the occupation of Paris, by *A. Acquesti*. The upper bas-relief on the rt. was begun by *G. Rusca*, and finished by his son; it represents the entry of the allied sovereigns into Paris. The large bas-relief below this represents the Peace of Paris; and the lowest one the entry of the Austrians into Milan in 1814; these two are by *G. Monti*. The four pedestals of the columns on this side represent Vigilance, by *Pizzi*; History, Poetry, and Lombardy, by *Acquesti*. On the eastern flank of the building is the battle of Leipsig, by *Marchesi*; on the western that of Arcis-sur-Aube, by *Somaini*. The key-stones of the arches are ornamented with allegorical busts. The grand frieze all round was modelled by *Monti* and *Marchesi*.

The total cost, including the lodges on each side and the iron railing, was 142,839*l*.; the bronze car and figures on the top 40,000*l*. alone. An easy staircase in the interior leads to the summit. The bas-reliefs have been much and justly criticised for a pedantic adherence in the costumes to classical models.

The *Arena* is an amphitheatre designed by *Canonica*. It is an ellipse whose greater diameter is 780 ft., and lesser 390, and is capable of containing 30,000 spectators. It is surrounded by ten rows of seats, arranged in the manner of an ancient amphitheatre, and which were intended to be of stone, but for economy were made of turf. At one end of the greater diameter are the Carceres, flanked by towers, at the other a triumphal Doric gateway of granite, of which the design is good. At one side of the lesser diameter is a portico of eight Corinthian columns of polished granite. The arena can be flooded for aquatic exhibitions. It was commenced in 1805, and opened the following year. The Portico, Gateway, and Carceres have been added since. The first races took place the 17th June, 1807; and in the following December there was a regatta in the presence of Napoleon. Races, balloon ascents, rope-dancing, and fireworks, take place here frequently.

Churches.

The *Duomo*. The present building is the third, perhaps the fourth, re-edification of the original structure, which St. Ambrose, in his letter to his sister Marcellina, calls the great new Basilica. The primitive cathedral was destroyed by Attila. When rebuilt it was burnt by accident, in 1075, and again destroyed by Frederick I. in

1162; but this demolition was, it is said, only partial, being caused by the fall upon the church of a lofty bell-tower, which was destroyed in order to prevent its being used as a fortress. Lastly arose the present structure.

The first stone of the present Duomo was laid by Gian' Galeazzo Visconti, in 1387. Some historians say that the undertaking was in fulfilment of a vow; others ascribe it to a wish to encourage the arts. It was beyond the Alps that the Duke sought an architect. He had recourse to the freemasons of Germany; and it is in vain that Italian patriotism has sought to impugn the claims of *Heinrich Ahrler* of *Gmünden*, or "*Enrico di Gamodia*," the Italian version of his name. To him, between the years 1388-99, were associated other brethren from Germany, Paris, and Normandy, from Friburg, Ulm, and Bruges. Italians were afterwards called in; amongst others, the celebrated Brunelleschi of Florence. But Germany still continued to be considered as the school of the architects of the cathedral; and as late as 1486 Gian' Galeazzo Sforza addressed letters to the magistrates of Strasburg, requesting them to send him the master mason of their *Domkirche*, Hammerer, for the purpose of advising upon some difficulties which had been apprehended in the construction of the central tower.

The building has been often interrupted, and has, when resumed, been often carried on slowly, and it is yet unfinished in some of its details. The octagon cupola was vaulted by the *Omodei* (father and son), 1490, 1522; the three western divisions or arches of the nave were left unfinished after the extinction of the Sforza dynasty, and not completed till 1685. The central tower and the spire, of great beauty, which crowns it, were completed in 1772, from the designs of *Croce;* and the gable and upper range of windows of the front, as well as very many of the buttresses and pinnacles, by *Amati, Zanoja*, and others, between 1806, when the works were resumed by order of Napoleon, and the present time. In this long succession of years many of the first artists of this favoured country, amongst whom may be named *Bramante, Leonardo da Vinci,* and *Giulio Romano,* gave their advice and assistance. The dates only of some of the principal constructions are here noticed; but, since the first stone was laid, the scaffolds have always been standing on some part of the edifice.

It seems that the original designs for the façade had been long lost, and the portion of the nave, as erected, wanted three of its arches. A façade of black and white marble, built considerably within the line of the present structure, curtailed the nave by one-third of its just length; and, as far as this had been raised, it was unfinished and inelegant. Pellegrini was employed in 1560 by St. Carlo Borromeo to complete the front, and he designed an Italian façade upon a magnificent scale. San Carlo died; Pellegrini was summoned to Spain by Philip II. to paint the Escurial, and the work was carried on very leisurely by other hands, amongst them by *Castelli* and *Francesco Ricchino*, who, altering the designs of Pellegrini, gave to the Roman doors and windows that exuberance of ornament which they now exhibit; but the plans of Pellegrini—according to one of which the front was to have been composed of a gigantic modern Roman portico—had given rise to numerous discussions, which were continued, revived, and resumed during the 17th and 18th centuries. Some of the architects of Lombardy strongly protested against the admixture of Roman architecture begun by Pellegrini, and advocated the reconstruction of the façade in the Pointed style.

Thus, in 1635, two Gothic designs were proposed by *Carlo Buzzi,* and a third by *Francesco Castelli,* all three of considerable merit. It will be sufficient to observe that, about the year 1790, it was determined by the Syndics to

Gothicise the façade, preserving, however, the doors and windows of Pellegrini and Ricchini, on account of their elaborate elegance; and, in order to apologise for the discrepancy of the styles, they caused an inscription stating this reason to be engraved on the corner buttress of the front.

To these works Napoleon gave great impulse, and their continuation was intrusted to a commission, under whom the façade was brought to its present form, chiefly by the insertion of three Gothic windows; and the greater number of the pinnacles and flying buttresses of the rest of the building were completed. The cost of these undertakings during the French government amounted to about 3½ millions of francs. 1½ millions of this sum were derived from the sale of the lands belonging to the Duomo, the remainder from the property of the suppressed monastic institutions. After the revolution of 1848 the supplies were for a time cut off; still a good deal has been done during the Austrian occupation.

A magnificent Gothic campanile was projected by the Marquis Cagnola. Others proposed flanking the front with belfry towers. The designs for the latter were sent to Napoleon at Moscow, and lost in that calamitous campaign. At present nothing further is in progress as to this part of the edifice; but, when Amati inserted the Gothic windows, he supported them by what are called bearing-arches of granite; so that, if it should hereafter be thought expedient to remove the Romanised doors and windows, the operation may be performed without injury to the superstructure.

When Gian' Galeazzo endowed the Duomo, he included in his donations the marble-quarries of la Gandoglia, in the valley of the Toccia, on the Simplon road, and of that material the building is entirely constructed. Time gives to this marble a fine warm yellow tint.

In the tracery there is an unusual approximation to what has been called the *flamboyant* style. This was probably owing to the influence of the French Gothic, as it is most apparent in the great E. window, which was built by Campania from the designs of Nicholas Bonaventure of Paris (1391).

The E. end, or tribune, is probably the most ancient or original portion of the structure. It is calculated that the niches and pinnacles of the exterior will require a *population* of 4500 statues. Of these more than 3000 are executed, besides the bas-reliefs. The excellent sculptures of the central door, by *Bono*, *Castelli*, and *Vismara* (about 1635), may be especially pointed out. The tympanum contains a bas-relief representing the creation of Eve. The arabesques in the pilasters are allusive to the works of the other days of the creation.

In the compartments for the bas-reliefs there is a great variety of detail. Many of the artists were from Como. A careful observer will discover in them not a few of the symbolical representations of an earlier age in modern forms. Amongst the minor *capricci* is a female head covered by a veil, all the features being seen, as it were, through the transparent covering. The Caryatides, by *Rusca* and *Carabelli*, are in finely varied attitudes.

The traveller, in order fully to understand the details of the building, should ascend the summit. A staircase, the entrance to which is at the W. corner of the S. transept, where a charge of 25 centimes is made, leads by 158 steps to the roof. The best time to enjoy the magnificent panoramic view is the evening, the plains being generally covered with mist at an earlier hour.

Steps upon the flying buttresses afford an ascent to the different levels. Two staircases, winding in turrets of open tracery, as at Strasburg, bring you to the platform of the octagon, and a similar staircase in the spire conducts to the belvedere or gallery, at the foot of the pyramid, or flèche, which crowns it. These turrets were executed by *Antonio Omodei* between 1490 and 1494. The sculpture, as well as the architecture, is from his design. The open tracery was executed by *Amici* of Cremona. The whole is of exquisite finish. There were to have been two others of similar workmanship at the opposite angles of the octagon. The larger number of the pinnacles of the nave and aisles have been completed since 1805. The smaller ornaments — baskets of fruit, cherubs' heads, sunflowers, lilies — are admirable, and much superior to anything which results from the *rigorism* now inculcated by Gothic architects.

All the main pinnacles, 3 on each buttress, are completed; a very perceptible progress has been made in the course of the last few years.

From the octagon gallery you gain a noble view of the plain of Lombardy, studded with cities and villages and church towers; the whole walled in, on the N. and E., by the snowy Alps. To the eastward, in a line with the cupola of Sta. Maria della Passione, is the plain watered by the Lambro, called the Martesana, and beyond are the mountains of the province of Brescia, which towards the N. are connected with those of the Seriana and Brembana valleys, and then with the Resegone, which rises above Lecco, and is distinguished by the serrated or sawlike form of its summit. The lower ridges to the W. of this form the hilly country of the Brianza, behind which, and in a line with the Porta Nuova, rises the mountain of S. Primo, which stands between the two southern arms of the lake of Como. To the l. of S. Primo rise the mountains which encircle the lakes of Como, Varese, and Lugano, with the snowy peaks about the S. Gothard beyond. Still further to the westward, the Simplon is distinguished, and then Monte Rosa, with its summits sparkling with eternal snow, and showing at sunset those hues from which it derives its name. Exactly W., Mt. Cenis may be seen, and still further to the l. the sharp snow-capped pyramid of Monte Viso. In a line with the Porta Ticinese the Apennines begin, among which the most remarkable point is the Penice. Advancing towards the S.E., and in the line of the Porta Romana, is the insulated group of hills of S. Columbano, and then the vast plain of the Po, in which may be distinctly seen on a clear day Lodi, Cremona, and Crema. By ascending to the gallery just before sunrise, the visitor may sometimes enjoy the striking spectacle of the rays of the sun catching successively the snow-clad peaks of the Alps long before the orb itself has appeared on the horizon.

The ground-plan of the Duomo is a Latin cross, terminated by an apse or tribune, in the form of five sides of an octagon. The body is divided into a nave and four aisles, by four ranges of colossal clustered pillars, with nine inter-columniations. The transepts and the chancel end are divided into three aisles. There is no triforium gallery, nor any division corresponding with it. The vaultings of the roof spring at once from the pillars: hence arises an appearance of great loftiness. Fifty-two pillars, each formed by a cluster of eight shafts, support the pointed arches on which the roof rests. The total height of each pillar of the nave and chancel is 80 ft. The diameter of the shaft is 8 ft. 3½ in. The diameter of the four great pillars which support the octagonal cupola is one-fifth greater. The beautiful capitals of the nave and choir were designed by *Filippino* of *Modena* in 1500; the lower part is formed by a wreath of foliage, mixed with figures of children and animals; above is a circle of eight niches, corresponding to the intervals between the eight shafts of the clustered pillar, and each containing a statue covered by a canopy. The shafts which divide the niches terminate in a pinnacle, surmounted by a small statue. The design, however, is varied in different pillars. The roof is painted to represent an elaborate fretwork. The execution is modern, but the design, as well as this mode of ornament, is ancient. The five doorways on the inside were designed by Fabio

Mangoni in 1548. Flanking the great centre doorway are two granite columns, each of a single black: they were given by San Carlo, and brought from the quarries of Baveno. They have been called the largest monoliths in Europe; and, perhaps, were so until the erection of the church of St. Isaac at Petersburg. The height of each shaft is 35 ft., the diameter 3 ft. 10¾ in.; the cost of quarrying and finishing them amounted to 1948*l*.

The principal dimensions of the Duomo are as follows, omitting fractions:—

	English Feet.
Extreme length	486
Breadth of the body	252
Between the ends of the transepts	288
Width of the nave, from centre to centre of the columns, which is double the width of the aisles measured in the same way	63
Height of the crown of the vaulting in the nave from the pavement	153
Height from the pavement to the top of the statue of the Madonna, which crowns the spire	355

Just beyond the entrance the pavement, which is of a mosaic pattern of red, blue, and white marble, is crossed by a meridian line, laid down by the astronomers of Brera in 1786. The sun's rays, passing through a small aperture in the roof, cross it, of course, at noonday. Originally all the windows were filled with painted glass. Pellegrini designed those in the nave: much glass remains of extraordinary brilliancy, but a great deal is lost. The restoration of the painted windows is amongst the works now in progress, 3 only in the N. aisle remaining unfinished; the windows of the apse have been already completed by Milanese artists: the lower ranges contain subjects from the Apocalypse. Parts of the glass, too, in the S. transept, and the W. window, are modern. These restorations are poor in design. Two of the great pillars supporting the octagonal cupola, between which you enter the choir, are encircled by pulpits, partly of bronze, begun by direction of San Carlo, and completed by his nephew, Cardinal Frederigo Borromeo. These are covered with bas-reliefs by *Andrea Pellizone*, and rest on colossal caryatides, representing the symbols of the four Evangelists, and the four Doctors of the Church, SS. Gregory, Jerome, Ambrose, and Augustine, modelled by *Brambilla*, and cast by *Busca*, bending and spreading forwards to support the superstructure. Behind the altar are seen the three gigantic windows of the tribune. The best time of day for contemplating this scene is when the morning sun is streaming through the eastern windows. The effect of the brilliant background is much heightened by the dark bronzes of the pulpits. Suspended from the vaulting of the octagon over the altar, is a reliquary, said to contain one of the nails of the cross, which annually, on the feast of the Invention of the Holy Cross (3rd May), is exposed upon the altar, and carried in solemn procession through the city.

"With some feeling of disappointment, from having heard so much of this building, it was impossible not to acknowledge the sublime effect of the interior. The first particulars which strike you on passing to the interior are, that it is dark and gloomy, and that the leading lines are very much interrupted by the shrines introduced in the capitals of the piers, which injure also the apparent solidity of the building.

"The style does not correspond with any of our English modes of pointed architecture. The vaulting is simple, without any branching ribs, or any ridge-piece; it is so much supervaulted, that each bay appears to be the portion of a dome; and the disposition of the materials in concentric circles, or in portions of such circles, makes me believe that this is nearly the case. * * * The lower part of the capitals has something of the running foliage of the 14th centy. in England: but the shrine-work which forms the upper part is perfectly unique; at least, I know nothing parallel, either in the work itself, or in the manner it is here introduced. The bases and the plans of the pillars are equally anomalous, and I think any person would be baffled in attempting to determine the date from the architecture, only he might safely decide that it could not be very early." — *Woods' Letters of an Architect.*

To point out in detail the more remarkable objects to be seen in the Duomo, beginning from the western end and on the rt.-hand side :—First is the monument of Marco Carelli, a benefactor of the Duomo, a work of A.D. 1394. It is an altar-tomb, with small figures in niches. Next follows the altar of St. Agatha, with a picture by *Federigo Zucchero;* then that of St. John the Evangelist, by *Melchior Gherardini.* In the next is a picture by *Fiammenghino.* These altars were erected in the time of the Borromeos.

According to the strict Ambrosian rule, there ought, as in the Greek Church, to be only one altar in the cathedral, and the Duomo was planned accordingly. Other altars have been introduced, but there are fewer than is usual in Roman Catholic cathedrals; and the chapels are much less prominent than in similar buildings.

In the S. transept is the tomb of Giovanni Giacomo de' Medici, Marquis of Marignano (d. 1555), and uncle of San Carlo, executed in bronze by *Leon Leoni,* and said by Vasari to have been designed by *Michael Angelo.* The principal statue of Medici is not unworthy in its general design of the great master who is supposed to have sketched it. In the splendid window near this tomb, proceeding eastward, the armorial bearings of the deceased are introduced. This Medici, often called *il Medichino,* was not related to the Ducal House of Florence, though the armorial bearings are the same.

In the tribune at the end of the S. transept is the chapel of San Giovanni Bono. The pilasters of the arch and its archivolt are covered with exceedingly elaborate bas-reliefs by *Simonetta, San Petro, Zarabatta, Brunelli, Bussola,* and others. The figures of Justice and Temperance, by *Vismara,* are good, but the chief merit is rather to be found in the exuberance of composition and high finish of the groups and tablets—of which some are taken from the life of San Giov. Bono. The statue of the Guardian Angel is by *Buzzi,* that of St. Michael by *Giov. Milanti.* On one side is the entrance to the subterranean way leading to the archbishop's palace, and, on the other, that of the staircase which leads to the roof. Next is the altar of the Presentation of the Virgin, by *Bambaja* (1510), who has attempted a difficult representation of perspective in sculpture.

The tomb, close by, of *Giovanni Andrea Vimercati,* a canon of the cathedral, has two fine heads in bas-relief by *Bambaja* (1537-48).

The Martyrdom of Santa Apollonia, by *Ercole Procaccini,* is rather injured. The statues of San Satiro, by *Cacciatori,* and St. Ambrose, by *Gaetano Monti,* were placed here in 1842. The elaborate Gothic doorway, composed of foliage intermixed with imagery, on the rt. hand, is the entrance to the southern sacristy. Then comes a sitting statue of Pope Martin V. by *Jacopino di Tradate,* erected by Filippo Maria Visconti, to commemorate the consecration of the high altar by that pontiff. The much celebrated statue of St. Bartholomew, formerly on the outside of the cathedral, and vaunted above its deserts, has been lately removed into the S. transept. The inscription, "*Non me Praxiteles, sed Marcus finxit Agrates,*" is adopted from an epigram in the Greek Anthology.

The tomb of *Cardinal Caracciolo,* governor of Milan (d. 1538), also by *Bambaja,* is striking in its general effect.

On the wall beneath the great E. window is a tablet of marble, with a monogram of high antiquity, called the "*Chrismon Sancti Ambrosii*," and which contains the A and Ω, together with other symbols. Some suppose it to be a Gnostic monument. Near this, engraved on a marble tablet, is a long list of relics of saints, fingers, toes, teeth, &c., possessed by this church.

North side.—The tomb of *Ottone Visconti*, Archbishop and *Signore* of Milan (d. 1295), is earlier than the foundation of the present building. It is striking from its singularity of form and colour, being of bright red Verona marble. He left his moveable goods and chattels to the knights of St. John, who erected this mausoleum. The same tomb, by a singular economy, serves as the memorial of Archbishop Giovanni Visconti (d. 1354), who also united in his person the temporal and spiritual supremacy of Milan.

Immediately above this tomb is the sitting statue of Pope Pius IV. (1559-1565), the brother of the Marquis of Marignano, and uncle of San Carlo. It is by *Angelo de Manis*, a Sicilian (1560). The semi-Gothic bracket which supports it, by *Brambilla*, is full of elegant fancy in the groups which compose it. An inscription, recently found under a house near the Cathedral, stating that it was erected in 1386, has been placed on the wall near Ottone Visconti's tomb.

Many defaced armorial bearings are seen in this and other churches of Milan; this was done during the three years' republic, by the Milanese themselves, and not, as is generally supposed, by the French.

The circuit wall of the choir, towards the aisles, is covered with bas-reliefs, representing the history of the Virgin. The subjects are divided into compartments by angels, whose attitudes are finely varied.

Entering the N. transept we come to the altar of San Praxedes, with a bas-relief by *Marc' Antonio Prestinari*.

The Annunciation is a copy of that of *Giotto* at Florence. The chapel of the Holy Sacrament, at the end of the N. transept, called *dell' albero*, from the splendid bronze candelabrum which stands before it, the gift in 1562 of Giovanni Battista Trivulzio, archpriest of the cathedral, contains some fine bas-reliefs, and a statue of the Madonna, by *Buzzi*. In front of this altar are the slab tombs of the Cardinal Federigo Borromeo, the nephew of S. Carlo, of Card. Caietani, and of two archbishops of the Visconti family. In the chapel of St. Catherine the Gothic altar is delicately executed. In the altars which come next, the picture of St. Ambrose absolving Theodosius is by *F. Baroccio*, and the Marriage of the Virgin is by *F. Zucchero*. Then follows a crucifix which was carried about the city, before St. Carlo, during the time of the plague. Two modern statues, St. Martha, by *Cacciatore*, and St. Magdalen, by *Monti*, have been placed in front of it. The next space contains an altar-tomb, erected in 1480, and restored in 1832; it has a bas-relief by *Marchesi*. The Baptistery,—a small square temple supported by four columns of *macchia-vecchia* marble—is by *Pellegrini*. It contains an ancient *labrum*, used as a font, from a bath of the lower Empire, the Ambrosian ritual requiring baptism by immersion. Behind the Baptistery, in the N. wall, are eight statues of saints, with a circular bas-relief of the Virgin and Child. The saints, in Verona marble, are of an early mediæval date.

The choir was designed by *Pellegrini*. The richly carved stalls of walnut-wood, with bas-reliefs, represent the history of St. Augustine and St. Ambrose. The organ-cases are rich with gilded carving and paintings of *Figini*, *Camillo Procaccini*, and *Giuseppe Meda*.

On the high altar is a magnificent tabernacle of gilt bronze, adorned with figures of our Saviour and the Twelve Apostles, the work of the *Solari*, and the gift of Pius IV. A Gothic candelabrum of wood covered with metal hangs from the roof of the choir, to carry the paschal candle. Beneath the choir is the subterranean church, in which service is celebrated during the winter season, as being warmer than the vast one above. This lower church is from the designs of *Pellegrini*. From it is the entrance into the chapel of St. Carlo, rebuilt in 1817, from the designs of *Pestagalli*, in the form of a lengthened octagon. This subterranean chapel is lighted by an opening in the pavement of the church above, but not sufficiently to allow of the objects in it being seen without the aid of tapers. The walls are covered with 8 oval bas-reliefs, in silver gilt, representing the principal events of the life of the saint, viz.—The Birth of San Carlo; his presiding at the Provincial Council of Milan (1505), in which canons were enacted virtually protesting against some of the worst abuses of the Roman Church; San Carlo's distribution to the poor of the proceeds of the sale of the principality of Oria. He had a life-interest in this domain, which he sold for 40,000 crowns; and he ordered his almoner to distribute it amongst the poor and the hospitals of his diocese. The almoner made out a list of the items, how the donations were to be bestowed, which, when added up, amounted to 42,000 crowns. But when he found out the mistake, he began to revise the figures. "Nay," said San Carlo, "let it remain for their benefit;" and the whole was distributed in one day.—San Carlo's administration of the Sacrament during the great plague.—The attempt made to assassinate him. San Carlo had laboured to introduce salutary reforms into the order of *Humiliati*, whose scandalous mode of living had given great offence. Some members of the order conspired to murder him. A priest named Farina was hired to execute the deed. He gained access to his private chapel, and, as San Carlo was kneeling before the altar, fired at him point blank with an arquebuse. At this moment they were singing the verse, "Let not your heart be troubled, neither be ye afraid." The bullet struck San Carlo on the back, but did not penetrate his silken and embroidered cope, and dropped harmless on the ground; and the failure of the attempt was considered as an interposition of Providence. San Carlo continued in prayer, while all around him were in consternation. The assassin escaped for a time, but was ultimately executed, though San Carlo endeavoured to save him.—The great translation of relics effected by him. —The death of San Carlo. He died 4th November, 1584, aged 46 years, his life having been unquestionably shortened by his austerities.—His reception into Paradise. These tablets are surrounded by fanciful ornaments. Thus (*e. g.*) round a tablet given by the money-changers are cornucopias pouring out money, the coins being real golden florins, pistoles, ducats, &c., fastened together by wire, or some similar contrivance. Jewels, crosses, rings, and other votive gifts are hung around: some are very recent.

The body of the saint is deposited in a gorgeous shrine of gold and gilded silver, the gift of Philip IV. of Spain. The front can be lowered, and displays the corpse dressed in full pontificals, reposing in an inner shrine, or coffin, and seen through panes of rock crystal. These panes are so large as to excite some doubt whether they are not of very fine glass, and whether the manufacturers of Murano may not have furnished the material supposed to be the production of nature. The skill of modern embalmers has not been able to preserve the body from decay. The brown and shrivelled flesh of the mouldering countenance scarcely covers the bone; the head is all but a skull, and the face, alone uncovered, offers a touching aspect amidst the splendid robes and ornaments in which the figure is shrouded. Upon the sarcophagus, and all around, worked upon the rich arras, is repeated in golden letters San Carlo's favourite motto, "*Humilitas*," which long before his time had been borne by the Borromeo family. The interior of the shrine

N. Italy—1860.

may be seen on paying 5 lire to the sacristano in attendance.

On the anniversary of this saint (Nov. 4) large pictures are suspended between the pillars of the transepts and nave, representing the events of his life and the miracles which he is supposed to have performed.

The principal or southern sacristy contains some objects of interest, the remains of a much larger collection. Amongst those most deserving of notice are the following :—*The Evangelisterium*, the cover richly worked in enamel, and containing a MS. copy of the Gospels, from which the archbishop reads portions on certain great festivals. It was given to the Duomo by Archbishop Aribert, 1018, but is probably of much older date than his time, the workmanship of the enamel appearing to be of the Carlovingian era.

A small *vessel of ivory*, ornamented with whole-length figures, the Virgin and Child, and the Evangelists, is placed beneath Lombard arches. It was given to the church by Archbishop Godfrey, by whom it was used at the coronation of the Emp. Otho II., A.D. 978.

Two *diptychs* of the Lower Empire, of good workmanship, representing events in the history of our Lord; Greek inscriptions, not all correct in their orthography, and one almost inexplicable.

Full-length *statues of St. Ambrose* and *San Carlo* on silver. The first was given by the city in 1698, and was the work of Scarpoletti, and twenty other goldsmiths. There are small statues of gold in the pastoral staff, and events in the history of the saint are delineated on his chasuble. The statue of San Carlo was given by the goldsmiths in 1610.

Several *busts* of the same material and character.

A *mitre*, said to have been worn by San Carlo during the pestilence. It is embroidered with the brightest feathers, and was probably brought from some of the Spanish American convents.

There are also some splendid specimens of modern jewellery, particularly a *Pax*, by *Caradosso*, the gift of Pius IV. It contains many figures ; the principal group represents a Deposition from the Cross ; the figures are worked with the utmost delicacy. *Ambrogio Foppa*, nicknamed *Caradosso*, was a Milanese, the contemporary of Cellini, and earned the deserved praise of the jealous Tuscan. He was also a die-sinker, in which art he excelled, and an architect. Foppa was not handsome : and a Spanish grandee having in contempt called him " Cara d'osso," or Bear's face, he very innocently adopted the name, without understanding it, perhaps thinking it a compliment.

The Ambrosian rite is almost the only national liturgy in the West which has been spared by the Roman Church, and it is probably much older than the Roman Liturgy. The *Rito* or *Culto Ambrogiano* is in use throughout the whole of the ancient archbishopric of Milan. Several attempts have been made to introduce the Roman service in its place, but they have been foiled by the attachment of the clergy and people to their ancient rite; and even in the present age " *noi Ambrogiani* " is an expression employed with a certain warmth of national feeling. The service is longer than the Roman. The Scriptures are not read from the Vulgate, but from the ancient version called the *Italica*, which preceded that made by St. Jerome. No musical instrument is permitted except the organ; the melodies of modern music are rarely introduced, and the monotonous chant maintains its supremacy. There are many minor differences in the ceremonies which are anxiously retained, extending even to the shape of the censers or *turiboli*.

A species of tunnel connects the Duomo with the *Archiepiscopal Palace*. Annexed to it is a workshop belonging to the fabric, in which is the model, or rather the wreck of the model, of one of the plans for completing the front of the Duomo. It is so large that a man can stand up in it; but it is sadly broken and neglected. According to this plan the front would have had a noble portal of Gothic arches, not unlike Peterborough, and much more appropriate than the present one.

There are many churches besides the cathedral deserving notice. Several of them are interesting from their antiquity; from their connexion with events recorded in history; or for the works of art which they contain. Some of them have lost their interest, however, by being modernized, particularly the interiors; and this seems to have been done chiefly about the time of St. Carlo, and during the Spanish rule.

Sant' Ambrogio. This basilica was founded by St. Ambrose, when Bishop of Milan, and dedicated by him, June 19th, 387, to the Martyrs *SS. Gervasius* and *Protasius,* whose bones he removed to this church. Posterity has transferred the dedication to the founder. This structure exhibits many of those arrangements which were adopted in the early ages of the Church. In front is the atrium, beyond whose precincts the catechumens were not to pass. As it now stands, it was built by Archbishop Anspertus (about 868-881), as appears from his epitaph in the choir. It is, therefore, the most ancient mediæval structure in Milan. When repaired in 1631 by the architect *Richini,* by order of Cardinal Federigo Borromeo, an operation rendered indispensable by its impending ruin, all its features were preserved without alteration.

The square court in front is acknowledged to date from the 9th century, and the church exhibits very much of the same style of art. This atrium is an oblong square surrounded by arcades, having 3 arches at each end, and 6 on each side, supported by pilasters with half-columns; the sculpture on the capitals of which, animals and runic knots, are good specimens of early Christian art. There is nothing in the details of the design, or in the execution, to demand admiration; and yet it is beautiful, from the mere simplicity and harmony of the general disposition.

The architecture of Sant' Ambrogio may be called Lombard (*i. e.* with circular arches), that style which it has been of late years the fashion to call Romanesque, but singularly rude. The five arches of the front are very characteristic; those above enclosing a gallery which stands over the peristyle. Fragments of frescoes still remain on the walls of the atrium, round which are arranged slab tombs, urns, altars, votive and sepulchral inscriptions, found in 1813, when the pavement of the Basilica was taken up and repaired. Some of the inscriptions are remarkable from the corruption of the Latin, exhibiting, perhaps, specimens of the colloquial dialect. Two small panels,—one at the top of each of the folding doors,—are shown as part of the gates which St. Ambrose closed against the Emperor Theodosius after his merciless slaughter of the inhabitants of Thessalonica. These relics are of cypress-wood, and, though not decayed, bear the marks of extreme age. The doors, scarcely visible through a close grating, are ornamented with foliage and Scripture histories. The general costume and treatment of many of the figures is that of the Lower Empire: they were executed most probably in the 9th century, and were restored in 1750, when the two bronze masks were added. As for the remarkable event to which the tradition refers, it took place at the gate of the Basilica Portiana, now the ch. of San Vittore al Corpo.

With respect to the architecture of the interior, it was, like the atrium, Lombard; but in the 13th century pointed arches were built up under the circular ones which support the roof, in order to strengthen them.

The inside of the church was originally divided on the plan into square portions, each division having two semicircularly arched openings on each side below, and two above in the gallery, and a vaulting of semicircular groined arches, groinings being added on the

I 2

roof. The first two squares remain nearly in the original state, but the third has double pointed groins springing from a lower point; the strong ribs which separate the squares unite likewise in a point so as to form a pointed arch. The fourth square is covered by the lantern, which is probably an addition of the 13th century. There is no transept. The parallel walls of the building continue a little beyond the lantern, and terminate in the ancient tribune, between which and the nave is seen the Baldachino over the high altar, supported by 4 columns of porphyry. Beneath are deposited the bodies of St. Ambrose and of Saints Gervasius and Protasius. But the great curiosity of the Basilica is the splendid facing of the altar, which is one of the most remarkable monuments of goldsmith's art of the middle ages. It was presented by Archbishop Angilbertus II. (about 835), and its interest is increased by the preservation of the name of the artist "Volvinius," who describes himself as "Magister Faber," or Master Smith, just as the famous "Wieland" is styled *Meister Schmied* in the Niebelungen lay. His name seems to indicate that he was of Teutonic race—a circumstance which has excited much controversy amongst the modern Italian antiquaries. The front of the altar is of plates of gold; the back and sides are of silver, all richly enamelled and set with precious stones: the latter are all rough, at least not polished according to our present mode. The golden front is in three great compartments, each containing smaller tablets: in the centre compartment are eight, containing our Lord, the emblems of the Four Evangelists, and the Twelve Apostles. The two lateral compartments contain the principal events of the life of our Lord. The Transfiguration is represented according to the type followed, without any variation, in all the early Greek and in most of the Latin delineations of that miracle. The sides and the back of the altar, though less valuable in material, are perhaps more beautiful than the front, from the greater variety of colour which they exhibit. The bas-reliefs on them are the following (we add the descriptions, because the inscriptions are not easily read, and the Custode explains them *ad libitum*):—

l.-hand side. Eight angels bearing vials; four whole-length figures, not appropriated; and four medallions, representing SS. Ambrose, Simplicianus, Gervasius, and Protasius.

rt.-hand side. The four archangels, Michael, Gabriel, Raphael, and Uriel. Four angels with vials, and four saints, SS. Martin, Maternus, Nabor, who suffered martyrdom with St. Felix, at Milan, A.D. 304, and St. Nazarius.

But the back is the most interesting part, for here are represented the principal events of the life of St. Ambrose, and here the artist has left his portraiture. Like the front, it consists of three grand compartments divided into smaller tablets. These are separated by enamelled borders. *Centre:* The archangels Michael and Gabriel. St. Ambrose bestowing his blessing upon the Archbishop Angilbert; and, in the pendant, he is also blessing the master smith Wolvinus. *Lateral tablets.* The history begins with the lowest tablet at the l. corner, and thus we shall accordingly describe them, proceeding upwards. (1.) The bees swarming around the sleeping child. St. Ambrose, born A.D. 340, was the son of the prefect of the Gauls. The legend tells us that the swarm thus flew about the infant's cradle, whilst he was lying in one of the courts of his father's palace at Arles. This was considered a presage of future eloquence. Nearly the same story is told of St. Dominick, and of Pindar. (2.) Ambrose proceeds to take the command of the eastern and Ligurian provinces of Italy. (3.) St. Ambrose, having been chosen Archbishop of Milan by acclamation (A.D. 375), attempts to escape his promotion by flight. (4.) His baptism, which did not take place until *after* he was nominated by the people to the archbishopric. (5.) Ambrose is ordained bishop. (6, 7.) Whilst entranced, he is present, in spirit, at the funeral of St. Martin of Tours—a legend, of which the futility has been pointed out by Baronius. (8.) St. Ambrose preaching, but prompted by angels. (9.) Heals the lame. (10.) He is visited by our Lord. (11.) The apparition of the angel calling St. Honorat Bishop of Vercelli to administer the viaticum to St. Ambrose, then on his deathbed. (12.) His death; angels receiving his soul. This monument is important as an authentic record of ecclesiastical costume. It narrowly escaped being seized and melted down by the revolutionary commissioners in 1797. Except upon high festivals, it is covered up, but it is shown upon payment of a fee of about 5 frs. to the sacristan.

Near the end of the singing gallery, towards the altar, is a half-length figure in bas-relief, with shaven head and chin, long pallium, and pontifical garments, the right hand being raised in the act of giving benediction, the left holding an open book on which is written Sanctus Ambrosius. It is an ancient representation of the saint.

In the nave of the church, placed upon a granite pillar, is a serpent of bronze, the subject of strange traditions. It is said to be the brazen serpent of the desert (in spite of the Scripture account of the destruction of that type), and as such was given, in 1001, to the Archbishop Arnulphus by the Emperor of Constantinople. It is probably an Alexandrian talisman of the 3rd or 4th century.

The pulpit is a curious structure, standing upon eight arches. It is said to have been rebuilt in 1201; but most of the ornaments are so evidently of the earliest Lombard period, that it can only have been repaired. A remarkable bas-relief, representing the *Agape*, or love-feast, should be particularly noticed. The bronze eagle for supporting the book is of the workmanship of the lower empire. Beneath it is a fine early Christian sarcophagus in the highest state of preservation. It is called the tomb of Stilicho; but this is an antiquarian whim, there not being the slightest foundation for the opinion.

Near the entrance of the choir are two slabs with inscriptions, the one covering the tomb of Archbishop Anspertus, the other of the Emperor Louis II., who died 875.

The tribune, or eastern termination, is the most unaltered portion of the edifice. The vaulting is covered with mosaic upon a gold ground—a splendid specimen of the Byzantine style, and the first which the traveller sees in this part of Italy. It represents the Saviour, and SS. Protasius, Gervasius, Satirus, Marcellina, Candida, and the two cities of Milan and Tours, in allusion to the legend of St. Ambrose being present at the death of St. Martin without leaving Milan. The inscriptions are partly in Greek, exhibiting in its spelling the present Romaic pronunciation, and partly in Latin. A monogram, conjecturally deciphered, probably contains the name of the donor and the dedication of the work; and in the hieroglyphics, contained within a square cartouche, the erudite may discover the names of the Abbot Gaudentius, the Archbishop Angelbert, and the Emperor Louis II. But whether the interpretation be correct or not, the character of the work is certainly not later than the 9th century, and probably of an earlier period.

In the centre of the tribune is a very curious marble chair or throne, called the chair of St. Ambrose, of an ancient form, decorated with lions at the arms, and a simple scrollwork. It is, in fact, the primitive throne of the Archbishops of Milan, on which they sat, according to the ancient practice of the Church, in the midst of the 18 suffragans of the province, of whom the most northern was the Bishop of Chur or Coire, and the most southern, of Genoa. The chairs of the bishops remained until the 16th century, when they were replaced by wood stalls for the canons, carved in a rich Flemish style, but so as to make us regret the loss of antique simplicity. When the traveller reaches Torcello (see p. 382) he will find the ancient arrangement still unaltered. The brick campanile is probably of the 13th century.

The chapel of *San Satiro* contains by far the most interesting mosaics in this church. This chapel was, in the time of St. Ambrose, the basilica of Fausta, but afterwards received the name of " St. Vittore in cielo d' oro," from the mosaic on the ceiling. It originally stood separated from the edifice of St. Ambrogio by a narrow street,' but was united when the basilica was rebuilt. The mosaics represent in full-length figures Ambrose, Protasius, Gervasius, Felix, Maternus, and Nabor: none are designated as saints, or crowned with the *nimbus:* in the centre is a medallion, supposed to represent St. Victor. The probability is, that they were executed not long after the age of St. Ambrose himself, perhaps in the 5th century. The nimbi and letters which are seen are a clumsy addition of a later period. Behind the high altar is a good fresco of our Saviour between Angels by *Borgognone*, and in a chapel close by a Gloria by *G. Tiepolo*.

The church contains several good paintings: in the 1st chapel on the rt. a Holy Family by *Luini*, seen with difficulty from the bad light; in the 2nd, now forming an entrance, frescoes of the Maries weeping over the dead Saviour, by *Gaudenzio Ferrari*; in the 7th, St. George destroying the Dragon, and the Martyrdom of the Saint, attributed to *Luini, Lanini,* and *Borgognone;* the vault and arches, beautifully decorated with flowers, arabesques, and children, and the Christ in the oratory outside, in the midst of angels, are probably by the same artists. The atrium leading to the sacristy has a Christ disputing with the Doctors, a feeble work by *Borgognone;* and a Virgin and Child on panel, of the very early Lombard school. A modern chapel has a statue by *Marchesi*. If the traveller descends into the once curious crypt, or *scurolo*, he will find it modernised by the munificence of Cardinal Borromeo. The roof is supported by 26 modern pillars of red and white marble. There is some fine church plate in the sacristy, especially an *ostensorium*, in the form of the handsome campanile of the church of S. Gottardo, given by Azzo Visconti. In the archives of the chapter are several diplomas of the 8th and 9th centuries, and a missal, with fine miniatures, of 1398, a gift of Gian' Galeazzo. The archives of San Ambrogio were removed to the General Record Office, and its library to Brera, in 1799.

The adjoining *Convent* of Sant' Ambrogio, now used as a military hospital, was built about 1495 by *Bramante*, and retains vestiges of its ancient magnificence. The splendid cloister has been destroyed. The refectory is a fine specimen of an interior in the decorated Italian style: it is painted in fresco by *Calisto da Lodi*, 1545. This sumptuous hall is used as a ward for patients affected with loathsome diseases; and whilst this occupation of the chamber prevents its being examined with any degree of pleasure, the exhalations have greatly altered the colours of the paintings.

Just without the precinct of Sant' Ambrogio stands a solitary shivered Corinthian column, a relic of Roman Milan. It has been found by recent excavations that this pillar did not belong to a building formerly standing here, but had been placed here singly, probably to support a statue.

Ch. of *S. Alessandro*. This church belonged to the Barnabites, by whom it was rebuilt in 1602, from a design of one of their order, Lorenzo Binaghi. The interior is very rich in painting and decoration, without containing any work deserving of being particularly noted. The façade, with its 2 bell-towers, is incomplete. The Barnabites, in 1723, established here, in emulation of the Jesuits, a college for noble families; whence the neighbouring street acquired the name of Contrada dei Nobili.

Ch. of *San Antonio*, built in 1632, from the designs of *F. Richini*. It contains 7 chapels richly ornamented with marbles and paintings. The vault of the nave is painted in fresco, by *Carlone*; the subjects relate to the Crucifixion and the Miracles of the Cross. The choir is painted by *Moncalvo*: the subjects are taken from the history of St. Paul the Hermit, and St. Anthony the patron saint. In the first chapel on the rt. hand the picture of St. Andrea di Avellino is by *Cerano*. The Nativity, in the 2nd chapel, is by *B. Campi*, and another further on by one of the *Caracci*. In the principal chapel on the l., Christ bearing his Cross is by *Palma Giovane*. In the chapel of the Annunciation are various works of *G. C. Procaccini*.

San' Bernardino del Monte, in the Piazza del Verzaro; an octagonal church, with a cupola; attached to it is a sepulchral chapel, entirely walled with skulls and bones symmetrically disposed. Some say that they are the remains of the Catholics slain by the Arians in the time of St. Ambrose. They are not, however, considered as relics; and the exhibition of these gloomy tokens of mortality is merely intended to excite devotional feelings. The oblations for masses are said to amount annually to between 10,000 and 15,000 lire.

San Carlo Borromeo, in the Corso Francesco, built by contributions raised amongst the inhabitants of Milan after the first invasion of the cholera, from the designs of *Amati*. The first stone was laid on the 29th of Dec. 1838. It is an extensive circular edifice, surmounted by a dome, and only second in size to the Pantheon at Rome, its diameter being 105 feet, its height 120 feet, and with the lantern 150; it is consequently larger than either the domes of Possagno or Ghisalba. In front is a fine Corinthian peristyle, opening on a square, surrounded by a portico of granite columns of the same order. The interior has still an unfinished, bare look, notwithstanding the 24 magnificent columns of red Baveno granite which decorate it. Amongst the works of art which it contains, the most remarkable are *Marchesi's* group of the Saviour and Virgin, called il Venerdi Santo: and in an opposite chapel, San Carlo administering the Sacrament to young people, by the same artist. The outer appearance of the edifice is poor, from the disproportion of the immense dome with the low peristyle and colonnade. The old church of the *Servi*, which contained some good paintings, was pulled down to make room for the portico.

San Celso, in the Borgo San Celso. In a field called "ad tres moros" St. Ambrose, in 396, discovered the bodies of SS. Nazarus and Celsus, martyrs. St. Nazarus he dug up and deposited in the church of the Sant' Apostoli: but over that of S. Celsus, which was allowed to remain in its original resting-place, he built a small ch., afterwards enlarged, and restored in 1651. There only now remains the choir, an ancient painting in a lunette, and a door with symbolical ornaments of the 10th century. The square brick campanile is a fine specimen of this class of edifices of the 13th or 14th centy. During the recent repairs several fragments of early Christian sculpture, which were dug up in the neighbourhood, have been placed on the walls, and the front painted to represent an atrium, which is supposed to have stood in front of this ch., similar to that of St. Ambrogio. Adjoining this is the fine ch. of La Madonna di S. Celso (see p. 179).

St. Eufemia, in the Corso di San Celso, with an Ionic vestibule, contains, in the first chapel on the left, a picture by *Marco d' Oggione*. The Death of St. Eufemia is asserted to be by *Titian*.

S. Eustorgio, situated at the end of the Borgo di Cittadella, near the Porta Ticinese. The suburb of the Porta Ticinese was first surrounded with a wall by the Viscontis, and called Cittadella, a name which thus remains. This church is one of the oldest in Milan, having been dedicated in the fourth century, A.D. 320, by Archbishop Eustorgius, who is said to have deposited in it the bodies of the three Magi, presented to him by the Emperor Constantine. It is one of the few remains of ancient Milan which escaped destruction from Barbarossa. After many vicissitudes it was attached to a Dominican monastery. This order established themselves, and the tribunal of the Inquisition, here, in 1218. At their expense the church, or rather aggregation of churches, which is now called S. Eustorgio, was reduced to its present form by *Tomaso Lombardino*. The campanile was built between 1297 and 1309. The church was finally completed by *F. Richini*. As a repository of monuments it is the most interesting in Milan. These are pointed to by Cicognara as worthy of more notice than they generally receive. All have suffered more or less from Vandalism during the early occupation of the French, and of the Cisalpine Republic. The armorial bearings have been completely defaced, the inscriptions of titles of nobility and honour chiseled out. In their present state it is very difficult to make out to whom the several tombs belong. In the first chapel on the rt. the monument of Stefano Brivio (ob. 1485) is of very delicate cinquecento work. It is said to be from a design of *Bramante*. Over the altar are 3 paintings in compartments by *Borgognone:* the subjects are the Virgin, the Infant Saviour, St. James and other Saints. Beyond the next pilaster is the chapel of St. Dominick, with a marble monument to Pietro, a son of Guido Torelli, Lord of Guastalla, of 1416. The next chapel, of the Rosary, is of 1733. In the 4th chapel, erected towards the conclusion of the 13th century, and dedicated to St. Thomas, is the tomb of Stefano Visconti, son of Matteo Magno. The sarcophagus is supported by eight spiral columns resting on marble lions, with bas-reliefs remarkable for the age. In the 5th chapel are the mausoleums of Uberto Visconti, brother, and of Bonacossa Borri, wife of Matteo Magno. The 6th chapel, dedicated to *St. Martin*, was built by the della Torre family. The fine tomb of Gasparo Visconti exists, though mutilated, and the bearings upon the shields have been obliterated by the republicans of 1796; but some traces of the insignia of the Order of the Garter may yet be discerned. Gasparo obtained this distinction in consequence of his having been repeatedly despatched to the court of Edward III., upon the negotiations for the matrimonial alliances effected or proposed between our Royal Family and the Visconti's: he died about 1430. The opposite tomb of Agnes, the wife of Gaspar, has been also much injured. It appears to have been taken down and the fragments rebuilt, but not exactly in their original position. The costume of the principal figure is curious: she holds an immense rosary. In the chapel on the right of the high altar is an enormous sarcophagus, destitute of sculptures or inscriptions, which once held the relics of the three kings of the East. When we say that it has no inscription, we exclude a modern one in large gilt letters,—"Sepulchrum trium magorum." At the approach of Frederick Barbarossa the citizens removed the relics from this church, which then stood without the walls, to another, deemed more secure. But in vain; upon the fall of the city the relics became the trophies of the victor, and Archbishop Rinaldus, of Cologne, carried them off to his own city. Opposite is a bas-relief representing the Nativity, and the Arrival of the three Kings, which, as appears from the chronicles of the monastery, was put up in 1347. It is supposed to have been executed by some of the scholars of *Balduccio di Pisa*. A passage leads from the subterranean chapel under the choir to the chapel of S. Pietro Martire. It was erected to him by a Florentine, *Pigello de' Portinari*, in 1460, and in it has been placed the shrine or sepulchre of this saint, a work of *Balduccio* himself, which is an exceedingly beautiful specimen of Tuscan art. Cicognara considers it as a masterpiece. *Balduccio* was one of the artists invited by Azzo Visconti for the adornment of his metropolis. The general plan is like that of the shrine of the Confessor in Westminster Abbey; a lower story, a base supported by eight beautiful columns, and the sepulchre above. Statues, full of simplicity, stand in the Gothic arches below; the Doctors of the Church, St. Thomas and St. Eustorgius. More interesting to the stranger, because more novel, are the allegorical representations of the Virtues. Beyond the Alps such allegories are but rare; not occurring very often in the Gothic buildings of France, and still more seldom in England, but they are amongst the peculiar characteristics of the Pisan school;—Charity,—Faith,—Fortitude. —Prudence represented as having three faces, contemplating past, present, and future. — Hope looking upwards and grasping a nosegay of budding flowers. —Obedience holding a Bible.—Temperance pouring forth water from a vase. On the tomb above are eight bas-reliefs, representing the life and miracles of San Pietro Martire. *Balduccio* has subscribed his name and date to this monument,—" Magister Johannes Balducci de Pisis, sculpsit hanc archam, anno Domini 1339." The material is white marble. A likeness of *Pigello* is preserved in an ancient painting above the door. The high altar was erected by Uberto Visconti in 1316. The nine bas-reliefs were added by Gian' Galeazzo. The barbarous rock-work additions to represent Mount Calvary were made in 1540. The silver busts on the altar contain relics of saints of the order of St. Dominick. On the outside of the church is a pulpit, from which it is said that San Pietro Martire preached to the multitude against the Cathari and other heresies which then abounded in Milan. It is a species of Paul's Cross pulpit, or like that at Magdalen College. Fra' Pietro did not, however, content himself with preaching, but worked out in practice what has been approvingly styled " the theory of persecution." He exercised without mercy the office of inquisitor in the monastery of the Dominicans formerly attached to this church, and fell a victim quite as much to the fears as to the revenge of those who slew him near Barlassina, 6th of April, 1252. The Church of Rome, in admiration of his principles and practice, canonised him only 13 years after his death. The adjoining convent was, in 1798, turned into a barrack. In the Piazza opposite is a statue of Peter Martyr, on an elevated granite column.

S. Fedele, one of the most elegant churches in Milan, built for the Jesuits by S. Carlo, by whom they were established here. It is from the designs of *Pellegrini*. The bas-reliefs of the front are by *Gaetano Monti of Ravenna* and his pupils, and have considerable merit. Since the suppression of the Jesuits the adjoining college has been converted into the *Repository of the Public Archives*, which contains many documents of great interest on the mediæval history of Italy. San Fedele may be called the fashionable church of Milan, as the visitor will see by going there at high mass on Sundays.

S. Giorgio in Palazzo was founded in 750, by Saint Natalis. The façade was restored in 1800, by *B. Ferrari*. The interior in 1821, by *Canonica*. It has thus been much modernized. The frescoes on the ceiling of the choir are by *S. Montalto*. It also contains, in the 1st chapel on the rt., a St. Jerome, by *Gaudenzio Ferrari*, and, in the 3rd on the same side, a Deposition and Ecce Homo, by *B. Luini*, amongst the best pictures of the master. Both are very fine, and in good preservation ; there are some fair frescoes on the arch of this chapel.

San Giovanni in Conca, shut up and desecrated. The front exhibits a curious mixture of the circular and pointed styles. Here were the tombs of the Visconti family. The monument of Bernabo has been removed to the Brera museum. Adjoining the ch. is a lofty bell-tower, long used as a meteorological observatory. To the l. of this church is what was the Casa Sforza ; and on the rt. a house called Dei Cani, from the dogs which Bernabo Visconti kept in it.

S. Lorenzo. In the Corso di P. T:-

I 3

cinese, close to this church, stand the Colonne di San Lorenzo, the most considerable vestige of the architectural magnificence of Roman Milan. These columns, 16 in number, are of the Corinthian order. Mouldering, fire-scathed, shattered by violence, these relics contrast strangely with the bustle and vivacity of the street in which they stand. According to the earliest Milanese historians, they are portions of the Temple of Hercules, built by Maximinian in honour of his tutelary deity. Modern antiquaries consider them as portions of the peristyle of the baths of Hercules, commemorated by Ausonius in the epigram which we have before cited; and the constructions which can yet be traced in the adjoining church seem to confirm this conclusion. An inscription in honour of Lucius Verus, built into a pier, has evidently no concern with the columns, and another, containing the N. following letters, A. P., on what is T. I. S. supposed to be a part of the original edifice, does not afford much explanation. The style has been assigned to the 3rd century. The increased intercolumniation of the 8 columns on the l. is an irregularity found in the nearly contemporary palace at Spalatro. The ancient church of San Lorenzo fell down in 1573. It had previously sustained many mischances, particularly in 1071, when it was burnt. It was by this fire that the columns were so much damaged. *Pellegrini*, the builder of the Escurial, a good painter as well as an architect, was employed by San Carlo Borromeo to give the designs for the new structure, but they were partly altered by *Martino Bassi*. The interior was rebuilt upon the plan of *San Vitale*, at Ravenna, and has 8 sides, 4 being filled by lofty arches enclosing recesses. The arches which fill the intervals are smaller; 2 orders are employed, the lower is Doric, the higher Ionic. The arches are surmounted by a Doric cornice, which serves as the impost to the cupola, a regular octagon, having a window in each compartment. On the rt. the basilica communicates with the octagonal chapel of St. Aquilinus, founded by Ataulphus, the King of the Goths and successor of Alaric, but who aspired to the glory of being the restorer, not the destroyer, of Rome. In this chapel, which, excepting the cupola, is ancient, although entirely modernised on the surface, is the remarkable tomb of Ataulphus, who married Galla Placidia, daughter of Theodosius the Great, whose part in the history of the decline of the Roman empire is that of a heroine of romance conquering her victor by her charms. The tomb bears a considerable resemblance to that of his wife at Ravenna, and, like hers, without an inscription, and of very plain workmanship. The monogram of Christ (with the descending dove over a cross) and a species of Runic knot, with two lambs, are the only ornaments. In the chapel are two very early Christian mosaics, perhaps amongst the oldest existing specimens of Christian art: they represent—that on the right, our Lord in the midst of the Apostles—a fountain gushes from his feet as an emblem of the living waters; and on the left, Shepherds and their flocks, and the Sacrifice of Isaac. It is thought, and with some probability, that this part of the building was originally one of the chambers of the ancient baths. The shrine of St. Aquilinus is a rich specimen of pietra-dura work. The entrance door of the chapel is of the lower empire, and covered with sculpture. In a chapel behind the high altar is the fine mausoleum erected by Gasparo Visconti to Gio. Conti in 1538. At the first altar on the l. hand the pictures are by *A. Luini*. The Baptism of our Saviour is pleasing. There are also, the Martyrdom of SS. Hippolytus and Cassianus, by *Ercole Procaccini*—the Visitation, by an unknown artist, *Morazzone*—and a good fresco, representing the discovery of the body of Sta. Natalia, by *E. Procaccini*.

S. Marco. Built in 1254. The façade is Gothic, the interior is modernized. It contains many fresco paintings by *Lomazzo*; the best of which is the Madonna and Infant, with saints, in the third chapel. The picture of the Trinity is attributed to *Luini*. Over the altar is a rich modern tabernacle in the form of a Corinthian temple. The large pictures by the side of the high altar are by *C. Procaccini* and *Cerano*. In the vestibule facing the Naviglio are some Gothic monuments: one in white marble, with the figure of Lanfranco Septala, the first general of the Augustinian Order, who died in 1243, is attributed to *Balduccio* of Pisa—he is represented sitting amidst his pupils; and another of 1344 to one of the Aliprandi family.

Sta. Maria del Carmine. This church has undergone two transformations. It was built by the Carmelites in 1446, in a Gothic style. In 1660 this was altered, as far as possible, into Roman by *Richini*, and restored to its original state by *Pizzagalli* in 1835. It contains two ancient Lombard pictures, and a Madonna in fresco, by *B. Luini*. The chapel at the side incrusted with marbles and gilt stucco contains on the walls two pictures by *Camillo Procaccini*.

Sta. Maria presso San Celso, more generally known as *La Madonna*. A very splendid building, one of the richest churches of Milan.

According to tradition, St. Ambrose, on the spot on which he found the remains of St. Nazarus and St. Celsus, placed a picture of the Madonna, who afterwards, on the 30th December, 1483, appeared there. The miracle drew so many persons to the small church which had been built in 1429 by Filippo Maria, that it was resolved to erect a splendid church on the spot, and this was commenced in 1491 from the plans of *Bramante*. In front of the ch. is a handsome square court, 3 of the sides formed of 5 Corinthian arches, the capitals of the half-columns as well as of the pilasters in bronze. The façade was begun by *Bramante*, or, as others say, by *Gobbo Solaro*, carried on and altered in 1572 by *Martin Bassi*, and completed by *Alessio*, to whom the present design is principally due. The sculptures of the façade are remarkable. The two statues of Adam and Eve, and the bas-reliefs of the Annunciation, the Adoration of the Magi, and the Flight into Egypt, are by *Stoldo Lorenzi*, a Florentine; the rest are by *Annibale Fontana*, a Milanese. The capitals of the columns of the interior are of bronze. The rich organ over the entrance has statues of prophets on each side, by *Fontana*, and is supported by caryatides by *Bassi*. 12 statues stand round the 12-sided cupola. The pendentives, and the lunettes beneath, were painted by *Appiani* in 1797. Below, on the pilasters which support the dome, is a statue of St. John the Baptist, by *Fontana*, and two others by *Lorenzi*. The 4th space is occupied by the rich altar of the Virgin, on which the miraculous painting is preserved. The altar is rich in silver and gold, the sculptures by *Fontana*. The wood-work of the stalls is by *Taurini*. According to the original design there should only have been 2 altars, but several have been since added. In the 1st recess on the rt. hand is a Deposition by *G. C. Procaccini*; the side pictures are by *Nuvolone*. Over the altar next to it is the Martyrdom of St. Nazarus and St. Celsus, also by *G. C. Procaccini*. They were beheaded at Milan, under Nero, A.D. 69. The mother of San Nazarus was Perpetua, who had received the faith from St. Peter. Under the altar is a rude sepulchral urn, with a bas-relief of the 4th century. The roof of the nave is richly decorated with sunken and gilt circular and octagonal panels. At the altar of the Crucifixion the St. Joseph is by *E. Procaccini*. The Baptism in the Jordan, 4th chapel on rt., is by *Gaudenzio Ferrari*. In the principal chapel of the rt.-hand transept are, a fine picture representing St. Jerome kneeling before the Infant Saviour, and some small pictures, by *Paris Bordone*. In the spaces of the circuit behind the high altar it is difficult to see the pictures for want of light. The Resurrection in the 1st is by *A. Campi*. The pictures in the 2nd, 3rd, and 5th are by *Carlo Urbino*. St. Catherine in the central one is by *Cerano*. St. Jerome in the 6th is by *Calisto Piazza*. The Conversion of St. Paul in the 7th, by *Moretto*. In the principal chapel of the l. transept the Assumption is by *C. Procaccini*. There is also a picture by *Borgognone*.

Close to here is the very ancient ch. of St. Celso. (p. 175.)

Santa Maria delle Grazie. In the Borgo delle Grazie, which leads to the P. Vercellina.—This church, with the convent of Dominicans to which it was annexed, was founded (1463) upon the site of the barracks belonging to the troops of Francesco Sforza I., by Count Gasparo Vimercati, then commander-in-chief of the ducal army. A considerable portion of the military buildings was converted, in the first instance, into an habitation for the friars; the church was built afterwards.

In a small chapel in the house of Vimercati, which is still preserved on the l. of the nave, was a miraculous image of the Virgin. This, together with his house, Vimercati bestowed on the Dominicans, who, pulling down the whole, built the present church on its site. The first stone was laid in 1464. Its progress was slow, not having been completed till after 1493. Ludovico il Moro and his wife Beatrice were liberal contributors to the church, and she was buried here.

The front is a fair specimen of Lombard Gothic of brick, with ornaments in terracotta. The interior consists of a good Gothic nave, separated from the aisles by 7 pointed arches, surmounted by a Gothic groined vault; and although dirty, dilapidated, and forlorn, is still grand. At the end of the nave rises the cupola by *Bramante*. In the second chapel on the rt. is a St. John the Baptist, attributed to *Francesco d'Adda*. In the fourth are some noble frescoes by *Gaudenzio Ferrari*. Three compartments, dated 1542, contain the principal events of the Passion of our Lord, but are unfortunately much injured: The Crucifixion has been much admired. The Flagellation, opposite, exhibits peculiar power and freedom. This fresco, and Our Saviour Crowned with Thorns, in a compartment above, have been injured by damp. The vaulting of the chapel retains its paintings in their original full and vigorous tone. The figures introduced — Angels bearing the instruments of the Passion—are very fine. Gaudenzio exerted his utmost skill in these paintings, expecting to have an order for the altarpiece, but Titian was preferred, his celebrated Saviour crowned with Thorns, now in the Louvre, having stood here. Amongst the other frescoes are, in the 5th chapel on rt., a Crucifixion and Angels on the vaulting, by *Carlo di Crema :* and several on the roof of the last chapel on the rt., and upon the vaults of the choir, by the school of *Leonardo da Vinci*. The choir itself is richly painted by *Maleotto*. The high altar is a fine specimen of richly inlaid marble work. In the sacristy are some presses for holding the priests' vestments, handsomely painted with arabesques and the shields of the Viscontis and Sforzas. These paintings, in imitation of intarsia-work, are very beautiful, but have been erroneously attributed to B. Luini.

When the friars were expelled, the monastery again reverted to its primitive destination of military quarters; but part of the conventual buildings not occupied by the soldiers continue to communicate with the church. Two deserted cloisters have portraits of the celebrities of the order, the Glorification of St. Thomas Aquinas, and other similar subjects.

In the refectory is the celebrated CENACOLO, or LAST SUPPER, of LEONARDO DA VINCI. Perhaps no one work of art has had more written about it, and none deserving higher praise. "This picture of the Last Supper has not only been grievously injured by time, but parts are said to have been painted over again. These niceties may be left to connoisseurs—I speak of it as I felt. The copy exhibited in London some years ago, and the engraving by Morghen, are both admirable; but in the original is a power which neither of those works has attained, or even approached." — *Wordsworth.*

The history of the painting and its mischances may be briefly stated. It was begun in 1493, being among the first works which Leonardo executed under the patronage of Ludovico il Moro. An anecdote is told by Vasari concerning the composition: that Leonardo told the Duke he must leave the head of the Saviour imperfect because he could not realise his conception of the celestial beauty it ought to possess: "Ancor gli mancava due teste da fare, quella di Cristo, della quale non voleva cercare in terra c non poteva tanto pensare, che nella imaginazione gli paresse poter concepire quella belezza e celeste grazia, che dovette essere in quella della divinità incarnata." And yet this very head, which Leonardo is so said to have left imperfect, is now one of the finest portions of the whole. Leonardo employed sixteen years upon the work; but he used a new process, which proved its ruin. The ground is plaster, impregnated with mastic or pitch, melted in by means of a hot iron. This ground he covered with a species of priming, composed of a mixture of white lead and some earthy colours, which took a fine polish, but from which the oil colour flaked off.

The materials with which the wall was built are of a very bad quality, rendering it susceptible of injury from damp. As early as 1500 the refectory seems to have been flooded, owing to its low situation. The vicinity of the kitchen smoked the painting, which exhibited early symptoms of decay. Armenini, who saw it about 50 years after it was painted, said it was then half spoiled, and Scanelli, who saw it in 1642, speaking hyperbolically, observed that it was then difficult to discover the subject. In 1652 the monks, wishing to enlarge the door, cut away Christ's feet and those of some of the Apostles, and, by shaking the wall in cutting it away, brought off parts of the surface. In 1726, Bellotti, an indifferent artist of much pretension, who painted the fresco over the door of the adjoining church, persuaded the monks he was possessed of a secret method which would entirely restore the faded painting. He concealed himself behind planks, and painted it all over. In 1770, Mazza, a wretched dauber, was employed to go over the whole of it again. The three heads, however, to the extreme right of the spectator, escaped, in consequence of the outcry which the proceeding raised.

When Napoleon was at Milan in 1796 he visited the refectory; and, sitting on the ground, he wrote, placing his pocket-book upon his knee, an order that the spot should be exempted from being occupied by the military. This order was disobeyed, and the room was employed as a cavalry stable, and afterwards as a hay magazine. The door was then for some time built up in order effectively to exclude the military. In 1800, owing to the drain being blocked up, and rain falling for 15 days, the refectory was flooded to a considerable depth. In 1801, on the instance of Bossi, the secretary of the Academy, it was reopened, and in 1807 the Viceroy Eugene caused the refectory to be repaired and drained, and everything done which might in any way tend to preserve the remains of the painting. It is, however, now again scaling off, not very rapidly, but incessantly; and this is, perhaps, the last generation whose eyes will behold its beauties, even yet so transcendent in their irreparable decay. Professor Barozzi of Parma is said to have discovered a means of preventing the painting flaking off, which he has only yet applied to a small portion of it.

The late Professor Phillips, R.A., in 1825, "examined its condition with careful and minute attention, and could with difficulty find a portion of its original surface. The little I did find exhibited an exceedingly well prepared ground, smooth in the highest degree, and the painting upon it free, firm, and pure."

"Till this time all paintings on walls had been wrought in fresco; but oil painting, which had become known and practised in smaller works, better suited da Vinci's mode of proceeding, as it admits of retouching or repeating: and, unfortunately, he adopted it here. He was not, however, the first who had employed it in that way; Domenico Veneziano, and one or two others, had made tempting examples for him, and thus led to a result so unfavourable to his reputation.

"It would appear that the vehicle which he employed, whatever it were, had no union with the ground, and therefore the surface cracked; and whenever damp found its way through those cracks, and between the painting and the ground, small parts of the former were thrown off, till at length large blotches were formed, exhibiting the white preparation beneath. These have at various times been filled up; and it had been well if with that filling up had rested the efforts of the restorers. But their attempts to match the remaining colours failing, as I suppose, they have taken the shorter method of cure, by repainting the whole surface of the part they were required to mend; so that, at the present time, little or nothing, it may be said, remains of Leonardo, save the composition and the forms generally."

"Of the heads, there is not one untouched, and many are totally ruined. Fortunately, that of the Saviour is the most pure, being but faintly retouched; and it presents even yet a most perfect image of that divine character. Whence arose the story of its not having been finished it is now difficult to conceive; and the history itself varies among the writers who have mentioned it. But perhaps a man so scrupulous as Leonardo in the definement of character and expression, and so ardent in his pursuit of them, might have expressed himself unsatisfied, where all others could see only perfection."—*Phillips' Lectures*, p. 65.

"That part which is to the rt. hand of the large dish, under the figure of our Saviour, including an orange, a glass of wine, a portion of two loaves, and a large piece of the tablecloth just about and under these objects, are, in my opinion, the only part of this great work which have been untouched. These parts have all the beauty of finish to be found in da Vinci's oil pictures."—*J. C. H.*

In his treatment of the subject, Leonardo adhered to the traditional style of composition, handed down from an early period, and peculiarly adapted to the position chosen for the picture. Placed at the upper end of the refectory, down the sides of which are ranged the tables of the monks, it connects itself with their circle, while it is, at the same time, exalted above them by its elevated position and the greater size of its figures. "This mode of composition, which betrayed the earlier artists into a disagreeably stiff and monotonous representation, and seems so unfavourable to the development of an animated action, is here enlivened in the most varied manner, while a most naturally imagined connection reduces it to an harmonious whole. The figure of Christ forms the centre; he sits in a tranquil attitude, a little apart from the others; the disciples are ranged three and three together, and they form two separate groups on each side of the Saviour. These four groups in their general treatment indicate a certain correspondence of emotion and a harmony in movement, united, however, with the greatest variety in gesture and in the expression of the heads."—*Kugler.*

The figures of the Apostles are thus placed. The standing figure to the extreme left of the spectator, and on the right of the Saviour, is St. Bartholomew; then they come in order thus: St. James the Less, St. Andrew, Judas, St. Peter, St. John. On the left of our Lord, beginning with the figure next to him are St. Thomas (with the forefinger raised), St. James the Greater, St. Philip, St. Matthew, St. Thaddæus, St. Simon. "The well-known words of Christ, 'One of you shall betray me,' have caused the liveliest emotion. * * * The two groups to the left of Christ are full of unpassioned excitement, the figures in the first turning to the Saviour, those in the second speaking to each other; horror, astonishment, suspicion, doubt, alternate in the various expressions. On the other hand, stillness, low whispers, indirect observation, are the prevailing expressions in the groups on the right. In the middle of the first group sits the betrayer, a cunning sharp profile: he looks up hastily to Christ, as if speaking the words 'Rabbi, is it I?' while true to the scriptural account, his left hand and Christ's right hand approach, as if unconsciously, the dish that stands between them."—*Kugler.*

Copies have been at various times made of this celebrated work: the best of which is, one by Marco d'Oggiono, a pupil of da Vinci, now happily preserved in the Royal Academy, London. Another by Bianchi, made by order of Cardinal F. Borromeo, is in the Ambrosian Library. Bossi, by direction of the Viceroy Eugene, in 1807, made with great care a cartoon drawing of the size of the original, and afterwards an oil painting, from which a mosaic was executed. This mosaic is now at Vienna; the cartoon is in the Leuchtenberg gallery at Munich; the oil-painting in the Brera.

At the opposite end of the refectory is a painting which, anywhere else, would attract great attention, but which is generally overlooked in consequence of its vicinity to the Cenacolo. It is a very large and well-preserved fresco of the Crucifixion by *Montorfano*, with his name and the date 1495. It contains a great number of figures grouped without any confusion, one of the best conceptions of a multitude we have almost ever seen, and full of merit. The good condition of this painting causes one the more to regret that Leonardo did not employ fresco. His error is very curiously exemplified on this same wall. You see two white spaces in the corners. Here Leonardo painted in oil the portraits of the donors of the Cenacolo, but only a trace of the figures can be discerned.

Santa Maria Incoronata. Built 1451, at the expense of Francesco Sforza. It contains a good picture by *C. Procaccini*, and the monument of Gabriele Sforza, 1458. The bas-reliefs, also, in the Capella Bossi, should be noticed.

Sta. Maria della Passione. Opposite to the end of the Stradone della Passione, close to the Archinto palace, and between the Porta Orientale and Porta Tosa, stands this church, built in 1485. The fine cupola was raised in 1530, from the design of *Solaro.* Its height from the pavement is 160 ft. The façade was added in 1692. It is heavy and overloaded: upon it are 3 fine high-reliefs, representing the Scourging of our Lord—the Crowning with Thorns—the Entombment. The interior is divided into a nave and two aisles, and the original design of a Greek cross has been altered into a Latin one, with 8 chapels in each aisle. On the rt. at the end of the transept, is a Crucifixion, by *G. Campi;* the roof above it is painted in fresco, by his brother *Antonio;* near this is the tomb of the two Biraghi, Daniel, Bishop of Mytélene, on the urn above, Francis below; a work of *Andrea Fusina.* It is the only specimen which can certainly be attributed to this artist, almost unknown, but who was amongst the best sculptors of Lombardy. Cicognara, speaking of this monument, says, "its general proportions, the grace of its ornaments, the beauty of the several parts, all are in the best taste and the utmost elegance." On the l. the baptistery contains the supper of San Carlo, by *Daniel Crespi;* the first chapel, a St. Ubaldo, by *Bianchi;* the fifth on l., a St. Francis, by *Camillo Procaccini;* the last, Christ going to Calvary, a work of the school of *L. da Vinci.* In the chapel of the l. transept is a Last Supper by *Gaudenzio Ferrari*, and Christ in the Garden, one of the best works of *Salmeggia*. The Flagellation, the Resurrection, and the long pictures on the pilasters of the high altar are also by him. Much expense has been bestowed upon the high altar; the ciborium is of pietra dura; and behind it is a painting, almost a miniature, upon marble, by *Camillo Procaccini*, representing the Deposition of our Lord. The principal ornament, however, is the altarpiece, a *Pietà*, by *B. Luini*, in his first manner. The doors of the organ are painted in chiar'-oscuro by *Crespi* and *Carlo Urbino*. Those on the rt.-hand side are by *Urbino*. By *Crespi* also are the small pictures of the Four Doctors of the Church, and the 8 pictures fixed to the great pillars, and representing the History of our Lord's Passion. The interior of the cupola is painted by *Nuvolone*. The sacristy is a noble apartment. In the lunettes are paintings of the saints and prelates who have belonged to the order, worthy of Borgognone.

The monastery connected with this church has, since 1808, been occupied by the Conservatorio di Musica, the most celebrated training school of Italy for theatrical music.

San Maurizio Maggiore, in the Corso di Porta Vercellina, called also the *Monasterio Maggiore*, on account of its rich endowments and the numerous privileges bestowed upon it by King Desiderius and the Emperor Otho. It is said to stand upon the site of a temple of Jupiter, from whence the columns supporting the tribune of Sant' Ambrogio were brought, and to have been one of the three buildings exempted by Barbarossa from the general destruction of Milan. Of the building of that early period, however, few traces remain, except in the two towers, the one round the other square (used as prisons for some of the Lombard martyrs), which are embellished with some coarse paintings and niches. One of the towers is traditionally asserted to have been of the 300 erected by the Romans which defended the city, and a fragment of Roman wall may be discovered in the monastery. The present construction is chiefly the work of *Dolcebono* (1497-1506), a pupil of *Bramante*; the façade is by *Perovano* (1565). The church is divided into two parts by a solid screen reaching to the height of the principal cornice. The half which serves for public worship is arranged in the same manner as the inner church, which belongs exclusively to the monastery. Great elegance of proportion is displayed in a triforium above a row of small chapels which are unconnected with each other, while the triforium leads round the whole church. The architecture is of a refined Tuscan order, and Bramantesque in the truest sense. The screen dividing the two churches is painted on both sides. On the outer side, or towards the church for the public, the whole of the paintings are attributed to *Luini*. At the bottom are 4 large female figures of saints, with angels bearing torches between; above in lunettes are portraits of the founders, and still higher up the Martyrdom of St. Maurus and St. Sigismund. The 1st chapel on rt. is painted by *Gnocchi;* the 2nd has two saints and *Putti*, attributed to *Luini;* the 4th chapel, perhaps the most interesting of the whole, is entirely painted by *Luini*, representing Christ bound between St. Catherine and St. Stephen, and the founder of the chapel kneeling before the former, on the side walls her Martyrdom, and on the vaults angels with the instruments of the Passion; on the l. side in 2nd chapel is St. Stephen preaching and martyrized, by *Aurelio Luini;* in the 3rd, the Birth and Martyrdom of St. John the Baptist, by the same painter; and in the 4th, a Descent from the Cross, by pupils of *Luini*. The *inner* ch. or choir:—the lower part of the screen has been converted into a chapel; in the lunettes are paintings of Christ mocked, his Crucifixion, and Deposition in the sepulchre; and on the side-walls, our Saviour in the Garden, with 3 sleeping Apostles, and the Resurrection, admirable works of *B. Luini;* the Almighty with the 4 Evangelists, and Angels singing, are probably by *Borgognone*, as also the beautiful half-figures in the gallery that runs round the church.

San Nazaro Maggiore, in the Corso di Porta Romana. This basilica was founded by St. Ambrose (A.D. 382), and dedicated to the 12 Apostles. It was burnt in 1075, enlarged upon its being rebuilt, and again by San Carlo: the two principal chapels were added in 1653. The most interesting part of the ch. is the vestibule by which it is entered. This is the sepulchral chapel of the Trivulzis, and contains an interesting series of monuments of that illustrious family. They are remarkably simple, figures as large as life, in the armour, dress, and garb of the times, true portraits in marble, resting upon their sarcophagi in stucco.—Antonio (d. 1454), the father of the great Trivulzio, who, upon the death of the last Sforza, turned the dubious scale in favour of the Viscontis.—The great Gian' Giacomo (died 1518), Marquess of Vigevano, his laurel-crowned head pillowed upon his corslet, with the inscription "Johannes Jacobus Magnus Trivultius Antonii filius, qui nunquam quievit quiescit, tace." This was the Trivulzio who, banished from Milan, returned at the head of the French army, and may be said to have been the main cause of the ruin of his country. Those who had profited by his treason respected him not: the old warrior died broken-hearted, at the age of 80 years, and was buried, as the French say, at Bourg de Chartres, near Montlhery. He was the founder of the chapel, as appears from an inscription yet remaining. — The two wives of the Marquis, Margareta Colleoni, died 1488, and Beatrice d'Avalos, sister of the Marquis of Pescara.—Gian' Nicolo, died 1512, the only legitimate son of the Marquis; as zealous as his father in the interests of France, and who, had he lived, would probably have equalled him in military fame.—Paula Gonzaga, the wife of Giannicolo; Ippolita, Luigi, and Margherita—maiden, boy, and infant, children of Giannicolo, all lying side by side; and, lastly, Gian' Francesco, died 1573, the son of Giannicolo, who served both Francis I. and Charles V., changing sides as was most convenient to him. It was he by whom these monuments were erected, as commemorated by him in an inscription which seems to apply to the whole series. All the monuments, however, are cenotaphs, the bodies being deposited in the vault below. The chapel is said to have been designed by *Bramante*, and altogether is one of the most remarkable of its kind in Milan. On the cupola and four spandrils are frescoes by *Vitale Sala*. There is a copy of Gaudenzio Ferrari's Cena, by *Lanini*, in the church. A good fresco, representing the Martyrdom of St. Catherine, in the oratory of St. Caterina della Ruota, adjoining the church, was executed by the same painter in 1546. In the principal compartment, near the pilaster of an arch, on the rt. hand, he has introduced himself between Gaudenzio Ferrari and Della Cerva.

S. Paolo, on the S. side of the open space in front of St. Eufemia. The side towards the piazza, coupled with Corinthian pillars above Doric, projecting from the wall, is from the design of *Alessio*. The front, which is in bad taste, has a bas-relief over the door, la Madonna di Loreto in the tympanum, and some long perpendicular compartments with emblems, beautifully executed. The interior is divided transversely by a screen, as at S. Maurizio, rising as high as the cornice, the further part being occupied by the Augustinian nuns called the Angeliche.

San' Pietro in Gessate (in a street leading from the Corso di Porta Tosa to the Borgo of the same name), so called from the Gessate family, who here founded a convent for the order of the Umiliati. The interior, consisting of a nave and two aisles, with painted arches supported by monolith columns of grey granite, preserves its original construction unaltered. The date of the present arrangement of the choir is 1640. In the third chapel on the rt. is a

Madonna of *Luini*, in 6 compartments, with Saints and Donatarii. *D. Crespi* painted the S. Mauro, to whom persons afflicted with the sciatica performed pilgrimages in this church. The actions of the saint at the sides are by *Moncalvo*. The frescoes in the 2nd chapel, on the l., representing St. Ambrose as archbishop, are attributed to *B. Zenale* and *B. Buttinoni* of Treviglio. In the altar of the 3rd chapel on l., a Madonna, in the middle of six compartments of very ancient paintings, is by *Bramantino* or *Vincenzio Foppa*. The monastery adjoining this church was erected in 1509, and is in the style of the school of Bramante: it has 2 cloisters, with Doric columns, with arches and a frieze of brick. It is now used as an Orphan Asylum.

San Satiro, in the Contrada del Falcone, nearly surrounded by houses, is without façade or choir, but is a very graceful building inside. The original church was built by Archbishop Anspertus on the site of his own house, in the 9th centy.: the only remains of this is the chapel in the l. transept, with four larger and several smaller columns of different materials and dimensions, and with different capitals, all taken from earlier buildings, as was then usual. The present church was erected about 1480. It was intended to be in the usual shape of a Latin cross; but, from want of space, the choir is wanting, and its place is supplied by a perspective painted on the wall. This painting is as old as the church, but it has lately been retouched and refreshed. It can hardly be called a work of art, but, as a specimen of perspective, the deception is marvellous. Annexed to the church is a small very elegant octagon sacristy, by *Bramante*. The bas-reliefs, arabesques, and sculpture are by *Caradosso*, and are very beautiful.

S. Sebastiano has a good painting of the martyrdom of the patron saint by *Bramantino*.

San Sepolcro (close to the Ambrosian library) retains its ancient towers built in the 11th century; the rest is modern. Over the door is a celebrated painting by *Bramantino*—a Dead Christ mourned by the Marys — but it is so shut up in glass and grating, to protect it from the weather, that it is difficult to examine it. This church was the centre of the congregation of the Oblati, a body of priests founded by San Carlo, in order that they might, by stricter lives and more exemplary performance of their duties, check the Protestant Reformation. The congregation has ceased to exist.

S. Simpliciano. St. Ambrose erected a chapel here, over the burial-place of some saints, and S. Simplicianus deposited here the bodies of Sisinius, Martirius, and Alexander. The Milanese, when they defeated Barbarossa at *Legnano*, believed that they were assisted by these martyrs, and that three doves, flying from their altar, perched themselves upon the mast of the Caroccio. In consequence of this, a fine Lombard church was built here, which, after having undergone some alterations in 1582, in a different style, has been recently restored, preserving the Lombard portal. In the choir is a Coronation of the Virgin in fresco, by *Borgognone*, a remarkable work for the simplicity and grace of the figures, approaching to the style of Fra Angelico; it has been much injured.

San' Stefano in Brolio, in the Piazza del Verzaro, the market for vegetables ("verzee") and fish, a very ancient basilica, rebuilt by Archbishop Visconti, the successor of San Carlo, and completed by Cardinal Federigo Borromeo. It was also called *St. Zaccaria alla Ruota*, from a species of wheel of terracotta, with the inscription "*Rota sanguinis fidelium,*" formerly fixed against a pillar, and afterwards deposited in the sacristy, but recently again concealed or removed. Near the pillar is a species of rude urn, now buried in the pavement up to its rim, and covered with a grating. This is called the "Pietra degli innocenti." Who the innocents were is a subject of great discussion, and so also with respect to the "rota;" some say it commemorates martyrdoms in the earliest ages of the Church. In the modern history of Milan an important fact is connected with the "Pietra degli innocenti." Hard by perished one to whom that name did not apply, Galeazzo Maria Sforza, slain December 26, 1476, by the three conspirators—Carlo Visconti, Girolamo Olgiato, and Giovann' Andrea Lampugnano. They were instigated by Cola Montano, a man of letters, who, fanaticised by the study of ancient history, urged his disciples — and he had many — to imitate the examples of those who had perished in the extirpation of tyranny. This church was judiciously restored in 1829. The rich Corinthian chapel to the rt. of the high altar built by Cardinal Trivulzio, governor of Milan, (1656) was restored in 1844. The baptistery has been lately fitted up with modern stained glass by Oldrino, a manufacturer in Milan. The ancient campanile having fallen down, the present one was built in 1642.

San Tomaso in terra mala, or terra amara. The date of the present form of this church is 1580. The hexastyle portico was added in 1825. It contains a Magdalen by *A. Luini*, a S. Carlo by *G. C. Procaccini*, and a St. Anthony by the younger *Sabatelli*. It is said to derive its name from one of those acts so characteristic of the tyrants of Italy. The priest of the parish had refused to read the funeral service over one of his poor parishioners, unless his widow would previously pay the fees. The woman burst out in loud lamentations; when Giovanni Visconti, riding by, asked the cause of the disturbance.—" Bury him gratis," exclaimed he to the priest, who complied; but, like the choristers in the ballad of the Old Woman of Berkeley, repeated the dirge with a quaver of consternation. And, when the service was finished, "Now," said Visconti, "throw him in." And the miserable priest was buried alive with his parishioner. The story adds that, as they were casting the earth over the priest, he cried out, "Come questa terra è amara!" from which the church derives its present name.

San Vittore al Corpo, in the Stradone di San Vittore: formerly the Basilica Porziana, vying in dignity with the cathedral. According to the traditions of the Church of Rome, an early convert, the Senator Oldanus, had two sons, Portius and Faustus; the latter built the basilica, which was incorporated afterwards in the Ambrosian. The former built this basilica, from him called Porziana. It was the scene of the Emperor Theodosius' exclusion from the church by St. Ambrose, and of the latter's victory over the Arians, and of the introduction of the *canto alterno* of the Ambrosian rite. At that time it was also known by the name of the "*basilica extramurana.*" It was first assigned to the Benedictines; in 1507 to the Olivetans, by whom it was rebuilt in 1560, from the designs of Alessio. The façade is simpler than the usual style of this architect. He intended to add a magnificent cortile, but this part of the design was stopped in its progress. The interior is splendid. The vaulting exhibits that union of plastic work and colour which, almost peculiar to Italy, produces such an effect of elaborate magnificence. It is divided into compartments of raised work, foliage and figures, within which are paintings of saints, martyrs, and angels, not so small as to fritter away the general aspect, and not so large as to intrude upon the architecture. St. John and St. Luke, in the cupola, were painted by *D. Crespi*; the other evangelists and the sibyls are by *Moncalvo*. The roof of the choir is by *A. Figino:* *Erc. Procaccini* painted the compartments of the roof of the nave, and St. Bernardo above the door. St. Christopher is by *Ciocca;* St. Peter by *Gnocchi*. The paintings in the choir on each side of the high altar are by *Salmeggia;* St. Bernard, and St. Victor, the patron saint, on horseback, the horse leaping forward with much effect. Another painting by *Salmeggia* represents Sta. Francisca Romana, the foundress of the order of the Oblate or Collatine Nuns, comforted by the apparition of her guardian angel. Five Victors are honoured as saints by the western churches. The patron of this church suffered martyrdom upon the site which it now occupies. He was a soldier in the army of Maximinian, by whose command he was tortured and beheaded, A.D. 303.

In the Capella Arese, designed by *G. Quadri*, with its fine black marble columns, the Madonna, angels, and prophets were sculptured by *Vismara*. It contains the sepulchres of the Arese family. In the last chapel on the rt. hand are three pictures by *Camillo Procaccini*, subjects from the life of St. Gregory the Great, —his Litanies during the great pestilence,—his attending on the poor, —and the feast given by him after the cessation of the plague. In this composition the table is placed in singular angular perspective; the sons of Totila are falling down before him. In the chapel of St. Benedict are some good paintings by *Figino*. The stalls of the choir are of the 17th century. They are of walnut-tree, and the carvings represent events in the life of St. Benedict. The sacristy is a fine room with noble wood carvings; it also contains several good pictures, of which the best is the Martyrdom of Saint Victor, by *Camillo Procaccini*.

THE SECULAR EDIFICES OF MILAN.

Palazzo della Reale Corte, close to the cathedral. This palace, which was the residence of the viceroys under the Austrian rule, and now of the King when he visits Milan, is built upon the site of the very magnificent one raised by Azzo Visconti about 1330, which was one of the largest and finest palaces in Italy, and decorated with paintings by *Giotto*. After repeated partial demolitions, the whole, excepting the church of *San Gotardo*, included in the present palace as its chapel, was pulled down towards the close of the last century.

"The steeple of *St. Gothard*, built in 1336, is a curious specimen of that age; it is of brick, except the little shafts which decorate it, and these are of stone. The four lower stories appearing above the roof of the church are plain octagons, with unequal faces, with a row of ornamental intersecting arches to each cornice, and a shaft or bead at each angle, which interrupts all the cornices. There is a little window in the lowest but one, but it appears to have been broken through at a later period; the fourth has on each face a window divided into two parts by a little column, and each part finishes in a small semicircular arch. This sort of arrangement occurs in the early architecture of France, of the 11th, and perhaps of part of the 12th centy., but I think not later. In the fifth story, the angular shafts receive their capitals, and unite with other shafts on the faces of the octagon to support a series of little arches; but as the angular shafts intersect the little cornices of each story, and consequently pass beyond the upright of the plain faces, while the intermediate shafts are within that line, the latter are broken into two heights, one projecting before the other. Over this are two stories, rather smaller than those below, and forming an equal-sided octagon; and above all is a spire, cut to indicate scales or shingles, terminating in a globe, and a little winged figure supporting a weather-cock. I have dwelt more fully on these details, because they so strongly distinguish the Lombard buildings from similar edifices of the same period in France or England; and because also they show the necessity of a new system of dates, when we would determine the epoch of a building by the peculiarities of its architecture. Though built in the 14th centy., it exhibits more of what we call Norman than of the Gothic; and perhaps the Italians never entirely abandoned that mode of building for any consistent style, till the restoration of the Roman architecture in the 15th centy., under Brunelleschi. There are several steeples at Milan of this sort, but this is the best. It was highly extolled by contemporary writers; and it derives more additional interest from having contained the first clock which ever sounded the hours."—*Woods' Letters of an Architect.* From the circumstance of the first striking clock having been placed in this tower the neighbouring street acquired the name of "Dell' ore." A singular story is connected with the gilt brass angel on the summit. A bombardier, in 1333, being condemned to die, offered to strike off the head of the figure at one shot, and, being allowed his trial, he succeeded; and his skill purchased his pardon. The angel continued without a head till 1735, when it was restored. It was when proceeding to the church of San Gotardo that Giovanni Maria Visconti was slain, 16th May, 1412. The diabolical ferocity of this tyrant had continued unchecked for ten years. It was his regular pastime to feed his bloodhounds with human victims, delighting in the spectacle as he saw the animals tear the quivering flesh from the bones. That his unbridled cruelty at last terminated in perfect insanity cannot be doubted. It *is* a curious fact that Giovanni Maria began his reign by granting a kind of Magna Charta to the Milanese, and that he was a liberal patron of literature. He is buried in the chapel, near the altar, but his tomb was destroyed by the French, and the interior of the chapel is now entirely modernised. The exterior of the tribune retains its ancient aspect.

The ROYAL PALACE contains many modern frescoes. The show parts of the palace worthy of mention, are the following:—*Saloon:* Night and Morning, by *Martin Knoller*, a Tyrolese, a scholar of Mengs. *Salle-à-manger:* ceiling, the Four Seasons, by *Treballesi.* *Small Dining Room:* a very elegant cabinet, with medallions on chiar'-oscuro. *Sala di Rappresentazione:* ceiling by *Appiani* and *Hayez,* Jupiter and Mercury. *Sala di Audienza:* ceiling by *Appiani*—History inscribing the deeds of Napoleon upon the shield of Minerva; in the four angles, the four quarters of the globe. *Imperial Throne Room:* by *Appiani*—the Apotheosis of Napoleon, he being represented as Jupiter upon an eagle: considered the best of the series. *Present Throne Room:* Marriage of Napoleon and Maria Louisa, by *Hayez.* *Ball Room:* the Coronation of the Emperor Francis as King of the Lombardo-Venetian Kingdom, also by *Hayez.* The *Great Ball Room* is a splendid old-fashioned apartment. Its principal feature is a gallery supported by caryatides, executed by *Calano,* an artist from Parma. They are cleverly varied. *Small Ball Room,* an Egyptian Hall; *i. e.* a hall supported by ranges of columns, like that at our London Mansion House. Lastly, a room hung with tapestry from the designs of Raphael.

The *Arcivescovado,* or Archbishop's Palace (between the Piazza Fontana and the cathedral), contains a very good collection of paintings, bequeathed to the see by Cardinal Monti, and increased by his successors. A few have been transferred to the Brera Gallery. The following are the best:— *Giulio Campi:* the Madonna, supported by Angels; originally a church-banner, or gonfalon. *Bernardino Campi:* St. John the Evangelist, with his symbol the Eagle. *Leonardo da Vinci:* a Sketch,—the Virgin contemplating our Lord, who is holding a Lamb. *Gaudenzio Ferrari:* a Nativity,—many saints introduced. *Titian:* an Adoration of the Magi. *Camillo Procaccini:* the Heads of the Twelve Apostles. *Cerano:* the Circumcision of our Lord. *Sarzana:* the naked Infant Saviour sleeping on the Cross. *Bramantino:* a Virgin and Child,—the Virgin dressed in blue, with a turban. *Andrea del Sarto:* a Magdalene holding the Vase of Ointment. *Leonardo da Vinci:* a Virgin and Child. *Morazzone:* the Murder of the Innocents. *Palma Vecchio:* the Woman taken in Adultery; our Lord is pointing to the writing on the ground, the Pharisees looking on. *Guido*: St. Joseph holding and contemplating the Infant Saviour. *Michael Angelo*: a Battle-piece, with many naked figures. *Titian*: a Portrait of Pope Julius III. *Giulio Cesare Procaccini*: St. Jerome, half naked,—an angel above is in the act of speaking to the saint; the Marriage of St. Catherine. *Bernardino Campi*: a Design in chiar'-oscuro, representing St. Sigismund of Cremona, and other Saints. *After Raphael*: the Adoration of the Shepherds, a piece of tapestry woven in gold and silk. *Morazzone*: the Angel wrestling with Jacob. *Antonio Campi*: our Lord's Agony in the Garden. *Andrea del Sarto*: the Lord of the Vineyard paying the Hire of his Labourers. *Raphael*: a Design, on paper, of several naked figures in the act of shooting at a mark. *Leonardo da Vinci*: two Designs, in chiar'-oscuro, of naked children. *Camillo Procaccini*: the Raising of Lazarus, and the Martyrdom of SS. Nazaro and Celso; Designs in chiar'-oscuro, with many figures. *Mabuse*: a Virgin and Child. *Antonio Campi*: the Circumcision of our Lord. *Albert Durer*: St. Jerome. *Paris Bordone*: two Holy Families, one including St. Ambrose, and another with St. Catherine. *Bernardino Campi*: our Lord bearing his Cross. *Morazzone*: a Holy Family. *Pordenone*: the Virgin and Child. *Titian*: a Holy Family, with St. George in armour.

The *Palazzo della Città*, or *Broletto*, in the Corso del Broletto. Broletto was the name formerly given to the town-hall or palace of the municipality. It first stood on the site of the Corte, afterwards in the Piazza de' Tribunali. The present building, which is extensive, with two courts and colonnades, is a specimen of the architecture of the revival previous to the time of Bramante. It was built by *Filippo Maria Visconti* for the celebrated Count Carmagnola. It now contains the several municipal offices.

The *Piazza de' Tribunali* is remarkable as containing some remains of mediæval Milan. In the centre rises a large square building, standing upon open arches, of which the upper portion serves as a depository for the Notarial archives of the city, whilst the arched space below was used as a species of market. The latter has been handsomely restored and enclosed in glass, and serves as the general rendezvous of the mercantile community, and especially as a corn exchange. This building was the *Palazzo della Ragione*, where, in earlier times, the magistrates of the commonwealth of Milan assembled, and where the ducal courts of justice sat in after times. It was begun in 1228 by the Podestà Aliprando, and completed 1233 by his successor, Oldrado Grosso di Tresseno, who is represented on the S. side mounted on his steed in full armour, very curious for the costume, but still more so perhaps for the inscription, which recounts his good and doughty deeds in extirpating heresy:—

"Qui solium struxit, Catharos ut debuit uxit."

The Cathari here mentioned were Manichœan sectaries, whose name, corrupted into *Gazzari*, was transformed by the Germans into *Ketzer*. The last word should be *ussit*; but the author of the inscription took the poetical licence of altering it into uxit, in order to rhyme. On the archivolt of the second arch, on the N. side, is a mysterious figure, which belonged to a much older structure, and was thus preserved in the 13th century, out of respect for its then remote antiquity. It is no other than the once celebrated *half-fleeced* or *half-fleecy* sow, by whose augury *Mediolanum* was founded, and from which the city derives its name (In medio lanæ). Belovesus the Gaul was guided to place his settlement, just as the sow and thirty young pigs settled the site of Alba.

Claudian, in his Epithalamium upon the marriage of the Emperor Honorius with Maria the daughter of Stilicho, thus describes Venus as repairing to Milan, where, as it would seem, the hide of the woolly sow was still preserved:—

"Continuò sublime volans, ad mœnia Gallis
Condita, lanigerm Suis ostentantia pellem
Pervenit."

And Sidonius Appollinaris, by the description of "the city named after the woolly sow," includes in one distich Ravenna and Milan:—

"Rura paludicolæ temnis populosa Ravennæ,
Et quæ lanigera de sue nomen habet."

The Piazza de' Tribunali is surrounded by other buildings, possessing much historical interest, and not devoid of picturesque beauty. Of these, the most curious in aspect is that on the S. side called the *Loggia degli Ossi*, from the family who defrayed much of the expense of the structure, which was begun in 1316. From the balcony, or "*ringhiera*" (or, in the language of the common people, *parléra*), in the front, the assent of the citizens was asked by the Podestà to the acts of government, and the sentences passed upon criminals were proclaimed. A row of shields with armorial bearings decorate the façade, being those of the six quarters of the city, and of the Visconti-Sforzas. It is of an elegant Italian Gothic, in black and white marble, and as such was much admired by Mr. Hope. Alongside the *Loggia degli Ossi* is the ancient Scuola Palatina, now converted into an office for mortgage-deeds, in front of which are statues of Ausonius and of St. Augustin. On the opposite side of the Piazza is the ancient college, formerly belonging to the doctors of civil law. It was built by Pope Pius IV. about 1564. The interior has some tolerable paintings of the 17th centy. On the opposite side of the Piazza from the Loggia degli Ossi is the old *Palazzo della Città*, or, as we should say, the Town Hall, a building of the 16th century. The statue of St. Ambrose occupies the place of that of Philip II. of Spain, which was converted into a Brutus in 1797, and destroyed during the riots of 1813. The lower part has been recently enclosed as the Bolsa or Exchange. The tower that rises on it is of the 13th cent., having been erected by Napoleone della Torre.

This part of the city is the heart of business. Opening out of it are the goldsmiths' street; the *Contrada di Santa Margherita*, the Paternoster Row of Milan, full of booksellers' shops (Guides, prints, and excellent maps, including those of the Austrian Ordnance survey, are to be had at Artaria's, who has also establishments at Vienna and Mannheim); and the Contrada dei Borsinari, leading to the Cathedral, the seat of some of the best shops in Milan.

BRERA. *Palazzo delle Scienze e delle Arti* is the *official* name of the great establishment which, when it belonged to the Jesuits, was called the *Collegio di Sta. Maria in Brera*, or, more shortly, *Brera*, by which name it is still generally known. It might be called St. Mary's in the Fields, for the old Lombard word *Brera*, or more properly *Breda*, is a corruption of *Prædium*. The establishment originally belonged to the order of the *Umiliati*, some of the principal members of which having conspired against the life of San Carlo Borromeo, it was suppressed. Their dissolute conduct had already excited great scandal. The Jesuits were put in possession of the Brera in 1572, upon condition that they should establish both what we may term a high school and a college, a duty which they executed with their usual ability till they were expelled in their turn. The church was pulled down in 1810 to make room for the academy. The present buildings are very extensive, and now contain within their walls (besides a chapel) the apartments occupied by the "Reale Academia," the schools of various branches of the fine arts, apartments for the "Real Instituto delle Scienze," a very extensive gallery of paintings, the *Pinacoteca*, the Library, a rich collection of fine medals and coins, many curious Chinese manuscripts, a small botanic garden, &c. In the great court have been erected statues of Verri the historian, of Cavallieri the mathematician, of the Marquis Cagnola the celebrated architect, of Grossi the historical novelist, and of Count Castiglione, an eminent Orientalist; on the stairs leading to the library, are busts of Oriani and others, and statues of Beccaria and Parini by G. Monti and Marchesi; and under the corridor on the first floor, which runs round three sides of the building, busts of Monti, Manzoni, Gen. Vaccani, and of several other Milanese celebrities, &c. Out of the S.E. corner of this corridor opens

The *Pinacoteca*, or gallery of paintings, a collection which, though somewhat deficient in particular schools, is nevertheless of great value. The pictures, however, gain nothing by their arrangement. There is no attempt at classification, and they are indifferently lighted. The names of the painters, with the numbers of the pictures, in large characters, are appended to each, which renders the purchase of the incomplete

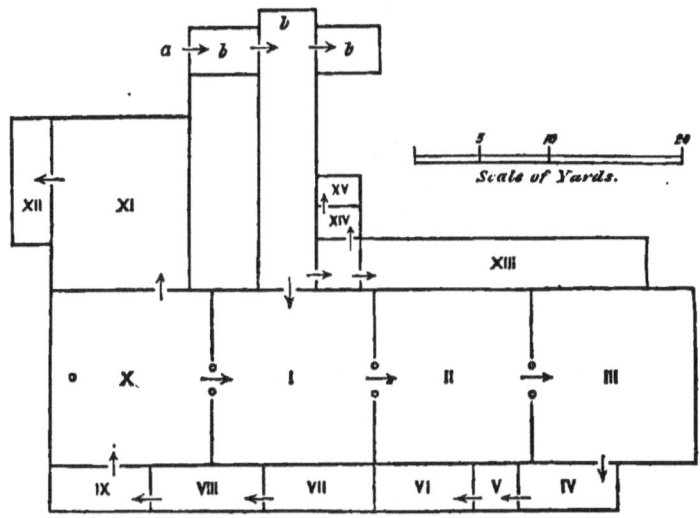

PLAN OF THE BRERA GALLERY.

a Entrance. *b b b* Halls of the Frescoes. *c* Bust of King. I. to XIII. Halls of Paintings. XIV., XV. Rooms of Engravings.

and unsatisfactory catalogue unnecessary: a new one is in preparation. The gallery is open daily, from 9 to 2.

In the two entrance halls (*b b*) are a number of frescoes by different early Lombard masters; some on the walls, which have been sawn from their places, and others which have been transferred to panel and canvas. The most important are those by *Luini*.

Among these frescoes the following are most worthy of notice:—By *Bernardino Luini*: 1, three Girls playing apparently at the game of hot cockles; 2, a Youth riding on a white horse; 4, a Child seated amongst vines and grapes; 5, St. Sebastian; 7, the Virgin and St. Joseph proceeding to their marriage at the temple. —8, *Bramantino:* the Virgin and Child and two Angels.—9, *B. Luini:* Two Minstrels, such as used to accompany wedding processions, and probably intended as a portion of No. 7; 10, a Sacrifice to Pan; 11, the Metamorphosis of Daphne; 15, the Dream of St. Joseph.— 16, *Aur. Luini:* a large fresco of the

Martyrdom of St. Andrew.—17, *Vincenzio Foppa*: the Martyrdom of St. Sebastian; the earliest in date of the frescoes exhibited here.—18, *B. Luini*: the Israelites preparing to depart from Egypt; 19, the Presentation in the Temple; 20, an Angel; 26, the Infancy of the Virgin; 27, of his school also is a San Lazzaro.—22 and 28, *Bernardino Lanini*: Mary Magdalene, and Sta. Marta.—29, Sta. Marcella, school of *Luini*; and by *Luini* again are—30, the Birth of Adonis; 31, an Angel; 32, St. Anna and St. Joachim; 33, the Birth of the Virgin; 34, the Body of St. Catherine carried by three Angels to the Sepulchre—a lovely work, reproduced in chromo-lithography by our Arundel Society of London; 35, a Cherub; 36, the Virgin and Child, with Saints, and an Angel tuning a lute, painted in 1521. This very fine fresco bears his name, and the date 1521. 37, the Almighty; 38, a Cherub; 39, the Presentation of the Virgin in the Temple; 40, the Prophet Habakkuk awakened by the Angel; 41, St. Anna; 42, St. Anthony of Padua.—By *Gaudenzio Ferrari* are—43, the History of Joachim and Anna, in 3 connected paintings; 48, the Salutation; 49, the Dedication in the Temple; 50, the Adoration of the Magi, in 3 compartments.—*B. Luini*, 51, Two Angels; 56, the Transfiguration; 57, St. Ursula; 59, St. Joseph; 61, the Redeemer; 62, a Portrait of a Young Lady; 65, another Portrait of a Lady; and, 66, an Angel flying, very beautiful.

In the first room (I.) the pictures most worthy of attention are:—5, *Parmigianino*: the Virgin and Child, with St. Margaret, St. Jerome, St. Petronio, and an Angel, probably a copy.—6, *Titian*: St. Jerome in the Desert. The saint is kneeling, with his eyes fixed on the crucifix, and grasps a stone, with which he appears in the act of striking his breast. The action of the saint, and the tone of the landscape, are fine. A larger picture of the same subject is in the Escurial, of which this has been thought to be the first design.—10, *Vandyke*: the Virgin and Child, with St. Anthony

N. Italy—1860.

of Padua.—11, *Paris Bordone*: the Virgin and the Twelve Apostles.—16, *Guercino*: St. Clara and St. Catherine. —17, *Rubens*: the Institution of the Lord's Supper.—18, *Domenichino*: the Virgin and Child, with St. John the Evangelist, St. Petronio, and many Cherubs.—19, *Albani*: a small Madonna.—20, *Guercino*: the Virgin, St. Joseph, and St. Theresa.—21, *Agostino Caracci*: the Woman taken in Adultery, with many figures.—22, *Ludovico Caracci*: the Woman of Canaan at our Lord's feet, with several Apostles. —26, *Paris Bordone*: the Baptism of our Lord.—27, *Annibale Caracci*: the Woman of Samaria at the Well.—32, *Procaccini*: the Magdalene, with an Angel.—33, *Trotti*, called Il *Malosso*: the Entombment.—35, *Procaccini*: St. Cecilia sinking from her wounds, but her eyes fixed on heaven, supported by two Angels.—36, *Daniel Crespi*: Our Lord going to Mount Calvary.—41, *Campi*: the Holy Family, with St. Theresa and St. Catherine; good.— 43, *Daniel Crespi*: the Martyrdom of St. Stephen—a picture crowded with figures. — 44, the Adoration of the Magi, called a *Titian*, but more probably by *Bonifazio*.

The second room (II.) contains from Nos. 44 to 71.—45, *Garofalo*, a Pietà, with many figures —47, *Tintoretto*: another Pietà.—48, *Moroni*: the Assumption of the Virgin.—49, 50, and 51, *Paul Veronese*: St. Gregory and St. Jerome, St. Ambrose and St. Augustine with a glory of Angels around, and an Adoration of the Magi.—52, *Palma Giovane*: St. Benedict under temptation. — 53, *Bassano*: St. Roch visiting the Sufferers from Plague, the Virgin above.—55, *Foschi*: Virgin and Child, with four Saints and Angels.—56, *Moretto*: the Virgin and Child above, in glory; below, St. Jerome, St. Francis, and St. Anthony the Hermit.—58, *Tim. della Vite*: the Virgin, St. John the Baptist, and St. Sebastian. — 59, *Romanino*: Virgin and Child, St. Francis, Saints, and Angels.—60, *Palma Vecchio*: the Adoration of the Magi, with St. Helen.

K

—61, *Paul Veronese*: the Marriage of Cana.—62, *Geronimo Savoldo*, called *il Cavaliere Bresciano*: the Virgin and Child, with two Angels in glory; and below, St. Peter, St. Paul, St. Jerome, and St. Dominick.—63, *Carpaccio*; St Stephen; beautiful.—65 and 66, *Moretto*: St. Clara and St. Catherine, and St. Jerome and an Apostle; 68, St. Francis.— 70, *Tintoretto*: the Holy Cross, with many Saints; St. Helen and St. Catherine are the chief figures; St. Andrew and St. Dominick are amongst the others.—71, *Paul Veronese*: St. Cornelius (a pope), St. Anthony the Abbot, St. Cyprian, a page and priest.

The third room (III.) contains from 72 to 128. 73, *Stefano da Ferrara.*— 75, *Gentile da Fabriano*: the Virgin with the Holy Trinity and many Angels; figures about half the size of life—a curious and good picture.—77, *Niccolò da Foligno*: the Virgin and Child surrounded by Angels; with his name, and the date 1465.—78, CARLO CRIVELLI: a picture divided by architectural ornaments into 3 compartments; in the 1st is the Virgin and Child; on her rt. hand are St. Peter and St. Dominick, and on the l. St. Peter Martyr and San Geminiano. The name and date (1482) are on this curious old picture.—79, *id.*, a Sainted Bishop and a Cardinal: all these works of Crivelli are first-rate specimens of the master.—86, *Bartolommeo Montagna*: the Virgin and Child, with St. Andrew, St. Monica, the Emp. Sigismund, St. Ursula, and three Angels below, playing on different instruments. A curious specimen of this early and rather stiff master; it is full of character in the actions and expressions of the saints. The date (1499) is on the base of the picture, with the name of Montagna. —88, *Giottino*: Events in the Life of St. Jerome, in two parts.—90, *Gentile Bellini*: St. Mark preaching at Alexandria in Egypt: a striking picture, remarkable for its great size, as well as for the variety of figures and costume. In the background the Basilica of S. Marco at Venice, and before it camels; and a camelopard is introduced, which Bellini probably saw and drew when he was in the East. 91, *Luca Signorelli*: the Flagellation.—96, *Cima da Conegliano*: St. Peter Martyr, St. Nicholas, St. Augustine, and an Angel tuning his lute.—97, *Giovanni Sanzio*, father to Raphael: the Annunciation, a remarkable picture. It has much of that grace and delicacy which his son afterwards manifested so largely. The colour is rich, and in parts good, but inharmonious.—98, *Luca Longhi*: Madonna and Child, St. Paul and St. Anthony, the work of a rare master.—101 and 109, *Giacomo Francia*: Virgin and Child, with Saints.—103, *Palmezzano*: the Nativity, with Angels, very peculiar.—105, *Andrea Mantegna*: divided by columns into 12 compartments, St. Mark in the centre, and various Saints around. 107, *Corradini*, called *Frate Carnevale*: the Virgin and Child, with many surrounding figures; many portraits, especially of Federigo da Montefeltro, Duke of Urbino, are introduced into this curious picture. —111, *A. Mantegna*: beautiful distemper, S. Bernardino, with two Angels.—112, *Paul Veronese*: our Lord in the house of Simon the Pharisee, a fine picture, and full of figures.— 113, *Gio. Cariani*, a rare master: Madonna and many Saints.—116, *Ben. Montagna*: Madonna and Saints.—117. *Martino da Udine*: St. Ursula, surrounded by attendant Virgins.—118, *Garofalo*: a large Crucifixion.—121, *Stefano di Ferrara*: the Virgin enthroned, with Saints. — 123, *C. Crivelli*: a Crucifixion.—125, *Giotto*: the Virgin and Child, signed.—126, *Marco Basaiti*: St. Jerome, highly finished. —127, *Palmezzano di Forli*: Virgin and four Saints, with name and date 1493.—128, *Carlo Crivelli*: Virgin and Child, with exuberant ornamentation.

The fourth room (IV.) contains from 129 to 164. 130, *Garofalo*: a Landscape, with two small figures, representing St. Francis and St. Anthony of Padua.—131, a joint production of *Van Thielen* and *Poelemburg*, the first, whose name the picture bears, for the flowers, the second for the figures.—136, *Vandyke*: a female portrait.—137, one of the finest portraits by *Moroni d'Albino*: a half-length of a Bergamasc Magistrate. —139, a picture attributed to *Correggio* on very doubtful grounds, the Virgin and Child, Mary Magdalene, and St. Lucia, in a Landscape.—142, *Francia:* the Annunciation; injured and much retouched.—144, *Carpaccio:* St. Stephen disputing with the Pharisees (1514).—146 and 151, *Hobbema:* Landscapes.—155 and 161, *Breughel:* the Descent of Æneas into the Infernal Regions, and the Burning of Troy, on copper, with a multitude of minute figures.—154, *Bloemen:* a Landscape. —157, *Poelemburg:* Women bathing.— 153 and 163, *Aurelio Luini:* parts of a Holy Family.—*G. F. Moroni:* Virgin and Four Saints, from S. Zenone at Verona.

The fifth room (V.) contains from 166 to 175. 166, *Palmezzano:* a good Coronation of the Virgin and two Saints. 167, *Liberale da Verona,* curious from the scarceness of the artist; 176, LANINI, Madonna and Saints, with the Donatario.

The sixth room (VI.) contains from 177 to 209. 180, *Vittore Carpaccio:* A Bishop, in a green and purple robe, good in tone and colour."— 182, *Carpaccio:* St. Anthony of Padua, a figure of a Monk, reading, and holding a lily in his hand.—184, *Cesare da Sesto:* the Virgin and Child.— 185, ALBANI: the Dance of Cupids, or the Triumph of Love over Pluto: a most graceful and pleasing specimen: one of *Albani's* finest works, and in excellent condition.—187, *Annibale Caracci:* the Virgin and Child, St. Francis, an Angel, and St. Joseph in the distance: whole-length figures, rather affected.—188, *Giovanni Bellini:* a Pietà, with the artist's name, very early.—191 and 197, *Fyt:* Dead Game.—192, *Van Goyen:* a Sea View. —193, *Gio. Pedrini,* one of the rarer pupils of L. da Vinci: Magdalene.— 195, *Poussin:* a Landscape.—199 and 200, Sketches of two Girls, attributed to *Tintoretto.*—202, *Annibale Caracci:* the Portrait of the Artist and three other Heads: very clever.—206, *Garofalo:* Madonna and Child, in a glory of Angels.—208, *Moroni:* the Virgin and Child, St. Catherine, St. Francis, and the Donor: figures half-length.— 209, *Giovanni Bellini:* the Virgin and Child; signed and dated 1510; a good picture.—354, 358, *Andrea di Salerno:* two good specimens of the master.

The seventh room (VII.) includes from 210 to 230. 210, *Marco d' Oggionno:* the Virgin and Child, St. Paul, St. John the Baptist, and an Angel playing on a violin: a good specimen of this rare artist; the heads are full of expression, especially that of the Virgin, which is beautiful and tender. Marco d'Oggione was a pupil or imitator of Leonardo da Vinci, and he made two or three excellent copies of the Cenacolo.—214, GUERCINO: Abraham dismissing Hagar: perhaps the most praised amongst the pictures in the Brera. Ever since Lord Byron was so much struck by this picture, numberless travellers have been struck too; it has been beautifully engraved by Jesi.—213, 217, *Cima da Conegliano:* two pretty small pictures of the Madonna.—219, *Andr. Previtali,* a rare master, a Bergamasc, pupil of *Gio. Bellini:* Christ on the Mount of Olives: very fine; it has a date, 1513.—218 and 222, *Carpaccio:* the Marriage of the Virgin, and the Dedication: pictures full of figures, very interesting for the costume of the period.—230, RAPHAEL: the "Sposalizio," or Marriage of the Virgin. This celebrated picture was originally at Città di Castello. It is in the artist's early style, and bears much resemblance to that of Perugino in the architectural perspective, arrangement of the figures, and a certain degree of hardness in the outline; yet the design and action are very graceful, and it is a most interesting specimen of one of Raphael's early works, bearing his name, and the date, RAPHAEL URBINAS, MDIIII. "Mary and Joseph stand opposite to each other in the

K 2

centre; the high priest between them joins their hands; Joseph is in the act of placing the ring on the finger of the bride: beside Mary is a group of the Virgins of the Temple; near Joseph are the suitors, who break their barren wands—that which Joseph holds in his hand has blossomed into a lily, which, according to the legend, was the sign that he was the chosen one."—*Kugler*. This lovely painting has been recently much improved by removing the old varnish; many fine details, both of design and colouring, concealed by years of neglect, have been brought out, some of which escaped Longhi in his celebrated engraving of it, especially the delicate landscape in the background. 247, *Luini*: the Virgin and Child, a very fine and characteristic picture.—358, *Andrea da Milano*: the Holy Family, with a venerable portrait of an aged man, perhaps the donor of the picture, introduced: the name, and date, 1495, are given. — 416, *Leonardo da Vinci*: the Head of our Lord, a design in black and red chalk, heightened a little by white, and believed to be the study for the head in the celebrated *Cenacolo*: extremely beautiful.

The eighth room (VIII.) contains from 231 to 255. 231, *Fran. Verla*, rare: Madonna on Throne, and Saints.—234, *Titian*: An old Man's Head, bald, and with a large beard; fine.—235, *Raphael*: Sketch, in sepia, of an allegorical group of naked figures, on paper. At the bottom of this very clever design is written, as it is thought, by Raphael, the name of *Michello Angelo Bonarotus*. This bistre drawing is the original sketch for the fresco formerly in the Casino Olgiati at the Villa Borghese, and now in the Borghese Gallery at Rome.—236, *Cesare da Sesto*: a good portrait. — 237, *Guido*: St. Peter and St. Paul. It was formerly in the Zampieri Gallery of Bologna.—239, *Giovanni Kupetzki*: A Head of a Man, believed to be that of the artist.—240, *And. del Sarto*: A bistre drawing, called "Il Padre di Famiglia," the Man in the Gospel paying the Workmen.—241, *Filippo Mazzuolo*: a Head.—242, *Ambrogio Figino*: a Soldier; a clever portrait, thought to be that of Marshal Foppa. —243, A very fine specimen of the German school, in three compartments; the Adoration of the Magi in the middle. —244, St. Sebastian, once attributed to *Giorgione*.—246 and 248, *Canaletti*: two Landscapes. — 252, *Alessandro Turchi*, called *l' Orbetto*: whole-length Magdalene; fine for this master and school.—254, *Velasquez*: Portrait of a sleeping Monk, excellent.—226, ANDREA MANTEGNA: a Dead Christ and the two Marys; in distemper: singular and forcible effect of foreshortening, and executed with great power.

The ninth room (IX.) contains from 256 to 279. 256, *Simone da Pesaro*: a Madonna and Saint presenting Acorns. —257, *Bonifazio*: the Presentation of the Infant Moses to Pharaoh's Daughter; until of late years attributed to Giorgione.—258, *Sandrart*: the Good Samaritan.—259, *Luini*: Noah drunk, and his Sons.—263, *Rubens*: a Female Portrait. — 264, *Vandyke*: the Portrait of a Man.— 268, *Franz Hals*: a most beautiful male Portrait.—269, a Portrait, said to be by *Titian*. — 270, *Geldorp* or *Gualdrop*: a Female Portrait.—271, *Rubens*: the Portrait of a Man. — 272, *Raphael Mengs*: another, three quarters length.—274, *Guercino*: La Sacra Sindone.—277, *Giovanni Bellini*: the Virgin and Child, surrounded by Cherubim.—278, *Moretto*: the Assumption of the Virgin. —279, *Sassoferrato*: the Virgin and the Infant sleeping; above, a Glory of Cherubim; a poor picture.

The tenth room (X.) contains from 280 to 333. 280, *Luca Giordano*: the Virgin and Child, St. Anthony of Padua, St. Joseph, and many Angels and Cherubim.—284, *Gaspar Poussin*: St. John the Baptist in the Desert; St. John is represented as a child of about ten years old.—285, *Deiner*: the Portrait of an Artist, three quarters length; a very theatrical picture.—290, *Baroccio*: the Martyrdom of San Vitale, with many figures; "the best specimen of this most *baroque* master."—*L. G.*— 292, *Zuccheri*: The Descent of the Saviour into Hades, with his name, and the date 1585.—293, *Sneyders*: a Staghunt.—294, *Pietro da Cortona*: the Virgin and Child, St. Joseph, St. Catherine, St. John the Baptist, and St. Gaetano.—296, *Lattanzio Gambara*: Portrait of a Man. A fine specimen of this great fresco-painter, whose oil paintings are extremely rare. —297, *Daniele Crespi*: half-length Portrait of a Sculptor.—299, *Pietro Subleyras*: the Crucifixion, with St. Mary Magdalene and two other figures, with the artist's name, and the date 1744.—300, St. Jerome in the Desert, by the same artist.—301, *Procaccini*: a curious specimen of a picture designed for a gonfalon or church banner, and painted on both sides. On that now exposed is the Virgin and Child, with San Carlo and Sant' Ambrogio and Seven Angels: the other side also has the Virgin and Child with other Saints and Angels.—302, *Pompeo Battoni*: a Holy Family, with many Angels. — 308, *Guido*: the Head of a Philosopher. — 311 to 318 inclusive: all portraits, and considered those of the artists themselves. They are interesting, especially 316, the portrait of *C. F. Nuvolone*; and 317, *Martin Knoller*: Portrait of Mengs.—321, *Bonifazio*: the Disciples at Emmaus.— 322, *Salvator Rosa*: the Souls in Purgatory. Salvator Rosa was not equal to this subject.—325, *Castiglione*: the Departure of the Israelites for the Holy Land.—326, *Andrea Porta*: the Portrait of the Artist.—327, *Scarsellino*: the Virgin and Child, with the Doctors of the Church and a glory of Angels.—331, *Francesco del Cairo*: a Portrait, believed to be that of Scaramuccia Perugino; a fine picture.—332, *Salvator Rosa*: St. Paul the first Hermit; a remarkably fine and clearly painted scene.

The eleventh room (XI.) contains from 334 to 397. 335, *Bernardino Lanini*: The Virgin and Child, seated on the knees of St. Anne; a design full of grace, though not without affectation. — 336, *Beltraffio*: St. John the Baptist, on wood — 337, *And. Salaini*: the Virgin and Child, with St. Peter and St. Paul.—338, *Callisto da Lodi*: the Virgin and Child, St. John the Baptist, St. Jerome, and an Angel.—339 and 342, *Marco d' Oggiono*: the Assumption of the Virgin; and St. Michael conquering Lucifer, with two angels; curious, especially the latter, in which the drawing of the figures and the tranquil unmoved expression of the countenances of the angels deserve attention.—343, GAUDENZIO FERRARI: the Martyrdom of St. Catherine, an admirable work, perhaps the finest work in oils of this master; the Saint, tranquil and resigned, looks up towards heaven awaiting her martyrdom, whilst the executioners at the wheel have their eyes fixed on their superior, waiting his commands to commence their cruel task.—344, *Bernardo Zenale*: the Virgin and Child, with the Fathers of the Church, SS. Gregory, Ambrose, Jerome, and Augustine. Many of the figures evidently portraits of the family for whom this very interesting picture was painted; amongst others, Ludovico Sforza (il Moro), and his wife Beatrice Visconti, with their two daughters, are introduced; it bears the date of 1515. —345, *Bernardino Luini*: the Virgin and Child, St. Philip, and others. The Saints are in the act of presenting a man and two women, kneeling, and only partly seen, to the Virgin.—346, *Caravaggio*: the Samaritan Woman at the Well. — 348, *Marco d' Oggione*: the Last Supper: this picture is a study for the same subject in fresco, and perhaps for the picture in the Louvre. — 350, *Nicola Appiani*: the Adoration of the Magi, valuable as one of the only two pictures of this rare artist.— 354, *B. Crespi*, called "il Bustino:" the Presentation in the Temple, "very bold and fine drawing." *L. G.*—355, *Enea Salmeggia*, called *il Talpino*, with his name and the date 1604: the Virgin and Child, St. Roch, St. Francis, and St. Sebastian. — 362, *Andrea da Milano*: the Virgin and Child. This and another, 358, in Room VII., are two of the best specimens of this rare artist, who lived towards the close of the 15th centy., a contemporary of Gio. Bellini.—360, *Cesare da Sesto:* the Virgin and Child, with St. Joseph, St. Joachim, and the Infant St. John.— 361, *Leonardo da Vinci:* the Virgin and Child, with a Lamb, an unfinished work: beautiful, particularly the head of the Virgin.—363, *Bramante:* Presentation in the Temple.—364, *Andrea Salaino:* the Virgin and Child.—365, *copy of Raphael:* the Virgin and Child, with St. Joseph.— 366, *Dan. Crespi:* the Virgin and Child, with several Saints.—369, *Camillo Procaccini:* the Nativity, with the Adoration of the Shepherds. The scene is illuminated by the light radiating from the Infant Saviour, as in the celebrated "Notte" of Correggio. — 370, *Ambrogio Borgognone:* the Assumption of the Virgin, with the Apostles, and SS. Ambrose and Augustine, Gervasius and Protasius, surrounded by Angels and Cherubs; with his name, and the date 1522.—371, *Giulio Cesare Procaccini:* the Adoration of the Magi. — 375, *Bevilacqua:* the Virgin and Child, with St. Peter Martyr, and another Saint, called by some King David, by others Job, and a devotee kneeling. The date 1502 is on the base of this picture, which is simple, and a curious specimen of the early style which preceded Leonardo, in which there is much of dignity in the character of the figures. — 376, *Carlo Francesco Nuvolone:* a Family, believed to be that of the artist, and considered one of his best works. — 377 and 379, *C. F. Nuvolone:* the Angel Gabriel in the act of giving, and the Virgin in that of receiving, the Annunciation. — 378, *Ambrogio Borgognone:* an Ecce Homo. — 382, by the same artist, Lazarus, St. Martha, St. Mary Magdalene, and other Saints. This picture represents an early legend of a miracle worked by St. Martha, on founding the first church at Marseilles. — 384, *Gio. Battista Crespi:* the Madonna and Child, St. Dominick, St. Catherine of Sienna, and many Angels. The Virgin is in the act of giving the rosary to St. Dominick, while the Infant Saviour places a crown of thorns on the head of St. Catherine. —385, *Gio. Battista Discepoli,* called *lo Zoppo di Lugano:* the Adoration of the Magi.—387, *Marco d' Oggione:* St. Francis and a Nun.—388 and 390, *Francesco Londonio:* two good specimens of the Milanese Berghem.—389, *Francesco del Cairo:* a Head; believed to be that of the artist.—391, *Ercole Procaccini:* the Crucifixion; full of figures.—393, *Michael Angelo Cerrutti:* Fruit. — 397, *Marco d' Oggione:* St. Anthony of Padua and a young Lady. An interesting collection of Studies of Animals and groups of Peasants, by *Francesco Londonio,* a painter of the 18th century, celebrated for this class of works—presented to the gallery by his grand-nephew.

The twelfth room (XII.) contains from 398 to 428 of modern artists. 398 and 400, *Andrea Appiani* and *Gaetano Tambroni:* Landscapes, with groups of figures.— 402, *Andrea Appiani:* Jupiter, Juno, Hebe, Ganymede, &c. — 406, 407, 408, *Marco Gozzi,* Landscapes. — 410, *Giuseppe Appiani:* an Old Man's Head. — 412, *Francesco Fidanza,* an artist celebrated for this kind of scenery: a Winter Landscape.—414, *Andrea Appiani:* a Portrait, of the artist.—417, 418, 420, 421, 422, 423, *Marco Gozzi:* Landscapes.—424, *Bernardino Galliari:* a Nativity, in distemper. — 426, *Luigi Basiletti,* a living artist at Brescia: a Waterfall.—427, *Gaspar Galliari:* a View of Venice by Moonlight; in distemper.— 447, *Londonio:* several studies of poor people and animals.— 68 and 69, *Appiani:* two portions of frescoes.

An apartment (XIII.) has been recently opened, called the Galleria Oggionni, which contains a large collection of second-rate pictures, bequeathed by a person of that name, amongst which a Coronation of the Virgin, with a Pietà in the lunette above, by *C. Crevelli,* painted in 1493, some Canalettis and Garofalos, are the most remarkable.

The *Museo Lapidario* is in a room on the ground-floor. It contains some ancient inscriptions and sculptures, amongst which the bronze *Statue of Napoleon*, by Canova, intended for the Arco della Pace, a repetition of that possessed by the Duke of Wellington; the *tomb of Bernabo Visconti*, surmounted by his equestrian statue, brought from the ch. of S. Giovanni in Conca. He is in the full armour of the age, the biscia, or viper, being prominently displayed upon his back. It is evidently a good portrait of this prince, whose cruelty was such as to convey the idea that he was actuated by insanity. This is not the place to speak of the tortures and horrible deaths which he inflicted upon his subjects, but one passage will exemplify his ingenious tyranny. He kept upwards of 5000 hounds, which were quartered upon the richest citizens, who were bound to board and lodge them. Every two months a dog-inspection was held. If, in the opinion of the *Canetero*, a dog was too lean, the host was fined heavily for having neglected the canine inmate. If the dog was declared to be too fat, then the citizen was fined much more heavily for having over-fed the dog, and thus injured his health. But if the dog was dead, then the host was punished by imprisonment and loss of all his property. Bernabo was dethroned by his nephew Gian Galeazzo, in 1385. The interest of this monument is increased by its being the earliest modern equestrian statue in Europe. Many fragments of sculpture and architecture from ruined churches and monasteries; the original models for the Napoleon bas-reliefs of the Arco della Pace; Roman remains, including an altar *with paintings upon it*, said to have been found near San Lorenzo, but for which it is not being over sceptical to demand a certificate of origin. The recumbent statue of Gaston de Foix: a fragment of his magnificent monument, the *chef-d'œuvre* of the celebrated Agostino Busti or Bambaja, erected by the French, when in possession of Milan, in the 16th centy.; it formerly stood in the Ch. of Sta. Martha, attached to an Augustinian monastery. The monument was considerably advanced in 1522, when, Francesco Sforza regaining his dominions, the work was suspended; and the church being afterwards pulled down for the purpose of being rebuilt, it was broken up and the portions dispersed. Other fragments are to be met with in different collections, some of the best in that of the Marchese Trivulzio at Milan.

Another fine monument by *Bambaja* is that of Lanino Curzio, the poet.

In other parts of this palace are the usual appurtenances of an academy: model-rooms, collections of casts, &c. The *Library*, of which the main part belonged to that of the Jesuits, but to which great additions have been made, is very extensive and well selected; better adapted for general study than the Ambrosian, as far as printed books are concerned. The collection of manuscripts is not extensive, but curious. It contains a great number of Chronicles and other materials for Venetian history, which were brought here during the French occupation, and which have not been sent back to Venice. Amongst them is a copy of the celebrated "Libro d'Oro," which the republicans burnt in honour of liberty. Amongst the show volumes are the magnificently illuminated choir-books of the Certosa at Pavia. With this library of manuscripts is connected a very valuable and select collection of coins and medals. The *Observatory*, or *la Specola di Brera*, was founded in 1762, under the direction of the celebrated Jesuit Father Boscovich. When the building was planned, all the nuns in the city remonstrated against it, alleging that they would be constantly spied at by the astronomers when walking, as they were wont to do, upon the terraces of their convents. The Observatory is well provided with instruments, and the observations annually published by its director Carlini are highly appreciated by the scientific world.

Not so the Botanical Garden, which is very indifferent; not at all worthy of the institution to which it is annexed.

Every second year there is an "exposition" of native art in the Brera. The exhibition takes place in the autumn.

The *Biblioteca Ambrosiana*.—This justly celebrated collection was founded by the Cardinal Federigo Borromeo (1609), Archbishop of Milan. The library is under the direction of a "congregation" of ecclesiastics, presided over by a clerical member, or, if there be none, by the head, of the Borromeo family. The chief acting officer is the Prefetto. This dignity was held by the celebrated Cardinal Maï, who was previously professor of Oriental languages, and who, by the discovery which he made of the *palimpsests* in this collection, laid the foundation of his high reputation. The Prefetto and the three other principal librarians are honorary canons of Sant' Ambrogio. The library is open daily from 10 to 3, except on Sundays and festivals. The librarians are very civil and attentive, but the catalogues are imperfect and incomplete. It has been erroneously said that the want of proper catalogues results from the will of the cardinal founder, and that there is a papal bull prohibiting the making of them: but the reason is to be sought in causes which operate full as forcibly in other libraries. Cardinal Borromeo's regulations were liberal in the truest and largest sense of the term. The Ambrosian was, in fact, the earliest public library in Europe; that is to say, a library not attached to any college or cathedral for the use of its own members, but open to all students or to the public, and for whom, what was then unexampled, writing materials were provided.

The collection of manuscripts is of the highest importance, consisting of 5500 volumes. Many were purchased by the founder, but the principal stores have been brought from suppressed monasteries or convents, particularly from that of Bobbio. This was founded by St. Columbanus and Irish missionaries in the 7th centy., and from this ancient Cœnobium have proceeded several manuscripts of extreme value to the Celtic scholar, inasmuch as they contain some of the earliest specimens of the Gaelic language in existence. They consist principally of interlineary translations and commentaries of portions of Scripture, in general beautifully written. Of these one of the most remarkable is a Psalter of the 8th centy., with the commentary of St. Jerome. This is filled with Gaelic glosses, beside a page at the beginning, probably containing a preface or dedicatory epistle. The whole is in the ancient Irish character, and very legible. And a MS. of the Gospels, with Gaelic notes, of high antiquity.

The *palimpsests* are ancient manuscripts written upon vellum, from which the characters of a previous manuscript have been rubbed off, or partially effaced. The existence of this practice was long known; but Cardinal Maï was the first who ever endeavoured to recover the classics below from the superincumbent *strata* of legends or homilies. The original writing is generally in bold, uncial characters, imperfectly erased, and the scribes of the second period usually crossed the older writing, as ladies do their letters, though sometimes they took the intervals between the lines. Of course much patience is required; but the principal difficulty lies in the transposition of the leaves, and it is in connecting the separated leaves that Maï has shown his great skill. Amongst the specimens which are generally shown are the fragments of the version of the Bible, made A.D. 360-80, by Ulfila Bishop of the Mœsogoths. The gospels are at Upsala; a portion of the epistles was found at Wolfenbuttell; whilst from these palimpsests Maï has extracted large fragments of the Acts of the Apostles, and portions of the Old Testament—a singular dispersion; and perhaps many more of these Sibylline leaves may be hidden even in England. The letters of Fronto and Marcus Aurelius, and various fragments of Orations, and of the Treatise de Republicâ of Cicero, were also published from palimpsests in this library.

Amongst other literary curiosities, the following may be pointed out :—Virgil, copied and annotated by Petrarch, and with one miniature by Simone Memmi representing Virgil, and an allegorical personification of Poetry, of great beauty. The handwriting is fine and clear. Prefixed to this manuscript is the note in which Petrarch is supposed to describe his first interview with Laura. The manuscript, which afterwards belonged to Galeazzo Visconti, may be authentic, but the note is suspicious, and we may be tempted to doubt whether it deserves much more credit than the sonnet of Petrarch found in Laura's tomb at Avignon. —The autograph correspondence between Cardinal Bembo and Lucretia Borgia. A lock of her beautiful flaxen hair, which was annexed to one of the letters, is now in the Museum up stairs.

Josephus translated into Latin by Rufinus, who died in 410, upon papyrus, probably of the 5th centy.: manuscript books upon this material are of the greatest rarity.

Homer: fragments of a manuscript, perhaps of the 4th centy., with fifty-eight illuminated miniatures, highly interesting both for the art and the costume which they exhibit. "This MS., with the Virgil of the Vatican and the Book of Genesis at Vienna, disputes the palm of being the most ancient volume containing illuminations that has come down to our days." Lucano di Parma's treatise 'De Regimine Principis,' presented to Galeazzo Sforza, with a very curious and characteristic portrait of the donee.

Twelve volumes of heads of sermons by San Carlo; and his correspondence during the Council of Trent, all in his own handwriting.

A very large volume filled with clear neat drawings by *Leonardo da Vinci:* a most singular miscellany—machines, ordnance diagrams, caricatures, fancies: the descriptions are written by himself from right to left, so that they can only be read with facility by being placed before a looking-glass. There were originally twelve of these volumes, which were presented to the library in 1637 by Galeazzo Arconate, after having refused 3000 doubloons offered for one volume of them by the King of England, as we are told by an inscription on the stairs; but the other eleven have been retained in the library of the Institute at Paris, to which they were removed during the French occupation of Lombardy.

A small volume, with architectural designs by Bramante, and some manuscript descriptions.

Vite degli Arcivescovi di Milano, with fine miniatures of the time of Luini.

Livy, translated into Italian by Boccaccio.

The Missal used by San Carlo Borromeo, very finely illuminated, and with his motto, *Humilitas.* Printing was of course common in the days of San Carlo; but there continued to be a feeling of preference for manuscript prayer-books, and some were executed for the royal family even as late as the reign of Louis XIV. A very fine and early Dante. In a room on the ground-floor is a fresco by *B. Luini,* of the Crowning with Thorns.

The printed books are principally in one lofty hall. They amount to about 100,000 volumes. The arrangement is not by classes, but strictly by sizes, and the volumes are built in with so much accuracy that hardly a chink or a cranny can be discovered.

The great or principal room is a fine apartment. It is ornamented with a frieze of portraits of individuals distinguished for holiness or for knowledge; principally, however, prelates or fathers of the Church. Forming part of the library is a hall in which have been placed several modern marbles, and busts of Lord Byron, Thorwaldsen, and Oriani, and some beautiful bas-

K 3

reliefs by Thorwaldsen, and monuments to the late Count Borromeo, by Cacciatori, and to the Marquis Fagnani, who left his valuable collection of printed books to the Ambrosian.

The *gallery* and *museum* annexed to the library are not extensive, but valuable, containing many important historical monuments and works of art. Amongst the first are to be placed the collection of portraits made by *Paolo Giovio*, and partly, though only to a small extent, employed by him in his well-known work, 'Vitæ Illustrium Virorum.' Paolo Giovio was the first who formed the plan of illustrating biography by portraits. Many are ideal; but with respect to contemporaries, or those who were not of a remote period, he took great pains to have them as authentic as possible. To these have been since added many others, but these are not, as they ought to be, distinguished from the Giovio collection; this is to be regretted; but possibly the curators may have the means of so doing when they publish a catalogue of their gallery. Amongst the more remarkable are Machiavelli, Scanderbeg, Sigonius, Cardinal Pole, Cardinals Bembo and Baronius, Vida, Alciatus, Card. Noris, Budæus, Sixtus V. These are in the ante-rooms. The first of these rooms also contains a copy, by *Andrea Bianchi*, of L. da Vinci's Last Supper, painted by order of Card. F. Borromeo. It has only the upper half of the figures.

In the first gallery is the Profile of *Leonardo da Vinci*, by himself, in red chalks. Seven valuable Miniatures.— Two drawings by *Caravaggio*, our Saviour appearing to Mary Magdalene: and some fine studies by *Luini* and *Cesare da Sesto*.—*Raphael*, two Men on Horseback, an early work, 1505.— *Hemling*, a beautiful picture of Madonna and Child.—*A. Luini*, St. John, an Infant, playing with a Lamb.— *L. da Vinci*, an exquisite Female Head. —Two pictures attributed to *Titian*, a Holy Family, and our Saviour dead: of the latter the authorship is very doubtful.—*Marco d' Oggiono*, the Virgin nursing the Saviour.—Twelve coloured drawings for the painted glass of the Cathedral, by *Pellegrini*.

In the second gallery is Raphael's cartoon for the School of Athens: it is executed with black chalk on grey paper, and contains the figures only, without the architecture. " It is one of the most interesting examples of the nature and extent of the alterations introduced in a composition prepared for fresco. The changes are mostly additions. The figure of Epictetus, represented in the fresco, sitting in the foreground on the left, leaning his head on his hand, is wanting in the cartoon. This figure was added to fill up a vacant space, and thus the change, though a considerable improvement, involved no inconvenience. Some less important alterations in the same fresco, such as covering the head of Aspasia with drapery instead of showing her flowing tresses (for thus she appears in the cartoon), might have been made on the wall without any change in the drawing. That this cartoon was the identical one which served for the execution of the fresco is proved by the exact conformity of every part, except the additions above mentioned, with the painting."—*Eastlake*. In a room opening out of this are arranged the original Drawings of the great masters:—Many studies, by *Michael Angelo*, for the Last Judgment. Two exquisite portraits in red chalk, by *L. da Vinci*. Also by him, three portraits: the profile of Beatrice d'Este, who died in childbirth at 27, and whose monument is in the Certosa at Pavia. Head of St. John: a drawing of part of the Triumph of Julius Cæsar, by *Mantegna*. The Annunciation, attributed to *Parmigiano*. *Sandro Botticelli*: Madonna, Child, and Angels; a round picture. *B. Luini*: Holy Family; a masterpiece, and the design for which is attributed to *L. da Vinci*. *L. da Vinci*: beautiful Portrait of a Physician, half figure. *Benvenuto Garofalo*: Holy Family, with Angels, small. A Holy Family, said to be by *Titian*. *Giacomo Bassano*: Flight into Egypt.

Guido: Christ on the Cross. *Titian:* the Adoration of the Magi. *B. Luini:* the Young Saviour, half-length. Holy Family, with Saints, half figures; attributed to *Titian. Raphael:* part of the cartoon for the Battle of Constantine. *Luini:* Young Tobit returning with the Angel; an exquisite drawing. *Gaudenzio Ferrari:* the Marriage of the Virgin.

In the next room, containing the original drawings of the ancient masters, are several modern works in gilt bronze, exhibited as specimens of Milanese manufacture: amongst others, a model of an intended Porta Orientale, by *Cagnola.* Here are also drawings by *Giulio Romano, Caravaggio, Michael Angelo, Alb. Durer, Mantegna, Guercino, Luca Cambiaso,* the two *Luinis, Raphael, Leon. da Vinci,* &c. &c.; and a portion of *Raphael's* cartoon for the battle between Constantine and Maxentius.

A cabinet has been formed for the gilt bronzes left by E. Pecis to the library. This cabinet also contains two of Holbein's finest portraits. *Basaiti:* our Saviour with a standard. *Giorgione:* St. Sebastian, full length, with Rome in the background. *Mengs:* Portrait of Clement XIII. *Velasquez:* a portrait. *Bronzino:* a portrait, called that of B. Cellini. *Lucas van Leyden:* Adoration of the Magi. *Albani:* Galatea borne by Dolphins. *Carlo Dolce:* a Madonna. *B. Luini:* St. John.

In a small garden opening on a side street is the stump of the *tin* palm-tree, which Lalande, in his description of Italy, has noted with great accuracy, as a proof of the mildness of the climate of Milan. The cortile, as you enter, contains many Roman and mediæval inscriptions let into the walls. Some of the most interesting are the early Christian ones.

Among the scientific establishments at Milan, the most remarkable is the *Museo Civico di Storia Naturale,* which contains a very good collection of Zoology and Paleontology: the latter is particularly rich in fossils from the tertiary subapennine formations of the duchies of Parma and Piacenza. The museum is liberally endowed and supported by the municipality, which deserves the greatest credit for the encouragement it has given to the teaching of science, and of natural history in particular. The extensive collections of the suppressed *Scuola delle Miniere,* consisting of fossil remains of gigantic animals, found S. of Parma and Piacenza, and purchased by E. Beauharnois, and of the fossil tertiary shells described by Brocchi, in his classical *Conchiologia Fossile Subapennina,* have been recently removed to the *Museo Civico.*

Ospedale Maggiore, or Great Hospital of Milan.—This splendid establishment was founded by Francesco Sforza, and his duchess Bianca Maria, in 1456. They gave for its site an ancient palace which had belonged to Bernabo Visconti. The funds for its maintenance were partly supplied by the duke and his consort, and partly by the union of the endowments of several other hospitals previously existing in the city. To these have been added from time to time, and still continue to be added, legacies and donations of the Milanese, who have a great affection for the institution, which has had an unusual exemption from spoliation in every political vicissitude. The building was begun on the 4th of April, 1457, the first stone being laid by the hands of the duke and duchess. Antonio Filarete, a Florentine, was the architect; the southern portion of the edifice was alone executed from his designs. The ground-plan of this original portion of the foundation is a square, the central space being the grand quadrangle. The windows of the façade are beautifully ornamented with reliefs of children and foliage in moulded terracotta; and the numerous niches and lunettes contain busts of Saints and allegorical figures. The central portion of the hospital is also of moulded brick, but was erected at a later period, in 1621, by a donation of a liberal citizen, Gian Pietro Carcano. The architects were Fabio Mangone and F. Richini.

On entering by the Great Gateway, a very noble quadrangle presents itself: it is surrounded by a double colonnade, having 21 arches on two sides, and 19 on the others: the columns of the upper order are composite, of the lower modern Ionic, with archivolts and entablatures ornamented with arabesques and figures in relief between circular niches, from the designs of *Camillo Procaccini*. The upper colonnade has been partly walled in to gain space; the lower is formed by 80 columns of red granite. This quadrangle measures 250 ft. by 280, not including the depth of colonnade, which is 19 ft. In the small church opposite the entrance is a good Annunciation, by *Guercino*. In 1797 Giuseppe Macchi, a notary who had led the life of a miser, left an immense property to the hospital, by means of which it was completed. The N. wing is from the design of *Castelli*, who, unfortunately, abandoned the style of the earlier part of the building, so that this wing is out of keeping with the rest. The average number of patients admitted annually is about 20,500; the deaths, 2700; the mean mortality being 13 per cent. The hospital can accommodate 2000 patients, but has seldom more than 1600. Monuments have been raised under the porticoes of the great quadrangle to Recorsi, Locadelli, and other eminent medical teachers who were attached to the establishment.

The *Ospizio Trivulzi* is a noble monument of pious charity. It was founded in 1771 by Antonio Trivulzio, who for that purpose gave up his palace. The endowment has since received very considerable additions, and the building has been recently enlarged to nearly double its original size. It now contains 600 inmates, all above seventy years of age, who are well fed and clothed at the expense of the institution.

Milan contains as many as eighty-five hospitals and institutions of charity, possessing property to the amount of 200 millions of lire, nearly of 7 millions sterling.

The vast *Lazaretto* is just out of the Porta Orientale; it is interesting both from its magnitude and from the recollection of the scenes which have been witnessed within its walls. It consists of a square cloister of red brick; measuring, outside the arcade, 404½ yds. by 393. From these arcades surrounding the quadrangle opened 280 small rooms or cells; in the centre is a chapel designed by *Pellegrini*, and possessing much beauty. This building was founded by Lodovico il Moro about 1461, when governing in the name of his nephew Gian Galeazzo, but not completed till the end of the 15th century. It was the scene of some of the finest episodes of the *Promessi Sposi*.

Milan has few squares. The largest is the *Piazza della Fontana*, in front of the archbishop's palace. In it is one of the few fountains in Milan. The *Piazza Borromeo* has a statue of San Carlo, by *Bussola*, formerly in the Cardusio; it stands in front of the small ch. of Santa Maria Podone, belonging to the Borromeos, whose palaces form two sides of the piazza. The *Piazza del Marino*, with the handsome palace of that name on one side, and the newly opened *Piazza della Scala*, opposite the theatre, with the *Palazzo Brambilla*, a remarkable specimen of modern decoration in terracotta and moulded brick-work.

There were formerly many crosses and similar monuments in the streets and crossways, but most of them have been removed. Of those that remain, the "*Leone di Porta Orientale*," a small column in that street, is the principal. It is said to commemorate some victory gained by the Milanese over the Venetians; but the lion is not the lion of St. Mark.

Of older street architecture, the principal relic is, the *Coperto de' Figini*, in the Piazza del Duomo. It was built by Pietro Figini, in honour of the marriage of Gian' Galeazzo Visconti with Isabella the daughter of John King of France. The Gothic arches remain: the upper stories have been modernised.

Palazzo Trivulzi.—Built by the Marquis Alessandro Trivulzi. Here is a very select and valuable library of printed books and manuscripts, and a choice collection of coins, and of Greek, Roman, and mediæval antiquities, including the monument of Azzo Visconti, formerly in the Church of San Gottardo at Milan. There are also some good pictures.

Casa Archinito.—Some good frescoes by *Tiepolo* and other Venetian artists. Here, also, is a very good library and collection of antiquities.

Casa Andriani, now *Sormani.*—The garden is one of the largest in Milan. In the collection in this mansion is a pleasing *Mantegna,* — the Virgin and Child between St. John and St. Mary Magdalene.

Casa Pianca contains a very precious series of portraits of the Sforza family in fresco by *Luini,* all apparently taken from originals.

Casa Melzi.—A large library, and some good modern pictures.

There is another *Casa Melzi* in the Borgo Nuovo, originally the house of the painter *Bramantino,* who has left some frescoes in what is now a coach-house; and in the court is a good fresco by *B. Luini,* of an Atlas supporting a Globe, in his last and best manner.

Palazzo Castelbarco, opposite the Brera, contains a large collection of pictures, many of which are good, and some attributed to Raphael, L. da Vinci, Correggio, &c.

Palazzo Litta.—This was built by *Richini,* and is one of the finest in Milan. Here is a small collection of paintings; amongst others, a *Correggio,* originally the lid or cover of a spinet, or some similar instrument, of which the subject is Apollo and Marsyas. It is most highly finished. It was painted by *Correggio* when he was very young, and it has a better certificate of origin than such productions usually possess, having been engraved by Sanuto in 1562. There are other paintings by *Leonardo* and *Luini;* but the principal ornaments of the collection are, perhaps, the frescoes by *Luini,* cut out of the walls of a demolished villa and chapel near Milan. They are, — The Adoration of the Magi. The kneeling king is supposed to be a portrait of Luini himself.—The Crucifixion. Two saints are introduced, St. Thomas Aquinas and St. Jerome.—A fine picture from St. John, chap. xvi. v. 23, 24, " Whatsoever ye shall ask the Father in my name, he shall give it you." A single admirable figure.—Our Lord holding the globe in his left hand, and in the attitude of blessing with his right. There are several repetitions of this fresco; a very bad one in the convent of the Grazie, and a very good one (attributed to Leonardo da Vinci) in the collection of Mr. Miles.—One subject is taken from profane history. Curius Dentatus rejecting the presents of the Sabines.—Another more doubtful *Luini* in this collection is the Birth of the Virgin.—*Titian:* the portrait usually called his mistress, probably only a good copy.—*Sasso Ferrato:* a praying Head.—An old painting of the Castle of Milan is curious, as showing its state at the close of the 17th centy.;—there are some modern paintings by *Appiani* and others, worthy of notice. The great saloon is splendidly fitted up in the style of Louis XIV. There is also a valuable library of 30,000 vols. in this palace, which, during the banishment of its owner, is said to have suffered from its occupation by the Austrians.

Palazzo Vismara, in the Via de Bossi, remarkable for its handsome portal from the designs of Michelozzi. This house, which was given to Cosimo de' Medici in 1456 by Francesco Sforza, is supposed to have been the seat of a Branch bank of that celebrated Florentine family in the 15th century. Over the archway are the armorial bearings of the Dukes of Milan, with the two dogs of the Sforzas, and the portraits of Francesco and his wife Bona Visconti.

Palazzo Borromeo.—The exterior is one of the few remaining specimens of the Gothic style, having belonged to the family since 1444: the interior is modernised, and contained a fine collection of minerals, formed originally by Breislack, and a valuable series of paintings by *B. Luini;* but on the banishment of this noble family, arising out of the events of 1848, the palace had been seized upon and converted into a barrack by the Austrian authorities, since which it has remained uninhabited.

Palazzo Pozzi.—This palace was designed and built by *Leone Leoni,* of Arezzo, a capital medallist or die-sinker. Leone was a sculptor and an architect, and much patronised by Charles V., by whom he was knighted. Hence he is often called "Il Cavaliere Aretino." He became very opulent; and this building is a monument of the riches he had acquired, as well as of his genius. It is, however, rather odd than elegant: colossal statues support the front, to which the Milanese have given the name of *Omenoni* (i. e. big men), and to account for which there are many strange stories.

Theatres.—Milan is of all the cities in Italy the most celebrated for its theatres and theatrical amusements; the principal house is *La Scala,* so called from its having been erected upon the site of the Church of St. Maria della Scala. It was built from the designs of *Piermarini,* and was opened in the autumn of 1779. It contends with *S. Carlo* at Naples for being the largest theatre in Italy, and has always been admired for the excellence of its internal arrangements. The house is capable of containing 3600 spectators. The number of boxes in each row is 41: each has a small room attached to it; the greater number are private property. The form of the house is a semicircle, with the ends produced and made to approach each other; the greatest width is 72 ft., the length, including the proscenium, that is to say, from the front of the centre box to the curtain, is 95½ ft. The width of the opening between the columns of the proscenium is 54 ft., and the depth of the stage behind the curtain is 150 ft. This theatre also contains a Sala di Ridotto, where concerts are given, and masked balls during the Carnival.

The other Royal Theatre is *La Canobiana,* connected by a species of viaduct with the palace. It was built from the designs of *Piermarini,* and opened in 1780. The pit contains 450 seats, and the house will hold 2200 spectators.

These two Royal Theatres are under one management, and receive an annual subvention from the government, subject to the expense of maintaining the Academy of Dancing. The theatrical year is divided into three seasons; the Carnival, which extends from St. Stephen's day to the 20th of March; the spring, from Easter to the end of June; the autumn, from the beginning of September till the end of November.

Teatro Carcano.—This Theatre was built in 1803, from the designs of *Canonica,* on the site of the Monastery of S. Lazzaro. Every part of the interior is constructed of wood; it is in the form of a horseshoe, with a convex ceiling, and it is considered very favourable for hearing. The pit contains 300 seats, and the house can hold 1800 spectators. Operas and comedies are performed here.

Teatro Rè, near the Piazza del Duomo, was built in the year 1812, by Carlo Re, from the designs of *Canonica.* It stands on the site where the Archpriest Dateo, in 787, erected the church of San Salvatore, and the first foundling hospital that ever existed. The comedies of Goldoni, Nota, &c., are often well represented here. The pit holds 120, and the whole house is capable of containing 1000 spectators.

Teatro Filodrammatico. — Antolini, in the theatre which he designed for the Foro Bonaparte, declared his intention to banish everything by which the attention is distracted, and that he would not therefore have boxes as a retreat for noisy chattering. He said the audience would behave and attend better if every one was seen, and that pretty women would not have to complain of being shut up in cages where they were half hidden. These classical opinions, which were called republican, prevailed when the Teatro dei Filodrammatici was built from the designs of *Polack* and *Canonica*, on the site of S. Damiano alla Scala, and it hence received the appellation of "patriotico." The pit contains 245, the open boxes 630 persons. The tickets of admission are distributed gratuitously by the members, who are formed into a regular academical body, have a school of declamation, and give prizes. The company is entirely composed of amateurs, young men engaged in trade or in the public offices, and young women belonging to respectable families of the city. Actors who have appeared in public are not allowed to play on this stage. Vincenzo Monti, Carlo Porta, and other distinguished authors and actors, appeared here, and here Pasta commenced her career.

Teatro Fiando, Fantoccini, Marionetti or *Puppets.*—This theatre was built by one Fiando, from the design of *Canonica*, in the Oratorio or Chapel of Bellarmine. It is called also the Teatro Girolamo, from the comic character who always appears as one of the principal personages in every drama represented here. Girolamo is a Piedmontese from the Duchy of Montferrat, always frightened and hungry, but jesting and babbling. The performances are exceedingly droll and amusing, consisting usually of a play, which is apt to be very pathetic, and a ballet. But strangers will not hear there the language and humour of the people, as at the Cassandrino at Rome, or the San Carlino at Naples.

The *Giardino Publico* is a pleasant public promenade near the Porta Orientale. It contains a theatre, ballroom, and some other buildings for similar purposes; it has been recently enlarged, and a building erected in the centre for a café-restaurant.

Amongst the places of amusement were two club-houses, the *Casino dei Nobili*, and the *Casino dei Negozianti*, called also *Società del Giardino*. Both contained reading-rooms, ball-rooms, coffee-rooms, and the like; and an introduction to either could be easily obtained. Both have been closed since 1848, and that of the nobles converted by the Austrians into a barrack.

The *Casino degli Artisti* is on the same system as our English clubs.

The *Galleria de Cristoferis*, a species of Burlington Arcade, forming a passage between the Corso Francesco and the Via del Monte, is one of the novelties of Milan. It contains some good shops, coffee-houses, &c. &c.

Plan for visiting the Sights of Milan in 3 days.

1st day.—Duomo; Royal Palace; Archbishop's Pal.; Ch. of San Fedele and Piazza di Marino; Piazza della Scala; Brera Gallery, Library, and other Collections; Pal. Castelbarco; Ch. of S. Marco; Ch. of S. Simpliciano; Arena; Arco della Pace; Castello.

2nd day.—Ch. of San Carlo; Piazza dei Tribunali; Chs. of Maurizio Maggiore, of San Tomasso; Palazzo Litta; Chs. of Sta. Maria delle Grazie, of S. Vittore, of S. Ambrogio; Museo Civico di Storia Naturale; Piazza Borromeo; Ambrosian Library; Chs. of S. Giorgio, S. Satiro, S. Giovanni in Conca; Pal. Trivulzi; Ch. of S. Alessandro.

3rd day.—Chs. of S. Lorenzo and S. Eustorgio; Porta Ticinese; Chs. of La Madonna di S. Celso, SS. Celso and Nazzaro, S. Paolo, and S. Eufemia; Great Hospital; Chs. of S. Stefano, S. Bernardino, S. Pedro in Gessate, Sta. Maria della Passione; Giardino Pubblico; Corso di Porta Orientale; Lazzaretto.

In the *neighbourhood of Milan*, besides the places described upon the different routes, the following may be noticed:—About 3½ m. from the Porta Vercellina, and on the l. of the high road leading to Vercelli, near a village called Quarto Cagnino, is

Linterno, memorable as the solitude to which Petrarch retired after the death of Laura, and where he composed his poetical lamentations for her loss. Its original name was *Inferno*, or *Inrerno*; but the laureate, out of love for Cicero, changed it into the classical *Linternum*, the retreat of Scipio.

ROUTE 22.

MILAN TO VARESE, BY SARONNO.

About 34 m. Diligences run by this route daily, performing the distance in 4 hours; persons may leave by it in the morning, visit Saronno, and return from Varese at 3½ P.M.; there is also a diligence to Saronno only, leaving Milan at 2¼ P.M., and returning every morning; but the traveller whose object is to visit Varese only will find it more convenient to take the Rly. to Camerlata, and thence by diligence, which starts on the arrival of each train. See Rte. 21.

This road to Saronno leaves Milan by the Porta Tanaglia, passing through the Suburb degli Ortolani. A road which turns off to the rt., at a short distance from the gate, leads to the *Palazzo della Simonetta*, noted for its remarkable echo. The front presents three colonnades, one over another, with arches and small columns, and paintings in the cinquecento style. The interior is not remarkable. The façade towards the garden was constructed with a very intricate arrangement of angles, and from a window on the second floor, on the l. hand, is an echo which is said formerly to have repeated the sound of the discharge of a pistol 50 times. An alteration in the building has diminished its powers, but the echo will still repeat a clear sharp sound nearly 30 times.

3½ m. from the Porta Tanaglia, and about ½ m. on the l. of the road, is the village of Garegnano, near which is the *Certosa of Garegnano*, a once celebrated Carthusian monastery, in the midst of a territory which the labours of the monks reclaimed. It was founded by the Archbishop Otho Visconti, Lord of Milan. The conventual buildings are desecrated; the church contains some frescoes by *Crespi*. Those on the walls represent the principal events of the life of St. Bruno, those on the ceiling subjects from the New Testament. Some have been much injured by the wet penetrating when the lead was stripped off the roof in 1796.

Caronno.—In the parish church are some frescoes, attributed to *Aurelio Luini*, the son of *Bernardino*.

2 *Saronno*, about 15 m. from Milan: on the rt.-hand side of the road is the church of the *Santuario della Madonna di Saronno*. It is close to the posthouse, and on the opposite side of the road is an inn, where a fair dinner may be had. The town of Saronno itself lies ½ m. distant to the east. This church contains celebrated works in fresco, by *Gaudenzio Ferrari* and *Bernardino Luini*, in excellent preservation. It was commenced in 1498, from the designs of *Vincenzo dell' Orto*. The campanile, the cupola, the high altar, and the two side chapels, were erected by *Paolo Porta*, in the 16th century. The façade, which is overloaded with ornament, was built in 1666, from the design of *Carlo Buzzi*. Owing to this change of architects the interior is somewhat irregular. The cupola is painted in fresco, by *Gaudenzio Ferrari*. The subject is the heavenly host playing upon various instruments, with a circle of cherubs above them singing. Below is a series of painted statues, in 12 niches, two figures in each, consisting, for the most part, of Prophets and Sibyls, as Sibylla Delphica and David, &c.; 24 in all; there are also groups representing the Calvary, the Last Supper, &c.

Below, in circles in the pendentives, are eight subjects from Genesis,—the Creation of Eve; Eating the Forbidden Fruit; the Expulsion from Paradise (much injured); Tilling the Ground after the Fall; Adam and Eve in the Garden, very fine; Abel tending his flocks; the Remorse of Cain; and Adam blessing his posterity: these are also by *Ferrari*. The lunettes below are by *Lanini*. All these frescoes may be more easily seen from the gallery which runs round three sides beneath the cupola. In that part of the church which connects the nave and the choir are two large frescoes by *Luini*, the Marriage of Joseph and Mary on the l.-hand, and Christ disputing with the Doctors on the rt. On the wall on the l.-hand side of the high altar is the Presentation in the Temple, with a view of the Ch. of Saronno, and opposite is the Adoration of the Magi. These 4 large frescoes are well preserved, and are, according to Lanzi, among the greatest of his works; and certainly they are very superior to anything at Milan, with the exception, perhaps, of one or two small portions of fresco in the Brera; for instance, (34) in the entrance hall, the body of St. Catherine carried by three Angels to the Sepulchre.

The 4 great frescoes of Luini in the ch. of Saronno afford admirable examples of this style of painting, and are in excellent preservation: in the Adoration of the Magi, perhaps the best of the four, the Virgin and Child are exquisite examples of that union of beauty and tenderness which distinguishes Luini's best works; the heads of the two kneeling kings are admirable, and the transparency of the colours throughout affords the best example of fresco-painting. In the Christ disputing with the Doctors, although the figures of our Saviour and the Virgin are wanting perhaps in dignity, the whole is finely conceived; the heads of the Doctors are admirable. Luini's own portrait, which he has introduced, is very fine. In the fresco of the Marriage of the Virgin the principal figure is perhaps too much of a Venetian character, and wanting in youth and simplicity.

There are many smaller frescoes by *Luini* on the walls and ceiling of the choir; amongst others, the Evangelists, and the four Doctors of the Church (which have been retouched), with St. Catherine, and St. Apollonia; and two Angels remarkable for the transparency of their colours. In the sacristy is a picture by *G. C. Procaccini*. On the wall of the cloister leading from the church to the priest's house is a Nativity by *Luini*. He was paid for the single figures of saints a sum corresponding to 25 Austr. lire, and received besides wine, bread, and lodging. For the other works he was paid so much a-day, together with bread and wine, and was so well pleased with his pay that he painted this last fresco for nothing.

Beyond Saronno the level of the country rises, and the road, after passing through Mozzate, Carbonate, and *Tradate*, a large village, where, on a hill, are the remains of an ancient castle, crosses the Olona, [a short way lower down the river is the village of Castiglione di Olona, an interesting place from its many mediæval remains, but chiefly from the frescoes by *Massolino da Panicale* recently discovered in one of the churches: C. di O. is about half-way between Saronno and Varese] from which there is a continuous ascent to

2 Varese. See Route 18.

ROUTE 23.
MILAN TO GENOA, BY PAVIA.

3 Austrian posts to Pavia, 20 kil. to Casteggio, and from thence 114 kil. by Rly.; in all about 110 miles. The postmaster charges ½ a post extra for going down to the Certosa.

Persons wishing to visit Pavia and the Certosa, without proceeding farther, will find public conveyances which start several times a day, employing about 3 hrs., and returning to Milan in the afternoon. Ask for the diligence that passes through Binasco, as many of the public conveyances take the more direct road, but by much the least interesting, through Campo Morte, Pontelungo, and *Ponte Curate*, in which case the traveller will be set down nearly 2 m. from the Certosa, and have to find his way with some difficulty to it, which is then approached from behind. The inn from which they set out is in the Piazza del

Duomo: visitors to the Certosa, by setting out early, can be set down at *Torre di Mangano*, one of the diligences passing by there, and, having secured their places, be taken up there on its return in the afternoon, having plenty of time to visit the monastery, &c. Quitting Milan by the Porta Ticinese, the road enters what may be termed the most Flemish portion of the plain of Lombardy. Meadows, rich in clover, yield two or three crops a year; thick rows of sallows and poplars bespeak the humidity of the soil, luxuriant even to rankness. On either side are frequent transverse or longitudinal cuts and canals. Of these, the largest is the *Naviglio di Pavia*, completed during the French occupation, which joins the Ticino at Pavia. The road skirts this canal all the way. From the gate of Milan to Pavia, the canal descends 182 ft. 8 in.; there are 13 locks, the whole descent of which is 167 ft. 8 in.; leaving for the descent of the canal alone 15 ft. The length is 20¼ m., the breadth 42½ ft. At first it forms a considerable stream, but is continually giving off part of its waters for the purposes of irrigation, and becomes very sluggish on its arrival at Pavia.

1½ *Binasco*, a town of 5000 Inhab., remarkable for its castle, much modernised, still exhibiting the shield of the Viscontis. It was in this castle that the unhappy Beatrice di Tenda, widow of Facino Cane, and wife of Duke Filippo Maria, was, by his orders, beheaded in the night of September 13th, 1418. Beatrice was a lady of irreproachable virtue; but, in the agonies of the torture, she confessed to the crime of infidelity imputed to her by the Duke; or, as some say, she was convicted by the false testimony of *Orombello*, who, accused as her paramour, inculpated her in the hopes of saving his own life, but in vain. Beatrice had been not only a most affectionate wife, but a wise and faithful counsellor to her husband, to whom she brought vast domains; and it is difficult to account for his conduct.

He was much addicted to astrology, and a probable conjecture is, that, timid and cruel, some prediction that Beatrice would cause his death instigated him to the crime.

19 m. from Milan, and 5 from Pavia, is *Torre del Mangano*, nearly opposite to which is a straight road leading to the *Certosa della Beata Vergine delle Grazie*, commonly called the *Certosa of Pavia*, the most splendid monastery in the world, founded by Gian Galeazzo Visconti, the first Duke of Milan. It was built by him as an atonement for guilt, to relieve his conscience of the murder of his uncle and father-in-law, Bernabo Visconti, and his family, who, having by treachery made himself master of Milan, he sent to the castle of Trezzo, where they were poisoned. The foundation was laid 8th September, 1396. 25 Carthusian monks were appointed to take charge of this sanctuary, and executed, down to their expulsion in 1782, the task imposed on them, of augmenting the glory of the Madonna, by adding to the beauty of the Certosa. From 1782 to 1810 the Certosa was occupied by other orders, and in the latter year it was finally closed. Exaggerated reports have prevailed of the subsequent neglect of this splendid monument; blame, however, must be thrown on the Republican authorities, by whose order, in 1797, the lead was stripped from the roof. The monks were re-established in 1843, and the building is now well cared for, and kept in good order, by the produce of the monks' garden and casual offerings, and for more extensive repairs by the munificence of some wealthy Milanese families; little is done by the Government. There were in 1854, 25 monks,

Ladies are admitted into the nave, but are not allowed to enter the side chapels, or the choir.

The vestibule or principal entrance to the monastery is covered with frescoes, principally by *Luini*. Its front towards the road is a spacious arch, flanked by two pilasters, and crowned with a widely projecting but low roof, beneath which are also numerous frescoes. They are all much injured by exposure to the weather.

Through this vestibule a quadrangular court (109 yds. long, 45¼ yds. wide) is entered, at the opposite end of which is the gorgeous façade of the church.

The architect of the church, excepting the front, is said to have been Heinrich von Gmunden, or, as the Italians write it, Enrico da Gamodia, the same who began the Cathedral of Milan eleven years previously. "The style of the edifices is so different as almost to preclude the possibility of their being the productions of one man; the present offers no indication of the taste of our northern artists, while the cathedral above mentioned abounds with them." — *Woods*. The outer walls, the buttresses, the wide niches on the exterior of the transept, and the dome are of the fine brickwork peculiar to the Lombard buildings of that epoch: the interior and façade are of marble. *Ambrogio da Fossano*, called *Borgognone*, known also as an excellent painter, designed the richly decorated façade, which was begun in 1473. "It is an immense heap of little parts, in the taste of the *cinque-cento*, often beautiful in themselves, but leaving no impression as a whole, except an undefined sentiment of its immense prodigality of riches."—*Id*. This front rises from an extensive platform of three steps: four pilasters and two square turrets, corresponding with the general internal arrangement, divide it into five spaces of nearly equal breadth; upon these spaces that profusion of sculpture is displayed which forms one of the principal features and attractions of this edifice. The central portion is occupied by a richly decorated portico, formed of an arched roof resting upon four isolated Corinthian columns; above this is a kind of triforium of the Tuscan order, extending over the whole front, and serving as a base to a sort of shrine, on the frieze of which is the dedication to "Mary the Virgin, mother, daughter, bride of God." A second triforium, extending over the three central divisions, terminates the front, which, after all, it appears was never finished. The otherwise inevitably striking defect of accumulation of objects is much lessened by openings judiciously introduced; and where the play of light and shade which is the result was unattainable, the artist has produced the same effect by stained marbles.

Each of the pilasters and turrets is adorned with six statues; the masterpieces, however, of sculpture on this façade are to be found on and about the portico, and the four beautiful windows near it. The bas-reliefs on the walls of the portico represent, on the rt.-hand side, the ceremony of laying the foundation stone of the church; on the l. the funeral procession bringing the body of Giovanni Galeazzo from Melegnano to the Certosa (Nov. 9, 1443); and above, Alexander III. granting a charter to the Certosini. The small bas-reliefs represent actions of St. Ambrose, St. John Bapt., St. Siro, and the Virgin, and are, according to Cicognara, "oltre ognicredere degni d' ammirazione." The base is full of curious medallions, with heads of classic heroes and Roman emperors, sacred and profane personages, intermixed with arms, trophies, &c.

Many first-rate sculptors contributed to the plastic and marble works of the *Certosa;* among whom were Giov. Ant. Amadeo, Andr. Fusina, Agostino Busti, named il Bambaja, Marco Agrate, and Christofano Solari, called il Gobbo, to whom are ascribed the exquisite chiselings in the candelabra, between the windows, and the bas-reliefs on each side the door.

Interior.—The ground-plan of the church is a Latin cross, of which the length is 249 ft., and the width 173. The nave has four square divisions, each subdivided on the vault, and with oblique groins. The groining of the side aisles is singular, each space being, in fact, covered with five unequal pointed vaults, meeting in a common centre. Beyond the side aisles, on each side, two chapels open towards each square division of the nave. The choir and arms of the cross have each two square divisions, so that there are seven on the whole length of the church, and five on that of the transept. "On a critical examination, the traces of the various ages in which this edifice was erected become obvious. The most ancient portion dates from a period when the fundamental rules of architecture were by no means settled, and the romantic style was no longer satisfactory: then follows the style of the revival; then, as the building became more advanced, the proportions of Bramante were adopted, and more attention was given to the ornamental part; and thus age after age, each leaving the imprint of its characteristics."— *Gruner.* The eight statues before the pillars represent the four Evangelists and the Doctors of the Church; they are works of the best artists of the 16th centy. Rich bronze gates divide the nave from the transept. Every part of the interior is most richly decorated. The altars are inlaid with pietra-dura work, executed in the finest manner, and in which the most rare and costly materials are employed. Many good paintings which were in the church have been removed. The best of those which remain are—1st, Chapel on the rt., *Borgognone*, small fresco; the Madonna, and Angels adoring the infant Saviour; —2nd, *Giovan' Giacomo Fava*, called also *Macrino d'Alba*, a very rare master, 1496, an altar-piece in six compartments; 3rd, *Carlo Cornara*, S. Benedict, in a vision, sees his sister Sta. Scolastica ascending to heaven, with the date 1668;—4th, *Borgognone*, Christ on the Cross;—5th, the altar-piece, and the fresco in the vaulting, are by *Borgognone;* and some stained glass, representing St. Michael, by *Antonio da Pandino;*—6th, the altarpiece of this chapel is by *Guercino*. On the other side of the nave, in the 2nd chapel from the W. end, is an altar once decorated with a painting in six compartments, all by *Pietro Perugino*. Of these only one remains. It is above the centre, and represents God the Father. The 4 Doctors of the Church are attributed to *Borgognone*. In the 6th chapel is a splendid painting, St. Ambrogio on a throne and 4 Saints, by *Borgognone.*

The transepts.—In the S. transept is the tomb of Gian' Galeazzo, the founder, designed by *Galeazzo Pellegrino*, in 1490, but not completed till 1562. Many artists of unequal merit worked upon it during this long period. Over his statue, recumbent upon a sarcophagus, rises a canopy of the richest cinque-cento workmanship. Observe the trophies upon the pilasters. In the second story are six fine historical bas-reliefs:—Gian' Galeazzo receiving the baton of command from his father —his creation as Duke of Milan by the Emperor Wenceslaus—his foundation of the Certosa—the like of the Citadel of Milan—his victory over the Imperialists at Brescia (1402)—and the refoundation or dotation of the university of Pavia. These are attributed to *Gio. Ant. Amadeo.* Other parts are said to be by *Gio. Giac. della Porta.* It seems from the inscription that the monument was constructed by *Gian' Cristoforo Romano;* the statues of Fame and Victory, at the extremities of the tomb, are by *Bernardino da Novi.* That of the Virgin and Child is by *Bernardino de' Brioschi.* The monument, however, was, in a manner, executed in vain. Gian' Galeazzo died at Marignano, 3rd Sept. 1402; and his funeral was celebrated with extraordinary pomp in the Cathedral of Milan. Afterwards the body was moved, and the place where it was provisionally deposited was forgotten.

At the end of the S. transept is the altar of S. Bruno, above which is a fresco, representing the family of Gian' Galeazzo Visconti on their knees before the Virgin: he is offering her a model of the church, Filippo kneels behind, and his two other sons, Giovanni and Gabriele Macia, on the opposite side. This fresco is by *Bramantino*, by whom are also the 4 saints on each side of the arch, and the angels on the entablature above, supporting shields on which the arms of the Viscontis are blended with the mottoes of the Carthusians. Here also are two fine bronze candelabra, by *Fontana*, and some brilliant stained glass.

In the N. transept are, the monuments of the unfortunate Ludovico il Moro, and that of his beloved wife, Beatrice d'Este. She was a lady of very singular talent and beauty; and having died in childbirth, Jan. 2, 1497, he caused this monument to be erected at an expense of 50,000 ducats. Her body was interred here; but the monument was first placed in the church of St. Maria delle Grazie at Milan, and removed here in 1564. Both are said to be by *Solari*, and are finely executed: the costume is curious. Before the altar, at the end of the N. transept, are also two fine candelabra, by *Fontana;* and in the apsis are frescoes, by *Borgognone*.

The choir.—The fine doors with intaglios, and bas-reliefs representing the principal events of the life of S. Bruno, are by *Virgilio de' Conti ;* and the intarsiatura work in the seats by *Bartolomeo da Pola*, 1486; the fine balustrade, on which stand 4 bronze candlesticks, is by *Fontana*, as also the bas-reliefs on the walls, on each side of the altar, and the richly adorned high altar. The frescoes are the last work of *D. Crespi.*

By the side of the altar, which is at the end of the S. transept, is an entrance into

The *Sagrestia Nova*, covered with frescoes by *Pietro Sorri* (1600). Here is an excellent altar-piece, the lower part by *Andrea Solari*, the upper by *Bernardo Campi*. The pictures on each side are by *Solari*. Also, *Luini*, St. Ambrose, and St. Martin dividing his cloak with the Beggar.—*Morazzone*, S. Teresa with St. Peter and St. Paul.—*Montagna*, the Virgin with 2 saints and a Choir of Angels.—Some small pictures of *Borgognone*.

The *Lavatoio de' Monaci*, on the S. side of the choir, is as rich in gold and ultramarine as the church. Above the richly-sculptured doorway are seven medallions of Duchesses of Milan. Over the Lavatory is a bust, said to be that of *Heinrich* of *Gmunden*, the architect. Observe also—*Alberto Carrara*, two bas-reliefs, the Kiss of Judas, and the Washing of the Feet of the Disciples.—*B. Luini*, a fresco, of the Virgin and Child, the latter holding a pink flower. The stained glass is by *Cristoforo de' Motis*, 1477; a very beautiful work. From here you may ascend to the roof, and examine the construction of the building.

The *Sagrestia Vecchia*. — Over the door are fine medallions of the Dukes of Milan; and, on each side, a Choir of Angels, by *Amadeo*, considered amongst his best productions. The Sacristy corresponds in style with the Lavatory: in it is a curious ancient altar-piece, worked in the ivory of the teeth of the hippopotamus, containing 67 bassorilievos and 80 statues—all subjects from the New Testament, by *Bernardo degli Ubbriachi*. Several paintings ; the best are a portrait of Cardinal Colonna, by *Guido*, and a St. Augustine, by *Borgognone*.

In the cloister called *della Fontana* may be noticed numberless bas-reliefs of terra-cotta, much prized by Cicognara: our Lord and the Woman of Samaria ; Children playing upon musical Instruments. The doorway of white marble, leading into the church, is a masterpiece of *Amadeo*.

The *great cloister* is 412 ft. long by 334 ft. wide. The arches are of moulded brick, in the finest cinquecento style. Three sides are surrounded by 24 cells of the monks. Each is a separate dwelling, containing 4 good-sized rooms, 2 above and 2 below, with a small garden behind.

A very beautiful work on the Certosa, containing architectural drawings of the building, and minute details of its various parts and rich decorations (about 70 plates), has been published by the brothers Gaetano and Francesco Durelli of Milan.

The battle of Pavia, Feb. 24, 1525, in which Francis I. was taken prisoner was fought in the neighbourhood of the Certosa.

1¼ PAVIA (*Inns:* Albergo del Pozzo, clean and comfortable; La Croce Bianca, tolerable). Pop. 28,000. *Pavia la Dotta* was the capital of the Lombard kings, and the gloomy *Castello* has been thought to stand on the site of their palace. The present building, however, was raised in 1460, and completed in 1469. When perfect, it formed an ample quadrangle, flanked by 4 towers. The interior was surrounded by a double cloister, or loggia: in the upper one the arches were filled in by the most delicate tracery in brickwork: the whole was crowned by elegant forked battlements. In the towers were deposited the treasures of literature and art which Gian' Galeazzo had collected;— ancient armour; upwards of 1000 manuscripts, which Petrarch had assisted in selecting; and many natural curiosities.

All these Visconti collections were carried to France in 1499 by Louis XII., and nothing was left but the bare walls. One side of the palace or castle was demolished during the siege by Lautrec in 1527; but in other respects it continued perfect, though deserted, till 1796, when it was again put into a state of defence by the French. They took off the roof, and covered the vaultings with earth; and when the rains came on in autumn, the moisture and the weight broke down the vaultings and ruined great part of the edifice. It has since been fitted up as a barrack: in some parts the tracery of the interior arches is tolerably perfect; and the great ruined gateway, once entered by a drawbridge crossing the fosse, is still a fine object.

The *Duomo*, or cathedral, was commenced in 1488, but never finished. It was erected upon the site of an ancient Lombard basilica, of which there are some small remains now in course of demolition.

The first stone was laid by Galeazzo Maria Sforza, and his brother Ludovico; the captivity of the latter was one of the causes which prevented the prosecution of the edifice. The architect was *Christoforo Rocchi*, a pupil of Bramante. A spacious octagon occupies the centre, and a nave and side aisles, extending in each direction, were to have formed the cross; the side aisles opening into the oblique sides of the octagon, which are smaller than the others. The pulpit is of great size, surrounding one of the large clustered columns. The colossal Terms, representing the Fathers of the Church, bent forwards, and supporting the pulpit on their backs and shoulders, are finely executed in dark wood. A curious reminiscence of the age of romance is found in the lance of Orlando, a decayed shaft as large as a boat's mast, suspended from the roof of the cathedral.

In a side chapel is the tomb of St. Augustine, the greatest of the Fathers of the Latin Church. It was preserved and brought hither when the church of St. Pietro in Cœlo Aureo, where Liutprand King of the Lombards deposited the body in 700, was destroyed. Its date is about the 14th century. The body of St. Augustine (ob. 430) was removed from Hippo, a suffragan see of Carthage, during the Arian persecutions, when the Catholic clergy, being banished by King Thrasimund to Sardinia, transported the relic thither with them. Here it continued until Liutprand purchased it from the inhabitants, who, exposed to the constant invasions of the Saracens, could no longer ensure safety to the pilgrims who resorted to the shrine. The body was deposited by Liutprand in a species of catacomb or sepulchral chapel, where, when opened in 1090, the bones were found, wrapped in a silken veil, together with some of his episcopal ornaments, all contained in a silver shrine, of which the exterior is now exposed to view in the lower part of the present tomb. There is some uncertainty as to the names of the artists by whom this magnificent pile was erected. Cicognara, who says it must be reckoned amongst the most "magnificent and

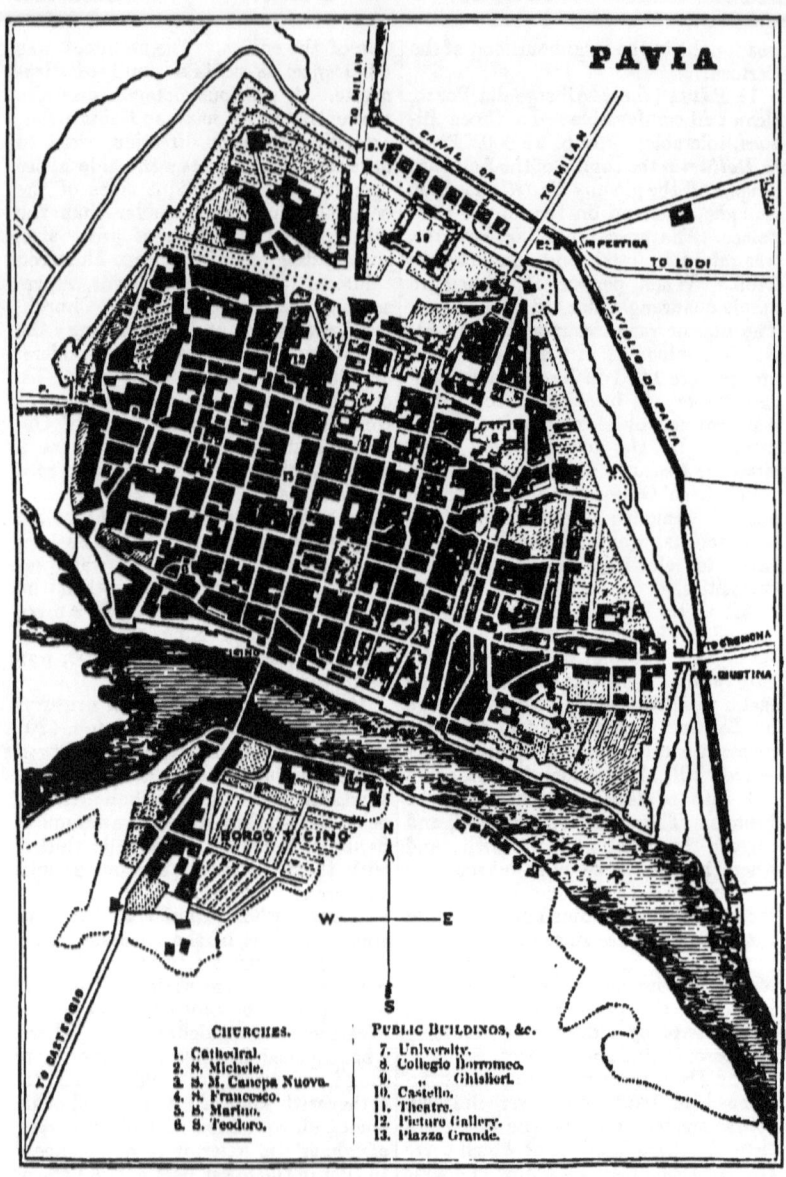

grandiose" of the 14th century, supposes it was executed by *Pietro Paolo* and *Jacobello delle Masegne*. Vasari, on the contrary, attributes it to *Agostino* and *Agnolo* of *Siena*. This assertion Cicognara supposes to be contradicted by the date of its supposed erection, stated in the books of the priory to have been 1362. The tomb consists of four *stories*: the basement, the sarcophagus, properly so called, upon which is extended the saint in his episcopal robes, the canopy, and the surmounting statues and pinnacles. Great invention and variety are displayed in the smaller statues and bas-reliefs. Round St. Augustine are the saints whom his order produced. Angels adjust the shroud around him; the Liberal Arts and the Cardinal Virtues, the principal events of the history of the saint during his life, and the miracles operated by his intercession after his death, adorn other portions of the tomb—290 figures in all; and Giovan' Galeazzo Visconti proposed to have added more. The mechanical execution corresponds with the beauty of the design.

Some good pictures exist in the cathedral, but the darkness of the building makes it rather difficult to distinguish them. The chief are, *D. Crespi*, the Virgin and Child, St. Syrus and St. Anthony of Padua; *H. Sojaro*, the Virgin of the Rosary; and *G. B. Crespi*, the Wise Men's Offering. The campanile is a noble massy tower of brick, not much altered from Gothic times.

The church of *San Michele* ranks before the cathedral in age. "The exact date of the construction of this church is not accurately known. The first time it is mentioned is by Paulus Diaconus, who incidentally relates that, in 661, Unulfus took sanctuary in this church to escape the vengeance of King Grimoaldus. The probability, however, is that it had only been recently finished at that time; because the particular veneration for the Archangel Michael, which commenced in Apulia in 503, did not reach the North of Italy till a century later. In addition to which we find that, during the whole of the 6th century, the inhabitants of Pavia were occupied with the construction of their cathedral, San Stefano; and it is not likely that they would have carried on two works of such magnitude at the same time. San Michele is 189 ft. long by 81 ft. wide; the nave is as much as 45 ft. wide. The plan is that of a Basilica, with the addition of transepts. The chancel is approached by several steps, which was probably an alteration introduced in later times than those in which the church was built. Above the aisles, on each side of the nave, there is a triforium or gallery; and above the intersection of the nave and the transepts there is a Byzantine cupola. Under the chancel there is a crypt. The arches on either side of the nave are supported by compound piers. All the capitals of the piers are enriched with images and symbols. The roof is remarkable. Unlike that of the old Basilicas, it is not of wood, but vaulted with stone; but the pilasters which run up to support the vault are of a later character than the other portions of the building, and confirm the impression, suggested by the nature of the roof itself, that the present vaulted roof must have been substituted for an older roof of wood. The walls of the building are of stone, massive and thick. The exterior is ornamented with small open galleries, which follow the shape of the gable in front, and crown the semicircular apse. The portals exhibit the complete adoption of the round form instead of the square, with the addition of several mouldings, and a profusion of imagery; nor are the ornaments confined to the portals. Bands, enriched with imagery, are carried along the whole of the front, and modillions are let into the walls. The windows are roundheaded, and divided by small pillars. The ornaments of the portals are a mixture derived from Christian, Pagan, and Scandinavian sources, together with some which are merely introduced for the purpose of decoration, and afford a good example of their peculiar style. San Michele may be taken as a specimen of a style which the Lombards adopted for their own."—*G. Knight.*

In the choir are some early frescoes by *Antonio di Edessa,* a contemporary of Giotto's; and there is also a tolerable painting by *Moncalvo.*

Santa Maria del Carmine, or *S. Pantaleone,* built in 1325, is a church deserving of notice as a beautiful specimen of the finest brickwork, and for its pointed style more akin to English-Gothic than almost any ch. in Italy: in the cornice are intersecting ornamental arches, and the W. front has a large rose-window, four pointed windows, and three pointed doors, all formed in finely-moulded terra-cotta, the whole surmounted by an elaborate, although perhaps heavy cornice, with 7 elegant pinnacles. "The brick pillars of the inside deserve notice; three squares form the nave, each of which is covered by a simple groin, but opens by two small arches into the side aisles, and has a very small circular window above. The beautiful brickwork has been hacked, to retain a coat of stucco or whitewash. The walls and vaults are also of brickwork, but of very different quality. These were evidently intended to be covered. The upper capitals are of stone, ornamented with detached leaves; the lower are of brick, cut into escutcheon faces."—*Woods.*

San Francesco is another fine church of the same material and style. "The upper part of the front, with one large central arch, surrounded by a number of plain and enriched bands, is finely composed."—*Woods.* The fine pointed arch of the W. front is very elaborate, a great number of terra-cotta ornaments introduced. The inside has been modernised, and done badly. A painting by *Campi* is the only picture worthy of notice.

Santa Maria di Canepanora is a fine specimen of the cinque-cento style, by *Bramante.* It was begun in 1492 by Giovanni Galeazzo Maria Sforza, and contains some indifferent frescoes, and

N. Italy—1860.

others pretty good by *Moncalvo,* and several subjects from the Old Testament by *Giulio Cesare* and *Camillo Procaccini.*

Of the celebrated church of *San Pietro in Cielo d'Oro* some portions remain, partly in ruins, and partly used as a storehouse. Here was one of the most interesting monuments in Italy, the tomb of Boethius.

The churches of *San Teodoro* and of *San Marino* were erected in the 8th and 9th centuries; but the interiors of both have been so entirely modernised that there is little in either to observe. In the latter is a good painting by *Cesare da Sesto,* the Virgin and Child.

The curious covered bridge over the Ticino was built by Gian' Galeazzo, and from his time to the present has been a favourite promenade of the inhabitants of Pavia. The body of the work is brick, with stone quoins to the arches. Its roof is supported by 100 columns of rough granite.

A little way outside the gates is the fine Lombard church of *San Lanfranco.* It offers a beautifully varied outline.

Outside the city is the ch. of *San Salvatore.* In the inside Corinthian pilasters support pointed arches. The whole is richly gilt and painted. Here is a school for children in connexion with the university.

The *University of Pavia* claims a high antiquity. It is said to have been founded by Charlemagne in 774; and, though this assertion is not susceptible of strict historical proof, it is certain that the civil law was professed at Pavia at a very early period. That great restorer and reformer of the Church of England, Lanfranc, Archbishop of Canterbury in the reign of the Conqueror, was born at Pavia of a family who possessed by inheritance the right of administering the civil laws, perhaps derived from their senatorial dignity in the Roman period. The splendour of the University, however, arose mainly from Gian' Galeazzo, who, about 1390, granted it so many additional privileges that he is usually honoured as the founder. But the parchment might

L

have been a dead letter, had not the duke wisely called in the great Baldus as a professor of civil law. He was a man of wonderful acuteness and diligence, and possessed what would now be termed an European reputation, to the highest extent. Kings and princes consulted him upon points of public law, and his commentaries

"on the Corpus,
Big and lumpy as a porpoise,"

contain a mine of learning. In more modern times Pavia has been principally distinguished as a medical school; and in this branch of knowledge it has produced men of great eminence. It is yet in considerable repute, containing about 1600 students. The anatomical theatre is well contrived, and the professors of anatomy have always enjoyed a high reputation.

Little can be seen of the ancient buildings of the University. Maria Theresa, in 1779, and the Emperor Joseph, in 1787, fronted and adorned much of the old part, and built two new quadrangles; and still more recently (1816) the principal façade was erected by *Marchese*, by order of the Emperor Francis I. The museums of anatomical preparations and of specimens of natural history are both remarkably good. It also contains a library of 50,000 vols., and a collection of coins. To this university also is annexed a school of the fine arts, in which drawing and engraving are taught. The utility of this institution has been much increased by the liberality of the late Marquis Malaspina, who bequeathed to it a very valuable collection of paintings, prints, and other objects illustrative of the history of art, placed in a building which he erected in his lifetime to contain them.

There are five fine courts, against the walls of two of which are placed monuments of early professors, some of them when the churches where they had been originally erected were suppressed. One of these is of the celebrated jurist *Alciat*. Most of the older monuments are on the same model — representing the professor seated in the midst of his pupils, who are listening to his lectures. Though often venerable-looking, long-bearded men, the pupils, to denote their inferiority, are made about half the size of their masters, which gives them the appearance of old boys. Their countenances and attitudes generally denote intense attention. Some eminent men of more recent times have monuments here—*Spalanzani, Fontana,* and *Scopoli, Volta, Scarpa,* and *Mascherini,* all of whom were professors in this university.

Of the many colleges formerly annexed to the university, two only have remained, the *Collegio Borromeo*, founded and supported by that family for the gratuitous education of about 40 students, and resembling some of the Halls or Colleges of our English Universities, and the *Collegio Ghislieri*. In front of the latter is a bronze statue of its founder, Pope Pius V.

From the university, four of the high and gloomy towers by so many of which Pavia was once adorned, defended, or tyrannised over, are well seen. These have been lowered, and one of them is surmounted by bells, and converted into a kind of town belfry. They are still from 200 to 250 ft. high, uniform in aspect, square, with small apertures all the way up, and adding much to the character of the city by their singular appearance. If the accounts of historians are to be credited, Pavia, the "Civitas Turrigera," at one time possessed 525 of these towers.

The façade of the Casa Botticelli, in the Corsia di Porta Marengo, is a fine specimen of cinquecento ornamental architecture.

Pavia is not healthy; the water from the Ticino is bad, and, whatever may be the cause, individuals who are stunted in their growth, or deformed, are so numerous as to force themselves upon the observation.

Amongst the *notabilia* of Pavia must be noticed the ancient costume of the ladies, which is rather declining at Milan. It is a *black* silken veil, thrown over the uncovered head in the same manner as the white veil is used at Genoa.

On quitting Pavia we cross the Ticino by the covered bridge, and enter the suburb called Borgo Ticino. Shortly after another branch of the Ticino is passed before reaching San Martino, about 2 m. from Pavia. 4 m. further on, the Po is crossed by a bridge of boats. A toll of 2¼ fr. is paid for each carriage at the Ticino bridge on quitting Pavia, and 3 fr. 40 c. on crossing the Po at Mezzana Corti.
20 kil. Casteggio. (Rte. 7.)
26 kil. Tortona. (Rte. 7.)
19 kil. Novi. (Rte. 5.)

The route from Pavia to Alessandria may also be performed by way of Mortara, to which the Rly. extends. The distance to Mortara is about 16 m. After leaving San Martino the road runs parallel to the Ticino, but at some distance, passing through Garlasco halfway; there are public conveyances from Pavia to meet the Rly.-trains to and from Genoa, Turin, and Piacenza, at Casteggio.

GENOA. (Rte. 13.)

ROUTE 24.

MILAN TO PIACENZA, BY MELEGNANO AND LODI.

(54 m.)

6¼ posts. Milan to Lodi, 24 m. Lodi to Piacenza, 30 m. Coaches leave Milan for Piacenza at 7 A.M. and 6 P.M., performing the journey in 8½ hours.

Leaving Milan by the *Porta Romana*, the road is for most part of the way of the same character as that to Pavia; in some parts exceedingly marshy, intersected with numerous canals and streams. It is perhaps the least agreeable side of Milan. If the traveller is coming from the S. he will miss the festoons of the vines, which, even before he reaches Lodi, will have almost entirely disappeared. The maize, though beautiful in flower and in ear, is, when ripe, arid in appearance and ungraceful. The rice plantations, below the level of the road, and where the cultivators labour in black mud above the ankle, convey the idea of unhealthiness; but the meadows are beautiful. Châteauvieux says, "The cultivation of rice in Lombardy is remarkably unhealthy; sickly labourers are seen walking along the banks to superintend the distribution of the water. They are clad like miners, in coarse clothing, and wander about, pale as spectres, among the reeds and near the sluices, which they have barely strength to open and shut. When crossing a canal they are frequently obliged to plunge into the water, out of which they come wet and covered with mud, carrying with them germs of fever, which invariably attacks them. They are not the only victims, for the harvest labourers seldom gather in the crop without being seized with *rigors*, the air in all the environs being polluted by the stagnant waters. The cultivation of the rice-planters is consequently restrained by law, and they are prohibited to extend its culture beyond prescribed limits."

At 3 m. from Porta Romana, on the Vetabbia, a short way on the rt. of the road, is the very ancient church of *San Giorgio di Nosedo*, annexed to what was a residence of the Archbishop. The mansion is now an inn. The church was founded in 571, by Alboin King of the Lombards: it is still standing, and has the remains of a curious fresco.

About 1 m. lower down the river, and 1½ m. to the rt. of the road, stands the Abbey of *Chiaravalle*, a Cistercian monastery, suppressed in 1797. A cross road, which leaves the post-route about 1 m. from the Porta Romana, passing by Nosedo, leads to it. "This was the church of the first Cistercian monastery that was established in Italy. The Cistercian reform was first introduced by St. Bernard, who was Abbot of Clairvaux in France. In 1134 St. Bernard crossed the Alps to attend a council at Pisa, and, on his way back, paid a visit to Milan. The citizens of Milan advanced 7 miles beyond their gates to receive him. His presence excited the most enthusiastic feelings; and within a year after his departure a monastery was built at the distance of about 4 miles from the city, which was to be governed by St. Bernard's rules, and to receive a name from the parent institution. The monastery was inhabited in 1136, but it was not till nearly the close of the twelfth century that the church was completed. It is in the Lombard style, and deserves consideration, as an architectural composition, for the importance of its central tower. The body of the fabric is left perfectly plain, and, in effect, serves only as a base for the leading feature of the design. The tower alone is enriched. Octagonal in its form up to a certain height, it becomes a spire above. Both the octagonal and spiral portions are enriched with Lombard galleries, which give an appearance of lightness, and attract the eye to that part of the building on which it is intended to rest. It is evident that the architect must have made the central tower his chief object; and whenever an architect has had a peculiar object, and has succeeded in producing the effect which he desired, his work deserves to be studied."—*G. Knight.*

This monastery was the favourite retirement of Ottone Visconti, who died here. What is called his tomb is still shown; beneath the inscription are shields of arms, amongst which are the fleurs-de-lys of France.

In the cemetery which adjoins the church are still several monuments of the powerful family of the Torriani, who selected it for their last resting-place. Here lies the great *Pagano della Torre* (who died 1241), the most distinguished of his race; and near him several of his descendants. This family was at the head of the popular party, and for two or three generations governed Milan, keeping the nobles in subjection. Having conspired against the Emperor in the year 1311, they were defeated, proscribed, and banished; and by their fall made way for their rivals the Viscontis, who were at the head of the aristocracy.

Here also is shown the tomb of the celebrated but ill-famed Wilhelmina. Her name passed into a once popular saying—*egli ha da fare peggio che la Guglielmina.*—She died in 1282, and during her lifetime she was regarded as a saint; but after her death it was discovered that she had been the foundress of a secret sect, whose tenets involved the most fearful blasphemies in doctrine, as well as the most abominable sins in practice. Her bones were taken up and burned, and her accomplices put to death. The cruelties inflicted upon them were most atrocious.

The country round this monastery was reclaimed by the labours of the Cistercians, who were in agriculture almost what the Benedictines were in literature. They invented the system of artificial meadows, called "*prati di Marcita*," to which Lombardy owes so much of its prosperity.

Returning to the post-road we pass through

San Donato.
San Giuliano.

1½ **Melegnano** or *Marignano*, on the river Lambro: Pop. 4000. Here, on the 14th Sept. 1515, Francis I. won, in the first year of his reign, the victory by which he acquired a transient and delusive glory. Having invaded the Milanese for the purpose of asserting his chimerical rights, he was attacked at Melegnano by the Swiss, to whom the defence of the Milanese territory had been intrusted. The battle was continued with great obstinacy during three entire days, and the Swiss were at length compelled to retreat, in good order, but leaving 15,000 dead upon the field, a slaughter which, if we may judge by the feelings expressed by Ariosto, occasioned great delight to the Italian heart :—

" Vedete il lte Francesco innanzi a tutti,
Che cosi rompe a' Svizzeri le corna,
Che poco resta a non gli aver distrutti ;
Si che 'l titolo mai più non gli adorna,
Ch' usurpato s' avran quei villan brutti,
Che domator de' Principi, e difesa
Si nomeran della Cristiana Chiesa."
Canto xxxiii. 43.

Melegnano was also the scene of a hard-fought battle on the 7th June, 1859, between the French and Austrians, in which both sides suffered severely : the French commanded by Marshal Baraguay d'Hilliers, the Austrians by Benedek, forming the rear-guard of the army retreating after the disaster of Magenta.

Cross the Muzza, one of the many canals of irrigation with which this district abounds. The approach to Lodi from Milan is somewhat singular, from the height of causeway on which the road is carried. A fine avenue of plane-trees borders it on either side.

1¼ LODI. (*Inns :* Il Sole, good, civil people ; L'Europa ; I tre Re, very fair.) The original settlement of the citizens, *Lodi Vecchio*, is about 5 m. off, to the westward. It was founded by the Boii, and, having been colonised by Cneius Pompeius Strabo, the father of Pompey the Great, the citizens called it *Laus Pompeia*. Cicero calls it simply *Laus*. The conversion of *Laus* into *Lodi* shows how, by the employment of the oblique cases, the Latin language was corrupted into the modern dialect.

The men of Lodi were the great and constant rivals of the Milanese, who, in 1111, entirely destroyed the city. "The animosity between Milan and Lodi was of very old standing. It originated, according to Arnulf, in the resistance made by the inhabitants of the latter city to an attempt made by Archbishop Eribert to force a bishop of his own nomination upon them. The bloodshed, plunder, and conflagrations which had ensued would, he says, fill a volume if they were related at length."—*Hallam*.

After the destruction of Milan, the Lodigiani, who had fled to Pizzighettone, came (1158) before Barbarossa, as suppliants, weeping and bearing crosses, and requesting a home ; and accordingly he gave them a village then called Monteguizone, granting them investiture by the delivery of a banner. The spot is said to have been fixed upon by Frederick himself ; it was defended by the river Adda, and lies in a tract of exuberant fertility : thus arose the modern city, containing now upwards of 18,000 Inhab.

The inhabitants of Lodi removed from their ancient city the relics of their patron saint, Bassianus, which they deposited in the Duomo, a fine Lombard building. The porch is supported by fine griffins ; perhaps not only the design, but even a part of the materials, may have been brought from old Lodi. This is certainly the case with respect to a bas-relief representing the Last Supper, a remarkable monument of early Christian art, anterior to the settlement of the Lombards. The eyes are of enamel. Some fine paintings in *tempera* are on the walls near the high altar. They are by *Guglielmo* and *Alberto di Lodi*, and were covered up till within the last few years.

The ch. of the *Incoronata*, by Bramante, begun in 1476, is a very beautiful specimen of the Renaissance. It is an octagon, and contains some good paintings of *Calisto da Lodi*, an imitator of Titian. The subjects are taken from the events of the Passion of our Lord, the Life of St. John the Baptist, and the Life of the Virgin: the heads have great beauty. It is said that some of the pictures were executed by Titian, who, passing through Lodi, gave this help to his pupil.

The great Piazza, surrounded by arches, is fine of its kind. The entrance of the convent formerly belonging to the *Padri dell' Oratorio* is formed by an arch said to have been brought from old Lodi. On it is inscribed *Ignorantiæ et Paupertati*: neither the form of the letters nor the nature of the inscription sanctions its supposed antiquity. The terrible passage of the bridge of Lodi, and the heroic conduct of the young Buonaparte at the head of his grenadiers, May 10th, 1796, need no commemoration. The bridge is on the eastern side of the city, over the Adda.

The Lodi district is the chief country for the production of the cheese usually called *Parmesan*. In the country it is called *Grana*. The territory in which the cheese is produced is 20 m. wide from Pavia to Milan and Lodi, and double that in length from Abbiategrasso, near the Ticino, to Codogno, near the confluence of the Adda and Po. The cows set apart for this production are about 80,000. It is seldom found profitable to rear them in the country; they come from the Swiss cantons of Unterwald, Uri, Zug, Luzern, and Schweitz. They are brought at the age of from 3 to 4 years, between October and March, and give milk abundantly for about 7 years. More than 12,000 are imported every year; the price of each is from 14*l*. to 18*l*., sometimes as high as 20*l*. After 7 yrs. they are sold, when worn out. The cheese produced from a cow is, on an average, 340 lbs. avoirdupois in the course of a year, which is weighed after 6 months. It is sold twice a year; that called la Sorte Maggenga (May lot) is that which is made between St. George's day and St. Michael's, 24th April to 29th Sept.; the other is called la Sorte Invernenga (the winter lot), which is made between the 29th Sept. and the 24th April. The average price is from 92 to 100 fr. (*i. e.* from 3*l*. 13*s*. 8*d*. to 4*l*.) for 171 lbs. avoirdupois. The total production of the year will be 27,568,500 lbs. avoirdupois. After two or three years' seasoning in the warehouses of the merchants, which are principally at Codogno, province of Lodi, and Corsico, province of Milan, the weight of the cheese is diminished 5 per cent. About the half comprehends two inferior sorts. The first of these is cheese of a bad quality; the other inferior sort, although of a good quality, from some defect in the shape cannot be exported, and is consumed in the country. The whole of the better kind is sent out of the country. The quantity exported to Great Britain is comparatively small.

Three kinds of pasture are used for the cows; viz. the *marcito* (or constantly flooded meadow-land); *irrigatorie stabile* (the merely irrigated grounds); *erbatico* (rotative meadowgrounds). The *marcito* consists in dividing the land into many small parallelograms, sensibly inclined to one side. The water which fills the little canals amongst them overflows these spots slowly; it spreads like a veil over these spaces, and by the inclination of the ground falls again into the opposite canal. From this it is diffused over other parts, so that the whole meadow country is continually flooded; from which there is maintained a rapid and continual vegetation in the heats of summer and the frosts of winter; at the same time no marshy weeds prevail. The grass is cut five times a year; and in some parts below Milan, in the meadows (along the Vettabbia), even nine times. When cut on the 31st May it is 32 inches high; at every subsequent cutting it is less — the second 10, the third 8, the fourth 6, &c. It is quite tasteless and insipid, and horses refuse to eat it, which proves the opinion of many strangers to be erroneous, who attribute the fine taste of the cheese to the flavour of the pasture. The *marciti* meadows require a constant supply of water; when there is not enough, the simple irrigating system is adopted; the grounds are then watered at the interval of several days. The *erbatico*, or rotation meadow, alternates with the cultivation of rice, grain, flax, Indian corn, and oats.

1½ *Casal Pusterlengo*, a good-sized town, where the road divides; one branch leads to Cremona and Mantua (see Rte. 25); the other, which we follow, continues to *Fombio, S. Rocco* and *la Ca Rossa*. Shortly afterwards the Po is crossed by two bridges of boats, connected by an island in the centre of the stream, a short drive from which brings us to the gate (Porta di Fodesta) of

2 PIACENZA (see Rte. 40).

ROUTE 25.

MILAN TO MANTUA, BY CREMONA.

Milan to Cremona, 63½ m. Milan to Mantua, 111 m.

1½ Melegnano. } See preceding
1¼ Lodi.   } Route.
1½ Casal Pusterlengo. }

Codogno, principally remarkable as a great cheese-mart.

Maleo.

Gera.

The country called the *Gera* or *Ghiara d'Adda* is hereabouts traditionally supposed to have been once covered by a lake, called the Lago Gerondo, and dried up, partly by drainage, and partly by evaporation. There is much in the aspect of the country to confirm this opinion.

1. *Pizzighettone* (Pop. 4000), once a fortress of importance. It was originally built by the men of Cremona in 1125 as a point of defence against the Milanese. Here Francis I. was detained after the battle of Pavia. The fortifications still look strong, though they have been partially dismantled. The place offers no object of interest, except some frescoes by *Campi* in the principal church. The Adda, which runs through the town, is here a fine rapid stream.

Aqua Negra, where the Cremonese sustained a signal defeat in 1166.

2 CREMONA. (*Inns:* none good. The Sole d'Oro is the best. There are diligences between Cremona and Pavia 3 days a week, in about 9 hrs.; daily to Parma, in 7 hrs.; and 2 from the Inn of the Capello to Brescia every day in 6 hrs. (See Route 41.)

Cremona ran the same course, and underwent the same vicissitudes, which befel most of the principal cities of Italy during the middle ages. Captured and destroyed by the northern barbarians in the 5th centy., it remained in a state of abandonment till the 7th, when, at the command of the Lombard king, Agilulfus, it was rebuilt. During the nominal rule of the German emperors, and the anarchy which ensued, Cremona obtained municipal rights. No sooner were the Cremonese independent than, like the other enfranchised towns of Italy, they quarrelled with their neighbours. Cremona was always at war either with Crema, Brescia, or Piacenza — but especially with Milan. When Frederick Barbarossa vented his wrath on Milan, the Cremonese aided him in the subversion of their ancient rival, and in return obtained a new charter. But internal disorders were now added to foreign wars. The nobles quarrelled; Guelph and Ghibelline factions fought in the streets. In the latter half of the 13th centy., Cremona, in common with many other cities of Italy, had recourse to the singular expedient of calling in a Dictator, under the name of Podestà, who was never to be a native, that he might be entirely unconnected with any of the various parties whom he had to control. The Podestà was so far of use that he preserved internal peace. But, after a time, an end was put to this anomalous, though beneficial domination, and a republican form of government was established. So much disorder, however, was the consequence, that the people, wearied with the strife of their rulers, again called out for a chief. The republican party were compelled to withdraw, but in strength enough to return to the charge. Civil war thinned the population, and exhausted the resources of this unfortunate district. The Emperor Henry VII., who came into Italy to vindicate the imperial authority, completed the ruin of Cremona when he attacked it in 1312; and in 1322 Galeazzo Visconti had little difficulty in avenging the former injuries of Milan by taking possession of Cremona, and incorporating it with the duchy of that city. It is now a thriving place, containing about 37,000 Inhab. It has a good trade, and a fair is held here about the end of September, a time when the noncommercial traveller will do well to keep away. Cremona was once celebrated for the manufacture of musical instruments. The business was hereditary in families: and the remote ancestors of *Amati*, the most renowned of these modern makers who flourished 1704-1739, had supplied Charles IX. of France with excellent lutes and violins. The instruments of the last Amati are yet in great repute, and fetch high prices. He was succeeded in reputation by Stradivarius and Guarnieri; at present the instruments made here have no peculiar excellence.

The public works of Cremona were undertaken in the short intervals of tranquillity which that city enjoyed. In 1107, after a sharp struggle with Brescia, the Cremonese began their *Cathedral*, which, however, was not consecrated till 1190, by which time the nave and the aisles were completed. Little more was done till after Cremona had become united to the duchy of Milan. In 1342 the transepts were commenced, but the choir was not finished till 1479. The façade was begun in 1274, continued in 1491, ornamented in 1525, and terminated in 1606. The various times at which the fabric was constructed sufficiently account for the different styles of its architecture. In the front, which is of marble, the Lombard predominates, and the pillars of the porch rest upon the usual griffonised lions, of which one grasps the serpent, the other an animal which holds a bird between its paws. The zodiac is over the door, and Count Von Hammer Purgstall has made good use of it in one of his treatises upon the Mithraic mysteries. The noble rose-window, surrounded by a rich and delicately carved vine-leaf moulding, was built by *Giacinto Porata* of Como in 1274. Other parts of the exterior are of moulded brick, and worked with much beauty. The front of the N. transept, which is entered by a porch supported by lions, is a fine specimen of the pointed style. It has three good rose windows. The interior is one mass of colouring and gilding. Lanzi considers this interior as rivalling the Sixtine Chapel, not, of course, as to the merit of the paintings, but in its pictorial magnificence. The frescoes in the nave occur in the following order, extending to the end of the choir:— On the l. 8 paintings representing events in the history of the Virgin by *B. Bocaccino;* next 2 of the Adoration of the Magi by *Bembo,* signed and dated 1451; beyond the organ the Flight into Egypt, and the Massacre of the Innocents, by *Altobello di Melone,* dated 1517; followed by Christ disputing with the Doctors, by *Bocaccino,* probably the best of the series. On the opposite side of the ch., and next the door, is the Last Supper, with four scenes of the Passion of our Lord, by *Altobello;* the two next, Christ bound, and before Pilate, by *C. Moretti,* followed by the Saviour shown to the People, by *Romanino:* the last three, and the great subject of the Crucifixion, at the end, are by *Pordenone.* The frescoes on either side of the principal entrance, representing a Dead Christ and the Maries, are by the same painter; the Resurrection, by *Getti;* the vault of the choir is painted by *Bocaccino.* In the 1st chapel on the rt. is a Madonna and Child, by *Pordenone,* surrounded by Saints, and the portrait of the Donatorio, one of the Schizzi family. The painting over the high altar is the last work of *Gatti (il Sojaro),* the Assumption of the Virgin. It is said that, being rendered infirm by age, he added the last touches to the painting with his left hand. It was unfinished at the time of his death, and it was completed by *Sommacchino* of Bologna. Four large frescoes have been lately added by *Diotti,* a living artist. "The southern transept has frescoes of subjects from the Old Testament, attributed to *Giorgio Casselli,* and said to have been executed about the year 1363; they are more curious than fine in art, but interesting, from the fact of their having lasted so well, especially considering the dampness of the situation. The *intarsiatura,* or inlaid work of the stalls of the choir (1489-90), by *Giovan' Maria Platina,* is very elaborate. There are some good specimens of mediæval sculpture in the chapel of San Nicolo, of San Pietro, and San Marcellino. In the transept is a singular ancient vessel, apparently of the 9th or 10th centy., ornamented at the 4 corners with winged and tailed monsters, in which, according to the sacristan, St. Albert was accustomed to knead bread for the poor. St. Albert was born at Castel Gualtieri in this neighbourhood; and, after filling the episcopal chair of Vercelli, was, in 1204, appointed patriarch of Jerusalem. He was the founder of the Carmelite Order, and distinguished for humility and kindness to the poor. The *Sacristy* still contains a few curious articles, ancient crosses, and the like; amongst others a large silver crucifix by Pozzi and Sacchi of Milan, made in 1475. Beneath the Duomo is a fine, though not very ancient crypt, with the tombs of the patron saints of the city.

The *Battisterio,* built, some say about the year 800, others a centy. later, is in a plain and simple Lombard style. It has, what is very rare in this class of edifices, a fine projecting porch, supported by lions. The windows, by which it is scantily lighted, might serve for a Norman castle. The walls within are covered with ranges of Lombard arches, and fragments of frescoes are seen in the gloom. In the centre is a noble font hewn out of a single block of marble. By the side of the Duomo, connected by a line of *loggie,* rises *the great tower,* which has obtained for Cremona its architectural celebrity. It was begun in 1283; in that year peace was made between Cremona, Milan, Piacenza, and Brescia; and in celebration of this event this tower was undertaken at the common expense of the Guelphs, or partisans of the Pope, not only of Cremona, but of all northern Italy. It is said to have been carried up to the square in the space of two years. The *Torazzo*, as it is called, is the highest of all the towers in the N. of Italy, 396 ft. 498 steps lead to its summit, from whence the eye surveys the extensive plains of the Milanese, intersected by the Po, and distinguishes the Alps to the N. and the Apennines to the S.W. In 1518 the bells were cast which hang in this tower, at which time it may be concluded the octagonal cupola was added. In the third story is an enormous clock, put up in 1594. The custode of the Torazzo lives in it. The staircase is not in the best repair; but it can be ascended without difficulty. The ancient doggrel rhyme—

"*Unus Petrus est in Roma,
Una turris in Cremona,*"—

is an illustration of the popular celebrity of this *campanile*. It had a chance of becoming even still more celebrated. In 1414 the Emperor Sigismund and the Pope visited Cremona, then subject to the usurped authority of Gabrino Fondulo. The Signore was cruel and treacherous, but wise and talented. The sovereign and pontiff consulted with him; and, by his advice, Constance was fixed upon as the place where the great council was to be held for the purpose of restoring the peace of Christendom; and Sigismund, besides other marks of favour, gave to Gabrino, in Cremona, the authority of a vicar of the empire. Gabrino invited his illustrious guests to mount the Torazzo and enjoy the prospect, and he alone accompanied them. They all came down in safety; but when Gabrino was brought to the scaffold at Milan in 1425, he said that only one thing in the course of his life did he regret—that he had not had quite courage enough to push Pope and Emperor over the battlements, in order that he might have profited by the confusion which such a catastrophe would have occasioned in Italy.

Near the cathedral is what is called the *Campo Santo*, though now used as the repository of the archives, and where the functionaries of the cathedral assemble. It contains a vault, to which you descend by about 14 steps; in it is an exceedingly curious but puzzling mosaic pavement, with allegorical figures representing a Centaur fighting against a figure representing Cruelty, Faith and a figure kneeling before her, and Pity conquered by Impiety. It seems to be an early Christian work. The place was evidently an ancient Christian cemetery, as appears not only from its name, but from the bones and the inscriptions found there.

Cremona had many convents, almost all of which are demolished. The churches are generally of dark red brick: those which have escaped demolition or modernisation are usually Gothic.

Santa Agata is one of these; and the architectural traveller will here find what we should call the earliest Norman capitals, from which spring the latest Gothic arches. This church contains several excellent specimens of *Giulio Campi;* one, the Martyrdom of Sta. Agata, dated 1537, has obtained high commendations from Vasari, usually so sparing in his commendations of Lombard artists.

Santa Margherita, annexed to the episcopal seminary. At an earlier period it was a priory, and has much interest, as having been built under the directions of the celebrated Jerome Vida. Vida employed *Giulio Campi* to decorate the church with his paintings, of which there are many; the best is the Circumcision.

San Nazaro. The cupola painted partly by *Giulio Campi*, and partly by *Malosso* from his designs. Over the high altar is a good picture by *Altobello.*

Sant' Agostino, and *San Giacomo* in *Breda*, a fine Gothic church with some remarkable paintings.—*Perugino*, the Virgin and Saints, a picture of great merit, carried off by the French, and restored in 1815.—*G. B. Zupelli*, the Virgin and Child in a beautiful landscape.—*Malosso*, a Deposition from the Cross; the Temptation of St. Anthony.—*Masserotti*, St. Augustine, and personifications of the Orders supposed to have arisen out of the rules constituted by the Saint.

San Giorgio, a sumptuous building with numerous paintings. — *Campi* and *Ermenegildo di Lodi*, the Christian Virtues in the vaulting of the nave.— *A. Campi*, a Holy Family, the Infant playing with a Bird.—The piece over the high altar. The Virgin and Child surrounded by Saints, by *Bembo*, dated 1527. It was originally painted for the Servites in the suppressed church of San Vittore. The price for which Campi stipulated was 250 Milanese *lire*, and a mass *per diem* during seven months.— *Bernardino Gatti*, or *Sojaro*, a Nativity; the main idea taken from the celebrated *Notte* of Correggio, retaining nearly the whole general composition, but illuminated by the light of day.

The *Palazzo Publico*, a relic of ancient Cremona, was begun in 1206, and is supported by lofty arches. Two towers are annexed to the building. The ancient gates of brass are said to have been put up in 1245, in the expectation of a visit from the Pope and the Emperor. The exterior has recently lost much of its character, owing to repairs. The interior, now used for the *Town Hall*, contains several paintings.—*Grazio Cossale*, the Descent of the Manna, dated 1597.— *A. Campi*, the Visitation.—*Malosso*, the Protectors of the City, Saints Himerius and Homobonus. In the antechamber is a chimney-piece of alabaster, brought from the Raimondi Palace, sculptured in Arabesque style by *Pedoni*, in which the artist has introduced a portrait of Marshal Trivulzio: it is much praised by Cicognara.

Near this Palazzo is another and better example of the Italian-Gothic applied to civil purposes, in which the College of Jurisconsults used to hold their sittings. It is now a boys' school. It is built of finely moulded brick.

There are many private residences in Cremona; some of the older ones are fair specimens of the cinque-cento style. Such is the *Palazzo San Secundo*; the sculptures on the exterior are by *Bernardo Sacchi*. The *Palazzo Raimondi* is by *Pedoni*; the pilasters are of a most fanciful style, and adorned with arabesques.

There are some tolerably good collections of pictures at Cremona.

Marchese Pallavicini, a Presentation by *Bernardino Campi*; an excellent library and some curious manuscripts.

Count Schizzi, many specimens of the Cremonese school. *B. Campi*, a Nativity, considered as one of his best works.

Count Ala Ponzoni, a rich collection of drawings (some by *Michel Angelo*), paintings, and coins.

The district round Cremona produces flax of a superior quality. Numerous remains of ancient castles are scattered over it.

Diligences run at 6 and 8½ A.M. from Cremona to Mantua, Parma, and Piacenza.

Just out of Cremona, on the Mantuan side, but not exactly on the road, is the noble church of *San Sigismondo*. It was in this church that Francesco Sforza married Beatrice, the only child of Filippo Maria Visconti (Oct. 25, 1441); and thus, after the death of his father-in-law, became the founder of the new dynasty. Cremona was the dowry of the bride; and Francesco, as a token of affection both to her and to the city, rebuilt the church as it now stands. It consists of a single nave with twelve chapels, and is full of the works of native artists.—*A. Campi*, the Decollation of St. John the Baptist. The vaulting of the chapel in which this picture is placed, as well as the bas-reliefs, are all by *Campi*, and he claims them by an inscription dated 1577. — *Bernardino Campi*, St. Philip and St. James. The vaulting is by him: the chapel was finished by *Malosso*.—*Giulio Campi*, an interesting picture for its portraits, over the high altar; the Virgin and Child, and Francesco Sforza and Bianca Maria Visconti presented to them by St. Sigismund with St. Chrysanthus by his side. The painter has introduced his own likeness and that of his mistress in the faces of the latter saint and of Santa Daria. Campi has subscribed his name and date, 1540. He was paid 200 *scudi d'oro* for the work. The vaulting is entirely covered with paintings, principally by *Bernardino Gatti*: the smaller ornaments, angels, foliage, and the like, by him, are graceful and beautiful.—By *Camillo Boccaccino* are the paintings in the tribune and round the high altar. Of these Lanzi says, "the finest are the four Evangelists; three are seated; St. John is standing, his figure thrown backwards, as if by a movement of surprise, and skilful in the drawing and perspective. It seems strange that so young a man as Camillo, and one who never frequented the school of Correggio, should so well have caught his style: this work, which is a model in perspective and the optical delusion of effect, was finished in 1537. The two side pictures are also much-esteemed works of Camillo. One represents the resurrection of Lazarus; the other, the Woman taken in Adultery: both are surrounded by an elegant frieze, in which the angels sporting with a crozier and other sacred emblems are admirable for their life and grace.

"The church of St. Sigismund is literally covered with the works of the brothers *Campi*; hardly a square inch has been left vacant. These frescoes, bearing date many of them 1566-77, are all vigorous and brilliant, and are perhaps, on the whole, some of the best that could be adduced in favour of the material. Among other colours, a green of an emerald kind, and a most vivid blue, I have never before seen equally well preserved: they are especially brilliant here in an Ascension by *Bernardino Gatto*, called *il Sojaro*, a pupil of Correggio. Probably this church was built of better materials and on a drier soil, as the walls with their decorations are in perfect preservation down to the very pavement."
—*S. A. Hart, R.A.*

1 *Cigognolo*. Near this place is an ancient castle, modernised, but still a fine object.

⸺ Pass *Villa Picinardi*, which has a gallery and library, and gardens possessing local celebrity.

San Lorenzo.

1¼ *Piadena*, a small town. In Latin it is called *Platina*, and as such it has given its name to Bartolomeo Sacchi, the historian of the popes, this being his birthplace. [Here a road branches off on the rt. to *Casal Maggiore.*]

Pass *Calvatone*, said to be on the site of the city of Vegra, destroyed by Attila.

¾ *Bozzolo*, a good-sized town of 5000 Inhab., anciently a small independent republic.

San Martino dell' Argine; a mile beyond which cross the *Oglio* at *Marcaria*, where is an ancient castle.

1½ *Castellucchio*, 2 m.; after passing which, and about 7 m. from Mantua, we reach the Austrian frontier at Le Grazie. Here is the church of *Sta. Maria delle Grazie*, consecrated in 1406, and built by Francesco Gonzaga, Lord of Mantua, as the sanctuary of a supposed miraculous painting of the Madonna, which had previously been venerated in a small church situated upon the bank of the adjoining marshy lake. The chief votaries of this sacred object were the boatmen of the lake. But in 1399 Gonzaga addressed his vows to the image, praying that the Virgin would intercede for the deliverance of Mantua from the pestilence which then desolated Italy, and the result was the erection of this church, together with the now suppressed monastery, of which only a small portion remains, tenanted by the two chaplains by whom divine service is performed. The architecture is good Italian-Gothic; the church contains a strange array of votive images arranged on each side of the nave above the arches, upon columns richly gilt and carved. They are as large as, and coloured to life, in every kind of costume, representing the individuals whose gratitude is commemorated in the verses beneath. Here may be seen the Emperor Charles V., Federigo Gonzaga, Pope Pius II., the Connétable de Bourbon, and a host of other celebrities. Others represent the trials and perils from which the votaries have been delivered, torture, anguish, death. All testify their gratitude to the Virgin for the help they have obtained through her intercession.

The choir is painted by *Lattanzio Gambara*, of Brescia, and there are also several curious paintings in the numerous side chapels. There are also some interesting monuments. One of the most remarkable is that of Baltassare Castiglione (ob. 1529), the celebrated author of the 'Cortigiano:' the epitaph was written by Cardinal Bembo, and the monument designed by *Giulio Romano*. The mausoleum is simple and noble—a plain sarcophagus, surmounted by a statue of our Lord. Baltassare's wife, Ippolita Torelli, had previously been buried here; a touching epitaph declares her beauty and virtues. Camillo, their son, lies in the same chapel. The supposed miraculous picture of the Virgin is an Italian painting, apparently not older than the 15th century. A long dark cloister, much dilapidated, leads to the church. It is still annually visited by large numbers of pilgrims, yet it looks deserted and decayed.

Curtatone, on the Lago Superiore, formed by the widening of the Mincio. Here was fought, on the 29th May, 1848, a very sanguinary action between the Austrians and the Tuscan auxiliaries of Carlo Alberto, the latter composed chiefly of volunteers, who defended themselves heroically against a superior force before retreating. In this battle the students of the university of Pisa took a distinguished part.

The tract around *Mantua* is called the *Serraglio*, from the ancient walls built to defend the city against the tyrant Eccelino da Romano. The country is very fertile, but not agreeable, from the marshes upon which it borders. The gnats and mosquitoes, the "*zanzare*" and the "*papatasse*," are numerous and annoying in summer.

Donatus informs us that Virgil was born at *Andes;* a local and very ancient tradition has identified this place with *Pietole*, about 2 m. from Mantua, at the S. extremity of the Lago Inferiore, surrounded by woods and groves, in which the willow predominates. One of the Gonzagas built a palace here, to which he gave the name of the *Virgiliana*.

1 *Mantua* (see Rte. 30).

ROUTE 27.

MILAN TO THE AUSTRIAN FRONTIER AT PESCHIERA, BY TREVIGLIO, BERGAMO, BRESCIA, SOLFERINO, ETC.—RAIL.

KIL.		KIL.	
10	Limito Stat.	80	Coccaglio.
17	Melzo.	88	Ospedalletto.
28	Cassano.	99	BRESCIA.
30	Treviglio.	108	Rezzato.
40	Verdello.	116	Ponte S. Marco.
51	BERGAMO.	123	Lonato.
55	Seriate.	127	Desenzano.
62	Gorlago.		Pozzolengo.
68	Grumello.	141	Peschiera.
72	Palazzolo.		

141 kil. = 87¼ Eng. m.

The Rly., being now completed the whole way from Milan to Venice, offers the most convenient means of visiting Bergamo and Brescia, and the Alpine valleys, of considerable beauty and interest, that open into the plains of Lombardy between the lakes of Como and Garda. Trains start 4 times a day from Milan, employing 1 hr. 48 min. to Bergamo, 3·20 to Brescia, and 4·20 to Desenzano, near which the territory of the new Italian kingdom ends; two of which continue onwards to Peschiera, Verona, and Venice; the latter starting from Milan at 6·10 and 11·15 a.m., and reaching Venice at 5·55 and 10·30 p.m. The station at Milan is outside of the Porta Tosa.

The Rly. follows in a straight line to the Adda, passing by

11 kil. *Limito Stat.*,

7 kil. *Melzo Stat.*, descending as it approaches the Adda, before reaching

10 kil. *Cassano Stat.*, a little way below the town, and crossing the river on a handsome bridge. Cassano is a large town full of silk-works. There are some ruins of an ancient castle. Cassano occupies an important military position on the Adda, at which were fought two sanguinary battles, between Vendôme and Prince Eugene, in 1705, and between Suwarrow and Moreau the 27th April, 1799. Crossing the plain for 3 m., we arrive at

5 kil. *Treviglio Stat.*, near the town of the same name of 6000 Inhab., a long, straggling place. The church is rather a remarkable building, and there are some good second-rate pictures in it. Diligences start for Caravaggio and Chiari, making the journey in 2 hrs.

The more direct road to Brescia, along which a rly. is projected, passes by Caravaggio and Chiari, but, except its passing through a very rich district, offers little interest, whilst the present line of rly. makes a considerable détour to include Bergamo, running through a more picturesque country.

[*Caravaggio*, 3 m. from Treviglio, a town of about 6000 Inhab. In the principal church, with a Lombard façade and high bell-tower, are some good paintings by Campi: near the town is the sanctuary of the Madonna, built in 1575 from the designs of Pellegrini. The name of this town is more generally known from the two painters, both called "da Caravaggio," who were born here in 1495 and 1569—*Polidoro Caldara*, the scholar of Raphael, and *Michel Angelo Merigi*, who has sometimes been compared to *the* great Michael Angelo.

Mozzonica, near the river Serio, a small village.

1¼ *Antignate*.

5 m. on l. is Romano, a large town in the midst of a fertile district; it is the country of Rubini, the celebrated tenor, who built himself a handsome villa there.

Calcio, near the rt. bank of the Oglio, once a small and independent community, and still a flourishing place; on the opposite side of the river, on a rising ground, is *Urago d'Oglio*.

1 *Chiari*, a town of 10,000 Inhab., whose ruined walls mark its ancient importance. Many Roman remains are found here. The principal church is a building of considerable size. Much trade is carried on, especially in silk. 2¾ m. beyond Chiari is *Coccaglio*, on the rly. between Bergamo and Brescia.]

On leaving Treviglio the rly. runs parallel to the course of the Adda and Brembo, but at a distance of some miles, as far as Bergamo, through a country richly cultivated in mulberry plantations, especially on approaching the hilly region.

10 kil. *Verdello* Stat., near the large village of that name on the l. From here the hills behind Bergamo, and the Alps beyond, come finely into view, the line ascending gradually to

11 kil. *Bergamo* Stat.

BERGAMO. (*Inns*: the only ones are in the lower town; the Albergo d'Italia the best, obliging people, and a good restaurant; the trout of the Lake of Iseo is particularly good; La Fenice.) There are public conveyances to Lecco daily in 4 hrs.; to *Edolo* and the Val Camonica on Monday, Wednesday, and Friday, by Railway as far as Gorlago, and then, ascending by the Val Cavallina, the road passes by *Lovere* and *Breno*, and reaches Edolo the same evening, returning on the intermediate days: or the tourist may go from Edolo to Brescia without returning to Bergamo, on Tues., Thurs., and Sat.; to *Zogno* and *Piazza* in the Val Brembana daily.

Bergamo, which contains upwards of 38,000 Inhab., consists of an upper, the CITTA, and a lower town, the latter called the Borgo of *San Leonardo*, half a mile distant from each other. Travellers should not fail to visit the former, in which the most interesting objects are contained, the lower town being the seat of business.

The Città or old town of Bergamo, the *Pergamus* of ancient writers, stands upon a steep and lofty hill, one of the last spurs of the Alps towards the plain; two roads lead to it from the lower town—that from the Prato, good and lined with trees, easy of access to carriages, and that from the Piazza de' Mercanti, but steeper and more direct, both uniting at the huge Doric Porta di S. Giacomo.

The position of Bergamo caused it to be strongly fortified by the Venetians, the greater part of the walls, although dismantled, still standing, and now converted into beautiful boulevards, commanding views of extraordinary beauty and extent; the walk near the Porta S. Giacomo on the S. side of the town is particularly interesting in this respect, extending to the Alps and Apennines, over the plains of Lombardy, in which the steeples of Milan, Monza, and Cremona are so conspicuous objects: there are two principal gates—of S. Giacomo on the E., above which is the Rocca, now converted into a barrack; and the Porta di S. Alessandro on the W., over which rises the bastion once connected with the Castello, and which, commanding the town, was included in its outworks.

The houses of the *Città* are solid and lofty: narrow streets and narrower *vicoli*, the sides often joined together by arches. In every part of the *Città* are vestiges of the middle ages—pointed archways, cortiles surrounded by arcades upon massive columns, seen in perspective through the gateways. The *Città* is almost wholly inhabited by the Bergamase nobility, who keep themselves apart from the traders of the lower town. Amongst themselves they maintain the use of the Bergamase dialect, the most inharmonious perhaps of northern Italy.

Harlequin, according to the traditional cast of the ancient Italian drama, was a Bergamase, and the personification of the manners, accent, and jargon of the inhabitants of the Val Brembana.

The principal objects of interest in the upper town are included in a very limited space surrounding the great square, viz. the *Palazzo Nuovo* or *della Ragione*, the *Palazzo Vecchio*, and the *Public Library*; the ch. of *Sta. Maria Maggiore* and the *Colleoni* chapel opening out of it; the *Cathedral* and the ch. of *Santa Grata* in one of the adjoining streets. A few hours will suffice to see everything here, including an excursion to the hill of the Castello, which no one fond of fine scenery should omit to visit; all this may be done between the arrival and departure of two successive railway trains, by taking a carriage at the station.

The *Palazzo Nuovo* or *della Ragione* was erected from the designs of Scamozzi, and has never been finished, the only parts completed being the Doric portico and the left wing, on the front of which is a figure of B. Colleoni; this palace is now occupied by the municipal authorities and offices, and forms one side of the Piazza Maggiore; opposite to it stands the *Palazzo Vecchio*, or *Broletto*, resting upon 3 lofty Gothic arches, with a projecting *ringhiera;* in front of it has been placed a statue of Tasso, whom Bergamo claims for one of its citizens, as, although born elsewhere (Sorrento), his father was a native of the town, and compelled by proscription to leave it; the statue does not offer the most remote resemblance to the great poet. The Public Library fills the apartment on the first floor of the P. Vecchio; passing under one of its arches, we find ourselves in front of the ch. of *Santa Maria Maggiore* and the fine façade of the *Colleoni* chapel annexed to it.

Ch. of Sta. Maria Maggiore. A portion of it is in the early Lombard style, others more recent; the more ancient portion dates from 1134: the N. part was erected in 1360 by Giovanni di Campello: it is of black and white marble. The southern porch, elaborately worked, is surmounted by a turret containing a statue of a saint, whilst over the principal entrance is a statue of King Lupus, who in the middle ages enjoyed a great reputation at Bergamo. The interior of Sta. Maria Maggiore is rich in stucco decorations and paintings; the cupola in the form of an elongated octagon; the tribune and transepts supported on high Italo-Gothic arches. The only sepulchral monument worth noticing is that of an Archbishop de Longis (ob. 1317) in alabaster; a monument by the eminent Swiss sculptor Vela has been recently erected here to the celebrated composer Donizetti, a Bergamasc. To the rt. of the principal entry, upon the outer circular projection of a chapel, are remains of old frescoes of the early Lombard school, some supposed to be as early as the 14th centy. The sacristy, an octangular building, erected, as appears from the inscription, in 1430, is among the earliest examples of the introduction of the Roman or classical style in juxtaposition with Gothic. The dado has pointed arches, but the two upper stories are Composite, accurately worked. The campanile, which is upwards of 300 ft. in height, is one of the towers so conspicuous in the view of the *Città*. Adjoining Sta. Maria Maggiore, and opening out of it, is the *Capella Colleoni*, the sepulchral chapel of Bartolommeo Colleoni, the celebrated condottiere of the 15th centy.; the façade, which has lately been restored, is very beautiful, ornamented with different coloured marbles, most elaborately worked; in two round spaces are busts of Julius Cæsar and Trajan, with their pagan designation of Divus, strange ornaments for a Christian edifice; the bronze doors are modern; the windows are divided by candelabra stems, with varied capitals and arabesques, placed so close to each other that the apertures for light are narrower than the diameter of these columns. The interior of the Colleoni chapel has been painted chiefly by *Tiepolo*; there is a picture by *D. Crespi* of one of Colleoni's battles, and a Madonna with the infant Saviour, St. John, and St. Joseph, by *Angelica Kauffman*, but the principal ornament is the sepulchral monument of the founder (who died in 1475) by *Amadeo*. The bas-reliefs of Christ led to Mount Calvary, the Crucifixion and Entombment, and of the Nativity, Epiphany, and Annunciation, are very good; upon the urn above stands the gilt equestrian statue of the great Condottiere. The fine tomb of Medea Colleoni, the child of Bartolommeo, which formerly stood in the ch. of Basella on the Serio, has been recently removed to her father's chapel; several branches of the Colleoni family still exist in the province of Brescia, collaterally descended from Bartolommeo, whose principal possessions were situated on the Serio, near Malpaga, where he retired in his older days in almost regal splendour, the last of the great Italian leaders of that troubled period.

The *Duomo* has a fine cupola, a conspicuous object; and the proportions and general character of the building are good, but as a whole it has a bare, undecorated look. It was designed by *Antonio Filarete*, but has since been much altered. It contains several paintings, but of little interest. There is a curious and ancient Baptistery, said to be as old as the 5th centy.

Santa Grata is the church of a restored nunnery, which has been newly gilt and decorated. The altarpiece, by *Salmeggia*, 1623, represents the Virgin and several Saints, amongst them Santa Grata bearing the head of St. Alexander. This picture, considered as the masterpiece of the artist, was carried off to Paris. There are some handsome mosaics in this elegant little building.

San Spirito contains some paintings of interest. At the 4th altar on the l. a Holy Family with Saints, by *L. Lotto*, signed and dated 1521; 5th altar, an Ancona, in 10 compartments, by *A. Previtale*; at the 1st altar on l., St. John between Saints, one of the finest works of *Previtale*; and at the 2nd altar on the same side, an Ancona, in 10 compartments, by *Borgognone*.

Other churches are *Sant' Andrea.*— In the vaulting are frescoes by *Padovanino*—The Virgin and Saints, by *Moretti*. *Church of Sant' Alessandro in Colonna*—St. John the Baptist, by the younger *Palma*. *Church of San Bartolommeo*—A Virgin; one of the best works of *L. Lotto*. *Church of San Michele al Pozzo*—a Virgin and Child, by *L. Lotto*.

There is a grand view from the terrace of the Casa Terzi, one of the finest palaces in the upper city.

There is rather a good public library in the *Broletto*; and the *Accademia Carrera*, with a collection of paintings, lately enriched by *Count Lochi's* bequest of his gallery to his native town.

Bergamo contains some private collections of paintings—the Museo Sopi, the Albani, Camozzi, and Verdos Galleries.

The situation of the upper town of Bergamo is remarkably fine. A walk of less than half an hour will take the traveller to the hill of the Castello W. of it, by the road emerging from the Porta di S. Alessandro; the fortress which stood here is now in ruins, but the panoramic view from it will amply repay the trouble of the excursion; it embraces the course of the Brembo on the W., the plain of Milan, the Brianza, and the innumerable towers scattered over them, with the steeples of Milan, Monza, and, farther still, the Monte Rosa, and even Monte Viso, 152 m. off. The Apennines beyond the Po are well defined in clear weather, with Crema and Cremona in the foreground.

The lower town is the seat of business. In ordinary times it offers little to interest the traveller; it consists of two principal streets, that by which it is entered from Milan, from which another, in which are the hotels and principal shops, branches off to the Prato, a large open square, where the fair is held, and which contains the theatre, barracks, and the fine gate leading to Crema. An important fair is held here. It begins about the middle of August, and lasts a month. This mart, called the *Fiera di Sant' Alessandro*, which has been known to have been held since the 10th centy., is the Leipsic fair of northern Italy. It is not only a very large business, but also a great pleasure fair, to which the gentry of all the country about resort.

Bergamo is celebrated in the annals of music by the number of good composers which it has produced—amongst them Rubini (d. 1854) and Donizetti.

Neighbourhood of Bergamo. The country around is one of the most renowned in Lombardy for its silk, the great source of the wealth of its landed proprietors. The province contains some of the most beautiful landscapes in the Lombardo-Venetian territory. The soil is of the greatest fertility, and is exceedingly well watered, the river *Serio* being the main trunk of irrigation.

Some other pleasant excursions may be noticed. There are many fine feudal castles dotted about the country on all sides, memorials of the contests of the Guelphs and Ghibellines; such as the *Castello di Trezzo* upon the Adda, about 12 m. by the road to the S.W. of Bergamo, and others to the eastward, near the lake Isco. The

Santuario *d'Alzano*, 4 m. from Bergamo to the N.E., at the opening into the plain of the Val Seriana, has some fair paintings and sculptures.

"About 8 m. to the N. of Bergamo is the church of *San Tomaso in Limine*. It stands alone on the brow of a hill, from whence there is a beautiful view. Its extreme age is obvious from its external appearance, but it is still in good preservation, for which it is indebted to the excellence of its construction. No record of the date of *San Tomaso* has come down to our time. The evidence of style, however, places it among the buildings of the 7th century, during which this part of Italy was at rest, and a great zeal for church-building prevailed. The plan is nearly identical with that of *San Vitale* at Ravenna, a rotunda crowned with a cupola. The cupola is not supported by pendentives, but by the walls themselves, assisted by the lateral resistance of the arches of the wings. The pillars are stunted and thick, and their capitals exhibit the usual imagery of the Lombards: the manner of construction of the walls is in their style. The Lombards were fond of the circular or octagonal form, and employed it in their churches, as they did that of the Basilica. If the round form is to be adopted there can hardly be found a more graceful model than is afforded by *San Tomaso*."—*G. Knight.*

Travellers by the Stelvio or Splugen roads, who wish to reach Venice without passing through Milan, may conveniently take the road from Como to Lecco, and from the latter to Bergamo, which is heavy, and with long ascents and descents, but affords pleasing scenery. (See Rte. 19.)

[A pleasant excursion may be made from Bergamo to the lake of *Iseo*. A good road to *Sarnico*, which is situated at the S. end of the lake where the Oglio leaves it, turns off from the Rly. Stat. at Grumello, from which the distance to Sarnico is about 6 m. At less than halfway, near where the rly. crosses the Cherio, *Gorlago* is about a mile to the l. of the road, which has a church containing some valuable paintings, and a saloon painted in fresco by *Giulio Romano*, and now used as a hayloft. About 4 m. before reaching Sarnico, on the rt. of the road, is the old castle of *Calepio*, built in 1430, and finely placed on the steep banks of the Oglio. There is a poorish Inn at Sarnico. The lake of Iseo presents some beautiful scenery. The "Monte dell' Isola" rises boldly from its surface. It is very deep, and abounds in fish. The vegetation of the shores is rich, and the olive-tree flourishes in the more sunny exposures. Many towers, castles, and villas are dotted round its shores. The *Villa Fenaroli, at Tavernola*, on the W. shore, opposite to the Monte dell' Isola, commands a fine prospect of the lake and of the small town of Iseo on the opposite shore..

The lake of Iseo (Lacus Sevinus) is the fourth in size of the subalpine lakes of Lombardy, occupying an area of 22 Eng. m. It has the same elongated form as those of Como and Garda, and, like them, fills the bottom of a great trough or transverse valley. Its principal feeders are the rivers Borlezza and Oglio, that descend from the Alps through the Val Camonica, and its only exit is by the Oglio at Sarnico; it is 700 ft. deep in some parts, and its surface is 680 ft. above the level of the sea; near its centre is an island, about 1½ m. long, with two villages, Siviana and Peschiera. The climate of the shores of Iseo is nearly the same as that of the lakes of Como and Maggiore, but, from its greater elevation above the sea, of a more alpine character than that of the Lago di Garda. The town Iseo has extensive silk-works; it is said to owe its name to a temple of Isis. It is about 7 miles by the footpath along the shore of the lake from Sarnico to Iseo, which is the principal port on the lake, and from whence a steamer starts twice a day for Lovere, at 10 A.M. and 6 P.M., returning at 4 A.M. and 4 P.M., from May to September, taking about

2 hrs. to run the distance. There is a tidy Inn at Iseo, by the water-side, kept by Angelo Ferrari. At the foot of the mountain, nearly opposite to Iseo, to the northward, is *Predore*, where there are some plantations of orange and lemon trees.

Lovere may also be reached by a road which turns off to the l., out of the high road at Albano, about 5 m. from Bergamo, and passes through the baths of Trescorre, where there is a villa of Count *Gianforte*, and a chapel painted by *Lorenzo Lotto*. The principal ch. of Trescorre contains a good picture by *Salmeggia*. Hence the road runs up the Val Cavallina by the side of the Cherio torrent, and along the W. shore of two small lakes, Spinone and Gajano. The distance from Bergamo to Lovere by this road is about 26 Eng. m. (*Inn:* il Canone d'Oro, poor.)

Lovere is well known as the residence during several years of Lady Mary Wortley Montagu, who thus describes it in a letter to Lady Bute, her daughter, dated the 21st July, 1747:—" I am now in a place the most beautifully romantic I ever saw in my life; it is the Tunbridge of this part of the world, to which I was sent by the doctor's order, my ague often returning. I found a very good lodging, a great deal of good company, and a village in many respects resembling Tunbridge Wells, not only in the quality of the waters, which is the same, but in the manner of the buildings, most of the houses being separate at little distances, and all built on the sides of hills, which indeed are far different from those of Tunbridge, being six times as high: they are really vast rocks of different figures, covered with green moss or short grass, diversified by tufts of trees, little woods, and here and there vineyards, but no other cultivation, except gardens like those on Richmond-hill. —The fountain where we drink the waters rises between two hanging hills, and is over-shadowed with large trees that give a freshness in the hottest time of the day." In a subsequent letter she describes part of her residence:—

" I have been these six weeks, and still am, at my dairy-house, which joins to my garden. I believe I have already told you it is a long mile from the castle, which is situate in the midst of a very large village, once a considerable town, part of the walls still remaining, and has not vacant ground enough about it to make a garden, which is my greatest amusement. This spot of ground is so beautiful, I am afraid you will scarce credit the description, which, however, I can assure you shall be very literal, without any embellishment from imagination. It is on a bank, forming a kind of peninsula, raised from the river Oglio 50 ft., to which you may descend by easy stairs cut in the turf, and either take the air on the river, which is as large as the Thames at Richmond, or, by walking up an avenue 200 yards on the side of it, you find a wood of 100 acres, which was all ready cut into walks and ridings when I took it. I have only added 15 bowers, in different views, with seats of turf. They were easily made, here being a large quantity of underwood and a great number of wild vines, which twist to the top of the highest trees, and from which they make a very good sort of wine they call brusco. I am now writing to you in one of these arbours, which is so thick-shaded the sun is not troublesome, even at noon. Another is on the side of the river, where I have made a camp-kitchen, that I may take the fish, dress and eat it immediately, and at the same time see the barks, which ascend or descend every day to or from Mantua, Guastalla, or Pont de Vie, all considerable towns. This wood is carpeted in their succeeding seasons with violets and strawberries, inhabited by a nation of nightingales, and filled with game of all kinds, excepting deer and wild boar, the first being unknown here, and not being large enough for the other." More modern travellers do not agree in Lady W. Montagu's enthusiastic description of Lovere, and suppose she must have mixed up in it that of some other sites on or about the lake of Isco.

Lovere has two large churches with pictures, and a fine cenotaph by *Canova*, one of the repetitions of that of Volpato, erected by Count Tadini to his son, who was crushed by the fall of an arch. At some distance from Castro, about 2 m. to the S. of Lovere, on the shore of the lake, is a narrow abyss called the Orrido di Tinazzo, where the torrent precipates itself with a roaring noise. It is a very singular place. The road from Lovere to Bergamo is carried along it for several yards on arches; the water below is out of sight. To the N. of Lovere is the Val Camonica, through which the Oglio flows, and along which there is a good road as far as Edolo, near the head of the valley. (See *Handbook of S. Germany*, Rte. 231.)

The traveller who does not wish to return from Lovere to Bergamo will find a very fair road on the E. side of the lake, through the villages of Pisogne, Sale, and Sulzano, to Iseo, and which from thence joins the old post-road from Bergamo, 3 m. before reaching Brescia.]

BERGAMO TO BRESCIA.

The distance from Bergamo to Brescia is 30 m. through generally a fine country, crossing the several large water-courses descending from the Alps, which bring fertility with them to the plains at their base. Leaving the lower town by the long and dirty suburb of San Antonio,

[5 kil. from Bergamo by the Rly. the *Serio* is crossed, near the village of Seriate, with a large modern church.

A road branches off from here on the l., leading to the alpine *Val Seriana*, and another to the rt., to Martinengo and Romano, passing to *Malpaga*, whose castle, built on Roman ruins by Bartolommeo Colleoni, still retains its gateways and drawbridges; the inside is decorated with historical frescoes—one saloon filled with those by *Carianni*, a pupil of *Giorgione's*, representing the visit of Christian II. of Denmark to Bartolommeo, highly interesting for the costumes. 1½ m. between Malpaga and Martinengo is a curious belfry, rich in architecture and sculpture, and the celebrated *Rotonda of Ghisalba*, one of the masterpieces of Cagnola.

About 2 m. W. of Malpaga, on the other side of the *Serio*, is a chapel called *La Basella*, formerly containing a masterpiece by *Amadeo*, the sepulchral monument of Medea, only child of Bartolommeo Colleoni, which is now in the chapel of the family at Bergamo.] (See p. 232.)

5 kil. *Seriate Stat*. From this station we cross the plain between the last declivities of the Alps and the small detached range of hills of Monticelli on rt.; similar to that of Mont' Orfano between Como and Bergamo, and formed of the same conglomerate (p. 151): there are some picturesque ruins on its E. extremity.

7½ kil. *Gorlago Stat.*, not far from the Cherio torrent, descending from the Val Cavallina. A road strikes off here on the l. up this valley to *Lovere*, at the N. extremity of the lake of Iseo, passing by the smaller one of *Spinone*.

6 kil. *Grumello Stat*. From here the best road to Iseo branches off to *Sarnico* at its S. extremity, which is 6 m. distant. From Grumello the rly. runs in a more S. direction, crossing the rich plain of the Oglio. Before reaching the station at Palazzuolo the line crosses the latter river on a fine high bridge and viaduct, from which the view of the town at some distance on the rt., with the river flowing at the bottom of the valley far below, and of the high tower, which forms so conspicuous an object, is very fine.

4 kil. *Palazzolo* (*Stat.*). The town stands on both sides of the river, which runs in a depression below the surrounding country, and from its situation was an important military position in the wars of the Brescians and Bergamaschi; on both sides are considerable mediæval remains; on the W. an old black castle, now built into a church, and on the E. an extensive fortress, upon which

has been erected a very high modern bell-tower, surmounted by a statue of St. George, from which the view includes Milan, Cremona, &c. Beyond Palazzuolo we re-enter on the great plain extending to Brescia, the road running at the base of the insulated ridge of hills of *Calogne* and *Montorfano*, on the l., at the S.E. extremity of which lies

8 kil. *Coccaglio* (*Stat.*). The mountain above it (*Monte Orfano*, on which there is a church, and a convent higher up) commands a noble view. The traveller who can spare a couple of hours will be well repaid for walking up to its summit by the splendid panorama discovered from it.

Rovato, in the plain on l., the birthplace of the painters *Moretto* and *Richino*.

8 kil. *Ospedaletto*. (*Stat.*)

11 kil. BRESCIA (STAT.) : just outside the Porta San Nazzaro, on the S.W. side of the town. (*Inns:* Albergo Reale della Posta, in the Contrada Larga, fair ; il Gambaro, resorted to by Italian families. Stables in the inns here render them all disagreeable.) This is a fine and flourishing city, now containing 40,000 Inhab., and appearing very prosperous. "*Brescia l'armata*" has been anciently celebrated equally for the strength of her fortifications, the valour of her inhabitants, and the excellence of the arms and weapons here manufactured. The Brescians have not degenerated from their ancestors in bravery ; but the fortifications are dismantled and the manufacture of firearms in the adjacent alpine valleys has almost ceased in consequence of the opposition of the Austrian authorities.—Brescia has 5 gates : 1, Porta di S. Giovanni, leading to Milan —2, San Nazzaro, to the Railway-station and Crema — 3, San Alessandro, to Cremona—4, Torlunga, to Verona and Mantua—5, Porta Pile, to Val Trompia and the other mountain valleys. — Brescia was anciently considered as one of the most opulent cities of Lombardy, second only to Milan. But the capture of the city by Gaston de Foix, the "gentil Duc de Nemours," the nephew of Louis XII. (1512), inflicted a blow upon its prosperity from which it never recovered. When in pursuance of the League of Cambrai the French overran the Venetian states, Brescia fell like the rest of the Venetian possessions, but was recovered by the vigour of the Count Luigi Avogadro. The inhabitants detested the French, and the standard of St. Mark being hoisted the whole district was in a state of insurrection The castle, however, was still held by the French, and Gaston de Foix marched against Brescia with an army of 12,000 men, the flower, says the 'Loyal Serviteur,' of French chivalry. Amongst them was the "Chevalier sans peur et sans reproche," the celebrated Bayard, who, in the attack of the breach by which the French entered, received a wound which he thought to be mortal. The French poured in, and the city was taken by storm ; the Venetian troops made a desperate but ineffectual resistance in the "Piazza del Broletto" to which they retreated, and the inhabitants emulated the soldiers in valour. The city was given up to pillage, and the French, the "flower of chivalry," under the guidance of the "gentil" Gaston de Foix, truly termed by Sismondi the most ferocious of the chieftains who ever commanded an army, indulged during seven days in pillage, lust, and slaughter. The French boasted that 46,000 of the inhab. perished.

The spirit of the warfare may be illustrated by two celebrated passages in the history of the siege of Brescia, —the *escape of Tartaglia* and the *generosity of Bayard*. Amongst the crowds who vainly sought refuge in the churches was a poor woman of the lowest class with a child in her arms. The French chivalry cut at mother and child, and the boy received in the arms of his mother five sabre wounds ; his skull was fractured and his upper lip split In spite of this treatment he lived, yet the wound in his lip was so severe that he never fully recovered his speech ;

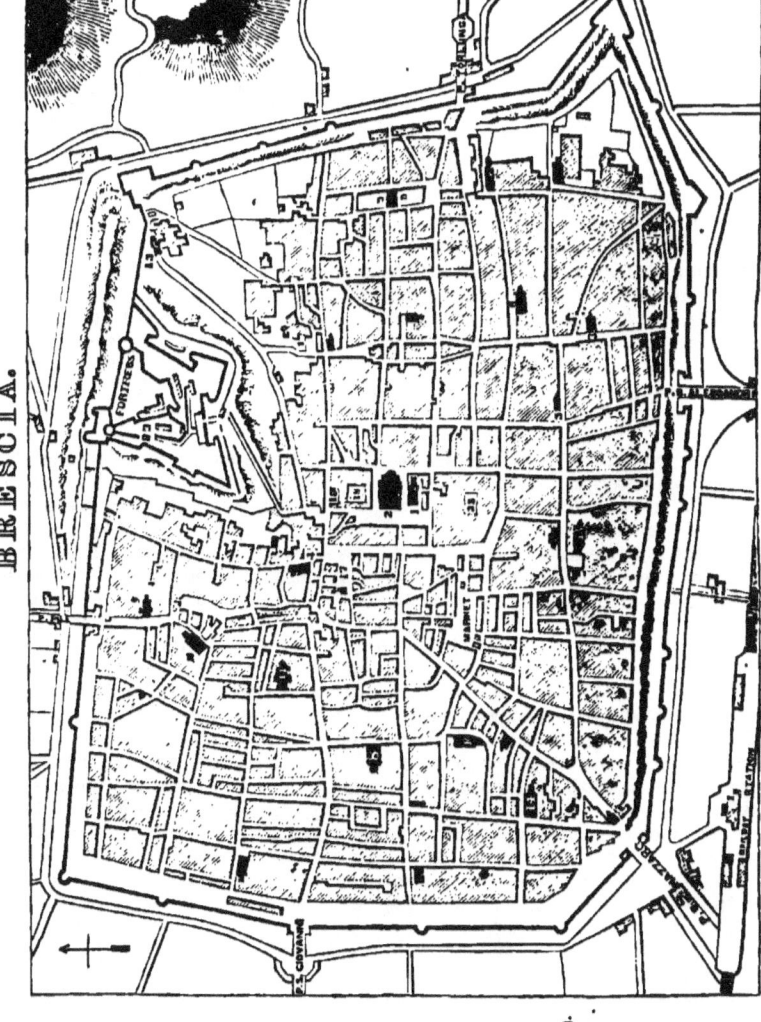

BRESCIA.

CHURCHES.
1. Duomo Vecchio.
2. Duomo Nuovo, Cathedral.
3. S. Afra.
4. S. Agatha.
5. S. Alessandro.
6. S. Barnaba.
7. S. Eufemia.
8. S. Domenico.
9. S. Faustino Maggiore.
10. S. Francesco.
11. S. Giovanni Ev.
12. S. Giuseppe.
13. S. Maria delle Grazie.
14. SS. Nazzaro e Celso.
15. S. Pietro.

PUBLIC BUILDINGS, &c.
17. Pal. Municipale.
18. Pal. del Broletto.
19. Biblioteca Quiriniana.
20. Museo Patrio (Antiquities).
21. Museo Civico (Pictures).
22. Theatre.

hence he was called *Tartaglia*, or the stutterer: but his memory has been preserved, not by the injuries which he shared with so many others, but by his talent as one of the greatest mathematicians of the 16th century.

With respect to Bayard, he was placed by 2 archers upon a door torn from its hinges, and carried to the best-looking house at hand, believed to be that of the Cigola family in the Giardini Publici, formerly the Mercato Vecchio. Its owner was "a rich gentleman who had fled to a monastery; but his wife and 2 fair daughters remained at home, in the Lord's keeping, and were hid in a hayloft under the hay." The mother, when she heard the knocking at the wicket, opened it, "as awaiting the mercy of God with constancy;" and Bayard, notwithstanding his own great pain, observing her piteous agony, placed sentinels at the gate, and ordered them to prohibit all entrance, well knowing that his name was a defence. He then assured the noble lady of protection, inquired into her condition, and, despatching some archers to her husband's relief, received him courteously, and intreated him to believe that he lodged none other than a friend. His wound confined him for 5 weeks, nor was it closed when he remounted his horse and rejoined the army. Before his departure, the lady of the house, still considering herself and her family as prisoners, and her mansion and whole property as the lawful prize of her guest, yet perceiving his gentleness of demeanour, thought to prevail upon him to compound for a moderate ransom, and having placed 2500 ducats in a casket, she besought his acceptance of it on her knees. Bayard raised her at the moment, seated her beside himself, and inquired the sum. He then assured her that if she had presented him with 100,000 crowns, they would not gratify him so much as the good cheer which he had tasted under her roof; at first he refused to take them, but upon her earnestly pressing him, and seeing " that she made the present with her whole heart," he requested permission to bid adieu to her daughters. "The damsels," says the 'Loyal Scrviteur,' "were exceedingly fair, virtuous, and well-trained, and had greatly solaced the good knight during his illness by their choice singing, and playing on the lute and virginals, and their much-cunning needlework. When they entered the chamber, they thanked him with deep gratitude as the guardian of their honour; and the good knight, almost weeping at their gentleness and humility, answered:—'Fair maidens, you are doing that which it is rather my part to do, to thank you for the good company which you have afforded me, and for which I am greatly bound and obliged to you. You know that we knight-adventurers are ill provided with goodly toys for ladies' eyes, and for my part I am sorely grieved not to be better furnished, in order that I might offer you some such as is my duty. But your lady mother here has given me 2500 ducats, which lie on that table, and I present each of you with 1000 in aid of your marriage portions; for my recompence I ask no more than that you will be pleased to pray God for my welfare.' So he put the ducats into their aprons, whether they would or no: then turning to the lady of the house, he said, 'These remaining 500 ducats I take, madam, to my own use; and I request you to distribute them among the poor nuns who have been pillaged, and with whose necessities no one can be better acquainted than yourself: and herewith I take my leave!' After having dined, as he quitted his chamber to take horse, the two fair damsels met him, each bearing a little offering which she had worked during his illness; one consisted of 2 rich bracelets woven with marvellous delicacy from her own beauteous hair, and fine gold and silver threads; the other was a crimson satin purse embroidered with much subtilty. Greatly did the brave knight thank them for this last courtesy, saying that such presents from so lovely hands were worth 10,000 crowns; then gallantly fastening the bracelets on his arm and the purse on his sleeve, he vowed to wear them both, for the honour of their fair donors, while his life endured; and so he mounted and rode on."

"The booty," says the 'Loyal Serviteur,' "was rated at 3,000,000 of crowns. Certain it is that the taking of Brescia was the ruin of the French cause in Italy: for they had gained so much that a great part of them returning home forsook the war, and were much needed afterwards at the battle of Ravenna." As for the unfortunate city, famine and pestilence followed the ravages of war, and the void of population has scarcely yet been replaced.

The inhabitants of Brescia, and especially of the neighbouring mountain valleys, have always been remarkable for their military spirit and bravery, which were again manifested during the political agitation of 1849. Upon the renewal, by the Piedmontese Government, of the hostilities which had been suspended by the armistice of the preceding year, a general rising of the people of Brescia took place, and putting at their head one of their fellow-citizens, Count Martinengo, they held the town for several days against the Austrian garrison in the castle above and a considerable force detached from Verona for the reduction of the town. The cannon of the besiegers, aided by the artillery of the fortress pouring shot and shell from the heights, at length compelled them to submit. The traveller as he goes through the town will see on all sides traces of the havoc committed by the cannon on its public edifices and palaces.

Brescia is pleasantly situated, and there are lovely views from the heights above the city. It is not far from the torrent Mella, the ancient *Mela*, noticed in the verses of Catullus.

" Brixia, Cycneæ supposita speculæ,
Flavus quam molli percurrit flumine Mela,
Brixia Veronæ mater amata meæ."

The Mela here mentioned is supposed to be the river of which Virgil speaks:—

". . . . . "tonsis in vallibus illum
Pastores, et curva legunt prope flumina
Mellæ."

Brixia is known to have become a Roman colony, but we are not informed at what period this event took place. It was also a municipium, as ancient inscriptions attest. Strabo speaks of it as inferior in size to Mediolanum and Verona.

The antiquities of Brescia were investigated in the 17th century by Rossi, who describes them in his *Memorie Bresciane*, but who trusted more to his fancy than to his observation. A tall Corinthian column was then protruding through the soil, and Rossi in his treatise gave the drawing of the whole temple to which it had belonged. The column escaped demolition, but no one paid much attention to it except *Girolamo Ioli*, who from a child was accustomed to wonder at the relic; and, mainly by his persuasion and exertions, the municipal authorities were persuaded to institute an excavation; the result was the discovery of the entire portico, and of much of the adjoining structure. The columns, with the exception of the one which so long declared the existence of the rest, are broken at various heights, but the portions remaining are very perfect, and so are the stairs and the basement, which are entirely in their original state. The latter is composed of upright blocks of marble, one block composing its whole height. The masonry indeed throughout is magnificent. The columns are elegant, both in proportion and execution, and good workmanship is visible in the sharply-cut capitals and mouldings which lie around. Where the outer casing is removed you may observe the bands of brick binding the structure. The architecture has many peculiarities, and, like almost every Roman building of the same period, shows that the architects considered themselves as by no means bound by such rules as those which Vitruvius has laid down. The building is called a temple, and is supposed from some fragments of inscriptions to have been erected or restored by Vespasian in the year 72 of our era, and dedicated to Hercules: but its form seems to indicate that it was intended for some other purpose, perhaps a court of justice; and it is not even certain whether the mutilated inscription upon which the conjecture is founded belonged to the building. Be this as it may, it is raised upon the foundations of an older structure, of which many vestiges may be seen in the passages and vaults included in the basement story. They have tessellated pavements, and the walls are of the "opus reticulatum," over which a fine and hard compact and polished stucco has been laid. Large portions of this remain quite perfect; it was painted in compartments as at Pompeii, and the colours are very fresh. When these passages were opened, the excavators discovered a heap of bronzes, some nearly whole, others broken, but none injured except by fracture, and which had evidently been deposited there all at one time—how or when, it is difficult to conjecture; but the most reasonable supposition is, that, when the emblems of paganism were removed by law from the temples, these were hidden by the adherents of idolatry, and forgotten in the dark vaults in which they were concealed.

The Museum of *Antiquities* (*Museo Patrio*) has been formed within the walls of this ancient building, to preserve these and other curiosities. The finest work in it is the bronze winged statue discovered in 1826, which, from its attitude, has been supposed to be either a Fame or a Victory. The shield under the left hand is a restoration; so also is the helmet upon which the left foot rests. The figure is rather larger than life. The head is encircled by a garland of laurel-leaves, inlaid with silver. The drapery and wings are executed with the greatest delicacy. When discovered the wings were found lying at the feet of the statue, evidently having been taken off for the purpose of better stowing the figure in its place of concealment. The head, the drapery,

N. Italy—1860.

the elegance of the limbs, are as fine as can be conceived. A reduction having been made from the statue, a copy was cast in bronze by the desire of the Emperor of Austria. It is erected at Culm. Found together with the Victory, and now in the same room, are six heads, with traces of gilding: one of them is supposed to represent the Empress Faustina. Also a small statue, fully gilt, representing a captive Barbarian. The workmanship is inferior to that of the Victory.

Portions of harness, with very fine figures in relief.

A female hand and arm, larger than life; very fine.

Many fragments of mouldings and ornaments, some gilt, all of great elegance; and probably decorations of the monument of which the Victory formed a part.

The Roman inscriptions in the museum are numerous. The citizens of Brescia began to preserve these remains at an early period; earlier indeed than any other city in Europe. By a special ordinance, passed in 1480, they required that all who, in digging or otherwise, might discover ancient inscriptions, should preserve them, and fix them on the walls of their houses, or place them where they could be the objects of study. The inscriptions thus brought together would form a large and curious volume: many are early Christian; one is to the memory of a certain Cecilia, who is singularly described as "Mater Synagogæ Brixianorum." There are good specimens of Venetian glass and Majolica ware, and several objects of *cinquecento* work, presented by liberal citizens of the town. The museum is open daily from 11 till 3.

There are several architectural fragments; some exhibit rich varieties of the composite. An Ionic capital with fine angular volutes supports a good Etruscan vase from Vulci, representing Hercules killing the Nemean lion in the presence of Minerva. Many other objects of interest are dispersed

M

over the museum:—votive altars and cippi; a portion of a beautiful mosaic pavement; specimens of pottery and articles of bronze. One apartment is devoted to mediæval antiquities: those of the Lombard era are interesting.—Several columns removed from the partly ruined ch. of Santa Giulia; fragments covered with runic knots, some apparently slabs and door-jambs, one the base of a cross; a runic cross bisecting an epitaph in Roman characters; the monument of a Count of Pitigliano.

Near these ruins are the supposed remains of a theatre. Not much is seen, as they are concealed by a private dwelling-house. Under another house, near the museum, in a kind of cellar, are some Corinthian columns, buried up to their capitals, and supporting architraves sculptured with foliage. These are conjectured to be parts of the Forum. Many other vestiges are found in other parts of the city. The *Monte di Pietà* contains several inscriptions and fragments built into the walls; and the columns and pavements dug up in various parts of the town attest its ancient magnificence. A folio volume of plates (62) of the most remarkable objects has been published and may now be had at the Museo; a second volume contains the inscriptions, which have been illustrated by Cav. Labus.

Brescia has two cathedrals. The *Duomo Vecchio*, also called the *Rotonda*, from its form, was built, according to some historians, between the years 662 and 671, by Marquard and Frodoard, two Lombard dukes, father and son, with the assistance of Grimoald King of the Lombards. Others attribute it to a Count Raymond, who governed Brescia under Charlemagne in 774. The walls are of stone; the circuit on the outside is divided by pilasters into 24 portions, surmounted by a brick cornice. Within there is a circular colonnade of 8 piers, bearing round arches, which support the dome, in conjunction with the outer circle of walls. The interior has been much altered; the presbytery and choir were added in the 13th and 15th centuries, and the lateral chapels as late as 1571. Some curious mediæval tombs are still left.—High up on the wall, over the 2nd chapel on rt., is the monument of Lambertus de Bononia, bishop of this see in 1349. A slabtomb covers the remains of Nicolo Durando, Archdeacon of Brescia in 1541; the effigies, in low relief, are expressive. The sarcophagus of Bishop Maggi is a good specimen of the style of the revival; by its side is the tomb of Cardinal Morosini, by Antonio Carra, a Brescian artist.

The best paintings in this cathedral are: 1st chapel on rt., *Pietro Rosa*, St. Martin dividing his Cloak with the Beggar.—*Bernardino Gandini*, the Guardian Angel. 4th chapel on rt., of the Sacrament, *Il Moretto*, Abraham and Melchisedec; the Last Supper; St. Luke and St. Mark; Elijah asleep; and Abraham and Isaac.—*Romanino*, the descent of the Manna, much injured. Over the high altar is a fine Assumption, by *Il Moretto*; the pictures of the Nativity of the Virgin and of the Visitation in the same chapel are by *Romanino*. Under glass is a Flagellation, attributed to Morone. A good *Giorgione* has been lately given by Count Averoldi; it represents the Nativity, and is hung on one of the pilasters of the Rotonda. In the chapel of the Santissimi Croci are two large paintings by *Cossali* and *Gandini:* the first represents the miraculous Apparition of the Cross to Constantine; the second " Duke Namo " delivering the ancient crosses, still preserved as relics in this chapel, to the magistrates of Brescia. The origin of these crosses is quite uncertain, inasmuch as the existence of Duke Namo rests only upon the authority of Ariosto and the romancers of the Dozepeers. Yet the curious casket in which they are enclosed bears unquestionable marks of respectable Byzantine antiquity. It represents Constantine and Helena, with their names in Greek letters. The crosses are known to have been in the possession of the citizens as far back as 1295. It is supposed by some authorities that they were brought from the East by Bishop Albert, who, between 1221 and 1226, was successively leader of the Brescian crusaders at the siege of Damietta, patriarch of Antioch, and apostolic legate in Syria. One of the crosses, indeed, is thought to have been the staff of his standard, but it seems much too small for any such purpose. In this chapel are also preserved the pastoral staff of St. Philasterius, Bishop of Brescia in 384, and several other relics. The statues of Faith and Charity near the pulpit are by *Alessandro Vittoria*. Under the cathedral is a subterranean ch. or crypt, entered by stairs near the 4th pillar on the rt., sometimes called the Basilica of St. Philasterius, supported by 42 marble columns: many of the shafts appear to be ancient: the capitals, which are Lombard, indicate an earlier style than the superincumbent structure. There are some very ancient frescoes on the walls—one, on that of the apse, of Our Saviour with Constantine and St. Helena, has been supposed to date from the 9th centy.; the other, in the small transept, of St. Michael and 3 bishops, from the 13th.

The *New Cathedral*, or *Duomo Nuovo*, was begun in 1604, from the designs of *Giovanni Battista Lantana*, on the site of the baptistery of S. Pietro di Dom., built by Queen Theodolinda, but the vault of the cupola was only closed in 1825. The dome, from the design of B. Mazzoli, a Roman architect, is said to be the *third* as to size in Italy; St. Peter's being the first, and that of the Cathedral at Florence the second. The architecture is fine. The Cathedral has some pictures by second-rate artists:—4th chapel on l., *Palma Giovane*, the Virgin, with San Carlo Borromeo and San Francesco; Bishop Marin Georgi, the donor, is introduced as a devotee. In the chapel (3rd on rt.) is the tomb or urn of S. Apollonius and S. Philasterius, bishops of Brescia, ornamented with bas-reliefs in three compartments, and in a good style of the 15th centy. The picture of the Assumption over the high altar is by Zoboli; the statues of SS. Philasterius and Gaudentius, the patron saints of the city, by *Caligari*; the bust of Cardinal Quirini by *Pincellotti*. The archives of the Canons are rich in ancient manuscripts. In the centre of the piazza, before the Duomo, is a fountain with an allegorical statue of the city, an armed female (Brescia armata), by *Caligari*.

Ch. of *Sta. Afra*, erected upon the site of a temple of Saturn. The present church dates from 1580, and is rich in frescoes and paintings. The latter were kept together at the period of the suppression of the collegiate establishment by the exertions of Canon Martinengo.—The frescoes of the roof are by *Bagnadore* and *Rossi*. — The great ornament of the church is, the painting of the Woman taken in Adultery, by *Titian*, near the 4th altar on l. The colouring is excellent. Whether this picture is entirely by *the* Titian has been the subject of considerable controversy; some have attributed it to his son *Orazio*: the prevailing opinion, however, now is, that it is by the father, and one of his best works. There are two or three repetitions of it in England.—*Paolo Veronese*: 2nd altar on l., the Martyrdom of Sta. Afra, over the altar, under which is the body of the saint, one of the finest pictures of the master. The severed heads of SS. Faustinus and Jovitus lie at the foot of the scaffold; that in front is the portrait of Paul Veronese himself, and is very fine. The picture has suffered from modern restoration. It bears the name of the artist, "Paolo Caliari, V. F."—*Tintoretto*: the Transfiguration, at the high altar. The lateral pictures of SS. Faustinus and Jovianus are by *Palma Giovane*; the dead Christ by *Baroccio*. Faustinus and Jovita, who so repeatedly appear in the Brescian paintings, were brothers of a Patrician family, who preached Christianity at Brescia whilst the bishop of the city lay concealed during the persecution. They suffered martyrdom, A.D. 121, by the command and in the

M 2

presence of the Emperor Hadrian. The Annunciation by *G. Rossi;* the Nativity under the organ by *Carlo Cagliari.—Bassano* (2nd chapel on rt.): the Baptism of Sta. Afra ; the rite is administered by torchlight by St. Apollonius, and Faustinus and Jovianus are distributing the Eucharist.—*Giulio Cesare Procaccini* (4th chapel on rt.): the Virgin, San Carlo Borromeo, and St. Latinus.—*Palma Giovane* (1st chapel on l.): the Martyrdom of St. Felix and his Companions—injured by restoration. This church is one of the most ancient in the city, and has sustained innumerable changes. One of the adjoining cloisters, in the style of Sansovino, is good: another is in an earlier one. The crypt is curious from its antiquity.

Ch. of *St. Agata,* supposed to have been founded by Queen Theodolinda. The walls and roof richly painted by *Sorisene* and *Ghitti.* Amongst many other paintings are:—*Foppa* the younger, the Adoration of the Magi, at the 1st altar on the l.; and over the high altar, the Martyrdom of S. Agata, by *Calisto da Lodi* (with St. Peter, St. Paul, Sta. Barbara, and St. Catherine below), the masterpiece of the artist, and a picture of great beauty.

Ch. of *S. Alessandro,* an ancient foundation, belonging to the order of the Servites, is now only remarkable for a painting of the Annunciation by *Fra Angelico da Fiesole,* painted in 1432, as appears from the books of the monastery, in which it is stated that the painter received 9 ducats for his labour, and 11 for the gold leaf employed on it.

Ch. of *San Barnaba,* erected on the site of a temple of Hercules: this is the tradition, and the remains found on the spot confirm it. It was founded in the 13th centy. by Bishop Maggi for the Friars of S. Augustin. It is now annexed to a foundling hospital. Paintings in 3rd chapel on rt.: *Palma Vecchio,* Sant' Onophrius the Hermit.—*Girolamo Savoldo,* the Shepherds at the Nativity; one of the best pictures of this little-known artist. The picture of the Martyrdom of S. Barnabas at the high altar is by *G. Panfilo.*—In an upper apartment, formerly the Library, now a printing-office, are some good specimens of the elder Foppa, in particular a Last Supper.

Ch. of *S. Clemente* contains five paintings by *Moretto;* the best, perhaps only second to his Coronation of the Virgin at S. Nazaro, is the group of female saints known as the Five Virgins, in a chapel on rt.; the Assumption of the Virgin, with St. Clement and other saints, over the high altar; the Offering of Melchisedeck, and St. Jerome, at altars on the l. The painter is buried in this church; the bust over his tomb is by *San Giorgio.* There is a fine Nativity (dated 1524) by *Callisto da Lodi* in the Sacristy.

Ch. of *Il S. Corpo di Cristo.*—This church contains a very fine monument of the 16th century, of which the principal ornaments are Scriptural histories. It is supposed to contain the remains of Marcantonio Martinengo, a very able commander in the Venetian service, slain in a skirmish with the Spaniards, 1526.

Ch. of *San Domenico,* a fine building, of a single nave and richly decorated with frescoes.—They are by various hands, *Sandrini, Fiaminghino,* and *Giugno.* — *Romanino* (over the high altar): the Coronation of the Virgin with many Saints introduced: the colouring is excellent. — *Ghitti:* the Resurrection.—*Antonio Gandini* (2nd chapel on l.): the Crucifixion, with the three Maries: and in the next chapel, on the side wall, *Palma Giovane,* two large pieces; in one are introduced portraits of Pope Pius V., Philip II. of Spain, and the Doge Veniero, returning thanks for the victory gained by their combined fleets over the Ottomans at Curzola in 1571; the other is allegorical, and represents the deliverance of souls from purgatory by the virtue of papal indulgences. The altarpiece is by *Gandini.*

Ch. of *S. Eufemia* has over its high altar a good painting by Il Moretto of the Virgin and Child with SS.

Eufemia, Justina, and John the Baptist.

Ch. of *San Faustino Maggiore*, one of the oldest monasteries of Brescia. The bodies of St. Faustinus and St. Jovita were translated here in 843. Three years after, some monks of the then recent order of S. Benedict were placed in it, and they continued in possession of the monastery till its suppression by the French: the present building is of the early part of the 17th century, after the designs of *Calegari*. The walls and roof are covered with frescoes. The tomb of the Patron Saints, behind the high altar, by *Carra*, is fine of its kind, being of black and white marble in the heavy style of the 17th century. Amongst other pictures is an excellent Nativity, over the 2nd altar on rt., by *Gambara*; one of the largest and best of his oil paintings.—*Romanino*, the Resurrection, with Saints, in the next chapel.—*Gandini*, St. Honorius. The angels in the 1st chapel on the rt. are by *Monti* of Ravenna. In the cloisters adjoining is a vaulted passage with a good fresco by *Gambara*; and in the conventual buildings, now used as a college, a very curious picture by *Cossale*, representing the supposed miracle worked by saints Faustinus and Jovita when Brescia was besieged by Nicolo Piccinino, on which occasion they were believed to hurl back the cannon-balls of the enemy.

San Francesco, founded in 1254; but only a small portion of the original edifice remains, the W. front, which is Lombard, with a good rose window, and the bell-tower. Within its precincts the Brescians took the oath of fidelity to the republic of Venice, March 17th, 1421. Paintings:—over the high altar, *Romanino*, the Virgin and Child, surrounded by St. Francis, St. Anthony of Padua, St. Bonaventura, and St. Louis. —*Cossali*, the Immaculate Conception, and St. John the Baptist and St. Apollonia, in the 4th chapel on l.—*Moretto*, St. Francis, St. Jerome, and St. Margaret, dated 1530, in the 3rd chapel on rt.—*Francesco da Prato di Caravaggio*, the Marriage of the Virgin, dated 1547,

1st chapel on l.: great beauty of expression and colouring. The works of this painter are exceedingly rare.—In the 2nd chapel on rt. is a *St. Michael*, by *Gandini*, and a fresco, probably of the 14th century.

Ch. of *San Giovanni Evangelista*. This is the primitive church of Brescia, having been founded in the 4th centy. by St. Gaudentius; but it was rebuilt in the 16th. It contains many of *Il Moretto's* productions: (3rd chapel on rt.) the Massacre of the Innocents. The Nativity, and the Presentation in the Temple, over the door of the Sacristy, are by *Cossali*. Over the high altar a group, in oils, of the Virgin and Child, with St. John, St. Augustine, and St. Agnes, and in tempera SS. John the Evangelist, the Baptist, and Zacharias, the Almighty and a prophet above, are all by *Moretto*; the two prophets on the side doors by *Maganza*. —*Giovanni Bellini*, the Three Maries weeping over the Body of the Saviour (excellent), in the chapel of the *Sacrament* (4th on l.): in the same chapel are the competing pictures of Moretto and Romanino; to the former belong (on the rt.) the Fall of the Manna, Elijah, the Last Supper, two Evangelists, and the Prophets on the roof; to Romanino (on the l.), the Resurrection of Lazarus, the Magdalen in the House of the Pharisee, the Presentation of the Holy Sacrament, two Evangelists and Prophets on the roof; another by Romanino (1st chapel on l.), the Marriage of the Virgin, is considered one of his best works. —*Cossali*, an Apocalyptic Vision—a striking composition, over the door of the ch. In the Baptistery is a good picture of Saints adoring the Trinity, in the style of *Francia*.

Ch. of *San Giuseppe*. Paintings: —*Romanino*, the three Maries round the dead body of the Saviour at the 2nd altar, the Nativity at the 4th, and St. Catherine, S. Paul, and S. Jerome at the 8th.—*Moretto*, the Descent of the Holy Ghost, at the 3rd. On rt. St. Francis, the Virgin, and a portrait of the donor of the painting, at the 6th.— *Palma Giovane*, St. Anthony of Padua, at the 6th (on l.).—*Luca Mombelli*, St. Joseph and St. Sebastian, in the 1st on 1.—*Avogadro*, the Martyrdom of SS. Crispin and Crispinianus, at the entrance into the Sacristy. Lanzi cites this picture as his *chef-d'œuvre*.

Ch. of *S. Maria Calchera* has beneath the pulpit a painting of our Saviour with SS. Jerome and Dorothy by *il Moretto*; at the 3rd altar on rt. SS. Apollonius, Faustinus, and Jovita, by *Romanino*; over the high altar the Visitation by *Callisto da Lodi*; and in the 1st chapel on l. a painting of Jesus and the Magdalen by *il Moretto*.

Ch. of *Santa Maria delle Grazie*, successively tenanted by the Umiliati, the Hieronymites, and the Jesuits. Curiously ornamented with very rich compartments of gilded stucco work, and ample frescoes by *Antonio Gandini, Fiamminghino, Morone, Pilati, Rossi*, and *Rama*. Other paintings:— *Pietro Rosa*, St. Barbara kneeling before her Father in Expectation of Death, scarcely inferior to Titian (in 1st chapel on rt.).—*Moretto*, the Nativity, over the high altar, an excellent picture; and St. Antony of Padua at the 4th, and SS. Roch, Sebastian, and Martin at the 7th altar, by the same.—*Ferramola* (1st chapel on l.), the Virgin and Child.—*Gandini sen.*, the Purification, and the Nativity by *C. Procaccini*, in the 6th chapel on l. There is a good modern painted glass window over the entrance. Attached to the ch. are a small cloister and a chapel, both hung round with votive offerings of every kind for favours received from the Virgin.

Ch. of *SS. Nazaro e Celso*, near the gate of the same name, at the S.W. extremity of the city. A suppressed collegiate establishment. The church was rebuilt in 1780; and as an edifice is not remarkable, but it is very rich in paintings. The picture behind the high altar, by *Titian*, consists of five distinct subjects, but united into one composition, and executed when he was in the full vigour of his powers.—The Annunciation forms the subject of the first and second pictures above.—The central one represents the Resurrection; the subject being spread over the compartments on either side. Amongst the figures the painter has introduced, in the lower compartment on the left, the portrait of Altobello Averoldo, by whom the picture was presented to the church, together with the patron saints, St. Nazaro and St. Celso, in armour;—on the other side is St. Sebastian, a magnificent figure, and in the distance St. Roch healed by the Angel; the introduction of these two Saints probably showing that the painting was a votive offering after a pestilence: at the foot of the column to which the saint is bound the painter has subscribed his name and the date of the work—"Ticianus faciebat, MDXXII." Another very fine painting is the Coronation of the Virgin, by *il Moretto*. It is in the 1st chapel on l., our Lord in the Clouds crowning the Virgin, above, with St. Michael the Archangel, St. Joseph, St. Nicholas, and St. Francis, below; the whole picture is beautifully harmonious in light and colour; the head of St. Nicholas is perfectly angelic. The Redeemer and the Angels, bearing the instruments of the Passion, in the 3rd chapel on rt., is also by *Moretto*. The other paintings are—the Nativity, with SS. Nazzaro and Celso, by *Moretto* (2nd chapel on l.).—*Gandini*: St. Roch.—*Foppa* the younger: Martyrdom of the Patron Saints.—And, near the side doors, *Romanino*: the Adoration of the Magi. In the sacristy are paintings by *Foppa* the younger, of the Annunciation; of the Nativity of the Virgin in tempera, by *il Moretto*, and a Sta. Barbara, with the Donatorio, P. Duca, by *L. Gambara*.

Ch. of *San Pietro in Oliveto*, at the N.E. extremity of the town, beyond the fortress, altered and partly rebuilt by Sansovino. Successively possessed by the Celestines, by the canons regular of the order of the Beato Lorenzo Giustiniani, and by the Carmelites, it was afterwards used as a chapel of the ecclesiastical seminary, but, the latter having been converted into a barrack, admission is now obtained with difficulty. It is rich in specimens of the Brescian school.—In the sacristy, *Foppa the elder*, St. Ursula, St. Peter, and St. Paul, upon gold grounds; and in 2nd chapel on l., *Vincenzio Foppa*, Our Lord bearing the Cross, considered as the *chef-d'œuvre* of this artist.—*Moretto*, at the high altar, a singular but fine composition; above are the Virgin and the Trinity, between Justice and Peace; below, St. Peter receiving the Keys, and St. Paul a tablet, signifying his commission to preach the Gospel. Over the first altar on the rt. is an allegorical composition—St. John the Evangelist and the Beato Lorenzo Giustiniani listening to the Advice of Wisdom; and over the confessionals 2 paintings by the same of the Fall of Simon Magus, and of St. Peter and St. Paul.—*Ricchino*, 4 large subjects from the life of Moses, in the choir.

Ch. of *San Salvatore*, annexed to the monastery of St. Michael and St. Peter. This noble building, in the form of an ancient Basilica, was erected by Desiderius King of the Lombards, in the middle of the 8th century, and is now turned into a military store. There is a curious crypt beneath the choir, with frescoes by *Romanino* and *Foppa*. The monastic buildings no longer exist.

Besides the above-mentioned churches, all of which possess many more paintings than we have noticed, there are several others containing objects worthy of notice.

Palazzo della Municipalita or *La Loggia*, in the Piazza Vecchia. Several of the first architects of the 15th and 16th centuries have successively worked upon this beautiful building, which was intended for the palace of the municipality, or town-hall. The decree for its erection was passed in 1467; but it does not appear to have been commenced until 1492. Although some have attributed the first design to Bramante, it appears that Tomasso Formentone was the architect who raised the edifice to the first floor. It was continued by Sansovino, who erected the second, and completed by Palladio, who finished the windows; yet the rich, varied, cinquecento style predominates, and it is one of the finest specimens of the kind. The general outline is that of the old Lombard town-hall: 3 rich arches form the ground-floor; an arcaded court is seen receding beneath them. Above is the council-chamber, with the projecting *Ringhiera* towards the piazza: an open staircase is on the side of the building. The order is a fanciful composite; the pilasters and friezes are covered with rich-sculptured scalework, foliage, and capricci, in the style of the baths of Titus. The entrance to the lower chambers is a small triumphal arch, composed, like the whole building, of the richest marbles.

The exterior is covered with sculpture. The fine series of medallions, representing Roman emperors in borders of coloured marble, are by *Gasparo di Milano* and by *Antonio della Porta*. The fanciful candelabra trophies by *Fostinello, Casella, Colla, Martino della Pesa*, and *Giovanni da Lugano;* Justice, and Saints Faustinus and Giovita, by *Bonometti;* Faith, by *Frederico da Bagno*—all artists of high merit, though their reputation is lost amidst the greater names of Italy. The magnificence of the interior originally fully corresponded with the outside; but, on the 18th of January, 1575, the whole was in flames. The proclamation issued by the governor attributed the fire to design. But it was believed at the time that the real instigators were in the Palace of St. Mark, and that the illustrious Signoria had paid the incendiary. The motive attributed for the act was the wish to destroy certain charters of liberties granted to the Brescians by the emperors, and confirmed by the republic. Some very fine paintings by Titian were destroyed by this fire. The beautiful façade suffered from the bombardment by General Haynau in April 1849, the marks of several cannon-balls being still visible. In the great but neglected chambers used for business there were some paintings which have been removed to the Museo *Civico*, where they are at present deposited.

The *Torre del' Orologio*. This tower rises upon a picturesque portico and arch. It is a fine structure, and has an enormous dial, with the numbers from 1 to 24. It marks the course of the sun and the moon; and two men of metal, as at old St. Dunstan's, strike the hours. It was put up in 1522.

The *Torre della Pallata*: this tower is also called *Torre dei Palladini*. Antiquaries differ about the derivation of these names. It is a fine and perfect specimen of castellated architecture, with a great projecting base and lofty battlements: it now serves as the town belfry. At the base is a fountain (1596), from the designs of Bagnadoro, the sculptures by Boncsino and Carra.

The *Broletto*, near the Cathedral, the ancient palace of the republic, is a huge pile of brick. A tower, called the Torre del Popolo, rises at the S. corner of the building, surmounted by a rude belfry and deeply-cleft Italian battlements. Some of the terracotta ornaments in the great court are very beautiful, particularly on a great circular window. The arcade or corridor is supported by round and pointed arches. The style is characteristic of the times in which it was erected, between 1187 and 1213. Here, as everywhere in Brescia, the armorial bearings were very wantonly effaced in 1796. Before the invasion of the French the interior contained excellent paintings, and many objects of historical interest; but the best were sold, others destroyed, and the Broletto turned into a barrack. It is now employed for public offices and prisons. One fine chamber retains its paintings on the ceiling; the subjects are from the Apocalypse, by *Lattanzio Gambara;* Venice triumphant, and St. Nicolas of Bari, by *Gandini*.

The *Biblioteca Quiriniana*, near the Broletto, was founded about 1750 by Cardinal Quirini, a diligent cultivator and munificent encourager of literature. To him we owe the collection of the works of Cardinal Pole, so useful as documents for the history of England. Here he placed his most ample collections, adding a noble endowment, which is partly employed in increasing the library, which now contains upwards of 30,000 volumes, including many early printed books and curious manuscripts, besides objects of antiquity. A few may be noticed:—The *Evangelerium*, or copy of the Gospels, according to the ancient Italian version, written in gold and silver upon purple vellum, of the 9th century. The *Codice Diplomatico Bresciano*, consisting of various charters from the 9th to the 11th century, formerly in the archives of the monastery of *Santa Giulia*. A Koran, upon cotton paper, of early date and great beauty. The "Croce Magna," set with ancient gems, called also the Cross of Galla Placidia, from having on it miniatures of that Empress and of her children Honoria and Valentinian III.; it is supposed to be of the 5th centy., and belonged also to the convent of St. Giulia. Four valuable ivory diptychs—the first in honour of Manlius Boetius, who became consul in 510, and who was the father of the celebrated Severinus Boetius: on the back are some curious Christian miniatures of the 6th centy., representing the Raising of Lazarus, and 3 Saints: on one side the Consul is represented in his consular robes; on the other presiding at the games of the Circus. Another diptych of Lampadius, consul A.D. 530: he also is represented as presiding at the games. A third, called the *Dittico Quiriniano*, is said to have belonged to Pope Paul II., afterwards passing into the possession of the Cardinal, with mythological subjects—Paris and Helen on one side, and a group of Paris and Helen crowned by Love on the other. Many have suspected that it is of comparatively recent date: the workmanship at all events is beautiful. The *Lipsanoteca*, a series of sculptured ivory plates, which formed a box in the form of a cross, to contain relics; the bas-reliefs represent subjects of the Old and New Testaments, and are referred to the 4th or 5th century. There is much doubt, however, as to the origin of this piece of antiquity. There are a few paintings in this library:—*Titian:* the Virgin, painted on a slab of lapislazuli. *Zuccarelli:* Saint Jerome taking care of Orphans. A very extensive collection of engravings, both wood and copper, from the first invention of the art, formed by Count Martinengo, and bought by the government for the library. The Biblioteca Quiriniana contains about 200 manuscripts, amongst which the Codex Eusebianus of the 11th centy., with miniatures, the Liber Poteris Brixiæ, containing the proceedings of the Municipality of Brescia during the 11th, 12th, and 13th centuries, and the *Statute Bresciane,* interesting for local history between 1200 and 1385.

Galleria Tosi, or *Museo Civico.*—This handsome palace, with the large collections contained in it, have been recently bequeathed to his native town by one of its distinguished citizens, Count Tosi, well known for his taste and patronage of the arts; the gallery is now therefore public, and the property of the municipality. It is extremely well arranged, and distributed over ten rooms; there are good hand catalogues in each (indeed the names are marked on many of the pictures), we shall therefore only notice the most remarkable. At the top of the stairs are two busts by Monti of Ravenna—one of Count Tosi, and another of Galileo; and on the walls some large pictures of the Brescian school, formerly in the Palazzo della Municipalita—a Holy Family and an Ecce Homo, by *il Moretto;* Christ bearing his Cross, by *Foppa;* 2 historical pieces by *Campi,* &c. In this gallery the most remarkable work is the celebrated *Pieta,* by *Raphael,* formerly belonging to the Mosca family of Pesaro, and which was purchased by Count Tosi for 24,000 francs—a small picture, charmingly executed, and admirably preserved: it represents our Saviour crowned with Thorns, with one of those fine masculine Italian faces of fair complexion which we sometimes meet among the peasantry of the Apennines: it was painted about 1505. A Holy Family, by *Frà Bartolommeo,* once belonging to the Salviati gallery; a Holy Family, by *Andrea del Sarto;* a good Battlepiece, by *Borgognone;* Venus attired by the Graces, by *Albani.* The Nativity, by *Lorenzo Lotto,* the Angels and Virgin being portraits of the Gussoni family, for whom it was painted; a Madonna, by *Francia,* and another by *Giulio Romano;* a portrait of Henri III. of France, by *Clouet;* a drawing of the Rape of the Sabines, by *Polidoro da Caravaggio;* a Madonna, by *Simone da Pesaro;* St. Francis, by *An. Caracci.* There are several portraits by *Morone, Titian, Tintoretto,* &c. In a small cabinet there is a collection of ancient and modern drawings by Raphael (?), Giulio Romano, Guercino, Appiani, Palaggi, Bossi, &c. Among the modern works are two Landscapes by *Massimo d' Azeglio;* one, the Uomo di Ferro of the Orlando; a Choir of Friars, by *Granet;* a composition by *Hayez,* representing the departure of the Exiles from Parga; a picture of Sir Isaac Newton studying the effects of light on soap bubbles, by *Palaggi;* Tasso reading the Gerusalemme at the Court of Ferrara, by *Podesti;* and Count Ugolino, by *Diotti,* &c. A long gallery is hung with engravings from the best masters; at the extremity of which is a chapel, with a fine statue of Christ disputing with the Doctors, by *Marchesi,* over the altar. There are also some illuminated MSS. by *G. Libri.* In different parts of the palace are works of sculpture; a young Bacchus, by *Bartolini;* bas-reliefs of Ganymede, and of Night and Morning, by *Thorwaldsen;* a bust of Eleonora d'Este, by *Canova;* copies, by *Gandolfi,* of Canova's bust of himself, and of his bust of Napoleon; and Pampaloni's lovely statue of a Child praying, so well known by its numerous copies. The bronzes and objects of *virtù* have been removed to the Museo Patrio, and the medals, coins, &c., to the Biblioteca Quiriniana.

M 3

Brescia contains some good private collections of pictures.

Galleria Averoldi (Contrada di S. Carlo, No. 1715). The Palazzo Averoldi was built in 1544, and the family have been long distinguished as cultivators and protectors of art. Amongst the pictures are fine portraits by *Morone*, *Paris Bordone*, *Callisto da Lodi*, *Girolamo Savoldo*, *Romanino*, *Richino*, &c.; landscapes by *Paul Brill* and *Tempesta;* and by *Titian* a Virgin with two Saints, probably Faustinus and Jovita, by *Carpaccio;* this fine picture is signed and dated 1515 : a Virgin and Child, by *Giovanni Bellini;* several specimens by *Romanino*—the painter's own portrait, a Nativity, and a fine portrait of Gherardo Averoldi, who contributed so materially to the expulsion of the Milanese in 1426 ; a Holy Family, by *Salaino;* and several *Morettos*, &c. In the house of another member of the Averoldi family (Contrada del Lauro, No. 1848) is the celebrated *Ecce Homo* by Titian, a legacy of the painter to one of the family. There are, besides, pictures by *Romanino*, *Foppa*, and other Brescian painters.

Galleria Fenaroli (Contrada del Pesce, 2689), belonging to Count Fenaroli. A Holy Family, by *Cima da Conegliano;* the same subject with St. John, by *il Moretto:* St. Roch attended by the Angels, St. John the Evangelist, a Madonna and Child, by the same; a Magdalen, or, as some will have it, a Gipsy, by *Titian;* specimens of *il Moretto;* fine portraits and other pictures by *Morone;* portraits by *Velasquez*, *Vandyke*, *Giorgione*, &c.; landscapes by *Poussin*, *Tempesta*, *Sal. Rosa;* views of Venice, by *Canaletti;* the Adoration of the Magi, by *Paul Veronese*, *Callisto da Lodi*, *Guercino*, &c. Also several paintings by modern artists; amongst which Venturo Fenaroli dragged to prison, from the ch. of il Carmine, in 1511, by *Hayez;* and specimens of sculpture by *Thorwaldsen*, *Tenerani*, &c.

The *Galleria Erizzo Maffei* (Contrada delle Grazie, No. 2731). The pictures in this palace once formed a part of the Fenaroli Gallery. The best are : a Martyrdom of St. Catherine, and a Madonna with 3 Saints, by *Romanino;* St. Agnes, and a portrait of a Man holding a Book, by *Moretto;* the Fates, by *Tintoretto;* Ecce Homo, by *Cesare da Sesto;* a Crucifixion, by *Bassano;* and Andromeda, attributed to Titian.

Casa Brozzoni, Via di San Francesco, No. 1977, contains some good modern pictures : Jacob and Esau by *Hayez;* a hunting scene by *Massimo di Azeglio;* a Magdalen by *Palaggi;* the Flight of Bianca Capello by *Appiani;* and a view of the Piazza di S. Marco at Venice, the last work of *Migliara*. There are also some paintings of the Brescian and Venetian schools, and the Mazzuchellian collection of coins and medals.

Among the palaces of Brescia the following are most worthy of notice :—

Palazzo Martinengo Sant' Angelo, at the end of the Giardini Publici, now abandoned, having been nearly destroyed by the Austrian cannon in 1849.

Palazzo, or *Casa Ducco,* in the Contrada di S. Antonio, has a fine gateway surrounded by bas-reliefs of military ornaments, a man on horseback crossing a bridge, said to be Bart. Colleoni, forming the central one.

The gay external decorations of the houses of Brescia form, or rather formed, a peculiar feature of the city ; but they are rapidly disappearing, from time and from neglect. In the *Strada del Gambaro* are some curious frescoes, on which Romanino was first employed; but *Gambara* having married his daughter, Romanino transferred the order to his son-in-law as part of the young lady's fortune. They represent various classical subjects :—the Rape of the Sabines ; passages from the Iliad ; Æneas and Dido ; Europa and Jupiter ; the Continence of Scipio ; Mutius Scævola ; Lucretia ; Asdrubal at the feet of Scipio ; and some others, with a great variety of accessary ornaments, showing wonderful fancy, and, though less grace, yet perhaps even more originality, than exhibited by

Pierino del Vaga in decorations not dissimilar in character.

In the *Corso de' Mercanti* is a house covered with frescoes by *Gambara;* the subjects are allegorical, and seem to represent the three principal stages of life, youth, manhood, and age. *Contrada della Loggia,* also allegorical, by the same artist: these have been nearly all whitewashed.

"A whole street, *Il Corso del Teatro,* has the fronts of the second-floor story painted with a series of scriptural, mythological, and historical subjects, attributed to the Cavaliere Sabatti. They have suffered much owing to their exposure to the weather, but the warm colours have remained, and in many portions are thoroughly well preserved. Some of the actions of the figures in these subjects, judging from their remains, are very grand, and equally so is the style in which they were drawn; many of the deep but brilliant lake tones are worthy a Venetian."—*S. A. Hart, R.A.*

Palazzo Martinengo Cesaresco, 358, Contrada S. Brigida, near the Museum, is remarkable for its fine architecture, probably by *Lud. Beretta,* the figures on the sides of the entrance by *Jacopo Medici,* a pupil of Sansovino's.

Palazzo Martinengo della Fabrica, an extensive and sumptuous edifice, with a fine gate entrance; one chamber is painted by *il Moretto.*

Palazzo Cigola, near the *Giardini Publici,* a good specimen of domestic architecture. It is supposed to have been here that the wounded Bayard was so hospitably received in 1512.

The *Citadel* or *Fortress* of Brescia occupies the summit of the hill round the sides of which the town is built, and is supposed to stand on the site of the *Specula Cydnea* of Catullus, erected by the Viscontis in the 14th century, it was much strengthened by the Venetians, and in later years by the Austrians, so as to completely command the city; it was from it that the notorious Gen. Haynau so barbarously bombarded Brescia in 1849.

The *Campo Santo* is well worth a visit, as one of the earliest establishments of the kind in Italy, and worthy of imitation in our own country; it is situated a short way outside the Porta di S. Giovanni, leading towards Milan on the l., and is approached by a fine allée of cypresses. Vantini, a native of Brescia, was the architect, in 1810, and deserves the greatest credit for having originated, and with great taste, the first of these useful foundations in Italy. The *Campo Santo* consists of a semicircular area in front, surrounded by tombs, and a row of cypresses. From this outer area two gates lead into the inner cemetery, between which is a very handsome chapel with a Doric portico, having over the altar a good statue, by *Gandolfi,* of the Angel Gabriel ascending to heaven, and over the cornice busts of the different saints of Brescian origin. On either side of this chapel, under the porticos which flank it, are the sepulchral vaults of the principal families of the province. The monuments of the Countess Erizzo Maffei, of the Countess Martinengo Cesaresco di Barco, and of Count Tosi, the patriotic founder of the Museum that bears his name, are deserving of notice; the two first are by San Giorgio, the last by Monti of Ravenna. The cemetery is kept in admirable order; the poorer classes have each a head-stone, of an uniform shape and size, with a number attached for more easy reference, the cost of which, including all charges for burial expenses, only amounts to about 6 francs. The high pyramidal monument in the centre is to *Bossini,* a benevolent curate of Brescia.

Plan for visiting in topographical order the principal Sights at Brescia. —This can scarcely be done in one day; the artist will find ample occupation for three or four.

Duomo Vecchio; Cathedral; Broletto; Biblioteca Quiriniana; Museo Patrio; Galleria Tosi; Ch. of S. Pietro; Citadel; Chs. of *S. Faustino Maggiore,* of *S. Giovanni Evangelista,* of *S.*

Francesco; Pal. Municipale; Chs. of *SS. Nazzaro e Celso,* S. Alessandro, *S. Afra, S. Barnaba,* and S. Eufemia; *Giardini Publici; Galleria Feneroli* and *Erizzo Maffei; Campo Santo.*

There are diligences from Brescia to Gargnano on the Lago di Garda daily at 8 A.M., arriving at 2 P.M., in time for the afternoon steamer, which calls there on its voyage from Peschiera to Riva (see p. 257); and to Edolo in the Val Camonica, on Mon., Wed., and Fri. at 5 A.M., passing by *Iseo, Pisogne,* and *Breno,* returning to Brescia on the intermediate days. Fares to and from Edolo, 9 lire; by this conveyance the traveller can visit the eastern shores of the Lago d' Iseo. To Cremona at 6 a.m. in 6 hrs.

BRESCHIA TO PESCHIERA.

The *Station* at Brescia is immediately outside the *Porta Sant' Nazaro,* from which the Rly. runs parallel to, and at a short distance on the rt. of the post-road, through a very rich and fertile country at the foot of the last declivities of the Alps; 3 trains daily each way as far as Desenzano, 2 of which continue to Peschiera only.

9 kil. *Rezzato Stat.* Cross an extensive plain for 6 miles to

8 kil. *Ponte San Marco Stat.*, on the Chiese, which empties the Lake of Idro: roads lead from this station to Salo and Gargnano on the l., and to the large villages of Monte Chiaro and Castiglione on the rt. After crossing the Chiese, *Monte Chiaro* is seen on the eastern acclivity of the hills on the rt., and a continuous ascent of 4 m. brings us to

7 kil. *Lonato* (*Stat.* S. of the town), which is situated on the summit level of a range of hills that separate the plains bordering on the Chiese from the Lago di Garda, and which extend to Castiglione and Volta. There is a large church with a dome in the centre of the town, and a high square mediæval tower, which command a fine view over the lake of Garda; and towards Verona are considerable remains of mediæval walls, which, seen from the road to Desenzano, form very picturesque objects in the landscape. Lonato is celebrated in the early military career of Napoleon as the scene of one of his most brilliant actions. Here, on the 3rd Aug. 1796, he defeated the rt. wing of the Austrian army commanded by Marshal Wurmser, following it up two days after by the still more decisive battle of Castiglione, which at the time sealed the fate of the Austrians in Italy.

Leaving Lonato, the rly. at first passes through very deep cuttings in the gravel-beds, and through a short *tunnel*, about 1½ m. beyond which we reach the *viaduct* of Desenzano, a bridge consisting of 15 pointed arches, a strange fancy of the Austrian engineers—the cause, probably, of the insecurity of this great work; it is built of red Verona marble. Before arriving at the viaduct the lake first bursts on the traveller; nothing can be more magnificent than the panorama on the l. from this spot; below us, Desenzano with its mediæval castle; further on, the long sandy spit of Sermione terminated by its Scaligerian fortress; and beyond, the Monte Baldo towering over the N.E. shores of the lake of Garda, with the hilly region between the latter and the Adige, covered with towns and villas. Immediately after crossing the viaduct we arrive at

4 kil. *Desenzano Stat.*, nearly a mile from the town and the shores of the lake, and at some elevation above the latter. Omnibuses are in waiting on the arrival of each train. The North Italian custom-house station is here, where luggage is examined on arriving from the Austrian provinces beyond the Mincio.

Desenzano. (*Inns:* Albergo Imperiale, not over clean; and Posta Vecchia: both overlooking the lake, and indifferent.) The town of Desenzano, which contains a Pop. of 5000 souls, is situated on the shores of the lake; immediately above rises a fine old castle, which in mediæval times commanded the road between Brescia and Verona. Desenzano will be the point from which the island or promontory of Sermione can be most easily visited. The distance by water is 5, and by land between 6 and 7 m. In fine weather the row across will occupy 1¼ hr.

" Peninsularum Sirmio insularumque
Ocella, quascunque in liquentibus stagnis,
Mari vasto fert, uterque Neptunus."
—CATULLUS, *Peninsulæ Sirmionis laudis.*

" Salve, o Venusta Sirmio ——." *Ib.*

The Peninsula of Sermione, which is now virtually an island since the cutting of the ditch which separates it from the long sandy spit at the extremity of which it is situated, is well worth a visit; it consists of a ridge of limestone, having at its S. extremity the village and the picturesque castle, which forms so fine an object of the landscape of the Lake of Garda, and at the N. point some very extensive Roman ruins, which tradition has attributed to the Villa of Catullus. There is an Osteria, *La Scaligera,* in the village, where the tourist, if inclined to prolong his stay, will find a decent bed and tolerable fare. The village is entered by a drawbridge and a mediæval gate on the S. On the opposite side is a fortified wall that separates it from the N. portion of the island, and through which opens the only gate in that direction. The old castle, in the form of a quadrangle, with a high square tower, was entered on the side of the N. by a drawbridge. This entrance is still well preserved, as well as its small port or *darsena,* surrounded by crenelated battlements; but the principal entrance is now on the side of the village by a gate over which are shields bearing the arms of the Scaligers, and which, having on each side the letters A. A., shows that the edifice dates from Alboino or Alberico della Scala, and was erected in the 14th cent. The castle, which belongs to the government, is tenanted by half a dozen soldiers, whilst the war-steamers of the N. Italian kingdom lie moored off it. In the village church there is nothing worthy of notice. There is a curious fragment of an early Christian bas-relief in the wall of a house adjoining. The town of Sermione is chiefly inhabited by fishermen. As the tourist proceeds into the interior of the island he will see under the gate a mutilated Roman altar dedicated to Jupiter, and a fragment of another inscription. The whole of the island is one extensive olive-garden, the olive-tree here flourishing luxuriantly, some of the trees attaining a size equal to those of the Lucchese or Roman territories. About the centre of the island is an old ch. dedicated to St. Peter, which contains some curious frescoes of the 14th or 15th centy., representing the Crucifixion, the Virgin and Child, St. George, &c. Proceeding from thence towards the N. extremity, we come upon an oblong square building, the walls of which are of Roman construction, called by the local cicerone the Baths of Catullus. A short way beyond this is a subterranean arched passage, and farther on a second one, but more extensive, which formed evidently the substructions of an extensive edifice, no trace of which remains above ground except a portion of the pavement of a court formed of bricks laid edgeways and diagonally. It is at the N. extremity of the island that the most extensive ruins exist, and which are really of Roman grandeur. They consist of massive pilasters and arches in a grand style of Roman masonry, formed of alternate layers of brick and of the slaty limestone of the locality. They evidently supported a very extensive edifice, the position of which is one of the finest on the whole Lake of Garda, commanding a view of a great portion of its N. prolongation into the mountains of the Tyrol, here wild and savage; the shores of the most fertile portion from Gargnano to Desenzano on one side, and from Torri and Pont St. Vigilio to Peschiera on the other; with the Monte Baldo, the gorge of the Adige, and the peaks above *Recoaro* in the background; whilst in the fore are the hilly region between the Adige and the Benacus, and the lovely villages of Garda, Bardolino, Lazzise, Pacengo, &c., bordering the shores of the lake. The high pointed peak on the l. of the Upper Lake is the Monte Fraine, overhanging the valley of Toscalano: the abrupt point beyond Manerba on our l. shuts out the view of the Bay of Salo: near the extremity of this point is the island of S. Francesco, covered with orange-groves, surrounding the Villa Lecchi, one of the finest situations on the lake. S. of Manerba are the villages of Moniga and Padenghe, remarkable for their fine mediæval castles, square structures, with towers at their angles, and still well preserved.

The *Lago di Garda*, the Benacus of classical writers, is formed chiefly by the river Mincio descending from the Italian Tyrol. Although receiving less water than the Lago Maggiore or Lake of Como, it is much more extensive; indeed more so than any of the Italian lakes. Its surface is 227 ft. above the level of the sea, and its greatest hitherto ascertained depth 1900 Eng. ft. Its upper portion is surrounded by high mountains, and except at the delta of the Mincio near Riva its sides are bold and precipitous. The lower portion, in the midst of the less elevated subalpine region, widens out, and its shores are fertile and covered with villages. Here the climate is milder than upon the other Lombard lakes, owing to its less elevated position above the sea. The olive is much cultivated, and extensive plantations of lemon-trees, which however it is necessary to cover during the winter-season. From its greater extent and the prevailing winds the Lake of Garda is more subject to violent storms than either those of Como or Maggiore, and, from the larger expanse of water, the waves rise to a greater height, which have rendered it celebrated for its storms, giving to its waters the appearance of an agitated sea—

" teque
Fluctibus et fremitu assurgens Benace Marino."

The Lake of Garda abounds in fish, the principal of which are the trout, pike, tench, eel, two or three species of the carp genus, with the *Sardella* and the *Agone*, which are different ages of the delicious fresh-water herring that exists in the other Lombard lakes. By a strange anomaly the perch is entirely wanting here, although so abundant in the more western lakes, where it is justly considered one of the finest species for the table.

The only outlet is the Mincio at Peschiera, which is not navigable, being intercepted by weirs, where great numbers of trout are caught. The recent introduction of trawling on the Lake of Garda, as on the Lago Maggiore, is soon likely to exterminate this fish now rapidly decreasing in consequence.

EXCURSION TO SOLFERINO.

Ponte S. Marco, or Desenzano, will be the most convenient points from which Solferino battle-field can be visited by travellers arriving from Brescia and Milan; the former is the nearest of the two, but vehicles are more easily procured at the latter station. In every case, should the traveller proceed from S. Marco, he will do well to stipulate that after visiting Solferino he shall be carried to the Desenzano or Peschiera station if he be proceeding to Venice, or back to S. Marco or Lonato if he be going towards Milan. A carriage with 2 horses will cost from 12 to 15 fr. Leaving Ponte S. Marco, a good road leads to Monte Chiaro, Castiglione, Solferino, S. Cassiano, La Volta, and Borghetto on the Mincio, at which the river may be crossed with the permission of the Austrian authorities; but as this has been lately attended with difficulty, it will be better to ascend along the l. bank as far as *Monzambano*, where there is a very curious Scaligerian Castle, and to cross from there by a hilly road to Pozzolengo and S. Martino, the scene of the heroic resistance of the Piedmontese, and from thence to Desenzano. The route from Desenzano will be somewhat different, avoiding Monte Chiaro and Castiglione. In either case, the excursion will occupy from 6 to 8 hrs.

The hilly region which extends from the southern extremity of the lake of Garda for about 10 m., and between the Chiese and Mincio, consists of a gravel deposit, forming a kind of great terminal *Moraine* of an enormous glacier, which, according to some geologists, may at a remote period have filled up this beautiful basin. These hills are covered with towns and villages, with vineyards and plantations of mulberry-trees, the principal centres of population being Lonato, Castiglione delle Steviere, San Cassiano, Cavriano, and Volta; places which have acquired a certain celebrity during the late war, as having witnessed the last scenes in the great struggle which closed with the Peace of Villafranca. A few words may be said therefore on the events that preceded the great battle to which the name of Solferino has been given by the Emp. of the French.

In other parts of this volume (pp. 38, 42) we have noticed the earlier operations during the campaign of 1859. After the victory at Magenta, which opened Lombardy to the Emperor Napoleon, the Austrian army found itself constrained to retreat, abandoning Milan, Pavia, Piacenza, &c., and to place itself in a strong defensive position behind the Mincio. The French, on the other hand, were not slow in following up their successes on the Ticino. A second victory over the retreating army at Melegnano, on the 7th June, was the first result of this onward movement (p. 221). The Austrians, however, succeeded in making good their retrograde movement, in crossing the river, and in placing themselves under the protection of Verona, Peschiera, and Mantua—the strongholds of the celebrated Quadrilateral of their military writers, between the Adige and the Mincio. The Emp. Francis Joseph, having assumed the command of his army, and having received large reinforcements, instead of shutting himself up in Verona, determined, towards the end of June, to reassume the offensive, and thereby to repair the successive disasters of his generals in the earlier part of the campaign. On the evening of June 23rd the whole Austrian army sallied out from Verona and Mantua, recrossed the Mincio, and occupied the principal points of the hilly region, from Pozzolengo on the N.E., by Solferino and Cavriana, to Giudizzolo in the plain of the Chiese; their line of battle being nearly 12 m. in length; the village of Solferino, perched on a high hill overlooking the plain, being its centre; the French being posted from Lonato to Carpendolo by Castiglione; and the Piedmontese, who formed the left wing of the Allied Army, from Desenzano to Rivoltella, on the S. shores of the lake. The number of Austrians engaged has been estimated at 150,000; of the Allied Franco-Sardinians, 145,000.

On the 24th of June, at 5 A.M., the French commenced the battle by attacking the left wing of the Austrians in the plain of Medole, and soon after the centre of the Imperialists at Solferino; whilst the Piedmontese, commanded by their gallant King, engaged the enemy's right, under Marshal Benedek, the most experienced of the Austrian commanders, between Pozzolengo and S. Martino. The battle, or rather the several almost independent actions, lasted with varying successes until 4 P.M., although for the Allies with hourly increasing advantage, when by a supreme effort the French succeeded in carrying Solferino, the key of the position, and establishing themselves solidly on its heights, thus cutting the Austrian line into two; the result was a general retreat, which was effected with considerable order on the same evening, by recrossing the Mincio at Monzambano, Borghetto, and Goito; the Piedmontese at the same time repulsing Benedek, and obliging him to retire under the guns of Peschiera. The Austrian army is said to have amounted to 150,000 men, the French to a nearly equal number. The losses of the former have been estimated at 20,000 killed and wounded, and 7000 prisoners, with 30 pieces of cannon. The immediate consequence of this victory was the investment of Peschiera by the Piedmontese, and the establishment of the French on the l. bank of the Mincio, preparatory to their laying siege to Verona and Mantua, each party preparing for fresh onslaughts, when the Treaty of Villafranca (June 11th), so hastily and unexpectedly concluded between the two Emperors, put an end to the war, leaving unattained the object for which it was undertaken as declared by Napoleon III.—the liberation of Italy from the yoke of Austria from the Alps to the Adriatic—the Venetian provinces, with their great military strongholds, remaining in the hands of the defeated Emperor.

The village of Solferino is remarkable for a high mediæval tower, probably of the age of the Scaligers, which is known by the name of *La Spia d'Italia* — the look-out or watch-tower of Italy— from the extensive view it commands, extending from the Alps to the Apennines, and along the Lake of Garda nearly to its termination in the heart of the Tyrolese Alps. Of Lonato and Castiglione we have already spoken. S. Cassiano and Cavriana are villages of little importance: it was in the latter that the Emperor Francis Joseph passed the night preceding the batttle, and Napoleon the night after. Volta, which derives it name from the turn in the direction of the road leading to the passage of the Mincio at Borghetto, is upon the edge of the plain. The three passages of the river between Peschiera and Mantua by bridges are at Monzambano, Borghetto, and Goito; the latter celebrated for a brilliant success of the Piedmontese army, commanded by their King Charles Albert, during the campaign of 1849.

As before stated, the battle-fields of the 24th of June 1859 can be most conveniently visited, by persons arriving from Milan and proceeding to Venice, from Ponte di S. Marco and Desenzano; from Peschiera by tourists proceeding in an opposite direction; and from Villafranca and Borghetto by travellers from Verona who wish afterwards to proceed to Mantua, Parma, and Bologna.

———

From the Desenzano Stat. the Rly. follows the plain which is bordered by the amphitheatre of low hills which bound the lake on the S. The views over it in this part of the journey are extremely fine: none more beautiful than its first burst on the traveller before reaching the Desenzano viaduct. A very gradual incline of about 120 ft. in 5 m. brings us to—

6 kil. *Pozzolengo Stát.*, about 2 m. from the village of the same name. Before reaching this station the village of San Martino is left on the rt. S. Martino was the scene of one of the most brilliant victories of the Piedmontese, on June 24, who, attacked by the whole rt. wing of the Austrian army under Marshal Benedek, drove him back, and ultimately obliged him to retire under the guns of Peschiera. 3 m. beyond this the first detached forts of Peschiera are passed on the rt. and l., and soon after the town and fortress, close to which the Mincio is crossed on a fine stone bridge of 5 arches, with a road for carriages beneath, the bridge being more than 50 ft. above the river. A short distance beyond this is the

3½ m. *Peschiera Stat.* (There is a poor Inn within the fortress, the *Albergo delle Tre Corone*, where a tolerable bed however may be procured.) At the Rly. Stat. the traveller proceeding to Riva by the steamer will find an omnibus in attendance to carry him to the borders of the lake, and carriages to any other point he may wish to visit. Peschiera, which is situated partly on an island, formed by the Mincio where it issues from the Lake of Garda, has been very strongly fortified of late years, first by Napoleon, and since by the Austrians; and has been the scene of many sanguinary conflicts: it underwent a siege of seven weeks in 1848, when it surrendered to the Piedmontese under

Carlo Alberto. Since that time the works have been greatly strengthened by the erection of several detached forts, especially on the W. side, and extensive barracks forming 3 sides of a square in the island-quarter of the town. It was again invested in June 1859 by the Piedmontese after the battle of Solferino, but its siege was cut short by the Treaty of Villafranca. The town itself, on the rt. bank of the Mincio, is a miserable place.

Peschiera being now the frontier town of the Austro-Italian provinces, passports and luggage are examined here, operations that take up about an hour, during which the railway-trains are detained. It is also the station for the Austrian *Government steamers*, which ply upon the Lago di Garda; they start regularly for Riva, calling at the different towns on either side; their time of arrival and departure corresponds with that of the railway trains to Verona and Brescia, thus establishing an expeditious communication between the Tyrol and Venetian Lombardy; the hours and days of starting being— for Riva, Mondays, Wednesdays, and Fridays, at 1 P.M., corresponding with the early trains from Milan, Verona, and Venice. The boats employ 3½ to 4 hrs.: the fares 4½ and 3 lire. The same boats leave Riva for Peschiera at an early hour, reaching Peschiera in time for the afternoon trains to Milan, Verona, and Venice. They call at *Limone, Tremesine, Gargnano, Malcesine, Torri, Castelletto,* and *Bardolino.* By these arrangements the traveller leaving Venice and Milan by the early morning-trains, can reach Trent, the capital of the Italian Tyrol, on the same evening; but these arrangements vary with the season as to days and hours. A boat runs from Riva to Desenzano on Mondays, calling at Limone, Tremosine, Gargnano, and Maderno; returning from Desenzano on the following day, calling at Maderno, Gargnano, Limone, and Tremosine. There is a fair *restaurant* on board these steamers. Omnibuses start from Riva for *Roveredo* and *Trento* on the arrival of the steamers, places in which ought to be secured on board.

The battle-fields of San Martino and Solferino may be also conveniently visited from *Peschiera;* in which case the itinerary will be to S. Martino, Pozzolengo, Solferino, and Cavriana, returning by San Cassiano and Castiglione to Lonato or Desenzano; or, should the traveller be proceeding to Mantua, from Cavriana to Volta, crossing the Mincio at Borghetto, and Valeggio to Villafranca station on the rly. Carriages for the excursion can be procured from a person named Nuto, to be heard of at the inn of the Tre Corone. A carriage with 2 horses will cost from 15 to 20 francs, according to the number of persons, but, in making the bargain, it must be distinctly understood that the Vetturino will bring back the tourists either to the Peschiera, Lonato, or Desenzano stations, or to Villafranca.

Several agreeable *excursions* may be made from Peschiera. 3 m. from it is the village of Cola, very beautifully situated on a hill (Colle); 2 m. farther is Luzise on the E. shores of the lake, surrounded with very picturesque mediæval walls, and a Scaligerian castle; 3 m. further N. is Bardolino, also on the lake. Here the traveller will do well to take boat to visit the picturesque promontory of San Vigilio, on which is a handsome villa; he may then return to the village of Garda, one of the most beautifully situated places on the Lake to which it gives its name, and enjoying a climate much milder than any other on its shores. At Garda is the villa of Count Albertini, with handsome gardens and plantations. A ride of an hour from Garda will bring the tourist to the plateau of Rivoli; from which, descending the rt. bank of the Adige, he may visit *Pastrengo,* celebrated in all the Italian wars as a military position.

ROUTE 28.

MILAN TO BERGAMO, BY THE POST-ROAD THROUGH GORGONZOLA AND VAPRIO.

About 29 m.

This, which was formerly the most direct line of communication with Bergamo, is now seldom followed by travellers since the opening of the Railway; still it offers interest, as it passes through one of the richest agricultural districts of Lombardy. It can only be performed by means of vetturini or hired horses, as the post stations have been removed. It follows the line of the Martesana canal nearly all the way to the Adda.

Quit Milan by *Porta Orientale*.

Crescenzago, a pleasant village, with many villas and gardens around.

1½ *Cascina de Pecchi*. This is a famous cheese district, of less extent than that about Lodi, but nevertheless of considerable importance. The cheese is called *Stracchino*. The road continues as far as *Le Fornaci*, along the *Martesana* canal. This canal was first excavated in 1457, by Francesco Sforza; but the levels being ill calculated, it was nearly useless. Leonardo da Vinci was afterwards called in, and he gave plans for improving the cut: and when the duchy was occupied by the French, Francis I. assigned 5000 zecchins annually for the works. In the 16th centy., under Philip II. of Spain, other surveys were made; but the *naviglio* was almost entirely re-excavated in 1776.

Gorgonzola, a flourishing town, with a new church and cemetery. Here the Milanese suffered a signal defeat from Frederick Barbarossa in 1158, a little before the destruction of Milan; and here King *Heinz*, whom the Italians call *Enzio*, the illegitimate son of Frederick II., was taken prisoner (1245) by the Milanese, but released upon his swearing that he never again would enter their territory, an escape which only renewed for him the captivity which ended with his life. About Gorgonzola the best *stracchino* is made from cream and unskimmed cows' milk. It derives its name from having been originally made from the milk of the cows of the migrating herds, called *bergamini* (perhaps from the German word *berg*, a mountain), which came down from the mountain pastures (*alpi*) in the autumn, to feed during the winter in the plains, and who arrived *stracche*, tired. Since the consumption has become very great, it has been made also from the milk of cows which pasture always in the plain country. Two sorts are produced, one in a square form, which is eaten fresh, or when not more than 6 months' old; the other round, and of a considerable size, which is kept from 3 to 12 months. It is valued in proportion as it is duly streaked and spotted with green marks, called *erborine*, and which are produced by mixing the curd of one day with that of the previous one. Although a mild rich cheese at first, it becomes very strong by keeping. Old stracchino is greatly esteemed. The stracchino is sold fresh at about 1 fr. the large pound, *i. e.* about 5*d*. a lb. avoirdupois. It is estimated that the cow which yields the milk for stracchino affords a double gain over that yielding the Parmesan cheese.

Le Fornaci: here a road branches off on the rt. to *Cassano d'Adda* and *Treviglio*; the road to *Bergamo* runs on to *Vaprio*, in a beautiful situation on the *Adda*: the country around is studded with villas. One of these, belonging to the Duke of Melzi, is interesting on account of its containing a remarkable painting, a colossal Virgin, now extending through two stories of the dwelling. There is much beauty in the figure, and it has been attributed, upon old authority, to Leonardo da Vinci; yet many doubt the tradition, on account of the unusual size.

The Villa Castelbarco, at Monisterolo, near Vaprio, is worth a visit.

Cross the Martesana and then the Adda: *Vaprio* and *Canonica* are only divided by the river.

1 *Canonica.* (*Inn:* Albergo de' Tre Rè.) From this point the views become very beautiful. Bergamo is seen on its hill, crowned by its domes and lofty towers; and in the foreground the landscape is of exceeding richness. A short way above Canonica the Brembo torrent empties itself into the Adda.

Boltiere.
Osio di Sotto.
Grumello del Diano.
1 *Bergamo.* (See Rte. 27.)

SECTION IV.

VENETIAN PROVINCES.*

1. *Territory; Population.*—2. *Passports.*—3. *Money.*—4. *Weights and Measures.*—5. *Posting.*—6. *Railways.*

ROUTES.

ROUTE.	PAGE.	ROUTE.	PAGE.
29. Peschiera to *Verona*—Rail	- 263	gnano, *Este, Montagnana,*	
30. Verona to *Mantua,* by *Villafranca*—Rail	- - - 287	*Monselice,* and *Abano*	- 385
		33. Padua to Ferrara, by *Rovigo*	- 390
31. Verona to *Venice,* by *Caldiero, Vicenza,* and *Padua*—Rail	299	34. Venice to Trieste, by *Treviso, Pordenone, Casarsa,* and	
32. Mantua to Padua, by *Legnano, Este, Montagnana,*		*Udine* - - - -	- 391

PRELIMINARY OBSERVATIONS.

§ 1. TERRITORY—POPULATION.

Under the name of the Lombardo-Venetian Provinces, now almost a misnomer since the separation of Lombardy, are included all the possessions now remaining to Austria in Italy since the Treaties of Villafranca and Zurich. They embrace the whole of the territory of the republic of Venice, ceded to Austria by Napoleon by the Treaty of Campo Formio, and confirmed by the treaty of Vienna; the possessions of the Dukes of Mantua E. of the Mincio; the triangular space between the Lower Mincio and the Po, once a part of Lombardy; and some small enclavures on the S. of the Po, belonging to the territory of Gonzaga, retained after the annexation of the Duchies of Parma and Modena, and of the Legation of Ferrara, to the North Italian kingdom in 1860. The population of the Austro-Italian Provinces scarcely reaches 2,400,000 inhab.

§ 2. PASSPORTS.

Here, as in every other part of the Austrian dominions, *no person can cross the frontier without a passport signed by an Austrian minister.* No exceptions are made. It is important to have the number of persons of which the family is composed, and the names of servants, whether English or foreign, inserted in the passport. By a recent regulation of the police, all foreigners remaining more than 3 days at Milan, Verona, and Venice, are obliged to take out a *Carta di Soggiorno,* which costs 6 lire, a very onerous tax on travellers; and on quitting Venice, the passport must be *viséd* by the police, and the signature of the Consul of the North-Italian Kingdom obtained if the territory of that power is to be entered. The latter visa is not however required to passports issued by the British Secretary of State.

§ 3. MONEY.

Money calculations are rather perplexing in consequence of payments being made in two currencies—in Lire Austriache and Lire Italiane. The Lira Austriaca, or third of an Austrian florin, is that now used in all official and commercial transactions.

---

* For the greater convenience of the traveller, we have introduced here the Austrian Provinces of Italy, although forming a break in those of the kingdom of Northern Italy.

The following are the comparative average values of these coins:—

Lira Italiana, or French Franc.		Lira Austriaca, or Zwanziger.		L. Austriache.		L. Ital.	
Lir.	Cent.	Lir.	Cent.	Lir.	Cent.	Lir.	Cent.
1	—	1	19	1	—	—	84
2	—	2	38	2	—	1	68
3	—	3	57	3	—	2	52
4	—	4	76	4	—	3	36
5	—	5	95	5	—	4	20
10	—	11	90	10	—	8	40

4. WEIGHTS AND MEASURES.

Weights.—Although the metrical division is now generally in use throughout the Venetian territory, at *Venice* other weights and measures are in use. The pound, by which all, except very heavy materials, are purchased, is the libbra, peso sottile; it is divided into 12 oncie, 72 sazi, or 1728 carati, and equals 4650 English grains; hence 100lb. peso sottile equal 66·4lb. avoirdupois.

§ 5. POSTING.

The extension of railways in the Austro-Italian provinces not having been carried to the great extent it is in Piedmont and Lombardy, there are still some roads which can only be travelled by post-horses: we insert therefore the regulations in force, and which were formerly those of the Lombardo-Venetian kingdom, premising that the Austrian post is equal to $8\frac{84}{100}$ English miles.

For each horse per post	3	16
Postilion	1	0
Hostler for each pair of horses per post	0	30
Calesse, if furnished by the maestro di posta	0	92

Austrian lire.

The following are the general regulations:—The postmaster is bound to furnish a *calessa* from station to station—very rumble-tumble concerns they are—at the price stated above. The postilions are, of course, not contented with the regulation fee; usually, if there are two horses, you pay the tariff of a third horse to the postilion, but they always grumble, even if you offer them more than double; and usually, the older the postilion is, the less likely he is to be satisfied.

Carriages are divided into three classes, which, with their load, must not exceed the following weights, all calculated according to the Vienna standard. 100 pounds Vienna weight = 123½ lbs. avoirdp. =56·01 kilogrammes.

Species of Carriage.	Lbs. of Vienna weight.	Horses.
A. of the lightest build, as open calèches with four seats, or half open with two — not exceeding	600	2
exceeding	600	3
B. of a medium size, as close carriages with two seats, and half closed with four, or with a small head, not exceeding	500	2
from 500 to	800	3
exceeding	800	4

5. *Posting.* 6. *Railways.* Sect. IV.

Species of Carriage.

	Lbs. of Vienna weight.	Horses.
C. of a heavy build, as carriages, whether with two or four seats, entirely covered and enclosed, not exceeding	600	3
from 600 and not exceeding	800	4
exceeding	800	6

§ I. In calculating the weight, the passengers are reckoned at the following rates:—

	Lbs. of Vienna weight.
An individual of twelve years and upwards	100
A child from five to twelve years	50
Two children, under the age of five years	40

A single child of five years, or under, is not reckoned. With respect to the ages of children, the declaration of the traveller suffices without further proof. The postilion is not calculated in the weight of the load.

§ II. The luggage is reckoned thus:—

	Lbs. of Vienna weight.
A bundle, a carpet-bag, and an imperial, when this occupies all the top of a covered carriage with four seats, each at	100
An imperial, occupying all the top of a covered carriage with two seats, or a half-closed carriage, or half an imperial, &c., fastened to the carriage, each at	50
A valise or portmanteau, when fastened outside the carriage, and 2 ft. long, 1¼ wide, not more (1 Vienna ft. = 12·45 inches Engl.), each at	50

§ III. Bags or boxes for caps and hats, if hung on the outside, or any parcels or small bundles placed within the carriage, are not reckoned.

These regulations as to weight look troublesome upon paper, but they are rarely insisted upon.

The following table may assist the traveller in his calculation as to horses:—

Post.	2.		3.		4.		5.		6.	
	Aust. l. c.	Ital. l. c.	Aust. l. c.	Ital. l. c.	Aust. l. c.	Ital. l. c.	Aust. l. c.	Ital. l. c.	Aust. l. c.	Ital. l. c.
1	6 32	5 50	9 48	8 25	12 64	11 00	15 80	13 75	18 96	16 50
1¼	7 90	6 88	11 85	10 32	15 80	13 75	19 75	17 19	23 70	20 63
1½	9 48	8 25	14 22	12 38	18 96	16 50	22 70	20 63	28 44	24 75
1¾	11 06	9 63	16 59	14 44	22 12	19 25	27 65	24 07	33 18	28 88
2	12 64	11 00	18 96	16 50	25 28	22 00	31 60	27 50	37 92	33 00
2¼	14 22	12 38	21 33	18 57	28 44	24 75	35 55	30 94	42 66	37 13
2½	15 80	13 75	23 70	20 63	31 60	27 50	39 50	34 38	47 40	41 25
2¾	17 38	15 13	26 07	22 69	34 76	30 25	43 45	37 82	52 14	45 38
3	18 96	16 50	28 44	24 75	37 92	33 00	47 40	41 25	56 88	49 50

§ 6. RAILWAYS.

The Railways at present opened in the Austro-Italian Provinces are—the continuation of the Great Lombardo-Venetian line from Peschiera to Venice; the lines from Verona to Mantua; from Verona to Botzen; and from Venice to Udine and Trieste, by Treviso, Conegliano, and Pordenone.

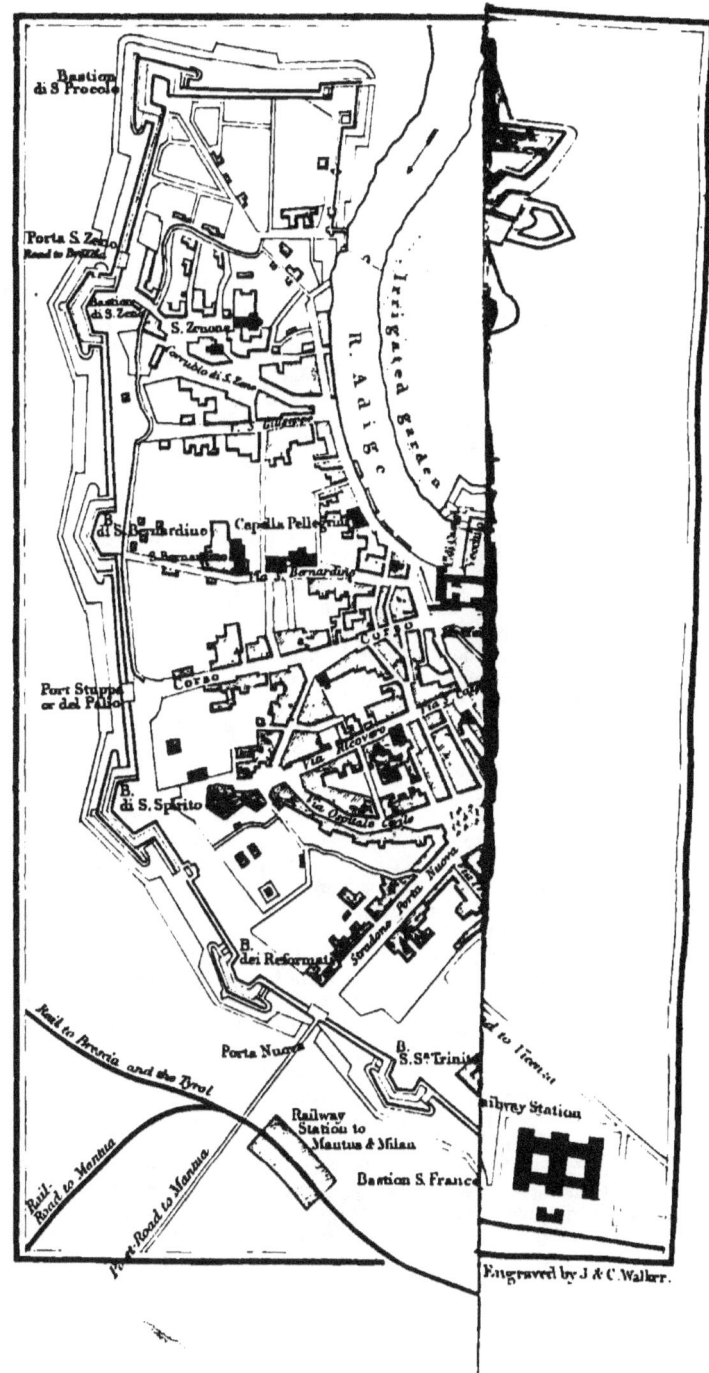

ROUTES.

ROUTE 29.

PESCHIERA TO VERONA—RAILWAY.

Castel-nuovo	4 m.
Somma Campagna	6
Verona	8

2 trains daily. 23 kil.=18 Eng. m.

Leaving the Peschiera Stat., the road proceeds by Cavalcaselle, through deep cuttings for 4 miles, to

4 m. *Castel-nuovo Stat.*, situated ½ m. S. of the village, above which are the ruins of a mediæval fortress. Castel-nuovo is now only rising from its ruins, having been sacked and burned by the Austrians in 1848, under circumstances of great atrocity, for having allowed itself to be occupied by one of the Lombard free corps, which, having landed at Lazise, succeeded in getting between Verona and Peschiera, and in destroying the powder magazines of the latter fortress: only two houses and the church remained intact after this act of military vengeance. [A good road leads from Castel-nuovo to Ponton on the Adige by Pastrengo, by which the traveller can join the old post-road or the rly. to the Tyrol without entering Verona, and being subjected to the annoyances regarding passports inseparable from fortified towns.] The village of Somma Campagna is in a high position on the l.; after leaving it, that of *Custozza* is seen about 2 m. on the rt., celebrated for a very sanguinary action in 1849, between the Austrians and the Piedmontese, in which the latter were worsted.

6 m. *Somma Campagna, Stat.* A good deal of deep cutting has been necessary in carrying the railroad between these two stations. From this place there is a gradual descent over a richly cultivated district, until we enter the Plain of the Adige, across which the railway runs to the Verona station, situated outside the Porta Nuova. Omnibuses are in attendance to convey passengers to the different hotels on the arrival of each train, and good broughams, the fare in which to any part of the city is only a lira.

8 m. VERONA. *Inns:* Albergo delle Due Torri; comfortable, and the best; a good table-d'hôte at 3 and 5 o'clock 3½ francs—(Luigi Bellini, the head waiter, is an intelligent fellow about everything worth seeing at Verona. The Strangers' Book here, kept since 1794, will be worth looking over by persons interested in autographs.)—La Torre di Londra; and Gran Parigi; also good. Verona is now the point from which diverge all the communications between Austrian Italy and Germany, and the centre of all military movements in the Venetian Provinces.

Malleposte daily for the Tyrol and Vienna by railway as far as Bolzano, from which there are regular public conveyances to Inspruck in 16 hours. Another similar conveyance leaves Inspruck for Munich immediately on the arrival of that from Bolzano. There is a railroad communication with Vicenza, Venice, Treviso, and Udine, with diligences from the latter to Trieste; to Mantua, from which there are diligences to Parma and Cremona.

Verona now contains 60,000 Inhab., not including its very large garrison. From its vicinity to the Alps the climate is somewhat sharp, but healthy. Fruit and flowers are excellent, as may be seen in the Piazza delle Erbe every morning. The city is divided into two unequal portions by the Adige. The treaty of Luneville, 1801, gave the smaller portion on the l. bank to Austria, the remainder to the Cisalpine republic. This division of one city occasioned great inconvenience to the inhabitants, who, in crossing the middle arch of the bridge, entered into a foreign territory; but their trouble soon ended by the French getting the whole. The site of Verona has been considered as the finest in the N. of Italy. Such superlatives are always matters of fancy; but the blue hills and mountains beyond, the rushing stream, and the finely varied landscape, dotted with villas, surrounded by groves, in which the tall dark cypress contrasts with the other trees, deserve the vivid picture which they have received from Berni:—

"Rapido fiume, che d'alpestra vena,
Impetuosamente a noi discendi,
E quella terra sovra ogn' altra amena
Per mezzo, a guisa di Meandro, fendi;
Quella chedi valor, d' ingegno è piena,
Per cui tu con più lume, Italia, splendi,
Di cui la fama in te chiara risuona,
Eccelsa, graziosa, alma Verona.
Terra antica, gentil, madre, e nutrice
Di spirti, di virtù, di discipline;
Sito che lieto fanno anzi felice
L' amenissime valli, e le colline,
Onde ben a ragion giudica e dice
Per questo, e per l'antiche tue ruine,
Per la tua onda altiera che la parte,
Quei che l' aguaglia alla città di Marte."

The river *Adige*, called *Etsch* in the German Tyrol, flows through the city. It is crossed by four bridges, and turns numerous floating watermills moored across the stream. The floods of the Adige are tremendous. One, which took place in the 13th centy., is commemorated in the ancient frescoes of the cathedral. By such a flood in 1757 the *Ponte delle Nave* was entirely carried away. On the 31st of August, 1845, after three days' hard rain, the greater part of the town could only be traversed in boats.

The distant aspect of "*Verona la Degna*," with its serrated walls and lofty towers, is very peculiar; it contains several remarkable objects.

Of these, the first to attract the attention of the traveller is the *Amphitheatre*. It is supposed to have been built between the years 81 and 117 of our era, consequently contemporaneous with the Coliseum. The interior is nearly perfect, which it owes to the continuous care bestowed upon it. Most of the other Roman amphitheatres have suffered exceedingly from having been converted into fortresses, as at Arles and Nismes, or considered as quarries for materials, as the Coliseum. The outer circuit was greatly damaged by an earthquake in 1184. The ruined portions appear to have been carried away and employed on other edifices, but the mass itself was diligently preserved. By a statute passed in 1228 it was enacted that every podestà, upon taking office, should spend 500 *lire* upon the repairs of the *Arena*. In 1475 penalties were decreed against any one who should remove any of the stone; in 1545 a special officer was appointed to take care of it; in 1568 a voluntary subscription was raised for its support; and in 1579 a tax was imposed for its reparation. Other decrees in its favour have been since made; yet, notwithstanding all this care, 4 arches only are preserved of the outer circuit, which consisted originally of 72, being 8 less than in the Coliseum. The internal aspect of the arena is complete: and though a great number of the seats have been restored, some as late as 1805, yet, the operation having been performed gradually, the restorations are not apparent. The greater diameter of the Amphitheatre is 511 ft.; of the arena 262½ ft. The lesser diameter of the Amphitheatre is 404½ ft.; and of the arena 146 ft. The circumference is 1429½ ft., and the height of what remains is, from the original pavement, 100 ft.; it is calculated that it could have contained 22,000 spectators. It is built of Verona marble, the substructions and vaultings beneath the seats being of good Roman brickwork. "The seats continue nearly in one slope from top to bottom, nor is there any evidence that they were divided by *præcinctiones* (i. e. broader steps, leaving a passage behind the seated spectators) into *mæniana*, or stories, as was usual. However, immediately above the *podium* (the terrace immediately above the arena, just wide enough to contain two or three ranges of moveable seats) is a wide space which, though never called by that name, is precisely of the nature of a *præcinctio*, and the sixth step from this is very narrow; and as it could not be used as a seat, the back of the step immediately below would become a means of communication: it is uncertain, however, whether this is anything more than a bungling restoration.* The steps now existing are 43, each, on an average, as nearly as I could determine it, 16 inches high and 28 wide, and sloping two inches from back to front. I will not undertake to say that this latter circumstance arises from anything but the settlement of the work; yet I think, from the ancient steps which remain, that these were originally laid with a small slope, to throw off the rain-water. The part which still exists of the outer circuit of the amphitheatre is unconnected with the steps, and, at the upper part, is entirely detached from the rest of the fabric; so that, if we have, therefore, no direct proof of the existence of a wooden gallery, there is at least no evidence against it. The building is much larger than that at Nismes."— *Woods.* So much remains perfect of the corridors and entrances by the vomitories, that a very clear idea of the arrangements of an ancient amphitheatre may be obtained. Some portions of the underground arrangements of the arena have been cleared out within a few years, but these do not afford any sufficient data for solving the much-debated questions respecting the object of these substructions. The numbers sculptured on the arches of the outer circuit to guide the spectators where to present their tickets remain quite distinct—LXIIII. LXV. LXVI. LXVII. Many of the arcades are now occupied by smiths, farriers, and small tradesmen. The interior is frequently used for exhibitions of horsemanship, dancing on the tight rope, fireworks, &c., &c. In the 13th century it was used for judicial combats; and it is recorded of some of the Visconti, that they received 25 Venetian lire for every duel fought there.

The *Roman Theatre* is on the l. bank of the Adige; its destruction began at a very early period. A curious decree of King Berengarius, dated 895, describes it as dilapidated, and permits all persons to demolish the ruinous portions; yet much of it was standing as late as the 16th century, and Caroto, the painter, delighted himself with drawing and studying its remains. There is now little above ground, excepting fragments principally incorporated in other buildings (between the base of the hill S. Pietro and the Adige); but numerous fragments of sculpture have been dug up about it.

Besides the amphitheatre, Verona still contains some remarkable monuments of the imperial age. The arch commonly called the *Porta dei Borsari*, like the Roman gates of Trèves, of Autun, and that which once stood at Chester, is double. From the traces of the inscriptions in the friezes, it appears to have been built under the Emperor Gallienus, together with the walls of the city in which it was inserted, about the year 265. The style of the architecture is very remarkable; pillars with spiral flutings, small arches or windows between columns and surrounded by pediments, and numerous other anomalies, rendering it a connecting link between the style of the Antonines and that of the darkest portion of the middle ages. The inscriptions were composed of bronze letters in relief, fastened to the stones as in the frieze of the *Maison Carrée* at Nismes, and the words have been deciphered by the marks which they have left behind. But some antiquaries are of opinion that Gallienus merely caused the gateway to be fronted and ornamented, and that the mass of the building, the 2 lower arches in particular, belongs to an earlier age. Be this as it may, the Porta dei Borsari, a monument 1600 years old, stands in full solidity athwart the crowded street of a living city.

Another fine Roman gateway is called the *Arco de' Leoni*: this, however, is much less perfect than the Porta dei Borsari. It is in better taste, and probably of about the same age.

Verona exhibits a remarkable series of *fortifications*, of various periods. The

---

* There can be little doubt that this narrow step is an imperfect restoration, as it is carried only half way round the amphitheatre.— P. C. H.

earliest are those built by the Emperor Gallienus, of which the *Porta dei Borsari* and the *Arco di Gavi*, pulled down in 1805, were 2 of the gates: large masses of this wall remain, but generally incorporated in other buildings. The most apparent portion is in a lane called the *Viottolo di San Matteo*. To these imperial walls succeed, in point of date, those attributed to Theodoric, and probably not much later than his time. They are of great extent, built of alternate triplets of courses of stone and brick; that is to say, three of each, the bricks placed in what is called herring-bone fashion, also employed in the churches of this city, and doubtless imitated from this structure. Another line is popularly attributed to Charlemagne: that is beyond the Adige. The fourth was begun by the Scaligers, who crowned them with the forked battlements which render them so picturesque, especially the part beyond the Adige, and the towers which rise upon the bold and precipitate hills add much to the beauty of the town. These last walls are built upon those of Theodoric. Lastly are the outworks of the Scaligerian walls, begun by the Venetians about 1520, according to the plans of several engineers. Ultimately they were completed by, or at least after the plans of, the celebrated Sanmicheli (born at Verona 1484), who may be considered as the father of the science of modern fortification. Square and circular bastions had previously been introduced: of the latter kind a very remarkable one is yet subsisting, called the *Bastione Boccare*, containing within it a vast bomb-proof casemate, of which the vault is supported by a central pillar. But a circular bastion can never be perfectly flanked; and Sanmicheli, considering this defect, introduced the triangular and pentangular bastion; and the *Bastione della Maddalena* of this city was the first specimen of the defence which has become the basis of the present system of fortification. Sanmicheli also not only flanked the curtain, but all the fosse to the next bastion, the covered way, and the glacis. The mystery of this art consisted in defending every part of the enclosure by the flank of a bastion.

The modern fortifications of Verona are amongst the most remarkable works of military engineering in Europe. Since 1815, when the city devolved to Austria, every effort has been made to render it a stronghold of the first order, but especially since the outbreaks in 1849, when it became not only the military but the civil capital of the Austrian possessions in Italy. Not only have its former walls been greatly strengthened, but a very extensive system of detached forts erected on every assailable point in its vicinity, so as to render it impregnable; every summit commanding the town has been fortified, extensive barracks erected within the fortifications, and a new arsenal on an immense scale formed in the plain opposite that founded by the Scaligers. Verona has thus become the key to the Austrian power in Italy, with its communications easily maintained by the valley of the Adige with Germany. It can at present accommodate a garrison of 20,000 men, and it is believed could only fall after a prolonged blockade, before an army greatly exceeding the number of its defenders.

The fortification gates designed by Sanmicheli yet remain. *Porta Stuppa*, or *del Palio*, is near the centre of the line of the fortifications on the W. and S. sides of the city. "In this gate the mode in which Sanmicheli combined pure and beautiful architecture with the requisites called for in fortification may be seen displayed to great advantage. It is an instance of his wonderful ingenuity and taste."— *Gwilt*. This gate was so called from the game of the *Pallone*, which used to be played near it. Vasari terms this gate a miracle of architecture.

Porta Nuova.—Through which passes the road to Mantua. "This gate has great architectural merit. It is a square edifice, supported within by a number of piers of stone, with enclosures or apartments for the guards, artillery, &c. The proportions as a whole are pleasing. It is of the Doric order, devoid of all extraneous ornament, solid, strong, and suitable to the purposes of the building.—For beauty, however, this gate is not equal to that of del Palio."—*Gwilt.* The Porta Nuova has been much injured as regards its architectural beauty, by enlarging the side entrances, rendered necessary for the traffic to one of the railway stations, which is just outside it.

Piazza dei Signori. Here are the palaces formerly inhabited by the *Scaligeri,* the lords of Verona, which upon their expulsion became the seats of the municipal government.

The *Palazzo del Consiglio,* in the mixed style of the 15th centy., was probably built by *Frà Giocondo.* His portrait exists in bas-relief on the building close to the *Volto delle foggie.* Frà Giocondo (d. 1499) was an excellent scholar as well as an architect. He was the first who gave a correct edition of Vitruvius. He discovered at Paris the letters of Pliny. He was also an exceedingly able engraver. Coupled windows and arches supported upon columns, pilasters with elegant arabesques, in a style similar to the Colleoni chapel of Bergamo, adorn other portions, all full of the merit of the cinque-cento style. The Annunciation in bronze, in front of this palace, is a fine work of Giovanni Campagna. This building is surmounted by statues of those whom Verona claims as her own; and all celebrated men are claimed as Veronese, who were born within the municipal jurisdiction. They are as follow:—*Pliny the younger,* though stoutly contested by Como, and apparently upon good grounds; for, though he speaks in his epistle of " our Verona," this probably refers only to his rights of citizenship in the city.—*Cornelius Nepos.*—*Macer,* the author of the poem upon the qualities and poisons of herbs and serpents.—*L. Vetruvius Cerdo.*—But, above all, *Catullus,* who reflected as much credit upon Verona as Virgil did upon Mantua, this value being assigned to him by Ovid and Martial:—

" Mantua Virgilio gaudet, Verona Catullo."
        Ovid. *Amor.* iii. el. 15, l. 7.
"Tantum magna suo debet Verona Catullo,
Quantum parva suo Mantua Virgilio."
        Mart. xiv. ep. 195.

Of the modern period, and on the *Volto delle foggie,* is *Fracastoro,* equally eminent as a poet and a physician, but who, unfortunately, chose disease as the subject of his didactic poem: he is one of the three great masters of modern Latin poetry, Vida and Sannazaro being the other two; and Hallam thinks that, though Vida excelled in the structure of his verse, yet that Fracastorius was the greatest poet of the three. And, lastly, on the side towards the Piazza delle Erbe, stands *Scipione Maffei,* the historian of his native city.

The two palaces on the opposite side of the Piazza, now occupied by the law courts and public offices, were built by Mastino (1272), and Alberto della Scala his son; but having been several times re-modernised, no traces remain of their ancient splendour, of Giotto's frescoes, or of where once lived the " Altissimo poeta" during his sojourn at the court of the Scaligers. The Campanile of the *Piazza dei Signori* is a magnificent, lofty, and simple unbroken piece of brickwork, nearly 300 feet high.

Communicating with the *Piazza dei Signori* on the S.W. side is the *Piazza delle Erbe,* or vegetable-market, which was the Forum in the republican times of Verona, and contains many old and picturesque buildings connected with its history. The small open tribune near the market-cross occupies the place of an older building to which the newly elected Capitano del Popolo of the Free City, after having heard mass at the cathedral, was conducted, and in which, after he had addressed the people, he was invested with the insignia of office. In after-times the sentences of condemned criminals were pronounced from this tribune. Proclamations were made from it, and debtors were here compelled to submit to a humiliating punishment. If the fountain, in the centre of the Piazza, was first erected by King Berengarius, in

N 2

916, it was restored and provided with an additional supply of water by Cansignorio, the ninth ruler of the Scaliger family, in 1368. The same Cansignorio erected the tower which is seen at the further end of the square, and placed in it the first clock erected at Verona. The building on one of the sides of the Piazza, with arcades and pointed windows, is an Exchange, called the Casa dei Mercanti, and was built for that purpose, by Alberto della Scala, in 1301. On it is a good statue of the Virgin, by Campagna. The pillar at the end of the Piazza was set up in 1524 by the Venetians, to whom Verona was then subject, to support the lion of St. Mark. The pillar consists of a single block of Veronese marble. The name of the architect, as may still be read on the base, was *Michael Leo*. The bronze lion was thrown down when the republic of Venice expired in 1799. At the end of the Piazza near this pillar is the Palazzo Maffei (now Tresa), once the residence of the patrician family of which the historian of Verona was a member. It is a highly enriched specimen of the Italian style of the 17th centy. The fronts of several of the more considerable houses in this Piazza are decorated with frescoes.

Near the Piazza dei Signori are the *Tombs of the Scaligers*. These singular monuments stand close to the church of *Santa Maria l' Antica*. They are in a small churchyard enclosed by a beautiful iron railing or trellis-work, consisting of open quatrefoils, in the centre of each of which is the *scala*, or ladder, the armorial bearings of the family. The origin of the family of the Scaligers, or more properly of the *Della Scalas*, is not known. We find them at Verona in 1035. In 1257 two brothers, Bonifacio and Frederico della Scala, of the patrician order, were beheaded by Eccelino da Romano. Their fate first gave the name a place in history. In 1261, after the death of Eccelino, the unanimous voice of the people of Verona, then a free town, raised *Mastino della Scala* to the office of " Capitano del Popolo." He had been a soldier of fortune in the army of the tyrant. He governed Verona wisely and moderately for 15 years. After escaping several state conspiracies, he was killed by some of the members of a disaffected family, who considered that he had aggrieved them by delaying the punishment of an offender against their honour (1277). This assassination took place under the archway in the Piazza dei Signori; which retains from that circumstance the name of *"il volto barbaro"* to the present day.

The tomb of *Mastino*, as it now exists, is a plain sarcophagus, ornamented only with a cross. The canopy which covered it has been destroyed, and the stones employed for paving the church, whilst the sarcophagus itself was afterwards appropriated by a member of the Nogarola family. The original inscription is, however, preserved.

Mastino was succeeded by his brother Alberto I., who, during 24 years, kept the turbulent factions in order, and sowed the seeds of commercial prosperity. These two superior men were the founders of the greatness of their house. Alberto, who had served as Podestà of Mantua, was exceedingly esteemed and loved for his pacific virtues; and he was installed amidst the shouts of " Viva Alberto, assoluto oggi e per sempre;" and if any portion of the legal power of the old commonwealth had still existed, it now wholly expired. Alberto died in 1301.

A sarcophagus standing on the ground, without inscription, is attributed to *Alberto* by immemorial tradition. Upon it is sculptured the Signore, riding in full state, with sword in hand.

To Alberto succeeded, in 1301, his second son, *Bartolommeo*, a gentle and humane prince, who died in 1304. In his time (in 1302) lived Romeo de' Montecchi, and Giulietta de' Cappelletti, or de' Capelli, immortalized by Shakspeare.

Upon the death of Bartolommeo, *Alboino* I. was called by acclamation to the supreme authority. Henry of Luxemburg was then prosecuting his plans for the re-establishment of the imperial prerogative; and Alboino in 1311, surrendering his authority as Capitano del Popolo, received it back from the Emperor as Imperial Vicar in Verona; a concession by which the dignity was confirmed to the family. Alboino, who had been originally intended for the church, was not well able to sustain the government, and he called in the assistance of his brother, Francesco, better known by the name *Can Grande*, who was associated with him by the Emperor Henry VII. as joint vicar of the empire. Cangrande was a Ghibelline in heart and soul; and, whilst he acquired the possession of Vicenza, Padua, Feltre, Belluno, and Bassano, by force or policy, the grant of the vicarial powers gave a legitimate character to the dominions which he had thus obtained.

The court of Cangrande was the most magnificent of the age in Italy, and exhibited a combination of military splendour and profuse hospitality and liberality to the stranger, and encouragement to literature. His palace became the refuge for all who, embracing his political opinions, had in anywise subjected themselves to persecution; and it was here that Dante found an asylum, having been first received by Alboino. Cacciaguida foretells to Dante his retreat, and describes the Court of Verona, and character of Cangrande, in these lines:—

" Lo primo tuo rifugio, e il primo ostello
 Sarà la cortesia del gran Lombardo
Che in su la Scala porta il santo uccello;
 Ch'avrà in te sì benigno riguardo
Che del fare e del chieder, tra voi due,
 Fia primo quel che tra gli altri è più tardo.
Con lui vedrai colui che impresso fue,
Nascendo, sì da questa stella forte,
 Che notabili fien l' opere sue.
Non se ne sono ancor le genti accorte
Per la novella età; che pur nove anni
Son queste ruote intorno di lui torte.
Ma pria che'l Guasco l'alto Arrigo inganni
Parran faville della sua virtute
In non curar d'argento, nè d'affanni.
Le sue magnificenze conosciute
Saranno ancora sì, che i suoi nimici
Non ne potran tener le lingue mute.
A lui t' aspetta, ed a suoi benefici:
Per lui fia trasmutata molta gente,
Cambiando condizion ricchi e mendici;
E porteràne scritto nella mente
Di lui, ma nol dirai."—*Paradiso*, xvii. 55, 92.

" Thy first retreat,—first refuge from despair,—
 Shall be the mighty Lombard's courtesy,
 Whose arms the eagle on a ladder bear.
His looks on thee so kindly shall be cast,
 That asking and conceding shall change place;
And that, wont first to be,'twixt you be last.
With him shall one be found, who, at his birth,
 Was by this ardent star so fraught with grace,
 His deeds of valour shall display his worth.
Not yet his virtue by the world is known,
 So tender is his age; for scarce nine years
 Around him have these rolling circles flown;
But ere the Gascon's artifice deceive
 Great Henry, he, all sordid hopes and fears
 Despising, shall a glorious name achieve.
His deeds magnificent shall still proclaim
 His praise so loudly that his very foes
 Shall be compell'd to celebrate his fame.
Look thou to his beneficence; for he
 Of fortunes in such manner shall dispose,
 Rich shall be poor, and poor exalted be.
Stamp in thy mind these words of prophecy,
 But be they not divulged."
 WRIGHT'S *Dante*.

Can Grande, or the Great Dog, died in 1329. Many conjectures have been made to account for his strange name.

The tomb of Cangrande I. forms a species of portal to the church of Sta. M. Antica. It is composed of three stories; columns support it; upon the sarcophagus the Signore is extended in his peaceful robes, girt with his sword: above, on a pyramid, is the equestrian statue of the warrior, in full armour. The sarcophagus rests upon figures of mastiff dogs supporting the shield charged with the ladder, the armorial bearing of the family of *La Scala*; and the mastiff's head equally appears as the crest of the helmet.

Cangrande was succeeded by Alberto II., his nephew, the sixth della Scala who ruled Verona. The seventh was Mastino II., the nephew of Alberto. With him commenced the decline of his house; and from his time the history of the family, instead of exhibiting statesmen and heroes, becomes a melancholy and revolting picture of misfortune and crime. Mastino II. was vain, weak, and unprincipled. He was surrounded by a brilliant court: Treviso, Vicenza, Bassano, Brescia, Parma, Reggio, and Lucca, all acknowledged him as their lord; and he won Padua from the powerful family of the Carraras. Having abandoned the imperial party, he was fixed upon by Pope Benedict

XII. as the head of the league or alliance of the Guelphs against the Viscontis, the leaders of the Ghibellines. But he lost several of the most important of the possessions which had been united under his authority. He died in 1351.

The tomb of Mastino II., at one corner of the churchyard, also exhibits the double effigy; the equestrian warrior on the pyramid, and the recumbent sovereign on the sarcophagus.

The eighth ruler, *Cangrande II.*, who built the Castel Vecchio, and the great adjoining bridge over the Adige, after a troubled reign of eight years, was murdered by his own brother, Can Signorio, 1359: and it shows in what a demoralised state Italy must then have been, when we find that such a crime did not prevent the perpetrator of it from succeeding to the government. He committed a second fratricide on his deathbed, the crime being instigated by his desire of preserving the succession in his own descendants, which he feared might be endangered if Paolo Alboino, another brother, had been suffered to survive him. Next to ensuring the inheritance of Verona to his sons, his most earnest passion in his latter days (he died in 1375) was the erection of his most sumptuous mausoleum.

The tomb of Can Signorio, which forms four stories, also surmounted by an equestrian statue, is exceedingly elaborate. The plan is hexagonal; and 6 Corinthianised Gothic columns support the lower story. The basement is surrounded by an iron trellis, of richer pattern than that of the rest of the cemetery. Upon the pilasters which support it are the six warrior-saints, St. Quirinus, St. Valentine, St. Martin, St. George, St. Sigismund, and St. Louis. Beneath the gable of the third story are allegorical figures of virtues: Faith, with the star upon her breast; Prudence, Charity, and three others. The figure is recumbent upon a sumptuous sarcophagus. An inscription, in Gothic letters, preserves the name of Bonino di Campilione, who was both the sculptor and the architect of this sumptuous pile.

These tombs stand in the old cemetery of Sta. Maria Antica, which had been the parish ch., the family burial-place of the Scaligers before they rose to power. The monuments are of white marble, in a style which is a mixture of the Pointed and the Lombard. There are four other sarcophagi of the Scaligers in this cemetery, of the very early part of the 14th centy., two belonging probably to Alberto (ob. 1301) and to his son Bartolommeo (ob. 1304).

Pinacoteca, the *Picture Gallery*, until lately in the Palazzo del Consiglio, has been removed to the Palazzo Pompei alla Victoria, in the Via di Porta al Campo Marzo, facing the Adige, and immediately below the Ponte alle Navi, the lowest of the bridges on the river. The palace, a handsome edifice, the front consisting of a Tuscan or rustic basement, surmounted by an elegant Doric portico, was bequeathed by its last owner to his native town a few years since for its present purpose. Strangers are admitted to the gallery on application to the custode, who will of course expect a fee. As yet there is no catalogue, or even names on the several paintings, which are arranged in a handsome suite of apartments forming the upper floor; in the lower one, are a series of casts from Canova's principal works, bequeathed by the Marquis Pindemonte; and in the Vestibule the great Bell formerly on the tower of the Piazza delle Erbe, and which was cast in 1370.

The paintings, chiefly by artists of the Veronese school, and rarely to be met with elsewhere, are just such as will particularly interest the artistic traveller. The following are those most worthy of notice:—

ROOM I. *Titian*: the Transfiguration.—*Bonifazio*: a Doge of Venice receiving the keys of Verona; a magnificent composition, and interesting for the grouping of the figures and the costumes.—*D. Brusasorsi*: Christ in the Garden.—*Farinati*: St. Peter

Martyr.—*Orlando Flacco*: the Virgin enthroned, with SS. Catherine and Helena below.—*Orbetto*: the Flagellation.—*Orlando Flacco*, an allegorical painting of Verona, with its patron saints Zeno and Peter Martyr.

ROOM II. *Paul Veronese*: a fine full-length portrait of Count Guarienti.—*Girolamo dai Libri*: 5 paintings, of the Virgin enthroned, with SS. Andrew and Peter; the Baptism in the Jordan; the Virgin and Child worshipped by S. Joseph, and Tobit with the Angel, a fine work signed and dated 1530; another Madonna, with SS. Roch and Sebastian; and a fourth, called the *Madonna del Coniglio*, from the rabbits in the foreground.—*F. Carotti*: S. Catherine of Alexandria, with the portrait of the Donor; and the Washing of the Feet of the Pilgrims.—*Carlo Crivelli*: a small painting of the Virgin, with wreaths of fruit and flowers, and several small figures.

ROOM III. *Giov. Badile*: the Raising of Lazarus.—*Giov. Mansueti*: the Madonna, with S. Jerome and the Baptist.—*Giov. Bellini*: the Baptism in the Jordan, very doubtful, and greatly inferior to the same subject in the ch. of Santa Corona at Vicenza (p. 305).—*G. Badile*: SS. Andrew and Peter.—*Giolfino*: a Virgin enthroned, with SS. Paul, Roch, Sebastian, and Charles Borromeo, and the Donor below.—*Paul Veronese*: the Deposition; a small but good painting.—*Gir. di Santa Croce*: the Adoration of the Shepherds.—*G. Mansueti*: the Epiphany.

ROOM IV. The paintings here are all by the Veronese master Morandi, called *Cavajola*: the best are 4 heads of Saints, a Deposition, Christ in the Garden, and an Ecce Homo.

ROOM V. *Girolamo Banaglia*: the Virgin and SS. Peter and Roch, and the heads of various Saints, with their instruments of torture, on the predella beneath.—*Liberale di Verona*: the Virgin and S. Joseph adoring the infant Saviour.—*Pisanello*: the Virgin in the midst of groups of angels, in a kind of bower, with S. Catherine, and two full-length figures of S. Fermus and S. Rusticus.—*G. Banaglia*: the Virgin and S. Catherine, with a good predella beneath.—*Badile*: a good ancona of the Madonna with three Saints on either side.—*Turoni*: a curious painting of 1360, having the Crucifixion in the centre; a picture of 25 subjects of the life of Christ, of a very early period, erroneously attributed to *Cimabue*.—*Falconetti*: the Sibyl foretelling to Augustus the advent of Our Saviour, the ornamental drapery in gilt relief.

ROOM VI. contains a collection of very second-rate engravings.

ROOM VII. *Pasqualetto*: the Discovery of the bodies of SS. Fermus and Rusticus.—*An. Caracci*: the Virgin and S. Joseph before the infant Christ.—*Carotto*: a good painting of the Virgin, with SS. Zeno and Peter Martyr.—*Orbetto*: the same subject, with SS. John and Peter Martyr.—*Brusasorzi*: SS. Cecilia, Orsola, Rosa, Catherine, Apollonia, and Barbara.—*Bernardino d' India*: the Descent of the Holy Spirit on the Apostles.—*Pasqualotto*: the Marriage of S. Catherine.

ROOM VIII. Little worthy of notice.

ROOM IX. *Brusasorzi*: the Baptism of Constantine.—*P. Farinati*: the Virgin, with S. Jerome, and portraits of the Donors.—*Pasqualotto*: a good Deposition.—*Brusasorzi*: a very large painting of a battle between the Veronese and the Brescians, and opposite to it an equally large one by *Farinati* of the Victory of the Lombard League over Frederick Barbarossa, and his expulsion from Milan.—*Ridolfi*: the Circumcision.—*Brusasorzi*: the Virgin, with SS. Orsola and Monica.

It is proposed to remove to the palace of the Pinacoteca the ancient marbles now in the *Museo Lapidario*, and other smaller collections, especially that in the Pal. Canossa bequeathed by Count C. to his native town.

The *Museo Lapidario* contains a valuable collection of ancient marbles, disposed in a cortile adjoining the *Teatro Filarmonico*. It was begun by the *Accademia Filarmonica* in 1617; but it acquired its present importance from the exertions of the celebrated Scipione Maffei, who bestowed upon it his collections, adding to their value by the description which he published of them in the *Museum Veronense*. Many important additions have been subsequently made. This collection does not contain any objects of great merit as works of art; but it is full of monuments illustrating points of archæology, and of local interest. The porticoes under which these antiquities stand were built by the Philharmonics, each member contributing an arcade.

The *Castel Vecchio* was erected in 1355 by Cangrande II. It is still a noble and picturesque pile, battlemented at the top. Within, the quadrangle has been much modernised, and some fine towers have been demolished, in adapting it to its present use as a military arsenal.

Immediately adjoining the castle, which is on the banks of the Adige, is the coeval bridge, the *Ponte del Castello*, also a picturesque object. It is of brick, turreted and battlemented. The arches are of unequal size; the largest is about 161 feet in span. The views of and from this bridge are very fine.

Upon the l. bank of the Adige rose the *Castel' San Pietro*, where formerly stood the palace of Theodoric; built in part of Roman materials. Late in the middle ages it retained much of its pristine splendour; and, as the most prominent structure of their city, the inhabitants caused it to be engraved upon their seal. As far as the character of this representation is intelligible, it agrees with the early descriptions, which state the palace to have been surrounded by porticos. Many parts of the building were demolished for the purpose of building the church of San Pietro, which contained several capitals, columns, and other fragments of the *Gothic* structure. In more recent periods (1393) Theodoric's palace was turned into a castle by Gian' Galeazzo, who obtained the lordship of Verona in 1387, when the dominion of the Scaligers came to an end. But the Viscontis lost Verona in 1405, and other fortifications were added by the Venetians, to whom Verona then became subject. The remains of the building were blown up by the French in March 1801. What remained after the explosion has been removed, and a fine barrack erected on the site, which forms a striking object in all the views of Verona. A very convenient flight of steps leads from opposite the Ponte di Pietra, and no traveller who wishes to enjoy the magnificent panorama over the surrounding country ought to omit to ascend to the terrace, from which, in fine weather, may be descried the great plain of the Adige and Po, studded with innumerable towns and villages, with the Tuscan and Modenese Apennines in the background. Beyond the ruins of the church of San Pietro are the remains of the *Castel San Felice*, now crowned by a very strong fortress, which formed the summit of the angle in the old system of defences. This also was the work of Sanmicheli. The limestone of the hill abounds in fossil remains; and in the history of geology they are remarkable, as being amongst the first which excited curiosity, when a specimen of them was presented to the celebrated Fracastoro. He had read about them in Pliny and Theophrastus, and he came to the conclusion that they were not semblances, generated by the plastic force of nature, as was the opinion at the time, but had one day been real animals living in, and deposited by the sea.

Churches.—The *Duomo* or *Cathedral*, also called *Sta. Maria Matricolare*, is attributed to Charlemagne, though it cannot be clearly shown by whom, or at what time exactly, the existing fabric was commenced. A church had been erected before the time of Charlemagne on the spot where the cathedral now stands, in honour of the Virgin, on the site, and with the materials, of a temple of Minerva. This church was repaired thirty years after Charle.

magne's death by the Archdeacon Pacificus, as is mentioned in the inscription on his tomb. Had Charlemagne built a new church, it would not so soon have wanted repair, except owing to some accident, of which, however, there is no mention. The tradition of this church having been built in the time of Charlemagne may perhaps be accounted for by the episcopal chair having been transferred here in 806. A new sacristy was built in 1160, and in 1187 Urban III. reconsecrated the existing cathedral. We may conclude, therefore, that the greater part of the existing cathedral was rebuilt in the first half of the 12th centy. The apse at the E. end, and a portion of its sides, are in a very different style from the rest of the building; so near a resemblance to the Roman as to induce us to believe that these portions are a remnant of the original church. The vaulting of the *Duomo* was begun in 1402, but not finished till 1514. In 1534 further alterations (the choir, screen, and the chapels placed along the S. wall) were made under the direction of *Sanmicheli*.

The handsome porch must have formed part of the new building, and belongs, therefore, to the 12th centy. Four columns, supporting two arches, one over the other, and the lower columns resting on griffons, support the porch. This mode of supporting columns seems to have been common in Italy in the 12th and 13th centuries. The celebrated Paladins, Roland and Oliver, who guard the entrance, may be supposed to have been introduced with reference to the traditionary connection of Charlemagne with this building. The Lombard imagery no longer appears as an ornament of the mouldings, but the underside of the arch which forms the vault of the porch exhibits a variety of grotesque images and symbols.

On the l. of the door, Orlando in his rt. hand holds his celebrated sword, upon the blade whereof its name is inscribed, divided thus into its four syllables, Du-rin-dar-da. His shield, straight at top, is pointed at the bottom, and ornamented with a species of Etruscan scroll-work. His l. leg and l. foot are armed in mail; the rt. leg and rt. foot are bare. Opposite to him is his companion Oliver: his shield is like that of Orlando; and he is armed not with a sword, but with a truncheon or mace, to which is appended a ball held by a chain. Such a weapon, supposed to have belonged to him, was until the last age preserved in the monastery of Roncesvalles, thus showing the *authority* of the traditions according to which the sculptures were formed. But the most remarkable circumstance is, that the combined peculiarities of the arms and armour of Roland and Oliver are found in Livy's account of the Samnite warriors; and the description which he gives is so singularly applicable to the costume of these statues, that we think it best to give the very words of the historian, in order that the traveller may compare them with the effigies which he will see before him.— "The shape of their shield was this; broad above to cover the breast and shoulders, embossed with silver or with gold, flat at top, and wedgelike below, — 'spongia pectori tegumentum,' — and the l. leg covered by the ocrea."— The "spongia" has puzzled the commentators, and Baker translates it by "a loose coat of mail;" but Maffei supposes that the *spongia* is the ball wielded by Oliver, and which represents, to a certain degree, a sponge in its form.

In the semicircle over the entrance is an ancient bas-relief, representing the Adoration of the Magi; it has been coloured, and the blue ground is yet visible: beneath are three female heads, well executed, inscribed *Fides, Spes, Caritas*. Among the grotesques of this portal may be noticed a hog standing upright on his hind legs, dressed in a monk's robe and cowl, and holding in his fore paws an open book, upon which is inscribed A. B. PORCEL—evidently a satire of the middle ages against the monks.

The porch on the S. side of the ch. consists of two ranges of columns, with strange mystical or satirical sculptures.

The more modern portions of the Duomo are exceedingly rich. Amongst the chapels, those of the Maffei family, and of St. Agatha, are peculiarly elegant. In and about the Duomo are some remarkable monuments.—One inscription commemorates the death and the works of the celebrated Pacificus Archdeacon of Verona (778-846). His name is written in three languages,—*Pacificus, Salomon, Irenæus*. Seven churches were founded by him at Verona. He had great skill as an artist in wood, stone, and metal, and he also invented some machine for telling the hour by night; but there is no reason to suppose that a striking clock was intended. His epitaph also claims for him the merit of having been the first glossator of the Holy Scriptures.—Pope Lucius III., like many other of the mediæval pontiffs, was driven from his see by the disturbances of the unruly Romans, and compelled to take refuge at Verona, where, after holding a very important ecclesiastical council, he died (1185), and is buried here. A curious epitaph marks the place of his interment.—An ancient sarcophagus, with the head of Medusa, was afterwards used as the tomb of a noble Venetian. Such adaptations often take place: at Pisa we shall find several. Amongst the more modern monuments is that of the Poet de Cesaris, with good statues of Religion and Poetry, and surmounted by his bust. The Duomo formerly boasted of many fine paintings; but several have been removed. The Assumption, by *Titian*, in the 1st chapel on l., has resumed its place here after travelling to Paris. This picture needs no praise, for its beauties would strike the most careless observer. The manner in which the Virgin is represented as floating upwards is admirable. Others worthy of notice are,—*Moroni*, St. Peter and St. Paul; —*Giolfino*, the Last Supper;—*Farinati*, the Virgin and Child;—*Liberale*, the Adoration of the Three Kings.

The bronze statue of our Saviour is by *Giovanni Battista di Verona* (fl. 1500). The presbytery in which it stands is by Sanmicheli, and the walls and mouldings are painted in fresco by *Francesco Torbido il Moro*, from the designs of Giulio Romano. The *Baptistery*, also called the church of *San Giovanni in Fonte*, is said to have been built between the years 1122 and 1135; the older baptistery having been destroyed by an earthquake in 1116. In the centre is a large octangular font, 31 ft. in circumference, hewn out of a single block of Verona marble. A frieze of small Lombard arches, supported by grotesque heads, runs round the summit. On the faces are represented the following subjects: the Annunciation, the Visitation, the Birth of our Lord, the Angels appearing to the Shepherds, the Adoration of the Magi, Herod commanding the Slaughter of the Innocents, the Execution of his Decree, the Flight into Egypt, the Baptism in the Jordan. The sculpture is in a rude but forcible style. The picture of the Baptism of our Lord, over the high altar, is by *Paul Farinati*.

The *Cloister* of the cathedral has been modernised in the upper story, for it had originally a double arcade. It has two ranges of arches in the height of the gallery; each arch rests on a pair of columns, and each pair is of a single stone, the capitals and bases being united. Adjoining is a fragment of what is said to have been a church before the erection of the present cathedral. It is merely a rectangular room, with a groined vault supported on columns.

The *Biblioteca Capitolare*, which is entered from the cloister, is one of the important collections in Italy for sacred and Patristic literature. It was first formed by Pacificus, and contains a large proportion of very early manuscripts, some of the 4th and 5th centuries. Here Petrarch first read the Epistles of Cicero; and the library is yet an unexplored mine for the historical, ecclesiastical, and liturgical inquirer. Many of the manuscripts are palimpsests, and one of them furnished the 'Institutes of Caius,' compiled in the reign of Caracalla. It was known that this treatise was the foundation of the 'Institutes of Justinian,' but not a fragment of it could be found. "A rumour, devoid of evidence," says Gibbon, "has been propagated by the enemies of Justinian, that the jurisprudence of ancient Rome was reduced to ashes by the author of the Pandects, from the vain persuasion that it was now either false or superfluous. Without usurping an office so invidious, the Emperor might safely commit to ignorance and time the accomplishment of this destructive wish. Before the invention of printing and paper, the labour and the materials of writing could be purchased only by the rich; and it may reasonably be computed that the price of books was an hundredfold their present value. Copies were slowly multiplied and cautiously renewed: the hopes of profit tempted the sacrilegious scribes to erase the characters of antiquity, and Sophocles or Tacitus were compelled to resign the parchment to missals, homilies, and the golden legend. If such was the fate of the most beautiful compositions of genius, what stability could be expected for the dull and barren works of an obsolete science."—*Gibbon.* Years after the death of Gibbon his sagacity was verified by the zeal of Niebuhr, who, when on his way to Rome in 1816, examined this library: two small fragments relating to jurisprudence, not palimpsests, had been published by Maffei, but he had not ascertained their author. Niebuhr suspected that they were parts of the 'Institutes of Caius;' and upon further examination he discovered the whole remainder, or nearly so, of this ancient text-book of the Roman law palimpsested beneath the homilies of St. Jerome, literally verifying Gibbon's words. At the instance of Niebuhr a learned German jurist was despatched to Verona by the Prussian Government, and the result has been the publication of the lost work. Of the other palimpsests is a Virgil of the 3rd or 4th centy., under a commentary by St. Gregory on the Book of Job, in Longobardic writing of the 8th. It may be older than the Virgil in the Laurentian Library at Florence. The Biblioteca Capitolare also contains inedited poems by Dante. Here also may be seen the baptismal certificate of Prince Charles Edward Stuart, the young Pretender, dated "Roma, ultima Decemb. 1720;" and a Diptych of the Consul Anastasius in the 6th centy.

The *Vescovado*, or bishop's palace, has been altered and rebuilt at various periods, but principally about the year 1356. One of the courts with fanciful columns is striking, and this edifice exhibits in its more modern portions many curious modifications of the cinque-cento style, particularly in the portals attributed to *Fra Giocondo.* Many of the paintings have been carried off, but in the *Sala dei Vescovi* a series still remains of the portraits, by *Brusasorzi*, of the bishops of Verona from Euprepius to Cardinal Agostino Valerio in 1566; of course the greater number are imaginary. In the principal court of the Vescovado stands a fine colossal statue of a crowned female, with the artist's name, *Alessandro Vittoria.*

Altogether there are about 40 churches in Verona; the following are the most remarkable:—

Ch. of *Sant' Anastasia*, close to the Albergo delle due Torri, one of the most beautiful Gothic churches in Italy. "It would, if the front were finished, probably be the most perfect specimen in existence of the style to which it belongs. It was built at the beginning of the 13th century, by the *Dominicans.*" The main fabric was begun in 1260, but the casing of the front not till 1426. The façade was to have been enriched with bas-reliefs, but this work had been only begun. The inside consists of a nave and 2 narrow aisles separated by 6 pointed arches, terminated by an apse of 5 sides. The transepts are short, with 2 chapels opening out of each, and in the angle between one of them and the choir is a square tower, terminating in an octagonal spire. All the arches and vaultings are obtusely pointed. The springing of the middle vault hardly exceeds the points of the arches into the aisles; and the windows of the clerestory are circular and very small. Its dimensions are 75 ft. wide, and 300 ft. long. The church is rich in paintings and altars; and it appears to have been originally entirely covered with frescoes, but many of them are almost destroyed; those, however, in the spandrils of the vaulting are very remarkable on account of their beauty and fine preservation. A few of the principal objects which it contains may be enumerated:— The two urns for holy water, supported by grotesque figures; the one on the l. is by *Gabriele Cagliari*, the father of Paolo Veronese.— The *Fregoso Altar* and Chapel, which Vasari, usually scanty in his account of Lombard art, considers as one of the finest in Italy; *Danese Cataneo*, 1565, was at once the architect and sculptor of this monument.—The *Altar of St. Vincent*, built of rich grey marble, the pillars on each side of Fior di Persico; the Patron Saint is by *Rotari*: above is a curious fresco, in tolerable preservation.—The *Altar of the Bevilaqua Laise Family*: *Caroto*, the Body of our Lord, with the Maries weeping around. —The *Pindemonte Altar*.—*Caroto*, St. Martin: beyond it from the roof hangs the lower jaw-bone of a spermaceti whale.—*Chapel of the Crucifix*, a curious ancient piece of sculpture: a Deposition from the Cross.—*Altar of the Centrago Family*: the Virgin between St. Augustine and St. Thomas Aquinas; an excellent picture by *Francesco Morone*.—The *Chapel of S. Gemignano* has fine frescoes (probably by *Altichieri*) connected with the Cavalli family, and a Gothic tomb.—*Pellegrini Chapel*: curious bas-reliefs, in terracotta, of the life of our Saviour; they are of the 15th century. The Descent from the Cross is the best, in which the artist has introduced a fine figure of one of the Pellegrini family.

Here are also two good Gothic monuments of the Pelegrinis, and some curious ancient frescoes, in which portraits are introduced of members of the Alighcri and Bevilaqua families; the best is that of the Virgin surrounded by Saints, with the Donatorio presented to her. Over the arch of the chapel is a St. George, by *Vittorio Pisanelli;* the foreshortenings and projections, as usual, remarkably skilful.—*High Altar: Torelli*, the Death of St. Peter Martyr, imitated from Titian; tomb of *Cortesia Serego* (1432), the brother-in-law and general of Antonio della Scala.—The *Lavagnoli Chapel*: curious frescoes in the style of Mantegna; and a fine tomb of the family.—*Sacristy:* over the door, a huge ugly picture, the Council of Trent, by *Falcieri*, with no merit as a work of art, but curious as a nearly contemporary memorial of that assembly. Within are some good pictures by *Brusasorzi*: the altarpiece with Saints, and portraits of members of the Dominican order.—*Chapel of the Rosary*, built from the designs of *Sanmicheli*: the altarpiece, in distemper, in a Giottesque style, contains portraits of Mastino II. della Scala, and his wife Taddea Carrara, kneeling before the Virgin, injured by time; the features of Mastino are remarkably expressive of his character.— The *Miniscalchi Chapel*: Amongst its many decorations the principal is the Descent of the Holy Spirit, by *Giolfino*.—Several cenotaphs have been erected in the ch. of S. Anastasia: of *Cossali*, the author of the *Storia Critica dell' Algebra*, a work of great merit; *Cagnoli*, the mathematician; *Targa*, the translator of Celsus; and of *Lorenzi*, a poet. Much of the marble called *bronzino* is introduced into the ornaments of this church: it is not so called from its colour, but from the metallic sound which it emits when struck. The pavement is extremely varied and beautiful, being formed of most tasteful designs in white, gray, and red marbles; the woodwork of the principal door well deserving of notice from its chaste design.

On the N. side of the square, before

this church, is the interesting Gothic Chapel of *San Pietro Martire*, which, with the adjoining buildings, formed a part of the convent of *Sant' Anastasia*. The edifice is now the *Liceo*, or college, an institution in which upwards of 500 pupils were educated, before they were driven from it by the Austrians to convert it into a barrack. Over the entrance, on the side of the square, is the monument of *Guglielmo da Castelbarco* (ob. 1320), the friend and adviser of the Scaligers, and one of the benefactors of S. Anastasia, a lofty Gothic canopy, beneath which stands the sarcophagus. There are other tombs of the same description within the court-yard of the convent.

Ch. of *San Bernardino:* monastic in its outward aspect, and flanked by cloisters full of decayed and broken tombs. It is now closed, being converted into a military storehouse, and most of the paintings removed to the Pinacoteca. The ch. was built about 1499, after the great pestilence. The principal pictures which it contained were—*Bonsignori*, the Virgin between St. Jerome and St. George, dated 1488. His paintings are rare out of Mantua.—A very beautiful and interesting painting, the joint work of *Morone* and *Paolo Cavazzolo*, the latter of whom died at the age of 31 (1522), while engaged on this work. The lower portion is by him. The upper division, by *Morone*, consists of the Virgin and Child, SS. Francis and Anthony, and Angels; a group of Saints, including St. Elizabeth, who, according to the legend, sees the bread which she has distributed to the poor changed into roses: he has also introduced the portrait of the female donor. The Chapel of the Holy Cross has a Deposition, and other good paintings, by *Cavazzolo.—Giolfino*, some beautiful though damaged frescoes. In one of them the painter has introduced a view of the Piazza di Brà, as it stood in his time, an interesting topographical memorial. Annexed to the church is the *Capella Pellegrini*, one of the finest works of *Sanmicheli*. "The gem of this great master is the little circular chapel at San Bernardino, whose beauty, we think, has scarcely ever been surpassed, and which exhibits, in a striking degree, the early perfection of the Venetian school. It was not finished under Sanmicheli, and blemishes are to be found in it; it is, nevertheless, an exquisite production, and, in a surprisingly small space, exhibits a refinement which elsewhere we scarcely know equalled."—*Gwilt*. The material is of a greyish white, showing exquisite workmanship: in the pavement some coloured marbles are introduced. In the upper cloisters, and in what was once the library, are some frescoes by *Morone*.

Ch. of *Sta. Elena*, adjoining the baptistery of the cathedral: some curious ancient tombs and inscriptions; amongst others that of Theodorius, one of the cardinals of the time of Lucius III.; about 1177. Paintings: *Felice Brusasorzi*, St. Helen and other Saints, a pleasing composition.—*Liberale*, St. Helen and St. Catherine, dated 1490. In the crypt is a curious early Christian mosaic.

Ch. of *Sant' Eufemia*, a building of the time of the Scaligers, but modernised. It contains several frescoes and paintings of the Veronese school, of which the best are those by *Caroto*, in the Chapel *degli Spolrerini*. They are considered as the finest of his productions. In the middle picture of the altar are represented the three archangels; in the side panels two female saints. On the side wall Caroto painted the History of Tobias: of these pictures the lower one is graceful; the mother of Tobias embraces her daughter-in-law, while Tobias himself heals the eyes of his blind father. These frescoes are in some parts painted over and much injured.—Besides these are some good fragments by *Stefano da Zevio*, over a side door; they are principally heads of saints in fresco.— In 3rd chapel on l., *D. Brusasorzi*, the Virgin in Glory; below, St. Roch, St. Sebastian, and others.—In 1st chapel on l., *Il Moretto*, St. Onoprius and St. Anthony. There are also several monuments in this church. That of

Marco and Pier Antonio Verita, by Sanmicheli, has much merit. Two are remarkable from their connection with Petrarch—the tomb of *Rinaldo di Villa Franca*, one of Petrarch's correspondents, and that of *Pietro del Verme* and *Lucchino* his son. The latter was a Condottiere of considerable fame, to whom Petrarch dedicated his treatise upon the virtues needed for a commander. The cloister is from the designs of Sanmicheli; but it is now used as a barrack. The celebrated antiquarian and historian Panvinio and Cardinal Noris were Austin friars in the convent of Sta. Eufemia.

Ch. of *San Fermo Maggiore*. This church has the epithet of "*Maggiore*" from its size: it is, perhaps, the most interesting in Verona after the cathedral and San Zenone. Its foundation may be traced as far back as 751. The crypt appears to have been built in 1065; and the massive piers and heavy vaulting are perhaps unaltered. The church is of brick with a good deal of ornament, and the rows of little arches are some of them trefoil-headed. The door in the façade is round-headed, with a profusion of ornamented mouldings. It has no rose in the front, but, instead, are four lancet windows with trefoil heads. Over these is a smaller window, divided by little shafts into three parts, and a small circular opening on each side of it. There is no tracery. The building ends in a gable, whose cornice is loaded with ornament, with three pinnacles rising above it. The interior is in a fine and bold Gothic style, built between 1313 and 1332. The ceiling is of wood, but spoiled by modern restorations and painting. There is a curious sepulchral monument of the 14th centy. in one of the chapels out of the rt. aisle. San Fermo, originally belonging to the monks of St. Benedict, passed to the Franciscan friars in the 13th centy.

San Fermo has some remarkable monuments in the S. transept. In the chapel of the Alighieris are two urns of the last members of the family of Dante. They were erected by Francesco Alighieri, sixth in descent from the poet, to the memory of his brothers Pietro and Ludovico. Francesco was eminent for his literary acquirements; he was also much addicted to the study of architecture, and made an excellent translation of Vitruvius. Until its extinction this family continued in great prosperity and honour at Verona. Two of the descendants of Dante took his name; and hence on the epitaph the father of Francesco and his brother are designated as "Dante terzo." The wing, or *Ala*, in the shield of the Alighieris, is what is called in French heraldry an " armoirie parlante." It was a daughter of Francesco who married into the noble family of Serego of Verona, and which, under the name of Serego Alighieri, still represents the descendants of the great poet. *Torello Saraina* chapel, built by the historian of Verona of that name in 1523. An excellent cinque-cento specimen.—*Tomb of the Torriani*, erected about the beginning of the 16th century, by Giulio, Battista, and Raimondo della Torre, to the memory of their father Girolamo and their brother Marc Antonio. Both father and son were professors at Padua, and enjoyed the highest reputation. The monument, a lofty altar-tomb, was decorated with bronzes, by *Andrea Riccio* or *Briosco*, the architect, of the church of Sta. Giustina at Padua. The few ornaments, the bronze sphinxes and the portraits of the Torriani, which remain, are of great beauty: the principal bas-reliefs were carried off to Paris, where they are fixed into a door of painted wood at the Louvre; here the broken and disfigured panels remain as accusers of this Vandalism. There is a curious monument to the memory of *Antonio Pelacani* (or, skin the dogs), who appropriately took for wife *Mabilia Pelavicini* (or, skin the neighbours). He was a professor of medicine, who died in 1327, and is represented teaching, surrounded by his pupils.

Many ancient paintings in and about the church have been whitewashed over. Among those which remain are the following:—a Crucifixion, supposed to be earlier than the time of Cimabue.—*Vittorio Pisanello*, an Annunciation, executed about 1430: the angel is represented as kneeling before the Virgin. The Adoration of the Magi: this painting is in a bad light.—*Benaglia*, the same subject.—*Domenico Morone*, St. Anthony of Padua.—*Orbetto*, the Nativity.—*Caroto*, the Virgin and Saints, dated in 1528.—*Barca*, a Pietà.—*Coppa*, an emblematical composition,—Verona supplicating the Virgin for deliverance from the Pestilence.—*Doudoli*, the last Supper.—*Giovan Battista del Moro*, St. Nicholas and St. Agostino.—*Torbido*, the Virgin and Saints. —*Crema*, the Virgin with St. Anthony and St. Brandan.—*Caneiro*, the Virgin with St. Peter and St. Paul.—*Francesco Bonsignore*, the Virgin, with the Lady by whom the painting was presented kneeling before her, date 1484.—*D. Brusasorzi*, a Crucifixion, with the Virgin and Saints and the Magdalene. The Gothic pulpit, with fine frescoes of Saints and Prophets, by *Stefano da Zevio*, is remarkable. The sacristy and cloisters should also be visited. So also the crypt, with curious fragments of frescoes freed from the whitewash with which they had been long covered.

Ch. of *San Giorgio Maggiore*, at the N. extremity of the town, on the l. side of the Adige, of very ancient foundation. The interior, by *Sanmicheli*, exhibits his talent and exuberant richness of fancy. The adjoining convent was sold by the French, and is now almost wholly demolished. In the church the following objects are worthy of notice: The High Altar is by *Brugnoli*, the nephew of Sanmicheli: the details are exquisitely sculptured.—*Paolo Veronese*, the Martyrdom of St. George.— *Farinati*, the Miracle of the Loaves and Fishes, painted by the artist in 1603, at the age of 79. With many defects, this picture, which is of great size, is a remarkable performance.— The fall of the Manna in the Desert, begun by *Felice Brusasorzi*, and completed by *Ottini* and *Orbetto*, his pupils.—*Caroto*, the Annunciation; St. Ursula, in distemper.—*Il Moretto*, the Virgin and Saints. — *Girolamo de' Libri*, the Virgin, two Bishops, and three Angels. Lanzi points this out as being a masterpiece in delicacy of work and beauty of design.—*Brusasorzi*, the Three Archangels, supposed to have been executed in rivalry of the preceding picture.—*Jacopo Tintoretto*, the Baptism in the Jordan. This church contains a profusion of other paintings, statues, and architectural ornaments. The campanile, by *Sanmicheli*, is a noble structure.

Ch. of *San Giovanni in Valle*, on the hill beyond the Adige: principally remarkable for its crypt, which contains two very curious Christian tombs, in white marble, of an early date. Both are covered with sculptures: upon the one believed to be the most ancient, the prominent group includes our Lord upon a hill, whence issue four streams, which represent the four rivers of Paradise. Nearly the same occurs in the several ancient mosaics at Milan, Ravenna, and Rome. St. Peter is on one side and St. Andrew on the other;—our Lord and the Woman of Samaria;—the Cure of the Demoniac; —Moses receiving the Law;—Daniel in the Lion's Den. What might puzzle the antiquary are two figures of monks; but these appear to have been added about the year 1495, when the tomb was discovered. The other is in a better taste as to art, but far less interesting as to subjects: it represents a deceased husband and wife, with St. Peter and St. Paul.

Ch. of *Santa Maria in Organo*, also on the l. bank of the Adige, a very old church, upon the site of some still more ancient building, called the *Organum*, of the time of the Lower Empire. What this building has been much disputed by antiquaries. It is doubtful whether it was an arsenal or a prison. The present edifice was principally built in 1481, as appears by an inscription upon the first column on the rt. hand towards the entry: the façade is by *Sanmicheli*. Within the church, the following objects are worthy of remark:—the *intarsiatura*, or inlaid wood-work of the choir, by *Fra' Giovanni*, an Olivetan friar, to which order this church belonged, was executed in 1499. *Fra' Giovanni* is considered as the greatest master in this branch of art. In the Chapel of the Holy Sacrament is a candelabrum of walnut-tree wood, carved with beautiful grotesques. Paintings: *G. de Libri*, the Virgin, in fresco.—*Brentana*, the Discovery of the Holy Cross by the Empress Helena.—*Giolfino*, Subjects from the Old and New Testament.—*Farinati*, St. Peter sinking on the Waters; St. Gregory feeding the Poor.—*Domenico Brusasorzi*, the Resurrection of Lazarus; the Pool of Bethesda; St. Jerome and St. John.—*Caroto*, the Virgin, St. Vincent, and St. Maur. The sacristy, according to Vasari one of the most beautiful in Italy, besides the *intarsiatura* and carving of *Fra' Giovanni*, contains some "beautiful studies, three half-figures in every compartment (of which there are fourteen) of monks of the Olivetan order, all in white dresses, hooded, relieved on blue grounds, and all in the most perfect condition. Eighteen lunettes contain each two portraits of the popes who have been elected out of this order. The blue grounds have been relieved by gilding, and have stood perfectly. These works are all by *Moroni*." Among the portraits is that of *Fra' Giovanni*, over the door leading to the altar. In the adjoining cemetery are curious ancient tombs. The campanile was erected in 1533 by the same Fra' Giovanni.

Sta. Maria della Scala. The exterior is in a cinquecento style, by *Fra' Giocondo*. It was first founded by Cangrande, and a fresco upon a wall which formed part of the original structure displays curious portraits of his nephews Alberto and Mastino. The church contains the tomb of Scipione Maffei, the historian of Verona, perhaps the most able and judicious of Italian antiquaries, and who was also a dramatic poet of considerable merit. He died in 1755.

Ch. of *SS. Nazaro e Celso*, not far from the Porta Vescovo, in the suburb leading to Vicenza. The ancient monastery to which this church belonged is partly destroyed, but in and about it are some remarkable relics of antiquity. In a small chapel, excavated in the side of an adjoining hill, are frescoes, probably of the sixth century, and good specimens of the style of that age. The subjects also which they represent are more than usually varied. The church is partly from the designs of Sanmicheli, but unfortunately mutilated in their execution, the five arches which he contemplated having been reduced to three. It is filled with paintings by *Brusasorzi*;—amongst these his favourite subject of a Choir of Angels, painted on the doors of the organ.—*Paolo Farinati* also contributed much to the adornment of this church. His fresco of Adam and Eve is thought to be one of his best productions.—*Caneriu*, the Descent of the Holy Ghost. The handsome chapel of S. Biagio (St. Blaise) at the extremity of the l. transept, is preceded by another of more recent date, painted by *Falconetti*. The chapel of St. Biagio is Gothic, its walls covered with frescoes, some of which have been attributed to *Mantegna*. The fine picture of St. Biagio and St. Sebastian, over the altar, is by *Monsignori*: the figures of the female saints, and especially of the patron saint holding a card (the instrument of his martyrdom), are very beautiful; the predella beneath, representing the martyrdom of several saints, is a good work by *Girolamo dai Libri*.

Ch. of *San Sebastiano*, formerly belonging to the Jesuits, and exhibiting that excess of decoration for which the churches of this order are remarkable. The front is after the designs of *Sanmicheli*, and very magnificent. Almost all the marbles found in the province of Verona are employed in the sumptuous columns and decorations of the altars, the principal one being from the design of Padre Pozzi. There are several paintings, but none of great note. In the adjoining buildings is the municipal library, containing about 12,000 volumes.

Ch. of *San Stefano*, on the l. bank of the Adige, near the Ponte di Pietra, built in the 11th century, has been much modernized. Its porch resembles that of the cathedral; and the central octagon tower also retains its original appearance. Twenty of the Bishops of Verona are buried here; and it has been doubted whether it was not the original cathedral. There is a marble throne for the bishop still existing. The crypt may, perhaps, date from the 7th century, having every mark of early Christian antiquity: so have also two very remarkable sarcophagi; the one of Placidia, daughter of Eudoxia and Valentinian III., and wife of Olibrius Emperor of the East; the other (as is supposed) contains the remains of Marcian, a patrician, A.D. 427.—Amongst the paintings are—*Caroto*, the Virgin between St. Peter and St. Andrew.—*Giolfino*, the Virgin with St. Maur and St. Simplicianus, and St. Placidus.—*Dom. Brusasorzi*, a very fine fresco: St. Stephen preceded by the Holy Innocents; above, a choir of angels. Our Lord bearing the Cross. The Adoration of the Magi.—*Ottini*, the Massacre of the Innocents.—*Orbetto*, the Forty Martyrs; one of his best works.

Ch. of *San Tomaso Cantuariense*, in the island of the Adige. Tebaldo, a Bishop of Verona, chose Thomas à Becket for the patron of this church in 1316, which has been repeatedly altered. The front is of the 15th century, partly from the designs of *Sanmicheli*: had these been followed the church would have been one of the finest of his productions. Here is the tomb of *Giovan' Battista Beket Fabriano*, who claims to be of the family of the Archbishop, perhaps a descendant of some of those who followed him into exile. Paintings: *Orbetto*, Martha and Mary.—*Felice Brusasorzi*, the high-altar piece; the Virgin, with St. Thomas and St. Catherine.—*Farinati*, St. Jerome in Meditation: good. In the sacristy is a fine painting, which has been ascribed either to *Caroto* or *Garofalo*. It represents the Infant Saviour and St. John playing before the Virgin. The foreground is rich in flowers, the pink or *garofalino* being conspicuous amongst them.

Ch. of *San Zenone*.—This is the most interesting example in Verona of the Ecclesiastical architecture of the middle ages, and that which has undergone least change in the interior. It stands at the W. end of the city near the gate leading to Brescia. The first church which was built on the site was erected in the beginning of the 9th century, by Rotaldus Bishop of Verona. This was much injured by the Hungarians in 924. In 961 Otho II. passed through Verona on his way to Rome, and left a rich donation in the hands of the bishop for its restoration. The new church, however, was not begun till 1138, and not finished before 1178. The plan of the edifice is that of the Latin Basilica, without transepts: the style is Lombard. The front is of marble: the sides are constructed with alternate layers of marble and brick.—"The front may be cited as a good example of the early architecture of this part of Italy: the general idea is that of a lofty gable with a lean-to on each side, which, being the natural result of the construction, is, if well proportioned, a pleasing form."—*Woods*. The principal feature of the front is one of the earliest wheel of fortune windows. It was executed by a sculptor of the name of *Briolotus*, who also built the baptistery. An inscription in the baptistery records this fact, and speaks of the window as a work which excited wonder in those times. Its allegorical meaning is here made sufficiently clear by the King at the top of the wheel, and the prostrate wretch at the bottom, and the verses both within and without, by which Fortune speaks and addresses the beholders. Maffei gives the inscriptions:—

En ego fortuna moderor mortalibus una
Elevo, depono, bona cunctis, vel mala dono.

This is on the outer circumference; within is—

Induo nudatos, denudo veste paratos,
In me confidit, si quis, derisus abibit.

The portal is a very rich specimen of those of the Italian churches in the 12th century. If in its decorations some ludicrous images are retained, the greater part of them attempt to imitate the more correct models of the Roman bas-reliefs. All the figures are rudely sculptured; but the arabesques, which enrich the divisions of the different compartments, are beautifully designed, and not badly executed. The rude bas-relief over the door is said to represent a deputation which was sent to San Zeno by the Emperor Gallienus. Immediately above the arch of the porch is a hand with the fore and middle fingers extended, and the two others bent, in the act of the *Latin Benediction*. On the flanks of the portal appear subjects taken from the Old and New Testament,—the history of Adam and Eve on the rt. hand, the principal events in the life of our Saviour on the other, explained in leonine verses in short epigraphs. With these are blended, as usual, subjects taken from ordinary life, and illustrating the manners of the times,—knights jousting at each other; and below the first series is a representation of the chace, popularly called the Chace of Theodoric. The feet of the hunter, who is in Roman costume, are placed in stirrups; and this, according to Maffei, is the most ancient piece of sculpture in which they are exhibited. The dogs have seized the stag, and at the extremity is a grinning demon waiting for the hunter. Some lines underneath designate him as Theodoric, and, according to the vulgar notion, the infernal spirits furnished him with dogs and horses. This arose probably from his being an Arian. The old bronze doors are very curious, consisting of a series of plates, 48 in all, fixed on a pinewood frame; the reliefs on them represent, in the rudest style of art, scriptural subjects, and are perhaps amongst the earliest specimens, as they are amongst the rudest, of Christian sculpture. The pillars of the portal, as usual, rest on the backs of animals —lions, symbolical of the vigilance and strength of the church. Round the arch of the portal are symbolical representations of the months of the year, beginning with March. It is to be regretted that this porch is much neglected; and the group of Theodoric and the demon, in particular, is defaced by the urchins who have punched holes in the marble, in order to "smell the brimstone" which it is popularly supposed the fiend gives out by this process.

The interior of the church is striking, from the grandeur of its proportions and its elevation. The nave is high, and is divided from the aisles, which are low, by alternate pillars and piers supporting semicircular arches in pairs. From the piers ascend ribs, in the form of rude Doric pilasters, to support the roof of the nave; two only of these ascending shafts support a direct arch across the nave, and the arrangement is not calculated to support any vaulting. The wooden roof is exceedingly curious, and elaborately ornamented, painted in faint colours; at the extremity of the nave is the raised ch., which is reached by a double flight of handsome steps, as in some of the ancient basilicas; the choir or tribune which terminates it is in the pointed style, and covered with frescoes; but this part of the ch. was rebuilt in the 15th centy. The windows, like those in the early basilicas, are of small dimensions. Many curious relics of antiquity are disposed about the interior. Of these, the strangest is the statue of San Zeno, sitting in a chair, in the upper ch. San Zeno is the patron of Verona; he became its bishop in A.D. 362, in the reign of Julian the Apostate. He was an African by birth; and the painted statue represents him as brown as a mulatto, though not with a negro physiognomy. He is in the attitude of giving his benediction. On the opposite side is St. Proculus, executed in 1392. On the l. on entering the church is the *Coppa di San Zenone*, a vase formed out of a single block of red porphyry, the outer diameter of which is 13 ft. 4 in., the inner 8 ft. 8 in.; and the pedestal is formed out of another mass of the same material. It is of high antiquity, and, according to the legend, was brought by the fiend from Syria, at the behest of the bishop. It originally stood on the outside of the church, and Maffei supposes it to have been intended for washing the feet of the pilgrims before entering the sacred edifice. On the wall of the S. aisle are a series of rude statues of Christ and the Apostles, of the 14th century.

Many of the altars are adorned with pillars, taken, probably, from some more ancient edifice. In particular, the Altar of the Virgin, 2nd on l., may be remarked; the columns here are composed of four smaller pillars fastened in a kind of true-lovers' knot, and resting on winged bulls and lions. A Roman inscription of Augusta Atilia Valeria, on the steps leading to the Tribune, is one of the few early Christian ones which formerly abounded in this city. Several frescoes, one representing the great flood of the Adige in 1239, and probably coeval with the event. A bas-relief, representing two cocks carrying a fox dangling from a pole, considered as symbolical of vigilance overcoming craft. There are few pictures worthy of notice. The best is by *Mantegna*, behind the high altar, at the end of the choir, and amongst the finest works of the master, consisting originally of six compartments, which were all carried to Paris; only three have been restored, but these the most important. The centre one represents the Virgin having the infant Christ on her knees, enthroned with Angels; rich architecture, adorned in front with festoons of fruit, surrounds the composition; the second, SS. Peter, Paul, and John; and the third, SS. John the Baptist, Lawrence, and Benedict. There is also a remarkable sarcophagus, perhaps of the 9th century, serving as an altar-table: it has sculptures on three of its sides.

Under the choir there is a spacious crypt, the semicircular groined roof of which is supported by 40 pillars, with capitals of various forms, the main piers on each side of the choir being continued downwards through it. In its recesses are dispersed numerous fragments of ancient frescoes and bas-reliefs, the tombs of Euprephrius and Cricinus, and of SS. Proculus and Agabius, bishops of Verona, and the stone sarcophagus containing the bones of St. Zeno, discovered in 1838. The double flights of steps leading from the nave to the crypt deserve notice from the handsome coupled shafts of red Verona marble which support the two arches on the N. side. The ch. of St. Zeno is so much below the level of the surrounding ground, that it is entered by 13 descending steps. The effect on entering by the principal door, and looking down into and along the nave below, is very grand.

The *cloister* of S. Zenone consists of brick arches, pointed on the E. and W. sides, circular on the two others, supported on coupled columns of red marble, united by a little appendage of the same substance at the necking of the column and at the upper torus of the base. On the N. side is a projecting edifice, sustained by double columns of different diameters, those at the corners being more massive. It served as a lavatory, and formerly contained a large basin for the monks to wash before entering the refectory. The cloister contains many tombs, some which always stood here, others brought of late years from suppressed churches. Here are the tombs of *Giuseppe della Scala*, of whom Dante speaks, and of *Ubertino della Scala*, superior of the Benedictines, and prior of this monastery. This beautiful cloister is falling into ruin; the pavement destroyed, and the monuments mutilated. On one of the walls is a fresco of the Infant Saviour by Mantegna.

Adjoining the cloisters is an old church, built in the same manner as the one which stands close by the cathedral, with groined semicircular arches supported on four pillars, all unlike, dividing it into nine equal squares.

The campanile or bell-tower of Zan Zenone is one of the most beautiful edifices of its kind, and one of the finest objects in the very varied landscape about Verona. Begun by Abbot Albericus in 1045, it was completed in 1178, and is entirely detached from the ch. at its eastern extremity; it is built of alternate zones of brick and marble, surmounted by a double gallery of Lombard arches, and these again by a low conical spire and 4 turrets.

The adjoining cemetery, from which the church and its campanile may be conveniently examined, contains an ancient and singular mausoleum. Descending by a flight of steps, at the bottom stands an ancient sarcophagus. Over the entrance is an inscription, appropriating it to Pepin King of Italy, the son of Charlemagne, who died at Milan A.D. 810. The urn is remarkable, and evidently belonged to some person of distinction; but the inscription is modern, and was put up by a priest in the course of the last century. The water found in the tomb, caused by the percolation of the rain, is thought to possess medicinal virtues by the lower orders.

"Sanmicheli's most admired works are his *Palaces* at Verona; the general style of composition, very different from that of the palaces of Florence and Rome, is marked by the use of a basement of rustic work, wherefrom an order rises, often with arched windows, in which he greatly delighted, and these were connected with the order after the manner of an arcade, the whole being crowned with the proper entablature. The façade of the *Pompei* palace is a good example."— *Gwilt.*

Palazzo Bevilaqua, in the Corso, would have been beautiful; but, like our Whitehall, it stands merely as a specimen of an entire design. It did contain a splendid collection of antiquities, which have been dispersed. They are now chiefly in the Glyptotheca at Munich. Near it stands the

Palazzo Canossa, also by *Sanmicheli*. This palace, belonging to one of the most influential families of Verona, was begun in 1527, by Ludovico di Canossa, Bishop of Bayeux, in France. His armorial bearings are on the front. It was not completed till 1560. It contains some tolerable paintings; the best are by *Brusasorci*, *Farinati*, *Orbetti*, *Giolfino*, *Pisanello*, &c. The collection of Monte Bolca fishes and other fossil remains here has been transferred to the Pinacoteca.

Palazzo Portalupi, near the latter. Its Ionic front, which is of the 18th centy., is handsome, but overcharged with ornament.

Palazzo Maffei, now Tresa, in the Piazza delle Erbe, a noble elevation of three stories, more laboured than the style of Sanmicheli, but very effective; the construction of the staircase is remarkably bold. The collection of the Maffei family is dispersed, but one good statue of Scrapis remains. The Maffei family of Verona has recently become extinct in the male line.

Opposite to the amphitheatre, in the Piazza di Brà, is the *Palazzo della Gran Guardia*, a fine building. It was built by Andrea Midano, a pupil of Sanmicheli, as appears from an inscription lately discovered.

Palazzo Giusti, on the declivity of the hill overlooking the Adige. The gardens are well laid out, and the view over Verona is very fine. The front was painted by *P. Farinati*. It is now occupied by public offices.

Palazzo degli Emilii, near the ch. of S. Anastasia. Some good pictures; amongst them the Adoration of the Magi, by *Orbetto*.

Palazzo Miniscalchi. The exterior is painted in fresco by *Tullio d'India* and *Aleprandi*. Amongst other subjects is the feast of Damocles. Under the stables of this palace are Roman vaults used as prisons by *Eccelino da Romano*. The Moscardi Collection or Museum, a good collection of armour, amongst which is that of Cangrande della Scala, is now here. The son of the present owner, Count Miniscalchi Erizzo, has also added to the treasures of his parental house a valuable collection of Oriental MSS. made during his travels in the East.

Palazzo Catarinetti, near the latter, is a good specimen of the house architecture of the 15th and 16th centuries; the balcony at the corner of the street is very handsome.

Palazzo Guastaverza, now *Sparavieri*. One of the most graceful productions of *Sanmicheli*: the management of the rustic work is peculiarly able.

Palazzo Guarienti. Painted on the outside by *Farinati*.

Palazzo Sagramoso. Several good pieces by *Orbetto* and *Felice Brusasorci*. Near it are some remains of Roman walls.

Palazzo Gazzola. An extensive collection of Monte Bolca fishes, and other geological specimens.

Theatres. The *Teatro Filarmonico* is open during the autumn and Carnival: for operas only during the former, for operas and ballets during the latter season.

The other theatres are the *Teatro Nuovo*, in the Piazza Navona, and the *Teatro Valle*.

Verona and Shakspeare are, of course, associated in the mind. The *Montecchi* belonged to the Ghibellines; and as they joined with the *Cappelletti* in expelling Azo di Ferrara (some short time previous to 1207), it is probable that both were of the same party. The laconic mention of their families, which Dante places in the mouth of Sordello, proves their celebrity:—

" Vieni a veder Montecchi e Cappelletti
Monaldi e Filippeschi, uom senza cura,
Color già tristi, e custor con sospetti."
Purgatorio, vi. 107.

' Come, see the Capulets and Montagues,—
Monaldi—Filippeschi, reckless one!
These now in fear—already wretched those."
WRIGHT'S *Dante*.

The tragic history of Romeo and Juliet cannot be traced higher in any written document than the time of Lungi di Porto, a novelist of the 16th cent. The *Casa de' Cappelletti*, now *Osteria del Cappello*, an inn for vetturini, in the *Via Cappello*, may have been the dwelling of the family. With respect to the tomb of Juliet, it certainly was shown in the last century, before Shakspeare became generally known to the Italians. That tomb, however, has long since been destroyed; but the present one, in the garden of the *Orfanotrofio*, does just as well. It is of red Verona marble, and, before it was promoted to its present honour, was used as a washing-trough. Maria Louisa got a bit of it, which she caused to be divided into *hearts* and *gems*, elegant necklaces, bracelets, &c., and many other sentimental young and elderly ladies have followed her Majesty's example.

The *Public Cemetery*, outside the Porta Vittoria, contains several good modern monuments; like those of Brescia and Vicenza, it is in the form of a large square surrounded by arcades with vaults and monuments, the poorer classes being interred in the centre.

Plan for visiting the Sights of Verona in 1 or 2 days, and in topographical order.

Ch. of *S. Anastasia;* DUOMO; Vescovado, and Biblioteca Capitolare; Ch. of S. Eufemia; *Piazza dei Signori; Pal. del Consiglio; Piazza delle Erbe;* Ch. of S. Maria l'Antica, and TOMBS OF THE SCALIGERS; Corso; *Arco dei Borsari;* Piazza Bra; *Arena;* Arco de' Gavi; Museo Lapidario; Castel Vecchio, and Bridge; Chs. of *S. Zenone,* of *S. Bernardino;* Porta Nuova.

Ch. of *S. Fermo Maggiore;* Ponte alle Navi; Pal. Pompei; PINACOTECA, and other collections in it; Campo Santo; Ch. of *S. Tomaso Cantuarense; Pal. Giusti* and *Gardens;* Chs. of *SS. Nazzaro e Celso, S. Maria in Organo, S. Giorgio,* and *S. Giovanni in Valle;* Barracks and Castel di S. Pietro; Ch. of *S. Giorgio Maggiore;* Castel di S. Felice; Ponte di Pietra.

Neighbourhood of Verona.

Towards the Adige, and on the N., are *Gargagnano,* where Dante is said to have composed his Purgatorio, and where he possessed some property, a villa, which afterwards passed into the *Serego Alighieri* family. It is in a wild and picturesque situation.

Sant' Ambrogio, a little to the E. of the road, about 2 m. before reaching Volargne, on the road from Verona to the Tyrol: near it are quarries from whence much of the red marble of Verona is obtained. The workmen of these quarries are remarkable for their cleverness as masons and sculptors, which arts, as at Como, they follow from father to son.

San Giorgio, a mile and a half N.E. of St. Ambrogio, upon a lofty hill, apparently easy of ascent, but in fact very difficult, whence it has the name of "*Inganna poltrone*." Here is a good Lombard church, where columns and inscriptions of Liutprand were found.

The mountainous districts to the N., the *Monti Lessini*, afford a variety of interesting excursions, such as that to the *Ponte di Veja*, to which a road passes up the *Val Pantena*, through the pleasant villages of *Quinto*, *Grezzano*, and *Lugo*. It can be taken on horseback or in a light carriage.

At *Quinto*, on his way to the *Ponte*, the traveller should stop for the purpose of visiting the sanctuary of *Santa Maria della Stella*. Beneath the church is a very curious Roman crypt, which the Italian antiquaries have supposed to be a cave dedicated to *Mercurius Trophonius* (a creation of their own), but which, in 1187, was consecrated by Pope Urban III. A heathen altar or Roman sarcophagus, now in the crypt, may have been brought from its vicinity. The floor exhibits the remains of a beautiful mosaic: a stream of very pure and limpid water, which still flows into the crypt in the original Roman conduit, and the remains of other Roman constructions adjoining, may possibly lead to the supposition that the cave of Trophonius was originally a bath.

Grezzana, in the Val Pantena.

The *Villa Cuzzano*, near Grezzana, is a good and unaltered specimen of an old Italian mansion, and contains frescoes by *Paolo Veronese*.

In the vicinity of *Marzana* are Roman remains, an aqueduct, and other buildings.

Val Policella and *Val Pantena* are filled with villas, the summer residences of the rich Veronese. The wines of the Val Policella have a local celebrity. The chief place in it is the large village of *S. Pietro in Cariano*.

In a deep ravine, near the head of the Val Pantena, is the *Ponte della Veja*, a natural arch, beneath which rushes a cascade. The span of the arch is about 150 ft.: you can walk along the summit, of which the breadth varies from 10 to 15 ft. Beyond is the village of *Sant' Anna*, a secluded spot.

An excursion to the *Monte Bolca*, which, going and returning, will be about 40 m., also includes many objects of varied interest.

Soave, the town nearest the Vicenza road, is a good specimen of *Scaligerian* fortification: the surrounding walls and gates, as well as the castle, are more than usually perfect.

Diverging by the by-road which branches off on the l. at the St. Bonifacio Rlwy. Stat. to *Monteforte*, following the Alpone torrent 4 m. farther, you approach the valley of *Ronca*. The rocks of the *Val Cunella*, which opens into that of the Alpone, are composed almost wholly of beds of shells, whilst the neighbourhood possesses some very remarkable basaltic formations. Returning to the Alpone, and following it upwards to *S. Giovanni Ilarione*, from which a road, still following the torrent, leads to Bolca, passing the Monte del Diavolo, a mass of basaltic columns: here the pillars are mostly inclined at a considerable angle; others are curved, and others broken off, so as to form an horizontal pavement. Continuing onwards, at *Vestena Nova* the basaltic prisms are very lofty and erect. In one part they form a cliff nearly 50 ft. in height, down which the torrent *Alpone* pours a beautiful cascade. The basaltic columns are called the *Stanghellini*, a name similar in its etymology to the Hebrides *Staffa*, for *Stanga* means a pole or staff.

About 3 m. further is the *Monte Bolca*, called La Purga, the largest and most singular deposit of fossil fishes yet discovered. The mountain, which is of a conical form, is partly formed of basalt. The impressions of the fish are found in the schistose strata, which gives out, when broken, a bituminous smell. A lignite of inferior quality is found here in the same tertiary marine strata under the basalt.

With respect to the fossil fishes, it must be observed that the same ingenuity which supplies the antiquary with Othos, equally insures to the geologist the rarest and most extraordinary specimens; that is to say, they are imitated in such a manner as to deceive any ordinary eye; they are cleverly manufactured out of the disjointed fragments of several different species. Good specimens may be bought of the *custode* of the Amphitheatre at Verona; but they are not cheap: and the high price is explained by telling you, which is tolerably correct, that it is a rare occurrence, amidst the numberless fragments imbedded in the schistus, to find anything approaching to an entire individual.

The province of Verona abounds in objects of great singularity and interest. Amongst the works of art the ancient feudal castles are remarkable. Of those which are of the era of the Scaligers, and more or less in the style of the Castle of Verona, some are noticed in the different routes; but there are many more in parts of the country out of the beaten track of travellers.

ROUTE 30.

VERONA TO MANTUA, BY VILLAFRANCA.
—RAIL.

MILES.		MILES.	
4	Dossobuono.	16	Roverbella.
8¾	Villafranca.	20	Mantua.
11¼	Mozzecane.		

20 Ital. m.=23 Eng. m.

4 trains daily, at 7·55 A.M.; 12·12, 5·0, and 9·30 P.M.

The country on the rt. of the road is celebrated as the scene of some of the most bloody actions between the Piedmontese and Austrians in 1848. It passes near to Santa Lucia and Somma Campagna, from which Charles Albert blockaded Radetsky in Verona, to Custozza, where, after a most sanguinary and protracted contest, the Piedmontese were worsted on the 25th of July, and obliged to recross the Mincio; and by Villafranca, the head-quarters of the King of Sardinia during a part of his invasion of the country beyond the Mincio.

4 m. *Dossobuono, Stat.*, near a straggling village on right.

3¾ m. *Villafranca. Stat.*

At Villafranca is a fine castellated structure. It was founded in 1199 by the Veronese; but the present building is of the 14th century. Villafranca has acquired a celebrity in the diplomatic history of Europe as the site of the negotiations between the Emperors of France and Austria, which ended in the conclusion of the convention which put an end to the late war on the 11th July, 1859. [From here a cross-road of 5 m. leads to *Valeggio* and *Borghetto*, on the Mincio. Overlooking Borghetto, and on the opposite side (east) of the river, is the Scaligerian Castle of Valeggio, with a very lofty dungeon. Valleggio and Borghetto constitute an important military position, as affording an easy passage of the Mincio. Here the French crossed in August, 1796, after the battle of Castiglione; the Piedmontese in 1848—the Austrians on both occasions retreating to Verona; and again the French in pursuit of the Austrians, after their defeat at Solferino on the 24th June, 1859. Valeggio, a village of 2000 inhabitants, in the midst of a rich silk district, is on the edge of the great plain of Mantua. But the most remarkable feature of the place is the fortified bridge or causeway between it and Borghetto, built in 1393 by Gian' Galeazzo Visconti, who has in this fabric exhibited his favourite passion for architectural magnificence. His engineers availed themselves of a Roman substructure, upon which they erected this raised causeway or viaduct, at each end of which was a lofty gate tower, and in the centre the bridge over the Mincio; the latter has long been broken down. The length of the causeway is 602 yards, battlemented on either side like the bridge at Verona, and defended by lofty turrets. It cost 108,182 golden zecchins of Venice.]

2¾ m. *Mozzecane, Stat.* The country about, and hence to Mantua, consists chiefly of irrigated meadow-land.

3½ m. *Roverbella, Stat.* The town, a large wealthy place, is at some distance on the right of the stat.: here they show the house in which Napoleon lodged in 1796, during the military operations between the Adige and the Mincio, and the siege of Mantua.

4 m. *Mantua, Stat.*

1 MANTUA: Italian, Mantova.— (*Inns:* La Fenice, united to la Croce Verde, good, kept by Maria Trevisani. There is a good Servitore di Piazza, called Giovanni Casagrande, who will take the visitor over the sights in a few hours. L'Aquila d'Oro is also good. Both these inns are in the Contrada della Croce Verde. Lo Scudo di Francia.)

The railroad stat. is 2 m. from the town, but omnibuses start to meet each train to and from the different hotels; fare ½ a lira.

Diligences.—In consequence of the interruption of friendly relations between the Government of Austria and the annexed states of N. Italy, the communications have been in great measure suspended by public conveyances, the only one being to Parma daily in 8 hrs., by way of Casalmaggiore, corresponding with Cremona.

Moretti Foggia, a chemist, keeps English medicines.

Mantua is surrounded by lakes and marshes, adding at once to the strength of this ancient city and to its insalubrity. The latter, however, has somewhat diminished, the marshes having been partially drained. This was effected by the French. The three portions of the lake are called the *Lago di Mezzo*, *Lago Inferiore*, and *Lago Superiore*, formed by the swelling out of the Mincio, and maintained by artificial dams and embankments; they are crossed by six bridges, or *chaussées*.

Mantua stands on the "smooth-sliding Mincius."

" Propter aquam, tardis ingens ubi flexibus errat
Mincius, et tenerâ praetexit arundine ripas."

In fact, the city is situated on two lands, between which the river flows, and from its situation amid the flat and sedgy banks of the Mincio its climate is anything but healthy: intermittent and low fevers are frequent in the autumn, and it has no claims to natural beauty; but it contains many fine buildings, and remains of works of art, called into existence by its former sovereigns.

The Gonzagas, first Lords, or Captains, in 1328; next Marquises, or Margraves, in 1433; and lastly, created by Charles V. Dukes of Mantua, in 1530, were men of great talent, and possessed extraordinary munificence and energy; and in the 16th centy. "*Mantova la Gloriosa*" was one of the most rich and gay of the

CHURCHES.
1. Duomo or Cathedral.
2. S. Andrea.
3. S. Barbara.
4. S. Barnaba.
5. S. Maurizio.
6. S. Sebastiano.

PUBLIC BUILDINGS, &c.
7. Palazzo Ducale.
8. Prisons; Archives.
9. Theatre of the Court.
10. Teatro Sociale.
11. Amphitheatre.
12. Piazza di S. Pietro
13.   „   delle Erbe.
14. Botanic Garden.
15. Palazzo del Te.

N. Italy—1860.

courts and cities of Italy. The Gonzagas, but more especially Giovanni Francesco II. (from 1484 to 1519), and Federico II. (1514-1540), who first obtained the ducal dignity, were magnificent patrons and promoters of the arts and of literature. Their successors continued to govern with much wisdom; and Mantua became one of the most opulent and flourishing cities of Lombardy, when the death of Vincenzio II. (1627) was followed by every kind of calamity. It seemed thenceforward as if the house had become fated. Francesco IV. having died without male issue after a reign of ten months, the duchy devolved upon Cardinal Ferdinando, his brother. It was more than doubtful whether he had any right to the duchy, for Mantua had not been declared a male fief; and it was considered that Maria, his niece, was the lawful heir. Ferdinand, having by papal licence resigned his cardinal's hat, married twice. By his first and secret marriage with Camilla Reticina he had one son; but Ferdinand procured the marriage to be dissolved; Jacintho Gonzaga was declared illegitimate, and his father married Catherine of Medicis; but he had no children by her; and, on his death in 1627, the duchy was claimed by the branch of the Gonzagas settled in France, then represented by Charles Duke of Nevers. The right was contested; and the Emperor Ferdinand II. claiming to dispose of the duchy of Mantua as an imperial fief, the country was invaded by Altringer, Colalto, and Gallas, names written in blood in the history of the thirty years' war. Duke Charles, was neglected, and almost betrayed, by the Venetians, and feebly supported by the French. On the 8th April, 1630, the imperialists laid siege to the town: famine and pestilence raged within; but the duke defended himself bravely; and the inhabitants, knowing what would be their fate, aided with the utmost valour and desperation. On the 18th July, when the garrison was reduced to 1000 fighting men, the city was taken by storm, and during three days was given up to plunder. The Germans on this occasion executed their work of devastation with great system and regularity; they got exceedingly drunk; they neither killed a man, nor insulted a woman, nor burnt a house: but they stripped the town of everything which it contained. The plunder was valued at 8,000,000 ducats. Previous to the siege the duke had sold large portions of the Gonzaga collections. The plunder of the city dispersed the remainder, with the exception of such of the marbles as remain in the museum. The best portions were taken to Prague. They were afterwards purchased by Christina Queen of Sweden, who carried them to Rome, where they remained until they were obtained by the Regent Duke of Orleans, and became the foundation of the Orleans gallery.

Carlo Gonzaga I. regained his duchy by submission to the emperor; but Mantua never recovered from the blow. Population has increased of late years; there are now about 35,000 Inhab., upwards of 3000 of whom are Jews, by whom a great proportion of the trade is carried on.

The Gonzagas were in the last century deprived of their possessions by the jurisprudence of the feudal ages. Carlo IV. having unfortunately joined the French in the war of the succession, the Emperor Joseph I. placed him under the ban of the empire, and seized his dominions. The duke fled, and died at Padua in 1707, not without suspicion of poison; and Joseph, declaring the fief to be forfeited, united it to his own dominions. The last of the Gonzagas, still a resident here, is now a pensioner of the Austrian government. The Austrians added to the fortifications, and Mantua became, what it is now, one of the strongest fortresses in Italy.

Hence, in 1796, after the fall of Milan, Napoleon immediately endeavoured to make himself master of Mantua, as the bulwark of the Austrian dominions, and without the possession of which the conquest of Lombardy never could be secure. The siege was begun 14th June, 1796, by a blockade; but the forces of Serrurier were only sufficient to keep the garrison in check, and the French could not prevent the occupation of the city by Wurmser, after his defeat at Bassano. About September the Austrians were shut within their walls. Wurmser then killed all his horses, and salted their carcases. Four unavailing attempts were made by the Austrians to relieve the garrison. After the failure of the last, Mantua could no longer hold out. One half of its numerous garrison was in the hospital: they had consumed all their horses, and the troops, placed for months on half-rations, had nearly exhausted all their provisions. In this extremity Wurmser proposed to Serrurier to capitulate: the French commander stated that he could give no definite answer till the arrival of the general-in-chief. Napoleon, in consequence, hastened to Roverbella, where he found Klenau, the Austrian aide-de-camp, expatiating with Serrurier on the powerful means of resistance which Wurmser enjoyed, and the great stores of provisions which still remained in the magazines. Wrapped in his cloak near the fire, he overheard the conversation without taking any part in it, or making himself known. When it was concluded, he approached the table, took up the pen, and wrote on the margin his answer to all the propositions of Wurmser; and when it was finished, said to Klenau, "If Wurmser had only provisions for fifteen days, and spoke of surrendering, he would not have merited an honourable capitulation; but as he has sent you, he must be reduced to extremities; but I respect his age, his valour, and his misfortunes. Here are the conditions which I offer him if he surrender tomorrow: should he delay a fortnight, a month, or two months, he shall have the same conditions: he may wait till he feels he can do so with honour to himself. I am now about to cross the Po to march upon Rome: return, and communicate my intentions to your general." The aide-de-camp, who now perceived that he was in the presence of Napoleon, finding that it was useless longer to dissemble, confessed that they had only provisions left for three days. The terms of capitulation were immediately agreed on; Napoleon set out himself to Florence, to conduct the expedition against Rome; and Serrurier had the honour of seeing the marshal, with all his staff, defile before him. On taking the city, the French committed many excesses. It was retaken after a bombardment of four days by the Austrians in 1799.

In the centre of the city there is much appearance of commercial activity; but the grass grows in the outskirts, and the marks of ruin, too visible upon many of the buildings, attest the misfortunes which Mantua has sustained. Yet many interesting memorials remain, to remind us of its ancient splendour. There are no large squares, but great masses of buildings, huge piles casting deep shadows, feudal towers crowned with their forked battlements, castles and Lombard arches, form a scene of peculiar and novel character.

The assemblage of buildings which, beginning at the *Porta di San Giorgio*, extends from the *Piazza di S. Pietro* to the *Lago Inferiore*, is almost unique in its kind. The first object is the ancient *Castello di Corte*, the palace and fortress of the Gonzagas, built by Francesco Gonzaga IV., Capitano of Mantua, between the years 1393 and 1406, the architect being Bertolino Novara. It is a vast pile, flanked by deeply machicolated and noble towers, but battered and decayed. It was used by the Austrians partly as a prison, chiefly for political offenders, and partly as public offices. The archives contain documents reaching as far back as the early part of the 11th centy., and all those relative to the Gonzagas are deposited here. The interior was richly decorated with frescoes, which were perfect till the conquest of Lombardy by the French: now only a few vestiges can be traced in some of the rooms, occupied by the public offices. Of these the most interesting are in one of the rooms now used as a council-room, 1, on the wall on l. of the entrance a man and boy holding a horse and dogs; 2, the fine picture of Ludovico Gonzaga, and his wife Barbara and three children; 3, over the door a beautiful group of 3 Angels holding an inscription: all these frescoes are by *Andrea Mantegna*. In the coves of the ceiling are heads in chiar'-oscuro of the Cæsars, also by *Mantegna*. Another smaller room has a border representing, in small but animated groups, chaces of wild animals and of fabulous creatures; and in the rest of the neglected chambers similar traces may be seen of past grandeur.

Adjoining the Castello di Corte is the immense edifice begun in 1302, by Guido Buonacolsi, surnamed Boticella, third sovereign lord of Mantua, now comprising the so-called Palazzo Imperiale, Palazzo Vecchio, and Corte Imperiale, and containing, it is said, 500 rooms. Of the older building, however, little besides the front, with its Gothic arches and windows surmounted by machicolated battlements, and the arms of the Buonacolsi in the capitals of some columns, is now in existence. Several artists had employed their talents upon it before *Giulio Romano* was called upon to transform it entirely, und exhibit new proofs of the inexhaustible powers of his genius. Since his time many other artists have contributed in various ways to its embellishment. In fact, for the grandeur of its masses, for propriety, invention, and decorations of every kind, for the solution of the most perplexing problems in architectural and pictorial arrangement, for the skilful adaptation of designs to the most uninviting and embarrassing spaces, we know no edifice of this kind either in or out of Italy which approaches this imperial residence, or which displays such varied resources to the student of decorative art. This Palace was the favourite residence of the later members of the ducal house. The Emperor Joseph bestowed much care upon it, several of the rooms were furnished anew during the French occupation and by the Austrians to receive the Emperor Francis; many retain much of their former splendour, but a great proportion have been converted into storehouses and barracks. The genius of *Giulio Romano*, whether as a painter or an architect, is nowhere displayed to greater advantage. The front of the Cavallerizza, and the Giardino pensile, on a terrace, so as to be on a level with the upper floor, and surrounded with richly painted *loggie*, are especially deserving of attention.

The order in which the state apartments are shown is nearly as follows:—

The *Camera del Zodiaco*, from the painting of the Signs of the Zodiac by *Giulio Romano*, and amongst which Orion is introduced: the two children representing the twin offspring of Orion and the Moon in the centre are very beautiful.

Camere degl' Arazzi, 4 in number: on the walls are extended a set of tapestries from the Cartoons of Raphael at Hampton Court, and the Conversion of St. Paul, and the Martyrdom of St. Peter; both fine, but not equal to that of St. Paul preaching at Athens. "The tapestries are surrounded by painted borders of allegorical imagery, and there is a painted ceiling: all have the finest effect."—*L. G.*

The stucco ornaments of the doors and wood carvings are from designs by Primaticcio.

On the opposite side of the courtyard to the Camere degl' Arazzi is the *Galleria degli Specchi*, or ball-room, with some fine Venetian glass painted by Giulio Romano's pupils. The great audience-chamber, whose ceiling is upborne by magnificent consoles, is interesting; and still more so is another, the *Galleria de Quadri*, containing the

PLAN OF THE BUILDINGS OF THE DUCAL PALACE IN MANTUA.

1 Piazza Arche.
2 Scuderie Reali.
3 Cda. Ducale.
4 Cda. Giorgio.
5 Cda. del Duomo.
6 Seminario.

References to the Apartments.

a Scalcheria.
b Camera degli Arazzi.
c Camera del Zodiaco.
d Galleria degli Specchi.
e Giardino pensile.
f Corridor leading to the Corte Vecchia.
g Sala de' Marmi.
h Sala and Appartamento di Troja.
i Corte Vecchia.
k l Castello, now Archives.
m Sala with portraits of the Gonzaga family.
n Gallery.
o Appartamento Stivali.
p Appartamento Paradiso.
q Passage leading to the Cathedral.
r House of B. Castiglione.

long series of *Capitani*, Marquises, Dukes, Princes, and Princesses of the Gonzaga family, and some very indifferent paintings, one attributed to *Luini*. A suite of rooms is kept well furnished, but the greater part are empty and desolate; and in the back part of the building, deserted cortiles, and blocked-up windows, and springing vegetation, are sad and dreary memorials of Mantua's decay.

In the interior, the chamber called the "*Appartamento di Troja*" is principally painted by *Giulio Romano*, perhaps partly by *Mantegna*. The works were begun in 1524, by Federigo Gonzaga, the first Duke of Mantua, and he employed *Baldassare Castiglione* to make the needful arrangements with the artists. It leads to the Sala di Troja, which is painted entirely by *Giulio Romano*. These chambers, as the name imports, contain passages from the history of the Trojan war, and are in tolerable preservation. " In this room, painted by *Giulio Romano*, in fresco, his characteristic invention is powerfully conveyed. Ajax, transfixed with a fiery arrow by Minerva, is strongly and vividly expressed. Minerva retiring looks back with scorn upon the impotent rival of her favourite Ulysses. When Paris conducts Helen to the ship, the natural feeling of the characters is admirably portrayed. The lover is manly, and is earnestly persuading his fair heroine to embark: she, though not unwilling, yet looks back to her attendants who bear her attire, with true female feeling, to see if her adornings are in security: all is bustle and activity. The frescoes of *Laocoon* and his sons, and of the completion of the Trojan Horse, are weak, and yet again, in that of Achilles dragging Hector at the back of his chariot, the very spirit of vengeance seems to inspire him. In colour and effect it is as bad as it can be, and this work is by no means so finished as his labours in the Palazzo del Tè."— *Phillips, R.A.*

Adjoining these chambers is the Sala de' Marmi (so called from a number of masterpieces of the Grecian chisel which once adorned it), very richly decorated. It is of the time of Giulio Romano. This is connected by a gallery, running along one side of the Cavallerizza, with the Appartamento Stivali, painted by *Giulio Romano* and *Primaticcio*. Near this last is the apartment called "Il Paradiso," containing some curious ancient cabinets, yet retaining the initials of *Isabella d'Este*, wife of Francis III. Marquis of Mantua, equally celebrated for her beauty and her intrepidity. The ceilings of most of the apartments are of wood, richly ornamented with carvings and stucco-work, by *Primaticcio*. They are very curiously varied: in one room the ceiling represents a labyrinth, with the inscription *"forse che sì, forse che no,"* repeated in each meander. The *Sala de' Mori* is the richest; it is blue and gold. The *Scalcheria*, or room of the seneschals, contains an exquisite specimen of a richly decorated ceiling, said to be one of the first paintings which Giulio Romano executed in Mantua. The conception is beautiful, and the execution most careful. The figure of a female, with a genius, in the centre, looking over a balustrade, is painted in oil, and attributed to Mantegna. The pleasures of the chace, or sports of Diana, in the lunettes, are amongst the most elegant inventions of Giulio Romano.

Opposite to the palace with its Gothic windows, stands the palace of B. Castiglione, the author of the *Cortegiano;* it has a fine gateway with sculptured arabesques; on one side of which is the bishop's palace, and on the other that of the Guerrieri family. Close to the latter is an ancient tower annexed to the palace which formerly belonged to the Buonacolsis; it was built in 1302 by Boticella. About half-way up projects an iron cage, from whence this building derives its name of *Torre della Gabbia*. According to the traditions of the city, when any criminal deserved to be put to shame, he was exposed in this cage for three successive days, and for three hours each day. The caging of criminals was very common in Italy (see Piacenza, p. 398). On the capture of the city by the French, the cage was taken down, but replaced afterwards by the direction of Napoleon; the tower itself commands a fine prospect over the town and the lake.

The *Torre dello Zuccaro*, hard by, is also fine of its kind, and interesting as a memorial of the ancient factions by whom the city was ruled and divided.

The *Palazzo della Ragione* was begun in 1198, in the age of Mantuan independence, and completed about

1250. It is a fine specimen of the civil architecture of the time. A large archway of brick and stone forms a prominent feature in this building. Inserted in the wall is a Gothic throne and canopy supported by twisted and facetted columns. Beneath this canopy is a sitting statue of Virgil, a crowned figure, the countenance grave but beautiful, holding an open book upon his knees; the inscription below is of the 12th or 13th century. From this building rises a lofty campanile with a curious astronomical clock upon the *Dondi* plan (see *Padua*), but of rather later date, having been put up in 1478. It has a great number of complicated movements, now out of order.

It is in the neighbourhood of this Palazzo that the city is most unchanged. In the neighbouring *Piazza d'Erba* may be seen a small but beautifully decorated house-front in terracotta resting on a portico supported by Corinthian columns.

The DUOMO, dedicated to St. Peter, has been much altered. One side-wall, exhibiting a series of Gothic gables, separated by pinnacles of moulded brick and all richly ornamented, shows the original style. The fine Lombard campanile is also standing. The interior was rebuilt by *Giulio Romano*. The arches of the aisles rest upon Corinthian pillars: the roof of the nave is flat, with richly ornamented compartments. Except a fresco by *Mantegna*, now covered with glass (and that partly covered by another picture), there are no paintings of any peculiar merit in this building. The Chapel *della Madonna Incoronata*, by *Alberti*, is fine The Chapel of the Virgin is richly decorated, in that of the Holy Sacrament, in the l. transept, is the fine monument of Pietro Strozzi by Giulio Romano.

The *Basilica di Sant' Andrea* is among the finest existing specimens of an interior in the Italian or revived Roman style. It was designed by *Leon Battista Alberti*. The cupola was added by *Juvara*; it was begun in 1732, but not completed till 1781. The church is about 310 ft. in length.

It contains many good frescoes by the scholars of Mantegna. In a crypt beneath the high altar is a shrine where is preserved the blood of our Lord collected by the Centurion. The vaultings of the aisles of this church are very bold and skilful. *Mantegna* is buried in the first chapelon the l. His bust in bronze by *Sperandio*, erected in 1516, ten years after Mantegna's death, is an excellent piece of workmanship. The eyes are said to have been formed of diamonds. In the chapel of the Virgin is a Holy Family, with St. Elizabeth, by *Mantegna*. The other good paintings are—*L. Costa*, a Holy Family;—*Guisoni*, a Crucifixion. Several of the monuments are worthy of notice, either for their beauty, or on account of the persons to whose memory they are raised. *Prospero Clementi of Reggio*, a pupil of Michael Angelo, sculptured the tomb of Giorgio Andreassi.—The *Cantelmi* monument, of curious architectural construction; the memorial of Pietro Pomponazzo, who enjoys an unfortunate celebrity—his renowned work on the Immortality of the Soul, published at Venice in 1516, having laid him under the imputation of atheism, a charge not diminished by his having had Cardinal Bembo as a defender. The great portal or entrance of the church is deeply recessed. It has also the remains of a fresco by *Mantegna*. The fine brick Gothic campanile belonged to the original basilica.

The *Ch. of Sta. Barbara*, within the Palace, was built by *Bertani*, a scholar of Giulio Romano. Over the high altar is the Martyrdom of the Patroness, by *Brusasorzi*. This is a collegiate church, exempted from the jurisdiction of the bishop, but immediately under the papal see; and the liturgy has some peculiarities of its own. The archives are extensive and curious. The once rich sacristy still contains a few objects of value; the most remarkable is a golden vase, delicately chased, attributed to *Benvenuto Cellini*.

San Maurizio, formerly S. Napoleone. Here is the Martyrdom of the Saint, by *Ludovico Caracci*: the figure of St. Margaret is beautiful. Near this is the ch. of *San Francesco*, a fine building of the 14th or 15th century, but now desecrated, and converted with its convent into artillery stores and barracks.

San Sebastiano, now closed, erected by *L. B. Alberti* in 1460; a specimen of the revived Roman style: it offers some good but dilapidated frescoes by *Mantegna*. Opposite stands the house of Mantegna, presented to him by the generous Gonzagas with an honorary inscription; by the side of which is the Porta Pusterla leading to the *Palazzo del T.*

A curious specimen of ancient engineering is the *Argine del Mulino*, the bridge, or rather dam, constructed in 1188 by *Alberto Pitentino*. It stands between two of the pieces of water which surround Mantua, one of which, being of a higher level than the other, serves as a great millpond, and turns the wheels of the twelve mills which flank the bridge and are severally dedicated to the twelve Apostles. Each mill has the statue of its apostle. The bridge itself is covered, and is entered by a fortified tower or gateway, in which is a beautiful pointed window, divided by a central mullion. Near the *Porta Mulina* is a saw-mill, which is, perhaps, the earliest example of such machinery. It was built by *Girolamo Arcari* in 1400, and it is still in active operation.

The *Beccheria* and the *Pescheria*, the shambles and the fish-market, stand upon the Mincio, so that they are always kept clean. They were built by *Giulio Romano;* and, whilst the plan is exceedingly simple, he has given them, and more especially the Beccheria, no inconsiderable degree of architectural beauty.

The *Palazzo Colloredo* in the Via Larga, the widest thoroughfare in Mantua, was built by *Bertani* from the designs of Giulio Romano. The front is supported by enormous caryatides of bold sculpture. Within is a profusion of frescoes by the *scholars of Giulio Romano*. Amongst them are introduced many curious portraits of sovereigns and princes: Francis I., Charles VIII., and other French kings; Giovanni de' Medici; Nicolo III. Marquis of Ferrara; and Francesco IV. Marquis of Mantua.

In the same street, and nearly opposite to the Palazzo Colloredo, is *Giulio Romano's* house; the front is of an elegant and chaste design. Over the door is a statue of Mercury, or rather a fragment restored by *Giulio Romano* and *Primaticcio*. The attributes of the heathen god are introduced in various parts of the building. Giulio Romano was buried in the neighbouring ch. of S. Barnaba, but the place of his grave is unknown.

The *Palazzo del Diavolo*, now having a dreary, deserted, and haunted look, is said to have been built by the fiend in the course of one night, he having been constrained thereto by the divining rod of hazel, which in Germany used to be employed for the discovery of treasures. The exterior was painted by *Pordenone*, but it is now cut up into shops and dwellings, and has little remarkable except its name. Near the Palazzo del Diavolo is the Teatro Sociale, built by Canonica, a handsome modern construction, in the Corso di Porta Pradella, a fine wide street leading to the gate of that name, and through which the road to Cremona passes.

The *Accademia delle Belle Arti*, founded in 1775, is now merely a drawing-school. It contains some pictures from suppressed churches and convents. There is a good copy of the "Notte" by *Correggio;* but the gallery does not pretend to great names. Our Lord bearing his cross, by *Francesco Monsignore*, is amongst the best in it.

The *Scuole Pubbliche* were formed out of the Jesuits' College. The library contains about 80,000 printed books, and a few curious MSS.: some beautiful missals, and one with pen-and-ink drawings by *Andrea Mantegna*. Here is a very fine Rubens, formerly in the church, representing four members of the Gonzaga family in the act of prayer.

The *Museo Antiquario* is a long and narrow gallery, filled with Roman and some few Greek statues and fragments, of which the greater portion, it is said, were part of the plunder collected by Lodovico Gonzaga at the sack of Rome. It used to be considered the first collection in Italy, a rank it can no longer maintain; though it certainly contains some good specimens.—Three fine bassirilievi, representing the submission of a province, a sacrifice, and the marriage of an emperor, supposed to be Lucius Verus. Several Imperial busts, amongst them a fine Caligula. The Battles of the Amazons; Death of Penthesilea. The Sun (not Apollo) surrounded by other divinities. Euripides. Thales. The Descent of Orpheus. Medea. A Cupid Sleeping, attributed to Michael Angelo, and also said, like some other of his productions, to have been passed off by him for an antique. Virgil's Chair, that is to say, a very ancient bishop's throne of marble. The bust of Virgil, a calm, beautiful countenance with long flowing hair. There was, anciently, in the market-place of Mantua, a statue said to be Virgil, and representing him sitting on a throne, holding his works in one hand, and raising the other, as in the act of declaiming. This statue became the object of a species of worship; and when Carlo Malatesta, in 1397, occupied Mantua, a conscientious scruple induced him to break the idol in pieces and cast its fragments into the lake, the head only being saved. It is evident, whatever may be thought of the story, that this head never could have belonged to a statue, inasmuch as it is part of a Term, and, in the next place, it is equally evident that it is not Virgil, but a young Bacchus, or some similar mythological personage.

The *Ponte di San Giorgio* crosses the entire lake, and is upwards of 2500 ft. in length. It was built in 1401, and was anciently covered like a Swiss bridge. The view of Mantua from hence, towers and cupolas, and the great mass of the castle, is peculiar.

The *Piazza Virgiliana* was formed out of a swamp, drained and planted by the French; it is yet dark and rather dreary. At one end is the *Anfiteatro Virgiliano*, built 1820, for shows and games, as a private speculation.

Outside the walls and a few hundred yards beyond the Porta Pusterla is the *Palazzo del Tè*. Various accounts have been given of the origin of the name of this palace, but the only one which seems to deserve credit is that of Gabrieli Bertolazzo (the author of a description of Mantua, the 2nd edition of which appeared in 1628), who ascribes it to the form of the roads and avenues by which it was approached, which were so arranged as to produce the capital letter T. All the old authors, beginning with Vasari, write it del T, and not, as in modern times, del Tè; which affords a confirmation of this view. The Palazzo consisted originally of stables, and the Marquis Federigo Gonzaga intended to make this building an unpretending country-house, with one single large room besides the necessary accommodation; but Giulio, in acquitting himself of his commission, showed so much taste, that the Marquis decided upon transforming and extending the new house into a splendid palace, and thus gave the artist an opportunity of applying, in harmonious combination, his powers as architect, painter, and sculptor. Giulio executed this great work, with the assistance of his pupils Primaticcio, G. B. Pagni, and Rinaldo Montorano, in the short space of five years. The principal building, with the large court in the centre, forms a square, each front being about 180 ft. outside, and about 120 ft. in the court. The order of architecture is throughout Doric, tastefully exhibiting all the variety of which this style is susceptible. The hall opposite the principal entrance leads over a bridge into an extensive parterre, which ends with a semicircular wall, portioned out into 15 niches, probably for statues. At each extremity of this wall was an exquisite apartment of small dimensions, composed of a grotto and a *loggia*, with

o 3

which a small flower-garden was connected. Of these the one on the l. is still in a tolerable state of preservation: the other was destroyed more than a century ago, by being used as a guardhouse.

The principal rooms of the palace are the following, in the order which the visitor is shown over them :—

Small apartment on rt. of entrance, with plaster reliefs by Primaticcio and his scholars.

Camera dei Cavalli.—Pictures of Gonzaga's horses. This is the oldest part of the building, and that which gave such delight to G. Romano's patron. The ceiling, which is of wood, is finely carved in compartments. "I was struck with the great truth shown in the imitation of the horses, six in number, of the natural size, painted in this room. The two bays are nearly as perfect in preservation as could be desired, while the three white, and remaining one, an iron grey, have suffered much. These are said to have been also painted by the pupils of Giulio Romano, B. Pagni and Rinaldo Montovano, from the designs of their master."—*S. A. Hart, R.A.*

Camera di Psiche.—Rich in frescoes, oil-paintings, and stuccoes, illustrating the story of Psyche from Apuleius. "Subjects of deep pathos, of sublime allegory, are here treated with the hand of a master, in all that relates to poetic imagination and invention in design. The pictorial is wanting to render them agreeable, though it is in this room that Giulio Romano has evidently put forth his strength in force and depth of colours, and in effects of light and shade, particularly in Psyche offering her fruits and flowers to Venus, in her receiving the grapes, in the discovery of Cupid by Psyche, and in some of the beautifully composed figures of the lunettes. These pictures are in oil, and therefore he could work on them to effect more fully than in fresco, and they are so treated, but are far too black. The large pictures below are in fresco, and are rich indeed in the important qualities of imagery, invention, and design, but woefully wanting in colour, effect, and harmony."—*Prof. Phillips, R.A.*

"G. Romano's pupils, Benedetto, Pagni, and Rinaldo Montovano, are said to have painted the ceiling in oil from the designs of their master. These paintings are turned black and heavy, especially in the shadows; a remark which cannot with equal truth be applied to the subjects in the room beneath in fresco, in which not more than a certain depth is indulged in, calculated to give space and light to the apartment. The ceiling, on the contrary, looks low."—*S. A. Hart, R.A.*

Camera dei Cesari contains 2 frescoes in the lunettes, by *Giulio Romano :* Alexander discovering the writings of Homer, and restoring the wife of Mardonius.

Camera di Faetonte.—So called from the oil-painting of the fall of Phaëton, on the vault. The distribution of this small room is as tasteful as its execution is exquisite.

Camera del Zodiaco, o dell' Astronomia.—On the ceiling, in stucco, are the winds and the 12 signs of the zodiac: the occupations of the seasons are painted in 16 medallions.

The *Atrio*, or Loggia forming the principal entrance.—Passages from the life of David, executed by Giulio's scholars. The medallions by *Primaticcio*. A cannon-ball fell through the vaulting during the siege of 1796, injuring the frescoes of the fall of Phaëton.

Sala de' Stucchi, in which there is a double frieze executed by *Primaticcio*, from designs of *Giulio Romano*, representing the triumphal entrance into Mantua of the Emperor Sigismund in 1433, who the year before had created Gian Francesco Gonzaga Marquis of Mantua. The arched ceiling is equally rich in stuccoes.

Sala de' Giganti.—The most celebrated of the series : it was chiefly executed by *Rinaldo Montovano;* a small portion only was the work of *Giulio Romano*, who furnished the designs. Jupiter, amidst the heathen gods, hurls his thunders upon the Titans, who, in different actions, terror, danger, and impending death, cover the four walls, down to the very floor. The giants in the foreground are represented 12 or 14 ft. high. Most contradictory judgments have been passed on these paintings. Vasari, Borghini, and all the earlier writers upon art, praise them exceedingly; and Lanzi considers him as rivalling Michael Angelo. Others have thought that they have been praised far beyond their deserts. "Colossal figures in a small room, even where the idea of a supernatural size is intended to be conveyed, are unsatisfactory, as the spectator is quite near enough to perceive details, and finds none, except those belonging to the execution of the work, which ought not to be visible. This unpleasant effect is produced in the 'Sala de' Giganti,' by Giulio Romano, at Mantua." —*Eastlake.*

"The hall of the Giants would occupy a month to understand, or convey thoroughly the quantity of matter, of feeling, of allegory, and poetry which it contains. . . . . The taste of the work is displeasing, and unfit for the adornment of a palace: but the power of imagination exhibited in it is of the most extraordinary kind. Most of the figures are of superior order in action and in form, though some are coarse and offensive. The grouping is often exceedingly beautiful, particularly so in that of Cybele, Ceres, Hercules, Mercury, &c., but the only head that has any pretension to beauty is that of Juno. The Hours staying the progress of the horses of Apollo are perhaps in the most perfect style of painting, as to colours and effect, of the whole."—*Prof. Phillips, R.A.*

For routes from Mantua to Parma, see Rte. 42; to Ferrara and Bologna, Rte. 56; to Cremona, Rte. 25.

Plan for visiting in one day, and in topographical order, the Sights at Mantua.

Piazza delle Erbe; Pal. della Ragione; Ch. *of S. Andrea;* Piazza di S. Pietro; *Duomo;* Ch. *of Santa Barbara; Castello di Corte; Archivio;* Accademia delle Belle Arti; Piazza Virgiliana; returning by Corso di Porta Pradella to Theatre; *Pal. del Diavolo;* Pal. Colloredo; Chs. of *S. Maurizio* and *S. Barnaba;* Houses of Giulio Romano and Mantegna; Ch. of S. Sebastiano; *Palazzo del Tè.*

ROUTE 31.

VERONA TO VENICE, BY CALDIERO, VICENZA, AND PADUA.—RAIL.

MILES.	MILES.
3¾ San Martino.	34 Pojana.
6½ Caldiero.	44 PADUA.
9½ Sambonifacio.	Ponte di Brenta.
13¼ Lonigo.	Dolo.
16¼ Montebello.	Marano.
20¼ Tavernelle.	Mestre.
25¼ VICENZA.	VENICE.

62½ Ital. = 71½ Eng. m.

Trains leave Verona 3 times a day. There are two stations, but the most convenient for persons going towards Vicenza will be that outside the *Porta Vescovo*, near the cemetery, on the l. bank of the Adige, from which trains start at 7·24 A.M., 2·2 and 6·39 P.M., employing about 1½ hr. to Vicenza, 2½ to Padua, and 3·50 to Venice.

The railroad, on leaving Verona, and in nearly its whole extent to Vicenza, runs parallel and near to the old postroad. It skirts the last spurs of the Alps. These hills are extremely picturesque, from the many villages which are situated upon them, with their Scaligerian castles. Looking back on the city, the view of Verona, with its mediæval walls, and its heights crowned by the modern fortifications, is beautiful. At a distance of 3 miles we pass the village of *San Michele.* Here was a very ancient monastery, which afterwards became a convent of Benedictine nuns. It has some interest as being the place where the three grand-daughters of

Dante, the children of his son Pietro, namely, Aligheria, Gemma, and Lucia, took the veil, the last having been abbess in 1402. The family of Dante became extinct in the male line in 1558, the last descendant who bore the name then holding a municipal office in Verona. In the church, which is modern, are some good second-rate pictures by *Lo Spadarino, Bellotti*, and *Il Gobbino*. Immediately beyond S. Michele, on the l. of the rly., is the church of the *Madonna di Campagna*, also from the designs of *Sanmicheli;* a circular building with a Tuscan colonnade, and crowned by a cupola of great beauty and originality. The contrivances of the vaulting, the winding staircase, and other portions of the fabric, show also great ingenuity. Within are some good paintings by *Brusasorzi* and *Farinati*, the latter a Nativity. Before the altar *Davila* the historian is interred: he was assassinated close to the church.

At a short distance from the road, but on the other side of the Adige, is the *Lazaretto*, built in 1591, and for which *Sanmicheli* gave the designs. It is said that they were not strictly followed, but altered for the sake of economy; yet the building, as it now stands, cost 80,000 zecchins. It is a noble cloister; a parallelogram of about 700 ft. by 300, containing 150 cells. In the centre is a very graceful circular chapel of marble. The building is now used as a powder-magazine.

About 3 m. from San Michele, on the l., is the village of *Montorio*, remarkable for its well-preserved Scaligerian defences.

3½ m. *San Martino, Stat.*, soon after leaving which the wide valley of Ilasi opens on the l.

6½ m. *Caldiero (Stat.)*, anciently called *Calidarium*, from its now neglected thermal springs. An inscription found here shows that the baths were built or repaired by Petronius Probus, A. U. C. 753, or the first year of the Christian era, and dedicated to Juno. The buildings stood and continued in use until 1240, when they were royed by Eccelino. The waters retained, however, so much reputation that the Venetian republic, more than two centuries afterwards (1483–1500), directed the building of a bath-house, and made regulations for preventing the waste or destruction of the salutary streams; but at present they are little visited. The principal spring is surrounded by a circular enclosure. Like all in this district, the water is strongly sulphureous. At *Caldiero*, and on the opposite heights of Colognola, the Austrians took their position, towards the beginning of November, 1796, where, on the 11th of the month, they were assailed by Napoleon, whom after an obstinate struggle they defeated. Napoleon then retreated to Verona, which he quitted suddenly two days afterwards with all his disposable forces; and by a rapid march along the right bank of the Adige, crossed that river at Ronco, a movement which was followed by the brilliant victory of Arcole.

After leaving Caldiero, the picturesque town of *Soave*, on the declivity of a hill, is passed on the left. The modern town is in the plain, but the mediæval walls, which are very perfect, are seen converging to the summit of the eminence, terminated by the ancient castle—the general disposition of all the fortresses in the hilly region of this part of Italy.

Villanuova is now passed. This hamlet possesses a church which is rather remarkable. The campanile is formed out of an ancient feudal tower, formerly part of the castle of the noble family of San Bonifacio, by whom the place was founded. The altar has a good bas-relief in the style of the 13th century, and the capitals of several of the columns seem to have belonged to some early Christian structure. The village at the foot of the hills on the l. is *Monforte*.

9½ m. *Sambonifacio, Stat.* A road leads from here on the l. to Monte Bolen. The group of Vicentine hills, or Monti Berici, now come into view. Sambonifacio is on the l. bank of the Alpone, 3 m. to the S. of which is *Arcole*. It was near this point that Napoleon, after his check at Caldiero, determined to assail the Austrians in flank; and he therefore stationed his army in the low grounds which extend from this village to the Adige. He thought, with reason, that, on the narrow causeways which traversed these marshes, the superiority of numbers on the part of the enemy would be unavailing, and everything would depend on the resolution of the heads of columns. The position which he had chosen was singularly well adapted for the purpose in view. Three chaussées branch off from Ronco; one, following the l. bank of the Adige, remounts that river to Verona; one in the centre leads straight to Arcole, by a stone bridge over the little stream of the Alpone; the third, on the rt., follows the descending course of the Adige to Albaredo. Three columns were moved forward on these chaussées: that on the l. was destined to approach Verona; that in the centre to attack the flank of the Austrian position by the village of Arcole; that on the rt. to cut off their retreat. At daybreak on the 15th Massena advanced on the first chaussée as far as a small eminence, which brought him in sight of the steeples of Verona, and removed all anxiety in that quarter. Augereau, with the division in the centre, pushed, without being perceived, as far as the bridge of Arcole; but his advanced guard was there met by three battalions of Croats, by whom the French were driven back. The Austrians despatched by Alvinzi passed through Arcole, crossed the bridge, and attacked the corps of Augereau; but they also were repulsed and followed to the bridge by the victorious French. There commenced a desperate struggle; the republican column advanced with the utmost intrepidity, but they were received with so tremendous a fire that they staggered and fell back. Napoleon, deeming the possession of Arcole indispensable, not only to his future operations, but to the safety of his own army, put himself with his generals at the head of the column, seized a standard, advanced without shrinking through a tempest of shot, and planted it on the middle of the bridge; but the fire there became so violent that his grenadiers hesitated, and, seizing the general in their arms, bore him back amidst a cloud of smoke, the dead and the dying. The Austrians instantly rushed over the bridge, and pushed the crowd of fugitives into the marsh, where Napoleon lay up to the middle in water, while the enemy's soldiers for a minute surrounded him on all sides. The French grenadiers soon perceived that their commander was left behind: the cry ran through their ranks, "Forward to save the general!" and, returning to the charge, they drove back the Austrians, and extricated Napoleon from his perilous situation. During this terrible strife Lannes received three wounds. His aide-de-camp, Meuron, was killed by his side when covering his general with his body, and almost all his personal staff were badly wounded.

The battle continued with various fluctuations through the 16th and 17th, when both parties advanced, with diminished numbers but undecaying fury. They met in the middle of the dikes, and fought with the utmost animosity. Towards noon, however, Napoleon, perceiving that the enemy were exhausted by fatigue, while his own soldiers were comparatively fresh, deemed the moment for decisive success arrived, and, ordering a general charge of all his forces, cleared them of the enemy, and formed his troops in order of battle at their extremity, having the rt. towards Legnago. By the orders of Napoleon the garrison of Legnago issued forth with four pieces of cannon, so as to take the enemy in rear; while a body of trumpeters was sent, under cover of the willows, to their extreme l. flank, with orders to sound a charge as soon as the action was fully engaged along the whole line. These measures were completely successful. The Austrian commander, while bravely resisting in front, hearing a cannonade in his rear, and the trumpets of a whole division of cavalry

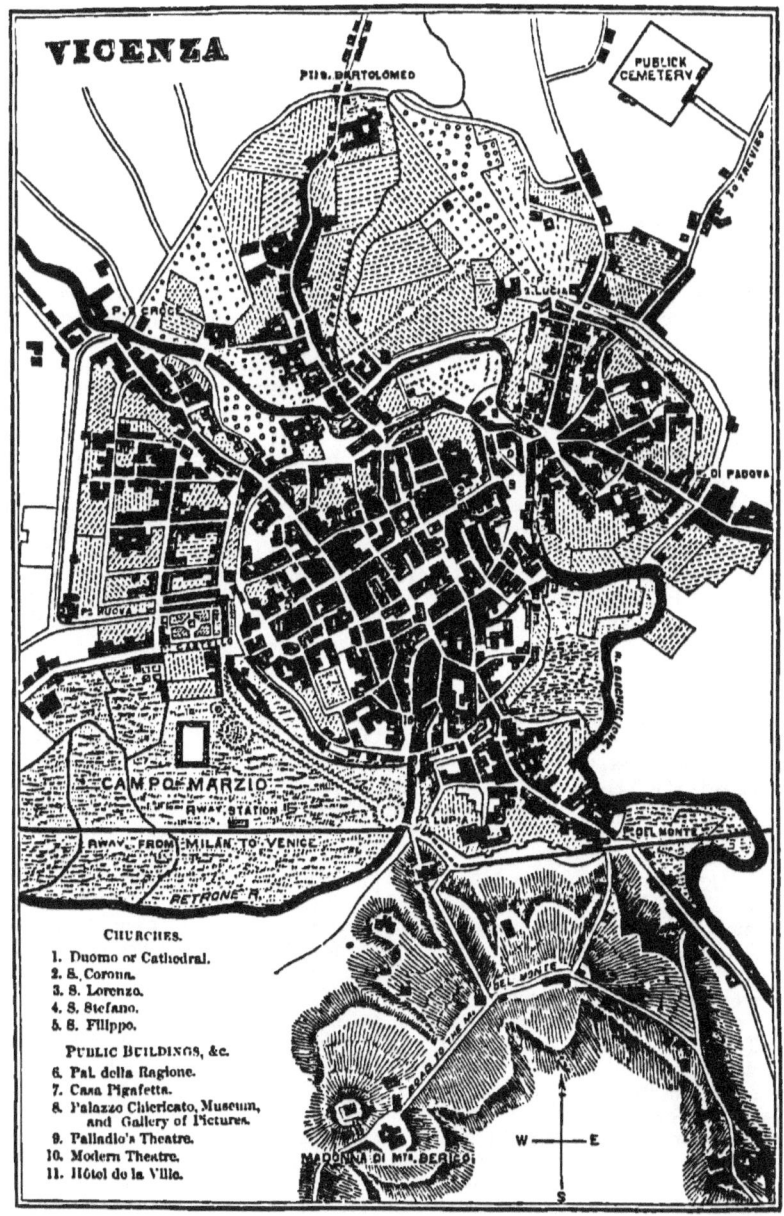

in his flank, ordered a retreat, and, after a desperate struggle of three days' duration, yielded the victory to his enemies.

An obelisk was erected near the bridge of Arcole in commemoration of the victory, and is yet standing, but it has been mutilated and disfigured.

13½ m. *Lonigo Stat.*, 2 m. from the town of the same name on rt.

16¾ m. *Montebello, Stat.* The village, on the l., a good-sized one, is at the base of the hill, on the summit of which are ruins of a mediæval stronghold; on the rt. are the Monti Berici. This Montebello must not be confounded with that near Casteggio (Rte. 7), the scene of the two great battles in 1800 and 1859. There are several handsome villas here. On quitting this station the two fine castles of *Montecchio* now come into view; and on the opposite side of the valley which leads towards Vicenza, the castle of *Brendola*, on one of the slopes of the Monti Berici. The castles of Montecchio were strongholds of the family of that name, rendered so celebrated by Shakspeare as the rivals of the Capulets.

20¼ m. *Tavernelle, Stat.*, in a rich plain between the hills of Montecchio and the Monte Berici.

25½ m. *Vicenza, Stat.* The station is outside the Verona gate, close to the shady promenade of the Campo di Marte.

VICENZA. (*Inns:* the Hôtel de la Ville, kept by Torresani; a large and fairly comfortable hotel just inside the Verona gate, and the nearest to the rly. station; le Due Ruote, and the Stella d'Oro, very fair, principally resorted to by the gentry of the country around. There is a *café* at the railway station, which will serve all the purposes of the traveller who may wish to spend only a few hours or the interval between two trains at Vicenza.)

The situation of this city, which, including the adjoining villages, contains upwards of 33,300 Inhab., is beautiful, particularly on the side of the *Monti Berici*. The rapid *Bacchiglione*, which runs through it, and which is joined within its walls by the *Retrone*, though small, sometimes does much mischief. Eight bridges cross these rivers, one of which, that of *San Michele*, a bold single arch, is attributed to *Palladio*. Vicenza is of great antiquity: of Roman remains, portions of a theatre have been recently discovered. There are not many structures of the middle ages: this is much owing to the influence of Palladio (born 1518, died 1580) in this his native town, and of those architects who more or less followed his school.

"*Palladio's* buildings are in general very beautiful; but most of them are at present in a very forlorn condition. The fronts and even the columns are of brick, the entablatures of wood, and the stucco, with which both have been covered, is peeling off. I am aware that this statement of their materials may lessen your respect for the palaces which make so fine a display on paper; but the circumstance does not diminish the merit of the architect, though it does the magnificence of the city. Palladio's columns are mostly mere ornaments; but in contemplating his buildings it is impossible to feel this to be a fault. The sculpture which loads the pediments of the windows is certainly ill placed; and still worse is the little panel of bas-relief so frequently introduced over the lower windows; dividing what ought to be one solid mass into two miserably weak arches. What is it then that pleases so much and so universally in the works of this artist? It seems to me to consist entirely in a certain justness of proportion with which he has distributed all the parts of his architecture; the basement being neither too high nor too low for the order above it; the windows of the right size, and well spaced; and all the parts and proportions suited to one another. The same excellence is found in his orders, and the relation of the columns, capitals, entablatures, &c. He has not adopted the theoretical rules of another, but has drawn them all from what he felt to be pleasing to himself, and suited to his own style of art; but they are not good when united to a more solid and less ornamental manner."—*Woods.*

Palladio was succeeded by Scamozzi, also a Vicentine (born 1552, died 1616). He was in a manner formed by the example of Palladio. This will be seen fully at Venice, where Scamozzi was principally employed, though some fine specimens of his talents are to be found in this his native city.

The *Piazza dei Signori* is remarkably fine. At one end of it are the two columns the Venetians used to erect in all the cities of their dominion, in imitation of those in the Piazza di San Marco. A lofty and slender campanile, the *Torre dell' Orologio*, is 270 ft. in height, though only 23 ft. wide; the range of shields on it are those of the ancient magistrates.

The *Basilica*, or *Palazzo della Ragione*, is a Gothic building, surrounded with or cased in galleries, on two tiers, Doric below, Ionic above, by Palladio, commenced in 1560. The great hall is a noble apartment, but rather dilapidated. The pictures formerly here have been recently removed to the *Pinacoteca*.

Palazzo del Comune, forming the continuation of the Basilica into the neighbouring *Piazza della Biada*, is partly from the designs of Scamozzi; it now contains the municipal offices and the law-courts. The *Torre dell' Orologio* is connected with it.

The *Palazzo Prefettizio*, opposite the Basilica, was designed also by Palladio, but, being at Rome when it was in the course of construction, it is said that those who had the direction of the work departed from his designs. It is Corinthian, rich and fanciful. A narrower front towards the E. is a Roman triumphal arch converted into a dwelling; and Palladio was so well pleased with his work that he has sculptured his *fecit* upon the architrave. In the *Sala Bernardo*, so called from Battista Bernardo, governor of the city at the time of the erection of the palace, are good paintings by *Fassolo;* the subjects are taken from Roman history. The building next to this palace is the *Monte di Pietà*.

The *Duomo*, or Cathedral, built in 1467, is a Gothic edifice : it has lately undergone a thorough repair. The nave is nearly 60 feet wide; the roof appears low. There are few objects of art in it that deserve notice. In the *Barbarin* Chapel (4th on l.) are some ancient frescoes representing the Martyrdom of Sta. Montana ; two pictures by *Zelotti*. In the 7th chapel on rt. a good picture of the Almighty with Christ crucified, by *Bart. Montagna;* SS. Catherine and Margaret, by *Alessandro Montagna*. In another chapel is a curious painting of the Virgin and Saints, by *Lorenzo*, dated 1366, in 31 compartments. The choir was erected in 1574. The Council of Trent held some of its meetings here.

Ch. of *San Lorenzo*, an elegant Gothic edifice, which, having for a long time been desecrated and converted into a military store-house, has been recently restored to its primitive destination. The front is divided by 7 high pointed arches, in the centre of which is the fine porch, having on either side canopied tombs of the 14th century. The interior contains several monuments, many of which have been removed here from desecrated churches. On the left hand of the entrance is the tomb of Scamozzi, with his bust; and beyond it the sepulchral tablet of B. Montagna, who died in 1572. The monument to Leonardo Porto is in the form of a handsome Ionic portico, having his urn in the centre, and those of two members of his family beneath. The tomb of Isabella Alledossi consists of a *cinquecento* urn. On the wall beyond is the slab tomb that formerly covered the grave of the celebrated Giovanni Giorgio Trissino. The monument of Ippolito Porto has some good bas-reliefs. Amongst the other sepulchral monuments in San Lorenzo are those of Ferreti, the historian of Vicenza, and of John of Schio, or

Scheldcrs, the contemporary and friend of St. Dominick, the "Angeli Pacis Nuncius," "Tyrannorum Gladius," and "Hereticorum Malleus," as his inscription tells us, "qui vigebat saeculo ferreo xiii."—Over the altar, dedicated to SS. *Lorenzo and Vincenzo*, is a painting of these saints by *Montagna*, with a view of the ch. in the background.

Ch. of *La Santa Corona*, near the Corso, also a Gothic edifice. Several sepulchral inscriptions and monuments have been removed here of late years from other churches. In the 2nd chapel on l. a good picture of the Virgin and 4 Saints by *B. Montagna*. The high altar is of Florentine mosaic work. In the chapel on the right of it are two fine Gothic tombs of the *Tiene* family, with recumbent statues in armour; the tombs and ornaments are richly gilt, each having a fresco of the Virgin and Child. —In the 5th chapel on the l. there is a magnificent picture of the Baptism in the Jordan, by *Giovanni Bellini*; the figure of Christ is exquisitely beautiful, and the expression angelic. Another chapel is that of the *Beato Bartolommeo de' Breganzé*. This Beato was a most fanatical follower of St. Dominick; he had been deputed to the court of St. Louis. From a second inscription in another part of the church, in which he is styled "Dux. Marchio. Comes, Barbarani Rex"—Barbarano being a village on the Monte Berico—he must have been a vain man. This estimable monk was beatified at Rome towards the close of the last century, at the instance and heavy cost of the Bourbon dynasty of Parma.—In the 3rd chapel on the rt. is a picture of the Adoration of the Magi by *Paolo Veronese*, scarcely visible, from its dark tints, and the bad light in which it is placed. Palladio, who died in 1580, was buried in this church, in a tomb prepared two years before, for himself and his sons: his remains were removed, as we shall see hereafter, to a more fitting monument in the new Campo Santo.

Church of *San Stefano* has a picture of the Virgin between S. Vincent and Sta. Lucia, by *Palma Vecchio*, over the altar of the l. transept: and a St. Paul, by *Tintoretto*, in the 1st chapel on l.

San Pietro, to which is annexed the *Ospizio de' Poveri*. Over the entrance of the Ospizio is a bas-relief by Canova, a female figure of Charity, writing on a pedestal which supports the bust of Ottavio Trento, the founder of the institution. The statues of Adam and Eve are by *Albanese*. In the church are some good pictures by *Maganza*, a king offering his son to St. Benedict, St. Placidus, and St. Maurus; a Pictà; Our Saviour presenting Garlands of Flowers to St. Peter and St. Paul.— *Zelotti*, Christ delivering the Keys to St. Peter.

Vicenza is more celebrated perhaps than any other town in Italy for its *palaces*. They may be classed under two heads; those built in what may be called the Venetian semi-Gothic style, and those by *Palladio* and his followers in the Classical. Of the former the principal are, the *P. del Conte Schio*, in the Corso, a fine specimen of the period: under the gateway and in the court-yard are several ancient inscriptions, the most interesting of which are 3 in what has been called the *Euganean* character; they were found at the foot of the hills about six miles S.E. of Vicenza, over the entrance of a cavern, and are supposed to have belonged to the Euganean tribes, who preceded the Romans in this part of Italy, as the Etruscans did beyond the Apennines.

P. Colleoni Porto. The two palaces belonging to this family are also in the Venetian style, and stand close to each other. One of them has a very handsome gateway, and contains a few second-rate pictures of the Venetian school.

Among the fine specimens of Palladian architecture in Vicenza, the following are the most remarkable:—

P. Barbarano, by *Palladio*, Ionic and Corinthian, with rich festoons.

P. Chiericati, in the Piazza dell' Isola, at the E. extremity of the Corso. Of the edifice *Palladio* was particularly proud, and with reason. The lower order has a fine Doric portico, the upper an Ionic, with two Loggie on the sides. This palace, which was falling into ruin, has been recently purchased by the Municipality, and beautifully restored according to the original plans of the great architect; it is now one of the finest of Palladio's palaces, and amongst the most remarkable in his native city; it has been converted into a museum and picture-gallery, of which we shall speak hereafter. The general design is very fine, and the interior arrangements are managed with great skill. It escaped narrowly in 1848, during the bombardment of Vicenza by the Austrians, a cannon-shot having pierced the roof and injured the vaulting of its great saloon.

P. Tiene. Had this been completed, it would have been the largest in the city. "The architect of this is said to have been the proprietor, Count Marc Antonio Tiene, the contemporary and friend of Palladio, from whom, no doubt, he has largely borrowed. Scamozzi seems to have completed it. It consists of two orders, Corinthian and Composite, and an attic; the lower order is partly rusticated, and an impost moulding contracts the heads of the windows, which are square. The upper windows are smaller at top than at bottom, but the diminution is slight; altogether the building is very beautiful. The back consists of an open colonnade of two orders, closed at each end; the middle intercolumniation is wider than the others, and has some masonry and an arch within it. The front has eight columns in each story; the back ten."—*Woods.*

P. del Conte Porto al Castello (but for which the stranger must inquire under the name Ca' del *Diavolo*). "This fragment is by some attributed to Palladio, by others to Scamozzi; but the latter disclaimed it, and it appears to me to be Palladian. Whoever was the architect, we may certainly pronounce it a noble design, although a very small part has been executed, and that fragment is nearly in ruins."—*Woods.*

P. Valmarana, by *Palladio,* only in part completed: Composite.

P. Trissino, in the Corso, by Scamozzi. "This is probably one of his best works, and is a noble edifice, though it wants something of that undefinable grace of proportion we admire in Palladio, and it stands in so narrow a street that one can hardly judge of it fairly. It has a range of nine windows on the principal floor, with intermediate pilasters doubled at the angles; but the change of design in the three middle divisions, the high unmeaning arch in the centre, and the double pilasters separating the centre from the wings are so many defects."—*Woods.* The Pal. Trissino was never completed, the front towards the Contrada di San Stefano being alone finished. It is now occupied by the Custom-house.

P. Trento is also by Scamozzi: much plainer than the preceding.

P. del Conte Orazio Porto. This was designed by Palladio for Conte Giuseppe Porto, and a great part of it executed under his eyes; but it has never been completed.

P. Cordellina, by Calderari, now occupied by the Elementary Schools.

Among the *remarkable houses* of Vicenza are those of Palladio and Pigafetta.

Casa di Palladio, in the Corso, supposed to have been built by the great architect for his own use, whilst by others it is attributed to Conte Pietro Cogollo, a Venetian patrician. It is a Palladian adaptation of a triumphal arch.

Casa Pigafetta. This is a beautiful edifice, but in a very different style. Being situated in a dark, dirty, and out-of-the-way street—a very Edinburgh *Wynd*—(the Contrada della Luna, below and behind the Basilica), it has little attracted the notice of travellers. It is a fine specimen of the highly decorated domestic architecture of the 15th centy., having been completed in 1481. It consists of a basement and 2 upper stories, surmounted by a cornice. On the basement are sculptured groups of roses, with the inscription in French, "Il n'est rose sans épines." Each of the 3 windows have elaborately-carved balconies and canopies, ornamented with griffons and other animals, the spaces between being covered with arabesques in low relief, flowers, eagles, &c. This *bijou* of architecture—for it is scarcely 8 yards in front—was inhabited by the celebrated navigator Antonio Pigafetta, one of the companions of Magellan; the family still exists at Vicenza. The name of the architect is not known.

Teatro Olimpico, if not the finest, yet the most curious of the works of Palladio. The Accademia Olimpica of Vicenza had been accustomed to act translations of the ancient Greek tragedies, and *Palladio* being a member they employed him to give the designs for this fabric, of which the first stone was laid on the 23rd of May, 1580; but in consequence of the death of the architect, which followed almost immediately afterwards, it was raised and completed by *Scilla Palladio*, his son. He followed, as strictly as he could, the text of Vitruvius and the remains which existed. The scenery, which is fixed, represents the side of a species of piazza, from which diverge streets of real elevation, but diminishing in size as they recede in the perspective. A considerable effect of distance is obtained, especially in the middle avenue. Daylight, however, by which a traveller usually sees it, is injurious to its effect. On the opening of the theatre the academicians performed the Œdipus Tyrannus, a play to which the scenery is entirely unadapted. It is such as would have been used for the comedies of Menander, and the other plays of the New Comedy. It would be admirably adapted for the representation of the comedies of Terence by the Queen's scholars at Westminster. The custode speaks English, and will prove a good guide for going over the sights at Vicenza.

The *Museum*, or *Pinacoteca Civica*, now placed in the Palazzo Chiericati, contains some good pictures, partly brought from the *Basilica* and *Palazzo del Comune*, but chiefly presented by 3 patriotic citizens—the Countess Pigafetta Vessari, Count Egidio di Velo (who erected the monument to Palladio in the cemetery), and Count Vicentino del Giglio,—whose names deserve to be recorded. It has been purchased by the Municipality, and magnificently restored in order to adapt it to its present destination. The palace is entered from the Piazza dell' Isola, under the Doric portico, by a handsome vestibule, paved with ancient marbles, discovered in the excavations of the neighbouring Roman theatre. From here a handsome staircase, lined with medallions of celebrated men of Vicenza, leads to the grand apartments; the great hall, a splendid room, and 4 adjoining ones on the N., are entirely filled with paintings. As there is a good catalogue of them, we shall merely notice the most remarkable:—*Giorgione*, the Portrait of Pietro di Abano; *L. Bassano*, the Madonna and Child, with G. Moro and S. Capello, the chief Magistrates of the City, kneeling before the Virgin, and some portraits, one of which is of Fracastoro; *Cima da Conegliano*, a Virgin and Child, bearing the painter's name and the date, May 1, 1489; *B. Montagna*, two pictures of the Virgin and Child, also signed, and the Martyrdom of St. Biagio, in 3 compartments; *Titian*, a half figure of the Magdalen, very expressive; *Tempesta*, 3 landscapes; *Perugino*, Santa Barbara, a pretty figure of a female saint; *Paulus de Venetiis*, a curious old picture of the Madonna and Saints, signed and dated 1323; *Gio. Bellini*, Virgin and Child; *P. Veronese*, same subject; *Luini*, an oblong picture of an Eastern king presenting gifts to the Virgin and Child, colouring good; *Luca Giordano*, 3 large pictures—Paris and the Graces, very good, and a supposed portrait of Ariosto; *Giacomo Tintoretto*, a Scene of the Plague; *Gio. Bellini*, what is called a Portrait of Cardinal Bembo; *Elisabetta Sirani*, the Portrait of a Young Lady.

In the great hall is now suspended what *was* once the magnificent picture of the Supper of St. Gregory, by *Paolo Veronese*. This celebrated work, only second in size to that of the Marriage of Cana in the Louvre, stood in the refectory of the Convent of the Madonna di Monte Berico, where it was most wantonly mutilated, literally hacked into 32 pieces, by the Austrian soldiery who occupied that building after the bombardment of Vicenza in 1848. The fragments have been since put together, after a good copy of the original, which had luckily been made some years before, and which is in another part of the Pinacoteca. Beyond the picture gallery, on the N. side of the palace, in two rooms, are placed an extensive series of engravings, and a collection of 56 original drawings, by the three great architects of Vicenza — *Palladio, Scamozzi*, and *Calderari*. Those of Palladio are particularly interesting. They consist of designs for some modern edifices, such as the palace at Vicenza, and the Rialto bridge at Venice; and of copies of ancient Roman edifices, triumphal arches, temples, thermæ, &c., as they existed at his time. Several of these valuable designs had been deposited in the archives of the Municipality; others were given by a Vicentine citizen, Pinali. In a series of small apartments on the opposite side of the Great Sala are placed the collections of natural history, consisting principally of objects from the neighbouring provinces. The series of quadrupeds and birds are very complete, as are also the minerals and fossil organic remains; amongst the latter will be worthy of the attention of the naturalist the remains of a rhinoceros in the bone breccia of Monte Zopea, near Soave, and a fine fossil shark from Monte Bolca; there is also an extensive herbarium, in which has been incorporated that of the Venetian provinces, formed by the celebrated Arduino. In an adjoining apartment are the coins, and the smaller specimens of ancient sculpture, discovered by Count Velo during his excavations at Rome, chiefly in the baths of Caracalla; and on the ground floor the larger objects, and several fragments dug out during the recent excavations of the neighbouring theatre.

The *Collegio Cordellino* is an educational establishment for the upper classes, on the same plan as the French Imperial Lycées. It is located in the suppressed convent of San Marcello. The first court (the former cloister) has been surrounded by a handsome double row of colonnades by the native architect, Malacarne.

Theatre.—The *Teatro Eretenio* is not very large, but is neatly fitted up; the performances in general are good.

The country about Vicenza is beautifully varied with hill and dale. About ¾ m. from the city is the *Monte Berico*, celebrated for its sanctuary erected upon the summit in 1420 in honour of a supposed apparition of the Virgin. It is joined to Vicenza by a continued range of arcades, 730 yards long, with 168 arches. Each of the arches of the *Portici del Monte* bears the shield, device, or name of the fraternity or individual at whose expense it was erected. There is no peculiar beauty in the architecture, but the long succession of arcades is striking.

The ch., which is called *Sta. Maria del Monte*, was small and of pointed architecture, erected in 1428, to commemorate the apparition of the Virgin to a lady of Vicenza, and the liberation of the town from the plague; but a large new part was added in 1688, in the form of a Greek cross, which internally is very beautiful. What was once the nave of the old ch. has thus become the transept of the new building, and the altar has been removed from the recess in the end of the former building to a place which was the middle of one of the aisles. It contains some good paintings of *B. Montagna*: at the altar of the Virgin, the Madonna with the dead Christ and Saints, signed and dated by the painter, 1500; another, the Adoration of the Magi, reckoned one of his best pictures, was destroyed in 1848. This edifice, and the adjoining conventual buildings, suffered much from their occupation by a Croat regiment in 1848, when the Cena of Paul Veronese so narrowly escaped total destruction. It was from the hill before it that the Austrians, after having driven away the Italian corps which occupied the town, so cruelly bombarded Vicenza on the 24th of May of that year, during 9 successive hours.

Although this church is not situated on the highest part of the hill, its elevation (320 feet above Vicenza) is such, that the view from its campanile, or from some of the villas near it, is most extensive. Looking to the N.E., but at a great distance, are seen the snow-capped peaks of Friuli; to the N. are the Alps beyond Bassano, the gorge through which the Brenta breaks into the plain, the serrated ridges which encircle the upper valley of the Adige, at the foot of which can be easily descried the large towns of Bassano, Schio, and Treviso, and, on a clear day, even the temple of Possagno raised by Canova, and in the foreground the Vicentine and Veronese hills; to the N.W. the two castles of Montecchio form very picturesque objects in the landscape; looking towards the E. you see the Euganean hills, separated from the Alps by the wide plain in which Padua is clearly visible, and extending to the Lagoons of Venice and to the shores of the Adriatic; between the Euganean group of hills and the equally insulated one of the Monti Berici, on which we stand, is the depression through which a portion of the waters of the Bacchiglione are carried to form the canal of Este, communicating with the Adige; behind and to the S. extend the Monti Berici towards Montagnano, covered with villas of the Vicentine gentry, amongst which that of Count Rambaldo, on the site of a Cistercian Convent, is worthy of a visit.

Near the *Porta del Castello*, just outside of Vicenza, is a remarkable tower, dark and deeply machicolated, which forms rather a prominent object in the view from the *Monte*. It was erected by the Scaligers as the *March Tower* between Lombardy and the Venetian states, and it is now used as the *campanile* of an adjoining church.

At the foot of Monte Berico is the *Rotonda Capra*, so well known as Palladio's Villa, copied by Lord Burlington at Chiswick. "It is a square building, containing a round saloon lighted from above. From the four sides you ascend on broad stairs, and reach at every side a porch formed by 6 Corinthian pillars. It may be that architecture never pushed splendour to a higher pitch. The space taken up by stairs and porches is far greater than that of the building, because every side would be quite sufficient for the entrance to any temple. The saloon exhibits the finest proportions, as well as the rooms. Every side presents itself from all parts of the adjoining country in a most magnificent manner."—*Goethe*. The Rotonda is now falling into ruin. Occupied, like the Convent of Monte Berico, by the Austrian soldiery in 1848, it was stripped of everything that could be carried away, its furniture dispersed, the statues mutilated. It presents now a sad picture of abandonment and dilapidation.

Not far from the Rotonda is the *Villa Valmarana*, surrounded by extensive gardens. The villa consists of 3 separate casinos; in the central or largest is a large saloon covered with frescoes by *Tiepolo*, who has also painted some rooms in the two others.

Just beyond the *Porta di San Bartolommeo* is the *Palazzo Trissine in Cricoli*, interesting, both on account of its beauty, and as having been the residence of the celebrated Giovanni Giorgio Trissino, whose name appears on the architraves of the upper windows. Trissino was a poet of considerable eminence, and it is said that the palace was built from his own designs. The honour is claimed also for Palladio.

The *Public Cemetery* is one of those useful establishments which do so much credit to the municipal bodies of the large towns in N. Italy. It is situated ½ m. beyond the town, the suburb leading to which bore until lately numerous marks of the military operations of 1848. The cemetery has been erected from the designs of the architect *Malacarne*, and includes a large square space surrounded by a high wall, round the interior of which run 4 porticoes with 124 arches, built of brick, and which, instead of being covered with cement, have been hacked, to give the whole a semi-ruined appearance, in harmony with their destination. Under the arcades are placed the vaults and monuments of the higher classes; in the centre, the graves of the poor. Many of the tombs are worthy of notice as works of art. In the centre of the N.W. arcade is the monument to Palladio, by *Fabris*, of Rome, raised at an expense of 15,000 dollars, by Count Velo. Palladio's remains, which formerly lay in the ch. of Santa Corona, have been recently removed here. Of the other monuments may be noticed that of Countess Isabella Velo, with a fine recumbent figure of the deceased on an urn; of her brother Count Velo, just mentioned; of the Toguzzaro family, by an artist of Padua; of Count Trissino; and of the Prince of La Tour et Taxis, an Austrian general, killed in 1848 in the conflict which took place close to the gates of this cemetery.

Plan for visiting (in one day) the principal Sights at Vicenza, in topographical order.

Duomo or *Cathedral*; Ch. of *San Lorenzo* dei Pal. Trissino; *Piazza dei Signori*; Palazzo Prefettizio; *Palazzo della Ragione*; *Casa Pigafetta*; Chs. of *San Stefano* and *Sta. Corona*; *House of Palladio*; *Pal. Chiericati and Museum*; *Teatro Olimpico*; Campo Santo; *Rotunda di Palladio*; Villa Valmarana; *Madonna di Monte Berico*.

[The baths of *Recoaro* are 26 m. from Vicenza to the N.W., at the head of the valley of the Agno; there are two intermediate relays, the first at *Montebello*, and the second at *Valdagno*; they are principally frequented during the months of July and August, during which a diligence leaves Vicenza at 9½ A.M. and 3 P.M., returning at 7 and 11 A.M. daily. There are several good Inns (that kept by Domenico Trettenero excellent), and every accommodation for persons frequenting the baths: indeed Recoaro may be resorted to as a very cool and agreeable summer residence, little inferior in this respect to the Baths of Lucca. The waters of Recoaro, which are ferruginous, are sent in bottles, properly sealed, to all parts of Italy. Persons using them should see that the small leaden seal bears the date of the current year: if kept beyond the year the iron precipitates. The season for bottling the water begins in May. Another mineral water, Aqua Catulliana, containing a rather strong solution of sulphate of iron, is also procured in the neighbourhood, and is sent to different parts of Italy. Very agreeable excursions may be made from Vicenza to Recoaro, the Sette Commune, &c., which, belonging more properly to the Italian Tyrol, are described in the *Handbook for S. Germany*.

The roads from Vicenza to Inspruck, by the Val de' Signori and the Val Sugana, through Schio, Bassano, &c., as well as those to Feltre and Belluno, including Possagno, the country of Canova, and Asolo, the retreat of the Queen of Cyprus, Caterina Cornaro, are described also in the *Handbook for South Germany* (Routes 222, 228, 232), in connection with the great lines of communication across the Alps, between the Tyrol and Italy. Public conveyances will be found from Vicenza daily to Schio, Bassano, Montagnano, and Este.]

Vicenza to Padua.

By railway, 16½ Ital.=18½ Eng. m.

Soon after leaving the station the rly. crosses the bridge over the Bachiglione. The country is well cultivated with vines, maize, mulberry-trees, &c.

8 m. *Pojano, Stat.* The road from

Vicenza to this stat., and indeed to Padua, is over a dead flat, in some places swampy. Before reaching Pajano the low hill of Monte Galdo may be seen on the rt.; and beyond, the Euganeans: the Ceresone, and afterwards the Brentella, which is carried into the Bachiglione of Este, are crossed before reaching

18 m. *Padua Station*, which is at some distance from the town, but where carriages and omnibuses will be found; the latter ill-appointed vehicles. The traveller will find it more expeditious to employ a light calèche, fare 1 to 1½ lira.

PADUA. *Inns:* Aquila d'Oro; good and in an airy situation, near the ch. of S. Antonio. La Stella d'Oro, in the Piazza de' Noli, kept by Fanti, much improved, good and clean: an obliging landlord and moderate charges: it is in the centre of the town, and close to the Post Office, the University, &c., and nearest to the Rlwy. Stat.

Cafés: the Café Pedrocchi, celebrated all over Italy, is the best; there is also a *restaurant*, and a fine assembly-room on the first floor. While the building of this café was in progress Pedrocchi was present every evening, and paid all the workmen ready money, and, it was said, always in old Venetian gold. He had been left in poor circumstances, and lived in a little old house upon the site of his present café, which, falling into decay, he was compelled to pull down. Suddenly he abounded in riches —as many stories were afloat concerning hidden treasures and yet more awful things as would furnish materials for a legend. The secret of his wealth appears to have been that he kept a gaming-house. In excavating for the foundation of an ice-house attached to the establishment portions of a Roman edifice were discovered, and the marbles found have been employed in the ornaments and pavement of the *salone*.

Booksellers. Zambecarri, near the University, has a good choice of old and new books.

Padua is perhaps the oldest city in the N. of Italy, and the one abounding most in traditions propagated from age to age. The foundation of Padua was attributed to Antenor by the Romans.

"Antenor potuit, mediis clapsus Achivis,
Illyricos penetrare sinus atque intima tutus
Regna Liburnorum, et fontes superare Timavi:
Unde per ora novem vasto cum murmure montis
It mare proruptum, et pelago premit arva sonanti.
Hic tamen ille urbem Patavi, sedesque locavit
Teucrorum, et genti nomen dedit, armaque fixit
Troia. Nunc placidâ compostus pace quiescit."
   Æneid, lib. i. 243, 249.

"Antenor from the midst of Grecian hosts
Could pass secure, and pierce th' Illyrian coasts:
Where, rolling down the steep, Timavus raves,
And through nine channels disembogues his waves.
At length he founded Padua's happy seat,
And gave his Trojans a secure retreat;
There fix'd their arms, and there renew'd their name,
And there in quiet rules, and crown'd with fame." DRYDEN's *Virgil*.

In the year 1274, when the workmen were laying the foundation of the Foundling Hospital, a large marble sarcophagus was discovered, containing a second of lead, and a third of cypress-wood. In the latter was a skeleton, of larger than the ordinary stature, grasping a sword in the bony hand; an inscription upon the sword, in barbarous Latin, was interpreted to indicate that the tomb belonged to Antenor. The discovery, like that of the bones of Livy, excited the greatest enthusiasm, and the remains of the founder of the city were deposited in the church of San Lorenzo. To the same church the sarcophagus was removed, and an inscription composed by Lovato, a doctor of laws and a poet, was engraved upon the monument, which still exists in excellent preservation. When Alberto della Scala governed Padua in 1334 the sarcophagus was opened, and he requested as a gift the sword of the Trojan hero. The church has been demolished, but the sarcophagus has been spared. It stands at the corner of a street, beyond

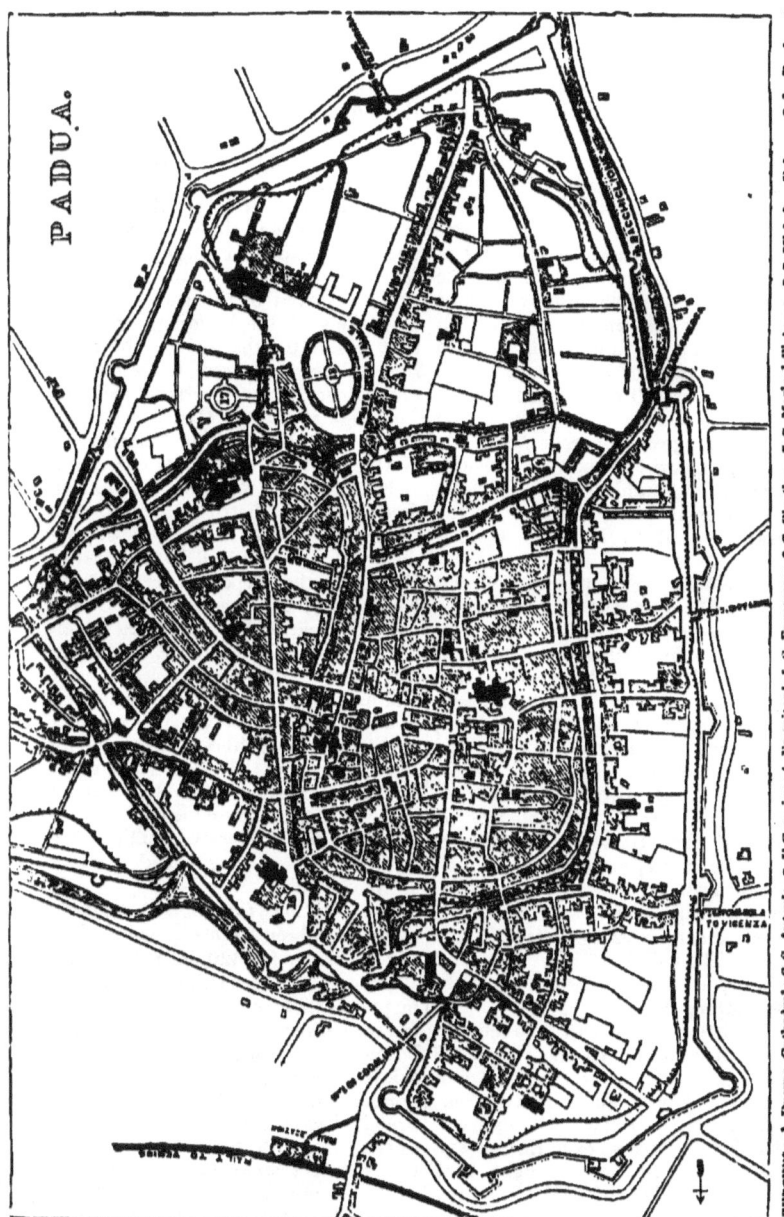

CHIEFUPGA.—1. Duomo, Cathedral; 2. S. Antonio; 3. Il Carmine; 4. Eremitani; 5. S. Francesco; 6. S. Giustina; 7. S. Maria dell' Arena; 8. S. Michele.—Palaces: 9. La Ragione; 10. La Municipalità; 11. Il Capitanio.—12. The University; 13. Library of University; 14. Great Hospital; 15. Tomb of Antenor; 16. Arena; 17. Botanic Garden; 18. Observatory; 19. Prato delle Valle; 20. Teatro Nuovo; 21. Teatro Novis-imo; 22. Post Office; 23. Hôtel Aquila d'Oro; 24. Hôtel Stella d'Oro; 25. Caffè Pedrocchi.

the bridge of St. Lorenzo, in front of the palace of the Delegazione Provinciale, beneath a canopy of brick, and, whatever may be thought of the story, is unquestionably antique, though of what age it is difficult to decide. The most probable solution is that it belonged to one of those Hungarian invaders who descended into Italy in the 9th century. The urn resembles in its form those of the time of the Lombard period at Ravenna; the canopy over it, and the stumpy columns that support the urn, are of the 13th centy., when it was discovered, similar to those of the tomb of Petrarch at Arqua. Near it is Lovato's own sarcophagus.

"Padova la Forte" contains 45,000 Inhab. Long rows of arches, generally pointed, support the houses. Irregular unoccupied ground — wide-stretching tracts of open spaces or piazze on the outskirts — add to its peculiar character.

The edifice the most peculiar and most national is the *Palazzo della Municipalita*, or *Palazzo della Ragione*, built by *Pietro Cozzo* between 1172 and 1219, which forms one side of the market-place: a vast building, standing entirely upon open arches, surrounded by a loggia. The E. end is covered with shields and armorial bearings. To the Broletto of the Lombard cities it has no resemblance. A vast roof, like that at Vicenza, towers above the edifice, rising, perhaps, half as high again as the walls upon which it rests. This roof is said to be the largest, unsupported by pillars, in the world. The hall is 267½ feet long, and 89 wide, as much in height, but not quite rectangular.

The history of this hall is as remarkable as its aspect. In the year 1306 there came to Padua a renowned architect and engineer, an Augustin friar, called *Frate Giovanni*. He had travelled far and wide, over Europe and in Asia, and he had brought back plans and drawings of all the buildings which he had seen; amongst others, one of the roof of a great palace in India. This design greatly pleased the Paduans, and they requested him to

N. Italy—1860.

roof their hall (which had previously formed three chambers) in like manner; and *Fra' Giovanni* assented, asking no other pay than the materials of the old roof, which he was to take down. The Loggia, or corridor, under arches, that surrounds it, is of the same period.

The interior of this hall is gloomy, and the whole is closely covered with strange mystical paintings, which have replaced those by Giotto, and which were destroyed by the successive conflagrations of the building, especially that of 1410; the authors of these frescoes are supposed to be anonymous Padovese and Ferrarese painters. The original ones by Giotto were executed according to the instructions of the great physician, astrologer, and alchemist, *Pietro di Abano* (born 1250, died 1316). Pietro di Abano was the first reviver of the art of medicine in Europe; and he travelled to Greece for the purpose of learning the language of Hippocrates and Galen, and of profiting by the stores which the Byzantine libraries yet contained. He practised with the greatest success; and his medical works were considered as amongst the most valuable volumes of the therapeutic library of the middle ages. He wrote the 'Conciliator differentiarum Medicorum.' His bust is over one of the doors of the hall: the inscription placed beneath it indignantly repudiates the magic and sorcery ascribed to him.

The paintings, forming 319 compartments, have been repeatedly damaged by fire and water, in 1420, 1608, 1744, and 1762; and have been entirely repainted; no part of those by Giotto remain. They fall into several classes. The constellations—sacred subjects—apostles and saints—the winds and elements—allegorical figures of Virtue;—but the principal series consists of the months of the year, with their ruling planets and constellations; the employments of the month; and the *temperaments*, assigned, according to astrological rules, to those who are born under the different astral combinations. The apertures, or windows, are said to be

P

so disposed that the solar rays in each month travel along the representatives of the signs and planets then in ruling activity. The following paintings may be remarked, either for their beauty or singularity:—Justice and Prudence; portrait of Dante, under the personification of Sagittarius; Pisces, under which is a young woman supporting an aged person with great tenderness; also a very beautiful kneeling figure; generally, the representations of the trades and occupations of human life. —The Coronation of the Virgin—the Magdalene—and St. Paul in prayer.

At one end of the hall is the so-called monument of Livy, erected in 1547. Like the astrologer, he was born at Abano. According to an immemorial tradition, the site of Livy's house can be pointed out in the Strada di San Giovanni; and in the year 1363 an inscription was found near the church of Santa Giustina, purporting to have been placed there by a certain Titus Livius Halys, erroneously attributed to the historian, although it is distinctly stated on it that he was a freedman of Livia Quarta. Some time afterwards, in 1413, a tesselated pavement was discovered, beneath which was found a leaden coffin containing a skeleton, which was immediately supposed to be that of the great historian himself. The discovery excited the greatest enthusiasm, and it was determined to place the remains in the Palazzo. The translation took place with as much pomp as if Livy had been a tutelary saint. The relics were divided: the jawbone was deposited in the Cancellaria; and Alfonso of Arragon, King of Naples, despatched (1450) a special embassy to request the gift of an armbone, which was conceded by the Paduans, as appears by an inscription on a marble tablet over the door. The inscription found at Sta. Giustina has been let into the wall; and statues of Minerva (or, as some say, Eternity) and Fame, the Tiber and the Brenta, have been added: above is a bust, upon which are engraved the letters P. T. L. E., which, with somewhat of Oldbuck's sagacity, are explained to signify *Patavini Tito Livio Erexerunt.* The bones are placed over one of the side doors leading to the Uffizio della Sanità. Over a third door is the bas-relief representing the celebrated jurist *Paulus*, who flourished in the age of Alexander Severus, and contributed much to the formation of the codes of the civil law. *Alberto Padovano*, commemorated over another doorway (died 1323), was a preacher of extraordinary eminence in his day: *Sperone Speroni* also has a statue. It was erected at the public expense in 1594. Hallam considers Speroni's tragedy of *Canace* as a work of genius; and his Dialogues, an humble imitation of Plato, which may have been valued when well-turned phrases were accepted as an equivalent for meaning. Such tributes to literary eminence are sufficiently common, but the bust erected, 1661, by the city to the memory of *Lucrezia Dondi*, is, perhaps, unique: it bears witness to her virtue and to her death, under circumstances nearly similar to those of her Roman namesake. Lastly, in this assembly, is the bust of *Belzoni*, by Rinaldi, represented in a Turkish costume, between the two Egyptian statues which he presented to his native city. No circumstance in poor Belzoni's life pleased him more than his being able to present these trophies to Padua. A medal was struck by the city as a token of their gratitude, in addition to the bust thus placed in its great hall.

At one end of the hall is the *Lapis Vituperii* et *Cessionis Bonorum*, of black granite, the altar of insolvency, upon which debtors cleared themselves by their exposure. At the other end of the hall stands the enormous wooden model of a horse, formerly in the Palazzo Emo, by *Donatello*, upon which *Vasari* has expatiated with much admiration. It was executed in 1466 for a certain A. Capodalista, to figure at some public rejoicings, and was to have borne a statue of Jupiter; the head is a modern restoration. A meridian line crosses the hall: the ray of the sun passes through a hole in the centre of a golden face on the roof.

Archivio Pubblico.—In a suite of apartments near the entrance to the Palazzo della Ragione, and forming a part of the municipal buildings, are placed the extensive series of *Paduan archives.* They have been lately well attended to, and are in process of being arranged and catalogued, thanks to the zeal of the then Podesta Cav. di Zigno. In addition to the documents of the time of the Carraras, when Padua had an independent political existence, an immense mass of diplomas and charters has been brought here from suppressed monastic establishments. Some of these rolls go back to the 9th century; a bull, in particular, of Pope Eugenius II., when the Roman pontiffs signed such documents, instead of, as at a later period, appending leaden *bullas.* There are several diplomas of the German emperors of the Franconian line. One of Henry V. is remarkable, as showing that he could not sign his name, and had recourse to the illiterate expedient of a +. The series of the statutes of Padua is very complete, including those of Ecceline (1276) and of the Carraras (1362). In another room of the municipality are some pictures by *Padovanino*, and a few good specimens of *Raphael* pottery; and in a 3rd room, called the Sala Verde, some pictures, by *Varotari, Damino,* and *Campagnola*, representing events connected with the history of Padua.

The *Palazzo del Capitanio*, which occupies the entire W. side of the Piazza de' Signori. It is in a mixed style: the exterior and the fine doorway are by *Falconetto* (1532); the staircase, attributed to *Palladio*, is remarkably fine.

The *Piazza dei Signori,* so called from the dwelling of the Carraras having been in it, and on the W. side of the P. della Ragione. At one extremity is the Ch. of S. Clemente, and at the opposite one the *P. del Capitanio*, with its celebrated clock-tower. The *Loggia del Consiglio*, near it, now a military post, was erected at the end of the 15th centy.; the great hall, with its three handsome windows, which formerly was the place of meeting of the municipal body, is now dilapidated. The ancient column in the piazza belonged to a Roman edifice discovered in making excavations near the Ch. of S. Giobbe, in the last centy.

The open spaces on the N. and S. sides of the Pal. della Ragione, are called the Piazze *delle Frutte* and *delle Erbe,* from the fruit and vegetable markets held here.

Striking clocks are said to have been invented at Padua; and that which stands in the great battlemented tower in the Piazza de' Signori is claimed as the contrivance of *Giacomo Dondo* or *Dondi.* It was erected in 1344, at the expense of Ubertino di Carrara; the works, however, having been made by Maestro Novello in 1428. Besides the four-and-twenty hours, it indicates the days of the month, the course of the sun in the Zodiac, and the phases of the moon. Dondi obtained such celebrity for his performance, that he acquired the surname of *Orologio.* It passed to his descendants, and the family of " Dondi dell' Orologio" still flourishes. This clock-tower forms the centre of the Pal. del Capitanio.

CHURCHES.

The Cathedral or *Duomo* claims *Michael Angelo* for its architect, at least of the choir and sacristy; but it was two centuries in progress, not having been completed until 1754; it is probable, from the bad taste displayed in some of the parts, that, if he was the designer, his plans were not carried out. The best picture in the church is a fine copy by *il Padovanino* from *Titian*, long supposed to be an original: it is in the Tribune, and represents the Virgin and Child. In the rt. aisle are two paintings, by *Francesco Bassano* : the Flight into Egypt and the Wise Men's Offering; both well coloured.—*Sassoferrato* : a Virgin.—And in the N. transept a Madonna, attributed by many to Giotto, by others to *Giusto Padovano.*—On each side of the door in the N. aisle are the tombs of *Sperone Speroni* and of *Giulia de' Conti,* his daughter. A modern bust of Petrarch, who held a canonry in the cathedral, by *Rinaldi*, a scholar of Canova's, has been recently placed here at the expense of Canon Concini; there are also two others, in the choir, in honour of Benedict XIV. and Cardinal Rezzonico. These last are curious monuments of priestly vanity. What had the pope done for the canons to deserve this token of gratitude? He graciously granted them the privilege of wearing their pontifical copes in the choir. And what had Rezzonico done? Why, he had asked that favour for them.

The *Sacristy* contains some early liturgical manuscripts, with miniatures of the 12th and 13th centuries—one, an *Evangeliarium*, painted by a certain Isodorus in 1170; the other an Epistolarium, with miniature histories from the Old and New Testaments, by *Giovanni Gaibana*, in 1259—and some curious *reliquiarii* of the 14th and 15th; in the subterranean ch. is preserved the body of St. Daniel, discovered in 1075.

The *Baptistery* is a Lombard building of the 13th centy., belonging to what may be termed the imitative class of these buildings, similar to those at Parma and Cremona. The walls and vaulting are entirely covered with frescoes, executed at the expense of Fina Buzzacarina, wife of Francesco di Carrara the elder. The frescoes on the outside, which have entirely disappeared, were by Giunto and Altichieri, and those inside, representing histories of the Old and New Testament, by Giovanni and Antonio of Padua; the cupola represents the Paradise, with numerous angels and saints upon it. Fina Carrara, her husband, with other members of the family, and Petrarch, are represented kneeling before the Virgin.

Biblioteca Capitolare. — Petrarch may be reckoned as one of its founders. It contains upwards of 10,000 vols., amongst which 450 of the 15th centy., and several inedited manuscripts. Amongst others, those of Sperone Speroni, with several letters of Tasso, a MS. of the 14th centy. containing the description of Dondi's clock, and some splendidly illuminated missals, and collections of decretals, also with miniatures, of the 14th and 15th cents.; in the entrance hall are some curious old paintings of 1367, by *Nicolo Semitecolo*, relative to the life of S. Sebastian, much valued as a document in the history of the Venetian school.

The *Palazzo Vescovile* has been modernised. It contains several frescoes by *J. Montagnana*, a pupil of Giovanni Bellini, painted about 1495. In one of the upper rooms the portraits of the Bishops of Padua to 1494. In the chapel are the 12 Apostles, in chiaro-scuro; the altarpiece, representing the Annunciation, is by the same artist; and in the bishop's private chapel, or oratory, are several small paintings, the best one by P. Veronese, representing the martyrdom of Santa Ginstina; and an *Ancona* of a double row of compartments, with S. Peter in the centre, and the Saviour on the Cross above, from the monastery of S. Peter. It is attributed to *Squarcione*.

Over the door of one of the rooms is a portrait of Petrarch, which was originally painted upon the walls of the house in which he dwelt when he resided at Padua under the protection of the Carraras. The house was demolished in 1581; but the fresco was cut from the wall, and thus preserved. This portrait is reckoned one of the most authentic of the poet, and is attributed to *Guariento*.

Church of *Sant' Antonio* or of *Il Santo*. "On the death of S. Antonio in the year 1231 the citizens of Padua decreed that a magnificent temple should be erected in honour of St. Anthony, their patron saint. To accomplish this object, they sent for Nicolo da Pisa, and intrusted to him the construction of the new church, and he produced one of the most remarkable buildings in Italy. The fashion of the day compelled him to adopt the Pointed style, but with this he combined some of the Byzantine features of St. Mark's at Venice. St. Anthony's is crowned with no less than 8 cupolas, which give it an oriental character. It is in the form of a Latin

VENETIAN PROV. *Route* 31.—*Padua—S. Antonio.* 317

cross, 230 ft. in length, 138 ft. in breadth to the extremity of the transepts. It was completed in 1307, with the exception of the cupola over the choir, which was not added till 1424. If the external features of this church are meagre, if the three great portals are bald when compared with the contemporary portals of the North, it must be remembered that Nicholas of Pisa was compelled, by the fashion of the day, to adopt a style which he did not like, and which, it must be confessed, he did not understand."—*G. Knight.* The W. front is divided into 4 pointed arches of unequal width, in the centre of which is a niche containing a statue of S. Antonio of the 14th centy. Over this rises a portico of pointed arches, with a balustrade, surmounted by a handsome Lombard turret; the fresco of SS. Antonio and Bernardino, in the lunette over the principal entrance, was painted, as stated in the inscription below, by *A. Mantegna*, in 1452; the two bell-towers beyond the transepts, on ranges of pointed arches, are very beautiful.

The church of S. Antonio is remarkable for the splendour and beauty of its internal decorations. Occupying the N. or l.-hand transept, stands the chapel of *the* Saint, "*il* Santo"—(for thus is Anthony honoured at Padua, where he died, having been born at Lisbon). It is illuminated day and night by the golden lamps, and silver candlesticks, and candelabras borne by angels, which burn before the shrine. The chapel was begun in 1500 by *Giovanni Minello*, and *Antonio* his son; continued by *Sansovino*, and completed by *Falconetto* in 1553. The two richly worked pilasters are by *Pironi* and *Matteo Aglio*. A large and singular series of bas-reliefs relative to histories of the Saint, by various artists, surround the walls. The best are: 1st on rt. by *P. Lombardo;* 3rd and 4th by *Tullio Lombardo;* the 6th, S. Antonio resuscitating a dead child, by *Sansovino*. In the centre is the shrine, as splendid as gold and marble can make it: the statues over the altar of St. Anthony,

St. Bonaventura, and St. Louis are by *Tiziano Aspetti.* The two fine sculptures on the sides of the sarcophagus are the work of *Orazio Marinali*, 1450, and *Filippo Parodi.* They support two of the candelabras. Beyond the chapel of St. Antonio is the curious Gothic chapel of the Black Virgin, the *Madonna Mora*, from the brown-complexioned picture over the altar; this ch. is a portion of the church of Santa Maria Maggiore, built in 1110, and pulled down in great part to make room for the present edifice. In it is an interesting sarcophagus of one of the Obizzo family. The sepulchral urn near it belongs to Raphael Fulgoso, an eminent jurisconsult of the 14th centy. Opening out of this chapel is another of the Beato Belludi, covered with frescoes relative to St. Philip and St. James, and attributed to Giunto Padovano: the Apparition of S. Antonio to the Beato, to announce the liberation of Padua from Eccelino, is historically interesting: they have been sadly injured by restoration in the last centy.

On the opposite side of the ch. is the chapel of *S. Felix* (5th on rt.). It was originally dedicated to St. James, and erected in 1376, but subsequently to St. Felix, when his remains were deposited here in 1504. It is separated from the body of the church by a screen of Gothic arches of red Veronese marble, above which rises a species of entablature of coloured marbles disposed in scales. The wall and vaulting are covered with excellent early frescoes, by *Jacopo Avanzi* and *Altichieri da Zevio*—the worse, however, for the injuries they received in clearing off the whitewash with which they had been covered, and for their restorations. The subjects are taken partly from the legendary history of St. James, and partly from the Gospels: they are striking even in their present state. The first seven frescoes are considered to be by the hand of *Altichieri.* They are full of life and expression. The wall behind the altar at the end of the chapel is divided into five spaces by columns and pointed arches, corresponding to those opposite which separate the chapel from the church. In the centre space the subject is the Crucifixion. To the rt. of this the soldiers are casting lots for the garments of Christ. The skill displayed in this composition seems almost in advance of the time (about 1376) of the painter. To the l. of the Crucifixion is the crowd following Jesus from the city; one group is beautiful: it is a woman supporting the fainting figure of the Virgin Mother, followed by another who is leading along her own infant son. Farther on, to the rt. of the Crucifixion, is the tomb of Bartolommea Scrovegna, wife of Marsilio Carrara, the second lord of Padua; the space above it is filled with the picture of the Resurrection. Two tombs on the opposite side contain the remains of the founder of the chapel, Bonifazio de' Lupi, Marquis of Soragna, a general in the service of the Carraras: the picture over it represents the Deposition from the Cross, and members of the Rossi family, contemporaneous lords of Parma. These five paintings by *Avanzi* and *Altichieri* fill the lower part of the side of the chapel opposite the entrances; they are each under a pointed arch. Over them the space is divided into three compartments, each also canopied by a pointed arch, and filled with a painting. The subject of that on the l. of the spectator is the Denial of St. Peter; of that in the centre the *via dolorosa*, or Christ led to be crucified; and of that on the rt. the Entombment. In the spandrils to the extreme rt. and l. of the five lower arches the Annunciation is painted. The angel Gabriel occupies the spandril to the extreme l.; and the Virgin that to the extreme rt. The head of the Virgin is very beautiful. A long narrow window is in the end of the chapel to the rt. of the entrance. One of the compartments on that side contains the picture of the Virgin and Child, engraved by D'Agincourt; the others are filled up with scenes from the lives of St. Christopher and other saints, now much effaced. The opposite end is divided into irregular compartments, and painted by the before-mentioned artists with subjects from the Scriptures and from legends. Above the altar are 5 statues of the 13th centy. Over the stalls which surround the chapel are good half-figures of saints.

The *Presbytery* and *Choir* are divided from the rest of the church by splendid marble balustrades and bronze doors. The statues of the saints, and of Faith, Temperance, Charity, and Force, are by *Tiziano Aspetti*. Donatello contributed the bronze reliefs which decorate the high altar, and the fine group of the Madonna and saints over it. The 8 bas-reliefs of subjects from the Old Testament, and the symbols of the Evangelists, under the Music Gallery, were cast by Velluti, his pupil, in 1488. By Donatello, also, are the great bronze crucifix, and a bas-relief in gilt terracotta of the Deposition over the door leading to the chapel of the relics behind it.

Cicognara points out as the finest work of art in this most sumptuous sanctuary the great *candelabrum* of bronze, standing on the rt. of the high altar, executed by *Andrea Riccio*, the result of ten years' labour. It is a species of cinque-cento adaptation of the antique form. The human figures possess exquisite grace and simplicity. Four emblematical figures upon the pedestal have occasioned much perplexity to the commentators. They have been explained as representing astrology, music, history, and cosmography. But these interpretations are more ingenious than satisfactory. In the presbytery are 2 fine bronze bas-reliefs by the same master: David and Goliath; and David dancing before the Ark. The objects most deserving of notice in the other chapels are in that of the Holy Sacrament (3rd on rt.), the bronze bas-reliefs on the altar, by *Donatello*, and the presses, with their fine inlaid or *intarsia* work, executed in the 15th century by the two Canozzis.

The sepulchral monuments, which are numerous, are many of them fine. The tombs of Gattamelata and of his son are in the chapel of the Sacrament (3rd on the rt.). The *monument* to Alessandro Contarini, erected in 1555, at the expense of the republic, is from the design of *Sanmicheli*, the sculptures being by *A. Vittoria* and *Danese Cattaneo*. *Sanmicheli* also designed the monument opposite to this, on the 3rd pedestal on the rt., to *Cardinal Bembo*, erected by Cardinal Quirini; the bust is by *Cattaneo*, and the inscription by *Paolo Giovio*.

Several fresco paintings still exist on the pilasters of the nave; those of the Crucifixion, with SS. Sebastian and Gregory, and numerous prophets (on the 6th on the rt.), by *J. Montagnana*, and of the Madonna (on the 2nd on the l.), attributed to *Stefano di Ferrara* or *Filippo Lippi*, are the most worthy of notice.

In the adjoining cloisters are several sepulchral monuments; that of Manno Donati (1370) is remarkable for its inscription by Petrarch; of Luigi Visconti (1553), by *Sanmicheli*. Many monuments have been brought here from desecrated churches, one of which, between the 2 cloisters, is a good Gothic tomb; out of these cloisters opens the library of Il Santo, containing nearly 15,000 vols. In one of the rooms of the convent is a good Holy Family by *Garofalo*.

In front of the church is an irregular and picturesque piazza, partly surrounded by the conventual buildings. In a corner of it, near the entrance to the cloisters, is the sepulchre of Rolando Piazzola, one of the stanchest defenders of his country's liberties against the Emperor Henry VII. In the centre stands the equestrian statue of "Gatta Melata," whose real name was Erasmo da Narni, by *Donatello*, a production full of vigour. It is the only equestrian statue he ever executed, and bears his name, "Opus Donatelli Flor." Opening out of the piazza is

The *Scuola del Santo*, now re-occupied for conventual purposes: it contains some frescoes by *Titian* and *Campagnola*, representing the miracles ascribed to St. Anthony.

Four are by *Titian*. The first, a miracle of St. Antonio, restoring to life a woman killed by her husband in a fit of jealousy. The female heads are very beautiful. This fresco has suffered much of late years. The second, over the door of the sacristy, the saint miraculously uniting a boy's foot, which had been cut off by accident. The third, the restoring to life of a boy who had fallen into a boiling caldron. The fourth, St. Antonio causing an infant to speak, in order to bear witness to his mother's innocence, in answer to an accusation of infidelity by her husband.

Close to *Sant' Antonio* is the small church of *San Giorgio*, erected as the sepulchral chapel of his family by Raimondino di Soragna in 1377; it contains some fine frescoes by *Avanzi*. *Altichieri* helped him here also; but the greater part are, without doubt, the work of Avanzi, whose style of conception is seen to much more advantage here than in the frescoes in the chapel of S. Felix. The subjects are from the New Testament; the miracles of SS. George, Catherine, James, and Lucia: the large painting of the Crucifixion behind the altar, and over it the Crowning of the Virgin, are very fine; the now bare sarcophagus was formerly surrounded by 10 gilt statues of members of the Soragna family, which were destroyed during the occupation by the French soldiery at the end of the last century: their portraits are seen in one of the paintings, kneeling before the Virgin, to whom they are presented by S. George their patron.

Ch. of *Santa Giustina* is supposed to have been erected on the site of a Temple of Concord. It was repeatedly built, and as frequently ruined. The edifice raised after the destruction of the city by Attila was thrown down by an earthquake in 1117. In the 13th centy. it was rebuilt. Two griffonised lions, standing at the top of the flight of steps in front of the present structure, are vestiges of the earlier church. The present edifice was begun in 1502, by *Padre Girolamo da Brescia*, and completed 1532-1549, by *Andrea Mo-*

rone. The façade is rough and unfinished; but the general style of the interior is good, from its proportions, its great expanse, and its many piers and lofty cupolas. The disposition of the aisles is rather that of a series of vaulted recesses opening into the nave, and nearly as high as that is, and communicating with one another by lower arched openings, than a continued aisle.

The Martyrdom of Sta. Giustina at the high altar, by *Paolo Veronese*, is the best picture in the church. The other paintings are:—*Carlino* and *Gabriele Cagliari* in 1st chapel on rt.: the Conversion of St. Paul.—*C. Rodolfi:* St. Benedict instituting his Order.—*Liberi:* St. Gertrude supported by Angels, in 2nd on rt.—*Luca Giordano:* The death of Sta. Scolastica, in 4th on rt.—*Palma Giovane:* St. Benedict with St. Placidio and St. Mauro, in 5th on rt.; and near the same chapel, *G. Maganza*, Totila King of the Goths falling before St. Benedict. The chapel on rt. of the high altar contains a beautiful group by Parodi, representing a dead Christ, with the Virgin, Mary Magdalene, and St. John. The fine sculptured woodwork of the choir was executed from designs of *A. Campagnola* in 1556; the stalls in the *Coro Vecchio*, the only portion of the older ch. that was preserved, date from a century earlier; they are by two artists of Parma and Piacenza. The painting over the altar in this choir, of the Virgin with 4 Saints, is a fine work of *Romanino's:* behind the altar in the l. transept is a sepulchral urn erected by Gualportino Mussato in 1316, in which is preserved the pretended body of St. Luke. A small chapel opening out of the rt. transept contains a miraculous image of the Virgin, supposed to have been brought from Constantinople by St. Urius, where it escaped the flames raised to destroy it by the Iconoclast Emp. Constantinus in the 8th centy.

There is a fine cloister annexed to this church. In a cortile adjoining is a piece of sculpture of the 11th centy., one of the earliest specimens of mediæval allegory. It represents Mercy and Justice. The large cloister is a part of the older monastery. It contains the few remains of a curious series of paintings of the life of St. Benedict, executed between 1489 and 1494, by *Bernardo Parentino, Campagnola*, and *Girolamo Padovano.* The French converted this monastery into a barrack; some of the paintings were whitewashed over, others spoiled by the soldiery.

The *Prato della Valle*, or *Piazza delle Statue*. The Church of Sta. Giustina stands at the extremity of a very large, irregular open space, the centre of which is occupied by the *Prato della Valle*, an oval, surrounded by a small canal, supplied with water from the Bacchiglione, and peopled with statues. It was intended to limit these memorials to the great men of Padua; but as even local fame could not supply a sufficient number of characters, they have been forced to enlist some celebrities of other countries—Antenor, Pietro di Abano, Petrarch, Tasso, Galileo; 78 in all; that of the Marquis Giovanni Poleni, a correspondent of Sir I. Newton, is one of the early works (1789) of Canova. Gustavus of Sweden, the "Lion of the North," has a full right to his station here, for in 1609 he studied at Padua, and attended the lectures of Galileo; and in consequence of this, when his unfortunate namesake visited Padua in 1783, he requested permission to erect this statue of his great ancestor.

The *Arena*, the form of which, and its name, sufficiently indicate that it was a Roman amphitheatre. No traces of seats can be found; they may have been constructed of wood, as at Pola. Here and there the Roman masonry can be distinguished; but, in the middle ages, the Roman circuit was, like the amphitheatres of Nimes and Arles, converted into a place of defence by the family of Dalesmanini, who crowned it with battlements. It afterwards passed to the Scrovegno family, in the person of Enrico Scrovegno, the son of Reginaldo, condemned by Dante for his usury and avarice.

Enrico, about 1303, built within its precinct the chapel of the *Annunziata*, commonly called *Santa Maria dell' Arena*; but, whether as a domestic chapel, or for the use of the order of the Cavallieri di Santa Maria, has been much contested. This order of religious chivalry was instituted, not for the defence of the faith in general, but for the worship of the Virgin in particular. They obtained large possessions, and thereupon abandoned themselves to worldly luxury, whence they were called *Frati Godenti;* but their career of vice and profligacy was cut short by papal authority; they were suppressed, and their property made over to other religious orders.

There is not, however, the slightest evidence that the chapel was ever appropriated to this order, or that the founder was a member of it. The inscription beneath his very curious statue in the sacristy,—" Propria figure Domini Henrici Scrovigni, militis da Arena,"—and probably put up in his lifetime, only shows that he was a knight; and his dress is merely the ordinary "abito civile" of the time. We must, therefore, adopt the supposition, that the chapel was erected for domestic worship. At this period (1306) *Giotto*, then young, was working at Padua, and Scrovegno employed him not only to build, but to decorate the edifice. The Chapel consists of a single aisle with a tribune at its extremity in a simple Gothic style. The unity of design apparent in the chapel and in the paintings no doubt resulted from both being designed by the same mind; and what adds to their interest is, that Dante lodged with Giotto when the works were in progress. Of all the existing productions of Giotto, none are so perfect and genuine, or so truly exemplify the character and beauties of his style. The subjects are taken partly from the New Testament, and partly from the Apocryphal Gospels.

Standing as the chapel does at the end of a green court-yard, backed by gardens growing vegetable stuff, without a single trace of the monastic buildings which formerly were attached to it, and which with it were, till late in the last centy., hermetically sealed from public gaze and curiosity, every association which might raise an emotion in the mind is removed, save that which is to be derived from the contemplation of its internal mural decoration. But let those who have so far cultivated a love and knowledge of art as to appreciate its high capabilities, most carefully study these frescoes of Giotto. They will there find Sacred History illustrated with a dignified as well as touching simplicity, eminently befitting the Divine theme. No artist of any period has been more successful than Giotto in telling his story in a striking and intelligible manner. Add to this indispensable ingredient in the composition of a great historical painter Giotto's exquisite feeling for graceful beauty and deeply pathetic expression, and you have the chief qualifications of works which, without using the language of middle-age mania, may be safely pronounced as possessing the very highest interest. Second in consideration, but equally remarkable, is Giotto's skill in ornamental design; in this light, the chapel may be considered as a perfect model of taste. The beauty of the ornaments, particularly those which divide the walls into panels to receive the various subjects, and the judgment which has kept everything not purely ornamental work from the ceiling, are some points of excellence, which it is to be regretted have not been, and are not, more frequently observed and imitated.

Over the entrance is The Last Judgment. This is much injured: some of the groups of the blessed have great beauty. The vices of the clergy are brought forward with peculiar prominence. In the centre, and not connected at all with the rest of the composition, Scrovigno is represented, offering his chapel, which is accepted by 3 angels.

The general series is distributed into 3 ranges, of which the uppermost, on the rt. hand, contains scenes from the Life of the Virgin, principally from the Apocryphal Gospel attributed to St. James the Less. 1, Joachim driven from the Temple by the Priests, because he had not begotten any issue in Israel. 2, Joachim returns to his sheepfolds, and prays during 40 days and 40 nights. 3, The Angel Gabriel appears to Anna, and reveals that the prayers of her husband have been heard. 4, The Angel announces to Joachim that his Prayers have been heard. 5, Joachim's Vision. 6, The meeting of Joachim and Anna at the gate of the Temple. "And Joachim went down, with the shepherds; and Anna stood by the gate, and saw Joachim coming with the shepherds; and she ran, and, falling on his neck, said, 'Now I know that the Lord hath blessed me,'"—a most graceful composition.— On the wall opposite. 7, The Birth of the Virgin. 8, The Presentation of the Virgin in the Temple. 9, The Priests having declared that the marriageable men of the House of David should bring their rods to the Temple, and that whosesoever rod should bud was to become the husband of Mary, they come, each man bringing his rod. 10, The Blessing of the Rods. 11, The Marriage of Joseph and Mary: the Virgin and the other female figures are graceful. 12, The Procession after the Marriage. This, perhaps the most beautiful painting in the series, is the one which has most suffered by damp. 13, The Salutation, in two divisions: here the grace which Giotto imparts to his female figures is peculiarly discernible. This compartment is under 14, and forms the connecting link between the Life of the Virgin and that of our Lord, which forms a second series.

Above.—1, The Nativity, injured; but the colouring yet in parts remarkably vigorous. 2, The Wise Men's Offering. 3, The Presentation of Jesus in the Temple. 4, The Flight into Egypt. 5, The Massacre of the Innocents. 6, Our Lord disputing amongst the Doctors; much injured, but some fine heads can yet be made out. 7, The Baptism in the Jordan. 8, The Marriage in Cana of Galilee. 9, The Raising of Lazarus: a magnificent composition; awe approaching to terror in the bystanders, death yet struggling with life in the resuscitated corpse. 10, The Entry into Jerusalem: groups full of animation and spirit. 11, Christ driving the Money-changers out of the Temple.

Below.—The third series begins with, 12, The Last Supper: much ornament, very minutely finished, is introduced into the architecture; each apostle has a marked and peculiar dress, either in colour or fashion, which is preserved in all the other paintings in which they are introduced. 13, Christ washing the Feet of the Apostles, a very beautiful composition. 14, Jesus betrayed by Judas. 15, Jesus before Caiaphas. 16, Jesus scourged and crowned with Thorns. 17, Jesus bearing the Cross: a full composition with some beautiful groups, particularly Mary and her companions pushed back by the Jews. 18, The Crucifixion: the thieves are omitted. 19, The Deposition from the Cross. In expression this is considered the finest of all the existing works of Giotto, here or elsewhere: the deep and tender affliction of the Virgin, the impassioned eagerness of St. John, and the steady composure of Nicodemus and Joseph of Arimathea, are all in accordance with their characters. 20, The Resurrection: the figure of St. Mary Magdalene is an admirable personification of devotion. 21, The Ascension: the Virgin is the most prominent figure. 22, The Descent of the Holy Ghost upon the Apostles: singular in its arrangement.

The lowest range of paintings consists of allegorical or symbolical figures, intermixed into architectural compartments, presenting imitations of marble, panelling, &c., with borders, exactly like those executed in mosaic upon the tomb of Edward the Confessor in Westminster Abbey. This species of decoration seems to have been a favourite amongst the Italian artists of the time of Giotto, as it is found in the papal chapel of Avignon, painted in his style, or by his school. Opposite to each virtue is the antagonistic vice; the figures are tinted in chiar'-oscuro. In many the allegory is very intelligible; in others obscure. Commencing on the rt.—*Hope:* winged, scarcely touching the earth which she is quitting, and eagerly stretching forwards and upwards to the celestial crown.—On the opposite wall. *Despair:* portrayed as a female, who, at the instigation of the Fiend, is in the act of hanging herself.—*Charity:* a triple flame issues from her head. Her countenance is beaming with joy. She holds up her right hand to receive gifts from heaven; and in her left is the vase from which she dispenses them.—*Envy:* standing in flames: a serpent issues from her mouth, and recoils on herself: she has the ears and claws of a wolf.—*Faith:* holding the creed, and trampling on a horoscope: in the other hand she grasps the cross. When we recollect the trust which, in the age of Giotto, was placed in astrologers, the boldness of thought which this figure discloses will be appreciated.—*Unbelief:* a Roman helmet upon her head; in her hand an ancient heathen idol, to which she is noosed, and by which she is dragged to the pit. — *Justice:* a crowned matron seated upon a throne; her countenance severe and thoughtful. The scales of the balance which she poises are perfectly even. In one an angel presents a laurel-wreath to the good; in the other is the destroyer, wielding the sword for the punishment of the wicked. Beneath is a composition with figures hunting, sporting; apparently indicating the ease and comfort enjoyed by those who live under a good government.—*Injustice:* an elderly man in the dress of a judge, of a harsh and forbidding countenance: he is "sitting in the gate;" but the path to his tribunal is overgrown with thorns and briers, and his fingers terminate in claws. In one hand he holds an unsheathed sword for punishment; in the other a hook (like that with which demons are usually represented), as the emblem of rapacity. In the compartment below, travellers assaulted and murdered, indicate, in apparent contrast to the figures on the opposite side, the miseries of living under an evil government. — *Temperance:* a female figure fully draped. She holds a sword, but it is bound into the scabbard: a bit is placed in her mouth—emblem of restraint.—*Anger:* a hideous crone, tearing her dress.—*Fortitude:* in ancient armour; the skin of a lion thrown over the armour. She rests tranquilly upon the shield which she opposes to her enemies.—*Inconstancy:* a young girl, and, with some touch of satire, represented in the dress of a Florentine damsel, falling backwards from a wheel, upon which she tries to balance herself; in allusion to Eccles. xxxiii. 5.—*Prudence:* sitting at a desk, and contemplating herself in a mirror. At the back of her head is the face of an old man, but apparently a mask, or part of her head-dress, and not a second face, as in the tomb of San Pietro Martire at Milan. Rafael adopted this mode of allegorising the Virtues.—*Folly:* in a fantastic dress, probably intended for that of a court fool, or jester.

The tribune, or choir, is painted with the history of the Virgin, by some supposed to be by *Taddeo di Bartolo* of Siena, but, from their close approach to Giotto's own style, with more likelihood by his pupil *Taddeo Gaddi:* be this as it may, they are much inferior to those of Giotto. They represent, 1. the visit of the Virgin to St. Elizabeth; 2, The Pact between the Devil and Judas; 3, The Virgin announcing her Death to St. John; 4, Her Death, and in the three lower compartments of the choir, 5, The Obsequies of the Virgin; 6, Her Ascent to Heaven; and 7, Her Coronation. Behind the altar is the tomb of Enrico Scrovegno, who died in exile at Venice in 1320. It is highly finished in the style of the Pisan school, surmounted by 3 small statues of the Virgin and 2 Angels. The sculptor is unknown, although on one of the statues is cut the name of Johannis Magistri Nicoli, whence it has been supposed the work of Giov. Pisano. The windows of the chapel mostly retain the ancient Venetian glazing—small circular panes of thick glass,—which adds to its antique effect. This glazing is not now often found in Italy; but it may be remarked that one example exists in England, at Chester, in a room overlooking the cloisters. In the small sacristy opening out of this tribune is the statue of the founder placed in a Gothic niche.*

The key of the chapel is kept at the dwelling-house in the Arena, where the proprietor resides. Inquiry should also be made for the key of the sacristy, which is often locked.

Ch. of *the Eremitani*. This church adjoins the Arena. It was erected between 1264 and 1276, the roof 30 years afterwards by the same Fra Giovanni who put up that of the Palazzo della Ragione, and who is said to have employed here the old one which he obtained for his labour. It is a most solemn and striking building, from its simplicity as well as its ornament. It consists of a single nave, nearly 300 ft. long, lighted from the extremities. The large choir has some curious frescoes, attributed to *Guariento*, and remarkable, not only for the beauty of the design, but for their mystical and allegorical character. The lower tier in chiaroscuro consist of the planets ruling the constellations more peculiarly appropriated to them.—The Earth appears crowned with the papal tiara, and placed between Industry and Idleness, an allegory of which it is difficult to hit the precise meaning.—Mercury is dressed like a friar.—Mars is mounted on a spirited steed, painted with much action.—Venus is adjusting her attire: and so on: all very strange.—Above are large paintings, in 6 compartments on either side, representing subjects from the lives of the saints; some of them have suffered from damp, time, and neglect. By *Mantegna* are fine frescoes in the large chapel of SS. Christopher and James on the rt. The best compartment, though unfortunately damaged, is that representing the death of St. Christopher, in which *Mantegna* has introduced himself in the character of a young Soldier, holding a spear. *Squarcione* appears as another soldier, in a green dress near him. The compartments of the upper row are by *Buono* and *Ansuino*, disciples of Squarcione; they have great merit, though inferior to their master's. The altar of this chapel has several figures of terracotta, painted of a bronze colour. They are by *Giovanni di Pisa*, a pupil of Donatello. Cicognara ranks them very high for their grace and movement as well as for the beauty of the drapery. Behind the altar are frescoes, by *N. Pizzolo*, of the school of Mantegna. The painting of the Assumption of the Virgin, with the Apostles below, is by *Niccolo Pizzolo*, a competitor of *Mantegna's*. The painting over the high altar of the church, by *Fiumicelli*, is a grand composition. It is a votive picture of the Madonna and four Saints, presented by the city of Padua: in it is introduced a portrait of the Doge Andrea Gritti, holding the city in his hand. On the altar of the sacristy is a good St. John the Baptist in the Desert by *Guido*.

The tombs in this church are interesting: none more so than that of Jacopo di Carrara, 5th Lord of Padua, the friend and patron of Petrarch, who composed the Latin epitaph upon it. The companion to this monument is that of Ubertino di Carrara (died 1354). Each is beneath a canopy as large as a church portal: the figures are of beautiful execution. The countenance of Ubertino, the hard old man, is expressive. These two monuments originally stood in the suppressed Ch. of S. Agostino. With the exception of these tombs, there are but few memorials of the once powerful lords of Padua. The extinction of the family is one of the most gloomy events in the history of Venice. After a valiant defence Francesco di Carrara and his two sons surrendered Padua to the Venetians

---

* The frescoes of the Arena chapel have been reproduced (1857) in a beautiful series of chromo-lithographs, accompanied by artistic details, by the Arundel Society. The general view of the chapel, from the pencil of one of our most talented amateur artists, Mrs. Higford Birr, is a remarkable work, whether considered as a most faithful copy, executed with consummate skill and feeling, or for the application of chromolithography in reproducing the now rapidly perishing works of the early Italian painters.

(1405): they were independent princes nowise subject to Venice; but by the Council of Ten they were condemned and strangled in the dungeons of St. Mark, 1406. Francesco made a desperate resistance in his cell, but was overpowered, and a member of the noble family of Priuli did not disdain to perform the task of the executioner.

The monument to the architect of the church is in the rt.-hand transept: he is represented by an odd half-length statue, clad in a robe. Near it are those of Spigelius and Valisnieri, two celebrated professors in the university. The splendid monument of Benavides, professor of law (1583), is by *Ammanati*: the artist has equally displayed his talents as a sculptor and as an architect. Benavides would not trust his executors, and therefore he erected this memorial in his own lifetime: it is decorated with allegorical figures of Wisdom and Labour, Honour and Fame.

In the passage leading from the l. transept to the sacristy is the slab tombstone of Pietro di Abano. (Petri Aponi Cineres, ætat. 66.) This ch. is considered as the chapel of the university, and the students attend divine service here on Sundays and holidays. As it received them when living, so it was their place of repose when dead; and there are many touching inscriptions to their memory. In the sacristy is a basrelief, by Canova, to the memory of William Frederick Prince of Orange, who died at Padua in 1799, at the age of 25 years. It represents the ever-recurring weeping female figure, near which is a pelican. The design has much beauty of form, and it is carefully executed. Near this is the Gothic monument of red marble to the memory of Paulus de Venetiis (ob. 1419), and upon which he is represented lecturing to his pupils, men as old as himself, and with cowls and hoods; but, as at Pavia, the dignity of the tutor is preserved by his being represented four times as large as his auditors.

Amongst the other churches of Padua may be noticed:—

Ch. of *Santa Sofia*, supposed to be the ancient cathedral of Padua. Some portions of the architecture and sculptures, especially about the principal portal, are of the 12th century, and in a rude style. It contains some early paintings.

Ch. of *San Michele*: a fragment preserved by the care of a private individual, and converted into an oratory. Here is a painting of the Adoration of the Magi, by *Jacopo da Verona*, dated 1397; it has merit in itself; but its principal interest consists in its portraits of several members of the Carrara family. In the painting of the Funeral of the Virgin opposite are said to be introduced those of Boccaccio, Dante, Petrarch, and Pietro di Abano. The body of the church, which was covered with excellent frescoes, has been pulled down.

Ch. of *San Gaetano*, not far from the Arena. The fine façade is by Scamozzi. Two paintings by *Maganza*, the Adoration of the Magi, and our Lord disputing in the Temple, and a small halffigure of the Virgin by *Titian*, are in the chapel of the Holy Sepulchre.

Ch. of *Sta. Maria in Vanzo*, erected in the 16th century. The painting over the high altar is by *Bartolommeo Montagna*: it represents the Virgin surrounded by a host of saints. The fresco of the Coronation of the Virgin on the vault is by the same painter. *Jacopo Bassano*, Our Lord carried to the Sepulchre, in the chapel on l. of the high altar, is a striking composition. The artist, according to his custom, has introduced the portraits of himself and his family. Annexed to this church is the *Seminario Vescovile*, or College for students in theology, which contains an excellent library of upwards of 40,000 printed books and several MSS., amongst which is an autograph letter of Petrarch to Jacopo Dondi, a curious Psalter of the 14th cent., and the original MS. copy by Forcellini for his great Latin Dictionary. Attached to the Seminary is an extensive printing office.

Ch. of *Il Carmine*, near the gate, on entering from the Railway station, formerly Gothic. In the *Scuola* adjoining, now neglected, are several paintings of considerable merit, by *Campagnola* and

Girolamo Padovano, and two which may be by Titian or Palma Vecchio.

The *University*, or, in more ancient language, the *Studio* of Padua, enjoyed considerable celebrity as early as 1221, when Frederic II. commanded the students of Bologna to forsake that city, which had incurred his displeasure, and to resort to the city of Antenor. At first it was pre-eminent in law, and the great Baldus here taught and professed what lawyers call the written reason."

Padua also greatly excelled in medicine; and the professorships of the university include some of the greatest medical names of the 16th and 17th centuries — *Vesalius* (1540), *Fallopius* (1551), *Fabricius ab Aquapendente* (1565), and *Spigelius* (1618). Here *Sanctorius* taught (1611); and, in times nearer our own, *Morgagni* continued to emulate their learning. The university, which was specially protected and encouraged by the Venetians, enjoys greater reputation as a medical school than any other in Italy. It has five faculties, theology, law, medicine, philosophy, and mathematics. Each faculty has a *Direttore* or *Dean*, one of the senior Professors, who, with the *Rettore Magnifico*, elected by the several faculties and approved by the government, constitute the *Senatus Academicus*. There are 46 professorships, and the students vary in number between 1500 and 2000. The public treasury contributes only about 10,000 lire annually towards the general expenses.

Attached to the University are several establishments in different parts of the town, such as 4 clinical schools for medicine, surgery, diseases of the eye, and midwifery; veterinary and agricultural schools; a botanic garden and an astronomical observatory.

The Palace of the *University* is called *il Bò*, or *the Ox*, as it is said from the sign of the inn upon the site of which it stands; something in the same way that the *Hog-market* is honoured at Oxford. Others dispute this origin of the name, and ascribe it to a different tradition, and point out the figure of the animal on a column within. The building was begun in 1493, at the expense of the republic of Venice. The great court, attributed to *Palladio*, but perhaps with more reason to *Sansovino*, is very handsome: the walls are entirely covered with the armorial bearings of the members. At the top of the staircase is the statue of *Elena Lucrezia Cornaro Piscopia*, who died 1684, aged 48 years. She spoke Hebrew, Arabic, Greek, Latin, Spanish, and French, with fluency, was a tolerable poetess, an excellent musician, wrote mathematical and astronomical dissertations, and received a doctor's degree from the university. She died unmarried, having refused many advantageous offers. The Anatomical Theatre was built by *Fabricius ab Aquapendente* in 1594. Although it only replaced a pre-existing one of the 15th centy., it still is the oldest in Europe. The design for it is said to have been given by Fra Paolo Sarpi. The *collection of anatomical preparations and models* is worthy of a visit. That of natural history was first founded by *Vallisnieri* in 1734: the mineralogical and paleontological divisions are the most complete; the latter particularly so in fossils of the Veronese and Vicentine hills, especially in fossil fishes from Monte Bolca. Galileo was professor of mathematics here for upwards of ten years; and in the *Gabinetto di Fisica* they exhibit one of his vertebræ, purloined probably when his remains were removed, in 1757, to their present resting-place in the church of Santa Croce at Florence. The *Gabinetto di Antiquaria e Numismatica*, opening out of the cortile, contains several Roman and Greek bronzes, inscriptions, &c., and a curious papyrus from Ravenna, of the years 616-619—a deed of sale.

As Padua can show the earliest anatomical theatre, so also does it possess the most ancient *botanic garden* in Europe, it having been instituted by the Venetian senate in 1543. The celebrated Prosper Alpinus professed here in 1545. It is situated near the churches of Il Santo and Sta. Giustina, and is laid out in the ancient formal style. The garden is interesting as containing some of the oldest specimens of exotic trees and plants now common in Europe, the patriarchs of our shrubberies, plantations, and conservatories. The Lebanon cedar, the oriental plane, and a *Gleditchia* 93 feet high, may be noticed. The magnolias are superb. Attached to the garden are a Botanical Museum with an extensive *herbarium*, and a Library of 5000 volumes with several MSS.

Bibliotheca Publica. This library, considered as that of the University, is situated at some distance from it, in the vast cortile of the *Palazzo del Capitanio*. The large hall, which formed a part of the palace of the Carraras, is the most extensive in Padua after that of the P. delle Ragione: the printed books amount to upwards of 100,000 volumes, and the MSS. to 1500. This hall, formerly covered with frescoes by *Avanzi* and *Guariento*, having fallen, the colossal frescoes of heroes and emperors which now decorate it were painted in 1540, chiefly by *D. Campagnola*, the portrait of Petrarch, much injured, alone remaining. The library is open, except on Wednesdays and feast-days from 9 a.m. to 3 p.m., from Nov. 3rd to Sept. 7th.

The *Specola*, or astronomical observatory, dates from 1767. It is situated in the mediæval tower of S. Tomaso, the principal defence of Padua on the W. side. Erected by Eccelino, it served as the prison in which many of his victims suffered. The Observatory, under the direction of Prof. Santini, is well supplied with instruments from London, Munich, and Vienna. The view from the summit is very fine over the N.E. Alps, the Lagune of Venice, and the Euganean hills.

Padua has many palaces and fine old houses.

Palazzo Giustiniani, anciently belonging to the Cornaro family. It is from the designs of *Falconetto*. Adjoining it is a rotonda, also erected by *Falconetto*, intended for musical entertainments, and built by the directions of the celebrated Luigi Cornaro, the writer on the mode of prolonging life. It is a very beautiful structure.

Palazzo Pappafava (now the property of Count Andrea Cittadella di Vicodazzere, the descendant of that family) contains a good collection of paintings; amongst others, some curious frescoes brought from suppressed convents. Also a strange group, in sculpture, of Lucifer and his companions cast down from heaven, by *Agostino Fasolata*. It consists of sixty figures, carved out of one block of marble. The figures are so twisted together that it is difficult to understand how the artist could have managed his tools. It is five feet high. The artist was employed upon it more than twelve years: it is a wonderful specimen of patience. The Pappafava family are descended from a branch of the Carraras before they became Lords of Padua; but the name being thought dangerous by the jealous republic, they were compelled to exchange it for a *sobriquet*, borne by one of their ancestors.

Palazzo Zigno. The geologist will find there a very interesting collection of fossils and rocks, generally of this neighbourhood, formed by its present owner, Cav. Zigno, one of the talented geologists of N. Italy.

The *House of Eccelino* is now converted into the Marionette or Puppet Theatre of Santa Lucia. It has some Gothic windows.

Theatres. The *Teatro Nuovo* is opened during a season styled "Fiera del Santo" (the fair of St. Anthony), which begins in June and ends in August; the *Teatro Nuovissimo*, near the cathedral, and the *Teatro Diurno* are for representations by daylight.

The ancient defences of "Padova la Forte" are much dilapidated: a few towers remain, and some gateways by *Falconetto*, in a good style.

Hospitals. The principal hospital, called the *Spedale Civile*, in the street behind the University, is a very extensive building, erected on the site of a suppressed college of the Jesuists in 1798. It can receive 500 patients. 5 of its wards belong to the University, and constitute the Clinical School: they

Padua to Venice.

29¼ Ital. =27 Eng. m.

The ... mode of performing the
... now is by railway, the post-
... ing no longer supplied with
... ssengers travelling in their
... will do well therefore to
... Padua, where they will in-
... than at Mestre, and
... terms. It is scarcely
... that taking them to
... attended with con-
... and inconvenience
... ould afford
... Trains leave Padua
... rming the journey
... hour. The rail-
... teresting country.

... Stat., situated
... ly. crosses

... tween this and
... the Friuli
... een. There
... tian nobility
... he banks
... t. of the

... own of
... about
... one
... which
... line

... 2 miles
... to Ve-
... line, and
... to the l.
... on the
... Ve-
... un-
... is hi
... sive
... the
... ter
... d
... rige,
... remains

can accommodate 50 medical and 25 surgical cases. Other wards are occupied by Obstetric and Ophthalmic cases. In the chapel of the Hospital is a monument to Bishop Giustiniani, the great benefactor of the charity, by Canova. One division of the Spedale Civile is set apart for lunatics.

The Hospital of *S. Giovanni di Dio* is under the management of the monks of that Order, and can receive a small number of acute medical and surgical cases. The *Foundling Hospital,* or *Istituto degli Esposti,* was founded under the denomination of the *Casa di Dio* in 1097. It is consequently the oldest institution of the kind in Europe. The annual admissions average about 400; there are upwards of 3000 children in all on the books, the deaths averaging on the latter number 15 per cent.

Plan for visiting in one day the Sights at Padua, in topographical order.

Palazzo della Ragione; Pal. della Municipalita; Pal. del. Consiglio, Library; Duomo, Baptistery, and *Pal. Vescovile; Observatory; Prato della Valle;* Ch. of *Sant' Antonio* and *Scuola;* Botanic Garden; Ch. of *Santa Giustina* and Chapel of *San Giorgio;* Ch. of *S. Michele; Tomb of Antenor; University* and its collections; *Arena* and *Sta. Maria dell' Arena;* Ch. of *gli Eremitani;* Ch. of *Il Carmine.*

Excursions can be more easily made from Padua to the different places in the Euganean hills than from any other point. Carriages can be hired for Battaglia, where there is a good inn, *Hôtel di Battaglia,* which is much frequented during the season of baths, July, August, and September. From Battaglia excursions may be easily made to Arqua, the retreat of Petrarch, to the Baths of Abano, &c. &c., which are described Rte. 32; and by the geologist amongst the volcanic formations of the adjoining group. For conveyances to Rovigo and Ferrara, see Rte. 32.

Padua to Venice.

23½ Ital.=27 Eng. m.

The only mode of performing the journey now is by railway, the postroad being no longer supplied with horses. *Passengers travelling in their own carriages will do well therefore to leave them at Padua, where they will be better taken care of than at Mestre, and on more economical terms.* It is scarcely necessary to add that taking them to Venice would be attended with considerable expense and inconvenience (as none of the hotels could afford them coach-room). Trains leave Padua 4 times a day, performing the journey in little more than an hour. The railway crosses a flat uninteresting country.

4 m. *Ponte di Brenta Stat.*, situated near the Brenta, which the rly. crosses near this.

10 m. *Dolo Stat.* Between this and the next stat. the Alps of the Friuli and Carinthia are well seen. There are some villas of the Venetian nobility about the town of Dolo, on the banks of the Brenta, 2 miles on rt. of the stat.

15 m. *Mirano Stat.* The town of Mirano, with its high steeple, is about 2 miles on the l. We here cross one of the principal canals, along which and from the bridge there is a fine vista.

21 m. *Mestre Stat.*, about 2 miles from the Laguna. The railway to Treviso, Conegliano, Pordenone, Udine, and Trieste strikes off from this stat. to the l. We now pass (on the l., and on the borders of the sea) the *Fort of Malghera,* a very strong position, which underwent a long siege in 1849 : its fall led to the surrender of Venice, since which, as the key to the Queen of the Adriatic on the land side, it has undergone considerable additions and repairs. We here enter on the bridge, which is traversed in about 6 minutes.

References

Principal Churches

1	S. Mark	F e
2	S. Giovanni e Paolo	F c
3	S. Giorgio Maggiore	F f
4	S. Maria dei Frari	C d
5	S. Maria della Salute	E f
6	Il Redentore	D g
7	S. Salvatore	E d
8	S. Zaccaria	F d

Public Buildings

9	Ducal Palace	F e
10	Academy of Fine Arts	C e
11	Palazzo Manfrini	B b
12	Grimani a	
	S. Maria Formosa	F d
13	Post Office	D d
14	Hospital	F c
15	Teatro della Fenice	D e
16	Gallo	D d
17	Apollo	E d
18	Malibran	E v
19	Entrance to the Arsenal	H d

Other Churches

20	S. Apostoli	E c
21	S. Francesco della Vigna	G e
22	Gesuiti	E b
23	S. Giovanni Crisostomo	E c
24	S. Giorgio de Greci	G d
25	S. Jacopo di Rialto	E c
26	S. Lucia	B c
27	Madonna dell'Orto	D a
28	S. Maria del Carmine	B e
29	S. Maria Formosa	F d
30	S. Maria de Miracoli	E c
31	S. Martino	H d
32	S. Nicolo	A e
33	S. Pantaleone	B d
34	S. Pietro di Castello	K d
35	S. Rocco	C d
36	Gli Scalzi	B c
37	S. Sebastiano	A e
38	S. Stefano	D e
39	Tolentini	B d
40	S. Trovaso	C f
41	Hotel Danieli	C d
42	dela Ville	F e
43	Police Office	F d
44	Museo Correr	

J. & C. Walker, Sculp.

This great work, which carries the railroad over the Lagoon, and enters Venice on the island of St. Lucia, is parallel to, and a little S. of, the channel connecting Venice with Mestre, and passes close to the fort of San Secondo: it occupied 4½ years in erecting, and was completed on the 27th of October, 1845. The length of the bridge is 3936 yds., or 2 m. and 416 yds. It consists of 222 circular arches, of 32 ft. 9½ in. span. The thickness of the single piers is 3¼ ft. The height of the top of the parapet above the mean level of the water of the Lagoon is 14 ft. The width of the bridge, where it passes over arches, is 29½ ft. In the centre is a large embankment, called *Piazza Maggiore*, 446 ft. in length, and in width 97 ft. 10 in. The depth of the water through which the bridge is carried varies from 13 to 3 ft. The soil of the bottom of the Lagoon, where it is built, is entirely of mud. The foundation is upon piles driven into the bed of the Lagoon. The piers from the platform on the heads of the piles up to the impost are of limestone, the arches and spandrils of brick, the cornice and parapet of Istrian stone. Close inside the parapet, on a level with the roadway, two channels are formed for carrying fresh water from the mainland to Venice.

It may give some idea of the magnitude of the work to mention that, amongst other materials, 80,000 larch piles were used in the foundations, and in the bridge itself 21 millions of bricks and 176,437 cubic ft. of Istrian stone; and that, on an average, 1000 men were employed daily. It cost 5,600,000 Austrian lire, = 186,666*l*. The bridge was much injured during the siege of Venice in 1849, when several of the arches were destroyed, and a battery formed of the Piazza Maggiore.

23½ m. VENICE *Stat*. Passports are taken by a police officer, and a receipt given at the station, which must be presented at the central Police Office before the traveller leaves the town, when the visa is granted gratuitously. Although Venice is a free port for everything but salt and tobacco, passengers' luggage is searched at the station, and books are sometimes examined. The examination is more rigorous on leaving Venice, and the confusion and bustle intolerable.

The rly. stat. is at a considerable distance from most of the hotels, but gondolas in abundance will be found on the arrival of each train. The Rly. Company has established a service of omnibus boats: the fare for conveying the traveller to the vicinity of the Piazza di San Marco is 25 centimes, and 25 centimes for every article of luggage which the traveller cannot carry in his hand, not including a fee to the boatman for carrying the latter to the traveller's apartment in the hotel; but as these omnibus boats are only bound to convey persons to certain stations, they may exact an additional sum for calling at the hotels; a gondola will be found the most expeditious, comfortable, and often as economical conveyance, the whole charge not exceeding 2 lire.

VENICE. Ital., *Venezia*: French, *Venise*: Germ., *Venedig*. Hotels : *Albergo Reale*, kept by Danieli, on the Riva dei Schiavoni. It was formerly the Nani-Mocenigo Palace, and is at a short distance from the ducal palace. Good table-d'hôte at 4 francs. Complaints have been made of the attendance and charges, which are higher than elsewhere at Venice. In the autumn mosquitoes are a great pest at Venice, and especially on the Riva dei Schiavoni.— *Hôtel de la Ville*, Palazzo Loredan, on the Grand Canal; *Hôtel Barbesi*, also on the Grand Canal: both these hotels have good table-d'hôtes at 5 P.M., at 4 fr. without wine; bed-rooms, 3 to 5 fr.; breakfasts, 1½ to 2 fr.; and baths in the house: as many persons frequent Venice for sea-bathing, they will find this very convenient. Arrangements during a prolonged stay may be made advantageously for board and lodging at the *Hôtel Barbesi* in the Palazzo Zucchelli, which has a garden with a southern aspect, a fine view over the Lagunes, is near the Piazza di San Marco, and in the best position as a winter residence: it is kept by the former proprietor of the Hôtel de la Ville, a very obliging man, who speaks English.—*Hôtel Bellevue*, in the Piazza S. Marco, lately established by Bauer, of Ischl and Vienna; this hotel is highly spoken of for cleanliness and comfort generally, with a table-d'hôte, and dinners served à la carte, and at so much a head.—*Albergo dell' Europa*, formerly the Giustiniani Palace, close to the Piazza di San Marco, much improved; clean and comfortable.—*Albergo della Regina Vittoria*, on a small canal near the Piazza di S. Marco, improved; from its situation to be preferred in the season of heat and mosquitos to the hotels on the Grand Canal: the landlord very civil, the house clean, charges moderate (en pension 9 lire a day, everything included).—*Albergo d' Italia*, a new house, at San Moisè, on a canal near the Fenice theatre. It has a table-d'hôte and is well recommended, and is in a convenient situation, being near the Piazza di S. Marco. *Albergo San Marco*, in the Piazza San Marco, kept by Padron, with a tolerable restaurant, moderate as to charges. *Luna*, close to the S.W. angle of the Place St. Mark. As a general rule, *come to an understanding beforehand at all the Venetian hotels as to the charges to be incurred during your stay!!* Travellers will do well not to listen to recommendations from agents and touters for hotels at the railway station.

To visit Venice with the greatest comfort and advantage, the best time of the year will be the spring, at which period the climate is delightful, the sky clear and unclouded, and the canals clean after their winter agitation; at this season there are no mosquitoes, the pest of the place in the autumn, when they are really intolerable, and when the stench from the canals, after the summer heats, is insupportable in some quarters. Thick fogs set in here, as throughout the N. of Italy, in October, which render the climate cold and disagreeable. During the winter the cold is at times intense, from the violent winds descending from the snow-capped Alps of the Tyrol and Friuli. (See Plan for visiting Venice in topographical order, at p. 380.)

Passports. All foreigners must deliver their passports, for which receipts are given, on arriving at the rly. stat., and apply at the head Police Office for the necessary visa before leaving the city, when they are examined at the station or on board the steamers. Persons going into the Bavarian territories by the Brenner or Ampezzo roads will do well to provide themselves with that of the consul of Bavaria at Venice. The Police office is on the Quay, called the Fundamenti di S. Lorenzo.

Restaurants. There are few good at Venice: the best is at the Hôtel Bellevue in the Piazza S. Marco. At the Restaurant Français, in the Piazza di San Marco, dinner may be had for 3 zwanzigers.

Cafés. Florian's has long enjoyed what may be called an European reputation. It is situated in the centre of the Procuratie Nuove, and has been lately fitted up with great elegance. Galignani and some French newspapers may be seen there, and breakfasts à-la-fourchette and suppers may be had. Close to Florian's is the *Café Suttil*, also very good, and equally fashionable, but more frequented by Austrian society. Nearly opposite to Florian's, in the Procuratie Vecchie, are the *Café de' Specchi*, handsomely fitted up and good, and the *Café Quadri*, the resort of the military and Austrians. Italian ladies rarely enter the cafés; they take their refreshment—ice or coffee—outside, especially when the military bands play, on Sundays, Tuesdays, and Thursdays.

The arcade outside Florian's is the rendezvous of the Venetian *beau monde* in the warm summer and autumnal evenings.

Gondolas. The tariff is as follows: For a gondola with one boatman, 1 lira for the first hour, and 60 centimes for every succeeding one; for the day, 6 lire; with 2 rowers 10 lire; 2 lire for the first hour, and 1 l. 20 c. for every subsequent one. If, however, a gondola is taken for the day or several hours, an abatement may be effected by previous agreement. It will be a good plan for a traveller, as long as he is occupied in sight-seeing, to hire a gondola by the day, which with one man may be had for 4 zwanzigers, with a trifling buonamano. The gondolier, being generally well acquainted with the situation of all the objects a traveller wishes to see, will thus save the annoyance and expense of a valet de place. From the Railway to the Piazzetta of S. Marco or vice versâ, 2 lire, and 30 c. for every parcel of luggage. All gondoliers are obliged to carry the Police tariff, which they must exhibit if required.

Railways. Three trains leave Venice daily, for Padua, Vicenza, Verona, at 4·40, 5·45, and 10·18 A.M., the two latter only continuing to Brescia, Bergamo, and Milan; 4 trains daily to Padua; and for Trieste at 7·20 and 11·20 A.M. and 5·41 P.M., passing by Treviso, Conegliano, Pordenone, and Udine.

Steamers to Trieste every morning at 6; average passage 6 hours in the best boats. The hours may however vary with the season, but they can be easily ascertained at the office in the Piazzetta di San Marco. The steamer from Trieste leaves at 7 A.M., and arrives at Venice about midday. Persons with return tickets to Trieste must have them changed at the office the day before starting.

Post Office. Letters for England are despatched daily at an early hour, *viâ* Milan and France; letters must be posted the night before; postage for a single letter, viâ France, 35 soldi; ½ oz. weight, 1 lira and 40 centimes, arriving in London on the fourth day: and by Vienna and Belgium at 6 a.m., but letters of ½ oz., or double the weight, may be sent by this route, arriving in 5 days, —postage 25 soldi. Letters arrive daily from England by both routes. The postage on newspapers is high—a London paper costing 16 soldi.

British Consulate. Mr. Perry, Consul General.

Bankers. Schielen Brothers, No. 5850, Santa Maria Formosa; S. and A. Blumenthal, 672, Freyrerin, Casa Aveseri.

Painters. Mr. Nerly, a Prussian, whose views of Venice are in great request, resides in the Palazzo Pisani, a S. Stefano. Madame Kartitz is a good copyist of the works of the old masters in the Academy. Sig. Molmenti is the most eminent of the painters of historical subjects and of portraits at the present day. Carlo Grubas, Calle dell' Erbe, No. 6120, paints small views of Venice, both in oils and body-colour, at a very reasonable rate. The best *views of Venice* are the *photographs*, to be had at Munster's and other printsellers in the Piazza San Marco, price 3 and 6 zwanzigers each, and at Ponti's 4180, Riva di Schiavoni.

Booksellers. Herman Munster, a very obliging man, who speaks English, Piazza San Marco, Nos. 72, 73, is well supplied with foreign and Italian works, maps, handbooks, guide-books, &c. Mr. M. also keeps a circulating library of French, English, German, and Italian books.

Physicians. Dr. Locatelli, Rio Terrao; Dr. Namias, Riva dei Carboni, near the Hôtel de la Ville; Dr. Minich, Ponte dei Barcaroli; Dr. Candeo, Calle San Benedetto, highly spoken of.

Apothecaries. There is a good apothecary near the post-office, in the Campo San Lucca, No. 3801, in correspondence with Savory and Son, London.

Valets de Place. Five zwanzigers for the first day, and about 4 for each succeeding one, is ample payment. At the churches ½ a zw. to the sacristan will be sufficient. At the Doge's Palace and the Academy somewhat more, but never exceeding 1 zw., except when the party is large.

For English goods the best shops are Trauner's, in the Merceria; he is said to have fixed prices, and to be very respectable (he and his son both speak English); and Prinoth's, behind the Piazza San Marco, in the street leading to S. Möse.

Venetian curiosities and objects of art and vertu. Zen, on the Canal opposite the Palazzo Vendramin. Richetti, Palazzo Marcello, Canal Grande. *Marchandes des Modes.* Madame Angelique Breant, Palazzo Capello, behind the church of St. Marco. Madame Julien, Ponte S. Moïse.

"The celebrated name of Venice, or Venetia, was formerly diffused over a large and fertile province of Italy, from the confines of Pannonia to the river Addua, and from the Po to the Rhetian and Julian Alps." Venetia was divided into *Prima* and *Secunda*, of which the first applied to the mainland, and the second to the islands and lagunes. In the first, "before the irruption of the Barbarians, 50 Venetian cities flourished in peace and prosperity: Aquileia was placed in the most conspicuous station: but the ancient dignity of Padua was supported by agriculture and manufactures."—*Gibbon.* Venetia Secunda, placed in the midst of canals at the mouth of several rivers, was occupied in fisheries, salt-works, and commerce.

Venice owes its existence as a city to the fugitives who, on the invasion of Italy by Attila, sought safety, after the fall of Aquileia, from the sword of the Huns, among the neighbouring islands. "At the extremity of the Gulf, where the Hadriatic feebly imitates the tides of the ocean, near a hundred small islands are separated by shallow water from the continent, and protected from the waves by several long slips of land, which admit the entrance of vessels through some secret and narrow channels."—*Gibbon.* This natural breakwater, or *aggere*, as it is termed, extending nearly 80 miles from the mouth of the Piave to Brondolo, has been formed by the deposit brought down by the rivers for ages, and not arrested till it meets the sea, where it has raised itself into impregnable ramparts (Littorali) against the inroads of the waves.

Between the Piave and the Adige 6 channels admit a passage from the Adriatic into the Lagune. Of these the most northern is the Porto di tre Porti, navigable only by the very smallest craft. The island of San Erasmo intervenes between this and the second opening, bearing the name of the saint just mentioned. The Porto di San Nicolo del Lido, a third channel, was formerly the most important, and might be called especially the Port of Venice: it is still much frequented by small vessels and the steamers from Trieste. South of this is the island of Lido, and the long sandy Littorale of Malamocco, extending for nearly 2 leagues, form an outwork in front of the city, and are separated from the Littorale of Pelestrina by the Porto di Malamocco, at present the deepest channel into the Lagunes. At the southern extremity of Pelestrina opens the Porto di Chioggia, taking its name from the town to which it leads, between which and the Porto di Brondolo, where the Brenta enters the sea, is the irregular island or *Littorale* of *Sotto Marina*; inside of this band is an extensive area of water of inconsiderable depth, navigable only for vessels of very slight draught, except where channels have been formed naturally by rivers which empty themselves into it, maintained by artificial means. In this expanse (the Laguna or Lagoon) are several small islands, the largest of which, called *Isola de Rialto* (which is abbreviated from *Rivo alto*—the deep stream), had long served as a port to Padua, and a few buildings for naval purposes had been constructed upon it. The fall of Aquileia, and the self-banishment of the neighbouring inhabitants of Concordia — Opitergium, now *Oderzo* — Altinum, *Altino* — and of Patavium, *Padua* — occurred in the year 452 of our era: but as early as 421 a church dedicated to St. James had been erected on the island of Rialto, and a decree had issued from Padua for forming a town on it, and collecting there the straggling inhabitants of the neighbouring island, under the government of annual magistrates with the title of consuls. Sabellico has preserved a tradition that the earliest buildings of this town were raised on the very spot now occupied by the cathedral of St. Mark, and that the first foundations were laid on the 25th March.

Venice is built upon 72 islands or shoals, the foundations for the buildings being formed with piles and stone. It is divided into two unequal portions by the *Canalazzo*, or grand canal, whose course through the city is in the form of an S, and is intersected in all directions by 146 smaller canals, crossed by 306 bridges. These bridges are frequent, and, being steep, are cut into easy steps. Three bridges only cross the Grand Canal: that of the Rialto, in stone, is the most celebrated; the other two in iron—one between the Campo di S. Stefano and the Accademia delle Belle Arti, and the other opposite to the Railway Station.

The smaller bridges are so numerous, and so well placed, that there is no part of the city—that is to say, no house—which cannot be walked to; but many of the finest buildings, as on the Canal Grande, can only be seen from the water, out of which they rise. A gondola is therefore all but indispensable to the stranger.

"The small canals, or *rii*, as they are termed, which are bestrid by these bridges, are the water-streets of Venice; but there is no part of either of the two divisions to which you may not also go by land, through narrow passages called *calli*. There are, besides, several small squares, entitled *campi*.

"The most considerable houses of Venice have each a door opening inland, and another towards the canal; but many, being built in the interior of these shoals, can have no immediate access by water. This is a considerable inconvenience, as it limits the use and comfort of a gondola.

"There is sometimes a wharf or a footway along the banks of the *rii* (called a *riva*), and usually secured by a parapet, bored for a wicket; but the *rii* oftener extend from house to house, and these then consequently rise on either side from out of the water. The same may be said of the Grand Canal as of the *rii*, though here and there is a small extent of terrace or *riva*, in front of the houses."—*Letters from the North of Italy.*

The larger and wider Rive are called *Fondamenti.*

As a general description of Venice, that of Rogers is pleasing, and was correct, but the railroad has superseded the passage from the mainland in a gondola, and, though it may jar with the prejudices of some, presents a scene not less singular.

"There is a glorious city in the sea.
The sea is in the broad, the narrow streets,
Ebbing and flowing; and the salt sea-weed
Clings to the marble of her palaces.
No track of men, no footsteps to and fro,
Lead to her gates. The path lies o'er the sea,
Invincible; and from the land we went,
As to a floating city—steering in,
And gliding up her streets, as in a dream,
So smoothly, silently—by many a dome,
Mosque-like, and many a stately portico,
The statues ranged along an azure sky;
By many a pile, in more than eastern pride,
Of old the residence of merchant-kings;
The fronts of some, tho' Time had shatter'd them,
Still glowing with the richest hues of art,
As though the wealth within them had run o'er."

The Venetians have laid aside the peculiarities of dress which marked their nationality in their days of independence. The national dresses, the red *Tabarro* of the men and the black *Zendale* of the women, so often mentioned in Goldoni's plays, have entirely disappeared. The gondolas still retain unchanged their black funereal appearance. Conjurors, storytellers, and Punch, may be often seen on the Riva dei Schiavoni.

"The Venetian dialect, or rather language, was formerly so much cherished as a token of nationality, that the speakers in the Senate were compelled to employ it to the exclusion of the Tuscan or *Volgare*. It possesses great softness and pleasantness of sound, and bears somewhat the same relation to the *Volgare* that the Portuguese does to the Castilian; the consonants are elided, and the whole softened down: as in *Padre, Pare; Madre, Mare; Figlio, Fio; Casa, Ca;* and some have regretted that it did not prevail instead of its more fortunate sister. It is softer and more winning than the Tuscan, though it falls far beneath it in dignity and force. The judgment, however, of a foreigner is of little weight. It has had better testimonies borne to its merits by *Bettinelli*, and a host of Italian writers who may naturally be supposed to have had a nicer and more discriminating sense of its perfections. In all the lighter and gayer walks of poetry it is delightful; and the Venetian verse is, compared with the verse of other nations, very much what Venetian painting is as to that of the rest of Europe."—*Rose's Letters.*

The manufactures of Venice are the glass-works, in which are produced magnificent mirrors, artificial pearls, gems, coloured beads, &c., employing about 4500 people; the women and children are employed in the various manufactures—beads, jewellery, gold and silver chains, gold and silver stuffs, silks, laces, and velvets; soap, earthenware, wax and spermaceti candles, sugar refineries, &c. Printing is extensively carried on. Ship and boat building to a considerable extent at Venice and Chioggia. The inhabitants are not, however, fully employed ashore, and a great number depend on fishing and on navigating the vessels belonging to the port. The latter, exclusive of fishing-boats, amount to about 30,000 tons of shipping, employed chiefly in the coasting trade.

The entrances to the port of Venice are intricate; the best ship entrance is by the Pass of Malamocco, by which vessels drawing from 18 to 20 ft. can enter easily since the prolongation of its two moles, outside of which, in the Gulf, there is good holding ground. It is absolutely necessary to have a pilot to enter. Although not actually on the decline, its trade has suffered greatly from the increasing prosperity of Trieste, which has met more favour and encouragement from the Austrian government than the Queen of the Adriatic. The railroad from Milan, and the re-establishment of the freedom of its port, will probably increase the trade, but not so far as to raise its commerce and navigation to that of a place of first-rate importance. The direct trade between England and Venice consists in some cargoes of fish, in large quantities of coal and iron, and a few of manufactured goods, although a great proportion of the latter are transhipped from Trieste.

Venice is a free port, and most of the articles for the use of the citizens are admitted duty free. There are, however, small dues levied to raise funds to defray the municipal expenses. Goods of various descriptions are exported from Venice, and carried chiefly by contraband into the Papal states, and into the kingdom of Naples. There is also a considerable trade carried on between Venice and Dalmatia, Albania, and parts of Greece. The Imperial Dockyard, formerly the celebrated arsenal of the Republic, has much fallen off in importance since the establishment by the Austrian Government of its naval stations at Trieste, and especially at Pola, on the coast of Istria.

Within a few years very extensive moles have been formed, with stone brought from Istria, near the Malamocco Pass, in order that by narrowing the waterway at ebb-tide the scour of the water flowing through might deepen the channel. The plan has been attended with great success. Vessels drawing 20 ft. now enter by this passage without difficulty, and without waiting for spring-tides. There is a regular tide of the Lagoon, the rise and fall at Venice being between 2 and 3 ft., so that at low water the Lagoon in some directions appears a vast expanse of mud. This is particularly observable on looking westward from the neighbourhood of the bridge which crosses the canal leading to the Arsenal, or from the top of the tower of S. Marco; the Lagoon under these circumstances offers a very strange aspect.

It is highly probable that the original depth of the Adriatic was greater than now. At present its greatest between the coast of Dalmatia and the mouths of the Po is 22 fathoms, and a large part of the Gulf of Trieste, and the Adriatic opposite Venice, is less than 12 fathoms deep. This decrease is caused by the deposits brought down by the numerous large rivers which, charged with alluvial matter, empty themselves into the N. extremity of the gulf.

The centre of business and amusement at Venice, and the spot which a traveller usually first visits and most often returns to, is the *Piazza di S. Marco*. With this it will be therefore better to commence our description of the city.

We will suppose the traveller standing in front of the church, and looking towards it.

On the E. side stands the basilica of St. Mark. On the N. or l.-hand side is the long line of buildings called the *Procuratie Vecchie* and the *Torre dell' Orologio*. On the S. side, and opposite, are the *Procuratie Nuove* and the *Libreria Vecchia*. Towards the W. the Piazza formerly extended only as far as a mark in red marble let into the pavement, near the 16th arch of the Procuratie Nuove, counting from the angle behind the campanile. This red mark indicates the position of a canal, on the bank of which formerly stood the *Church of St. Geminiano*. In the 12th centy. the canal was filled up and the church pulled down to afford space for enlarging the Piazza. The length of this Piazza is 576 ft.; its greatest width, *i. e.* from the corner close to the campanile to the opposite side, 269 ft.; its least width, which is at the W. end, 185 ft.

At right angles with the Piazza, at its eastern end, is the *Piazzetta*, extending from near the base of the campanile to the *Molo* or quay formed along the edge of the canal, from the newly-formed promenade behind the viceregal residence to the extremity of the southern front of the Doge's palace. On the W. side of the Piazzetta stands the *Libreria Vecchia*, and on the E. the Ducal palace; and on the Molo, near the southern end of the Piazzetta, the two famous granite columns, one surmounted by the bronze Lion of St. Mark, the other by the statue of St. Theodore, the Protector of the Republic.

A large flock of pigeons will always be seen frequenting the Piazza and the neighbouring buildings. They have existed here so long that their origin is forgotten; various explanations have been offered, too long and too unsatisfactory to insert, accounting for their existence, and for their having been fed at the expense of the government. They are protected by the almost superstitious care and affection of the Venetian people; they are fed at two o'clock, and it is a curious sight to see them arrive from every side on the striking of that hour by the great clock of the Torre dell' Orologio.

San Marco. This church did not become the cathedral until the year 1807, when the patriarchal seat was removed to it from San Pietro di Castello. Until then it was the Ducal Chapel, founded in the year 828, by the Doge Giustiniani Partecipiazio, for the purpose of receiving the relics of St. Mark, which had just been translated, or rather, in plain English, stolen from Alexandria, by *Bono*, the "Tribuno" of Malamocco, and *Rustico* of Torcello. These remains were deposited in the Chapel of St. Theodore: but the popular veneration was transferred, apparently without hesitation, from St. Theodore to the Evangelist, whose symbol became the emblem, and almost the palladium, of the republic; and the too humble Church of Narses was demolished to make room for the more splendid edifice of the newly chosen protector. Giustiniani died, leaving the church unfinished; but it was completed by his heirs, and stood until destroyed in the conflagration which terminated the life and reign of Pietro Candiano IV. in 976.

Pietro Orseolo I., the successor of Candiano, was the founder of the present edifice. The foundations were laid in 977; but nearly one hundred years elapsed before the walls were completed, under the reign of Domenico Contarini, 1043. Many precious adornments, and in particular the mosaics, were added by the Doge Domenico Salvo, 1071; and it was not consecrated till the time of Ordelafó Falier, on the 4th October, 1111.

Although it has been disputed to which of the several eras of construction the present Basilica is to be ascribed, and whether or not it is to be considered as a specimen of Byzantine art, it may be without much doubt said that the original design has undergone little alteration, and that it was due to Greek architects, or to artists who had studied in the school of Constantinople and the East.

"The plan of St. Mark's, like that of Santa Sophia, is a Greek cross, with the addition of spacious porticos. The centre of the building is covered with a dome, and over the centre of each of the arms of the cross rises a smaller cupola. All the remaining parts of the building are covered with vaults, in constructing which the Greeks had become expert, and which are much to be preferred to the wooden roofs of the old Basilicas.

"Colonnades and round arches separate the nave from the aisles in each of the four compartments, and support galleries above. The capitals of the pillars are of exquisite foliage, in some cases, as though blown about by the wind, and are free from the imagery which at that time abounded in other churches of Italy. It is computed that in the decoration of this building, without and within, above 500 pillars are employed. The pillars are all of marble, and were chiefly brought from Greece, and other parts of the Levant. Whilst St. Mark's was building, every vessel that cleared out of Venice for the East was obliged to bring back pillars and marbles for the work in which the republic took so general an interest.

"The defect of the interior of St. Mark's is, that it is not sufficiently light. The windows are few in proportion to the size of the building. Rich, therefore, as the interior is, it is gloomy to a fault, in spite of the brilliant rays of a southern sun."—*Gally Knight.*

In the façade are two rows of columns of verd-antique, porphyry, serpentine, and other marbles, some with Armenian and Syrian inscriptions deeply engraven, and showing by their variety of style and dimensions that they were brought from older buildings. Several tablets of ancient sculpture are inserted in the outer walls. They are of various ages and nations. One on the N. side, in the small square of the lions, represents Proserpine, or Ceres, holding a torch in either hand, and in a chariot drawn by two dragons, and of which a duplicate will be found at San Donino, near Parma. Cicognara judged it to be of Persian origin. In the opposite corner, towards the Ducal palace, is inserted a remarkable group of four full-length figures, in red porphyry, striking from their peculiar colour, and from their position. It is probably of the 10th or 11th centy.; but the absence of any inscription, as well as of all knowledge of its origin, forbids further conjectures; the tradition is that it had been brought from Acre, and ornamented the pedestal of an equestrian statue. Five large mosaics fill the recesses over the doorways. Beginning on the rt. of the spectator, the subject of the first and second is the removal of the body of St. Mark from the tomb at Alexandria, executed in 1650, from the designs of *Pietro Vecchio*: of the next, the Last Judgment, executed by Liborio Salandri; the following recess contains the Venetian Magistrates venerating the body of St. Mark, designed by *Sebn. Rizzi*, in 1728: the last recess contains the most ancient of these mosaics, a work probably of the 14th cent., representing the church of St. Mark. Four mosaics occupy the semicircular gables above, beginning with that which is above the one last mentioned in the lower row: they represent the Taking down from the Cross, the Descent into Hades, the Resurrection, and the Ascension, by *Luigi Gaetano*, 1617, from the drawings of *Maffeo Verona*. The archivolts of the centre doorway, and of the portal which encircles it, are embossed with Prophets and Evangelists, allegorical representations of the months of the year, trades and labours; to which, within and without, must be added several of those mystical figures which have been so often described, of lions and other animals devouring or prostrating human victims. The celebrated *bronze horses*, formerly gilt, stand over the central portal of the vestibule, in a situation which renders it difficult to see them well either from below or from the level on which they are placed. They were brought from the Hippodrome at Constantinople, being part of the share of the Venetians in the plunder when that city was taken by the Crusaders in the fourth crusade. They were removed to Paris for a short time, but brought back in 1815. Antiquaries hesitate concerning the date and even the country of these horses; for by some they have been assigned to the Roman period, and to the age of Nero; by others to the Greeks of Chios, and to the school of Lysippus. According to the most generally received opinion, that of Cicognara, Augustus brought them from Alexandria, after his victory over M. Antony, and erected them on a triumphal arch at Rome: they were successively removed by Nero, Domitian, Trajan, and Constantine, to arches of their own; and in each of these positions it is believed that they were attached to a chariot. Constantine in the end transferred them to his new capital.— A recent Greek writer, Mutoxidi, has endeavoured to prove that they were cast at Chios, and supposes they were removed to Constantinople by Theodosius. They are not in the highest style of art, and Cicognara says that the casting of them was so ill managed that the artist was compelled to finish them up by many solderings; the weight of each horse is 1932 lbs.

The five outer doors of the vestibule are of bronze: on that next to the central one, on the l. hand, is an inscription, showing that it was executed in the year 1300, by *Bertuccio*, a Venetian goldsmith.

Upon entering the vestibule, which extends along the whole front; by the central portal, there is seen in the pavement a lozenge of white and red marble, marking the spot where Pope Alexander III. and the Emperor Frederic Barbarossa were, on the 23rd July, 1177, reconciled, through the intervention of the Venetian republic. The Pope, it is said, but on very doubtful authority, placed his foot upon the head of the prostrate Emperor, repeating the words of the Psalm, "Thou shalt tread upon the lion and the adder." This is the story of the Church-writers; but the reconciliation of the Emperor is described by the cotemporary Archbishop of Salerno as of a much less humiliating character for the imperial penitent.

The vaulting of the vestibule is covered with mosaics, and around the walls are numerous columns of precious marbles, brought from the East. Among the mosaics may be noticed St. Mark, in pontifical robes, over the centre door of the church. It was executed in 1545 by Francesco and Valerio Zuccato, from the designs of Titian. Opposite to this is the Crucifixion, by the brothers Zuccati, in 1549. The Resurrection of Lazarus, the Annunciation, the Four Evangelists, the Eight Prophets, the Angels and Doctors in the frieze, are also by the Zuccati. This vestibule opens, on the rt. hand, into the *Zeno Chapel*, in which is the splendid tomb of Cardinal Zeno, cast in 1505-15, from the designs of the two *Lombardi*, and of *Alessandro Leopardi*.

Of the three doors which open from the vestibule into the church, the centre one, and that on the l. of it, are Venetian works executed between 1100 and 1112. That on the rt. is said to be of Byzantine workmanship, and to have been carried off from S. Sofia at Constantinople in 1203. The 8 marble columns on each side of this entrance were brought from Constantinople in 1205. In the N. corridor is the monument of Doge Marino Morosini, with a more ancient bas-relief of Christ between the 12 Apostles.

The interior is very rich: the walls and columns are of precious marbles, the vaulting is covered with mosaics upon a gold ground, and the pavement of tessellated marble. This marqueterie in marble, called *vermiculato*, is not only remarkable for the beauty and richness of the patterns, but for the symbols and allegories supposed to be contained in the various devices. The following are given as instances:—The round, well-fed, sleek Lion on the sea, and the lean, meagre Lion on the land, denoted what would be the fate of Venice if she deserted the profits of her maritime commerce for the vainglories of territorial conquest. Two cocks carrying off a fox indicate the conquest and capture of the crafty Ludovico Sforza by the two Gallic monarchs Charles VII. and Louis XII. It would far exceed the limits of this work to enter into a detail of the mosaics in San Marco: we shall only therefore notice a few of the most remarkable. Over the central door is a mosaic of the 11th century, the Virgin and St. Mark. Entering by this door, on the rt. hand is a porphyry basin for holy water; the base supporting which is an ancient Greek altar, with bas-reliefs of dolphins, children, &c. Further on the rt. is the *Baptistery*, adorned with marbles, bas-relief and mosaics, all executed about the 14th centy. In the middle is a basin, with a bronze cover adorned with low

reliefs by Tiziano Minio and Domenico da Firenze, pupils of Sansovino, in 1545; on the top is a statue in bronze of St. John the Baptist, by Francesco Segalla, in 1565. Behind the altar are reliefs of the 14th centy., representing the Baptism in the Jordan, St. George, and St. Theodore. The altar-table, behind the modern altar, is formed of a massive granite slab brought from Tyre in 1126, and upon which our Saviour is said to have stood when he preached to the inhabitants of that city. Against the wall is the monument of Doge Henry Dandolo, who died in 1354. He was the last doge who was buried in St. Mark's, the senate having decreed that none should in future be interred here. Dandolo, the fourth doge of his name, was the friend of Petrarch, the first historian of Venice, and descended from the celebrated blind hero of the crusades, who, elected doge in 1192, at the age of 45, commanded at the siege of Constantinople in his 97th year. The other tomb, in a Gothic style, is of Doge Soranzo (ob. 1328). The mosaics of the Crucifixion, over the altar, and representing several modes of baptism by immersion, on the cupola over the font, are curious as works of art, and in excellent preservation.

Returning into the church: near a pilaster of the N. aisle is the chapel of the Holy Cross, a small octagonal tribune supported by six columns; the one nearest the altar on the right is of a very rare variety of black and white Syenite.

At the end of the N. transept is the Chapel of the Madonna de' Mascoli, of which the marble altar, as well as the statues of the Madonna, of St. Mark, and St. John are works of the school of Nicolo Pisano; the angels in front are of a later date. The mosaics in this chapel are by Michele Giambono, in 1490; they represent the history of the Virgin. This artist was one of the first who abandoned the stiff and dry manner of his predecessors in this branch of art.

On the wall above the entrance to the chapel of *St. Isidore* (founded in

1550 to receive the body of the saint, brought from the island of Schio), and to the rt. of that of the M. de' Mascoli, is a curious mosaic, representing the genealogical tree of the Virgin.

The choir and its divisions rise in triple ascent. It is parted from the nave by a rich screen, after the Greek fashion, surmounted by fourteen statues executed by *Jacobello* and *Pietro Paolo dalle Massegne* (1393), pupils of the Pisan school: the cross over the centre, with the statue of Christ in silver, is by *Marco Benato* (1594). The presbytery contains the high altar, standing under a Baldacchino, supported by four columns, covered with bands of sculpture and Latin inscriptions, and supposed to be of the 11th century. These bands, nine upon each column, contain the principal events and traditions of the Gospel history, from the Marriage of St. Anna to the Ascension. At the sides of the high altar are eight bronze statues—the four Evangelists by *Sansovino*, and the four Doctors of the Church by *G. Cagliari*. Behind the high altar are 2 *Pale* or altar fronts. The innermost is not seen unless request is made for that purpose. The outer "Pala," in fourteen compartments, by *Messer Paolo* and his sons, in 1344, is very interesting, as one of the well-determined (as to date) specimens of Venetian art, although it has been almost ruined by successive restorations. It is more Greek and stiff than contemporary works at Florence. This covers the *Pala d' Oro*, or *Icone Bisantina*, one of the most remarkable specimens now existing of Byzantine art, made in 976 at Constantinople by order of Doge Pietro Orseolo; but repaired by the Doges Ordelafo Falier 1105, Pietro Zani 1209, and lastly by Andrea Dandolo 1345. By all these processes it has gained in splendour, but it has lost in originality. It exhibits a mixture of Byzantine and Gothic styles. Some of the inscriptions are in Greek, some in Latin. The material is silver gilt, encircled with coarse gems and enamels. The letters are in *niello*. The representations of sacred personages and subjects are of the usual description: some are from the legendary life of St. Mark. The most curious are of the Doge Falier and the Empress Irene. This *Pala* is now arranged in 2 horizontal rows of 83 panels. Taken as a whole, it is inferior in workmanship to the goldsmith's work and enamel of Lombardy, France, and Germany, at any of the periods to which it belongs. It has lately been thoroughly cleaned and put in order. Behind the high altar is another, called the Altar of the Holy Sacrament, with bas-reliefs, some of which (Jesus Christ and the Angels) are by *Sansovino*. It stands, like the great altar, under a canopy, supported by four fluted spiral pillars, said to have been brought from the Temple at Jerusalem. Two are of oriental alabaster.

By the side of this altar is the entrance to the sacristy, closed by the bronze door, upon which *Sansovino* is said to have exercised his talents during twenty years. The subjects of the bas-reliefs are the Deposition and Resurrection of our Lord. In the border are introduced small heads of the prophets and evangelists, starting forward with exceeding life and vivacity. Three of these are portraits—of Sansovino himself, of Titian, and of the notorious Pietro Aretino. The expense was defrayed by Federigo Contarini, one of the procurators of St. Mark. *Sansovino* has authenticated the work by engraving his name on it.

The *Sacristy* is a noble apartment, and was probably used also as the chapterhouse for the canons of the Basilica. The coved roof is richly covered with mosaics. The best are St. George and St. Theodore, by *Zuccato* after *Tintoretto*. The presses and seats are ornamented with *intarsia* work. Those by *Fra' Sebastiano*, *Schiavone*, and *Ferrando da Bergamo* are considered as amongst the best of this species of art.

In the S. transept a door opens into the *Treasury of St. Mark*, situated between the transept and the Baptistery, and which is carefully kept under lock and key, and can only be seen on Monday and Friday, from 12·30 until 2 o'clock, except by special permission. It is divided into two departments, one containing sacred reliquiaries, the other objects of art. This treasury became at various times very opulent, and formed a sort of reserve fund on which the state drew in great emergencies. In 1797 most of the available articles were turned into money, and the valuable objects of art which remain were deposited at the Zecca or Mint: they have been of late years arranged here, and offer the richest collection in existence of ancient Byzantine jewellery. The collection of relics is extensive, and some of the objects are rare, as a bit of the dress of our Saviour, a small quantity of earth imbibed with his blood, a fragment of the pillar to which he was bound: there is a portion of the genuine cross, of course. The reliquiary in which the latter is enclosed is a fine specimen of workmanship, presented in 1120 to Santa Sophia at Constantinople by the Empress Irene, wife of Alexis Comnenus. The episcopal seat in marble in the treasury was at one time supposed to have been given in the 7th centy. to the Patriarch of Grado by Heraclius Emperor of the East, but there is little doubt that it is of a later period, probably of the 11th. The Champleve enamels are amongst the very interesting objects in the Treasury.

In front of St. Mark are the 3 bronze pedestals, in which are inserted the masts from which once proudly floated the three *gonfalons* of silk and gold, emblematical of the three dominions of the republic—Venice, Cyprus, and the Morea. These *gonfalons*, after having given way to the *tricolor*, are now replaced by the Austrian standards. Of the beautiful bronze pedestals, in which the masts are inserted, with reliefs of sea-nymphs and Tritons elaborately finished, one was placed there by Paolo Barbo, a Procurator of St. Mark, in 1501; the others by Doge Loredano, 1505: all the work of *Alessandro Leopardi*.

To the rt. on coming out of St. Mark is the *Torre dell' Orologio*, so called from the dial in the centre, resplendent with gold and azure, the sun travelling round the zodiacal signs which decorate it, and marking the time of twice twelve hours. Above are two figures of bronze, called by the people Moors, who strike the hours upon the bell. In a writer of the last century there is a story of one of these bronze men having committed murder, by knocking an unfortunate workman, who stood within the swing of his hammer, off the parapet. The Virgin of gilt bronze, and, above, a gigantic lion of St. Mark, upon an azure and stellated ground, decorate the two upper stories. *Pietro Lombardo* was the architect of the tower, 1494. The clock, as appears by an inscription beneath, was made by *Giovan' Paolo Rinaldi* of Reggio, and *Gian Carlo*, his son. Having been injured by lightning in 1750, it was restored by Ferracina of Bassano, in 1755. The wings on each side of the tower, which are of the architecture of the school of Pietro Lombardo, were added at the beginning of the 16th century.

Beneath the clock-tower is the entrance to the *Merceria*, the part of Venice which exhibits most commercial activity. Here are the principal shops; and the best retail trade carried on in the city is nearly all concentrated in this quarter. The streets about the *Merceria*, and through which you may thread your way to the other main land of the Rialto, are very intricate, narrow, and much crowded.* Beyond the tower, the *Procuratie Vecchie*, standing upon 50 arches, forms nearly the entire N. side of the piazza of St. Mark. This fabric was raised by *Bartolommeo Buono da Bergamo*, in 1517, and was intended for the habitation of the procurators of St. Mark, who were amongst the most important dignitaries of the republic. They were originally the churchwardens or trustees of San Marco, having

* It may assist the pedestrian visitor to know that in the pavement of these streets he will see a white line of marble let in, by following which he will always reach the Ponte di Rialto. It extends to the most northern extremity of the city.

the care of the fabric, and the management of its property; Bartolommeo Tiepolo, elected in 1049, being the first upon record. With the increase of the riches of San Marco, their numbers were augmented, till at length they increased to about 34, and the enlargement of the board, or tribunal, was accompanied by a great extension of their powers. Amongst other duties, they constituted a court of orphans, being their official guardians and trustees. The procuratori were in such high repute for their integrity and good management, that it was a common practice for parents in other states of Italy to appoint them executors of their wills. And, generally speaking, the doge was elected from this body. The office was held for life, and, as the republic declined, a certain number of the places were sold as a means of filling the coffers of the state. This practice began during the disastrous war of Candia. They had two prices: the old nobility paid 30,000 ducats (6000*l*.) for their gown, the new 100,000 (20,000*l*.). For the accommodation of the increasing numbers the *Procuratie Nuove* were erected. This building is in the lower stories a continuation of the *Biblioteca : Scamozzi,* to whom it was intrusted, adopting for the most part the design of *Sansovino,* added a third story. " For this upper order of the Procuratie Nuove Scamozzi has often been unjustly reproached, because he did not confine himself to two stories, so as to complete the design of Sansovino. The design of Scamozzi, had it been continued in the Piazza San Marco, would have placed in the background every other square in Europe. The two lower stories of the Procuratie Nuove are similar in design to the Libreria : and it is greatly to be regretted that Scamozzi was so much otherwise occupied, that he had not the opportunity of watching the whole of its execution, which would have extended to 30 arcades, whose whole length would have been 426 ft. Scamozzi only superintended the first 13 ; the 3 built by Sansovino excepted, the rest were trusted to the care of builders rather than artists, and, from the little attention bestowed upon preserving the profiles, exhibit a negligence which indicates a decline in the arts at Venice." —*Gwilt.* The sculptures here are elegant, particularly the foliaged frieze of the Ionic story, interspersed with sea-gods and nymphs.

These Procuratie Nuove were converted into a palace by the Viceroy Eugene Beauharnois, and now constitute the *Palazzo Imperiale,* which is continued along the western side of the Piazza by a façade also built by the French. To make way for this addition to the palace the church of *San Geminiano,* one of the finest works of *Sansovino,* and his burial-place, was demolished. The history of the church of San Geminiano is curious. It was founded by Narses upon ground by the side of the great campanile of S. Marco, and now forming part of the piazza, which was enlarged to its present extent by the demolition of the ancient fabric. This demolition took place when Vital' Michiel was Doge; and the consent of the pope was solicited, but not obtained. " The apostolic see may pardon a wrong after it is committed, but never can sanction it beforehand," was the reply. Acting upon this guarded reply, they demolished the church, and rebuilt it upon the site which it afterwards occupied. But yearly the Doge came forth with his train to meet the parish priest, who, standing upon the desecrated spot, demanded of his Serenity that he would be pleased to rebuild the church upon its old foundations. " Next year," was the reply of the Doge; and thus was the promise renewed and broken until the republic was no more. The second church of San Geminiano, falling into decay, was replaced, about the year 1505, by the structure which disappeared in the present century.

The Imperial Palace contains some good paintings, dispersed through its several apartments: amongst others, in the octagon saloon, *Tintoretto,* the Adoration of the Magi, and Joachim driven from the Temple. In the chapel, Albert Durer, an Ecce Homo.—*Bassano*, the Presentation in the Temple. Several very clever pieces, and some showy modern frescoes, by *Hayez* and other modern artists.

The W. side of the Piazzetta is occupied by the *Libreria Vecchia*, now part of the Palazzo Imperiale, and united to the buildings of the Piazza. The donations of the MSS. of Petrarch and of Cardinal Bessarion induced the Senate to build the library in 1536; a task which they intrusted to *Sansovino*, who, in 1529, had been appointed architect to the republic. Petrarch appears to have contemplated his visits to the Lagunes with no ordinary satisfaction; and, in order more substantially to testify his grateful sense of the frequent hospitality of the republic, he offered his library as a legacy. In 1362, while the plague was raging at Padua, he had fixed his abode at Venice, which was free from it: his books accompanied him, and, for their conveyance, he was obliged to retain a numerous and extensive stud of baggage-horses. On the 4th of September in that year he wrote to the Senate,—" I wish, with the good-will of our Saviour, and of the Evangelist himself, to make St. Mark heir of my library." His chief stipulations were, that the books should neither be sold nor dispersed, and that a building should be provided in which they might be secure against fire and the weather. The Great Council gladly accepted this liberal donation, and addressed its thanks in terms of courtesy (perhaps not exaggerated, if we remember the times in which they were written), " to a scholar unrivalled in poetry, in moral philosophy, and in theology." A palace which belonged to the Molina family, and which in later years had been converted into a monastery for the nuns of St. Sepulchre, was assigned as a residence for the poet, and as a depository for his books. This collection, which formed the nucleus of the now inestimable library of St. Mark, though by no means extensive, still contained many treasures of no ordinary value. Among them are enumerated a MS. of Homer, given to Petrarch by Nicolaus Sigeros, ambassador from the Greek Emperor; a beautiful copy of Sophocles; the entire Iliad, and great part of the Odyssey, translated by Leontio Pilato, and copied in the writing of Boccaccio, whom the translator had instructed in Greek; an imperfect Quintilian; and most of the works of Cicero, transcribed by Petrarch himself, who professed most unbounded admiration for the great Roman orator. The Venetians, to their shame, grievously neglected the stipulations that accompanied the poet's gift. When Tomasini requested permission to inspect the books, in the early part of the 17th century, he was led to the roof of St. Mark's, where he found them, " partly reduced to dust, partly petrified "—dictu mirum! in saxa mutatos; and he adds a catalogue of such as were afterwards rescued from destruction; the whole of Petrarch's MSS. have been destroyed. About a century after the establishment of this first public library in Venice it was largely increased by the munificence of Cardinal Bessarion, who, as patriarch of Constantinople, possessed frequent opportunities of securing MSS. of great rarity, and who may be considered the founder of the present library; and afterwards by the collections of Cardinal Grimani and of Professor Melchior Wieland, a native of Marienburg, who, out of gratitude for benefits conferred by the republic, bequeathed his library to it. It now contains about 120,000 vols. and 10,000 MSS., which in 1812 were transferred from the *Libreria Vecchia* to the splendid saloon in the Ducal Palace, no longer required for the assemblies of the Grand Council, and to some rooms adjoining.

" The library of St. Mark is a building of noble design, notwithstanding the improprieties with which it is replete. It consists of two orders,—the lower one of highly ornamented Doric, and the upper one Ionic, and very graceful in effect. Of both these orders the entablatures are of inordinate comparative height. The upper one was expressly so set out for the purpose of exhibiting the beautiful sculptures with which it is decorated. The cornice is crowned with a balustrade, on whose piers statues were placed by the ablest scholars of Sansovino. A portico occupies the ground-floor, which is raised three steps from the level of the piazza. This portico consists of 21 arcades, whose piers are decorated with columns. In the interior are arches corresponding to the exterior ones, 16 whereof, with their internal apartments, are appropriated for shops. Opposite the centre arch is a magnificent staircase leading to the hall, beyond which is the library of St. Mark. The faults of this building, which are very many, are lost in its grace and elegance; and it is, perhaps, the *chef-d'œuvre* of the master."—*Gwilt*. The interior decorations are in keeping with the exterior. The ceiling of the great hall in which the books were deposited is filled with very fine ornaments in stucco, and with paintings by the best Venetian artists. Three compartments, honour, mathematics, and music, are by *Paolo Veronese*. Other subjects are —*Tintoretto*, St. Mark delivering a Saracen, and the furtive exportation of the relics of St. Mark from Alexandria; and the grand staircase; the latter has fine ornaments in stucco by *Vittoria*.

The *Zecca*, or Mint, adjoins the Libreria, on the Molo. Built by *Sansorino* in 1536, it is a noble specimen of Italian rustic-work, above which are two orders, Doric and Ionic. From this establishment the *Zecchino*, or Sequin, the ancient gold coin of the republic, derived its name; in the *Stamperia* of the Zecca is a Madonna in fresco by *Titian*, and in the room of the director 6 portraits by *Tintoretto*. The *Cortile* of the Zecca is by *Scamozzi*. Here is a singular figure of an Apollo, by *Cattaneo*, holding a golden ingot.

At the southern extremity of the Piazzetta are the *two granite columns*, the one surmounted by the lion of St. Mark, the other by St. Theodore, executed by *Pietro Guilombardo* (1329). These columns so completely formed a part of the *idea* of Venice, that they were repeated in most of the cities subject to its dominion. St. Theodore stands upon a crocodile: his head is covered by a nimbus. In his l. hand he wields a sword; a shield is on his rt. arm. This is considered, says Francesco Sansovino, as symbolical of the temper of our republic; and that she exerts her strong hand for her own defence, and not to attack others. St. Theodore Tyro was, as his surname imports, a young Syrian soldier, who suffered martyrdom under Maximin, and was much honoured by the Eastern Church. Narses, after expelling the Ostrogoths, visited (A.D. 553) the rising republic of the Venetians—for Venice, properly so called, did not then exist— and built a church or chapel in honour of St. Theodore, now included in that of St. Mark; and St. Theodore continued the patron of the republic until, as already mentioned, St. Mark supplanted him in the popular veneration.

The lion suffered during the republican rule of the French. From the book which he holds the words of the Gospel were effaced, and "*Droits de l'Homme et du Citoyen*" substituted in their stead. Upon this change a gondolier remarked that St. Mark, like all the rest of the world, had been compelled to turn over a new leaf. The lion was afterwards removed to the *Invalides* at Paris, but was restored at the peace of 1815.

The capitals of the columns bespeak their Byzantine origin. Three were brought from the Holy Land in 1127. One sank into the mud as they were landing it; the other two were safely lodged on the shore; but, as the story goes, there they lay, no one could raise them. Doge Sebastiano Ziani (1172-1180) having offered as a reward that he who should succeed should not lack any "*grazia onesta*," a certain Lombard, nicknamed Nicolò il Barattiere, or Nick the Blackleg, offered his services; and he placed the columns on their pedestals. Nicolò claimed as his reward that games of chance, prohibited elsewhere by the law, might be played with impunity between the columns. The concession, once made, could not be revoked; but the Council enacted that all public executions, which had hitherto taken place at *San Giovanni Bragola*, should be inflicted in the privileged gambling spot, by which means the space "between the columns" became so ill-omened, that even crossing it was thought to be a precursor of misfortune.

At the opposite end of the Piazzetta, near the Basilica of San Marco, are some other curious relics of ancient times.

The *Pietra del Bando*, at the corner of the church, a stumpy column of red porphyry, from which the laws of the Republic were promulgated; it is said to have been brought from Acre.

The *square pillars of St. John of Acre*, originally forming part of a gateway in the Ch. of Santa Saba at Ptolemais: after a contest between the Venetians and the Genoese for that ch., in 1256, and in which the former were successful, they brought away these piers as a trophy of their triumph. They are covered with fretwork and inscriptions, apparently formed of monograms, which have never been explained, and which are supposed to date from the 7th centy. The Latin cross sculptured on the base is of a much more recent date.

Near the angle of the Piazza and Piazzetta stands the great *Campanile* or Bell-tower of St. Mark: begun in 902, under the government of Domenico Tiepolo, it was not carried up to the belfry until the time of Domenico Morosini (1148-1155), whose epitaph is so ambiguously worded as to claim the honour of the entire edifice. The ascent is by a continuous inclined plane *a cordoni*, which winds round an inner hollow tower. The belfry, an open loggia of four arches in each face, was built in 1510, by *Maestro Buono*; the whole being surmounted by a lofty pyramid. The prospect hence is magnificent. A watchman is stationed in the belfry, who at stated times strikes the great bell. The height of the Campanile is 323 ft., and 42 ft. wide at the base. The Angel surmounting the tower, and serving as a weathercock, is said to be 30 ft. high. At the foot is the much criticised loggia of *Sansovino*, built about 1540, ornamented with four bronze statues of Pallas, Apollo, Mercury, and Peace—cast by him. The order is a fanciful Composite. The columns are of rich marbles. The elevation contains several bas-reliefs in marble, of which the three principal are in the attic, and represent in the centre Venice as Justice, with two rivers flowing at her feet: on the rt. of the spectator, Venus—the symbol of the Island of Cyprus; on the l., Jupiter—the symbol of Crete. The two bas-reliefs also beneath the bronze statues, on the side towards the flagstaffs, are much admired; the subjects are, the Fall of Helle from the Ram of Phryxus, and Tethys assisting Leander. In the interior, which was used as the station for the Procurators in command of the guard during the sitting of the Great Council, is a Madonna by *Sansovino*.

Palazzo Ducale. (Open from 9 to 4 daily, Sundays included.) On the eastern side of the Piazzetta stands the Doge's Palace, or Palazzo Ducale. The southern front extends along the *Molo* as far as the canal which separates the latter from the *Riva degli Schiavoni*. The first palace which was built on this spot was in 820. This having been destroyed in a sedition was replaced by another, built about 970, by the Doge Pietro Orseolo. This last was, 150 years afterwards, destroyed by a great fire, which consumed a third of Venice. A second fire having destroyed the palace, its reconstruction began under the Doge Marin Falier (1354-5); the architect, or at least the designer, being *Filippo Calendario*, the same, according to modern historians, who appears as a chief conspirator in Lord Byron's tragedy. That a person so named did take an active share in the plot, and that he was hanged with a gag in his mouth upon the red pillars of the balcony of the palace from which the duke was wont to view the shows in the *Piazzetta*, is unquestionable; but the contemporary chronicle describes him as a seaman; and it would seem that the real Filippo, at least the real artist, died in the preceding year whilst employed upon his works. Very little of Calendario's edifice now remains except the two large halls of the Maggior Consiglio and Scrutinio, the rest of the palace dating from the reconstruction commenced in 1420 under Doge Tomasso Mocenigo. In this reconstruction the family of Bon or Buono, native architects, or, as they are termed in a contemporary document, stonecutters (*Tajapieri*), bore the principal part: the most eminent of whom was one of the sons, Bartolommeo, who has left his name inscribed on the most beautiful portion of the façade, the *Porta della Carta* or principal entrance to the Palace on the side of the Piazzetta. To the period of the Bons belong the whole of the beautiful colonnades towards the Molo and Piazzetta, the Porta della Carta, and the passage leading from it to the Great Inner Court, which appears to have been completed about the year 1471. A great deal, particularly the sides of the Court, is of a later date—the interior of the building having been exceedingly damaged, or rather reduced to a shell, by two successive fires, in 1574 and 1577.

All the principal apartments were destroyed by these conflagrations. The paintings of Giovanni Bellini, Carpaccio, Pordenone, and Titian, representing the triumphs of the republic and the heroes of her annals, together with the vast halls whose walls they covered, perished in the flames. The walls were calcined and riven. One corner of the building had fallen, several columns and arches were shattered; and Palladio, who was consulted with other architects, maintained it would be dangerous, if not impracticable, to attempt the re-insertion of the floors, and proposed to rebuild the whole palace in a more uniform and elegant style. But after much consideration in the Senate, it was determined not to innovate, but to retain the fabric as much as possible in its ancient form. In the repairs and alterations, however, of the interior cortile, the later Italian style of the Renaissance is a good deal introduced.

The plan of the building is an irregular square: the 2 sides fronting the Piazzetta, and the *Molo* on a line with the *Riva degli Schiavoni*, are supported upon double ranges of arches. The columns of the lowest tier of arches are partly imbedded in the pavement, the level of which was raised (1732) about a foot, in consequence of the inundations to which the Piazzetta and Molo were subject, which gives them an undeserved appearance of clumsiness. They stand, however, not upon bases, but upon a continued stylobate, as discovered some years ago when the piazzetta was repaved.

It appears, from observations made with care, that the mean level of sea at Venice has risen about 3 in. in every century: so that, as these columns have been erected five centuries, about 15 in. of the lower part of them are now concealed, owing to the repeated and necessary elevation of the pavement.

Before the fire both the upper and lower loggie were only separated from the main cortile, as well as from the Piazza and Piazzetta, by ranges of open arches, but now these are closed. The whole of the loggia towards the Molo, and the first six of the columns on the side of the Piazzetta, being of larger diameter than the others in consequence of having to support a greater weight of the pre-existing edifice, are by the Bon family, Giovanni the father and his sons Pantaleone and Bartolommeo. The capitals, executed principally from the designs of the latter, are extremely curious for their varied designs, as they are elaborate from their execution. They contain figures and groups emblematical of good government and the due administra-

Q 3

tion of the law; such as the legendary story, so popular in the middle ages, of the Justice of Trajan, the Seven Sages, and a long train of analogous allegory. The 9th and 10th of the upper tier in the Piazzetta, reckoning from the angle at the door of entrance, called the *Porta della Carta*, are of red marble; from between these two columns, sentences on criminals were proclaimed. Dr. Moore, writing from Venice about 20 years previous to the fall of the republic, says, "The lower gallery, or piazza, under the palace, is called the Broglio. In this the noble Venetians walk and converse; it is only here, and at council, when they have opportunities of meeting together, for they seldom visit openly, or in a family way, at each other's houses, and secret meetings would give umbrage to the state inquisitors; they choose therefore to transact their business on this public walk. People of inferior rank seldom remain on the Broglio for any length of time when the nobility are there."

The front over the colonnades and the large window towards the Molo are rich in figures and bas-reliefs, executed probably towards the close of the 15th centy. by *Antonio Rizzo;* and the other large window, towards the Piazzetta (1523-1538), is as remarkable of its kind, having been executed by *Tullio Lombardo* and *Guglielmo Bergamasco:* all are wrought with the greatest care. The principal entrance to the Palazzo is from the Piazzetta through the *Porta della Carta,* which possesses great symmetry and delicacy. The inscription "Opus Bartholomæi" over the arch (1439-1443) declares the name of the architect. The 4 statues of Force, Prudence, Hope, and Charity, and the seated figure of Justice above, are good specimens of the sculpture of the 15th centy., and by members of the Bon family the statue of Doge Foscari, during whose reign this beautiful gate was erected, kneeling before the Lion of St. Mark, was brutally broken to pieces by the democratic rabble in 1797, the head of Foscari, now in the museum, being alone preserved.

Opposite to, and seen through, the *Porta della Carta* and the fine portal beyond it, which opens into the Grand Court of the Palace, is the *Scala dei Giganti,* the Giants' Staircase, erected towards 1483 by *A. Rizzo.* It derives its name from two colossal statues of Mars and Neptune by *Sansovino,* which stand on either side at the head of the staircase. The portals and arches are inlaid and incrusted with the finest marbles, most delicately worked, by *Bernardo* and *Domenico di Mantova;* and the steps themselves are inlaid in front with a species of metal *intarsiatura.* The statues of Adam and Eve, opposite the Scala dei Giganti, are by *Rizzo,* and are considered as having surpassed all previous productions of the Veneto-Lombard School. It was on the platform at the head of these stairs that the Doges were crowned—it was here also that Lord Byron, by a strange anachronism, has placed the closing scene of Marin Falier, for which there was no documentary authority.

Round the colonnade on the 1st floor have been placed busts of Venetian celebrities — Enrico Dandolo, Morosini, Bembo, Arduino, Lazzaro Moro, Marco Polo, Tintoretto, Fra Paolo Sarpi, Paruta; of Doges Zeno, Vittorio Pisani, Foscari, and Rinieri, the last but one of Venice's lords; of Galileo, Sebastian Cabot, &c.; some placed here by their descendants, but the greater number by a society of patriotic Venetian gentlemen.

In the courtyard are two finely sculptured bronze openings of cisterns or *Puteali,* one executed by *Nicolò de Conti* in 1556, the other by *Alfonso Alborghetti* in 1559. On the l. hand, when ascending the Giants' Staircase, is a beautiful façade of 2 stories, by *Guglielmo Bergamasco,* forming one side of the *Corte de' Senatori.* Opposite the top of the staircase, and close to it, against the wall of the loggia may be observed an inscription let into the wall, commemorating the visit of Henry III. of France to Venice in 1574. Passing along the corridor loggia, which surrounds three sides of the court, and in which have been lately placed busts and statues of celebrated Venetians, you find on the l. the great staircase, the *Scala d' Oro*. Sansovino had a considerable share in its construction. The ornaments in stucco are by *Alessandro Vittoria*, and the paintings by *Franco*; the whole was completed about the year 1577. There was much difficulty in adapting this staircase to the plan of the building. The adaptation of the fretwork to the cove of the ascending roof is particularly skilful: beyond this staircase are the *Stanze degli Avvogadori*, in one of which is a Pietà by *Giovanni Bellini;* it was here in former times that the celebrated Libbro d' Oro, or Roll of the Venetian Aristocracy, was preserved. Farther on is a second flight of stairs, which leads to the library, after ascending which a large door on the l. hand gives admission to the suite of rooms which occupy the façades of the Palace on the side of the Molo and Piazzetta. The first room entered is an antechamber, now filled with books, and having over the door the portrait of Card. Bessarion, and above the opposite one leading to the great hall a portrait of Paolo Sarpi, by *Leandro Bassano*. From this opens the reading-room of the library, and beyond, the door leading to the librarian's apartments, where are preserved the MS. treasures (upwards of 10,000) of this celebrated collection, amongst which may be mentioned the magnificent Grimani breviary with more than 100 splendid miniatures by Hemling, Vander Mere, &c., of the 16th centy.; it was purchased by Doge Grimani for 500 zequins, and is one of the finest works of art of the kind in the world; the MS. of the Divina Commedia of the 14th centy., with contemporary miniatures; the Herbarium of Rimo (1415); the Will of Marco Polo (1373); and many fine Greek MSS. bequeathed by Cardinal Bessarion; and amongst the books, the first printed at Venice, *Cicero ad Familiares*, 1469, and the Ed. Prin. of Homer (1488), printed on vellum. In this room may be seen two fine antique cameos of Jupiter Egyptiacus, illustrated by E. Q. Visconti. Re-entering the ante-room the door opposite leads into the

Sala del Maggior Consiglio. This truly magnificent Hall, 175¼ ft. long, 84¼ broad, and 51¼ ft. high, was begun in 1310, and completed in 1334. It was afterwards painted by *Titian, Bellini, Tintoretto,* and *Paul Veronese.* The fire of 1577 destroyed it, and the adjoining one, *dello Scrutinio,* and all the works of art they contained. It is now the *Bibliotheca di San Marco,* or *Marciana,* the library of the Republic having been transferred here from the old Library in the Piazzetta in 1812. It is open from 9 to 4 o'clock, daily, including Sundays, but not on certain Feast-days. The decorations of this hall of the Great Council remain unaltered, and the splendid paintings which adorn the walls are proud memorials of the opulence and power of the republic. In the history of art they are remarkable for a circumstance which had considerable influence on it. They are amongst the earliest large specimens of oil painting upon canvas. On the rt. as you enter, that is, upon the wall at the E. end of the hall, is

Tintoretto—Paradise. Damaged and blackened by time and picture-cleaners, yet still powerful and impressive; said to be the largest picture ever painted upon canvas, being 84½ ft. in width, and 34 ft. in height.

Proceeding round the hall, beginning with the picture next to this on the rt., at the E. end of the N. wall, the paintings occur in the following order.

1. *Carlo* and *Gabriele Cagliari,* sons of Paolo Veronese. Pope Alexander III. discovered by the Doge Ziani and the senate in the convent of La Carità, where he had concealed himself when flying from Frederic II. in 1177. According to one historian he was disguised as a scullion, according to another as a poor priest; in the painting his dress rather resembles the latter. Baronius takes great pains to refute this story, and he is particularly angry with this painting. It is full of action. The

group in the gondola in the foreground is good.

2. *By the same.* The Embassy despatched with powers from the Pope and the Republic to the Emperor; a small composition cut in two by columns, one in the light and the other in the shade: the groups are animated.

3. (Above the window.) *Leandro Bassano.* The Pope presenting the lighted taper to the Doge. By this act the Doge and his successors acquired the privilege of having such a taper borne before them.

4. *Tintoretto.* The ambassadors meet Frederic II. at Pavia, praying him to restore peace to Italy and the Church, when he made the proud answer, "that unless they delivered up the pope he would plant his eagles on the portal of St. Mark." The principal figures, the two ambassadors, have great grandeur.

5. *Francesco Bassano.* The Pope delivering the consecrated sword to the Doge previous to his embarkation. The scene is in the Piazza of San Marco, of which it is a representation as the buildings stood at the end of the 16th century.

6. (Above the window.) *Fiammingo.* The Doge departs from Venice receiving the Pope's blessing.

7. *Domenico Tintoretto.* The great naval battle which took place at Salvore off Pirano and Parenzo in Istria, when the Imperial fleet was entirely defeated, and Otho, the son of the Emperor, taken prisoner, an event which induced Frederic to treat for peace. This is a mere piece of national boasting, inasmuch as it appears, from the absolute silence of all contemporary writers, that no such battle was ever fought. The details of armour, costume, and equipments are curious.

8. (Over the door leading to the *Sala dello Scrutinio.*) *Il Vicentino.* Otho presented to the Pope.

9. *Jacopo Pulma.* The Pope releases Otho, and allows him to repair to his father.

10. *F. Zucchero.* The Emperor submitting to the Pope. This painting is amongst the finest in the series.

Amongst other beautiful portions is the group of the lady and her little boy.

11. (Over the door.) *Girolamo Gamberato.* The Doge, who had co-operated so strenuously in the Pope's cause, having embarked with him and the Emperor, they land in Ancona on their way to Rome. On this occasion, according to the Venetian chronicles, the Anconitans came out with two umbrellas or canopies, one for the Pope and the other for the Emperor, upon which the Pontiff desired that a third should be brought for the Doge, who had procured him the consolation of peace.

On the W. side of the hall, beginning with the picture next to that last mentioned, are—

1. *Giulio del Moro.* Consecrated banners bestowed upon the Doge by the Pope in the church of St. John Lateran: a composition in which the story is remarkably ill told. In the foreground are some strange grotesque figures, in particular a dwarf (without doubt, a portrait) leading a dog.

2. (Between the 2 windows.) *Paolo Veronese,* a fine work. The return of the Doge Contarini after the naval victory gained by the Venetians over the Genoese at Chioggia (1378).

3. *L'Aliense.* Baldwin of Flanders receives the Imperial crown from the hands of the Doge Dandolo at Constantinople. This is historically untrue, inasmuch as he was crowned by a legate.

On the S. side of the hall are—

1. (Next to the last picture.) *Il Vicentino.* Baldwin elected Emperor of the East by the Crusaders in the church of Sta. Sophia.

2. *Domenico Tintoretto.* The second conquest of Constantinople by the Crusaders and the Venetians (1204), which was followed by the pillage and conflagration of the city.

3. *Palma Giovane.* The first siege and conquest of Constantinople by the Crusaders (1203), the assault being led on by the Doge Dandolo, blind, and nearly 90 years of age.

4. *Il Vicentino.* Alexis Comnenus, the son of the dethroned Emperor of

Constantinople, Isaac, implores the aid of the Venetians on behalf of his father.

5. (Over the window.) *Domenico Tintoretto*. The surrender of Zara.

6. *Vicentino*. Assault of Zara (1202) by the Venetians, commanded by the Doge Dandolo and the Crusaders.

7. *Le Clerc*. The alliance between the Venetians and the Crusaders, concluded in the church of St. Mark, 1201. The ambassadors on the part of the Crusaders were Baldwin Count of Flanders, Louis Count of Blois, Geoffrey Count of Perche, Henry Count of St. Paul, Simon de Montfort, the two Counts of Brienne, and Matthew de Montmorency.

The ceiling is exceedingly rich in painting and gilding. Three larger paintings are placed in a line down the centre. That nearest to the great picture of Paradise is by *Paul Veronese*, and represents Venice amid the clouds and crowned by Glory. The centre painting, which is oblong, is by *Jacopo Tintoretto*, and consists of two parts: above, Venice is seen among the Deities; below, the Doge da Ponte with the senators receiving deputations from the cities who tender allegiance to the republic. The third picture is by *Palma Giovane*: the subject Venice seated, crowned by Victory, and surrounded by the Virtues. Some of the smaller paintings are worthy of notice. Two octagonal pictures, on either side of the first mentioned oval, are by *P. Veronese*. As you stand with your back to the picture of Paradise, the octagon on the rt. represents the taking of Smyrna; that on the l. the defence of Scutari. The two beyond these are the Venetian Cavalry routing the army of the Viscontis, by *Tintoretto*: that on the l., the Victory of the Venetians over the Duke of Ferrara, by *Bassano*. There are three octagonal pictures on each side of the last oval by *Palma*. The two middle ones are by *F. Bassano*: that on the rt. represents the victory gained by Vittore Barbaro over the Viscontis; that on the l., the victory by George Cornaro over the Germans at Cadore in 1507. Further on, on the l., Soranzo, in 1484, defeating the Ferrarese; on the rt., the Defence of Brescia by the Venetians; and on the l., the Capture of Gallipoli, in 1484; all three by *Tintoretto*. The two last compartments are painted by *Palma Giovane*, and represent, on rt., the Capture of Cremona, by F. Bembo, in 1427, and, on l., of Padua, by Andrea Gritti, in 1509.

Round the Hall is the celebrated frieze of portraits of the 72 Doges, commencing from A.D. 809, with the black veil covering the space which should have been occupied by the portrait of Marin Falier, with the well-known inscription. These portraits are, many of them, by *Tintoretto*, who must of course have painted the earlier ones from fancy.

A corridor connects this hall with the *Sala dello Scrutinio*, which occupies the rest of the façade towards the Piazzetta. In this fine hall, formerly used to elect the 41 nobles, who afterwards nominated the Doge, are now preserved the MSS. collections, the early printed books, and the Aldine editions of the library. The large painting opposite the entrance represents a triumphal arch erected in 1694 to Francesco Morosini, surnamed Il Peloponessiaco, from his having conquered the Morea. His ephemeral conquest is now principally recollected as connected with the destruction of the Parthenon. The three other sides are adorned with historical pictures: beginning on the rt. hand,—

E. wall: 1. The Taking of Zara in 1346, by *Tintoretto*; 2. The Capture of Cattaro in 1378, by *Vicentino*; 3. The Battle of Lepanto in 1571, by the same. Over the window: 4. The Demolition of Margaritino, in 1571, by *Bellotti*; 5. The Victory gained by Mocenigo at the Dardanelles, by *Liberi*. On the W. wall, or that towards the Piazzetta: 6. Pepin, son of Charlemagne, besieging the Rialto in 809; and 7, his defeat in the Canal Orfano, both by *Vicentino*; 8. The Egyptian Caliph defeated at Jaffa in 1128, by *Sante Peranda*; 9. The Capture of Tyre in

1125, by *Aliense;* and 10, The Defeat of Roger King of Sicily on the Coast of the Morea in 1141, by *Marco Vecellio*. On the wall opposite the Arch of il Peloponessiaco is Palma Giovane's Last Judgment, one of his finest works. The frieze of Doges is continued and concluded in this apartment. That of the last Doge, Ludovico Manin, under whom the republic perished, has recently been placed here. There are also several fine historical paintings on the ceiling, the best of which is nn oval in the line of the middle of the ceiling, next to Palma's Last Judgment, by *Francesco Bassano*, representing the Capture of Padua from the Carraras in 1405.

Returning to the vestibule from which we entered the Library, a door on the l. opens into the *Archæological Museum*, lately arranged in a series of rooms, which once formed the residence of the Doges.

The first room, a kind of corridor, contains some ancient marbles, a colossal Minerva, much repaired, and a statue of Esculapius, discovered at the baths of Abano. Opening out of this is the hall called the *Camera degli Scarlati*, from its being the robing-room, or where the scarlet robes of the members of the Maggiore Consiglio were kept. The most remarkable object here is the fine chimney-piece, richly ornamented with sculpture, executed for Doge Barberigo, about 1490. Over the door is a bas-relief of Doge Loredan at the feet of the Virgin, and several ancient marbles, with copies of others made in the 15th centy. *Sala dello Scudo*, so called from the shield or coat of arms of the Doge being placed here on his election. The walls are covered with maps of the countries explored by Venetian navigators and travellers: they were originally drawn by the learned geographer Ramusio in the 16th centy., but these having almost disappeared, the present ones only date from 1762. Here has been lately placed the celebrated Mappe-monde of *Frate Mauro*, a species of geographical encyclopædia of all that was known at the period of its construction, 1457. Fra Mauro was a Camaldolese monk of the Convent of St. Michael at Murano, who appears to have composed this curious work for Alphonso V., King of Portugal. It remained at Murano until the suppression of the convent in 1811, when it was removed to the Library of St. Mark; it has recently been published in fac simile by Viscount de Santarem, the eminent historian of early Portuguese geographical discoveries. There are several other maps here: one worthy of being remarked is a Turkish one of the earth, in the form of a heart, by the Tunisian *Hadgi Mahomed* (1559). Alongside is the engraved wood-block from which it was struck: it was found in a galley captured by the Venetians. *Sala dei Bassi-rilievi* contains some Greek marbles, among which a curious inscription of the Archons of Athens, and a sarcophagus with a bas-relief of Niobe and her children. The two latter halls may be considered as the ante-rooms of the Doge's residence. Opening out of the *Sala dello Scudo* are the two rooms which were really occupied by the Chief of the Republic until the end of the 16th centy. In each is a fine Lombard chimney-piece, of the end of the 15th centy. The inclined carved wooden roof in what was the Doge's bed-room is very beautiful. There are two other rooms containing ancient marbles and bronzes, with some fine specimens of Roman architectural decoration, and an extensive numismatic collection, formed out of several private cabinets, purchased or presented by their owners. The series of Venetian medals and coins, arranged separately, is unique. The last room of this suite of apartments (from which there is a good view over the Bridge of Sighs), and which opens on the Scala d'Oro, is the *Camera de' Stucchi*, from its ornaments in relief by A. Vittoria and his school. On the walls are some paintings:—*Tintoretto*, a portrait of Henry III. of France; *Bonifacio*, the Adoration of the Magi; *Pordenone*, a Deposition. Here also is preserved the marble head of F. Foscari, all that remains of the statue of that Doge which stood before the Porta della Carta (see p. 346).

Ascending the Scala d'Oro, a door on the l. opens into the suite of rooms which fill the upper story on the eastern side of the Palace. The first is the *Sala della Bussola*, the ante-room of the Council of Ten. At the entrance is an opening, on which was a lion's head, the celebrated LION'S MOUTH into which were thrown the secret denunciations. The ceiling is painted by *P. Veronese*. The paintings on the walls by *Aliense*, of the Surrender of Brescia and Bergamo to the Venetians in 1426 and 1427. Out of this opens

The *Sala dei Capi del Consiglio dei Dieci*, containing a fine marble chimney-piece, sculptured by *Pietro da Salò* in the 16th centy. The centre compartment of the ceiling has a painting of an Angel driving away the Vices, by *Paul Veronese*.

Sala del Consiglio dei Dieci. Opposite the windows is the Visit of the Wise Men, by *Aliense*. To the rt. the Doge Sebastian Ziani returning from the victory obtained over the Emperor Frederic Barbarossa, met by Pope Alexander III., by *Leandro Bassano*, who has introduced his own portrait in the figure carrying the umbrella behind the Pope. Opposite to this is the Congress held at Bologna in 1529, by Clement VII. and Charles V., when the peace of Italy was restored, by *Marco Vecellio*. The frieze is by *Zelotti*. In the very rich ceiling, an oval, containing a figure of an old man seated near a beautiful young woman, is a fine work of *P. Veronese*. Two paintings, one an oval representing Neptune drawn by sea-horses, and another oblong, Mercury and Peace, are by *Zelotti* and *Bazzacco*.

Sala delle Quattro Porte; so called from the four doors, designed by *Palladio*, remarkable for their symmetry. The ceiling is the joint production of *Palladio, Sansovino*, and *Vittoria;* the two first having given the designs, which were executed by the last. Here, as in the subsequent apartments, only a selection of the paintings can be noticed. Those of the ceiling are in fresco, by *J. Tintoretto*. On the walls, to the rt. as you enter, is the Doge Marino Grimani on his knees before Faith, a great work of *Titian's*. The two figures at the side are by *Marco Vecellio;* and Battle near Verona, by *Contarini:* opposite to this is the Doge Cicogna receiving the Persian ambassadors in 1585, and the arrival of Henry III. of France at the Lido, by *Andrea Vicentino*. The two first-mentioned pictures, by *Contarini* and *Titian*, went to Paris in 1797, and were brought back in 1815.

Sala dei Pregadi or *del Senato*. Between the windows is a picture said to be by *Marco Vecellio*, but by some attributed to *Bonifacio:* the Election of S. Lorenzo Giustiniani to the Patriarchate of Venice in 1451. On the wall above the throne is a great work of *J. Tintoretto:* the dead Saviour, with Saints and two Doges kneeling. The two figures at the side are also by him. Of the pictures on the side opposite to the windows, three—1, The Doge Francesco Venier before Venice; —2, The Doge Pasquale Cicogna kneeling before the Saviour;—3, The League of Cambrai, represented by Venice seated on a Lion, daring the rest of Europe. These three paintings are by *Palma Giovane;* the 4th, The Doge Pietro Loredan praying the Virgin to help Venice, is by *J. Tintoretto*. Above the door, opposite to the throne, is a fine work of *J. Palma*, the Doges Lorenzo and Girolamo Priuli adoring the Saviour. The paintings of the ceiling are by different artists; the best is the oval in the centre, representing Venice as Queen of the Sea, with many Deities, by *Tintoretto*.

A small corridor, on the same side as the throne, leads to the chapel through an antechamber, in which, between the windows, is a beautiful work of *Bonifacio*, Christ driving the Money-changers from the Temple.

The Chapel has little remarkable except the altar, by *Scamozzi*, and a Madonna and Child, sculptured by

Sansovino. This apartment, in fact, was merely a private oratory, the real chapel of the Palace being the Church of St. Mark. A small adjoining staircase contains the only fresco painting remaining in Venice by *Titian.* It is a single figure of St. Christopher: the head is fine. Returning to the *Sala delle Quattro Porte,* we pass into the

Sala del Collegio. This was the audience-chamber, in which the Doge and the *Grandi,* his Privy Council, received foreign ambassadors. The picture over the door, and the three to the rt. on entering, are by *J. Tintoretto.* The subjects are, — 1. Doge Andrea Gritti before the Madonna and Child. — 2. The Marriage of St. Catherine in the presence of Doge Dona. — 3. The Virgin with Saints and Angels, with the Doge da Ponte. — 4. Doge Alviso Mocenigo adoring the Saviour, by *C. Cagliari.* On the wall at the throne end of the chamber is a splendid work of *P. Veronese*—a grand but confused composition of Venice triumphant, or the Victory of Curzolari (1571), in which are introduced portraits of the General, afterwards Doge, Sebastian Venier, and the Proveditore Agostino Barbarigo. The two side figures in chiar'-oscuro are also by *P. Veronese.* The picture between the windows, representing Venice, is by *Carletto Cagliari.* The rich ceiling was designed by *Antonio da Ponte;* all the paintings are by *P. Veronese.* The compartment nearest to the door represents Neptune, Mars, and flying children. In the centre an oval, containing Faith; the next is, Venice seated on the world with Justice and Peace. These compartments are surrounded by 8 smaller, representing 8 Virtues; and by 16 in green chiar'-oscuro, with subjects from ancient history. A fine frieze runs round the room. The chimney-piece, with pilasters of verde-antique and statues, is by *G. Campagna,* the paintings by *P. Veronese.* There are two doors with columns of cipollino. A door in the side of this room opens into the

Anti-Collegio, a guard-room, containing four splendid paintings in *Tintoretto's* best style. They hang by the sides of the two doors. The subjects are, Mercury and the Graces; the Forge of Vulcan; Pallas driving away Mars; Ariadne crowned by Venus. On the wall opposite to the windows are, the Return of Jacob to the Land of Canaan, by *J. Bassano;* the Rape of Europa, by *Paul Veronese,* a very fine painting, which went to Paris. This room contains also a splendid fireplace, and a rich doorway with two pillars, one of verde-antico, the other of cipollino, said to have been brought from Santa Sofia; both were designed by *Scamozzi.* Over the door are 3 statues by *A. Vittoria.* The fresco in the centre of the ceiling is by *P. Veronese,* as well as the four chiar'-oscuro paintings: the latter have been repainted by *Rizzi.* From the Anti-Collegio opens a small room, called the Salotto di Ingresso, the ceiling of which is painted by *Tintoretto,* representing Venice offering the Sword and the Scales of Justice to Doge G. Priuli. From this room the visitor can ascend to

The famous *Sotto Piombi* at the top of the building, as their name denotes "under the leads." They were formerly used as prisons, and were represented to be very disagreeable places of residence; the heat in summer and the cold in winter being intense. Jacopo Casanova was shut up in them in 1775. Silvio Pellico was one of the last persons confined here: but it has been lately discovered by the defenders of the Venetian government that they must have been rather pleasant abodes. A few have been recently converted into dwelling apartments; the others are used for lumber-rooms.

The *Pozzi,* or dark cells in the two lower stories, are still open to the visitor; obscure and intricate passages lead to them, and the lowermost tier are perfectly dark, and correspond with the well-known and accurate description given by Sir J. C. Hobhouse in the notes to the fourth Canto of 'Childe Harold.' They were all lined with wood, but this wainscoting was chiefly destroyed when the cells were thrown open by the French.

The Ducal Palace is separated, on the eastern side, by a canal called the *Rio della Paglia*, or *di Palazzo*, from the public prisons, the *Carceri*, a fine building, which, on the side facing the palace, has a gloomy character suited to its destination. They were built in 1589, by *Antonio da Ponte*. The front towards the *Riva dei Schiavoni* is of a less severe character, owing to the architect placing in this part of the building the apartments intended for the *Signori di Notte*, the heads of the night police, which enabled him to introduce larger openings than in the portion intended for the security of criminals. This prison can now contain about 400 prisoners. It is a very handsome building, with rustic arches below, and above these a range of Doric columns on pedestals, and a large cornice with consoles in the frieze.

The Molo is connected with the *Riva dei Schiavoni* by the *Ponte della Paglia;* standing on which and looking up the Rio di Palazzo, a covered bridge is seen at an unusual height above the water. This is the celebrated *Ponte dei Sospiri*, or Bridge of Sighs. It served as a communication between the Ducal Palace and the prisons by a covered gallery, the interior being divided into a double passage. Prisoners, when taken out of the prisons to die, were conducted across this gallery to hear their sentences, from which they were led to execution: hence its name.

The Arsenal. The fifth bridge on the Riva dei Schiavoni, after crossing the Ponte della Paglia, is a small suspension one. This crosses the canal leading to the Arsenal. Just before you reach this bridge a passage on the l. leads to the gates of the Arsenal. If we consider the size of the vessels when Venice was a naval power, the extent, size, and completeness of the basins, yards, and buildings of the arsenal must convey a high idea of the greatness of the power of the Republic. Of late years there has been some difficulty in obtaining admission to see it from the Austrian authorities. Recently, however, foreigners have been admitted from 9 till 1 o'clock, on presentation of their passports.

The arsenal attained its present dimensions, nearly 2 miles in circuit, between 1307 and 1320. Walls and towers, battlemented and crenelated, surround it. They are attributed to *Andrea Pisano*. The principal gateway, erected in 1460, as appears from an inscription upon the column on the l. side, is an adaptation of a Roman triumphal arch. An attic with a pediment was added in 1581, surmounted by a statue of St. Giustina, by *Girolamo Campagna*, in commemoration of the great battle of Lepanto, fought on the festival of that Saint, 7 Oct. 1571. Near this entrance stand the two colossal marble lions brought by Morosini from Athens in 1687. The most remarkable of them, that which is erect, stood at the entrance of the Piræus, which from this image was commonly called the Porto Leone. It is of very ancient workmanship, and it has been conjectured, upon somewhat dubious grounds, to have been originally a memorial of the battle of Marathon. Engraven on this lion's shoulders and flanks are some Runic inscriptions, which have so much exercised the learning, and baffled the penetration of antiquaries. Professor Rahn of Copenhagen supposes they record the capture of Athens and the suppression of a revolt in the reign of the Emperor Michael (A.D. 1409), and contain the name of Harold the Tall. The head of the second of the lions is a restoration.

The noble armoury was in part dispersed by the French. It has recently been re-arranged, and still contains some very interesting objects, many of which were brought from the armoury at the Ducal Palace.—The great standard of the Turkish Admiral, taken in the battle of Lepanto, of red and yellow silk. Much fine and curious ancient armour, interesting both from its workmanship and the historical personages to whom they belonged. Among those which have more claim to be considered genuine are the shield, helmet, and sword of the Doge Sebastiano Ziani, 1172-1178. Upon the first is represented the Rape of Helen : upon the last, an Arabic cipher. The armour of *Gattamelata*, for man and horse, of fine Milanese workmanship of the 15th centy. The full suit of Henry IV. of France, given by him to the republic in 1603. This was brought from the Palazzo Ducale. The sword was stolen in 1797. *Arbalétes*, or cross-bows, of remarkable power. Helmets and shields of the ancient Venetian soldiery, and of very strange forms. Quivers yet filled with arrows, perhaps used by the Stradiotes and other semibarbarian troops of the republic. A press full of instruments of murder and torture. A species of spring pistol, in the shape of a key, with which it is said that Francesco di Carrara was accustomed to kill the objects of his suspicion, by shooting poisoned needles at them. In front of this press are some iron helmets of rough workmanship, without apertures for the eyes or mouth, so that the wretch enclosed in them could neither see nor breathe. Such being the case, it has been oddly conjectured that they were intended for the protection of the warriors who stood on the prows of the Venetian galleys. Others suppose that they were used as instruments of torture, or of restraint equivalent to torture, a conjecture less improbable. Ancient artillery and fire-arms: a springal of iron, not cast, but composed of fifteen pieces riveted together, and covered with exceedingly elegant arabesques, made by the son of the Doge Pasquale Cicogna, who flourished towards the close of the 16th centy. This also formed part of the ducal armoury. This armoury also contains the monument raised by the Republic in 1795 to the High-Admiral Emo (died 1792). The bas-reliefs from his tomb, representing naval subjects, were brought from the church of the Servites, when it was pulled down. The memorial, a rostral column surmounted by a bust, was made for the place where it now stands, and is interesting as being amongst the earliest works of Canova, executed at Rome in 1795. It is exquisitely finished. There is also here a statue of Vittorio Pisani, of the 14th centy.

The arsenal contains four basins, two large and two small. These are nearly surrounded by dry docks, building slips, and workshops. The roofs are supported by ancient arches, lofty and massive, some circular, some pointed, standing upon huge cylindrical pillars, with angular leafy capitals. The columns are sculptured with numerous shields and inscriptions, some of which are in the ancient Venetian dialect. The rope-walk, the *Corderia della Tana*, dates from 1579, having been erected by Doge N. da Ponte: it is 346 yards long, and is supported by 92 Doric pillars.

The model-room still contains some curious materials for the history of naval architecture. The collection was once exceedingly rich and important, but the revolutionists at the close of the last century destroyed a great portion. They also stripped of its ornaments the celebrated *Bucentoro*, the vessel from which the doge annually, on Ascension Day, espoused the Adriatic, and which, after having successively served as a gunboat and a prison, was burned in 1824. A model of it is preserved here. The ceremony of the espousal, which took place off the Lido entrance to the Laguna, and was intended as a continued assertion of the right of the republic to the dominion of the Adriatic, has been traced back to the time of Doge Pietro Orseolo in 998.

Long before the actual fall of Venice, the arsenal displayed all the decrepitude of the state. When the French entered Venice, they found thirteen men-of-war and seven frigates on the stocks. This enumeration seems respectable; but of these vessels, none of which were completed (nor were there any sufficient stores or materials for completing them), two had been begun in 1752, two in 1743, two in 1732, and the remainder at subsequent periods, so that, if the one most advanced could have been launched, she would have attained the respectable and mature age of 75 years. At present, the business of the arsenal is just kept alive, affording a scanty memorial of the operations which so struck the fancy of Dante as to furnish the subject for one of his most strange and striking similes :—

" Quale nell' arzanà de' Viniziani
Bolle l' inverno la tenace pece
A rimpalmar li legni lor non sani
Che navicar non ponno; e'n quella vece
Chi fa suo legno nuovo, e chi ristoppa
Le coste a quel che più viaggi fece;
Chi ribatte da proda, e chi da poppa;
Altri fa remi, e altri volge sarte;
Chi terzeruolo ed artimon rintoppa :
Tal, non per fuoco, ma per divina arte,
Bollìa laggiuso una pegola spessa."
Inferno, xxi. 7-18.

" As in the arsenal of Venice boils
Tenacious pitch in winter, to repair
The bark disabled by long watery toils;
For since to venture forth they are afraid,
One here a vessel builds, another there
Caulks that which many voyages hath made;
One strikes the prow—one hammers at the poop,—
One mends a main, and one a mizen sail,—
One shapes an oar, another twists a rope;
So, not by fire beneath, but art divine,
Boil'd up thick pitch throughout the gloomy vale." Wright's *Dante*.

Canal Grande. Palaces.—We will suppose the traveller to embark in a gondola at the stairs of the Piazzetta on the Molo, and to proceed up the Canal Grande or *Canalazzo;* and will pass in review the more remarkable palaces, as far as the limited nature of this work will allow. Nearly opposite to the Piazzetta is the island and church of *San Giorgio,* and adjoining this, and enclosed by a sort of mole with a lantern tower at each end, is the original *Porto Franco,* whose limits are now extended to a considerable circuit round Venice. To the westward of this is the long canal and *Island of La Giudecca.*

On entering the Grand Canal, the *Dogana del Mare,* built in 1682, is on the l. hand, on the point of land dividing the Grand Canal from that of the Giudecca: beyond this is the *Ch. of S. Maria della Salute.* On the rt., after passing the gardens of the Royal Palace, and the pavilion, in a Greek style, built by Napoleon, at the entrance of the canal is the *Palazzo Giustiniani,* now the *Albergo dell' Europa,* and beyond it the *Palazzo Trèves,* formerly *Emo,* containing a collection of pictures by modern artists, and two fine colossal statues by *Canova,* of Hector and Ajax. A little further is the *Palazzo Contarini Fasan,* which, although it has only two windows in front, with these beautiful balconies, is an exquisite specimen of the richest Venetian Gothic of the 14th centy. Further on, on the same side, is the *Palazzo Ferro* of the same period, and the *Palazzo Corner,* built by *Sansovino,* in 1532. The façade has three orders—Doric, Ionic, and Composite. It is now occupied by the Civil Governor of the province. Further on, but on the l., incrusted with coloured marbles, and bearing the inscription " Genio Urbis Johannes Darius," is the *Palazzo Dario,* in the style of the *Lombardi,* a fine specimen of the decorated fronts of the 15th cent., and contiguous to it the *P. Manzoni.* Beyond, with a quay in front, is the *Accademia delle belle Arti* and the ch. of *La Carita;* opposite to which is the *Tragetto* or ferry of *San Vitale,* once the busiest ferry on the Grand Canal, over which an iron bridge has been recently erected.

Proceeding—on the rt., *P. Cavalli,* now the residence of the Count de Chambord, with its fine Gothic windows of the 15th centy.; *P. Giustiniani Lolin* of the 17th, by *Longhena.* On the l., *P. Contarini degli Scrigni,* with three orders—Rustic, Ionic, and Corinthian, by *Scamozzi. P. Rezzonico,* Doric, Ionic, and Corinthian, by *Longhena.* Two palaces of the *Giustiniani* family, in the Venetian style of the 15th centy. *P. Foscari,* built towards the end of the 15th centy., and attributed to *Bartolommeo Bon,* the architect of the Doge's palace and of the Porta della Carta. Here, in 1574, Francis I. of France was lodged: it being then considered as the Palace which, in all Venice, was best adapted for the reception of royalty. The tragic history of the Doge Foscari and his son is well known. They were not a powerful family, for the power of a family depended upon its numbers, and they were few; hence, possibly, the extreme harshness and rigour exercised against them received so little mitigation. This beautiful edifice, which was falling into ruin, had been purchased by the Municipality of Venice to place in it a school of arts, but it has been seized upon by the military authorities, and converted into a barrack, and until recently tenanted by an Austrian regiment, from whom its decorations have much suffered. Next to the P. Foscari, but separated from it by the canal or Rio di San Pantaleone, is the

P. Balbi, by *Aless. Vittoria*, in 1582, with three orders—Rustic, Ionic, and Composite. Behind it is seen the Campanile of the church of the Frari. The temporary building for the public authorities, who distributed the prizes at the Regattas on the Grand Canal, was always erected by the side of the Balbi Palace, as it commands a view of both reaches of the great canal. On the rt. hand, after the P. Giustiniani Lolin, are the large *P. Grassi*, now the property of the Viennese banker, Sina, the *P. Morosini*, and the *P. Contarini*, built between 1504 and 1546. The architect is unknown, but seems to be of the school of the *Lombardi*. The elevation has much fancy and elegance. The *P. Corner-Spinelli*, also by *Lombardi*. On the l., *P. Pisani a S. Polo*, built at the beginning of the 15th centy.; arabesque Gothic, but the latest of its kind. In this palace was the celebrated "Family of Darius," by *Paolo Veronese*, purchased for our National Gallery at the price of 13,500l. The group of Icarus and Dædalus, by Canova, by which his rising reputation was established, and which was formerly in the Barberigo Palace, is now here. The Pisani, though belonging to the second class of Venetian nobility, and strangers by origin, were amongst the most illustrious families of the republic. To this family belonged Vittorio Pisani, the great naval commander, who died in 1380, just after his skill and valour had saved the republic from imminent peril. *Palazzo Grimani a San Toma*, a noble building of the 16th centy., probably by *Sanmicheli*, now dismantled. *P. Barberigo della Terrazza*: the façade and entrance are in the Rio di S. Polo; only a wing and terrace are on the Grand Canal. The Barberigo collection of pictures, so celebrated for its many Titians, has been recently sold to the Russian Government.

On the rt. *P. Grimani*, now the post-office, from the designs of Sanmicheli, who unfortunately died before it was completed, in consequence of which some alterations for the worse were made in the design. It consists of three Corinthian orders exquisitely worked. It is one of the finest of the more modern palaces. *Sanmicheli*, who was employed to build it by Girolamo, father of the Doge Marino Grimani, had great difficulties to contend with, in consequence of the irregular form of the site, of which the smallest side fronts the Grand Canal. Being now a public building, it is kept in good repair. The Grimanis were originally Vicentine nobles, but after their aggregation to Venice they rose to high dignities in the state. Two Doges were of this family, Antonio and Marino. Upon the election of the latter, 1595, his duchess, a lady of the Morosini family, was inaugurated with great splendour, according to the custom of Venice, in the case of a married doge. She was conducted from her palace to San Marco, clad in cloth of gold, wearing a golden crown, and, stepping into the Bucentoro, she was thus brought to the piazza, where she landed, amidst the strains of martial music and peals of artillery. In the ducal palace she was enthroned amidst her ladies, and the balls and festivals of rejoicing lasted for weeks afterwards. Pope Clement VIII. presented her with the golden rose, blessed by the pontiff every year. According to the usage of the court of Rome, this rose is given only to sovereign princes, and the gift awakened, if not the suspicion, at least the caution of the senate. It had hitherto escaped notice that, although the doge wore only the beretta, the crown of his consort was closed or arched, which was considered as the peculiar privilege of sovereign princes not owning any superior, and hence denied to the dukes of Milan, or the electors of the empire. The rose was, by the order of the senate, taken from the Dogaressa, and deposited in the treasury of St. Mark: and the coronation of her successors no longer took place. Opposite, and on the l.-hand side of the canal, the *P. Dona*, of the Bisantino-Lombard style of the 12th centy., and the *Palazzo Tiepolo*, of which the architecture is of the 16th centy. The façade is of the Doric, Ionic, and Composite orders, extending to the *Fabriche* of the *Rialto*.

Beyond the P. Grimani on the rt. of the canal is the *Palazzo Farsetti*, now the Congregazione Municipale: on the staircase are two baskets of fruit, almost the earliest works of *Canova*; executed when he was fifteen. Beyond this, P. Loredan, of the same style, now the Hôtel de la Ville; the P. Bembo, a fine building, erected between 1350 and 1380; on the site behind stood the P. Dandolo, built by the Doge Henry Dandolo, of which a small but rich Gothic edifice of the 13th centy. may have formed a part; and last of all, before reaching the Bridge of the Rialto, the *Palazzo Manin*, by *Sansovino*, restored by *Selva*. It has a Doric, Ionic, and Corinthian front. It belonged to the last Doge of Venice.

The land on the rt. hand in passing up the canal forms the island of *San Marco*, that on the l. the island of the *Rialto;* and at this part of the canal, near the Rialto bridge, on the l. hand is the spot on which Venice as a city first existed. Even till the 16th centy., and perhaps later, "*Rivo alto*" was considered as the city in all legal documents, and distinguished as such from the *State* of Venice: and of all the islands upon which the city now stands, it is the largest. After the population was extended into the other quarters, the Rialto continued to be the seat of all the establishments connected with trade and commerce. The *Fabriche*, a series of buildings, covering, perhaps, as much as a fifth of the island, and partly connected by arcades, were employed as warehouses and custom-houses; the exchange being held in the piazza, opposite the church of *San Jacopo* (the first church built in Venice), an irregular and now a neglected quadrangle. The whole place was the resort of the mercantile community; but if you seek to realize the locality of Shylock and Antonio, you must station yourself in the double portico at the end of the piazza opposite to the church, that being the spot where the "*Banco Giro*" was held, and where the merchants transacted the business of most weight and consequence. Sabellico tells us that this "nobilissima piazza" was crowded from morning to night.

In the night of the 10th of January, 1513, a fire broke out which destroyed all the buildings as well as their contents. The senate immediately decreed the reconstruction of the commercial buildings, and they were intrusted to *Antonio Scarpagnino*, whose designs were preferred to those of the celebrated Frate Giocondo. He was an artist of small reputation; and Vasari speaks most contemptuously of his productions. The *Fabbriche* are now principally converted into private houses. Many portions have been demolished; all are neglected and in decay; and the merchants no longer congregate here, but transact their business in their counting-houses.

There were several churches upon

the Rialto. *San Jacopo* is desecrated: *San Giovanni*, by *Scarpignano*, is not ill-planned. The only building on the island now possessing any splendour is the *Palazzo de' Camerlinghi*, only one side of which is upon the Grand Canal: to examine its architecture it will be necessary to land.

At the foot of this Palazzo is the *Ponte di Rialto*. This very celebrated edifice was begun in 1588, in the reign of the Doge Pasquale Cicogna, *Antonio da Ponte* being the architect. His design was preferred to those by Palladio and Scamozzi. Cicognara says he is not sufficiently estimated; but this edifice is more remarkable for its solidity and originality than for its beauty. There was an older bridge of wood, which was replaced by the present structure. Sabellico informs us it was so constantly thronged by passengers that there was hardly any hour of the day when you could get along without much difficulty. It was intended that the bridge should have been much more adorned than it is at present. The ornaments which it now exhibits are confined to the statues, in the spandrils, of the Angel and the Virgin, or the Annunciation, and of the patron saints of Venice, St. Theodore and St. Mark.

The span of the arch is about 91 ft., and the height from the level of the water is 24½ ft. The width of the bridge is 72 ft., and this width is divided longitudinally into 5 parts; that is, into 3 streets or passages, and 2 rows of shops. The middle street or passage is 21 ft. 8 in. wide, and the 2 side ones near 11 ft. The number of shops on it is 24.

The palace of the Treasurers, or *dei Camerlinghi*, now the *Tribunale d'Appello*, is on the l. hand immediately after having passed through the bridge. It was built by *Guglielmo Bergamasco* in the year 1525. It is irregular in figure owing to its site, but its architecture is much to be admired.

Opposite, on the rt. hand, is the *Fondaco dei Tedeschi*. The *Fondachi* form a curious portion of the reminiscences of the ancient commercial prosperity of Venice. They were the factories of the different nations, very similar in object to some still possessed by the Franks in the Levant, or by the Europeans at Canton, where the merchants of each language and race could dwell together under a domestic jurisdiction; where their business could be transacted, and their goods safely housed. It is hardly necessary to observe that they have long since ceased to be applied to their original use. Some are converted into public offices, but, generally speaking, they are falling into decay. The finest and the best preserved is the *Fondaco dei Tedeschi*, near the foot of the Rialto. It was built some time after 1505, when the older Fondaco was burnt down. The architect was a certain *Girolamo Tedesco*, of whose history nothing else is known. Coupled arches and arched porticoes mark it as one of the diversified channels by which the Veneto-Gothic style passed into the classical style. It has now a somewhat heavy character; but its walls were originally covered with frescoes by *Giorgione*, *Carpaccio*, and others, which have long since disappeared.

On the l. are the *Fabbriche Nuove di Rialto*, built by *Sansovino* in 1555. The façade has three orders, Rustic, Doric, and Ionic.

On the rt. *P. Valmarana*, *P. Michiel delle Colonne*, and *P. Sagredo*, of the 13th centy., and beyond

The *Casa* or *Ca' d'Oro*, perhaps the most remarkable of the Palaces of the 15th centy., and of which the ornaments are the most in the oriental style, particularly in the ogee or contrasted turns of the arches. It was gilded, and hence, according to some, its name; others say it was called after the Doro family. It was much dilapidated, but a few years since underwent a complete restoration by the proprietor, Madlle. Taglioni, the celebrated dancer: it now belongs to the Jew banker Herrera.

On the l. hand are the *Palazzo Corner della Regina*, now Monte di Pieta, built by *Rossi* in 1724, and the vast *Palazzo Pesaro*, now Bevilacqua, built by *Longhena*.

On the rt. are the *Palazzo Grimani*, attributed to Sanmicheli, and the *Palazzo Vendramin Calergi*. This, which in the 16th centy. was reckoned as the very finest of the Venetian palaces, was built in 1481 at the expense of the Doge Andrea Loredano, by *Pietro Lombardo*. But the circumstances of the family compelled them to alienate it, and it was sold in 1681 to the Duke of Brunswick for 60,000 ducats; and by the latter, not long afterwards, to the Calergis, and afterwards to the Vendramins. It now belongs to the Duchesse de Berri. The order is Corinthian; but columns are placed as mullions in the great arched windows which fill the front. It contains some works of art, amongst which are statues of *Adam* and *Eve* by *Tullio Lombardo*, removed from the Vendramin Mausoleum in San Giovanni e Paolo, and several interesting relics of the elder branch of the House of Bourbon. On the l. is the

Fondaco de Turchi: it dates from the 11th cent., and, having belonged to the House of Este, was purchased by the Republic to form a factory for the Turkish merchants: it is now the government tobacco warehouse. Immediately beyond it is

The *Museo Correr*, or *Municipal Museum*, on the Grand Canal, not far from the rly. stat., only open on Wed. and Sat. This fine collection, the result of individual exertion, was formed by Count Correr, who bequeathed it to the Municipality of Venice about 25 years ago, and by whom it is now very liberally supported. It consists of a series of ancient marbles, a collection of arms, and a gallery of pictures arranged in six rooms on the ground floor, forming the *Pinacoteca*, among which may be cited (room I.), *Stefano Pievano*, a Madonna (1369); *Mantegna*, the Transfiguration; *G. Bellini*, a portrait of Doge G. Mocenigo; and *Marco Palmezzano*, Christ bearing the Cross. On the second floor are the library; a good ornithological collection formed by Count Contarini; a series of engravings, amongst the very curious bird's-eye views of Venice, attributed to Albert Durer, but dating from the end of the 15th centy.; some interesting pictures of old Venetian masters (the pretended portrait of Cesar Borgia by *L. da Vinci*); an extensive series of original drawings, amongst which are several by *P. Veronese*, *Guercino*, *Longhi*, &c.; the fine collection of Correr coins and medals, and that of manuscripts, amongst which are worthy of special notice, some canzoni of Petrarch, and the Portulano, or collection of marine charts, by Pietro Visconti of Genoa, executed in 1318, the oldest work of this kind in existence with a certain date. The specimens of majolica, of about A.D. 1440, are well worthy of notice.

Beyond the P. Correr is the Ch. of S. Simeon Piccolo; and nearly opposite to the Rly. Stat., the P. Papadopolo, with its fine gardens, nearly at the extremity of the Canal Grande.

Further on to the rt., after the P. Vendramin, a canal, much wider than those hitherto passed, opens out of the Canal Grande, and leads to Mestre. On the angle formed by this canal, which is called the *Cannareggio* (*i. e.* canal regio), with the Grand Canal, stands the *Palazzo Labia*, built by *Cominelli*, much dilapidated. Proceeding up the Cannareggio, immediately after having passed under the bridge, we arrive, on the l., at the

Palazzo Manfrini, an elegant modern building. It once contained the best collection of paintings in Venice after that of the Academy: they filled ten rooms, but the best of them were sold (1856) to an English dealer, and those that remain will soon follow the same dispersion; they are to be seen on Mondays and Thursdays from 9 till 1. There are hand catalogues in each room; and as the pictures that remain are of very secondrate importance, we have omitted the list of the Manfrini gallery inserted in the former editions.

Other palaces, not upon the Grand Canal, which ought to be mentioned, are the *Palazzo Trevisan a S. Zaccaria* (Ponte di Canonica), by G. Bergamasco, richly incrusted with fine marbles, and marking the transition from the Gothic to the Italian. This palace afterwards passed to the Capello family, having been purchased by Bianca for her brother Vittore Capello, in 1577. The original Capello Palace is near the ch. of S. Apollinare: it was from the latter that Bianca fled with Pietro Bonaventuri, in 1563, who carried her to Florence, where she became the favourite, and subsequently the wife (1578), of Francesco de Medicis.

Palazzo Corner Mocenigo (Campo di San Paolo), built by Sanmicheli, remarkable for the boldness of its elevation and its grandeur.

Palazzo Morosini, in the Campo S. Stefano, of the 16th cent. Here was born F. Morosini, surnamed *Peloponesiaco;* and are still preserved his arms and other memorials. In the same *Campo* are the *P. Loredan*, now a military post, and the vast *P. Pisani*.

The *Palazzo Grimani a S. Maria Formosa*, in a narrow street (*Ruga Giuffa*) near the Campo of *S. Maria Formosa*, is attributed to Sanmicheli. It contains a collection of ancient statues, bas-reliefs, and inscriptions; but is chiefly remarkable for the colossal statue of Agrippa, which was formerly in the vestibule of the Pantheon at Rome: both arms and legs are restorations; it now stands in the court of the palace. The illustrious Roman is represented, his l. hand seizing a dolphin. On the opposite side of the quadrangle is a good torso in armour, of the time of the Antonines, restored as a colossal statue of Augustus. There are some second-rate paintings in the large rooms on the first floor, and a Christ crowned with Thorns, by *Palma Vecchio*, in the chapel.

Palazzo Badoër, in the Campo di S. Giovanni Bragola, a fine specimen of the Gothic of the 14th centy. (1310): the front is ornamented in coloured marbles, with a rude relief of an eagle. This palace has been lately restored, the front painted barbarously in white and red squares, like a chess-board.

Palazzo Giovanelli, a fine specimen of the pointed style of the 15th cent. It is situated near the Ch. of *S. Fosca*, and belongs to the wealthy patrician prince whose name it now bears. The modern decoration of the apartments is very rich.

Palazzo Falier, near the Bridge and Campo of the SS. Apostoli, in the Arabo-Byzantine style of the 13th centy.; it has 4 handsome pointed windows behind a modern balcony. It belonged to Marino, the decapitated Doge, and was confiscated to the State after his execution in 1355.

Amongst the *remarkable Houses* of Venice may be mentioned the *Palazzo Moro* (modernized), on the Campo del Carmine, the supposed residence of Cristoforo Moro, the Othello of Shakspeare: on the corner towards the Canal is the statue of a warrior of the 15th centy., probably by Rizzo. The *Palazzo dei Poli*, in the *Corte del Sabbion*, near the Teatro Malibran, of which little more remains than a handsome walled-up doorway, in the Arabo-Byzantine style. Here lived *Marco Polo*, the celebrated traveller of the 13th centy., who, after being taken prisoner at Curzola by the Genoese, died here in 1323. *Tintoretto's house* was on the Quay of the Campo dei Mori, near the Madonna del Orto; and Titian's, in the Calle di S. Cancino, at a place called Berigrande, opposite to the island of Murano.

Churches.—Generally speaking, the churches of Venice are fine, and very varied in their character; they fall into four principal styles, which, amongst themselves, are very uniform. The first is a peculiar Gothic, generally plain, massive, and solemn, unlike the arabesque richness of the ducal palace, and the secular structures of the same order. The second is a style which here they term Lombard, but which is a revival of the Roman style in the 15th centy. The third is classical—Italian, properly so called—of which the principal examples in the sacred edifices here are Palladian. The last is the modern Italian; sometimes overloaded with superfluous ornament. Perhaps no city in Italy, not even Rome itself, possessed formerly so many churches in proportion to its population. It was the policy of the Venetians that every shoal and island should have its mother church, surrounded by a host of minor oratories.

Ch. of *SS. Apostoli*, rebuilt in 1575, is a relic of an older building much modernized. It is chiefly remarkable for the sepulchral chapel of the Corner family. The architect was *Guglielmo Bergamasco* : fanciful Corinthian pillars, half fluted in the general way and half fluted spirally, support it. Here are the tombs of Marco Corner, father of Catherine Queen of Cyprus, and of Giorgio her brother. This church contains a dubious *Paolo Veronese*, near the high altar, the Fall of the Manna.

La Chiesa de' Carmini, or of *La Vergine del Carmelo*, a fine church of the 14th centy., but the façade is modern. It has several good paintings, among which are, at the first altar on the rt. hand, the presentation of the infant Saviour to Simeon, by *Tintoretto*, a very fine picture, and, at the third altar, the Nativity, by *Cima da Conegliano*. On the neighbouring piazza stood the Palazzo Moro, called the Casa di Otello, where Shakspeare's hero is supposed to have lived.

Ch. of *S. Cassano*, beyond the Bridge of the Rialto, remarkable for three fine paintings by Tintoretto at the high altar, the Resurrection, the Descent into Hades, and the Crucifixion — the latter perhaps one of the grandest works of the master.

San Francesco della Vigna. This magnificent, though still unfinished church, was built at the expense of the Doge Andrea Gritti, by whom the first stone was laid Aug. 15, 1554. *Sansovino* had made the designs; these were criticised, and differences of opinion arose, particularly with respect to the proportions of the building. The doge

N. Italy—1860.

was troubled, and opinions were taken; amongst others, Titian was consulted. The building was completed, but from the designs of *Palladio*, and much of what we now see, the façade, with its lofty portal, bears the impress of his style. The entrance is profusely ornamented. It contains 17 chapels; in the fourth chapel is the Resurrection, by *Paolo Veronese*; in the *Capella Santa* a Madonna by *Giov. Bellini*; in the sacristy a curious Ancona by *Jacobello del Fiore*. The *Capella Giustiniani* is in the sumptuous style of the Lombardi. There are several tombs of doges of the 16th and 17th centuries in this ch. The small bronze statues of St. John and St. Francis in the holy-water basin, are by *Al. Vittoria*.

The *Frari*, or *Sta. Maria Gloriosa de' Frari*, built, at least designed, by *Nicolo Pisano*, about 1250. The interior consists of a rather narrow nave and aisles, with two short transepts. Each aisle is separated from the nave by 6 pointed arches. Having belonged to the Franciscans, it contains several tombs of historical interest. In the basins for holy water are two small bronze statues by Girolamo Campagna; that on the l. represents St. Antony, that on the rt. Innocence. Commencing the circuit of the church, on the rt. hand as we enter is the colossal monument of Titian, completed at the expense of the Emperor of Austria. It had been the intention of Charles V. to erect a tomb over the remains of the great painter, but it was reserved to the Emperor Ferdinand I. to do so. The monument, which was uncovered in 1853, consists of a massive basement, on which rises a highly decorated Corinthian canopy, under which is a sitting statue of the painter crowned with laurel, and behind bas-reliefs copied from his three greatest works — the Assumption of the Virgin, the Death of St. Peter Martyr, and the Martyrdom of St. Lawrence. There are several statues allegorical to the Arts, on either side, and two on the basement; that holding the inscription "*Tiziano monumentum erectum sit Fer-*

R

dinandus I., 1839," is by Zandomeneghi: the statue of the old man holding a book, on which is written, "*Eques et Comes Titianus sit. Carolus V.* 1553," at whose feet is a volume inscribed, "*Canones et Decreta Concilii Tridentani*," is intended for Fra Paolo Sarpi, and is the last work executed by Zandomeneghi (1847). The statue of Titian and some of the others are by Zandomeneghi, who was also the principal designer of the monument. The marble slab with the verses—

"Qui giace il gran Tiziano de' Vecelli, Emulator de' Zeusi e degli Apelli,"

which for centuries was the only memorial on the artist's grave, still may be seen on the rt. of the present magnificent mausoleum. No trace of his remains were however discovered beneath. The statue of St. Jerome, over the 3rd altar, is by *Aless. Vittoria*. 4th Altar, *Palma Giovane*, Martyrdom of St. Catherine. Beyond this altar is a door, over which is a wooden case, supposed to contain the bones of Francesco Carmagnola, the celebrated condottiere, executed at Venice in 1432; but it is now well ascertained that his remains were carried to Milan. In the corner of the rt.-hand transept is a fine picture, in three compartments, by *B. Vivarini*, 1482. It represents the Virgin and four Saints, with a Pietà above. The Gothic monument of the Beato Pacifico over this was raised by his family in 1437. This Beato, originally the architect Scipione Bon, died in the middle of the preceding century. The monument of the Venetian general, Benedetto Pesaro, is a triumphal arch, and forms the decoration of the door of the sacristy. The principal figure is by *Lorenzo Bregni*; on his l. is a fine one of Mars, by *Baccio da Montelupo*. The *Bregni*, who flourished about the latter part of the 15th and the beginning of the 16th centuries, were members of one of the families of artists, of which there were many in Italy, amongst whom art was so successfully carried on by tradition. *Paolo* was an architect; *Antonio*, his brother, a sculptor; and both worked upon these tombs. *Lorenzo Bregni*, not less eminent, lived a generation later.

In the sacristy is a beautiful painting over the altar by *Giovanni Bellini*, in three portions, the Madonna and four Saints (1488). Also some high reliefs of the Crucifixion and Burial of our Lord.

Returning into the church, in the 2nd chapel on rt. of the choir, a good Gothic tomb, of the 14th century, of Duccio degli Alberti, a Florentine ambassador (ob. 1336). In the Tribune are two splendid monuments: on the rt. that of the unfortunate Doge Francesco Foscari (died 1457)—an exceedingly noble elevation by *Anto. Rizzo*. The columns support statues. Lord Byron's tragedy has rendered the history of the Foscari family familiar to the English reader. This monument was erected by the Doge's grandson Nicolo, who filled several important offices in the republic between 1480 and 1501. Opposite is the tomb of the Doge Nicolo Tron (died 1472), by *Antonio Rizzo*, which is perhaps 50 ft. in width and 70 in height, being composed of five stories, and adorned by 19 full-length figures, besides a profusion of bas-reliefs and other ornaments.

The screen before the choir deserves notice from its peculiar construction, and its low reliefs of saints of the 15th centy.

The high altar was erected in 1516. The picture, the Assumption of the Virgin, is by *Salviati*. The stalls of the choir, which extends as far as the 5th arch of the nave, are of the very finest wood-work, the backs most beautifully inlaid, or worked in *tarsia*, by Giovanni Paolo di Vicenza, 1468, or according to others by *Marco di Vicenza*. In the 7th chapel (1st on l. of high altar) is a painting of the Virgin Enthroned, by *B. Licinio*; in the 8th is the monument of Melchior Trevisan (died 1500), by *Dentone*: the statue above is in complete armour, standing boldly forth in simplicity of conception combined with great richness in execution. The St. John in wood, and in the niche over the altar, is by *Donatello.* There is some good painted glass by *Maestro Marco,* of 1335, in the corner chapel opening into the l. transept. In the 9th chapel is a good altarpiece by *Luigi Vivarini,* completed by *Basaiti,* the Crowning of the Virgin, with a group of Saints on either side.

In the l.-hand transept is a monument, the work of an unknown artist, at the end of the 15th century—it was raised by Maffeo Zen to his wife Generosa Orsini; and 3 paintings of S. Mark and 2 other saints, by *B. Vivarini* (1474). In the chapel of St. Peter, opening out of the N. aisle, are a font with a statue of St. John the Baptist, by *Sansorino;* some sculptures of the 15th centy.; an Ancona in compartments, containing statues of saints below, St. Peter in the centre, with the Virgin and 4 female saints above, by *Jacobello dalle Massegne* (1485); and the monument to Bishop Miani, with 5 statues, probably by the same artist (1464). Beyond the entrance to this chapel is the monument, rich in Oriental marbles, of Jacopo Pesaro, who died 1547. Over the Pesaro altar is a fine votive picture by *Titian,* called the *Pala dei Pesari.* It is the private property of the Pesaro family, and therefore was not taken to France. It represents the Virgin seated in an elevated situation, within noble architecture, with our Saviour in her arms, who turns to St. Francis: below is St. Peter with a book; on one side of him St. George bearing a standard, on which are emblazoned the Pesaro arms: below are five members of the Pesaro family, kneeling before the Virgin, one of whom, a young female, is particularly lovely. In composition this picture ranks next to the Peter Martyr. More full and deep colour belongs to the nature of the subject, if subject it may be called, and it possesses it. It is also an excellent specimen of background finished to character, but so well composed to receive that finish that it nowhere obtrudes on or interrupts the principal matter, though it has itself sufficient grandeur and interest, and is perfectly natural. Titian received, in 1519, 102 golden ducats for this magnificent work.

The monument of the Doge Giovanni Pesaro (died 1659) is also a stupendous fabric, but it is more remarkable for its singularity than its beauty. It is supported by colossal Moors or Negroes of black marble, dressed in white marble; their black elbows and knees protruding through the rents of their white jackets and trousers. In the centre sits the Doge. It is a curious specimen of the bad taste of the 17th century. The architect was *Longhena,* the sculptor *Barthel:* it was executed about 1669.

By the side of this, opposite that of Titian, is the monument erected to the memory of Canova (in 1827), a repetition of his own design for that of the Archduchess Christina at Vienna. A vast pyramid of white marble, into whose opened doors of bronze various mourners, Religion, Art, Genius, and so forth, are seen walking in funeral procession, with a crouching lion of St. Mark on the opposite side. This design of Canova's monument was at one time proposed to be erected to Titian.

On the altar which follows this is a large bas-relief of the Crucifixion. Between this and the principal door is an elegant monument, in marble, of Pietro Bernardo (who died 1568), by *Alessandro Leopardi.* The mediæval monument near it is of *Simeone Dandolo,* one of the judges of M. Falier (ob. 1360). The fine detached bell-tower was commenced in 1361 by *Jacopo,* and finished in 1396 by *Pietro Paolo dalle Massegne.* Several of the doors leading into the ch. of the Frari are fine specimens of the Pointed style of the 14th cent.

Venetian Archives. The conventual buildings attached to the ch. of the Frari have been converted into a depository for the archives of the ancient Venetian state. Their bulk is appalling: they are said to fill 295 rooms, and to consist of upwards of 14 millions of documents. They have been formed from the collections of suppressed monastic establishments, from the records of noble Venetian families, and from the ancient diplomatic archives of the Republic. The selections relating to Sanuto, and from the diplomatic correspondence of the Venetian envoys in England, made by Mr. Rawdon Brown, show to what good use they might be turned; but considerable difficulty is experienced in obtaining the necessary permission to examine them, from the Austrian authorities at Vienna.

San Giovanni Crisostomo, by *Tullio Lombardo*, 1489. Paintings—1st altar on rt., *Giovan' Bellini*, St. Jerome with 2 Saints; over the high altar, *Sebastian del Piombo*, St. Giovanni Crisostomo and Saints. The fine bas-relief of the Coronation of the Virgin, and the 12 Apostles, by *Tullio Lombardo*, in the 2nd chapel on l. In this the management of the perspective is very remarkable.

Ch. of *Santi Giovanni e Paolo*, better known as *San Zanipolo*, begun in 1246, but not finished till 1390. The architect's name is not known: he is supposed to have been of the school of Nicolo Pisano. Its length is 330½ ft., its width between the ends of the transepts 142½ ft., and in the body 91 ft.: its height 123 ft. The principal door, with columns and sculptures, is in the finest Pointed style of the 13th centy.; there are some rude bas-reliefs of the 7th and 8th cents. let into the wall of the façade, and in the niches on the side of the door some tombs of Doges of the 13th.

The interior is a fine specimen of the early Italian Gothic; the 5 wide pointed arches on either side of the nave give it a very light appearance, so different from our northern Gothic churches. The transept is very short in proportion to the length of the nave. The once handsome tribune has been sadly disfigured by the modern adaptation of Corinthian ornament.

On the rt. on entering is the monument of the Doge Pietro Mocenigo (died 1476), the work of *Pietro* (the father) and *Antonio* and *Tullio Lombardo* (the sons). At the first altar on the rt. is a picture of the Virgin and Child, by *G. Bellini*, with 5 Saints on either side, and 3 children singing below. At the 2nd altar, one in 9 compartments, attributed to *V. Carpaccio*. Outside the 6th chapel are the colossal monuments of the Doges Silvestro and Bertuccio Valier, 1658, 1700; and of the wife of the former, in the style of Bernini. The 7th chapel (dedicated to St. Dominick) contains 6 bas-reliefs representing the actions of St. Dominick, by *Camillo Mazza*; 5 of them are in bronze, the 6th in wood. In the rt.-hand transept, near the angle, is a picture of St. Augustine seated, by *B. Vivarini*, 1473.

Over the door of this transept are the tombs of the general Dionigi Naldo (died 1510) by *Lorenzo Bregno*, and of Nicolo Orsini Count of Pittigliano (died 1509), both in the service of Venice against the League of Cambray; these two monuments were raised at the expense of the Republic. The large window with good painted glass was executed by *Girolamo Mocetto* in 1473, from the designs of *B. Vivarini*. In a line with the high altar are 2 chapels, on each side. In the 1st are 2 paintings, by *Bonifazio*, of several Saints; and in the 2nd, that of the Magdalene washing the Feet of the Saviour is a fine work of the same painter; that of the Emperor Constantine, with SS. Vito and Ascanio, the Virgin and Saints, and some portraits of nobles, is by *Tintoretto;* the group of the Crucifixion over the altar by *Gug. Bergamasco*.

On the wall on the rt. hand of the high altar is the monument of the Doge Michele Morosini (ob. 1382), in a tolerably pure Pointed style. Morosini reigned only four months, but this short reign was illustrated by the capture of Tenedos. Next to this the monument of the Doge Leonardo Loredan (died 1521) commemorates one of the wisest of the princes of Venice, when her prudence and fortitude baffled the league of Cambrai. The design is by *Girolamo Grapiglia*, 1572. The statue of the Doge is by *G. Campagna*, the others by *Danese Cattaneo*. Opposite to this is the most splendid monument of its kind in Venice—that of the Doge Andrea Vendramin (died 1479). "The bas-reliefs and the *statuettes* round the sarcophagus seem as if taken from the intaglio of a Greek gem, so pure is the outline, so graceful the invention, and so dignified the style."—*Cicognara*. The statue of the deceased Doge, stretched on the bier, exhibits him as fallen asleep rather than as dead. In the architectural portion the arabesques of the pilasters and friezes are remarkable. They are attributed to *Alessandro Leopardi*. The elevation of Andrea Vendramin to the sovereignty (1478) marks the decline of the primitive policy of the state. He was the first of the newly ennobled families admitted to the honours heretofore monopolised by the descendants of the primitive aristocracy. The founder of the family was a banker or moneychanger, who, having fitted out a vessel at his own expense during the war of Chioggia, was inscribed on the Libro d'Oro as a reward for his patriotism. In the chapel of the Trinity are two good works of *Leandro Bassano*, one on the wall on the l. hand, the Disinterment of St. John; the other, over the altar, the Trinity, Madonna, and Saints. The sepulchral urns contain the remains of Doge Pietro Corner (ob. 1368), and of Andrea Morosini. After passing this chapel, on the wall on the rt. are the tombs of Jacopo Cavalli, by *Jacobello dalle Masseyne*, and opposite of Doge Delfin (ob. 1361). In the adjoining N. transept is a marble group representing Vittore Capello receiving the *baton* of command from S. Elena, by *Antonio Dentone* (1480). From the transept a door leads into the chapel of the Rosary, over which is the tomb of Doge Antonio Venier (ob. 1400). The chapel is splendidly decorated; over the door on the inside is a painting by *D. Tintoretto*, the Holy League of 1570; the altar is by *Campagna*, and the pictures of the Battle of Lepanto and of the Crucifixion by *J. Tintoretto*; the handsome carvings in wood, by *Brustolon*, were brought here from the Scuola della Carita. The series of marble bas-reliefs on the walls behind the altar, representing events in the life of our Saviour, are by *Bonazza* of Padua (1732). Returning to the church, in the Sacristy are paintings of Christ bearing the Cross, by *Aloise Vivarini*, of Honorius III. approving of the Order of St. Dominick, by *Bassano*, &c. Further on, beyond the door of the sacristy, is the monument of Doge Pasquale Malipiero (died 1461), and under it a painting of the Coronation of the Virgin, attributed to *Girolamo da' Udine*; in the subjacent niches are the tombs of Doge Michael Steno (in whose reign Padua was seized, and Francesco di Carrara barbarously murdered in his prison), with the painted statue of the deceased (ob. 1413) and of *Alvise Trevisan* (ob. 1528). Then follow monuments of doges and generals: an equestrian statue of Pompeo Giustiniani (ob. 1616); Doge Giovanni Dandolo (ob. 1289); Doge Tomasso Mocenigo, by *Pietro da Firenze* and *Martino da Fiesole* (1423); and of Doge Nicolo Marcello, a fine specimen of the Lombardi style, by *Alessandro Leopardi* (1474). At the altar, which is the second on the l. hand on entering the church, is the celebrated St. Peter Martyr, by *Titian*, perhaps his finest work, indeed considered by many the third picture in the world, coming after the Transfiguration of Raphael and the Communion of St. Jerome by Domenichino. It represents the martyrdom of the saint. At the last altar is a fine statue of St. Jerome, by *Alessandro Vittoria*. On the wall, on the l.-hand side on entering the principal door, is the monument of the Doge Giovanni Mocenigo (died 1485), a fine work of *Tullio Lombardo*. Amongst the other ducal monuments in this Westminster Abbey of

Venice are those of Marco Giustiniani (1347), with rude bas-reliefs of the Virgin (above is a picture of the Virgin with 3 Senators kneeling before her, by *J. Tintoretto*), of Doges Alvise Mocenigo (1576), and of Giovanni Bembo (1618), over the great entrance—the two latter by *Grapiglia*.

In the *Campo* in front of the church stands the celebrated statue of Bartolommeo Colleoni, the second equestrian statue raised in Italy after the revival of the arts, that of Gattemelata by Donatello being the first (see Padua). *Andrea Verrocchio* gave the design and model for it, but, according to the story, he died of grief because he could not complete it, in consequence of the failure of the mould. It was cast by *Alessandro Leopardi*, whose name can be traced in the inscription upon the girth beneath the horse's body: "Alexander Leopardus F. opus." This may be rendered "fusit opus." The handsome marble pedestal is lofty, supported and flanked by composite columns. Colleoni is said to have been the first who employed field-pieces in warfare. Although this is not strictly correct, he is nevertheless to be considered as one of the great teachers of the modern art of war. The statue is very animated. The beautiful building which forms the N. side of the Campo, the *Scuola de San Marco*, is a fine specimen of the rich decorated Venetian architecture of the 15th century, ornamented with coloured marbles in the style of Ca' Doro and Palazzo Dario; the elegant portal, surmounted by the Lion of St. Mark, with this again by a statue of the Saint, is very elegant. The Scuola as well as the conventual buildings behind the church have of late years been converted into an hospital, accommodating on an average one thousand patients. The two great halls of the Scuola are fine adaptations of Martino Lombardi's architecture; out of the lower one opened the chapel of Santa Maria della Pace, in which were discovered some years ago the sarcophagus (now destroyed) and the bones of Marin Falier.

Ch. of *San Giorgio Maggiore*. This fine edifice, beyond the Canal Grande, opposite to the Piazzetta and Riva degli Schiavoni, was designed by Palladio, and begun in 1556, though the front was not completed till 1610. The general proportions of the front are pleasing. "Internally the church has a nave and two side aisles, but the piers are very solid, and admit no oblique view between them on entering the great door. The nave itself is much inferior to that of the Redentore. It is too short, and the pedestals are too high. The transept cuts the lines disagreeably; and the want of some projection or alteration of plan at the intersection produces an effect of feebleness. The altars are all similar, simple, and good."—*Woods*. This church was finished under the directions of *Scamozzi*, who is believed to have made some alterations in the design of *Palladio*. It contains several good pictures: at the 1st altar on the rt. the Nativity, by *J. Bassano*: at the 2nd a crucifix by *Michelozzo*; at the 3rd, Martyrdom of Saints; at the 4th, the Virgin crowned; both by *Tintoretto*. On the walls of the central chapel, the Falling of the Manna and the Last Supper, by the same. The 48 seats in the choir are beautifully sculptured by *Albert de Brule*, a Fleming: they represent events in the life of St. Benedict. The group of figures in bronze over the high altar is by *Gir. Campagna*. A door on the rt. on entering the choir leads into a corridor, where is a monument erected in 1637, from the design of *Longhena*, to the memory of the Doge Domenico Michiel (died 1128). It was this doge who urged the Venetians to co-operate in the crusade. In the two chapels on the l. of the choir are pictures by *Tintoretto*, the Resurrection, and the Martyrdom of St. Stephen; in the 2nd altar on the l. a statue of the Virgin by *Campagna*; and in that next the door the Martyrdom of St. Lucia, by *Leandro Bassano*. As amongst the last works of *Palladio*, the portico and refectory in the monastery are interesting.

Ch. of *San Giorgio de' Greci*, the ch. of the Greek rite in Venice, is from the designs of *Sansovino*. It is well known that the Greeks do not admit of sculpture in their sacred edifices. Medallions of mosaic in the façade, and, within, paintings of which the ground is covered with silver plates, therefore constitute the principal ornaments. "On the division which separates the sanctuary from the body of the church are some paintings coated with silver, and having crowns and other ornaments of gold attached to them, and leaving hardly anything visible but the faces. I was assured that the painting was complete beneath this covering, and that the parts which were figured in low relief on the silver plate corresponded exactly with the drawings behind it."—*Woods*. The altar is hidden behind a screen, covered with paintings, and filling up the entire E. end of the ch.

Ch. of *S. Giacomo di Rialto*, at the foot of the bridge. On the site of this church stood the first church which was built in Venice, erected in 421. In its present form it was first built in 1194. It was entirely restored or rather rebuilt in 1531, but "precisely in the old form, as we are informed by an inscription in the portico; we may doubt the perfect accuracy of the imitation, but the six marble columns of the nave, with their capitals copied from the Corinthian, are probably parts of the ancient building. The middle space is about twice the width of the others, forming a transept, and a cupola rises at the intersection. I suspect that this was an innovation, but on the whole it is a pretty little thing."—*Woods*. It contains a fine bronze statue of St. Anthony the Abbot, by *G. Campagna*, and one at the high altar, of the patron saint, by *A. Vittoria*.

The *Chiesa de' Jesuiti*, built by *Fattoretto* and *Rossi* (1715-1730), is an extraordinary specimen of the theatrical and luxurious magnificence of the churches of this order. The walls are tabled with carved marble inlaid with verd'-antique and other coloured marbles in flowers. The twisted columns of the altar are solid blocks of verd'-antique mixed with brocatello, as is also the pavement within the altar-rails. The roof is finely coloured. Beneath a slab in front of the high altar is interred Manin, the last of the long line of Venice's Doges. The inscription, "ÆTERNITATI SUÆ MANINI CINERES," is singularly affecting. Manin, a weak and honest man, was unequal to the exigencies of the times he lived in, and when required to take the oath of allegiance to the Austrian Emperor he dropped senseless upon the ground, so poignantly did he feel his country's abjection and misfortunes. In the chapel, on the l. of the high altar, is the tomb of Doge Cicogna (ob. 1595), by *G. Campagna*, and, in that on the rt., the mausoleum erected to Ottavio Farnese by the senate in 1676.

Ch. of *La Madonna dell' Orto*, at the N. extremity of the city, facing the island of Murano. A fine Gothic edifice; the façade was erected in 1473, and approaches our Decorated style. Over the door are statues of St. Christopher, and, on the sides of the gables, of the twelve Apostles, by *Bartolommeo Bon*, who executed so much of the Palazzo Ducale. The interior consists of a nave and two aisles, separated by marble columns supporting pointed arches, probably of the end of the 14th centy. The roof, flat, and of wood, was formerly richly painted. The church contains several paintings by *Tintoretto*, the two principal ones being the Last Judgment, a most singular picture, and of enormous size, at least 60 ft. by 30. Nothing can be more strange than the composition, or more unlike the ordinary representations of the subject. Opposite to it, and of the same size, the Worshipping of the Golden Calf. The arrangement is peculiar, but it is nevertheless a picture of great power. These two great works are on the walls on each side of the high altar, behind which is a colossal statue of St. Christopher, by *Morazzone*. Besides these, the church contains, at the first altar on the rt.

of the entrance, a fine work of *Cima da Conegliano*, St. John the Baptist and four other Saints; at the fourth altar is the Martyrdom of St. Lorenzo, by *Vandyke*. On the organ are paintings, also by *Tintoretto*; and beneath, a small but fine Madonna and Child, by *Giovanni Bellini*. The fourth chapel on the l. hand is dedicated to St. Agnese. In it is the Martyrdom of the patron Saint; one of the most pleasing pictures of *Tintoretto*. St. Agnes, in white drapery and with her lamb, allusive to her name, is in a full bright light, looking upwards and awaiting her death. This painting was carried to Paris. Before its spoliation this church was the richest in Venice; but much has been carried off, and the neglect of repairs has caused the almost total destruction of the paintings which formerly existed on the roof. The best time for seeing this church to advantage is towards the afternoon. It is principally of brick, and the ornaments are formed out of that material. The upper portions were partly destroyed in 1828, by lightning. In La Madonna dell' Orto were buried Tintoretto, Alessandro Leopardi, and Ramusio, the celebrated geographer. The ch. has been long undergoing restoration, and in the mean time is used as a hay-store for the Austrian cavalry (1860).

Ch. of *S. Maria Formosa*, in the Piazza of the same name. This church was built in the 15th, but altered in the 17th century. The well-known story of the Brides of Venice who were carried off by the pirates of Istria took place in this church. The memory of the event was long kept alive by an annual procession of Venetian women on the 2nd of February, and by a solemn visit paid by the Doge to this church. Over the entrance is the sarcophagus of Vincenzo Capello (ob. 1541). Inside the ch. at the first altar on the rt. is by *Palma il Vecchio* a series of 6 paintings, with S. Barbara in the centre, and SS. Dominick, Sebastian, John the Baptist, and S. Luigi Gonzaga on each side, and a Dead Christ above. The Santa Barbara is, perhaps, the finest work of this master. At the 2nd altar 3 paintings on panel by *Vivarini* (1473); and at the 3rd a Dead Christ by *Palma Giovane*. Opposite to the great entrance to St. Maria Formosa is a beautiful Gothic arch of the 14th centy., overlooking a bridge (the Ponte del Paradiso).

Ch. of the *Madonna dei Miracoli*, built between 1480 and 1489. The plan was produced by competition. The name of the successful architect is not preserved; but he appears to have endeavoured to get the prize by novelty of style; and the exterior exhibits a very curious attempt to unite the Byzantine and Italian styles. The designs were carried into effect by *Pietro Lombardo*, and some portions are his own. Within, the ornaments of the raised presbytery, in the centre of which stands the high altar, have singular beauty, especially the arabesque reliefs on the columns and friezes. In its flourishing days the Madonna from whom it derived its name attracted to it abundant alms and offerings. The front is rich in marbles and decorations. Titian lived in the neighbourhood of this church, which was annexed to a Franciscan monastery.

Sta. Maria della Salute: founded pursuant to a decree of the senate in 1631, as a monument of thanksgiving after the cessation of the great pestilence, in which 60,000 of the inhabitants are said to have died. It is a great octagonal church, erected under the direction of Baldassare Longhena. "Internally, the dome is supported on eight pillars, the aisle continues all round it, and there are eight recesses, seven of which are chapels, and the eighth forms the entrance. The disposition produces a degree of intricacy without confusion; that is, without rendering it at all difficult to understand the design, which is very favourable to the expression of richness and splendour, and presents some very picturesque and even beautiful combinations; but the windows, disposed two on each side over the arches of the cen-

tral octagon, have a bad effect."—*Woods*.
The interior is splendidly decorated and contains many fine works of art. In the 3 first chapels on the rt. a series of paintings, by *Luca Giordano*, of the Presentation in the Temple, the Assumption, and the Nativity of the Virgin. The 4 large compartments on the roof, over the high altar, are by *Salviati*, and the 8 smaller ones, containing the Evangelists and Doctors of the Church, by *Titian*. He has represented himself in the figure of St. Matthew. In the passage leading to the sacristy St. Mark and 4 Saints, also by *Titian*, in his first manner. The vault of the sacristy is also painted by him, the frescoes representing the Death of Abel, the Sacrifice of Abraham, and David and Goliah. Over the altar is the Madonna della Salute, by *Padovanino*. On the side wall of the sacristy are the Marriage of Cana, by *Tintoretto*; Samson and Jonas, by *Palma Vecchio*; and 2 curious Anconas by *Cristoforo da Pamia* and *Andrea da Murano*, of the 14th centy. The Melchisedec and the Triumph of David on the opposite wall are by *Salviati*. Returning into the church, in the 3rd chapel on the l. is the fine picture of the Descent of the Holy Spirit, by *Titian*, painted when the artist was in the full vigour of his talent. The conventual buildings adjoining the church have been of late years converted into the Patriarch's Ecclesiastical Seminary, for which they are well suited. The library, formerly belonging to the Somaschi Fathers, a highly cultivated confraternity, is remarkably good. Several fragments of sculpture, sepulchral and others, of artistical and historical interest, have also been removed here from desecrated churches. In the oratory is the tomb of Sansovino, the sculptures by A. Vittoria. Sansovino's remains had lain for 250 years in the ch. of S. Geminiano. They were removed here in 1820 (see p. 341).

Ch. of *San Moïse*, near the Piazza di San Marco. A small marble slab in the floor opposite the entrance marks the grave of John Law, the celebrated originator of the S. Sea scheme, who died here in 1729. It was placed by his descendant, Marshal Lauriston, when he was Governor of Venice in 1808, when Law's remains were transferred here from the ch. of S. Geminiano. There is a Last Supper, by *Palma Giovane*, and Christ washing the feet of the Pilgrims, by *Tintoretto*, in the chapel on the l. of the high altar.

Ch. of *San Pantaleone*, built in 1668. In the second chapel on the rt. is St. Pantaleone healing a child, by *P. Veronese*; and in a chapel to the l. of the high altar, the Coronation of the Virgin, by *G.* and *A. da Murano* (1444), and a finely worked Gothic altar of the same period.

Ch. of *San Pietro di Castello*, at the E. extremity of the city, beyond the arsenal, interesting as being the mother church or cathedral of Venice, from the earliest times of the republic down to 1807. The campanile (1474) is fine. The façade, by Smeraldi, was erected in 1594; the interior, by Grapiglia, between that period and 1621. The church contains some paintings by *Basaiti*, *Liberi*, and *Lorenzini*, and a St. Peter and St. Paul, near the 3rd altar on the rt., by *P. Veronese*. The rich Vendramin chapel, incrusted with marble, is from the design of *Longhena*. Near the 2nd altar on the rt. is a curious relic, an ancient episcopal seat, said to have been that of St. Peter, at Antioch, and given in 1310 by the Emperor Michael Palæologus to Doge Gradenigo; the back is covered with Oriental inscriptions, which have exercised the sagacity of some recent antiquaries.

Ch. of *Il Redentore*, in the island of La Giudecca. This church, an ex-voto built by the republic after the staying of the plague of 1576, is considered by the common consent of architects as the finest of *Palladio's* ecclesiastical edifices. It has the advantage of a commanding situation upon the broad canal of the Giudecca; and the front exhibits all the peculiar characteristics and favourite arrangements of Palladio. It is entirely his design and was begun by him in 1577. "Internally, it has a fine, wide, single nave, and this simple disposition might be well imitated in our Protestant churches. The arrangement and colour of the lower part are beautiful, and if the vault were a semi instead of a segment, and panelled instead of whitewashed, it might be cited as a perfect model of this mode of architecture. The termination of the choir wants consequence, and the plain whitewashed wall, behind the semicircular screen of columns, is absolutely disagreeable. The supports of the dome are good, and have no appearance of insufficiency."—*Woods*. The church contains, at the 1st altar on the rt. the Nativity, by *F. Bassano*; at the 3rd the Flagellation, by *Tintoretto*;—at the 3rd on the l. a Deposition, by *J. Palma*; at the 2nd a Resurrection, by *F. Bassano*; and at the 1st on the l. the Ascension, by *Tintoretto*. In the sacristy are three fine works of *Giov. Bellini*: a Virgin and Child and two Angels; a Madonna between St. John and St. Catherine; and a third between St. Jerome and St. Francis. The island of *Giudecca*, on which this church stands, was originally called *Spinalonga*: it received its present name when the Jews obtained permission to settle on it.

Ch. of *San Rocco* (see p. 373).

Ch. of *San Salvatore*, near the Ponte di Rialto, commenced in 1506, and completed by *Tullio Lombardo* and *Sansovino* about 1534; the heavy façade was added at a much later period (1663) by Sardi. "The inside has a nave and side recesses, or, as Moschini has it, a nave with three transepts, the farthest of which is longer than the others; each intersection is covered with a little dome, and each dome is crowned with a small lantern. The piers which separate these transepts are perforated in both directions with a small arch. The lights are kept high, and the general effect is very good. Where there is a range of lower arches opening into the nave, surmounted by a continued cornice, the simple vault forms by far the finest finish; but in a case like this, where the side-arches are as high as the nave, the succession of domes is possibly superior, at least the upper and lower parts seem perfectly suited to each other."—*Woods*. Beyond the first altar on the rt. is a monument of Andrea Dolfin and his wife, by *Giulio dal Moro* (1602). The second altar, and the statue of the Madonna and Child, are by *Campagna*. Then comes the splendid monument of the Doge Francesco Venier (died 1556), by *Sansovino*, executed in his 80th year, but exhibiting no mark of decaying powers. The same remark cannot be applied to the Annunciation by *Titian*, painted by him when he was nearly 90 years of age, and which is placed at the altar, designed by *Sansovino*, which comes after this monument. It is said that this is the painting on the margin of which the artist wrote, "*Titianus fecit, fecit;*" in order to silence the critic who asserted that no one would believe that it was painted by him. In the rt.-hand transept in the centre of a Corinthian portico, flanked by tombs of 2 cardinals, is the monument of Catherine Corner, Queen of Cyprus; the bas-relief on it represents her delivering up her crown to the Doge Barberigo. It was by showing her portrait to the young Lusignan that her uncle Andrea Corner, then in exile at Cyprus, excited first the passion of the prince. Lusignan was then Archbishop of Nicosia, and, being illegitimate, without pretensions to the throne; but the protection of the Soldan of Egypt, the support of the republic, and the favour of the Pope (Pius V.), a strange combination, enabled him to win the crown. Catherine was solemnly adopted as the daughter of the republic, and given, with a rich dowry, to the archbishop, who had ascended the throne as King James Lusignan II. but died within two years after his marriage. A posthumous child was the fruit of this union, who, proclaimed as James III., died an infant in 1475; and the republic, as the grandfather of the minor, claiming his inheritance, the daughter of Venice was forced to abdicate, her *dear mother*, the republic, obtaining the sovereignty. This took place in 1489, when, abandoning her kingdom, she retired to the castle at Asolo with the empty title of Queen, which she retained until her death, surrounded by a diminutive court, of which the celebrated Pietro Bembo, afterwards Cardinal, formed a part.— See *Handbook for South Germany*, Rte. 222. Over the high altar is the Transfiguration by *Titian*, also a work of his declining years; behind this is a *pala* of embossed silver, with the Transfiguration in the centre, executed in 1290, a very remarkable specimen of Venetian goldsmith work of the period. In the chapel on the l. of the high altar is a very fine painting by *Giovanni Bellini* of Our Lord at Emmaus; in the l. transept are tombs of the Cornaros, called Corners in their native city, and between it and the entrance to the ch. the monuments of the doges Girolamo and Lorenzo Priuli, in black marble, after the designs of Cesare Franco, with statues of their patron saints, by *Giulio del Moro* (1559, 1567).

Ch. of *Gli Scalzi*, close to the Rly. Stat., built in 1680, the pride of the Venetians for its richness. *Longhena* was the architect. It abounds in rare and rich marbles, statues, bas-reliefs, and in gilding. Its principal treasure is the beautiful picture behind the high altar—a Madonna and Child, by *Giovanni Bellini*. There are several statues in bad taste; the best are 6 Sibyls by *Montuori*, on each side of the choir.

Ch. of *San Sebastiano*, near the Canale della Giudecca, was built by *F. Castiglione* of Cremona (1506), except the façade, which is attributed to *Sansovino* (1548). It is the burial-place of *Paolo Veronese*. For the inscription to his memory might be substituted the well-known epitaph of Wren, for the church contains some of the best productions in his first manner. The roof is almost covered with his paintings, of which the principal subjects are taken from the Book of Esther, the three compartments representing Esther before Ahasuerus, her Coronation, and the Triumph of Mordecai. Commencing on the rt., at the 1st altar is a St. Nicolas, painted by *Titian* in his 86th year; at the 2nd a Madonna by P. Veronese; at the 4th the Two Maries by the same. The fine monument to Bishop Podocataro is by Sansovino (1556). The Capella Maggiore is entirely painted by P. Veronese, viz. the picture over the altar, of the Virgin and four Saints, the Martyrdom of S. Sebastian on the rt., and of SS. Marcus and Marcellinus on the l. The doors of the organ are also by him; near the latter is his bust by *Bozzetti*; and beneath, a sepulchral slab with a most inflated inscription covering his grave. The roof of the sacristy has a fine series of frescoes of the Coronation of the Virgin, and the Four Evangelists. The Baptism in the Jordan, at the 3rd altar on the l., is also by P. Veronese.

Ch. of *San Stefano*. One of the finest churches in the Pointed style at Venice; it is situated in the Campo of the same name, at a short distance from the Piazza di S. Marco. It was built by the Augustinian friars at the end of the 13th centy. (1294-1320). The fine portal, so rich in ornament, is attributed to the *Dalle Massegne*. The interior consists of a nave and 2 aisles, with a fine wooden roof, and contains numerous sepulchral monuments. Of these, that of Jacopo Suriano, a physician of the 16th centy., in the good cinquecento style, deserves to be noticed. In the centre of the ch. is the slab tomb of Doge Morosini, surnamed il Peleponnesiaco (ob. 1694). The adjoining cloister, now converted into a kind of Monmouth-street market, was erected in 1532: in it is the sarcophagus of Andrea Contarini, Doge in 1367. It was during his reign that the Venetians recovered their supremacy over the Genoese by the victory of Chioggia (1380). Francesco, the last of the Carraras, was buried also here, but no trace remains of his tomb.

The Ch. *de' Tolentini* "is perhaps one of the best works of Scamozzi.

The front is a handsome portico of six Corinthian columns, but the leaves of the capital are uncut—perhaps they have never been finished; and an opening in the middle of the pediment is disagreeable. The inside consists of a nave with three chapels on each side, a transept with a dome at the intersection, and a choir somewhat narrower than the nave."—*Woods.* The design of the façade was, however, altered by *Andrea Tirali*, by whom the building was completed after the death of Scamozzi. In the first chapel on the rt. are two pictures on the side walls, by *il Padovanino*, representing actions of St. Andrea Avellino. And on the side walls of the 3rd chapel are Herod and Herodias, and the Beheading of John the Baptist, by *Bonifazio.* On the l. hand in the principal chapel is a monument to Patriarch Morosini (died 1678), by *Parodi*, a pupil of *Bernini.*

Ch. of *San Trovaso*, or more properly *San Gervasio e San Protasio* : a design of the Palladian school, built in 1583. There are many pictures. In the Chapel of the Holy Sacrament is a rich-sculptured altarpiece in the style of the *Renaissance*, probably by Lombardi. The Crucifixion over the high altar is by *Domenico Tintoretto*; the Temptation of St. Anthony, in a chapel on the l., and the Last Supper, in that of the Sacrament, are by *Jacopo Tintoretto.*

Ch. of *San Zaccaria.* This church is in a remarkable transition style, built between 1456 and 1515, by Antonio di Marco—Gothic in the choir, and semi-Byzantine in the nave. The continuation of the aisle round the great altar in the form of a five-sided tribune, with circular arches below and pointed ones above, is remarkable. The pointed arches are very beautiful. "The western front seems to belong to the latter date, or perhaps has been added still later, but the rest of the building is in a sort of pointed style..... The side aisles are very lofty, the clerestory windows very minute, so that this mode of arrangement seems to have been preserved to the last period of pointed architecture."—*Woods.* The statue of the patron saint over the entrance is by *A. Vittoria.* A fine picture of the Virgin and Child, and four Saints, by *Giovanni Bellini*, stands over the 2nd altar on l. It was taken to Paris, has suffered, and is badly restored, especially in the upper part of the Virgin and Angels. By *Tintoretto* is the Birth of St. John the Baptist. Another painting by *Giovanni Bellini* is the Circumcision, within the choir. The three altars in the side chapel of S. Tarasio are richly decorated with carvings and paintings, and are remarkably valuable specimens of early Venetian art; the Anconas or pictures in compartments over them are by *Ludovico dal Friuli*, and *Giovanni* and *Antonio da Murano* (1443). In the old ch. of S. Zaccaria were interred the 8 doges of Venice who lived between 836 and 1172; in the present one are the monuments of *N*. Sanudo by Leopardi, and of the sculptor Alessandro Vittoria (1595).

San Lazaro, the Armenian convent, stands on its own island, and beyond the precincts of the city. It was founded about the beginning of the last century by the Abbot Mechitar. The ch. and the conventual buildings are models of neatness and good order. Here, as is well known, Lord Byron amused himself by studying the Armenian language; and he has borne full testimony to the merits of the worthy inmates. They have an excellent library, with a great number of curious Oriental manuscripts; and the convent may be regarded as a centre of Armenian literature. They are enabled to print in 24 languages. Many important works, such as the translation of Eusebius, have been printed here, besides the greater portion of the liturgical and other religious books for the use of their widely dispersed co-religionists. The Armenians are amongst the most respectable and opulent native merchants at Calcutta, and they contribute liberally to the support of this national institution. *San Lazaro* is under the protection of Turkey, whose flag floated over it during the siege of 1849.

The *Scuole* of Venice were institutions of a very peculiar nature, and of which the intent could scarcely be collected from their name. They were associations, composed principally of laymen, but acting by authority of the Church, and they effected most of the objects for which our modern benevolent and charitable institutions are founded. They were "Blanket and Clothing Societies;" "Societies for visiting the Poor in their own Habitations;" "Mendicity Societies;" and provided places for boys, and dowries for maidens, of whom more than 1500 are said to have been annually married by their aid. These religious confraternities, of which there were five, became very opulent by the private contributions, gifts, and legacies which were bestowed upon them. The buildings in which they assembled are amongst the most remarkable monuments of ancient Venice; not of the government, but of the people; for the foundations were in the strictest sense voluntary and private.

Of these buildings, perhaps the *Scuola di San Marco* (which stands close to the church of *SS. Giovanni e Paolo*) is the most remarkable. The external decorations are singularly elegant, Byzantine richness blending itself with classical architecture. *Martino Lombardo* has in this building so much surpassed his former productions, that it is conjectured he was assisted by Frate Francesco Colonna, the author of the 'Sogno di Polifilo,' a work in which a great number of very singular and beautiful designs are introduced; and who lived in the adjoining monastery. The present building was erected soon after 1485, when a pre-existing one was destroyed by fire. The sculptures on the façade are by B. Bon and Tullio Lombardo. There is much fine work in the interior, particularly in the carvings of the ceilings. The building is now a part of the great civil hospital, formed also out of the adjoining convent of the Dominicans.

Scuola di San Rocco, near the church of Santa Maria dei Frari. This was begun in 1517, and completed by *Scarpagnino* (1550). The principal front towards the "*Campo*" is by the latter. The fraternity, in 1560, became the patrons of *Tintoretto*, who continued to paint here during 18 years. The lower *Sala* is a magnificent hall, the walls of which are covered with his paintings. The best are the Annunciation, and the Massacre of the Innocents. The others are the Adoration of the Magi, the Flight into Egypt, the Magdalene, Santa Maria Egizziaca, the Circumcision, and the Assumption. The statue of the Patron Saint on the altar is by *Campagna*. On the staircase, the Visitation, also by *Tintoretto;* the Annunciation, by *Titian*. The upper *Sala* is also filled with paintings by *Tintoretto;* of the nine, the Miracle of the Loaves and Fishes, the Last Supper, the Resurrection, may be particularly distinguished for their richness of grouping and invention. The picture at the altar represents S. Rocco in glory, also by *Tintoretto;* the statues at the side, St. John the Baptist and S. Sebastian, are by *G. Campagna*. Round this hall are sculptures in wood; those on the side opposite to the altar are by *Francesco Pianta*, and a certain *Michael Angelo*, of Florence. The ceiling is very fine. The 7 compartments, which are all by *Tintoretto*, contain subjects from the Old Testament, as well as the works in chiaro-scuro on the sides. Over the doorway is the portrait of *Tintoretto*, painted by himself, when he was 66 years of age. In the *Sala dell' Albergo*, so called because the fraternity received their guests here, is the Crucifixion, considered to be his chef-d'œuvre, showing great powers of invention and composition; it is exceedingly injured: the other subjects in this room being Christ before Pilate, our Saviour on Mount Calvary, and the Crowning with Thorns. The paintings on the roof, of St. Roch in glory, as well as all the others in this Sala, are by *Tintoretto*. The adjoining *Ch. of San Rocco* contains many paintings by *Tintoretto*. On the rt.-hand side of the nave is the

Pool of Bethesda.—In a chapel on rt. of high altar, *Titian*, our Lord dragged along by an executioner, much injured. In the chapel of the high altar, 4 large pictures of acts of charity of S. Rocco. This altar is from designs of *Bartolommeo Bon*, as well as the other architectural decorations of this chapel, a fine specimen of the 15th centy. (1495), the only part of the older ch. remaining. On the l. side of the nave,—*Pordenone*, St. Martin and St. Christopher.—*Moschino*, statues of St. Sebastian and Pantaleone.

Accademia delle Belle Arti (open every day from 12 to 3). The building in which the *Academy* is located is the ancient *Convent of la Carità*, and it was one of those upon which Palladio bestowed the greatest study; we have besides the advantage of his own explanation of his design, he having published an account of it in his work on Architecture. He intended that the habitable portion of the convent should represent a Roman mansion, at least according to the idea which (Pompeii being then undiscovered) he was enabled to form of such structures: but it has sustained many misfortunes. The greater part was burnt down in 1630, the only part of Palladio's edifice now standing being a well-proportioned square hall, formerly the sacristy of the ch., and now one of the drawing schools. On the suppression of the convent, the buildings were for some time occupied as a barrack, but in 1807, Napoleon having decreed the formation of an academy of fine arts, they were arranged for that purpose. The Accademia consists of the several schools necessary for such an institution, which occupy the ground floor round the ancient cloister; and of the *Pinacoteca*, consisting of a very extensive collection of pictures, chiefly of the Venetian school, such as is not to be found elsewhere; and though the present appropriation of the building

SKETCH OF THE GROUND-PLAN OF THE PINACOTECA AT VENICE.

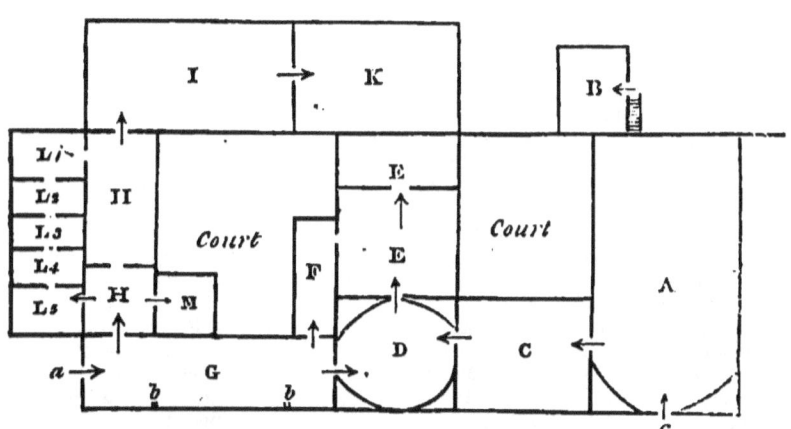

A. Sala dell' Asunta.
B. Collection of Drawings of the Old Masters.
C. Sala delle Antiche Pitture.
D. Vestibule with Statues.
E. 'Pin. Contarini.
F. Wood Sculptures and China.
G. Corridor, with Architectural Drawings.
H. Corridor leading to Sale Nuove.
I. Prima Sala Nuova.

K. Seconda Sala Nuova.
L. Sale Palladiane.
M. Recent acquisitions.

a. Entrance on private days.
b b. Entrance to Halls of Casts.
c. Entrance to S. dell' Asunta from the Campo della Carita.

was intended to preserve it from further degradation, still, to adapt it, several alterations were needed, by which what was left of the original plan and design has been much altered. The *Pinacoteca* is situated on the first floor, in a succession of fine rooms, to which considerable additions have been made of late years. The catalogue recently published gives merely the name of the painter, the subject, and the locality where the painting originally stood. The following are the objects most worthy of the visitor's attention, in the order in which he can best go over the collection.

Entering by the great staircase from the Campo della Caritù, the first hall, the *Sala dell' Assunta* (A), contains the chefs-d'œuvres of the Venetian school: —No. 24. *Titian :* The Assumption of the Virgin, somewhat blackened by candles and incense; it stood over an altar in the church of the Frari. Count Cicognara, suspecting its value, had himself drawn up to it, cleaned a small portion, and, having obtained it from the friars of the church, in exchange for a new and bright painting, placed it in this gallery. "In this picture Titian has employed the whole power of his palette, from its brightest and purest light to its richest and deepest tone. The composition divides itself into 3 compartments of unequal size; the largest in the centre, where is the subject of it, the Assumption of the Virgin. Her action is grand and devout, her character maternal, the arrangement of her drapery such as to produce a full and fine form. It is a glorious work, its power of colour is immense: far beyond that even of any other picture of Titian."—*Phillips, R.A.* — 25. *Tintoretto*, Adam and Eve taking the forbidden Fruit.—26. *Bonifacio*, St. Jerome, St. Margaret.—27. St. Mark.—28. St. Bruno and St. Catherine.—29. St. Barnabas and St. Silvester. These are pictures of great ability.—30. *Andrea Vicentino*, St. Francis receiving the Stigmata, and other Saints—a dignified and excellent specimen of the master; as also 31. *Marco Basaiti;* the Calling of the Sons of Zebedee.—32. *Tintoretto*, the Virgin and Child, with 3 Senators.—33. *Titian*, the Deposition; Titian's last work, when he was 98 years of age, finished by *Palma Giovane.*—34. *Bonifacio*, SS. Antonio and Mauro.—35. *Titian*, the Visitation of St. Elizabeth; Titian's earliest work, said to have been begun when he was only 14 years of age. We have thus here, almost juxtaposed, the works of the great chief of the Venetian school at an interval of more than 80 years; a circumstance unique in the history of painting.—36. *Tintoretto*, the Resurrection.—37. *Giorgione*, St. Mark staying miraculously the Tempest, one of the principal works of imagination of this painter. (See Kugler's *Handbook of Painting.*) The subject of this picture is a story so characteristic of the superstitious age in which it was believed, and so often referred to in the works of art at Venice, that we shall give it here. "In the year 1341 an inundation of many days' continuance had raised the water three cubits higher than it had ever before been seen in Venice, and during a stormy night, while the flood appeared to be still increasing, a poor old fisherman sought what refuge he could find by mooring his crazy bark close to the *Riva di San Marco.* The storm was yet raging, when a person approached and offered him a good fare if he would but ferry him over to *San Giorgio Maggiore.* 'Who,' said the fisherman, 'can reach *San Giorgio* on such a night as this? Heaven forbid that I should try!' But as the stranger earnestly persisted in his request and promised to guard him from harm, he at last consented. The passenger landed, and, having desired the boatman to wait a little, returned with a companion, and ordered him to row to *San Nicolo di Lido.* The astonished fisherman again refused, till he was prevailed upon by a further assurance of safety and excellent pay. At *San Nicolo* they picked up a third person, and then instructed the boatman to proceed to the Two Castles at Lido.

Though the waves ran fearfully high, the old man by this time had become accustomed to them, and, moreover there was something about his mysterious crew which either silenced his fears or diverted them from the tempest to his companions. Scarcely had they gained the strait when they saw a galley rather flying than sailing along the Adriatic, manned (if we may so say) with devils, who seemed hurrying, with fierce and threatening gestures, to sink Venice in the deep. The sea, which had hitherto been furiously agitated, in a moment became unruffled, and the strangers, crossing themselves, conjured the fiends to depart. At the word the demoniacal galley vanished, and the three passengers were quietly landed at the spots at which each respectively had been taken up. The boatman, it seems, was not quite easy about his fare, and, before parting, he implied pretty clearly that the sight of this miracle, after all, would be but bad pay. 'You are right, my friend,' said the first passenger; 'go to the Doge and the *Procuratori*, and assure them that, but for us three, Venice would have been drowned. I am St. Mark, my two comrades are St. George and St. Nicholas. Desire the magistrates to pay you; and add, that all this trouble has arisen from a schoolmaster at *San Felice*, who first bargained with the Devil for his soul, and then hanged himself in despair.' The fisherman, who seems to have had all his wits about him, answered that he might tell that story, but he much doubted whether he should be believed: upon which St. Mark pulled from his finger a gold ring, worth about five ducats, saying, 'Show them this ring, and bid them look for it in my Treasury, whence it will be found missing.' On the morrow the fisherman did as he was told. (See P. Bordone's picture in the first *Sala Nuova*, No. 493.) The ring was discovered to be absent from its usual custody, and the fortunate boatman not only received his fare, but an annual pension to boot. Moreover, a solemn procession and thanksgiving were appointed in gratitude to the three holy corpses which had rescued from such calamity the land affording them burial." —*Ven. Hist.*—38. *Giovanni Bellini,* the Holy Family, with 6 Saints, and 3 Angels playing on musical instruments. —39, 40, *Palma Giovane*, the Vision of 12,000, and the White Horse of the Revelations.—41. *Contarini*, portrait of a Doge.—42. *Bonifacio*, SS. Dominick and James.—43. *Palma Giovane*, S. Francis. — 44. *Paul Veronese*, the Prophet Ezekiel, in chiar'-oscuro.— 45. *Tintoretto*, the Venetian Slave delivered by St. Mark, one of the wonders of this school of painting. All is motion, animation, and energy. It is certainly one of the finest works of Tintoretto.—46. *Paolo Veronese*, Isaiah, in *chiar'-oscuro*.—47. *Padovanino*, the Marriage at Cana; considered his best work.—48. *id.*, a Madonna and Saints. — 49 and 50. *Bonifacio*, St. Francis of Assisi and St. Paul, and the Woman taken in Adultery.—53. Tintoretto, the Virgin with Saints, and the portrait of a Doge.—54. *Bonifacio*, the Judgment of Solomon.— 55. *P. Veronese*, the Virgin above, surrounded by Saints, amongst whom St. Dominick distributing roses, in allusion to the Rosary, and numerous portraits, probably of members of the confraternity for whom it was painted, was, like many of its neighbours, carried off to Paris.—56. *Carlo Caliari*, our Lord bearing his Cross.—57. *Bonifacio*, the Adoration of the Magi.—59. *Palma Vecchio*, the Assumption of the Virgin. (The upper part of the picture is unfinished.)—61. *Leandro Bassano*, the Incredulity of St. Thomas. — 62. *P. Veronese*, Santa Cristina.—63. *Tintoretto*, the Death of Abel. The fine gilt and carved roof of the Sala del Assunta is a splendid specimen, supposed to have been executed by *Fra Cherubino Ottali* in the 15th centy. The painting of St. Nicholas, Bishop of Mira, in the centre, is by *P. Veronese*, and the four Prophets by *D. Campagnola*. Round the cornice are portraits of the most celebrated artists of the Venetian school, by pupils of the Academy.

' Entering on the rt. from the Sala dell' Assunta is

The Sala delle Antiche Pitture (C), containing a very interesting series of the early Venetian school. 1. *Bartolommeo Vivarini* (1464), the Virgin and Saints.—2. *Michele Mattei da Bologna* (about 1469), an Ancona of many compartments.—3. *Michele Giambono* (died about 1450), the Saviour and four Saints.—5. *Lorenzo Veneziano* and *Francesco Bissolo*, dated 1357, another altarpiece in several compartments, the Annunciation in the centre. —4, 6, 7. *Marco Basaiti*, St. James, St. Anthony, and a dead Saviour.—8. *Giovanni* and *Antonio da Murano* (1440), Coronation of the Virgin.—9. *B. Vivarini*, St. Mary Magdalen.—11 and 13. *Vincenzo Catena*, St. Augustin and St. Jerome. The influence of Vivarini on this artist's style is perceptible.— 10, 15, 17-20. *Alvise Vivarini*, the younger, St. Matthew and other Saints. This artist flourished at the close of the 15th centy. He has much of the feeling and colouring of Carpaccio.— 14 and 22. *B. Vivarini*, Sta. Barbara and Sta. Chiara.—16. An altarpiece of many compartments: the central, representing the Coronation of the Virgin, is by Stefano Pievano, with the date 1386. The 8 histories of our Saviour around, by unknown artists, are very primitive and curious. — 22. *Giacomello del Fiore*, the Virgin and two Saints, signed and dated 1436; chiefly interesting as a specimen of a rare artist.—23. *Gio. di Alemagna* and *Antonio da Murano*, the Virgin enthroned, under a canopy supported by Angels, with the four Doctors of the Church by her side. This large picture, dated 1446, is curious. The roof of this hall is an elaborate specimen of very beautiful painted and gilt wood-carving of the Renaissance.

The circular Vestibule (O) beyond the preceding Sala contains a statue of our Saviour by *Tullio Lombardo*; a group of Chiron, a statue of Adonis, and a bust of Titian, by *Rinaldi*, &c.

Several rooms contain works of little interest: of these, some are inferior Flemish pictures, many by unknown artists: most are gifts, and of recent acquisition. Amongst them is

The *Pinacoteca Contarini* (E), a numerous collection of second-rate pictures, formed by a public-spirited nobleman, Count Girolamo Contarini, and bequeathed by him in 1843 to the academy. It consists of more than 270 specimens arranged in 2 rooms. The best are, 94. *Giov. Bellini*, a. Madonna.—96. *Marziali*, the Supper of Emmaus.—117. *Franc. Bessolo*, a Dead Christ.—125. *Cima da Conegliano*, a Madonna with Saints.—132. *Boccaccino da Cremona*, a Virgin and Child with Saints, a specimen of a rare master. In the inner room are a series of small allegorical paintings, 234-238, by Giov. Bellini, which were originally encased in a piece of furniture. In a corridor (F) opening out of the P. Contarini is a collection of sculptures in wood, chiefly ebony, executed by Brustolon, for the patrician Pietro Venier, &c.

In the *Corridors* (H) leading to the Sale Nuove.—295. *Tintoretto*, portrait of Antonio Capello.—300. *Schidone*, a Deposition.—301. *Titian*, head of an old woman, called Titian's Mother.—313. *Giov. Bellini*, a Madonna and Child.— 319. *Titian*, portraits of Jacopo Soranzo; and 350, of Priamo da Lezze.—356. *Antonello da Messina*, the Virgin reading; signed. This picture, having been in the Ducal Palace, appears authentic. About the middle of the 15th centy. this artist repaired to the Netherlands, and there, as it is said, learned Van Eyck's secret in the preparation and use of oil-colours, which knowledge he spread amongst the Venetians. At the extremity of the Corridor open the 2 Sale Nuove, containing the largest works of the Pinacoteca; in each the numbers commence on the wall opposite the entrance.

Prima Sala Nuova (I).—467. *A. Vicentino*, the Deposition.—470 to 478. —*Carlo Caliari*, Angels bearing the instruments of our Lord's Passion.— 475. *D. Tintoretto*, the Crowning with Thorns.—472. *Giorgione*, portrait of a Venetian noble; 476. *Contarini*, a

similar subject; and, 480. the same, by Bassano.—481. Padovanino, the Descent of the Holy Ghost.—489. Carpaccio, the Presentation in the Temple. —488. Titian, the Presentation of the Virgin in the Temple, very fine.—493. Paris Bordone, the Fisherman presenting the Miraculous Ring to the Doge. —497. P. Veronese, SS. Luke and John.—484, 500, 501, 505, 506. Bonifacio, a fine series of the master.—499. Tintoretto, the Assumption.—504. id., the Virgin, with portraits of 4 Senators. —508. Tintoretto, the Virgin in Glory, with SS. Cosmo and Damiano.—521. Bonifacio, the Virgin, with several Saints; and, 525, the Adoration of the Magi.—515. Tintoretto, the Crucifixion, with the 3 Marys; and, 518, Venice, with portraits of 6 Senators.—520. Paolo Veronese, the Virgin with St. Joseph and St. John the Baptist; and 522. Santa Christina forced to worship the Pagan idols. The painting on the roof of Santa Elena discovering the Cross is by G. B. Tiepolo.
Seconda Sala Nuova (K).—529. Donato Veneziano, the Crucifixion.—530. Gentile Bellini, the recovery of the cross dropped into the Canal near San Lorenzo. This is a very interesting picture, and a worthy pendant to the procession, No. 29, for the numerous portraits, and variety of costume, which it exhibits; it was painted in 1500. Amongst other portraits is that of Caterina Cornaro, Queen of Cyprus, a portly dame in black, on the l. of the painting, the only personage wearing a crown.—531, 532. Cima da Conegliano, Justice and Temperance.—533. Martino da Udine, the Annunciation, a picture of tranquil and noble beauty, by this rare master.—534, 538, 540, 543, 545, 547, 550, 553, 560, 561. V. Carpaccio; this series of paintings represent the history of St. Ursula and the 11,000 virgins, and were formerly in the Scuola of the Saint at Venice.— 536. Bartolommeo Montagna, our Lord between St. Roch and St. Sebastian.— 544.—Gentile Bellini, a Sanctuary.— 546. Lazzaro Sebastiani (a scholar of Carpaccio), the miraculous Appearance of the Holy Cross to Antonio Riccio.—

548. P. Veronese, our Saviour in the house of Levi; an immense picture, only second in size to the Marriage of Cana, in the Louvre, covering one end of the hall.—549. Giovanni Mansueti, miracle of the Holy Cross. Like Sebastiani, Mansueti was a scholar of Carpaccio, and his works also chiefly relate to the miracles supposed to have been wrought by means of the Cross.—552. Seb. Florigerio, 4 Saints, and the Madonna, with St. Augustin and Sta. Monaca.—556. Gentile Bellini, procession and Miraculous Cure in the Piazza di San Marco; very interesting, as showing the state of the piazza in 1491, and exhibiting the costume of the period in many animated figures. It bears the author's name, GENTILIS BELLINI VENETI EQUITIS, CRUCIS AMORE INCENSUS, OPUS 1491.—35. Vivarini, the Virgin and Child, with 4 Saints.—565. Carpaccio, a miracle performed by the Patriarch of Grado, healing a Demoniac by means of the relics of the Cross. There is a curious view of the old Ponte di Rialto in this picture. — 357. Florigero, Madonna with SS. Augustine and Monica.—563. Martino da Udine, a Madonna; and 564, an Annunciation.

A series of five rooms, called the Sale Palladiane (L), opening out of the corridor leading to the Sale Nuove, contain a very miscellaneous collection of smaller pictures, for the most part very second-rate.—ROOM [1]. 456, Cima da Conegliano, Our Saviour and two Saints; 441, 464, Tintoretto, two portraits; 443, Jacopo Bellini, a Madonna; 452, Garofalo, Virgin in Glory with Saints; a bust of the present Emperor of Austria has been lately placed here at the expense of the Venetian Academicians, and on the occasion of his escape from assassination.—ROOM [2] contains the collection bequeathed to the Academy by Countess Renier; 429, Cima da Conegliano, a Dead Christ; 430, V. Carpaccio, a Virgin and Child; 435, Bissolo, a Madonna with St. John; 436, Giov. Bellini, the Virgin with S. Catherine and the Magdalen.— ROOM [3]. 394, Semeticolo, N., the Virgin enthroned (1351); 410, *Jacopo Avanzi*, a Deposition (1367); 404, *A. Busati*, a Madonna; 407, *Jacopo da Valesa*, a Virgin and Child with Saints, signed and dated 1309, of a very rare master. —ROOM⁴. 387, *B. Vivarini*, Virgin and Child; 373, 374, 375, 389, 391, 393, *Lorenzo Veneziano*, an Annunciation (1371), and 5 Saints, which once formed a single Ancona; 381, *Andrea da Murano*, S. Sebastian; 382, *Gentile da Fabriano*, a Madonna.— ROOM⁵. 372, *Giov. Bellini*, Virgin and Child; 366, TITIAN, St. John in the Desert, a noble and vigorously drawn figure, in his best manner and colouring; 367, *Bassano*, a Holy Family; 368, *Bonifacio*, the Adoration of the Magi; 360, *Vigri Caterina*, Sta. Ursula and Virgins, signed and dated 1456.

The *Bossi* collection belonging to this Academy contains many and beautiful drawings by *Raphael*, *Michael Angelo*, *Leonardo da Vinci*. They are kept in a room (B) near the Sala dell' Asunta, open to the public on Tues. and Sat.

The *Sala delle Radunanze Accademiche*, or room in which the Academy holds its meetings, is a noble apartment, with 20 small paintings of Angels, Evangelical Symbols, &c., by *Titian*. Over the chair of the president is a vase of porphyry, containing the right hand of Canova, with his chisel above.

The *Pinacoteca Manfredini* is deposited in the buildings of the Ecclesiastical Seminary attached to the ch. of *Santa Maria della Salute* (see p. 369), to which establishment it was bequeathed by its late owner. It contains amongst other pictures a portrait of Pietro Aretino by *Titian*; a head of St. John the Baptist by *A. Durer*; a Holy Family by *L. da Vinci*, bearing the arms of the Sforza Pallavicinis; an Annunciation by *Daniele da Volterra*; a Virgin and Child by *Fra Bartolommeo*, and a Deposition by *Pietro Perugino* (?); some fine sketches by *Correggio* for the frescoes of the Duomo of Parma. The cloister of the Seminary is filled with monuments and inscriptions saved from demolished and desecrated churches, amongst which the sepulchral urn of Doge F. Dandolo, of the 14th centy., and the gravestone of the painter Giacomello del Fiore (1433). The keys of the gates of Padua, brought away when it was seized by the Venetians, are hung upon one of the walls.

Theatres. The principal theatre is *la Fenice*, originally built in 1791, but burned down in 1836. It is handsome and of a good size. It is open during the carnival, *i. e.* during the early months of winter, and sometimes in the spring, for the performance of operas and ballets. The office for places is, during the day, situated about the middle of the Procuratie Vecchie. The price of admission is 3 zwanzigers.

The next theatre after the Fenice is the *Teatro Gallo*, so called from the name of its proprietor, also known by the name of *Teatro San Benedetto*. In autumn, winter, and spring, a company, usually second-rate, perform operas at this theatre. When the Fenice is shut the performances are rather better.

The *Teatro Apollo, a San Luca*, is generally open for the drama.

The *Teatro San Samuele* is rarely open. It is a pretty theatre, well adapted for hearing. Opera buffas are performed here.

The *Teatro Malibran* is near the Rialto. It is opened during the day, evening, or night. It is large. The amusements consist of rope-dancing, sword-swallowing, and such-like performances.

The *Giardino Publico*, or Public Promenade, occupying the triangular space at the E. extremity of Venice, was laid out by the French, but has been extended and improved of late years. Its distance causes it to be little resorted to. The views from it over the Lido and the Islands are fine.

Artesian Wells—Supply of water.— Several Artesian wells have been sunk at Venice (in 1847), at the expense of the municipality, and under the direction of a French engineer, M. Degoussée. Situated in the midst of a salt marsh, Venice had hitherto been dependent on its cisterns for fresh water, or on its being brought from the mainland in large flat-bottomed boats, attended with great expense. M. Degoussée, who had executed several works of this kind in France, was led from geological considerations to conclude that an ample supply of fresh water might be obtained, at an inconsiderable depth and expense, and the result has fully confirmed his previsions. Before the Revolutionary movement in 1848 no less than seven Artesian wells were pouring forth unceasing streams of fresh water, and supplying fountains in several of the squares of Venice; and although at first prejudices were raised against it, from its slightly chalybeate quality, it has come into general use, and is greatly superior to that of ill-kept cisterns, or of the muddy rivers of the mainland. It will interest the traveller to visit some of these fountains, spouting on the borders of the Laguna, as in the Piazzas of Santa Maria Formosa, of the Gesuiti, &c. The water contains a small quantity of iron and some vegetable matter, the latter derived from the peaty stratum through which it filters. It is supposed, with great probability, that the water which rises to the surface through these borings has fallen in the form of rain upon the mountains bordering on the Lago di Garda. It has been lately proposed to carry into Venice, by means of pipes laid on the Rly. viaduct, an additional supply of water from the river Sele.

Plan for visiting the Sights at Venice and its Environs in six days, in topographical order.

1st day.—Piazza di S. Marco; Cathedral of S. Marco; Campanile; Ducal Palace, its Library, Collections, &c.; Zecca; Chs. of S. Giorgio de' Greci and S. Zaccaria; Campo della Bragola.

2nd day.—Ch. of Sta. Maria Formosa; Pal. Grimani; Chs. of S. Maria de' Miracoli, S. Salvatore; Ponte di Rialto'; Chs. of S. Giacomo di Rialto, SS. Giovanni e Paolo; Scuola di S. Marco, and Hospital; Ch. of i Jesuiti: returning by the Canals to the Ch. of Sta. Maria dei Frari; Archives; Scuola di S. Rocco; Chs. of S. Pantaleone and Il Carmine; house of Othello.

3rd day.—Chs. of S. Mosé and S. Stefano; Accademia delle Belle Arti; Ch. of Sta. Maria della Salute and Pinacoteca Manfredini; Chs. of S. Giorgio Maggiore, i Gesuati, S. Trovaso, and S. Sebastiano. Cross to the Island of La Giudecca: Ch. of Il Redentore.

4th day.—Arsenal; Ch. of S. Pietro di Castello; Giardino Pubblico; rounding from the Isola di S. Pietro to the Island of Murano; Public Cemetery; Chs. of S. Michele and S. Pietro Martire: returning to Venice by the Ch. of Sta. Maria in Orto; Pal. Manfrini; Ch. of i Scalzi; Museo Correr (Wed. and Sat.); and excursion down the Great Canal to the Piazzetta di S. Marco; Merceria.

5th day.—Excursion to Murano, if not previously seen, and Torcello.

6th day.—Excursion to the Islands of S. Giorgio, S. Lazzaro, the Lido, Malamocco, and Chioggia.

EXCURSIONS IN THE NEIGHBOURHOOD OF VENICE.

Some of the islands round Venice contain objects well deserving of a visit. They may be easily reached in a gondola. To Murano in half an hour; to Torcello in 1½ hours.

Murano is the largest, and was formerly the most flourishing, with a Pop. of 4500. The distance from the N. of the city is scarcely a mile. It is well known that the glass manufactures of Murano were the most renowned in Europe, not only during the middle ages, but even till the beginning of the present centy. Mirrors, flasks, drinking-cups, and an infinite variety of small articles for which Venice was so celebrated, were made here. At present it is carried on in six establishments, employing about 1000 hands, beads for the Eastern market and coloured glass constituting the principal articles manufactured.

The chief objects of interest at Murano are—

The *Duomo* or Cathedral, and the church of *St. Pietro Martire*.

"In the year 1125 Domenico Michael, 34th Doge of Venice, took the island of Cephalonia on his return from the Holy Land, and brought from thence the body of San Donato, once Bishop of Evorea, in Epirus. This treasure he deposited in the ancient church of *Sta. Maria*, at Murano. The probability is that the church was entirely rebuilt soon after this transaction, as the style of its architecture is in accordance with that of the 12th centy. The eastern apse exhibits one of the richest specimens of external decoration in the Lombard style. From the veneration of the saint the church of *Sta. Maria* was soon called *S. Donato*. In front of the high altar is a bas-relief of *San Donato*, carved in wood, which was executed by some Venetian artist at the beginning of the 14th centy."— *G. Knight*.

The vaulting over the altar, covered with gold, contains only one figure, a lengthened, ghastly Virgin, in the stiffest Byzantine style, with the Greek monogram, not later than the 12th cent. The columns which separate the nave from the two aisles are of white marble, with Corinthian capitals, and, like those of Torcello, were probably brought from the ruins of *Altinum*. The pavement resembles that of St. Mark. It exhibits various patterns; many are like what are found in the Roman tesselated pavements. An inscription in the centre gives us the exact date (1140). In other parts the church has been modernised. Behind the high altar is the curious wooden bas-relief above mentioned, of San Donato, including the portraits of the Podestà Memmo and his wife, dated 1310, and said to be amongst the earliest known specimens of the Venetian school, as the inscription is one of the oldest in the Venetian dialect. Before leaving this church, the visitor will do well to observe the outside of the pentagonal tribune, with its double row of rounded arches in the Arabo-Lombard style, and which by some is supposed to date as far back as the 10th centy.

The church of *S. Pietro Martire*, erected in the 15th centy., contains a picture of *Giov. Bellini*, a Madonna with two Saints, with the portrait of the Donor, Doge A. Barberigo (1488).

Between the group of islands of Murano and the N. part of Venice is the small island of S. Michele, on which stands the church of *San Michele di Murano*, erected in the 15th cent. by the architect Moro or Moretto. It is rich both within and without. The inscription to the memory of the Greek monk Eusebius was composed by Aldus Manutius; the ornaments which surround it are remarkable. The sepulchral slab which covered the grave of Fra Paolo Sarpi; it formerly stood in the church of the Servites at Venice, and was removed here after its desecration in 1796; the friars, however, to please the clergy, effaced the inscription, which the authorities have obliged them to restore. It is in the pavement close to the door. The statues on the monument of Doge G. Delfino are by *Bernini*. Connected with the church is the Capella Emiliana, a beautiful structure, by *Guglielmo Bergamasco*, built about 1530. The church of S. Michele formed a part of the large conventual establishment of the Camaldolese monks, which existed from 1210 until its suppression in 1810; it has now been transferred to the Franciscans, and the grounds of the monastery converted into the great public cemetery of Venice. Frate Mauro, the celebrated geographer (see p. 350) of the 15th centy., was a member of this community, and here he composed his celebrated Mappe-monde;

and in our own times the enlightened Cardinal Zurla, the historian of the Venetian Navigators, and the late Pope, Gregory XVI., as Fra Mauro Cappellari.

4 m. beyond Murano are the *Isola di Mazorbo* and *Isola di Burano*.—These islands contain much garden-ground: a large proportion of the vegetables consumed at Venice are grown upon them. The Inhab., about 5000, of whom one-half are fishermen, are industrious, and preserve some features of the ancient character of the Venetians. Beyond Burano, forming one of the same group, is

The *Isola di Torcello*.—" Torcello was the parent island of the Venetian states; the spot to which the unfortunate inhabitants of Altinum and Aquileia fled for safety when their homes were made desolate by the northern invaders. Torcello thus peopled became a town, and had its cathedral and its bishops, long before the existence of *St. Mark's*." Others sought refuge here from the desolating and persecuting arms of the Arian Lombards; and to escape their yoke Paul Bishop of Altino translated his see here about the year 635, taking with him the relics and treasures of the cathedral which he abandoned. The city seems to have decayed as early as the 11th centy.; but the succession of the Episcopal see continued until the revolution, as well as the *republic*. There was a podestà and senate of Torcello, in whom all the rights of the ancient community were vested, and who, amongst other privileges, conferred titles of nobility on such as were willing, like our primitive baronetcy, to assist the treasury of the state—in this instance, by the payment of ten zecchini, somewhat about five pounds sterling.—" In process of time Torcello was enriched with the remains of Sa. Fosca, a virgin of noble birth, who, together with her nurse, Maura, had, during the persecution of Decius, earned the palm of martyrdom at Ravenna, her native city.   *   *   *   *
The time at which the body of Sa. Fosca was brought to Torcello, and consequently the exact date of this building, is unknown; but the church must have existed before the year 1011, because in that year, as is proved by a deed cited by Cornelius, two sisters, Maria and Bona, natives of Torcello, endowed the church of Sa. Fosca with certain lands. The building itself presents all the appearance of remote antiquity. Upon the whole, we may safely assume that it is at least as old as the 10th centy. The plan of this building, whenever it was erected, must have been imported from the East; for Sa. Fosca is not a Latin Basilica, but the square church of the Greeks, surmounted by the Oriental cupola. The capitals of the pillars of the porticoes by which it is surrounded are very peculiar; neither formed after Roman models, nor admitting Lombard imagery. These were also probably of Byzantine extraction. The interior is gracefully designed, consisting of a peristyle of insulated columns and piers, which together support the dome. The church underwent restoration at different times—in 1247, and again at a later period; but the original character of the building has been preserved." *G. Knight.*

Near to the church of S. Fosca stands the Duomo, or *Cathedral of Torcello*, in the same state in which it was rebuilt in the beginning of the 11th centy., by Orso, Bishop of Torcello, and son of the celebrated Dogo Pietro Orseolo. This edifice neither resembles its Lombard contemporaries nor its Byzantine neighbour, but might be thought more ancient than it really is, as it is built on the Latin plan, and in the more Roman style of the old basilicas. The fact is that the Venetians, from their maritime and commercial pursuits, were always accustomed rather to look abroad than to Lombardy for their models; and if this cathedral is in the Roman and not in the Byzantine style (as were most of the Venetian buildings), it perhaps was copied from a church still existing on the opposite shores of the gulf—the cathedral of Parenzo, in Istria, which was built in the 6th centy., and to which the cathedral of Torcello bears a strong resemblance.

"The chancel of the cathedral of Torcello is very remarkable. In this instance, behind the principal apse, there are 5 additional apses, separated from the sanctuary by an intervening aisle, introducing a change which places the choir very much in that insulated position which it occupies in later buildings. Nor is this the only peculiarity of this chancel. The principal apse in this instance, and in this alone, has internally the appearance of a theatre. 8 semicircular steps of white marble rise above each other, forming seats for the clergy of different degrees, and conducting, as it were, to the bishop's throne, which occupies the central spot at the summit."—*G. Knight.*

The vaulting of the chancel is covered with figures of the Apostles in mosaic: above is that of our Lord, of the 12th centy. At the opposite end of the church, over the principal entrance, are a series of mosaic compartments of an earlier period, probably Byzantine, remarkably bright and crude. They are arranged in six rows, and represent the Crucifixion; Limbo or Hades; Christ in glory surrounded by Angels; the Last Judgment, where Kings and Emperors are introduced as usual, their costume Byzantine; Hell and Heaven, or the Happiness of the Blessed and Punishment of the Wicked. The Virgin on the arch of the door is of the same period. As works of art they are curious, because, like the monkish tales of equal merit, they must have been designed to excite the devotions of the pious, and the fears of the wicked. The choir retains its original reading-desks of marble, and the enclosure of marble worked in Greek patterns. The Pala or altar-table, of embossed silver, is of Greek workmanship; only some few compartments remain, and these are now affixed over the entrance of the choir. In a chapel on the l. of the choir are also some curious mosaics of the 11th and 12th centuries, with Latin inscriptions. The windows are not the least curious part of the structure. They were closed by slabs of stone. Some of the windows are now glazed, but those on the S. side of the ch. remain unchanged. The crypt is older than the ch., probably of the 7th centy.; it is semicircular, and surrounded by niches. The bell-tower, which stands quite detached from the ch., beyond the eastern end, may be ascended without difficulty. From the top a fine view is obtained of the Alps and of the Adriatic : and the character of the N. portion of the Lagoon, and of the islands in it, may be well observed from it.

Amongst the other curiosities of Torcello is the Palazzo del Commune, of the 13th cent., and a massive stone chair, standing in an open field, and called the "*Throne of Attila.*" It is perhaps the seat in which the chief magistrates of Torcello were inaugurated. About 6 m. from Torcello, through intricate canals, is the village of *Altino,* near one of the branches of the *Sele* where it enters the Lagoon; it is now a poor place, and, although occupying the site of the once-flourishing *Altinum,* offers nothing to attract the traveller.

The Lagoon, immediately opposite to Venice, is closed by a long sandy island, extending from the Pass of the Lido to that of Malamocco. The N.E. entrance into the Lagoon is protected by the *Forte di S. Nicolo,* constructed by Sanmicheli. The plan of the fortress is a pentagon; and the foundations were not laid without great difficulty. Sanmicheli was much censured, and it was bruited about that the edifice was insecure. Such an accusation might have cost the architect his head, but the senate, as the story goes, determined to *prove* the fortress. The 40 embrasures were mounted with the largest guns, double charged, and all were fired simultaneously, but not a stone was moved, and Sanmicheli's detractors were dismissed with deserved contumely.

The shore of this Litorale, towards the Adriatic, constitutes the *Lido,* now associated with the name of Byron, as the spot where he used to take his rides, and where he intended to have been buried. Tombs there are already; ancient Jewish sepultures, moss-grown, and half covered with drifted sand, adding to the gloomy feeling of the solitude; the few trees are old and stunted, the vegetation is harsh and arid, all around seems desolate. The sunrise as seen from here is magnificent. The Lido is much frequented during the bathing season, Aug. and Sept. The bathing is excellent. A steamer runs to it several times a day from the Piazetta.

Excursion to Chioggia; in Venetian, *Chiozza.*—During the summer, on Sundays and other days, steamboats frequently make excursions to Chioggia, leaving Venice between 9 and 10 a.m., and returning between 6 and 7 p.m. The distance between Venice and Chioggia is about 20 m., which is performed in 2 hrs. It is an excursion worth making, as thereby a good general view of the Lagoon, S. of Venice, of the small islands studded in it, and of the 2 long ones which separate the Lagoon from the Adriatic, is obtained. Chioggia, too, preserves those features of a fishing and mercantile settlement amid the waters, which in Venice disappeared under the splendour of the Capital. The excursion can hardly be made in the same day in a gondola, because even with 2 rowers between 4 and 5 hrs. would be required for the voyage.

The steamer, leaving her moorings opposite to the Riva dei Schiavoni, proceeds down the Orfano Canal, leaving on the l. the islands on which are the lunatic asylum, and S. Lazzaro which contains the Armenian convent, and on the rt. La Grazia: then entering the canal of S. Spirito, it passes on the l. S. Clemente and S. Spirito, and on the rt. the Lazzaretto di Poveglia. It then runs nearer to the long island of the Lido, where the pass bends round close to the village of Malamocco, which gives its name to this part of the channel. Further on, opposite the Fort Alboroni, which is at the extremity of the island, and guards the Malamocco entrance on the N., the steamer passes out from the Lagoon into the Adriatic by the Malamocco Pass, as there is no deep channel inside of the island of Palestrina. Extensive moles, formed with large blocks of stone brought from Istria, are seen on each side of the Malomocco entrance: these have been made of late years in order to increase the scour at the ebbing of the tide by contracting the width of the channel, and thereby produce a greater depth in the pass, and which has succeeded so well that vessels drawing 20 feet water can now enter the Lagunes through it. On entering the Adriatic the steamer coasts along and at a short distance from the long island of Palestrina, on which are a succession of small towns, S. Pietro in Volta Portosecco, and Pelistrina, a town of 7000 Inhab. The entrance to the Porto di Chioggia is wide, but not deep, protected on the S. by the Fort of *S. Felice:* the steamer enters, but it is necessary to disembark in boats.

Chioggia consists of a long and wide straight street, extending the whole length of the island on which the town is built, with smaller ones branching off from this at right angles. On the seaward side are canals, streets, and alleys filled with boats, masts, nets, and the usual implements of a fishing town. A wide arm of the Lagoon separates the town from the long bank or island which here divides the Lagoon from the open sea. On this island is the small town of *Sotto Marina,* between whose inhabitants and those of Chioggia there exist great rivalry and jealousy. In the principal street of Chioggia are several churches, two of considerable size, but having a faded and dilapidated appearance. There is also a mixture of large houses with small, and a few cafés, whose style is by no means splendid. At the end of this street a long low bridge of numerous small arches connects the town with the adjacent island. The population is engaged in the coasting trade, in fishing, and in piloting vessels into the harbour of Venice. Chioggia has a reputation for the beauty of its women, who are said to have furnished the models of the fine figures of the Venetian painters. The people of Chioggia are very proud of their descent: they are remarkable for their attention to dress. The Mantilla and Zendale may still be seen there, and the regular old Italian story-teller heard in the street. Goldoni's account of the inhabitants in his day drolly hints their decline in prosperity :—" In questo paese si divide tutta la populazione in due classi: ricchi, o poveri. Quelli che portano una parrucca ed un mantello, sono i ricchi; quelli che non hanno che un berretto, ed un cappotto, sono i poveri, e bene spesso questi ultimi hanno quattro volte più danaro degli altri."

In the voyage from the pass of Malamocco to that of Chioggia, the voyager will have an opportunity of seeing the Murazzi or great sea-walls, the object of which is to protect the long sandy spits that separate the Laguna from the Adriatic from the inroads of the latter; they consist of a great embankment of huge blocks of Istrian stone, rising 15 ft. above high water, presenting an inclined surface outwardly, or in the form of stairs; the whole length of the Murazzi, including those on the island of Sotto Marina, where they can be best seen, is 5720 yds. or 3¼ m.; they are a comparatively modern work, commenced in 1741, and completed in 1782; the slope towards the sea is as 1 to 4; the width of this pyramidal structure at its base, on the level of the sea, is 45 ft.

In returning from Chioggia to Venice, in the afternoon, the sunset as seen over the Lagoon, with the Euganean hills and the Veronese mountains in the distance through the golden haze, is very fine.

The traveller who wishes to proceed to Ravenna can do so from Chioggia, but it is an uninteresting route, and must be performed under circumstances of much discomfort, in a great part by canals. This route is fully described under Rte. 83 in this volume. The distance is nearly 90 miles.

N. Italy—1860.

ROUTE 32.

MANTUA TO PADUA, BY LEGNAGO, ESTE, MONTAGNANA, MONSELICE, AND ABANO.

POSTS.	POSTS.
1¼ Nogara.	1¼ Este.
1¼ Legnago.	1 Monselice.
1¼ Montagnana.	1¼ Padua.

8¼ Austrian posts=72¼ m.

Quitting Mantua by the *Porta di San Giorgio*, the road continues among the marshes; but the soil shows great fertility.

Castellaro.

Bonferraro. — In the church is a painting of the Immaculate Conception, by *Casti*, a second-rate artist. Cross the *Tartaro*, upon the l. bank of which is

1¾ *Nogara*, a good-sized town. Of the once strong and celebrated castle some ruins remain: it has an interest from its connection with the history of the Emperor Henry IV., who sought refuge in it during his contests with his son Conrad. *Palazzo Marogna* has a fine gateway; and parts of the walls are painted by *Brusasorzi*. The ancient churches of *San Silvestro* and *San Pietro* are worth visiting; but the latter has been modernised.

Sanguinetto: here also are the remains of a feudal castle. The road from here to Legnago skirts on the rt. an extensive marshy district, called the *Valli grandi Veronesi*, situated in the space between the Adige and the Po. Many attempts have been made to drain it, but hitherto in vain: a new project

s

has been lately sanctioned by the Austrian authorities, the government advancing a large sum towards its execution, which will, if successful, add a large tract of most fertile land to the province of Verona.

Cerea, a large straggling town of near 6000 Inhab., once an independent community, with the remains of an ancient castle. In the church of the *Vergine del Carmine* is a good painting by *Brusasorci*.

1½ *Legnago*, situated upon the Adige. Pop. 6000. The fortifications are remarkable, as having been in part planned and executed by *Sanmicheli*, the architect who most contributed to the invention of the art of modern military fortification. One of the gates designed by him, and of great beauty, has been pulled down, and partly rebuilt in another situation. Legnago is now one of the strongholds of Austria in Venetian-Lombardy, only second to Verona, Mantua, and Palma Nova, commanding as it does with the first the line of the Adige. It is one of the great markets of N. Italy for agricultural produce.

Bevilacqua; the capital of an ancient feudal barony. The castle was built in 1354, by a Count di Bevilacqua, who obtained a grant of the fullest rights of sovereignty; and who intended to render his "Rocca" worthy of his authority. It became a position which was often contested, and hence, after the peace of Cambrai, its then owner, Giovanni Francesco Bevilacqua, caused it to be dismantled and partly demolished. The portion of the edifice which remained, including 4 towers, was converted into a splendid palace. The great cortiles and the massive ornaments of rustic work unite picturesquely with the towers and drawbridges that yet subsist. The statues and architectural ornaments are beautifully executed; but the whole is exceedingly dilapidated, having suffered much during the revolutionary wars.

1¼ *Montagnana* (pop. 8200), remarkable as presenting a fine specimen of mediæval fortification, vast walls and lofty towers, all of the finest brickwork. The circuit towers are open towards the town: those which flank the gateways are lofty. A cross *fleurée* and *bottonée* appears conspicuously over the portals. In the town are some good old churches. One in the great square or Piazza is of the Italian-Gothic of the 14th centy., partly altered into the cinquecento style. The road from Montagnana to Este is heavy and sandy, in consequence of which the postmaster is entitled to add a third horse. The country, however, continues as rich as possible; vines in festoons, hemp with stalks as tall as small trees, and gourds of great diameter.

Saletto.

Ospetaletto. The fine range of the Euganean hills rise more and more as we advance.

1¼ ESTE.—(*Inn*: La Speranza, a small quiet house, clean and good.) Beautifully situated at the foot of the *Monte Murale* or *Monte Cero*, which forms the S. extremity of the Euganean group of hills. The "*Rocca*," or Castle of Este, is a fine and almost unaltered building, erected in 1343 by Ubertino Carrara, and repaired by the Scaligers during their temporary possession of it; a noble dungeon tower, with frowning embrasures and battlements, and standing at least upon the site of the original fortress, the seat of the family of Este, so celebrated in history. Alberto Azzo (born 996) must be considered as the more immediate founder of the house here on the death of the Emperor Henry III. The ancestry of Alberto may be traced in history to Bonifazio Duke or Marquis of Tuscany, in 811. Poetry carries it much higher. The magician, in the vision of the enchanted shield, enables Rinaldo to behold Caius Attius as his remote ancestor:—

" Mostragli Caio allor, ch' a strane genti
Va prima in preda il già inclinato Impero.
Prendere il fren de' popoli volenti,
E farsi d' Este il Principe primiero;
E a lui ricoverarsi i men potenti
Vicini, a cui Rettor facea mestiero,
Poscia, quando ripassi il varco noto,
A gli inviti d' Honorio il fero Goto."
Orlando Furioso.

Alberto Azzo, Marquis of Este, was twice married. His first wife was Cunegunda, a princess of the Suabian line, by whom he had Guelph Duke of Bavaria (succeeded 1071), and from whom all the branches of the House of Brunswick are descended.

Fulco I., Marquis of Italy and Lord of Este, the son of Alberto Azzo, by his second wife Garisenda, daughter of Herbert Count of Maine, was the founder of the Italian branch, from which the dukes of Ferrara and Modena descended; the male line of which became extinct at the end of the last century. The deposed Duke of Modena, who is of the House of Hapsburg-Lorraine, represents that of Este in the female line, his grandmother, Maria Beatrix, having been the last descendant of the Italian branch. Este continued in the possession of the descendants of Alberto until 1294, when it fell an easy conquest to the Carraras. Successively a dependency of Padua and of the Verona Scaligers, it passed to Venice in 1405, retaining its local government and municipal institutions.

The town of Este contains more than 10,000 Inhab. It has a Lombard aspect ; most of the houses are supported by picturesque arches. The exterior of the church of *San Martino* bears the appearance of high Romanesque antiquity, but the interior is modernised; in that of Sta. Maria delle Grazie is a Madonna by *Cima da Conegliano*. The campanile, in the same style, inclines as much as the leaning tower of Pisa. A fine belfry tower, with forked battlements, and a *Dondi* clock (see *Padua*) of the largest size, add to the antique adornments of this mediæval town. The hills all the way from beyond Este, sometimes nearer to, and sometimes more distant from the road, are very picturesque. The road follows the canal, leading the whole way, at the foot of the Eugancan hills, by *Merendole* on the l. to

1 *Monselice*, a town commanded by a *rocca*, or castle, of the 13th century, even more feudal in aspect than Este. Pop. 5400. It stands upon a noble rock. It has no dungeon, but long ranges of curtain walls with *stepped* battlements, studded with bold crenellated towers. They ascend and descend the hill-sides, intermingled with the richest vegetation. Monselice was a place of importance in the middle ages : in the 10th century it became a feudal possession of the House of Este, even before they had acquired the town whose name they subsequently adopted (1165). The hill of the Rocca, from which the town derives its name—mountain of silex, or more properly of paving-stone—is formed of a variety of *trachyte* or volcanic porphyry, known by the local designation of *masegna*, which is extensively quarried for building purposes. The palace on the hill belonging to the Duodo family, the church, and the 7 detached chapels in imitation of the 7 basilicas of Rome, were built from the designs of *Scamozzi*. There were some paintings by *Palma Giovane* in the church. In the Villa Cromer is preserved one of Canova's earliest works, a statue of Esculapius. All the country through which the road passes is exceedingly rich, but intersected by muddy canals. Monselice will be the best point to diverge from the main road to visit *Arqua*. The postmaster considers himself entitled to charge one post and a half, there and back, for this excursion, although the distance is less than 5 m.; but if the traveller professes indifference, he will be contented with 1 post, going and returning included.

Excursion to *Arqua*. This place is beautifully situated amongst the Euganean hills; here Petrarch retreated, dwelt, and died. The house shown was very probably his habitation, for as far back as 1650 the tradition was firmly believed : the paintings on the walls, of which the subjects are taken from his poems, date from the preceding centy.; and there is nothing in the architecture (Petrarch died in 1374) inconsistent with the story. It is inhabited by a farmer, and is somewhat

s 2

dilapidated. Here is Petrarch's chair, and his inkstand, in which you may dip your pen and add to the nonsense in the album. Petrarch's cat, or *"miccia,"* as he used to call her (and as all cats are still called in Italy), is here, stuffed, and in a small niche. The tomb of the Laureate, of the same form as that of Antenor at Padua (see p. 311), like it stands on 4 stumpy pillars in the chyard. It is of red Verona marble, and was raised by Francesco di Brossano, the husband of Francesca, one of the illegitimate children of the poet. The inscription is by Petrarch himself. Above is a bronze bust, placed there in 1677. The *Pozzo di Petrarca*, a walled cistern, is said to have been built at his expense for the use of the town. In the village church are two paintings attributed to Palma Giovane and Paul Veronese. Near Arqua is a spring, called (from the late viceroy) the *Fonte del Vicerè Rainieri*: its waters are strongly sulphurous. Very good figs and wine (for this country at least) are grown near Arqua, and may be had at the little *osteria* in the town.

Instead of returning to Monselice the traveller going to Padua may, by a cross road, join the post-road at Rivello 1 m. before reaching

Battaglia, with a good hotel, the *Albergo di Battaglia*, close to the high road, upon the canal of Monselice: it has some thermal springs, which are now in great vogue and much frequented in July and Aug. About 1 m. beyond Battaglia, on the l. of the road, is the castle of *Catajo*, which was bequeathed by its former proprietor, the Marquis Obizzi, to the Duke of Modena, upon condition that he should keep it in its present state. The old part of the castle may always be seen; it contains some frescoes, said to be by *Paul Veronese*. The designs are possibly by him, but the frescoes must have been executed by his scholars; they are very careless and slight. The museum, which is extensive, contains a vast collection of old armour and warlike weapons, ill-arranged; early inscriptions of the ch.; and some other curious antiques and relics.

About 2 m. on the rt. of the road after leaving Battagalia is *Carrara di S. Stefano*, once celebrated for its Benedictine Monastery founded in 1027. Several of the Carraras were buried in the ch. Marsilio, who died in 1330, has a monument in white marble, with reliefs of the Virgin, SS. Antony and Benedict. On a pilaster upon the S. wall of this edifice is an inscription in Lombard characters relative to the death of Ubertino Carrara in 1365, in which the family is designated by the name of *Papafava*, lords of Carrara and Padua. The bell-tower bears the date of 1293. The monastery was suppressed in 1777, and sold by the Venetian government to the Erizzo family.

Abano may be visited either from Padua or from Battaglia, being at an equal distance, about 6 Eng. m., from both. There are two very fair inns here, especially during the summer season, the Albergo dell Orologio and le Due Torri. Its baths have retained their celebrity from the time of the Romans; medals and other remains of antiquity are found here in abundance: the place is also remarkable as being the birthplace of Livy, of Valerius Flaccus, and of Pietro d'Abano, in whom the Paduans take almost equal pride. "This village is about 3 m. from the Euganean Hills; and the houses occupied by those who resort to this place for the benefit of its muds and waters are yet nearer, all situated in an extensive plain: from this rises a sort of natural *tumulus*, of a circular form, of about 15 ft. high, and above 100 in circumference. It appears to be of the same sort of composition as the neighbouring hills, consisting of materials indicative of a volcanic origin. From this mount burst two or three copious streams of hot water, varying from 77° to 185° Fahr: they contain a minute portion of muriates of soda, lime, and magnesia, and of sulphate of lime; the gaseous emanations with which they are accompanied consisting of azote and carbonic acid. A part of them serves to fill the baths and pits for heating the muds; a part loses itself in cuts and wet ditches, amidst the meadows; and a part turns the wheel of a mill, which whirls amidst volumes of smoke.

The meadows, which are of surprising fertility, extend about 2 m. without interruption, when they are broken by an insulated hill, entirely covered with trees, brushwood, and vines; from the foot of this issue smoking streams, and a little farther is another single hill, from whose roots issue hot mineral waters. The structure of the hills, and their character and position show evidently that they are outliers of the volcanic group of the Eugàneans.

There are other springs of the same nature, and having all of them more or less medicinal virtues; which procured apparently for this place the ancient name of *Aponon*, derived from a privative, and πονος, pain.

"It is celebrated for its muds, which are taken out of its hot basins, and applied either generally or partially, as the case of the patient may demand. These are thrown by after having been used, and, at the conclusion of the season, returned to the hot fountain, where they are left till the ensuing spring, that they may impregnate themselves anew with the mineral virtues which these are supposed to contain. The most obvious of these, to an ignorant man, are salt and sulphur. The muds are, on being taken out, intensely hot, and must be kneaded and stirred some time before they can be borne. When applied, an operation which very much resembles the taking a cast, they retain their heat without much sensible diminution for three quarters of an hour, having the effect of a slight *rubefacient* on the affected part, and producing a profuse perspiration from the whole body; a disposition which continues more particularly in the part to which they have been applied, when unchecked by cold. Hence heat is considered as so essentially seconding their operations, that this watering-place, or rather mudding-place, is usually nearly deserted by the end of August; though there are some who continue to wallow on through the whole of September.

"The baths, though sometimes considered as a remedy in themselves, are most generally held to be mere auxiliaries to the muds, and usually but serve as a prologue and interlude to the dirty performance which forms the subject of the preceding paragraph, they being supposed to open the pores and dispose the skin to greater susceptibility."—*Rose's Italy*.

Since Mr. Rose visited the place it has been much improved. A range of handsome bath-buildings has been erected, with all needful accommodations for visitors; a good *restaurateur's* and *café*. There are 16 baths well fitted up, besides those for the poor. The thermal springs in this district are very numerous. Besides those at Abano, there are others at *Caneda, Monte Gotardo, Sant' Elena, San Pietro Montagnone, Monte Grotto, San Bartolomeo, Monte Ortone, San Daniele in Monte*.

The road from Battaglia, which we now rejoin, continues along the bank of the canal, the hills retiring on the left, and after 6 m. we reach *Padua*. (Rte. 31.)

ROUTE 33.

PADUA TO FERRARA, BY ROVIGO.

POSTS.
1¼ Monselice.
1¼ Rovigo.

POSTS.
1 Polesella.
2 Ferrara.

6 Aust. posts = 53 m.

A Malleposte leaves Padua for Ferrara every evening at 9, reaching Santa Maria Maddalena on the Po at 5 a.m.; carriages will be found at the Ponte di Lago Scuro as far as Ferrara, from which a Diligence for Bologna starts at 10 a.m. (There has been great irregularity of late in the public conveyances from Padua to the frontier near Ferrara.)

On leaving Padua the road follows the canal.

6 miles beyond the city is Battaglia, a town of 2700 Inhab., at the foot of the Euganean hills, surrounded by villas: it is celebrated for its baths. A m. before reaching Battaglia, on the rt., is the villa of Catajo, belonging to the Duke of Modena. (See Rte. 32.)

1½ posts. Monselice, a town of 8000 souls at the foot of a hill, one of the most eastern spurs of the Euganeans, and on which once stood a castle celebrated in mediæval Italian history; the town derives its name from the lava (Selce) quarried here for the roads.

Cross the Gorzone canal and soon after the Adige (by a bridge) at Boara. The country is flat and marshy, but with the most luxuriant vegetation.

1½ Rovigo (in going from Rovigo to Monselice an additional horse is required at least in winter on account of the badness of the road). *Inns:* Cappa d'Oro; la Corona d'Oro. A small city, active and cheerful. Pop. near 10,000. The cathedral is now the seat of the Bishop of *Adria.* That ancient city lives only in the name of the Adriatic: its site, at a short distance from Rovigo, can scarcely be traced, and the excavations have not been productive of any objects of great interest. The *Duomo* of Rovigo is a plain building, with a few second-rate pictures. In the Piazza before the Palazzo del Podestà stands a column, which once bore the Lion of St. Mark. The *chapel of the Madonna*, a circular edifice, at the extremity of the city, contains a host of votive offerings and paintings, the latter principally by the inferior artists of the Venetian school.

The road continues through the flat country intersected by canals; part of it runs upon an embankment, and the country continues to display the same exuberant fertility. 8 m. beyond Rovigo we cross the Bianco canal, from which skirting on the rt. a branch of another canal, we soon afterwards reach

1 *Polesella,* where the canal enters the Po.

"To check the aberrations of the rivers in this part of the country from their channels, a catastrophe which used formerly frequently to occur, a general system of embankment has been adopted: and the Po, Adige, and almost all their tributaries, are now confined between high artificial banks. The increased velocity acquired by the streams thus closed in enables them to convey a much larger portion of foreign matter to the sea; and, consequently, the deltas of the Po and Adige have gained far more rapidly on the Adriatic since the practice of embankment became almost universal. But, although more sediment is borne to the sea, part of the sand and mud, which in the natural state of things would be spread out by annual inundations over the plain, now subsides in the bottom of the river channels; and their capacity being thereby diminished, it is necessary, in order to prevent inundations in the following spring, to extract matter from the bed, and to add it to the banks of the river. Hence it happens that these streams now traverse the plain on the top of high mounds, like the waters of aqueducts, and at Ferrara the surface of the Po has become more elevated than the roofs of the houses. The magnitude of these barriers is a subject of increasing expense and anxiety, it having been sometimes found necessary to give an additional height of nearly one foot to the banks of the Adige and Po in a single season."—*Lyell*. " The practice of embankment was adopted on some of the Italian rivers as early as the 13th centy. The deltas of the rivers falling into the upper part of the Adriatic have gone on rapidly increasing within the period of history. From the northernmost point of the Gulf of Trieste, where the Isonzo enters, down to the S. of Ravenna, there is an uninterrupted series of recent accessions of land, more than 100 m. in length, which within the last 2000 years have increased from 2 to 20 m. in breadth.

The Isonzo, Tagliamento, Piave, Brenta, Adige, and Po, besides many other smaller rivers, contribute to the advance of the coast-line, and to the shallowing of the gulf. The Po and the Adige and the Brenta may almost be considered as entering by one common delta.

" In consequence of the great concentration of the flooded waters of these streams since the system of embankment became general, the rate of encroachment of the new land upon the Adriatic, especially at that point where the Po and the Adige enter, is said to have been greatly accelerated. Adria was a seaport in the time of Augustus, and had in ancient times given its name to the gulf; it is now upwards of 12 geogr. miles inland, from the nearest point of the coast-line. Ravenna was also a seaport, and is now about 4 m. from the shore. Yet even before the practice of embankment was introduced, the alluvium of the Po advanced with rapidity on the Adriatic; for Spina, a very ancient city, originally built in the district of Ravenna, at the mouth of a great arm of the Po, was, so early as the commencement of our era, 11 m. distant from the sea."—*Prin. of Geol.*, i. 435. The length of the course of the Po is 410 m., and the superficial extent of the basin drained by it is 22,656 geo. sq. miles. (The basin drained by the Thames is 6400 geo. sq. miles, that by the Severn 4000.)

From Polesella the post-road follows the l. bank of the Po to the Austrian frontier station.

Cross to *Ponte di Lago Scuro*, the frontier station of the Emilian Provinces, by a ferry-boat, a tedious operation. The Dogana here will give but little trouble, and a civil word and a small bribe will remove all difficulty. In coming from Emilia the examination of passports by the Austrian authorities is rather a tedious operation.

2 Ferrara, see Rte. 58.

Inns: The Europa is now the best in Ferrara; it is opposite to the Post and Diligence offices. The Tre Corone.

ROUTE 34.

VENICE TO TRIESTE, BY TREVISO, PORDENONE, CASARSA, AND UDINE.

MILES.		MILES.	
5¼	Mestre.	53	Pordenone.
11¼	Mogliano.	62¼	Casarsa.
14	Preganziol.	70	Codroipo.
18	Treviso.	84	Udine.
22	Lancenigo.	93	Percotto.
26¼	Spresiano.	102	Romans.
30	Piave.	111	Monfalcone.
35	Conegliano.	116	Nabresina.
39	Pianzano.	128	Trieste.
45	Sacile.		

128 Eng. miles.

Steamers four times a week in winter, and daily in summer—the quickest and least fatiguing way; some performing the voyage in 6 hrs., and sailing at 6 A.M.

Railway trains leave Venice for *Casarsa* on the Tagliamento, about 62 m., 3 times a day (to be continued to Udine and Trieste in Oct. 1860), employing 3 h. 40 min., by way of Treviso; when the Railway has been opened to Udine, the journey to Trieste will be performed in 10 hours. The line of railroad to Treviso separates from that to Padua (Rte. 31) at Mestre, and from thence runs nearly N. through a very rich country by
5¼ m. *Mestre Stat.*
5¾ m. *Moglimo Stat.*
3 m. *Preganziol Stat.*
3½ m. TREVISO STAT. : the ancient Tarvisium (*Inns:* Quattro Corone, the best; Albergo Reale), a city of 18,600 Inhab., on the Sile, a tributary of the Piave. Treviso was formerly capital of the Trevisan Mark, as it still is of the province of the same name, and a Bishop's see ; it is situated in a very fertile territory, and possesses manufactures of cloth, paper, &c. The Duomo, or cathedral, dedicated to St. Peter, though unfinished, is a fine building, with its five cupolas. It contains a chapel covered with good frescoes, by *Pordenone*. There is an altarpiece of the Annunciation, by *Titian*, and a curious picture representing a procession of the Trevisan authorities, by *Domenici*, a native artist. The Gothic church of San Nicolo contains paintings by *Gian Bellini* and *Paris Bordone*, and a somewhat celebrated one by *Marco Pensabene*, erroneously attributed to *Sebastian del Piombo*. In the Monte di Pietà there is a celebrated picture by *Giorgione*, the Entombment of Christ, said to have been his last work, and even to have been finished by *Titian*. It is now nearly effaced in parts. The Palazzo Publico and Theatre are fine buildings ; the Villa Manfrini has extensive gardens.

The high road from Milan to Vienna, by the Ampezzo and Pontebba routes, joins that from Venice at Treviso; having crossed the great plain of the Trevigiano from Vicenza, through Cittadella on the Brenta, and Castelfranco, the country of Giorgione.

Three roads lead from Treviso towards Trieste, all joining again near Codroipo and Palma Nova. The first through
Oderzo, a large village, the ancient Opitergium.
Motta, a town of 5000 Inhab., on the Livenza, which is from this point navigable. Scarpa, the anatomical professor of Pavia, was a native of this place his collections of ancient armour and pictures are preserved here.
San Vito, 2 m. from the Tagliamento, a flourishing town of 5000 Inhab., with linen and silk manufactories : there are some good pictures by *Pompeo Amalteo* and his master *Licinio* in the choir of the hospital church.

The second, being a continuation of the former from Motta, is more direct still ; it passes through *Portogruaro*, *Latisana* on the Tagliamento, *S. Giorgio*, and *Ontagnano*, 2 m. from Palma Nova, where it falls into the post-road from Udine.

The third or upper road from Treviso, which is the only one upon which there are post-horse stations, and that followed by the Rly., runs along the foot of the last declivities of the subalpine hills, and is more picturesque and interesting. Leaving Treviso, it runs nearly due N. through the plain to the Piave, passing by
4½ m. *Lanceniyo Stat.*
4½ m. *Spresiano Stat.*, 3 m. beyond which we cross the Piave, on a bridge of several arches.
3¼ m. *Piave Stat.*, on the river-side ; from here the line follows the foot of the hills to
5 m. *Conegliano Stat.* (*Inn:* La Posta, good). Pop. 6500. The town is surmounted by an extensive castle, that gives a fine appearance to it as it is approached. There are frescoes by *Pordenone*, now nearly obliterated, on the outside of several private houses in the town ; in the Duomo an altar-piece of Cima da Conegliano, a native of the place. On leaving the town we pass under a triumphal arch, erected in honour of the late Emperor Francis I. of Austria. 3 m. farther the great road by Belluno, the valley of Cadore, and the Ampezzo pass to Inspruck, branches off to the l. (See *Handbook of S.*

Germany, Rte. 228.) Leaving Conegliano, the Rly. follows the line of the old post-road to

4½ m. *Pianzano Stat.*, to the l. of which opens the valley of Serravalle, through which passes the road to Belluno and Ampezzo, and 6 m. farther on reaches 6 m. *Sacile Stat.* (*Inn :* La Posta), a town of 3700 Inhab., on the Livenza. It retains some traces of its former importance, being surrounded by a good wall and ditch ; the palace of the Podestà is a considerable building.

8 m. *Pordenone Stat.* (*Inn :* La Posta, fair) contains 4000 Inhab., and is supposed to occupy the site of the Portus Naonis of the Romans. It contains large paper-works on the Noncello torrent. Giovanni Antonio Licinio Regillo, called Il Pordenone, was born here in 1483; there is a picture of St. Christopher by him in the principal church. Between Pordenone and *Casarsa* the Rly. crosses several torrents descending from the Alps. *Casarsa* is about 4 m. from the *Tagliamento*. The Rly. to Trieste will be opened in the course of the present year.

8 m. *Codroipo* (*Inn :* Il Imperatore). Here the two roads from Treviso join. 3 m. before reaching this place the Tagliamento is crossed upon a wooden bridge, 1130 yards, or nearly two-thirds of a m. long, the bed of the river being here upwards of a m. wide, and a real "Sea of Stones," showing the changeable nature of the river's course. From near the Ponte della Delizia, on the l. bank of the Tagliamento, a road branches off to the l., and, following it, leads to *Osoppo*, a fortified town, and *Venzone*, and by the Val di Ferro to Pontebba, and thence to Tarvis and Villach, and by the Valley of the Drave to Vienna. (See *Handbook of South Germany*, Rte. 250.) From Codroipo the post-road makes a considerable détour to Udine, but a more direct one passes across the plain to Palma Nova, a very strongly-fortified town, 3 m. W. of the river Torre. The road from Codroipo to Udine passes through Basagliapenta and

Campo Formio, or more properly Campo Formido, where the treaty between General Bonaparte and the Emperor of Austria was signed in October 1797, by which Venice was so shamefully sacrificed by the French general to Austria—one of the deepest blots in the political history of Napoleon. The mean house in which this disastrous treaty was signed is still pointed out.

14¼ m. *Udine Stat.* (*Inn :* L'Europa, good ; La Stella), a city of 20,000 Inhab., once a place of much importance as the capital of Friuli. It is still surrounded by its ancient walls. In the midst is the old town, also walled, and surrounded by a ditch. In the centre is the castle, on a height, said to have been founded by Attila. Udine presents so many features of resemblance in its buildings to the mother city, to whose rule it was so long subjected, as to merit the name of Venice in miniature : it has its grand square, its palazzo publico— a fine building on arches in imitation of the Doge's palace—the two columns, the winged lion of St. Mark, and the campanile with two figures to strike the hours. The cathedral, dedicated to the Virgin, in the Byzantine style of architecture, is the most interesting object in the town. The campanile dates from the 12th century. In the bishop's palace is a ceiling painted by *Giovanni da Udine*, whose house still exists, and is remarkable for being adorned within and without with stucco ornaments, probably by himself. The castle on the height is now used as a prison ; the view from here over the plains of Friuli is very fine. The Campo Santo is well deserving of a visit.

10 m. E. of Udine is Cividale, the ancient Forum Julii, interesting from its numerous Roman antiquities: its Duomo, or collegiate church, founded in 750, is a remarkable Gothic edifice. The archives contain some valuable ancient MSS.

Public conveyances leave Udine for Nabrasina on the rly. to Vienna, and for *Trieste* in correspondance with the early train from Venice, arriving at Trieste about 6 P.M.

8¾ m. *Percotto*.

8½ m. *Romans.* Between Percotto and this post the direct road from Codroipo by Palma Nova joins our route

s 3

1 m. W. of the passage of the Torre river. From Romans a road branches off on the l. to Gradisca and Gorizia, along the banks of the Isonzo; the road to Trieste crossing the same celebrated river, the theoretical boundary of Italy towards the N.E.

8½ m. *Monfalcone*. From here the road runs near the Adriatic through S. Giovanni on the Timavo, the ancient Timavus, ½ m. from the coast, the most northern point of the Adriatic, Duino, and Nabresina, the second station out of Trieste, from which it is 12 m. distant, on the rly. to Laibach and Vienna.

8½ m. *Santa Croce* } See *Handbook of*
8½ m. *Trieste*   } *South Germany*, Rtes. 248 & 254.

An interesting excursion may be made to Aquileja either from Monfalcone or Palma Nova, the former 15, the latter 10½ m. distant from it. From Palma Nova the road passes through Strasoldo (3 m.), Cervignano (2½ m.), Terzo (2 m.), Aquileja (3 m.). Aquileja was in ancient times one of the most important provincial cities of Rome, and one of its strongest frontier fortresses, the chief bulwark of Italy towards the N.E. Augustus often resided in it, and its population was then estimated at 100,000 souls. It was taken by Attila in 452, and reduced to ashes by that ferocious barbarian, who caused it to be levelled to the ground. It contains at present about 1500 Inhab. Its climate is pestilential at certain seasons from the marshes in the midst of which it is situated. The Duomo, built between 1019-42, is a splendid architectural monument of the middle ages, historically remarkable as the metropolitan church of the Patriarch of Aquileja, whose stone throne, in which he was installed, is still preserved behind the altar. The crypt is very curious. Among the remains of antiquity are fragments of the palace of the Patriarch Poppo, who built the cathedral or campanile and a detached tower. The Roman remains in the neighbourhood are very abundant; excavations are going on, and a local museum contains much of what has been discovered.

SECTION V.

DUCHIES OF PARMA AND PIACENZA.

1. *Government.*—2. *Nature of the Country, Inhabitants, Produce, Finances.*—3. *Money and Posting.*

ROUTES.

ROUTE	PAGE	ROUTE	PAGE
40. Piacenza to Parma, by Borgo San Donino.—Rail	396	42. Parma to Mantua, by *Guastalla*	421
41. Cremona to Parma, by *Casal Maggiore* and *Colorno*	420	43. Parma to Sarzana, by *Fornuovo* and *Pontremoli*	422
(TURIN to PIACENZA, by *Alessandria*. See Rte. 7.)		(MILAN to PIACENZA, 6¼ posts, Rte. 24.)	

PRELIMINARY INFORMATION.

§ 1. GOVERNMENT.

These two dismemberments of ancient Lombardy, ceded to Leo X. by Francesco Sforza in 1515, were bestowed by Pope Paul III. on his bastard son Pier Luigi Farnese, in 1545; they remained in the possession of his descendants until the extinction of the male branch of that celebrated family in 1731, when they devolved to the Spanish branch of the House of Bourbon, in virtue of the inheritance of Elizabeth Farnese, the daughter of the last duke, Ranuccio II., who left heirs, and who had married Philip V. This transfer was confirmed by the treaty of Aix-la-Chapelle. At the breaking out of the war which followed the French Revolution these duchies were governed by Ferdinand the grandson of Elizabeth, and were invaded by Bonaparte in 1796. After that period they may be considered as dependencies of France; they formed the Departments of the Trebbia and Taro of the Kingdom of Italy. On the fall of Napoleon, Parma and Piacenza, to which Guastalla had been annexed, were made over at the congress of Vienna to the Empress Maria Louisa for her life, to revert on her death to the descendants of the last duke of the House of Bourbon, to whom in the mean time the duchy of Lucca had been given in compensation. On the demise of Maria Louisa, in December, 1847, Charles II. of Bourbon became Duke of Parma and Piacenza; but abdicated in 1849 in favour of his son, Ferdinand III., who was assassinated in 1854, leaving several children. The eldest, Robert, being under age, the government of the duchies was assumed by his mother, as Regent, during his minority. In the event of failure of male issue in the reigning family, the duchy of Parma Proper was to have passed to Austria, and that of Piacenza to the King of Sardinia; when the events of 1859 upset the stipulations made at the Congress of Vienna, the provinces of Piacenza and Parma annexing themselves by an almost unanimous vote to the kingdom of Northern Italy, under the rule of Victor Emanuel.

The sovereignty of Parma from 1815 to 1859 embraced the duchy of that name, the duchy of Piacenza, and the district of Pontremoli, ceded by Tuscany on the sovereign of the latter coming into possession of the duchy of Lucca. Guastalla had been transferred to the Duke of Modena on the death of Maria Louisa.

§ 2. Nature of the Country.—Inhabitants.—Produce.—Finances.

The territory comprised in the two duchies of Parma and Piacenza, and the province of Lunigiana, has a population of 499,900 souls. It extends from the Po on the N. to near the Mediterranean on the S. The portion of its territory in the plain between the Apennines and the Po is fertile, and watered by numerous rivers descending from the mountains. The districts in the Apennines are dry and thinly peopled, and so inadequate to maintain their scanty population, that many of the inhabitants annually leave their homes to seek employment during the agricultural season in Lombardy and Tuscany, returning with the money thus earned to maintain themselves and their families; others, for a much longer period, as itinerant musicians, &c. Most of those Italians with organs, &c., whom we see about our streets, come from the districts of Parma and Modena bordering on the Apennines. Whenever we find this migration in search of employment abroad, the people may be considered as not in a favourable condition in their own country. This applies equally to the Irish and the Westphalian peasantry; the one leaves his country for England, the other for the Netherlands, during harvest-time.

The finances of this small state were not very flourishing. The public revenue was estimated during the last year of the Ducal Government at 9,686,000 fr. (387,480*l*.); the expenditure absorbed the whole of the receipts, and there was a public debt of 13,300,000 fr. (533,000*l*. sterling). Of late years Austria had maintained a large military force in the Duchies, and kept a garrison in the principal stronghold, Piacenza.

The trade of Parma is limited to the importation, through Trieste and Genoa, of colonial produce for its consumption, British and other foreign manufactures, and articles of luxury.

The exports consist chiefly of cattle, hemp, and cheese, some silk, and a good deal of wine to the neighbouring provinces of Lombardy and Sardinia.

§ 3. Money and Posting.

The coin struck by Maria Louisa is very beautiful, and is similar to the French and Sardinian. The old lira of Parma is still in circulation; 97 of these are equivalent to 20 francs; but in ordinary dealing 5 lire of Parma are equal to a franc, a lira being thus 20 centimes. The posting distances and regulations are the same as in other parts of the North Italian monarchy.

ROUTES.

ROUTE 40.

PIACENZA TO PARMA, BY BORGO SAN DONINO.—RAIL.

KIL.		KIL.	
2	Ponte Nura.	35	Borgo S. Donino.
21	Florenzuola.	45	Castel Guelfo.
28	Alseno.	57	Parma.

57 kil. = 35½ m.

PIACENZA. *Inns:* the San Marco, called the best, but dirty, and with uncivil and inattentive people (1860); the Croce d'Oro, said to be better; and the Albergo d'Italia, fair. As all the hotels are indifferent, and as everything can be seen in a short time, the less the traveller has to do with hotels here the better. By arriving early he will have ample time to visit everything of interest in the town, and continue by an evening train to where he will find more comfortable quarters, at Genoa or Turin, or at Parma.

The following itinerary will embrace everything worthy of notice at Piacenza, in the order they can be most easily visited—supposing the traveller to start from the railway station, where hackney coaches may be hired at the rate of 2 fr. an hour:—The *Duomo*, Ch. of *San Francesco*, *Piazza dei Cavalli*, and *Palazzo del Commune*; Ch. of *Sant' Antonino* and *Theatre*; Ch. of *Sant' Agostino*; the public Promenade; the *Fortress*; *Santa Maria di Campagna*: returning to the Rly. Stat. by the Ch. of *S. Sisto*, the *Citadella*, the Porta di Fagosta leading to the Po, the Bridge of Boats over the latter, &c. There are two good cafés in and near the Piazza dei Cavalli, where he can procure his breakfast.

Railways and Diligences.—There is now a rly. communication between Turin and Piacenza, corresponding with Genoa, Milan, the Lago Maggiore, &c., and with Bologna, by Parma and Modena — trains four times a-day. A diligence daily to Cremona in 4 h. early in the morning, so as to enable persons to reach Brescia by another on the same evening. To Milan daily, by way of Lodi and Marignano, in 8 h., starting at midnight in summer, and early in the morning in winter.

Piacenza la Fedele, founded by the Boian Gauls, received from the Romans the name of *Placentia*, on account of its pleasing situation. It was one of the places which revived the soonest after the invasions of the northern barbarians, and obtained an early share of the commerce which in the middle ages enriched the Italian towns. In the 10th century the fair of Placentia was one of the principal marts of the peninsula. This city now contains about 32,000 Inhab., a number which is not by any means in proportion to the ground it occupies.

The most busy part of Piacenza is in the neighbourhood of the *Piazza de' Cavalli*, so called from the bronze statues of the two dukes, *Alessandro* and *Ranuccio Farnese*, which stand in front of the *Palazzo del Commune*. "This building was erected by the merchants of Piacenza, and was begun in 1281. The lower part is of red and white limestone, and in the pointed style; the upper half is in the round style, and of brick, with terra-cotta mouldings and ornaments. This building is one of the many instances which prove that the Saracenic style, finding its way through Venice, had in the middle ages a partial influence upon the architecture of Italy. The windows and the forked battlements of this building are in a Saracenic manner, and the Saracenic passion for variety appears in the dissimilarity of its parts, for the windows of the front are varied, and the two ends of the building are purposely made unlike each other. It is a noble building, in spite of its anomalies and mixture of different styles and materials."—*G. Knight.*

The equestrian statues were designed by *Francesco Mocchi*, a scholar of Giovanni di Bologna, and cast by *Marcello*, a Roman artist. They were decreed by the city on the occasion of the public entrance of Margherita Aldobrandini, the wife of Ranuccio, and were executed at its expense, at a cost of 44,107 Roman scudi. The statue of Ranuccio was erected in 1620, that of Alessandro in 1624. Ranuccio is in an attitude of command; Alessandro is reining in his steed. The rider has pulled up the horse; but the speed with which they have been proceeding is seen by the flutter of his drapery and the housings and mane all carried out by the wind. Both the statues seem wanting in that repose and simplicity which constitute the truly beautiful in art. These colossal statues, instead of being formed of several pieces, have been cast at one jet.

The traveller here first becomes acquainted with the countenances of the Farnese family, whose elevation so deeply tarnishes the Papal tiara. Alessandro, who succeeded to his father Ottavio in 1586, is the "Prince of Parma" whose name was so familiar in England in the reign of Elizabeth, as spoken of in the famous old ballad on the "Armada:"—

*Their men were young, munition strong,
And, to do us more harm a,
They thought it meet to join their fleet
All with the Prince of Parma,
All with the Prince of Parma.*

He was bold and enterprising. Governor of the Low Countries, he served Spain wisely and prudently; and, as a general, was less sanguinary than the other captains of his times. He died in 1592 at Arras, in consequence of the wounds which he had received at the siege of Rouen, his services having been transferred to France for the purpose of assisting the party of the League. The very low reliefs upon the pedestal represent the attempt to burn the flying bridge thrown over the Scheldt by Farnese during the siege of Antwerp (1585), and the interview with the envoys of Queen Elizabeth, near Ypres, to negotiate the peace (1591). Alessandro was succeeded by his son Ranuccio. Gloomy, suspicious, covetous, and merciless, Ranuccio was constantly in dread of the vengeance of the nobility, whom he insulted and oppressed. One of the first acts of his reign was to burn nine women accused of witchcraft. A supposed conspiracy enabled him, in 1612, to wreak his vengeance upon them. On the 19th May the scaffold was raised before the windows of his palace; and Barbara San Vitale, Countess of Colorno, one of the most beautiful woman of her day, was brought forth, shown to the people, and beheaded; she was followed by Pio Torelli —his head fell also; San Vitale, Marquis of Sala, succeeded, and four others of the principal families. The execution lasted four hours, the duke looking on with savage delight. He wished to extirpate these families; and we dare not repeat the treatment inflicted upon the children of San Vitale. The son and nephew of Torelli escaped; and the latter, taking refuge in Poland, and having married the heiress of the family of Poniatowski, became the ancestor of the last King of that unhappy country.

The *Duomo* stands at the end of the long "Contrada dritta," which runs in a straight line from the Piazza. Though not of very remote date, having been consecrated by Pope Innocent II. in 1133, it is, excepting some additions in the 16th century, in the ancient Lombard style. The porches are curious; the central one dates from 1564. In the archivolt are sculptured various figures, emblematical of the heavenly bodies and elements; amongst them are the twelve signs of the zodiac; the sun and the moon; stars, planets, and comets, and winds. The two lateral ones, of an earlier period, are ornamented with rude bas-reliefs of the Annunciation, the Visitation, the Nativity, and Adoration of the Magi. The pillars that support these arches rest upon quaint crouching human figures, with a kind of saddle on which the columns rest, &c.; and the whole exterior is full of curious details. A window in the apse is remarkable, the moulding of the archivolt standing out from the wall, with which it is connected by four grotesque heads. The *Campanile*, about 200 ft. high, was erected in 1333, and consists of a square brick tower, with an open belfry on the summit: to a window in it is affixed an iron cage, like that at Mantua, placed there in 1495 by Ludovico il Moro, to expose to public view persons guilty of sacrilege and treason. The interior of the ch. (360 ft. in length, 210 wide between the transepts, and 125 high in the centre of the nave) is in a Lombard style, with wide-spreading arches rising from massive columns, with bold plain capitals: over the crown of each arch a statue is let into the wall, and on most of the pillars are small tablets, representing workmen of various descriptions—a wheelwright, a carpenter, a smith, and many others, denoting the *Crafts* who contributed to the expense of erecting the building. The choir retains its stalls of rich carving by Gian Giacomo, a Genoese (1471); massive, bossed choir-books; and its twenty-four canons, who, with diminished means, still retain their station in the cathedral. At the intersection of the nave and transepts rises the octagonal cupola, surrounded both without and within by a gallery of Lombard arches. The paintings on it are of a superior order. Six of the eight sides are painted in fresco by *Guercino*; two, namely, the E. and N.E. compartments—supposing the church to stand exactly E. and W.—are by *Morazzone*. A nearer view of them may be obtained from the colonnade which runs round the top of the drum, but the ledge is rather narrow, and has no rail. The subjects are — four Prophets, four Sibyls, choirs of Angels, and Biblical subjects. These frescoes have been injured in a peculiar manner,—birds getting into the dome have flown against and scratched them. "The Guercino frescoes are very remarkable for their great power in colour and skill in execution of fresco on a large scale, and have less of the heaviness usually pervading the works of this master. At the great distance from which they must be seen from the floor of the cathedral, they are quite satisfactory, and fine specimens of interior decoration."— *C. W. C.* Lower down, on each side of the windows, are figures of Charity, Truth, Chastity, and Humility, by *Franchini*. In the choir are frescoes by *Agostino* and *Ludovico Caracci*, full of academic power and skill, showing great knowledge of the human form and much grandeur of contour; the colours are distemperlike, but *in as perfect preservation as if but just done.* The Ascension of the Virgin, in the centre of the choir, as well as the Sibyls on either side, are by *C. Procaccini;* the two large subjects of the Burial of the Virgin, and the Apostles discovering her tomb empty, on the side walls, are by *Landi;* they replace the two pictures of the same subjects, now in the Pinacoteca at Parma, painted in 1609 by Lud. Caracci, and which had been carried off by the French to Paris in 1796. The Virgin surrounded by angels, on the vault of the apse, is a magnificent work of *Lud. Caracci*, in preservation and execution of its kind quite complete, and full of skill. The vault over the high altar is divided into four compartments: in one, the Virgin crowned by the Trinity is by *C. Procaccini;* the 3 others, representing choirs of angels, and the souls of the Fathers of the Church in Hades, are by *Lud. Caracci*—the figure of Moses in the latter is particularly worthy of notice; the Nativity of the Virgin and the Salutation, on the arch of the organ gallery, are by the same painter; the Visitation, and the Descent of the Holy Spirit, on the opposite side of the choir, are by *C. Procaccini*. The other paintings most worthy of notice in this cathedral are, St. Martin dividing his Garment with the Beggar, by *Lud. Caracci*, in the chapel on l. of the choir; in the 2nd chapel on the rt. is a strange painting, attributed to *Andrea and Elisabetta Sirani*, representing the 10,000 crucified Martyrs, who, according to the legend, consisted of an army of 9000 Roman soldiers miraculously converted to Christianity, and 1000 more troops sent against them, who followed their example,—an execution said to have occurred by the advice of Sapor, in the reign of Hadrian. Near the altar of Santa Lucia is a curious painting of the 13th centy., representing the Madonna and Child, by *Bartolino da Piacenza;* some of whose works we shall see in the Baptistery at Parma. The Diptychus, over the great door of the church, in low relief, formerly occupied the place of Procaccini's Ascension of the Virgin, in the choir; it was executed in 1479 by two artists, *B. Gropallo* for the painting, and *Antonio Burlenghi* for the sculpture, at the expense of a member of the Landi family; the Virgin that occupied the central compartment has been destroyed. A silver basin, weighing 400 ounces, formerly existed in the Sacristy, with a good bas-relief of the Assumption; the vase was sold, but the bas-relief remains—it is a good work of the beginning of the last centy.

The subterranean church or *Scurolo* is a complete church of itself, with transepts and choir, supported by numerous columns with varied capitals.

The *Ch. of San Francesco il Grande*, near the Piazza de' Cavalli, was built by the Franciscan Friars in 1278. The exterior is partly Lombard, the interior in the Pointed style. The painting of the Conception of the Virgin in the 2nd chapel on the rt., and the cupola over the altar, are by Malosso, of Cremona, executed in 1607.

Ch. of Sant' Antonino, the original Cathedral of Piacenza, founded A.D. 324, it is said upon the spot where St. Barnabas preached to the people, rebuilt in 903, and again 1104, and much altered at various subsequent periods (lastly in 1562), so that only portions of its mediæval architecture now remain, the Bell-tower and the curious porch on the N. side called "*Il Paradiso*," the proportions of which are very good (1350). The sanctuary and choir are painted by *Camillo Gavassetti* of Modena, who died in 1628, at a very early age, and few of whose works are found except in his native city. They are principally subjects from the Apocalypse, and were admired by Guercino. The drawing is exaggerated. Gavassetti is one of the numerous artists who, having painted but little in oil, are scarcely known. An ancient painting upon wood of the 14th centy. in the Sacristy should also be noticed; it represents incidents from the life of the patron saint. There are two mediæval sarcophagi outside the ch.

Behind S. Antonino is the small ch. of *San Vincenzo*, with two large paintings of David and Isaiah by *Camillo Bocaccino* (1530), in a grand and broad style.

Ch. of San Savino, founded in 903, and rebuilt in the 15th centy. The crypt is probably as old as the 10th centy.: the pavement is tessellated, representing the Signs of the Zodiac.

In the church are good specimens of *Nuvolone*.

Ch. of San Giovanni in Canale, founded by the Knights Templars. In the cloisters are some curious fragments of paintings of very early date. The building, which is spacious, contains a St. Hyacinth by *Malosso*, and some paintings of modern artists. There is a fine tomb of Orazio Scotti, Count of Montalbo, by *Algardi*, in the chapel of St. Catherine.

Ch. of Sant' Agostino, closed and falling into ruin. This church, by *Vignola*, has a grand and imposing façade. The nave is supported by 34 Doric columns, each shaft being of a single block of granite.

Ch. of the San Sepolcro, by *Bramante*, and a beautiful specimen of architecture (1531). It was converted by the Austrians into a military hospital.

Ch. of Sta. Maria della Campagna, near the gate leading to La Stradella and Alexandria, at the W. extremity of the town, was also erected from the designs of Bramante, originally in the form of a Greek cross: it was sadly spoiled towards the end of the last centy. by lengthening the choir. This alteration occasioned the destruction of several frescoes by *Campi*. The frescoes of this church, though little known, are excellent, and will probably be the first in a good style that the traveller from beyond the Alps will have seen in Italy, and, being placed in juxtaposition with oil paintings of the same masters, will show how much superior they are for effect, colouring, and mural decoration to the latter. "In this church is a cupola and chapel painted in fresco by *Pordenone*, showing to what extent colour may be carried in fresco. The orange and blue, azure and gold, purple and red, are as rich as in the Venetian pictures, and similar in treatment: the design not more severe, and with the same fierce dash in execution. On the l. of the western door on entering there is a fresco of St. Augustine (done as a specimen previously to his being engaged to put his hand to the larger works), more complete and careful in finish, and very beautiful in colour; the rosy tints and luscious fulness in the flesh are as fine as can be."—*C. W. C.* Some of these frescoes have suffered from the effects of damp and time, but they are generally very fine. On entering the ch., upon the wall on the l. is the fresco above alluded to of St. Augustine, beyond which is the chapel of the Magi, entirely painted by *Pordenone*. The subject over the altar represents the Adoration of the Magi, in the lunette above the Nativity, on the side wall the Birth of the Virgin, and above it the Flight into Egypt. The paintings of St. Sebastian and St. Roch at the next altar, as well as four subjects from the life of St. Francis, are by *Camillo Procaccini*. Beyond this is the Chapel of St. Catherine, entirely painted by *Pordenone*: the altarpiece in oils represents the Marriage of St. Catherine of Alexandria with the Infant Christ; the figure of St. Paul on one side is the portrait of the artist himself, and that of the Virgin the likeness of his wife. The French were unable to remove this picture; when they attempted to roll up the canvas, the painting, which was executed upon a prepared ground of plaster or *gesso* spread to the thickness of about ⅛th of an inch on the canvas, broke and fell off. On the side wall is the magnificent fresco of St. Catherine disputing with the Doctors, into which the painter has also introduced his portrait in the Doctor lying on the ground with an open book before him. These fine works were executed in 1516 for a Countess Scotti Fontana, at whose expense the chapel was erected. "The cupola is likewise by *Pordenone*; it is divided into 8 panels which contain Scripture subjects. Immediately under the circular opening of the lantern, upon which is painted the Almighty, and on the bands which divide the panels, are painted small compositions of children playing with animals among festoons of flowers of exquisite colour and fancy. Below the dome, on the frieze of the entablature, from which it springs, is a circle of small frescoes from the heathen mythology, in which the painter has evidently revelled."—*C. W. C.* Subjects which are thus so incongruously mixed with Scripture subjects are—1. Neptune and Amphitrite with sea monsters; 2. Rape of Europa; 3. Silenus drunk, borne by Fauns and Satyrs; 4. Bacchus with Fauns and Satyrs; 5. Hercules strangling the Serpents, and other figures expressive of his Labours; 6. Jupiter hurling lightning at the Giants; 7. Diana hunting with Nymphs and Satyrs; 8. Venus and Adonis, with Cupids, Nymphs, and Satyrs. On the piers, which alternate with pillars in supporting the entablature, are figures called apostles, said to be by Pordenone, but very inferior to the paintings in the dome, and resembling more the works of *Bernardino Gatti*, who painted the drum below these piers with subjects from the life of the Virgin. The pendentives are by *Pordenone*. These frescoes may be seen exceedingly well from the gallery which runs round the drum, behind the pillars and piers, and which is very wide. In a series of Scripture histories, forming a kind of frieze over the arches of nave and choir, the best are,—Tobias and the angel Raphael, by *Daniele Crespi;* Ruth and the Reapers, by *Tiarini;* several by *Gavassetti*, of which Rachel and Rebecca, and the Apparition of the Angel to Lot and his wife, near the music gallery, by *Guercino*, are the most striking. There are some paintings in the choir worthy of notice: a copy of Daniele da Volterra's Taking Down from the Cross by *Tintoretto;* a St. Catherine by *Pordenone*, with an Annunciation above by *Boccaccino*. On the rt. wall, on entering the ch., is the St. George, painted by *Gatti*, opposite to the St. Augustine, as a specimen when competing with Pordenone for the execution of the frescoes here.

The *Ch. of San Sisto*, at the N. extremity of the city, was rebuilt in the beginning of the 16th centy. It has a good nave, supported by columns of grey granite, but from the excess of decoration, in general in bad taste, it has a heavy look. It formerly contained, over the high altar, Raphael's celebrated *Madonna di San Sisto*, now in the gallery at Dresden, which, in 1754, the monks sold to the Elector of Saxony and King of Poland, Frederick Augustus III., for 12,000 sequins: a copy by *Avanzini* of Piacenza is now in its place. Amongst the paintings which remain are the Slaughter of the Innocents, by *Camillo Procaccini*; Sta. Barbara, by *Palma Giovane*; the Martyrdoms of Sta. Martina, by *Bassano*, and of St. Fabian and St. Benedict, by *Paolo* and *Orazio Farinato*, *degli Uberti*,—all on the walls of the choir. The immense monument, in the l. hand transept, of Margaret of Austria, wife of Ottavio Farnese (ob. 1586), is rich but heavy; it was sculptured by *Giacinto Fiorentino*. The *intarsiatura* of the stalls of the choir was very beautiful, but is now much injured; it represents views of towers, castles, villas, &c.

The *Citadella* or *Palazzo Farnese*, also at the N. extremity of the town, occupies a portion of the site of the citadel erected by Galeazzo Visconti, in 1395, to protect Piacenza on the side of the Po. The *Pal. Farnese*, which was erected in 1558 by Margaret of Austria, from the designs of *Vignola*, was once a most sumptuous edifice, and the remains of its splendid ornaments may be traced on its dilapidated walls. It has long been converted into a barrack. Of the part erected in the 14th cent. a portion only remains on the W. side, from the closed window in which the conspirators who assassinated Pier Luigi Farnese showed his corpse to the people, and afterwards hurled it into the ditch below.

The *Castello*, at the S.W. extremity of Piacenza, an irregular pentagon, was begun by Pier Luigi Farnese in 1547. It was permanently occupied by an Austrian garrison until 1859, and had been greatly strengthened since 1848.

The *Palazzo del Commune*, in the square of i Cavalli, dates from 1281; the tower and middle part in a good style of Lombard Pointed architecture; the great hall was completely altered by the Farneses in the 17th centy.

Palazzo dei Tribunali, formerly *Landi*, is remarkable for its fine façade in brickwork, with terracotta windows and cornices. The entrance and court are in an excellent cinquecento style. The Theatre opposite, formerly the Ch. of St. Eustachio, is also a good specimen of ornamental brickwork.

Palazo Mandelli, near the Hôtel S. Marco, a large pile, the residence of the late Ducal Court.

There are some private collections of paintings at Piacenza: in the Pal. Marazzani—a St. Jerome by *Guercino*; a Holy Family attributed to *F. Francia*; Herodias by *Lionello Spada*; an Adoration of the Shepherds by *G. Bellini*.

The charitable institutions of Piacenza are numerous. One may be instanced as interesting to the passing traveller: the *Instituto Gazzola*, founded by an officer of that name in the Spanish service for the maintenance and education of young females, who also receive marriage portions; and as a School of Design. The house contains a very good collection of objects useful for instruction in the fine arts.

The Great Hospital (*Ospedale Grande*), in the Contrada di Campagna, covers a considerable space of ground. It is well supported and managed, and can receive 300 patients. Annexed to it is a medical library, bequeathed by some of its former physicians.

The walk round the decayed ramparts of Piacenza offers some fine points of view—the masses of the churches and palaces within, the distant Alps and Apennines, and the glimpses of the Po, studded with its willowy islands.

Neighbourhood of Piacenza. An interesting excursion may be made to *Velleia*, the Pompeii of Northern Italy, which lies S.E. of Piacenza; but it cannot be reached with post-horses: indeed a part of the road is scarcely practicable for any carriage, excepting the vehicles of the country; the distance is about 20 miles. It passes through the following places.

San Polo, formerly a fief of the family of *Anguisola,* whose castle is still standing here.

San Giorgio, near the Nura torrent, with a large ancient castle, and a villa from the designs of *Vignola,* both belonging to the Scotti—a noble family said to be descended from a branch of the Scotch Douglasses long settled at Piacenza, where one was its *Signore* in 1290.

Rezzano, near which is also a feudal castle, now dismantled. *Badagnano,* where the carriage-road ends.

The track now leads to the valley of the Chiero, and passes by a spot about ¾ m. from Velleia, where flames formed by carburetted hydrogen gas, are constantly issuing from the ground; we soon come in sight of the *Monte Moria* and *Monte Rovinazzo,* anciently a single eminence, but severed by the fall of the masses by which the city was buried. It is conjectured that on the summit was a lake, and that the waters, percolating through a lower stratum of clay, detached the superincumbent rocks and soil, which, as at Goldau, slid down and covered Velleia. It is worthy of remark that the names of both the hills have reference to the catastrophe; Rovinazzo being derived from *rovina,* and Moria from *Morte.* No coins have been found of a later period than the reign of the Emperor Probus; and hence we may conclude that the catastrophe took place during or not long after his short reign.

Velleia, though it must have been a city of considerable note, is nowhere directly mentioned in any of the writings of ancient authors; but there is a curious indirect notice of it in Pliny, in relation to the census of the Roman empire taken by Trajan, on which occasion there were found to be at Velleia six persons exceeding 110 years of age, four of 120, and one of 140. The subterranean treasures were first obscurely known in the 17th century; and for a long time those who were in possession of the secret worked the mine with much profit: the larger bronzes went to the bell-founders, the coins and ornaments to the goldsmiths of Piacenza; but in 1760, the circumstances having been made known to the Infant Don Philip, then Duke of Parma, excavations were begun scientifically, and in the course of five years many statues, inscriptions, and smaller antique articles were found, which have filled the museum at Parma. An amphitheatre, temples, and a forum, have been discovered; none of the walls are more than 10 ft. in height, the mighty crush having thrown down the upper part. The excavations have not been continued for several years.

We now return to the rly. from Piacenza to Parma, which, upon quitting the gates of the city, runs at a short distance N. and parallel to the old post-road, the ancient Via Emilia, so called from Emilius Lepidus, who constructed it B. C. 187, which took a wide circuit from Bologna, passing through Modena, Parma, and Piacenza, to Milan. (See note at p. 532.) The rly. stats. are at very short distances from the several towns, and on their N. side also. One mile from Piacenza, on the rt., is

San Lazzaro, so called from an ancient hospital for lepers, upon the site of which is now erected an extensive ecclesiastical seminary. The celebrated Cardinal Alberoni, who was born in the neighbouring town of Fiorenzuola, left all his property to this institution. Besides the students, it supports many poor. The college contains some good pictures, in an apartment called the Cardinal's Saloon. The Apparition of our Lord to St. Francesca Romana, by *Taddeo Zucchero;* a Virgin and Child, attributed to *Pietro Perugino;* two paintings of Warriors on Horseback, by *Borgognone;* his own portrait, by *M. Polidoro di Caravaggio.* In the church is the monument of the Cardinal founder, and a good Christ on the Cross, by *C. Procaccini.* The library contains 20,000 volumes, amongst which a copy of Alberoni's works, with MS. additions and annotations. The whole institution is conducted upon most benevolent and liberal principles. Cross the river Nura, on a handsome bridge of five elliptical arches, 1 m. before reaching the *Ponte Nura Stat.*, near which were discovered the mosaic pavements now in the Museum at Parma. Between this and the next stat., not far from the line of rly. on the rt., are the villages *Cadeo*, whose name, like San Lazzaro, is a memorial of ancient piety; for here, in 1110, one Gisulphus, a citizen of Piacenza, founded an hospital, *Casa di Dio*, or *Ca' Deo*.

Fontana fredda, now a small place, but anciently a seat of the Gothic kings. Theodoric had here a palace, and the spring, answering to its present name, is in ancient chronicles called "Fons Theodorici." He is supposed to have founded the present parish church of San Salvatore.

Cross the *Arda* torrent, and soon after reach the

Fiorenzuola Stat., a small but rather active town. It is supposed to occupy the site of the Roman Fidentia. It has some mediæval relics. To one tower chains are pendent, to which, it is said, criminals were bound. Small as the place is, it was once rich in conventual and ecclesiastical establishments. The principal church, *San Fiorenzo*, is still collegiate. The carved work of the choir is worth notice; and the sacristy contains some curious relics of ancient art, amongst others a fine specimen of *Niello*.

3 m. on the left is the Monastery of Chiaravalle, founded by the Pallavicinis in 1136.

Velleia may also be reached from Fiorenzuola: the road is shorter than from Piacenza, but it is not so good. It passes through *Castel Arquato*, which stands on the bank of the Arda, a decayed but interesting little town. The *Palazzo Pubblico* is a good Gothic building. Near Castel Arquato is the *Monte Zago*, abounding in fossil shells and marine animal remains in a high state of preservation. The *Cortesi* palæontological collection, now in the university of Parma, where it has remained unpacked for a quarter of a century, was principally formed from fossils found in this neighbourhood.

From Fiorenzuola we continue to follow the line of Roman road through a territory remarkable for its fertility. The country on the l. extending to the Po was once called the Stato Pallavicino, from the celebrated family who held the sovereignty of it. It was erected into an imperial *Vicariato* in the 12th century, and extended from the Po to the Apennines, embracing the districts between the Chiavenna and Taro rivers. Its chief town, Bussseto, was honoured with the title of city by Charles V., and was the place of a conference between that sovereign and Paul III. The Rocca, a castellated building where this meeting was held, contains a large Gothic court. The other towns were Corte Maggiore—there is a fine tomb of Rinaldo di Pallavicini II. (1481) in the parish church here, removed from the Convent of St. Francis — and Soarza, near the Po.

Alseno Stat. There are fine views of the mountains on the rt. from the rly. hereabouts. [The geologist will observe that the higher chain of the Apennines is bordered towards the plain by a lower range of hills covered with vegetation; this is entirely formed of pliocene marls and sands, extremely abundant in fossil shells, whilst the more distant points are composed of eocene beds. The village of Castel Arquato, at the base of the Monte Zago, and commanding the entrance to the valley of the Arda, which runs far into the Apennines, forms from hereabouts a picturesque object in the landscape. The ravines round the village are celebrated as localities for the fossils of the pliocene series, described by Brocchi.] The large villa seen on the rt. of the Alseno stat. is that of S. Polo, belonging to the Anguisola family.

Borgo San Donino Stat., close to the town (*Inns:* Croce Bianca, opposite the Duomo, fairly good). This small city, often noticed in the mediæval history of Italy, contests with Fiorenzuola the honour of being the ancient Fidentia. It has now a population of 4000 Inhab. The castle and towers, which so often enabled the inhabitants to defy the power of Parma, have long been levelled with the ground.

The principal vestiges of mediæval antiquity which the city still retains are the Gothic *Palazzo Publico* and the *Duomo*. "San Donino, in whose honour this church was erected, was a soldier in the army of the Emperor Maximian, and served under his orders in Germany. Donino, with many others, became a Christian; and when Maximian issued an edict, ordering all persons to renounce the Christian faith on pain of death, Donino fled, but was overtaken near the river Strione, by the emissaries of the tyrant, and immediately put to death. Near that spot there was at that time a village called Julia.

"In 362 the Bishop of Parma, admonished by a dream, sallied forth and discovered the body of Donino—known to be that of the martyr by an inscription found on the spot, and by the sweet odour which issued from the grave. A chapel was immediately erected to receive the holy remains: and we learn from a letter from St. Ambrose to Faustinus that the village of Julia had changed its name into that of San Donino so early as 387.

"From that time the shrine of St. Donino became one of the most frequented in Italy, and received oblations which led to the construction of a temple on a larger scale. The existing church is a large building, and has undergone various alterations. The oldest part of it is in the Lombard style; but the very curious and rich façade belongs to times subsequent to those of the Lombard—to times when the imitation of the Roman bas-reliefs succeeded to the monstrous imagery of the 7th and 8th centuries. No record remains of the period at which this façade was erected; but there are various circumstances which give us reason to believe that it cannot be older than the 12th century. The barbarous character of the sculpture, the neglect of all proportions, the heads as large as the bodies, might seem to indicate a remoter antiquity; but there is a bas-relief over one of the gates at Milan, known to have been executed at the close of the 12th century, which is no less rude, and which proves that the arts of Italy, down to that period, continued to be in a state of the lowest depression. The projecting portals, the pediment over the doors, the pillars resting on animals, are all features of the latter part of the 11th and of the 12th century."—*G. Knight.*

There is a good deal of mediæval sculpture, curious to the antiquarian. In one of the lateral porches, called the porch of *Taurus*, the heads of bulls are introduced; in another, the porch of *Aries*, the pillars rest upon kneeling rams, and the ram's head is introduced in the capitals, while the sun—represented by a human head surrounded with rays—appears in the archivolt. Some sculptures of the porches are taken from Scripture history; others from Pagan. "Hercules" is wrestling with the lion. A square tablet, containing the figure of a woman in a chariot drawn by dragons, holding a torch in either hand, is the same design which at San Mark's at Venice is called Ceres or Proserpine. It is in the same singular low relief. Among the sculptures on the walls of the apse are the hunt of the soul by the Demons, under the emblems of the stag and the hounds; and the "Petra Solis," exhibiting the sun, followed by an inscription in uncial letters. The interior of the cathedral, which is scarcely altered, is as interesting as the outside. The crypt is well worth a visit.

Borgo San Donino contains a large Poorhouse, or Union Workhouse, established by the French in the buildings of a suppressed convent. On leaving the stat. cross the river on a handsome bridge.

Rovacchia Codura, on the torrent Rovacchia, where a church marks the site of a deserted village.

Parola. Here a certain Podestà of Parma built a castle, for the purpose of keeping the "Borghigiani" in check. The traces of the ruined building are in the fields to the S. of the road, and the situation so struck Ariosto, that he has described it in the following stanza:—

"Giacea non lungi da Parigi un loco,
Che volgea un miglio, o poco meno intorno,
Lo cingea tutto un argine non poco
Sublime, a guisa d' un teatro adorno.
Un castel già vi fu, ma a ferro, e a foco
Le mura e i tetti, ed a rovina andorno.
Un simil può vederne in su la strada,
Qual volta a Borgo al Parmigiano vada."
Orlando Furioso, cant. xxvii. 47.

Fontenellato. 3 m. beyond Parola, a road striking off on the l. leads to *Rocca di Fontenellato*, a village near the Rio Grande torrent, consisting chiefly of a villa belonging to the family of San Vitale, in which there is a room painted in fresco by *Parmigianino*, on the plan of Correggio's more celebrated Camera di San Paolo at Parma (p. 414). It is supposed the artist took refuge here when persecuted by the confraternity of *La Steccata*, and painted the room out of gratitude to his protectors. The subject is the fable of Actæon, represented in 13 lunettes, above which are children on the roof of the grotto. In one of the lunettes is the portrait of a beautiful Countess di San Vitale; in another two of the children embracing each other. One of the hunters in the second lunette is the painter's portrait. Diana throwing water in the face of Actæon is very graceful. The room, smaller than that of San Paolo, is badly lighted. The frescoes are in excellent preservation.

Castel Guelfo Stat., a small place, with the ancient castle from which it derives its name. One portion is in ruin, others are partly modernized; but the bold projecting machicolations still remain, as well as the original outline, testifying to its feudal grandeur. The walls are now covered with ivy. The castle was, at one time, called *Torre d' Orlando*, not from the Paladin, but from *Orlando Pallavicini*, who held it for the Ghibelline party; but being besieged and taken (1407) by *Ottone Terzi*, the lord of Parma, and a great leader of the opposite faction, he changed its name to *Castel Guelfo*, in honour of his victory.

From this spot, and during the remainder of the journey, the views of the Apennines, ranging along the southern horizon, are fine.

Soon afterwards we reach the banks of the *Taro*, in the winter season a fine and rapid torrent rushing to join the Po, whilst in the summer, the wide waste of the stony bed marks the extent of its stream at other seasons. This river is of considerable note in ancient geography, as having been the boundary between the Gaulish and the Ligurian tribes. In the autumn it swells with sudden and impetuous fury, and during the whole winter season the passage was here attended with much difficulty and peril. Such dangers so often occurred during the middle ages, that bridge-building was undertaken as a work of Christian charity: and, somewhat like the *Pont Saint Esprit*, the first bridge over the Taro was erected about 1170, by the exertions of a poor hermit of Nonantola, who, stationing himself by the side of the Via Emilia, begged until he collected sufficient money to build it. But, after sustaining repeated damage from the violence of the river, the hermit's bridge was finally carried away in 1345, and ill replaced by a dangerous and inconvenient ferry, even till our own times. The present magnificent bridge was begun by Maria Louisa in 1816, and completed in 1821, at a cost of 2,161,508 fr. It is 586 mètres (1922 ft.) in length, and composed of 20 arches. Colossal statues of the four principal streams of the state, the Parma, the Taro, the Enza, and the Stirone, resting upon their urns, adorn the abutments at each end; it is in many respects a work worthy of the best times of Italy. The rly. crosses the river on a separate bridge a little lower down the stream; from here the spires of Parma come into view. The river Parma is crossed on a new bridge, which contrasts favourably with the three older ones seen from it on the rt., and the line, after running along the Ducal gardens, soon brings us to the Parma stat., situated close to the city gate (Porta S. Bernardo), where omnibuses to the hotels and hackney carriages will be found waiting.

PARMA. (*Inns:* Albergo della Posta, in the main street: very fair, and improved since the stables have been removed. Il Pavone, said to be a well-conducted house, in an out-of-the-way corner of the Piazza.) This capital, whose population now exceeds 45,000, is of an oval shape, which it has retained from remote antiquity. Situated in the territory of the Boian Gauls, it was reduced to a Roman colony as early as B.C. 187; destroyed during the wars of the Triumvirate, it was rebuilt by Julius Cæsar and Augustus. In the middle ages, like most of the large towns in Italy, it was successively governed as a republic and by the heads of some of its great families — the most remarkable of the latter who tyrannized over it being the Terzis, the De' Rossis, the Pallavicinis, and the San Vitales. Julius II. obtained it from the Dukes of Milan in 1513; it remained a possession of the Popes until 1545, when Paul III. made it, as well as Piacenza, over to his natural son, Pier Luigi Farnese, with the title of duke. It is said to have been called *Parma* from its similarity to the form of a shield. When the city was under the authority of the Popes, it was represented by a female figure sitting upon a pile of shields, and holding a figure of Victory, with the inscription of *Parma aurea*. But the torrent Parma, which runs through the city, most probably gave its name to the buildings which arose upon its banks.

Parma suffered from the earthquake in 1832, and several houses were so much injured as to require being rebuilt.

The Via Emilia, which divides the city into two nearly equal portions, crosses, in the centre, the *Piazza Grande*, which has on the N. side the *Palazzo del Commune*, with its campanile. So complete has been the subversion of the ancient colony of Lepidus, that a few inscriptions, mutilated sculptures, and objects of jewellery are all that remain of Roman times. The name of Parma is connected with some of the principal events in the Lombard league; but little of its mediæval character remains, except in the fine group formed by the *Duomo* and the *Baptistery*, which stand close to one another at a short distance to the N. of the Piazza Grande.

Plan for visiting the Sights of Parma in a day, and in topographical order.

Cathedral; Baptistery; Ch. of San Giovanni Evangelista; Teatro Farnese; Galleria; Library; Museum of Antiquities; Printing Office; Camera di San Paolo; Ch. of S. Alessandro; Ch. of La Steccata; Piazza Grande; University; Ch. of the Annunziata; Giardino Ducale; Citadella; Stradone and Boulevards. The tourist will find hackney coaches at 2 fr. an hour, which will materially assist him in getting over so much work; or the landlord at the Posta will furnish carriages at the same rate.

The *Duomo* or *Cathedral:* the exterior of the W. front is almost unaltered. The transepts and the choir are Lombard, and the centre is crowned by an octagon tower and dome. In the great portal the peculiar Lombard style will be recognised. The building was consecrated by Pope Pascal II. A.D. 1106; many portions are much later. The principal entrance, forming the central door of the façade, has on each side colossal lions of red Verona marble, the one grasping the serpent, the other the ram: they were sculptured by *G. Bono da Bisone*, in 1281. The other sculptures of this portal are by *Bianchino*, in 1493. The sun mystically placed in the keystone of the circular

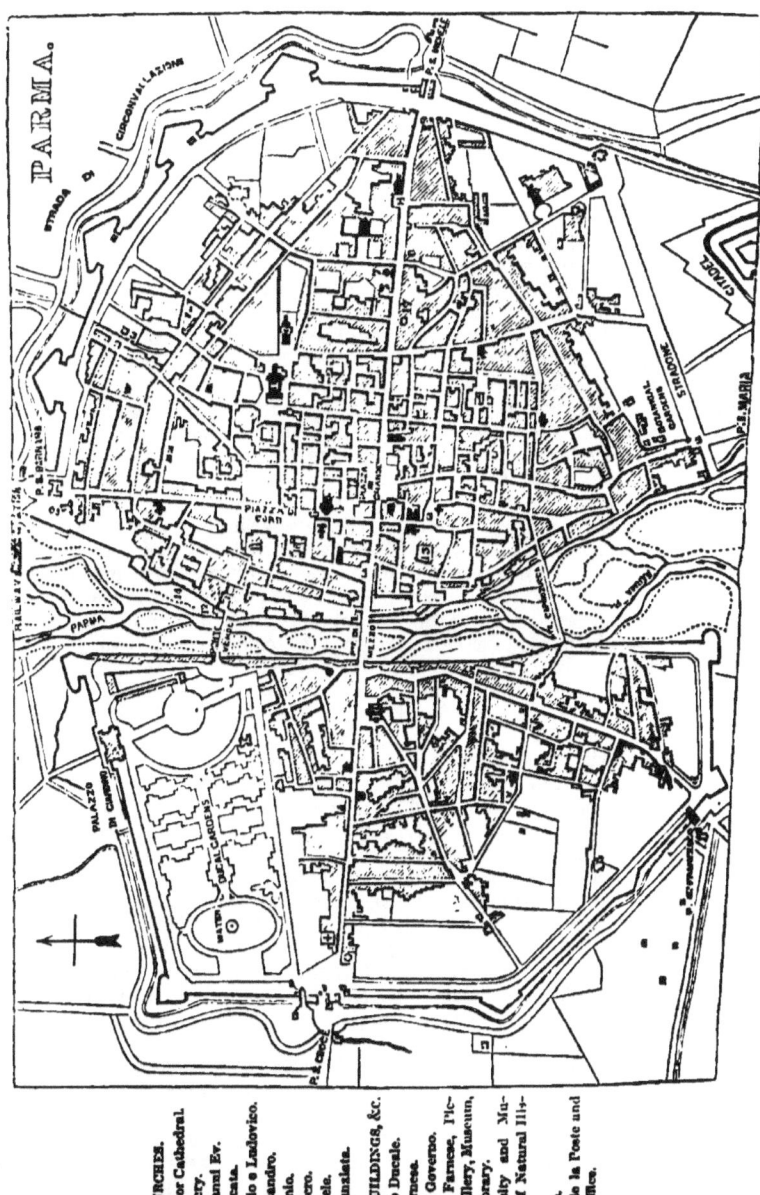

CHURCHES.
1. Duomo or Cathedral.
2. Baptistery.
3. S. Giovanni Ev.
4. La Steccata.
5. SS. Paolo e Ludovico.
6. S. Alessandro.
7. S. Antonio.
8. S. Sepolcro.
9. S. Michele.
10. L' Annunziata.

PUBLIC BUILDINGS, &c.
11. Palazzo Ducale.
12. Pal. Farnese.
13. Pal. del Governo.
14. Teatro Farnese, Picture Gallery, Museum, and Library.
15. University and Museum of Natural History.
16. Theatre.
17. Hôtel de la Poste and Post Office.

arch, the months by the principal occupations during each on either side; the hunt, the allegory of the pursuit of the soul by the fiend, over the lintel, are curious: a few Roman inscriptions are built up in the walls, indicating perhaps how many more are concealed in its core or beneath in the foundations.

The interior, excepting some Gothic interpolations and some modern additions, is in a fine Lombard style, and the arrangement of the triforium is remarkable: "The vaulting of the nave is elliptical; a circumstance I do not remember having met with elsewhere in a building of this era."—*Woods*. Magnificent but perishing frescoes cover the walls. The most important of these are upon the cupola, and were executed by *Correggio* between the years 1522 and 1530. The subject is the Assumption of the Virgin. The painter has imagined that the octagon form, or drum, from which the cupola rises, embraces the space on earth in which stood the sepulchre of the Virgin; for this purpose, upon the octagon itself, from whence the great vault springs, runs a balustrade, above which rises a candelabrum at each of the 8 angles, with a number of boys between engaged in lighting tapers, or burning incense and odoriferous herbs. On the balustrade, and in front of the base of the cupola, stand the Apostles disposed around looking upwards with astonishment, and as if dazzled by the great light of the Celestial host who transport the Virgin; and above, Heaven appears open to receive her. The Angel Gabriel descends to meet her, and the different hierarchies of the blessed circle around him. In the arches under the cupola, or on its pendentives, are represented the Four Protectors of the City of Parma—St. Hilary, St. Bernard, St. John the Baptist, and St. Thomas—attended by Angels symbolical of the virtues of the Saint, and with the emblems and ornaments of his dignity. St. John, holding a Lamb; angels around darting, as it were, through the clouds: St. Thomas, also surrounded by angels, some bearing exotic fruits, emblematical of this apostle's labours in India; St. Hilary, looking down upon the city with an expression of kindness and protection; while St. Bernard, kneeling, is imploring on its behalf. This magnificent work, which occupied so many years of the artist's life, was poorly paid for and inadequately appreciated. He was much teased and thwarted by the cathedral wardens: one of them, in allusion to the fact that many more limbs than bodies are visible from below, told him that he had made a "hash of frogs," *un guazzetto di rane*. The work is remarkable for its chiaro-scuro, confined indeed, as compared with Correggio's oil pictures, to a light scale, especially in the upper portions; for its wonderful foreshortenings; and for the extensive range in the size of the figures, in order to convey by their perspective diminution an impression of great space. "It must be evident that gradations in magnitude will be more full and varied when they comprehend, if only in a limited degree, the perspective diminution of forms. The great Italian artists seem to have considered this essential to distinguish painting, however severe in style, from basso-rilievo, in which the varieties of magnitude are real. But in the works by Michael Angelo and Raphael this perspective diminution of figures is confined to narrow limits; partly because the technical means may have been wanting to mark the relative distances of objects when the work was seen under the conditions required; but chiefly because figures much reduced in size cannot be consistently rendered expressive as actors or spectators. In the second compartment of the ceiling in the Sistine Chapel the effects of the perspective are expressed without restraint; but the indistinctness which was the consequence was probably among the causes that induced Michael Angelo to reduce the space in depth in the other compartments (as regards the figures) almost to the conditions of sculpture. In Raphael's Transfiguration the figures on the mount are supposed to be distant with reference to those below; but, had they been so re-

N. *Italy*—1860. T

presented, they would have been devoid of meaning and importance: they are, therefore, by a judicious liberty, brought within that range of vision where expression, action, and form are cognizable. One great exception is, however, not to be overlooked; Correggio, who was devoted to picturesque gradation under all circumstances, and sometimes at any sacrifice, adopted a different course. The perspective diminution in the cupolas at Parma (to say nothing of the objects being represented as if above the eye) is extreme; so that even the principal figures are altogether subservient to the expression of space. This was the chief object; but the grandeur of form and character which the nearer figures exhibit has been justly considered to place these works far above subsequent efforts of the kind, which in the hands of the 'machinists' soon degenerated to mere decoration.

"If the criticisms which the frescoes in the Duomo at Parma called forth on their completion had any foundation, it may be inferred that the great distance at which the figures were seen rendered it impossible, in some cases, to discern the nicer gradations of light and shade which are essential to make perspective appearances intelligible. Such considerations must, at all events, operate to restrict foreshortening under similar circumstances."—*Eastlake.*

"At first, and seen from below, this magnificent work appears extremely confused, but with great amenity of colours. This confusion is found to arise from two things, the destruction of the colours and consequent relief of the parts, and the blotches of white produced where the plaster has fallen, which I regret to say are neither few nor small. The lights too have doubtless changed somewhat of their tone, and become darker than they were originally. . . . The effect is extremely injured by the round window which is found in each of the eight compartments of the base of the dome, and the picture is well seen only when those lights are hidden.—*Prof. Phillip R.A.*

The decay of these frescoes is to be chiefly attributed to the old insufficient roof over the dome, which still exists under the new leaden one, added to save the wrecks of Correggio's works from destruction. Their present deteriorated state has also been partly attributed to Correggio having used an intonaco containing a proportion of sand. A closer inspection of them may be obtained by ascending to the roof of the church, from four small openings in the drum of the cupola. A good aid towards their study and comprehension will be the examination of the beautiful copies of them in the Pinacoteca (p. 417) by the late Professor Toschi and his pupils.

The vaultings of the choir and nave are by *Girolamo Mazzola*, the cousin and scholar of Parmigianino. The sides of the nave are by *Lattanzio Gambara*, who worked here from 1568 to 1573. Near the door he has introduced fine heads of Correggio and Parmigianino—evidently portraits. These frescoes, which are now in process of restoration, are academical in treatment; they want brightness, the subjects are confused, and not well adapted for mural decoration. By *G. Cesare Procaccini* are two good paintings of King David and St. Cecilia. The other works of art here worth noticing are, in the 4th chapel of the rt. aisle, belonging to the Commune of Parma, several paintings of the 15th centy. relative to SS. Fabianus and Sebastian, by *Jacopo Loschi* and *Bartolomeo Grossi*. They had been whitewashed over, and have only been lately rediscovered. The picture over the altar, of a Virgin and Saints, is by *Anselmi*. In a chapel near the southern door of the transept is a good Crucifixion with Saints by *B. Gatti*. The Valesi-Baganzola chapel, opening out of the N. aisle, is covered with frescoes of the 15th centy., by *Loschi* and *Grossi*, representing scenes in the lives of SS. Andrew, Christopher, Catherine, &c., and are interesting in the early history of the school of Parma. Amongst the minor objects of interest are the seats of the choir, finely carved, and the rich high altar; also fragments of a fine painted glass window, executed by *Gondrate* in 1574, from the designs of L. Gambara.

The inscription upon *Bodoni's* tomb is cut in imitation of his printing types. The tomb of *Bartolomeo Montini* (died 1507), by *di Grate*, should also be noticed.

Petrarch held preferment here. By his will, in which he most truly styles himself *inutile Archidiacono*, he directed that, if he died at Parma, he should be interred in this cathedral. In 1713 a cenotaph was erected in the chapel at the extremity of the rt. aisle to his memory by Nicolo Cicognari, one of the canons.

The subterranean Church is large and well lighted, and supported by 28 marble columns with varied capitals. It contains some good specimens of sculpture by *Prospero Clementi* of Reggio — the Altar and Shrine of *San Bernardino degli Uberti*, Bishop of Parma (died 1133). The saint is represented between angels supporting his mitre and pastoral staff. The bas-reliefs were designed by *Girolamo Mazzola*. The tomb of *Bartolommeo Prato*, erected in 1539. Two weeping figures are full of expression: the drapery is of good execution; the background is a mosaic upon a gold ground, rare in a work of such modern date. In a chapel opening on the rt. out of this subterranean ch. some curious early frescoes have been discovered under the whitewash; one, of the Madonna seated on a rich Gothic throne, is fine and broad in character, with the Donatorio, a Bishop, on her rt. The ornamental heads of saints in medallions round the base of the vault are very good specimens of the 15th centy.

The *Campanile* is in the ordinary square form of such Lombard edifices, divided into stories by 3 cornices, with an open belfry on the summit.

The *Battisterio*. This is one of the most splendid of the Baptisteries of Italy. It is entirely built of red and grey Verona marble, and was constructed after the designs of Benedetto Antelami, being begun in the year 1196. But the work experienced many interruptions, especially during the supremacy of the powerful and ferocious Eccelino da Romano, who, in the middle of the 13th century, governed the north of Italy in the name of the Emperor, and who, displeased with the inhabitants of Parma, forbade them access to the quarries of the Veronese territory, from which the marble with which the battisterio was built was obtained. In consequence of these interruptions the battisterio was not finished before 1281, which will sufficiently account for the appearance of the round style in the lower part of the building, and of the pointed above.

Externally the battisterio is encircled with four tiers of small columns, forming as many open galleries, which, with more observance of ancient rules than is usually found in the Lombard style, support continued architraves, the whole surmounted by a drum of as many pilasters. There are 3 portals, all very elegant and covered with sculptures; round the base of the tower is a band of sculptures in high relief of real and fabulous animals, dogs, bears, lions, centaurs, sphinxes, griffins, &c. The interior has 16 sides, from which spring converging ribs that form a pointed dome. In the centre stands a very large octagonal font, cut out from one block of yellowish-red marble. It appears from an inscription cut on the rim that this font was made by *Johannes Pallassonus* in 1298. In one corner of the building is a smaller font (or, at least, what is now used as such), covered with Runic foliage and strange animals; it stands upon a lion setting his paws upon a ram. All the children born in Parma are still brought here for baptism. The baptistery is a collegiate church, having a chapter of six canons and a provost, besides inferior officers; its registers go back to 1459. The vault of the Baptistery is lighted by 24 windows, the intervals covered with paintings supposed to have been executed soon after its completion or early in the 13th centy., whilst those

T 2

of the niches below are of a later date, as they bear the names of *Nicolo da Reggio* and *Bartolino da Piacenza*, who lived towards the middle and end of the 14th. These paintings, arranged in rows or compartments, represent the 12 Apostles, the Evangelists with their symbolic animals, and Doctors of the Church; the Virgin in a blue mantle, with the Prophets; scenes in the History of St. John the Baptist; various Saints and Prophets; and in the niches Prophets and Saints, and subjects from the life of Christ. Many of these paintings display a vivid colouring and a vehemence of action often carried to exaggeration. Besides the frescoes, there are—an altarpiece, representing St. John, by *Filippo Mazzola*, the father of Parmigianino; and St. Octavius, by *Lanfranco*. The stalls, of inlaid work, were made by *Bernardino Canoccio* in 1493.

The *Church and Convent of San Giovanni Evangelista*, immediately behind the Duomo, attached to a very extensive Benedictine monastery which dates from the 10th centy. The interior was designed by one *Zaccagni*, a native architect, and begun in 1510: the exterior is nearly a centy. later (1607), by *Simone Moschino* of Orvieto: the design is good and striking. The interior consists of a long nave and aisles, supported by fluted pilasters with Ionic capitals. The dark paintings on the vault give it a heavy look, which it has not in reality. The ch. contains frescoes on the cupola by *Correggio*, now damaged and obscured by damp and smoke, representing a vision of St. John. He, in extreme old age, and the last surviving apostle, beholds, in a moment of extacy, his companions in heaven, who form a circle around their Divine Master resplendent in glory. The saint is alone upon the earth, and is depicted below all the others at the extreme edge of the cupola. He kneels upon a rock, his arms leaning on a book, which is supported by a number of boys, of whom the very clouds are full. Each of the 4 pendentives contains an Evangelist, with a Doctor of the Church, viz. St. John with St. Augustine; St. Matthew with St. Jerome; St. Mark with St. Gregory; St. Luke with St. Ambrose; all seated in various attitudes upon clouds, and supported by graceful children. This is a much smaller work than that of the Duomo, and painted some time before, when Correggio was only 26 years of age, between 1520 and 1524. The style is extremely large, and the finish more complete than in that of the Duomo. The figures in the angles are much injured by the peeling off of the plaster: some parts appear very fine. The heads and expression of the saints in the group below are more complete and appropriate than in those of the Duomo. *Correggio* also painted the tribune behind the choir. When the church was enlarged in 1584 the monks thought that the frescoes could be detached, but they crumbled and broke in the operation. On that occasion was procured the fragment of the Coronation of the Virgin, now preserved in the Library. A copy made by *Aretusi* in some measure replaces the original, whilst a more accurate one still by *An. Caracci* may be seen in the Pinacoteca. By *Correggio* also is a small fresco of St. John writing his Gospel. It is over a door opening out of the l. hand transept into the monastery. The other works of art here are— in 2nd chapel on rt., the Virgin and St. Joseph in Adoration before the infant Saviour, by *G. Francia:* the figure of the Virgin adoring the Infant Saviour is good; it has been much restored, and is badly seen; so is one of the shepherds stretching forth both arms as he hears the song of the Angels. In the 4th chapel, a fine altarpiece of St. James at the feet of the Virgin, by *Gir. Mazzola*. In the 5th, frescoes by Anselmi on the roof, much restored. The Transfiguration, at the extremity of the choir, is by *Parmigianino*. The Christ on the Cross, in the 6th chapel, is by *Anselmi*. In the 5th chapel on l. a bad copy of Correggio's St. Jerome. In the 4th, the Virgin offering a palm-branch to St. Catherine and St. Nicholas, by *Parmigianino*. In the 2nd, S. George and 2 saints over the arch. And in the 1st on the l. on entering the church, 2 frescoes on the arches of Sta. Lucia and Sta. Apollonia before the Virgin, by the same. The arabesque paintings on the vault of the nave are by *Anselmi*.

The monastery, suppressed by the French, was restored some years ago for Benedictines. It is a stately building, containing three very handsome quadrangles, surrounded by cloisters. The outer walls were adorned with frescoes, which have all but disappeared from the effect either of time or of violence. The interior is fine: it is traversed by 4 long galleries, which in the form of a cross unite in the centre. At the point of junction are 4 statues in terra-cotta, executed by *Antonio Begarelli*, of Modena. The sculptured arabesques on their pedestals and those on the door of the chapter-house are by *Agresti*. The greater part of the conventual buildings are now tenanted by soldiers. The *Campanile*, the highest in Parma, and which is detached from the church, was erected in 1614. It is a fine edifice of the kind; square below, it is surmounted by an octagonal lantern and belfry, and a gallery, from which there is an extensive view over the surrounding country.

Ch. of the *Madonna della Steccata*, in the street leading from the Piazza Grande to the Ducal Palace, begun about 1521, from the designs of *Francesco Zaccagni*. A figure of the Virgin painted on the wall of a house first attracted the devotion of the people of Parma; and from a palisade (*Steccato*) built round it, it acquired the name of the *Steccata*. The present church, which stands on the site of an oratory, to which the miraculous picture had been removed, is in the form of a Greek cross, with a semicircular apse at the extremity of each branch. In each of the angles of the cross are smaller chapels. The chief paintings are by *Parmigianino*: Moses breaking the Tables of the Law, Adam and Eve, and the Sibyls, and the Virtues over the organ. The Moses, and Adam and Eve, which are executed in chiar'-oscuro on the soffit of the arches which form the entrance to the choir, have become so dark that it is difficult to see them; but the merit of the Moses has always been considered very great. "Parmigianino, when he painted the Moses, had so completely supplied his first defects, that we are here at a loss which to admire most, the correctness of drawing or the grandeur of conception. As a confirmation of its great excellence, and of the impression which it leaves on the minds of elegant spectators, I may observe, that our great lyric poet [Gray], when he conceived his sublime idea of the indignant Welsh bard, acknowledged that, though many years had intervened, he had warmed his imagination with the remembrance of this noble figure of Parmigianino."— *Sir J. Reynolds*. Parmigianino was employed by the Fraternity of the Annunciation, to whom the church then belonged, and by whom he was engaged at weekly wages. He was at this time much addicted to alchemy, to which he gave his time when he should have been employed at his work. His employers first warned him that such conduct would not do: then they sued him at law, and he ran away, and died soon afterwards (Aug. 24, 1540), of trouble and vexation, in the 37th year of his age. Upon his death, *Anselmi* was called in, some say at the instance and under the directions of Giulio Romano. *Anselmi's* principal painting here is a Coronation of the Virgin on the vault over the high-altar. The interior of the cupola, by *Sojaro* or *Gatti*, represents the Assumption, for which he was paid 1400 golden scudi in 1566. It is an imitation of Correggio. By *Girolamo Mazzola* are the frescoes of the Nativity, and of the Descent of the Holy Ghost, in the chapels on rt. and l. of the high altar: a picture of the Madonna and Child between St. John the Baptist and St. Luke is good, and attributed to *Francia*. There are some good sepulchral monuments here. In the chapels of St. Thomas and St. Paul are those of Sforzino Sforza, son of Francesco Sforza II. (died 1523), sleeping in death, his head resting on his helmet, by *Agrate*, and of Ottavio Farnese (died 1567), by *Brianti*, a fine bust. Count Guido da Correggio, a full-length statue, rising above a sarcophagus of yellow marble, executed by *Barbieri*, about 1568. In the S. arm of the cross or chapel over the altar, in which there is a large painting of St. George by *Franceschini*, has been placed a memorial to the Duchess Maria Louisa, consisting of a group of the Dead Christ, by *Bondoni*, a native artist, and at the expense of the city. In the vaults beneath the church are the sepulchres of the dukes of the house of Bourbon, and of some of their Farnese predecessors. The most interesting is that of Duke *Alessandro;* his name, *Alexander*, only appears upon the sarcophagus, upon which are lying his helmet and his long-bladed Spanish rapier. The remains of the other princes are in vaults bricked up in the wall, a marble tablet recording the name of each. A small vault with a grated door contains the heart of the last sovereign, placed in a little box, on a table. In the same street, and nearly opposite the Madonna della Steccata, is the ch. of

Sant' Alessandro, which dates from 1625, having been erected on the site of a ch. of the 9th centy. by Margaret daughter of Alessandro Farnese, and from the designs of *Magnani*. It consists in the interior of 3 divisions, separated by handsome Ionic columns of red Verona marble. The architectural views on the roof are by *M. A. Colonna;* and the cupola, on which is represented Christ conducting the Virgin to heaven, by *Tiarini*. The painting over the high altar, of the Virgin giving the palm of Martyrdom to Sta. Justina, is by *Parmigianino;* the St. Bertoldo in the 2nd chapel on rt. is by *Tiarini*.

Following the same street, passing the theatre, we soon arrive at the Piazza di Corte, near which, in a narrow one on the rt., stands the

Ch. of *San Lodovico*, formerly attached to a monastery of Benedictine nuns, restored of late years for purposes of education to the Jesuitical female order of the Sacré Cœur, recently suppressed. The ch. and buildings are not remarkable: the great object of attraction is the "*Camera di San Paolo*," painted by *Correggio* about the year 1519, by order of the Abbess, Giovanna di Piacenza, in the Parloir of the adjoining convent (the keys are kept at the Picture Gallery). It represents, over the chimney-piece, a grotto of Diana, beneath the level of the ground, covered with a roof of foliage, having 16 oval apertures corresponding in number with the spaces interposed between the sections of the vaulted roof. In each of these ovals children are seen peeping in and out as they pass around the grotto. The composition is varied in each of the ovals. They bear various symbols or attributes of the goddess, and implements of the chace. Under these medallions are 16 lunettes containing mythological subjects in chiar'-oscuro, —The Three Fates; the Suspension of Juno; Bacchus nursed by Leucothea-Lucina; Ceres; a group of Satyrs; Endymion and Adonis; Minerva; the Graces; and the like. Round the apartment runs an elegant frieze. On one side of the chamber is a projecting chimney, on which is painted Diana throwing off her veil as she mounts a car drawn by stags; these latter now effaced. An adjoining chamber, very similar in form, is painted by *Alessandro Araldi*, principally with groups of figures. In the 3 lunettes over each wall are different profane and Christian subjects. The roof is covered with very handsome arabesques, interspersed with portraits and small medallions; on the chimney are the arms of the abbess (3 half-moons), which are frequently introduced into the paintings here of Araldi and Correggio.

At the time when Giovanna lived great irregularities prevailed in the more opulent nunneries. The abbesses, even when untainted by grosser vices, indulged, without the least restraint, in the gaieties and pleasures of the world, setting at nought all ecclesiastical discipline. The Vatican was, however, alarmed by the progress of the Reformation; and, under the rigid Adrian VI., the nuns were commanded to observe the vows which they had made; disorders in the conventual establishments were reformed; the doors of San Paolo were closed, and the poor abbess died within a month afterwards. The paintings remained almost forgotten until about the year 1795, when the duke caused them to be examined, and a dissertation from the Padre Affò brought them out of their seclusion. In the church of S. Lodovico is the sepulchral monument to Count Niepperg, the second husband of Maria Louisa, by Bartolini of Florence.

Several ancient churches were demolished by the French. Those which remain are principally modern or modernised: a few may be noticed. *S. Andrea* has a painting of S. Bernardo by *Sebastian Conca*. *S. Sepolcro*, near the Porta S. Michele, leading towards Modena, a Madonna and Saints, in 1st chapel on rt., by *Parmigianino* (the celebrated picture of the Madonna della Scodella was formerly in this church). *S. Tomasso*, over the high altar, the Nativity, by *Alessandro Mazzola*. *S. Uldarico*, a very ancient conventual foundation on the site of the Roman theatre, the Nativity over the principal altar, by *Gir. Mazzola*. In the Ch. of the SS. *Annunziata*, beyond the bridge, founded by Ottavio Farnese, is a half-ruined fresco of the Annunciation, by *Correggio*, brought from a desecrated edifice. It has been engraved in Toschi's collection. The painting opposite to it, of the Madonna, with St. John the Evangelist, St. Bernard, and St. Francis, is by *Marchesi da Cotignola*, and highly prized by Lanzi.

The ancient *Farnese Palace*, called also *La Pilotta*, and the buildings connected with it, form a somewhat gloomy and rambling pile of great extent. One portion includes a cortile of fine proportions, but unfinished. It was begun by Ranuccio Farnese I., in 1597, and then adjoined the fine church of San Pietro Martire, which was pulled down to enlarge the cortile.

Entering under the gateway of the palace, by which passes the road to the bridge, and ascending the wide staircase, a rich heavy portal is seen in front. This is the entrance to the *Teatro Farnese*, built, in 1618, by Duke Ranuccio, and opened in 1628, upon occasion of the marriage of Duke Odoardo with the Princess Margaret of Tuscany. It is said to be the first theatre in which *boxes* as we build them were introduced. The whole is of wood; and, though some effort has been made to keep it in repair, it is in a most dilapidated state, and seems rapidly verging to complete ruin. The light shines through the rafters above, and the decayed floors are giving way below.

To the l. of the theatre are the apartments of the *Reale Accademia di Belle Arti*, founded in 1752. After many changes the Academy was re-established in 1822. It is now almost exclusively dedicated to the fine arts. Of this establishment the *Galleria* or *Pinacoteca* forms a portion. The collection contains nearly 600 pictures, several of the highest importance.

The *Pinacoteca* occupies a series of 14 rooms or divisions, as will be seen on reference to the annexed plan made on the spot in June of the present year.

There is no catalogue nor Nos. to the pictures, nor any indication of the subjects they represent, although the name of the painter is generally attached to each specimen.

Entering from the great staircase, a vestibule or kind of anteroom (I.) contains some modern works of Parma artists of very little interest. This hall opens into the *Great Gallery* (II. to VI.), divided off into 5 portions: here are some of the very fine works of the Pinacoteca. In the 1st division (II.) are the oldest paintings. A Madonna with St. Catherine, attri-

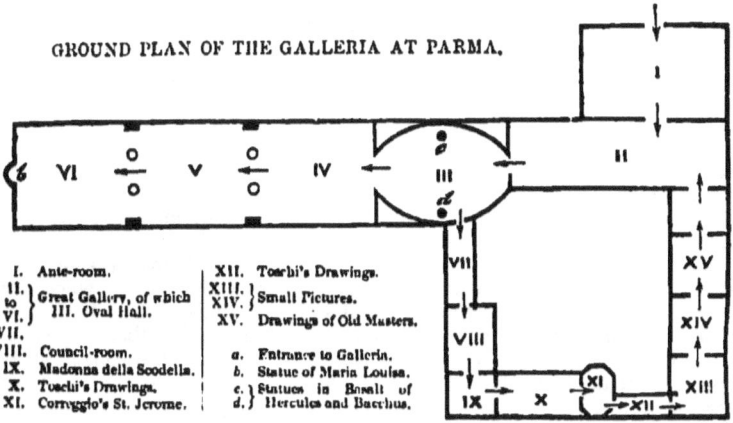

GROUND PLAN OF THE GALLERIA AT PARMA.

I. Ante-room.
II. to VI. } Great Gallery, of which III. Oval Hall.
VII.
VIII. Council-room.
IX. Madonna della Scodella.
X. Toschi's Drawings.
XI. Correggio's St. Jerome.
XII. Toschi's Drawings.
XIII. XIV. } Small Pictures.
XV. Drawings of Old Masters.
a. Entrance to Galleria.
b. Statue of Maria Louisa.
c. } Statues in Basalt of
d. } Hercules and Bacchus.

buted to *Luca di Parma*. A Virgin enthroned, by *Jacopo di Luschi* (1471). Two similar subjects, by *Temperello* (1499). A good Annunciation, by *A. Araldi*. *Correggio's* fine fresco of the Virgin, called *La Madonna della Scala*, painted originally over the town gate of San Michele. A Virgin and Child with St. Jerome and St. Benedict, by *Parmigianino*. Several paintings by *Gir. Mazzola* and *Anselmi*, excellent specimens of the school of Parma. And a Madonna and Child with San Bruno, by *Fran. Gatti*.

In the Oval Hall (III.) that follows are some works of modern artists of no great interest, but in which have been placed two colossal statues in green or Ethiopian basalt—one of Hercules, the other of Bacchus and Pan; they are perhaps the largest specimens known of this very hard and rare material, and in a good style of art. They were discovered in the 17th centy. in the gardens of the Palatine at Rome, then the property of the ruling family of Parma, the Farneses. There is some resemblance to Hadrian in the face of the Hercules, as there is in that of Bacchus to Antinous. Round this Oval Hall are eight senatorial statues, more or less mutilated, and in white marble from the ruins of Velleia.—*Room* IV. contains some of the chefs-d'œuvre of this part of the gallery. The SAN

VITALE MADONNA, and the DEPOSITION, by *F. Francia*; the first, a lovely picture, represents the Virgin and Child seated on a throne, with SS. Benedict, Placidus, Justina, and Scolastica on either side, with the infant St. John in the foreground; it is dated 1515, and long belonged to the San Vitale family. The Deposition represents the Dead Saviour on the knees of the Virgin, surrounded by saints; it is signed, but not dated. The other remarkable works here are *Ludovico Caracci's* large subjects of the Virgin carried to the tomb, and the latter found empty by the Apostles. The Dead Christ, by *An. Caracci*. A series of six copies of Correggio's magnificent frescoes in the ch. of S. Giovanni, including the justly celebrated Coronation of the Virgin, by *Ag. Carracci*. An Adoration of the Magi, by *Gir. Mazzola*. A Madonna and Child, by *Guercino;* and a good Descent from the Cross, by *Schidone*. The last division of the Great Gallery (*Room* VI.) contains Canova's sitting statue of Maria Louisa, as Concord; a curious St. Sebastian, by *Josephat Aldis;* two very fine Holy Families, by *Cima da Conegliano*, both signed by the painter. The Apparition of the Angel to the Apostles, by *Bassano;* a small Annunciation, by *Albano;* several Heads by *Spagnoletto*, &c.

Returning to the *Oval Hall* (III.), a

door leads from it into a series of smaller rooms on the side of the river. In the first (VII.) are some small genre paintings by *Tempesta, Viera, Canaletti*, &c. In the second (VIII.), where the Council of the Academy hold their meetings, are several portraits :—an Erasmus, by *Holbein;* Benvenuto Cellini, by *G. C. Amidoni;* Ag. Caracci, by himself; Alessandro Farnese and his Wife, by *Gir. Mazzola;* Petrarch, by *An. Caracci*; Correggio, Parmigianino, &c. From here we pass to the first room of Correggio's chefs-d'œuvre (IX.), the *Hall of the Madonna della Scodella*. A Flight into Egypt, deriving its name from the *scodella*—the small dish or bowl which the Virgin holds in her hand, the armorial bearings of the Scutellari or Scodellaris, for one of whom it was painted. Vasari calls this picture "divine." Beyond this is a kind of passage room (X.), hung with elaborate drawings of some of Correggio's great works in Parma. They were made by Toschi and his pupils for the purpose of being engraved, and which the traveller will do well to study here at his ease, before doing so on the originals, so much injured and effaced. From here we enter the *Hall of the St. Jerome* (XI.), hung, like that of the Madonna della Scodella, in green silk, with the letters A A (Antonio Allegri) worked into it. The celebrated picture called the *St. Jerome* is the only one here. It bears the name of St. Jerome in consequence of his being the most remarkable figure in the group, of which the centre is formed by the Madonna and Child; St. Mary Magdalen is opposite to St. Jerome, kissing the feet of the Infant. The history of this fine painting is curious. It was ordered by a widow lady, Briseis Bergonzi, who, in her contract with Correggio, made her stipulations as to what she was to have for her money with the utmost minuteness. The price was 47 sequins—about 22*l*. Correggio was employed during six months in the widow's house painting the picture, and, when it was finished, she was so well satisfied with it that she gave him, besides his board, two cartloads of faggots, a quantity of wheat, and a pig. The widow bestowed the painting upon the Convent of St. Anthony at Parma in 1527; and it speedily acquired an European reputation, so much so, that Don John V. of Portugal in 1549 opened a negotiation with the convent for the purchase of the painting, offering, as it is said, as much as 460,000 frs., a sum which appears incredible. The magistrates of Parma, hearing of the intended contract, and fearing lest their city should lose its treasure, gave notice to the duke, and he stopped the bargain by removing the picture and placing it in the cathedral. Here it continued till 1756, when one M. Jollain, a French painter, obtained an order from the then reigning duke, the Infant Don Philip, to make a copy of it. The chapter made some difficulties, upon which the duke sent a file of grenadiers and removed it, and after a lapse of a year placed it in his newly-founded Academy, paying at the same time the Prior of S. Antonio 1500 sequins in compensation. It was one of the earliest works of art carried off by the French. The Virgin is lovely; gentleness and entire devotion reign throughout her figure; but the children's heads are slightly exaggerated. The colouring is exquisite. "The Angel next to St. Jerome is extremely beautiful; other portions are, however, not quite free from affectation."—*Kugler*. The Italian writers upon art often call this picture "*Il Giorno*," from the wonderful effect of bright daylight which it exhibits, thus placing it in contrast with his celebrated *Notte*, above which it is placed by Mengs, who considered it as the finest of Correggio's works.

Another room (XII.), containing Toschi's drawings of the Correggios in the Camera di San Paolo and in the ch. of S. Giovanni, leads to Room XIII., which contains RAPHAEL'S JESUS GLORIFIED, the Virgin and St. Paul on one side, St. John the Baptist and St.

Catherine on the other. It was much restored at Paris, and Passavant speaks very doubtfully of its originality. Its early history is quite unknown, and it cannot be traced beyond the last century. Passavant thinks it is the work of some clever scholar of Raphael. *Correggio's* Martyrdom of SS. Flavia and Placidus, and its pendant the Dead Christ with the two Marys and St. Joseph of Arimathea. *Agostino Caracci*, a Madonna with three Saints. *Parmigianino*, the Marriage of St. Catherine. *Francia*, a lovely Holy Family with St. John. *Leon. da Vinci*, a bold sketch of a female head. And *Correggio*, a portrait of an Egyptian (?). In *Room* XIV. are several small paintings, of which the most worthy of notice are—*Mantegna*, the Martyrdom of St. Sebastian. *Bonifacio*, a Holy Family. *F. Baroccio*, St. Francis. Three small subjects by *Garofalo*. In the next *Room* (XV.) are several original drawings by masters of the Parma school, especially the Mazzolas.

The *Biblioteca* or *Library*, founded by Duke Philip of Bourbon in 1769, is said to contain 140,000 vols. It possesses the very valuable Hebrew and Syriac manuscripts of De Rossi, the great Oriental scholar, bought by Maria Louisa for 100,000 frs., as well as his printed books. It is altogether well selected, and is much frequented by readers. Amongst the literary curiosities are — Luther's Hebrew Psalter, with many autograph notes of the great reformer; evidently the copy from which he worked in making his translation of the Bible. A very beautiful MS. of Petrarch, which belonged to Francis I., and was found amongst his baggage at the battle of Pavia. The autograph collections of the great anatomist Morgagni. A map of the world made by Pizzicagni in 1367. The Koran found in the tent of the Grand Vizier Kara Mustapha, after the raising of the siege of Vienna. A MS. on the purity of the Virgin, of the 15th centy., with miniatures. The *Heures* which belonged to Henry II. of France, in each page of which is the emblem of Diana of Poictiers. Autograph letters from Voltaire, Galileo, Prince Eugene of Savoy, Emanuel Philibert, and of General Bonaparte to the Duke of Parma. The Library is fitted up with elegance, and is kept in admirable order for cleanliness and efficiency. In its second great hall is the fresco of the *Incoronata*, painted by *Correggio*, and removed from the demolished tribune in the church of San Giovanni : it represents our Saviour placing on the head of the Virgin a crown of stars. In a room opening out of the first hall are preserved the *matrices* of all Bodoni's types, 52,000 in number; and in another hall of the Library, a series of modern paintings of different episodes from the Divina Commedia, by Scaramuzza, a Parmesan painter. Attached to the Library is the rich collection of engravings, said to contain 85,000 specimens, of which a large proportion (60,000) were purchased of Massimiliano Ortalli, a few years ago, by Maria Louisa, for 45,000 francs.

The *Museum of Antiquities*, formerly called the *Museo Ducale*, is entered from the first landing-place on the great staircase. It has been formed principally by objects brought from Rome by the Farnese Princes, by several discovered at Velleia in the last century, and by some found amongst the ruins of Roman Parma. Like the Pinacoteca and the Library above, it is open to visitors daily from 10 A.M. until 3 P.M. It consists of four rooms. In the first are numerous Roman inscriptions : one dedicated by the *Respublica Velleiata* to a certain Proconsul Coelius Festus, its benefactor, is locally interesting. The Signa Tegulasia are numerous : one of A.U.C. 685 records the names of the Consuls, Q. Hortensius and Quintus Coelius. *Room* II. contains chiefly bronzes, many from Velleia, the most important being the great *Tabula Alimentaria* of Trajan, or the decree for the distribution of his gifts towards the maintenance of the children of the poor. He gives the sum of 1,144,000 sesterces, to be invested in lands, of which the proceeds are to be employed in maintaining 245 males and 45 females, all to be legitimate, together with one *spurius* and one *spuria*, a proof how much the Roman policy, even at that period, respected the sanctity of marriage; every boy was to receive 16 sesterces by month, and every girl 12, but the *spurius* and the *spuria* only 10 each. It appears that the whole sum invested produced about 5 per cent. The *Tabula* is nearly 12 ft. in length by about 5 in height; the writing is in seven columns. The names and situation of the lands are given, thus rendering it an interesting memorial of local topography.—Another inscription contains the fragments of laws to be observed in Cisalpine Gaul.—A small statue of a Drunken Hercules, on the marble pedestal of which is engraved a dedicatory inscription to the demigod by a certain Demetrius.—Three graceful statuettes of Mars, Apollo, and Bacchus.—A small statue of a Victory.—A full-sized gilt bust of Hadrian, and another of a Young Man with glass eyes inserted in the sockets; and numerous articles of domestic use. —*Room* III.—Some Egyptian articles: fragments of Comic Masks in marble, discovered in the ruins of the Roman theatre at Parma; two busts of Vitellius from Rome; a mutilated statue, called Agrippina, from Velleia; and a small group of Leda and the Swan, without the heads, found also at Parma, a rather indelicate subject, such as would be consigned at Rome or Naples to the cellars of the Vatican or Museo Borbonico.—*Room* IV. contains the collection of Coins and Medals, numbering nearly 30,000; four good draped Senatorial statues in marble, two with their heads perfect, from Velleia; a few Græco-Siculan Vases; and a very interesting series of gold ornaments, chains, bracelets, &c., discovered in 1821 in digging the foundation of the new theatre; with gold coins from the reign of Nero to that of Gallienus. The Colossal Bust of Maria Louisa in this room is by Canova.

The *University*, not far from the Piazza Grande, in the ancient College of San Rocco, which belonged to the Jesuits, contains the different schools, an astronomical observatory, and a cabinet of natural history. The average number of students of late years has been between 300 and 400.

The *Tipografia del Governo* (in the Farnese Palace, below the Galleries) is known to the bibliographical world as having been under the direction of the celebrated Bodoni. Among his collections may be seen various fine specimens of typography, and different methods of printing music. These, as well as the models or matrices of his types, have been deposited in a room set apart for the purpose in the Library.

The *Teatro Nuovo*, close to the Ducal Palace, begun in 1821, and opened in 1829, is a very showy building within. It cost 2,000,000 *lire Italiane*.

The *Botanic Garden* is on the l. bank of the river, not far from the Citadel on the S. side of the town, from which extends the *publio promenade* or *Stradone*, to the *Boulevards*, which, running along the ramparts, surround the whole of the eastern portion of Parma.

The late Cavalier Toschi and his school had been, for some time prior to his death, engaged on a series of elaborate drawings from the frescoes of Correggio; from which engravings are being executed, which will preserve a knowledge of these great works, now so decayed. They are executed with great care, and may be seen at Toschi's house in Parma; and in London, at Messrs. Colnaghi's.

In 1843 the remains of a Roman theatre were discovered at Parma, near the church of S. Uldarico.

The torrent Parma has here no beauty: it is crossed by three bridges. In the N.W. suburb is the *Palazzo del Giardino*. It was built by Ottavio Farnese, but was altered and enlarged in 1767. It is partly stuccoed and looks unfinished, but contains some curious frescoes, which about a century ago were covered with paper-hangings. Parts were uncovered by the French about 40 years ago, others very recently; some are still concealed. The frescoes in one room are by *Agostino Caracci;* but were left unfinished by him, as we learn from an inscription, which says that it is better to see them unfinished by his hand than finished by any other. They represent the Rape of Europa, the Triumph of Venus, the Marriage of Peleus and Thetis, in three large paintings occupying three sides of the room. On the window side is Apollo and Daphne. In the centre of the ceiling are three Cupids, and other subjects in lunettes above the four sides. "Although slight and coarse in execution, the classical stories they represent are pleasingly told and with much poetic feeling; particularly that one of Peleus and Thetis, where the coy modesty of the lady, the enjoyment of the Cupids, and the general languid voluptuousness are successfully treated."—*C. W. C.*

A second room is decorated with allegories representing various scenes of enjoyment; one the palace of Armida, with its columns and walls of crystal, like the *Palais de la Vérité* of Madame de Genlis, through which the figures are seen. A third room contains mythological subjects. There is also a large collection of portraits of the members of the houses by which Parma has been ruled, but which have little merit as works of art.

The *Giardino Ducale* is in the old-fashioned French style, with half-deserted look. The grounds are open at all times, and are most easily reached by crossing the bridge from the Farnese Palace.

ROUTE 41.

CREMONA TO PARMA, BY CASAL MAGGIORE AND COLORNO.

(5¼ posts = 48 m.)

Cremona,
1 Cicognolo, } Rte. 25.
1¼ Piadena,

Between Parma and Cremona there is a diligence daily, which leaves Parma at 8 A.M. There is also a daily diligence to Mantua by Casal Maggiore in 7 or 8 hours (fare, 9 francs), corresponding with those to and from Cremona, now the only public conveyance between the Austrian territory and the provinces S. of the Po.

1¼ *Casal Maggiore;* a small but important town, of 5000 Inhab., on the N. bank of the Po, here a mighty stream: the country is always at the mercy of its devastating waves.

"Sic pleno Padus ore tumens super aggere tutas
Excurrit ripas, et totos concutit agros.
Succubuit si qua tellus, cumulumque furentem
Undarum non passa, ruit; tum flumine toto
Transit, et ignotos aperit sibi gurgite campos.
Illos terrâ fugit dominos; his rura colonis
Accedunt, donante Pado."
Pharsalia, vi.

" So, raised by melting streams of Alpine snow,
Beyond his utmost margin swells the Po,
And loosely lets the spreading deluge flow:
Where'er the weaker banks oppress'd retreat,
And sink beneath the heapy waters' weight,
Forth gushing at the breach they burst their way,
And wasteful o'er the drowned country stray:
Far distant fields and meads they wander o'er,
And visit lands they never knew before.
Here, from its seat the mouldering earth is torn,
And by the flood to other masters borne;
While gathering there, it heaps the growing soil,
And loads the peasant with his neighbour's spoil."
ROWE'S *Lucan,* vi. 464-476.

The embankments, in many parts, look down upon the adjoining country; and from time to time "the king of rivers" fully asserts his devastating power.

"There is an old channel of the Po in the territory of Parma, called Po Vecchio, which was abandoned in the

12th centy., when a great number of towns were destroyed. There are records of parish churches, as those of Vico Belignano, Agojolo, and Martignana (which lie a little to the N. and N.W. of Casal Maggiore), having been pulled down, and afterwards rebuilt at a greater distance from the devouring stream. In the 15th centy. the main branch again resumed its deserted channel, and carried away a great island opposite Casal Maggiore. At the end of the same century it abandoned, a second time, the bed called 'Po Vecchio,' carrying away three streets of Casal Maggiore."—*Lyell.*

" Proluit insano contorquens vortice silvas
Fluviorum rex Eridanus, camposque per omnes
Cum stabulis armenta tulit."
Georg., l. 481.

" Then, rising in his might, the king of floods
Rush'd through the forests, tore the lofty woods,
And rolling onward, with a sweepy sway,
Bore houses, herds, and labouring hinds away."
DRYDEN's *Georgics*, l. 649-653.

The traveller will have full time to study, not only these quotations, but probably to read good part of the Georgics, in crossing the ferry, one of the clumsiest and worst ordered of its kind, the passage from land to land occupying a considerable time.

Shortly after, you reach *Sacca*. Here we enter the Parmesan territory.

Colorno, on the Parma, formerly a fief of the family of S. Vitale, of whom the beautiful Barbara di Colorno, sacrificed to the tyranny of Ranuccio I., was a member. Upon the execution of her husband the fief was confiscated, and the Palace became the principal *villegiatura* of the sovereigns: it is a large and stately, but somewhat neglected, building. Under the Farnese dukes it contained several remarkable specimens of antiquity and works of art. It has also some tolerable modern frescoes by *Borghetti*. The Church of *San Liborio*, near the Palace, is richly ornamented.

Cortile San Martino. Here is a desecrated building, once a Carthusian monastery, with a fine church in the Renaissance style, now falling into ruin.

The above is the only road on which there are post relays between Cremona and Parma; but there is a more direct one, which crosses the Po at the Porto di Cremona to Monticelli, from whence it branches off on the l. to Cortemaggiore, Busseto, Borgo San Donino, and Parma (see Rte. 40). From Corte Maggiore there is also a good road of 5 m. to S. Azuola, and another from Monticelli, through San Nazzaro, Caorso, and Roncaglia, to Piacenza, about 20 m.

2 PARMA (Route 40).

ROUTE 42.

PARMA TO MANTUA, BY GUASTALLA.

POSTS.	POSTS.
2 Brescello.	2 Borgoforte.
1 Guastalla.	1 Mantua.

(6 posts = 52 m.)

Vicopré, with a small church in the style of the Renaissance.

Sorbolo, on the Enza torrent, a village on the frontier of Modena.

2 *Brescello;* pleasantly situated near the rt. bank of the Po, here dotted with numerous islands. This town, which is now on the rt. bank of the river, is one of those of which the site was formerly on the l. "Subsequently to the year 1390, the Po deserted part of the territory of Cremona, and invaded that of Parma; its old channel being still recognisable, and bearing the name of Po Morto."—*Lyell.* Brescello is the birthplace of our eminent adopted countryman Mr. Panizzi, of the British Museum.

The road runs along the Po by Boretto and Gualtieri, and crosses the *Crostolo* river, which formerly separated Modena from Guastalla.

1 *Guastalla.*—(*Inns:* La Posta, Il Capello Verde, Il Leone d'Oro.) This small city on the Crostolo, containing between 2000 and 3000 Inhab., is quite in proportion to the duchy of which it is the capital. Guastalla belonged originally to the family of the Torellis as its Counts from 1406 to 1509, and afterwards to a younger branch of the Gonzagas of Mantua; in 1748 it was given to the Parma Bourbons by the treaty of Aix-la-Chapelle, the last of the Gonzagas of the Guastalla branch having died in 1746 without issue. Forming with those of Parma and Piacenza the sovereignty of Maria Louisa, it reverted to the Duke of Modena on the death of that princess. In the Lombard times it was known by the name of *Guardstall.* The statue in bronze of Ferrante Gonzaga I., by *Leone Leoni,* in the piazza, is the only work of art worthy of notice here. He is trampling upon Envy, represented in the shape of an ugly satyr. Don Ferrante had been accused of treason against the emperor, but he disproved the charge made by his enemies. The cathedral has only recently obtained a bishop, the see having been instituted in 1828. There are eight other churches in the town, and some charitable institutions. Guastalla is now the frontier town of the N. Italian kingdom towards the Austrian possessions on the Po.

Luzzara, a village on the banks of the Po, on the Austrian frontier. It is a point of some military importance; here, in August 1702, the imperialists under Prince Eugene suffered a memorable defeat from the French. Between Villa and Sailetto we traverse the territory of Gonzaga, which, by a strange oversight at Villafranca, was allowed to remain in the hands of Austria.

One mile beyond Sailletto we cross the Po by the ferry of

2 *Borgoforte,* so called from the *strong castle* built here by the Mantuans in 1211.

1 MANTUA (Rte. 30).

ROUTE 43.

PARMA TO SARZANA, BY PONTREMOLI.

POSTS.	POSTS.
Fornuovo.	Terra Rossa.
Berceto.	Sarzana.
Pontremoli.	

The road is kept in tolerable repair, but is heavy in winter, and at all times dull until it reaches the summit of the Apennines. It has been improved of late years, and a diligence travels by it daily, except on Sundays, carrying the mails, from Parma to Sarzana by Pontremoli, leaving at 5 A.M.: fare to Pontremoli 11 fr. and to Sarzana 19 fr. This road was much frequented in the middle ages by persons going to Rome from countries beyond the Alps; hence the names then given to it of *Strada Francesca* and *Romea.* Anciently a branch of the Via Clodia appears to have traversed this pass of the Apennines.

This route, perhaps the least interesting over the Apennines in a picturesque view, may prove convenient to persons desiring to reach the baths of Lucca, sea-bathing at Spezia, &c., from Lombardy, without going round by Bologna on the E., or by Genoa on the W.

The only tolerable sleeping-place will be found to be Pontremoli, which may be easily reached with vetturino horses in a summer's day from Parma.

Collecchio, a village pleasantly situated near the commencement of the hilly country; there is a good Gothic church with a baptistery here. From Collecchio the road runs along the hills which bound the valley of the Taro, gradually approaching that river, to

2 posts, *Fornuovo* (Forum Novanorum), at the foot of the Apennines, on the rt. bank of the Taro, at its junction with the Ceno, a considerable stream

flowing from the W.S.W. There are many vestiges of Roman antiquities in the more recent buildings of Fornuovo, particularly in the walls of the principal church and some of the adjoining houses. The church is rather a good Lombard structure; on the façade are some curious bas-reliefs, particularly one representing the Seven Mortal Sins. Fornuovo derives some celebrity from the battle fought here in 1495 between Charles VIII. of France on his return from Naples, and the Italian confederates under Francesco Gonzaga, Marquis of Mantua, when the latter were defeated with great loss, although numbering more than four-fold the victorious army. The roads leading from Parma to Borgo Taro and Bardi separate at Fornuovo. There is an indifferent Italian Inn here (Albergo Reale); the people civil. The road begins to ascend rapidly after Fornuovo, over a spur of the Apennines separating the Taro and Bagnanza valleys, winding round the high hill of *Monte Prinzera*, and passing through the villages of Piantogna and Cassio.

3 posts, *Berceto* (*Inn:* Albergo Reale, very poor; the Diligence and Vetturini generally stop here)—a picturesque ancient town in the midst of the mountains. The church is a Gothic building; the piazza in front, the fountain, and the whole scene around, are singular; this is the last town before crossing the Apennines. The road from hence ascends the Bagnanza torrent to the Cisa Pass, which is very wild and desolate, at an elevation of 3420 Eng. ft. above the sea; it is supposed that it was by this pass that Hannibal penetrated into Etruria, after having defeated Sempronius on the Trebbia. We here enter the province of Upper Lunigiana. The road descends rapidly by *Monte Lungo* and *Mignenza* on the Magra, the rt. bank of which it follows to

Pontremoli (*Inn:* Il Pavone, at the Posta: although not over clean, it is a tolerable house, with civil people, and the best stopping-place between Parma and Sarzana). This city, of 3400 Inhab., which derives its name probably from a shaky bridge over the Magra (Pons tremulus), offers a striking contrast to all the traveller has hitherto seen. He finds himself amongst a new race, and many buildings have a peculiar character. Situated in a triangle formed by the junction of the Magra and Verde torrents, it consists of an upper and lower town, the former surrounded by massive and picturesque fortifications. Pontremoli, being during the middle ages as it were the key to one of the most frequented passes of the chain between Tuscany and Lombardy, has repeatedly changed masters. Some of the old towers were raised in 1322 by Castruccio, the lord of Lucca; others by the Genoese, when they held possession of the Lunigiana. It also belonged for a time to Milan; and the armorial bearings of the Sforzas show its ancient union to that powerful duchy. The lower town of Pontremoli has a more modern aspect; the Duomo, unfinished, was begun in 1620. Sta. Annunziata in the S. suburb was built in 1471; within stands a small octagonal temple of white marble and good workmanship. The other churches are modernized. Pontremoli is 23 m. from Carrara.

The road, on leaving Pontremoli, runs parallel to, but at some distance from the Magra, passing *Villafranca*, where the Bagnone torrent enters it; several fine old castellated remains are scattered over the country on each side of the river.

Filattiera, between Pontremoli and Villafranca, has a fine old castle, once belonging to the Malaspinas, the feudal lords of the Lunigiana.

2 posts, *Terra Rossa* (no *Inn*), near the junction of the Coviglia and Tavarone torrents with the Magra, both of which must be crossed on leaving it for Sarzana. Do not let travellers allow themselves to be imposed upon by the people offering assistance to cross these torrents, as it is unnecessary. A new road has been recently opened from Terra Rossa to Sarzana by

Aulla (the Papagallo; a poor cabaret, outside the gate, is kept by civil people);

the country as far as Aulla is beautiful. After leaving this town the Auletta torrent is crossed in a ferry-boat, the landing from which is bad for carriages on both sides.

Sarzana; an extra horse between Sarzana and Terra Rossa, both ways, from Nov. 1 to May 1. (Rte. 14.)

[Travellers to Lucca and Florence need not go out of their way to Sarzana; after crossing the Auletta, on leaving Aulla, they may enter the duchy of Massa Carrara; the carriage-road ascends for 5 m. to

Ceserano, a small town, where a road branches off on the l. to Fivizzano; from Ceserano a hilly road leads by Terenzo and Tendola to

Fosdinovo, a town of 1850 Inhab., very finely situated on a projecting part of the Apennines, and offering fine views over the Mediterranean, the Gulf of Spezzia, and the shore to the eastward; myrtles grow wild in abundance between Fosdinovo and the plain to the S. There is a good road of about 5 m. from Fosdinovo to *Portone,* where it joins the high road from Sarzana to Lucca, 3 m. beyond the former.

From Fosdinovo a considerable ascent of nearly an hour to Monte Girone, and an equal distance to *Castelpoggio,* where there is a kind of *Inn* (the Pistola). From Castelpoggio the road is good and very picturesque as far as Carrara. (See Rte. 76.)]

SECTION VI.
DUCHY OF MODENA.
1. *Agriculture, Commerce, Finances.*—2. *Posting, Money.*

ROUTES.

ROUTE	PAGE	ROUTE	PAGE
50 Parma to *Reggio* and *Modena*—Rail	426	51 Modena to Pistoja, by Barigazzo and San Marcello	433

PRELIMINARY INFORMATION.

Francesco V., Duke of Modena (deposed in 1859), was born 1st June, 1819, and succeeded his father on the 21st January, 1846. In addition to his principal title, he is an Archduke of Austria, and Duke of Guastalla, Massa, and Carrara. His territories embraced the duchies of Modena Proper, Guastalla, and Reggio, on the N., and of Massa and Carrara, the districts of the Apennines, and Fivizzano, more recently acquired by exchange from Tuscany, on the S. The Modenese territory therefore extended from the Po to the Mediterranean, although the portion lying on the sea-coast is very small, and devoid of ports or harbours. Owing to his family ties with the House of Austria, Francesco V. espoused the imperial cause with ardour, the consequence of which has been, that, on the breaking out of the war with France and Piedmont in the spring of 1859, he was obliged to abandon his states, which, in the early part of the present year, by an almost unanimous vote, annexed themselves to the kingdom of Northern Italy, and of which they now form the provinces of Modena and Reggio, of the Emilian Confederation.

§ 1. AGRICULTURE.—COMMERCE.—FINANCES.

The Modenese territory was of somewhat greater extent than Parma. Its soil and productions are similar, except to the S. of the Apennines, where the olive and orange grow in the open air. The population by the last census amounted to 606,139 Inhab. The farms are small, and the métayer system prevails. Agriculture is the chief industry; chestnuts form the principal food of the peasantry in the mountain districts, *pollenta* or porridge of Indian cornmeal in the plain. Wheat, maize, wines, olives, silk, hemp, and some flax, are the principal objects of culture. The valley of La Garfagnana is that alone in which dairy pasture is followed to any extent. The Duke and a few of the principal landlords own the large flocks of sheep which pasture on the Apennines and the slopes of the mountains. On the latter, pine, oak, and chestnut trees abound. The vine is extensively cultivated about Reggio and Modena, from which a large quantity of wine, of a strong rough description, is exported to Lombardy. The marble of Carrara forms the most valuable article of its mineral riches. Some silk-works, linen and canvas, leather, paper, and pottery, all on an insignificant scale, comprise the manufacturing industry of this small state. Its trifling commerce is, like that of Parma, confined to an interchange of its few surplus products for colonial commodities and articles of luxury; all of which, from both, are comprised in the trade of the surrounding maritime states. The annual revenues of Modena as an independent state, in 1858, amounted to 8,413,622 francs (336,545*l.*); the expenditure, 8,728,133 francs (349,126*l.*); showing here, as everywhere in Italy, a deficit.

§ 2. POSTING.—MONEY.

The posting regulations and money are the same as in the other parts of the N. Italian Kingdom.

ROUTES.

ROUTE 50.
PARMA TO REGGIO AND MODENA, BY RAILWAY.

KIL.		KIL.
11 S. Ilario.		40 Rubiere.
28 Reggio.		53 Modena.

53 kil. = 33 m.

The railway continues nearly parallel to the Via Emilia.

On quitting Parma fine views of the purple Apennines in the distance open on the rt.

San Lazzaro; the name of this place indicates the existence of an ancient hospital. Lepers were strictly prohibited from entering the city of Parma, hence the necessity of this house of refuge. The Portone di San Lazzaro, an arch which crosses the post road on the rt., was erected to commemorate the arrival of Margaret of Medici, on the occasion of her marriage with Odoardo Farnese in 1628.

San Prospero, a village on the rt.; a mile further, we cross by a long bridge the Enza torrent, furious in winter, but in summer having its course marked only by a bed of stones. About a mile further on commenced the territory of Modena, soon after which we reach

11 kil. *Sant' Ilario Stat.,* about ½ a m. from the village of the same name. 5 m. S. of this lies *Montecchio,* celebrated for the birthplace of Attendolo Sforza, the father of Francesco, the founder of the great but unfortunate second dynasty of the Dukes of Milan. 1 m. N. of St. Ilario is *Taneto,* which preserves nearly unchanged the name of *Tanctum,* one of the Roman stations on the Via Æmilia.

2 m. further cross the *Crostolo,* which, under the French, gave its name to the department, before reaching

17 kil. *Reggio* (*Inns:* Posta, Giglio), a flourishing city, containing upwards of 16,000 Inhab. *Regium Lepidi* was founded by, or at least received the privileges of a Roman colony from, Æmilius Lepidus. The devastations of Alaric, and the restoration of the city by Charlemagne, have effaced almost every vestige of antiquity. A curious Roman statue of Janus, of fairly good workmanship, but lacking both arms, is built into the corner of a house near the *Palazzo dei Bechi.* A statue, which is called that of Lepidus, is preserved in the *Palazzo del Commune.* There are several curious Roman inscriptions and cippi in the cortile and porticoes of that building.

The great romantic poet of Italy was born at Reggio, and the house in which Ariosto first saw the light is, according to immemorial tradition pointed out near the Palazzo del Commune. Some, however, maintain that Ariosto *must* have been born within the precincts of the citadel. The house itself has no appearance of age, and has nothing but the tradition to render it remarkable.

The *Duomo* is of the 15th century. The façade, which is unfinished, is ornamented with marble columns, and recumbent on the pediment of the great door are good statues of Adam and Eve, by *Clementi.* They are larger than life, and *Clementi* has evidently imitated his master, Michael Angelo, in the position of the figures, which are like the "Morning and Evening" in the Medicean Chapel at Florence; there are also statues of SS. Chrysanthus and Darius, the patron saints.

Within the cathedral are several other works by *Clementi:*—The Tomb of Ugo Rangoni, Bishop of Reggio. He is represented larger than life, giving his blessing. By *Clementi* also is the bronze group at the high altar, representing Christ Triumphant, and the statues of Saints Prosper, Maximus, and Catherine in the choir. *Clementi* himself is buried in this cathedral, under a monument by his pupil, *Pacchione,* who was both a sculptor and an architect. In a chapel is a statue of Bishop Ficcarelli, who died in 1825. It is above the ordinary run of modern provincial sculpture in Italy. Another monument is that of Francesco Maria d'Este, late Bishop of Reggio, died 1820. He left all his property to the cathedral.

Madonna della Ghiara. The plan of this church is a Greek cross. It was begun in 1597 from the designs of *Balbi,* and completed by *Pacchione,* who added the vaulting of the cupola. The architectural details are good. The interior is covered with frescoes. Large and small there are upwards of 200 compartments thus decorated, and in good preservation. One series is by *Luca Ferrari* (1605-1654), a native of Reggio, the disciple of Guido. Amongst these are several Scripture histories, which, like all the paintings throughout the church, are explained or allegorised by short mottoes; as, for example, Rebecca at the Well, "*Hausit aquas in gaudio de fonte Salvatoris.*" Another series is by *Tiarini,* of Bologna (born 1577, died 1668). The painter, who lived during the greater part of his life at Reggio, was in some respects formed by the Caracci, yet preserved a distinct character. His compartments also are Scripture histories, intermixed with devices. A third series is by *Lionello Spada* (1576-1622), a friend, and yet in some degree a rival, of *Tiarini,* and to whom he was superior in colouring, but inferior in design. *Spada* was here in direct competition with *Tiarini,* and the series which he has left contains some of his most carefully executed works. By *Desani* (1594-1657), a pupil of *Spada,* and who established himself at Reggio, is a curious series of figures, representing eight religious orders, with the virtues supposed to belong more particularly to each. By *Gavassetti* (died 1628), several Prophets and Virtues. A Crucifixion, by *Guercino,* seems a fine picture, but it is dirty and ill seen. The original *Madonna della Ghiara,* once an old painting upon a garden wall, has long since perished. The present one w s painted in 1573, and placed in a magnificent shrine or altar, with beautiful lamps of silver suspended before it. The tomb of Maria Teresa, the last descendant of the house of Cibo Malaspina, Dukes of Massa Carrara, and wife of Ercole III., was erected by her daughter, Maria Beatrix, in 1820; over it is a good bust of the deceased.

The ancient Basilica of *San Prospero* (which stands behind the cathedral) was entirely rebuilt in the 16th century. The demolished building was in the Lombard style. Six colossal marble lions which supported the portals are still in front of the modern church. One grasps two skulls with his hind paws; others have the usual rams and serpents. Within, the structure is grand and regular. Fine, but damaged frescoes by *Campi* and *Procaccini*—amongst other subjects, the Last Judgment, Heaven, Purgatory, Hell—decorate the vaultings. Other paintings are by *Tiarini.* In the sanctuary are some statues, a crucifix, and massive ornaments, in silver.

Reggio has a good public library and a museum. In the latter are the collections of the celebrated Spallanzani: he was born at Scandiano, within the district, and therefore the inhabitants of the city consider him as their fellow-citizen. Reggio is also the country of Valisnieri, Toschi, and Paradisi. There is an active trade here in wine, silk, cheese, and hemp, so that the place has an air of prosperity.

A road much improved of late years, and with a military object, leads from Reggio to the shores of the Mediterranean by the Pass of Sassalbo, Fivizzano, and Sarzana, through a country offering little interest, with only one decent resting-place, at Castelnuovo nel Monte; there are no relays of post-horses upon it; it has been chiefly used hitherto by persons carrying fish from the coast of the Mediterranean to Reggio and Rubiera.

About 12 m. S.W. from Reggio is *Canossa,* celebrated as the place where the Emperor Henry IV., after supplicating during three days, barefooted and bareheaded, obtained absolution from Pope Gregory VII. in 1077.

12 kil. *Rubiera Stat.,* 1 m. before reaching the *Secchia.* This place, surrounded by fine fortifications, was a fief belonging to Bojardo, Lord of Scandiano, author of the 'Orlando Inna-

morato.' There are some remains of a Roman bridge over the Secchia.

The road continues through a plain, with many vines; but, in other respects, with somewhat diminished fertility. Before reaching the Modena Stat. the railway runs close to the fortified wall of the city on rt. 13 kil. *Modena Stat.*, close to the New Porta del Castello, leading by a wide street to the Ducal Palace, and into the city.

MODENA (*Inns:* Albergo S. Marco; Albergo Reale; a new house; dirty and dear—1859), the ancient *Mutina*, possesses nothing but the features of land and stream to recall its early history. The city is pleasantly situated between the rivers Secchia and Panaro. The verses of Tassoni well describe the locality:—

" Modana siede in una gran pianura,
Che da la parte d' Austro, e d' Occidente,
Cerchia di balze, e di scoscese mura
Del selvoso Apennin la schiena algente;
Apennin, ch' ivi tanto all' aria pura
S' alza a veder nel mare il Sol cadente,
Che su la fronte sua cinta di gelo
Par che s' incurvi, e che riposi il cielo.

Da l' Oriente ha le fiorite sponde
Del bel Panaro, e le sue limpid' acque,
Bologna incontro, e a la sinistra l' onde,
Dove il figlio del Sol già morto giacque,
Secchia ha da l' Aquilon, che si confonde
Ne' giri, che mutar sempre la piacque;
Divora i liti, e d' infeconde arene
Semina i prati, e le campagne amene."
Secchia Rapita, canto i., st. 8, 9.

[A few hours, indeed for many travellers the interval between two successive railway trains, will suffice to visit the most interesting objects at Modena: the best plan in that case will be to hire a carriage at the railway station, and to adopt the following itinerary:—Ducal Palace, *Pinacoteca* and *Library;* Ch. of S. Vincenzo; *Duomo;* Piazza Muratori; Ch. of S. Agostino; *Museo Lapidario;* Piazza d'Armi, and Citadel; returning by the Corso della Via Emilia, and along the ramparts.]

The city, which contains about 30,000 Inhab., is fortified, and the ramparts, though destitute of strength, offer a very pleasant walk. The views of the Appenines from them are peculiarly fine.

The Citadel, and its *Piazza d'Armi*, include perhaps one-third of the area of the city, which possesses a character differing much from the other Lombard towns in its domestic architecture, it being more of a German cast.

The *Duomo*. "This splendid building was begun in 1099, at the instance and with the assistance of the celebrated Countess Matilda, of whose vast possessions Modena formed a part. In 1108 the work was so far advanced that in that year the body of St. Geminianus, the patron saint of Modena, was translated into the new Basilica, which was at the same time consecrated by Pope Pascal II., in the presence of the Countess Matilda. The bulk of the fabric therefore belongs to the close of the 11th century. The name of the architect was Lanfrancus, as is shown by an inscription on one of the outer walls. The style is Lombard throughout. External arcades ornament both the W. end and the great semicircular apse. In the interior, monsters and grotesque images are still retained in the capitals of some of the pillars. But a feature which is not found in the old Lombard churches may be remarked here, in the large projecting porch, two stories in height, which advances before the principal entrance; and in the lions, on the backs of which the pillars of the porch rest. Though projecting porches were an essential part of the primitive churches, they seem to have been abandoned under the Lombard dynasty, and not to have been resumed till the 11th century, when they became universal. The lions are symbolical. They were intended to represent the strength and vigilance of the Church. At a later period the animals which were introduced in the porches often represented the arms of the state to which the building belonged. For example, the griffin is the crest of Perugia, and the wolf that of Sienna, Perugia and Sienna were constantly at war: in consequence, the doorway of the Palazzo Publico of Perugia is decorated with a griffin tearing a wolf."

"On either side of the nave there are galleries. Under the chancel is a

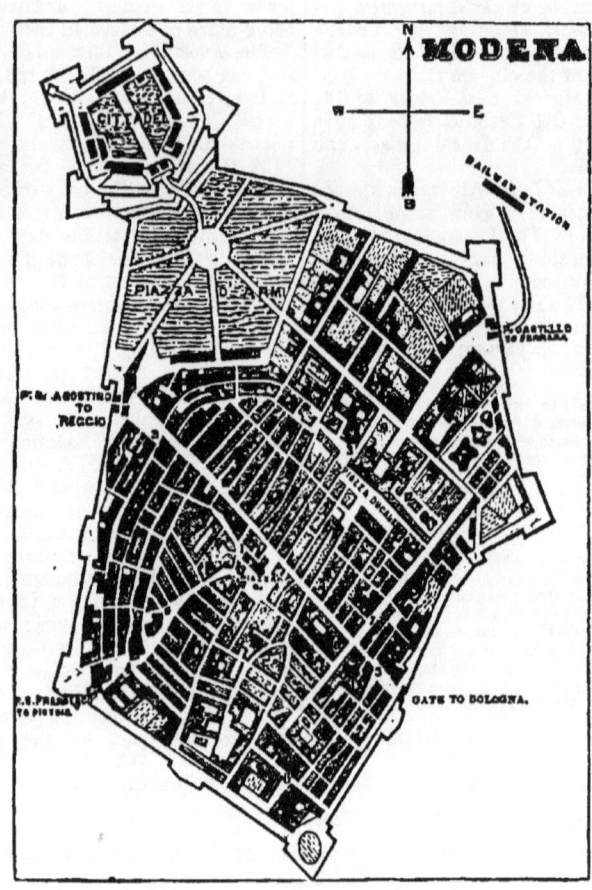

CHURCHES.
1. Duomo or Cathedral.
2. S. Agostino.
3. S. Domenico.
4. S. Francesco.
5. Il Carmine.
6. S. Pietro.
7. S. Vincenzo.

PUBLIC BUILDINGS, &c.
8. Ducal Palace.
9. Picture Gallery.
10. University.
11. Museo Lapidario.
12. Theatre.
13. Post Office.

lofty crypt. To gain elevation for the crypt, the chancel is approached by several steps, as at S. Miniato (near Florence) and elsewhere. The portals exhibit ornaments and bas-reliefs of different periods, from the 12th down to the 14th century. The earliest are executed with little skill, though they must have excited great admiration at the time, as an inscription preserves the name of the artist. Over the head of one of the figures, at one of the side-doors, appears the name of Artres de Bretaniâ—a proof that the legends of romance were popular in Italy in the 12th century."—*G. Knight.*

The sculptures on the doorway of the façade are extremely rude, and represent Adam and Eve, the Creation of Eve, the Fall, and other Scripture histories. A city walled and turreted, assailed by knights with the pointed shields and conical helmets of the 11th century, and whose names are written in barbarous characters. Here are the names of some of the heroes of the round table. Some ancient Roman inscriptions and tombs are built into the façade. Behind the altar of the crypt is the tomb of St. Geminianus. The crypt has been altered. The marble columns in the church itself have capitals approaching Corinthian.

The paintings in the Duomo are in general below mediocrity. It contains, however, some good works of art. The screen of red marble on either side of the choir, consisting of a range of small double columns, supporting a species of balustrade, is peculiar. An altarpiece in the 2nd chapel on l., in the style of the Renaissance, in terra-cotta, with abundance of curious small statues. Another altarpiece contains the earliest known specimen of Modenese art. It is by *Serafino dei Serafini* da Modena, and was executed 1385. It is hard and dry, and more than usually Byzantine. The pulpit is of marble, sculptured, 1322, by *Tomaso Ferri,* called also T. da Modena; the small statues on it are of a subsequent period; the *tarsia*-work of the stalls in the choir, executed in 1465, is worthy of notice.

Near the sacristy, in a niche behind and above an altar, is a beautiful group of the Nativity, in terracotta, by *Begarelli* (1518). So many of the works of this artist have perished, that this is kept shut up, but it will be opened by the *sacristano.* The tombs in this cathedral are interesting. Several, belonging to the Rangoni family, are of a good period of art. That of Claudio Rangoni, on l. of the choir, designed by *Giulio Romano,* consists simply of a sarcophagus beneath a canopy. Two angels, supporting a tablet on which the letters I.II.S. are inscribed, and a similar one below, constitute its only ornaments. Claudio, who died 1537, at the age of 29, succeeded his father, Francesco Maria, as Count of Castelvetro. He was a great protector of literature, and married Lucretia, a daughter of the celebrated Pico della Mirandola, who erected this monument to his memory. The tomb of Lucia Rusca Rangoni, his mother, is even more simple— a vase resting upon a sarcophagus. This is also from a design of Giulio Romano. In a recess, on the l. of the upper ch., is a monument to Ercole Rinaldo, the last duke of the House of Este in the male line. Deprived of his dominions by the French invasion, a principality was erected for him in the Brisgau, but he would not accept this compensation, and died as a private individual at Treviso, 14th Oct. 1803. He married Maria Teresa Cibo, Sovereign Princess of Massa Carrara, the last heiress of the House of Cibo Malaspina. They had an only child, Maria Beatrix, who married the Archduke Ferdinand of Austria. The duchy of Modena had been previously secured to her by the treaty of Versailles. She died at Vienna, 1829, at an advanced age. The lately deposed sovereign of Modena, Francesco V., is her grandson. The monument is by Pisani, a native sculptor.

The façade of the Duomo towards the S., overlooking the market-place, has two fine and deep portals; one with quadruple bound columns, and very elaborate ornamental work round the door. At the S.E. extremity of this side of the church are four bas-reliefs representing events in the life of S. Gemininnus; amongst others, his expelling the Devil from the Daughter of the Emperor Jovinian; they were sculptured, as we see by an inscription, in 1442, by a certain *Augustinus de Florentiá.*

"The *Campanile,* or *Ghirlandina,* as it is called, from the bronze garland which surrounds the weathercock, is 315 ft. high, and is one of the four towers of which the North of Italy has reason to be proud. Whether it was undertaken at the same time with the church is uncertain; but the square part of it must have been complete in 1224, for in that year it was seized upon by one of the factions who at that time disturbed the peace of Modena. The upper pyramidal part was only finished in 1319."—*G. Knight.*

In this tower is preserved suspended by an iron chain the old wormeaten *Secchia,* or the wooden bucket, taken by the Modenese from the Bolognese in the battle, or rather affray, of Zappolino, Nov. 15, 1325; it was deposited here by the victors, the *Geminiani,* as a trophy of the defeat of the *Petroniani,* with wonderful triumph, as described in Tassoni's celebrated poem :—

" Quivi Manfredi in su l'altar maggiore
Pose la Secchia con divozione :
E poi ch' egli, ed il clero, e Monsignore
Fecero al Santo lunga orazione,
Fu levata la notte a le tre ore,
E dentro una cassetta di cotone
Ne la torre maggior fu riserrata,
Dove si trova ancor vecchia e tarlata.

Ma la Secchia fu subito portata
Ne la torre maggior, dove ancor stassi
In alto per trofea posta, e legata
Con una gran catena a curvi sassi.
S' entra per cinque porte ov' è guardata,
E non ò cavalier, che di là passi,
Nè pellegrin di conto, il qual non voglia
Veder si degna e gloriosa spoglia."
Secchia Rapita, cant. i. 63.

The Modenese and Bolognese were respectively called *Geminiani* and *Petroniani,* from their patron saints Geminianus and Petronius.

Ch. of *S. Agostino,* near the gate leading to Reggio. In the 1st chapel on the rt. is the remarkable group of the Deposition from the Cross, in painted terra-cotta, by *Begarelli.* The figures, which are as large as life, are full of animation. " If this clay could become marble," exclaimed Michael Angelo, " woe to the antique!" " *Se la creta delle figure di costui dicentasse marmo, guai alle statue antiche !*" Muratori is buried in this ch. A statue has been raised to him in an open space off the Corso, called the Piazza Muratori, with the inscription, à L. A. Muratori—La Patria, 1853. Near the ch. of S. Agostino is the large Palace, called the *Monte dei Pegni,* which contains the offices of the charitable establishments of the city. Under the porticoes round the court, and on the ground floor, have been arranged a series of Roman and Mediæval monuments and sculptures which constitute the MUSEO LAPIDARIO. There are a good many Roman inscriptions, several huge Mediæval Sarcophagi, the greater number from desecrated churches.

Ch. of *S. Vincenzo* contains the tomb of the late Duchess of Modena, a work of merit, and of other members of the ducal family.

Ch. of *S. Domenico,* near the palace, was the Chapel Royal of the court.

The *Ducal Palace* was begun in the 17th century. Much was added by the late Duke, and it is now a fine building. It contains numerous courts, with open staircases, galleries, arches upon arches, such as are seen in the background of old Italian pictures.

The most interesting portion of this pile to the traveller is that containing the *Picture Gallery (Galleria Estense),* situated as well as the library in the uppermost story of the N.W. wing; the entrance is by a side door opening out of the Corso del Naviglio; both are open daily to strangers and students.

The collection of paintings is large, exceeding 500 specimens, arranged in 13 rooms. There is a very good catalogue ; each specimen has attached to it the name of the artist, and the period when he lived ; the description of the subject and the history will be found in the catalogue. Besides the paintings there is an extensive series of *original drawings* of the old masters. The following are the most worthy of notice:

ROOM I.—4. *Simone da Bologna:* a Madonna and Child.—6. *Masaccio:* a Portrait.—27. *Mantegna:* 3 Warriors and a female called Lucretia.—33. *Gherard of Haerlem:* a curious old painting of the Crucifixion.—34. *Montagna:* the Virgin with the two Saint Johns.—38. *Gior. Bellini:* a Holy Family.—39. *Giacomo Francia:* the Assumption.—42. *Lorenzo di Bicci:* an interesting Florentine Master of the 15th century; a Madonna and Child.—*Spinello Aretino:* a Marriage, interesting for the costumes. —5. *B. Loschi:* a Modenese Master little known out of his native district; the Madonna and Child, painted for Prince Pio di Carpi in 1515, as stated on the inscription.—58. *Marco Melloni;* another native painter; the same subject painted in 1504.

Room II.—*Nicolo dell' Abate:* eight Landscapes originally painted for a room in the feudal castle of the Boiardis, at Scandiano.—60. *Correggio:* the medallion on the vault, representing Endymion, was originally in the Castle or Rocca of Novellara, from which it was removed by the late Duke of Modena. There is another series of subjects from the Æneid in this room by *Nicolo dell' Abate*, also from the Castle of Scandiano. They contain some family portraits.

Room IV.—Chiefly subjects of the Venetian School. The five paintings on the roof are attributed to *Tintoretto*, as is 119. A Virgin and Saints. —123. *Giorgione:* the Portrait of a Female, not unlike the so-called Fornarina, in the Gallery of Florence.—125. *Paris Bordone:* the Adoration of the Magi.—128. *Paolo Veronese:* his own Portrait. —129. *Palma Vecchio:* the Madonna and Saints.—141. *Bonifazio Bembo:* the Adoration of the Magi.—143. *Cima da Coneglicano:* a good Deposition.—114, 117. *Titian:* Portraits attributed to him.

Room V.—Chiefly works of the Bolognese School.—145. *Gennari:* a good Half-figure.—147? *A. Sirani:* S. Francis. —149. *Guido:* a fine Crucifixion; the back-ground in awful darkness has a fine effect.—163. *Guercino:* St. Peter.—164. *Lud. Caracci:* the Assumption of the Virgin.—169. *Simone da Pesaro:* the Supper in Emmaus.

Room VI.—Chiefly of the School of Ferrara.—171. *Dosso Dossi:* Judith, and 176, the Nativity.—172. *Garofalo:* the Crucifixion; and 189, a Madonna and Saints, one of whom is San Contardo d'Este; it is signed and dated 1532.—196. A Female Portrait by the same; and 191, 192, 195. *Dosso Dossi:* portraits of Alphonso 1st and 2nd Dukes of Ferrara.

Room VII.—*Profane subjects of the Bolognese School.*—201. *Lud. Caracci:* Flora.—204. *An. Caracci:* Venus.—206. *Guercino:* Venus seated. —207. *id.*, Ammon and Thamas.—210. *Albani;* a lovely picture of Aurora.—*Lud. Caracci:* Galatea.—215, 218. Portraits by *Guercino:* the last of Cardinal Mazzarin.

Room VIII.—A large collection of Tableaux de Genre of different Schools. —237. Attributed to *Claude.*—246. A good Teniers, and 231, an interior of the same.—222. *Van Helmont:* an Ecclesiastic distributing Alms to the Poor; some *Canalettis,* &c. &c.

Room IX. — *Paintings of Different Schools.*—297. *Andrea del Sarto:* a Holy Family.—298. *B. Luini:* Our. Lord, the hand upon a Globe.—302. *Le Brun:* the Sons of Madian.—309. *Fo. Vanni:* the Marriage of St. Catherine.—320. *Luke of Leyden:* a good Madonna and Child.

Room X., or Grand Hall (Salon Grande).—This fine saloon contains all the larger paintings of the different schools.—327. *G. Procaccini:* the Circumcision. — 366. *Dosso Dossi:* the Virgin and Child.—*C. Procaccini:* the Adoration of the Magi.—341. *Guercino:* the Crucifixion of St. Peter.—342. *J. Tintoretto:* Daphne pursued by Apollo. —345. *Dosso Dossi:* a large Madonna. —348. *Leonello Spado:* Young Men in strange dresses, and 365, St. Francis offering flowers to the Virgin and Child. —353. *Turini:* a Crucifixion. — 355. *Guercino:* the same subject.—370. *Pomarancio:* the Dead Saviour on the Cross, with the Marys, and St. John; one of the painter's finest works.—373. *Guido:* St. Roch in prison.—371. *Guercino:* the Madonna and Child with a Capuchin Friar.—385. *Bern. Strozzi:* S. Francis.

Rooms XI. and XII. are devoted to the Modenese Masters.—391, 444, by *Donini of Correggio.*—397. *Sassuolo.*—400. *Carnevale.* — 450, 455. *Lelio Orsi di Novellara.*—402. *Nicolo dell' Abate.*—403.

Pellegrino da Modena.—423. *Bernardo Cervi.*

The last ROOM (XIII.) is filled with small paintings. — 456. *Cavedone:* a Virgin and Saints.—461. The Head of a Child, attributed to *Correggio.*—478. *Holbein:* Portrait of Henry VIII.— 452. *Fra Bartolommeo:* a Madonna.— 488. *Raphael?* a Virgin and Child blessing two Angels, in Raphael's first manner, but very doubtful; this picture belonged to the French General Miollis, who sold it to the Duke of Modena.

Beyond the collection of paintings, and leading to the library, is a long gallery, the walls of which are covered with *Drawings by the Old Masters.* There are specimens by Titian, Giulio Romano, Tintoretto, Michael Angelo, Pordenone, Molosso, Guido, the Caraccis, Parmegianino, Luca Cambiaso, Baroccio, Mantegna, Bronzino, Leonardo da Vinci, Passarotti; the whole length of the wall, on one side of this gallery, is occupied by a narrow series of drawings of the bas-reliefs on the column of Trajan, at Rome, executed by *Giulio Romano,* for Alfonso d'Este, Duke of Ferrara. This very interesting treasure of the House of Este was carried to Paris, with several of the paintings in the gallery, and restored in 1815 to its rightful owners.

The *Biblioteca Estense,* or library, brought from Ferrara by Cesare d'Este on his expulsion by Clement VIII., is rich in books (100,000 vols.) and manuscripts (3000). Three of the most learned men in Italy during the last century, Zaccaria, Tiraboschi, and Muratori, have been its librarians. Attached to the library was a large collection of 25,000 coins and medals, but it was carried off by the Duke of Modena, who was deposed in 1859, as well as 12 very valuable illuminated MSS.; those of the Divina Commedia, and the Bible amongst the number. The library is well arranged and very available for students. The Archivio Estense, containing several important documents of mediæval history, is in another part of the palace.

ROUTE 51.

MODENA TO PISTOJA, BY BARIGAZZO AND SAN MARCELLO.

This is a long dreary road, through a country offering little interest except to the geologist. It traverses the central chain of the Apennines three times. On the northern side of the Apennines it was, generally speaking, in bad repair where it runs through the Modenese territory; the contrary being the case with the Tuscan portion. There are no post-horses; but vetturini sometimes travel by it, employing two days and a half between Pistoja and Modenas and a diligence runs 3 times a week between Modena and Pistoja, performing the journey in a day. Were it kept in better repair it would offer, now that the railway is completed between Pistoja and Florence, advantages to the traveller going from Verona and the Italian Tyrol to the shores of the Mediterraneaan.

The road leaves Modena by the Porta di San Francesco.

Formigine, a town of 1800 Inhab., is the first stage, 9 m. from Modena, on the plain, in a district rich in grain, vines, and mulberry-trees.

Marinello, 5 m. farther, on entering the hilly region.

Paullo or *Pavullo,* a town, 35 m. from Modena. The Duke of Modena had a handsome villa near this. 4 m. further on, the road, which had hitherto run nearly S., changes its direction to W.S.W., turning abruptly round the picturesque hill of

Montecucullo, with a castle on the summit, the birthplace (in 1609) of the celebrated military commander Montecuculli, the rival of Turenne and Condé.

A dreary road of 15 m., through a pasture country, leads to

Barigazzo, a small hamlet, near to which are emanations of carburetted hydrogen gas, similar to those near Pietramala, on the road from Bologna to Florence, and which ignites on a light being applied to it. Ascending along the Scoltenna torrent we reach

Pieve Pelago, a village of 1800 Inhab., in a cold inhospitable region; and 7 m. higher up the hamlet of *Fiumalbo*. Here the principal ascent of the Apennines commences, having the Monte Cimone, the highest peak of this part of the chain, about 4 m. on the l. The most elevated point of the road is at the *Col dell' Abbetone*, or del Libro Aperto. Here we enter the Tuscan territory (Pistoja being 35 m. distant), and after a rapid descent of 7 m. reach

Cutigliano, a village of 1200 Inhab., on the Lima river, which we follow as far as

San Marcello, a prosperous town on the Limastre. There are several paper-mills in the neighbourhood. A road nearly completed will lead down the ravine of the Lima to the Baths of Lucca. There is a road of 22 m. through a beautiful country from San Marcello to Pescia by Petiglio.

From San Marcello the road to Pistoja runs easterly, ascending again the central chain by *Bardclone*, to descend to Ponte Petri, a bridge on the river Reno, near its source. Here we are again on the N. side of the Apennines.

From *Ponte Petri* (Pons Presbyteris) the road ascends along the Reno, here a mountain-torrent, to the hamlet of *Piastre*. By a slight ascent to Chireglio—from which the water runs towards the Ombrone—the central chain is crossed for a third time. The road now descends along the Ombrone, which it crosses by a bridge at Burgianico, 2 m. before arriving at

Pistoja. (See Rte. 77.)

SECTION VII.

LA ROMAGNA.

ROUTES.

ROUTE	PAGE
56. Mantua to Ferrara	436
57. Modena to Ferrara	437
58. Padua to *Ferrara*, by Rovigo	437
59. Ferrara to Bologna, by *Malalbergo*	452
60. Ferrara to Bologna, by *Cento*	453
61. Modena to *Bologna*—Rail	454
62. Bologna to Florence, by *Pietramala* and the *Pass of la Futa*	496
63. Bologna to Florence, by *La Porretta*, the *Pass of la Collina*, and Pistoia	499
64. Faenza to Florence, by *Marradi* and *Borgo S. Lorenzo*	502
65. Florence to Forli, by *Dicomano* and the *Pass of S. Benedetto*	503
66. Forli to Ravenna	504
67. Faenza to Ravenna	505
68. Venice to Ravenna, by the Canals and Comacchio	505
69. Bologna to *Ravenna*, by Imola and *Lugo*	508
70. Bologna to Ravenna, by *Medicina* and Lugo	531
71. Ravenna to Rimini, by *Cervia*	531
72. Bologna to the Papal Frontier, by *Imola, Faenza, Forli, Cesena, Rimini*, with Excursion to *San Marino*	532

PRELIMINARY INFORMATION.

History.—Passports.—Money.—Posting.—Railroads.

Under the name of Romagna are included all the former possessions of the Holy See on the northern side of the Apennines, which formed, according to the most recent division of the Pontifical States, the Legation of La Romagna, consisting of the four Delegations, now Provinces, of Bologna, Ferrara, Ravenna, and Forli. This territory, one of the most luxuriant in Italy, containing a population of more than one million, extends from the Duchy of Modena, on the W., to the Adriatic, and from the Po to the N. declivity of the Apennines, where it limits with Tuscany.

These provinces, which had been acquired at different times by the popes, partly by cessions from Pepin and Charlemagne (Ravenna), partly by a pretended suzerainty over some of their feudal rulers, on the extinction of their families in the male line (Ferrara), and others by violence, as in the case of the free towns of Bologna, Forli, &c., formed for upwards of three centuries the Northern Legations of the Holy See.

In consequence of the universal discontent that reigned amongst these populations, and the inability of the government of Rome to maintain its power over them without foreign intervention, the assistance of Austria had become necessary, and, in addition to the garrisons which that empire was authorized to maintain at Ferrara and Comacchio by the treaty of Vienna, she held military rule over the Romagna from 1848 until 1859, exercising a degree of tyranny which not only created a deadly animosity against the German protectors of the Holy See, but extreme hatred of the Papal rule. When, therefore, the Austrian protecting force was obliged, arising out of the military events of last year, to withdraw, a general rising against the pontifical authorities immediately followed. Juntas were formed in all the larger towns, and subsequently a central one at Bologna, which, during a period of considerable difficulty, governed the Romagna with great moderation and ability. In August, 1859, a parliament, elected by universal suffrage, was called together by this governing Junta, which met on the 2nd of September, and declared unanimously their separation for ever from the government of Rome. The same question having been re-submitted to universal suffrage on the 12th of March, 1860, the country declared, by an almost unanimous vote, its desire to form a part of the North Italian monarchy, instead of forming a separate state, a declaration which was accepted by King Victor Emanuel and the parliament of Piedmont.

The territorial delineations of the Romagna have undergone no alteration since its annexation to the kingdom of Northern Italy, consisting of the four provinces of Bologna, Ferrara, Ravenna, and Forli, each under the direction of a governor. Up to the present they form, with the former Duchies of Modena and Parma, the Emilian Confederation, the chief seat of which is at Modena; but in their government and administration they will be gradually assimilated to the other parts of the kingdom of Northern Italy.

Passports.—Same regulations as in Sardinia.

Money.—Officially speaking, the currency is the decimal one of Sardinia; but the most common coin of the country is still and will remain for some time that of the Papal government—scudi, pauls, and baiocchi; the scudo being equal to 4s. 3½d. or 5f. 37c., the paulo to 5½d. or 54 centimes, and the baiocco to ½d. or 5 centimes. The Austrian coinage has hitherto passed current in the Romagna; the florin at 4½ pauls or 1s. 11d., the swanziger at 1½ paul or 7¾d. It is probable, however, that in a few years the decimal coinage will be the only circulating medium in this new annexation of the North Italian kingdom.

Posting.—The posting regulations of Sardinia are now introduced into the Romagna.

Railroads.—The principal line is that which runs parallel to the Via Emilia from Piacenza to Parma, and which is now open as far as Bologna, and will probably be extended in all 1860 to Faenza, and to Rimini in 1861. Branch-lines are projected from Faenza or Forli to Ravenna. The works have been commenced on that which is to cross the Apennines, ascending the valley of the Reno, to gain the Maria Antonia Railway at Pistoia on their southern declivity; a line has been decreed between Ferrara and Bologna.

ROUTES.

ROUTE 56.
MANTUA TO FERRARA.

	POSTS.
Mantua to Governolo	1¾
Governolo to Sermide	1¾
Sermide to Bondeno	1¾
Bondeno to Ferrara	1¾

6¾ posts = 52¼ m.

The old post-road from Mantua to Ferrara followed that to Padua as far as Nogara (1 post), whence it turned southward to Ostiglia, crossing the Po between it and Revere.

The present route follows the l. bank of the Mincio to Governolo, near where it falls into the Po.

1½ Governolo. Leaving this place, the road skirts the l. bank of the Po as far as Ostiglia, which it crosses to Revere. It then follows the rt. bank, passing by Borgoforte, as far as

1¼ Sermide, a post station. 8 m. farther the frontier of the Austro-Italian Provinces is passed at Quatrelle; and a little farther on is *Stellata*, the North Italian Custom-house, where passports and luggage are examined. From here the road follows the l. bank of the Panaro to

1½ *Bondeno*, a town on the l. bank of the Panaro, formerly a fief of the house of Este. The road from here to Ferrara lies through a flat, well-irrigated country, passing along the canal or Po di Volano, by Vigarano, Cassana, and Mizzana, to

1¾ FERRARA, described in Rte. 58.

ROUTE 57.

MODENA TO FERRARA.

	POSTS.
Modena to Bomporto	1
Bomporto to Finale	2
Finale to Bondeno	1¼
Bondeno to Ferrara	1¾

6 posts = 57 m.

The road follows the banks of the Panaro for the first 3 posts.

1 *Bomporto*. From here it proceeds through Campo Santo and Cà de' Coppi to

2 *Finale*, situated on either side of the Panaro, which is here crossed. 3 m. farther on are Serragliolo and *Santa Bianca*, from which the road soon reaches Bondeno, where it falls into the post-road from Mantua. (Rte. 56.)

1¼ *Bondeno*. From here we follow the bank of the Po di Volano to

1¾ FERRARA (Rte. 58).

ROUTE 58.

PADUA TO FERRARA, BY ROVIGO.

	POSTS.
Padua to Monselice	1¼
Monselice to Rovigo	1½
Rovigo to Polesella	1
Polesella to Ferrara	2

6 posts = 51¾ m.

For first part of this Route see Rtes. 32 and 33.

The road between Padua and Rovigo follows the line of the canal, and in its interesting character contrasts with the monotonous flat which extends southward as far as Bologna. Before arriving at Rovigo the Adige is crossed by a bridge; and between it and Ferrara the Po is passed in a ferry-boat. The height of the embankments necessary to restrain the inundations of the Po will convince the traveller how much Ferrara and its plains are at the mercy of that river, the level of which is higher than the roofs of many of the houses in that city. The Austrian frontier station and Dogana is at Sta. Maria Maddalena, and the Italian at *Ponte Lagoscuro*, on the S. side of the river, called the "Port of the Po," from the considerable commerce it maintains with Lombardy in corn and wine, which are brought here for shipment. The Pamfilio Canal extends from Ponte Lagoscuro to the Porta S. Benedetto at Ferrara, distant 3 m. The city is entered by the Porta del Po, leaving the citadel on the rt.

FERRARA, the *Forum Allieni* of Tacitus.—(*Inns*: Albergo dell' Europa, opposite the Post and Diligence offices, is now the best in Ferrara: the Tre Corone, near the poste aux chevaux, an old inn, fallen off.) Few cities ranking among the ancient Italian capitals are so much neglected by travellers as Ferrara, and yet few are more associated with interesting recollections. It is situated in a fertile but unhealthy plain, at a level of only 6½ ft. above the sea, and at a short distance from the Po, which forms here the boundary between the Austro-Venetian and the North-Italian kingdoms. This plain, intersected only by irrigation canals from the river, presents an unbroken horizon, and extends, with little variation, up to the walls of Ferrara.

The aspect of the city, once the residence of a court celebrated throughout Europe, still retains many traces of its ancient grandeur. The broad, regular, and ample streets appear like those of a deserted capital; grass grows on the pavement, the palaces are falling into decay, and the walls, 7 miles in circuit, which once contained nearly 100,000 souls, now enclose scarcely one-third of that number. The population is collected together in the centre of the city, and thinly scattered over the remaining portion. Ravenna itself is hardly more fallen than Ferrara, although it was the great commercial emporium of Italy during the middle ages, the *città bene avventurosa* of Ariosto, the *gran donna del Pò* of Tassoni.

The modern city is supposed to have been founded in the 5th century, when the invasion of the Huns and the destruction of Aquileja drove the inhabitants into the marshes for security. Its walls were built in the 6th century by the Exarchs of Ravenna, and it was raised to the rank of a city in 661, when the bishopric of Vigovenza was transferred to it. But the chief interest of Ferrara arises from its connection with the house of Este. As far back as the 10th century we find this family connected with Ferrara; first as supreme magistrates, and afterwards as hereditary princes (1240), acknowledging generally the suzerainty of the Pope, though sometimes asserting their independence. It remained under their sway until the extinction of the legitimate branch in 1597, in the person of Alfonso II.; and in the following year it was annexed to the States of the Church by Clement VIII., on the pretext that Cesare d'Este, the representative of the family by a collateral line, was disqualified by illegitimacy. During the 16th centy. the Court of Ferrara was unsurpassed by any other in Europe for its refinement and intelligence; its University was renowned throughout Christendom, and so many English students were collected within its walls as to form, as they did in Bologna, a distinct nation in that learned body. But there are greater names associated with the history of Ferrara at this period than those of its princely sovereigns. "Melancholy as the city looks now, every lover of Italian poetry," says Forsyth, "must view with affection the retreat of an Ariosto, a Tasso, a Guarini. Such is the ascent of wealth over genius, that one or two princes could create an Athens in the midst of this Bœotia. The little courts of Ferrara and Urbino seemed to emulate those of Alexandria and Pergamos, contending for pre-eminence only in literature and elegance."

The Ferrara School of Painting, founded and patronised by the Este family, deserves some notice in connection with this tribute to the intellectual history of the city. It is observed by Lanzi that Ferrara boasts of a series of excellent painters, far superior to its fortunes and population; a circumstance which will not excite surprise when we consider the series of poets which it cherished, from Bojardo and Ariosto down to our own times, a sure criterion of accomplished and refined minds more than ordinarily disposed towards the fine arts. To this circumstance, and to the good taste of the inhabitants in their patronage of art, may be added the favourable position of the city, in its contiguity to Venice, Parma, and Bologna, and its convenient distance from Florence and Rome; so that its students were enabled to select from the different schools of Italy what was most congenial to the tastes of each, and to

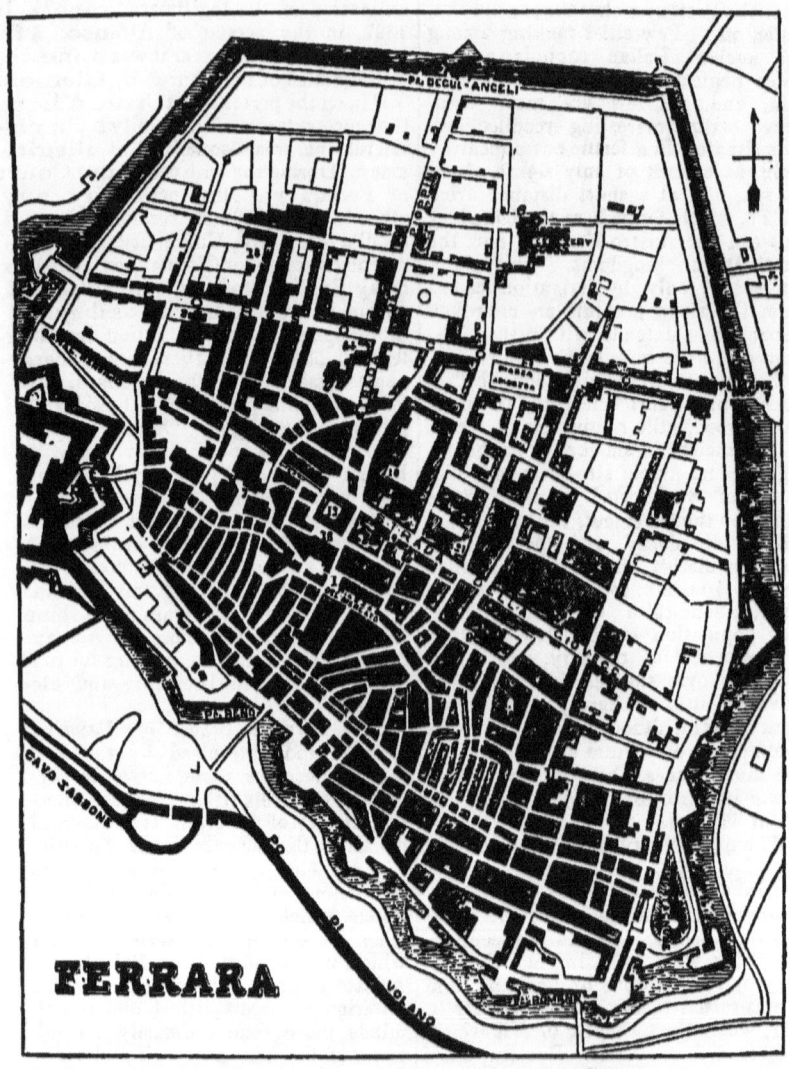

CHURCHES.

1. Duomo or Cathedral.
2. S. Andrea.
3. S. Benedetto.
4. Capuccini.
5. Corpus Domini.
6. S. Cristoforo.
7. S. Domenico.
8. S. Gaetano (Teatini).
9. S. Francesco.
10. Il Gesu.
11. S. M. in Vado.
12. S. Paolo.

PUBLIC BUILDINGS, &c.

13. Castle.
14. Pinacoteca and Ateneo.
15. University.
16. Accademia Ariostea.
17. Hospital and Prison of Tasso, and Pal. Roverella.
18. House of Ariosto.
19. Post Office.
20. Theatre.
21. Pal. Mazza.

profit by their several excellences. So great, indeed, was the influence of this latter circumstance, that Zanetti considered it doubtful whether, after the 5 great schools, Ferrara did not claim precedence over all the others. The first fact recorded in connection with the fine arts at Ferrara is the commission given by Azzo d'Este, in 1242, to the Venetian painter Gelasio di Niccolò, a pupil of the Greek artist Teofane of Constantinople, for a picture of the Fall of Phaëton. In the 14th century, when Giotto passed through Ferrara, on his way from Verona to Florence, he was employed by the Duke to paint some frescoes in his palace and in the church of St. Agostino, which were still in existence in the time of Vasari. After the lapse of some years, during which several names are mentioned which have survived their works, Galasso Galassi appeared early in the 15th century; his works are chiefly confined to Bologna, and none are now found in his native city. He was followed by Antonio da Ferrara, known by his works at Urbino and Città di Castello, who painted some chambers in the palace of Alberto d'Este in 1438, at the time when the General Council was held there for the union of the Greek and Latin churches, and which is supposed to have supplied him with his subject. But the most celebrated of the early painters was Cosimo Cosmè or Tura, the pupil of Galassi, employed at the court of Borso d'Este: his minute and elaborate work is admirably shown in the miniatures of the choir-books preserved in the cathedral. Among the painters of this period may be mentioned Lorenzo Costa, the reputed pupil of Francia, and Francesco Cossa, both known by their works at Bologna. Costa, indeed, may be regarded as the true father of the school; for the series of painters from his time may be clearly traced; and Lanzi classes him among the first masters of Italy. His most eminent pupil was Ercole Grandi, called by Vasari Ercole da Ferrara, whose great work, painted for the Gargauelli chapel, is now preserved in the Academy of Fine Arts at Bologna. Lodovico Mazzolino, better known as Mazzolini da Ferrara, another pupil of Costa, is known by his works in various galleries; and Domenico Panetti, the master of Garofalo, is remarkable for having become the pupil of his own scholar, and for the works he produced after his style had been remodelled on the example of Garofalo. The school of Ferrara was at its prime under the latter painter and the two Dossis, in the early part of the sixteenth century, when Alfonso d'Este was the patron of literature and art. This prince had invited Titian to decorate his palace; and, among other celebrated paintings, the "Cristo della Moneta," of the Dresden Gallery, was painted during his stay at Ferrara. Dosso Dossi, and his brother Giobattista, born at Dosso, in the vicinity of Ferrara, were among the earliest patronised by Alfonso and his successor Ercole II.; and their merit is sufficiently attested by the fact that Ariosto has mentioned them as amongst the best painters of Italy. Ortolano is another painter of this school, whose works are often confounded with those of Garofalo; he is known as a successful imitator of Raphael; some of his works are yet seen in his native city. Benvenuto Tisio, better known by the name of Garofalo, from the pink which he introduced into his paintings, stands at the head of the Ferrarese school, and is justly called the Raphael of Ferrara: some of his most celebrated works are still here. His pupil, Girolamo da Carpi, recommended to Ercole II. by Titian himself, and whose oil paintings were of extreme rarity in the time of Lanzi, may also be studied at Ferrara. While these two artists excelled in the graces of the art, Bastianino, or Bastiano Filippi, was introducing the style of Michel Angelo, as seen in the grand picture of the Last Judgment in the cathedral. Another painter of this school, Scarsellino, who was called the Paul Veronese of Ferrara, and who studied under that master, has left some works in his native place; he is, however, better known by those preserved in the galleries at Rome. Giuseppe Mazzuoli, known by the surname of Bastaruolo, and the contemporary of Bastianino, was called the Titian of Ferrara: we shall hereafter see that he has left behind him several works by which his claim to that title may be appreciated. Ferrara likewise contains some interesting examples of Domenico Mona, and of his able pupil Giulio Cromer, or Croma, who was selected to copy the principal paintings in the city, when the originals were transferred to Rome, after Clement VIII. had seized upon Ferrara and attached it to the Church. After this event the school rapidly declined for want of patronage. Some Bolognese masters endeavoured, with little success, to introduce the style of the Caracci; Carlo Bonone, the scholar of Bastaruolo, was perhaps the most celebrated follower of this new manner; his works in Sta. Maria in Vado are highly praised by Lanzi for that kind of foreshortening called *di sotto in su*, where figures are supposed to be seen above the eye. Another artist, worthy of mention as a follower of Bonone, is Chenda, or Alfonso Rivarola, who was employed, at the recommendation of Guido, to finish some of Bonone's works, but was better known by his decorations for public spectacles and tournaments. It is unnecessary to enumerate any of the painters whose names appear in the subsequent history of this school, for Ferrara never recovered the change of masters; and its school gradually declined, until, at length, in spite of the establishment of an academy, it became completely extinct. Notwithstanding, however, this decline and the loss of its political influence, Ferrara still retains many interesting examples of the school, which will be noticed in our description of the city.

In addition to the brilliancy of its court and the celebrity of its school of art, Ferrara offers no inconsiderable interest to the English traveller for the impulse which it gave to the Reformation. The names of Ariosto and Tasso have almost eclipsed the recollection of that event, and of the asylum given to Calvin and to Marot by the Duchess Renée, the high-minded daughter of Louis XII., and the wife of Ercole II. At an early period Ferrara afforded protection to numerous friends of the Reformed Faith who fled from other parts of Italy, and even from countries beyond the Alps, a circumstance to be ascribed to the influence of the accomplished princess just mentioned, who had become acquainted with the doctrines of the Reformers previous to her departure from France in 1527, by means of some of those learned persons who frequented the court of Margaret Queen of Navarre. "The first persons to whom she extended her protection and hospitality were her own countrymen, whom the violence of persecution had driven out of France. Mad. de Soubise, the governess of the duchess, had introduced several men of letters into the court of France during the late reign. She now resided at the court of Ferrara, along with her son, Jean de Parthenai, sieur de Soubise, afterwards a principal leader of the Protestant party in France; her daughter, Anne de Parthenai, distinguished for her elegant taste; and the future husband of this young lady, Antoine de Pons, Count de Marennes, who adhered to the reformed cause until the death of his wife. In the year 1534 the celebrated French poet Clement Marot fled from his native country, in consequence of the persecution excited by the affair of the *placards;* and, after residing for a short time at the court of the Queen of Navarre, in Bearn, came to Ferrara. He was recommended by Madame de Soubise to the duchess, who made him her secretary; and his friend Lyon Jamet, finding it necessary soon after to join him, met with a reception equally gracious. About the same time the celebrated reformer John Calvin visited Ferrara, where he spent some months under the assumed name of Charles Heppeville. He received the most distinguished attention from the duchess, who was confirmed in the Protestant faith by his instructions, and ever after retained the highest respect for his character and talents." Among the other learned personages assembled here at this time was Fulvio Peregrino Morata, who had been tutor to the two younger brothers of the duke, and who became still more celebrated as the father of Olympia Morata, the most enlightened female of her age; who first "acquired during her residence in the ducal palace that knowledge of the gospel which supported her mind under the privations and hardships which she afterwards had to endure."

The description of Ariosto, and the testimony of numerous contemporary authorities, proves that, under the sway of the house of Este, Ferrara was one of the great commercial cities of Italy. Its trade began to decline in the 16th century, and, although it has been much reduced even since that period, the city still carries on a considerable traffic in agricultural produce. A great deal of business was formerly done here in hemp, of which large quantities found its way into the English dockyards, the Ferrara growth being considered the best for cordage; but, from the heavy export duties and other circumstances, the trade has considerably declined. The high duties on manufactured articles have thrown the foreign trade into the hands of the Swiss and the merchants of Lombardy, and the circulating capital is to a great extent in the hands of the Jews, who are in Ferrara a very opulent body; their number is about 3000. They inhabited until lately, as in all the other Papal cities, a distinct quarter of the town called a *ghetto*; it was formerly usual at Rome and other places to lock them in at night; here, however, their importance has exempted them from the observance of that degrading regulation. At the present time Ferrara is the capital of a province comprehending 244,524 inhabitants; the population of the city and suburbs is 31,184.* In spite of their deserted appearance, the effect of its broad and handsome streets is particularly imposing; that of San Benedetto is 1¼ m. in length; and its palaces, though many of them are dilapidated, have an air of grandeur in accordance with the former celebrity of the city.

The Cathedral, dedicated to St. Paul, was consecrated in 1135; its Gothic exterior, with few exceptions, belongs to that period, but the interior has been altered and spoiled by modern renovations. The front is divided by small towers, crowned with pinnacles, into 3 equal portions, each surmounted with a gable containing a wheel window, and ornamented with a range of pointed arches. The porch is composed of a semicircular arch supported by columns; the flanks have also semicircular arches. The bas-reliefs with which this part is covered are in a good state of preservation; they represent the Last Judgment, various events in the life of Christ, the seven Mortal Sins, with numerous sacred, profane, and grotesque emblems. Over the right-hand door is a colossal marble bust of Donna Ferrara, the sister of the founder of the church. Over the central door is the long venerated miraculous Madonna attributed to *Nicolo da Pisa*. On the same side is a statue of Alberto d'Este, in the pilgrim's dress in which he returned from Rome in 1390, laden with bulls and indulgences. The interior, in the form of a Greek cross, had been modernised at various times; the semicircular choir was first added in 1499, by Rosette, a native architect, known as one of the earliest restorers of Italian architecture; the portion beyond the transept dates from 1637, and the remainder from between 1712 and 1735. There are several paintings worthy of notice. The Assumption, the St. Peter and St. Paul, and the superb picture of the Virgin throned with Saints, are by *Garofalo*. The chapel of the Holy Sacrament contains some remarkable sculptures of angels, &c.; and in another chapel good specimens of wood sculpture of SS. George and Maurillus with the Virgin, by *Andrea Ferreri*, an artist of the last century; the altarpiece is by *Parolini*, a native painter (1733), whom Lanzi describes as "l'ultimo nel cui sepolcro si sia inciso elogio di buon pittore; con lui fu sepolta per allora la gloria della

---

* These numbers, as all others respecting the population of the former States of the Church, &c., given in this volume, are taken from the last official returns published by the Government in 1857, made up, however, only to the end of 1853.

pittura Ferrarese." In the choir is the Last Judgment, by *Bastianino*, one of the favourite pupils and the best copyist of Michel Angelo. Lanzi says that it occupied him three years in painting, and describes it as "so near to that of Michael Angelo in the Sistine Chapel, that the whole Florentine school has nothing to compare with it. It is characterised," he says, "by grandeur of design, a great variety of figures, a good disposition of the groups, and by the pleasing repose which it presents to the eye of the spectator. It seems impossible that in a subject already occupied by Buonarroti, Filippo should have had the power of showing himself so original and so grand. We see that, like all true imitators, he copied not the figures, but the spirit and the genius of his example." Like Dante and Michel Angelo, Bastianino availed himself of the opportunity to put his friends among the elect, and his enemies among the damned; the picture consequently contains numerous portraits of both. Among the latter are pointed out the young woman who refused his hand, while the one whom he married is placed among the blessed, and is seen maliciously gazing at her early rival. It is much to be regretted that recent attempts to restore this fine work have injured the effect of the original colouring. The seventh chapel contains another painting by the same master, the St. Catherine, called by Lanzi "la gran tavola di S. Caterina." The Annunciation and the St. George are by *Cosimo Tura*, the painter of the 23 choir-books presented by Bishop Bartolommeo della Rovere, the execution of which has been so highly prized as to be preferred by many to that of the famous miniatures in the Library of Siena. On an adjoining altar are 5 bronze statues representing the Saviour on the Cross, the Virgin, St. John, and St. George, by *Bindelli* and *Marescotti*, much admired by Donatello. Over the sixth altar on the left is a Coronation of the Virgin, by *Francia*, a very beautiful work of the master. The cathedral contains the sepulchral monument of Urban III.,

who died of grief on hearing of the reverses of the second crusade, previous to the fall of Jerusalem; that of Lilio Gregorio Giraldi, the celebrated mythologist, has been removed to the Campo Santo; the inscription on the tablet, dated 1550, and written by himself, records the poverty which excited the compassion of Montaigne,

"Nihil
Opus ferente Apolline;"

but, in spite of his complaints, it appears from Tiraboschi that he was assisted by the Duchess Renée, and that he left at his death a sum of 10,000 crowns.

The Ch. of S. Andrea, near the Porta Romana and the Montagnone, at the extremity of the city, contained several good pictures, the greater number of which have been removed to the Pinacotheca: the Virgin Throned, with saints, by *Garofalo*, is supposed by some to have been executed with the assistance of Raphael; the Guardian Angel is by *Carlo Bonone*; the Resurrection is attributed by some to *Titian*, by others to *Garofalo*; the St. Andrew is by *Panetti*; and there is a fine statue of St. Nicholas of Tolentino, by *Alfonso Lombardo*. In the refectory was the grand allegorical picture by *Garofalo*, representing the Victory of the New Testament over the Old.

The Ch. and Monastery of San Benedetto, near the Porta di Po, classed among the finest buildings of Ferrara, have suffered more vicissitudes than perhaps any other edifice in the city. The monastery was occupied as barracks by Austrian, Russian, and French troops, and was afterwards converted into a military hospital; the church, during the political troubles of Italy, was shut up, and was only reopened for divine service in 1812. It was formerly celebrated for the tomb of Ariosto, transferred to the public library by the French in 1801; and for the fine paintings of the school of Ferrara which it still retains. The most remarkable of these are Christ on the Cross, with St. John and other Saints, by *Dosso Dossi*; the Martyrdom of St. Catherine, by *Scar-*

sellino, one of his finest works; and a Circumcision, by *Luca Longhi*, of Ravenna. The four Doctors of the Church, by *Giuseppe Cremonesi* (G. Caletti), are much praised by Lanzi, who applies the epithet "maraviglioso" to his grand and expressive figure of St. Mark, and extols the execution of the books, whose truth and nature gained for the artist the title of the "Painter of Books." On the ceiling of the vestibule of the refectory is the celebrated painting of Paradise, with the choir of angels, by *Dosso Dossi*. Ariosto was so enamoured of this work, that he requested Dossi to introduce his portrait, being desirous, he said, of securing a place in that paradise, since he was not very sure of reaching the real one. The poet was accordingly introduced, and his portrait is seen between the figures of St. Sebastian and St. Catherine. About the middle of the last centy. the bust which surmounted the tomb of Ariosto in this ch. was struck by lightning, and a crown of iron laurels which surrounded it was melted away; an incident which Lord Byron has happily embodied in his well-known stanza :—

"The lightning rent from Ariosto's bust
The iron crown of laurel's mimick'd leaves;
Nor was the ominous element unjust,
For the true laurel-wreath which Glory weaves
Is of the tree no bolt of thunder cleaves,
And the false semblance but disgraced his brow;
Yet still, if fondly Superstition grieves,
Know, that the lightning sanctifies below
Whate'er it strikes;—you bend is doubly sacred now."

The *Ch. of the Campo Santo*, whose fine architecture is attributed to Sansovino, is decorated with sculptures by that celebrated artist. The twelve chapels are remarkable for as many paintings of the Mysteries by *Niccolò Rosselli*, classed, doubtfully, among the Ferrarese school by Lanzi, who mentions these works as imitations of the style of Garofalo, Bagnacavallo, and others. The Nativity is by *Dielai;* S. Bruno praying, and the Marriage of Cana, are by *Carlo Bonone;* the S. Christopher, by *Bastianino*, is mentioned with the highest praise by Lanzi; the Descent of the Holy Ghost, and the Deposition from the Cross, are by *Bastaruolo;* the S. Bruno, by *Scarsellino;* the Last Supper, by *Cignaroli ;* and the Decollation of John the Baptist, by *Parolini*. The adjoining *Campo Santo* was the Convent of la Certosa. The cloisters are now covered with statues, bas-reliefs, and sepulchral monuments. Among the tombs are those of Borso d'Este, first Duke of Ferrara, the founder of the monastery; of Duke Venanziano Varano and his wife, by Rinaldini; of Lilio Giraldi, the mythologist, by *Lombardi*, removed from the cathedral; of the wife of Count Leopoldo Cicognara; and of the Bernardino Barbulejo, or Barbojo, said to have been the preceptor of Ariosto; &c. Amongst the other works of art in the cemetery may be noticed, the bust of Cicognara, Canova's last work; the tomb of Count Mosti, by *Tadolini;* and the monument of Garofalo, with his ashes beneath. Forming the entrance to one of the chapels, is a beautiful doorway by Sansovino; another chapel, intended to contain monuments of illustrious Ferrarese, contains good statues of Monti and Varano by *Ferari*, a native artist of merit.

The *Ch. of the Capuchin Convent*, in the Corso di Porta Po, has some fine paintings: the Virgin Throned, with saints; a similar subject, with Capuchin nuns, both by *Scarsellino;* S. Christopher and S. Antony the Abbot, S. Dominick, and S. Francis, in the sacristy, by *Bonone*. The small statue of the Conception is by *Ferreri*.

The *Ch. of the Convent of the Corpus Domini* contains several tombs of the d'Este family; that of Lucrezia Borgia was said to be among them, but there is no authority for the statement.

The *Ch. of S. Cristofero* (*gli Esposti*) contains a remarkable painting by *Costa*, the Virgin and Child, with St. Louis and St. Roch.

The *Ch. of San Domenico*, in the Piazza dell' Oca, between the castle and the citadel, is remarkable for the statues on its façade by *Andrea Ferreri*, and for some interesting works of Garofalo and Carlo Bonone. The dead man restored to life by a piece of the true cross, and the Martyrdom of S. Pietro di Rosini, are by *Garo-*

falo; the S. Dominick and S. Thomas Aquinas are by *Carlo Bonone*. The adjoining convent was once celebrated for the Library bequeathed to it by the celebrated Celio Calcagnini, "a poet, scholar, antiquarian, moralist, professor, ambassador, wit, and astronomer; one of the first who maintained the earth's movement round the sun; whose praises have been sung by Ariosto, his fellow traveller in Hungary, in the suite of Cardinal Ippolito d'Este. The number of volumes amounted to 3584, but most of them are now dispersed. Calcagnini also bequeathed fifty golden crowns for the repairs of the library, and to furnish the chairs, benches, and desks then in use."— *Valery.* Over the door of the library is the bust and dilapidated tomb of this eminent philosopher; the inscription is a remarkable testimony to the insufficiency of human learning:— *Ex diuturno studio in primis hoc didicit : mortalia omnia contemnere et ignorantiam suam non ignorare.* Ariosto, in the Orlando, records his astronomical discoveries in a beautiful passage:—

" Il dotto Celio Calcagnin lontana
Farà la gloria, e 'l bel nome di quella
Nel regno di Monese, in quel di Juba,
In India e Spagna udir con chiara tuba."
Or. Fur. xlii. 90, 5.

Ch. of S. Francesco, in a street out of the Corso near the Diligence-office, founded by the Duke Ercole I., is one of the most interesting in Ferrara. Among its pictures are the following, by *Garofalo*: the Betrayal of our Saviour, in fresco; the Virgin and Child, with St. John and St. Jerome, a charming picture; a beautiful Holy Family; the Raising of Lazarus, one of his best works; and the Massacre of the Innocents, one of the most touching representations of the subject. The Flight out of Egypt is by *Scarsellino*; there are 3 fine works by *Mona*, the Deposition, the Resurrection, and the Ascension; and a Holy Family, a very interesting work, by *Ortolano*. The church contains also the monument of the Marchese di Villa of Ferrara, celebrated for his defence of Candia against the Turks in 1676; several tombs of the princes of the house of Este; and that of Giambattista Pigna, the historian of the family, and the secretary of Duke Alfonso. Not the least remarkable curiosity of the church is the famous *echo*, said to reverberate 16 times, from every part of the edifice.

"The nave seems to have been intended to present a series of cupolas, as the side aisles actually do on a smaller scale: but in its present state, at the point where the square is reduced to a circle, a flat ceiling is introduced instead of a cupola. Standing under any one of these, the slightest footstep is repeated a great many times, but so rapidly that it is difficult to count the reverberations. I counted sixteen; but the effect is a continued clatter, rather than a succession of distinct sounds."— *Woods.*

The *Ch. of il Gesù* has a picture of the 3 Japanese Martyrs, by *Parolini*; and a ceiling painted by *Dielai*. In the choir is the mausoleum of the Duchess Barbara of Austria, wife of Alfonso II., so well known by the eloquent eulogies of Tasso.

The *Ch. of S. Giorgio* is celebrated as the scene of the General Council held at Ferrara by Pope Eugenius IV., in 1438, for the purpose of bringing about an union between the Greek and Latin Churches, and at which the Emperor John Palæologus was present. Even at that period the atmosphere of Ferrara was tainted by malaria, for it is recorded that the council was removed to Florence in consequence of the unhealthy climate of this city.

The *Ch. of Sta. Maria del Vado*, near S. Andrea and the Montagnone, one of the oldest in the city, is celebrated for a miracle resembling that of Bolsena, which the genius of Raphael has immortalized. The Church tradition relates that, the faith of the prior having failed at the moment of the consecration on Easter Sunday 1171, the host poured forth blood, and converted him from his disbelief. This church is also celebrated for its magnificent paintings by *Carlo Bonone*, whose talent can only, in Lanzi's opinion, be appreciated here. He relates that Guercino, when he removed from Cento to

Ferrara, spent hours in studying these works. Among them are the Marriage of Cana; the Visit of the Virgin to Elizabeth; the Crowning of the Virgin; the Paradise; the Miracle of the Host; the Marriage of the Virgin, left unfinished at his death, and completed at the suggestion of Guido by *Chendu*; the Ascension, copied from Garofalo, and the half figures on the pillars, one of which represents, under the form of St. Guarini, the portrait of the author of 'Il Pastor Fido.' The splendid painting of St. John in Patmos contemplating the harlot of Babylon is by *Dosso Dossi*; the head of St. John was considered by Lanzi a "prodigy of expression," but the picture has been disfigured by the green drapery added by some Bolognese artist to satisfy the fastidious scruples of the clergy. The Tribute Money, a graceful work in the Varano Chapel, is by *Palma Vecchio*. Opposite is the painting of Justice and Power, containing the celebrated Latin enigma of Alessandro Guarini, which has not yet been explained. The Visitation is by *Panetti*, the master of Garofalo; the Miracle of St. Antony is one of the best works of Garofalo's pupil, *Carpi*. In the sacristy are the Annunciation by *Panetti*, and a Flight out of Egypt, another work of the Venetian School. Most of the good paintings in this church have been recently removed to the Pinacotheca, and replaced by copies. Sta. Maria del Vado contains the tombs of some of the most remarkable artists of Ferrara, and of Tito Vespasiano Strozzi, and his celebrated son Ercole, classed by Ariosto himself among the first of poets. The painters whose ashes reposed here—Ortolano, Garofalo, Bonone, Bastianino, and Dielai—have been removed to the Cemeterio Comunale. The elder Strozzi is known also as the President of the Grand Council of Twelve, but he acquired a less enviable notoriety as a minister than as a poet, for it is recorded by Muratori that in his official capacity he was hated "più del diavolo."

The *Ch. of S. Paolo*, in the Strada di Porta Reno, near the cathedral, is remarkable for one of the masterpieces of *Scarsellino*, the Descent of the Holy Ghost. A Nativity, and the ceiling of one of the side chapels, are by the same master. The choir was painted by *Scarsellino* and *Bonone*. The Resurrection is by *Bastianino*. 2 painters of this school are buried here, Giambattista Dossi, and Bastaruolo, who perished while bathing in the Po. Another tomb in this church records the name of Antonio Montecatino, the friend and minister of Duke Alfonso, better known as a professor of Peripatetic philosophy. His bust, which is much admired, is by *Alessandro Vicentini*.

The *Ch. of the Theatins* (de' Teatini), close to the Diligence-office, contains a large painting of the Presentation in the Temple by *Guercino*; and a Resurrection, and a S. Gaetano, by *Chenda*.

The *Castle*, formerly the Ducal Palace, surrounded by its ample moat, and furnished with towers and bridges, carries the imagination back to the fortunes of Ferrara during the middle ages. "It stands," says Forsyth, "moated and flanked with towers, in the heart of the subjugated town, like a tyrant intrenched among slaves, and recalls to a stranger that gloomy period described by Dante:—

"Che le terre d'Italia tutte piene
Son di tiranni; ed un Marcel diventa
Ogni villan che parteggiando viene."
Purg. vi. 124.

It is a huge, square building, defended at the angles by 4 large towers; it retains few traces of the ducal family, and wears an air of melancholy, in accordance with the deserted aspect of the city. Its apartments were formerly decorated by the first masters of the Ferrarese school, but the paintings have entirely disappeared, excepting on the ceilings of the antechamber and the Saloon of Aurora, where some by *Dosso Dossi* still remain. In the dungeons of this castle Parisina and her guilty lover were put to death. The outlines of that dreadful tragedy have been made familiar to the English reader by the beautiful poem of Lord Byron, to whom the subject was suggested by a passage in Gibbon. A more complete account, however, is

Route 58.—Ferrara—Gallery of Pictures.

found in Frizzi's History of Ferrara, from which the following is an extract descriptive of the closing scene:—
"It was, then, in the prisons of the castle, and exactly in those frightful dungeons which are seen at this day beneath the chamber called the Aurora, at the foot of the Lion's Tower, at the top of the street of the Giovecca, that, on the night of the 21st of May, were beheaded, first Ugo, and afterwards Parisina. Zoese, he that accused her, conducted the latter under his arm to the place of punishment. She, all along, fancied that she was to be thrown into a pit, and asked at every step whether she was yet come to the spot? She was told that her punishment was to be by the axe. She inquired what was become of Ugo, and received for answer that he was already dead; at which, sighing grievously, she exclaimed, 'Now, then, I wish not myself to live;' and, being come to the block, she stripped herself with her own hands of all her ornaments, and, wrapping a cloth round her head, submitted to the fatal blow, which terminated the cruel scene. The same was done with Rangoni, who, together with the others, according to two records in the library of St. Francesco, was buried in the cemetery of that convent."

Gallery of Pictures, or *Pinacoteca Municipale*. — This collection, formerly at the Municipality, has been recently transferred to the fine Palazzo Villa, now the *Ateneo Civico*, in the Via di Pioppini, the wide street leading from the castle to the Campo Santo. The palace, once belonging to the Estes, is one of the finest in Ferrara, being entirely of stone, a rarity in this alluvial district: only the N. and W. fronts have been completed, and consist of diamond-shaped projecting layers, a very unusual style of construction. Some of the pictures in this collection are remarkable; the greater part have been brought from desecrated religious edifices, or churches falling into ruin, in and about Ferrara; they are arranged in a series of eight apartments on the upper floor, and may be seen at any time, on application to the custode.

1st room:—*Garofalo*, a copy of his celebrated fresco of the Last Supper; several portraits of members of the house of Este; head of St. Paul in fresco, by *Dosso Dossi*. 3rd room, the great saloon of the palace, with a fine unfinished wooden ceiling:—*Garofalo*, a large fresco of the Old and New Testament, called the Vecchia e Nova Religione, an immense composition; it formerly stood in the refectory of S. Andrea; it represents the victory of the New over the Old Testament, the ceremonies of the Mosaic being contrasted with those of the New Law; *Scarsellino*, a good Last Supper; *Rosselli*, a Transfiguration, with portraits of members of the Este family; *Carlo Bonone*, a Last Supper. 4th room:—*Palma Vecchio*, the Tribute Money, a fine picture; *Costa*, Virgin and Child and St. Jerome; *Dosso Dossi*, the Resurrection. 5th room:—*Dosso Dossi*, St. John; *Carpi*, S. Antonio and Infant Jesus; *Cortellini*, Virgin and Saints; *Stefano di Ferrara*, the Virgin, Child, and two Saints; *Garofalo*, the Adoration of the Magi; *Panetti*, the Annunciation, the Salutation; *Massolino da Ferrara*, the Adoration of the Infant Jesus, with S. Benedict and another Saint, one of his finest works; *Costa*, the Virgin, S. Petronius, and St. Jerome, very fine; *Galasso Galassi*, a Crucifixion; *Garofalo*, Christ in the Garden. 6th. room:—*Guercino*, St. Peter Martyr; *Vittorio Carpaccio*, a dead Madonna, signed, and dated 1508; *Ercole Grandi*, Adoration of the Magi; *Annibale Caracci*, 2 small pictures. *Bustiannino*, Santa Lucia; *Garofalo*, the Adoration of the Magi, his last work, dated 1548; *Stefano da Ferrara*, the Twelve Apostles; *V. Carpaccio*, the Death of the Virgin. 7th room:—*Garofalo*, the Holy Sacrament; *Francia* (?), Sta. Maria Egizziaca; *Pannetti*, San Andrew; *Coscia*, Decollation of St. Aurelius; *Cosimo Turra* (1406), good portrait of a Cardinal Saint; *Ortolano*, an Annunciation, the chiari-scuri by Garofalo. 8th room:—One wall of this apartment is entirely covered by *Dosso Dossi's* immense picture of the Madonna, with Infant Christ and Saints: it is a huge composition, full of talent;

unfortunately it has been overvarnished on its removal here from the ch. of S. Andrea, where it formerly stood: in the centre is seated the Virgin and Child; in the four angles, St. Augustin, St. Andrea, St. Sebastian, and St. George; and at the foot of the Madonna's throne, St. John, clad in green.

Beyond the Museo Civico is the half-ruined Palazzo Prosperi, with a very beautiful Decorated entrance of the 16th cent.; and farther, on the opposite side of the same street, that of the Ariostei.

Palazzo del Magistrato, in the Corso, near the Albergo di Europa. In a hall of this palace the *Accademia degli Ariostei* holds its sittings; it has succeeded to the *Accademia degli Intrepidi,* one of the first poetical societies of Italy, but it has now become more generally useful as a literary and scientific institution. Near its hall of assembly some small rooms are shown which were occupied by Calvin, when he found an asylum at the Court of the Duchess Renée under the assumed name of Charles Heppeville. It is impossible to visit them without carrying one's thoughts back to the meetings at which the stern reformer secretly expounded his doctrines to the small band of disciples whom the favour of his patroness had collected together. Among these were Anne de Parthenai, Olympia Morata, Marot, Francesco Porto Centese, and other Protestants whom persecution had driven from beyond the Alps, and who assembled in these apartments to derive instruction from the great teacher of Geneva.

The Studio Pubblico enjoys some celebrity as a school of medicine and jurisprudence. It contains a rich cabinet of medals, and a collection of Greek and Roman inscriptions and antiquities; among which is a colossal sarcophagus of Aurelia Eutychia. But its chief interest is the *Public Library,* containing 80,000 volumes and 900 MSS., among which are the Greek Palimpsests of Gregory Nazianzen, St. Chrysostom, &c. The most remarkable, however, and the most valuable of all its treasures, are the manuscripts of Ariosto and Tasso. Those of Ariosto are in an apartment where the poet's arm-chair of walnut-wood, the beautifully executed medal bearing his profile, which was found in his tomb, and his bronze inkstand surmounted by a Cupid enjoining silence, which he is said to have designed himself, are deposited. These manuscripts comprise a copy of some cantos of the *Orlando Furioso,* covered with corrections, and remarkable also for the following memorandum which Alfieri begged permission to inscribe— "Vittorio Alfieri vide e venerò 18 Giugno, 1783;" one of the Satires; the comedy of La Scolastica; and some highly interesting letters, among which is one from Titian to Ariosto. The manuscript of the *Gerusalemme* is one of the most touching records in Ferrara; it was corrected by Tasso during his captivity, and ends with the words *Laus Deo.* Like the Orlando, this is also remarkable for its corrections and cancelled passages, many of which are extremely curious, and worthy of being published. There are likewise nine letters of Tasso, written while confined in the hospital of St. Anna; and a small collection of his *Rime.* Another manuscript, which seems to lose its interest by the side of the two great Epic poems, is that of the *Pastor Fido* of Guarini. A valuable treasure, but of a different character, is the series of *Choir Books,* in 18 volumes, filled with beautiful miniatures, which formerly belonged to the Certosa. There is also a *Bible,* in one large volume, illustrated with miniatures in the same style, and apparently by the same hand.

Of the printed books in the library, we may mention 52 early editions of Ariosto, a fine collection of cinquecento editions, and a very perfect series of books printed at Ferrara, which was one of the first cities in which the printing press was established. Signor Antonelli, one of the curators of this library, in his work on the Ferrarese printers of the 15th century, states that during the first 30 years of the 15th century upwards of 100 editions were issued from the press of 9 printers in Ferrara. Among the most famous of these printers was Giambattista

Guarini, from whom Aldus, before settling at Venice, received instruction in printing Greek. The medical traveller will find here the exceedingly rare work of Giambattista Canani, "*Musculorum humani corporis picturata dissectio*," without date, but referable to the middle of the 16th century.

In one of the rooms of this library is a very interesting collection of *Portraits of Ferrarese Authors*, from the earliest period down to Cicognara and Monti; and in another, 18 *Portraits of Ferrarese Cardinals*, the most interesting of which, from his connection with Ariosto, is that of Cardinal Ippolito d'Este, in whose service the great poet had spent so many painful and unprofitable years;

"Aggiungi che dal giogo
Del Cardinal da Este oppresso fui."

In a third room, called the Sala d'Ariosto, is his *Tomb*, brought here by the French from the ch. of S. Benedetto, on the 6th of June, 1801, the anniversary of the poet's death. The inscriptions, recording the merits of Ariosto as a statesman as well as a poet, were written by Guarini. The library is open to the public from 8 to 12, and from 3 to 4.

The *Casa d'Ariosto* is marked by an inscription composed by the great poet himself:—

"Parva sed apta mihi, sed nulli obnoxia, sed non
Sordida, parta meo sed tamen ære domus."

Above it is the following, placed there by his favourite son and biographer, Virgilio:—

"Sic domus hæc Ariosta
Propitios habent deos, olim ut Pindarica."

Ariosto is said to have inhabited this house during the latter years of his life, and, when some visitor expressed surprise that one who had described so many palaces had not a finer house for himself, he replied that the palaces he built in verse cost him nothing. After his death nearly all the well-known characteristics of the house, described with so much interest by the poet, were destroyed by its subsequent proprietors. In 1811 Count Girolamo Cicognara, when chief magistrate, induced the town council to purchase it, as one of those national monuments which ought to be beyond the caprice of individuals. The chamber of the poet was then carefully restored, and the circumstance was recorded in the inscription placed under his bust:—*Lodovico Ariosto in questa camera scrisse e questa casa da lui abitata edificò, la quale* CCLXXX *anni dopo la morte del divino poeta, fu dal Conte Girolamo Cicognara Podestà co danari del comune comprata e ristaurata, perchè alla venerazione delle genti durasse.*

The *Casa degli Ariostei*, in the Via de' Piopponi, in which the poet was educated, is still preserved and is situated near the ch. of Sta. Maria de' Bocche. He lived there for the purpose of pursuing his legal studies under the superintendence of his paternal uncles; but he soon gave up law for the more congenial study of poetry and romance. It was in one of the chambers of this residence that Ariosto, with his brothers and sisters, performed the fable of Thisbe, and other comic pieces of his own composition. The apartment is still shown, and is well adapted for such representations. On the death of his father, the poet removed from this house to the one already described.

The *Casa Guarini*, still inhabited by the Marquises of that name, recalls the name of the author of the *Pastor Fido*, whose bust decorates the hall. On the corner of the house is the inscription: *Herculis et Musarum commercio favete linguis et animis.*

Some of the private palaces in Ferrara contain good pictures.

In the *Palazzo Mazza* is a fine Garafalo from the ch. of S. Guglielmo, some Dosso Dossis, and 2 Panettis; and in the *P. Strozzi* a few good pictures.

In the *Palazzo Schifanoia* are some curious frescoes by *Cosimo Turra*, representing events in the life of Borso d'Este under different months; 7 only are preserved. The Horse and Donkey Races are very spirited. In an adjoining room is a beautiful ceiling. The palace now belongs to the municipality.

The Piazza Grande, now the *Piazza di Ariosto*, formerly contained a statue of Pope Alexander VII.; but this was removed by the republicans of 1796 to make room for one of Napoleon, whose name the Piazza bore until the peace of 1814, when both the statue and the title gave way to those of the "Italian Homer."

One of the great objects of interest in Ferrara is the cell in the hospital of St. Anna, shown as *the prison of Tasso*, in the precincts of the hospital, and near the Hôtel de l'Europe. Over the door is the following inscription, placed there by General Miollis: *Rispettate, o Posteri, la celebrità di questa stanza, dove Torquato Tasso infermo più di tristezza che delirio, ditenuto dimorò anni* vii. *mesi* ii. *scrisse verse e prose, e fu rimesso in libertà ad istanza della città di Bergamo, nel giorno* vi. *Luglio,* 1586. It is below the ground floor, and is lighted by a grated window from the yard; its size is about 9 paces by 6 and about 7 feet high. "The bedstead, so they tell, has been carried off piecemeal, and the door half cut away, by the devotion of those whom 'the verse and prose' of the prisoner have brought to Ferrara. The poet was confined in this room from the middle of March 1579, to December 1580, when he was removed to a contiguous apartment, much larger, in which, to use his own expressions, he could philosophise and walk about. The inscription is incorrect as to the immediate cause of his enlargement, which was promised to the city of Bergamo, but was carried into effect at the intercession of Don Vincenzo Gonzaga, Prince of Mantua."—*Hobhouse.* Few questions have been more debated than the cause of the great poet's imprisonment, some believing that it was actual insanity, others that it was mere detention in a *Maison de Santé*, combined with vexatious annoyances of the police; while by far the greater number coincide in regarding Tasso as neither more nor less than a prisoner of state, whose sufferings were aggravated by the capricious tyranny of Alfonso. His biographer, the Abbate Serassi, has shown that the first cause of the poet's punishment was his desire to be occasionally, or altogether, free from his servitude at the court of Alfonso. In 1575 Tasso resolved to visit Rome, and avail himself of the indulgences of the jubilee; "and this error," says the Abbate, "increasing the suspicion already entertained that he was in search of another service, was the origin of his misfortunes. On his return to Ferrara the Duke refused to admit him to an audience, and he was repulsed from the houses of all the dependants of the court; and not one of the promises which Cardinal Albani had obtained for him was carried into effect. Then it was that Tasso—after having suffered these hardships for some time, seeing himself constantly discountenanced by the duke and the princesses, abandoned by his friends, and derided by his enemies—could no longer contain himself within the bounds of moderation, but, giving vent to his choler, publicly broke forth into the most injurious expressions imaginable, both against the duke and all the house of Este, cursing his past service, and retracting all the praises he had ever given in his verses to those princes, or to any individual connected with them, declaring that they were all a gang of poltroons, ingratefuls, and scoundrels (poltroni, ingrati, e ribaldi). For this offence he was arrested, conducted to the hospital of St. Anna, and confined in a solitary cell as a madman." His own correspondence furnishes the best evidence of the treatment he experienced;—for almost the first year of his imprisonment he endured nearly all the horrors of a solitary cell, and received from his gaoler, Agostino Mosti, although himself a poet, every kind of cruelty— "ogni sorte di rigore ed inumanità."

"On the walls of Tasso's prison are the names of Lord Byron, Casimir Delavigne, and Lamartine's verses on Tasso, written in pencil. Notwithstanding these poetical authorities, with the inscription *Ingresso alla prigione di Torquato Tasso* at the entrance, another inside, and the repairs of this pretended prison, in 1812, by the prefect of the department, it is impossible to recognise the real prison of Tasso in the kind of hole that is shown as such. How can any one for a moment suppose that Tasso could have lived in such a place for seven years and two months, revised his poem there, and composed his different philosophical dialogues in imitation of Plato? I had an opportunity of consulting several well-informed gentlemen of Ferrara on this subject, and I ascertained that not one of them believed this tradition, which is equally contradicted by historical facts and local appearances. There was enough in Tasso's fate to excite our compassion, without the extreme sufferings he must have experienced in this dungeon. Alfonso's ingratitude was sufficiently painful: a slight on the part of Louis XIV. hastened the death of Racine; and with such spirits mental afflictions are much more keenly felt than bodily pains. Madame de Staël, who was ever inclined to commiserate the misfortunes of genius, was not misled by the legend of the prison of Ferrara; Goethe, according to the statement of a sagacious traveller, maintains that the prison of Tasso is an idle tale, and that he had made extensive researches on the subject."—*Valery.*

Sir John Hobhouse, in reference to the inscription on the cell, says that "Common tradition had long before assigned the cell to Tasso: it was assuredly one of the prisons of the hospital; and in one of those prisons we know that Tasso was confined. Those," he adds, "who indulge in the dreams of earthly retribution will observe that the cruelty of Alfonso was not left without its recompence, even in his own person. He survived the affection of his subjects and of his dependants, who deserted him at his death, and suffered his body to be interred without princely or decent honours. His last wishes were neglected; his testament cancelled. His kinsman, Don Cæsar, shrank from the excommunication of the Vatican, and, after a short struggle, or rather suspense, Ferrara passed away for ever from the dominion of the house of Este."

"Ferrara! in thy wide and grass-grown streets
Whose symmetry was not for solitude,
There seems as 'twere a curse upon the seats
Of former sovereigns, and the antique brood
Of Este, which for many an age made good
Its strength within thy walls, and was of yore
Patron or tyrant, as the changing mood
Of petty power impell'd, of those who wore
The wreath which Dante's brow alone had worn
before.

And Tasso is their glory and their shame;
Hark to his strain! and then survey his cell!
And see how dearly earn'd Torquato's fame,
And where Alfonso bade his poet dwell:
The miserable despot could not quell
The insulted mind he sought to quench and blend
With the surrounding maniacs, in the hell
Where he had plunged it. Glory without end
Scatter'd the clouds away—and on that name attend
The tears and praises of all time; while thine
Would rot in its oblivion — in the sink
Of worthless dust, which from thy boasted line
Is shaken into nothing; but the link
Thou formest in his fortunes bids us think
Of thy poor malice, naming thee with scorn—
Alfonso! how thy ducal pageants shrink
From thee! If in another station born,
Scarce fit to be the slave of him thou mad'st to mourn." *Childe Harold.*

Next to the hospital, in which is Tasso's tomb, is the handsome Roverella palace, a good specimen of the terracotta Decorated style of the 16th cent.

The Theatre of Ferrara is one of the finest in the Romagna. The first opened in Italy is said to have been here.

The Citadel was founded in 1211. After Clement VIII. had seized the principality as a fief which had lapsed to the Church for want of heirs, it was entirely rebuilt; an expedient so successfully adopted at Perugia and Ancona, to resist the malcontents likely to rebel against the usurpations of the Holy See. It was completed by Paul V. By the treaty of Vienna, Austria acquired the right of occupying this citadel and the small neighbouring fortress of Comacchio; since which time it had been occupied by an Austrian garrison until 1859.

Ferrara is one of the 3 archbishoprics of the Romagna: the bishopric dates from A.D. 661; its archbishopric was founded by Clement XII. in 1735.

Plan for visiting in a day the principal objects of interest at Ferrara, and in topographical order.

DUOMO; *the Castle; Ch. of San Domenico; Fortress; Chs. of San Benedetto* and *Capuccini; Pinacoteca; House of Ariosto; Campo Santo* and *Ch. of San Cristofero;* returning by the *Piazza Ariostea* to the Strada della Giovecca; *Public Library; Prison of Tasso; Ch. of the Teutini; Ch. of San Francesco; Uni-*

versity; Botanic Garden; Chs. of Sta. Maria in Vado, S. Andrea; Promenade of the Montagnone; Porta Romana; Porta Reno; returning to the Duomo by the Ch. of S. Paolo.

Boats may be hired at Ferrara for Venice, a voyage of 20 hours. There is a procaccio twice a week to Bologna, by water. Travellers may also proceed by the canals to Ravenna. The canals from Ferrara are the following (these communicate with many others, by which a constant intercourse is maintained with the central towns of Northern Italy; but this mode of travelling is so tedious and full of inconvenience as not to be recommended): —The canal called the *Pò di Volano* leads from the Porta Romana to the Adriatic, by a course of 56 m., skirting the northern district of Comacchio: it is navigable all the year. The *Canalino di Cento*, 28 m. in length, keeps up a communication between Cento and Ferrara. From the Porta Po or di S. Benedetto the *Cavo Pamfilio* extends to Ponte di Lagoscuro, a course of 3 miles. From the Porta di S. Giorgio the *Pò di Primaro* empties itself into the Reno, the united waters of which, after running along the S. side of the marshes of Comacchio, empty themselves into the Adriatic at Porta Primaro: it is navigable all the year by boats of considerable burden.

There is a very good road of 45 m. from Ferrara to Comacchio, leaving the city by the *Borgo di S. Giorgio*, and passing by *Locomero, Cona, Quartesana, Rovereto, San Vito, Dogato*, and *Ostillato*. Travellers can proceed from Comacchio to Ravenna (25 m.), through Torre Bell' Occhi and *Mandriolo*, but the road is bad from the depth of the sand.

A post diligence leaves Ferrara every morning for Bologna, employing 4½ to 5 hours, and for Ponte Lago Scuro every evening at 3. Diligence from Sta. Maria Maddalena to Padua, but very irregular of late.

There is a British vice-consul at Ferrara, Mr. McAlister McDonald.

ROUTE 59.

FERRARA TO BOLOGNA, BY MALALBERGO.

	POSTS.
Ferra to Malalbergo	1½
Malalbergo to Capo d'Argine	1
Capo d'Argine to Bologna	1

3½ posts = 26 m.

This is the high post-road, which has superseded the old route through Cento. Close to the walls of Ferrara the canal called the Cavo Tassone, communicating with the Pò di Primaro, is crossed, and the road proceeds over a perfectly level plain, remarkable for its fertility and cultivation, but otherwise destitute of interest. From the walls of Ferrara to the gates of Bologna it is covered with hemp, corn, rice-grounds, and meadow-lands. About half a mile before arriving at Malalbergo the Reno, retained between high embankments, is crossed by a long wooden bridge.

1½ *Malalbergo* (Inn: La Posta), a large village. The road from here to *Altedo* follows a canal, the country on each side covered with rice-fields. There is a large locanda at Altedo, which is generally made the half-way stopping-place by vetturini. From here the road ascends to the level of an artificial canal of irrigation, which it follows through a most fertile district; and as the traveller approaches Bologna he cannot fail to be struck with the improved aspect of the country—the corn-fields, the maize-plantations, and the hemp-grounds denote the extreme fertility of the soil, and bespeak a careful and better system of husbandry. The cottages are neat, and the general appearance of the people indicates prosperity and industry.

1 Capo d'Argine.

1 BOLOGNA, described in Rte. 61.

ROUTE 60.

FERRARA TO BOLOGNA, BY CENTO.

About 32 Eng. m.

This was formerly the principal line of communication between Ferrara and Bologna, and it is still interesting on account of its passing through the birthplace of Guercino, which lovers of art may consider worthy of a pilgrimage. At a short distance from Ferrara it leaves the post-road to Mantua at Cassana and Porotto, and proceeds by Vigarano, Mirabello, S. Agostino, and along the Reno, by Dosso, to Cento.

Cento.—This interesting and pretty town is situated in a fertile plain not far from the Reno. It is said to have derived its name from an ancient settlement of fishermen, who were led to fix upon this spot by the great number of crawfish for which the neighbouring waters were celebrated. They are said to have built a hundred cottages (*cento capannucce*), which they surrounded with a deep fosse; and the number of their cottages thus became the appellation of the town which subsequently arose upon their site. The population of Cento is 5400. The town was formerly celebrated for the college of S. Biagio, which was suppressed on the establishment of the Kingdom of Italy; but its chief interest arises from its being the birthplace of *Guercino*. The ch. is full of the works of this great artist; and his house, which it was his delight to cover with his paintings, is still preserved without any alteration, save what has been produced by time. The *Casa di Guercino* has been correctly termed a real domestic museum. "In the little chapel is an admirable picture of *two pilgrims praying to the Virgin*. The extreme destitution, no less than the fervour of these pilgrims, is painted with great minuteness of detail (even to the patches of the least noble part of their habiliments), without in any way weakening the general effect of this pathetic composition. The ceiling of one room presents a series of horses of various breeds; there is one superb group of two horses; another horse at grass, nothing but skin and bone, is a living skeleton of this poor animal. A *Venus* suckling Cupid is less pleasing than the rest, despite its celebrity and the merit of the colouring.

"Guercino had for Cento that love of locality, if we may so say, of which Italian painters and sculptors have in all ages offered numerous examples: he preferred residing in his native town to the titles and offices of first painter to the kings of France and England; he had his school there, and remained in the town till driven away by the war between Odoardo Farnese, Duke of Parma, and Urban VIII., when Taddeo Barberini, nephew of the latter, general of the Pontifical troops, determined on fortifying Cento. The campaign and operations of these two combatants seem but mean at the present day beside the glory of the fugitive Guercino. The house of Guercino, in its present state, attests a simple, modest, laborious life, which inspires a kind of respect. This great artist, really born a painter, *the magician of painting* as he has been surnamed, was also a pious, moderate, disinterested, and charitable man; an excellent kinsman, whose comrade and first pupils were his brother and nephews: beloved by his master Gennari, praised and recommended by Lodovico Caracci, he seems to have escaped the enmity too frequent among such rivals. The house of Guercino is not, however, devoid of magnificence: it is easy to conceive that he might there receive and regale, *ad uno squisito banchetto*, those two cardinals who had come to the fair, when his most distinguished pupils served at table, and in the evening performed *una bella commedia*, an extemporised proverb, with which their eminences were enraptured. Christina of Sweden also visited Guercino at Cento; and after admiring his works, that queen wished to touch the hand that had produced such *chefs-d'œuvre*.

"The *Chiesa del Rosario* is called at Cento the *Galerie*, a profane title, partially justified by its appearance and the arrangement of the paintings. Guercino is not less resplendent there than at home. The ch. is full of his paintings: he is said to have given the design of the front and steeple, and to have worked at the wooden statue of the Virgin; he is consequently to be seen there as a painter, sculptor, and architect, but especially as a Christian. A chapel founded by him bears his name: he bequeathed a legacy for the celebration of mass there, and left a gold chain of great value to the image of the Virgin of the Rosary. This pious offering was stolen about the middle of the last century by a custode of the ch.; a double sacrilege in the town where his memory is still popular and venerated." — *Valery.*

The fair of Cento, above alluded to, formerly celebrated throughout the province, still takes place on the 7th of September; but it has much fallen off of late years.

On leaving Cento, the road crosses the Reno. A little distance beyond the river is *Pieve di Cento*, a town of 4000 souls, surrounded with walls, and formerly celebrated for its miraculous crucifix and the College of Sta. Maria Assunta. It possesses a fine Assumption by *Guido*, over the principal altar in the ch. This noble picture was under sentence of removal at the French invasion in 1797; but the people rose against the intended robbery, and effectually prevented it.

The road now proceeds through S. Giorgio and Castagnolo Maggiore to BOLOGNA, Rte. 61.

ROUTE 61.

MODENA TO BOLOGNA.—RAIL.

KIL.	KIL.
12 Castelfranco.	27 Lavino.
19 Samoggia.	37 Bologna.

37 kil. = 23 m.

The rly. follows the line of the Via Æmilia.

3 m. after leaving Modena the road crosses the Panaro by a fine modern bridge at *Ponte S. Ambrogio*. The Panaro formerly separated the duchy from the States of the Church. Here we enter the Romagna. Castelfranco is considered by Dr. Cramer to agree with the position of *Forum Gallorum*, the scene of several important actions during the siege of Mutina, A.U.C. 710, and particularly of the defeat of Antony by Hirtius and Octavian, after the rout of Pansa.

12 kil. *Castel Franco*, or *Forte Urbano*. The old walls and ramparts of the castle, called after Urban VIII., who built them, are picturesque. The church possesses a dubious *Guido*. The site of the battle between Mark Antony and the Consuls Hirtius and Pansa is supposed to have been in this neighbourhood.

7 kil. Samoggia stat. (*Inn*, 'La Posta), a village situated on the river of the same name, about midway between Modena and Bologna; considered to occupy the site of *Ad Medias*, one of the stations of the Æmilian Way. Beyond Anzola the road crosses the Lavino; and 2 m. before reaching Bologna the Reno is crossed by a long stone bridge. Between La Crocetta and Trebbo, 2 m. on the l., is an island in the Reno, which antiquaries regard as the scene of the meeting of the second Triumvirate, A.U.C. 709. The road passes through an open and finely-wooded country, diversified by meadows and rich pasture-grounds, beyond which the hills which bound the prospect are clothed with vegetation, sprinkled with handsome villas, and cultivated to their summits.

8 kil. *Laveno* stat. Soon after leav-

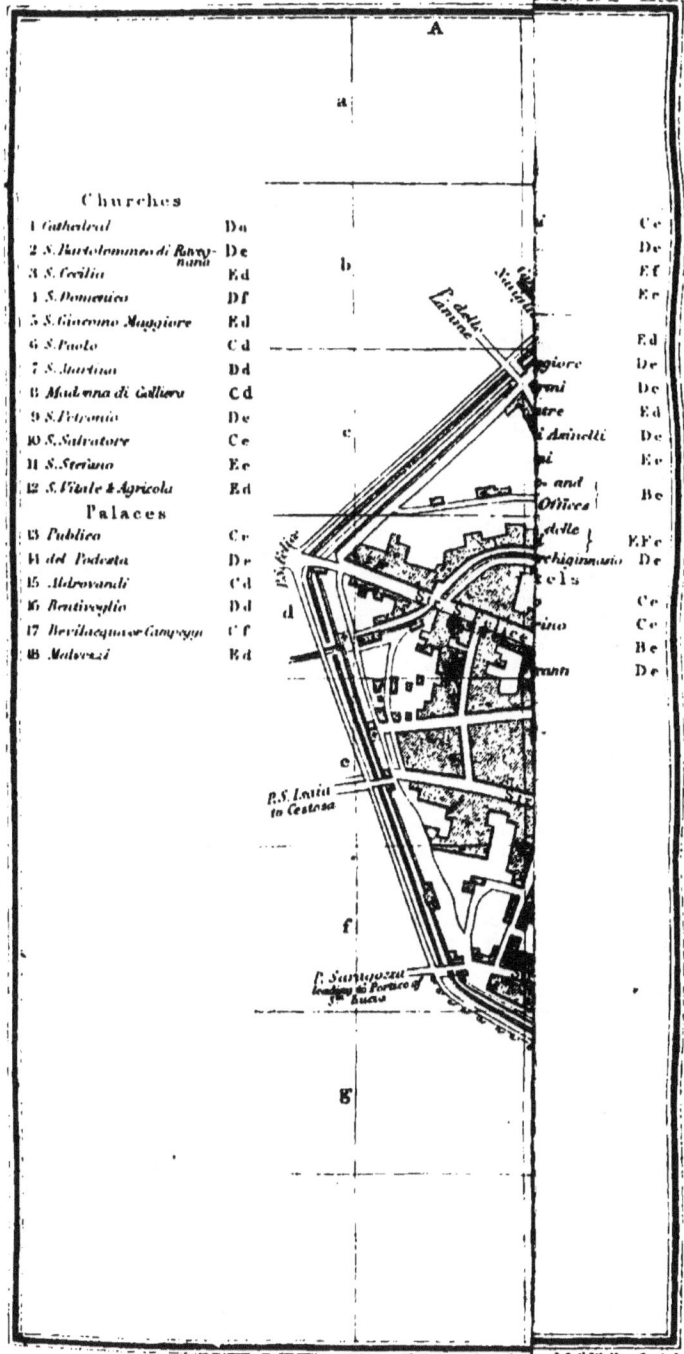

Churches

1 Cathedral	D a
2 S. Bartolommeo di Ravig- nana	D e
3 S. Cecilia	E d
4 S. Domenico	D f
5 S. Giacomo Maggiore	E d
6 S. Paolo	C d
7 S. Martino	D d
8 Madonna di Galliera	C d
9 S. Petronio	D e
10 S. Salvatore	C e
11 S. Steriano	E e
12 S. Vitale & Agricola	E d

Palaces

13 Publico	C e
14 del Podesta	D e
15 Aldrovandi	C d
16 Bentivoglio	D d
17 Bevilacqua e Campeggi	C f
18 Malvezzi	E d

this cross the Reno. The towers of Bologna now come into view, and Monte Guardia, crowned by the well-known ch. of the *Madonna di San Luca*, is a conspicuous object from the road on approaching the city; on the rt. is the Certosa, now the Campo Santo.

10 kil. *Bologna* stat. The station is near the city gate of La Galliera, where omnibuses and hackney coaches will be in attendance.

1½ BOLOGNA. (*Inns:* the Grande Albergo Svizzero, very comfortable, kept by Brun, a civil man; it is in the Malvasia Palace, and close to the post and diligence offices, with a table-d'hôte at 5½ pauls (wine included), one of the best in N. Italy; other charges moderate; single rooms 3 to 4 pauls; excellent cuisine. The San Marco, also comfortable; Il Pellegrino, both in the same street. I Tre Mori, and I Tre Re, second-rate inns.)

Hackney Coaches, Omnibuses, &c.— Omnibuses are in attendance to convey travellers from the rly. stat. to the different hotels. The hackney cabs are very good, with moderate fares. For a carriage with 1 horse, 1 paul the course within the city walls, and 2 pauls the hour; from the rly. 1½ pauls, with a small gratuity for luggage.

Booksellers.—The traveller will find a good supply of works of local interest, and of French books, at *Marsigli* and *Rocchi's*, in the Portico de' Banchi.

Cafés.—There are few towns in Europe that possess a greater number relative to the population. They are all mediocre and dirty. The best is that of Brunetti, with a restaurant, lately opened, beneath the portico of La Dogana Vecchia, near the Piazza del Nettuno.

Bologna, the second capital of the States of the Church, and one of the most ancient cities of Italy, is situated at the foot of the lower slopes of the Apennines in a beautiful and fertile plain; it is surrounded by a high wall without fortifications from 5 to 6 miles in circuit; the Savena washes its walls, and a canal from the Reno passes through the city. It was until recently the capital of the most important province of the Holy See. The city is about 2 m. long by 1¼ broad; it has 12 gates, and a population of 75,000 Inhab. It is the residence of the Governor of the Province, and the seat of an archbishop. It is one of those interesting provincial capitals which no country but Italy possesses in such abundance. With its rich and varied colonnades, affording a pleasant shelter from the sun and rain, with well-paved streets, noble institutions, and a flourishing, intelligent, and learned population, it rivals Rome in all except classical and religious interest, and the extent of its museums. It would do honour to any country in Europe as its metropolis; and the inhabitants still cherish in their love of freedom the recollections inspired by its ancient motto, "Libertas." Bologna has always been the most flourishing and the most advanced in an intellectual point of view of all the cities of the Papal States, although it has never been the residence of a court nor the seat of a Sovereign; and there can be no doubt that this prosperity is attributable to the long continuance of its privileges, and to the freedom of manners and opinions for which its people are remarkable.

On entering its principal streets the attention of the stranger is at once attracted by the covered porticoes, like those of Padua and Modena. The older quarters of Bologna, however, wear a heavy and antique aspect; their arcades are low and gloomy, and the streets are irregular and narrow; but these only serve as a contrast to the broad thoroughfares and noble arcades of the more modern part of the city.

The early history of Bologna carries us back to the time of the Etruscans. Its ancient name of *Felsina* is supposed to have been derived from the Etruscan king of that name, to whom its foundation as the capital of the 12 Etruscan cities, in 984 B.C., is attributed. His successor, Bonus, is said to have given it the name of Bononia, although some antiquaries refer it to the Boii, who occupied the city in the time of Tarquinius Priscus.

In the middle ages Bologna had become independent of the German Emperors during their contests with the Popes; and had obtained from the Emperor Hen. V., in 1112, not only an acknowledgment of its independence, but a charter granting to its citizens the choice of the consuls, judges, and other magistrates. It subsequently appeared among the foremost cities of the Guelphic league; and, after Frederick II. had left the war in Lombardy to the management of his illegitimate son Hensius King of Sardinia, it "undertook to make the Guelph party triumph throughout the Cispidine region. Bologna first attacked Romagna, and forced the towns of Imola, Faenza, Forlì, and Cervia to expel the Ghibelines and declare for the Church. The Bolognese next turned their arms against Modena. The Modenese cavalry, entering Bologna one day by surprise, carried off from a public fountain a bucket, which henceforth was preserved in the tower of Modena as a glorious trophy. The war which followed furnished Tassoni with the subject of his mock-heroic poem entitled 'La Secchia Rapita.' The vengeance of the Bolognese was, however, anything but burlesque; after several bloody battles the 2 armies finally met at Fossalto, on the 26th of May, 1249. Filippo Ugoni of Brescia, who was this year podestà of Bologna, commanded the Guelph army, consisting chiefly of detachments from all the cities of the Lombard league; the Ghibelines were led by Hensius: each army consisted of from 15,000 to 20,000 combatants. The battle was long and bloody, but ended in the complete defeat of the Ghibeline party: King Hensius himself fell into the hands of the conquerors; he was immediately taken to Bologna, and confined in the palace of the Podestà. The senate of that city rejected all offers of ransom, and all intercession in his favour. He was entertained in a splendid manner, but kept a prisoner during the rest of his life, which lasted for 22 years."—*Sismondi*. In the latter part of the 13th century the city became a prey to family feuds, arising out of the tragical death of the lovers Imelda Lambertazzi and Bonifazio Gieremei; and for many years it was harassed by the fierce contests for supremacy among these and other noble families. The Gieremei were the leaders of the Guelph party, and the Lambertazzi of the Ghibelines; but their mutual hatred was kept in check by the authorities until the occurrence of this domestic tragedy, which bears, in some respects, a strong similarity to the history of Edward of England and his devoted Eleanor. The Guelph party at length appealed to the Pope, then Nicholas III., whose mediation was so successful that the city acknowledged him as Suzerain; the tyranny of his legate, however, brought on a revolution in 1334, which ended in the supreme power being seized by the captain of the people, the celebrated Taddeo Pepoli, who subsequently sold it to the Viscontis. For upwards of a century after that event Bologna was subject either to the tyranny of the Viscontis and of the Popes, or to popular anarchy: the family of Bentivoglio, taking advantage of these feuds, seized and maintained the government in the Pope's name; but their power was too independent to be acceptable to the warlike Julius II., who dispossessed them; and, after a long struggle, established, by military force, the absolute supremacy of the Holy See.

Bologna is one of the few cities of Italy which have been occupied by British troops. During the last struggle with Napoleon in Italy, in 1814, the Austrian army was supported in its operations on the Adige by a body of English troops, under General Nugent, who landed at the mouth of the Po and occupied Bologna in February of that year.

In 1848 an unjustifiable attempt of the Austrian General Welden to take possession of Bologna was repulsed with great bravery by the Bolognese, and the invading force obliged to retreat to Ferrara. During the following year the Austrians were more successful. Having determined to seize on the capital of the Romagna, to counterbalance the occupation of Rome by the French, they attacked the city, posting themselves on the heights above it with a force of 15,000 men. The Italian party within the walls resisted bravely for 10 days, when they were obliged to surrender after an heroic defence. From that period Bologna, until 1859, had been occupied by the Austrians. On the breaking out of the war between Austria and Sardinia in the spring of that year, the Germans, who had rendered themselves excessively unpopular by every kind of intermeddling in the local administration, tyranny, and vexation, suddenly withdrew; when the townspeople formed a Provisional Government, which continued to govern the city and the province with great ability and moderation, declaring at the same time their determination never again to submit to the Papal rule. Called upon subsequently (March 12, 1860) to pronounce on their future political destinies, the Bolognese, like all the other cities of La Romagna, by an almost unanimous vote declared in favour of being annexed to the new kingdom of Northern Italy, under Victor Emanuel, a compact subsequently accepted by that sovereign and the Sardinian Legislature.

Bologna has been the seat of a bishopric since A.D. 270. It was raised to the rank of an archbishopric by Gregory XIII. It has had the honour of contributing more prelates to the sacred college perhaps than any other city of Italy except Rome; among the natives who have been raised to the pontificate were Honorius II., Lucius II., Gregory XIII., Innocent IX., Gregory XV., and Benedict XIV.

The School of Bologna in the history of painting occupies so prominent a place, and numbers among its masters so many great names, that it would be impossible in the limits of this work to enter into anything like a detailed account of its history; and the publication of an English translation of *Kugler's Handbook of Painting* will now render this less required. But while the traveller is referred to that learned work for the details of the school, it may be useful, as an introduction to a description of the works of art in the city, to give a brief general outline of its progress.

The first name of any eminence among the early followers of Giotto at Bologna is that of *Franco Bolognese*, supposed to have been the pupil of Oderigo da Gubbio, the missal painter, mentioned by Dante. He opened the first academy of art in Bologna in 1313, and is termed by Lanzi the Giotto of the Bolognese school. Among his successors were *Vitale da Bologna* (1320), *Jacopo Paolo* or *Avanzi* (1404), *Pietro* and *Orazio di Jacopo*, *Lippo di Dalmasio*, *Muso da Bologna*, *Marco Zoppo*, scholar of Lippo, and afterwards of Squarcione, at Padua (1474), who founded an academy of great celebrity at Bologna, and *Jacopo Forti*, the friend and imitator of Zoppo (1483). But the most celebrated name which occurs in the early history of the school is that of *Francesco Francia* (1518), who may perhaps be considered as its true founder. Of the style of this great master, whose works are now fully appreciated in England, Lanzi says, "It is, as it were, a middle course between Perugino and Bellini, partaking of them both;" and Raphael, in a letter printed in Malvasia's work, says that he had seen no Madonnas better designed, more beautiful, or characterised by a greater appearance of devotion, than those of Francia. Among the scholars of Francia, whose works may yet be studied at Bologna, were his son *Giacomo* (1575), *Lorenzo Costa* (1535), *Girolamo Marchesi da Cotignola* (1550), and *Amico* and *Guido Aspertini* (1491). From the time of Francia to that of the Caracci various styles were introduced by Bagnacavallo, 1542; Innocenzo da Imola, a pupil of Francia, 1542; Francesco Primaticcio, 1570; Niccolò Abate, 1571; and Pellegrino Tibaldi, 1600. The style introduced into the Bolognese school by *Bagnacavallo*, and adopted by *Innocenzo da Imola*, was that of Raphael; while that of Michel Angelo was adopted by *Pellegrino Tibaldi*. Their contemporaries *Primaticcio* and *Niccolò Abate* left Bologna to study under Giulio Romano at Mantua, and subsequently settled in France. The school was for a time supported by *Lavinia Fontana*, *Lorenzino* (Lorenzo Sabbatini), *Orazio Samacchini*, and *Passerotti;* but it gradually declined until the third and greatest epoch of the Bolognese School, which produced the Caracci and their pupils.

Before the close of the 16th century we find a new style created by the Caracci, which superseded the ancient maxims, and finally supplanted those of every other master. This revolution in art originated with *Lodovico Caracci*, "a young man," says Lanzi, "who, during his earlier years, appeared to be slow of understanding, and fitter to grind colours than to harmonise and apply them." After visiting the works of his predecessors in the different cities of Italy, he returned to Bologna, and, with the co-operation of his cousins, *Agostino* and *Annibale*, established an academy. By their judgment and kindliness of feeling, and by their mild conduct, in spite of opposition and ridicule from the artists who then monopolised public favour at Bologna, they succeeded in attracting a crowd of pupils.

The most distinguished scholar of the Caracci was *Domenichino* (*Domenico Zampieri*), considered by Poussin as the greatest painter next to Raphael. His friend *Albani* is another name imperishably associated with the school of the Caracci, and the traveller will not fail to recognise his powers in all the great galleries of Italy. But *Guido*, another disciple of this school, is frequently considered as its greatest genius; and it is well known that no pupil of the Caracci excited so much as he did the jealousy of his masters. Among the names which figure in the history of the Bolognese school at this period are those of *Guido Cagnacci*, *Simone Cantarini*, and *Francesco Gessi* (the best pupils of Guido), *Guercino*, and *Lanfranco*. Among the scholars of the Caracci who remained in Bologna after this time are *Sisto Badalocchi*, *Alessandro Tiarini*, *Lionello Spada*, *Lorenzo Garbieri*, *Giacomo Cavedone*, *Pietro Facini*, *Lucio Massari*, &c., all artists of considerable reputation, and *Gobbo de' Caracci*, so famous as a painter of fruit. The school of Bologna declined with that of the Caracci; the attempt of *Michel Angelo Colonna* arrested its downfall for a period, but was wholly inadequate to restore it to its ancient celebrity. The fourth and last period of the school boasts the names of *Pasinelli* and *Carlo Cignani*; the former aimed at uniting the design of Raphael with the colouring of Paolo Veronese, and the latter the grace of Correggio with the varied knowledge and correctness of the Caracci.

After this general sketch of the Bolognese school, which will be found useful to appreciate the paintings scattered over the city, we shall proceed at once to the

Accademia delle Belle Arti.—This noble institution, of recent origin, is situated near the N.E. extremity of the fine street of San Donato, beyond the Palace of the University, occupying the buildings of a suppressed convent of the Jesuits. The academy consists of schools for different branches of the fine arts, and contains the celebrated Gallery of Paintings, or *Pinacoteca*; the *Oplioteca*, or collection of arms; the hall where the members of the academy hold their meetings; a library of works chiefly connected with the fine arts; and on the ground floor the various schools, which are numerously attended : in the vestibule, formed out of a portion of the cloister of the convent, are several specimens of, and casts from, ancient and mediæval sculptures, and a statue of a Duke of Courland, who resided at Bologna, and was one of the protectors of the institution at its commencement. The great object of attraction, however, for the traveller will be the Gallery of Pictures, on the first floor, which is open to the public on Thursdays only, but a small gratuity to the *custode* will obtain admission at any other time.

The *Pinacoteca* has been formed chiefly of paintings from suppressed churches; of pictures which, belonging to the municipality, had been preserved in the Palazzo Pubblico; by gifts from several patriotic citizens; and, although fewer in number, but more valuable as chefs-d'œuvre of art, by the paintings carried off by the French in 1796 from the churches, and restored after the peace of Paris in 1815. A few good paintings were transferred

Route 61.—Bologna—Picture Gallery.

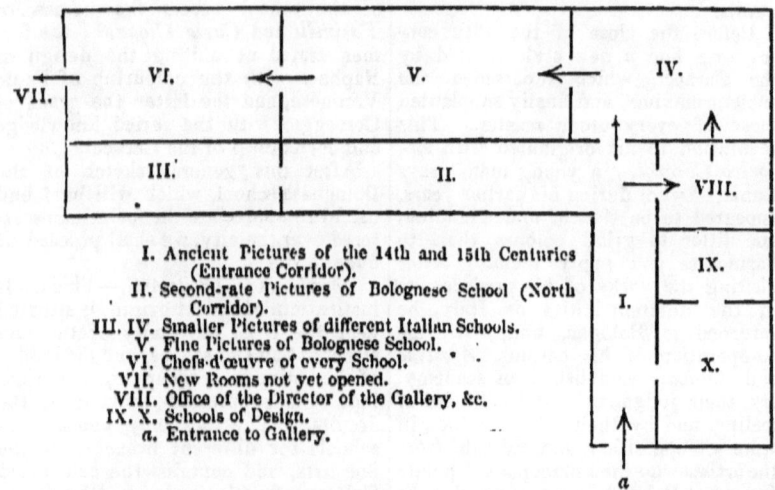

GROUND PLAN OF THE PINACOTECA OR PICTURE GALLERY OF THE ACCADEMIA AT BOLOGNA.

I. Ancient Pictures of the 14th and 15th Centuries (Entrance Corridor).
II. Second-rate Pictures of Bolognese School (North Corridor).
III. IV. Smaller Pictures of different Italian Schools.
V. Fine Pictures of Bolognese School.
VI. Chefs-d'œuvre of every School.
VII. New Rooms not yet opened.
VIII. Office of the Director of the Gallery, &c.
IX. X. Schools of Design.
a. Entrance to Gallery.

to the Brera Gallery at Milan when Bologna was annexed to the kingdom of Italy, and on being brought back were deposited here also.

The great value of the Bologna Gallery consists in what may be called its nationality, as it certainly contains the finest specimens, with very few exceptions, of the Bolognese school, or of what German writers have designated as the Academic: in this respect no city of Italy can compete with Bologna. In no place can the school of the Caracci be seen to such advantage as here; as Sir Joshua Reynolds, in recommending Ludovico Caracci as a model of style of painting, justly has observed: "It is our misfortune that the works of the Caracci, which I would recommend to the student, are not often to be found out of Bologna, . . . and I think those who travel would do well to allot a much greater portion of their time to that city than it has hitherto been the custom to bestow."

The pictures of the Pinacoteca are arranged in a series of eight rooms, the two first forming sides of the former monastic corridor: in the first of these, which forms the entrance hall, are arranged the works of the older masters; and in two large apartments fitted up in 1849 are placed the chefs-d'œuvre of the collection, which are admirably arranged, and lighted from above.

In noticing the more remarkable works of art we shall follow the order in which the traveller will generally visit the gallery in preference to the arrangement by schools, as was adopted in former editions of this work, as more likely to enable him to examine its contents in the shortest time possible. Although the different rooms bear no numbers, we shall affix one to each, in the order in which most persons will go over them.*

The annexed ground plan of the gallery may facilitate the traveller's examination of the treasures in the Pinacoteca.

I. ENTRANCE CORRIDOR.—Here are arranged a very interesting series of

* There is an indifferent catalogue sold at the gallery, but on the most unsatisfactory plan, of an alphabetical order of the artists' names, without any indication from where the pictures have been brought, their history, &c.; the latter defect may be supplied, as regards the most remarkable works, of which he has given engravings, by reference to Rosaspina's Pinacoteca dell' Accademia delle Belle Arti, 1 vol. folio, 1830. Two new halls are now (Aug. 1860) about to be added to the Gallery, the whole collection to undergo an entirely new arrangement, and a catalogue worthy of it to be published.

x 2

the earliest Bolognese school, with some of those of other Italian painters of the 14th and 15th centuries, and a few Byzantine works:—10, 11, *Jacopo Aranzi* (1408), a Crucifixion, and a Madonna and Child crowned; 159 to 174, and 340, *Simone da Bologna* (1400), an interesting series of the works of this old master: they are painted on wood, and often form *Anconas*, or subjects in various compartments. These subjects are for the most part Madonnas and Crucifixions, from which the painter was generally known as S. dei Crocefissi; many are signed and dated. 64, *F. Cossa* (1474), a Madonna with S. John, San Petronio, and the portrait of the person for whom it was painted: it is very much in the style of Mantegna, and formerly belonged to the Foro dei Mercanti. 102, *Giotto*, an Ancona, formerly in four compartments; the centre-piece is in the Brera gallery; in those here are represented SS. Paul, Peter, Michael, and Gabriel; 103 to 106, and 281, *Michele di Matteo*, a good *Ancona*, of Virgin and Saints, with its *Predella*, and figures of St. Francis and St. Dominick; 203, *Vitale da Bologna* (1320), a Madonna and Child, one of the oldest pictures of the Bolognese school, very elaborately executed (*signed*); 204, *T. della Vite*, a full-length figure of the Magdalena; 316 to 324, a series of Sacred Subjects by Byzantine artists, anterior probably to the Italian schools; 127, 128, *F. Pelosi* (1476), a Madonna, and a Deposition; 202, *Vigri-Caterina* (an Ursuline Nun), Santa Ursula, and other martyrs; 225, a charming *Giottino*; 205, *Ant.* and *Bart. Vivarini da Murano*, a very fine Gothic ancona or altarpiece, divided into numerous compartments, in the centre the Virgin and Child, in the others different Saints. The inscription states that it was painted for the Cardinal di Santa Croce in Gerusalemme, by the abovenamed artists, and in the reign of Nicholas V. (1450.)

II. N. CORRIDOR.—The pictures here are only second rate. 188, 189, *Tiarini*, a Holy Family and San Lorenzo; 191, an Ecce Homo; 32, *Canuti*, the Death of St. Benedict; 84, 89, *Giacomo Francia*, St. Francis and a Madonna; 173, 174, *Andrea Sirani*, the Virgin and Child, and S. Antony of Padua; 200, *Viani*, S. Bruno; 209, *Marco Zoppo* (1498), an Ancona, with small figures of the Virgin and Saints; 156, *Sementi*, Christ on the Cross; 126, *Passerotti*, the Virgin, with S. Francis and St. Dominick; 88, *Giulio Francia*, the Descent of the Holy Spirit on the Apostles; 131, *C. Procaccini*, the Nativity; 9, *Aspertini*, the Epiphany. In the middle of the corridor: *Nicolo Alunno*, a picture painted on both sides; on one the Annunciation, on the other the Virgin and St. Francis.

III.—Rooms opening out of Corridors 1 and 2.—61, *Cima da Conegliano*, the Madonna, with Infant Jesus and Angels; 54, *Lodovico Caracci*, a copy of the miraculous Madonna di S. Luca (see p. 493); 180, *Eliz. Sirani*, a Madonna and Angels; 18, *Guercino*, St. John; 332, *C. Procaccini*, the Annunciation; 276, *Mengs*, a small fresco of Christ and the Pharisee; 90, *Innocenzio da Imola*, the Holy Family, with St. John, St. Elizabeth, and the two Donatarii for whom the picture was painted: this lovely painting was copied for the late King of Prussia, on account of the resemblance of the principal figure to his beautiful Queen; 292, another Holy Family, by the same; 210, *Giulio Romano* (?), a copy of the St. John in the Wilderness, of the Borghese gallery at Rome; 1, *Albani*, the Madonna and Child, with SS. Catherine and Magdalen, one of his earliest productions, painted before he was 21; 14, *Guercino*, St. Peter Martyr; 15, St. John the Baptist; 16, St. Joseph; 19, the Magdalene; 31, *Simone da Pesaro*, St. Jerome; 39 and 40, *Ann. Caracci*, the Annunciation; 69, *G. M. Crespi*, St. John Nepomucene; 77, *Franceschini*, S. Anthony of Padua; 108, *Cotignola*, the Marriage of the Virgin; 157, *G. Sementi*, Sta. Eugenia.

IV. ROOM.—30, *Simone da Pesaro*, Portrait of Guido in his old age; 37, *Ann. Caracci*, Madonna throned with Saints, much injured; 38, the Assumption, with the Apostles; 51, *Lodovico Caracci*, three Saints; 52, St. Angelo; 53, St. Roch, painted in crayons; 82, *Francesco Francia*, scenes from the life of Christ; 83, a Dead Christ between Angels; 112, *Massari*, the Prodigal Son; 113, Santa Chiara; 115, the Destroying Angel; 142, *Guido*, a Head of Christ in crayons; 143, Portrait of Padre Dionisio, a Carthusian Monk; 141, the Virgin crowned by the Trinity and Four Saints, painted by *Guido*, when young, for the Ch. of San Bernardo; 146, *L. Sabatini*, the Assumption, and 148, a Dead Christ; 175, *Eliz. Sirani*, St. Antony of Padua; 179, the infant Saviour standing on a globe; 172, *Andrea Sirani*, Presentation at the Temple; 185, Ecstasy of St. Catherine; 181, *Leonello Spada*, Melchisedek blessing Abraham; 150, *Samacchini*, the Virgin, with Five Saints, Nabor, Felix, John, Catherine, and Mary Magdalene; 178, *Cotignola*, a Madonna, with Angels and Saints; 283, *Brizzi*, a Madonna with four Saints; 275, *Mengs*, Portrait of Clement XIII.; 199, *Giorgio Vasari*, Christ in the house of Martha, with the Magdalene at his feet; 74, *Prospero Fontana*, Christ laid in the tomb; 75, *Lavinia Fontana*, St. François de Paul blessing the infant Francis I. in the arms of his mother, Louisa of Savoy. 137, GUIDO, Samson having vanquished the Philistines. This fine picture, one of Guido's best works, was painted for Cardinal Ludovisi, to be placed over a chimney, which will explain its unusual form: on his death, the Cardinal bequeathed it to his native town, where it long formed one of the ornaments of the Senatorial Palace. 139, San Andrea Corsini in his Archiepiscopal Robes, a very expressive portrait; 140, S. Sebastian, a sketch, probably for a larger picture.

From Room IV. we enter two large halls, which contain the most valuable pictures of the Pinacoteca.

V. ROOM.—2, ALBANI, the Baptism of Christ, a fine picture, formerly in the Ch. of S. Giorgio; 3, the Virgin and infant Jesus, with SS. John, Francis, and Matthew below, painted in his old age; 12, GUERCINO, William Duke of Aquitaine receiving the religious habit from St. Felix, with the Madonna above, and SS. Philip and James the Apostles: a fine picture, formerly in the Ch. of S. Gregorio, from which it was removed to Paris in 1796. 13, San Bruno, formerly in the Certosa; 44, LODOVICO CARACCI, the Calling of St. Matthew, painted for the Chapel of the Corporation of the Meat Salters, from which it was carried to Paris in 1796; 43, the Transfiguration; 45, the Nativity of St. John the Baptist. The portrait below is of Monsignore Ratta, who presented the picture to the Monastery of St. John the Baptist. 47, the Conversion of St. Paul; 34, AGOSTINO CARACCI, the Communion of St. Jerome, one of his finest paintings: it was formerly at the Certosa, and was carried to Paris, with the following: 35, the Assumption; 36, *Annib. Caracci*, the Virgin and infant Jesus in glory above, and SS. Louis, Alexis, John the Baptist, Francis, Chiara, and Catherine below. This is considered one of the artist's finest works, and stood over the high altar in the Ch. of SS. Ludovico e Alessio. 41, St. Augustine; 95, *C. Gennari*, a Holy Family with four Saints; 98, *Gessi*, a Holy Family, with Angels; 135, GUIDO, the Murder of the Innocents; 136, the Crucifixion, with the Virgin, St. John, and the Magdalene at the foot of the Cross. This picture, generally known as the *Cristo de' Capucini*, is one of Guido's finest works: it formerly stood over the high altar in the Ch. of the Capucins. 138, the Virgin of the Rosary above, and the Protecting Saints of Bologna beneath. This painting was executed by Guido in 1630, and is painted on silk to be carried as a banner in a procession, to invoke the Virgin, on the occasion of the plague which desolated the city at the time; it was formerly preserved in the Senatorial Palace, having been executed at the public expense; 182, *Tiarini*, the Deposition; 206, DOMENICHINO, the Martyrdom of St. Agnes, one of the painter's finest productions. It was painted for the Convent of St. Agnese, where it stood until 1796. 207, the Madonna of the Rosary, with St. Dominick, and Angels carrying the emblems of the Rosary, with a Pope and several other figures praying beneath; it formerly stood in the Ratta Chapel at S. Giovanni in

Monte, from which it was carried to Paris.

VI. GREAT HALL of the Chefs-d'œuvre, or Tribune.—8, *Ansaloni*, the Madonna and Child in glory; 4, *Albani*, a fine Head of the Almighty; 17, *Guercino*, a similar Head; 134, *Guido*, La Madonna della Pieta, so called from the Virgin weeping over the dead body of Our Saviour, which forms the upper half of this large and very fine picture; below stand the five Saints, Protectors of Bologna—Petronius, Carlo Borromeo, Dominick, Francis, and Proculus; and in the background, a bird's-eye view of the city with its towers, &c. This celebrated painting was executed in 1616 or the municipality, who were so pleased with it, that, in addition to the price agreed upon, they bestowed a gold chain and a medal of gratitude on the artist. 42, LODOVICO CARACCI, the Madonna and infant Jesus throned, with SS. Dominick, Francis, Clara, and Mary Magdalene; the four latter are portraits of members of the Bargellini family, at whose expense the picture was painted. 46, St. John preaching to the Multitude; 48, the Madonna of the Conception: the Virgin standing on a half-moon in the midst of a glory of Angels, "an inimitable painting, in which the artist has displayed the richest stores of genius." This fine painting belonged to the Bentivoglio chapel, in the Ch. of the *Scalzi*.—49, the Flagellation of Christ, from the Ch. of the Certosa; 50, Christ crowned with Thorns, from the same place; 55, *Carcdone*, the Virgin and Child in glory, beneath SS. Alo, or Eloi, and Petronius. St. Alo, one of the patrons of Bologna, was a blacksmith, which explains the introduction of the instruments of his trade beside him. 65, *Costa*, St. Petronius, Bishop of Bologna, between St. Francis and St. Thomas Aquinas; 78, FRANCESCO FRANCIA, the Madonna, with SS. Augustine, Francis, John the Baptist, Sebastian, and Proculus. This painting, on wood, is one of Francia's finest works: it was executed in 1490 for B. Felicini, and is said to have procured for the painter the patronage of the Bentivoglios. 79, the Annunciation;

81, our Saviour in the cradle, adored by Angels and Saints; the Knight of Malta kneeling is Antonio Bentivoglio; the Shepherd, Pandolfo Cassio, a rich jeweller and poet, and a friend of the painter's; 80, the Madonna and Child between four Saints, with an Angel bearing a lily. This has always been looked upon as one of Francia's finest paintings. 86, GIACOMO FRANCIA, S. Frediano, Bishop of Lucca, and other Saints, with the painter's own portrait; 87, the Virgin in glory; 89, *Innocenzo da Imola*, the Virgin and Angels in the clouds, with SS. Peter, Michael, and Benedict beneath, from the Ch. of S. Michele in Bosco; 96, *Gessi*, the Miracle of S. Bonaventura restoring to life a new-born child at Lyons; 111, *Massari*, the Deposition; 116, *Parmigiano*, the Virgin and Child caressed by S. Marguerite, painted on wood, and for the ch. of that Saint in Bologna: it is looked upon as one of Parmigiano's finest works; it was carried to the Louvre; 122, *Niccolò da Cremona*, the Deposition of our Saviour in the Sepulchre, in presence of the Disciples and the two Marys; 133, *Baguacavallo*, a Holy Family, with three Saints; 145, *Tintoretto*, the Visitation; 152, RAPHAEL, Santa Cecilia in Ecstasy on hearing the heavenly music of the Angels, and surrounded by St. Paul, St. John the Evangelist, St. Augustin, and St. Mary Magdalene. "Santa Cecilia is represented with a lyre, held by both hands, carelessly dropped; the head, turned up towards heaven, with a beautiful pensive countenance, having an expression of concentrated and exalted feeling, as if devoting the best faculties and gifts of God to God, is deeply and touchingly impressive; her drapery is of finely enriched yellow, thrown over a close-drawn tunic; St. Paul, a superb dignified figure, fills one corner; St. John, drawn with a greater expression of simplicity and delicacy of form, is next to him; St. Augustine, another grand figure, and Mary Magdalene, like sister of the heaven-devoted Cecilia, stand close by her. All the figures are in a line, but so finely composed, and the disposition of the lights and shades such, as to produce the effect of a beautiful central group, consisting of Santa Cecilia, Mary Magdalene, and St. Peter. Musical instruments, scattered on the foreground, fill it up, but without attracting the eye; a pure blue element forms the horizon, while high in the heavens a choir of angels, touched with the softest tints, is indistinctly seen."—*Bell*. This beautiful picture was painted for the Bentivoglio chapel at San Giovanni in Monte. The story, as told by Vasari, of Francia's dying of mortification on seeing it after its arrival in Bologna, is very unlikely: indeed it is disproved by the friendly terms on which he and Raphael were, as evidenced by their correspondence. The lower part of the picture is supposed to have been painted by Raphael's scholar, Giov. da Udine. The Santa Cecilia remained at the Louvre until 1815.—183, *Tiarini*, the Marriage of St. Catherine, in the presence of SS. Joseph, Barbara, and Margaret. 197, *Perugino*, the Virgin in Glory, with SS. Michael, John the Evangelist, Catherine, and Apollonia: this picture, in Perugino's best style, stood at the Vezzini chapel in the ch. of S. Giovanni in Monte, and formed part of the French spoils in 1796.—198, *Vasari*, the Supper of St. Gregory the Great, entertaining the twelve poor Pilgrims, amongst whom our Saviour, as we are told by the Church legend, appeared as the 13th. This painting, not equal to many of the master, was executed for the Convent of S. Michele in Bosco: it is chiefly interesting as representing the portraits of several of the artist's contemporaries and patrons; Clement VII. as St. Gregory, Duke Alexander de Medicis, &c. &c., and even the butler of the convent. 208, *Domenichino*, the Death of St. Peter Martyr; this fine specimen of the master was painted for two nuns of the Spada family for their convent, le Monache Dominicane. 177, *Luca Cambiaso*, the Nativity. 27, *Calvaert*, Christ appearing to the Magdalene. A new hall is now in progress beyond this.

Opening out of the same corridor from which the Pinacoteca is entered is the *Oplioteca*, a collection of arms and warlike implements, formed chiefly out of those belonging to Count Marsigli : it possesses little to interest the traveller who has visited those of Turin, Venice, and Genoa. This collection will soon be removed into Rooms IX. and X. on plan.

Beyond the *Oplioteca* is the library, and the apartment in which the members of the academy hold their meetings: in it are some interesting drawings of the Bolognese school, and portraits of its celebrities ; a few fine specimens of niello work, two of which by *F. Francia*, and relics of the Caracci.

The University of Bologna, celebrated as the oldest in Italy, and as the first in which academical degrees were conferred, was long the glory of its citizens. It was founded in 1119 by Irnerius, or Wernerus, a learned civilian, who taught the law with such reputation in his native city, that he acquired the title of "Lucerna Juris." During the troubled period of the 12th century the fame of this university attracted students from all parts of Europe; no less than 10,000 are said to have assembled there in 1262, and it became necessary to appoint regents and professors for the students of each country. Irnerius succeeded in introducing the Justinian code; his disciples were called Glossators, who, treading in the footsteps of their master for nearly 2 centuries, spread the study of the Roman law over Europe, and sent to England Vacarius, one of the ablest of their body. At this period civil and canon law formed almost the exclusive study at Bologna ; the faculties of medicine and arts were added before the commencement of the 14th century; and Innocent VI. instituted a theological faculty some years later. In the 14th century also it acquired celebrity as the first school where dissection of the human body was practised; and in more recent times it became renowned for the discovery of Galvanism within its walls. The University of Bologna has also been remarkable for an honour peculiarly its own—the number of its learned female professors. In the 14th century, Novella d'Andrea, daughter of the celebrated canonist, frequently occupied her father's chair; and it is recorded by Christina de Pisan, that her beauty was so striking that a curtain was drawn before her in order not to distract the attention of the students.

"Drawn before her,
Lest, if her charms were seen, the students
Should let their young eyes wander o'er her,
And quite forget their jurisprudence."—*Moore*.

The name of Laura Bassi, professor of Mathematics and Natural Philosophy, is of more recent date; she had the degree of Doctor of Laws, and her lectures were regularly attended by many learned ladies of France and Germany, who were members of the University. Another, and, as our English travellers may consider, more surprising instance, is that of Madonna Mauzolina, who graduated in surgery and was Professor of Anatomy; and nearer our own times, the Greek chair was filled by the learned Matilda Tambroni, the friend and immediate predecessor, we believe, of Cardinal Mezzofanti. At the present time the university has lost its high reputation as a school of law, and the traveller who is interested in the early history of the Glossators will be disappointed in his researches at Bologna. Medical studies appear to have the superiority, and the name of Tommasini has given a reputation to it as a clinical school, which has been well maintained by other professors since his removal to Parma. The number of students scarcely now (June, 1860) reaches 700.

The noble Palace in the Strada S. Donato, which includes the University, the Institute, the Museum of Natural History, &c., was formerly the Palazzo Cellesi. It was built by Cardinal Poggi, the front being designed by Pellegrino Tibaldi, and the fine and imposing court by Bartolommeo Triachini, a native architect of the 16th century. It was purchased in 1714 by the Senate of Bologna, to receive the library and the collections of natural history and scientific instruments presented to the city, as the foundation of a national institute, by Count Marsigli, the friend of Sir Isaac Newton, and a fellow of the Royal Society of London.

The Palace at first included the Academy of Sciences, or the Instituto delle Scienze di Bologna, founded in the 17th century, by a noble youth named Maufredi, at the age of 16, who formed a literary society at his house, and assembled there all the men of talent in the city. In 1803 the university was transferred here, under the general name of the "Pontificia Universita."

The halls of the loggiato and the adjoining chambers are remarkable for their frescoes, by *Pellegrino Tibaldi* and *Niccolò Abbate*. In the court is a statue of Hercules in grey stone, by Angelo Pio, a sculptor of some repute in the 17th cent. In the upper corridor are several memorials, erected in honour of celebrated professors and others, natives of the city.

The Cabinet of Natural Philosophy contains some paintings by Niccolò Abbate. The Anatomical Museum is rich; and the various branches of pathological, general, and obstetrical anatomy are well illustrated by preparations and wax models. The Museum of Natural History has been considerably augmented of late years, and the rooms in which it is contained newly fitted up a few years ago at the expense of Cardinal Opizzoni, Archbishop of Bologna; it is well arranged, and contains a good geological collection of the country around. Upon one of the walls are suspended the chains by which Count Marsigli was bound when a prisoner with the Turks. The Museum of Antiquities, on the ground-floor, is small, but possesses some curious and interesting fragments. The first apartment contains the inscriptions, among which is that belonging to the sacred well, which gave rise to the commentary of Paciaudi on the "Puteus Sacer;" 2 milestones from the Via Æmilia, numbered CC. and CCXXCVI.; 2 fragments of *latercoli*, or military registers; and a large number of sepulchral tablets. The second chamber contains some Egyptian and Etruscan antiquities; among the latter is the fragment of the celebrated engraved plate, or, according to Chev. Inghirami, of a mystic mirror, called, from the

name of its first possessor, the Cospiana Patera. It represents the birth of Minerva, who issues armed from the head of Jupiter, while Venus is caressing him. The names of the figures are in Etruscan characters. Another mirror represents, but in relief, Philoctetes healed by Machaon, the names of which are also in Etruscan characters. The following are worthy of examination. A semi-colossal bronze foot and a Bacchic vase in marble, both found in the island of Capri; a series of Roman weights in black stone, and some metal weights of the middle ages; among which is one of the time of Charlemagne, with the inscription "Pondus Caroli." In the third chamber are some architectural remains, with 2 fragments of marble torsi, the one of a Venus coming out of the bath, the other of the same goddess standing; a male torso, attributed to Augustus, found in the Via di S. Mamolo; an Isiac table of black basalt, found on the Aventine in 1709, and an elliptical vase of porphyry. In the next chamber are works after the Revival, among which is the bronze statue of Boniface VIII., by Andrea da Pisa, erected by the Bolognese in 1301; it is remarkable only as showing the low state of art at that early period. Some carved ivories and Majolica plates are worthy of notice. The collection of Medals contains some ancient Roman coins, Greek pieces from Sicily, a collection of Italian and foreign moneys, and a good series of modern medals of sovereigns and illustrious men. There is also a small collection of gems, among which is the Maffei agate, representing Achilles and Ulysses, highly prized by archæologists. It would be an omission in an account of the antiquities of Bologna not to mention the celebrated Latin inscription discovered in some excavations of the city. This famous riddle, which gave rise to so much learned controversy in the 17th century, is as follows:—
"D. M. ÆLIA LÆLIA CRISPIS, nec vir, nec mvlier, nec androgyna, nec pvella, nec jvvenis, nec anvs, nec casta, nec meretrix, nec pvdica, sed omnia; svblata neqve fame, neqve ferro, neqve veneno, sed omnibvs; nec cœlo, nec aqvis, nec terris, sed vbiqve jacet. Lvcivs Agatho Priscivs, nec maritvs, nec amator, nec necessarivs, neqve mœrens, neqve gavdens, neqve flens, hanc nec molem, nec pyramidem, nec sepvlchrvm, sed omnia, scit et nescit cvi posverit." At the top of the building of the University is the Observatory, containing some good astronomical instruments. The view from the terrace of its tower is most extensive, and no traveller should leave Bologna without ascending to it, which is easily done on application to the Custode of the University.

The *University Library* occupies a building constructed by Carlo Dotti, and added to the Institute by Benedict XIV. It contains about 150,000 volumes and 7000 manuscripts; of these, not less, it is said, than 20,000 volumes were presented by that pope, who also induced Cardinal Monti, another native of Bologna, to follow his patriotic example. Among the printed books are the following: the first edition of Henry VIII.'s famous *Assertio Septem Sacramentorum adversus Martinum Lutherum*, Lond. *in Œdibus Pynsonianis*, 1512, dedicated to Leo X., with the autograph signature "Henricus Rex;" and about 200 volumes of scientific MSS. by Ulisse Aldrovandi.

It is scarcely possible to consider any record of this library complete which fails to commemorate its connexion with one of the extraordinary men of our age, the late Cardinal Mezzofanti, who commenced his career as its librarian. He was the son of an humble tradesman of Bologna, and had become celebrated throughout Europe for his knowledge of languages, even while he filled the chair of professor of Greek and Oriental literature in this university; but it remained for the late pope (Gregory XVI.) to raise him from the humbler dignity of an abbé to the highest honours which it was in his power to confer. At the age of 36 Mezzofanti is said to have been able to read 20, and to converse fluently in 18 languages; at the time of his death in 1849 he spoke 42. Mezzofanti was called to Rome by the late pope, and appointed to a post in the Vatican Library, under Mai; and when that illustrious scholar was created a cardinal, Mezzofanti was raised to the same dignity. Perhaps the English traveller may desire no higher evidence of the unequalled powers of Cardinal Mezzofanti than the following extract from the 'Detached Thoughts' of Lord Byron:— "I do not recollect," he says, "a single foreign literary character that I wished to see twice, except, perhaps, Mezzofanti, who is a prodigy of language, a Briareus of the parts of speech, a walking library, who ought to have lived at the time of the tower of Babel, as universal interpreter; a real miracle, and without pretension too. I tried him in all the languages of which I knew only an oath or adjuration of the gods against postilions, savages, pirates, boatmen, sailors, pilots, gondoliers, muleteers, camel-drivers, vetturini, postmasters, horses, and houses, and everything in post! and, by Heaven! he puzzled me in my own idiom." A new hall has been recently added to the library, dedicated to Mezzofanti, to contain the manuscripts; amongst which are some interesting ones of Tasso, a number of Voltaire's letters to Frederick of Prussia, letters of Metastasio, Mezzofanti's Catalogues, &c.

In connexion with the University, there remain to be noticed the Botanical and Agrario Gardens, and the Public Hospitals. The *Botanical Garden* was formed in 1804, on the site of the ancient Collegio Ferrerio de' Piemontesi. The Agrario Garden, *Orto Agrario*, one of the results of the French occupation, was commenced in 1805 as a practical school for agricultural students, for whom a course of theoretical and experimental lectures on agriculture are delivered. The lecture-room is the ancient Palazzino della Viola, formerly the villa of Giovanni II., Bentivoglio, and celebrated for its frescoes by *Innocenzo da Imola*. These fine works represent Diana and Endymion; Actæon metamorphosed into a stag; Marsyas, Apollo, and Cybele. There were originally other frescoes by Costa, Chiodarolo, Aspertini, Prospero Fontana, and Niccolò dell' Abbate, but they have all been destroyed for the purpose of building additional apartments. The Great Hospital (*Ospedale Grande*) was founded in 1667; the clinical cases are received in a separate building, near the university, called the *Ospedale Azzolini*, from the Senator Francesco Azzolini, by whom it was founded, in 1706, for the sick and infirm poor of the parish of S. M. Maddalena. In the Borgo di S. Giuseppe is the *Ospedale de' Settuagenari*, for the aged poor; and in the ancient Benedictine Monastery of S. Procolo is the *Ospedale degli Esposti*, for foundlings, recently enlarged. Dr. Fraser conveys the following information of the Ospedale Grande:—"A good hospital and a separate building for clinical cases. There are at present 500 students. There is a large collection of anatomical figures, but it is inferior to that at Florence."

Churches. — Among the hundred churches of Bologna there are few which do not contain some painting which, if not itself a masterpiece, supplies an episode in the history of art. In the following pages we have given such details as will enable the traveller to select and judge for himself amidst the multiplicity of riches; at the same time the artist will bear in mind that there are very few of them from which he will fail to derive instruction.

The Duomo, or *Cathedral*, dedicated to St. Peter, is a very ancient foundation, but it has been several times rebuilt. The present edifice was begun in 1605; the front and some of the chapels were added in 1748 by Benedict XIV., from the designs of Torreggiani. The interior is in the Corinthian style, imposing in its effect; on each side of the door are rude lions in red Verona marble, on which stand vases for holy water; they probably supported the columns of the portal of the ancient edifice, and are attributed to Ventura di Bologna. In the 2nd chapel on the rt. is preserved the skull of St. Anna, presented in 1435 by King Henry VI. of England to the Blessed Niccolò Albergati. In the 3rd chapel is the fine work of *Graziani*, a native painter of the 18th century, representing St.

Peter consecrating St. Apollinaris. In the cupola before the 4th chapel is the St. Peter commanding Pope Celestin to elect S. Petronius bishop of Bologna, by *Bigari*; and over the altar a Holy Family, and frescoes of S. Pancras and S. Petronius, by *Franceschini*, painted in his 80th year. The *Sacristy* contains, among other works, a Crucifixion, by *Bagnacavallo*; and in the Camera del Capitolo, opening out of it, a St. Peter mourning with the Virgin for the death of the Saviour, a strange invention, by *Lodovico Caracci*. In the passage leading to the Sacristy there is a curious bas-relief of the 16th century on the tomb of Lorenzo Pini, a Doctor of Laws, of a professor teaching. The choir, designed by *Domenico Tibaldi*, contains on the vault a fine picture designed by *Fiorini* and coloured by *Aretusi*, representing our Saviour giving the keys to St. Peter in the presence of the 12 apostles; and on the arch above the high altar the celebrated painting of the Annunciation, the last work of *Lodovico Caracci*. The foot of the angel bending before the Virgin was a little crooked, and it is related that, when the aged artist made the discovery, he offered to defray the expense of re-erecting the scaffold in order that he might re-touch it, but the request was refused, and Lodovico died of grief a few days after. In 1830 the error was corrected by Prof. Faucelli, who was employed to clean and restore the paintings in this chapel and in the Sacristy. Returning towards the entrance, the chapels of the opposite side remain to be examined. The chapel of the SS. Sacramento contains a work by *Donato Creti* which has been much admired: it represents the Virgin with the infant Saviour in the clouds, surrounded by angels, with S. Ignatius before her. The gilt bronze ornaments were executed at the cost of Benedict XIV., when archbishop of this his native city. On the adjoining pier is the monument of Cardinal Oppizzoni. In the Baptistery is a finely composed painting of the Baptism of our Saviour, by *Ercole Grazini*. On St. Peter's day some fine tapestries are exhibited in this church, executed at Rome from the designs of Raphael Mengs, and presented by the same pontiff. The ch. beneath the choir is curious: it contains numerous relics, and some works of art, among which the two Marys weeping over the dead body of Christ is by *Alfonso Lombardo*. Behind the cathedral is the archbishop's palace, a fine and spacious modern edifice. There are some good slab tombs from the floor of the old cathedral in the passage leading from the church to the episcopal residence.

The elegant *Ch. of S. Bartolommeo di Porta Ravegnana*, behind the Torre degl' Asinelli, was commenced in 1653, on the site of a more ancient building erected in 1530, from the designs of Andrea da Formigine. The original site was occupied by an ancient ch. built in the 5th century by S. Petronius on the foundations of one of the early Christians. The portico of Formigine is still preserved; and the bas-reliefs of its pilasters, the work of Lombard sculptors, are well worthy of observation. The ch. contains some interesting paintings: in the 2nd chapel on the rt. is S. Carlo Borromeo kneeling before the tomb at Varallo, by *Lod. Caracci*. 4th. An Annunciation, significantly called "del bell' Angelo," a beautiful and expressive work of *Albano*; by whom also are the lateral pictures of the Birth of the Saviour and the Angel warning Joseph to fly out of Egypt. 7th, "The picture in the choir behind the high altar is by *Franceschini*, representing the Martyrdom of St. Bartholomew, a grand but horrible picture, yet less savage than the statue at Milan of the same subject, as here at least the actual representation of torture is spared. The saint is tied and drawn up high to a tree for sacrifice; two ferocious figures are seen tightening the ropes, while a third is deliberately preparing to excoriate one of his legs, where a little blood appears, but there only."—*Bell*. The frescoes, representing the events in the life of S. Gaetano, are by the pupils of *Cignani*. 2nd on the l., S. Antony of Padua, by *Tiarini*. 13th, the St. Bartholomew, the altarpiece of the old church, is by

Aretusi. The roof of the nave was painted by *Colonna*, into which are introduced numerous members of the order of the Theatins, to whom the ch. formerly belonged. The artist is said to have received in payment the 3rd chapel on the rt., which he also decorated with his frescoes.

The *Ch. of S. Bartolommeo di Reno* is remarkable for some works of the Caracci. In the 6th chapel is the Nativity, by *Agostino Caracci*, painted at the age of 27. The two Prophets on the vault of the chapel are by the same master. The two fine pictures of the Circumcision and the Adoration of the Magi are by *Lod. Caracci*; the last of these has been engraved by his cousin Annibale. The marble ornaments are by *Gabriele Fiorini*. The Capella Maggiore contains a miraculous image of the Virgin, of very high antiquity, called "La Madonna della Pioggia." Opposite the stairs leading to the oratory is a large landscape by *Mattioli*, an engraver. The oratory contains a St. Bartholomew, by *Alfonso Lombardo*.

The *Ch. of S. Benedetto*, near the Porta di Galliera, has, in the 1st chapel, the Marriage of St. Catherine in the presence of 4 Saints, by *Lucio Massari*. In the 2nd, the 4 Prophets are by *Giacomo Cavedone*, and the Annunciation by *E. Procaccini*. In the 4th, S. Antonio Abate beaten by demons, the beautiful "Charity" on the ceiling, and the Virtues of God the Father, are also by *Cavedone*. 5th, S. Francesco di Paolá, by *Gabriele Ferrantini*, one of the masters of Guido. The descent from the Cross, over the high altar, is by *Fiorini* and *Aretusi*. 7th, S. Antony of Padua, by *Cavedone*. 11th, the Virgin holding the crown of thorns, and conversing with the Magdalen on her son's death, an expressive work of *Tiarini*; by whom are also the Prophets and the Angels on the side walls. In the Sacristy is a picture of the Crucifixion, with the Virgin, the Archangel Michael, and St. Catherine, by *Andrea*, the father of Elisabetta, *Sirani*, retouched by Guido.

The *Ch. of Santa Maria della Caritá*, in the Strada di S. Felice, attached to a Franciscan convent, suppressed in 1798, and converted into a military hospital, contains, in the 1st chapel, the Visitation by *Galanino*, extolled by Malvasia. The 3rd chapel contains the picture of St. Elizabeth of Hungary in a swoon at the Saviour's appearing to her, by *Franceschini*. Over the high altar are the Virgin and Child, and Charity and St. Francis, another joint work of *Fiorini* and *Aretusi*. 5th, the Virgin and Child, St. Joseph and St. Antony of Padua, by *Felice*, son of *Carlo Cignani*. 6th, Sta. Anna, by the elder *Bibiena*.

The ancient *Oratory of Sta. Cecilia*, behind the ch. of S. Giacomo Maggiore. (p. 472, the Sacristano of which has the keys), erected in 1481 at the expense of Giovanni II. Bentivoglio, once celebrated for its frescoes by early painters of Bologna, was desecrated during the French occupation, but it still exhibits many interesting fragments for study. The following enumeration of the subjects, commencing on the rt. hand, may be useful, although, from the state of ruin in which the edifice is, it will be difficult to recognise many of them:— 1, The Marriage of St. Valerian with Sta. Cecilia, by *F. Francia*. 2, Valerian instructed in the faith by St. Urban, by *Lor. Costa*. 3, The Baptism of Valerian, by *Giacomo Francia* (?). 4, the Angel crowning the betrothed Saints with garlands of roses, by *Chiodarolo*. 5, the brothers Valerian and Tiburtius beheaded in the presence of the Prefect. 6, Their Funeral. 7, Sta. Cecilia and the Prefect: these three subjects are by *Amico Aspertini*. 8, Sta. Cecilia placed in the boiling bath, by *Giacomo Francia*. 9, the Saint distributing her riches to the poor, by *Costa*. 10, her Funeral, a very graceful composition, by *Francesco Francia*. In order to preserve what remains of these interesting works the late government repaired the chapel, and handed it over to the Accademia delle Belle Arti, to be in future used in its religious ceremonies. In the interior of the suppressed convent are some good specimens of terra-cotta ornaments.

The *Ch. of the Celestini*, behind

S. Petronio, with a façade from the designs of Francesco Tadolini, 1765, has in its 1st chapel one of the best works of *Lucio Massari* — the Saviour appearing to the Magdalen in the form of a dove. The painting at the high altar, representing the Virgin and Child, with John the Baptist, St. Luke, and S. Pietro Celestino, is by *Franceschini*. The paintings on the vault of the ch. are by *Boni*.

The *Ch. of the Corpus Domini*, in the street leading to and near the Porta S. Mamolo, called also *La Santa* from Sta. Caterina Vigri of Bologna, is attached to a very extensive nunnery. The frescoes of the cupola, the roof, and the walls, are by *Marcantonio Franceschini* and *Luigi Quaini*. 1st chapel, St. Francis, with a fine landscape, by *Calvart*. 4th, the Saviour appearing to the Virgin, with the Patriarchs; and the Apostles engaged in the burial of the Virgin, are by *Lodovico Caracci*. The statues of the Virgin and Child, the bas-reliefs of the mysteries of the Rosary which surround them, and the two large Angels, are by *Giuseppe Mazza*, by whom are also the bas-reliefs over the high altar. The picture representing the Last Supper is a celebrated work by *Marcantonio Franceschini*. The Annunciation, in the 2nd ch. on the l., is by *Franceschini*, whose masterpiece, the Death of St. Joseph, is in the next, the ceiling of which is also painted in fresco by him. The unfinished façade of this ch. has a good door in moulded terra-cotta.

The *Ch. of S. Cristina*, attached to an Augustinian Convent, is decorated with paintings executed almost entirely at the expense of different nuns. The Ascension, at the high altar, is by *Lodovico Caracci*; the Nativity and the Journey of the Magi, in the 1st chapel, are by *Giacomo Francia*. The figures of St. Peter and St. Paul, in the niches between the pilasters, are the production of *Guido* in his youth.

The *Ch. of San Domenico*, celebrated as containing the tombs of St. Dominick, the founder of the order of Preaching Friars and of the Inquisition, of King Hensius, of Taddeo Pepoli, and of Guido, is also rich in works of art. The *Tomb of San Dominick*, the early triumph of *Niccolò di Pisa's* genius, in the large chapel out of the rt. aisle, forms in itself an epoch in the history of art, which ought to be closely studied by those interested in the early history of modern sculpture as extremely beautiful, whether viewed as a whole or in its details. This great master, who has been justly called the precursor of the revival of sculpture, did not complete the pulpit at Pisa until 35 years after the date of the present work (1225), and consequently we may regard this as the foundation of a new era in that branch of art. The bas-reliefs by Niccolò di Pisa represent various events in the life of the saint and the miracles performed by him; they surround the four sides of the urn, and are full of character and truth. In front, the knight thrown from his horse and brought to life by St. Dominick in the presence of his family, who are deploring his death, and the St. Peter and St. Paul in heaven, presenting the saint with the constitutions and baton of the order, are among the most remarkable of these graceful compositions. Below them is another interesting series by *Alfonso Lombardo*, forming a kind of predella, executed 3 centuries later, and not superior in delicacy or feeling. One of the small statues in front of the urn, that of S. Petronius, with his ch. in his hand, is a work of *Michel Angelo* in his youth, as is likewise the beautiful angel on the left, now made to hold a very indifferent candlestick. It is recorded in the city annals, that the great artist received 12 ducats for the angel, and 18 for the S. Petronius! The other angel and the statues of SS. Francis and Procolus are, according to Vasari, by *Nicolò dell' Arca*. The architecture of this (the 6th chapel, on the rt.) is by Terribilia; the 1st picture on the rt. hand, the Child brought to life, is one of the masterpieces of *Tiarini*, and was much admired by Lodovico Caracci. The great painting, representing a Storm at Sea, in which St. Dominick is rescuing the sailors by praying to the Virgin; the knight thrown from his horse, and brought to life by the saint; the stories in the lunettes, and the graceful figures representing his virtues, are by *Mastelletta*. The fresco on the vault above the altar, representing the glory of Paradise, with the Saviour and the Virgin receiving the saint, amidst a host of angels, is by *Guido*. "In the highest circle; of the dome, a soft radiance, emanating from the Holy Spirit, illuminates the picture, touching, with partial lights, the heads of our Saviour, of Mary, and the saint, who are placed at equal distances, while a choir of angels, exquisitely designed, and finely coloured, fills the space below. The composition of the whole rises in a fine pyramidical form, harmonising at once with the subject and the proportions of the dome."—*Bell*. The saint burning the books of the converted heretics, a fine painting, is esteemed the masterpiece of *Leonello Spada*.

The other chapels of this church present additional objects of interest: 1st, the Madonna, called "Del Velluto," by *Lippo di Dalmasio*. 3rd, St. Antoninus with the Saviour and the Virgin appearing to St. Francis, by *Facini*, a pupil of Annibale Caracci. Below it is a Virgin, attributed to *Francia*. 4th, St. Andrew the Apostle preparing for his martyrdom, by *Antonio Rossi*. 5th, the Madonna della Febbre, a good picture of the 15th century, brought here from the ch. of St. George, where it had a reputation for curing fever patients, as its name indicates. 9th, St. Catherine of Siena, by *Brizzi*. 10th, or rt.-hand transept, St. Thomas Aquinas writing on the subject of the eucharist, with 2 inspiring angels, by *Guercino*. Near the entrance of the Sacristy is the monument erected by the Clementine Academy to the memory of Count Marsigli, the founder of the Institute, whose patriotic zeal for the welfare of Bologna, and whose connexion with the science of England, have been noticed in a previous page. In the Sacristy is a S. Jerome, by *Leonello Spada*; and in its chapel, on l. of the observer, the Marriage of St. Catherine, by *Filippino Lippi*, signed and dated (1501).

The choir has a good picture by *Bartolommeo Cesi*, the Adoration of the Magi. The stalls of the choir present interesting examples of *intarsia* works, of the 15th century, by Fra Damiano da Bergamo, and by Fra Antonio Asinelli, both Domenican monks; the subjects are taken from the Old and New Testaments. In the left-hand transept is the inscription to Hensius, King of Sardinia, the son of the Emperor Frederick II., made prisoner by the Bolognese in 1249, and detained here in captivity until his death in 1272, in which the haughty republic makes the record of its royal captive the object of a higher compliment to itself; the present record replaced in 1731 a more ancient one. In singular and striking contrast to this tomb, the adjoining chapel contains the monument of Taddeo Pepoli (ob. 1337), the celebrated ruler of Bologna, by the Venetian artist Jacopo Lanfrani: the urn, of an elegant form, rests on a basement, covered with black and white checker-work, the armorial shield of the family. The sculptures upon it represent Pepoli rendering justice to his fellow-citizens. The altarpiece, with St. Michael, St. Dominick, St. Francis, and the Saviour with Angels above, is by *Giacomo Francia*. 15th, the Chapel of the Relics: among the other relics here preserved is the head of St. Dominick, in a silver case of 114 lbs. weight, made in 1383, at the joint expense of the city, of Benedict XI., and of Card. Matteo Orsini. The body of the Beato Giacomo da Ulma, the painter on glass, is also preserved here. On the wall of this chapel is the disgusting mummy of the Venerabile Serafino Capponi. Opposite the monument of King Hensius is the portrait of St. Thomas Aquinas, by *Simone da Bologna*, proved by the annals of the Order to be an authentic likeness, and preserved here, as the inscription under it conveys, during the last 400 years. 17th: the Annunciation, by *Calvaert*. The magnificent chapel dedicated to the *Madonna del Rosario*, opening out of the l. aisle, contains inscriptions painted on the wall, which inspire very different feelings from that of the founder of the

Inquisition, or those of King Hensius and Pepoli: those of Guido, and of Elisabetta Sirani, who died of poison in her 26th year; they are both buried here. Over the altar is a series of small paintings representing the 15 mysteries of the Rosary; the Presentation in the Temple is by *Calvaert*; the Descent of the Holy Spirit, by *Cesi;* the Visitation, and the Flagellation of our Saviour, are by *Lod. Caracci;* the Assumption is by *Guido*. The statues over the altarpiece are by *Angelo Piò;* the painting of St. John the Evangelist is by *Giuseppe Marchesi*. The roof, painted in 1656, is an able work of *Michel Angelo Colonna* and *Agostino Mitelli*. In the vestibule leading to the side door is the tomb of Alessandro Tartagni, of Imola, a celebrated jurisconsult, by the Florentine sculptor Francesco di Simone; and opposite that of the Volta family, with a statue of S. Procolus, by Lazzaro Casario. 22nd chapel, St. Raimondo crossing the sea on his mantle, is by *Lod. Caracci*. 23rd. This chapel contains a bust of S. Filippo Neri, from a cast taken after his death.

The *Sacristy* has also some pictures and other objects of interest: the Birth of the Saviour, or "La Notte," by *Luca Cangiasi*, is a repetition of the smaller painting preserved in the academy. The Paschal Lamb is attributed to *Vasari*. The S. Jerome is by *Leonello Spada*. The *intarsia*-work of the *armadie* or presses and of the entrance door are by the artists who executed those in the choir. The large statues of the Virgin and of San Domenico are of cypress wood, and, according to the verses inscribed underneath, were carved out of a tree which St. Dominick himself had planted —one of those, perhaps, which Evelyn saw growing in the quadrangle of the convent at the period of his visit.

The Cloisters of the adjoining convent of San Domenico are extensive: the outer one, supposed to be that erected in 1231 by Niccolò di Pisa, contains some inscriptions and ancient tombs, among which are to be noticed those of Gio. d'Andrea Calderini, the work of the Venetian Jacopo Lanfrani, in 1238; and of Bartolommeo Salicetti, by Andrea da Fiesole, in 1412. There is preserved here a portion of a painting by *Lippo di Dalmasio*, representing the Magdalen at the feet of Christ, which Malvasia describes as his earliest work; the head of the Magdalen is lost. Beyond this, in the same corridor, is a Crucifixion, with S. Lorenzo presenting a Doctor kneeling; it bears the inscription *Petrus Joanis* (Pietro di Giovanni Lianori?), and is of the 14th century. On leaving the convent, under the portico built by Niccola Barella, leading up the Via di S. Domenico, on the l. hand, is a picture of the Virgin and Child, with St. John, by *Bagnacavallo*.

In the *Piazza* surrounding the *Church of San Domenico* are some interesting objects. The gilt bronze statue of S. Domenick, standing on a red brick column, was cast at Milan in 1623; the Madonna del Rosario is by Giulio Cesare Conventi; and two sepulchral monuments, one, in the centre of the square, the tomb of the learned jurist Rolandino Passaggeri, *Correlaro* of the corporation of Notaries, who, while holding the office of town-clerk, was selected to write the reply of the Republic to the haughty letter of the Emperor Frederick II., demanding the release of his son King Hensius. The other is the tomb of a member of the family of Foscherari, and was raised by Egidio Foscherari in 1289. The early Christian bas-reliefs forming the arch of the canopy are more ancient, and not unlike some of those of the 8th centy. which we shall see at Ravenna. Both tombs stand under canopies supported by columns, and were restored in 1833.

Ch. of S. Francesco, behind the Post and Diligence offices.—This ch., one of the most extensive of the ecclesiastical edifices of Bologna, was desecrated in 1798, and converted into the Dogana or custom-house. It has been restored of late years to its primitive destination, and the walls painted in gaudy colours with execrable taste; the transepts have been restored in the most modern style of classical architecture—a sad eyesore in an edifice of such a pure kind of Italian Gothic; the many interesting sepulchral monuments it contained—the churches of St. Francis throughout Italy being the favourite burying-places—have been destroyed, or transferred to the Campo Santo. The principal object worth notice in the restored edifice is the marble decoration or screen over the high altar, a fine work of the 14th century by *Giacobello* and *Pietro dalle Massegne*, and for which they received 2150 golden ducats, a very large sum for the period (1388). The bas-reliefs on it represent the Coronation of the Virgin, in the centre, with figures of saints on either side. Amongst other celebrated individuals buried here was Pope Alexander V. (1410). In the adjoining portico are frescoes relating to the life of S. Antonio di Padova, by *Tiarini, Tamburini, Gessi*, &c. The mutilated Sarcophagus near the door of the Convent bears the inscription of the celebrated Glossator Accursius. The Bell Tower, of the 13th century, is one of the finest in Bologna.

The *Ch. of S. Giacomo Maggiore*, in the Strada di S. Donato, belonging to the Augustine hermits, was founded in 1267, enlarged in 1497, but never completed. Some of its existing details, however, are interesting, as illustrations of early Italian Gothic. The doorway has a canopy in which the shafts supporting it rest on lions. On each side are arched recesses for tombs. An ugly square window has replaced an elegant wheel one; whilst the two handsome Gothic ones, which admitted light into the nave, have been barbarously walled up. The beautiful portico adjoining, and which forms one side of the Via di S. Donato, was erected in 1477 by Giovanni di Bentivoglio. The immense vaulted roof of the ch., divided into 3 portions by cross arches, has been much admired for the boldness of its execution. The paintings in the different chapels which open directly from the central nave are the chief objects of attraction. In the 1st chapel on rt., the small fresco of the Virgin, "della Cintura," is covered up by a more modern one of Cherubim. 4th. The fall of St. Paul, by *Ercole Procaccini*. 5th. Christ appearing to Gio. da S. Facondo, by *Cavedone*, who also painted the side walls. 6th. The Virgin throned, surrounded by John the Baptist, St. Stephen, St. Augustin, St. Anthony, and St. Nicholas; a fine work, by *Bartolommeo Passerotti*, much praised by the Caracci. 7th. St. Alexis bestowing alms on the poor, and the frescoes of the arch, by *Prospero Fontana*. 8th. The Marriage of St. Catherine, by *Innocenzo da Imola*, justly called an "opera Raffaelesca," for it is almost worthy of that great master: this is really a magnificent picture. The small Nativity, on the *gradino* underneath, is another beautiful work by the same painter. 10th. St. Roch struck with the plague, and comforted by an angel, by *Lodovico Caracci*: the glory of angels above, and the saints by the side, are by *Francesco Brizzi*. 11th. The four Doctors of the Church are by *Lorenzo Sabbatini*; the Angel Michael, over the altar, by his scholar *Calvart*. Its merit was so much appreciated by Agostino Caracci, that he engraved it. 12th. The chapel of the Poggi family, designed by Pellegrino Tibaldi. The altarpiece, representing the Baptism of our Lord, was finished by *Prospero Fontana*, by desire of Tibaldi. The compartments of the roof are also fine works of Fontana. The grand picture of St. John baptizing, and that in illustration of "Many are called, but few are chosen," are by *Pellegrino Tibaldi*: they are characterised by great power of composition and expression, and are said to have been much studied by the Caracci and their school. 13th. The Virgin, with St. Catherine and St. Lucia, and the Beato Rinieri below, is by *Calvaert*. 14th. The Virgin and Child in the air, with SS. Cosimo and Damiano and S. Catherine below, and the portrait of one of the Calcina family, patrons of this chapel, are by *Lavinia Fontana*. 15th, said to contain a fragment of the true cross. Over the altar of this chapel is a large Ancona, in several compartments, of the Coronation of the Virgin with Saints, which is worthy of observation as bearing the name of *Jacopo Avanzi*, on which, in the group of St. George and the Dragon, the head of the horse is wonderfully well drawn for the period. The Crucifix on the side wall bears that of *Simone* (da Bologna), with the date 1370. 18th. The celebrated chapel of the Bentivoglio family, the ancient lords of Bologna, is, on many accounts, the most interesting in this ch. The Virgin and Child, with 4 angels and 4 saints, over the altar, is one of the most celebrated works of *Francesco Francia*, "painter to Giovanni II., a Bentivoglio." The Ecce Homo in the lunette above is also attributed to this master. In another lunette, one of the visions, the Apocalypse, in fresco, is by *Lorenzo Costa*, retouched by *Felice Cignani*, who painted the Annunciation. The oil painting, on the side wall on rt. of the altar, of the Virgin throned, with Gio. II., Bentivoglio, and his numerous family in adoration, interesting as a study of costume and character, is by *Lorenzo Costa*, Francia's able scholar (1488). The 2 curious ones opposite, representing triumphs, are also by *Costa* : one is a procession of Death drawn on a car by 2 buffaloes, and the other, a beautiful female figure, by black elephants; the numerous figures which follow in these processions are interesting for the costumes of the period. The alto-relievo of Annibale Bentivoglio within the chapel (*ob.* 1458) on horseback is by *Nicolò dall' Arca*. The expressive bas-relief of Giovanni II., on one of the pilasters, is said to have been sculptured by *Francesco Francia*. Outside the Bentivoglio chapel is the fine monument of Antonio Bentivoglio, who perished on the scaffold in 1435, the father of Annibale I.; it is supposed to have been executed by *Jacopo della Quercia* : the other tomb near it is of Nicolo Fava, an eminent medical professor of the 15th century. 19th. The Christ in the Garden, and in the 20th chapel the St. Peter, St. Paul, and King Sigismund, are by *Ercole Procaccini*. 21st. The Virgin, with John the Baptist, S. Francis, and S. Benedict, by *Cesi*, one of his most pleasing works. 23rd. The Martyrdom of St. Catherine, by *Tiburzio Passerotti*. 25th. The Presentation in the Temple is the masterpiece of *Orazio Samacchini*; it was engraved by Agostino Caracci. The figures on the side walls are also by Samacchini. 29th. The monument to Cardinal Agucci, over the side door of the ch., with the statues and bas-reliefs, is by *Gabriele Fiorini*, from the design, it is said, of Domenichino. 31st. The Last Supper is supposed to be a repetition of the celebrated picture by *Baroccio*, in the Ch. di S. M. sopra Minerva, at Rome, by the painter himself. The frescoes of Melchisedek and Elijah, and the Angels of the ceiling, are good works of *Cavedone*. In the 33rd chapel is a miraculous crucifix in wood, the history of which can be traced as far back as the year 980. [As St. Giacomo Maggiore is now (June 1860) undergoing extensive repairs, it is very possible that some alterations may take place in the position of the different works of art above noticed.] Behind and communicating with the convent is the chapel of Santa Cecilia (described at p. 468); it is entered through the convent, and will be opened by the Sacristano of the church.

The Ch. of San Giorgio, built by the Servite Fathers, contains a few interesting pictures. In the 4th chapel, S. Filippo Benizio, kneeling before the Virgin and Child in the midst of Angels, was begun by *Simone Cantarini*, and finished in the lower part by *Albani*. The St. George, at the high altar, is by *Camillo Procaccini*. In the 5th chapel on l., the Annunciation is by *Lodovico Caracci*, and the graceful paintings underneath are by *Camillo Procaccini*. 4th. The Probatica Piscina in this chapel is also by *Lodovico Caracci*. 1st. The Flight out of Egypt, by *Tiarini*.

The Ch. of S. Giovanni in Monte, a fine Gothic edifice with a groined roof, so called from its being on a slight rising, the highest point within the walls of the city, one of the most ancient in Bologna, founded by St. Petronius in 433, and rebuilt in 1221, was restored in 1824, without disturbing the general style of its ancient architecture. The great entrance dates from 1527; the eagle in painted terracotta over it is by *Nicolò dall'*

Arca. The interior consists of a nave separated from the aisles by four wide round arches originally pointed; the arches of the tribune and transepts being still in the latter style. 1st chapel on rt. The Saviour appearing to the Magdalen, by *Giacomo Francia*. 2nd. The Crucifixion, by *Cesi*. 3rd. The St. Joseph and St. Jerome, in the ovals on the side walls, are by *Guercino*. 6th. A small oval Madonna, almost hidden by ex-voto offerings, placed below Mazzoni's picture of the Liberation of St. Peter, is by *Lippo di Dalmasio*. 7th. The Virgin throned with Saints is a fine work of *Lorenzo Costa*. 8th. The miraculous figure of the Virgin here, originally in the ancient church of S. Eutropio, was formerly celebrated for its powers in curing the sick: it is of high antiquity. 9th. The S. Ubaldo is a good work of *Gio. Battista Bolognini*. The picture in the choir, of the Virgin with the Almighty and the Saviour above, and John the Evangelist, St. Augustin, St. Victor, and other saints below, is by *Lorenzo Costa*. The busts of the Apostles over the stalls are by *Alfonso Lombardo*, and the 2 Evangelists by *Fra Ubaldo Farina*; the *intarsia* work is by *Paolo Sacca*, 1525. The ancient Madonna, on a pilaster, to the l. of the high altar, a fresco detached from some suppressed church, is said to be anterior to the year 1000, but it has lost all its original character. 12th, or l.-hand transept, the picture of Sta. Cecilia, by *Raphael*, now in the Pinacoteca, was over the altar in this chapel until 1796; there is now an indifferent copy in its place. Beneath the altar is buried the Beata Elena Duglioli dall' Olio, at whose expense the Sta. Cecilia was painted. 6th on l. The figure of the Saviour, carved out of a single block of a fig-tree, is attributed to *Pietro da Pavia*, 1430. 17th. In the 2nd chapel on the l., the St. Francis kneeling, adoring a crucifix, is a powerful and expressive work by *Guercino*. The adjoining convent, whose cloisters were designed by *Terribilia* in 1548, has been converted into a prison. On the stairs leading from the ch. to the Via di S. Stefano are several tombstones and inscriptions formerly on the floor of its nave and aisles.

The Ch. of *St. Gregorio*, near the Cathedral, almost entirely rebuilt after the earthquake of 1779, contains, in the 6th chapel, one of the early oil paintings of *Annibale Caracci*: the Baptism of the Saviour. In the 8th chapel, the St. George delivering the Queen from the Dragon, with the Archangel Michael above pursuing the demons, and likewise the picture of God the Father, are by *Lodovico Caracci*. The picture over the high altar, representing St. Gregory's miracle of the Corporale, is by *Calvaert*. Albani is buried in this ch.

The Ch. of *S. Leonardo* contains, in its 1st chapel, the Annunciation, by *Tiarini*, in which the Almighty, holding a dove as the symbol of the Holy Spirit, is represented as awaiting the answer of the Virgin to the announcement of the Angel. The altarpiece, the Martyrdom of St. Ursula, and the St. Catherine in prison, converting Porphyrius and the wife of Maximianus to Christianity, are both excellent works by *Lodovico Caracci*.

The Ch. of *Sta. Lucia*, in the Strada Castiglione, a large modernized edifice with a very bare look, is, perhaps, more remarkable for a curious literary relic preserved there—a long letter written by St. Francis Xavier, in Portuguese, which is exposed with singular homage on the festival of that saint— than for its works of art, although there are several pictures which deserve notice, among which may be specified the Sta. Lucia and Sta. Anna, with the Virgin and Child, at the high altar, by *Ercole Procaccini;* the Death of St. Francis Xavier, considered the best work of *Carlo Antonio Rambaldi*, in the 6th chapel; the Virgin and Child, with John the Baptist, S. Carlo, and Sta. Teresa, by *Carlo Cignani*, in the 7th chapel; and in the Sacristy, the Crucifixion by *Lavinia Fontana*; and the Conception, one of the first works of *Calvart* while yet a pupil of Sabbatini.

The Ch. of the *Madonna del Baraccano* was so called from a Confraternith, established in 1403, in honour of the miracles performed by a picture of the Virgin painted on a bastion of the city walls, called "Il Baraccano di Strada Santo Stefano." Over the portico, constructed from the designs of Agostino Barella, is a statue of the Virgin by *Alfonso Lombardo*. At the high altar the miraculous picture of the Virgin, *Francesco Cossa*, of Ferrara, repainted it in 1450, with the addition of 2 portraits, of Gio. I. Bentivoglio, and of Maria Vinciguerra. The frieze of flowers which adorns this altar, and other sculptures of the chapel, are graceful works by *Properzia de' Rossi*. The Virgin and Child, with SS. Joseph and Joachim, in the 4th chapel, is by *Lavinia Fontana;* and the St. Catherine, in the 5th, is by *Prospero Fontana*.

The *Madonna di S. Colombano* is remarkable for being covered internally by frescoes, painted by various pupils of Lodovico Caracci. The St. Francis on the rt. wall is by *Antonio*, son of *Agostino Caracci;* the Virgin and Child, with Joseph gathering dates, is by *Spada;* the Sibyl over the side door, and the Coronation of St. Catherine, are by *Lorenzo Garbieri;* the Sta. Marta conversing with the Saviour, before whom the Magdalen is kneeling, is by *Lucio Massari*, on the vault above; by whom are also the Sibyl over the other door, and the angel bearing the palm of martyrdom to Sta. Ursula; the infant Saviour playing with St. John in the presence of little angels is by *Paolo*, brother of *Lodovico Caracci*, who gave the design. In the upper oratory, the frescoes representing the Passion were all, it is said, the result of a trial of skill among the younger pupils of the Caracci; among them, the fine picture of St. Peter going out weeping from Pilate's house, by *Albani*, may be particularly noticed. The Virgin, over the altar of this ch., is by *Lippo Dalmasio*.

The Ch. of the *Madonna di Galliera*, near the Cathedral, a very handsome ch. inside, contains some interesting paintings. In the 1st chapel (del Crocifisso) the frescoes on the ceiling, representing the Death of Abel, and the Sacrifice of Abraham, are the last works of *M. Angelo Colonna*. In the 2nd, the St. Antony of Padua is by *Girolamo Donnini*, the pupil of Cignani. In the 3rd, the Virgin and Child, with Joseph, S. Francesco di Sales, and S. Francesco d'Assisi, is by *Franceschini*, who painted the frescoes of this chapel. The Capella Maggiore contains a very ancient painting of the Virgin and Child, generally concealed from view; the figures of the angels round this painting are by *Giuseppe Mazza*. In the 4th, the Incredulity of St. Thomas is by *Teresa Muratori*, celebrated as much for her talent in music as in painting; the angels above, frequently praised for their delicacy and grace, are said to have been added by her master, Gio. Giuseppe dal Sole. The 2nd chapel on l. contains the picture of the infant Christ between the Virgin and St. Joseph, a lovely painting by *Albani;* the Adam and Eve in oil, the Cherubim and the Virtues in fresco, are by the same master. In the 1st is S. Filippo Neri in ecstacy, surrounded by Angels, by *Guercino*. In the Sacristy, St. Philip, the Beato Ghislieri, the Conception, and the S. Francesco di Sales, are by *Elisabetta Sirani*. The Celestial Love, and the St. Elizabeth Queen of Hungary, are by *G. Andrea Sirani*. The Assumption is by *Albani*. The adjoining oratory, built from the designs of Torreggiani, has over the entrance door a fresco of an Ecce Homo by *Lodovico Caracci*.

Sta. Maria Maddalena, near la Porta Mascarella, contains, at the first altar, a Madonna, S. Onofrio, and S. Vitale, by *Tiburzio Passerotti;* and at the 3rd, St. Francis, and St. James, by the same. The Virgin, with S. Sebastian and S. Roch, is by *Bagnacavallo*. The oratory contains an altarpiece by *Ercole Procaccini*, restored by Giovannini; the Archangel Gabriel and the Virgin by *Giuseppe Crespi*, and other works by his two sons.

Sta. Maria Maggiore, in the street leading to the Porta Galliera, one of the ancient churches of the city, contains some good works by *Tiarini*. At the 1st altar, St. John the Evangelist dictating to St. Jerome is a pleasing example of this master. The 3rd altar has a very ancient wooden crucifix. The 5th has a Madonna and Child, with St. James and St. Antony, by *Orazio*

Samacchini. The 7th was decorated by *Carlo Francesco Dotti.* The 5th on l. has a Virgin, Child, and St. John, painted by *Franceschino Caracci*; the 1st on l. a picture of the Madonna with 2 saints of the 15th centy., attributed on very doubtful grounds to *Carlo Crivelli.*
The Ch. of *Sta. Maria della Pietà,* better known as *I Mendicanti,* near the Porta di San Vitale, which the great masters of the Bolognese school had enriched with some of their finest works, was stripped of its most valuable treasures at the first invasion by the French; the Madonna della Pietà by Guido, the St. Matthew by Lodovico Caracci, the S. Alò and S. Petronius of Cavedone, are in the Pinacoteca; and the Job of Guido, which accompanied them to France, has never been restored. Among the most interesting paintings which remain are the following: at the 1st altar, the Sta. Ursula, by *Bartolommeo Passerotti*. 3rd on l., Christ feeding the Multitude, by *Lavinia Fontana*. 4th, the Flight out of Egypt, with a fine landscape, and the paintings on the side walls, by *G. A. Donducci*. 2nd, the St. Anna adoring the Virgin in a vision, by *Bartolommeo Cesi.* 1st, the Crucifixion, with the Virgin, St. John, and other saints, by the same master.
The Ch. of *Sta. Maria della Vita,* in the Via Clavature, near the Pepoli Palace, founded in 1260, by the Beato Riniero of Perugia, who devoted himself on this spot to the relief of the sick, was entirely remodelled in the last centy. In the 2nd chapel are preserved the bones of the Beato Buonaparte Ghisilieri, brought here, in 1718, from the suppressed ch. of S. Eligio. The picture representing the Beato Buonaparte and St. Jerome is by *Aureliano Milani*. The 3rd chapel contains an Annunciation, with S. Lorenzo underneath, painted by *Tamburini* from a design of *Guido*, who is said to have retouched it. Over the high altar is a fresco of the Virgin and Child by *Simone da Bologna;* the marble ornaments are by *Angelo Venturoli*. The two statues by the side are by *Petronio Tadolini;* and those in plaster by *Giacomo Rossi*. In the 3rd chapel on l. is another gift of Count Malvasia, the bust of S. Carlo Borromeo, the head of which is of silver. In the Sacristy is a picture of S. Eligio, attributed to *Annibale Caracci*, and in the oratory is the masterpiece of *Alfonso Lombardo,* a bas-relief representing the death of the Virgin in the presence of the apostles, whose heads are said to have inspired many painters of the Bolognese school. The Beato Riniero healing the sick, in the 2nd chapel on l., during the plague, is by *Cavedone,* whose history is scarcely less affecting than that of Properzia de' Rossi. Cavedone, at the death of his son, was so much oppressed with grief that he lost his talent, and with it his employment: his old age was passed in beggary, and, after having contributed so much in early life to the decoration of the churches and palaces of his native city, he was allowed to die in a stable.
The fine ch. of *S. Martino Maggiore,* in the Piazza S. Martino and near the Via di S. Donato, belonged to the Carmelite Friars from the 14th centy. to the period of the French invasion. The Adoration of the Magi, in the 1st chapel, is one of the most graceful works of *Girolamo de' Carpi;* the Annunciation, over the side door, is by *Bartolommeo Passerotti,* and the alto-rilievo of S. Martin by *Manzini,* 1530. In the 4th chapel is a picture of St. Joachim and St. Anna, with the date 1558, by *Giovanni Taraschi.* In the 5th is the picture of the Virgin and Child, with a sainted bishop on one side, and Sta. Lucia on the other, with St. Nicholas below, giving their dowry to 3 young girls, by *Amico Aspertini,* the pupil of Francia, called "dai due pennelle," because he worked with both hands, holding at the same time a brush for light and another for dark tints. The 7th chapel contains the only work in Bologna by *Girolamo Sicciolante,* the imitator of Raphael: it represents the Virgin and Child, with St. Martin, St. Jerome, &c., and contains a portrait of Matteo Malvezzi, for whom it was painted. Near the door of the Sacristy is the monument and bust of the eloquent Filippo Beroaldi the elder, by *Vincenzo Onofrio.* Above it is the Ascension, by *Cavedone.* In the 8th chapel is an Assumption, attributed to *Perugino.* In the 9th is the grand picture of St.

Jerome imploring the Divine assistance in the explanation of the Scriptures, by *Lodovico Caracci*. In the 10th is the Crucifixion, with St. Andrew, and the Beato Pietro Toma, by *Cesi*. The 11th was entirely painted by *Mauro Tesi*, an eminent artist of the last centy. In the 12th chapel is the Madonna and Child, with several saints, by *F. Francia*, as well as the paintings of the Saviour above, and bearing the Cross below. The St. Roch in the painted glass of the window over the altar is by the Beato *Giacomo da Ulmo*. The oratory, formerly the conventual library, was painted by *Dentone;* the Dispute of St. Cyril is by *Lucio Massari*. The altarpiece, representing the Incredulity of St. Thomas, is a fine work of *Giampietro Zanotti*, painted for the suppressed ch. of S. Tommaso del Mercato. In the cloister are several sepulchral monuments, among which may be particularly noticed those of 2 Professors of Law of the Saliceti family; the one bearing the date of 1403 has in front a curious bas-relief of a Professor lecturing, and is attributed to *Andrea da Fiesole;* the second, of a certain Petrus, having a similar bas-relief with 6 bearded students, is of 1503.

S. *Nicolò,* modernised in the last centy., has a fine painting in the 9th chapel by *Annibale Caracci,* the Crucifixion, with the Madonna and 4 Saints. Over the entrance door is a head by *Alfonso Lombardo.*

The Ch. of *S. Paolo,* in the Via di Aposa, behind the Piazza Maggiore, built by the Barnabite fathers in 1611, was restored in 1819. The marble statues of St. Peter and St. Paul on the façade are by *Mirandola* and *Conventi.* At the 1st altar, the Christ in the Garden, and the Christ bearing the Cross, on the side walls, are by *Mastelletta.* At the 2nd is the fine painting of Paradise, by *Lodovico Caracci.* The small Madonna underneath is by *Lippo di Dalmasio.* In the 3rd are the Nativity, and the Adoration of the Magi, by *Cavedone,* which is regarded as his masterpiece. The frescoes on the vault, representing the Circumcision, the Flight out of Egypt, and the Dispute with the Doctors, are by the same painter. At the altar in the rt. transept is the Purgatory by *Guercino,* in which St. Gregory shows to the souls the Almighty, the Saviour, and the Virgin in the heavens. Above the high altar the 2 statues of St. Paul and the Executioner are by *Alessandro Algardi,* who is said to have given Facchetti the design of the Tribune, and to have sculptured the ivory Crucifix on it: the tabernacle in jasper is in the form of a basilica. At the 3rd on l., the S. Carlo Borromeo carrying the cross through Milan during the plague, and the other pictures of the same saint on the side walls, are by *Lorenzo Garbieri*. At the 2nd, the Communion of St. Jerome, and the other paintings of this chapel, are by *Massari.* At the 1st, the Baptism of the Saviour, and the Birth and Burial of St. John the Baptist, are by *Cavedone.*

The *Ch.,* or *Basilica, of San Petronio,* the largest in Bologna, and, though unfinished, one of the most interesting and remarkable, is a fine monument of the religious munificence which characterised the period of Italian freedom. It was founded in 1390, while Bologna was a free city, the architect being Antonio Vincenzi, celebrated as one of the 16 *Riformatori,* and as the ambassador of the Bolognese to the Venetian Republic in 1396. The original plan was a Latin cross, and, if the building had been completed, it would have been 750 Eng. ft. long, or 136 more than St. Peter's at Rome. The portion we now see consists merely of what was intended for the nave and aisles, as may be seen on the outside, where the construction of the transept had been just commenced when the work was abandoned. Of the exterior, a small portion of its front alone is finished, and of the interior little more than the nave has been completed. In spite of these deficiencies, San Petronio is one of the finest specimens of the Italian Pointed style of the 14th century. The 3 canopied doorways of the unfinished façade are pure, and amongst the finest examples of the Italian Gothic; they are covered with bas-reliefs representing various events of Scripture history from the Creation to the time of the apostles, and are ornamented with busts of prophets and sibyls which recall the taste and designs of Raphael. The *central doorway* and its bas-reliefs were justly considered the masterpiece of Jacopo dalla Quercia, and were entirely executed by him. They must be carefully studied to appreciate their details; there are 32 half figures of patriarchs and prophets, with the Almighty in the centre of the arch; 5 subjects from the New Testament in the architrave, and 5 from the Old Testament, from the Creation to the Deluge, on each pilaster. Over the architrave are statues of the Virgin and Child, San Petronius, and St. Ambrose. It is recorded that the artist was commissioned to execute this door for the sum of 3600 golden florins, the Reverenda Fabbrica providing the stone (grey limestone); Vasari says that he devoted 12 years to the work, and that its completion filled the Bolognese with astonishment. The *l.-hand doorway*, supposing the spectator looking from the Piazza, is remarkable for the angels and sibyls round the arch, by Tribolo, well known as the friend of Benvenuto Cellini, who has left an amusing record of him in his most entertaining biography. Of the 4 subjects on the l. pilaster, the 1st, 3rd, and 4th are by Tribolo, as well as the 4th on the rt. pilaster, supposing the spectator to be looking at the door. Tribolo was assisted in these works by Seccadenari, Properzia de' Rossi, the Bolognese Sappho; and by Cioli and Solosmeo, pupils of Sansovino. The 3 other subjects on the rt. pilaster are by Alfonso Lombardo, and represent different events of the Old Testament. The second subject of the l. pilaster, representing Jacob giving his blessing to Isaac, is by an unknown artist. Under the arch is the superb sculpture of the Resurrection, by Alfonso Lombardo, praised by Vasari, and admirable for its simple dignity and truth. The *rt.-hand doorway* is another monument of the taste and purity of Tribolo. The angels of the arch, the sibyls, and the 8 subjects from the Old Testament on the pilasters, are by this master. Under the arch is the group of Nicodemus with the dead body of Christ, by Amico; the Virgin is by Tribolo; and the St. John the Evangelist by Ercole Seccadenari.

The interior of San Petronio is particularly imposing, and never fails to excite regret that it has not been completed on its original extensive plan. Some fault might be found with the proportion of the edifice; but the size and peculiar simplicity of the design produce an effect which reminds the English traveller of the purer Gothic of the north. "It possesses in a high degree the various peculiarities which characterise the arrangements of the Italian Gothic, such as the wide and low pier arches whose span equals the breadth of the nave, the absence of the triforium and of the clerestory string, the great empty circles which occupy the space of the clerestory, the extensive doming of the vaults, the shallowness of the side aisles, the heavy capitals which surround the piers and half piers like a band of leaves, and the squareness of the piers with their nook shafts; all these serve to make a wide distinction between this example and those of the genuine Gothic; and they are rarely found so completely united even in Italian churches. Each compartment of the side aisle has two arches, which open into shallow chapels."— *Willis.*

On entering the ch., the ornaments in relief round the great doorway are by Francesco and Petronio Tadolini. Over the side doors are the fine circular bas-reliefs by Lombardo, one representing the Annunciation, the other Adam and Eve in Paradise, formerly attributed to Tribolo. In the chapels on the rt. there are several objects to engage attention. The 2nd is the chapel of the Pepolis, so celebrated in the history of Bologna; and some of the pictures contain portraits, it is said, of members of that illustrious family. The painting of the Assumption has been attributed to *Guido;* but it was more probably only retouched by him. Those on the side walls, painted between 1417 and 1431, are curious; the figure praying on the l. bears the inscription, *Sofia de Inghilterra fe fa;* evidently representing the Donatoria, or the person at whose expense the work was executed; that opposite was painted by *Luca da Perugia*, in 1417, and represents the Virgin, Child, and Saints, with portrait of the Donatorio Bartolommeo di Milano, a merchant. Between this and the next chapel is a monument, raised by the municipal authorities, to the memory of Cardinal Opizzoni, more than 50 years Bishop of Bologna, who, after charities most liberal during his lifetime, left all he possessed to his adopted city for beneficent purposes. The fine painted glass in the 4th chapel is by the *Beato Giac.da Ulma.* 6th—St. Jerome, by *Lorenzo Costa*, spoiled by retouching. 8th, belonging to the Malvezzi Campeggi families. The marble ornaments of this chapel were designed by *Vignola*, and are said to have cost him the loss of his situation as architect to the ch. through the jealousy of his rival Ranuccio. The St. Francis is by *Mustelletta;* and the St. Antony raising the dead man to liberate the father, who is unjustly condemned, is by *Lorenzo Pasinelli:* the intarsia-work on the sides was formerly in the choir of the ch. of San Michele in Bosco, and was executed by *Fra Raffaele da Brescia*. 9th—Chapel of St. Antony of Padua. The marble statue of the Saint over the altar is by *Sansovino*. The miracles of the Saint painted in chiaro-scuro are fine works by *Girolamo da Treviso*. The beautiful windows of painted glass are celebrated as having been made from the designs of *Michel Angelo;* they contain 8 figures of Saints, and S. Antony in a lunette above. 10th—the large painting of the Coronation of the Madonna del Borgo S. Pietro, and the frescoes in chiaro-scuro opposite it, are by *Francesco Brizzi*, a favourite pupil of the Caracci: he commenced life as a journeyman shoemaker, and became the principal assistant of Lodovico. 11th—The bas-relief of the Assumption, by *Tribolo*, stood formerly at the high altar in the ch. of La Madonna di Galliera. The angels over the altar by the side are by *Properzia de' Rossi*. The walls of this chapel support the entire weight of the Campanile. On each side of the high altar the two marble statues of St. Francis and St. Dominick are by *D. Aimo;* the large picture in the choir by *Franceschini*. Crossing to the l. aisle—10th chapel, reckoning from the great entrance to the ch. (l.) —Sta. Barbara, considered the best work of *Tiarini*. 9th—the Archangel Michael, by *Calvaert* (Fiammingo), which may in some degree explain the celebrated picture by his pupil Guido in the Capuchins at Rome; the 8th chapel has a handsome iron railing of the 15th century, erected by Antonio Barbaca and his wife Margarita Pepoli. 16th—St. Roch, a portrait of Fabrizio da Milano, by *Parmegianino*. 7th—the Chapel of the Baciocchi family, contains the Tombs of the Princess Eliza Baciocchi, the sister of Napoleon, of her husband, on the rt., and opposite of 3 of her children, with a beautiful altarpiece by *Costa*, of the Madonna and Saints; and a fine painted glass window. 5th—the Annunciation, upon the wall in front, and the 12 Apostles on the side ones, are among the finest works of *Costa;* over the altar the martyrdom of St. Sebastian is in his earlier manner. The Magdalen, by *F. Brizzi*. The intarsia-work beneath was executed in 1495, by *Agostino da Crema*. The pavement of enamelled tiles dates from the earliest times of its manufacture, 1487. On the pilaster between this and the next chapel is a statue in wood of S. Petronius, believed to be the most ancient likeness of that saint extant, but it has been so altered by frequent restorations that little probably of the original countenance now remains. 4th chapel — the paintings of the Magi, and of the Paradiso and Inferno here, formerly attributed to Giotto, and subsequently by Vasari to Buffalmacco, are now generally considered to have been painted by Simone da Bologna, very early in the 15th centy. 2nd—in this chapel, rebuilt by Torreggiani at the expense of Cardinal Aldrovandi, whose tomb is placed in it, is preserved the head of S. Petronius, removed by order of Benedict XIV. from the ch. of S. Stefano. This chapel was gaudily restored in 1743, when the head was brought to it, and is also that in which divine service was first performed in 1392. Some very ancient frescoes of the Crucifixion and Adoration of the Magi have been lately discovered on the walls of the chapel next to this and to the entrance to the church.

On the floor of S. Petronio is traced the celebrated meridian line of Gian Domenico Cassini, 220 Eng. ft. long: it was substituted in 1653 for that of P. Ignazio Danti. It was in the ch. of S. Petronio that the Emperor Charles V. was crowned by Clement VII. on the 24th February, 1530. The halls of the *Reverenda Fabbrica*, adjoining, contain a highly interesting series of original designs for the still unfinished façade, by the first architects of the period. 3 of these are by Palladio; another bears the following inscription in his own hand, "Laudo il presente disegno," and has, no doubt erroneously, been attributed to him. There are 2 by Vignola; 1 by Giacomo Ranuccio, his great rival; 1 by Domenico Tibaldi; 3 by Baldassare Peruzzi; 1 by Giulio Romano and Cristoforo Lombardo; 1 by Girolamo Rainaldi; 1 by Francesco Terribilia, which received the approbation of the senate in 1580, and was published by Cicognara in his History of Sculpture; 1 by Varignano; 1 by Giacomo di Andrea da Formigine; 1 by Alberto Alberti, of Borgo San Sepolcro; and 3 by unknown artists. Over the entrance door is the marble bust of Count Guido Pepoli, by *Properzia de' Rossi*, supposed to be that ordered by his son Alessandro, to prove the powers of that extraordinary woman, as mentioned by Vasari. In the 2nd chamber is her masterpiece, the bas-relief of the Temptation of Joseph, believed to allude to the history of her own misfortunes. The life of that celebrated and accomplished woman, at once a painter, sculptor, engraver, and musician, is one of the most tragical episodes in the annals of art; "Finalmente," says Vasari, in a passage which will hardly bear translating, "alla povera inamorata giovane ogni cosa riuscì perfettissimamente, eccetto il suo infelicissimo amore." She died of love at the very moment when Clement VII. after performing the coronation of Charles V. in this church, where he had seen and appreciated her genius, expressed his desire to take her with him to Rome. Vasari records the touching answer given to his Holiness: *Sta in chiesa, e gli si fa il funerale!*

The *Sacristy* contains a series of 22 pictures, representing various events in the history of S. Petronius from his baptism to his death, by Ferrari, Francesco Colonna, Mazzoni, and others. The inside of the ch. of San Petronio has lately undergone a thorough repair, during which some early frescoes of the 14th century have been discovered under the whitewash on the 4 first columns of the nave, since removed.

Over the great door of this ch. stood the celebrated colossal bronze statue of Julius II. executed by Michel Angelo after their reconciliation on the subject of the Moses. The pope was represented with the keys of St. Peter and a sword in his l. hand, and in the act of blessing or reprimanding the Bolognese with his rt. But this great masterpiece existed for only 3 years. In 1511, on the return of the Bentivoglio party to power, it was destroyed by the people, and the bronze, said to have weighed 17,500 lbs., was sold to the Duke of Ferrara, who converted it into a piece of ordnance, under the appropriate name of the *Julian*. It is recorded of this statue, the loss of which will ever be deplored by the lovers of art, that, when Michel Angelo asked the warlike pontiff whether he should put a book in his left hand, he replied, "A book! no: let me grasp a sword; I know nothing of letters."

The Ch. of *S. Procolo* in the Via di S. Mammolo, belonged before the French occupation to the Benedictine monks of Monte Cassino; its foundation is of very ancient date, but the present one was built in 1536. Over the principal entrance is a Virgin and Child with S. Sixtus and S. Benedict, a beautiful example of *Lippo di Dalmasio*, painted in *oil*, and therefore adduced by Malvasia and Tiarini as a proof of the much higher antiquity of oil-painting than Vasari had supposed.

Beneath the organ is the Almighty surrounded by a glory of Angels over the Magi, in relief, copied by *Cesi* from a design of Baldassare Peruzzi, formerly in the Bentivoglio palace. In the 2nd chapel on rt., the St. Benedict in ecstasy is also by *Cesi*, who is buried in this ch. In the 4th on l., the Virgin in glory, with St. Benedict below, is one of the last works of *Ercole Graziani* the younger. In the 2nd chapel, designed by Torreggiani, is the marble urn over the altar in which are preserved the bodies of the 2 martyrs who gave their names to this ch.—S. Proculus, a soldier, and S. Proculus, a bishop, found in the ancient subterranean ch. in 1390. In the 1st chapel on l., the S. Maurus is by *Ercole Graziani*. On a wall near the door of the ch. the following inscription to the memory of a person called Procolo, buried in the ch., who was killed by one of the bells falling on him as he was passing under the campanile, was much admired in the last century, when this kind of play upon words was more in fashion than it is now:—

: " Si procul a Proculo Proculi campana fuisset,
Nunc procul a Proculo Proculus ipse foret."

The Ch. of *S. Rocco*, near the Porta Isaiii, converted in 1801 into a "Camera Mortuaria," where the dead are deposited before being carried to the Campo Santo, is remarkable for one of those agreeable examples of generous and patriotic rivalry for which the school of Bologna was particularly distinguished. The *oratory* is covered with the frescoes of the young artists of the period, who, for no greater sum than two pistoles each, adorned its walls with paintings illustrating the life of S. Roch, and other suitable subjects. Their zealous emulation has been justly described as a "tournament of painting." They represent events in the life of the saint, and of the patron saints of Bologna.

The Ch. of the *Santissimo Salvatore*, in the street leading from the Piazza S. Francesco to the P. Maggiore, has some interesting paintings. In the 1st chapel is the Beato A. Canetoli refusing the Archbishopric of Florence, by *Ercole Graziani*. In the 2nd is a Resurrection, by *Mastelletta*. In the 4th, the Adoration of the Magi, by *Prospero Fontana*. The Miracle of the Crucifix bears the inscription, "*Jacobi Coppi*, civis Florentini, opus, 1579," and is mentioned by Lanzi as one of the best pictures in Bologna prior to the time of the Caracci. A picture of the Virgin and St. Thomas, by *Girolamo da Treviso*, formerly at the altar "de' Scolari Inglesi" in the old ch. The Judith going to meet the Hebrew Damsels with the Head of Holofernes is by *Mastelletta*. The Virgin holding the Infant Saviour to St. Catherine, with St. Sebastian and St. Roch, is a fine work of *Girolamo de' Carpi*. The finely-preserved painting of the Virgin crowned, underneath this picture, is of the 14th century. In the choir, the Saviour bearing his cross was designed by *Guido*, who painted the head, and retouched the whole picture, after it was finished by *Gessi*. Of the 4 Prophets, the David is by *Cavedone*. The subjects illustrating the miraculous crucifix are by *Brizzi*, and the St. Jerome is by *Carlo Bonone*. In the 6th chapel is a striking Nativity by *Tiarini*; in the 7th, a fine Crucifixion surrounded by Saints, by *Innocenzo da Imola*; in the 8th, the Ascension, by *Carlo Bonone*; in the 9th, St. John kneeling before the aged Zacharias, by *Garofalo*. The 4 doctors of the Church, painted over the 4 small chapels, are by *Cavedone*. The large picture over the door, representing the Marriage of Cana, is by *Gaetano Gandolfi*, a modern painter of Bologna. In the Sacristy, the frescoes of the roof are by *Cavedone*; and in an adjoining room the S. Dominick is attributed to *Guercino*; and the St. John the Baptist, with the Lamb, to *Simone Cantarini*; the Madonna is by *Mastelletta*. Guercino was buried in this ch., but without any inscription or monument. There are several interesting MSS. regarding the history of Bologna in the Library of the adjoining Convent.

The Ch. of the *Servi*, or *Sta. Maria de' Servi*, in the Via Maggiore. In front, and flanking it towards the street, is the grand *Portico de' Servi*, built upon marble columns, in 1392, by Fra

N. *Italy*—1860. Y

Andrea Manfredi of Faenza, General of the Servites, which has a series of frescoes in the lunettes, illustrating various events in the life of S. Filippo Benizzi. Of these 20 subjects, the principal are by *Cignani Giovanni Viani, Peruzzini, Giuseppe Mitelli, Lorenzo Borgonzoni*, &c. The ch. is remarkable for some fine paintings. In the 2nd chapel on the rt., the Virgin giving the conventual dress to the 7 founders of the order is one of the last works of *Franceschini*, painted by him when nearly 85 years of age. 4th, the Death of Sta. Giuliana Falconieri is by *Ercole Graziani*. 5th, the Paradise, a large and elaborate work, by *Calvaert*. 7th, the Madonna di Mondovì, with angels and saints, John the Baptist, S. James, and S. Francesco di Paolo, by *Tiarini*. 8th, the Virgin appearing to S. Filippo Benizzi. In the 10th chapel is preserved a marble pitcher, said to have been used at the marriage of Cana, presented by Fra Vitale Baccilieri, General of the Servites, who had been ambassador to the Sultan of Egypt in 1350. The monument of Lodovico Leoni, over the door of the Sacristy, is by *Giacomo Ranuccio*. In the 12th chapel, the miracle of S. Gregory at mass is by *Aretusi* and *Fiorini*. In the 14th, the Virgin and Child painted on the wall, and 2 saints by the side, are by *Lippo di Dalmasio* ; opposite, the Beato Gioacchino Piccolomini fainting during the celebration of mass is by *Ercole Graziani* ; the Madonna above it is another work of *Dalmasio*. 15th, St. Joachim and St. Anna, by *Tiarini*. On the opposite wall is a painting of the Virgin enthroned, of the 14th centy. On the back wall of the choir is the slab-tomb of Fra Andrea Manfredi of Faenza, the eminent architect and general of the order, by whom the ch. was founded (ob. 1396). 16th, S. Onofrio, by *Calvaert*. In the 9th chapel on l., the fresco representing S. Carlo in heaven was painted by *Guido*, gratuitously, in one day. 7th, the Annunciation, a fine work by *Innocenzo da Imola*. The frescoes of the roof and side walls are by *Bagnacavallo*. 24th, or 5th on l., the St. Andrew adoring the Cross prepared for his martyrdom, a fine picture by *Albani*. The monument of the Cardinal Ulisse Gozzadini in this chapel has a portrait of that prelate in Roman mosaic. 3rd on l., the Noli-me-tangere is another fine work of *Albani*. The large painting of the Nativity of the Virgin, with numerous figures, over the principal entrance, was the last work of *Tiarini*.

The most ancient ecclesiastical edifice in Bologna, and one of the oldest in Italy, is that of *San Stefano*, quite a labyrinth, formed by the union of 7 churches. Entering from the piazza by the large portal is what is called the church of the Crocifisso, from a painting of the Crucifixion over the high altar. This, as well as another of our Saviour bearing the Cross, is probably of the 15th cent. On the l.-hand wall is a painting by *Teresa Muratori* and her master *Giuseppe Dal Sole*, representing a father supplicating St. Benedict to intercede for his dying son. Descending some steps, on the l. is the *Banzi Chapel*, in which a Roman marble sarcophagus contains the body of the Beata Giuliana de' Banzi. This is called the second church. The third, *del Santo Sepolcro*, is a circular building, supposed to have been the ancient Lombard Baptistery. The marble columns are said to have been derived from a neighbouring temple of Isis. The upper gallery has been closed ; but the well for immersion sufficiently shows its original destination. The marble sepulchre beneath the altar, with its ancient symbols, was erected to receive the body of S. Petronius, who is said to have imparted miraculous qualities to the water of the well. The ancient paintings which covered the walls of its circular aisle have entirely disappeared under a series of modern daubs. There is a very ancient rude ambone behind the altar. The fourth church, dedicated to SS. Peter and Paul, is supposed to have been the primitive Cathedral, founded by S. Faustinianus, A.D. 330. It contains, near the high altar, a Crucifixion, by *Simone da Bologna*, known also as Simone dai Crocifissi, from the excellence with which he treated this subject; it bears his name, "Simon fecit hoc opus." There is an Ionic capital in this ch., apparently antique. The Madonna and Child, with St. Nicholas, and St. John, is by *Sabbatini*. The St. James, St. John, and St. Francis is referred to *Lippo di Dalmasio*. This ch. has some general resemblance to our old Norman buildings, from its massive piers and columns, on some of which early frescoes of saints have been lately discovered under the whitewash. The fifth church is formed out of the cloister called the Atrio di Pilato. In the centre of it is a mediæval font, called of Liutprand, which once stood in the centre of the Lombard Baptistery: opening out of this atrio is a ch. with a good painting of St. Jerome adoring the Crucifix, by *Giacomo Francia*, and the hall of the *Compagnia dei Lombardi*, which was erected by Benedict XIV; the keys of the gates of Imola, captured by the Bolognese in 1322, are preserved here. From the Atrio di Pilato opens another ch., and from it we enter into a cloister which has 2 rows of galleries: the upper one is very elegant, and enclosed by coupled columns, with fanciful capitals, composed of monsters supporting small circular arches, over which is a frieze with other whimsical ornaments of the same kind; 2 sides of the lower portion are enclosed, and on the walls are several saints of Bologna, painted in the 15th century, which were removed from other places. From this enclosed corridor the 6th church (La Confessione) is entered, a kind of crypt, remarkable only for its ancient columns with bas-reliefs, and as containing the bodies of 2 native saints and martyrs, Vitalis and Agricola. The Madonna in the wall is said to have been placed here, in 488, by S. Giocondo, bishop of the diocese. One of the pillars professes to represent the exact height of our Saviour. The 7th church, called la SS. Trinità, also contains some interesting works of ancient art, a few of which are regarded as contemporaneous with S. Petronius. The St. Martin, bishop, praying for the restoration of a dead child to life, is by *Tiarini*, a repetition of the same subject painted for the ch. of S. Rocco. The S. Ursula, on a pillar, is by *Simone da Bologna*; and the Holy Trinity is by *Samacchini*. This ch. is celebrated for its relics, among which are the bodies of 40 martyrs, brought by S. Petronius from Jerusalem. In the chapel of the Relics is a curious reliquiary, with enamels, by *Jacopo Rossetti*, 1380. Outside these churches are two marble sarcophagi, appropriated in former times by the Orsi and Bertuccini families; one of them at least is an ancient Christian sarcophagus, and is an interesting relic. Near the entrance opposite the Via di Gerusalemme is an inscription recording the existence of a Temple of Isis, already mentioned as occupying this site.

The Ch. of the *SS. Trinità*, in the Strada S. Stefano, not far from the gate, has, at the 2nd altar, the Birth of the Virgin, by *Lavinia Fontana*. At the high altar is the S. Roch supplicating the Virgin, by *Guercino*. At the 7th altar is the Madonna in glory, with SS. Jerome, Francis, Doninus, and Apollonia, and some children playing with the cardinal's hat, by *Gio. Battista Gennari*, of Cento.

The very ancient ch. of *SS. Vitale ed Agricola*, giving its name to the street leading towards Ravenna, consecrated in 428 by St. Petronius and St. Ambrose, has a graceful painting of *F. Francia*, covering the ancient image of the Madonna in the 1st chapel on l. Beside it are 2 fine frescoes, one representing the Nativity, by his son *Giacomo*, and the other the Visitation, with portraits of the Donatorii, by *Bagnacavallo*. Opposite is an inscription recording the consecration of the ch.: the column, with a cross of the early Christians, brought here in 1832, formerly stood on the spot in the adjoining street where S. Vitalis and S. Agricola suffered martyrdom. The 2nd chapel on rt. has a picture by *Tiarini*, the Virgin dismounting from the ass during the flight from Egypt.

Opposite to the Ch. of S. Vitale is the Fantuzzi Palace, now the property of a retired opera singer; at each extremity is the armoirie parlante of the

Y 2

first owners, an elephant with a castle on his back.

The PIAZZA MAGGIORE was the Forum of Bologna in the middle ages: it is still surrounded by remarkable edifices rich in historical associations, the relics of the once formidable republic. It was considered by Evelyn, in his time, as the most stately piazza in Italy, with the single exception of that of San Marco at Venice. The ch. of San Petronio has been already described; the other buildings which give an interest to this square are the Palazzo Pubblico, the Palazzo del Podestà, and the Portico de' Banchi. On entering the Piazza, the attention of the traveller is arrested by the magnificent fountain called The *Fontana Pubblica*, or the *Fontana di Nettuno*, constructed in 1564, while Cardinal (since S. Carlo) Borromeo was legate: the general design is by *Lauretti*; the pedestal and the basin are by *Antonio Lupi*; and the Neptune, with the other figures and bronze ornaments, are by *Giovanni di Bologna*. The Neptune, one of the most celebrated works of that great sculptor, is 8 ft. high, and the weight of the bronze employed in the figures is said to be 20,012 Bolognese pounds. The cost of the fountain, with its pipes and aqueducts, amounted to 70,000 golden scudi. The merits of the Neptune have been very differently estimated by different critics. Forsyth says he "saw nothing so grand in sculpture" at Bologna: "the Neptune is admired for the style, anatomy, and technical details: his air and expression are truly noble, powerful, commanding—perhaps too commanding for his situation." Bell, on the other hand (a high authority on such a subject), says, "Neptune, who presides over the fountain, is a colossal heavy figure, in the act of preaching and wondering at, rather than commanding, the waves of the ocean; boys in the 4 corners are represented as having bathed small dolphins, which they are holding by the tail to make them spout water; while 4 female Tritons fill the space beneath; these fold their marine extremities between their limbs, and press their bosom with their hands, to cause the water to flow. The whole composition and manner is quaint, somewhat in the French style, and such as I should have been less surprised to find at Versailles than at Bologna."

The *Palazzo Pubblico*, or *del Governo*, begun at the end of the 13th century, is one of the great public monuments of the city. Prior to 1848 it was the residence of the Legate and of the Senator, as it is now of the Civil Governor. Its façade still exhibits some traces of the Pointed style in its eight walled-up windows, but the building has been so altered at various periods, that little uniformity remains. In the upper part of the façade, under a canopy, is a Madonna in relief, by *Nicolò dell' Arca*, in gilt terra-cotta. The ornaments of the clock are by *Tadolini*. The entrance gateway is by *Galeazzo Alessi* (1570): the bronze statue of Gregory XIII. (a native of Bologna), in the niche over the gateway, was erected at the cost of his fellow-citizens; it is by *Alessandro Menganti*, called by Agostino Caracci the "unknown Michael Angelo." After the revolution of 1796, in order to save the statue by converting it into that of the patron saint of the Bolognese, the tiara was changed for a mitre, and a pastoral staff placed in the right hand, with the inscription "Divus Petronius Protector et Pater." The pastoral staff is quite out of proportion with the dimensions of the statue. On entering the building is the great court, recently handsomely restored, and beyond in the 3rd court, formerly a garden, we find the beautiful cistern constructed by *Terribilia*, at the cost of 6000 scudi.

A grand staircase *à cordoni* of 53 steps, by *Bramante*, leads us to the upper halls. The bronze bust of Benedict XIV., and the ornaments over the door where it is placed, are by *Giobattista Bolognini*. The great Saloon of Hercules takes its name from his colossal statue by *Alfonso Lombardo*. On the rt. is a hall, covered with frescoes, the architectural portions of which are by *Antonio Bibiena*; the figures on the ceiling are by *Angelo Bigari*, and those on the walls by *Sca-*

rabelli. In the adjoining chapel is a fresco of the Virgin, called the Madonna del Terremoto, supposed to have been painted by the school of Francia in 1505. The gallery leading out of the Hall of Hercules is covered with frescoes illustrating the glories of Bologna by *Colonna* and *Pizzoli.* The Sala Farnese, so called from a bronze statue of Paul III., is perhaps the most magnificent. Its roof and walls are covered with paintings representing the history of the city, by Cignani, Francesco Quaini, Scaramuccia, Pasinelli, the elder Bibiena, and other eminent artists.

The *Palazzo del Podestà* was begun in 1201, the façade added in 1485 by Bartolommeo Fioravanti: although still an unfinished building, it has an air of grandeur which accords with its character as the ancient seat of municipal authority. Its greatest interest, however, is derived from its having been the prison of Hensius, King of Sardinia, and natural son of the Emp. Frederick II., captured by the Bolognese in 1249, and kept here a prisoner until his death in 1272. The history of this unfortunate monarch, whose monument we have already noticed in the account of the ch. of S. Domenico, offers a singular illustration of the manners of the middle ages. The haughty republic rejected all the overtures of the emperor for the restitution of his son, and his threats and treasures were of no avail in the attempt to obtain his liberty. During his long imprisonment the prince employed his time in poetical compositions, some of which are marked by considerable taste. The young king moreover was beloved in his captivity by a fair damsel of Bologna, Lucia Vendagoli, who succeeded in visiting him under various disguises; and the Bentivoglio family are believed to derive its origin from these mysterious meetings. The great hall is still called *Sala del Re Enzio*, although there is no proof that it was occupied by him; its size, 170 feet by 74, would almost seem conclusive against such a belief. This hall has likewise had its vicissitudes: in 1410 the conclave for the election of Pope John XXIII. was held here; in the last century it was converted into a theatre; it was afterwards used for the game of *pallone;* and was latterly degraded into a workshop. In other parts of the building are the Archives of the Notaries and other public offices. The former are rich in rare and inedited materials for the history of Bologna, and indeed of Italy during the middle ages; among them is pointed out the Bull called 'Dello Spirito Santo,' published at Florence, July 6, 1439, by Eugenius IV., for the union of the Greek and Latin Churches. The lofty tower, called *Torrazzo dell' Aringo*, rises upon arcades, is a massive and imposing pile: it was erected in 1264, for the purpose, it is said, of watching Hensius. The statues in terra-cotta of the 4 Saints protectors of the city, on the pilasters which support its arcades, are by *Alfonso Lombardo*. The name of their new sovereign Vittorio Emanuele has been given by the Bolognese to the market-place or piazza between this palace and the ch. of S. Petronio.

The *Portico de' Banchi*, occupying one side of the Piazza, and the whole length of the ch. of S. Petronio on the E. 300 ft. in length, was designed and executed by *Vignola*, who had to adapt it to the irregularities of an older building. Here are some of the most showy shops in Bologna. Opening out of it is the building called *Il Registro*, formerly the College of Notaries, presented to that body in 1283 by the learned jurisconsult and chief magistrate Rolandino Passaggeri. The hall, now converted into a chapel, has a Madonna by *Passerotti;* the Sacristy contains, among other documents, a Diploma of the Emperor Frederick III., confirmed by a Bull of Julius II., granting to the Correttore de' Notari the power of creating apostolical and imperial notaries, and the singular privilege of legitimatizing natural children.

Private Palaces.—The Palaces of Bologna are numerous, but they are with few exceptions scarcely deserving of a visit; the works of art which formerly gave them celebrity are gradually disappearing; so that it would be difficult to give any description of their moveable contents. Their frescoes, however, like their architecture, cannot be exported; and in both these respects there is much to engage the attention of the traveller.

Palazzo Albergati in the Strada di Saragozza, is a good example of the architecture of *Baldassare Peruzzi* (1540). Under this palace some foundations or Roman baths have been discovered.

Palazzo Aldrovandi, now *Montanari*, in the Strada di Galliera, was almost entirely rebuilt in 1748, by Card. Pompeo Aldrovandi, on a scale of grandeur worthy of that eminent scholar. The library and the gallery of pictures collected by the Cardinal, and augmented by his successors, have been nearly all dispersed.

Palazzo Arcivescovile, behind the Cathedral, the residence of the archbishop, was built in 1577 by Tibaldi, and has been recently restored and decorated with considerable taste at the cost of Cardinal Oppizzoni, Archbp. of Bologna. The apartments are painted by the most eminent modern artists of Bologna, Professors Frulli, Pedrini, Fancelli, Fantuzzi, Zanotti, &c.

The *Palazzo Baciocchi*, now *Grabinski*, behind the Piazza of S. Domenico, formerly *Ruini*, is one of the most imposing specimens of domestic architecture in Bologna: its principal façade is by *Palladio*, by whom some of the other details were probably designed. The grand hall is ornamented by *Bibiena*.

The *Palazzo Bentivoglio*, in the Borgo della Paglia, beyond the Cathedral, has been frequently the residence of sovereign princes during their visits to Bologna; it recalls the magnificence of the ancient palace of the Bentivoglios, destroyed by the populace at the instigation of Julius II., who adopted this mode of revenging himself on his great rival Annibale Bentivoglio. In the reprisals which followed, the vengeance of the populace and their chief fell, as we have already stated, on the statue of the pope, one of the masterpieces of Michel Angelo.

Palazzo Bevilacqua Vincenzi, in the Via S. Mammolo (formerly belonging to the Campeggi family), whose architecture is attributed to *Bramantino*, yields to few in the magnificence of its court. The front is a fine specimen of the Diamond Rustic style, surmounted by a good cornice, with 2 handsome round-headed gateways opening into a court, surrounded by a double colonnade, the upper one partly enclosed, of round arches. There is a very handsome balcony in this palace towards the street. In one of the chambers is an inscription recording that the Council of Trent assembled here in 1547, having removed to Bologna by the advice of the celebrated physician Fracastorius, under the pretext of contagion.

Palazzo de' Bianchi, in the Strada di San Stefano, has a fine ceiling by *Guido*, representing the Harpies infesting the table of Æneas.

Palazzo Fantuzzi, in the Via di S. Vitale (see p. 483).

Palazzo Fava, opposite the Ch. of the Madonna di Galliera, is rich in frescoes by the *Caracci*. The great hall contains the first fresco painted by *Agostino* and *Annibale*, under the direction of Lodovico, after their return from Parma and Venice: it represents, in a series of 18 pictures, the Expedition of Jason, and is one of the most interesting examples of the Eclectic School. The small chamber adjoining is painted by *Lodovico*, who has represented the Voyage of Æneas in 12 pictures; 2 of them, the Polyphemus and the Harpies, were coloured by Annibale. The next chamber is painted by *Albani*, with the assistance of Lodovico Caracci: it presents 16 subjects, also from the Æneid. The chamber beyond is painted by *Lucio Massari*, with the assistance of the same great master. The decorations of the other chambers are by his pupils, the last room being by *Cesi*; subjects of the Æneid prevail throughout the whole. The paintings of a cabinet representing the Rape of Europa are by *Annibale Caracci*.

Palazzo Grassi, in the Via di Mezzo, has the magnificent fresco by *Lodovico*

Caracci, representing Hercules armed with a flambeau treading on the Hydra; and some curious cameos by *Properzia de' Rossi*, engraved on peach-stones, and illustrating different events of Scripture history.

Palazzo Guidotti, at the extremity of the Portico de' Banchi, formerly *Magnani*, is an imposing design of *Domenico Tibaldi*. It is celebrated for the frescoes of the *Caracci*, representing the history of Romulus and Remus, and not inferior either in composition or in colour to those in the Farnese palace. They are called by Lanzi "the miracle of Caraccescan art."

Palazzo Hercolani, in the Via Maggiore, restored at the close of the last century from the designs of *Venturoli*, was famous throughout Europe for its pictures, sculptures, and library, rich in MSS. and printed books; but they have nearly all disappeared.

Palazzo Malvezzi Bonfioli, in the Strada Maggiore, a fine specimen of palace architecture, by *Vignola*, has in its second court an interesting series of frescoes illustrating the Gerusalemme Liberata, by *Leonello Spada*, *Lucio Massari*, and *Francesco Brizzi*. In the gallery is a portrait by *Domenichino*, and a Sibyl by *Guido* in his early youth, and some other good works of the Bolognese school.

Palazzo Malvezzi Campeggi, in the Via di S. Donato (the other 2 Malvezzi palaces are opposite the ch. of S. Giacomo, in the same street), designed by the Formigini, is remarkable for some tapestries from designs of Lucas von Leyden, presented by Henry VIII. to Cardinal Campeggi, the papal legate in England.

Palazzo Marchesini, formerly *Leoni*, has a façade designed by Girolamo da Treviso. Under this portico is a fine Nativity by *Niccolò dell' Abate*: it was damaged, however, by restoration in 1819. In the great hall and the adjoining chamber is a series of very beautiful paintings by the same master, illustrating the history of Æneas.

Palazzo Marescalchi, in the Via delle Asse, opposite the ch. of S. Salvatore, formerly so celebrated for its pictures by Correggio, the St. Peter of Guido,

the St. Cecilia of Domenichino, and other masterpieces, has been despoiled of its principal treasures. The façade is by *Do. Tibaldi*; the vestibule at the top of the stairs is painted in chiaroscuro by *Brizzi*; and so profusely has art lavished her resources here, that even the chimney-pieces are painted by the *Caracci*, *Guido*, and *Tibaldi*.

Palazzo Pepoli, one of the few specimens of domestic mediæval architecture in Bologna that remain, a huge brick edifice, consisting of an agglomeration of several dwellings. It is situated in the Strada di Castiglione, in the rear of the Foro de' Mercanti. It was erected in 1344, and was long the residence of the Pepoli family; it has more the appearance of a castle than a palace, from its height surmounted by machicolated defences; the two Gothic gateways leading into it are good specimens of the decorated terra-cotta work of the 14th centy. On the opposite side of the street is another palace of the same name, but of more modern architecture, built from the designs of *Torri* in the beginning of the last century, occupying the site of the ancient palace of the great captain Taddeo Pepoli. It is a fine building, with frescoes of *Colonna* and *Canuti*, illustrating the history of Taddeo Pepoli.

Palazzo Piella, formerly the *Bocchi* Palace, was built by *Vignola* for the learned Achille Bocchi, who is said to have had some share in its design. The hall on the ground floor has a ceiling painted by *Prospero Fontana*; its chief interest consists in its connexion with Bocchi, the historiographer of Bologna and founder of the Academy.

Palazzo Ranuzzi, formerly *Lambertini*, in the Via di S. Stefano, built from the designs of Bartolommeo Triachini, is interesting for its paintings by Bolognese masters prior to the Caracci. The most remarkable of these works are the ceiling of the upper hall by *Tommaso Laurelli*, the Virtues by *Lorenzo Sabbatini*, the Fall of Icarus by *Orazio Samacchini*, and the Death of Hercules by *Tibaldi*.

Palazzo Sampieri, in the Strada Maggiore, 244, once so celebrated for the treasures of its gallery; its famous pictures have been sold; the greater part have been transferred to the Brera Gallery at Milan. But its fine ceilings and chimney-pieces, by the Caracci and Guercino, are well preserved and will amply repay a visit.—I. In the 1st hall, the ceiling, painted by *Lodovico Caracci*, represents Jupiter with the Eagle and Hercules; "in form, dignity of feature, and magnificence of character," says John Bell, "finely suited to harmonise as a group. The muscular figure and gigantic bulk of Hercules is imposing without extravagance; a perfect acquaintance with the human figure is displayed with admirable foreshortening and great skill and boldness in composition and execution. The artist's knowledge of anatomy is discoverable from his correct proportions and fine bendings, but is not obtruded on the eye by caricatured or forced lines." The chimney-piece of the same apartment had a painting by *Agostino Caracci*, representing Ceres with her torch in search of Proserpine, and, in the background, the Rape of the latter.—II. The 2nd hall has a ceiling by *Annibale Caracci*, representing the Apotheosis of Hercules, conducted by Virtue.—III. The ceiling of the 3rd hall, by *Agostino Caracci*, represents Hercules and Atlas supporting the Globe. The chimney-piece of this hall, by the same master, represents Hercules holding down Cacus, preparing to pierce him with the sharp end of his club.—IV. In the 4th hall, the ceiling, representing Hercules strangling Antæus, is by *Guercino*. "A superb piece, with fine deep-toned colouring, and wonderful power of chiaroscuro. The figure of Hercules is very grand, but seems to have occupied rather too much of the artist's care. Antæus is wanting in vigour; the resisting arm is not drawn with force or bulk corresponding to the action; neither are the figures sufficiently connected. But the whole piece, although liable to these criticisms, is a work of great vigour and unquestionable merit. In one of the accompanying ornaments of the ceiling of the next rooms there is a beautiful little painting by *Guercino*, of Love (I think it should have been Ganymede) carrying off the spoils of Hercules, the skin of the Nemean lion, and the club. The motto under it is 'Iter ad superos gloria pandet.'"—*Bell*. Everything that could find a buyer has been removed, even to some of the beautiful works on the chimney-pieces above mentioned.

Palazzo Zambeccari, in the Piazetta di S. Paolo, had a fine gallery, rich in works of the Caracci and other masters. Among those that remain may be noticed Jacob's Ladder, and Abraham at table with the Angels, by *Lodovico Caracci*; the Dead Christ, by *Agostino*; the Sibyl, the Elijah, and the Madonna and Child, by *Guercino*; the Marriage of St. Catherine, by *Albani*; portrait of Cardinal de' Medici, by *Domenichino*; his own portrait, by *Baroccio*; St. John, by *Cararaggio*; a St. Sebastian, and the portrait of Charles V., by *Titian*; a fine Landscape by *Salvator Rosa*; the Marriage of Anne Boleyn, by *Giulio Romano*; and the 6 Mistresses of Charles II., by *Sir Peter Lely*. Besides these works, there is a Crucifixion, in silver, a very beautiful work attributed to *Benvenuto Cellini*. On the entrance-door are 2 bronze Lion-headed knockers by *Giovanni di Bologna*.

One or two of the great halls have been converted into a receptacle or kind of bazaar for the sale of pictures, of which a vast number of bad ones may always be found there.

An interesting modern residence is the *Casa Rossini*, in the Via Maggiore, built in 1825 for the great "Maestro," who resided here until the Austrian occupation, when he voluntarily removed to Florence. It is covered with Latin inscriptions in large gold letters, taken chiefly from classic writers. In the front is the following from Cicero:—

"Non domo dominus, sed domino domus."

On the side is an inscription from the Æneid:—

"Obliquitur numeris septem discrimina vocum Inter odoratum lauri nemus."

Another interesting house is that of Guercino, in which the great painter lived during his residence at Bologna: it is in the small piazza behind the Ch. of St. Nicolò degli Albári, No. 449. The house of Guido has a fresco of 2 angels holding a crown, painted by him, on the exterior. The house in which *Galvani*, the discoverer of that species of electricity to which he has given his name, was born, is in the Borgo delle Casse, No. 1347; over the door is the following inscription:—

" Galvanum exceps natum luxique peremptum
Cujus ab invento junctus uterque polus."

Of the other public buildings and institutions of Bologna, one of the most interesting to the architectural antiquary is the *Foro de' Mercanti*, or Palazzo della Mercanzia, the best preserved example of the ornamented Italian Gothic in the city. It was built in 1294 of moulded brickwork, and restored as it now stands in 1439 by the Bentivoglios during their political ascendency. The interior contains the Exchange and the Tribunal of Commerce. On the stairs are painted, commencing from the top, the shields of the ten corporations of the city— *Cambiatores, Mercanti, Macellari, Merciari, Orefici, Tallegari, Drappi a lana, Drappi e Strazzioluri, Speziali*, and *Bambiriari*—and of the Consuls of Commerce from A.D. 1441 to 1813.

Near the *Foro de' Mercanti* is a large open space, from which branch off four streets leading to the principal gates of the city. Here are the 2 celebrated leaning towers, called the Torre degli Asinelli and the Torre Garisenda, the most remarkable edifices in Bologna, but so destitute of architectural attractions, that Mr. Matthews compares them to the " chimney of a steam-engine, blown a little out of the perpendicular." The *Torre degli Asinelli*, begun in 1109 by Gherardo degli Asinelli, was shown, by the investigations of Tadolini, to have been finished at different periods. It is a square and of massive brickwork, divided into 3 portions: the lowest has a projecting battlement, which is occupied by shops; the others diminish from below upwards in their outward diameter, whilst the inner one increases, owing to the lesser solidity and thickness of the walls as they ascend. The height of the tower is 292¾ feet (89·2 mètres), and to the top of the lantern 321 ft., according to measurements made in 1857 by Prof. Respighi. The inclination was ascertained at the same time to be 1° 16' from the vertical, or equal to 6 ft. 10¼ in. from the centre of gravity; that of 3 ft. 4 in., stated on the marble tablet on the W. front, having been evidently obtained by erroneous means. The direction of the inclination is to the W., quite opposite to that of the neighbouring T. Garisenda. Professor Respighi also found that the amount of inclination was different in the three portions of the shaft; the largest in the lower one as high as the machicolated projection, less in the central one, and very small in the highest. The T. degli Asinelli can be ascended without danger, the stairs being perfectly safe. There are 449 steps in all, divided into flights of 10 each, between which there are convenient landing-places. The lower stairs are for a short way round an axis, the remainder placed against the inner walls. Near the summit are two cross-groined arches, on which rests the terminal terrace, to strengthen which two others have been more recently added. On the top is a kind of lantern or belfry, containing a bell of no large dimensions, which is only tolled on very solemn or important occasions.

It does not appear that the inclination of the tower has undergone any change of late years. As to its use, there is every reason for believing that, like many others in Bologna, it was reared from family vanity; as, from its mode of construction, it could scarcely have served for retreat or defence, and, being almost without windows for the admission of light, it could not have served as a place of habitation. The view from the summit is most interesting, and the panorama which it embraces so magnificent that no traveller visiting Bologna should omit ascending. It is entered by a low door on the S. side, where the keeper, an obliging cobbler, will be found, and who will accompany the visitor to the summit and point out the different localities seen from it. He will discover at his feet the whole city spread before him; the richly-clad hilly range, at the N. foot of which Bologna lies; the Via Emilia stretching in a straight

Y 3

line for 22 m. to Castel Bolognese on one side (the E.), and on the other to Modena, with the rich plain of the Romagna towards the N. and E., and, in clear weather, the Euganean and Veronese hills beyond, and still farther the snow-capped peaks of the Tyrolese, Styrian, and Carinthian Alps. The other tower, *La Garisenda*, built by the brothers Filippo and Oddo Garisendi, in 1110, is 161 feet high. Its inclination, in 1792, was 8 Bolognese feet to the E., and 3 to the S.; but some measurements made by Professors Bacelli and Antolini, in 1813, showed an increase of an inch and a half over the former observations. Alidosi and other writers have endeavoured to maintain that the inclination of the Garisenda tower is the effect of art; as if Italy did not present an abundance of such examples in situations where the ground is liable to gradual sinking, and earthquakes are of common occurrence. The best answer to this absurd idea is that the courses of brick and the holes to receive the timbers of the floors are also inclined, which they certainly would not have been if the tower had been built in its present inclined form. The Garisenda, however, has a higher interest than that derived from this question, since it supplied Dante with a fine simile, in which he compares the giant Antæus, stooping to seize him and his guide, to this tower, as it is seen from beneath when the clouds are flying over it :—

" Qual pare a riguardar la Carisenda
Sotto il chinato, quando un nuvol vada
Sovra essa si, ch' ella in contrario penda,
Tal parve Anteo a me, che stava a vada
Di vederlo chinare, e fu tal ora
Che io avrei voluto ir per altra strada."
Inf. xxxi.

There are remains of some other similar towers in different parts of Bologna, especially two on either side of the Archbishop's Palace, the bases of which are built of blocks of gypsum; being mutilated, neither attain a great height.
The noble building in the street adjoining San Petronio, on the E. side, called the *Archiginnassio*, once the seat of the university, then designated as the *Scuole* and *Studio Pubblico*, before it was transferred to its present site, is one of the finest edifices in Bologna. It was designed in 1562, by *Terribilia*. The building has been recently restored at the expense of the municipality, for the purpose of placing the public library, or *Biblioteca del Comune*, formed chiefly by a learned ecclesiastic, Magnani, who bequeathed it to his native city. The apartments appropriated to the schools have some good paintings by *Samacchini*, *Sabbatini*, and their scholars. In the loggie above are several interesting memorials of deceased professors: that of the physician Muratori is by his daughter Teresa; that of the Canonico Peggi, the philosopher, erected by his pupils, is by Giuseppe Terzi; that of the celebrated anatomist Malpighi is by Franceschini; that of Mariani is by Carlo Cignani; and that of the philosopher Sbaraglia is by Donato Creti. In the adjoining chapel of Sta. Maria de' Bulgari are some paintings which deserve to be seen: the Annunciation at the high altar is by *Calvaert*, and the frescoes on the walls, representing the history of the Virgin, sibyls, and prophets, are by *Cesi*. All the halls, galleries, and loggie are decorated with the coats of arms of the students of the ancient university, forming a pleasant and interesting mode of decoration: there are many hundreds of these escutcheons, with the names and country of their owners.

The *Collegio di Spagna*, in the Via di Saragoza, the Spanish college, was founded in 1364, by Cardinal Albornoz. It was formerly remarkable for the frescoes of its portico by *Annibale Caracci*, in his youth, but they have almost disappeared. In the upper loggia is the fine fresco by *Bagnacavallo*, representing the Virgin and Child, St. Elizabeth, St. John, and St. Joseph, with an angel above scattering flowers, and the Cardinal founder kneeling in veneration. But the great fresco of Bagnacavallo, representing Charles V. crowned in S. Petronio by Clement VII., although much injured, is by far the most interesting work, because it is a contemporary record. From this circumstance we may regard the picture as a series of authentic portraits, in the precise costume of the period. In the ch. annexed to the college are some frescoes by *C. Procaccini*; a St. Marguerite, with Saints Jerome and Francis, by *G. Francia*; and in the Sacristy an Ancona in 21 compartments, by *Marco Zoppo*.

The *Collegio Venturoli*, so called from the eminent architect of Bologna, who founded it for architectural studies in 1825, occupies the building formerly used as the Hungarian College. The pupils are educated here until their 20th year. The establishment is well managed, and tends to keep alive the arts of design among the young students of Bologna. The marble bust of Venturoli is by Professor *Demaria*.

The *Teatro Comunale*, in the Strada di San Donato, was built in 1756, on the site of the ancient palace of Giovanni II. Bentivoglio, which was destroyed by the populace at the instigation of Pope Julius II. The design of the theatre is by *Bibiena*, but it has been frequently altered and adapted to the purposes of the modern opera. The curtain, representing the Apotheosis of Felsina or Bononia is by *N. Angiolini*.

The *Teatro Contavalli* was built in 1814, in a part of the suppressed Carmelite convent of S. Martino Maggiore. The old convent stairs serve for the approach to the modern theatre—another of those strange contrasts so frequently met with in Italy.

The *Teatro del Corso* was built in 1805, from the designs of Santini, and is one of the most popular places of amusement in the city.

In the Palazzo Bolognini, near the Strada S. Stefano, a *Casino*, supplied with literary and political journals, was formed a few years ago for the convenience of the upper classes; musical parties, conversazioni, and balls are given here.

The *Accademia Filarmonica*, No. 614, Cartoleria Nova, and the *Liceo Filarmonico*, in the Via delle Campane, institutions peculiarly appropriate to a city which boasts of being the most musical in Italy, have acquired an European reputation. The academy was founded by Vincenzo Carrati, in 1666, and has numbered among its members the most eminent professors of the 2 last centuries. The Lyceum, founded in 1805, by the municipality, as a school of music, is enriched with the unrivalled musical library and collections of the celebrated Padre Martini. The library contains no less than 17,000 volumes of printed music, and the finest collection of ancient manuscript music in existence. There is an interesting collection of portraits of professors and dilettanti, another of antique instruments, and a fine series of choir-books with miniatures.

The *Montagnuola*, a slight elevation at the N. extremity of the town, was converted, during the occupation of the French, into a handsome promenade, the only one within the walls.

Environs of Bologna.—Outside the Porta di Castiglione is the ch. of *La Misericordia*, ruined in the wars of the 15th century, and partly rebuilt with little regard to the uniformity of the original plan. It contains some pictures of interest. The Annunciation, on the wall over the entrance, is by *Passerotti*; the Virgin, called La Madonna della Consolazione, at the 2nd altar, is by *Lippo di Dalmasio*; at the 5th is the Descent of the Holy Spirit, by *Cesi*; at the 6th, an Annunciation, by *U. Gandolfi*; in the choir, a picture in 3 portions,—the upper, consisting of a half figure of the Saviour, and 2 good female heads, is probably by *F. Francia*—the central portion, a Nativity, and the lower one, a Virgin and Saints, by a very inferior hand; 8th, or l.-hand transept, the Tabernacle, supported by 4 Doctors of the Church, is carved in cypress wood by *Marco Tedesco* of Cremona, an able sculptor in wood of the 17th century, who also executed the ornaments of the organ and singing gallery.

Close to the Porta di S. Mammolo is the ch. of the *Annunziata*, attached to a Franciscan convent. It has some interesting paintings, particularly by *F. Francia*. In the 2nd chapel is the Madonna and Child, with St.

John, St. Paul, and St. Francis, by that celebrated master. In the 3rd is the Crucifixion, with the Magdalen, the Virgin, St. Jerome, and St. Francis, by the same, with the ordinary inscription "Francia Aurifex" at the foot of the Cross. 4th, the Nuptials of the Virgin, by *Costa*. 5th, St. Francis in ecstasy, by *Gessi*, a superb painting worthy of Guido. 3rd on l., the Madonna del Monte, by *Lippo di Dalmasio*. The Annunciation, with 4 saints, in the choir, is another beautiful work of *Francia*. In the Sacristy a Dead Christ, by *G. Francia*, and several portraits. D. Tibaldi is buried in this ch. Outside the church is a long portico, painted in fresco by *Giacomo Lippi* and other pupils of the Caracci. The Shepherds worshipping the newly-born Saviour is by *Paolo Caracci*, from a design by his brother Lodovico. Not far from the ch. of the Annunziata, towards the Piazza di Castiglione, was

The ancient little church of the *Madonna di Mezzaratta*, built in 1106, formerly one of the depositories of sacred Italian art. A considerable part of the building had fallen down, and what remained, having been purchased by Cav. Minghetti, has been cleaned and restored. The frescoes are attributed to *Jacopo Avanzi, Galasso Galassi, Simone da Bologna*, and other early artists of the Bolognese school, and are interesting as its earliest efforts, although as works of art far behind their contemporaries of the Tuscan, Umbrian, and Lombard. The Marriage of Jacob and Rachel, attributed to *Galasso Galassi*, is one of the most curious. The frescoes here are, however, worth a visit.

Not far from this are the *Bagni di Mario*, an octagonal building, constructed in 1564, by Tommaso Lauretti, for the purpose of collecting and purifying the water for the Fountain of Neptune. It derives its name from the ruins of the ancient aqueduct, built, it is said, by Marius, and restored by Hadrian and Antoninus Pius, as shown by inscriptions in the Museum.

On the hill above Bologna, beautifully situated, stands the ch. of San *Michele in Bosco*, attached to the suppressed monastery of the Olivetans. This great establishment, in the time of Bishop Burnet one of the finest examples of monastic splendour in Italy, was suppressed at the French invasion ; its magnificent halls were converted into barracks and prisons for condemned criminals, and its best pictures were carried to Paris. The walls and ceilings, painted by Ludovico Caracci and his school, are gradually falling into ruin, and the famous cloister, which was entirely decorated by 37 subjects by these great artists, is now a melancholy wreck. Many of the paintings have entirely disappeared, and of those which remain the subjects are hardly to be distinguished. They represented the history of St. Benedict and St. Cecilia, St. Tiburtius and Sta. Valeriana: the one by Guido was retouched by himself only a few years before his death.

The library of the convent, built from the designs of Giovanni Giacomo Monti, had in its several compartments paintings illustrating the subjects of the works contained in them ; they were executed by *Canuti*, a pupil of Guido, at the suggestion of the Abbate Pepoli, but they have shared in the general ruin. In the splendid dormitory, 427 ft. in length, are preserved the dial of the clock painted by *Innocenzo da Imola* with figures and festoons of fruit ; several models of sculpture, amongst others of a horse by Canova, and of Gian di Bologna's Neptune ; and several pictures belonging to the Pinacotheca, which, for want of room at the Accademia, have been brought here.

The ch. contains some good paintings. In the 1st chapel, a copy of Guercino's Beato Tolomeo, which is now in France, and once stood here. 2nd, the Death of San Carlo, and, 3rd, the S. Francesca Romana, both by *Fiorini*. 4th. In this chapel is the monument of Ramazzotti, a condottiere in the service of the Popes in the 16th century, by *A. Lombardo*. The 4 medallions on the roof are by *Cignani*. The large lunette of S. Michael at the high altar, and the cupola over it, are by *Canuti*. In the sacristy are frescoes of 13 saints by *Bagnacavallo*. The other paintings have suffered greatly, the apartment having long been used as a hay-store. The conventual buildings of S. Michele in Bosco were converted into a barrack, and the fine halls of the Ulivetan monks occupied by soldiery, during the Austrian occupation. The ch. is generally closed; the grounds and gardens have been converted into a promenade; and a fine road leads to the convent from the Porta di S. Mammolo, constructed by the municipality, obliged to do so by the Austrian authorities, to connect it with their park of artillery below, St. Michele being a strong military position commanding the city. On the hill opposite rises a Grecian mansion, built by Aldini, one of Napoleon's ministers under the kingdom of Italy. Its proprietor was forced to abandon it, to allow of its being converted into an Austrian military position. The view of the city, and of the plain of the Romagna, is very fine from this point.

Outside the gate called La Porta di Saragozza, lately restored by the municipality, is the fine arch designed by Monti in 1675 as a propylæum or entrance to the celebrated *Portico* leading to the *Madonna di S. Luca*. This extraordinary example of public spirit and devotion, which we regret to say sustained damage from the Austrian soldiery in 1849, was projected by the Canon Zeneroli of Pieve di Cento, who presented to the senate his memorial on the subject in 1672. On the 28th June, 1674, the first stone was laid between what are now the 130th and 131st arches. The portico is 12ft. broad and 15ft. high, and consists of 2 portions, one called the Portico della Pianura, the other the P. della Salita; it is not in a straight line, but has several angles or turnings in consequence of the irregularity of the ground. In 1676 the whole portico of the plain, consisting of 306 arches, was completed at the cost of 90,900 scudi. Here the Portico della Salita begins, and is united to the 1st portico by the grand arch, called, from the neighbouring torrent, the "Arco di Meloncello," built at the cost of the Monti family, from the designs of Bibiena. The difficulties of the ascent were skilfully overcome; and the money was raised by the voluntary contributions of the inhabitants, aided by the donations of the corporation and religious communities, as is shown by the inscriptions recording their benefactions. The theatres even promoted the work by presenting the proceeds of several performances given for the purpose. From 1676 to 1730, 329 arches of the ascent were finished, with the 15 chapels of the Rosary, at the cost of 170,300 scudi; and in 1739 the entire portico was completed, including, from the Porta di Saragozza to the ch., no less than 635 arches, occupying a space little short of 3 m. in length.

The magnificent ch., occupying the summit of the Monte della Guardia, derives its name of the *Madonna di S. Luca* from one of those numerous black images of the Virgin traditionally attributed to St. Luke. It is said to have been brought to this spot in 1160, by a hermit from Constantinople; and is still regarded with so much veneration, that its annual visit to the city is the scene of one of the greatest public festivals of the Bolognese. The church was built in the last century from the designs of Dotti, but not in the purest taste. It contains numerous paintings by modern artists, but none of the great Bolognese masters, excepting a Madonna with S. Dominick, and the 15 Mysteries of the Rosary, in the 3rd chapel on the rt., by *Guido*, one of his earliest productions. The miraculous image of the Virgin is preserved in a recess above the high altar, in a case of marble and gilt bronze, and is still the object of pilgrimages. The view from Monte della Guardia is alone sufficient to repay a visit to the ch. The rich and glowing plains, from the Adriatic to the Alps and Apennines, are seen spread out like a map in the foreground, studded with villages, churches, convents, and cities, among which Ferrara, Modena, and Imola may be distinctly recognised. Towards the E. the prospect is bounded by the Adriatic, and on the W. and S. the eye ranges along the picturesque and broken line of Apennines. It is impossible to imagine a scene more charming or more beautiful.

Public Cemetery.—In returning to the city, and about ½ m. from the gates of S. Felice and S. Isaïah, is the ancient *Certosa*, built in 1335 by the Carthusian monks, and suppressed in 1797. It was consecrated in 1801 as the public cemetery, and has been much praised as one of the finest models for an extensive modern Campo Santo. It was the first result of the government of Napoleon, who forbad the burial of the dead within the city; and its regulations are remarkable as establishing no exclusion of sect, although a separate enclosure is set apart for Protestants and Jews. The ch. of the convent, which has been preserved, retains many remarkable paintings: in the 1st chapel on the rt. hand, the Last Judgment, and the 2 saints by the side, are by *Canuti;* the S. Bruno, at the altar, is by *Cesi.* The other large picture, representing the Ascension, is by *Bibiena.* Opposite to the latter is the Supper in the House of the Pharisee, and the Magdalen at the feet of Christ, by *Andrea Sirani.* The Baptism of Christ is a large composition by his daughter *Elisabetta,* painted in her 20th year, with her portrait sitting, and her name. The Miraculous Draught of Fishes, Christ driving the money-changers from the Temple, and the 4 Carthusian Saints were the last works of *Gessi.* The 2 pictures representing Christ entering Jerusalem, and appearing to the Virgin with the host of patriarchs after the resurrection, are by *Lorenzo Pasinelli.* At the high altar, the Crucifixion, the Christ praying in the garden, and the Deposition, are by *Cesi.* In an inner chapel are the Annunciation, by *Cesi;* Christ bearing the Cross, a half-length in fresco, by *Lodovico Caracci;* S. Bernardino in fresco, by *Amico Aspertini;* and another Christ with the Cross, by *Massari.*

The *Cemetery* occupies the spacious corridors and cloisters of the convent, in which niches in the walls have been built to receive the dead. The general effect is very fine, and some of the tombs and monuments are remarkable not only for the names they record, but for the character of their design. Three collections of engravings from these monuments have been published, as well as two volumes of inscriptions, composed by Professor Schiassi, and much admired for their pure Latinity.

Several monuments from churches desecrated during the revolution have been removed here,—some of a very remote period, as may be seen in the corridor opposite the entrance. Others are extremely beautiful as works of art, amongst which may be cited the monument to Francesco Abbergato, a very fine specimen of cinque-cento style (ob. 1517). The cemetery now consists of two sets of cloisters or arcades; the larger one has been recently added. In its centre are the graves of the poorer classes; near the chapel in the latter are the monuments of Vigano and Vestris, of theatrical celebrity.

On the right of the principal entrance to the cemetery is a small walled-in space, destined as the last resting-place of our Protestant countrymen, and of all creeds not Roman Catholic.

Leaving the city in the opposite direction, by the Porta Maggiore is the *Portico degli Scalzi,* consisting of 167 arches, and 1700 feet in length, leading to the ch. called *Gli Scalzi,* or the Madonna di Strada Maggiore. The ch. has some good paintings, among which may be mentioned a good Holy Family by *Pasinelli;* the Sta. Teresa praying, by *Canuti;* the Assumption of the Virgin, by *Sabbatini,* and other works of the Bolognese school.

The epithet of *Grassa,* given to Bologna by the historian Paul Van Merle, of Leyden, in the 15th century, applies as much to the *living* and culinary delicacies of the inhabitants as to the productions of its fertile territory. The wines of its neighbourhood are very tolerable, and the fruits, particularly the grapes, are much esteemed. The *mortadella,* everywhere known as the Bologna sausage, still keeps up its reputation: and the *cervellato*, a kind of plum pudding, is peculiar to the city. It is only made in the winter.

Mr. Beckford has designated Bologna as "a city of puppy-dogs and sausages." The dogs of Bologna, so celebrated in the middle ages, which still figure in the city arms, and are alluded to in the epitaph on King Enzius in the ch. of S. Domenico, were worthy of more respect than is implied in this flippant remark; they have unfortunately disappeared, and a trace of their pure breed can scarcely now be discovered.

In a University town, so celebrated for its medical professors, the invalid can never be at a loss for good advice; the ordinary fee, either for physicians or surgeons, is 5 pauls, and for consultations 2 scudi.

The climate is considered healthy, but in winter Bologna is reputed to be cold and in summer the hottest city in Italy. In other respects, amply provided with the necessaries and luxuries of life, with an intellectual society, to say nothing of its works of art, Bologna is peculiarly calculated to be an agreeable and economical residence.

The Bolognese dialect, of all the forms of Italian which the traveller will meet with, is most puzzling. It was aptly described by the learned grammarian of the 16th centy., Aulus Gellius Parrhasius, as the *raucida Bononensium loquacitas*. Forsyth says, "with all the learning in its bosom, Bologna has suffered its dialect, that dialect which Dante admired as the purest of Italy, to degenerate into a coarse, thick, truncated jargon, full of apocope, and unintelligible to strangers."

In regard to the character of the Bolognese, we may refer to the well-known description by Tassoni:

"Il Bolognese e un popol del demonio
Che non si puo frenar con alcun freno."

This character, at first sight so formidable, would seem to refer to the independent spirit, and to the love of political freedom imbibed from their ancient republican institutions. It has been a fashion with many passing tourists of our own time to depreciate the Bolognese; but the calumny, if there ever were any foundation for it, applies no longer; and in education, in character, and in the arts of civilisation, Bologna stands prominently forward amongst European cities, as its inhabitants do amongst the bravest, most patriotic and public-spirited of regenerated Italy.

Diligences.—Diligences run twice a-week, Sunday and Thursday, between Bologna and Rome, performing the journey in 84 hours, by way of Ancona and Macerata; but as the carriage from Bologna now does not proceed beyond Rimini, the traveller must get on from there by vetturino to Pesaro, from where the Roman diligence now starts (Malleposte to Rimini in correspondence with Rome every day except Thursday);—daily by Covigliajo in 16 hours, and by La Porretta and Pistoia on Tuesday, Thursday, Saturday, performing the whole trajet in 14 hours; fares, by both routes, 45, 40, and 35 pauls. A diligence daily to Ferrara and Ponte Lago Scuro; another in continuation starts from Sta. Maria Maddalena, on the opposite bank of the Po, in 15 hours, for Padua, and thence to Venice by rly. Diligences every day to Ravenna in 10 hours, by way of Medecina and Lugo.

Travellers going from Bologna to Verona and the Tyrol must now proceed to Parma by the early train, from which a diligence, that starts at 8 a.m., arrives in 8 hours at Mantua. Here the traveller must remain for the night. Since the annexation of the Emilian Provinces to the N. Italian kingdom the Austrian authorities have closed all other routes for reaching their territories by public conveyances except from Ferrara to Padua and from Parma to Mantua.

Travellers who are desirous of proceeding from Bologna to Rome, without passing through Florence, can follow the road through Forlì (Rte. 72), and along the Adriatic to Ancona (Rte. 87), from whence, or from Fano by Fossombrone, good roads traverse the Apennines to Foligno (Rtes. 88 and 89), and from thence to the capital (Rte. 107).

Plan for visiting, in topographical order, everything most worthy of notice at Bologna in 3 days.

1st day.—Piazza and Fontana di Nettuno; *Palazzo Pubblico*; Ch. of SAN PETRONIO; *Pal. del Podesta*; *Portico de' Banchi*; *Archiginnasio and Biblioteca*; Ch. of S. *Maria della Vita*; Chs. of SAN DOMENICO, of *Santa Lucia*; Pal. Ranuzzi; Chs. of *San Giovanni in Monte*, of *San Stefano*; Pal. *de' Bianchi*; *Pal. Pepoli*; Ch. of *S. Maria de' Servi*; *House of Rossini*; Pal. *Sampieri*; Ch. of *San Bartolommeo in Ruregnana*; TORRE DEGL' ASINELLI; Chs. of *San Vitale* and *I Mendicanti*; Pal. *Fantuzzi*; Via di San Donato.; Pal. *Malvezzi*, *Malvasia*, &c.; Ch. of S. GIACOMO MAGGIORE; Oratory of *Santa Cecilia*; UNIVERSITY; *Great Theatre.*

2nd day.—CATHEDRAL.; Ch of *Madonna di Galliera*; Pal. *Fava*; Chs. of *San Giorgio* and *San Martino*; Pal. *Aldrovandi*; Ch. of S. *Bartolommeo in Reno*; *House of Galvani*; *Arena*; Ch. of *San Benedetto*; *Montagnola*; Pal. *Bentivoglio*; ACCADEMIA DELLE BELLE ARTI AND COLLECTIONS; *Botanic Garden*; *Collections and Library at University*; Drive in the afternoon to the CERTOSA and CAMPO SANTO, by the Porta Sant' Isaïa, returning by that of Santa Felice.

3rd day.—Chs. of SAN FRANCESCO and *S. Salvatore*; Pal. *Marescalchi*, *Zambeccari*, and *Bevilacqua Vincenzi*; Chs. of *S. Paolo, La Sagra*, and *San Procolo*; Porta San Mammolo; Chs. of *l' Annunziata* and *Misericordia*; S. MICHELE IN BOSCO; *Villa Aldini*: Porta di Saragozza, and excursion to the Ch. of the MADONNA DI S. LUCA, returning by the Via di Saragozza, *Collegio di Spagna*, and *Pal. Albergati*.

ROUTE 62.

BOLOGNA TO FLORENCE, BY PIETRAMALA AND THE PASS OF LA FUTA.

	POSTS.
Bologna to Pianoro	1½
Pianoro to Lojano	1¼
Lojano to Filigare	1
Filigare to Covigliajo	1
Covigliajo to Monte Carelli	1
Monte Carelli to Cafaggiolo	1
Cafaggiolo to Fontebuona	1
Fontebuona to Florence	1

9 posts = 71 m.

There is a very good diligence 3 times a week to Florence in winter, and daily in summer, performing the journey in 16 hours; it leaves at a very early hour on Monday, Wednesday, and Friday, so as to reach Florence about 8 P.M.

The road from Bologna to Florence crosses the central chain of the Apennines. It is in general in good repair, but in many places the ascents are so rapid that, in addition to the ordinary extra horses, oxen are required. The time occupied in performing the journey is from 12 to 15 hours by post, and from 18 to 20 by vetturino. The scenery of this part of the Apennines is often picturesque, but they want the grandeur and boldness of the Alps.

Leaving Bologna, the road soon enters the valley of the Savena, which it crosses at S. Rufillo, rising very gradually along the rt. bank of the river, through a fertile district, and passing by the villages of Rastigniano and Musiano to

1½ *Pianoro*, situated close to the Savena, which the post-road quits here, and from whence the ascent of the Apennines may be said to commence. From here to Lojano an additional horse is required for every pair, with oxen for the very steep ascents. The price of the extra horse is 6 pauls. Between this and the next post the road offers several fine points of view over the plains of Bologna and the valley of the Po.

1½ *Lojano*. A post station with a poor inn. From this elevated spot the view is very striking and extensive; the eye ranges along the chain of distant Alps, embracing the vast plain of the Po to the Adriatic, Mantua, Verona, Padua, Bologna. The papal frontier, before the annexation of the Emilian Provinces to the kingdom of N. Italy, was at *La Cà*, where there is a clean inn.

1 *Filigare*. There is a tolerable inn at Pietramala, 3 m. further on. This upper portion of the Pass is much exposed to storms, and is bitterly cold in winter. About 1½ m. E. of Pietramala is a singular phenomenon, called the "i Fuochi," which deserves a visit. It occurs at the base of the Monte di Fo, in a very limited space, and consists of emanations of inflammable gas, which being ignited present at first something of a volcanic appearance. The flames rise about a foot from the ground, and to be seen to advantage must be visited by night: they burn most brightly and rise to a greater elevation in rainy or stormy weather, owing probably to the diminished atmospheric pressure. Round the orifices from which the gas issues, a carbonaceous deposit like soot is formed, as occurs in the ordinary gas-burners of our houses. Volta, who was the first to investigate these phenomena, very properly attributed these flames to emanations of carburetted hydrogen (coal-gas) from the subjacent arenaceous rock, which here, as elsewhere, contains vegetable remains, from the decomposition of which this gas is probably derived. Similar phenomena are met with in other parts of the Apennines, and from the same causes—at Barigazzo, La Porretta, &c. (see Rte. 63). The flames vary in colour, from blue to yellow, according to the light in which, and the time of the day when they are seen, and emit an odour of burning spirits of wine. The Acqua Buja, 1 m. to the W. of Pietramala, is a similar phenomenon, but here the inflammable gas, passing through water, only becomes ignited on the approach of a light to the bubbles as they reach the surface.

From Pietramala a gradual ascent of 3 m., at the base of the Peaks of Monte Beni and Sasso di Castro, leads to Covigliajo. The geologist will find much to interest him in this part of the route—the above-named mountains, which attain respectively elevations of 4080 and 4135 English feet above the sea, being formed of serpentine, which has broken through the subjacent stratified rocks of the cretaceous formation.

1 *Covigliajo*, at the foot of Monte Beni, a solitary post-house, which had in former days a bad reputation, but which is now a very comfortable inn, much more so indeed than the traveller has a right to expect in such a situation; from its great elevation the climate is very cold, and warm clothing is at all seasons advisable on this journey. A further ascent of 4 m. brings us to the summit of the Pass of la Futa, the highest point of the road between Bologna and Florence, 2987 feet above the sea. From this pass, which in the winter season is at times impassable from accumulations of snow, a rapid but well-managed descent leads to

1 *Monte Carelli*. From this post-station to Covigliajo, a third horse, or oxen, are required by the tariff. The road now runs on the summit of a spur of the Apennines, before descending into the valley of the Sieve, which is so celebrated in the history of the middle ages and in Italian poetry, under the general name of Val di Mugello. Here a road on the rt. leads to Barberino, and thence to Prato and Pistoja. On approaching the valley of the Sieve, about 3 m. from Cafaggiolo is *Le Maschere*, formerly a country-seat, now converted into an inn, and so picturesquely situated that many travellers, desirous of seeing more of the beauties of this part of the Apennines, make it their halting-place. "It overlooks the brow of a mountain which, although covered with trees, is almost perpendicular; while on the plain far below lies the beautiful vale of Arno, bounded by a circle of magnificent hills, sometimes rising in acclivities, sometimes in polished knolls or bold promontories, cultivated to the very summit with the vine and olive, interspersed with fruit and forest trees, and thickly studded with villas, convents, and churches, presenting an aspect of extraordinary animation and beauty. Turning from the contemplation of this rich, lively,

and cultivated landscape, to the bold country spread abroad among the Apennines behind the Maschere, you behold a prospect finely contrasting nature in all its most polished splendour with the wild and majestic grandeur of mountain scenery."—*John Bell.*

1 *Caffaggiolo*, a post station on the rt. bank of the Sieve. A short distance beyond it the old road from Bologna to Florence through Firenzuola and Scarperia falls into this route. About midway between this and the next station we pass the village of Vaglia, on the Carza torrent, whose left bank the road follows to Fontebuona. On an eminence on the l., surrounded by cypress plantations, is seen the Servite convent of Monte Senario, which forms so remarkable an object in the landscape N. of Florence.

1 *Fontebuona*. A third horse is necessary from Florence to this station; the ascent on leaving the post-house is very steep. A short distance beyond Fontebuona on the l. is *Pratolino*, once the favourite seat of the Grand Dukes of Tuscany, situated on the southern slopes of a hill, embosomed in fine trees. The beautiful villa, designed by Buontalenti, for Francesco de' Medici, son of Cosimo I., to receive his mistress Bianca Capello, has long been demolished. The money lavished upon its decorations, its *giuochi d'acqua*, &c., amounted to no less a sum than 782,000 crowns, an expenditure upon which the Grand Duke Ferdinand II. gave an expressive commentary when he said that the money there wasted would have built a hundred hospitals. Besides the grottoes, fountains, and labyrinths of Pratolino, there is a colossal monster, called the Statue of the Apennines, 60 feet in height. The artist's name is unknown. The beauties of Pratolino and of Bianca are frequently celebrated by Tasso:—

"Dianzi all' ombra di fama occulta e bruna,
Quasi giacesti, Pratolino, ascoso;
Or la tua donna tanto onor t' aggiunge,
Che piega alla seconda alta fortuna
Gli antichi gioghi l' Apennin nevoso;
Ed Atlante, ed Olimpo, ancor si lungo,
Nè confin la tua gloria asconde e serra;
Ma del tuo picciol nome empi la terra."
Rime, 360.

The rapid descent hence to Florence, along an excellent road, is one of the most interesting drives in Europe. Every eminence is studded with villas; the country, rich in vineyards and olive-groves, seems literally "a land of oil and wine;" cultivation appears in its highest perfection; the Etruscan fortress of Fiesole, consecrated by the genius of Milton, with its Arx now occupied by the Franciscan Convent, rises magnificently over the opposite bank of the Mugnone; and Florence, with its domes, campaniles, and battlemented towers, bursts upon the view. This approach recalls the remark of Ariosto, that if all the villas which are scattered as if the soil produced them over the hills of the Val d'Arno were collected within one wall, two Romes could not vie with Florence.

"A veder pien di tante ville i colli,
Per che'l terren vele germogli, come
Vermene germogliar suole, e rampolli.
Se dentro un mur, sotto un medesmo nome
Fosser raccolti i tuoi palazzi sparsi,
Non ti sarian da pareggiar due Rome."
Rime, cap. xvi.

Florence is entered by the Porta di San Gallo, where passports are demanded, and a receipt given.

1 FLORENCE; described in *Handbook for Central Italy* (Rte. 80).—*Hotels:* Baldi's Hôtel de l'Italie on the Lungo Arno, excellent. Hôtel de l'Europe, comfortable, quiet, and moderate as to charges, with a good table-d'hôte—the landlord speaks English; Hôtel du Nord; both these hotels are in the Piazza di Santa Trinita, the most central situation in the city, and close to the diligence office, reading-room, Lungo Arno, &c., cool in the spring and summer. Hôtels de la Grande Bretagne and dell' Arno, on the quay, central, and very good. Hôtel de York, near the Cathedral, also good. Hôtel de la Ville, on the western prolongation of the Lungo Arno, a new hotel on the German system. Hôtel Victoria, near the latter, clean and comfortable. Hôtel de New York, in the same quarter. H. de la Pension Suisse, di Porta Rossa, dello Scudo di Francia, and della Luna, second-rate, frequented by commercial men and Italian families.

The hotels on the Lungo Arno are generally to be preferred during the winter months on account of the sun; they have, however, few small apartments or bachelors' rooms looking south, and are inconvenient in the summer from the heat, the exhalations from the river and the sewers which empty themselves into it, and from the greater abundance of mosquitoes, at which season the Europe, Nord, and York are perhaps to be preferred. Most of the hotels have now good tables-d'hôtes, and leave little to be desired as regards cleanliness and general comfort.

ROUTE 63.

BOLOGNA TO FLORENCE, BY LA PORRETTA, THE PASS OF LA COLLINA, AND PISTOJA.—70 m.

This route, which has been opened of late years, now forms the most direct line of communication between Bologna and Florence: it is certainly more agreeable and picturesque than that by Pietramala and the Pass of La Futa; and by it travellers can easily reach Florence in one day. There are no post-stations on it beyond Castel del Vescovo, but persons travelling in their own carriages can make arrangements at the diligence office to have the use of their horses at the ordinary posting rates; by this means, and starting early from Bologna, they will reach Pistoja in time for the latest railway train, which arrives at Florence the same evening.

An excellent diligence starts 3 times a-week at from 3 to 4 A.M., performing the journey to Pistoja in 14 hours, and arriving in time for the last train to Florence by the Maria Antonia Railway. Vetturini perform the same in 2 days, including the transit by railway, sleeping the first night at La Porretta; or in a long summer's day can go the whole way to Pistoia.

A railway is in progress from Bologna to Pistoia.

The road follows the bank of the Reno nearly to its source; it is kept in tolerable repair in the Bolognese portion, where the nature of the soil renders this difficult; whereas, as soon as it enters the Tuscan territory, it is excellent.

The diligence-stations are, reckoning the distances from Bologna,—

	MILES.
Cervia, or Borgo di Sasso	9
Vergato	22
La Porretta	34
La Collina Pass	43
Pistoja	52

Leaving Bologna by the Porta di San Felice, the road skirts the walls of the town, and afterwards (on the l.) the hill on which the ch. of the Madonna di S. Luca is situated. 3 miles farther it crosses the Reno, over a handsome 4-arched bridge, at the village of Casalecchio, where the mountain-valley in which the Reno runs opens into the great plain of the Po.

Casalecchio was the scene of the battle in which Giovanni Bentivoglio was defeated by the army of Gian Galeazzo, on June 26, 1402. The allied army of Florence and Bologna, under Bentivoglio and Bernardo de Serres, had encamped at Casalecchio, contrary to the judgment of the latter general, who was anxious to have retired within the walls of the city. While they were waiting for reinforcements from Florence, the Milanese, under Alberigo da Barbiano, gave them battle. The Bolognese troops, weary of the tyranny of Bentivoglio, refused to fight; Bernardo de Serres was taken prisoner; the inhabitants, encouraged by the faithless promises made by Gian Galeazzo that he would restore their republic, opened the gates to the Milanese, and 2 days afterwards Bentivoglio was murdered by order of Barbiano. In 1511 Casalecchio was the scene of the victory gained by the Sieur de Chaumont, general of Louis XII., over the troops of Julius II., commanded by F. M. della Rovere, Duke of Urbino. It was fought on the 21st of May, and was called the "day of the ass-drivers," because the French knights returned driving asses laden with their booty.

From Casalecchio the road may be said to enter the valley of the Reno, and runs along the base of the low hills that border it on the W. to Cervia or Borgo di Sasso, or Castel del Vescovo, a village situated above the river, where the only accommodation is a poor café. The road, on leaving it, runs through the narrow defile of Il Sasso, cut in the tertiary sandstone, along a deep cliff overhanging the torrent. This part of the road is not without danger in the rainy season, being in some parts ill protected on the side of the precipice, the ravine only allowing sufficient room for the river to pass. Immediately beyond the valley widens; a broad torrent, the Setta, here nearly equal in size to the Reno, joins the latter from the S. From the summit of the Pass of Il Sasso the view up the valley of the Setta is very fine. Following the l. bank of the Reno, often along a high cliff above it, the road crosses several ravines, which, being excavated in the tertiary marls, offer some disagreeable passes in the rainy season; passing through the hamlet of Marzabotto, composed of a series of very neat farm-buildings, near the river, and in the midst of meadowlands; above which is a large villa belonging to the Ario family.

Vergato, an inconsiderable village near the Reno; on leaving it, a rapid, and in the winter season a dangerous, torrent, the Vergatello, is forded, as there is no bridge, the bed being so extensive, and the rolled masses of rock so large and numerous, as to render the construction of one very difficult; indeed, all along this road from Il Sasso to La Porretta, one of the great drawbacks is the want of bridges. On leaving Vergato the appearance of the country changes; the valley of the Reno, hitherto enclosed between precipitous mountains, now widens; the hills on either side becoming rounded and less precipitous—a circumstance arising from the change in the geological nature of the soil, from the tertiary marls and sandstones to the calcareous rocks of the cretaceous or eocenic period. 5 m. beyond Vergato is Sibana, opposite which and on the other side of the Reno rise the rugged peaks of Monte Ovolo and Monte Vigese; at the foot of the latter the village of Vigo was overwhelmed, in 1851, by a terrific landslip. Continuing along the l. bank of the Reno, the recently restored castle of Savignano is a picturesque object, in the angle formed by the junction of the Reno and Limentra on the l.; from thence, crossing a spur of hills, the traveller discovers another reach of the Reno, at the head of which the village of Porretta is seen in the distance. This part of the valley forms a picturesque amphitheatre surrounded by verdant hills, on the summit of which are seen, on the rt., ruins of some mediæval towers. 2 m. before reaching Porretta the Sella torrent is crossed on a new and handsome bridge, one of the finest works of art upon the whole line of this road.

La Porretta, a village of 1010 Inhab., celebrated for its mineral waters and baths, which are much frequented in the summer months. There are several inns and lodging-houses; that which appears to be most convenient for travellers is the Locanda Nova d' Italia, kept by Gennasi; there is a second during the bathing season, il Palazzino, nearer the road; for persons travelling in their own carriages this place may be made the breakfast-station, as it forms the sleeping-place for those employing vetturino horses between Bologna and Pistoja, and vice versá. During the bathing season, June, July, and August, a public conveyance runs daily between La Porretta and Bologna—fare, 15 pauls.

The waters of La Porretta have long been celebrated for their medicinal qualities, and are much resorted to from July to September; they issue from the sandstone-rock of the cretaceous period, and reach the surface at temperatures varying, according to the springs, from 89° to 101° Fahr.; they contain a variable portion of sulphuretted hydrogen and carbonic acid gases, and in some localities so large a quantity of carburetted hydrogen as to make its collection profitable for lighting purposes. Strange to say, in this remote district of the Apennines, this application of natural gas was first made by an ingenious shoemaker, named Spiga ; since which a part of the village is lighted by it. Besides these gaseous contents, the waters of La Porretta contain muriate, bromate, and carbonate of soda, and a peculiar pseudo-organic matter; they are used both in the form of baths and internally, and are considered to be very efficacious in chronic glandular obstructions, in rheumatism, paralysis, and nervous affections generally.

During the heats of summer, La Porretta, from its elevation above the sea (1130 English feet), is cool ; the situation is considered healthy; fevers, which exist lower down the valley of the Reno, are unknown here.

The Monte Cardo, which rises behind the village, offers several emanations of carburetted hydrogen from the fissures in the sandstone, which ignite on the approach of a light. They are entirely similar to those of Pietramala and Barigazzo. (See Rte. 62.)

Leaving La Porretta, the road passes through a narrow limestone defile, barely affording room for the Reno to pass, and is necessarily cut along the side of the precipice. The mineral spring, called La Porretta Vecchia, is situated in this defile, and is principally resorted to by drinkers, the temperature being 89°. Having passed this defile, the valley expands ; woods of oaks clothe the sides of the hills. The road ascends more rapidly than it has hitherto done, and Le Capanne, formerly the Papal frontier station, is soon reached. The river Reno, which is crossed by a bridge, formed here the boundary between Tuscany and the States of the Church; from this point the road leaves it, the river running to the S.S.W. The ascent of the Apennines may be said to commence from this point, although, for the first 2 m., it is very gradual along the Limentra ; here the road enters a deep, narrow ravine, and for the next 5 m. ascends continually, crossing the river several times, but so excellently constructed is it, and in such good repair, that it is easily surmounted. About 7 m. from La Porretta the torrent divides into 2 branches ; at the point of junction is seen, far below the road, Lo Spedaleto, formerly an *hospice* for travellers crossing this part of the Apennines. An extremely well-managed ascent of about 2 m. leads from this point to the Collina Pass, a low saddleback over the central chain of the Apennines. On the summit of the pass is a large inn, where passengers by diligence *from* Bologna dine, but in general badly supplied with comforts. The most elevated point of the Via Leopolda, as the road is called, at the Collina Pass, is 3350 English feet above the sea.

The view from the Collina Pass, or, better still, from a point a few hundred yards lower down, is perhaps as fine as from any place in the Apennines, and will well repay a short delay on the part of the traveller. Looking towards the S. and Pistoja, you have on the rt. the highest peaks of the Modenese and Lucca mountains, generally covered with snow ; the serrated pinnacles about the Cisa and Abetone passes (see Rtes. 43 and 51) ; the mountains of La Pania ;—to the S.W. the Lakes of Fucecchio and Bientina and the Pisan group of hills, with the upper valley of the Ombrone in the fore, the valley of the Arno beyond, and the distant hills S. of the Arno in the background ;—the whole valley of the Ombrone, with Pistoja in the centre, and the chain of hills which separate it from the Val d'Arno Inferiore and the plains of Pisa on one side ;—whilst the Val d'Arno, extending to Florence, and the Apennines of Valombrosa, close the view to the E. "I seldom have witnessed a grander panorama of Italian scenery than from the Collina Pass on a fine clear November's evening."

About 1 m. to the rt. of the pass of La Collina is seen the lower pass of Peacchia, under which the rly. will pass by a long tunnel.

A rapid and well-managed descent of 6 m., by a series of zigzags, leads into the valley of the Ombrone, passing rapidly through every zone of Italian vegetation, from pasturage and pines, through woods of oaks to chesnut-trees, and then through vineyards to olive-groves, which are here first met with by the traveller arriving from Northern Italy. From the foot of the descent, above which is seen a picturesque modern tower, supposed to mark the site of Catiline's defeat (n.c. 60), a level road of 2 m., through neat farm-houses and villas, leads to the gates of Pistoja; ½ m. before reaching which, are passed on the l. the handsome grounds of the Villa Puccini.

Instead of passing through the town of Pistoja, to avoid the annoying visit at the gates, travellers drive round the walls to the railway-station, situated near the Florentine gate, and close to which is the *Hôtel de Londres*, with clean beds and moderate charges, the best in the place.

Railway trains from Pistoja to Florence start 4 times a day, by the Maria Antonia Railway, performing the journey in an hour. The stations are, reckoning the distances from Pistoja—

	Tuscan miles.
San Piero	4¼
Prato	9¼
Sesto	15¼
Castello	17
Riffredi	18¼
Florence	20

For a description of this part of the route see *Handbook for Central Italy*, Rte. 77.

ROUTE 64.

FAENZA TO FLORENCE, BY MARRADI AND BORGO SAN LORENZO.—69 m.

This road, which was opened in 1844, establishes a convenient communication between Florence and Ravenna. It passes through a picturesque country.

Leaving Faenza, it soon reaches the foot of the first sub-Apennine hills at San Prospero, from whence it follows the l. bank of the Lamone by San Ruffilo to Brisighella, a picturesque village overlooking the plain of the Lamone, to 12 m. *Fognano*, an inconsiderable village on the l. bank of the river, with a wretched inn. The views of the Apennines, in their lower elevations, covered with woods of chesnut-trees, are very pleasing. The Lamone, here nearly dry during the summer months, is an impetuous and dangerous torrent in the rainy season. Following its l. bank, the road crosses it at S. Eufemia; and 7 m. still farther we arrive at 18 m. *Marradi*. Marradi is one of those strange Italian villages often met with out of the high roads. It contains 2200 Inhab. The Locanda del Lamone is indifferent. The valley here becomes very narrow; the precipices on each side merely allowing room for the passage of the river and the road.

1 m. beyond Marradi, at a hamlet called *La Biforca*, the Lamone receives the Compigno torrent on the l.; the road continues along the Lamone for 5 or 6 m., until it reaches Crespino, formerly the seat of a suppressed Vallombrosian monastery. Not far from it is the picturesque cascade of Valbura. From Casaglia commences the ascent of the central chain, which is crossed at Casa di Alpe or Colla di Casaglia, 2980 English feet above the level of the sea. On ascending from Marradi the chesnut woods gradually disappear, the mountains become nearly bare. It requires 3½ hours to reach the highest part of the pass, as it does 2 more to descend to Borgo San Lorenzo. From the pass of Casaglia the road descends rapidly along the Razotta torrent to Puliciano on the Elsa, and from thence to 20 m. *Borgo San Lorenzo* (*Inns*: Locanda della Rivola, clean and civil; Locanda del Sole). Borgo San Lorenzo, situated near the l. bank of the river, is the principal town in the upper part of the valley of the Sieve, generally called the Mugello. It is in a fertile plain, and contains a population of 3500 souls. Its ch., dedicated to San Lorenzo, is an edifice of the 13th century, as appears

from an inscription bearing the date of 1263; the campanile is nearly a century later. 2 roads lead from Borgo San Lorenzo to Florence: the first and most direct, 15 m. up the valley of the Fistona to near its source, and from thence descending along the Mugnone to the gates of the city. 5 m. from Borgo San Lorenzo the mountain of Monte Senario is passed 3 m. on the rt. Before reaching Florence the Mugnone cuts through a deep glen, having on the l. the hill on which the Etruscan arx of the ancient Fesulæ stood, and the Monte Rinaldi, celebrated amongst the Tuscan architects for its quarries of building-stone, on the rt. Emerging from this ravine, we cross the Ponte della Badia, so called from the neighbouring convent, founded by Cosimo de Medicis, from which the road is bordered by lines of farm-houses and villas to the Porta di San Gallo, before reaching which it is joined by the high road from Bologna by Covigliajo. (Rte. 62.)

The second route, from Borgo San Lorenzo, although longer by 3 m., is to be preferred, being less hilly and more suited for carriages, following the l. bank of the Sieve to San Piero, a large village in one of the most fertile districts of the Mugello, near the juction of the Carza and Sieve, and, a mile farther, joining the high road from Bologna to Florence (Rte. 62), not far from Caffaggiolo.

ROUTE 65.

FLORENCE TO FORLI, BY DICOMANO AND THE PASS OF S. BENEDETTO.

	MILES.
Florence to Pontassieve	10
Pontassieve to Dicomano	10
Dicomano to S. Benedetto	16
S. Benedetto to Rocca S. Casciano	12
Rocca San Casciano to Forlì	16

64 miles.

This road, opened of late years by the Tuscan government, for the purpose of establishing a direct communication across the Apennines between Florence and the Romagna, is in good repair, and constructed on the best principles of modern engineering.

A diligence, or rather a vetturino carriage, leaves Florence daily for Forlì, and Forlì for Florence, employing about 16 hours on the road. The fares 30 and 40 pauls. (When the railway is open to Pontassieve, the public conveyances will start for Forlì from the latter place.) As there are no post stations, the only other means of travelling over this route will be by vetturino, which will require 2 days, in which case San Benedetto would be the best halting-place for the first night. A party would find it more agreeable to hire a carriage for the journey than to travel by the diligence; and not much more expensive.

Leaving Florence, we proceed along the rt. bank of the Arno as far as Pontassieve, on the road to Arezzo, where the Forlì road strikes off to the N.E., and ascends the valley of the Sieve as far as Dicomano. The scenery is very fine in many parts, especially for the first 10 m., when it is repeatedly crossed by the line of rly. to Pontassieve; but it becomes wild as we approach the lofty chain of Apennines over which the road is carried.

10 m. *Dicomano.* (*Inns:* Locanda Passerine, and the Leone d'Oro.) It is an old town, prettily situated at the junction of the Sieve and Dicomano torrents, but has little beyond its position to attract the attention of a passing traveller. On leaving it the road proceeds up the valley and along the river of *San Godenzo* to near its source, where extra horses are put on, in order to master the ascent, which is extremely steep. The village of *San Godenzo,* through which the road passes, is situated at the southern base of the central chain, among wooded scenery. Here the ascent of the Apennines, properly speaking, commences, but the road is admirably constructed. The descent is gradual and well managed; the Osteria Nuova, 2 m. below the

pass, is soon reached, and the road shortly attains the banks of the Montone, which it follows to Forlì.

16 m. *San Benedetto.* This place is about half-way between Florence and Forlì; it has a very fair inn, the Leone d'Oro, the best on the road, and it would be the most eligible resting-place for travellers in a private carriage. Between this village and Rocca San Casciano the road passes through *Portico*, an old fortified town, with a ruined castle, which once commanded the road from the Romagna. There are some emanations of inflammable gas, similar to those at Pietramala, near the hamlet of Querciolano on the l. of the road.

12 m. *Rocca San Casciano* (*Inn:* the Locando del Giglio, tolerable), a village of 1600 Inhab., on the rt. bank of the Montone. It is the most important town of the Tuscan Romagna; but contains little to detain the traveller. A road has of late years been opened from it across the pass of *Le Forche* to *Galeata* and *Santa Sofia*, in the upper valley of the Ronco. Leaving San Casciano, the road continues along the Montone, between Monte Grosso on the rt. and Monte Torcella on the l. Before arriving at *Dovadola*, a good road across the pass of Monte Trebbio, of 10 m. on the l., leads to *Modigliana*, a very ancient town of 3000 Inhab., probably the Castrum Mutilum of Livy. *Dovadola* has an old castle in ruins. (Near here commence the Miocene deposits, which are seen forming precipices of almost horizontal strata behind the village: they rest on the Eocene limestones and marls which form the centre of the chain, and are succeeded by the Pliocene or Subapennine marls and sands which extend to the valley of the Po; the mineral waters of Castroaro issue from the Miocene beds). Between Dovadola and Terra del Sole is the village of *Castro Caro*—the ancient Salsubium—celebrated for its mineral waters, which contain a considerable portion of iodine, and have proved very efficacious in glandular and scrofulous affections. Castro Caro derives its name from its picturesque mediæval castle, situated on a mass of marine breccia or *Panchina*, which rises precipitately above the town. 5 m. beyond this is

Terra del Sole, formerly the frontier station of Tuscany, a walled town on the l. bank of the Montone. 1½ m. farther is Rovere, until lately the Papal frontier station. From this a pleasant drive of about 2 m. across the plain—during which Bertinoro, perched on one of the last spurs of the Apennines, is seen picturesquely on the summit of its hill, at some distance on the rt.—brings us to the bridge over the Montone and

16 m. FORLÌ (described in Rte. 72).

ROUTE 66.

FORLÌ TO RAVENNA.

20 m.

As there is no regular public conveyance on this route, persons proceeding to Ravenna must hire a vehicle for the journey. Paolo Traversaro, an obliging vetturino, who may be heard of at the diligence office, has a good carriage, and can be recommended; the charge to Ravenna will be about 10 francs, and the time occupied in the journey 3 hours.

An excellent road of about 20 m,. parallel to the l. bank of the Ronco, which from here to the sea is confined in its channel by high banks. Like the following, this route presents a succession of farm-houses thickly scattered over a country which is surpassed by none in Italy for fertility or

cultivation. Soon after leaving Forli, a road to Cervia and Rimini branches off on the rt.: before reaching Ravenna, the canal formed by the united waters of the Montone and Ronco is passed, and the city is entered by the Porta Sisi.
20 m. RAVENNA (Rte. 69).

ROUTE 67.

FAENZA TO RAVENNA.

A cross-road of 22 m.
An agreeable drive of about 3 hours over a level road, through a country of extraordinary fertility. 4 m. after leaving Faenza the road crosses the Lamone at the Ponte della Castellina. Between Russi and Godo, which lie on the rt., the present route falls into the high road from Bologna to Ravenna through Lugo and Medecina.
2½ RAVENNA (Rte. 69).

ROUTE 68.

VENICE TO RAVENNA, BY THE CANALS AND COMACCHIO.

	POSTS.
Venice to Chioggia, 20 m.	
Chioggia to Cavanella	2
Cavanella to Mesola	2
Mesola to Pomposa	2
Pomposa to Magnavacca	2
Magnavacca to Primaro	1
Primaro to Ravenna	2

11 posts = about 90 m.

The traveller who is desirous of proceeding from Venice to Ravenna by the shortest route may do so by the canals which intersect the vast lagunes between the 2 cities. Although only a short portion of the route can be performed in a carriage, there is a series of post stations from Chioggia to Ravenna, the route being estimated at 11 posts.

A person having his own carriage must be prepared to run all risks of trans-shipment from the ferry-boats; but a traveller not so encumbered will do well to rely on the canal-boats and on the carriages of the country, which he will find at Mesola to convey him to Ravenna.

Persons proceeding by this route will have a good opportunity of seeing the famous *Murazze*, or great sea-wall of Venice, as the boat must pass along it whether it follows the canal inside the island of Malamocco, or takes the outer or seaward route.

The ordinary course, if in a gondola, is to proceed down the deeper channel of the Laguna, called the Malamocco canal, and from thence inside the long narrow island which lies beyond it: a steamer leaves Venice every morning during the summer for Chioggia.

Chioggia or *Chiozza*. This would be the best resting-place for the first night. The time occupied in rowing the distance in a 6-oared boat is about 6 hours; it would, of course, be much shorter in a sailing one, with a fair wind. *Chioggia* is a well-built town, with a convenient port, much frequented by the small coasting vessels of the Adriatic. Its history and association with the naval achievements of Venice, recalling " the Doria's menace," so beautifully sung in 'Childe Harold,' belong to the description of that city, and need not be particularised here. Leaving the town, we proceed to Brondolo, on the Brenta, and from thence by the Canal di Valle, which connects the latter river and the Adige, to *Cavanella dell' Adige*, ascend the Adige for 2 m., and then follow the Canal di Loreo to *Cavanella di Pò*, on the l. bank of that branch of the Po called the Pò Grande, or della Maestra. The other branch farther S. is the Pò di Goro, and between the point of bifurcation at Punta di Sta. Maria and the sea these two arms of the river enclose an island, called *Isola d' Ariano*, frequently subject to the destructive inundations of both its branches. On the northern shore of this island, and about 3 m. lower down, is *Taglio del Pò*, to which, if the island can be traversed, the traveller should proceed, and there leave his boat; otherwise he must ascend the northern branch of the Po, and make a tedious *détour* round the western angle of the island to Sta. Maria, near the town of Ariano; in either case he will arrive at *Mesola*, the frontier town of the North Italian kingdom. The difference of time occupied by these two modes is considerable: from Chioggia to Taglio the voyage, *direct*, occupies about 8 hours; from Taglio to Mesola, across the island, is little more than 1 hour: whereas the route from Chioggia to Mesola, going round by the Po and Sta. Maria, requires at least 14 hours.

Mesola, on the rt. bank of the *Pò di Goro*. This should be made the sleeping-place on the second day; there is a tolerable inn here; and a country carriage, quite good enough for the roads, may be hired for the next day's journey. Mesola has a population of 1917 souls: it appears to have been considered important as a frontier town, since it is recorded that it has been twice purchased of the House of Austria by the Church—by Pius VI., for a million of scudi, and by Leo XII., in 1822, for 467,000. The difficulty and expenses of keeping up the embankments of the canals and rivers in this part of Italy, which are admirably constructed and managed, as the traveller will not fail to observe during his journey, are said by the inhabitants to have made the acquisition an onerous one to the Papal government.

Leaving Mesola, the road proceeds along the flat sandy tract to *Pomposa*, near the Pò di Volano, which is crossed by a ferry, and afterwards passes over the sandy strip which encloses on the E., separating from the sea, the shallow Lagune, or, as it is called, the *Valle di Comacchio*, to *Magnavacca*. W. of Magnavacca is the town of *Comacchio*, with 6600 souls. The Lagunes of Comacchio, similar to those of Venice in their mode of formation, occupy an extensive area between the Pò di Volano on the N., and the Pò Primaro or Reno on the S., separated from the sea by a long sandy spit which has only one communication with it by the cut of Magnavacca. These Lagunes have from time immemorial been celebrated for their fisheries, consisting chiefly of eels and grey mullet: by means of a most ingenious system the' rivers which encircle them at a certain period of the year are allowed to flow in, and thus to introduce the young fry which ascend these streams from the sea; the fish are allowed to increase in size, and, as all exit is prevented by nets and sluices, at a particular time the fishing commences. The fishery employs a population of nearly 6000 persons, who are located about Comacchio, and is farmed out from the government at present by the banker Torlonia of Rome, who pays 18,000 scudi annually; the average production has been 1,800,000 lbs. annually. The fish is cured on the spot, and exported to every part of Italy. The contrivances for *enticing* the young fish, and for *retaining* the old returning to the sea, which are very ingenious, have been described by Tasso and Ariosto.

" Come il pesce colà, dove impaluda
Ne' seni di Comacchio il nostro mare,
Fugge dall' onde impetuosa e cruda,
Cercando in placide acque, ove ripare.
E vien, che da sè stesso ei si rinchiuda
In palustre prigion, nè può tornare ;
Chè quel serraglio è con mirabil uso
Sempre all' entrar aperto, all' uscir chiuso."
Gerus. Lib. vii. 46.

Ariosto calls *Comacchio*
" La città, che in mezzo alle piscose
Paludi del Pò teme ambe le foci."
Orl. Fur. iii. 41, 3.

The town of Comacchio was formerly fortified, and occupied, in virtue of a stipulation in the Treaty of Vienna, by an Austrian force; but the defences were destroyed in 1848. It is on an elongated island, having the Convent of the Capuccini at one end, and the remains of its citadel at the other. The depth of the Laguna varies from 3 to 6 feet.

About 7 m. S. of Magnavacca the road crosses the southern branch of the Po, called the Pò di Primaro, at Il Passo, the supposed *Spineticum Ostium* of the ancients, leaving on the l. the town of Primaro and its small port, defended by the Torre Gregoriana.

1 m. beyond Primaro the Lamone is crossed, and we soon enter the northern extremity of the *Pineta*, described in the account of Ravenna, in the succeeding Route. After a drive of a few miles through this venerable forest, we enter Ravenna near the tomb of Theodoric, by the Porta Serrata. The journey from Mesola to Ravenna will occupy about 10 hours, and be a fair day's work.

RAVENNA, described in the next Route.

[A recent traveller, Dr. Fraser, who performed the journey from Ravenna to Venice, gives the following account of his progress:—" This route is not devoid of interest, although it is seldom followed. On leaving Ravenna, the road passes by the tomb of Theodoric, and soon after enters the Pineta. The deep silence of the forest is unbroken by the noise of the carriage, which now passes over the green turf, scarcely marked, and in some places not at all, by any track; and the traveller soon feels that without the aid of a guide, or the instinct of the North American, his path would soon be lost. We were told that wild boars abound in the recesses of the forest; but we saw no game, nor indeed any other living thing. After threading its mazes for 2 hours, we observed with regret a thinning of the trees, and gradually entered on the open country. An uninteresting drive brought us to Magnavacca, where, in addition to our own stock of provisions (for every person taking this route ought to carry a supply), we found the means of making a tolerable breakfast. We changed horses and carriage at this place, by which we neither improved our vehicle nor the quality of the horses. We were now given to understand that no one would take a good carriage by this road, so that we had been deceived by the innkeeper at Ravenna, who had agreed to convey us to Mesola in his snug barouche; whereas the one to which we were now transferred was somewhat ruder in construction than a tax-cart. We had, however, no alternative, and were given to understand that next day we should obtain a better carriage at Mesola, which we reached at sunset.

We slept there, although our original intention was to make Ariano our resting-place for the first night; but the usual road was cut up by the late floods, and that which we were to follow so increased the distance, that the landlord would not furnish us with horses that evening. As he had everything in his own hands, we submitted with as good grace as possible. Mesola is the frontier town of the Papal States, and consists of a large building, the residence of the governor, apparently constructed so as to be turned into a fort if necessary, and a few straggling houses, all lying below the level of the river, which is here magnificently embanked. During this day's journey we crossed five streams by means of ferry-boats; but the steepness of their banks, and the bad arrangements of the boats, convinced us that no English carriage could be safely transported without improved means. On one occasion, indeed, our carriage, from its impetus in descending, was nearly thrown into the river, dragging the men and everything after it. If this accident had happened, we should have had our baggage destroyed, if not lost, and should have been compelled to proceed for some distance on foot. We started from Mesola the next morning at daybreak, and drove along the S. bank of the Pò di Goro, or Pò Piccolo, to the point opposite Vicolo, where we found numerous boatmen, and soon made an arrangement for our conveyance to Chioggia. We were now dragged, as in a canal boat, by two men, up the Po to Sta. Maria in Ponto, without landing at Ariano. Before arriving at Sta. Maria we left the boat in order to avoid the tiresome navigation round the western point of the island. We reached Sta. Maria in this way, after a walk of a mile, while the boat did not arrive for 3 hours. Sta. Maria is the Austrian frontier station: we found the officers extremely civil and obliging, and were subjected to far less inconvenience than we had met with in many petty towns of the Papal States. The effects of the floods on this island of Ariano were still visible in the broken banks, and in the vast masses of shingle thrown up on various parts of the surface. The inhabitants were unable to leave their houses for 15 days during the great flood of November, 1839. On the arrival of our boat we proceeded on our voyage, passing through numerous canals, and seldom encountering a lock, in consequence of the level character of the country. We crossed the branch of the Po called Pò Maestra, the Adige, and the Brenta, during the day; but the only towns we passed were Cavanella di Pò and Loreo. We arrived at Chioggia at 8 in the evening, and our anxiety to reach Venice was so great that we immediately hired a boat, and landed in that city at 2 in the morning. We ought to have slept at Chioggia, as we suffered much from cold in passing the lagunes, and had but an imperfect view of the great wall, which is so well seen on this passage. Our route altogether, in spite of the drawbacks mentioned, was far from being uninteresting; the swamps, canals, and rivers were so unlike anything we had seen before, that we were amused by the novelty of the scene; the time passed away pleasantly under the awning of the boat, or in walking along the banks of the canals, which the slow movement of our boat permitted; we were struck by the simple manners of the peasantry, and still more by the extreme beauty of the women; we were not annoyed by beggars; we enjoyed a freedom unknown to travellers in a diligence; and at the close of our journey we almost regretted that it was the only one, and the last of the kind."]

Travellers will perceive from this that it is desirable to divide the journey into 3 days, sleeping at Mesola or Ariano on the first night, and at Chioggia on the second. They would thus reach Venice early on the third day.

ROUTE 69.

BOLOGNA TO RAVENNA, BY IMOLA AND LUGO.

	POSTS.
Bologna to S. Niccolò	1¼
S. Niccolò to Imola	1¼
Imola to Lugo	2
Lugo to Ravenna	3

7½ posts = 55½ m.

This route, being longer than that by Medecina, is seldom taken by persons proceeding from Bologna to Ravenna, and there are no public conveyances upon it; it has, however, the advantage for persons travelling in their own carriages of enabling them to perform the whole with post-horses, and to see Imola. When the rly. has been opened as far as the latter town, it will afford the most rapid mode of reaching the city of the Exarchs from the capital of the Emilian Provinces.

The first 2 stages, between Bologna and Imola, are described in Rte. 72, where an account of Imola will be found. The route from Imola to Ravenna is somewhat longer than that from Faenza; but the road is excellent, and the country through which it passes is interesting on account of its high state of cultivation.

Leaving Imola, the road proceeds along the l. bank of the Santerno as far as Mordano. After crossing the Santerno it turns towards Lugo. 3 m. N.W. from this is the walled town of *Massa Lombarda*, supposed to have derived its name from the Mantuan and Brescian emigrants who fled from the persecutions of Frederick Barbarossa, and settled here in 1232. There is no doubt that the establishment of this colony contributed to the prosperity of the district; and it is recorded that Francesco d'Este, one of the generals of the Emp. Charles V., on his deathbed at Ferrara in 1573, directed that the Lombards of Massa should carry his body from Ferrara to this town, where, in accordance with his wishes, it was buried. The present population is about 5000. On the l. bank of the Santerno, a branch road from Ferrara through the marshes of Argenta falls into this route.

2 *Lugo* (*Inn:* Albergo di San Marco, tolerable), situated in the plain, nearly midway between the Santerno and the Senio rivers, supposed to occupy the site of *Lucus Dianæ*, whose temple was in the neighbourhood. Lugo, now an important provincial town of 8474 souls, was raised to municipal rank by Julius II., and was confirmed in its privileges by Pius VII. It contains nothing to detain the traveller, unless he happen to visit it at the period of its fair, which commences September 1st, and lasts till the 19th of the month. This fair is said to date from the time of Marcus Æmilius, a proconsul of Ravenna. In the vicinity of Lugo are 2 small towns, each of which is interesting as the birthplace of personages whose names occupy a distinguished place in Italian history. The first of these, *Cotignola*, 3 m. to the S.E. of Lugo, on the banks of the Senio, was the birthplace of Attendolo Sforza, the founder of that illustrious house which subsequently played so important a part. It was here that he threw his pickaxe into the branches of an oak, in order that it might decide by its fall, or by remaining fixed, whether he should remain a tiller of the ground, or join a company of condottieri. The other town, *Fusignano*, about 4 m. N., also on the l. bank of the Senio, is memorable as the birthplace of Vincenzo Monti the poet, and of Angelo Corelli the composer. The castle of Cunio, celebrated as one of the strongholds of Romagna in the middle ages, was in the neighbourhood of Cotignola: its ruins still exist.

A short distance from Lugo the road crosses the Senio, and passes through *Bagnacavallo*, a town of 4011 souls, originally called Tiberiacum, in honour of Tiberius. Several Roman inscriptions, and other antiquities of the time of the Empire, discovered there in 1605, prove its existence at that period as a Roman city. The present town is walled, and was formerly famous for its strong castle. It has a cathedral dedicated to St. Michael the Archangel, and a circus for the game of pallone, but it contains little to interest the stranger. 2 m. beyond Bagnacavallo the road crosses the Lamone, and proceeds across the plain to Ravenna. Near Godo that from Faenza falls into this route.

3 RAVENNA.—(*Inn:* La Spada Nova, or Spada d'Oro, very good for Ravenna, the best in the place, in the Palazzo Raize, near the Piazza, Theatre, and principal sights, charges reasonable; the owner, Ranzini, an obliging old fellow, is well acquainted with what is to be seen, and will serve as a guide to them if required, for there are no professed laquais de place here. La Bella Emilia, on the Via di Porta Adriana, more moderate and tolerably good,) Ravenna, the capital of the Western Empire, the seat of the Gothic and Longobardic kings, and the metropolis of the Greek Exarchs, is one of those historical cities which are best illustrated by their own monuments. Within its walls repose the remains of the children of Theodosius, and amidst the tombs of exarchs and patriarchs rests all that was mortal of Dante. A short distance beyond the gates is the sepulchre of Theodoric, king of the Goths: the city ramparts still bear evidence of the breaches made in them by the barbarians who invaded Italy, and the deserted streets are filled with Christian antiquities which have undergone scarcely any change since the time of Justinian. As the traveller wanders through the streets, their unbroken solitude recalls the feelings with which he may have ridden round the walls of Constantinople; but Ravenna has preserved more memorials of her imperial masters, and possesses a far higher interest for the Christian antiquary, than even that celebrated seat of empire. "Whoever loves early Christian monuments, whoever desires to see them in greater perfection than the lapse of 14 centuries could warrant

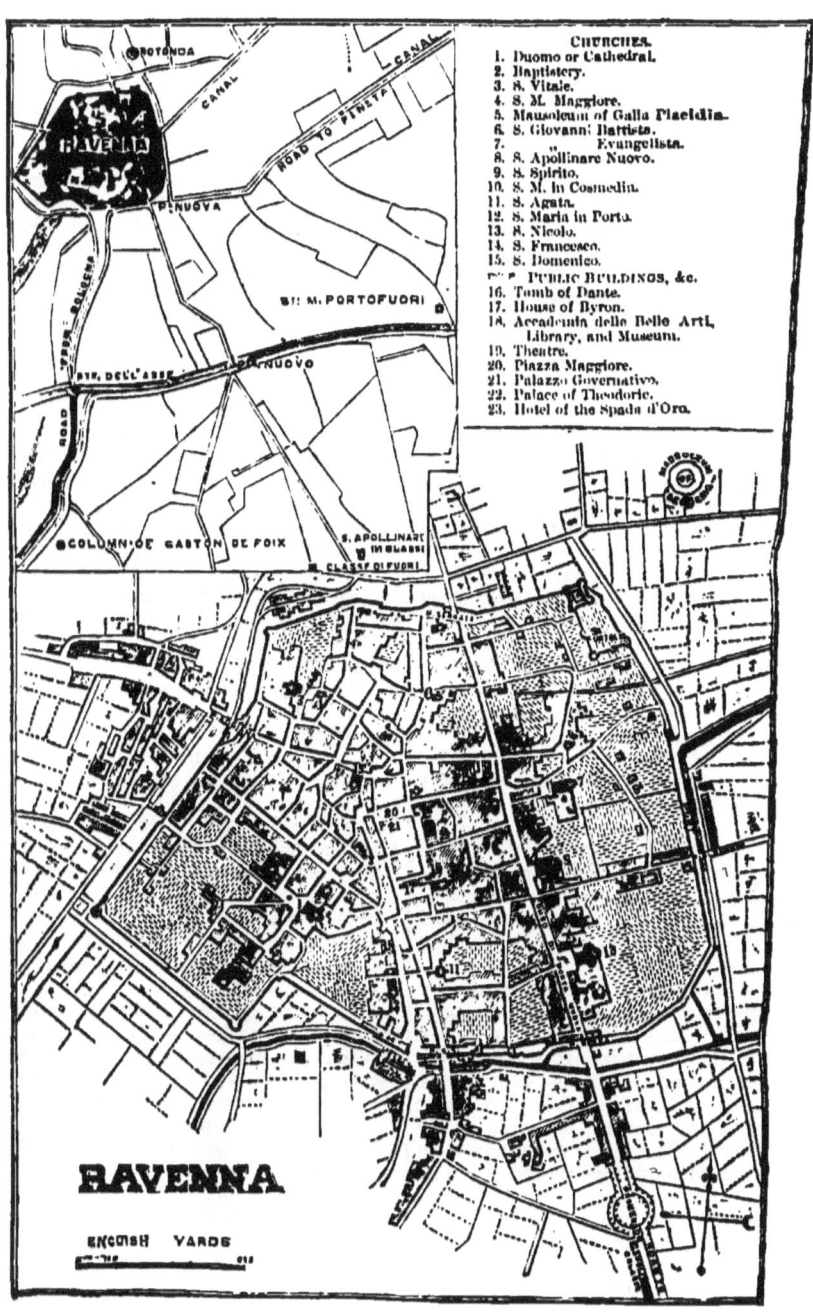

us in expecting, whoever desires to study them unaided by the remains of heathen antiquity, should make every effort to spend some days at least in this noble and imperial city. From Rome it differs mainly in this—that your meditations on its ornaments are not disturbed by the constant recurrence of pagan remains, nor your researches perplexed by the necessity of inquiring what was built and what was borrowed by the faithful. Ravenna has only one antiquity, and that is Christian. Seated like Rome in the midst of an unhealthy, desolate plain, except when its unrivalled pine-forests cast a shade of deeper solitude and melancholy over it; quiet and lonely, without the sound of wheels upon its grass-grown pavement; it has not merely to lament over the decay of ancient magnificence, but upon its total destruction—except what Religion has erected for herself. She was not in time to apply her saving as well as purifying unction to the basilicas and temples of preceding ages; or rather, she seemed to occupy what she could replace, and therefore, in the strength of imperial favour, raised new buildings for the Christian worship, such as no other city but Rome could boast of."— *Cardinal Wiseman.*

The history of Ravenna embraces a considerable portion of that not only of Italy during the middle ages, but also of the Eastern and Western Empires. Without entering into these details, it will be useful for the appreciation of its antiquities to give a rapid sketch of its history under its ancient masters.

The accounts of the classical writers prove that the ancient city was built on wooden piles in the midst of a vast *laguna*, and so intersected with marshes that communication was kept up by numerous bridges, not only throughout the adjacent country, but even in the city itself. The sea, which is now from 3 to 4 m. distant, then flowed up to its walls. Ravenna became early a Roman colony. In the contests between Sylla and Marius it espoused the cause of the latter, for which it subsequently severely suffered; and, judging from an expression in Cicero, was an important naval station at the time of Pompey. Cæsar occupied it previous to his invasion of Italy. Under Augustus its consequence was increased by the construction of an ample port at the mouth of the Candianus, capable of affording shelter to 250 ships, and which superseded the old harbour at the mouth of the Ronco. He connected the new port with the Po by means of a canal, and carried a causeway to it from the city, which he made his frequent residence, and embellished with magnificent buildings. The new harbour was called *Portus Classis*, a name still retained in the distinctive title of the basilica of S. Apollinaris; and the intermediate settlement which arose from the establishment of the port was called *Cæsarea*, whose name also was perpetuated until a comparatively recent period by the church of S. Lorenzo in Cesarea. Subsequent emperors added to the natural strength of Ravenna by fortifying and maintaining its importance as a naval station. But its true interest does not commence until after the classical age. On the decline of the Roman empire, Honorius chose Ravenna as the seat of the Western Empire, A.D. 404. As early as then the alluvial deposits of the Po had begun to accumulate on the coast; the port of Augustus had been gradually filled up, and the forest of pines which supplied the Roman fleet with timber had usurped the site where that fleet had once rode at anchor, and spread far along the shore, thus extending gradually to a greater distance from the city. These and other circumstances combined to make it a place of security; and Honorius, afraid of remaining defenceless at Milan, chose Ravenna as his residence, where his personal safety was secure amidst the canals and morasses, which were then too shallow to admit the large vessels of the enemy. He availed himself of these changes to strengthen the city with additional fortifications, and so far succeeded that its impregnable position saved it from the inroads of the barbarians under Radagaldus and Alaric. Without entering into details of the

Imperial rule at Ravenna under Placidia, the sister of Honorius, during the minority of her son Valentinian, it may suffice to state that under her feeble successors even the natural advantages of the city were unable to offer an effectual resistance to the hordes under Odoacer, who, in little more than 70 years after the arrival of Honorius, made himself master of Ravenna, and extinguished the Empire of the West, by deposing Romulus Augustulus, the last of the Cæsars. His rule, however, had lasted but 15 years when Theodoric, king of the Ostro-Goths, crossed the Alps with a powerful army, and after several gallant struggles overthrew Odoacer, and made Ravenna the capital of the Gothic kingdom. Theodoric was succeeded in the sovereignty of Italy by two of his descendants, and they in turn by a series of elective kings, from Vitiges, the last of whom, Justinian endeavoured to reconquer the lost provinces, aided by the military genius of Belisarius. The campaign of that celebrated general, and his siege and capture of Ravenna, are familiar to every reader of the 'Decline and Fall of the Roman Empire.'

It would be out of place to dwell upon the circumstances which led to the recall of Belisarius, and the appointment of Narses, the new general of Justinian, who drove the Goths out of Italy, and was intrusted with the administration of the Italian kingdom with the title of EXARCH. The rank thus conferred upon the favourite lieutenant of the emperor was extended to his successors during the continuance of the Greek sovereignty: the functions of the exarchs corresponded in some measure to those of the ancient prætorian prefects. Their government comprised the entire kingdom of Italy, including Rome itself, and the pope or bishop of the Christian capital was regarded as subject to their authority, possessing merely a temporal barony in Rome dependent on the exarchate. The territory understood to be comprised in the *Exarchate* embraced modern Romagna, the districts of Ferrara and Comacchio, the maritime Pentapolis or towns extending along the Adriatic from Rimini to Ancona, and a second or inland Pentapolis, including several towns on the eastern declivities of the Apennines. The exarchate lasted 185 years, during which the people of Rome erected a kind of republic under their bishop; and Astaulphus, king of the Lombards, seeing that Ravenna would be an easy prey, drove out Eutychius, the last exarch, became master of the city, and made it the metropolis of the Longobardic kingdom (A.D. 754). The attempt of the Lombards to seize Rome also, as a dependency of the exarchate, brought to the aid of the Church the powerful army of the Franks under Pepin and Charlemagne, by whom the Lombards were expelled, and Ravenna with the exarchate made over to the Holy See as a temporal possession; "and the world beheld for the first time a Christian bishop invested with the prerogatives of a temporal prince, the choice of magistrates, the exercise of justice, the imposition of taxes, and the wealth of the palace of Ravenna."

After the transfer of the exarchate to Rome by the Carlovingian princes, the fortunes of Ravenna began rapidly to decline; its archbishops frequently seized the government, and it was the scene of repeated commotions among its own citizens. In the 13th century the constitution of Ravenna strongly tended to an aristocracy; its general council was composed of 250, and its special council of 70 persons. In the contests of the Guelphs and Ghibelines, Pietro Traversari, an ally of the former, declared himself Duke of Ravenna (1218), without changing the municipal institutions of the city. His son and successor quarrelled with the emperor Frederick II., who reduced Ravenna to obedience and despoiled it of many of its treasures. The city was shortly after seized upon by Innocent IV., and reduced again to the authority of the Roman pontiffs, who governed it by vicars. In 1275 it was ruled by the family of Polenta, whose connection with it is commemorated by Dante under the image of an eagle which figured in their coat of arms:—

" Ravenna sta com' è stata molti anni:
L'aquila da Polenta là si cova,
Sì, che Cervia ricopre col suoi vanni."
Inf. xxvii.

" The state
Ravenna hath maintain'd this many a year
Is steadfast. There Polenta's eagle broods:
And in her broad circumference of plumes
O'ershadows Cervia." *Cary's Trans.*

After some subsequent changes the inhabitants were induced by civil tumults, arising from the ambition or cupidity of its powerful citizens, to throw themselves under the protection of Venice, by which the government was seized in 1441. Ravenna flourished under the republic; its public buildings were restored, its fortress was strengthened, and the laws were administered with justice and wisdom. After retaining it for 68 years, the Venetians finally ceded it to the Roman See in 1509 under Julius II.; and it then became the capital of Romagna, and was governed by the papal legates. In less than 3 years after this event the general Italian war which followed the league of Cambray brought into Italy the army of Louis XII. under Gaston de Foix, who began his campaign of Romagna by the siege of Ravenna. After a vain attempt to carry it by assault, in which he was bravely repulsed by the inhabitants, the arrival of the papal and Spanish troops induced him to give battle, on Easter Sunday, April 11, 1512. Italy had never seen so bloody a combat; little short of 20,000 men are said to have lain dead upon the field, when the Spanish infantry, yet unbroken, slowly retreated. Gaston de Foix, furious at seeing them escape, rushed upon the formidable host in the vain hope of throwing them into disorder, and perished in the attempt about 3 m. from the walls of Ravenna. The French gained the victory, but it was dearly purchased by the loss of their chivalrous commander.

At the French invasion of 1796 Ravenna was deprived of its rank as the capital of Romagna, which was given to Forlì; but it was restored by Austria in 1799, only to be again transferred by the French in the following year. On the fall of the Kingdom of Italy, Ravenna was again made the chief city of the province, but its ancient glory had passed for ever, and only 3 towns and a few villages were left subject to its authority.

Ravenna, at the present time, is the chief city of a province comprehending a pop. of 175,995 Inhab., including the suburbs, and a surface of 528 square m.; the city is inhabited by 21,056 persons, and its immediate territory irrigated by numerous rivers and torrents. It is the seat of an archbishop, to whom most of the bishops of Romagna are suffragans. Its bishopric, one of the most ancient in the Christian world, was founded A.D. 44, by S. Apollinaris, a disciple of Peter; and it obtained the dignity of an archiepiscopal see as early as 439, under Sixtus III. The circuit of the city is about 3 m., but nearly one-half of the enclosed space consists of gardens. Besides its churches and other objects of antiquarian interest, it contains a college, a museum, public schools, and an academy of the fine arts. Its port, communicating with the Adriatic by a canal, is still considered one of the great outlets of Romagna, and carries on a considerable trade with the Venetian kingdom, the Austrian possessions in Istria and Dalmatia, and the Papal States on the Adriatic.

To visit everything of interest at Ravenna will not occupy the traveller less than two days: to facilitate his doing so a carriage with one horse may be procured at the hotel for 1½ scudi per diem. There are no hackney-coaches in the town.

The following topographical order will be perhaps the most useful to follow:—

1st day: Piazza Maggiore; Duomo; BAPTISTERY; ARCHBISHOP'S PALACE; Palazzo Rasponi and Gallery; Porta Adriana and Boulevart near it; CH. OF SAN VITALE and Santa Maria Maggiore; TOMB OF GALLA PLACIDIA; Ch. of San Giovanni Battista; Porta Serrata; MAUSOLEUM OF THEODORIC; returning into the city by the Port of Ravenna and Porta Alberoni; PALACE OF THEODORIC; Ch. of S. APOLLINARE NUOVO; Ch. of S. GIOVANNI EVANGELISTA; Chs. of S. Spirito and S. MARIA IN COSMEDIN; TORRE DEL

PUBBLICO, &c. 2nd day: TOMB OF DANTE; CH. OF S. FRANCESCO; House of Lord Byron; ACCADEMIA DELLE BELLE ARTI; LIBRARY; Ch. of S. Nicolo; CH. OF S. AGATA; Porta Sisi; SANTA MARIA IN PORTO; Porta Nuova; S. APOLLINARE IN CLASSE; SANTA MARIA IN PORTO FUORI; driving back THROUGH THE PINETA to the embouchure of the Canal in the Adriatic, and from thence along the former to the Porta Alberoni at Ravenna.

The *Cathedral*, once a remarkable example of the ancient Basilica, has lost all traces of its original character. It was built by S. Ursus, archbishop of the see, in the 4th century, and called from him " Basilica Ursiana." It was almost entirely rebuilt in the last century; the cylindrical campanile alone remains of the original foundation. Amongst the objects of interest in the present ch. are the celebrated paintings by *Guido* in the chapel of the Holy Sacrament representing the fall of the manna, and in the lunette above the meeting of Melchizedek and Abraham; these are classed by Lanzi among Guido's best works. The frescoes of the Cupola, with the exception of the Archangel Michael, are attributed to his pupils, as well as the four Prophets on the pendentives below. Near this, in a lunette, over an arch at the entrance of the sacristy, is Guido's fresco of the Angel bringing food to Elijah, the latter a fine sleeping figure. Among the other pictures which deserve notice are the grand Banquet of Ahasuerus, over the great entrance, by *Carlo Bonone*, well known by the minute description of Lanzi, and the modern paintings in the choir, of the death of St. Peter Chrysologus by *Benevenuti*, and of the Consecration of the ch. by St. Ursus, by *Camuccini*. The high altar contains a marble urn, in which are deposited the remains of several early bishops of the see. The silver crucifix of St. Agnellus on this altar is covered with sculptures of the 6th century. The chapel of the Madonna del Sudore contains two large marble urns covered with bas-reliefs, in one of which, as related by the inscription, are the ashes of St. Barbatian, confessor of Galla Placidia; in the other those of San Rinaldus. Behind the choir are 3 semicircular marble slabs with symbolical representations of birds and animals, which formed part of the ancient *ambo* or pulpit, a work of the 6th century, as shown by the inscription stating that it was erected by St. Agnellus. Near these slabs is a bas-relief of St. Mark by Lombardi. In the sacristy is a *Paschal calendar* on marble, a remarkable monument of astronomical knowledge in the early times of Christianity. It was calculated for 95 years, beginning with 532, and ending in 626. The *Sacristy* also contains the *pastoral chair of St. Maximian*, formed entirely of ivory, with his monogram in front. The bas-reliefs below the monogram represent the Saviour in the character of a shepherd and priest in the midst of the 4 evangelists: on the 2 ends is the history of Joseph, and those which remain on the back represent various events in the life of the Saviour, with arabesque designs of animals. It is precious as a specimen of art in the 6th century, but it has evidently suffered from injudicious cleaning. Enclosed within the grand door of the cathedral are still preserved some fragments of its celebrated *Door of vine-wood*, which has been superseded by one of modern construction. The original planks are said to have been 13 feet long and nearly 1¼ wide—a proof that the ancients were correct in stating that the vine attains a great size, and confirmatory of the assertion that the statue of Diana of Ephesus was made of the vine-wood of Cyprus. It is probable that the wood of the Ravenna doors was imported from Constantinople.

The ancient Baptistery, called also " S. Giovanni in Fonte," separated from the cathedral by a street, is supposed to have been likewise founded by S. Ursus: it was repaired in 451 by archbishop Neo, and dedicated to St. John the Baptist. It is, like many baptisteries of the early Christians, an octagonal building; the interior has 2 ranges of arcades, the lower resting on 8 columns of different orders with marble capitals, placed in the angles of the building; the upper, 24 in number, are dissimilar in dimensions as well as in the style of the capitals. The lower columns are considerably sunk in the ground, and both these and the upper series are supposed to have belonged to some ancient temple. The cupola is adorned with well-preserved mosaics of the 5th century, representing in the centre Christ baptized in the Jordan by St. John, with a representation of the river, having its name placed over it, and in the circumference the 12 apostles, each with his name and bearing wreaths or crowns, and below emblems, of the Gospels, bishops, thrones, and with other ornaments. (The most correct representations of these, as well as most of the other ancient mosaics of Ravenna, will be found in Ciampini, Vetera Monumenta, 3 vols. fol., Roma, 1757, and of those of the tomb of Galla Placidia in Quast's 'Alt. Christlichen Bauwerke von Ravenna,' 1 vol. fol. Berlin, 1842.) The grand vase under the cupola, which was formerly used for baptism by immersion, is of slabs of white marble and porphyry, with a recess or ambo for the officiating priest. A chapel in one of the recesses of the building contains under its altar a sculptured marble of the 6th century, which formerly belonged to the ciborium of the old cathedral; and in another a beautiful urn of Parian marble covered with symbols supposed to relate to the ancient nuptial purifications; it was found in the temple of Jupiter at Cæsarea. The ancient metal cross of the summit of the building merits notice on account of its antiquity: it bears an inscription recording that it was erected in 688 by Archbishop Theodorus. It has recently been removed, and now stands in front of the church, but an exact representation of it has been let into the inner wall of the baptistery. In the adjoining square are several mediæval and sepulchral urns in marble.

The *Ch. of Sta. Agata*, in the street leading to the Porta Sisi, another ancient edifice, dating from the 5th century, has a nave and 2 aisles divided by 20 columns, partly of granite, of cipolino, and of other marbles, in general with ancient composite capitals, the imposts over which have the cross sculptured upon them. The wall which rises over them was formerly pierced with numerous windows, as we see in the smaller Christian basilicas. The choir contains a painting of the Crucifixion, by *Francesco da Cotignola*; and the chapel at the end of the rt. aisle one of *Luca Longhi's* best works, representing S. Agata, St. Catherine, and St. Cecilia. The altar of this chapel contains the bodies of S. Sergius martyr, and S. Agnellus archbishop, and bears the two monograms of *Sergius Diaconus*. The corresponding chapel in the opposite aisle has a good painting of the Virgin and St. Peter by *Barbiani*. The tribune was once covered with mosaics of the 6th centy., but which were destroyed by an earthquake in 1688. The very ancient pulpit is worthy of notice; it is formed of a hollowed-out section of a huge fluted column of cipolino marble from some gigantic pagan edifice.

The *Ch. of S. Apollinare Nuovo*, in the Corso or long street leading from Porta Nuova to P. Serrata, built by Theodoric in the beginning of the sixth century as the cathedral for his Arian bishops, was consecrated for Catholic worship by archbishop S. Agnellus, at the close of the Gothic kingdom, and dedicated to *S. Martin*. It was also called *San Martino in Celo Aureo*, on account of its magnificent decorations, and Sacellum Arii from its original destination. It assumed its present name in the 9th century, from the belief that the body of S. Apollinaris had been transferred within its walls, in order to secure it in its real resting-place at Classe from the attacks of the Saracens. The 24 marble columns of grey cippolino supporting the rounded arches dividing the nave from the aisles were brought from Constantinople; they have composite capitals, on each of which is an impost with Latin crosses sculptured on it. The walls of the nave, which rest on these arches, are covered with superb mosaics, executed about A.D. 570. On the l. is represented the city of Classis, with the sea and ships; then come 22 virgins, each holding in her hand a crown, preceded by the magi, in the act of presenting their offerings to the Virgin and Child seated upon a throne with 2 angels on either side. "This superb mosaic, the finest in the whole of Ravenna, may deserve attention on another account: the earliest monuments of Christian art give little countenance to Mariolatry, or the peculiar veneration to the Virgin, which has so long distinguished the Greek and Roman churches. In this mosaic, however, though the presence of the magi with offerings may seem to denote some relation to the Nativity as an historical fact, the 22 Virgins in their company, the 4 Angels as it were guarding the Mother and Child, and especially the Glory round her head, exclude all but an allegorical or symbolical meaning, and lead to the conclusion that this great corruption of Christianity was established in the Church before the end of the 6th centy., while the absence of similar representations in earlier works would lead to an opposite inference."—*H. Hallam.*

On the opposite side of the nave, the mosaic presents us with a picture of Ravenna at that period, in which we distinguish the Basilica of S. Vitale, and an edifice supposed to represent the palace of Theodoric from its bearing the word *Palatium* on the façade: and 25 saints holding crowns, each having a glory round the head, and receiving the benediction of the Saviour sitting on a throne between 4 angels. The first in the procession is in a violet instead of white tunic, and bears the name of Martinus, the patron of the ch. The rest of these walls, as high as the roof, are covered with mosaics representing the fathers of the Old and New Testaments, and various miracles of the Saviour. Another mosaic, in tolerable preservation, representing the emperor Justinian, is concealed behind the organ. In the nave is the ancient marble pulpit covered with early Christian sculptures, supported by a mass of grey granite. The altars of this ch. are rich in marbles. In the last chapel, opening out of the l. aisle, are some ancient relics—the urn in which are said to be preserved the remains of St. Apollinaris, and beneath the ancient marble chair of the Benedictine abbots, to whom the ch. formerly belonged: it is supposed to be a work of the 10th cent.

The *Ch. of Santa Croce*, built by Galla Placidia in the 5th century, and near her mausoleum, and consecrated by St. Peter Chrysologus, has been sadly ruined.

The *Ch. of San Domenico*, a restoration of an ancient basilica founded by the exarchs, contains some works by *Niccolò Rondinello*, of Ravenna, a pupil of Giov. Bellini. The Virgin and Child with S. Jerome, S. Dominick, S. Joseph, and S. Francis of Assisi, the Annunciation, the S. Domenico and St. Peter in the choir, and the Virgin and Child with the Magdalen and other saints. In the chapel on l. of the high altar is an ancient wooden crucifix curiously covered with fine linen in imitation of human skin, which is said to have sweated blood during the battle of Ravenna under Gaston de Foix. The 2nd chapel on the l. contains, in small circular paintings, the Fifteen Mysteries of the Rosary, by *Luca Longhi:* and the 3rd chapel on the rt. has a picture by the same artist representing the Invention of the Cross. A large painting on panel in the choir, of the Virgin and Child with saints, bears the name of *Benedictus Armini.* Longhi the painter is buried in this ch.

The *Ch. of S. Francesco*, near the Piazza and the Albergo della Spada d'Oro, supposed to have been erected in the middle of the 5th cent., by St. Peter Chrysologus, on the site of a temple of Neptune, has suffered from modern restorations. It has a nave and 2 aisles divided by 22 columns of white and cippolino marble. In the chapel at the extremity of the rt. aisle is the urn containing the remains of S. Liberius, archbishop of the see, a fine work, referred to the 4th or 5th century; on it is a series of bas-reliefs of the 12 Apostles, with the Saviour in the centre. The chapel of the Crucifix contains 2 beautiful columns of Greek marble, decorated with capitals sculptured by *Pietro Lombardo*, by whom likewise are the rich arabesques of the frieze and pilasters. In the l. aisle is the tomb of Luffo Numai, of Forli, secretary of Pino Ordelaffi, lord of that city, the work of *Tommaso Flamberti*. In the 4th chapel on rt. a picture of the Madonna, with the *Donatoria*, by *Sacchi d'Imola*, a rare master. Upon the wall on the rt. of the entrance door is a sepulchral slab tomb, formerly on the floor, with the figure in bas-relief of Ostasio da Polenta, lord of Ravenna, clothed in the dress of a Franciscan monk, and bearing the following inscription in Gothic characters: " Hic jacet magnificus Dominus Hostasius de Polenta qui ante diem felix obiens occubuit MCCCLXXXXVI die xiv mensis Martii, cujus anima requiescat in pace." The head of Ostasio is beautiful. The Polenta family, so celebrated for their hospitality to Dante and for the fate of Francesca da Rimini, are buried in this ch. On the l. side of the doorway is a similar sepulchral stone, on which is sculptured the figure of Enrico Alfieri, general of the Franciscan order, who died at the age of 92, in 1405, as recorded by a long inscription in hexameters. He was of Asti, and probably of the family of the great poet who has given immortality to the name. In the Piazza before this ch. is a statue of Pope Alexander VII. The house which forms the corner of the little square is that which Lord Byron inhabited for several months on his first arrival at Ravenna in 1819.

The *Church of S. Giovanni Battista*, near the Porta Serrata, also called *St. G. dalle Catine*, erected by Galla Placidia for her confessor St. Barbatian in 438, was consecrated by St. Peter Chrysologus, but it was almost entirely rebuilt in 1683. In the Piazzetta before it are 3 huge sarcophagi, the largest of which contains the ashes of Pietro Traversari, lord of Ravenna, who died in 1225. The columns of the interior are chiefly adapted from the ancient building; some of them, however, were found in the neighbourhood of the ch. on the supposed site of the imperial palace in which Galla Placidia resided. The ch. contains 2 paintings by *Francesco Longhi*, one in the l. transept representing the Virgin and Child with St. Clement and St. Jerome; the other, in the 1st chapel on l., the Virgin and Child with St. Matthew and St. Francis of Assisi. The circular Campanile of this ch. is one of the best preserved specimens of this class of Bell-towers, so peculiar to Ravenna; it has six tiers of openings; the upper one of narrow arches, with its terminal cornice and its pyramidal roof entire.

The *Basilica of S. Giovanni Evangelista*, also called *S. Giovanni della Sagra*, in a recess off the Corso di Porta Serrata, was founded in 414 by the Empress Galla Placidia, in fulfilment of a vow made in a tempest during the voyage from Constantinople to Ravenna with her children. Like the cathedral it has lost much of its ancient character by restorations, and most of its mosaics have disappeared. The Church tradition relates that, not knowing with what relic to enrich the church, the empress was praying on the subject when St. John appeared to her in a vision; she threw herself at his feet for the purpose of embracing them, but the evangelist disappeared, leaving one of his sandals as a relic. This vision is represented in a beautiful bas-relief over the pointed doorway, a work probably of the 12th centy.; the lower part shows St. John incensing the altar, with the empress embracing his feet; in the upper part she appears offering the sandal to the Saviour and St. John, while S. Barbatian and his attendants are seen on the other side. The doorway, especially in the small niches, is richly sculptured with figures of saints, and is a very fine specimen of the architecture of the period. The interior of the church, consisting of a nave and aisles, supported by 24 ancient columns, contains the high altar, beneath which repose the remains of SS. Canzius, Canzianus, and Canzianilla, martyrs; in the chapel of St. Bartholomew, at the extremity of the l. aisle, are some fragments of a mosaic representing the storm and the vow of Galla Placidia. The vault of the fourth chapel on the same side is painted by *Giotto*, representing the four Evangelists with their symbols, and St. Gregory, St. Ambrose, St. Augustin, and St. Jerome.

All these frescoes have been more or less repainted, the SS. John, Matthew, and Gregory the least. The walls of the chapel, once covered with frescoes, have been whitewashed over. Beneath the choir is the ancient altar of the confessional, in marble, porphyry, and serpentine, a work of the fifth century. The old quadrangular *Campanile*, the articulations of which were ornamented with white and green mosaics, is remarkable for its 2 bells cast by Robert of Saxony in 1208.

The *Ch.*, or *Oratory of Santa Maria in Cosmedin*, which opens out of the court of the ch. of S. Spirito, near here (see below), was the ancient Arian baptistery: its vault was decorated with mosaics in the 6th century, after it had passed to the Catholic worship. It is an octagonal building. The mosaics of the roof represent the Baptism in the Jordan in the centre, the river issuing from the urn of a river god; the Saviour half immersed in it, and who alone has a glory round the head: lower down, forming a circular band, are the Twelve Apostles, each bearing a crown in his hand, with the exception of St. Peter, who carries the keys, and St. Paul, who bears 2 scrolls, advancing towards a throne covered with a veil and cushion, and occupied by a cross only. Upon the large round block of granite in the centre of the floor is supposed to have stood the ancient baptismal font.

The *Ch. of Sta. Maria in Porto*, near the Porta Nuova, built of the materials from the Basilica of S. Lorenzo in Cesarea, in 1553, with a façade erected in the last century, is perhaps the finest ch. of recent date in Ravenna. It is celebrated for an image of the Virgin, in the chapel of the rt. transept, in marble, in an oriental costume, and in the act of praying—a very early specimen of Christian art, originally placed in the ch. of Sta. Maria in Porto Fuori, and transferred here in the sixteenth century. The 4th chapel on the rt. contains the masterpiece of *Palma Giovane*, the Martyrdom of St. Mark. The 5th chapel of the opposite aisle has a painting by *Luca Longhi*, representing the Virgin, with St. Augustin and other saints.

In the choir is an ancient vase in red porphyry, beautifully worked, supposed to have been a Roman sepulchral urn. The *Ch. of S. Nicolò*, built by Archbishop Sergius, in 768, in fulfilment of a vow, contains numerous paintings by *Padre Cesare Pronti*, an Augustinian monk, sometimes called *P. Cesare di Ravenna*. Among these may be mentioned the St. Thomas of Villanova; the St. Nicholas; the St. Augustin; the Virgin; Sta. Monica, considered his masterpiece; and the San Francesco di Paola. The large painting of the Nativity over the entrance door, the St. Sebastian on the l. wall of the choir towards the nave, and the St. Catherine on the rt., are by *Francesco da Cotignola*, and good specimens of this master; the archangel Raphael is by *Girolamo Genga*. Outside this ch. is one of the largest mediæval sarcophagi in Ravenna. On it are sculptures of the Saviour, of the Annunciation, &c.

The *Ch. of S. Romualdo*, or *Classe*, originally belonging to the Camaldolese order, is now the chapel of the college of Ravenna. The cupola is painted in fresco by *Giambattista Barbiani*, who was also the painter of the S. Romualdo in the choir, and of the frescoes in the 1st chapel on the l. of the entrance. The 2nd chapel contains a picture of S. Romualdo, by *Guercino*. The 1st chapel on the rt. has a painting of S. Bartholomew and S. Severus, by *Franceschini*; and the 2nd a picture of S. Benedict, by *Carlo Cignani*. The sacristy contains 2 fine columns of red porphyry, found near St. Apollinare in Classe; and the picture of the Raising of Lazarus, by *Francesco da Cotignola*. The frescoes of the roof are by *P. Cesare Pronti*. In the refectory of the adjoining convent, now the college, is a fresco of the marriage of Cana, by *Luca Longhi* and his son *Francesco*. The altars of this ch. almost surpass in brilliancy and riches all the others in the city.

The *Ch. of the Santo Spirito*, called also that of *S. Teodoro*, was built in the 6th century by Theodoric, for the Arian bishops; it assumed the name of S. Theodore after its consecration to the Catholic worship by S. Agnellus, and afterwards took the present name.

It is in the form of a small basilica; the arches of its nave being on columns of grey and other marbles, with composite capitals and Latin crosses on their imposts. In front of the ch. is a portico, and near it the Oratory of Sta. Maria in Cosmedin (see p. 518), the once Arian baptistery. Besides its rich marble columns, it contains in the 1st chapel on l. a curious pulpit, or *ambo*, with rude sculptures of the 6th century.

The magnificent *Church of San Vitale* (in a small square, near the ch. of Sta. Maria Maggiore, and the Mausoleum of Galla Placidia) exhibits the octagonal form with all the accessories of Eastern splendour. As one of the earliest Christian temples, it is of the highest interest in the history of art. It was built in the reign of Justinian by S. Ecclesius, the archbishop of the see, on the spot where St. Vitalis suffered martyrdom, and was consecrated by St. Maximianus in 547. It was an imitation of Sta. Sophia at Constantinople, and was adopted by Charlemagne as the model of his church at Aix-la-Chapelle. The original pavement is considerably below the present floor, and is covered with water at times. The architecture of the interior exhibits 8 arches resting on as many piers, between which are semicircular recesses of 2 stories, each divided into 3 small arches by 2 columns between the principal piers. The spaces between the lower columns open into the circular aisle, and those between the upper into a gallery. Above, the building becomes circular. The fourteen columns of the upper story have complicated capitals, some of which bear an anchor, supposed to indicate that they belonged to a temple of Neptune. The 14 columns of the lower range have also Byzantine capitals; and on each of the imposts of these columns are 2 monograms. The pilasters and the walls are covered with large plates of Grecian marble, on which are still to be traced some fragments of a frieze. The colossal dome was painted, in the early part of the 18th century, with frescoes representing the fathers of the Old and New Testaments, with various decorations, such as festoons of roses hanging from the roof; all in the most barbarous taste, and at variance with the architectural character of the building. The dome is constructed of earthen pots, and is perhaps the most perfect specimen known of this kind of work. They are small twisted vessels, having the point of one inserted in the mouth of the other in a continued spiral, and placed horizontally. The spandrils are partially filled with others of larger size, twisted only at the point, and arranged vertically. The walls and vault of the choir are covered with mosaics of the time of Justinian, as beautiful and as fresh as on the day when they were placed there; invaluable as specimens of art, no less than as studies of costume. The most elaborate of these mosaics are those of the tribune, representing in the larger compartments on the l. the Emperor Justinian holding a vase containing consecrated offerings; he is surrounded by courtiers and soldiers, and by St. Maximianus and two priests. In the compartment on the opposite wall is the Empress Theodora with a similar vase, which she offers to two courtiers, attended by the ladies of her court, in varied and elegant costumes; the expression of some of the figures is remarkable, considering the material in which they are represented. In the vault above is the Saviour throned on the globe between the archangels; on his rt. is S. Vitalis receiving the crown of martyrdom; and on the l. S. Eutychius in the act of offering a model of the ch., both saints being without glories round the heads. The roof is decorated with arabesques, urns, the 12 Apostles, and other ornamental devices. The mosaics on the concavity of the arch represent half figures of the Saviour and the 12 Apostles, with St. Gervasius and S. Protasius, sons of S. Vitalis. The semicircular mosaic on the rt. of the altar represents the sacrifices of the Old Law, the Offering of Abel, and of Melchizedek; beyond it Moses, with the sheep of Madan; Moses on Mount Horeb; Moses in the act of taking off his sandals at the command of the Almighty, represented by a hand in the heavens. The corresponding compartments on the opposite wall have reference to the sacrifice by Abraham; the three Angels entertained by the latter on foretelling the birth of a child, while Sarah stands in the doorway ridiculing the prediction; on the sides and above, Moses on Mount Sinai; the prophets Isaiah and Jeremiah; and on a level with the music galleries the four Evangelists with their emblems. The preservation of these extraordinary mosaics, still retaining the freshness of their colours, amidst all the revolutions of Ravenna, is truly wonderful; they have been the admiration of every writer, and they cannot fail to afford the highest interest not merely to the Christian antiquary, but to all travellers of taste. The splendid columns are mostly of Greek marble. On the imposts of the arches of the upper columns on the sides of this choir are two monograms of *Julianus*, written on one of them in the reverse. Near the high altar, on each side, are the celebrated bas-reliefs called the "Throne of Neptune," compared for their execution and design to the finest works of antiquity. In them are seen the throne of the god, with a sea-monster extended beneath it; a winged genius holds a trident on the rt., and on the l. two other genii are seen bearing a large conque shell. The ornaments of these sculptures are pilasters of the Corinthian order, a cornice with tridents, dolphins, shells, and two sea-horses. The columns of verde antico and Egyptian breccia on each side of these bas-reliefs supported the canopy over the high altar of the original ch. Several chapels surround the circular aisle of the basilica: that of the Holy Sacrament has on the altar a gilded ciborium attributed to *Michel Angelo*, and a picture of St. Benedict by *Francesco Gessi*, a pupil of Guido. The Assumption of St. Gertrude in another is by *Andrea Barbiani*. In that of La Pietà is a huge marble group of the Dead Saviour and Marys, by *Foschini* and *Bartos*. Next follows an opening of 3 arches in the outer wall, and immediately opposite to the tribune; this was the entrance to the basilica; it was preceded by a grand portico covered with mosaics, which, as well as the adjoining circular towers, were destroyed by the great earthquake of 1688. The chapel of S. Vitale has a statue by the before-mentioned sculptors. We next reach the *vestibule of the Sacristy*, with a good bas-relief of a sacrifice; it is supposed to have been one of the decorations of a temple dedicated to Augustus. The pictures in the Sacristy are the Virgin and Child throned, with St. Sebastian and other saints, by *Luca Longhi*, a native artist; the Sta. Agata is by his daughter *Barbara*, and the Annunciation by his son *Francesco*; the Martyrdom of S. Erasmus is by another native painter, *Giambattista Barbiani*; the Martyrdom of St. James and St. Philip is by *Camillo Procaccini*. The *Tomb of the Exarch Isaac*, "the great ornament of Armenia," remains to be noticed. It is in a recess off the passage from the side door of the basilica leading towards the street. It was erected to his memory by his wife Susanna, and bears a Greek inscription recording the fame he acquired in the east and in the west, and comparing her widowhood to that of the turtle dove. The urn containing his ashes is of marble, with bas-reliefs of the Adoration of the Magi (it is worthy of remark that there is no glory round the head of the Virgin), the Raising of Lazarus, and Daniel in the Lions' Den. Isaac was the 8th exarch of Ravenna, and died in that city, according to Muratori, A.D. 644. In the same recess are some Roman and early Christian sculptures and inscriptions. A short way beyond here is the

Mausoleum of Galla Placidia, called also the Ch. of SS. Nazario e Celso. This once magnificent sepulchre was built by the Empress Galla Placidia, the daughter of Theodosius the Great, and the mother of Valentinian III., the third and fifth emperors of the West, towards the middle of the 5th century. It is in the form of a Latin cross, 46 English ft. in length and 39¾ in width, and is paved with rich marbles. The cupola is entirely covered with mosaics of the time of the empress, in which we see the four evangelists with their symbols, and on each of the walls two full-length figures of prophets. The arch over the door has a representation of the Good Shepherd; behind the tomb of the empress is the Saviour with the gospels in his hand: and in each of the lateral arches are two stags at a fountain, surrounded by arabesques and other ornaments. The high altar, in the centre of the mausoleum, composed of three massive slabs of Oriental alabaster, was formerly in the ch. of St. Vitale, and is referred to the sixth century. It has reliefs of an early Christian period. The great object of attraction however is the massive marble sarcophagus which contains the ashes of Galla Placidia. It was once covered with silver plates; but these have disappeared, together with the other ornaments with which it was originally decorated. In the side next the wall was formerly a small aperture, through which the body of the empress might be seen, sitting in a chair of cypress wood, clothed in her imperial robes. Some children having introduced a lighted candle, in 1577, the robes took fire, and the body was reduced to ashes; since that time the aperture has remained closed. In the recess on the rt. side of the Mausoleum is another marble sarcophagus with Christian symbols, which contains the remains of the Emperor Honorius II., the brother of Galla Placidia; and on the l. is that of Constantius III., her second husband, and the father of Valentinian III. On each side of the entrance door are two smaller sarcophagi, said to contain the remains of the tutors of Valentinian, and of Honoria, his sister. These sarcophagi are the only tombs of the Cæsars, oriental or occidental, which now remain in their original places. The subterranean mausoleum of Galla Placidia is as a monument of the dreadful catastrophes of the Lower Empire. This daughter of Theodosius, sister of Honorius, mother of Valentinian III., who was born at Constantinople, and died at Rome, was a slave twice, a queen, an empress; first the wife of the King of the Goths, Alaric's brother-in-law, who fell in love with his captive, and afterwards of one of her brother's generals, whom she was equally successful in subjecting to her will: a talented woman, but without generosity or greatness, who hastened the fall of the empire—whose ambition and vices have obscured and, as it were, polluted her misfortunes.

Palace of Theodoric, in the Corso leading from the Porta Serrata to the P. Nuova, and near the ch. of St. Apollinare. Of the palace of the Gothic king, which served as the residence of his successors, of the Exarchs, and of the Lombard kings, the only portion remaining is a high wall, in the upper part of which are eight small marble columns, supporting round arches and a wide recess over the entrance gate. On one side of the latter is a large porphyry urn let into the wall, on which an inscription was placed in 1564, stating that it formerly contained the ashes of Theodoric, and that it was originally placed on the top of his mausoleum. Most antiquaries, however, now consider that it was a bath; the only argument in favour of its having been the sarcophagus of Theodoric is that it was found near his mausoleum. The palace was chiefly ruined by Charlemagne, who, with the consent of the pope, carried away its ornaments and mosaics, and removed to France the equestrian statue of the king which stood near it.

The *Tomb of Dante*, behind the Ch. of S. Francesco, and in the street which bears the name of the poet.—The key is kept at the Palazzo Pubblico, the Custode of which will open it, and of course expect his fee. Of all the monuments of Ravenna, there is none which excites a more profound interest than the tomb of DANTE. In spite of the taste of the building in which it is placed, it is impossible to approach the last resting-place of the great poet without feeling that it is one of the most hallowed monuments of Italy.

" Ungrateful Florence! Dante sleeps afar,
Like Scipio, buried by the upbraiding shore;
Thy factions, in their worse than civil war,
Proscribed the bard, whose name for evermore
Their children's children would in vain adore
With the remorse of ages; and the crown
Which Petrarch's laureate brow supremely
   wore,
Upon a far and foreign soil had grown,
His life, his fame, his grave, though rifled—
not thine own."   *Byron*.

The remains of the poet, who died here on the 14th Sept. 1321, at the age of 56, were originally interred in the ch. of San Francesco; but on the expulsion of his patron Guido da Polenta from Ravenna, they were with difficulty protected from the persecution of the Florentines and the excommunication of the pope. Cardinal Beltramo del Poggetto ordered his bones to be burnt with his tract on Monarchy, and they narrowly escaped the profanation of a disinterment. In 1482 Bernardo Bembo,' Podestà of Ravenna for the republic of Venice, and father of the celebrated cardinal, did honour to his memory by erecting a mausoleum on the present site, from the designs of Pietro Lombardo. In 1692 this building was repaired and restored at the public expense by the legate, Cardinal Corsi of Florence, and rebuilt in its present form in 1780, at the cost of Cardinal Gonzaga. It is a square edifice, with a small dome, internally decorated with stucco ornaments little worthy of such a sepulchre. On the vault of the cupola are four medallions of Virgil, Brunetto Latini (the master of the poet), Can Grande della Scala, and Guido da Polenta, his patron. On the walls are two Latin inscriptions, one in verse, recording the foundation by Bembo, the other the dedication of Cardinal Gonzaga to the "Poetæ sui temporis primo restitutori." Above the marble sarcophagus which contains the ashes of the poet is a bas-relief of his half-figure by Lombardi; he is represented sitting at his desk with his book; is surmounted by a crown of laurel with the motto *Virtuti et honori*. The inscription is said to have been left by himself. Below it, in a marble case, is a long Latin history of the tomb, to which it is not necessary to refer more particularly, as all the leading facts it records have been given above.

The feelings with which this sepulchre was visited by three of the greatest names in modern literature deserve to be mentioned. Chateaubriand is said to have knelt bareheaded at the door before he entered; Byron deposited on the tomb a copy of his works; and Alfieri prostrated himself before it, and embodied his emotions in one of the finest sonnets in the Italian language :—

" O gran padre Alighieri, se dal ciel miri
Me tuo discepol non indegno starmi,
Dal cor traendo profondi sospiri,
Prostrato innanzi a' tuoi funerei marmi," &c.

Lord Byron's lines commemorating the tomb of the poet and the monumental column of Gaston de Foix will scarcely fail to suggest themselves to the reader :—

" I canter by the spot each afternoon
 Where perished in his fame the l er >-boy
Who lived too long for men, but di d t >o soon
 For human vanity, the young De Foix!
A broken pillar, not uncouthly hewn,
 But which neglect is hastening to destroy,
Records Ravenna's carnage on its face,
 While weeds and ordure rankle round the base.

" I pass each day where Dante's bones are laid :
 A little cupola, more neat than solemn,
Protects his dust, but reverence here is paid
 To the bard's tomb, and not the warrior's column ;
The time must come when both, alike decay'd
 The chieftain's trophy, and the poet's volume,
Will sink where lie the songs and wars of earth,
 Before Pelides' death, or Homer's birth.

" With human blood that column was cemented,
 With human filth that column is defiled,
As if the peasant's coarse contempt were vented
 To show his loathing of the spot he soil'd :
Thus is the trophy used, and thus lamented
 Should ever be those bloodhounds, from whose wild
Instinct of gore and glory earth has known
Those sufferings Dante saw in hell alone."

Near the tomb of Dante is the house occupied by *Lord Byron*, whose name and memory are almost as much associated with Ravenna as those of the great "Poet-Sire of Italy." He declared himself more attached to Ravenna than to any other place, except Greece; he praised "its delightful climate," and says he was never tired of his rides in the pine-forest; he liked Ravenna, moreover, because it was out of the beaten track of travellers, and because he found the higher classes of its society well educated and liberal beyond what was usually the case in other continental cities. He resided in it rather more than two years, " and quitted it with the deepest regret, and with a presentiment that his departure would be the forerunner of a thousand evils. He was continually performing generous actions: many families owed to him the few prosperous days they ever enjoyed: his arrival was spoken of as a piece of public good fortune, and his departure as a public calamity." The house of Lord Byron now forms No. 295 in the Strada di Porta Sisi; it was here that our great poet resided for 8 months after his arrival in Ravenna on the 10th of June, 1819. Over the entrance has been recently placed the following inscription commemorative of the fact: — " Il x Giugno MDCCCXIX, come appena giunse in Ravenna, entrava questa casa, allora Grande Albergo, e que otto mese abitava, GIORGIO BYRON, Poeta Inglese, Lieto delle Vicenanze al Sepolcro di Dante, Impaziente di visitare l' Antica Selva, che inspiro gia il Divino e Giovanni Boccaccio." He subsequently removed to the Palazzo Guiccioli, in the Via di Porta Adriana (No. 328), where he continued to reside until his departure for Pisa at the end of Oct. 1821. The 'Prophecy of Dante' was composed here, at the suggestion of the Countess Guiccioli; and the translation of the tale of 'Francesca da Rimini' was " executed at Ravenna, where just five centuries before, and in the very house in which the unfortunate lady was born, Dante's poem had been composed." The 'Morgante Maggiore,' 'Marino Faliero,' the fifth canto of 'Don Juan,' 'The Blues,' 'Sardanapalus,' 'The Two Foscari,' 'Cain,' 'Heaven and Earth,' and the 'Vision of Judgment,' were also written during his residence at

" that place
Of old renown, once in the Adrian sea,
Ravenna! where from Dante's sacred tomb
He had so oft, as many a verse declares,
Drawn inspiration." *Rogers.*

Palaces. — The *Archbishop's Palace*, near the cathedral, is one of the most interesting edifices in Ravenna to the Christian antiquary. The chapel, still used by the archbishops, is the one which was built and used by St. Peter Chrysologus in the 5th century, without the slightest alteration or change: no profaning hand has yet been laid on its altar or mosaics. The walls are covered with large slabs of marble, and the ceiling still retains its mosaics as fresh as when they were first executed. In the middle they represent the symbols of the evangelists; and below, arranged in circles, the Saviour, the apostles, and various saints. The altar has some mosaics which belonged to the tribune of the cathedral previous to its re-erection. In one of the halls of the palace is a collection of ancient Roman and Christian inscriptions, with other fragments of antiquity. In the hall called the " Appartamento Nobile " is a bust of Cardinal Capponi by Bernini, and one of S. Apollinaris by Thorwaldsen. On the 3rd floor is the small *Archiepiscopal library,* formerly celebrated for its records; but most of these disappeared during the political calamities of the city. It still, however, retains the celebrated MS. whose extraordinary size and preservation have made it known to most literary antiquaries: it is a brief of the 12th century, by which Pope Pascal II. confirmed the privileges of the archbishops. The most ancient diplomas preserved in these archives are said to date from the 5th century.

Palazzo del Governo, in the Piazza Maggiore, a building of the 17th century, recently restored, contains nothing to interest the stranger. The portico is supported by 8 granite columns, on 4 of the capitals of which is the monogram of THEODORIC.

Palazzo Comunale, in the same Piazza, has marble busts of 7 cardinal legates, and a portion of the gates of Pavia, captured from that city by the inhab. of Ravenna. The public archives formerly contained a large collection of historical documents, but most of them have disappeared.

Palazzo Cavalli, the *P. Lovatelli,* the *P. Spreti,* &c., had all of them small galleries of paintings. The ceiling of the Pal. Giulio Rasponi, representing the death of Camilla, queen of the Volsci, by *Agricola,* is interesting because the figure of the queen is the portrait of Queen Caroline Murat, one of whose daughters married into the Rasponi family. The *Galleria Rasponi,* liberally open to visitors, has a few good pictures, amongst which may be noticed—*Palmezzano*, Christ on an altar with St. James of Compostello, and St. Sebastian, a fine figure; *Cotignola*, a Virgin and Child; *Luini*, St. Catherine, &c.

The *Biblioteca Comunale*, forming part of the *Collegio*, which occupies the buildings of the Carthusian monastery of Classe, adjoining the ch. of St. Romualdo. The library was founded by the Abbot Caneti in 1714, and subsequently enriched by private munificence and by the libraries of suppressed convents. It consists of a fine hall, followed by several smaller ones, and contains upwards of 50,000 volumes, 700 manuscripts, and a large collection of first editions of the 15th century. Among its MS. collections, the most precious is the celebrated *Aristophanes*, copied in the 10th century by Cyrillus Machirius, a Florentine, long known as unique. It is recorded of this MS. that Eugene Beauharnois wished to purchase it; but the inhab., being resolved not to lose so great a treasure, concealed the volume. A MS. of *Dante*, on vellum, with good initial miniatures of the 14th century; another Dante, of still earlier date; a small *Officium*, most beautifully written on parchment, with lovely miniatures of histories of Christ, of the 14th centy., ending with an invocation to all the saints to relieve its writer from his worldly ailments, amongst which his toothache is particularly alluded to; and another Officium, with numerous illuminations, &c., on violet vellum, especially one of the Crucifixion. Among the *princeps* editions, which range from 1465 to 1500, are the *Decretals of Boniface VIII.*, on *vellum*, 1465; the *Pliny the Younger*, on *vellum*, 2 vols. *Venice*, 1468; the *Bible, with miniatures, on kid*, 1478; the *St. Augustin, De Civitate Dei*, 1468; the *Dante of Lodovico and Alberto Piemontesi*, 1478. Among the miscellaneous collection may be noticed, the *History of the Old and New Testament, in Chinese, printed on silk*, and a series of upwards of 4000 rolls, beginning with the 11th and ending with the last centy., chiefly relating to the order of the Canons of Sta. Maria in Porto.

The *Refettorio del Collegio*, a fine hall, with good carved wood ceiling and doors, contains one of the elder *Lunghi's* best works, a fresco of the Marriage of Cana, into which he has introduced his own portrait, and those of several of his Ravennese cotemporaries. The veil thrown over the woman on the l. of Christ was added by his daughter Barbara, to satisfy the scruples of S. Carlo Borromeo, then Legate here.

The *Museum* consists of several rooms, forming a suite to those of the Library, and, besides a good miscellaneous collection of vases, idols, bronzes, majolica, and carved work in ivory, contains a rich cabinet of *medals*, ancient and modern. The ancient are arranged in 3 classes: 1. Medals of the free cities: 2. Consular; and 3. Imperial. In the 2nd class is a bronze one of Cicero, struck by the town of Magnesia, in Lydia: it bears on one side his profile and name in Greek characters, and on the other a hand holding a crown with a branch of laurel, an ear of corn, a bough of the vine bearing a bunch of grapes, with the inscription in Greek "Theodore of the Magnesians, near Mount Sipylus." It is supposed to be an unique specimen. There is a very interesting series of the coins of the Sovereigns of the Western Empire found about Ravenna, especially golden ones of Galla Placidia with a cross on the obverse, of Valentinian III., Anastasius, Heraclius, &c., with Christian emblems. The modern collection is also arranged in 3 classes: 1. Medals of the Popes from Gregory III.; 2. Medals of illustrious personages and of royal dynasties; 3. Coins of various Italian cities. In the 1st class is a fine medal of Benedict III., interesting because it is considered conclusive as to the fable of Pope Joan. In the 2nd class is a complete series of bronze medals of the House of Medici, 84 in number, of an uniform size. Among the ivories one is remarkable as representing several of the miracles which are seen in the paintings on the Catacombs at Rome: such as Jonas, the raising of Lazarus, the raising of the Paralytic, &c., with two venerable figures in the centre. The Museum also contains portions of beautiful gold ornaments of ancient armour, discovered some years ago in excavating the new docks on the canal; they are supposed to have belonged to Odoacer, whose tomb may have been hereabouts; unfortunately the greater part of them were melted down.

Galleria Lapidaria.—In one of the lower corridors of the College have been placed several inscriptions, both pagan and early Christian, most of which were found about Ravenna; and a series of Roman tiles, or *Signa Tegularia*, bearing the makers' names. On one of these tiles is the impression of a sandal, very like the sole of a modern shoe with its hob-nails.

The *Academy of the Fine Arts*, in the building adjoining the Collegio, formerly the offices of the convent of Classe, is an institution that does honour to its founder and first director, Ignazio Sarti, and to the patriotic and enlightened feelings of the citizens. It contains a Pinacoteca or museum of pictures, and a good collection of plaster casts of celebrated masterpieces of ancient and modern sculpture; attached to it are schools of design for young artists, &c. Many of the resident nobility, desirous of promoting the design, had removed their family collections from their palaces and deposited them in this public museum, but most have been since returned to their owners. As a whole, the Pinacoteca is far behind those of Ferrara, Forli, &c. The Municipality has contributed the pictures in its possession. Among the works it contains may be mentioned—*Daniele da Volterra*, the Crucifixion; *Luca Lunghi*, the Holy Family, Portrait called erroneously of Charles V., the Deposition, the Nativity, Virgin and Child throned, Portrait of Giovanni Arrigone (one of *Lunghi's* best works); *Vasari*, the Deposition; *Luca Giordano*, the Flight out of Egypt; *Francesco da Cotignola*, the Virgin throned; *Innocenzo da Imola*, Descent of the Holy Spirit; *Vandevelde* and *Berghem*, landscapes. There are a great number of small paintings of the Byzantine school. In one of the rooms on the upper floor is a fine mosaic pavement, found at Classe, with a vase of flowers and peacocks in the centre, and the beautiful recumbent statue of Guidarello Guidarelli, called Bracciaforte, formerly in the church of San Francesco.

The *Hospital*, formerly the convent of S. Giovanni Evangelista, near the Porta Serrata, was founded by Archbishop Codronchi at his own expense, in order to supersede the old hospital in the Via del Griotto. In the court is a cistern said to have been designed by Michel Angelo.

Theatre.—A new and magnificent one, the *Teatro Alighieri*, was opened in 1850, near the Piazza Maggiore, in the street in which is situated the Albergo della Spada d'Oro.

The *Piazza Maggiore*, supposed to correspond with the ancient Forum, has 2 granite columns erected by the Venetians, one of which bears the statue of S. Apollinaris by Pietro Lombardo; the other S. Vitalis by Clemente Molli, which replaced a figure of St. Mark by Lombardo, in 1509, when Ravenna was restored to the Church. Between them is the sitting statue of Clement XII., with an inscription recording that it was erected by the "S. P. Q." of Ravenna, in gratitude for the service rendered by that pontiff in diverting the channel of the Ronco and Moutone; from the inundations of which the city was threatened. At one extremity of the Piazza is the *Palazzo Communativo*, or Guildhall; at the other the Dogana, formerly a ch. Between these two, forming one of the long sides of the Piazza, are the *Palazzo Governativo*, the seat of the Provincial Administration, and an open portico of wide arches on ancient columns of granite, with ill-adapted marble capitals, upon some of which is a monogram believed to be that of Theodoric.

The *Piazza dell' Aquila* is so called from the column of grey granite surmounted by an eagle, the arms of Cardinal Caetani, to whose memory it was erected in 1609.

The *Piazza del Duomo* has a similar column of grey granite, surmounted with a statue of the Virgin, placed there in 1659.

The *Torre del Pubblico*, near the Piazza Maggiore, a large square leaning tower, cannot fail to attract the notice of the stranger: nothing is known of its history or origin.

The *Six Gates* of Ravenna merit notice; the *Porta Adriana*, at the W. extremity of the city, a handsome entrance of the Doric order, was erected in 1585, on the supposed site of the famous Porta Aurea built under Claudian and ruined by the Emperor Frederick II. It derives its name from being placed on the road leading to Adria. The *Porta Alberoni*, on the E., also called P. Corsini in honour of Clement XII., was built by Cardinal Alberoni in 1739. Immediately outside of it are the modern port of Ravenna, and the road leading to the harbour on the Adriatic and to the Pineta. On the S. side of the town the *Porta S. Mamante*, of the Tuscan order, so called from a neighbouring monastery dedicated to S. Mama, was built in 1612, and called P. Borghesia, in honour of Paul V. Near this the French army of 1512 effected the breach in the walls by which they entered and sacked the city. The *Porta Nuova*, designed by Bernini, in the Corinthian order, occupies the site of the P. San Lorenzo, rebuilt in 1653 under the name of P. Pamfilia, in honour of Innocent X., by whose arms it is surmounted. The road from it leads through the Borgo of Porta Nuova to the public promenade, the Ponte Nuovo, the Basilica of S. Apollinare in Classe, and to Rimini. The *Porta Sisi*, in the Doric style, was rebuilt in its present form in 1568, on the site of an ancient gateway, the name of which is unknown. The *Porta Serrata*, at the N. extremity, so called because it was closed by the Venetians during their possession of Ravenna, was re-opened by Julius II. under the name of P. Giulia.

The *Fortress* of Ravenna was erected by the Venetians in 1457, and then esteemed one of the strongest in Italy: it was partly demolished in 1735 to furnish materials for the Ponte Nuovo over the united stream of the Ronco and Montone, and little now remains but the foundations.

The *Port of Ravenna*, immediately outside of the Porta Alberoni, is still much frequented by the coasting craft of the Adriatic. It consists of a long basin, with quays on either side; from it commences the canal that leads to the Adriatic. The old Porto Candiano being rendered useless by the diversion of the Ronco and Montone, the *Naviglio* or Canal was opened in 1737, for the purpose of effecting a direct communication with the sea at the new *Porto Corsini*. The length of this canal is about 7 miles, and a broad road has been made along its rt. bank, which contributes much to the accommodation of the city. Boats may be hired here for the passage by the canals to Chioggia or Venice. (See Rte. 68.)

About half a mile beyond the Porta Serrata, taking the road on the rt. immediately beyond the gate, is the *Mausoleum of Theodoric*, more generally known as the *Rotonda*: it was built by Theodoric himself, in the beginning of the 6th cent. On the expulsion of the Arians, the zeal of the Church in promoting the Catholic worship ejected the ashes of the king as an Arian heretic, and despoiled his sepulchre of its ornaments. It has successively borne the names of *Sta. Maria in Memoriam Regis*, of *Sta. Maria ad Farum*, and *Sta. Maria Rotonda*. It is a rotunda, built of blocks of limestone from Istria, resting on a decagonal basement, each side of which has a recess surmounted by an arch formed of 11 blocks of stone curiously notched into each other. A double oblique flight of steps leads to the upper story, or sepulchral chamber; they were added to the building in 1780. The upper story is also decagonal externally, and appears to have been surrounded by columns forming a circular portico, several of the bases of which were discovered in digging out the ditch that now surrounds the building. In one of the sides is the door. Over this is a broad projecting band encircling the monument, above which is a row of small windows, the whole surmounted by a massive cornice, with rudely-sculptured reliefs. The vault stones of the doorway are curiously notched into each other, forming a straight arch or lintel. The roof is formed by a single block of limestone containing fossil shells, 36 feet in its internal diameter, hollowed out to the depth of 10, in the shape of an inverted calotte or shallow bowl; the thickness of the centre is about 4 feet, and of the edges about 2 feet 9 inches. The weight of this enormous mass is estimated at above 200 tons. On the outside are 12 pointed projections perforated as if designed for handles: they bear the names of the 12 apostles, but it is difficult to conceive how any statues could have stood on them; they more probably served in moving this huge solid mass of Istrian marble, —indeed, these names look comparatively recent. The summit is flat, and upon it may have stood a statue of the Gothic king. It is now divided into two unequal portions by a large crack, produced, it is supposed, by lightning. The chamber in the basement is filled with water to the depth of 4 feet, so that, notwithstanding the excavations of late years, a considerable portion of its lower story and of the fine arched niches that encircle it still remain buried. The interior of the upper chamber is circular, with a niche opposite the door, in which probably stood a sepulchral urn, although when carefully examined on the outside it appears to have been added after the mausoleum was finished. The chamber in the basement is in the form of a Greek cross; the fine door opening into it, as well as that to the sepulchral one above, is turned towards the west.

About 2 m. from the city, beyond the Porta Alberoni, is the *Ch. of Sta. Maria in Porto Fuori*, built towards the end of the 11th century by B. Pietro Onesti, called *Il Peccatore*, in fulfilment of a vow to the Virgin made during a storm at sea. The l. nave on entering the ch. contains the ancient sarcophagus in which the body of the founder was deposited in 1119. The chief interest of this ch. arises from its frescoes attributed erroneously to *Giotto*, although probably by some of his pupils, in noticing which Lanzi justly alludes to the honour conferred upon Ravenna by the family of the Polentas, in leaving behind them at their fall the memory of the two great names of Dante and Giotto. It was believed that the entire ch. was covered with the frescoes of that great master; and the lateral chapels, part of the l. wall of the middle aisle, and other parts of the ch., still retain sufficient to give some weight to the belief that they are by his scholars. The *Choir* is completely covered with them; on the l. wall are the Nativity, and the Presentation of the Virgin; the rt. wall contains the Death, Assumption, and Coronation of the Virgin, and the Massacre of the Innocents. The frescoes of the tribune represent various events in the life of the Saviour; under the arches are different Fathers and Martyrs; and on the ceiling are the four Evangelists with their symbols, and four Doctors of the Church. The quadrangular basement of the *Campanile* is considered to be the lower part of the Pharos or Torre Farea, the ancient lighthouse of the port, which is supposed to have been situated at this spot; from this circumstance the ch. derives the name of "*di Porto* without the walls."

Basilica of S. Apollinare in Classe.— No traveller should leave Ravenna without visiting this magnificent basilica, which is a purer specimen of Christian art than any which can be found even in Rome. It lies on the road to Rimini, and may therefore be visited by persons proceeding there; but the distance from the city-gate (Porta Nuova), about 2½ m., will not deter the traveller interested in early Christian antiquities from devoting an hour or two to it, as a separate excursion. About ¼ m. beyond the gate, after passing the Borgo, a Greek cross, called *la Crocetta*, on a small fluted marble column, in the public walk, marks the site of the once splendid Basilica of S. Lorenzo in *Cesarea*, founded (A.D. 396) by Lauritius, chamberlain of the Emperor Honorius, and destroyed in 1553 to supply materials for the ch. of Sta. Maria in Porto within the city. This act of spoliation was opposed by the citizens; but the monks to whom the basilica belonged had obtained the consent of the pope, and the cardinal legate, Capo di Ferro, completed the work of Vandalism by sending all its columns excepting the two now on the façade of Sta. Maria in Porto, together with its precious marbles, to Rome. The ancient basilica was the last relic of the city of *Cesarea*, which had existed from the time of Augustus. A short distance beyond, the united stream of the Ronco and Montone is crossed by the *Ponte Nuovo*, a bridge of 5 arches, erected whilst Cardinal Alberoni was legate of Romagna. From this bridge the view is extremely interesting, embracing from the Alps to the Apennines, with the tower of Santa Maria in Porto fuori and the Pineta on the l., and the ch. of S. Apollinare to the S., surrounded by rice-fields and marshes. The road crosses the marshy plain for about 1¼ m.; and about 1 m. from the pine-forest is *S. Apollinare in Classe*. This grand basilica was erected in 534, by Julianus Argentarius, on the site of a temple of Apollo, and was consecrated by archbishop St. Maximianus in 549. It formerly had a quadriporticus in front, but of which no portion now remains. It is built of thin bricks or tiles, in the manner of Roman edifices of classical times. Over the door may be seen the bronze hooks used to sustain the awning on festivals. The interior, 172¾ ft. long by 92¾ wide, is divided by 24 elegant columns of grey Cipolino marble into a nave and two aisles of lofty and imposing proportions. These columns, which rest on elegant square pedestals, are surmounted by complicated capitals, on which again rest quadrangular imposts, with crosses sculptured on the sides towards the nave, and support roundheaded arches and a wall, with double semicircular windows. From the nave a flight of broad steps leads to the high altar, placed above a crypt, and to the choir and tribune, which is circular internally, and polygonal on the outside. The floor of the nave is green with damp, and many times in the year the subterranean chapel of the saint is filled with water. The walls of the nave, and part of those of the aisles, are decorated with a chronological series of portraits of the bishops and archbishops of Ravenna, beginning with St. Apollinaris of Antioch, a follower of St. Peter, who suffered martyrdom under Vespasian, A.D. 74. These portraits are painted; they come down in unbroken succession to the last archbishop, who is the 129th prelate from the commencement. They have a common character, and do not seem to have been executed for the archbishops successively; the earlier, of course, are apocryphal. The mosaics of the nave have disappeared, and the marbles which once covered the walls of the aisles were carried off by Sigismundo Malatesta, to adorn the ch. of S. Francesco, at Rimini. In the middle of the nave is a small marble altar, dedicated to the Virgin, " Martyrum Reginæ," by St. Maximianus, in the 6th century; beneath lay the body of St. Apollinaris, until removd to the crypt in 1173. *In the l. aisle* are 4 marble sarcophagi, covered with basreliefs and Christian symbols, in which are buried 4 of the archbishops of Ravenna ; of two only the owners are known—the first to Felix, with an inscription, the fourth to Johannes V. On the wall there is an inscription, which seems not to be older than the 18th century, beginning, "Отно III. Rom. Imp.," recording, as a proof of his remorse for the murder of Crescentius, that, "ob patrata crimina," he walked barefooted from Rome to Monte Gargano, and passed 40 days in penance in this basilica, "expiating his sins with sackcloth and voluntary scourging." At the extremity of the l. aisle is the undecorated chapel of the Holy Cross, and near its entrance a very curious tabernacle of the 9th centy., over the altar of S. Felicola, raised by a certain Petrus, a Presbyter. *In the rt. aisle* are 4 sarcophagi, similar to those just described, and likewise containing the remains of early archbishops of the diocese. All these tombs were placed in the early ages of the Church under the portico in the fore court, and were removed to their present sites long subsequently. An inscription in the wall of this aisle records that the body of St. Apollinaris formerly was deposited behind a grating in it. On each side of the grand entrance is a sarcophagus of marble, larger than the preceding, but covered with similar ornaments and symbols. The high altar, beneath which rests the body of the saint, is

Route 69.—Ravenna—The Pineta.

rich in marbles and other ornaments; the modern canopy over it is supported by 4 columns of the rare marble known by the modern name of *bianco e nero antico*. The *tribune*, and the arch in front of it, are covered with *mosaics* of the 6th century, in fine preservation. The upper part on the vault represents the Transfiguration; the hand of the Almighty is seen pointing to a small figure of the Saviour introduced into the centre of a large cross, surrounded by a blue circle studded with stars. On the top of the cross are the 5 Greek letters expressing, "Jesus Christ, the Saviour, the Son of God." On the arms are the Alpha and Omega; and at the foot the words, "Salus Mundi." Outside the circle, and on either side of the hand, are Moses and Elijah; and below are 3 sheep, indicating the 3 apostles — Peter, James, and John, who witnessed the Transfiguration. In the middle mosaic is St. Apollinaris, in his episcopal robes, preaching to a flock of sheep, a common emblem of a Christian congregation. Between the windows are the portraits of S. Ecclesius, S. Severus, S. Ursus, and S. Ursicinus, in pontifical robes, in the act of blessing the people. On the rt. hand wall is represented Archbishop Reparatus obtaining privileges for his diocese from the Emperor Constantinus Pogonotus, who is seen in the centre of the composition, with Reparatus attended by 3 ecclesiastics, to whom the Emperor delivers a scroll, on which is inscribed the word *Privilegium*. On the rt. wall are represented the sacrifices of the Old Law: Abel, who offers the lamb, Melchisedek the bread and wine, and Abraham his son Isaac. On the arch is a series of 5 mosaics; that in the middle represents the Saviour, and the symbols of the 4 evangelists; in the second are seen the cities of Bethlehem and Jerusalem, from which a number of the faithful, under the form of sheep, are ascending towards our Lord; in the third is a palm, as a symbol of victory; the fourth contains the archangels Michael and Gabriel; and the fifth, half-figures of St. Matthew and St. Luke; the lower edge of the arch has handsome mosaics of arabesque ornaments.

In the crypt beneath the choir, to which the entrance is by two passages from the base of the stairs, is the sepulchral urn of St. Apollinaris. This urn contained the remains of the saint until 1725, when they were placed beneath the high altar. The crypt is damp and green from being frequently inundated. The stone book by the side, near one of the doors leading to the crypt, is called the breviary of Gregory the Great. The Bell-tower of St. Apollinare is a fine example of those circular Campaniles which are so peculiar to Ravenna; it is 120 ft. high and 33 in diameter at the base. This tower can be ascended (through the sacristy) by a series of ladders to a height of 100 feet; from the top the view is very fine, embracing the pine forest and the sea beyond to the E.; to the S. the Apennines, with Cesena and Bertinoro at their base; and, in fine weather, the Alps of the Tyrol and Styria on the N. This tower contains only two small bells. It is entirely built of brick.

The ancient town of *Classis*, of which this noble basilica is the representative, was one of the 3 quarters of Ravenna in the time of Augustus. It was, as its name imports, the station of the Roman fleet and then close to the sea, which is now 4 m. distant. With the exception of the present ch., the town was totally destroyed in 728 by Liutprand, king of the Lombards. Attached to the ch. are some farm-buildings, through which admittance to the Basilica will be obtained, as it is only open to the public at a very early hour, when a priest from Ravenna arrives to celebrate mass.

The celebrated *Pineta*, or Pine (*Pinus Pinea*) *Forest*, is reached not far beyond the basilica, and the road to Rimini skirts it as far as Cervia; although the most convenient will be that which passes by the Tomb of Theodoric, or through the Porta Alberoni, reaching it beyond the ch. of Sta. Maria in Porto fuori. This venerable forest extends along the shores of the Adriatic for a distance of 25 m., from the Lamone N. of Ravenna to Cervia on the S., and covers a sandy tract, varying in breadth from 1 to 3 m., thrown up by the sea, and separating it, as along the Pontine marshes, from the inundated region on the W. It affords abundant sport; and the produce of its cones, said to average 2000 rubbii annually, yields a considerable revenue. No forest is more renowned in classical and poetical interest: its praises have been sung by Dante, Boccaccio, Dryden, and Byron; it supplied Rome with timber for her fleets; and upon the masts which it produced the banner of Venice floated in the days of her supremacy. One part of the forest still retains the name of the *Vicolo de' Poeti*, from a tradition that it is the spot where Dante loved to meditate:—

> "Tal, qual di ramo in ramo si raccoglie,
> Per la pineta in sul lito di Chiassi,
> Quando Eolo scirocco for discioglie."
> *Purg.* xxviii. 20.

Boccaccio made the Pineta the scene of his singular tale *Nastagio degli Onesti*; the incidents of which, ending in the amorous conversion of the ladies of Ravenna, have been made familiar to the English reader by Dryden's adoption of them in his *Theodore and Honoria*. Count Gamba relates that the first time he had a conversation with Lord Byron on the subject of religion was while riding through this forest in 1820. "The scene," he says, "invited to religious meditation; it was a fine day in spring. 'How,' said Byron, 'raising our eyes to heaven, or directing them to the earth, can we doubt of the existence of God?—or how, turning them to what is within us, can we doubt that there is something more noble and durable than the clay of which we are formed?'" The Pineta inspired also those beautiful lines in the 3rd canto of Don Juan:—

> "Sweet hour of twilight!—In the solitude
> Of the pine-forest, and the silent shore
> Which bounds Ravenna's immemorial wood,
> Rooted where once the Adrian wave flow'd o'er,
> To where the last Cæsarean fortress stood,
> Evergreen forest! which Boccaccio's lore
> And Dryden's lay made haunted ground to me,
> How have I loved the twilight hour and thee!
>
> The shrill cicalas, people of the pine,
> Making their summer lives one ceaseless song,
> Were the sole echoes, save my steed's and mine,
> And vesper bells that rose the boughs along:

> The spectre huntsman of Onesti's line,
> His bell-dogs, and their chase, and the fair throng
> Which learn'd from his example not to fly
> From a true lover,—shadow'd my mind's eye."

The Pineta is a vast succession of lovely avenues and glades, upon which you can drive for miles over the turf: in doing so, however, it will be advisable to have one of the keepers for guide, as they will point out all the picturesque spots; they may be found at the ferry.

La Colonna de' Francesi. Beyond the Porta Sisi, about 2 m. from Ravenna, on the banks of the Ronco, is a square pillar erected in 1557 by Pietro Cesi, president of Romagna, as a memorial of the battle gained by the combined army of Louis XII. and the Duke of Ferrara over the troops of Julius II. and the King of Spain, April 11, 1512. Four inscriptions on the medallions of the pilaster, and an equal number on the 4 sides of the pedestal, record the events of that memorable day. Lord Byron mentions the engagement and the column in a passage quoted in the description of the tomb of Dante, and commemorates the untimely fate of the heroic Gaston de Foix, who fell in the very moment of victory. "The monument of such a terrible engagement, which left 20,000 men dead on the field, and made the Chevalier Bayard write from the spot, 'If the king has gained the battle, the poor gentlemen have truly lost it,' is little funereal or military; it is ornamented with elegant arabesques of vases, fruit, festoons, dolphins, and loaded with 8 long tautological inscriptions, and one of them is a rather ridiculous *jeu de mots*. The speech that Guicciardini makes Gaston address to the soldiers on the banks of the Ronco is one of the most lauded of those pieces, diffuse imitations of the harangues of ancient historians. Besides the illustrious captains present at this battle, such as Vittorio and Fabrizio Colonna, the Marquis della Palude, the celebrated engineer Pedro Navarra, taken prisoners by the French, and Anne de Montmorency, yet a youth, afterwards constable of France under 4 kings, who began his long military career amid this triumph, several persons eminent in letters were there—Castiglione and Ariosto; Leo X., then Cardinal de' Medici, as papal legate to the Spaniards, was taken prisoner. The bard of the Orlando, who has alluded to the horrible carnage he witnessed, must have been powerfully impressed by it, to paint his battles with so much fire. In several passages of his poem Ariosto attributes the victory on this occasion to the skill and courage of the Duke of Ferrara. It has been stated that Alfonso, in reply to an observation that part of the French army was as much exposed to his artillery as the army of the allies, said to his gunners, in the heat of the conflict, 'Fire away! fear no mistake —they are all our enemies!' Leo X. redeemed the Turkish horse which he rode on that day, and used it in the ceremony of his *possesso* (taking possession of the tiara at St. John Lateran), celebrated April 11, 1513, the anniversary of the battle. He had this horse carefully tended till it died, and permitted no one to mount it."— *Valery.*

ROUTE 70.

BOLOGNA TO RAVENNA, BY MEDICINA AND LUGO.
About 50 m.

This is the most direct route, A diligence runs every day from Bologna to Ravenna: fares 15 pauls, coupé 18: it employs 10 hours, and starts early in the morning in winter and at midnight in summer, from the Albergo dei Tre Rè and from the Albergo delle Due Torri at Bologna. This conveyance offers the most convenient means of reaching Ravenna. Vetturini will be found for about 8 scudi, which will perform the journey in 10 to 12 hours.

The distance from Bologna to Medicina is about 18 English m.; the road passing through one of the richest agricultural districts of La Romagna, crossing successively the Idice, Quaderna, and Gajana streams, flowing towards the Po; about 10 m. beyond Medecina it leaves, on the l., Massa Lombarda, and, after crossing the river Santerno, joins the road from Imola to Ravenna at Lugo (see Rte. 69).

ROUTE 71.

RAVENNA TO RIMINI, BY CERVIA.
4½ posts = 35 m.

This is a good road, although not supplied with post-horses. (The postmaster at Ravenna will send a relay of horses to Cesenatico, or will convey travellers the whole way to Rimini with the same horses, by allowing a halt of two hours at the latter place.) It follows the shores of the Adriatic, but presents few objects of interest, and the sea is generally concealed by banks of sand.

The first portion of this route, as far as S. Apollinare, has been described in the account of that basilica. After passing through the Pineta for several m., the road crosses the Savio at S. Saverio, and through *Cervia*, an episcopal town of 2230 souls on the Adriatic, in an unhealthy situation close to very extensive salt-works, upon which its prosperity depends. Farther S. is the town of *Cesenatico,* partly surrounded with walls, but presenting no object of any interest to detain the traveller. It is about half way between Ravenna and Rimini, and is therefore the usual resting-place of the vetturini. (Inn clean, with good bed-rooms.— *T. B.*, 1859.)

Beyond this we pass some small torrents which have been erroneously supposed to be the Rubicon. Farther on, at the distance of 9 m. from Rimini, near San Martino, we cross a wooden bridge spanning the Uso, a considerable and rapid stream, descending to the sea from Sant' Arcangelo, and called by the people on the spot *Il Rubicone.* The reasons for regarding this as the Rubicon, to the exclusion of the numerous streams whose pretensions to that distinction have been advocated by former travellers, will be stated at length in the next route.

The present route falls into the high post-road at Celle shortly before it reaches the Marecchia, and Rimini is entered by the Bridge of Augustus. 35 m. RIMINI (Rte. 72).

ROUTE 72.

BOLOGNA TO RIMINI, BY IMOLA, FAENZA, FORLI, CESENA, AND SAVIGNANO, WITH EXCURSION TO SAN MARINO.

	POSTS.
Bologna to S. Niccolò	1¼
S. Niccolò to Imola	1¼
Imola to Faenza	1
Faenza to Forlì	1
Forlì to Cesena	1¼
Cesena to Savignano	1
Savignano to Rimini	1

7½ posts = 59½ miles.

The road from Bologna to Forlì follows the line of the ancient *Via Æmilia*, which extended from Piacenza to Rimini.* It is the high post-road, is perfectly level, and runs in a straight line through Imola and Faenza to Forlì. The country through which it passes is highly cultivated, and is one of the most productive districts in Northern Italy. A railway is now in progress: it will be opened as far as Faenza early in next year and to Rimini in all 1861.

* The Via Æmilia, commenced by the Consul Marcus Æmilius Lepidus (B.C. an. 87), formed the continuation of the Via Flaminia towards Cisalpine Gaul. The principal stations, with their respective distances, were—

	M. P.
Placentia (Piacenza) to	
Florentia (Firenzuola)	XV.
Fidentia (Borgo S. Donino)	X.
Parma (Parma)	XV.
Tametum (Taneto)	VII.
Regium Lepidi (Reggio)	XI.
Mutina (Modena)	XVII.
Forum Gallorum (nr. Castel Franco)	VIII.
Bononia (Bologna)	XVII.
Claterna (Quaderna)	X.
Forum Cornelii (Imola)	XIV.
Faventia (Faenza)	X.
Forum Livii (Forlì)	X.
Forum Populii (Forlimpopoli)	VII.
Cæsena (Cesena)	VII.
Ad Confluentes (nr. Savignano)	VIII.
Ariminum (Rimini)	XII.

Leaving Bologna, the road crosses the Savena and the Idice (*Idex*), and proceeds through the village of S. Lazzaro, to

1¼ S. Nicolò, a village near the site of the Roman station of Claternum. Between this and Imola we pass through *Castel S. Pietro*, a fortified town on the Silaro (*Silurus*), whose castle was built by the Bolognese in the 13th century.

1¼ *Imola* (*Inns:* S. Marco, good; i Tre Mori, kept by Lama, newly fitted up, clean, 1857). This town, on the Santerno, the ancient Vartrenus, occupies the site of Forum Cornelii. It is generally considered to have been founded by the Lombards. In the middle ages its position between Bologna and Romagna made it an important acquisition in the contests for power: it was successively held by the different chiefs who exercised their sway in the cities of central Italy, and was united to the States of the Church under Julius II. As Forum Cornelii, and one of the stations of the Emilian Way, it was a place of some importance; it is mentioned by Cicero, and by Martial in his 3rd Ep.—

" Si veneris unde requiret,
Æmiliæ dices de regione viæ.
Si quibus in terris, qua simus in urbe rogabit,
Corneli referas me, licet, esse Foro."

The present town, with a pop. of 9320, contains little to detain the traveller. Among its public establishments are the *Hospital*, a *Theatre*, and a small *Public Library*, containing a MS. Hebrew Bible on parchment, of the 13th century, much prized by Cardinal Mezzofanti.

The *Cathedral*, dedicated to S. Cassianus the Martyr, contains the bodies of that saint, and of St. Peter Chrysologus, archbishop of Ravenna, who was born here about A.D. 400. Vassalva, the celebrated anatomist, was also born at Imola in 1666. The bishopric dates from 422, in the pontificate of Celestin I.; S. Cornelius was its first bishop. Pius VII. was bishop of Imola at the period of his elevation to the pontificate in 1900, as well as the reigning pontiff, Pius IX., in 1847.

The works of Innocenzo da Imola

must not be looked for in this his native own; the Palazzo Pubblico contained 2 of his paintings, but, as he lived almost entirely in Bologna, he probably found little patronage in the city of his birth.

[At Riola, 11 m. from Imola, in a picturesque valley of the Apennines, are some ferruginous mineral springs frequented in July and August.]

[A road leads from Imola to Ravenna, through Lugo, 5 posts (Rte. 69); but travellers not desirous of visiting *Lugo* will find a shorter and more convenient one from Faenza to the city of the Exarchs. See Rte. 67.]

Leaving Imola, we pass the Santerno by a handsome modern bridge. Midway between it and Faenza is *Castel Bolognese*, so called from the fortress built there by the Bolognese in 1380. In 1434 it was the scene of a decisive battle between the Florentines and the Milanese commanded by Piccinino, and the Florentines by Nicolò da Tolentino and Gattamelata. The army of the Florentines, amounting to 9000 men, was completely overthrown; Tolentino, Orsini, and Astorre Manfredi lord of Faenza, were made prisoners, together with the entire army, with the exception of 1000 horse; and what was more remarkable, only 4 were left dead on the field, and 30 wounded. Beyond Castel Bolognese, the Senio (*Sinnus*) is crossed.

1 FAENZA (*Inn:* La Corona or la Posta) occupies the site of the ancient *Faventia*, celebrated in the history of the civil wars for the victory of Sylla over the party of Carbo. It is on the Lamone (*Anemo*), and contains a population of 19,942 souls. It has several handsome edifices, and is built in a quadrangular form, divided by 4 principal streets which meet in the Piazza: it is surrounded by walls. Faenza is memorable in Italian history for its capture by the English condottiere, Sir John Hawkswood, then in the service of Gregory XI.: he entered the town March 29, 1376, and delivered it up to a frightful military execution and pillage; 4000 persons, says Sismondi, were put to death, and their property pillaged. Among the masters under whose sovereignty Faenza figures in the middle ages, the Pagani will not fail to suggest themselves to the reader of Dante. The poet, in the beautiful passage alluding to Machinardo Pagano under his armorial bearings, a lion azure on a field argent, says, in reply to the inquiry of Guido da Montefeltro,

" La città di Lamone e di Santerno
Conduce il leoncel dal nido bianco,
Che muta parte dalla state al verno."
Inf. xxvii.

" Lamone's city and Santerno's range
Under the lion of the snowy lair,
Inconstant partisan, that changeth sides,
Or ever summer yields to winter's frost."
Cary's Trans.

The tradition that Faenza takes its name from Phaëton is thus alluded to by a modern poet:

" Ecco l'eccelsa
Città che prese nome di colui
Chi si mal carreggiò in via ◆ sole
E cadde in Val di Po."
Count Carlo Pepoli's Eremo, canto ii.

Faenza is supposed to have been one of the first Italian cities in modern times where the manufacture of earthenware was introduced; whence the adoption of the name *faïence* for such pottery into the French language. The manufacture still exists, although it has been long surpassed by the productions of Umbria and the north. Another branch of industry inherited by the inhabitants from their ancestors, and still flourishing, is the spinning and weaving of silk: the art is said to have been introduced into Faenza by 2 monks on their return from India, who erected their spinning machine here in 1559.

The *Liceo,* or College, contains some examples of *Jacomone* of Faenza, an imitator of Raphael, and the supposed painter of the cupola of S. Vitale at Ravenna.

The *Cathedral,* dedicated to S. Costantius, the first bishop of the see, A.D. 313, is remarkable for the picture of the Holy Family by *Innocenzo da Imola,* and for bas-reliefs representing events in the life of San Savino, by *Benedetto da Majano.* The Capuchin Convent outside the town has a good picture of the Virgin and St. John by *Guido,* which was removed in 1797 to the Louvre. Faenza has produced many painters of note. Among these Lanzi mentions Jacomone. It also claims the honour of being the birthplace of Torricelli, the celebrated natural philosopher and mathematician, the inventor of the barometer.

Some of the churches of Faenza contain interesting objects of art: *S.in Majlorio* has a Madonna, attributed to Giorgione, but more probably by *Girolamo da Treviso*. In the ch. attached to the *Orfanotrofio delle Femmine* is a good picture by *Palmezzano*. In the sacristy of the ch. of the *Serti* are two good frescoes by *Bertucci*. In the *Commenda*, a church in the Borgo, is a fresco by *Girolamo da Treviso*, dated 1533, of the Virgin and Child, SS. Mary Magdalene and Catherine, with the Donatorio kneeling, a fine specimen of this rare master, and a remarkable work; a bust of St. John the Baptist, by *Donatello* (1420), which formerly belonged to the Knights of Malta, of great beauty and expression, is kept in the house of the priest adjoining.

Among the public establishments of Faenza, the *Hospital* and *Lunatic Asylum* may engage the attention of, at least, the professional traveller.

The *Pinacotheca* contains a few pictures by native artists, especially of the elder *Bertuccio*, among his few authentic works; of *Scaletta*, *Ottaviano Pace*, *Palmezzano*, &c.

The *Palazzo Comunale* was formerly the palace of the Manfredis, lords of Faenza. Its middle window, now closed by an iron grating, is pointed out as the scene of one of those domestic atrocities which figure so frequently in the annals of Italian families during the middle ages. It recalls the fate of Galeotto Manfredi, killed by his wife Francesca Bentivoglio, a jealous and injured woman, who, seeing that he was getting the advantage of the 4 assassins she had employed to murder him, leaped out of her bed, snatched a sword, and despatched him herself. Monti has written a fine tragedy on Galeotto Manfredi, The window of the chamber that witnessed the murder is that alluded to; the marks of the blood are said to have disappeared within these few years under Italian whitewashing. Lorenzo de' Medici subsequently interested himself in the fate of Francesca, kept imprisoned by the inhabitants of Faenza, and obtained her release.

The *Zanelli Canal*, so called from Signor Zanelli, by whom it was opened in 1782, connects Faenza with the Adriatic. It commences at the Porta Pia, and, after traversing the plain for 34 m., falls into the Pò di Primaro at S. Alberto.

The country around Faenza is not to be surpassed in richness and fertility; it was praised by Pliny, Varro, and Columella, and is still the object of admiration to every agricultural traveller.

[An excellent road leads from Faenza to Ravenna, distant about 24 m. (Rte. 67); and another across the Apennines to Florence, by Marradi and Borgo San Lorenzo. Rte. 64.]

Leaving Faenza, the Lamone is crossed, and the road proceeds over the plain, passing the Montone (Aries or Vernex) before entering Forlì, and which, uniting with the Ronco (*Bedesis*) near Ravenna, falls into the Adriatic soon afterwards.

1 FORLÌ (*Inn*, La Posta, in the Corso, very fair). This city, situated at the foot of the Apennines, in a pleasant and fertile plain, watered by the Ronco and Montone, is the capital of a province comprehending 541 sq. m., and 218,433 Inhab. The city itself contains a population of 17,000. It is built on the site of the *Forum Livii* founded by Livius Salinator after the defeat of Asdrubal on the banks of the Metaurus. During the middle ages it was a place of some importance as a free city, but at length fell into the hands of the Malatestas and the Ordelaffis. The latter, so well known in the 14th and 15th cents. as princes of Forlì, became extinct in the person of Luigi Ordelaffi, who died in exile at Venice in 1504, after having in vain offered to sell the principality to that republic. Forlì became a fief of the Church almost immediately after that event, in 1504, under Julius II. The Ordelaffis are mentioned by Dante under the figure of the green lion borne on their coat of arms, in a passage

containing an allusion to the defeat of
the French army at Forlì by Guido da
Montefeltro:—

"La terra, che fe' già la lunga prova,
E di Franceschi sanguinoso mucchio,
Sotto le branche verdi si ritrova"
Inf. xxvii.

"The green talons grasp
The land that stood erewhile the proof so long
And piled in bloody heap the host of France."
Cary's Trans.

Forlì is a handsome and well-built town; its architecture, particularly in some of its palaces, is imposing: the Palazzo Guarini, after the designs of Michael Angelo, the *Palazzo del Governo*, formerly *Apostolico*, and the Monte di Pietà may be mentioned among its most remarkable public edifices. It has a circus for the game of *pallone*, and a public promenade, both outside the Porta Pia, on the road leading to Rimini.

A day will amply suffice to see everything worthy of notice at Forlì, proceeding in the following order, supposing the tourist has taken up his quarters at the Albergo della Posta: *Piazza Maggiore*; ch. of *San Mercuriale*; ch. of the *Carmine*; *Duomo*; ch. of *S. Girolamo*; ch. of *San Filippo*; ch. of *Santa Trinita*; ch. of the *Dominicani*; *Citadel*; ch. of the *Servi*; *Pinacoteca*, or Picture Gallery; *Ginnasio and Library*; *Passeggiata Pubblica*; and *Giuocco di Palone*.

The *Cathedral of Santa Croce* is celebrated for the chapel of the Madonna del Fuoco, forming the l. transept, almost a ch. of itself, the cupola of which was painted by *Carlo Cignani* after 20 years' labour. "He passed," says Lanzi, "the last years of his long life at Forlì, where he established his family, and left the grandest monument of his genius in that fine cupola, which is perhaps the most remarkable work of art which the 18th century produced. The subject, like that in the cathedral of Parma, is the Assumption of the Virgin; and here, as there, is painted a *true paradise*, which is admired the more it is contemplated. He spent 36 years on his work, visiting Ravenna from time to time to study the cupola of Guido in the Cathedral, from which he borrowed the fine St. Michael and some other groups. It is said that the scaffolding was removed against his will, as he never made an end of retouching and finishing his work in his accustomed style of excellence. He is buried in this chapel." A *ciborium* in this cathedral is shown as the design of Michel Angelo, with a *reliquiary* of carved and enamelled work of the 14th century, supposed to be the work of German artists. The cathedral is now undergoing so entire a restoration that a considerable part of it has been rebuilt, the several paintings once in it having been removed to the Pinacoteca.

The *Ch. of S. Filippo Neri* contains a picture of S. Francesco di Sales, by *Carlo Maratta*, in the 2nd chapel on l.; a St. Joseph, by *Cignani*; and 2 fine works by *Guercino*—the Christ, and the Annunciation—at the 2nd altar on the rt.

The *Ch. of S. Girolamo* contains in the large chapel opening out of the rt. aisle the very fine picture of the Conception, one of the masterpieces of *Guido*; it represents the Madonna surrounded by a host of angels. The first chapel on rt. is painted in fresco by *Melozzo* and *Palmezzano*: the lower part, attributed to Palmezzano, is very beautiful; in the upper portion are introduced the portraits of Girolamo Riario and Caterina Sforza, dressed as pilgrims, and those of both the painters in the composition beneath. The vault and ornaments of the pilasters are very handsome: in this chapel is the tomb of Barbara Ordelaffi (1466). The 4th chapel has a picture over the altar of the Virgin and Saints, by *Palmezzano*; the Donatorii are supposed to be portraits of G. Riario and Caterina Sforza, with their two sons: the predella, representing the Last Supper, with beautiful figures of saints in the intervals of its 3 compartments, is by the same painter in the roof was painted by *Melozzo*: the whole of the other frescoes in this chapel have been covered with whitewash. The 5th chapel has some frescoes by *Agresti*, a native artist; the 2nd chapel on l. an Ancona of a Crucifixion, by *F. Menzocchi*. This ch. contains the tomb of Morgagni, the celebrated anatomist.

The *Ch. of S. Mercuriale*, in the form of a basilica and dedicated to SS. Thomas and Mercurialis, the first bishop of Forli, Capella de' Ferri, has a good painting by *Innocenzo da Imola*, and is decorated with sculptures of 1536. There are also several good paintings by *Marco Palmezzano*. Over the entrance is a curious bas-relief of the story of the Three Kings, erroneously attributed to *Sansovino*. The 4th chapel on l. contains a fine Almighty by *Palmezzano*, with a host of Angels kneeling: under it is a good Predella, in the style of *Pinturricchio*; on the lunette over the altar is the Resurrection. In 5th chapel on rt. is a good Madonna and Child, by *Palmezzano*, with a charming landscape. The *Campanile*, a fine quadrangular tower with a spire, remarkable for its architecture and great height, was erected in 1180.

The *Ch. of Il Carmine* has over the 1st altar on the l. what is considered *Melozzo da Forli's* finest painting in his native city—S. Antony the Abbot between St. John the Baptist and St. Sebastian. In an Annunciation behind the high altar, by the same painter, the figure of the Angel, as well as the whole of the composition, is very fine.

The *Ch. of the Servi*, in the Piazza di San Pellegrino: in 1st chapel on rt. is a monument with a bas-relief representing the Adoration of the Shepherds, erected during his life by *Luffo Numai*, for himself and wife Caterina Paulucci. Over the altar of the sacristy is an Annunciation by *Palmezzano*, and in the Chapter-house a fresco, wrongly given to *Giotto*. The frescoes by *Agresti* here are now almost destroyed.

The *Ch. of Santa Trinita*: in the 4th chapel is a Virgin and Saints, by *Menzocchi* (1500); and in the sacristy a Madonna with S. Bartholomew and S. Antony of Padua, by *Morolini* (1503).

The *Ch. of S. Antonio Abbate*: a Visitation, by *Palmezzano*, in the sacristy.

The house adjoining the *Spezeria Morandi* still exhibits some traces of the frescoes with which its exterior was adorned by Melozzo. This painter was a native of the city; and is supposed to have been a pupil of Pietro della Francesca. Lanzi, describing these frescoes, says he covered "the front of a *spezeria* with arabesques of the best style, and over the entrance a half-figure remarkably well painted, in the act of pounding drugs." It is much to be regretted that these remains of so interesting a master have not been more carefully preserved: they are now nearly destroyed.

GROUND PLAN OF THE PINACOTECA AT FORLI.

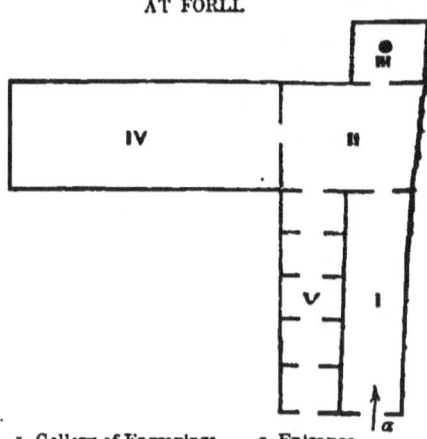

I. Gallery of Engravings.   a. Entrance.
II. Sala degli Arazzi.
III. Gabinetto.
IV. Sala di Palmeggiani.
V. A series of small Rooms, containing some Antiquities and objects of Natural History.

The *Pinacoteca*, or Gallery of Paintings, is placed in the *Collegio*, or *Ginnasio Comunale*, formerly a convent of missionaries, in the Piazza di San Pellegrino. It has been recently arranged, and contains several good works, especially of the school of Palmezzano. Many of the paintings have been presented by noble families of the town, others procured by exchange, but some —and those perhaps the best—from the cathedral and other churches. The gallery can be visited every day, on application to the custode of the Library at the Collegio. Entering from the principal staircase, a long room contains numerous engravings, amongst which a few by *Marc Antonio* and some frescoes by *Agresti* from the cathedral, and by *Menzocchi* from the banqueting-hall in the Palazzo Municipale. Out of this opens the *Sala degli Arazzi* (II.), so called from two specimens of Flemish tapestry. It contains several second-rate paintings, amongst which two (42 and 46) are attributed to *Giotto*, and two others (43 and 45), with more reason, to *Fra Angelico*. At the end of this hall is a cabinet (III.), containing 3 portfolios of drawings and sketches by *Canova*; they belonged to Cav. Missirini, the secretary of that great sculptor, and were presented by him to the museum of his native town. On the walls are several sketches and drawings by *Carlo Cignani*, especially for the paintings which he executed in the chapel of the Madonna del Fuoco in the cathedral. In the centre of this cabinet is a fine bust of Pino Ordelaffi, attributed to *Donatello*. From the *Sala degli Arazzi* we enter the Great Hall (IV.), called the *Sala di Palmeggiani*, a fine room, nearly 40 yards long, where are preserved the largest and most valuable works of the collection, of which the following are most worthy of notice:—77 and 142. *Carlo Cignacci*, two fine pictures of SS. Valerianus and Merculiaris, formerly in the cathedral. 78 and 141. *Damiano di Zotto*, a little-known painter of Forlì, SS. Sebastian and Roch. 85. *Vanni*, St. Catherine. 87. *Vandi*, a good portrait of Nessoli. 87. *Tintoretto*, a portrait. 89. *B. Carulli*, Coronation of the Virgin, signed and dated 1512. 92. *Agresti*, a Crucifixion, the head of Christ very fine. 93. *Rondinelli*, of Ravenna, a Madonna. 97. *Bagnacavallo*, a Holy Family. 99. *Lor. Credi*, portrait of Caterina Sforza. 101. *C. Cignani*, St. Gregory the Great. 106. *Felice Cignani*, his own portrait. 110. *Carlo Cignani*, Santa Rosa. 111. *Cotignola*, a good St. Jerome. 112. *Gennari*, the Virgin of the Rosary, with St. Dominick. 121. *Albani*, St. Sebastian. *Palmezzano*, several paintings by him—120. A Madonna, in his early manner; 125. Christ bearing the Cross; 127. The Last Supper; 128. His portrait, at the age of 80; and 129, 130. The Flight into Egypt and the Presentation in the Temple. 126. *Melozzo da Forlì*, the Almighty. 131. *Guercino*, St. John : this picture was removed to Paris by the French. 133. *C. Cignani*, his portrait. *A. Sacchi*, St. Peter, from the cathedral. 137. *Modigliana*, S. Valerian and his fellow-martyrs. 138. *C. Cignani*, a sketch for his picture of *La Notte di San Giuseppe*.

Forlì has a fine *Piazza*, and numerous good palaces. The *Palazzo del Governo* dates from the 14th centy. In the Casa Manzoni is a monument to a member of the family, with a bas-relief by Canova. Cornelius Gallus the poet, Flavio Biondo the historian, and Morgagni the anatomist, were natives of this town.

The *Citadel*, called the *Rocca di Ravaldino*, on the S. side of the town, was founded by Cardinal Albernoz in 1359, and enlarged by the Ordelaffis and the Riarios (1472-1481); it is now used as a prison. The ruined *Ramparts* recall many historical associations of the middle ages. In the 15th century the sovereignty of Forlì and Rimini was vested in Girolamo Riario, the nephew of Sixtus IV. He was one of the chief actors in the conspiracy of the Pazzi, and had married Catherine Sforza, the natural daughter of Gian Galeazzo, an alliance by which he secured the powerful protection of the Dukes of Milan. His enemies did not venture to attack openly a prince so protected; but at the instigation, it is said, of Lorenzo de' Medici, the captain of his guard and 2 of his own officers stabbed him while at dinner in his palace of Forlì. The conspirators threw the body out of the window, and the populace dragged it round the walls. The insurgents, having seized his wife and children, and thrown them into prison, proceeded to demand the keys of the citadel; but the commander refused to surrender unless ordered to do so by Catherine herself. The conspirators accordingly allowed her to enter the gates, retaining her children as hostages for her return; but she had no sooner entered within the walls, than she gave orders to fire on the besiegers. When they threatened to resent this by inflicting summary vengeance on her children, she mounted the ramparts and exclaimed, "If you kill them, I have a son at Imola; I am pregnant of another, who will grow up to avenge such an execrable act." The populace, intimidated by her courage, did not execute their threat, and the house of Sforza shortly afterwards avenged the indignities she had suffered. In 1499 Catherine again defended Forlì against the combined forces of France and the Church under Cæsar Borgia and Ives d'Allegre; but after an heroic struggle, in which she is described as contesting every inch of ground, retreating before her assailants from tower to tower, she was captured and sent a prisoner to Rome. Machiavelli, although the counsellor of the alliance with Borgia, celebrates the "magnanimous resolution" of this remarkable woman, and her conduct is recorded with admiration by most of the contemporary historians. The citadel, consisting of 4 low round towers, and of a central square castle or *keep*, is the only portion of the old defences in tolerable preservation.

[A road leads from Forlì along the l. bank of the Ronco to Ravenna, about 20 m. distant (Rte. 66); and there is an excellent road across the Apennines to Florence, Rte. 65, which is traversed by a diligence daily.]

The road to Rimini crosses the Ronco (*Ufens*) 3 m. after leaving Forlì, beyond which is the small town of *Forlimpopoli*, with a Pop. of 2324, which almost retains its ancient name of Forum Populii. It was ruined, by Grimoaldus king of the Lombards, in 700. 4 m. S.S.E. is *Bertinoro*, an episcopal town of 1546 Inhab., picturesquely situated on a hill, whose slopes are famous for their vines. It was one of the ancient fiefs of the Malatestas, by whom it was surrendered to the Church. Under Alexander VI. it became the property of Cæsar Borgia. It now contains a large educational establishment and a palace belonging to the Roman Duke Massimo. The view from Bertinoro, over the valley of the Po, extending to the Alps, is very fine. At the village of *Polenta*, 4 m. farther S., originated the family of the Polentas of Ravenna, celebrated as the lords of that city and as ᷉e protectors of Dante in his exile.

The river Savio (*Sapis*) is crossed under the walls of Cesena by a fine bridge constructed of Istrian limestone by Clement VIII.

1½ Cesena (*Inn*, Posta, called also Leone Bianco; civil people), still retaining the name of the last town of Cisalpine Gaul on the Æmilian Way. It is a neat city of 8684 Inhab., prettily situated in an agreeable and fertile country, on the slopes of a hill overlooking the plain watered by the Savio. This description of its position will not fail to recall the lines of Dante:—

" E quella, a cui il Savio bagna il fianco,
Così com' ella sie' tra il piano e il monte,
Tra tirannia si vive e stato franco "
Inf. xxvii.

" And she whose flank is wash'd of Savio's wave,
As 'twixt the level and the steep she lies,
Lives so 'twixt tyrant power and liberty."
Cary's Trans.

The *Palazzo Pubblico* in the great square is a fine building, and is ornamented with a statue of Pius VI., who was a native of the town, as was also his successor Pius VII. In the interior of the palace is a remarkable picture of the Virgin and Saints, by *Francesco Francia*. The *Capuchin Ch.* contains a good work of *Guercino*. The principal object of interest in Cesena is the Library, founded by Domenico Malatesta Novello, brother of Sigismund lord of Rimini, in 1452: it contains 4000 MSS. Many of them were executed by order of Malatesta himself. The oldest and most curious in the collection are the Etymologies of S. Isidore, of the 8th or 9th century. It was in this library that Paulus Manutius shut himself up to collect materials for his editions. The collection was formed by Malatesta, when that illustrious warrior returned to Cesena, severely wounded, and was bequeathed by him to the Franciscan friars, with an annuity of 200 golden ducats to keep it up.

Cesena is one of the earliest episcopal sees in Italy; the first bishop was St. Philemon, A.D. 92. In the turbulent pontificate of Gregory XI. the town was ferociously pillaged by the cruel cardinal Robert of Geneva, whom the pope sent into Italy from Avignon with a company of foreign adventurers. He entered Cesena, February 1, 1377, and ordered all the inhabitants to be massacred. Sismondi says that he was heard to call out during the fearful scene, "I will have more blood! Kill all! Blood! blood!"

About a mile from Cesena, on a commanding hill, is the handsome ch. of the Madonna or Santa Maria del Monte, the work of Bramante, where many Roman urns and other relics have been found. Pius VII. took the vows as a Benedictine monk in the adjoining monastery, and was long known there as the Padre Chiaramonte.

There is a road from Cesena into Tuscany, following the valley of the Savio to S. Pietro in Bagno, from which it crosses the central chain of the Apennines, into the upper valley of the Casentino at Bibiena; but it is only practicable for horses or pedestrians.

A few miles S. of Cesena are the sulphur-mines, which in a great measure supply the sulphuric acid works of Bologna, and the sulphur refinery at Rimini. The sulphur is beautifully crystallised, and is imbedded in the tertiary marine marls. The sulphur-deposits which exist throughout the hills between Cesena and Pesaro are so rich that the quantity now produced might be greatly increased.

2 m. after leaving Cesena, the little river Pisciatello, supposed by many to be the Rubicon, is crossed, and 3 m. farther on the Rigossa; between Cesena and Savignano by the roadside stands a column on which is inscribed a *Senatus-Consultum*, denouncing as sacrilegious any one who should presume to cross the Rubicon with a legion, army, or cohort. It was considered authentic by Montesquieu, but no doubt is now entertained that it is apocryphal. Beyond it the road crosses the Fiumicino, by the bridge of Savignano, a remarkable Roman work, built of travertine, little noticed by travellers. The small stream which flows under it, the Fiumicino, has had almost as many advocates as the Pisciatello as the true representative of the Rubicon, the line of separation between ancient Italy and Cisalpine Gaul. It unites with the Rigossa and Pisciatello, and falls into the Adriatic about 6 m. lower down. Dr. Cramer, following Cluverius, thought that these united streams, which are here known as the Fiumicino, must be identified with the Rubicon; the strongest argument in favour of which is the distance of 12 m. given in the Peutingerian Table; but we shall presently arrive at one which has much more claim than either of them to be identified with that celebrated stream.

1 *Savignano*, a town of 2393 Inhab. (*Inn*, Posta.) Savignano has been considered to mark the site of *Compitum Viæ Æmiliæ;* but many antiquaries are disposed to place that ancient station at Longiano, a village a few miles farther inland, where ruins with several relics confirming this opinion have been found. The town was fortified by Innocent VI. in 1361.

A few miles beyond this place, before arriving at the town of Sant' Arcangelo, the birthplace of Clement XIV., the road crosses, by a Roman bridge, the Uso, a considerable stream, which is called to this day *Il Rubicone*. It flows directly into the Adriatic, after a course of about 25 m. from its source between Monte Tiffi and Sarsina, rising about midway between the Savio and the Marecchia, and running parallel to the latter river for several miles. At its mouth it is a copious stream, and, if its course be carefully examined, the traveller can hardly avoid arriving at the conclusion that it is more likely to have formed a boundary than any of the others he has passed. A further confirmatory reason is the fact that the peasantry, who can have no interest in upholding the theories of antiquaries, to this day give it the name of Il Rubicone. From these circumstances we cannot but consider this stream to be the Rubicon of the ancients. It may, perhaps, be useful to give a summary of the several streams between Cesena and Rimini which have been considered to be the Rubicon, that travellers may prosecute the investigation for themselves:—1st, the Pisciatello, rising near Monte Farnetto; 2nd, the Rigossa, near Roncofreddo; 3rd, the Fiumicino, or River of Savignano, near Sogliano; all 3 uniting into a single channel before entering the sea, where it is crossed by the high road from Ravenna to Rimini (Rte. 71); and 4th, the Uso, rising near to the Tuscan frontier, and flowing direct into the Adriatic, receiving some minor torrents in its course, and becoming an ample stream at its embouchure.

Before entering Rimini we cross the *Bridge of Augustus*, erected over the Marecchia, the ancient Ariminus, more than 18 centuries ago, and still one of the best preserved Roman constructions of its kind in Italy. It was begun by Augustus in the last year of his life, and completed by Tiberius; it has 5 arches, and is entirely built of white Istrian limestone. The principal have a span of 27 feet, and the width of the piers is nearly 13. The inscriptions on it are scarcely to be made out, but a copy is preserved on a tablet under the Porta S. Giuliano. The river at this point separates Romagna from the ancient province of the Pentapolis, the modern Legations of Urbino and Pesaro; the Via Æmilia from Piacenza and Bologna here joins the Via Flaminia.

1 RIMINI (*Inn*: Tre Re, clean rooms, and moderate if you make your bargain), an interesting episcopal city of 16,216 souls, situated in a rich plain between the rivers Marecchia and Ausa; it is resorted to for sea-bathing in the summer. Rimini occupies the site of the Umbrian city of Ariminum. It became a Roman colony at an early period, and was patronized and embellished by Julius Cæsar, Augustus, and many of their successors. During the Lower Empire it was the most northern of the 5 cities which gave to a lieutenant of the Emperor of Constantinople the title of "Exarch of the Pentapolis." The cities governed by this exarch were Rimini, Pesaro, Fano, Sinigallia, and Ancona: his jurisdiction comprised nearly all that portion of the shores of the Adriatic embraced by the modern provinces of La Romagna and La Marca. There was another and more inland Pentapolis, from which this was often distinguished by the epithet "maritima." In 1200, when Rimini belonged to the German Empire, Otho III. sent into the Marca as his viceroy Malatesta, the ancestor of that illustrious family to which Rimini is indebted for its subsequent importance. His descendant Galeotto was created lord of Rimini by Clement VI. It passed from the Malatesta family to the Venetians by sale, and reverted to the pope after the battle of Gera d'Adda. The Malatestas often endeavoured to regain it, but in vain, and the treaties of Tolentino and of Vienna confirmed it to the Church. The name of Malatesta recalls the fine passage of the Inferno, in which Dante describes the lord of Rimini as "the old mastiff:"—

'E il mastin vecchio, e il nuovo da Verucchio,
Che fecer di Montagna il mal governo,
Là dove soglion, fan dei denti succhio."
Inf. xxvii.

"The old mastiff of Verucchio and the young,
That tore Montagna in their wrath, still make,
Where they are wont, an auger of their fangs."
Cary's Trans.

The celebrated council between the Arians and Athanasians was held here in 359.

The principal object of classical interest at Rimini, after the bridge, is the *Arch of Augustus*, now the Porta Romana, under which the road to Rome passes. It is one of the most remarkable monuments on the eastern coast of Italy, and is built of travertine. It was erected in honour of Augustus, and commemorates the gratitude of the inhabitants for the repairing of their roads. Its architecture is simple and massive, with 2 Corinthian columns on each side; above the arch are medallions, with the heads of Neptune and Venus on one side, and of Jupiter and Minerva, with a fine bull's head, on the other. The pediment is proportionately small, being scarcely larger than the breadth of the arch: a great part of the machicolated superstructure is of the middle ages.

The great attraction of the town is the *Ch. of S. Francesco*, now the cathedral. This noble edifice, originally built in the 14th century in the Italian-Gothic style, was reduced into its present form by Sigismundo Pandolfo Malatesta, from the designs of Leon Battista Alberti, in 1450. It is the masterpiece of that great architect, and is an interesting link in the history of art, made by Alberti to conceal the Gothic, and to revive the classical style. The front, consisting of 4 columns and 3 arches, is unfinished, but the side is masked by a series of 7 grand and simple arches on panelled piers detached from the wall of the ch., elevated on a continued basement, concealing without altering the Gothic windows. The whole building is covered with the armorial bearings of the Malatestas and their alliances; the most striking and frequent of these ornaments are the rose and elephant, and the united ciphers of Sigismundo and his wife Isotta. Under the arches above mentioned, on the side of the building, are 7 large sarcophagi in the mediæval style, wherein are deposited the ashes of the eminent men whom Malatesta had collected around him, poets, orators, philosophers, and soldiers. The effect produced by these tombs is as grand as the idea of making them an ornament to his ch. was generous and noble. The interior retains much of its original architecture in the pointed arches of the nave, and is full of interesting memorials of the Malatesta family.

The chapels are rich in bas-reliefs, many of which are of great beauty: as works of art they deserve an attentive study. The elephants of the first chapel which support the elaborately worked arch give an Oriental character to the building. Among the sepulchral monuments those of Sigismund himself, between the entrance and the chapel of S. Sigismund, the first on the rt.; of his favourite wife Isotta, in the chapel of S. Michael, in which the statue of the archangel is said to present her likeness; of his brother "olim principi nunc protectori," his stepson (1468), and of the illustrious females of his house "Malatestorum domûs heroidum sepulcrum," are the most remarkable; that of Sigismund bears the date of 1468, and is the finest in taste and execution. The bronze fruits and flowers on the columns of the chapel of the SS. Sacramento are supposed to be by Ghiberti. In the Chapel of the Relics is an interesting fresco, by *Pietro della Francesca*, of Sigismund kneeling before his patron saint, St. Sigismund of Hungary; behind him are two greyhounds; with a view of the castle of Rimini, erected by him, in a medallion above, signed "Petri di Burgo opus, 1481." In the 2nd chapel on l. is St. Francis receiving the Stigmata by *Vasari*; and in the sacristy a Marriage of the Virgin by *Benedetto Coda*.

Of the other churches of Rimini, that *of S. Giuliano* contains a fine altarpiece, representing the martyrdom of St. Julian, by *Paolo Veronese*, and a curious early picture of the life of that saint, in compartments, by *Lattanzio della Marca*, dated 1357. The ch. of *S. Girolamo* has a good painting of the Saint by *Guercino*; the chapel is painted by *Pronti*. Rimini was erected into a bishopric A.D. 260; its first prelate is supposed to have been S. Gaudentius. At the *Capuccini* are some ruins, said, without much foundation, to belong to an amphitheatre erected by Publius Sempronius.

The *Palazzo del Comune* contains a beautiful altarpiece by *Domenico del Ghirlandaio*, a picture by *Simone da Pesaro*, and an interesting early Pieta by *G. Bellini*, painted about 1470. The *Palace of the Marchese Diottolevi* also contains some good pictures.

In the market-place is a pedestal with the following inscription, recording that it served as the *suggestum* from which Cæsar harangued his army after the passage of the Rubicon:— C. CAESAR DICT. RUBICONE SUPERATO CIVILI BEL. COMMILIT. SUOS HIC IN FORO AR. ADLOCUT. This is probably as apocryphal as the Senatus Consultum on the column at Savignano. Near this is pointed out the spot where St. Anthony preached to the people, and near the canal is a chapel where the saint is said to have preached to the fishes because the people would not listen to him. In the square of the Palazzo Pubblico may be noticed a handsome fountain and a bronze statue of Pope Paul V. The ancient port of Rimini, situated at the mouth of the Marecchia, has been gradually destroyed by the sands brought down by that stream; and the marbles of the Roman harbour were appropriated by Sigismund Malatesta to the construction of his cathedral. Theodoric is said to have embarked his army in this port for the siege of Ravenna. It is now the resort of numerous small vessels occupied in the fisheries; half the population of Rimini are said to be fishermen.

The *Castel Malatesta*, or the fortress, now mutilated and disfigured by unsightly barracks, bears the name of its founder: the rose and elephant are still traceable upon its walls.

The *Library* was founded in 1617, by Gambalunga the jurist. It contains about 23,000 volumes. With the exception of a few classical MSS., and a papyrus known by Marini's commentary, the interest of its manuscript collection is chiefly local.

The house of *Francesca da Rimini* is identified with that occupied by Count Cisterni, formerly the Palazzo Ruffi; or rather, it is supposed to have occupied the site of the existing building. There is no part of the Divina Commedia so full of touching feeling and tenderness as the tale of guilty love in which Francesca reveals to Dante the secret of her soul, and of her soul's master. Its interest is increased by the recollection that Francesca was the daughter of Guido da Polenta, lord of Ravenna, who was the friend and generous protector of Dante in his exile. The delicacy with which she conveys in a single sentence the story of her crime is surpassed only by the passage where the poet represents the bitter weeping of the condemned shades as so far overcoming his feelings that he faints with compassion for their misery:—

"Noi leggiavamo un giorno per diletto
Di Lancilotto, come Amor lo strinse:
Soli eravamo, e senz' alcun sospetto.
Per più fiate li occhi ci sospinse
Quella lettura, e scolorocci 'l viso:
Ma solo un punto fu quel che ci vinse.
Quando leggemmo il disiato riso
Esser baciato da cotanto amante,
Questi, che mai da me non fia diviso,
La bocca, mi baciò tutto tremante:
Galeotto fu il libro, e chi lo scrisse—
Quel giorno più non vi leggemmo avante.
Mentre che lo uno spirto questo disse,
L' altro plangeva sì, che di pietade
Io venni men così come io mor'esse,
E caddi, come corpo morto cade."

"'We read one day for pastime, seated nigh,
Of Lancilot, how love enchain'd him too.
We were alone, quite unsuspiciously.
But oft our eyes met, and our cheeks in hue
All o'er discolour'd by that reading were;
But one point only wholly us o'erthrew;
When we read the long-sigh'd-for smile of her.
To be thus kiss'd by such devoted lover,
He who from me can be divided ne'er
Kiss'd my mouth, trembling in the act all over.
Accursed was the book and he who wrote.'
That day no further leaf we did uncover.'
While thus one spirit told us of their lot,
The other wept, so that with pity's thralls
I swoon'd as if by death I had been smote,
And fell down even as a dead body falls."
Trans. by Lord Byron.

The *Castel di S. Leo*, to the westward of Rimini, is remarkable as the place where Cagliostro, the celebrated impostor, died in exile in 1794.

There is a bridle-road to S. Leo, and from thence up the valley of the Marecchia, by Badia Tedalda, to Pieve S. Stefano in the upper valley of the Tiber, and from thence by the sanctuary of Alvernia to Bibiena and Florence, by which the fishermen at times supply the Tuscan capital with the produce of the Adriatic. The mountains over which it passes—the Alpe della Luna—are highly picturesque; the road is said at its highest point to command a view of the Adriatic and Mediterranean.

EXCURSION TO SAN MARINO.

About 13 m. from Rimini, isolated in the heart of the Emilian Provinces, like the rock on which it stands, is SAN MARINO, long the only surviving representative of Italian liberty. This miniature State, the smallest which the world has seen since the days of ancient Greece, and whose unwritten constitution has lasted for 14 centuries, has retained its independence while all the rest of the peninsula, from the spurs of the Alps to the gulf of Taranto, has been convulsed by political changes. Yet, with all this, the republic, until the year 1847, made but little progress, rather studying to preserve itself unaltered by communication with its neighbours, than keeping pace with the improvements of the age. The printing press had not then found its way into its territory, mendicity was common, and a gaming-table had very recently contributed its share to the public revenues. The constitution of this singular republic underwent an important change in 1847 amidst the universal agitation of the Italian States. The general council, which had hitherto been composed promiscuously of 60 nobles and plebeians, elected by the people, was then transformed into a chamber of representatives. Every citizen was declared an elector, and the sittings of the chamber were ordered to be public. This chamber constitutes the legislative body. The voting is by ballot, and two-thirds are necessary to confirm all official acts. A council of 12, two-thirds of whom are changed every year, communicate between the legislative body and 2 captains — 1 appointed for the town, the other for the country—who are charged with the executive power, and are elected every 6 months. The judicial office, like in the free towns of Italy in the middle ages, is not confided to a citizen of the republic, but a stranger, possessing a diploma of doctor of laws, is appointed to discharge its functions, and is elected for 3 years; a physician and surgeon are also chosen from persons who are not citizens, and are elected for a similar period. In a state so constituted it might be expected that great simplicity of manners would prevail; hence the chief magistrate will often be found farming his own land, and the senators pruning their own vines. The territory of the republic is 17 sq. m. in extent, its population is under 7000, and its miniature army does not number more than 40 men. It has 3 castles, 4 convents, and 5 churches, 1 very recently built, with a handsome portico.

The city occupies the crest of the rocky mountain which forms so conspicuous an object from the high road, and contains about 700 Inhab. Only one road, that from Rimini, leads to it; although steep and rugged, it is broad and practicable for carriages. It runs up the valley of the Ausa, which rises in the hills of S. Marino. The territory of the latter is entered 1 m. before reaching Serravalle.

The town, or as it is called *il Borgo*, situated on the declivity of the hill, is the place where the principal inhab. reside ; it contains about 500 souls. The soil of the lower grounds is fertile, and the little town of Serravalle, at the foot of the mountain, 9 m. from Rimini, has a thriving trade with the several towns in the plain. S. Marino itself, on the crest of the mountain, from its high situation, is exposed to a cold and variable climate, and snow frequently lies there when the lowlands enjoy a comparatively summer temperature.

The origin of the republic is as romantic as its position. According to the legend, a stonemason from Dalmatia, called Marinus, who embraced Christianity, after working 30 years at Rimini withdrew to this mountain to escape the persecutions under Diocletian. Leading the life of an austere anchorite, his fame soon spread, and he obtained disciples, as well as a reputation for sanctity. The princess to whom the mountain belonged presented it to him, and instead of founding a convent, after the example of the time, he established a republic. During the middle ages the independence of the state was often threatened by the dangerous vicinity of the Malatestas. In the last century Cardinal Alberoni, then legate of Romagna, intrigued against it, and, on the pretence that the government had become an oligarchy, invaded and took possession of its territory in the name of the Church. An appeal to Clement XII. obtained an order that the citizens should determine how they would be governed ; at a general assembly they unanimously voted against submission to the Church, and the papal troops were withdrawn. But the events which subsequently convulsed Europe threatened the republic more than the intrigues of the Church; and it would doubtless have long since ceased to exist except in history, if it had not been saved by the magnanimous conduct of Antonio Onofri, who deserved the title of "Father of his country," inscribed by his fellow-citizens upon his tomb. This remarkable man spent his life in its service, and by his bold and decided patriotism induced Napoleon to rescind his decree for the suppression of the republic. When summoned before the emperor, he said, "Sire, the only thing you can do for us is to leave us just where we are." In spite of all subsequent overtures, Onofri maintained so perfect a neutrality, that he was enabled to vindicate his country before the Congress of Vienna, and obtain the recognition of its independence. Unlike other republics, San Marino did not forget its debt of gratitude to the preserver of its liberties, for, besides the inscription on Onofri's tomb, a marble bust in the council-chamber records his services, and their acknowledgment by the state. In more recent times San Marino has not in vain solicited the protection and support of the First Napoleon's successor on the Imperial throne.

There are few objects of interest to be found in San Marino, if we except a picture of the Holy Family in the council-chamber, attributed to *Giulio Romano*. At Borgo there is a singular cavern, into which a strong and dangerous current of cold air perpetually rushes from the crevices of the rock. The view from the summit of the mountain, and from various points of its declivities, is sufficient to repay a visit; on a clear day, the deep gulf of the Adriatic is traced as far as the coast of Dalmatia, and a wide prospect of the chain of Apennines is commanded, singularly in contrast with the sea view. But the interest of San Marino in our own time, independently of its historical associations, has been derived from the late Cav. Borghesi; one of the first scholars of modern Italy, who made it his place of residence for nearly 40 years. This learned man, a native of Savignano, was an adopted citizen, and his archæological acquirements made a pilgrimage to San Marino a labour of love to the most eminent antiquarian travellers. The house in which Melchiore Delfico composed his historical memoir of San Marino is marked by an inscription expressive of the author's gratitude for the hospitality he experienced there during his exile.

INDEX.

HANDBOOK OF NORTH ITALY.

LATEST INFORMATION.

ROUTE 13.

GENOA.—A new line of steamers, under contract with the government, has been just established between Genoa, Leghorn, and Naples, starting every second evening on the arrival of the last railway train from Turin and Milan. The boats that leave on the Tues. and Thurs. call at Leghorn; that of Sat. proceeds direct to Naples. The steamers arrive at Leghorn at an early hour, and sail again at midday for Naples: they return from Naples every Mon., Wed., and Sat., at 6 P.M.; those of Mon. and Sat. calling at Leghorn, and leaving again at 9 A.M., thus performing the voyage to Genoa by daylight. The new line of steamers is in correspondence with others to Messina, Palermo, &c. There is also *now* a direct service between Genoa and Palermo.

ROUTE 34.

The Railway between Venice and Trieste was opened the whole way in Oct. 1860. There are two trains daily; the distance 29 Aust. leagues (134 Eng. m.); the fares $10\frac{1}{2}$, $7\frac{3}{4}$, and $5\frac{1}{4}$ florins. The evening train is in correspondence with that which leaves Turin at 8 and Milan in the forenoon on the one hand, and with the train to Vienna on the other; so that the whole distance to the Austrian capital is performed in 47 hrs. from Turin, 48 from Genoa, 43 from Milan, and 30 from Venice; and between Genoa, Turin, Milan, Venice, and Trieste, in 26, 25, and 21 hrs. There is a third train every day, which does not go farther than Udine.

The stations between Venice and Trieste, with the distances in Austrian leagues of $4\frac{1}{2}$ Eng. m., are—

A. L.		A. L.	
1	Mestre	16	Pasian-Schiavonesco
$2\frac{1}{4}$	Mogliano		
3	Preganziol	18	Udine
4	Treviso	19	Buttrio
5	Lancenigo	20	San Giov. Manzano
6	Spresiano		
$6\frac{1}{4}$	Piave	$20\frac{1}{4}$	Cormons
$7\frac{1}{4}$	Conegliano	22	Gorizzia
$8\frac{1}{2}$	Pianzano	23	Rubbia
10	Sacile	24	Sagrado
$11\frac{1}{4}$	Pordenone	25	Monfalcone
$13\frac{1}{4}$	Casarsa	27	Nabresina
15	Codroipo	29	Trieste.

INDEX.

₊ In order to facilitate reference to the Routes, most of them are repeated twice in the Index thus, Turin to Milan is also mentioned under the head of *Milan to Turin; such *reversed* Routes are marked in the Index with an asterisk.

ADANO.

A.

ABANO, baths of, 388
Abbey of Novalesa, 9
—— San Michele, 10
—— Chiaravalle, 220
Abbetone, col dell', 414
Abbiategrasso, 47
Academy of Fine Arts at Bologna, 458
—— at Ferrara, 447
—— at Genoa, 118
—— at Parma, 415
—— at Ravenna, 525
—— at Turin, 25
—— at Venice, 374
Acqui, city of, and baths, 68
Adda river, 151
Adige river, 257, 264, 390, 437, 505
Adria, 390
Aglie, castle of, 33
Agno, valley of, 310
Agogna torrent, 39
Agojolo, 421
Agrario Garden at Bologna, 466
Alassio, 92
Alba, 64
Albano, 235
Albaro, 122
Albenga, 93
—— valley, 92
Albese, 151
Albium Intermelium, 90
Albissola, 96
Aleramo, cavern of, 66
Alessandria, city of, 50. Citadel, 51. Cathedral, churches, fairs, 51
—— to Arona, 53
—— to Placenza, 54
—— to Savona, 67
Alpignano, stat., 12
Alpone torrent, 286
Alseno, 404
Alserio, lake of, 151
Altare, village, 70
Altedo, 452
Altino, 383

N. *Italy.*—1860.

ARMOURY.

Alzano, Santuario d', 234
Ambrogio, Sant', church of, 171
—— quarries of, 286
—— , stat., 11
Ambrosian library, 200
Amphitheatre at Milan, 161
—— near Nice, 83
—— at Padua, 320
—— at Verona, 264
Andes, village, 229
Andora castle and river, 92
Anone, 5c
Anone lake, 151
Antignate, 230
Antonino, St., town of, 9
Appio, Monte, 90
Aqua Negra, 223
Aquæ Statiellæ, 68
Aquileja, 394
Arboroso stream, 53
Arch at Susa, 7
—— at Milan, 161
—— of Augustus at Rimini, 540
—— at Verona, 265
Architecture, xxv
Architecture, domestic, in Italy, xxv. Military, xxvi
—— Lombard, xxv. Gothic, xxv
Archives at Bologna, 485
—— at Mantua, 291
—— at Modena, 433
—— at Novara, 40
—— at Padua, 315
—— at Ravenna, 524
—— at Turin, 20
—— at Venice, 363
Arcola town, 129
Arcole, battle of, 300
Arcore, 152
Arda river, 404
Arena Po stat., 57
Arenzana, 97
Ariano, island, 505
Arimiuum, 540
Arma, 91
Armenian convent at Venice, 372
Armoury at Turin, 19
—— at Venice, 353

BARDELONE.

Arno river, 503
Arona, stat., 54
Arqua, excursion to, 387
Arquata, stat., 52
Arrosia river, 66
Arsenal at Venice, 353
—— Genoa, 102
Art, school of, at Bologna, 457
—— at Ferrara, 438
—— at Genoa, 75
Asinelli tower at Bologna, 489
Asti, county of, 2
——, stat. and city of, 49. Cathedral—Churches—Palazzo Alfieri, 49
——, wines of, 49
Astigiano territory, 49
Augusta Bagiennorum, ruins, 65
Aulla, 423
Auletta torrent, 424
Ausa river, 540, 543
Austrian Dominions. *See* Venetian Provinces.
Avenza, 130
Avigliana, stat. and castle at, 11

B.

Bacchiglione river, 303
Badagnano, 403
Bagnacavallo, town, 509
Bagnanza torrent, 423
Bagnasco, 65
Bagnone torrent, 423
Baldichieri, stat., 49
Baldo, Monte, 252
Baptistery at Como, 147
—— at Cremona, 225
—— at Genoa, 114
—— at Novara, 39
—— at Padua, 316
—— at Parma, 411
—— at Ravenna, 514
—— at Venice, 338
—— at Verona, 274
Baradello tower, 144, 145, 149
Bardelone, 434

INDEX.

BARDOLINO.
Bardolino, 257
Barigazzo, 414
Barlassina, 150
Basella, 216
Basilica of La Superga, 11
—— of St. Marco, description of, 335
—— of S. Petronio at Bologna, 477
—— of S. Apollinare in Classe at Ravenna, 527
Bassano, city of, 309
Baths of Abano, 388
—— of Acqui, 68
—— of Battaglia, 388
—— of Caldiero, 300
—— of Castro Caro, 504
—— of La Poretta, 500
—— of Recoaro, 310
—— of Riola, 533
—— of Valdieri, 61
Battaglia, 388, 390
——, baths at, 388
Battle of Arcole, 300
—— of Caldiero, 300
—— of Casalecchio, 499
—— of Cassano, 210
—— of Castiglione, 252
—— of Curtatone, 228
—— of Custozza, 263
—— of Dego, 69
—— of Loano, 94
—— of Lodi, 222
—— of Lonato, 252
—— of Magenta, 43
—— of Marengo, 54
—— of S. Martino, 256
—— of Melegnano, 221
—— of Mondovi, 67
—— of Montebello, 57
—— of Montenotte, 69
—— of Mortara, 46
—— of Novara, 41
—— of Palestro, 38
—— of Ravenna, 530
—— of Solferino, 255
—— of Turin, 14, 32
—— of Vinaglio, 38
Baveno, 142
Bayard, anecdote of, 239
Beaulieu, 84
Bellinzago, stat., 53
Benacus, lake, 254
Bene, 65
Berceto town, 423
Bergamo, 230. Views from—Houses—Harlequin—Palazzo della Ragione or Nuovo—Town-hall—Statue of Tasso, 231. Cathedral—Churches, 232. Library—Collections of paintings — Situation — Castello—Neighbourhood of, 233
—— to Brescia, 236
*—— to Lecco and Como, 150
*—— to the Lake Iseo, 234
*—— to Milan, 229
Bergeggi, 94
Berico, Madonna di Monte, 308
Berici, hills, 300

BOLOGNA.
Bernardo, Col di, 66
Bertinoro, 518
Bevera torrent, 63
Bevilacqua, 186
Blanze, stat., 34
Bicocca, 153
Biella, railway to, 34
Biforca, la, 502
Binasco, 210
Bisagno torrent, 121
Bistagno, village, 68
Biume, 144
Boara, 190
Bogliase, 122
Bolca, Monte, 287
Bologna:—Inns, 455. Situation, importance, and prosperity, 455. Historical notice, 455. School of art, 457. Accademia delle Belle Arti, 458. Pinacoteca, 458. University, 463. Museums, 464. Observatory, 465. University library, 465. Botanic and Agrario Gardens, 466. Hospitals, 466.
Churches, 466:—S. Bartolommeo di Porta Ravegnana, 567; S. Bartolommeo di Reno, 468; S. Benedetto, 468; della Carità, 468; Cathedral, 466; Sta. Cecilia, 468; Celestini, 468; Corpus Domini, 469; S. Cristina, 469; S. Domenico, 469; S. Francesco, 471; S. Giacomo Maggiore, 472; S. Giorgio, 473; S. Giovanni in Monte, 473; S. Gregorio, 474; S. Leonardo, 474; Sta. Lucia, 474; Madonna del Baraccano, 474; Madonna di S. Colombano, 475; Madonna di Galliera, 475; Sta. Maria Maddalena, 475; Sta. Maria Maggiore, 475; Sta. Maria della Vita, 476; S. Martino Maggiore, 476; I Mendicanti, 476; S. Nicolò, 477; S. Paolo, 477; S. Petronio, 477; S. Procolo, 480; S. Rocco, 481; Santissimo Salvatore, 481; Servi, 481; S. Stefano, 482; SS. Trinità, 483; SS. Vitale ed Agricola, 483.
Piazza di S. Domenico, 471.
Convent of S. Domenico, 471.
Piazza Maggiore, 484. Fontana Pubblica, 484. Palazzo Pubblico, 484. Palazzo del Podestà, 485. Portico de' Banchi, 485. Il Registro, 485. Private palaces, 485-488. Foro de' Mercanti, 489. Torre Asinelli, 489. Torre Garisenda, 490. Biblioteca Comunale, 490. Archiginnasio, 490. Colleges, 490. Theatres, 491. Casino, 491. Accademia Filarmonica, 491. Liceo Filarmonico, 491. Montagnuola, 491. Dogs, 495.

BRENTA.
Climate, 495. Dialect, 495. Character of the people, 495. Conveyances, 495. Plan for visiting, 496.
Environs.—Churches: Misericordia, 491; Annunziata, 491; Madonna di Mezzaratta, 492; S. Michele in Bosco, 492; Madonna di S. Luca, 493; Scalzi, 494. Bagni di Mario, 492. Certosa, 494. Cemetery, 494. Portico degli Scalzi, 494.
*Bologna to Ferrara, 452, 453.
—— to Florence by Pietramala, &c., 496.
—— by La Porretta, &c., 499
*—— to Modena, 454.
—— to Ravenna by Imola and Lugo, 508.
—— by Medicina and Lugo, 531.
—— to Rimini, 512.
Boltiere, 259
Bolzanetto, stat., 52
Bomporto, 437
Bondeno, 437
Bonferraro, 185
Bononia and Felsina, 455
Books on Italy in general, xx.
Bordighiera, 90
Borghetto in Liguria, 126
—— on the Mincio, 288
—— di S. Spirito, 94
Borgo, at S. Marino, town, 543.
Cavern at, 544
—— Lavezzara, stat., 53
—— di San Dalmazzo, 62
—— San Donino, 405
—— San Lorenzo, 502
—— di Sasso, 500
—— Ticino, stat., 54
—— Vercelli, stat., 39
Borgoforte, 422, 437
Borgone, stat., 9
Borgorato, 67
Bormida, and valley of the, 68
Borromean Islands to Milan, 142
Bosco, 51
Botanic garden at Bologna, 466
—— at Genoa, 111
—— at Milan, 200
—— at Nice, 81
—— at Padua, 326
—— at Parma, 419
—— at Rivoli, 12
—— at Turin, 33
Bovisio, 150
Bozzolo, 228
Brà, 64
Bracco, pass of, 125
Brandizzo, 33
Braus, col di, 63
Breglio, 63
Brembana valley, 152
Brembo river, 152
Brendola, 303
Breno, 252
Brenta, river, 328, 505

INDEX. 547

BRENTELLA.

Brentella torrent, 111
Brera Gallery at Milan, 191
Brescello, 421
Brescia, stat., 237. Inns — Gates — Capture by the French, 237. Plan of, 238. Bayard, 239. Siege in 1849 —Roman remains—Antiquities, 240. Museo Patrio, 241. Cathedrals, 242. Churches, 243. Palazzo della Loggia, 247. Broletto—Library, 248. GalleriaTosi or Museo Civico, 249. Other galleries — Palaces, 250. Citadel—Campo Santo, 251. Plan for visiting, 251
Brescia to Milan, 229
—— to Bergamo, 236
—— to Peschiera, 252
—— to Verona, railway, 252
—— to Lake of Iseo and Val Camonica, 237, 252
Brianza, la, 152
Bridge of Augustus, 540
Brisighella, 502
Broletto at Bergamo, 233
—— at Brescia, 248
—— at Como, 147
—— at Milan, 190
—— at Monza, 154
Brondolo, 505
Broni, 57
Brouis, mountain of, 63
Brunetta Fort, la, ruins of, 8
Buco del Piombo, 151
Buonaparte family, origin of, 130
Burano, Isola di, 382
Burgianico, 414
Busalla, stat. and tunnel, 52
Busseto, town, 404
Bussoleno, stat., 9
Busto Arsizio, 142
Byron, Lord, at the tomb of Dante, 522. His residence at Ravenna, 522

C.

Ca, la, 497
Cà de' Coppi, 417
Cadeo, 404
Cadibona pass, 70
Caffaggiolo, 498
Cairo, 69
Calcio, 230
Caldiero, stat., baths of, 300. Battle at, 300
Calepio, castle of, 234
Calogna, 237
Calvatone, 228
Cambiano, stat., 48
Cameriata, railway from, to Milan, 144
Camnago, 151, 154
Camogli, village, 123
Camonica, Val di, 236
Campigno torrent, 502
Campo Formio, 393

CATHEDRAL.

Candia, 46
Canonica, d' Adda, 259
Canossa, 427
Cantalupo, 67
Cantu, or Canturio, 153
Canzo, 151
Caorso, 421
Capanne, le, 501
Cape of the Lame Goat, 94
Capo d' Argine, 452
—— Corvo, 129
—— della Croce, 92
—— delle Mele, 92
—— di Noli, 94
—— di Vado, 94
—— Verde, 91
Caprasio, Monte, 9
Caprino, 151
Carate, 154
Caravaggio, town, 230
Carbonate, 209
Carcare, 70
Carignano, principality of, 2
—— town, 58
Carmagnola, stat., 59
Caronno, 208
Ca Rossa, 223
Carrara, duchy of, 425
—— di St. Stefano, 388
Carriages for posting, classification of, in Piedmont, 5.
Carsaniga, 152
Carza torrent, 498, 503
Casaglia, pass of, 502
Casal Maggiore, 420
—— Pusterlengo, 223
Casale, city of, 45. Cathedral, 45. Churches, 46. Ancient edifices, 46
Casalecchio, 499
Casarsa, stat., 393
Cascina Bon Jesu, 142
Cascina de' Pecchi, 258
Cassana, 427
Cassano Albese, 151
—— d' Adda, 230
Cassine, 68
Cassio, 423
Casteggio, 56
Castel Alfieri, 49
—— Arquato, 404
—— Bolognese, 533
—— Ceriolo, 54
—— Franco, 454
—— Gavone, 94
—— Guelfo, town, 406
—— S. Pietro, 532
—— del Vescovo, 500
—— S. Giovanni, 57
—— Nuovo, stat., 263
Castellanza, 142
Castellaro, 185
Castelluchio, 228
Castelpoggio, 424
Castiglione, and battle, 252
—— di Olona, 209
Castro, 236
—— Caro baths, 504
Catajo, 388
Cathedral of Acqui, 68

CERTOSA.

Cathedral of Albenga, 93
—— Aquileja, 394
—— Asti, 49
—— Bergamo, 232
—— Bologna, 466
—— Borgo San Donino, 405
—— Brescia, 242, 243
—— Casale, 45
—— Como, 145
—— Conegliano, 392
—— Coni, 61
—— Cremona, 224
—— Faenza, 533
—— Ferrara, 442
—— Forli, 533
—— Fossano, 66
—— Genoa, 112
—— Imola, 532
—— Lodi, 221
—— Mantua, 295
—— Milan, 162
—— Modena, 428
—— Mondovi, 66
—— Monza, 154
—— Nice, 81
—— Novara, 39
—— Padua, 315
—— Parma, 407
—— Pavia, 213
—— Piacenza, 398
—— Ravenna, 514
—— Reggio, 426
—— Rimini, 540
—— Rovigo, 390
—— Savona, 95
—— Susa, 8
—— Torcello, 382
—— Treviso, 392
—— Turin, 15
—— Udine, 393
—— Venice, 335
—— Ventimiglia, 90
—— Vercelli, 35
—— Verona, 272
—— Vicenza, 304
Catullus, villa of, at Sermione, 253
Cavalcaselle, 263
Cavaller Maggiore, 60
Cavallina, Val, 235
Cavanella dell' Adige, 505
—— di Pò, 505
Cavo Pamfilio, 452
—— Tassone, 452
Celle, 96, 532
Cemenelum, anct., 83
Ceno, river, 422
Centa, river, 92
Centallo, stat., 60
Cento, 453. Casa di Guercino, 453. Chiesa del Rosario, 454. Fair, 454
—— Pieve di, 454
Cerea, 386
Ceresone torrent, 311
Ceriale, 94
Cernobbio, 144
Cerro, stat., 50
Certosa of Bologna, 494
—— of Garignano, 208

CERTOSA.

Certosa of Pavia, 210
— of Val Pesio, 61
Cervara, 123
Cervia, 500, 511
Cervignano, 394
Cervo, 92
Cesano, 150
Cesena : — Palazzo Pubblico, library, 538; sulphur-mines near, 539
Cesenatico, 531
Ceserano, 424
Ceva, marquisate of, 2
—, town, 65
Cherasco, 64
Cherio torrent, 235
Chiaravalle, abbey of, 220
Chiari, 230
Chiavari, 124
Chieri, 47
Chiero, valley of, 403
Chiese river, 252
Chioggia, 505. Excursion to, 384
Chireglio, 434
Chiusa, la, 9
Chivasso city, 33
Ciceroni, xvii
Cigliano, 34
Cigognolo, 228
Cimies, 83
Cinque Terre, le, 126
Cisa, pass of the Apennines, 423
Cisano, 151
Cividale, 393
Classis, ancient town of, 529
Clastidium, ancient, 56
Claternum, 533
Climate of Bologna, 495
— Genoa, 101
— Nice, 82
— Turin, 15
— Venice, 330
— Villafranca, 85
Coccaglio, 230, 237
Codogno, 223
Codrolpo, town, 393
Cogoletto, 97
Coins current in Italy, xviii
—, tables of, xxxi-xxxiii
Col, or Pass, dell' Abbetone, 434
— di Casaglia, 502
— delle Cerese, 61
— de Cisa, 423
— delle Finistre, 61
— di Giove, 52
— di San Bartolomeo, 66
— di Tenda, 62
Cola, 257
Collegno, stat., 12
Collecchio, 422
Collina pass, 501
Collina di Torino, 15
Colognola, 300
Colorno, 421
Columbus, birthplace of, 97
Comabbio lake, 143
Comacchio, 506
Comerio, 143
Como : Inns — Diligences — Steamboats, 144. Situation

DOLO.

— Trade — Duomo, 145.
Paintings, 146. Monuments —Baptistery—Broletto, 147. Theatre—Port, 148
Como to Lecco, road from, 150
— to Milan, 153
Compigno torrent, 502
Condove, stat., 9
Conegliano, town, 392
Coni, 60
Corniglia, 126
Corniche road, 87
Cornigliano, town, 98
Corsaglia, 67
Corsico, 47
Corte Maggiore, 404
Corte Olona, 57
Cortile San Martino, 421
Cotignola, 509.
Couriers, xvi.
Covigliajo, 498
Cozzo, 46
Cremona, history of, 223. Cathedral, 224. Baptistery—Tower, 225. Campo Santo —Churches, 226. Palaces— Collections of Pictures, 227. San Sigismondo, 227.
Cremona to Brescia, 227
— to Mantua, 227
*— to Milan, 223
— to Parma, 420
Crescentino, 45
Crescenzago, 258
Crespino, 402
Crostolo torrent, 421,426
Crown, the iron, 156
Cucciago, 153
Cunella valley, 286
Cuneo, or Coni, 60
Cunio castle, ruins of, 509
Currency, tables of, xxxi-xxxiii
Curtatone, battle at, 228
Custom-houses, x.
Custozza, battle of, 263, 287.
Cutigliano, village, 434

D.

Dante, tomb of, 521
Dego, and battle, 69
Dertona, ancient, 56
Desenzano, town, stat., 252
— to the Promontory of Sermione, 252
Desio, stat., 154
Dessaix, death of, 55
Diano Castello, 92
— Marino, 92
— valley, 92
Dicomano, 503
Diligences, xv.
Dockyard at Villafranca, 85
— at Genoa, 102, 121
— at Venice, 353
Dogliani, 65
Dolo, stat., 328

FERRARA.

Domenico, San, tomb of, 4
Bologna, 469
Domestic architecture in Italy, xxvi.
Dora-Baltea, 45
Dora-Riparia river, 15
Dossobuono, stat., 287
Dovadola, 504
Drap, 87
Duchies of Parma and Placenza, 395
— of Massa and Carrara, 425
— of Modena, 425

E.

Edolo, 236, 252
Egyptian Museum at Turin, 25
Ellero, the, 66
Elsa river, 502
Emilia, Via, 403
Enza torrent, 421, 426
Erba, 151
Esa, 87
Este, castle of, 386 ; town, 387
Este, house of, 538. Their patronage of art, 440
Euganean hills, 327, 386, 388
Exarchs of Ravenna, 512

F.

Faenza:—Inns, history, cathedral, 533. Churches, Pinacoteca, Palazzo Comunale, 534.
— to Florence, 502
— to Ravenna, 505
Falicon, 84
Faventia, site of (Faenza), 533
Felizzano, stat., 50
Felsina (Bologna), 455.
Fergusson, Mr., his Handbook of Architecture, xxv.
Ferrara :—Inns, 437. Historical notice, 438. School of art, 438. Plan of city, 439. Reformation at, 441
Churches:—Cathedral, 442; S. Andrea, 443 ; S. Benedetto, 443½; Campo Santo, 444 ; Capuchins, 444; Corpus Domini, 444 ; S. Cristofero, 444 ; S. Domenico, 444 ; S. Francesco, 445 ; Gesu, 445 ; S. Giorgio, 445; Sta. Maria del Vado, 445; S. Paolo, 446 ; Theatins, 446. Castle, 446. Gallery of Pictures, 447. Palazzo del Magistrato, 448. Studio Pubblico, 448. Public Library, 448. Casa di Ariosto, 449. C. Guarini, 449. Piazza di Ariosto, 449. Tasso's prison, 450. Theatre, 451. Citadel, 451. Canals, 451. Plan for visiting, 451.

INDEX. 549

FERRARA.
'errara to Bologna, by Malalbergo, 452.
—— by Cento, 453
—— to Comacchio, 452
—— to Mantua, 436
—— to Modena, 437
—— to Padua, 390, 437
Filattiera, 423
Filigare, 497
Finale, 437
——, Marina, 94
——, Borgo, 94
Fino, 149
Florenzuola town, 404
Fistona valley, 503
Fiumalbo, hamlet, 434
Fiumicino, the, 539
Fivizzano, 424
Floods of the Adige, 264
Florence, 498
*—— to Bologna, 496, 499
*—— to Faenza, 502
—— to Forlì, 503
Foce di Spezia, 126
Fognano, 502
Fombio S. Rocco, 223
Fontana fredda, 404
Fontebuona, 498
Fontenellato, 406
Forche, le, 504
Forlì, historical notice, 534; Circus, public garden, cathedral, churches, 535; Pinacoteca, Palazzo del Governo, citadel, historical associations, 537
* Forlì to Florence, 503
—— to Ravenna, 504
Forlimpopoli, 538
Formigine, 433
Fornaci, le, 258
Fornuovo, 422
Forte Urbano, 454
Forum Allieni, 437
—— Cornelii, 532
—— Licinii, 151
—— Livii, 514
—— Populii, 538
Fosdinovo, 424
Fossano, 60, 66
Fraine, mount, 254
Frugarolo, stat., 51
Fusignano, 509
Futa, la, col or pass, 497

G.
GALLA Placidia, mausoleum of, at Ravenna, 520.
Gaggiano, 47
Gajana stream, 531
Gajano lake, 235
Galatea, 504
Gallarate, 141
Galleries, public, at Bergamo, 233
—— Bologna, 458
—— Brescia, 249, 250
—— Faenza, 534

GRADISCA.
Galleries, public, at Ferrara, 447
—— at Forlì, 536
—— Milan (Brera), 191
—— Modena, 431
—— Parma, 415
—— Ravenna, 525
—— Turin, 21
—— Venice, 374
—— Verona, 270
—— Vicenza, 307
Galliano, 153
Gallinaria, island of, 92
Gamalero, 68
Garda lake, 254
—— village, 257
Garegnano, 208
Garessio, 65
Gargagnano, 285
Garisenda tower, 490
Garlasco, 219
Garlenda, 93
Gavirate, 143
Geminiani, 431
Genoa, "la Superba," 98. Inns, 98. Cafés—Consuls—Steamers—Diligences—Vetturini, 99. Railway—Post-office—English Church—Bankers—Physicians—Port regulations—Passports—Boatmen—Shops, 100. Sedan-chairs—House-rent—Provisions—Climate—Harbour—Population—Manufactures, 101. Costume—Streets—Piers—Lighthouse—Arsenal—Bagne, 102. Navy—Porto Franco—Custom-house—City walls—Gates—Ramparts—Public Gardens—Fortifications, 103. —Siege of—Garrison—Description of the city, 104. Palaces—Collections of paintings, 105. University, 111. Cathedral,112. Churches,114. Buildings — Hospitals, 117. Conservatorio — Academy of Fine Arts — Public Library, 118. Ducal Palace—Exchange—Goldsmiths' Street, 119. Bank of San Giorgio, 120. Dockyards, 102, 121
*Genoa to Turin, 48
*—— to Nice, 76, 87
—— to Sarzana, 121
*—— to Pavia and Milan, 209
Geology of country about Nice, 81, 85-87
Gera d' Adda, 223—torrent, 151
Ghiara d' Adda, 223
Ghisalba, 236
Giandola, 63
Godo, 505
Golden Legend, 97
Gonzagas, history of, 289
Gorgonzola, 258
Gorlago, 234, 236
Gorzone, canal, 390
Governolo, 436
Gradisca, 394

JULIUS.
Gravellona, 53
Greghentino, 152
Grezzana village, 286
Grumello, 236, 259
Guastalla, 422
Gulf of Spezia, 127

H.
Handbook of Painting, xxii.
—— of Architecture, xxv.
Hannibal, his passage over the Apennines, 423
Hobhouse, Sir John, ou Tasso's prison, 451
Hospice, St., peninsula of, 85

I.
Idice, the (Idex), 531, 532
Imola, public establishments and cathedral, 532
Impera, torrent, 66
Incino, 151
Industria, the ancient, 45
Inns in general, xviii
Inverigo, 151, 154
Iron Crown of Lombardy, 156
Iseo, lake and town of, 234
—— to Brescia, 234
*—— to Bergamo, 234
Isiac table, 27
Island of Ariano, 505
—— Bergeggi, 94
—— Burano, 382
—— Malamocco, 384
—— Mazorbo, 382
—— S. Michele, 381
—— Murano, 380
—— Paimaria, 128
—— Pelestrina, 384
—— Tinetto, 128
—— Tino, 128
—— Torcello, 382
Islands, Borromean, 142
Isola del Cantone, stat., 52
Isonzo river, 394
ITALY (North)—Passports and Custom-houses, x. Routes, xii. Modes of travelling—expenses, xiv. Couriers, xvii. Laquais de Place and Ciceroni, xvii. Money, xviii. Inns and accommodations, xviii. Books upon, xx. Maps of, xxiii. Objects to be noticed — Antiquities — Architecture, xxiv. Music, xxvii. Skeleton tours, xxix. Tables of currency, xxxi. Tables of measures of distances, xxxiv.
Ivrea, marquisate of, 2
——, railway to, 34

J.
Jean, St., 84, 85
Juliet, tomb of, 285
Julius II., birthplace, 96

KUGLER.

K.

Kugler's Handbook of Painting, xxii

L.

Laigueglia, 92
Lake of Anone, 151
—— San Bartolommeo, 11
—— Comabbio, 143
—— Como, 145
—— Garda, 254
—— Idro, 252
—— Iseo, 234
—— Madonna, 11
—— Maggiore to Milan, and steamers on the, 141
—— Monate, 143
—— Olginate, 151
—— Pisogne, 236
—— Pusiano, 151
—— Sale and Sulzano, 236
—— Varese, 143
Lambro, river, 151
Lamone, the, 502, 507, 533
Lancenigo, stat., 392
Laquais de place, xvii
Latisana, 392
Lavagna, 125
Lavagnaro river, 124
Laveno, town, 142. Stat. 454
—— to Como and Milan, 142
Lavino river, 454
Lazise, 257
Lecco, 151
—— to Bergamo, 151
*—— to Como, 150
—— to Milan, 152
Legnago, 386
Leira, 97
Lerici, 128
Lessini, monte, 286
Levanto, 126
Libraries at Bergamo, 233
—— at Bologna, 465, 490
—— at Brescia, 248
—— at Cesena, 538
—— at Ferrara, 448
—— at Genoa, 111, 118
—— at Imola, 532
—— at San Lazzaro 403
—— at Mantua, 296
—— at Milan, 200
—— at Modena, 433
—— at Nice, 81
—— at Padua, 316, 327
—— at Parma, 418
—— at Pavia, 218
—— at Ravenna, 524
—— at Reggio, 427
—— at Rimini, 542
—— at Turin, 19, 28
—— of St. Mark's at Venice, 342
—— at Vercelli, 35
—— at Verona, 274
Lido, island and forts, 383
Lima, river, 414

MANTUA.

Limastre, torrent, 414
Limentra, the, 500, 501
Limito, stat., 230
Limone, 62
Linterno, 207
Livenza, river, 392
Livorno, stat., 34
Loano, 94
Lodi, 221, 222
——, battle of, 222
*—— to Milan, 219
*—— to Piacenza, 223
Lojano, 496
Lombard league, 50
Lombardy:—Passports—Posting—Money, 111. Weights—Measures — Territory, 133. Nature of the country—Agriculture — Productions, 134. Language—Fine arts, 138
Lonato, stat., and battle of, 252
Longiano, 539
Lonigo, stat., 303
Lovere, 235. Description of, by Lady M. W. Montagu, 235
Lugo, village, 286
——, town, 509
Luinate, 143
Lunigiana, province of, 129, 423
Lura, 142
Lusignano, 92
Luzzara, 422

M.

Maddalena, la, stat., 60
Madonna del Bosco, sanctuary of, 61
—— della Guardia, 91
—— del Laghetto, sanctuary of, 87
—— di Misericordia, sanctuary of, 96
—— del Monte of Varese, sanctuary, 143
—— del Pilone, 32
—— di Saronno, 208
—— di Soviore, sanctuary of, 126
—— di Vico, sanctuary of, 67
Magenta, 42. Battle, 43
Magnavacca, 506
Magra, river, 129, 423
Malalbergo, 452
Malamocco island — village of —pass, 384. Canal, 505
Maleo, 223
Malgrate, 151
Malghera fort, 328
Malnate, 144
Malone torrent, 33
Malpaga, 236
Manarola, 126
Mangano, Torre del, 210
Mantua, stat. and city, 288. Inns — Railroads — Diligences — Situation, 288. History — Plan of the city, 289. Sieges, 290. Buildings: Castello di

MILAN.

Corte, 291. Palazzo Imperiale or Ducal Palace, 292. Plan of Ducal Palace, 293. Cathedral, 295. Churches, 295. Palaces, 296. Accademia-Scuole Pubbliche, 296. Museo Antiquario, 297. Ponte di San Giorgio, 297. Piazza Virgiliana, 297. Palazzo del Tè, 297. Plan for visiting, 299.
Mantua to Ferrara, 436
*—— to Milan, 223
*—— to Parma, 421
—— to Padua, 385
*—— to Verona, 287
Maps of Italy, xxiii
Marcaria, 228
Marcello, San, 434
Marecchia river, 539
Marengo village, and battle of, 54
Marignano, 221
Marinello, 433
Marquisate of Ceva, 2
—— Ivrea, 2
—— Saluzzo, 2
—— Susa, 2
Marradi, 502
Martesana, canal of, 258
Martignana, 421
Martinengo, 236
Marzabotto, 500
Marzana, Roman remains at, 286
Maschere, le, 497
Massa Lombarda, 508
Matarana, 126
Mausoleum of Galla Placidia, 520
—— of Theodoric, 526
Mazorbo, island, 382
Mazzonica, village of, 230
Measures of distance, xxxiv
Meda, 154
Mela torrent, 240
Melegnano, 221; battles, 221
Melzo, stat., 230
Mentone, 89
Merendole, 387
Merula, river, 92
Mesola, 506
Mestre, stat., 328, 392
Mezzana Corti, 57
Mignenza, 423
MILAN, city—Railway station —Inns, 44, 157. Vetturini —Post-office, 157 — Public conveyances — Physicians — Cafés, Booksellers' shops, &c.—Population of—Foundation of—History of, 158. Roman remains, 159. Gates, 160. Castello—Arco della Pace, 161. Arena, 162. Duomo, 162.
Churches:—S. Alessandro, 174. S. Ambrogio, 171. S. Antonio, 174. S. Bernardino, 175. S. Carlo Borromeo, 175. S. Celso, 175. S. Eufemia, 175. S. Eustorgio, 175. S. Fedele,

INDEX. 551

MILAN.

177. S. Giorgio in Palazzo, 177.
177. S. Giovanni in Conca, 177.
177. S. Lorenzo, 177. S. Marco, 178. S. Maria del Carmine, 179. S. Maria presso S. Celso, 179. S. Maria delle Grazie, 180. S. Maria Incoronata, 183. S. Maria della Passione, 183. S. Maurizio Maggiore, 184. S. Nazaro, 185. S. Paolo, 185. S. Pietro in Gessate, 185. S. Satiro, 186. S. Sebastiano, 186. S. Sepolcro, 186. S. Simpliciano, 186. S. Stefano in Brolio, 186. S. Tomaso in terra mala, 187. S. Vittore al Corpo, 187.
Public buildings : — Ambrosian library, 200. Arcivescovado, 189. Botanic garden, 200. Brera, 191. Pinacoteca, 192. Sculpture gallery, 199. Brera library, 199. Coperto de' Figini, 204. Observatory, 199. Ospedale Maggiore, 203. Ospizio Trivulzi, 204. Palazzo della Reale Corte, 188. Palazzo della Citta, or Broletto, 190. Piazza Borromeo, 204 ; della Fontana, 204 ; de Tribunali, 190 ; Museo Civico di Storia Naturale, 203. Lazzaretto, 204.
Private buildings: — Palaces: Andriani, 205 ; Archinto, 205 ; Borromeo, 205 ; Trivulzi, 205 ; Litta, 205 ; Castelbarco, 205 ; Vismara, 205 ; Pozzi, 206.
Theatres : — Arena, 162 ; Canobiana — Carcano — Filodrammatico — Rè, 206. La Scala, 206. Fiando, 207
Public garden, 207. Casinos (club-houses), 207. Galleria de Cristoferis, 207. Plan for visiting, 207. Environs, 207
*Milan to Turin, 33, 44
*— to Como, 153
*— to Monza, 153
— to Varese by Saronno, 208
— to Genoa, 209
— to Pavia, 209
— to Lodi and Piacenza, 219
— to Cremona and Mantua, 223
—— to the Austrian Frontier, at Peschiera, 229
·— to Venice, 229
— to Bergamo, 229, 258
— to Brescia, 229
Military architecture in Italy, xxvi
Millesimo, battle at, 70
Mincio river, 256
Mirano, 128
Mizzana, 417

MONTE.

Modena, duchy of — Agriculture, commerce, finances— Posting—Money, 425
MODENA, city—Cathedral, 428. Plan of the city, 429. Secchia Rapita, 431. Churches, 431. Palace, 431. Gallery, 431. Library, 433
— to Pistoia, 433
— to Ferrara, 437
— to Bologna, 454
Modigliana, 504
Mogliano, stat., 392
Mombello, villa at, 150
Monaco, territory of the prince of, 88. Town, 89
Monate, 143
Moncalieri, 48
Mondovi, 66
—, battle of, 67
Moneglia, 126
MONEY, xviii
— in Piedmont, 6
— in Riviera, 73
— in Lombardy, 111
— in Austrian Italy, 260
— in Parma, 396
— in Modena, 425
— in la Romagna, 436
Money, Tables of, xxxi
Monfalcone, 394. Excursion from, to Aquileia, 394
Monforte, 100
Monisterolo, 259
Monselice, 387, 390
Montagnana, 386
Montalbano, 84
Montalegro, sanctuary, 123
Montboron, 84
Mont Canferrat, 85
Montebello, battles of, 57
—, village, and stat., 303
Montecchio, castles of, 303, 426
Montecucullo, 433
Monte Appio, 90
— Baldo, 252
— Beni, 497
— Berico, 308
— Bolca, 287
— Calvo, 69
— Caprasio, 9
— Cardo, 501
— Carelli, 498
— Cavo, near Nice, 84
— Chiaro, 252
— Cimone, 414
— del Diavolo, 286
— di Fo, 497
— Fraine, 254
— Galdo, 311
— Girone, 424
— Guardia, 455
— Lungo, 423
— Moria, 403
— Musino, 11
— Orfano, 237
— Pirchiriano, 9
— Prinzera, 423
— Rovinazzo, 403
— Senario, convent of, 498

NERVI.

Monte Stregone, 68
— Trebbio, pass of, 504
— Viso, 48, 62
— Zago, 404
Montemore, 70
Montenotte, pass and battle of, 69
Monterosso, 126
Monteu Po, 45
Montezzemolo, 70
Montferrat, duchy of, 2
Monti Lessini, excursions on, 286
Monticelli, 421
Montone river, 504, 528
Montorfano, 151, 237
Montorio, 100
Monza, stat.—city, 154. Townhall—Cathedral, 154. Relics, 154. Ivory diptychs—Iron Crown—Bas-reliefs, 156. Palace and gardens, 157
*Monza to Como, 153
*— to Lecco, 152
— to Milan, 157
Monzambano, 254
Mordano, 508
Mortara, town and battle of, 46, 53
Motta, town, 392
Mozzate, 209
Mozzecane, stat., 288
Mozzonica, 230
Mugello, the, 497, 502
Mugnone, the, 503
Municipal buildings in Lombardy, xxvi
Murano island, 380
Murazze, the, 505
Museums: at Battaglia, 388
— Bologna, 464
— Brescia, 241, 249
— Genoa, 111
— Mantua, 297
— Milan, 199, 202, 203
— Modena, 431
— Nice, 81
— Padua, 327
— Parma, 418
— Pavia, 218
— Ravenna, 524
— Reggio, 427
— Turin, 25, 28
— Venice, 359
— Verona, 271
— Vicenza, 307
Musiano, 496
Music, xxvii
Musino, Monte, 11
Musocco, 44
Muzza, canal, 221

N.

Naviglio Grande, 42
— di Pavia, 210
Nervi, 122

NERVIA.

Nervia, river, 90
Nice, 76. Inns, 76. Lodgings—Servants — Cafés — Carriages—Vetturini, 77. Passports—Bankers—Physicians—Apothecaries -Libraries and reading-rooms — Diligences, 78. Steamers — Tradesmen — Straw hat and inlaid woodwork — House-agents, 79. English church and buryinggrounds, 79. Masters, 79. History of, 79. Castle, ruins of, 80. Cathedral, 81. Library and museum, 81. Geology of, 81. Climate, 82. Environs of, 83.
Nice to Genoa, 76, 87
——, county of, 2
Nicholas V., birthplace of, 130
Nogara, 385
Noli, 94
Nosedo, San G. di, church of, 220
Novara, 39. Cathedral, 39. Baptistery, 39. Churches, 40. Buildings, &c., 41. Battle of, 41
Novara to Arona by rly., 53
—— to Milan, 42
*—— to Alessandria, 53
Novalesa abbey, 9
Novi, stat., town, 51
Nura river, 404

O.

Obscure, Vallée, 84
Observatory at Bologna, 465
—— Milan, 199
—— Padua, 326
—— Parma, 419
—— Turin, 25
Oderzo, village, 392
Oglio river, 228, 235
Oleggio, stat., 53
Olegno, 53
Olevano, 53
Olgiate, 144
Olginate, lake of, 151
Olona, 44, 142
Oltro Po Pavese, 2
Ombrone di Pistoia, river, 434. Valley, 501
Oneglia, 92
Ontagnano, 392
*—— to Turin, 63, 66
Orco river, 33
Ormea, 66
Orrido di Tinazzo, torrent, 236
Oslo, 259
Osoppo, 393
Ospedaletto, stat., 237
Ospetaletto, 386
Ospizio, Peninsula di Sant', 85
Ostiglia, 437

PASSES.

P.

Padua, stat., 311
PADUA, city:—Inns—Cafés—Antiquities, 311. Plan of the city, 312. Palazzo della Ragione, 313. Archives, 315. Clocks, 315. Cathedral, 315. Baptistery, 316. Biblioteca Capitolare, 316. Palazzo Vescovile, 316. Churches, 316. Prato della Valle, 320. Arena, 320. Giotto's Chapel, or Santa Maria dell' Arena, 321. University, 326. Public library, 327. Observatory, 327. Palaces, 327. Theatres, 327. Hospitals, 327. Plan for visiting, 328. Excursions from, 328
Padua to Ferrara, 390, 437
—— to Venice, 328
*—— to Vicenza, 310
Paglione, valley and river, 63
Palestro, battle of, 38
Palestrina, island, 384
Pallarea, 87
Palazzolo, 236
Pallavicino, state of, 404
Palma Nova, fortress of, 393
Palmaria, island of, 128
Panaro river, 454
Panfilio canal, 437
Pania, la, peaks of, 501
Pantena, Val, 286
PARMA, 407. History—Plan for visiting, 407. Cathedral, 407. Plan of the city, 408. Baptistery, 411. Churches: San Giovanni, 412. Steccata, 413. Sant' Alessandro, 414. San Lodovico, 414. The Annunziata, 415. Farnese Palace, 415. Academy of Fine Arts, 415. Pinacoteca, 415. Library, 418. Museum, 418. University, 419. Tipografia del Governo, 419. Theatre, 419. Botanic garden, 419. Pal. del Giardino, 419. Giardino Ducale, 420
Parma and Piacenza, duchies of, 395.. Government, 395. Nature of the country—inhabitants — produce — finances —money, and posting, 396
*Parma to Cremona, 420
—— to Mantua, 421
—— to Lucca, 422
—— to Reggio and Modena, 426
—— to Sarzana and Lucca, 422
*—— to Piacenza, 396
—— torrent, 407, 419
Parola, 406
Passable, 85
Passes of the Apennines (see Cols)

PO.

Passo, il, 506
Passporta, x
Pastrengo, 257
Paullo, 433
PAVIA, Certosa of, 210. Case of, 214. City of, its history. Cathedral, 214. Plan of the city, 215. Churches, 21 University, 217. Insalubri of, 218
*Pavia to Milan, 209
—— to Genoa, 219
——, Naviglio di, 210
Peacchia, Monte, pass and tu nel, 501
Pegli, villas at, 97
Pelestrina, 384
Peninsula di Sant' Ospizio, 8:
Percotto, 393
Perinaldo, 90
Peschiera, stat., 256. Austria Gov. steamers at, 257
—— to Verona, 263
—— in Lake of Iseo, 234
Pesio, valley, 61
Pessione, stat., 48
Petiglio, 434
PIACENZA, Inns, 396. Objects worthy of notice, railways and diligences, 397. Piazza de' Cavalli, 397. Cathedral, 398. Churches, 400. Citadel—Palaces—Charitable Institutions, 402. Neighbourhood of, 402. Excursion from to Velleia, 402
——, duchy of, 395
*—— to Turin, 54
—— to Parma, 396
Pladena, 228
Plan d'Erba, 151
—— di S. Primo, 151
Pianoro, 496
Piantogna, 423
Pianzano, stat., 393
Plastre, hamlet, 434
Piave river and stat., 392
Piedmont: Territory—Government, 1. Nature of the country — extent — population, 3. Language—fine arts —literature, 4. Posting, 5. Railways— money—weights and measures, 6
Pletola, la, 229
Pietra, 94
Pietramala, 497
Pieve, 66
—— di Cento, 454
—— Pelago, 434
Pineta, the, near Ravenna, 529
Pino, 47
Pirchiriano, Monte, 9
Pisciatello, the, 539
Pisogne, 236
Pizzighettone, 223
Po, the, 417
—— di Goro, 505
—— Grande, 505
—— Vecchio, 420

PO.

Po di Primaro, 452, 506
—— di Volàno, 437, 452, 506
Pujano, stat., 310
Polcevera river, 98
Polenta, village, 518
Polesella di Rovigo, 390
Pollenzo, the ancient Pollentia, 64
Pomposa, 506
Ponte S. Ambrogio, 454
—— di Brenta, stat., 328
—— Carata, 209
—— della Castellina, 505
—— Curone, 56
—— Decimo, 52
—— di Lago Scuro, 391, 437
—— San Marco, stat., 252
—— di Nava, 67
—— Nura, 404
—— Petri, 434
—— San Pietro, 152
—— di Veja, 286
Pontremoli, 423
Ponzana, stat., 39
Pordenone, town and stat., 393
Poretta, la, and waters of, 500
Portalbera, ferry of, 57
Port of Como, 148
—— of Chioggia, 384
—— of Genoa, 102
—— of Nice, 81
—— of Malamocco, 384
—— of Primaro, 506
—— of Ravenna, 526
—— of Rimini, 541
—— of Sermione, 253
—— of Venice, 334
Porto Maurizio, 91
—— Secco, 384
—— Venere, 128
Portoguaro, 392
Portone, 424
Possagno, country of Canova, 310
Pozzolengo, stat., 256
Pra, 97
Pratolino, 498
Predore, 235
Preganziol, stat., 392
Primaro, 506
Puliciano, 502
Punta Bianca, 129
—— delle Chiappe, 123
—— del Corvo, 129
—— di S. Vigilio, 257
Purga di Bolca, 287
Pusiano lake, 151

Q.

Quaderna stream, 531
Quarto and Quinto villages, near Genoa, 122
Quatrelle, 437
Querciolano, 504
Quinto village, near Verona, 286

RAVENNA.

R.

Racconigi stat. and palace, 59
Railways open, xv, 6, 262, 436
Susa to Turin, 7
Turin to Genoa, 48
Turin to Ivrea, 34
Turin to Biella, 34
Turin to Milan through Alessandria as far as Mortara, 48, 53
Turin to Vercelli and Novara, 33
Turin to Pinerolo, 14
Between Alessandria and the Lago Maggiore by Mortara, and thence to Novara and Arona, 51, 53
Turin and Cuneo, 58
*Genoa to Turin, 48
*Genoa to Alessandria, 48
Genoa to Voltri, 100
Como to Monza and Milan, 153
*Milan to Monza and Como, 153
*Mortara, through Alessandria and Novi, to Genoa, 48
Milan to Brescia and Venice, 229; and at the other extremity, Coccaglio to Brescia, Verona, Padua, and Venice, 237, 252, 299
Milan to Venice, 229
Verona to Mantua, 287
*Mantua to Verona, 287
Brescia to Verona, 252
Verona to Vicenza, 299
Vicenza to Padua, 310
Padua to Venice, 328
Venice to Treviso and Casarsa, 392
Rapallo, 123
Rastigniano, 496
Ravenna :—Inns, 509. Historical notice, 509. Plan of the city, 510. Plan for visiting, 513. Churches :—Sta. Agata, 515; S. Apollinare Nuovo, 515; Baptistery, 514; Cathedral, 514; Sta. Croce, 516; S. Domenico, 516; S. Francesco, 516; S. Giovanni Battista, 517; S. Giovanni Evangelista, 517; Sta. Maria in Cosmedin, 518; Sta. Maria in Porto, 518; S. Nicolò, 518; S. Romualdo, 518; Santo Spirito, 518; S. Vitale, 519 Mausoleum of Galla Placidia, 520. Palace of Theodoric, 521. Tomb of Dante, 521. House of Lord Byron, 522. Palaces, 523. Library, 524. Museum, 524. Academy of the Fine Arts, 525. Hospital, 525. Theatre, 525. Piazze, 525. Torre del Pubblico, 525. Gates, 526. Fortress, 526. Port, 526.

ROSTA.

Ravenna :—
Environs :—Mausoleum of Theodoric, 526. Sta. Maria in Porto Fuori, 527. S. Apollinare in Classe, 527. Pineta, 529. Colonna de' Francesi and battle of Ravenna, 530.
*Ravenna to Faenza, 505.
*—— to Forlì, 504.
*—— to Venice, 505.
*—— to Bologna, 508, 531.
—— to Rimini, 531.
Razotta torrent, 502
Recco, 122
Recoaro, baths of, 310
Reggio, city, 426
Renaissance style, xxvi
Reno, river, 434, 452, 454, 500
—— valley, 500
Resegone di Lecco, mountain, 151
Retrone torrent, 303
Revere, 434
Rezzano, 403
Rezzato, stat., 252
Rho, 44, 142
Rialto at Venice, 357. Bridge, 358
Rigossa river, 539
Rimini :—Historical notice, 540. Arch of Augustus, 540. Cathedral, 540. Churches, palaces, port, 541. Fortress, library, house of Francesca da Rimini, 542.
*Rimini to Ravenna, 531.
—— to Bologna, 532
Rio Grande, 406
Rio Maggiore, 126
Riola, mineral springs at, 533
Ritorto stream, 151
Riva di Chieri, 47
—— on Lake of Garda, steamers to and from, 257
—— di Taggia, 91
Rivarolo, stat., 52
Rivello, 388
Riviera road, 87, 121
Rivoli, in Piedmont, 11
—— plateau of, 257
Robarello, village, 143
Robilante, 62
Rocca di Fontenellato, 426
—— San Casciano, 504
Roccabruna, 89
Roccia Melone, Monte di, 9
Rochetta di Tanaro, 50
Romagna, la, 435. History, 435. Passports—Money—Posting—Railroads, 436
Romano, 230
Romans, 393
Romeo and Juliet, story of, 285
Ronca, valley of, 286
Roncaglia, 421
Ronco, stat., 52
—— village, 300
—— river, 504, 505, 528, 538
Rosta, stat., 11

N. Italy.—1860.

2 B

ROTONDA.

Rotonda Capra, the, of Palladio, 309
Rottofreno stat., 57
Routes, xii.
Rovacchia Codura, 406
Rovato, 237
Roverbella, stat., 288
Roveglia, 65
Rovere, 504
Rovigo, city, 390, 437
Roya, torrent, 63, 90
Rubicon, the, or Uso river, 531, 539
Rubiera, 427
Russi, 505
Ruta, tunnel of, 123

S.

Sacca, 421
Sacile, town, 393
Sacro Monte di Varese, 143
Sagra di San Michele, 10
Sale, 236
Saletto, 386
Salmour, 65
Salto della Bella Alda, 10
Saluggia, stat., 34
Saluzzo, marquisate of, 2
Sambonifacio, stat., 300
Samoggia, 454
San Benedetto, 504
San Bernardo, valley of, 96
San Dalmazzo, village and abbey of, 62, 63
San Damiano, stat., 49
San Donato, 221
San Donino, Borgo, 405
San Fedele, 93
San Frutuoso, 123
San Germano, stat., 34
San Giorgio, 286, 403
San Giorio, stat., 9
San Giovanni Ilarione, 286
San Giuliano, 221. Stat., 56
San Godenzo, river and village, 503
Sanguinetto, 385
San Lazzaro, 403, 426, 532
San Leo, 542
San Lorenzo, 91, 228
—— della Costa, 123
—— de' Picinardi, 228
San Marcello, 434
San Marco, island, 357
San Marino, republic of, 542. Its constitution, 542. Hamlet of Borgo, 543. Origin and history of the republic, 543
San Martino, 42
——, village and battle, 256
—— d' Albaro, 122
—— dell' Argine, 228
—— di Lantosca, 61
——, stat., 300
—— di Ticino, 219
San Michele, tower of, 10. Village near Verona, 299

SAVONA.

San Nazzaro, 421
San Niccolò, 432
San Nicolo, stat., 57
San Pier d'Arena, 52, 98
San Piero, village, 503
San Pietro in Cariano, 286
San Pietro in Volta, 384
San Polo, 403
San Pona, 83
San Primo, erratic blocks at, 151
San Prospero, 426
San Remo, 91
San Rufillo, 496
San Salvatore di Lugano, 144
San Saverio, 531
San Stefano, 91
San Tomaso in Limine, church of, 234
San Vigilio point, 257
San Vito, 392
Sant' Ambrogio, 454
——, ch. at Milan, 171
——, near Verona, 286
——, stat., 11
Sant' André, near Nice, 84
Sant' Anna, village, 286
Sant' Antonino, stat., 9
Sant' Antonio di Rinverso, 11
Sant' Arcangelo, 539
Santa Bianca, 437
Santa Croce, post, 394
Santa Eufemia, 502
Santa Giulietta, stat., 57
Sant' Ilario, 426
Santa Lucia, near Verona, 287
Santa Margherita, 123
Santa Maria Maddalena, 437
Santa Maria della Stella, sanctuary of, 286
Sant' Ospizio, cape, 85
Santa Sofia, 504
Santerno, the, 508, 531, 532
Sauthia, stat., 34
Saorgia, town of, 63
Sardinian possessions on the Mediterranean — political changes, 71. Character of the country, 71. Agriculture— Towns, 72. Roads, 73. Posting, &c. — Money—Weights and Measures, 73. Character of the population, 74. Inns —Fine Arts, 75
Sarmato, stat., 57
Sarnico, 234
Saronno, 208
Sartirana, stat., 53
Sarzana, city, 129
*—— to Genoa, 121
Sarzanetta, 130
Sasso, il, pass of, 500
—— di Castro, mount of, 497
Savena river, 496, 532
Savigliano, stat., 60
Savignano, 539
—— castle, ruins of, 500
Savio, the, 531, 538
Savona, city of, 95
*—— to Turin, 70

STEAMERS.

*Savona to Alessandria, 67
Savoy, dukes of, 2
Scaligers, history of, 268
——, tombs of the, 268
Scarena, 63
Schio, town of, 309
Scoltenna river, 434
SCULPTURE in Italy, Lombardy, and Tuscany, xxvi
Secchia Rapita, la, 431, 456
—— river, 428
Sele, the, 383
Sella torrent, 500
Senio, the, 509, 533
Seregno, stat., 154
Seriana, val, 236
Seriate, village of, 236
Serio river, 236
Sermide, 437
Sermione, 253
Serraglio, 229
Serragliolo, 437
Serravalle, stat., 51
—— town, 543
—— valley, 393
Sesia river, 38
Sesto Calende, 141
—— to Milan, 141
Sesto, stat., 157
Sestri di Ponente, 98
—— à Levante, 125
—— to La Spezia, coast-road, 126
Setta, valley and torrent, 500
Sette Commune, district of, 310
Settimo, 33
Sezze, stat., 68
Shakspeare and Verona, 285
Sibana, 500
Sieve valley, 497, 502, 503
Sight-seeing, xvii
Silaro, the, 532
Silk, production of, in Lombardy, 138
Siviana, 234
Soarza, 404
Soave town, 286, 300
Solero, stat., 50
Solferino, 256
——, battle, 255
Somma, village, 141
—— Campagna, stat., 263
Sorbolo, 421
Sori, 123
Sospello, 63
Sotto Marina, town, 384; island, 385
Spezia, town and gulf of, 127
Spigno, 69
Spineticum, 506
Spinetta, la, stat., 56
Spinone, lake, 235
Spotorno, 94
Spresiano, stat., 392
Stained glass of Italy, xxvii
Steamers between Nice and Genoa, 79
—— between Nice and Marseilles, 79

STEAMERS.

Steamers between Genoa and Sardinia, 99
—— between Genoa and Leghorn, &c., 99
—— between Venice and Trieste, 331, 391
—— on the lake Maggiore, 54, 141
—— on the lake of Como, 144
—— on the lake of Iseo, 234
—— on the lake of Garda, 257
Stellata, 437
Stradella, 57
Strasoldo, 394
Stregone, Monte, 68
Strevi, stat., 68
Stupinigi villa, 33
Stura river, 64
Sturla torrent, 122
Suello, 151
Sulzano, 236
Superga, la, hill and church, 31
Susa to Turin, 7
——, arch at, 7
——, marquisate of, 2

T.

Taggia, 91
Tagliamento river, 393
Taglio del Pò, 506
Tanarelo mountain, 66
Tanaro river, source of, 66
Taneto, 426
Taro river, and bridge over, 406
Tartaro river, 385
Tasso's prison, 450
Tavarone, 423
Tavernerio, 151
Tavernola, 234
Tavernelle, stat., 303
Tenda, village, and Col di, 62
Tendola, 424
Terenzo, 424
Terra Rossa, 423
—— del Sole, 504
Terzo, 68, 394
Theodoric, palace of, at Ravenna, 521
——, mausoleum of, 526
Ticino river, 42. Bridges over, 42, 219
Tidone river, 57
Timavo river, 394
Tino and Tinetto, islands of, 128
Toirano, 94
Torazzo, stat., 34
Torcello island, 382
Torre Beretti, stat., 53
Torrion Balducco, 39
Tortona, town and fortress of, 36
Tours, skeleton, xxix
Tradate, village, 209
Travelling, modes of, in Italy, xiv
Trebbia river, 57

USO.

Trebbiano, 129
Trecate, 42
Trescorre, baths of, 235
Treviglio, stat., 230
Treviso, 392
Trezzo, 233
Trieste, 394
Trinita, la, 66, 87
Trino, 45
Trivella, castle of, 63
Troffarello, stat., 48, 58
Tronzano, stat., 34
Trophæa Augusti at Turbia, ruins of, 88
Tunnel of Busalla, 52
Tunny fishery, 85
Turbia, and ruins at, 87
Turin, battle of, 14, 32
TURIN, 12. Inns—Cafés—Restaurateurs—Post-office, 12. Diligences, vetturini, 13. Railways, physicians, population, 14. History, 14. Climate, 15. Buildings—Cathedral, 15. Santo Sudario—Relics, 16. Churches, 17. Protestant church, 18. Royal Palace, 18. King's Library—Armoury, 19. Archives—Military Academy, 20. Castle—Royal Gallery of Pictures, 21. Academy of Fine Arts—Acad. of Science—Museum of Antiquities — Egyptian Collection, 25. Medals—Museum of Nat. Hist.—University and library, 28. Piazzas—Palaces, 29. Theatres, 21, 30. Charitable Institutions, 30. Environs—Superga, 31.
Royal Villas, 32.
Turin to Asti, 47, 48
—— to Cormayeur, 33
—— to Genoa, 48
—— to Milan, 33, 44
—— to Nice, 58
—— to Oneglia, 63, 66
—— to Piacenza, 54
—— to Pinerolo, 14
—— to Romagnano, 33
—— to Savona, 67, 70
*—— to Susa, 7
—— to Val d'Aosta, 33

U.

Udine, town, 393
Ufens, river, 538
University of Bologna, 463
—— Genoa, 111
—— Padua, 326
—— Parma, 419
—— Pavia, 217
—— Turin, 18
Urago d' Oglio, 230
Urbano, Fort, 454
Uso river, the Rubicon, 531, 539

VENICE.

V.

Vado, 94
Vaglia, 498
Val d' Andona, fossil organic remains at, 49
Val Camonica, 236
Val Cavallina, 235
Val Cunella, 286
Val Madonna, stat., 53
Val Pantena, 286
Val Pesio, 61
Val Policella, 286
Val Seriana, 236
Valbura cascade, 502
Valdagno, 310
Valdechiesa, stat., 48
Valdieri baths, 61
Valeggio, village and castle of, 288
Valenza, stat., 53
Vallassina, 151
Valle, stat., 53
—— di Comacchio, 506
Valley of Ronca, 286
Valli grandi Veronesi, 385
Vallone Oscuro, il, 84
Vanestra torrent, 70
Vaprio, 258
Vara river, 126
Varallo Pombia, stat., 53
Varazze, 96
Varese, 143. Roads from, to the Simplon, Laveno, Como, Porto, and Milan, 144. Public conveyances to the Camerlata stat. and Como, 143. To Lago Maggiore, 144
Varese, lake, 143
·Varigotti, 94
Velleia, ruins of, 403. Objects of antiquity found at, 403
Velva or Bracco pass, 125
Venetian Provinces : Population, passports, money, 260. Weights and measures, posting, 261. Railways, 262
Venice, stat., 329
VENICE, city, 329. Hotels, 329. Passports, Restaurants, Cafés, Gondolas, 330. Railways, Steamers, Post-office, Shops, Valets de Place, 331. Description and History, 332. Costume, Dialect, 333. Manufactures, 334. Piazza of St. Marco, 335. Cathedral, 335. Clock Tower, 340. Merceria, 340. Procuratie Vecchie, 340. Procuratie Nuove — Palazzo Imperiale, 341. Libreria, 342. Zecca, 343. Columns, 343. Lion of St. Mark, 343. Piers of St. John of Acre, 344. Campanile, 344. Doge's Palace, 344. Bridge of Sighs, 353. Arsenal and Dockyard, 353. Canal Grande, 355. Palaces, 355–360. Rialto,

VENICE.

357. Fabbriche, 357. Ponte di Rialto, 358. Fondachi, 358. Churches, 360. Archives, 363. Scuole, 373. Academy of Fine Arts, 374. Museo Correr, 359. Pinacoteca Manfrini, 359. Theatres, 379. Artesian wells, 379. Plan for visiting the city, 380. Islands, 380. Churches: St. Mark (Cathedral), 335. SS. Apostoli, 361. La Vergine dei Carmelo, 361. S. Cassano, 361. S. Francesco della Vigna, 361. S. Giovanni Crisostomo, 364. SS. Giovanni e Paolo, 364. S. Giorgio de' Greci, 367. S. Giorgio Maggiore, 366. S. Giacomo di Rialto, 367. Jesuiti, 367. S. Lazaro, 372. Madonna dell' Orto, 367. S. Maria Formosa, 368. S. Maria Gloriosa dei Frari, 361. The Madonna de' Miracoli, 368. S. Maria della Salute, 368. S. Moise, 369. S. Pantaleone, 369. S. Pietro di Castello, 369. Il Redentore, 369. S. Rocco, 373. S. Salvatore, 370. Gli Scalzi, 371. S. Sebastiano, 371. S. Stefano, 371. Toleutini, 371. S. Trovaso, 372. S. Zaccaria, 372. Islands: — Murano, 380; Burano and Mazorbo, 382; Torcello, 382; Lido, 383; Pelestrina, 384. Malamocco pass, 384. Chioggia, 384 Venice to Chioggia, excursion, 384
*—— to Padua, Vicenza, Verona, and Brescia, 299
—— to Ravenna, 505
—— to Treviso, 391
—— to Trieste, 391
Ventimiglia, 90
Venzone, 393
Vercelli, lordship of, 2
——- city, 34. Its library, 35. Cathedral, 35. Churches, 36
*—— to Turin, 33
—— to Novara, 38
Verdello, 230
Vergatello torrent, 500
Vergato, 500

VEZZANO.

Vernazza, 126
Verolengo, 45
Verona, city of, 263. Inns, diligences, climate, divisions, site, 263. Ancient buildings: — Amphitheatre, 264. Roman theatre, 265. Porta de' Borsari, 265. Arco de' Leoni, Fortifications, 265. Gallery of pictures, 270. Cathedral, 272. Baptistery, 274. Biblioteca Capitolare, 274. Castel' Vecchio, 272. Castel' San Pietro, 272. Castel' San Felice, 272. Museo Lapidario, 271. Palazzo del Consiglio, 267. Piazza delle Erbe, 267. Piazza dei Signori, 267. Pinacoteca, 270. Theatres, 285. Tombs of the Scaligers, 268. Vescovado, or bishop's palace, 275. Neighbourhood of Verona, 285.
Churches: S. Anastasia, 275. S. Bernardino, 277. S. Elena, 277. S. Eufemia, 277. S. Fermo Maggiore, 278. S. Giorgio Maggiore, 279. S. Giovanni in Valle, 279. S. Maria in Organo, 279. S. Maria della Scala, 280. SS. Nazaro e Celso, 280. S. Pietro Martire, 272. S. Sebastiano, 280. S. Stefano, 281. S. Tomaso Cantuarense, 281. S. Zenone, 281 Palaces: — Canossa, Giusti, Miniscalchi, Guarienti, Maffei, Gazzola, &c., 284, 285
Tomb of Juliet, Verona and Shakspeare, &c., 285
Theatres, 285. Cemetery, 285
Plan for visiting, 285
Verona, environs of, 285
*—— to Brescia, 252
—— to Mantua, 287
—— to Vicenza, Padua, and Venice, 299
Verrua, 45
Vespolate, stat., 53
Vestena Nova, 286
Vettuone, 44
Vetturini, xiv
Vezzano, 129

ZAPPOLINO.

Via Æmilia, 403, 454, 532, 538
Roman stations on, 532
Vicentine hills, 308
Vicenza, stat., 303
VICENZA, the ancient: Plan of the city, 302. Inns — Situation — Bridges — Roman remains — Palladio's buildings, 303. Piazza de' Signori — Basilica — Palazzo Prefettizio — Cathedral — Churches, 304. Palaces, 305. Casa Pigafetta, 306. Teatro Olimpico — Pinacoteca Civica, 307. Cemetery, 309. Collegio Cordellino, 308. Neighbourhood of, 308. Madonna di Monte Berico, 308. Rotonda of Palladio, 309. Plan for visiting, 310
Vicenza to Padua, 310
*—— to Recoaro, 310
*—— to Verona, 299
Vico, sub. of Como, 148
Vico Belegnano, 421
Vicopré, 421
Vigevano, 47
Vigarano, 437
Vigo, 500
Villafranca, harbour, climate, &c., 85. Stat. 49, 287, 423. Treaty of, 256, 287.
Villanova, stat., 49
Villanuova, 93
——, stat., 300
Villastellone, stat., 58
Vinaglio, battle of, 38
Voghera, 56
Voltri, 97
Voragine, 96

W.

Wooden bucket (la Secchia Rapita) of Modena, 431, 456

Zanelli canal, 534
Zappolino, battle of, 431

THE END.

PRINTED BY W. CLOWES AND SONS, STAMFORD STREET, AND CHARING CROSS.

MURRAY'S HANDBOOK ADVERTISER,
1861.

The great advantage of this medium of Advertising for those who are desirous of communicating information to Travellers can scarcely be questioned, as it enables Steam, Railway, and other Public Companies, Landlords of Inns, Tradesmen, and others, to bring under the immediate notice of the great mass of English and American Tourists who resort to France, Belgium, Germany, Switzerland, Italy, Spain and Portugal, Sweden, Norway, Denmark, Russia, the East, and other parts of the world every Season, in the most direct way, the various merits of their Railways, Steamers, Hotels, Taverns, Articles of Merchandise, Works of Art, and such other information as they may desire to make known.

Annual Circulation, 12,000.
Advertisements must be paid in advance and sent to the Publisher's before May.
The Charges are—A Page, 4*l.* Half-page, 2*l.* 2*s.* A Column, 2*l.* 2*s.* Half a Column, 1*l.* 2*s.*

INDEX TO ADVERTISEMENTS.

GERMANY.
	Page
BERLIN.—Harsch's Glass Warehouse	15
BONN.—Golden Star Hotel	51
BREMEN.—Hillman's Hotel	34
CARLSBAD.—Wolf's Glass Manufactory	11
COLOGNE.—Farina's Eau de Cologne	10
FRANKFORT.—Tacchi's Glass Warehouse	9
Böhler's Manufactory of Staghorn	12, 13
Roman Emperor Hotel	14
MÜHLBAD.—Family Hotel	35
MUNICH.—Wimmer's Magazine	7
Four Seasons Hotel	49
NUREMBERG.—Stein's Magazine	33
Nuremberg Manufactures	34
PRAGUE and VIENNA.—Hofmann's Glass Manufactory	11
VIENNA.—Hôtel Wandl	35
Lobmeyr's Glass Manufactory	14

FRANCE, SWITZERLAND, & ITALY.
BAGNÈRES.—Hôtel de France	33
BERNE.—Bernerhof (Hotel)	36
BRIENZ.—Grossmann's Wood Sculpture	6
FLORENCE.—Bianchini's Mosaic	6
Mannaioni's Marble Works	14
Costa and Conti, Artists	16
Viguier, née Mauche	16
Bacciotti's Picture-rooms	16
Roberts, Perfumer	31
Lace, &c., Depôt	36
GENEVA.—Liodet, Watchmaker	30
Hôtel Byron	31
INTERLAKEN.—Pharmacie Anglaise	34
LEGHORN.—Micali's Marble Works	11
LUCERNE.—Englischer Hof	36
LYONS.—Grand Hotel de Lyon	27
NICE.—How's Hôtel de l'Univers	7
Pension Anglaise	34
School for Young Gentlemen	37
PARIS.—Hôtel de Deux Mondes	35
PISA.—Huguet and Van Lint, Sculptors	6
ROME.—Fabri, Forwarding Agent	8
House Agency	40
ZURICH.—Kerez, Chemist	33

HOLLAND.
AMSTERDAM.—Doelen Hotel	36
ROTTERDAM.—Dutch Rhenish Railway	32
Kramers, Bookseller	46

MALTA.
VALETTA.—Kingston, Chemist	35

EGYPT.
	Page
ALEXANDRIA.—Hôtel Abbatt	34
General Agency	44

ENGLAND.
Custom House Agents—McCracken	2-5
Cary's Telescope	7
Swiss Couriers' Society	11
Whitty, Geographer	15
White, Watchmaker	17
Olivier and Carr, General Agents	18, 19
Chubb and Son's Locks and Safes	20
Mudie's Library	21
Athenæum	21
Locock's Pulmonic Wafers	22
Burrow's Landscape Glasses	22
Black's Guide Books	23
Measom's Railway Guide-books	24, 25
Danube and Black Sea Railway Co.	26
Adams's Passport Agency Office	27
Books of Voyages and Travels	28
Brown and Polson's Patent Flour	29
Blackwood's Maps	29
Pelican Life Insurance	30
London and Westminster Bank	30
Travels in Denmark	33
Epps, Homœopathic Chemist	34
Thresher's Essentials for Travelling	34
Spiers' Ornamental Manufactures	34
Thimm, Foreign Bookseller	37
Rowland's Perfumery	37
Heal's Bedsteads	38
Southgate's Portmanteaus	39
South Coast Railway—Paris direct	41
Norwich Union Insurance	42
South-Eastern Railway	43
Hull Steamers	44
Galignani's Paris Guide	44
Whitburn's Foreign Pharmacy	44
Handbook for Paris	44
Durrell and Son's Passport Agency	45
Letts' Passport Agency	46
Glaciers of the Alps	46
Italian Valleys of the Alps	46
Tennant, Geologist	47
Murray's English Handbooks	47
Works on Iceland, &c.	48
South-Western Railway	50
Art of Travel	50
Lee and Carter's Guide Depôt	52

May, 1861.

B

NEW BRITISH TARIFF, 1861.

LONDON, *May* 1, 1861.

MESSRS. J. & R. M^cCRACKEN,

7, OLD JEWRY, LONDON,

AGENTS, BY APPOINTMENT, TO THE ROYAL ACADEMY, NATIONAL GALLERY AND GOVERNMENT DEPARTMENT OF SCIENCE AND ART,

EAST INDIA AGENTS,

AND

AGENTS GENERALLY FOR THE RECEPTION AND SHIPMENT OF WORKS OF ART, BAGGAGE, &C.,

FROM AND TO ALL PARTS OF THE WORLD,

Avail themselves of this opportunity to return their sincere acknowledgments to the Nobility and Gentry for the Patronage hitherto conferred on them, and hope, by the **MODERATION OF THEIR CHARGES**, and unremitting care in passing through the Custom-house Property confided to them, to merit a continuance of the favours heretofore enjoyed.

Their Establishment comprises

DRY AND SPACIOUS WAREHOUSES,

Where Works of Art and all descriptions of Property can be kept during the Owners' absence, at most moderate rates of rent.

Parties favouring J. and R. McC. with their Consignments are requested to be particular in having the Bills of Lading sent to them DIRECT by Post, and also to forward their Keys with the Packages, as, although the contents may be free of Duty, all Packages are still EXAMINED by the Customs immediately on arrival. Packages sent by Steamers or otherwise to Southampton and Liverpool also attended to; but all Letters of Advice and Bills of Lading to be addressed to 7, OLD JEWRY, LONDON.

MESSRS. J. AND R. M^cCRACKEN,

Having been solicited by many friends to extend their Agency to the East, have resolved to add to their other business that of

EAST INDIA AGENCY IN ALL ITS BRANCHES,

And they solicit the support and patronage of their Friends and Clients to this new Branch. They undertake all Banking and Financial Transactions; to execute Commissions for every description of Goods, Supplies, Personal Requisites, and Wines, which latter they are enabled to supply on the most favourable terms, as they are the Agents in England of several of the most eminent houses on the Continent for the sale of their Wines.

MESSRS. J. AND R. McCRACKEN
ARE THE APPOINTED AGENTS IN ENGLAND OF MR. J. M. FARINA,
GEGENÜBER DEM JULICHS PLATZ, COLOGNE,

FOR HIS

CELEBRATED EAU DE COLOGNE,
AND MESSRS. A. DELGADO & SON, OF CADIZ,

FOR THEIR

SHERRY AND AMONTILLADO WINES,
AND ARE ALSO

GENERAL IMPORTERS OF FRENCH AND ALL OTHER WINES,

For Prices of which, see separate List.

LIST OF DUTIES.

All kinds of Merchandise, Works of Art, Antiquities, Curiosities, &c., are now admitted into England **FREE OF DUTY**, except the following (and a few others not of sufficient interest to enumerate here), which are still liable to Duty, viz. :—

		£	s.	d.
ARQUEBUSADE WATER	the gallon	0	14	0
BOOKS printed in and since 1801	the cwt.	0	16	0
—— imported under International Treaties of Copyright	ditto	0	15	0
Pirated Editions of English Works are totally prohibited.				
—— English, reimported (unless declared that no Drawback was claimed on Export)	the lb.	0	0	1½
CIGARS and TOBACCO, manufactured (3 lbs. only allowed in a passenger's baggage, with 5 per cent. additional)	the lb.	0	9	0
TOBACCO, unmanufactured	ditto	0	3	0
COFFEE	ditto	0	0	3
CONFECTIONERY (Sweetmeats and Succades)	ditto	0	0	2
CORDIALS and LIQUEURS	the gallon	0	12	0
EAU DE COLOGNE, in long flasks	each	0	0	6
—— in other bottles	the gallon	0	14	0
MACCARONI and VERMICELLI	the cwt.	0	0	4½
PERFUMED SPIRITS	the gallon	0	14	0
PAPER-HANGINGS	the cwt.	0	14	0
PLATE, of Gold	the oz. troy	0	17	0
—— of Silver	ditto	0	1	6
PRINTS and DRAWINGS	the lb.	0	0	3
TEA	ditto	0	1	5
WINES in Cask, under 18° of strength	the gallon	0	1	0
—— ,, above 18° and under 25° of strength	ditto	0	1	9
—— ,, ,, 25° ,, 40° ,,	ditto	0	2	5
—— ,, ,, 40° ,, 45° ,,	ditto	0	2	11
—— in Bottle (6 bottles to the gallon)	ditto	0	2	5
SPIRITS in Cask and in Bottle	ditto	0	8	0

Spirits in Casks must contain not less than 21 gallons.

MESSRS. J. AND R. M^CCRACKEN'S

PRINCIPAL CORRESPONDENTS ARE AT

ALEXANDRIA.....	Messrs, BRIGGS & Co. Mr. E. St. J. FAIRMAN.
ALICANTE	Messrs. JASPER WHITE & Co.
ANCONA	Messrs. MOORE, MERELLET, & Co.
ANTWERP	{ Messrs. F. MACK & Co., Kipdorp, No. 1748. Mr. P. VAN ZEEBROECK, Picture Dealer, &c., Rue des Rècollets, 2076. }
ATHENS, PIRÆUS	Mr. J. J. BUCHERER.
BADEN BADEN...	Messrs. STUFFER & BINDER. Mr. F. PELIKAN'S Successor.
BAD EMS........	Mr. H. W. THIEL. Messrs. BECKER & JUNG.
BAGNERES DE BI-GORRE (Hautes Pyrénées).........	Mr. LÉON GÉRUZET, Marble Works.
BASLE	{ Messrs. JEAN PREISWERK & FILS. Mr. JEAN THOMMEN, Fils. Messrs. SCHNEWLIN & Co. }
BERLIN	{ Messrs. SCHICKLER Brothers. Mr. LION M. COHN, Comm^{re}. Expéditeur. Messrs. C. HARSCH & Co., Glass Manufacturers, 67, Unter den Linden. }
BERNE	Mr. ALBERT TRUMPY.
BEYROUT	Mr. HENRY HEALD.
BOLOGNA	Sig. G. B. RENOLI. Sig. L. MENI.
BOMBAY	Messrs. LECKIE & Co.
BORDEAUX	{ Messrs. J. H. SABATIER & Co. Messrs. J. SANSOT & FILS, Hôtel des Princes et de la Paix. Mr. LÉON GÉRUZET, 44, Allées de Tourny. }
BOULOGNE S. M...	Messrs. CHARTIER, MORY, & VOGUE. Mr. A. SIRE.
CALAIS...........	Messrs. CHARTIER, MORY, & VOGUE.
CALCUTTA	Messrs. GRANT, SMITH, & Co.
CARLSBAD.......	{ Mr. THOMAS WOLF, Glass Manufacturer. Mr. CARL KNOLL, au Lion Blanc. }
CARRARA........	Sig. F. BIENAIMÉ, Sculptor. Sig. VINCENZO LIVY, Sculptor.
CIVITA VECCHIA .	Messrs. LOWE BROTHERS, British Vice-Consulate.
COBLENTZ	Messrs. SACHS & HOCHREIMER, Wine Merchants. Mr. P. J. CASSINONE.
COLOGNE.........	{ Mr. J. M. FARINA, gegenüber dem Julichs Platz. Messrs. G^{me}. TILMES & Co. Mr. P. J. CASSINONE. }
CONSTANCE......	Messrs. ZOLLIKOFFER & HOZ.
CONSTANTINOPLE	Messrs. C, S. HANSON & Co.
CORFU	Mr. J. W. TAYLOR.
DRESDEN.........	{ Messrs. H. W. BASSENGE & Co. Mr. E. ARNOLD, Printseller. Mr. TH. UHMANN, Royal Porcelain Manufactory Depôt. Mr. J. KREISS, Glass Manufacturer. Madame HELENA WOLFSOHN, Schössergasse, No. 5. Mr. A. L. MENDE. }
FLORENCE	{ Messrs. EMM^{le}. FENZI & Co. Messrs. FRENCH & Co. Messrs. MAQUAY & PAKENHAM. Mr. E. GOODBAN. Mr. J. TOUGH. Messrs. NESTI, CIARDI, & Co. Mr. ANT^o. DI LUIGI PIACENTI. Mr. S. LOWE. Mr. GAET^o. BIANCHINI, Mosaic Worker. Messrs. P. BAZZANTI & FIG., Sculptors, Lungo l'Arno. Heirs of F. L. PISANI, Sculptor, No. 1, sul Prato. Mr. P. MANNAJONI, Sculptor in Alabaster, Lung'Arno, North Side, No. 2036A. Sig. CARLO NOCCIOLI. Sig. LUIGI RAMACCI. }
FRANKFORT O. M.	{ Mr. P. A. TACCHI'S Successor, Glass Manufacturer, Zeil. Messrs. BING, Jun., & Co. Mr. F. BÜHLER, Zeil D, 17. Mr. G. A. ZIPF. }
FRANZENSBAD....	Mr. C. J. HOFMANN.
GENEVA	Mr. AUG^{ste}. SNELL. Mr. F. PELIKAN'S Successor, Grand Quai, No. 171.
GENOA	{ Messrs. GIBBS & Co, Messrs. G. VIGNOLO & FIG^l. Mr. A. MOSSA, Croce di Malte. }
GHENT	Mr. J. DE BUYSER, Dealer in Antiquities, Marché au Beurre, No. 21.
GIBRALTAR	Messrs. ARCHBOLD, JOHNSTON, & POWERS. Messrs. TURNER & Co.
HAMBURG	Messrs. SCHAAR & CLAUSS. Mr. G. F. RODE.
HAVRE...........	Messrs. P. DEVOT & Co. Mr. A. CHAUMONT.

McCRACKEN'S LIST OF CORRESPONDENTS—continued.

HEIDELBERG ..... { Mr. PH. ZIMMERMANN. SCHULZE & MATTER, Successors to Mr. M. LIEBER.
HONFLEUR .... Mr. J. WAGNER.
INTERLACKEN.... Mr. J. GROSSMANN. Mr. CLEMENT SESTI.
LAUSANNE .... Mr. LONGCHAMPS. Mr. DUBOIS RENOU, Fils.
LEGHORN .... { Messrs. W. MACBEAN & Co. Messrs. HENDERSON BROTHERS. Messrs. THOMAS PATE & SONS. Messrs. MAQUAT, PAKENHAM, & SMITH. Messrs. GIAC°. MICALI & FIG°, Sculptors in Alabaster and Marble. Mr. M. RISTORI. Mr. CARLO CAROCCI, Uffizio della Strada Ferrata. Messrs. G¹⁰. GALLIANI & Co. Mr. ULISSE COTREMAN.
LISBON .... { Mr. ARTHUR VAN ZELLER, in the Peninsular and Oriental Steam Navigation Company's Offices.
LUCERNE .... Mr. J. KESSELBACH-UNTERFINGER. Messrs. F. KNORR & Fils.
MADRAS........... Messrs. BINNY & Co.
MADRID........... Messrs. HENRY O'SHEA & Co., 57, Calle de Fuencarral.
MALAGA........... Mr. GEORGE HODGSON.
MALTA .... { Mr. EMANUEL ZAMMIT. Messrs. Josʰ. DARMANIN & SONS, 45, Strada Levante, Mosaic Workers. Mr. FORTUNATO TESTA, 92, Strada Stᵃ Lucia. Mr. CARMELO DIMECH. Mr. L. FRANCALANZA, 123, Strada St. Giovanni.
MANNHEIM ...... Mr. DINKELSPIEL. Messrs. EYSSEN & CLAUS.
MARIENBAD ...... Mr. J. T. ADLER, Glass Manufacturer.
MARSEILLES ..... { Messrs. CLAUDE CLERC & Co. Messrs. HORACE BOUCHET & Co. Mr. PHILIORET, 8, Rue Suffren.
MAYENCE ....: Mr. G. L. KAYSER, Expéditeur. Mr. W. KNUSSMANN, Cabinet Maker.
MESSINA.......... Messrs. CAILLER & Co.
MILAN .... Messrs. BUFFET & BERUTO, Piazzale di S. Sepolcro, No. 3176.
MUNICH........... { Mr. HY. WIMMER, Printseller, Promenade St. No. 12. Heirs of SEB. PICHLER. Messrs. MAY & WIDMAYER, Printsellers. Messrs. L. NEGRIOLI & Co.
NAPLES .... Messrs. IGGULDEN & Co. Messrs. W. J. TURNER & Co.
NEW YORK .... Messrs. WILBUR & PRICE. Mr. THOMAS SCOTT.
NICE .... { Messrs. A. LACROIX & Co., British Consulate. Messrs. E. CARLONE & Co. Mr. T. W. HOW. Mr. CH. GIORDAN.
NUREMBERG..... { Mr. PAOLO GALIMBERTI, at the Red Horse, Dealer in Antiquities. Mr. JOHN CONRAD CNOPF, Banker and Forwarding Agent. Mr. A. PICKERT.
OSTEND .... Messrs. BACH & Co.
PALERMO .... Messrs. THOMAS BROTHERS.
PARIS .... Mr. L. CHENUE, Packer, Rue Croix Petits Champs, No. 24.
PAU .... Mr. BERGEROT.
PISA............... Messrs. HUGUET & VAN LINT, Sculptors in Alabaster and Marble.
PRAGUE.......... { Mr. W. HOFMANN, Glass Manufacturer, Blauern Stern. Mr. P. CZERMAK, ditto. Mr. A. V. LEBEDA, Gun Maker.
ROME .... { Messrs. TORLONIA & Co. Messrs. FREEBORN & Co. Messrs. MAC-BEAN & Co. Messrs. PLOWDEN, CHOLMELEY, & Co. Messrs. PAKENHAM, HOOKER, & Co. Mr. E. TREBBI. Mr. LUIGI BRANCHINI, at the English College. Mr. J. P. SHEA.
ROTTERDAM..... { Messrs. PRESTON & Co. Messrs. C. HEMMANN & Co. Messrs. BOUTMY & Co.
SCHAFFHAUSEN .. Messrs. ZOLLIKOFFER & HOZ.
SEVILLE .... { Mr. JULIAN B. WILLIAMS, British Vice-Consulate. Den JUAN ANT. BAILLY.
SMYRNA .... Messrs. HANSON & Co.
ST. PETERSBURG. Messrs. THOMSON, BONAR, & Co.
SYRA .... Mr. WILKINSON, British Consul.
THOUNE .... { Mr. A. H. J. WALD, Bazaar. Mr. EBB, Fils. Messrs. BUZBERGER & LANZREIN. Mr. ALBERT TRUMPY.
TRIESTE .... Messrs. MOORE & Co.
TURIN .... Messrs. J. A. LACHAISE & FERRERA, Rue de l'Arsenal, No. 4.
VENICE .... { Messrs. FREERS SCHIELIN. Mr. ANTONIO ZEN. Messrs. S. & A. BLUMENTHAL & Co. Mr. L. BOVARDI, Campo S. Fantine, No. 2000, rosso.
VEVAY .... Mr. JULES GETAZ.
VIENNA.......... { Mr. W. HOFMANN, Glass Manufacturer, am Lugeck, No. 768. Messrs. J. & L. LOBMEYER, Glass Manufacturers, 940, Kärntner
VOLTERRA ...... Sig. OTTO. CALLAJ, and Messrs. G. CHERICI & Figl. [Strasse.
WALDSHÜTT..... Messrs. ZOLLIKOFFER & HOZ.
ZÜRICH .... Messrs. WEISS zum BRACKEN.

FLORENCE.

G. BIANCHINI,

MANUFACTURER OF TABLES AND LADIES' ORNAMENTS OF FLORENTINE MOSAIC,

No. 4844, VIA DE' NELLI,
Opposite the Royal Chapel of the Medici,

INVITES the English Nobility and Gentry to visit his Establishment, where may always be seen numerous specimens of this celebrated and beautiful Manufacture, in every description of Rare and Precious Stones. Orders for Tables and other Ornaments executed to any Design.

G. BIANCHINI'S Agents in England are Messrs. J. & R. M'CRACKEN, 7, Old Jewry, London.

BRIENZ — INTERLACKEN.

J. GROSSMANN,

SCULPTOR IN WOOD, AND MANUFACTURER OF SWISS WOOD MODELS AND ORNAMENTS,

AT INTERLACKEN.

HIS WAREHOUSE is situated between the Belvedere Hotel and Schweizerhof, where he keeps the largest and best assortment of the above objects to be found in Switzerland. He undertakes to forward Goods to England and elsewhere.

Correspondents in England, Messrs. J. & R. McCRACKEN, 7, Old Jewry.

PISA.

HUGUET AND VAN LINT,

SCULPTORS IN MARBLE AND ALABASTER,

Lung' Arno, under the Hotel Peverada.

THE oldest established house in Pisa, where may be found the best assortment of Models of the Duomo, Baptistry, and Tower. Also Figures and other local objects illustrative of the Agriculture and Customs of the country, executed in the highest style of art.

Their extensive Show Rooms are always open to Visitors.

Correspondents in England, Messrs. J. & R. McCRACKEN, 7, Old Jewry, London.

NICE.

HOTEL DE L'UNIVERS.
T. W. HOW,
FROM LONDON, PROPRIETOR.

This Hotel, most eligibly situated in one of the most central positions in the town, on the south side of the Place St. Dominique, and close to the Corso, Cercle, Public Libraries, Theatre, Sea-Baths, &c., has been entirely renovated, and furnished with the comforts necessary to English travellers.

Apartments or single rooms on most moderate terms.

Table d'hôte. THE TIMES and GALIGNANI taken in.

Correspondents in London, Messrs. J. and R. M'CRACKEN, 7, Old Jewry.

CARY'S IMPROVED POCKET TOURIST'S TELESCOPE.
(See 'Murray's Handbook.')

Manufacturer of all descriptions of Mathematical, Surveying, and Optical Instruments, for the use of Naval and Military Officers, &c. Also the Binocular Reconnoitring Field Glass, so highly spoken of by officers and other gentlemen; price, with best sling-case, 5l. 5s. Cary's improved Achromatic Microscope, with two sets of choice lenses, capable of defining the severe test objects, 16l. 16s. and 18l. 18s. Travelling Spectacles of all kinds.

Mathematical and Optical Instrument Maker to the Admiralty, Royal Military College, Sandhurst, Christ's Hospital, and East India College, Agra, &c.

181, STRAND, LONDON.
Established upwards of a Century.

MUNICH.

HENRY WIMMER,

SUCCESSOR TO

J. M. DE HERMANN,

PRINT AND PICTURE SELLER TO HIS MAJESTY THE KING OF BAVARIA,

ROYAL PROMENADE STRASSE, No. 12,

MAGAZINE OF OBJECTS OF FINE ARTS,

PICTURES, PRINTS, DRAWINGS, AND LITHOGRAPHS,

INVITES the Nobility and Gentry to visit his Establishment, where he has always on Sale an extensive collection of Pictures by Modern Artists, Paintings on Glass and Porcelain, Miniatures, Drawings, Engravings, and Lithographs, the latter comprising the Complete Collections of the various Galleries, of which Single Copies may be selected.

He has also on Sale all that relates to the Fine Arts.

H. WIMMER undertakes to forward to England all purchases made at his Establishment, through his Correspondents, Messrs. J. & R. M'CRACKEN, 7, Old Jewry, London.

L. FABRI,
CAPO LE CASE, No. 3, ROME,
Forwarding Agent
TO
GREAT BRITAIN, FRANCE, RUSSIA, GERMANY, AND AMERICA.

L. FABRI, Commissionnaire and Forwarding Agent, undertakes the forwarding of Works of Art, Pictures, Statuary, and Baggage, the expense of which can be paid through rates on arrival of the packages at their destination.

M. FABRI, in order to save trouble to travellers or others who wish to forward articles, attends to their removal, packing, shipping, and marine insurance at moderate fixed rates, and fulfils all the formalities required by the Roman Customs on exportations.

M. FABRI employs skilled workmen for packing Statuary, Marble, and fragile articles, and has correspondents in all the principal Cities of the World, to whom packages are consigned, and who pass them through the Customs with the greatest possible care, and deliver them to the Consignees.

Messrs. LIGHTLY & SIMON,
123, FENCHURCH STREET, LONDON,
are M. FABRI's Correspondents in Great Britain.

M. FABRI also undertakes the purchase of Pictures, &c., and payments to Artists or others, as well as any other commission business.

M. L. FABRI has commodious warehouses specially adapted for the reception of Pictures and other works of Art.

RATES BY SAILING VESSELS.

From			To	Per cubic foot.
From Ripa Grande (Rome)			to New York	40 cents.
,,	,,	,,	Boston	50 ,,
,,	,,	,,	Philadelphia	50 ,,
,,	,,	,,	London, Dublin, and other English ports	1s. 10d.
,,	,,	,,	By STEAMER	2s. 9d.

FRANKFORT O. M.

P. A. TACCHI'S SUCCESSOR,

(LATE FRANCIS STEIGERWALD,)

ZEIL D, No. 17,

BOHEMIAN FANCY GLASS AND CRYSTAL WAREHOUSE.

P. A. TACCHI'S SUCCESSOR begs to acquaint the Public that he has become the Purchaser of Mr. F. STEIGERWALD'S ESTABLISHMENT in this Town, for the Sale of Bohemian Fancy Cut Glass and Crystals.

He has always an extensive and choice Assortment of the Newest and most Elegant Patterns of

ORNAMENTAL CUT, ENGRAVED, GILT, & PAINTED GLASS,

BOTH WHITE AND COLOURED,

In Dessert Services, Chandeliers, Articles for the Table and Toilet, and every possible variety of objects in this beautiful branch of manufacture. He solicits, and will endeavour to merit, a continuance of the favours of the Public, which the late well-known House enjoyed in an eminent degree during a considerable number of years.

P. A. TACCHI'S SUCCESSOR has BRANCH ESTABLISHMENTS during the Season at

WIESBADEN AND EMS,

Where will always be found Selections of the newest Articles from his principal Establishment.

His Agents in England, to whom he undertakes to forward Purchases made of him, are Messrs. J. & R. M'CRACKEN, 7, Old Jewry, London.

COLOGNE O. RHINE.

JOHN MARIA FARINA,

GEGENÜBER DEM JÜLICHS PLATZ

(Opposite the Julich's Place),

PURVEYOR TO H. M. QUEEN VICTORIA;
TO H. M. F. W. III., KING OF PRUSSIA; THE EMPEROR OF RUSSIA;
THE KING OF HANOVER, ETC. ETC.,

OF THE

ONLY GENUINE EAU DE COLOGNE.

THE frequency of mistakes, which are sometimes accidental, but for the most part the result of deception practised by interested individuals, induces me to request the attention of English travellers to the following statement:—

Since the first establishment of my house in 1709, there has never been any partner in the business who did not bear the name of FARINA, nor has the manufacture of a second and cheaper quality of EAU DE COLOGNE ever been attempted. Since 1828, however, several inhabitants of Cologne have entered into engagements with Italians of the name of Farina, and, by employing that name, have succeeded to a very great extent in foisting an inferior and spurious article upon the Public.

But they have in this rivalry in trade not been satisfied with the mere usurpation of my name; the concluding phrase, "*opposite the Julich's Place*," which had so long existed my special property, was not allowed to remain in its integrity. To deceive and lead astray again those of the public who are not fully conversant with the locality and circumstances, the competition seized hold of the word "*opposite*," and more than once settled in my immediate neighbourhood, that they might avail themselves to the full extent of the phrase "*opposite the Julich's Place*." When tried before the courts, the use only of the word "*opposite*" was forbidden, which, however, has been supplied by the word "*at*" or "*near*," with the addition of the number of their houses. It is true, another less flagrant, but not less deceitful invention was, that several of my imitators established the sites of their manufactories in other public places of the town, to enable them to make use of the phrase "*opposite —— Place,* or *Market*," on their address cards or labels, speculating, with respect to the proper name "*Julich*," on the carelessness or forgetfulness of the consumer. I therefore beg to inform all strangers visiting Cologne that my establishment, which has existed since 1709, is exactly opposite the Julich's Place, forming the corner of the two streets, Unter Goldschmidt and Oben Marspforten, No. 23; and that it may be the more easily recognised, I have put up the arms of England, Russia, &c. &c., in the front of my house. By calling the attention of the public to this notice, I hope to check that system of imposition which has been so long practised towards foreigners by coachmen, valets-de-place, and others, who receive bribes from the vendors of the many spurious compounds sold under my name.

A new proof of the excellence of MY manufacture has been put beyond all doubt by the fact of the Jury of the Great Exhibition in London having awarded ME the Prize Medal.— See the Official Statement in No. 20,934, page 6, of the '*Times*' of this month.

COLOGNE, *October*, 1851. J. M. FARINA,

Gegenüber dem Julichs Platz.

*** *My Agents in London are* MESSRS. J. & R. M'CRACKEN, 7, *Old Jewry, by whom orders are received for me.*

SWISS COURIERS'
AND
TRAVELLING SERVANTS' SOCIETY

BEG to inform the Nobility and Gentry, should they require the services of a Courier or Travelling Servant, only those whose characters have borne the strictest investigation, both as regards sobriety, honesty, and general good conduct, have been admitted into the Society, and who are capable of fulfilling their duties efficiently. The Society therefore ventures to solicit your patronage, and hopes to deserve your future favours.

All information may be obtained of the Secretary,
HENRY MASSEY, Stationer,
103, PARK STREET, GROSVENOR SQUARE.
Established 1856.

WILLIAM HOFMANN,
BOHEMIAN GLASS MANUFACTURER,
TO HIS MAJESTY THE EMPEROR OF AUSTRIA,

RECOMMENDS his great assortment of Glass Ware, from his own Manufactories in Bohemia. The choicest Articles in every Colour, Shape, and Description, are sold, at the same moderate prices, at both his Establishments—

At Prague, Hotel Blue Star; at Vienna, 768, Lugeck.

Agents in London, Messrs. J. and R. M'CRACKEN, 7, Old Jewry.

Goods forwarded direct to England, America, &c.

LEGHORN.

HIACINTH MICALI AND SON,
Via Ferdinanda, No. 1230.

Manufactory of Marble, Alabaster, and Scagliola Tables, and Depôt of objects of Fine Arts.

Their extensive Show-rooms are always open to Visitors.

THEIR AGENTS IN ENGLAND ARE
MESSRS. J. AND R. M'CRACKEN,
7, Old Jewry, London.

CARLSBAD.

THOMAS WOLF,
MANUFACTURER OF
ORNAMENTAL GLASS WARES.

THOMAS WOLF begs to inform the Visitors to Carlsbad that at his Establishment will be found the finest and richest Assortment of the Crystal and Glass Wares of Bohemia— especially Table and Dessert Services— all at reasonable and fixed prices.

CORRESPONDENTS IN ENGLAND:
Messrs. J. & R. M'CRACKEN, 7, Old Jewry.

FRANKFORT O. M.

SILBERNE MEDAILLE.

STEMPEL, bewilligt vom

SENAT der freien Stadt, **FRANKFURT.**

FRIEDRICH BÖHLER,

MANUFACTORY OF STAGHORN,

Zeil No. 54 (next door to the Post-Office).

FURNITURE OF EVERY DESCRIPTION, as Sofas, Chairs, Tables, &c. &c. CHANDELIERS, Table and Hand Candlesticks, Shooting-tackle, INKSTANDS, Paper-knives, Penholders, Seals, &c. KNIVES, RIDING-WHIPS, Cigar-cases and Holders, Pipes, Match-boxes, Porte-monnaies, Card-cases, Thermometers, GOBLETS, Candle-screens, Figures and Groups of Animals executed after Riedinger and others. BROOCHES, Bracelets, Earrings, Shirt-pins, Studs, and Buttons. STAG AND DEER HEADS with Antlers attached to the Skull. Sofa-rugs or Foot-cloths of Skins of Wild Animals with Head preserved.

Orders for a Complete Set or for any quantity of FURNITURE will be promptly executed.

The Agents in London are Messrs. J. and R. M^cCRACKEN, 7, Old Jewry.

FRANKFORT O. M.

FRIEDRICH BÖHLER,

Zeil, 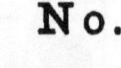 No. 54,

dicht neben der Post,

Stempel, bewilligt vom Senat der freien Stadt, Frankfurt

PENDULES (Ornamental Clocks) of every description, VASES, Goblets, ANTIQUE and MODERN STATUETTES and GROUPS, Groups of Animals, INKSTANDS, Paper-weights, &c. &c., in Bronze, Cast Iron, Galvano-plastic, &c.

CROWN-CHANDELIERS; Branch, Table, and Hand Candlesticks, in Bronze, &c.; Lamps of every description.

PORCELAIN and Britannia-metal Goods, Liqueur-chests.

TRAVELLING DRESSING-CASES, Railroad Companions, Picnic-baskets, Travelling Bags, Brushes, Combs.

WORK-TABLES and Boxes, Tapestries, Fans, Ball-books, Smelling-bottles, Opera-Glasses, &c. &c.

Superior Copies of the ARIADNE by Dannecker, and the AMAZON by Kiss.

Genuine Eau de Cologne of Jean Maria Farina, opposite the Jülichsplatz.

The Agents in London are Messrs. J. and R. M^CCRACKEN, 7, Old Jewry.

VIENNA.

Bohemian White and Coloured Crystal Glass Warehouse.

J. & L. LOBMEYR,
GLASS MANUFACTURERS,
No. 940, KÄRNTHNERSTRASSE,

BEG to inform Visitors to Vienna that they have considerably enlarged their Establishment. The most complete assortment of all kinds of Bohemian White and Coloured Crystal Glass, and of all articles in this branch of industry, in the newest and most elegant style, is always on hand. The rich collections of all Articles of Luxury, viz. Table, Dessert, and other Services, Vases, Candelabras, Lustres, Looking-glasses, &c. &c., will, they feel assured, satisfy every visitor.

The prices are fixed at very moderate and reasonable charges.—The English language is spoken.

Their Correspondents in England, Messrs. J. and R. M'CRACKEN, No. 7, Old Jewry, London, will execute all orders with the greatest care and attention.

FLORENCE.

PETER MANNAIONI,
SCULPTOR IN MARBLE AND ALABASTER, AND WORKER IN FLORENTINE MOSAIC,
LUNG' ARNO, NORTH SIDE, No. 2036a.

A vast collection of objects of Art of every kind is to be seen in this establishment, such as Marble and Alabaster Statues and Vases, Ancient and Modern Pictures, Miniatures, Engravings, and Drawings, Objects of Antiquity, Bronzes, &c. Artists' Books and Florentine Mosaic. Commissions taken for Marble Busts and Portrait Painting, and generally for all kinds of Architectural Works, as Monuments, Chimney Pieces, Furniture, &c.

Correspondents in London, Messrs. J. and R. M'CRACKEN, 7, Old Jewry.

FRANKFORT O. M.

MESSRS. LÖHR & ALTEN,
PROPRIETORS OF
THE ROMAN EMPEROR HOTEL,
Beg to recommend their House to English Travellers.

This large and well-situated Establishment is conducted under the immediate superintendence of the Proprietors, and newly furnished with every comfort, and a new splendid Dining-room.

The "ROMAN EMPEROR" is often honoured by Royal Families and other high personages. The following have lately honoured this Hotel—

H.M. THE KING AND QUEEN OF WURTEMBERG.
H.M. THE QUEEN OF HOLLAND.
H.R.H. THE CROWN PRINCE AND PRINCESS OLGA OF WURTEMBERG.
H.I.H. THE ARCHDUKE OF AUSTRIA. &c. &c. &c.

Table-d'hôte at 1, **1fl. 30kr.**   Breakfast, **42kr.**
       "   "   5, **2fl.**   Tea, **42kr.**
Bed Rooms, from **1fl.** to **3fl.**

BERLIN.

C. HARSCH & CO.,
67, Unter den Linden,

FANCY GLASS WAREHOUSE,

BEG to call the attention of VISITORS to their EXTENSIVE ASSORTMENT of

BOHEMIAN, BAVARIAN, AND SILESIAN GLASS,

CONSISTING OF

ARTICLES OF EVERY DESCRIPTION,

OF THE NEWEST AND MOST ELEGANT PATTERNS.

Their Correspondents in London are Messrs. J. & R. M'CRACKEN, 7, Old Jewry.

J. IRWINE WHITTY, D.C.L., LL.D., M.A., F.R.G.S.,
GEOGRAPHER,

English and Foreign Map Seller,

AGENT TO THE GOVERNMENT

FOR THE SALE OF THE

ORDNANCE MAPS AND RECORDS.

MAP-MOUNTING DONE ON THE PREMISES.

Spring Roller Maps, Case Maps, &c. Globes, Atlases, Charts.
GEOLOGICAL MAPS. GUIDE BOOKS.
TRAVELLING MAPS. SCHOOL MAPS. LARGE WALL-MAPS.
GEOGRAPHICAL WORKS. MILITARY SKETCHES, &c.

GEOGRAPHICAL WAREHOUSE,
35, Parliament Street, London.

FLORENCE.

MESSRS. COSTA & CONTI,
ARTISTS,

No. 1318, VIA DEI BARDI (Studio on the First Floor).

Messrs. COSTA and CONTI keep the largest collection in Florence of original Ancient and Modern Pictures, as well as copies of all the most celebrated masters.

N.B.—English spoken.

Correspondents in England, Messrs. J. and R. M'CRACKEN, 7, Old Jewry, London.

FLORENCE.

VIGUIER, NÉE MAUCHE,
PIAZZA SANTA MARIA NOVELLA, No. 4253, First Floor;
Next door to the Casa Libri.

Linen and Linen Articles, ready-made Shirts and Shirt-fronts, plain and embroidered.

Handkerchiefs, in Cambric and Linen, plain and embroidered, white and coloured.

Stockings and Socks, for Ladies and Gentlemen.

Damask Napkins and Table Linen.

Every kind of Novelty in Ladies' Dresses, &c.

This Establishment, selling for account of the first English and French Houses, furnishes articles of the best quality at Manufacturers' prices.—Fixed Prices.

FLORENCE.

PICTURE ROOMS.

MR. E. BACCIOTTI,
Via Legnajoli, No. 1,
OPPOSITE THE STROZZI PALACE,

THE best Copies of the Florentine Galleries may be found there. If desired, arrangements can be made for prices to include delivery free of charges in London or New York.

Correspondents in London, Messrs. J. and R. M'CRACKEN, 7, Old Jewry.

EDWARD WHITE,

(FROM DENT'S,)

CHRONOMETER,

WATCH, AND CLOCK

MANUFACTURER.

E. WHITE,

For several years principal assistant at Messrs. DENT'S, of Cockspur Street, having taken the premises formerly occupied by Messrs. Green and Ward, respectfully solicits an inspection of his Stock, comprising a choice selection of

CHRONOMETERS, WATCHES, CLOCKS, &c.,

Which have been recently manufactured, on the most improved principles, by workmen of the first talent.

20, COCKSPUR STREET, PALL MALL, LONDON, S.W.

TO VISITORS TO THE CONTINENT.

LONDON, 1ST MAY, 1861.

OLIVIER & CARR,
37, Finsbury Square, London,

COMMISSION MERCHANTS AND GENERAL AGENTS

For Shipment and Reception of Goods to and from all Parts of the World.

Agents to **Mr. F. BEYERMAN**, Bordeaux, and
Mr. T. FOWLE, Mareuil, near Ay, Champagne, and 8, Rue Pernelle, Paris,
FOR THE SALE OF THEIR BORDEAUX AND CHAMPAGNE WINES.

UNDERTAKE to receive, and pass through the Customhouse in London, Liverpool, Southampton, &c., packages of every description, particularly **THE WORKS OF ART AND OTHER PROPERTY, THE PURCHASES OF VISITORS TO THE CONTINENT,** assuring those who may favour them with their patronage that the greatest attention will be combined with **Moderate Charges.**

The Bills of Lading and Letters of Advice of Packages sent to Liverpool and Southampton should be addressed to O. & C. in London, and keys of locked Packages should be sent to them, as everything must be opened immediately on arrival.

O. & C. also undertake the execution of orders at a moderate commission for **THE PURCHASE OF GOODS OF EVERY DESCRIPTION,** being enabled from their long experience as Commission Merchants, and thorough knowledge of all the Markets, to purchase on the most advantageous terms.

In order to comply with the frequently expressed desire on the part of Travellers to know in anticipation to what expenses their Packages are liable on arrival in England, OLIVIER & CARR have established the following

Rates of Charges on the Reception of Packages.

For Landing from the Ship, clearing through the Customhouse, Delivery in any part of London, Agency included :—

On Trunks or Cases of Baggage and Personal Effects, if sent singly . **9s.** each.
   If 3 Packages sent at one time. . . . . **7s.** ,,
   If 6 ,, ,, ,, ... **5s. 6d.** ,,
On Cases containing Works of Art or other objects, the purchases of
   Travellers, of moderate size and value, if sent singly . . . . **15s.** ,,
   If 3 Cases sent at one time . . . . **12s.** ,,
   If 6 ,, ,, ,, ... **9s.** ,,
On large Cases of valuable Pictures, Statuary, &c., the charges will depend on the care and trouble required, but they will be on the same moderate scale as above.

Their Mr. C. H. OLIVIER having been established at the above address as a Commission Merchant for thirty years, and their Mr. C. CARR having been upwards of nineteen years in the house of Messrs. J. & R. M'Cracken, General Agents, No. 7, Old Jewry, they can offer the results of long experience and a determination to render themselves worthy of the patronage which they respectfully solicit. Their principal Correspondents are as follows.

OLIVIER & CARR'S Correspondents are—

At	Aix-la-Chapelle...	Messrs. A. SOUHEUR & CO.
,,	Alexandria	Mr. E. St. J. FAIRMAN.
,,	Antwerp	Mr. F. VERELLEN BEERNAERT.
,,	Basle	Mr. J. J. FREY.
,,	Bordeaux	Mr. F. BEYERMAN, to whom O. & C. are Agents for the Sale of his Wines.
,,	Boulogne	Mr. L. BRANLY.
,,	Calais..............	Messrs. CHARTIER, MORY, & VOGUE
,,	Cologne	Messrs. G. TILMES & CO.; Mr. C. H. VAN ZÜTPHEN.
,,	Constantinople ...	Messrs. VALSAMACHY & CO., Galata.
,,	Dresden............	Mr. JOHANN CARL SEEBE.
,,	Florence	Messrs. W. H. WOOD & CO.; Mr. J. TOUGH.
,,	Frankfort	Mr. H. HENLÉ.
		Mr. MORITZ B. GOLDSCHMIDT, Banker.
,,	Geneva	Messrs. JOLIMAY & CO.
,,	Genoa	Mr. J. NIMMO, 12, Strada Ponte Reale.
,,	Hamburg	Messrs. JULIUS WÜSTENFELD & CO.
,,	Havre............	Messrs. H. L. MULLER & STEHELIN.
,,	Interlacken	Messrs. RITSCHARD & BURKI.
,,	Leipzig	Messrs. GERHARD & HEY.
,,	Leghorn............	Mr. MARIO GIOVANNETTI, 13, Scali della Darsena Nuova.
,,	Marseilles	{ Messrs. GIRAUD FRÈRES. { Messrs. HORACE BOUCHET & CO.
,,	Milan..............	Mr. LOUIS MALEGUE, Rue de l'Agneau, No. 8 rouge.
,,	Munich	Mr. J. GUTLEBEN.
,,	Nice	Messrs. LES FILS DE CH. GIORDAN.
,,	Ostend	Mr. J. DUCLOS ASSANDRI.
,,	Paris	Messrs. VICTOR GRAND & CO., Bankers, 14, Rue de Trevise.
		Messrs. DELASSUS & LEDOUX, Packers and Forwarding Agents, 6, Rue Neuve St. Augustin, près la Bourse.
		Mr. T. FOWLE, 8, Rue Pernelle, and at Mareuil, near Ay, to whom O. & C. are Agents for the Sale of his Champagne Wines.
,,	Prague	Mr. J. J. SEIDL, Hibernergasse, No. 1000.
,,	Rome	Messrs. G. DALLEIZETTE & CO.; Mr. J. P. SHEA.
,,	Rotterdam.........	Mr. J. A. HOUWENS.
,,	Trieste	Messrs. MARTIN FRÈRES.
,,	Turin	Mr. C. REMONDINI.
,,	Venice	Mr. HENRY DECOPPET.
,,	Vienna	Messrs. ARNSTEIN & KRAUS.

O. & C. have a Stock in London of

Pure Bordeaux and Rhine Wines imported direct, from 18s. to 96s. per doz.

WINES IN WOOD CAN BE PROCURED AT SHORT NOTICE.

OLIVIER & CARR, 37, FINSBURY SQUARE, LONDON.

CHUBB'S PATENT DETECTOR LOCKS.

CHUBB'S LOCKS afford the greatest security from all Picklocks, or false Keys; also detect any attempt to open them, are extremely simple and durable, and of all sizes and for every purpose to which locks can be applied.

Trunks, Portmanteaus, Travelling Bags, Dressing Cases, Writing Desks, &c., fitted with only the usual common and utterly insecure locks, can have the place of these supplied by Chubb's Patent without alteration or injury.

Travellers' Lock-Protectors and Portable Scutcheon Locks for securing Doors that may be found fastened only by common locks.

CHUBB & SON have always in stock a variety of Writing and Despatch Boxes in Morocco or Russia leather, and japanned Tin; the latter being particularly recommended for lightness, room, durability, and freedom from damage by insects or hot climates. Writing Boxes fitted with trays and stationery complete, and japanned either plain or in imitation of oak, rosewood, and other woods. All are secured by the Detector Locks.

Travelling Covers for Writing Boxes kept in readiness.

Best Black Enamelled Leather Travelling Bags of various sizes, all with Chubb's Patent Locks.

Cash, Deed, and Paper Boxes of all dimensions.

CHUBB'S FIREPROOF SAFES.

THESE SAFES are constructed in the very best manner, of the strongest wrought-iron, fitted with Chubb's Patent Drill-preventive and their Gunpowder-proof Steel-plated Detector Locks, are the most secure from fire and burglary, and form the most complete safeguard for Books, Papers, Deeds, Jewels, Plate, and other valuable property.

CHUBB & SON have also Safes not fireproof, but equally secure in all other respects, intended for holding plate where protection from fire is not an object, and affording much more room inside than the Fireproof Safes. They are recommended specially in place of the ordinary wooden cases for plate, which may so easily be broken open.

Complete Illustrated Priced Lists of Chubb's Locks, Boxes, Safes, and other Manufactures, gratis and post-free.

CHUBB and SON, 57, St. Paul's Churchyard, London, E.C.

MUDIE'S SELECT LIBRARY.

A REVISED LIST
OF THE
Principal New and Choice Books
IN CIRCULATION AT THIS EXTENSIVE LIBRARY
IS NOW READY,
AND MAY BE OBTAINED ON APPLICATION.

This List will serve to indicate the INCLUSIVE character of the whole Collection, which now exceeds **Six Hundred Thousand Volumes**, and to which all Books of acknowledged merit and general interest are added, in large numbers, on the day of publication.

Single Subscription, ONE GUINEA per Annum,
COMMENCING AT ANY DATE.

First-Class Country Subscription (Fifteen Volumes at One Time) Five Guineas per Annum, of the best and newest Works; exchangeable (in sets) at pleasure.

CHARLES EDWARD MUDIE,
509, 510, & 511, New Oxford Street, and 20, 21, & 22, Museum Street, London; 74 & 76, Cross Street, Manchester; and 45, New Street, Birmingham.

THE ATHENÆUM.

It having been represented to the Proprietors that when the ATHENÆUM started in its career its yearly volume consisted of 840 pages, whilst now it has increased to double that number of pages, the Proprietors resolved that the ATHENÆUM should be paged in half-yearly volumes, and an enlarged Index is now given with each volume in January and July.

EVERY SATURDAY, PRICE FOURPENCE, OF ANY BOOKSELLER,

THE ATHENÆUM
JOURNAL OF LITERATURE, SCIENCE, AND ART.
(STAMPED TO GO FREE BY POST, 5*d*.) CONTAINS:—

Reviews, with extracts, of every important New English Book, and of the more important Foreign Works.
Reports of the Proceedings of the Learned Societies, with Abstracts of Papers of Interest.
Authentic Accounts of Scientific Voyages and Expeditions.
Foreign Correspondence on subjects relating to Literature, Science, and Art.
Criticisms on Art, with Critical Notices of Exhibitions, Picture Collections, New Prints, &c.
Music and Drama, including Reports on the Opera, Concerts, Theatres, New Music, &c.
Biographical Notices of Men distinguished in Literature, Science, and Art.
Original Papers and Poems.
Weekly Gossip.
Miscellanea, including all that is likely to interest the informed.

THE ATHENÆUM
Is so conducted that the reader, however distant, is, in respect to Literature, Science, and the Arts, on an equality in point of information with the best-informed circles of the Metropolis.

Office for Advertisements, 20, WELLINGTON STREET, STRAND, LONDON, W. C.

PERFECT FREEDOM FROM COUGHS IN TEN MINUTES AFTER USE,

And Instant Relief and a Rapid Cure of Asthma, Consumption, Coughs, Colds,
AND ALL DISORDERS OF THE BREATH AND LUNGS, ARE INSURED BY

Interesting Testimonial in favour of DR. LOCOCK'S PULMONIC WAFERS.

From Mr. T. J. Davies, Chemist, Rhosmaen Street, Llandilo.—"Gentlemen, I send you the enclosed testimonial, which you can depend upon. Mr. Jenkins is well known as a minister of the Gospel throughout the principality for thirty years. I sell more of Dr. Locock's Wafers than any other Patent Medicine.—Truly yours, T. J. DAVIES."

"Marry's Cottage, near Llandilo.

"Sir,—I have been for fifteen months afflicted with confirmed Asthma, attended with violent coughing. I have tried nearly all supposed remedies without any relief; but, providentially, I am happy to inform you that I was considerably relieved by taking two boxes of Dr. Locock's Pulmonic Wafers. You can make this public.—I am, Sir, yours faithfully,

"WILLIAM JENKINS,
"To Mr. T. J. Davies, Chemist, Llandilo." Calvinistic Methodist Minister."

To Singers and Public Speakers they are invaluable for clearing and strengthening the voice. THEY HAVE A PLEASANT TASTE. Price 1s. 1½d., 2s. 9d., and 11s. per box. Sold by all Druggists. Also,

DR. LOCOCK'S COSMETIC.

A delightfully fragrant preparation for improving and beautifying the complexion, rendering the skin clear, soft, and transparent, removing all eruptions, freckles, sunburn, tan, pimples, and roughness. Sold in bottles at 1s. 1½d., 2s. 9d., and 4s. 6d. each. Beware of counterfeits. Observe the words "Dr. Locock's Cosmetic" on the government stamp outside the wrapper. Sold by all Chemists.

NOTICE.

TRAVELLERS and TOURISTS should be provided with "BURROW'S LANDSCAPE GLASSES," if they desire to really enjoy the scenery of the country they intend traversing. The Press have unanimously praised these Glasses as the best yet produced, and the leading literary and scientific journal thus speaks of them:—

"Alp-climbers, yachters, naturalists, riflemen, pedestrians, summer tourists of all kinds have an interest in the art of making field-glasses. We have recently tried on the hill-side and at the butts a landscape-glass, made by Messrs. Burrow, of Great Malvern; and though the price is moderate, we can speak well of its powers. It is small in the pocket, light in the hand, easily adjusted, and renders the form and colour of the object more than a mile off with distinctness. At the sea-side, at a review, or among the moors, such a companion as the Malvern Landscape Glass must be valuable to many men. It is also available at the Opera."—*Athenæum.*

In sling cases, price Three and a Half and Six Guineas, forwarded on receipt of Post-office Orders, W. & J. BURROW, Great Malvern.

"This is the best binocular Telescope yet invented."—*Bell's Life.*
"The most compact, accurate, and powerful Glass we have met with."—*Field.*
"Excellent glasses, admirably adapted for deer-stalkers, yachtsmen, and sportsmen."—*Illustrated London News.*

CAUTION.—W. and J. BURROW find it necessary to warn the public against deception, as unprincipled persons are selling **inferior Glasses** under the **same** or **similar names**.

The **GENUINE MALVERN GLASSES** can **ONLY** be obtained from Messrs. **BURROW'S ESTABLISHMENT**, Belle Vue Place, Great Malvern.

ORDERS BY POST, ENCLOSING REMITTANCE, EXECUTED THE SAME DAY.

To Tourists in Britain. {BLACK'S GUIDE-BOOKS & TRAVELLING MAPS.

In neat Portable Volumes, illustrated with Maps, Charts, and Views of Scenery, and containing full particulars regarding Hotels, Distances, &c. &c.

England, 10/6.	**Scotland, 8/6.**
English Lake District, 5/.	**Highlands (Anderson's), 10/6.**
Wales, North and South, 5/.	**Trosachs, 1/6.**
North Wales, separately, 3/6.	**Skye, 1/.**
Derby and Warwick, each 2/.	**Staffa and Iona, 1/6.**
Hampshire (Isle of Wight), 2/.	**Sutherlandshire, 1/.**
Gloucester and Hereford, 2/.	**Edinburgh, 3/6 & 1/6.**
Yorkshire, 2/6.	**Glasgow, 2/6 & 1/.**
Surrey, 5/.	**Ireland, 5/.**
Kent, 2/.	**Dublin, Killarney,** each 1/6.
Sussex, 1/.	**Belfast, 1/6.**

BLACK'S ROAD AND RAILWAY TRAVELLING MAPS,

Carefully constructed from the Maps of the Ordnance Survey and other Authorities, neatly bound in portable cases, price 4s. 6d. each.

England, 32 × 22½. **4/6.**	**Scotland,** 32 × 22½. **4/6.**
English Lakes, 19 × 14. **2/6.**	**Scotch Counties,** each **1/.**
Wales, N. & S., 14 × 11¼. each **1/6.**	**Ireland,** 20 × 14½. **2/6.**
Derbyshire, 1/.	**Kent and Sussex, 1/6.**

Smaller Maps at 2s. 6d. and 1s. each.

THE ENCYCLOPÆDIA BRITANNICA.

EIGHTH EDITION.

A Dictionary of Arts, Sciences, and General Literature.

WITH UPWARDS OF FIVE THOUSAND ILLUSTRATIONS ON WOOD AND STEEL AND A COMPLETE INDEX.

21 Volumes 4to. cloth, price £25 12s.; or handsomely half-bound in Russia leather, £32.

BLACK'S GENERAL ATLAS of the WORLD.

A Series of Fifty-Six Maps

OF THE PRINCIPAL COUNTRIES OF THE WORLD, WITH ALL THE MOST RECENT DISCOVERIES, NEW BOUNDARIES, &c.

And accompanied by an **Index of 65,000 Names,** forming a ready Key to the Places mentioned in the Maps. Price £3, half-bound morocco, gilt leaves.

EDINBURGH: ADAM AND CHARLES BLACK.

OFFICIAL
Illustrated Railway Guide-Books,
By GEORGE MEASOM.

Second Editions.

North-Western Railway and its Branches. Three Hundred and Sixty Engravings. **ONE SHILLING.**

Lancaster and Carlisle, Edinburgh and Glasgow, and Caledonian Railways. One Hundred and Fifty Engravings. **ONE SHILLING.**

All the above bound together, 3s. 6d.

"It is certainly the most perfect Railway Guide that has yet appeared. As an 'official' work, it has authority when speaking of the history and statistics of the line: *all is done well*. Few books descriptive of tours contrive to tell so much, describing all that is worthy of description by the way, and conducting the traveller along each branch as the points are arrived at where each branch diverges from the trunk."—ATHENÆUM.

"A marvel of cheapness—being, perhaps, *the cheapest book ever produced under any circumstances*; and, whether as a guide-book or a work of reference, it is *worthy a place in every library*."—NEWS OF THE WORLD.

"*This useful and delightful volume*, which is *a perfect marvel of cheapness*, is prefaced with many interesting railway statistics, and useful directions to the traveller. The book, indeed, is so useful and entertaining, that every one who has travelled, or intends to travel, ought to have it, while he who has made up his mind to stay at home can find no better substitute for travel."—LIVERPOOL MERCURY.

The South-Eastern Railway and its Branches. 200 Engravings. **ONE SHILLING.**

Northern of France, with Six Days in Paris. 100 Engravings and splendid Map. **ONE SHILLING.**

The above two Works, bound together, with Map, 3s. 6d.

"Invest the sum of a shilling for each of the two guide-books above mentioned; *and he will have not only an amusing and instructive companion for the whole route, but save as many pounds as he has spent preliminary pence*. The Northern of France and Paris is by far the *best guide-book we have yet seen of Paris*, and the route there by Boulogne. The books, in fact, are well worthy a place in any library."—NEWS OF THE WORLD.

"Mr. George Measom maintains his credit as a railway topographer for travellers this summer with two Official Illustrated Guides—one to the South-Eastern Railway and its Branches, *a most liberal shilling's worth of edification*; the other to the Northern Railway in France. The latter of these includes a very *clever* illustrated summary of what may be seen in six days in Paris."—EXAMINER.

The Brighton and South-Coast Railway. One Shilling.
The South-Western Railway and its Branches. One Shilling.

R. GRIFFIN, BOHN, & CO., Stationers' Hall Court, Paternoster Row.
W. H. SMITH & SON, Euston, and all Stations on the Line.

OFFICIAL ILLUSTRATED RAILWAY GUIDE-BOOKS—*continued.*

Second Editions.
Great Western Railway and its Branches. 500 Engravings.
ONE SHILLING.
Bristol and Exeter, North and South Devon, Cornwall, and
SOUTH WALES RAILWAYS. 300 Engravings. 500 Pages of Letterpress.
ONE SHILLING.
The above two Works bound together, 3s. 6d.

" Mr. George Measom's *Official Illustrated Guide to the Great Western Railway* is the continuation of a *remarkable series* of illustrations, literary and pictorial, of country crossed by our great English railway lines. The abundance and *excellence* of the information, and the good woodcuts given in these works for a shilling, is one of the literary marvels of our day. The shilling official guide to the Great Western itself contains 872 pages of letterpress, with a woodcut or several woodcuts upon almost every leaf."—EXAMINER.
" The largest shilling's worth of reading we ever saw. This interesting publication is a marvel of cheapness. The illustrations are well chosen and well executed, and the letterpress is written in the plain unvarnished style which characterises the previous works of the *observant* traveller, Mr. Measom."—BRISTOL MIRROR.
" *The Official Illustrated Guide to the Bristol and Exeter Railways.*—This valuable guide is exactly similar in style and construction to the larger companion volume noticed above, giving descriptive illustrated notices of the different places on the various lines. No person travelling in South Wales and the West of England should be without this new official guide."—BRISTOL MIRROR.
" *Illustrated Railway Guides.*—Mr. George Measom has just added to his previous achievements one which cannot fail to excite the greatest astonishment. He has published *The Official Guide to the Great Western Railway*—a bulky volume, containing nearly 900 pages of well-printed descriptive matter, and 300 well-executed engravings—the charge for which is the absurdly low sum of one shilling! *The book is the cheapest book ever published in the world*, and the editor may well speak of the 'studious toil' necessary to get up such a mass of information relative to such a multitude of places. Mr. Measom has also published *The Official Illustrated Guide to the Bristol and Exeter, South and North Devon, South Wales, and Cornwall Railways*. If it were not for its gigantic companion, this Guide must be pronounced marvellously cheap."—LIVERPOOL MERCURY.

In the Press, ready in June, 1861.
Great Northern ; Manchester, Sheffield, and Lincolnshire ; and
MIDLAND RAILWAYS. 300 Engravings. 600 Pages of Letterpress.
ONE SHILLING.

In the Press, ready in June, 1861.
North-Eastern ; North British ; Edinburgh and Glasgow ;
SCOTTISH CENTRAL; EDINBURGH, PERTH, AND DUNDEE; SCOTTISH NORTH-EASTERN; and GREAT NORTH OF SCOTLAND RAILWAYS. 200 Engravings. 500 Pages of Letterpress.
ONE SHILLING.
The above two Works bound together, 3s. 6d.

Messrs. R. GRIFFIN & CO., Stationers' Hall Court, Paternoster Row.

⁎ Mr. GEORGE MEASOM will feel obliged for any local information of public general interest for embodiment in future Editions of the above Works.

Offices—74, Charrington Street, St. Pancras,
London, N.W.—May, 1861.

DIRECT INTERNATIONAL SERVICE

IN CORRESPONDENCE

Between Vienna and Constantinople,

VIA PESTH, BASIAZ, TCHERNAVODA, AND KUSTENDJIE,

Placing Constantinople within 6 Days' Journey from London.

SEA-PASSAGE ABOUT 20 HOURS.

Tickets available for 30 *days, with liberty to stop at intermediate Stations.*

TWO SERVICES WEEKLY.

Departures from Vienna by Railway to Basiaz, thence by Steamer of Danube Navigation Company to Tchernavoda, Railway to Kustendjie, and Austrian Lloyd's to Constantinople, **every Monday and Thursday** at 2 P.M., due at Constantinople Friday and Monday at 8 A.M.

FARES IN FRANCS.

First-Class. . 325   Second-Class . . 226·65   Mixed . . 304·30

Mixed Tickets are First-Class between Constantinople and Basiaz, and Second-Class by Rail or Steamer between Basiaz and Vienna.

The Express Boat of the Danube Steam Navigation Company leaves Vienna every Sunday at 6·30 A.M. The traveller can go by it to Basiaz instead of by the Railway on the following day at equal cost.

The Traveller leaving SOUTH-EASTERN STATION, LONDON BRIDGE, on SATURDAY or TUESDAY at 6·55 A.M., either viâ Paris, Strasbourg, and Munich, or viâ Calais, Brussels, Cologne, Mayence, arrives at Vienna mid-day MONDAY or THURSDAY, and may leave again at 2 P.M. same day for Constantinople.

Return from Constantinople every Monday and Saturday at 9 A.M., due at Vienna every Friday and Wednesday at 1·52 P.M.

The DANUBE STEAMER in correspondence with the Saturday Service from Constantinople is due in Vienna the following Friday about noon.

The Traveller can leave Vienna for England the day of his arrival, at 4 P.M. or 7·30 P.M. according to the Route chosen.

FARES, IN FRANCS, BETWEEN LONDON AND CONSTANTINOPLE.

	1st Class.	2nd Class.	Mixed.
Viâ Paris and Strasbourg	563·20	400·5	477·70
Viâ Cologne and Mayence	539·80	384·15	461·80

The food on board the Danube Boats and Austrian Lloyd's is included in the fare.

TICKETS OBTAINABLE AT THE SOUTH-EASTERN RAILWAY STATION, LONDON.

For further particulars apply in England to the SECRETARY of the Danube and Black Sea Railway and Kustendjie Harbour Company (Limited),

24, ABINGDON STREET, LONDON, S.W.

➥ A GOOD HOTEL AT KUSTENDJIE, WHERE ALL INFORMATION AS TO ROUTES MAY BE OBTAINED.

PASSPORT AGENCY OFFICE,
LONDON, 59, FLEET STREET, E. C.

Regulations for obtaining Foreign Office Passports gratis.

RESIDENTS in the United Kingdom or London, who desire to avoid trouble, can have their PASSPORTS obtained and viséd with expedition, upon application to W. J. ADAMS, 59, Fleet Street.

Country Residents, by this arrangement, are saved the trouble of coming to London, as the Passport can be forwarded to them by Post (*en Règle*).

Fee obtaining Passport, 1s. 6d.; Visas, 1s. each.

Passports carefully Mounted and Cased, and Names lettered thereon in Gold.

Passport Cases from 1s. 6d. to 6s. each.

The countersignature of the American Minister in London obtained to United States Passports.

Every Description of Stationery for Travellers.

THE LATEST EDITIONS OF MURRAY'S HANDBOOKS.

Phrase Books and Dictionaries.

BRADSHAW'S BRITISH and CONTINENTAL GUIDES and HANDBOOKS to France, Belgium, Switzerland, Paris, London, &c.

KELLAR'S Map of Switzerland, Original Edition, 6s. 6d. and 10s. 6d.

INDIA.

BRADSHAW'S Overland and Through Route Guide to India, China, and Australia, 5s.

BRADSHAW'S Handbook to the Bombay Presidency and the North-West Provinces, Madras, and Bengal, 10s. 6d. each.

EXPERIENCED COURIERS MAY BE HAD ON APPLICATION TO
W. J. ADAMS (Bradshaw's British and Continental Guide Office),
LONDON, 59, FLEET STREET, E.C.
OFFICE HOURS 8 TO 7.   SATURDAYS 8 TO 3.

GRAND HOTEL DE LYON,
RUE IMPERIAL, AND PLACE DE LA BOURSE, LYONS.

TWO HUNDRED BEDROOMS, and TWENTY SALOONS, in every Variety; Large and Small Apartments for Families, elegantly furnished; Saloons for Official Receptions; Conversational and Reading Rooms; Coffee and Smoking Divan; Baths; Private Carriages, Omnibuses, Restaurant; Service in the Apartments, *à la Carte*, or at fixed prices.

ALL LANGUAGES SPOKEN.

The GRAND HOTEL DE LYON is too important and too well known to require injudicious praise: It suffices to state that it cost nearly THREE MILLIONS OF FRANCS, and that the accommodation is of so comfortable and luxurious a character as to attract the notice of all visitors.

Although the GRAND HOTEL DE LYON affords the most elegant accommodation for the highest classes, it is frequented by visitors of the humblest pretensions. Rooms at 2 frs., very comfortably furnished.

TABLE D'HOTE at 4 frs. In consequence of the Proprietors having contracted with the Bordeaux and Burgundy Wine-growers for supplies of their Best Wines, qualities of the first vintages may be had at this Hotel at moderate prices. Since the Hotel has been in the hands of new Proprietors, instead of a Company, the reduction they have made in the prices precludes them from paying Fees to the Cab and Coach Drivers at the Railway Station. Travellers are therefore requested to bear in mind that the Grand Hotel de Lyon is situated in the centre of the Rue Impérial, near the Bank of France, and opposite the Palace of the Bourse.

Books of Voyages and Travels, Works on Natural History, &c.

MAY, 1861.

TEN WEEKS in JAPAN. By the BISHOP of VICTORIA (Hong Kong). With a Map and 8 Illustrations in Chromo-xylography. 8vo. 14s.

THE NATURAL HISTORY of CEYLON: comprising Anecdotes illustrative of the Habits and Instincts of the Mammalia, Birds, Reptiles, Fishes, Insects, &c., of the Island; also a Monograph of the Elephant, and a Description of the Modes of Capturing and Training it. By Sir J. EMERSON TENNENT, K.C.S., LL.D., &c. Republished from 'An Account of Ceylon,' &c., with copious Additions, and new Illustrations from Original Drawings. Post 8vo. [Nearly ready.

WILD LIFE on the FJELDS of NORWAY. By FRANCIS M. WYNDHAM. With 5 Illustrations in Chromo-lithography, 2 Maps, and 5 Woodcuts. Post 8vo. 10s. 6d.

ALPINE BYWAYS. By a LADY. With a Map and several Illustrations in Chromo-lithography. Post 8vo. [Nearly ready.

THE ALPS; or, Sketches of Life and Nature in the Mountains. By H. BERLEPSCH. Translated by the Rev. LESLIE STEPHEN, M.A. 8vo. with 17 Plates. [Nearly Ready.

NARRATIVE of the CANADIAN RED RIVER EXPLORING EXPEDITION of 1857, and of the ASSINNIBOINE and SASKATCHEWAN EXPLORING EXPEDITION of 1858. By HENRY YOULE HIND, M.A., F.R.G.S., &c. With 20 Chromo-xylographs, 76 Woodcuts, 3 Maps, &c. 2 vols. 8vo. 42s.

SEVEN YEARS' RESIDENCE in the GREAT DESERTS of NORTH AMERICA. By the Abbé DOMENECH. With above 60 Illustrations. 2 vols. 8vo. 36s.

ANAHUAC; or, Mexico and the Mexicans, Ancient and Modern. By EDWARD B. TYLOR. Pp. 356; with Route Map, 4 Illustrations in Chromo-lithography, and 26 Engravings on Wood. 8vo. 12s.

THE SEA and ITS LIVING WONDERS. By Dr. GEORGE HARTWIG, Author of 'The Life of the Tropics.' With several Hundred Woodcuts, a Physical Map, and 12 Chromo-xylographs, from designs by H. N. HUMPHREYS. Second Edition. 8vo. 18s.

THE LIFE of the TROPICS: a Popular Scientific Account of the Natural History of the Animal and Vegetable Kingdoms in Tropical Regions. By Dr. GEORGE HARTWIG, Author of 'The Sea and Its Living Wonders.' [In preparation.

A WEEK at the LAND'S END. By J. T. BLIGHT, Author of 'Ancient Crosses and other Antiquities of Cornwall:' assisted, in Ornithology, by E. H. RODD, Esq.; in Ichthyology, by R. Q. COUCH, Esq., M.R.C.S.; and, in Botany, by J. RALFS, Esq., M.R.C.S. With a Map, geologically coloured, and numerous Illustrations drawn and engraved on the Wood by the Author. Square fcp. 8vo. [Nearly ready.

GLENCREGGAN; or, a Highland Home in Cantire. By CUTHBERT BEDE. With 3 Maps, 8 Chromo-lithographs, and numerous Woodcuts from Designs by the Author. 2 vols. post 8vo. [Nearly ready.

TWO MONTHS in the HIGHLANDS, ORCADIA, and SKYE. By CHARLES RICHARD WELD, Barrister-at-Law. With 8 Illustrations. Post 8vo. 12s. 6d.

THE AFRICANS at HOME: being a popular Description of Africa and the Africans, condensed from the Accounts of African Travellers from the time of Mungo Park to the Present Day. By the Rev. R. M. MAC-BRAIR, M.A., Author of the 'Mandingo and Foola Grammars,' &c. With a new Map and about 70 Woodcut Illustrations. Square fcap. 8vo. 7s. 6d.

THE LAKE REGIONS of CENTRAL AFRICA. By R. F. BURTON, Captain H.M. Indian Army. Map and Illustrations. 2 vols. 8vo. 31s. 6d.

THE COMPARATIVE ANATOMY and PHYSIOLOGY of the VERTEBRATE ANIMALS. By RICHARD OWEN, F.R.S., D.C.L., Superintendent of the Natural History Department, British Museum; Fullerian Professor of Physiology in the Royal Institution of Great Britain; Foreign Associate of the Institute of France, &c. In One thick Volume, 8vo. With upwards of 1200 Engravings on Wood. [In the press.

SOCIAL LIFE and MANNERS in AUSTRALIA: Being the Result of Eight Years' Experience. By a RESIDENT. Post 8vo. [Just ready.

London: LONGMAN, GREEN, and CO., Paternoster Row.

1861. MURRAY'S HANDBOOK ADVERTISER. 29

VOYAGES AND TRAVELS, NATURAL HISTORY, &c.

PEAKS, PASSES, and GLACIERS. By Members of the Alpine Club. Edited by JOHN BALL, M.R.I.A., President. Traveller's Edition, comprising the Mountain Expeditions and the Maps printed in a condensed form. 16mo. 5s. 6d.
*** The Fourth Edition of 'Peaks, Passes, and Glaciers,' with 8 coloured Illustrations, may still be had, in One Volume, square crown 8vo., price 21s.

THE OLD GLACIERS of NORTH WALES and SWITZERLAND. By A. C. RAMSAY, F.R.S. and G.S., Local Director of the Geological Survey of Great Britain. Reprinted from 'Peaks, Passes, and Glaciers;' with Map and Woodcuts. Fcap. 8vo. 4s. 6d.

'THE EAGLE'S NEST' in the Valley of Sixt: a Summer Home among the Alps. By ALFRED WILLS, Barrister-at-Law. Second Edition. With 12 Illustrations on Stone, and 2 Maps. Post 8vo. 12s. 6d.

RAMBLES in the ISLANDS of SARDINIA and CORSICA: with Notices of their History, Antiquities, and Present Condition. By THOMAS FORESTER. With a Map and many Illustrations from Sketches by Lieut.-Col. BIDDULPH, R.A. Second Edition; with a New Preface. Imp. 8vo. 18s.

FOREST CREATURES: 1. The Wild Boar; 2. The Roe, a New Wonder in Natural History; 3. The Red Deer; 4. The Fallow Deer; 5. The Cock of the Woods; 6. The Black Cock; 7. The Eagle; 8. Homer a Sportsman; 9. Hints. By CHARLES BONER, Author of 'Chamois Hunting in the Mountains of Bavaria.' With Illustrations by Guido Hammer, of Dresden. Post 8vo. [*Just ready.*

London: LONGMAN, GREEN, and CO., Paternoster Row.

The LANCET states:—"This is Superior to anything of the kind known."

BROWN & POLSON'S
TRADE MARK
PATENT CORN FLOUR

The First Manufactured in the United Kingdom and France.

Paisley, Manchester, Dublin, & London.
Sold by Grocers, Chemists, &c., in Packets, 2d., 4d., and 8d., and Tins, 1s., 5s., and 9s. 6d.

NEW GENERAL ATLAS. Dedicated by Special Permission to the Queen.
One Volume, imperial folio, half-bound morocco, price 5l. 15s. 6d.,

Royal Atlas of Modern Geography:

In a Series of entirely original and authentic Maps. With an INDEX to each Map, Arranged so as to obviate the inconvenient method of reference by Degrees and Minutes of Longitude and Latitude.

BY ALEX. KEITH JOHNSTON, F.R.S.E., F.R.G.S., &c.,
Geographer in Ordinary to Her Majesty for Scotland, Author of the 'Physical Atlas,' &c.

W. BLACKWOOD & SONS, EDINBURGH AND LONDON.

*** Each Plate of the above Atlas may be had separately, with a special Index, price 4s. 6d. mounted in Case for the Pocket; or in Sheets at 3s.

SPECIAL NOTICE.

PELICAN LIFE INSURANCE OFFICE. Established in 1797. No. 70, Lombard Street, E.C., and 57, Charing Cross, S.W.

DIRECTORS.

Octavius E. Coope, Esq.	Henry Lancelot Holland, Esq.
William Cotton, Esq., D.C.L., F.R.S.	William James Lancaster, Esq.
John Davis, Esq.	John Lubbock, Esq., F.R.S.
Jas. A. Gordon, Esq., M.D., F.R.S.	Benjamin Shaw, Esq.
Edward Hawkins, jun., Esq.	Matthew Whiting, Esq.
Kirkman D. Hodgson, Esq., M.P.	Marmaduke Wyvill, jun., Esq., M.P.

Robert Tucker, *Secretary and Actuary.*

BONUS.—All Policies effected on the Return System, and existing on the 1st July, 1861, will participate in the next division of Profits, subject to such of them as have not then been in force for five years being continued until the completion of that period.

LOANS.—On Life Interests in possession or reversion: also upon other approved Security in connection with Life Assurance.

*** For Prospectuses, Forms of Proposal, &c., apply at the Offices as above, or to any of the Company's Agents.

THE LONDON and WESTMINSTER BANK issues Circular Notes of £10 each, payable at every important place in Europe. These Notes are issued without charge, and they are cashed abroad free of commission. The Bank also issues, free of charge, Letters of Credit on all the principal cities and towns in Europe. The Letters of Credit are issued only at the head office, in Lothbury. The Circular Notes may be obtained at the head office, in Lothbury, or at any of the Branches, viz.:—

Westminster Branch,	1, St. James's Square.	
Bloomsbury	,,	214, High Holborn.
Southwark	,,	3, Wellington Street, Borough.
Eastern	,,	87, High Street, Whitechapel.
Marylebone	,,	4, Stratford Place, Oxford Street.
Temple Bar	,,	217, Strand.

May 1, 1861. WM. EWINGS, General Manager.

GENEVA.

LIODET,

WATCHMAKER AND JEWELLER,

64, Rue du Rhone.

WATCHES OF EVERY DESCRIPTION, manufactured entirely on the Premises, and none sold that cannot be warranted PERFECT TIMEKEEPERS.

Travellers will always find a large choice of the newest style of

JEWELLERY, MUSICAL BOXES, MECHANICAL FIGURES, SINGING-BIRD BOXES, &c.,

only to be seen in the few old-established Firms of Geneva.

N.B.—All their Goods are warranted to their London, Paris, and New York Agents, who are responsible for their answering the Guarantee given at the time of Sale.

FLORENTINE BOUQUET,

Distilled from a combination of those delicious flowers for which Florence is so highly celebrated, by

ROBERTS & CO.,
DISTILLERS OF ESSENCES,
AND
PHARMACIENS TO THE BRITISH LEGATION,
4190, VIA TORNABUONI (Opposite the Corsi Palace),

FLORENCE.

In consequence of the daily increasing demands from England for this now fashionable bouquet the proprietors have established a depôt in LONDON at

A. Whitburn's, Foreign Chemist, 174, Regent Street,

Where it may be obtained in any quantities; as also at their depôts in

LEGHORN, H. Dunn, Via Grande.
TURIN, Mondo, Via Madonna degli Angeli, No. 9.
MILAN, Pozzi, Ponte di Porta Orientale.
GENOA, Bruzza, Piazza Nuova.
PISA, Carrai, Lungo l'Arno.
LUCCA, Farmacia Militare, Via Grande.
BOLOGNA, Melloni, Via Vetturini.
SIENA, Cicoli, Piazza Tolomei.
ANCONA, Belluigi, Vincenzo.

MODENA, Vandini, Via Emilia.
AREZZO, Ceccherelli, Via Vallelunga.
VERONA, Scudellari.
BORGO SAN SEPOLCRO, Gigli.
PISTOIA, Ferdinando Masi.
CITTA DI CASTELLO, Vegni.
PADOVA, Gasparini.
VICENZA, Curti.   [Toledo.
NAPLES, Lonardo e Romano, 303, Via
ROME, Sinimberghi.

Travellers are informed that at the above Pharmacy a supply of the following goods is kept. All English and French approved Patent Medicines and Medicated Lozenges; English and French Plain and highly Perfumed Soaps in great variety; Pure Cod Liver Oil from Newfoundland; Dr. de Jongh's ditto; Seidlitz Powders; Robinson's Patent Groats; Taylor's Homœopathic Cocoa; Oatmeal; Racahout des Arabes; Soda and Seltzer Water in Syphoide Vases; Congress Water direct from the Spring; India-rubber Goods of every description; Finest Turkey Sponge; Sponge Bags; Metcalfe's Tooth Brushes, Hair Brushes, and Nail ditto; Epps's Homœopathic Globules; Marrow Oil.

Depôt for the Genuine Eau de Cologne of Jean Maria Farina (gegenüber dem Jülichs Platz); Rowland's Macassar Oil, Odonto, and Kalydor; Henry's Calcined Magnesia.

LAKE OF GENEVA.

GRAND HOTEL BYRON, AT VILLENEUVE,
NEAR THE CHATEAU CHILLON.

One of the most delightful situations in Europe, enjoying a grand and spacious panorama of the Lake of Geneva and the beautiful and picturesque mountains which surround it. The rooms are large, well-aired, and fitted up most comfortably. The hotel also possesses a large public salon and reading-room, with beautiful promenades in its own grounds. The new proprietor, Mr. Wolff, will endeavour by particular attention in the service and by a good direction of the house, as well as by moderate charges, to deserve the confidence of the families and tourists who honour him with their visits. He will do his best to provide them with all the comforts of a first-rate hotel.

Pension on very moderate terms from 15th October to 1st June.

Dutch Rhenish Railway.

COLOGNE, THE RHINE, NORTHERN AND EASTERN GERMANY, AND SWITZERLAND, viâ HOLLAND.

The shortest and cheapest route between England and the above-named places is by the Boats of the

General Steam Navigation Company,
FROM LONDON TO ROTTERDAM,
AND THENCE BY THE
DUTCH RHENISH RAILWAY.

One of the General Steam Navigation Company's First-Class Steamers 'COLOGNE,' 'LEO,' or 'CONCORDIA,' leaves St. Katharine's Wharf for Rotterdam, every Tuesday, Thursday, and Saturday. The average passage is 18 hours, of which 10 hours are on the Rivers Thames and Maas, and 8 at Sea. An Agent of the Dutch Rhenish Company will attend the arrival of the Steamers at Rotterdam to assist the Passengers in transhipping to the Railway.

Passengers adopting this Route will not only avoid the landing in small Boats at Ostend, and crossing the Rhine at Cologne or Ruhrort, but will also effect a large saving in distance and expense.

Through Tickets are issued in London for the following Places:

AIX-LA-CHAPELLE.	DUSSELDORF.
AMSTERDAM.	HAMM.
BASLE.	HANOVER.
BERLIN.	HARBURG FOR HAMBURG.
BINGEN.	LEIPZIG.
BREMEN.	MANHEIM.
BRUNSWICK.	MAYENCE.
COBLENTZ.	MAGDEBURG.
COLOGNE.	MINDEN.
DRESDEN.	OBERHAUSEN, &c. &c.

The Direct Tickets are available for One Month from the date of issue, and enable the holders to break the journey at the chief intermediate places.

Return Tickets are also issued at a considerable reduction of price, and conferring the same privileges as the Direct Tickets.

From Dusseldorf and Cologne Steamers run several times daily, passing through the whole of the celebrated scenery of the Rhine. There are frequent daily communications between Cologne, Bonn, Aix-la-Chapelle, Wiesbaden, Baden-Baden, Frankfort, Carlsruhe, &c.

Tickets for the above places, Lists of Fares, and every information as to hours of departure, &c., can be obtained at the OFFICE OF THE DUTCH RHENISH RAILWAY, 40, GRACECHURCH STREET; the Offices of Messrs. Chaplin and Horne—Universal Office, Regent Circus, Piccadilly; Golden Cross, Charing Cross; Railway Office, 216, Oxford Street; Swan with Two Necks, Gresham Street: and Tickets for Amsterdam, Cologne, and Dusseldorf, at the Offices of the General Steam Navigation Company, 37, Regent Circus, Piccadilly, and 71, Lombard Street.

Very reduced throughout Rates for Parcels and Merchandize to the above Places and all the principal Towns of the Rhine, Germany, and Austria. Lists of these Rates can be obtained at the

LONDON OFFICE, 40, Gracechurch Street, E.C.

DENMARK.

Now ready, with Map and Illustrations, 2 vols. 8vo. 24s.

A RESIDENCE OF TWO YEARS IN JUTLAND, THE DANISH ISLES, AND COPENHAGEN. By HORACE MARRYAT.

'Mr. Marryat goes from town to town, from building to building, and stamps upon each the story or legend that gives it an interest. His volumes abound in amusing passages, and his ground is comparatively new.'—*Daily News.*

'It is refreshing to meet with a work like this, which is as void of pretension as it is replete with interesting information. Mr. Marryat describes what he has seen vividly and effectively, and in a style which is perfectly his own.'—*Press.*

'Mr. Marryat combines the discerning eye of the archæologist, the ready hand of an artist, and the knowledge of the historian.'—*Literary Gazette.*

JOHN MURRAY, Albemarle Street.

BAGNERES DE BIGORRE.

Is a delightfully situated town at the foot of the Pyrenees, possessing a large thermal establishment and waters of much celebrity. It is the most central of all the watering-places in the Pyrenees, and possesses the most resources and the best accommodation alike for summer and winter.

There is an English episcopal church and resident chaplain at Bagnères, where several English families permanently reside.

THE HOTEL DE FRANCE
Is a large and spacious establishment, well situated, clean, and comfortable. The cuisine is first-rate. The proprietor, MONAL, is accustomed to receive English families, and always uses his best endeavours to attend to the wants of his guests and treat them with great liberality.

ZURICH.

J. H. KEREZ,
CHEMIST AND DRUGGIST,

RESPECTFULLY announces to Tourists and Visitors that he prepares and dispenses Medicines and Prescriptions according to the English Pharmacopœia with the purest and choicest Drugs and Chemicals.

J. H. KEREZ, having been a principal dispensing Assistant at one of the first Houses in England, hopes that his experience and attention will merit the support and confidence of the English Nobility and Gentry.

J. H. K. keeps constantly on hand a well-selected Stock of the most popular English Patent Medicines and Perfumery.

NUREMBERG.

J. A. STEIN

(C. A. DEMPWOLFF),

Magazine of Library, Photographs, and Objects of Art,

BAIERISCHER HOF.

MR. DEMPWOLFF begs leave to recommend his Magazine—Photographs, Library, and Objects of Art—to the notice of Travellers visiting Nuremberg. They will find a large collection of all indispensable Works, Photographs, Views, Engravings, Maps, &c., of Nuremberg and other towns. All necessary information will be given to travellers with the greatest pleasure. Great collection of reproductions of old and rare Engravings in Photography.

To the year 1806 John Palm, famed for his deplorable death, was possessed of the old establishment of J. A. Stein.

Epps's Guinea Homœopathic Medicine Case

Contains Twenty-four Remedies, and a Guide giving full instructions for their use. This Case, leather-covered and specially adapted for the pocket, is always available in cases of emergency, as sea-sickness, sore throat, and all common complaints.

JAMES EPPS,
HOMŒOPATHIC CHEMIST,
112, GREAT RUSSELL STREET; 170, PICCADILLY; AND 48, THREADNEEDLE STREET, LONDON.
Established 1838.

NUREMBERG.
GREAT EXHIBITION
OF
MANUFACTURES.
—o—
Warehouse for Toys of every kind, and for Works in Wood, Ivory, and Horn, &c. &c. Can be viewed gratis at

A. WAHNSCHAFFE,
PLACE JOSEPH L., No. 292,
Where articles are sold at the Lowest Price.

ESSENTIALS
FOR
TRAVELLING.
—o—
Thresher's India Tweed Suits.
Thresher's Kashmir Flannel Shirts.
Thresher's Kashmir Woollen Socks.
Thresher's Coloured Flannel Shirts.
Thresher's Travelling Bags.

SOLD ONLY BY
THRESHER & GLENNY,
152, STRAND, LONDON.

BREMEN.
HILLMAN'S HOTEL,
The first Hotel at Bremen, is situated on the most beautiful part of the Rampart, and in the immediate vicinity of the Terminus, Theatre, and Exchange.

Superior accommodation and comfort will be found here for families and gentlemen.

The elegant Coffee Room attached to the Hotel is supplied with a large selection of English, French, and German Newspapers.

NICE.
Villa Visconti Cimies.
PENSION ANGLAISE.

Conducted by an English Lady and Gentleman. A charming modern residence, winter or summer, the air of Cimies Hill being recommended by medical men as preferable to Nice for delicate persons.

Frequented by the first English Families.
SUPERIOR ACCOMMODATION.

ALEXANDRIA, EGYPT.
HOTEL ABBATT,

Situate in a fine large airy square, **Place Ste. Catherine**, will be found by all families and gentlemen who should patronise it to be replete with every comfort.

French Table d'Hôte or English Living at option.

GOOD WINES, &c.

OXFORD.
SPIERS AND SON,
102 & 103, HIGH STREET,

Respectfully invite TOURISTS to VISIT their Extensive Warehouses for Useful and Ornamental Manufactures, suitable for Presents and remembrances of OXFORD.

All the GUIDE-BOOKS, MAPS, &c., of Oxford and its neighbourhood kept in stock, as well as Views, Photographs, Stereoscopic Pictures, &c.

INTERLAKEN.
PHARMACIE ANGLAISE
DE
AUG. F. DENNLER,
ENGLISH DRUGGIST,
DISPENSING CHEMIST.
SPÉCIALITÉS FRANÇAISES.
EAUX MINÉRALES,
NATURELLES ET ARTIFICIELLES,
PATENT MEDICINES.

PARIS.

Hotel des Deux Mondes et d'Angleterre,
8, RUE D'ANTIN.
Near the Tuileries, Place Vendôme, and the Boulevards.

THIS Magnificent First-class Hotel, recently constructed and elegantly furnished in the newest and most fashionable style, surrounded by Gardens, justifies the preference accorded to it by Families and Gentlemen, for the splendour and comfort of its Apartments, its excellent *Cuisine*, and the care and attention shown to all who honour the Hotel with their patronage. Large and small Apartments, and single Rooms at moderate Charges. Private Restaurant, splendid Coffee-Rooms, Saloons, Reading and Smoking Rooms. Letter-box, Interpreters, Horses, elegant Carriages, Omnibuses for the Railways.

VALETTA, MALTA.

W. KINGSTON,
CHEMIST AND DRUGGIST,
English Dispensary, 44, Strada Teatro
(Opposite the Palace Square).

Physicians' Prescriptions and Family Recipes carefully dispensed from the best and purest Drugs.

All Pharmaceutical Preparations made according to the Formulas of the British Pharmacopœins.

Genuine Patent Medicines.

BOPPARD ON THE RHINE.

Family Hotel, Rhine Baths,
VIZ.,
HYDROPATHIC ESTABLISHMENT OF MUHLBAD.

THE HYDROPATHIC ESTABLISHMENT of MUHLBAD merits attention, being well kept, and in a delightful locality. Its apparatus is excellent, under an experienced Physician who speaks English. The Water, 10° Réaumur, never varies in temperature. The Terms are very reasonable; and Tourists who do not require treatment may be boarded and lodged comfortably here.

HOTEL WANDL,
The largest Hotel in the centre of the Inner Town of Vienna,

CAN BE RECOMMENDED FOR

CAREFUL ATTENDANCE AND MODERATE PRICES.

THIS FIRST-RATE HOTEL, with 200 Rooms, among which are several Apartments for the Nobility, possesses new and comfortable accommodation, and is one of the most frequented and best situated of the Imperial Residences.

Dinners *à la carte* are served at any time of the day in the peculiarly-decorated Dining Saloon and Room.

The Owner will use his best endeavours to preserve the good reputation of the Establishment.

JOHANN WANDL,

Vienna.   HOTEL KEEPER.

BERNE.

BERNERHOF (HOTEL).
MR. KRAFT, Proprietor.

THIS New and First-class Hotel for Families and Gentlemen is highly recommended. It has 150 Rooms, commands from its windows a most extensive and splendid view of the whole chain of the Alps and of the beautiful environs of Berne; as also the Government Palace, the charming Promenade, the Ramparts, and Railway Terminus. The Hotel has excellent accommodation, combining elegance and comfort, and offers to Tourists a desirable place of temporary residence. From October 1st to July 1st families can be accommodated with board and lodging at reasonable terms.

Baths in the Hotel.

Reading-rooms supplied with the Times, Galignani's Messenger, Punch, and New York Herald.

LUCERNE.

ENGLISCHER HOF.
Proprietor, JEAN REBER.

THIS First-rate Establishment, very well recommended by the best class of Travellers, is situated close to the Steamers' Landing-place, and vis-à-vis the Railway Stations, on the loveliest position of the Lake, with superb views of the Rigi, Pilatus, Alps, and Glaciers; contains several Saloons, 62 comfortable Rooms, Smoking and Reading Rooms, where are French and English Newspapers.

Chamber, $1\frac{1}{2}$ fr. up to 3 frs. Breakfast, $1\frac{1}{4}$ fr.

Tables d'Hôte at 1, 4, and 7 o'clock. The prices are 3, 4, and $2\frac{1}{2}$ frs. In case of a longer stay, guests are received *en pension.*

Omnibuses and Droskies are at command.

AMSTERDAM.
BRACK'S DOELEN HOTEL,
Situated in the Centre of the Town, and most convenient for Visitors on Pleasure or Business.

IT commands a splendid View of the Quays, &c.; and, being conducted on a liberal scale, it is patronised by the highest classes of society in Holland. It is also much frequented by English Travellers for the comfort and first-rate accommodation it affords, as well as for the invariable civility shown to visitors.

Cold and Warm Baths may be had at any hour.

CARRIAGES FOR HIRE.

Table-d'Hôte at half-past 4, or Dinner à la carte.

FLORENCE.

AUX VILLES DE FLANDRE.
PLACE STA. MARIA MAGGIORE, No. 4662.

DENTELLES, BRODERIES, LINGERIES, ET CONFECTIONS.

Ce Magasin tient un Dépôt spécial d'Applications de Bruxelles.

Dentelles noires, Valenciennes, Imitations fines, Tuls unis et brodés. Broderies de l'Etranger et Fabrique de Broderies de Florence.

Trousseaux en Lingeries et Parures complètes en Dentelles.

NICE, FRANCE.

School for Young Gentlemen.
MR. J. NASH,
**MAISON PONS,
2, CROIX DE MARBRE.**

During the Summer Months (1st June to 1st Sept.) the School is carried on in the neighbouring mountains; the address being, Bollène, près Lantosque, Alpes Maritimes.

FOREIGN LANGUAGES.

FRANZ THIMM'S
SERIES OF
European Grammars,
AFTER AHN'S METHOD.

	s.	d.
German Grammar, by Meissner	3	6
French Grammar, by Ahn	3	6
Italian Grammar, by Marchetti	4	0
Spanish Grammar, by Salvo	4	0
Portuguese Grammar, by Cabano	4	0
Swedish Grammar, by Lenström	4	0
Danish Grammar, by Lund	4	0
Dutch Grammar, by Ahn	4	0
Latin Grammar, by Sckienszücker	3	0
Hebrew Grammar, by Herxheimer	4	0

The method adopted in this original Series of Grammars is most simple and rational, and is eminently adapted for Self-tuition, for School use, and for a comparative study of European Languages.

FOREIGN DIALOGUES,
On an entirely new and practical plan, calculated to insure a rapid acquisition of Foreign Languages, 12mo. cloth.

	s.	d.
Meissner's German and English	2	6
Dudevant's French and English	2	6
Marchetti's Italian and English	2	6
Salvo's Spanish and English	2	6
Monteiro's Portuguese and English	2	6
Lenström's Swedish and English	2	6
Lund's Danish and English	2	6
Haelen's Dutch and English	2	6
Turkish, Russian, & English Vocabulary	2	6
German Self-Taught	1	0
French Self-Taught	1	0
Italian Self-Taught	1	0

Published by Mr. FRANZ THIMM, Foreign Bookseller and Publisher, 3, Brook Street, Grosvenor Square, London; and at 32, Princess Street, Manchester.

Tourists and Travellers,
Visitors to the Seaside,
and others exposed to the scorching rays of the Sun and heated particles of Dust, will find

ROWLANDS' KALYDOR
a most refreshing preparation for the Complexion, dispelling the cloud of languor and relaxation, allaying all heat and irritability, and immediately affording the pleasing sensation attending restored elasticity and healthful state of the skin.

Freckles, Tan, Spots, Pimples, Flushes, and Discolouration, fly before its application, and give place to delicate clearness, with the glow of beauty and of bloom. In cases of sunburn, or stings of insects, its virtues have long been acknowledged.

Price 4s. 6d. and 8s. 6d. per Bottle.

The heat of summer also frequently communicates a dryness to the hair, and a tendency to fall off, which may be completely obviated by the use of

ROWLANDS' MACASSAR OIL,
a delightfully fragrant and transparent preparation for the Hair, and as an invigorator and purifier beyond all precedent.

Price 3s. 6d., 7s., 10s. 6d. (equal to four small), and double that size 21s. per Bottle.

Nor can we be too careful to preserve the Teeth from the deleterious effects of vegetable acids (an immediate cause of toothache), by a systematic employment, night and morning, of

ROWLANDS' ODONTO,
OR, PEARL DENTIFRICE,

a White Powder, compounded of the choicest and most fragrant exotics. It bestows on the Teeth a pearl-like whiteness, frees them from Tartar, and imparts to the Gums a healthy firmness, and to the Breath a grateful purity and fragrance.

Price 2s. 9d. per Box.

SOLD AT

20, HATTON GARDEN;
And by Chemists and Perfumers.

*** Ask for ROWLAND'S Articles.

HANDSOME BRASS AND IRON BEDSTEADS.

HEAL and SON'S SHOW ROOMS contain a large assortment of Brass Bedsteads, suitable both for Home use and for Tropical Climates; handsome Iron Bedsteads with Brass Mountings and elegantly Japanned; plain Iron Bedsteads for Servants; every description of Wood Bedstead that is manufactured, in Mahogany, Birch, Walnut Tree Woods, Polished Deal and Japanned; all fitted with Bedding and Furniture complete, as well as every description of Bedroom Furniture.

HEAL AND SON'S NEW ILLUSTRATED CATALOGUE CONTAINS DESIGNS AND PRICES OF 150 DIFFERENT ARTICLES OF BEDROOM FURNITURE, AS WELL AS OF 100 BEDSTEADS, AND PRICES OF EVERY DESCRIPTION OF BEDDING, SENT FREE BY POST. HEAL AND SON, BEDSTEAD, BEDDING, AND BEDROOM FURNITURE MANUFACTURERS, 196, TOTTENHAM COURT ROAD, LONDON.

LE SOMMIER ELASTIQUE PORTATIF.

HEAL and SON have patented a method of making a Spring Mattress portable. The great objection to the usual Spring Mattress is its being so heavy and cumbersome. The '**Sommier Elastique Portatif**' is made in three separate parts, and when joined together has all the elasticity of the best Spring Mattress. As it has no stuffing of wool or horse-hair, it cannot harbour moth, to which the usual Spring Mattress is very liable; the prices, also, are much below those of the best Spring Mattresses.

HEAL AND SON, 196, TOTTENHAM COURT ROAD, W.

JOHN SOUTHGATE,
Solid Leather Portmanteau Manufacturer,
76, WATLING STREET, LONDON.

HIS REGISTERED
WARDROBE PORTMANTEAU

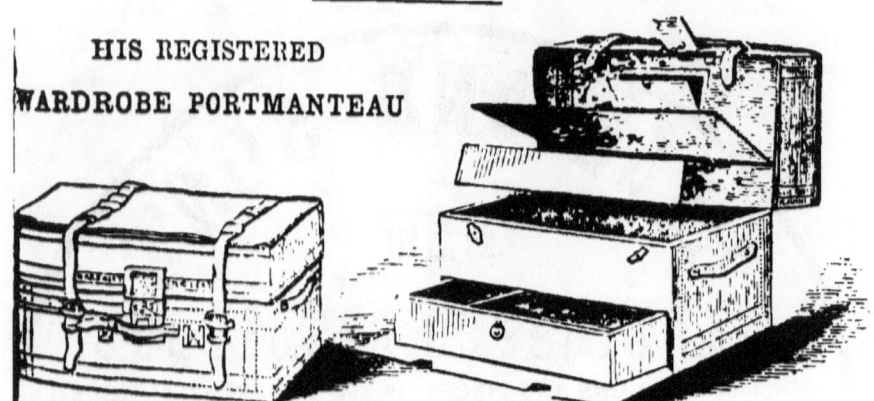

Is found by every one who has used it to be the most PERFECT and USEFUL of any yet invented, and to combine all the advantages so long desired by those who travel.

Its peculiar conveniences consist in its containing SEPARATE COMPARTMENTS or drawers for each description of Clothes, Boots, &c.; each is kept entirely distinct, and is immediately accessible on opening the Portmanteau, without lifting or disturbing anything else.

SOUTHGATE'S FOLDING PORTMANTEAU.

Also with separate divisions for Shirts, Linen, Clothes, and Boots; the whole of which are immediately accessible on opening the Portmanteau.

Both of these Portmanteaus are admirably adapted for Continental travelling on account of the facility they offer for Custom-house examination, without disarranging the wardrobe.

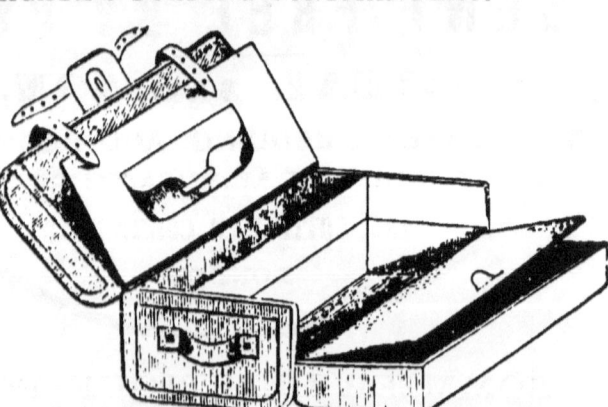

John Southgate's Ladies' Portmanteaus, Ladies' Dress and Bonnet Trunks, Ladies' Imperials, and Ladies' Travelling Trunks.

All with Trays and Moveable Divisions for Bonnets, and containing every convenience for packing separately Dresses, Bonnets, Linen, &c., and made in various styles and sizes.

They may be obtained of any Saddler or Outfitter throughout the kingdom; and of the Manufacturer,

JOHN SOUTHGATE, 76, WATLING STREET, LONDON.

ROME.

J. P. SHEA,

ENGLISH HOUSE-AGENT,

FORWARDING AGENT
TO H.R.H. THE PRINCE OF WALES.

11, PIAZZA DI SPAGNA.

At this Office persons applying for **Large or Small Furnished Apartments** invariably obtain correct and unbiassed information on all matters connected with **Lodging-Houses, Boarding-Houses,** and **Household Management,** while **Low and Fixed Charges** for practical services offer safe and satisfactory assistance to Proprietor and Tenant, as testified by the increasing confidence of English and American Travellers since the opening of the establishment in 1852. **Plans and Lists of Apartments sent by Post** to persons who wish to secure accommodation, or avoid inconvenience at the approach of Carnival or the Holy Week.

Mr. Shea, being a Custom-house Agent, clears and warehouses **Baggage and other effects** for persons who, to avoid the expense of quick transit, send their things by sea or luggage-train, directed to his care, through the following, or any other agent.

CORRESPONDENTS—

LONDON..................Messrs. J. & R. M'CRACKEN, 7, Old Jewry.
          Messrs. OLIVIER & CARR, 37, Finsbury Square.
DUBLIN ....Messrs. C. & R. ELLIOTT.
LIVERPOOL ....Messrs. C. & R. ELLIOTT, 17, Goree Piazza.
FOLKESTONE ....Mr. FAULKNER.
BOULOGNE S.M.......Mr. BERNARD, 18, Quai des Paquebots.
PARIS ....Messrs. LANSING & CO., 8, Place de la Bourse.
MARSEILLES ....Messrs. GIRAUD FRERES, 44, Rue Sainte.

PARIS

AND ALL PARTS OF THE

CONTINENT,

VIÂ NEWHAVEN AND DIEPPE.

LONDON, BRIGHTON, AND SOUTH COAST
RAILWAY.

THE SHORTEST AND CHEAPEST ROUTE.

From the London Bridge and Victoria Termini.

FARES THROUGHOUT:
First Class .... 28s. | Second Class .... 20s.
TICKETS AVAILABLE FOR FOUR DAYS.

RETURN TICKETS:
First Class .... 50s. | Second Class .... 36s.
AVAILABLE FOR ONE MONTH.

FOR Times of Sailing, the Summer Tidal Service, and full particulars, see Advertisements in 'Bradshaw's Guide for Great Britain and Ireland;' also 'Bradshaw's Continental Guide;' the 'Times' newspaper; and the Time Tables of the BRIGHTON AND SOUTH COAST COMPANY.

Every information may be obtained respecting this *pleasant and beautiful route*, on application in London to A. D. BOSSON, 4, Arthur Street East (opposite the Monument), London Bridge; and at the London and Brighton Railway Offices, London Bridge and Victoria Termini; and at all their various Stations; also at the Company's Offices, 43, Regent Circus, Piccadilly.—In Paris, to A. D. BOSSON, 7, Rue de la Paix; and at 35, Quai Henri IV., Dieppe.

Norwich Union
FIRE INSURANCE SOCIETY.
Instituted 1797.
DIRECTORS.

CHARLES EVANS, Esq., *President.*   EDWARD STEWARD, Esq. *Vice-President.*

GEORGE DURRANT, Esq.	JOHN WRIGHT, Esq.	D. DALRYMPLE, Esq.
ROBERT JOHN HARVEY	HENRY BROWNE, Esq.	M. D.
HARVEY, Esq.	W. C. HOTSON, Esq.	W. R. CLARKE, Esq.
H. S. PATTESON, Esq.	C. E. TUCK, Esq.	G. E. SIMPSON, Esq.

Secretary.—Sir SAMUEL BIGNOLD.   *London Agent.*—C. J. BUNYON, Esq.

INSURANCES are granted by this Society on buildings, goods, merchandise, and effects, ships in port, harbour, or dock, from loss, or damage by fire, in any part of the United Kingdom of Great Britain and Ireland.

It is provided by the constitution of the Society that the Insured shall be free from all responsibility; and to guarantee the engagements of the office, a fund of £550,000 has been subscribed by a numerous and opulent Proprietary, which fund has been further increased by the accumulation of an additional reserve, now exceeding £100,000. **Three-Fifths of the Profits of the Company are periodically distributed as a Bonus to parties insuring,** who have thus from time to time received from the Society sums amounting in the aggregate to nearly **£400,000.**

A further sum is applicable for a Bonus upon policies renewed in 1861.
The Rates of Premium are in no case higher than those charged by the other principal Offices giving no Bonus to their Insurers.

No charge is made for the Policy or Stamp when the insurance exceeds £300.

The business of the Company exceeds **£68,000,000,** and, owing to the liberality with which its engagements have been performed, is rapidly increasing. The Duty paid to Government for the year 1859 was **£80,639. 10s. 11d.;** the amount insured on Farming Stock was **£10,149,636.**

The Norwich Union Office is, therefore, **now third in order of magnitude** among the Fire Offices of Great Britain.

Norwich Union
LIFE INSURANCE SOCIETY.
Instituted 1808. Upon the principle of Mutual Assurance.
DIRECTORS.

JOHN WRIGHT, Esq., *President.*		C. M. GIBSON, Esq., F.R.C.S.
G. DURRANT, Esq., *Vice-President.*	*Committee.*	W. R. CLARKE, Esq.
JOHN HILLING BARNARD, Esq.		DR. RANKING.
FRANK NOVERRE, Esq.	JOHN BARWELL, Esq.	ROBERT FITCH, Esq.
RICHARD GRIFFIN, Esq.	FRANCIS PARMETER, Esq.	Rev. S. F. BIGNOLD.
THOMAS BREVOR, Esq.	R. W. HAWKES, Esq.	W. H. CLABBURN, Esq.
R. BLAKE HUMFREY, Esq.	G. E. FRERE, Esq., F.R.S.	THOMAS LUCAS, Esq.
Dr. GOODWIN.	R. JOHN WRIGHT, Esq.	Rev. WILLIAM WAYMAN.

Auditors.—Mr. E. WILLETT, Mr. A. BAILEY, and Mr. J. R. HARDY.
Secretary.—Sir SAMUEL BIGNOLD.   *London Agent.*—C. J. BUNYON, Esq.

The whole of the Profits belong to the Assured.
The Accumulations exceed **£2,000,000.**
The Income of the Society exceeds **£237,000.**
The Amount assured is upwards of **£5,078,000.**

Since its commencement, **32,700** Policies have been issued, and **£5,666,555** paid to the representatives of **6854** deceased Members.

The Bonuses may be applied at the option of the Assured in reduction of the future Annual Premium, or their cash value received.

One-half of the first five Annual Premiums may remain as a permanent charge upon Polices effected for the whole duration of Life.

Annuities and special risks are undertaken upon favourable terms.

This Society is entirely distinct from the Norwich Union Fire Office. The aggregate Annual Income of the two Societies is nearly **Half a Million Sterling.**

For Prospectuses apply to the Society's Offices,
6, CRESCENT, NEW BRIDGE STREET, BLACKFRIARS; and
SURREY STREET, NORWICH.

SEASON, 1861.

The only Short Sea Route to the Continent.
SEA PASSAGE UNDER TWO HOURS.—FOUR THROUGH SERVICES DAILY.

Commencement of a Paris through Night Service, viâ Folkestone and Boulogne, in addition to the Special Day Service.

LONDON AND PARIS in 10¼ HOURS,
By the Accelerated Special Express Daily Direct Tidal Service,
Viâ FOLKESTONE and BOULOGNE.

SMALL BOATS NEVER USED. AN INTERPRETING CONDUCTOR.

Marseilles	in 34 hours.	Switzerland [Bale]	in 37½ hours.
Bordeaux	38 "	Italy [Turin]	60 "

A Through Night Service between London and Paris,
By the Regular Trains and Special Boats,
VIA FOLKESTONE and BOULOGNE.

For Hours of Departure (which are variable), of both the above Services, see Time Book and Bills.

PARIS RETURN TICKETS (Viâ Boulogne) AT REDUCED RATES.

NEW ROUTE TO GERMANY and the EAST:
London to Vienna, Pesth, Basiasch, Kustendje, Constantinople,
VIA COLOGNE or PARIS, SALZBURG, and MUNICH.

BELGIUM, GERMANY, HOLLAND, &c. &c.,
By the Mail Trains.

TWO SERVICES DAILY, viâ Dover and Calais;
And A SERVICE EVERY NIGHT, viâ Dover and Ostend.

THROUGH TICKETS ISSUED AND BAGGAGE REGISTERED (with a free allowance of 56 lbs. each Passenger), to and from the **PRINCIPAL CONTINENTAL CITIES AND TOWNS**, in many of which there is an Agent of the Company.

In consequence of the opening of the Salzburg Railway between Munich and Vienna, Passengers can now be booked through, viâ Paris, to *Vienna*; and there also, as heretofore, via Cologne. Through Tickets are now, for the first time, issued to *Mannheim, Carlsruhe, Salzburg, Munich, Kustendje*, and *Constantinople*, via Paris; and to Baden-Baden and *Heidelberg*, via Paris; as well as by the Cologne route, as formerly.

THE PARCELS EXPRESSES convey Parcels to nearly all Continental Destinations, at through Rates, as quickly as the Mails.

A new System of Through Rates for Parcels up to 200 lbs. weight, viâ Folkestone and Boulogne, for Paris, Lyons, Marseilles, and other Principal Towns in France, from London and the Large Towns of the United Kingdom. The Parcels are also now forwarded with increased rapidity.

MERCHANDISE FORWARDED TO BOULOGNE.

For all information, see Time-Book and Book of Tariffs.

PASSPORTS.—British Subjects can now enter and travel through France without Passports.

LONDON BRIDGE STATION,
SEASON, 1861. C. W. EBORALL, General Manager.

STEAM COMMUNICATION BETWEEN HULL AND HAMBURG.

Helen M'Gregor, Knowles; **Emerald Isle**, Foster; are intended to leave the Humber Dock for Hamburg every Saturday evening after arrival of the 9·30 P.M. Train, one of these Boats returning from Hamburg every Saturday night. Particulars as to the hour of sailing from Hamburg may be learned from KIRSTEN and Co., Admiralität Strasse.

PASSAGE MONEY.—1*l*. 10*s*. First Cabin; Return Ticket, 2*l*. Second Cabin, 15*s*.; Return Ticket, 1*l*. 2*s*. 6*d*. Allowing four weeks on the Continent. Average Passage, 38 hours.

HULL AND DUNKIRK, AND VICE VERSA.

Transit and **Gazelle**, every WEDNESDAY and SATURDAY, according to Tide. PASSAGE MONEY.—15*s*. First Cabin; Return Ticket 1*l*. 2*s*. 6*d*. Average Passage, 20 hours. The very best accommodation for Passengers, Carriages, and Horses. Dunkirk Agents, C. BOURDON and Co. For further information apply to the Agents, LOFTHOUSE, GLOVER, and CO.—Hull, 1st April, 1861.

GALIGNANI'S
NEW PARIS GUIDE.
—o—

Compiled from the best authorities, revised and verified by personal inspection, and arranged on an entirely new plan, with Map and Plates. Royal 18mo. 10*s*. 6*d*. bound; or without Plates, 7*s*. 6*d*. bound.

London: SIMPKIN, MARSHALL, & CO.

WHITBURN'S
Foreign Pharmacy,
174, Regent Street, London,

Opposite New Burlington Street.

AUGUSTUS WHITBURN (late GRIGNON), Pharmaceutical Chemist, from Paris, Florence, and Rome, begs to inform English Tourists returning to London from the Continent that in his Establishment all Foreign Prescriptions and Recipes are prepared with the greatest accuracy. General Depôt of French, Italian, and other Patent Medicines, Plants, and Medicinal Waters.

EGYPT.
ALEXANDRIA and CAIRO.
E. ST. JOHN FAIRMAN,
GENERAL AGENT, AND MERCHANT, &c.,
Begs to place his services at the disposal of Visitors to Egypt.
AGENT FOR SEVERAL CONTINENTAL HOUSES.

Offices in **Alexandria**—Next Door to the Bank of Egypt, in the street immediately in a line with the P. and O. Co.'s Offices. In **Cairo**—In the Esbekié, a few Doors from the P. and O. Co.'s Offices.

PARIS.

Shortly, uniform with 'Handbook for Modern London,'

MURRAY'S HANDBOOK FOR PARIS.

BEING A GUIDE FOR VISITORS TO ALL OBJECTS OF INTEREST IN THAT METROPOLIS AND ITS ENVIRONS.

With a detailed Clue Map of Paris, and Plans. Post 8vo.

JOHN MURRAY, Albemarle Street.

DORRELL & SON'S
PASSPORT AGENCY,
15, CHARING CROSS,
IMMEDIATELY OPPOSITE DRUMMOND'S BANK.

French and Italian spoken, and Correspondence carried on in either Language.

BRITISH SUBJECTS who purpose visiting the Continent will save much trouble and expense by obtaining their Passports and Visas through the above Agency. No personal attendance is required, and persons residing at a distance from the Metropolis may have their Passports —with the necessary Visas—forwarded to them through the Post. Messrs. DORRELL and SON will send their "Passport Prospectus," containing every particular in detail relating to Passports, by Post, on application.

Passports Mounted, and enclosed in Cases, with the name of the Bearer impressed in Gold on the outside; thus affording security  against injury or loss, and preventing delay in the frequent examination of the Passport when travelling.

LIST OF CHARGES.

Foreign Office charge	2/0.	Agents' charge for Passport ... 1/0.
French Visa	4/3.	———— for each Visa ... 1/0.
Bavarian Visa	2/6.	Pocket Case, Russia leather ... 4/0.
Russian Visa	1/7.	———— Morocco ... 2/6.
Portuguese Visa	4/6.	———— Roan ... 1/6.
Sicilian Visa (Naples)	4/0.	Mounting the Passport on Muslin, and
Tuscan Visa	4/6.	Lettering Case with Bearer's Name 1/6.

THE LATEST EDITIONS OF MURRAY'S HANDBOOKS.

Travel Talk — North Germany — South Germany — Switzerland — France — Paris — Spain — Portugal — Central Italy — Rome and its Environs — North Italy — South Italy — Egypt — Syria and Palestine — India — Greece — Denmark — Russia. —— English Handbooks.

English and Foreign Stationery, Dialogue Books, Couriers' Bags, Pocket-books and Purses of every description, Journal and Cash Books with Lock and Key, Travelling Writing Cases and Inkstands, and a variety of other Articles useful for Travellers.

DORRELL and SON'S PASSPORT AGENCY,
15, Charing Cross, London, S.W.

NOTICE

Tourist's & Passport Agency,
8, ROYAL EXCHANGE, LONDON, E.C.

MESSRS. LETTS undertake to supply intended Excursionists either through this or Foreign Countries with every information that can be of service to them on their route—relative to times and means of Conveyance, Currency, &c.— and to provide PASSPORTS with the requisite *visés* with the utmost promptitude and regard to economy. The Passports being mounted on strong, *thin* linen, and inserted in Russia, Morocco, or Roan Cases, with the Proprietor's name lettered on the outside, are rendered sufficiently durable to last many seasons and facilitate their examination by the Police authorities. **TRAVELLERS to INDIA or the CONTINENT** may be provided with the *Newest Editions of*
MURRAY'S AND BRADSHAW'S GUIDES, and with the most approved Maps, as also with Dictionaries, Books of Travel-Talk, Polyglot Washing-Books, &c.
Trustworthy Couriers will be recommended by giving sufficient notice.

TOURISTS in the UNITED KINGDOM will find the following articles extremely valuable (many *indispensable*):—

MAPS AND GUIDES.
y Murray, Black, Stanford, and Johnston, or England, English Counties and Lakes, Isle of Wight, Wales (North and South), Scotland and Scotch Counties, and Ireland, together with the beautiful series of ORDNANCE MAPS (without which no Pedestrian should commence his tour), in neat and portable Cases, from 1s. each. Also **LETTS'** series of ROAD, RAILWAY, and RIVER MAPS, for Pedestrians through the most interesting parts of England.

Every description of STATIONERY required by the Traveller, of which the undermentioned may form a sample, kept in stock, and forwarded on application:—
Travelling Desks, Flexible Writing Cases, Metallic Books, Students' and Tourists' Cases, Perpetual Diaries, Luggage Labels, Foreign Paper (lined, waved, or quadrilled) and Envelopes, Cash Belts, Purses, Bags, Compasses, Artists' Colours, Brushes, Paper, and other Materials.

The best selection of Stereoscopic Slides of all the spots most interesting to the Traveller, and the most scientific and compact Stereoscope yet introduced, can be supplied to order, or a Dozen sorted Slides forwarded upon receipt of Post-office Order for 12s., payable to

LETTS, SON, & CO.,
8, ROYAL EXCHANGE, LONDON, E.C., Stationers, Travelling Desk Manufacturers, Lithographers, and Agents to H.M. Board of Ordnance and the Geological Society.

Illustrated Catalogues of Ordnance and other Maps, Guides, and Atlases, forwarded per return of Post, upon receipt of One Postage Stamp.

ROTTERDAM.

H. A. KRAMERS,
Importer of Foreign Books.

Mr. MURRAY'S 'Handbooks for Travellers,' BAEDEKER'S 'Reisehandbücher,' and JOANNE'S 'Guides pour les Voyageurs,' always in Stock.
English, French, and *German* Books imported Weekly, and a great variety of New Books kept in Store.

107, 108, VISSCHERSDYK.

THE ALPS.

With Illustrations, post 8vo., 14s.,

THE GLACIERS OF THE ALPS.

Being a Narrative of Excursions and Ascents; an Account of the Origin and Phenomena of Glaciers; and an exposition of the Physical Principles to which they are related.

By JOHN TYNDALL, F.R.S.,
Professor of Natural Philosophy in the Royal Institution of Great Britain.

'A work of sound and varied science: but rarely has science found a votary so bold of heart, so agile in hand and foot, and so dexterous with pen.'—*Guardian.*

II.

With Illustrations, crown 8vo., 18s.,

ITALIAN VALLEYS OF THE ALPS.

A Tour through all the romantic and less-frequented 'Vals' of Northern Piedmont, from the Tarantaise to the Gries.

By Rev. S. W. KING.

'Mr. King explored the less-frequented valleys of Northern Piedmont, and is an intelligent companion, and in his tour there is a great deal of agreeable reading. He has gone into regions comparatively unknown, and returned laden with spoil. We thank him for his pictures of snowy Alps, and mighty glaciers, and thundering avalanches.'—*Daily News.*

JOHN MURRAY, ALBEMARLE STREET.

GEOLOGY AND MINERALOGY.

A KNOWLEDGE of these interesting branches of Science adds greatly to the pleasure of the traveller in all parts of the world, and may lead to important discoveries.

Mr. TENNANT, Mineralogist to Her Majesty, 149, STRAND, gives *Practical Instruction to Travellers*, in MINERALOGY and GEOLOGY. He can supply Geological Maps, Hammers, Magnifying Glasses, Acid Bottles, Microscopic Objects, Blowpipes, and all the recent Works on Mineralogy, Conchology, Chemistry, Botany, and Geology; also Models of Crystals.

Elementary Collections of Minerals, Rocks, and Fossils, at Two, Five, Ten, Twenty, Fifty, and One Hundred Guineas each.

A Collection for Five Guineas, which will illustrate the recent works on Geology by Lyell, Ansted, Mantell, and others, contains 200 Specimens, in a plain Mahogany Cabinet, with five Trays, comprising the following specimens, viz. :—

MINERALS which are either the components of Rocks, or occasionally embedded in them: Quartz, Agate, Chalcedony, Jasper, Garnet, Zeolite, Hornblende, Augite, Asbestus, Felspar, Mica, Talc, Tourmaline, Calcareous Spar, Fluor, Selenite, Baryta, Strontia, Salt, Cryolite, Sulphur, Plumbago, Bitumen, Jet, Amber, &c.

NATIVE METALS, or METALLIFEROUS MINERALS; these are found in masses or beds, in veins, and occasionally in the beds of rivers. Specimens of the following metallic ores are put in the Cabinet: Iron, Manganese, Lead, Tin, Zinc, Copper, Antimony, Silver, Gold, Platina, &c.

ROCKS: Granite, Gneiss, Mica-slate, Clay-slate, Porphyry, Serpentine, Sandstones, Limestones, Basalt, Lavas, &c.

PALÆOZOIC FOSSILS from the Llandeilo, Wenlock, Ludlow, Devonian, and Carboniferous Rocks.

SECONDARY FOSSILS from the Lias, Oolite, Wealden, and Cretaceous Groups.

TERTIARY FOSSILS from the Woolwich, Barton, and Bracklesham Beds, London-clay, Crag, &c.

In the more expensive collections some of the specimens are rare, and all more select. Mr. TENNANT has on sale the Duke of Buckingham's Collection of Minerals from Stowe. It contains upwards of 3000 specimens, and has been greatly enriched since the purchase by a collection of coloured Diamonds, Australian Gold, &c. Price 2000 guineas.

J. TENNANT, Geologist, No. 149, Strand, London, W. C.

MURRAY'S
HANDBOOKS FOR ENGLAND.

I. **MODERN LONDON.** A COMPLETE GUIDE FOR STRANGERS TO THE METROPOLIS. Map. 16mo. 5s.

II. **KENT AND SUSSEX.** Map. Post 8vo. 10s.

III. **SURREY, HANTS, and ISLE of WIGHT.** Map. Post 8vo. 7s. 6d.

IV. **WILTS, DORSET, AND SOMERSET.** Map. Post 8vo. 7s. 6d.

V. **DEVON AND CORNWALL.** Maps. Post 8vo. 7s. 6d.

VI. **BUCKS, OXFORDSHIRE, AND BERKS.** Map. Post 8vo. 7s. 6d.

VII., VIII. **NORTH AND SOUTH WALES.** Maps. 2 vols. Post 8vo.

ICELAND.

This day, with Map and numerous Illustrations, Post 8vo., 14s.

THE VOLCANOES, GEYSERS, AND GLACIERS OF ICELAND.

BY COMMANDER S. C. FORBES, R.N.

'Capt. Forbes's book upon Iceland has more than the usual interest attaching to the adventures of British travellers in this marvellous island; for the author remained in it for several weeks.'—*Times.*

'Captain Forbes has thrown a new light around the northern island, and has found materials there for a most spirited and entertaining book of travel. A portion of this range of ice mountains has never, Captain Forbes avers, been trodden by the foot of man. Here is a fine field for our Alpine climbers.'—*John Bull.*

'Capt. Forbes heartily enjoyed his trip to Iceland, and we have heartily enjoyed his book.'—*Spectator.*

'An agreeable volume. By meting out science, history, legend, and literature, and personal adventure, in fair and nearly equal portions, Captain Forbes has consulted the general taste, and rendered himself an acceptable companion.'—*Athenæum.*

JOHN MURRAY, ALBEMARLE STREET.

EVERYTHING FOR THE TOURIST.

DRESSING-CASES.—At MECHI and BAZIN'S Establishments, 112, Regent Street, 4, Leadenhall Street, and Crystal Palace, are EXHIBITED the FINEST SPECIMENS of BRITISH MANUFACTURES, in Dressing-Cases, Work Boxes, Writing Cases, Dressing Bags, and other articles of utility or luxury, suitable for presentation. A separate Department for Papier Mâché Manufactures and Bagatelle Tables. Table Cutlery, Razors, Scissors, Pen-knives, Strops, Paste, &c. Shipping orders executed. An extensive assortment of superior Hair and other Toilet Brushes.

F. LAUSBERG & CO.,
ROSSMARKT, NO. 10, FRANCFORT O.M.,

Beg to recommend to English Travellers visiting this part of the Continent their Stock of all kinds of

HAVANNA, BREMEN, AND HAMBURGH CIGARS, TOBACCO, SPIRITS, AND FOREIGN WINES, EAU DE COLOGNE, ALL SORTS OF TEAS,

of which their genuine

"CARAVANE TEA"

merits a special attention.

Agency and Office of the Netherland Steamboat Company. Sale of direct Tickets to London available for one year. Goods forwarded to and from England and all other Countries.

MUNICH.

THE FOUR SEASONS HOTEL,
No. 2, MAXIMILIANS STRASSE.

⁎ The Maximilian Street, which is now being built at the express commands of His Majesty the King of Bavaria, will after its completion be one of the finest streets in Germany, both for its magnificent and grand Buildings, as well as for its beautiful ornamental Promenades.

AUGUST SCHIMON, Proprietor.

THIS spacious new Hotel, situated in the most healthy part of the town, has been recently constructed and elegantly furnished in the newest and most fashionable style by the present proprietor, who will spare no effort to promote the comforts and satisfaction of those who may do him the honour of frequenting his Hotel. The Hotel is situated in the most central part of the town, and near to the Royal Palace, the Royal Theatres, and the Post-office. The Hotel contains 120 large and small Apartments, all of them having the view of the above-mentioned handsome Street on the south side; together with two large Dining Saloons, Coffee-rooms, Smoking-rooms, and Billiard Tables.

The lovers of News will find at the Reading-rooms belonging to the Hotel (where smoking is not permitted) the best German, French, English, American, and Italian Newspapers and Periodical Literature.

HOT AND COLD BATHS ALWAYS READY.

ELEGANT CARRIAGES ON HIRE.

An Omnibus from the Hotel attends the arrival of the Trains.

A Fixed Charge for Attendance.

The Hotel was opened on the 1st of July, 1858.

London and South-Western Railway.
LONDON STATION, WATERLOO BRIDGE.

PARIS,
Via SOUTHAMPTON and HAVRE.
The Cheapest Route.

FARES THROUGHOUT—FIRST CLASS, 28/0; SECOND CLASS 20/0.
RETURN TICKETS (available for one month)—FIRST CLASS, 50/0; SECOND CLASS, 36/0.

For times of sailing, see The Times *Newspaper daily.*

Offices—Waterloo Bridge Station—No. 53, King William Street, City—Universal Office, Regent Circus—No. 216, Oxford Street (West)—Golden Cross, Charing Cross—Swan-Two-Necks, Gresham Street, London. — Southampton, Railway Station. — Havre, 47, Grand Quai.—Paris, 3, Place Vendôme, or 30, Rue Bergère.

JERSEY AND GUERNSEY,
MAIL SERVICE,
Via SOUTHAMPTON.
Every Monday, Wednesday, and Friday.

FARES THROUGHOUT, 31/0 FIRST, or 21/0 SECOND CLASS.
RETURN TICKETS, 45/0 FIRST, or 35/0 SECOND CLASS, available for one Month.

The Last Train from London is at 8.30 p.m.

Offices as above.

JERSEY AGENT, Mr. G. H. Millais. GUERNSEY AGENT, Mr. J. B. Barbat.

THE ART OF TRAVEL.

Now Ready, Third Edition, revised and enlarged, with many additional Woodcuts.
Post 8vo. 7s. 6d.

HINTS on the SHIFTS and CONTRIVANCES available in WILD COUNTRIES. By FRANCIS GALTON, Author of 'The Narrative of an Explorer in Tropical South Africa.'

'Mr. Galton's handbook might prove a friend in need, even to an old traveller, while to a young one, who intends to venture beyond railways, it must be valuable.'—*Athenæum.*

'Mr. Galton has collected much valuable and practical information. His own experience has supplied the substance of the book, while he has extracted from the works of travellers in every climate and region materials which add to its usefulness. For travellers the book will have a permanent value, and will be found a useful supplement to Murray's Handbooks.'—*Literary Gazette.*

JOHN MURRAY, ALBEMARLE STREET.

BONN ON THE RHINE.

MR. SCHMITZ,

PROPRIETOR OF THE GOLDEN STAR HOTEL,

BEGS leave to recommend his Hotel to English Travellers. The apartments are furnished throughout in the English style; the rooms are carpeted; and the attendance, as well as the kitchen and the wine-cellar, is well provided. MR. SCHMITZ begs to add that at no first-rate Hotel on the Rhine will be found more moderate charges and more cleanliness.

The STAR HOTEL has been honoured by the visits of the following Members of the English Royal Family:—

1857.	Oct. 16	H. R. H. the Prince of WALES, accompanied by General Sir W. CODRINGTON, Colonel PONSONBY, Sir Frederic STANLEY, Dr. ARMSTRONG, Rev. F. C. TARVER, Mr. GIBBS, etc.
1857.	Aug. 20	H. R. H. the Prince of WALES and his Suite paying a visit *at the Golden Star Hotel* to His Majesty the King of the BELGIANS.
1857.	Aug. 8	H. R. H. the Prince of WALES and his Suite.
1857.	July 29	T. R. H. the Duchess of CAMBRIDGE and Princess MARY of CAMBRIDGE, accompanied by the Baron KNESEBECK and Suite.
1857.	July 29	H. R. H. the Prince of WALES paying a visit *at the Golden Star Hotel* to T. R. H. the Duchess of CAMBRIDGE and Princess MARY of CAMBRIDGE.
1857.	July 15	H. R. H. the Prince of WALES, accompanied by the Right Honourable C. GREY, General MAJOR, Colonel PONSONBY, Sir Frederic STANLEY, Dr. ARMSTRONG, Rev. F. C. TARVER, Mr. GIBBS, etc.
1856.	Nov.	H. R. H. Prince ALFRED of GREAT BRITAIN, accompanied by Lieutenant-General Sir Frederick STOVIN and Lieutenant COWELL.
1846.	June 18	H. M. ADELAIDE, QUEEN DOWAGER OF GREAT BRITAIN, accompanied by His Highness Prince EDWARD of SAXE WEIMAR, Lord and Lady BARRINGTON, Sir DAVID DAVIES, M.D., Rev. J. R. WOOD, M.A., Captain TAYLOR, &c. &c., honoured the above establishment with a THREE DAYS' VISIT.
1818.	May	H. R. H. the Duke of CAMBRIDGE and Suite.
1825.	March and Sept.	H. R. H. the Duke and Duchess of CLARENCE (King WILLIAM IV. and Queen ADELAIDE) and Suite.
1834.	July	H. M. QUEEN ADELAIDE, accompanied by the Earl and Countess of ERROL, Earl and Countess of DENBIGH, Earl and Countess HOWE, &c.
1836.	Aug.	H. R. H. the Duchess of GLOUCESTER and Suite.
1837.	July	H. R. H. the Duchess of CAMBRIDGE and Suite.
1839.	Nov.	H. R. H. the Prince GEORGE of CAMBRIDGE and Suite.
—	Nov.	H. R. H. Prince ALBERT of SAXE COBURG GOTHA, accompanied by Prince ERNEST of SAXE COBURG GOTHA, and their Suite.
1840.		H. R. H. the Duchess of CAMBRIDGE, accompanied by the Princess AUGUSTA of CAMBRIDGE, and their Suite.
1841.		H. R. H. the Duchess of KENT and Suite, accompanied by H. S. H. the Prince of LEININGEN.
1841.		H. R. H. the Duchess of CAMBRIDGE and Suite.
—		H. R. H. Princess CAROLINA of CAMBRIDGE.
1844.		H. R. H. the Duchess of CAMBRIDGE and Suite.
—		H. R. H. Princess MARY of CAMBRIDGE.
1845.	June	H. R. H. the Duchess of KENT and Suite, accompanied by H. S. H. the Prince of LEININGEN.
1847.	July	T. R. H. the Duke and Duchess of CAMBRIDGE, with their Family and Suite.

PASSPORTS

Obtained through the medium of Bankers' Letters, carefully mounted and inserted in morocco cases, with name lettered in gold.

Ambassadors' Signatures obtained to British Secretary of State's and American Passports, at One Shilling each.

The latest editions of all MURRAY'S HAND-BOOKS.

COURIERS, or TRAVELLING SERVANTS, can be obtained at

Foreign Letter Paper,
Extra Large Size,
VERY THIN,
1s. per Quire.

BOOKS FOR JOURNALS, &c.

LUGGAGE LABELS.

DOOR FASTENERS.

BERRY'S PATENT INKSTANDS.

Leather Money-Bags.

LEE'S Polyglot Washing Books,
(To save Travellers the trouble of translating their Washing Bills)
For Ladies.
DITTO
ForGentlemen.
English & French.
English & Italian.
English & German.
English & Spanish.
English & Portuguese.
1s. each.

Metallic Soap Boxes.

LEE & CARTER'S GUIDE DEPÔT,
440, WEST STRAND, W.C.
TWO DOORS WEST OF LOWTHER ARCADE,

Where an EXTENSIVE COLLECTION OF GUIDES, HAND-BOOKS, MAPS, DICTIONARIES, DIALOGUES, GRAMMARS, INTERPRETERS, &c., useful for Travellers upon the Continent and elsewhere, and much useful information concerning PASSPORTS, can be obtained.

MURRAY'S HAND-BOOKS, rendered convenient POCKET-BOOKS by J. LEE's limp leather binding, at 2s. additional charge.

MOROCCO and RUSSIA PORTABLE ROLL-UP CASES, containing every essential for Writing.

Moore's German Interpreter.
With the exact Pronunciation in English on a separate column, price 5s. cloth, 6s. in leather.

LONDON: W. CLOWES AND SONS, STAMFORD STREET, AND CHARING CROSS.

www.ingramcontent.com/pod-product-compliance
Lightning Source LLC
Chambersburg PA
CBHW021221300426
44111CB00007B/385

*9 7 8 3 7 4 2 8 9 2 8 8 1 *